Principles of Risk Management and Insurance

The Addison-Wesley Series in Finance

Principles of Risk Management and Insurance

Seventh Edition

George E. Rejda

Addison
Wesley

Boston   San Francisco   New York
London   Toronto   Sydney   Tokyo   Singapore   Madrid
Mexico City   Munich   Paris   Cape Town   Hong Kong   Montreal

Executive Editor: Denise Clinton
Development Editor: Rebecca Ferris
Editorial Assistant: Christine Houde
Senior Production Supervisor: Juliet Silveri
Marketing Manager: Dara Lanier
Manufacturing Supervisor: Hugh Crawford
Cover Design: Regina Hagen and Leslie Haimes
Text Design: Delgado Design, Inc.
Project Coordinator: Heather Bingham

Cover photo © Tom Sanders/Adventure Photo and Film

Library of Congress Cataloging-in-Publication Data

Rejda, George E., 1931-
    Principles of risk management and insurance / George E. Rejda.—
  7th ed.
      p. cm.
    Includes index.
    ISBN 0-321-05065-7
    1. Insurance.   2. Insurance—United States.   3. Risk (Insurance).
4. Risk management.   I. Title.
HG8051.R44   2000
368—dc21
                              00-041633

2 3 4 5 6 7 8 9 10—CRW—04 03 02 01

Contents

Preface

In the three years since the sixth edition of *Principles of Risk Management and Insurance* was published, newspapers across the nation carried disturbing headlines that shocked and saddened Americans. Congress impeached President William J. Clinton for perjury and obstruction of justice; two teenage shooters entered Columbine High School in Littleton, Colorado, killing 12 classmates, one teacher, and then themselves; earthquakes in Turkey killed more than 1000 people; and Hurricane Floyd devastated parts of the Carolinas and other seaboard states, causing billions of dollars of property damage and enormous personal hardship. Speculators and day traders went on a frantic feeding frenzy, rocketing the prices of several Internet stocks to atmospheric levels; the nation feared a Y2K computer meltdown going into the new millennium; Microsoft Corporation faced a federal anti-trust suit because of an alleged software monopoly; and, on the bright side, Mark McGwire of the St. Louis Cardinals belted 70 home runs for a new major league record.

The U.S. Senate went on to acquit President Clinton in his impeachment trial; the media continues to grapple with why school children turn into rogue killers; earthquakes, hurricanes, tornadoes, and floods continue their awesome destruction; Y2K brought few problems; and Mark McGwire still hits home runs. To say that a lot has happened since the publication of the sixth edition might be an understatement.

Likewise, the insurance industry has experienced rapid changes in the last three years. Significant changes include a growing use of the Internet by insurance consumers; convergence of financial services; mergers and acquisitions; and demutualization of several large insurers. New federal legislation now allows banks, insurers, and investment companies to compete in each other's markets with fewer obstacles. In addition, insurers continue to settle class action suits by disgruntled policyowners regarding deceptive sales practices; commercial lines have been deregulated in many states; and new forms of risk management are emerging, such as enterprise risk management. The problem of paying catastrophic losses from natural disasters continues to challenge the industry. Finally, the Insurance Services Office (ISO) introduced a new homeowners policy and new personal auto policy (PAP).

The seventh edition of *Principles of Risk Management and Insurance* reflects these changes and others. Like earlier editions, the text is designed for a beginning undergraduate course in risk management and insurance with no prerequisites. Thoroughly revised and updated, the seventh edition provides complete and current coverage of the major areas in risk management and insurance. Coverage includes basic concepts of risk and insurance, risk management, legal principles, property and liability insurance, life and health insurance, employee benefits, social insurance, and functional and financial operations of insurers. The seventh edition also emphasizes the changing nature of insurance regulation and current public policy issues, especially those affecting consumers.

As with previous editions, the seventh edition emphasizes the insurance consumer and blends basic risk management and insurance principles with consumer considerations. Further, it addresses personal risk management and financial planning, so that students can apply basic concepts immediately to their own lives.

MAJOR CHANGES IN THE SEVENTH EDITION

1. **Increased emphasis on the Internet.** In recognition of the importance of the Internet as a powerful learning tool and source of insurance information to consumers, each chapter contains a number of Web sites that students can access. The seventh edition has an Internet site (*www.awlonline*

.com/rejda) that will be updated periodically as new developments in insurance occur. The site also provides Internet Exercises corresponding to each chapter that instructors can assign. In addition, after studying each chapter, students can take a self-administered test online and get instant feedback on how well they have mastered the material.

2. **New "Insight" boxes.** Instructors and students have enthusiastically endorsed the "Insight" boxes in each chapter in previous editions. "Insights" are effective learning tools that provide real-world applications of principles. Most "Insights" have been replaced with compelling new ones, such as the following examples:

   - "More Bad News for Widows"
   - "Parts Case May Hike Premiums, Auto Insurers Say Generic Parts Have Helped to Keep Costs Down"
   - "Genetic Testing Threatens to Alter Fundamentally the Whole Notion of Insurance"
   - "Report Says Mistakes in Medicine Too Frequent"
   - "New Life Study Reveals Crisis of Underinsurance"
   - "Look for Term Insurance Rates to Rise in the Future"
   - "For-Profit HMOs Score Lower on Care"
   - "Rising Numbers of Doctors Cut Links to HMOs"
   - "Ten Common Causes of Errors in Pension Calculations"
   - "Are Professional Football and Baseball Players Eligible for Workers Compensation?"
   - "Boundaries Blurring for Financial Services"

3. **Clarity in writing.** Insurance as a subject can intimidate students if set forth in a disjointed or abstract way. Since readability is crucial, I persist in presenting concepts clearly and directly, for the most user friendly of texts.

4. **Technical accuracy.** As in past editions, numerous insurance specialists and experts have reviewed the text for technical accuracy, especially in areas where changes have occurred rapidly or dramatically. The seventh edition offers the most technically accurate and up-to-date information available.

CONTENT CHANGES

Thoroughly updated, the seventh edition provides an in-depth analysis of current issues, which readers expect from *Principles of Risk Management and Insurance*. Timely content changes include the following:

1. **Heightened coverage of risk management.** In response to instructors' requests for more emphasis on risk management, the seventh edition contains a new stand-alone chapter on advanced topics in risk management (Chapter 4). Topics discussed include enterprise risk management, financial risk management, loss forecasting, financial analysis in decision making, and the application of new technology to risk management programs. In addition, Chapter 3 now includes a discussion of personal risk management for instructors who prefer this approach.

2. **New homeowners policy.** Chapters 8 and 9 discuss the major provisions in the new homeowners policies drafted by the ISO.

3. **New personal auto policy (PAP).** Chapter 10 discusses the basic provisions of the 1998 PAP drafted by the ISO. The chapter contains an appendix that summarizes the basic coverages in the new PAP, for the benefit of students.

4. **Consolidation of life insurance planning.** Discussion of life insurance planning and the needs approach has been streamlined and condensed into one chapter (16) to enable instructors to discuss the needs approach quickly and easily.

5. **Life insurance premiums quotes.** Chapters 16–19 contain a number of Internet sites that will enable students to obtain life insurance quotes conveniently (for example, see Exhibit 19.5 on page 404).

6. **Elimination of estate planning chapter.** Because few instructors teach estate planning in the introductory course, coverage of estate planning, which appeared in a separate chapter in earlier editions, has been substantially reduced and integrated with the material on the taxation of life insurance (Chapter 19).

7. **New chapter on annuities and individual retirement accounts (IRAs).** Because of their importance, annuities and IRAs are now discussed in a new chapter (20) dealing with retirement plans. The chapter contains a number of interesting Internet sites that provide additional material on annuities and IRAs.

8. **Managed care plans.** The important area of managed care plans has been updated to discuss physicians' widespread dissatisfaction with managed care plans and proposals for patients' bill of rights.

9. **Social Security and Medicare financial problems.** Chapter 24 outlines the various proposals for dealing with the financial problems plaguing Social Security and Medicare.

10. **Convergence of financial services.** Chapter 25 examines the important and timely topic of the convergence of financial services in the insurance industry. Chapter 25 also discusses demutualization of large insurers and the formation of mutual holding companies as a response to the trend toward "one-stop shopping."

11. **Life insurance distribution systems.** Material dealing with life insurance distribution systems has been substantially revised. Chapter 25 discusses the major life insurance distribution systems that life insurers are now using.

12. **Timely issues in insurance regulation.** Chapter 28 examines a number of timely issues in insurance regulation, including the new Financial Modernization Act of 1999, the convergence of financial services, the increase in mergers and acquisitions, the growth of the Internet, the insolvency of insurers, the quality of insurance regulation, and the deregulation of commercial lines.

SUPPLEMENTS

The seventh edition contains a number of new supplementary materials—specifically an Instructor's Resource CD-ROM and a Companion Web site—to help busy instructors save time and teach more effectively. The following items are available to qualified domestic adopters but in some cases may not be available to international adopters:

Companion Web Site   As noted earlier, the seventh edition provides an Internet site (available at *www.awlonline.com/rejda*) that will be updated periodically. The site offers self-administered quizzes and Internet exercises corresponding to each chapter. The Companion Web site system provides an online syllabus builder that allows instructors to create a calendar of assignments for each class and to track student activity with an electronic gradebook.

Instructor's Manual with Transparency Masters Designed to reduce start-up costs and class preparation time for busy instructors, this comprehensive manual contains teaching notes; lecture outlines; answers to all in-text review, application, and case questions; and transparency masters that illustrate key points.

Test Bank   Prepared by Michael J. McNamara, Washington State University, this new test bank enables instructors to construct objective exams quickly and easily. The test bank contains new mini-case objective questions to test students' critical thinking skills and analytical abilities.

Study Guide   Prepared by Michael J. McNamara, Washington State University, this study tool is an improvement over traditional study guides. The guide contains exercises that enable students to apply basic concepts to their own personal risk management program. Each chapter contains objective questions similar to test bank questions, worksheets (where appropriate) for solving end-of-chapter cases, and answers to all questions at the end of each chapter for quick reference and self testing.

Instructor's Resource CD-ROM   Fully compatible with the Windows NT, 95, and higher platforms and Macintosh computers, this CD-ROM provides a number of resources. First, PowerPoint lecture slides of all figures and tables from the book enhance classroom presentations. Instructors with Microsoft PowerPoint 97, 98, or higher can customize the slides by adding their personal lecture notes. Second, for added convenience, the CD-ROM contains Microsoft Word files for the entire contents of the instructor's manual. Finally, the CD-ROM includes computerized test bank files. The easy-to-use software (TestGen-EQ with QuizMaster-EQ for Windows and Macintosh) is a valuable test preparation tool that allows professors to view, edit, and add questions.

ACKNOWLEDGMENTS

A market-leading textbook is never written alone. I owe an enormous intellectual debt to many people for their gracious assistance. Numerous educators and insurance experts have taken time out of their busy schedules to review part or all of the seventh edition, to provide supplementary materials, or to make valuable comments. They include the following:

Vickie L. Bajtelsmit, Colorado State University

Burton T. Beam, Jr., The American College

Joseph M. Belth, professor emeritus, Indiana University

James O. Brown, Delta State University

William L. Ferguson, University of Southwestern Louisiana

Beverly Frickel, University of Central Oklahoma

Deborah S. Gaunt, Georgia State University

Edward E. Graves, The American College

Dan C. Jones, University of Houston

Robert W. Klein, Georgia State University

Gene C. Lai, Washington State University

Ralph A. Maffei, Insurance Services Office, Inc.

Joe P. McHaney, University of Texas at Arlington

Kerri D. McMillan, Clemson University

Michael J. McNamara, Washington State University

Peter Mikolaj, Indiana State University

Phyllis S. Myers, Virginia Commonwealth University

Robert J. Myers, former chief actuary, Social Security Administration

Jack Nelson, The College of Insurance

Donald R. Oakes, American Institute for Chartered Property Casualty Underwriters

Donald E. Sanders, Southwest State University

John L. Southall, Morgan State University

Kenn B. Tacchino, Widener University

Brenda P. Wells, University of North Texas

Eric A. Wiening, American Institute for Chartered Property Casualty Underwriters

Millicent W. Workman, Mueller Industries, Inc.

Emily Norman Zietz, Middle Tennessee State University

Special thanks are due to Michael J. McNamara of Washington State University. Professor McNamara wrote the new chapter (4) on advanced topics in risk management and the study guide. He also developed a new test bank and reviewed each chapter for clarity and accuracy. As a result, the seventh edition is a substantially improved product.

I also wish to acknowledge the technical assistance of Rebecca Ferris, who served as the development editor for the seventh edition. Her keen editorial insights and numerous suggestions have been invaluable.

Finally, the fundamental objective of the seventh edition remains the same as earlier editions—I have attempted to write an intellectually stimulating and visually attractive textbook from which students can learn and professors can teach.

George E. Rejda, PhD, CLU
V.J. Skutt Distinguished Professor of Insurance
University of Nebraska-Lincoln

Part One

Basic Concepts in Risk Management and Insurance

Chapter 1

Risk in Our Society

❝When we take a risk, we are betting on an outcome that will result from a decision we have made, though we do not know for certain what the outcome will be. ❞

Peter L. Bernstein
Against the Gods, The Remarkable Story of Risk

Learning Objectives

After studying this chapter, you should be able to:

▲ Explain the meaning of risk.

▲ Distinguish between pure risk and speculative risk.

▲ Identify the major pure risks that are associated with financial insecurity.

▲ Understand how risk is a burden to society.

▲ Explain the major methods of handling risk.

▲ Access an Internet site to obtain and analyze information dealing with risk.

Internet Resources

- ARIAWeb is the Web site of the **American Risk and Insurance Association (ARIA)**. ARIA is the premier professional association of risk management and insurance scholars and professionals. ARIA is the publisher of *The Journal of Risk and Insurance* and *Risk Management and Insurance Review*. Links are provided to research, teaching, and other risk and insurance sites. Visit the site at:

  http://www.aria.org/

- The **Federal Emergency Management Agency (FEMA)** is a federal agency that deals with natural disasters. Its mission is to reduce the loss of life and property and protect the nation's infrastructure through a comprehensive, risk-based, emergency management program of mitigation, preparedness, response, and recovery. Visit the site at:

  http://www.fema.gov/

- The **Insurance Information Institute** is a trade association that provides consumers with information on catastrophic losses, including hurricanes, floods, earthquakes, brush fires, and other natural disasters. Visit the site at:

  http://www.iii.org/

*M*egan, age 24, is a registered nurse who works at a community hospital in Dallas, Texas. After working the second shift, she drove home in a blinding rainstorm. A drunk driver crossed the center line, smashed head-on into Megan's car, and was killed instantly. Megan was more fortunate. She lived, but was unable to work for six months. During that time, she incurred medical bills in excess of $150,000 and lost about $20,000 in wages.

Megan's tragic accident shows clearly that we live in a risky world. Similar tragedies occur daily. Motorists die or become severely injured in auto accidents. Homeowners lose their homes and personal property because of fires, floods, hurricanes, earthquakes, or other disasters. Some people experience catastrophic medical bills and the loss of earnings because of heart disease, cancer, AIDS, or some other illness. Still others face financial ruin because they negligently injure someone and cannot pay a liability judgment.

This chapter discusses the nature and treatment of risk in our society. Topics discussed include the meaning of risk, the major types of risk that threaten our financial security, and the basic methods for handling risk.

MEANING OF RISK

There is no single definition of risk. Economists, behavioral scientists, risk theorists, statisticians, and actuaries each have their own concept of risk. However, risk traditionally has been defined in terms of uncertainty. Based on this concept, **risk** *is defined here as uncertainty concerning the occurrence of a loss.*[1] For example, the risk of being killed in an auto accident is present because uncertainty is present. The risk of lung cancer for smokers is present because uncertainty is present. And the risk of flunking a college course is present because uncertainty is present.

Although risk is defined as uncertainty in this text, employees in the insurance industry often use the term *risk* to identify the property or life being insured. Thus, in the insurance industry, it is common to hear statements such as "that driver is a poor risk" or "that building is an unacceptable risk."

Finally, when risk is defined as uncertainty, some authors make a careful distinction between objective risk and subjective risk.

Objective Risk

Objective risk *is defined as the relative variation of actual loss from expected loss.* For example, assume that a property insurer has 10,000 houses insured over a long period and, on average, 1 percent, or 100 houses, burn each year. However, it would be rare for exactly 100 houses to burn each year. In some years, as few as 90 houses may burn; in other years, as many as 110 houses may burn. Thus, there is a variation of 10 houses from the expected number of 100, or a variation of 10 percent. This relative variation of actual loss from expected loss is known as objective risk.

Objective risk declines as the number of exposures increases. More specifically, *objective risk varies inversely with the square root of the number of cases under observation.* In our previous example, 10,000 houses were insured, and objective risk was 10/100, or 10 percent. Now assume that 1 million houses are insured. The expected number of houses that will burn is now 10,000, but the variation of actual loss from expected loss is only 100. Objective risk is now 100/10,000, or 1 percent. Thus, as the square root of the number of houses increased from 100 in the first example to 1000 in the second example (10 times), objective risk declined to one-tenth of its former level.

Objective risk can be statistically measured by some measure of dispersion, such as the standard deviation or the coefficient of variation. Because objective risk can be measured, it is an extremely useful concept for an insurer or a corporate risk manager. As the number of exposures increases, an insurer can predict its future loss experience more accurately because it can rely on the law of large numbers. The **law of large numbers** states that as the number of exposure units increases, the more closely the actual loss experience will approach the expected loss experience. For example, as the number of homes under observation increases, the greater is the degree of accuracy in predicting the proportion of homes that will burn. The law of large numbers is discussed in greater detail in Chapter 2.

Subjective Risk

Subjective risk *is defined as uncertainty based on a person's mental condition or state of mind.* For example, a customer who was drinking heavily in a bar may foolishly attempt to drive home. The driver may be uncertain whether he will arrive home safely without being arrested by the police for drunk driving. This mental uncertainty is called subjective risk.

The impact of subjective risk varies depending on the individual. Two persons in the same situation can have a different perception of risk, and their behavior may be altered accordingly. If an individual experiences great mental uncertainty concerning the occurrence of a loss, that person's behavior may be affected. High subjective risk often results in conservative and prudent behavior, while low subjective risk may result in less conservative behavior. For example, a motorist previously arrested for drunk driving is aware that she has consumed too much alcohol. The driver may then compensate for the mental uncertainty by getting someone else to drive the car home or by taking a cab. Another driver in the same situation may perceive the risk of being arrested as slight. This second driver may drive in a more careless and reckless manner; a low subjective risk results in less conservative driving behavior.

CHANCE OF LOSS

Chance of loss is closely related to the concept of risk. **Chance of loss** *is defined as the probability that an event will occur.* Like risk, "probability" has both objective and subjective aspects.

Objective Probability

Objective probability *refers to the long-run relative frequency of an event based on the assumptions of an infinite number of observations and of no change in the underlying conditions.* Objective probabilities can be determined in two ways. First, they can be determined by deductive reasoning. These probabilities are called *a priori probabilities.* For example, the probability of getting a head from the toss of a perfectly balanced coin is 1/2 because there are two sides, and only one is a head. Likewise, the probability of rolling a 6 with a single dice is 1/6, since there are six sides and only one side has six dots on it.

Second, objective probabilities can be determined by inductive reasoning, rather than by deduction. For example, the probability that a person age 21 will die before age 26 cannot be logically deduced. However, by a careful analysis of past mortality experience, life insurers can estimate the probability of death and sell a five-year term life insurance policy issued at age 21.

Subjective Probability

Subjective probability *is the individual's personal estimate of the chance of loss.* Subjective probability need not coincide with objective probability. For example, people who buy a lottery ticket on their birthday may believe it is their lucky day and overestimate the small chance of winning. A wide variety of factors can influence subjective probability, including a person's age, gender, intelligence, education, and the use of alcohol.

In addition, a person's estimate of a loss may differ from objective probability because there may be ambiguity in the way in which the probability is perceived. For example, assume that a slot machine in a gambling casino requires three lemons to win. The person playing the machine may perceive the probability of winning to be quite high. But if there are ten symbols on each reel and only one is a lemon, the objective probability of hitting the jackpot with three lemons is quite small. Assuming that each reel spins independently of the others, the probability that all three will simultaneously show a lemon is the product of their individual probabilities ($1/10 \times 1/10 \times 1/10 = 1/1000$). This knowledge is advantageous to casino owners, who know that most gamblers are not trained statisticians and are therefore likely to overestimate the objective probabilities of winning.

Chance of Loss Distinguished from Risk

Chance of loss can be distinguished from objective risk. Chance of loss is the probability that an event that causes a loss will occur. Objective risk is the relative variation of actual loss from expected loss. *The chance of loss may be identical for two different groups, but objective risk may be quite different.* For example, assume that a property insurer has 10,000 homes insured in Los Angeles and 10,000 homes insured in Philadelphia and that the chance of loss in each city is 1 percent. Thus, on average, 100 homes should burn annually in each city. However, if the annual variation in losses ranges from 75 to 125 in Philadelphia, but only from 90 to 110 in Los

Angeles, objective risk is greater in Philadelphia even though the chance of loss in both cities is the same.

PERIL AND HAZARD

The terms *peril* and *hazard* should not be confused with the concept of risk discussed earlier.

Peril

Peril *is defined as the cause of loss.* If your house burns because of a fire, the peril, or cause of loss, is the fire. If your car is damaged in a collision with another car, collision is the peril, or cause of loss. Common perils that cause property damage include fire, lightning, windstorm, hail, tornadoes, earthquakes, theft, and burglary.

Hazard

A **hazard** *is a condition that creates or increases the chance of loss.* There are three major types of hazards:

- Physical hazard
- Moral hazard
- Morale hazard

Physical Hazard A **physical hazard** *is a physical condition that increases the chance of loss.* Examples of physical hazards include icy roads that increase the chance of an auto accident, defective wiring in a building that increases the chance of fire, and a defective lock on a door that increases the chance of theft.

Moral Hazard **Moral hazard** *is dishonesty or character defects in an individual that increase the frequency or severity of loss.* Examples of moral hazard include faking an accident to collect from the insurer, submitting a fraudulent claim, inflating the amount of a claim, and intentionally burning unsold merchandise that is insured.

Moral hazard is present in all forms of insurance, and it is difficult to control. Dishonest individuals often rationalize their actions on the grounds that "the insurer has plenty of money." This view is incorrect because the insurer can pay claims only by collecting premiums from other insureds. Because of moral hazard, premiums are higher for everyone.

Insurers attempt to control moral hazard by careful underwriting of applicants for insurance and by various policy provisions, such as deductibles, waiting periods, exclusions, and riders. These provisions are examined in Chapter 6.

Morale Hazard Some insurance authors draw a subtle distinction between moral hazard and morale hazard. Moral hazard refers to dishonesty by an insured that increases the frequency or severity of loss. **Morale hazard** *is carelessness or indifference to a loss because of the existence of insurance.* Some insureds are careless or indifferent to a loss because they have insurance. Examples of morale hazard include leaving car keys in an unlocked car, which increases the chance of theft; leaving a door unlocked that allows a burglar to enter; and changing lanes suddenly on a congested interstate highway without signaling. Careless acts like these increase the chance of loss.

BASIC CATEGORIES OF RISK

Risk can be classified into several distinct categories. The major categories of risk are as follows:

- Pure and speculative risks
- Fundamental and particular risks

Pure and Speculative Risks

Pure risk *is defined as a situation in which there are only the possibilities of loss or no loss.* The only possible outcomes are adverse (loss) and neutral (no loss). Examples of pure risks include premature death, job-related accidents, catastrophic medical expenses, and damage to property from fire, lightning, flood, or earthquake.

Speculative risk *is defined as a situation in which either profit or loss is possible.* For example, if you purchase 100 shares of common stock, you would profit if the price of the stock increases but would lose if the price declines. Other examples of speculative risks include betting on a horse race, investing in real estate, and going into business for yourself. In these situations, both profit and loss are possible.

It is important to distinguish between pure and speculative risks for three reasons. First, private insurers generally insure only pure risks. With certain exceptions, speculative risks are not considered insurable, and other techniques for coping with risk must be used. (One exception is that some insurers will insure institutional portfolio investments and municipal bonds against loss.)

Second, the law of large numbers can be applied more easily to pure risks than to speculative risks. The law of large numbers is important because it enables insurers to predict future loss experience. In contrast, it is generally more difficult to apply the law of large numbers to speculative risks to predict future loss experience. An exception is the speculative risk of gambling, where casino operators can apply the law of large numbers in a most efficient manner.

Finally, society may benefit from a speculative risk even though a loss occurs, but it is harmed if a pure risk is present and a loss occurs. For example, a firm may develop new technology for producing inexpensive computers. As a result, some competitors may be forced into bankruptcy. Despite the bankruptcy, society benefits because the computers are produced at a lower cost. However, society normally does not benefit when a loss from a pure risk occurs, such as a flood or earthquake that devastates an area.

Fundamental and Particular Risks

A **fundamental risk** *is a risk that affects the entire economy or large numbers of persons or groups within the economy.* Examples include rapid inflation, cyclical unemployment, and war because large numbers of individuals are affected.

The risk of a natural disaster is another important fundamental risk. Hurricanes, tornadoes, earthquakes, floods, and forest and grass fires can result in billions of dollars of property damage and numerous deaths. For example, in 1999, Hurricane Floyd caused $1.8 billion in insured damages and became the fifth most costly catastrophe in the U.S. history (see Exhibit 1.1). In 1998, Hurricane Georges caused insured losses of $2.9 billion. In 1992, Hurricane Andrew, the most costly natural disaster ever in the United States, devastated South Florida and caused insured damages of $15.5 billion, which resulted in the failure of a number of property insurers.

Floods and earthquakes also cause enormous property damage. In 1997, raging flood waters in Grand Forks, North Dakota, ravaged thousands of homes and buildings, which resulted in millions of dollars in property damage and enormous personal hardship. In 1994, a major earthquake in Northridge, California caused billions of dollars of property damage and the loss of numerous lives. Grass and brush fires and mud slides also occur frequently, often resulting in severe property damage, the loss of life, and intense personal suffering.

In contrast to a fundamental risk, a **particular risk** *is a risk that affects only individuals and not the entire community.* Examples include car thefts, bank

---

EXHIBIT 1.1

The 10 Most Costly U.S. Hurricanes (Insured Losses Only)

Hurricane	Year	Place	Estimated insured loss
Andrew	1992 (August 23–26)	Florida, Louisiana, Mississippi	$15,500,000,000
Hugo	1989 (September 17–18, 21–22)	U.S. Virgin Islands, Puerto Rico, Georgia, South Carolina, North Carolina, Virginia	4,195,000,000
Georges	1998 (September 21–28)	U.S. Virgin Islands, Puerto Rico, Alabama, Florida, Louisiana, Mississippi	2,900,000,000
Opal	1995 (October 4)	Florida, Alabama, Georgia, South Carolina, North Carolina, Tennessee	2,100,000,000
Floyd	1999 (September 15)	Florida, Georgia, South Carolina, North Carolina, Virginia, Maryland, Delaware, New Jersey, New York, Connecticut, Massachusetts, Maine	1,800,000,000
Iniki	1992 (September 11)	Kauai and Oahu, Hawaii	1,600,000,000
Fran	1996 (September 5)	South Carolina, North Carolina, Virginia, Maryland, West Virginia, Pennsylvania, Ohio	1,600,000,000
Marilyn	1995 (September 15–16)	Puerto Rico, U.S. Virgin Islands	875,000,000
Frederic	1979 (September 12–14)	Mississippi, Alabama, Louisiana, Florida, Tennessee, Kentucky, West Virginia, Ohio, Pennsylvania, New York	752,500,000
Alicia	1983 (August 17–20)	Texas	675,500,000

NOTE: Insurance Information Institute from estimates provided prior to 1984 by the American Insurance Association; thereafter by the Property Claim Services division of the Insurance Services Office, Inc.

SOURCE: Insurance Information Institute.

robberies, and dwelling fires. Only individuals experiencing such losses are affected, not the entire economy.

The distinction between a fundamental and a particular risk is important because government assistance may be necessary to insure a fundamental risk. Social insurance and government insurance programs, as well as government guarantees and subsidies, may be necessary to insure certain fundamental risks in the United States. For example, the risk of unemployment generally is not insurable by private insurers but can be insured publicly by state unemployment compensation programs. In addition, flood insurance subsidized by the federal government is available to business firms and individuals in flood areas.

TYPES OF PURE RISK

The major types of pure risk that can create great financial insecurity include personal risks, property risks, and liability risks.

Personal Risks

Personal risks *are risks that directly affect an individual*; they involve the possibility of the complete loss or reduction of earned income, extra expenses, and the depletion of financial assets. There are four major personal risks:[2]

- Risk of premature death
- Risk of insufficient income during retirement
- Risk of poor health
- Risk of unemployment

Risk of Premature Death **Premature death** *is defined as the death of a household head with unfulfilled financial obligations*. These obligations can include dependents to support, a mortgage to be paid off, or children to educate. If the surviving family members receive an insufficient amount of replacement income from other sources or have insufficient financial assets to replace the lost income, they may be financially insecure.

Premature death can cause financial problems only if the deceased has dependents to support or

dies with unsatisfied financial obligations. Thus, the death of a child age 10 is not "premature" in the economic sense.

There are at least four costs that result from the premature death of a household head. First, the human life value of the family head is lost forever. The **human life value** *is defined as the present value of the family's share of the deceased breadwinner's future earnings*. This loss can be substantial; the actual or potential human life value of most college graduates can easily exceed $500,000. Second, additional expenses may be incurred because of funeral expenses, uninsured medical bills, probate and estate settlement costs, and estate and inheritance taxes for larger estates. Third, because of insufficient income, some families may have trouble making ends meet or covering expenses (see Insight 1.1). Finally, certain noneconomic costs are also incurred, including emotional grief, loss of a role model, and counseling and guidance for the children.

Risk of Insufficient Income During Retirement

The major risk associated with old age is insufficient income during retirement. The vast majority of workers in the United States retire before age 65. When they retire, they lose their earned income. Unless they have sufficient financial assets on which to draw, or have access to other sources of retirement income, such as Social Security or a private pension, they will be exposed to financial insecurity during retirement.

How are older people, age 65 and over, doing financially? In answering this question, it is a mistake to assume that all aged are wealthy; it is equally wrong to assume all aged are poor. *The aged are an economically diverse group, and their total money incomes are far from uniform.* In 1998, about 18 percent of the households with an aged householder age 65 and over had incomes of less than $10,000. At the other extreme, 8 percent of the aged households had incomes of $75,000 or more. The median income for all aged households was only $21,589.[3] This amount is relatively low and is generally insufficient for retired workers who have substantial additional expenses, such as high uninsured medical bills, or the cost of long-term care in a nursing facility or high property taxes.

Insight 1.1

More Bad News for Widows

Most people think they have enough life insurance so that their survivors can get along just fine. But they may be fooling themselves—at least according to a new study sponsored by LIMRA International, the research arm of the insurance industry.

The study looked at the finances of men and women who lost a spouse "prematurely" (between ages 25 and 54). *"Widows—not widowers—were having trouble making ends meet or covering expenses,"* says Cheryl Retzloff, the project director. Although the women received more than double the average death benefit that was paid to the men—$162,600 versus $73,100—widows reported more financial problems. On average, the death benefit for widows was approxi-mately three times the total household income; widowers averaged only one year's household income. Interestingly, survivors generally spent the insurance benefit on short-term needs, such as paying off debts or paying down a mortgage.

LIMRA says that insurance agents need to do more thorough needs analysis, especially for wives. If a wife's earning potential is more limited, the agent should recommend higher levels of coverage and make sure it covers the costs associated with death (funeral, medical expenses, plus access to health benefits).

Source: Adapted from "More Bad News for Widows," *On Investing* (Fall 1999), p. 14.

In addition, many workers are not saving enough for a comfortable retirement. A *Wall Street Journal*/NBC poll of adults in late 1997 showed that many workers will not be financially prepared to retire. The poll revealed that 57 percent had not calculated or did not know how much they must save annually for retirement, and 55 percent stated they were dissatisfied with the amounts they were saving.[4] *For many workers, savings are meager and inadequate. The survey showed that for workers who are saving for old age, 26 percent have saved less than $10,000* (see Exhibit 1.2).

Risk of Poor Health Poor health is another important personal risk. The risk of poor health includes both the payment of catastrophic medical bills and the loss of earned income. The costs of major surgery have increased substantially in recent years. For example, an open heart operation can cost more than $200,000, a kidney or heart transplant can cost more than $400,000, and the costs of a crippling accident requiring several major operations, plastic surgery, and rehabilitation can exceed $500,000. In addition, long-term care in a nursing home can cost $50,000 or more each year. Unless these persons have adequate health insurance, private savings and

EXHIBIT 1.2
Retirement Savings

How much money have you saved for retirement? (asked of current savers)

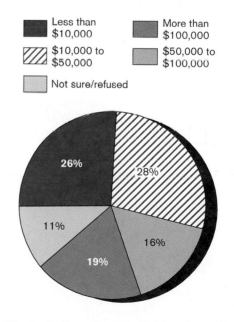

■ Less than $10,000	▨ More than $100,000
▨ $10,000 to $50,000	▨ $50,000 to $100,000
▨ Not sure/refused	

Source: "Gauging the Generations," *The Wall Street Journal*, December 12, 1997, p. R1.

financial assets, or other sources of income to meet these expenditures, they will be financially insecure. In particular, the inability of some persons to pay catastrophic medical bills is an important cause of personal bankruptcy.

The loss of earned income is another major cause of financial insecurity if the disability is severe. In cases of long-term disability, there is a substantial loss of earned income, medical bills are incurred, employee benefits may be lost or reduced, savings are often depleted, and someone must take care of the disabled person.

Most workers seldom think about the financial consequences of long-term disability. The probability of becoming disabled before age 65 is much higher than is commonly believed, especially at the younger ages. *For individuals age 25, the 1985 Commissioners Disability Table shows that the probability of being totally disabled for 90 or more days prior to age 65 is 54 percent.*[5] The loss of earned income during an extended disability can be financially very painful. Even if the disabled person carries disability income insurance, the financial consequences can be severe if the insurer refuses to pay the claim.

Risk of Unemployment   The risk of unemployment is another major threat to financial security. Unemployment can result from business cycle downswings, technological and structural changes in the economy, seasonal factors, and imperfections in the labor market.

At the time of this writing, the unemployment rate in the United States was low. However, unemployment at times can be a serious problem because of several important trends. To hold down labor costs, large corporations have downsized, and their work force has been permanently reduced; employers are increasingly hiring temporary or part-time workers to reduce labor costs; and millions of jobs have been lost to foreign nations because of global competition.

Regardless of the reason, unemployment can cause financial insecurity in at least three ways. First, workers lose their earned income and employee benefits. Unless there is adequate replacement income or past savings on which to draw, the unemployed worker will be financially insecure. Second, because

of economic conditions, the worker may be able to work only part-time. The reduced income may be insufficient in terms of the worker's needs. Finally, if the duration of unemployment is extended over a long period, past savings may be exhausted.

Property Risks

Persons owning property are exposed to the risk of having their property damaged or lost from numerous causes. Real estate and personal property can be damaged or destroyed because of fire, lightning, tornadoes, windstorms, and numerous other causes. There are two major types of loss associated with the destruction or theft of property: direct loss and indirect or consequential loss.

Direct Loss   A **direct loss** *is defined as a financial loss that results from the physical damage, destruction, or theft of the property.* For example, if you own a restaurant that is damaged by a fire, the physical damage to the restaurant is known as a direct loss.

Indirect or Consequential Loss   An **indirect loss** *is a financial loss that results indirectly from the occurrence of a direct physical damage or theft loss.* Thus, in addition to the physical damage loss, the restaurant would lose profits for several months while the restaurant is being rebuilt. The loss of profits would be a consequential loss. Other examples of a consequential loss would be the loss of rents, the loss of the use of the building, and the loss of a local market.

Extra expenses are another type of indirect, or consequential, loss. For example, suppose you own a newspaper, bank, or dairy. If a loss occurs, you must continue to operate regardless of cost; otherwise, you will lose customers to your competitors. It may be necessary to set up a temporary operation at some alternative location, and substantial extra expenses would then be incurred.

Liability Risks

Liability risks are another important type of pure risk that most persons face. Under our legal system,

Insight 1.2

Rottweiler Mauls Four-Year-Old Boy in Back Yard

Moments after a Rottweiler named Grizzly viciously mauled and critically injured a 4-year-old Omaha boy playing in his back yard Monday, the dog tried to attack a police officer.

Officer Robert Hauptman shot the dog four times before it finally fell dead. The animal, weighing about 100 pounds, had charged him after he shot it twice, Hauptman said in an interview.

The dog's owner was cited by animal-control officers for harboring a dangerous dog and failure to restrain the dog. Each is a violation of a city ordinance and carries a maximum penalty of six months in jail and a $500 fine.

When Hauptman arrived at the house, he saw the boy unconscious on the kitchen floor, bleeding heavily from multiple bites to his head and arms, Hauptman said. He said paramedics were working hard to save the boy's life.

[He] had no other choice but to shoot the charging Rottweiler. "I saw what that dog had done to the boy," Hauptman said. "I figured he didn't intend to lick me. That dog had to be destroyed."

According to the police, the boy was playing in the back yard of his home when the dog, kept at a residence to the north, came through a hole in the fence separating the properties. The dog then mauled the boy.

The boy's mother was inside her house and did not witness the attack. She later called 911 when she found her son in the back yard. Police did not know how long the attack lasted.

The Omaha chapter of the Nebraska Humane Society had no prior reports on file about Grizzly or its home address, said Darcy Beck, an agency spokeswoman.

Some dog owners obtain large guarding dogs that are territorial, such as Rottweilers or shepherd breeds, and then relegate them to back yards, she said.

"Then we have an accident waiting to happen," Beck said.

Guard dogs feel provoked, she said, even by people walking back and forth near a fence. Other reasons for dog attacks include the dog owner's failure to go through obedience training with the dog or to socialize so that the dog is comfortable around children, neighbors and friends, Beck said.

The Nebraska Humane Society in Omaha receives reports of about 1000 dog bites per year, Beck said.

Nationally, the number of dog bites needing medical attention rose 37 percent between 1986 and 1996, reaching 800,000, according to the National Center for Injury Prevention and Control, a division of the federal Centers for Disease Control and Prevention. During that same time, the number of dogs as pets increased 2 percent.

SOURCE: Adaptation of Toni Heinzl, "Boy in Critical Condition, Dog Is Shot Four Times After Charging Officer," *Omaha World Herald*, March 16, 1999, pp. 1–2.

you can be held legally liable if you do something that results in bodily injury or property damage to someone else. A court of law may order you to pay substantial damages to the person you have injured.

The United States is a litigious society, and lawsuits are common. Motorists can be held legally liable for the negligent operation of their vehicles; operators of boats and lake owners can be held legally liable because of bodily injury to boat occupants, swimmers, and water skiers. Owners of large dogs that severely injure small children are especially vulnerable to catastrophic lawsuits (see Insight 1.2).

Business firms can be held legally liable for defective products that harm or injure customers; physicians, attorneys, accountants, engineers, and other professionals can be sued by patients and clients because of alleged acts of malpractice. In addition, new types of lawsuits are constantly emerging. For example, some ministers have faced lawsuits brought by church members because of improper counseling.

Liability risks are of great importance for several reasons. *First, there is no maximum upper limit with respect to the amount of the loss.* You can be sued for any amount. In contrast, if you own property, there is a maximum limit on the loss. For example, if your car has an actual cash value of $10,000, the maximum physical damage loss is $10,000. But if you are negligent and cause an accident that results in serious bodily injury to the other driver, you can be sued for any amount—$50,000, $500,000, or $1 million or more—by the person you have injured.

Second, a lien can be placed on your income and financial assets to satisfy a legal judgment. For example, assume that you injure someone, and a court of law orders you to pay damages to the injured party. If you cannot pay the judgment, a lien may be placed on your income and financial assets to satisfy the judgment. If you declare bankruptcy to avoid payment of the judgment, your credit rating will be impaired.

Finally, legal defense costs can be enormous. If you have no liability insurance, the cost of hiring an attorney to defend you can be staggering. If the suit goes to trial, attorney fees and other legal expenses can be substantial.

BURDEN OF RISK ON SOCIETY

The presence of risk results in certain undesirable social and economic effects. Risk entails three major burdens on society:

- The size of an emergency fund must be increased.
- Society is deprived of certain goods and services.
- Worry and fear are present.

Larger Emergency Fund

It is prudent to set aside funds for an emergency. However, in the absence of insurance, individuals and business firms would have to increase the size of their emergency fund to pay for unexpected losses. For example, assume you have purchased a $100,000 home and want to accumulate a fund for repairs if the home is damaged by fire, hail, windstorm, or some other peril. Without insurance, you would have to save at least $20,000 annually to build up an adequate fund within a relatively short period of time. Even then, an early loss could occur, and your emergency fund may be insufficient to pay the loss. If you are a middle-income wage earner, you would find such saving difficult. In any event, the higher the amount that must be saved, the more current consumption spending must be reduced, which results in a lower standard of living.

Loss of Certain Goods and Services

A second burden of risk is that society is deprived of certain goods and services. For example, because of the risk of a liability lawsuit, many corporations have discontinued manufacturing certain products. Numerous examples can be given. Some 250 companies in the world once manufactured childhood vaccines; today, only a small number of firms manufacture vaccines, due in part to the threat of liability suits. Other firms have discontinued the manufacture of certain products, including asbestos products, football helmets, silicone-gel breast implants, and certain birth-control devices.

Worry and Fear

A final burden of risk is that worry and fear are present. Numerous examples can illustrate the mental unrest and fear caused by risk. Parents may be fearful if a teenage son or daughter departs on a skiing trip during a blinding snowstorm because the risk of being killed on an icy road is present. Some passengers in a commercial jet may become extremely nervous and fearful if the jet encounters severe turbulence during the flight. A college student who needs a grade of C in a course to graduate may enter the final examination room with a feeling of apprehension and fear.

METHODS OF HANDLING RISK

As we stressed earlier, risk is a burden not only to the individual but to society as well. Thus, it is important to examine some techniques for meeting the problem of risk. There are five major methods of handling risk:

- Avoidance
- Loss control
- Retention
- Noninsurance transfers
- Insurance

Avoidance

Avoidance is one method of handling risk. For example, you can avoid the risk of being mugged in a high-crime rate area by staying out of the area; you can avoid the risk of divorce by not marrying; and a business firm can avoid the risk of being sued for a defective product by not producing the product.

Not all risks should be avoided, however. For example, you can avoid the risk of death or disability in a plane crash by refusing to fly. But is this choice practical or desirable? The alternatives—driving or taking a bus or train—often are not appealing. Although the risk of a plane crash is present, the safety record of commercial airlines is excellent, and flying is a reasonable risk to assume.

Loss Control

Loss control is another important method for handling risk. Loss control consists of certain activities that reduce both the frequency and severity of losses. Thus, loss control has two major objectives: loss prevention and loss reduction.

Loss Prevention Loss prevention aims at reducing the probability of loss so that the frequency of losses is reduced. Several examples of personal loss prevention can be given. Auto accidents can be reduced if motorists take a safe-driving course and drive defensively. The number of heart attacks can be reduced if individuals control their weight, give up smoking, and eat healthy diets.

Loss prevention is also important for business firms. For example, a boiler explosion can be prevented by periodic inspections by a safety engineer; occupational accidents can be reduced by the elimination of unsafe working conditions and by strong enforcement of safety rules; and fires can be prevented by forbidding workers to smoke in a building where highly flammable materials are used. In short, the goal of loss prevention is to prevent the loss from occurring.

Loss Reduction Strict loss-prevention efforts can reduce the frequency of losses, yet some losses will inevitably occur. Thus, the second objective of loss control is to reduce the severity of a loss after it oc-curs. For example, a department store can install a sprinkler system so that a fire will be promptly extinguished, thereby reducing the loss; a plant can be constructed with fire-resistant materials to minimize fire damage; fire doors and fire walls can be used to prevent a fire from spreading; and a community warning system can reduce the number of injuries and deaths from an approaching tornado.

From the viewpoint of society, loss control is highly desirable for two reasons. *First, the indirect costs of losses may be large, and in some instances can easily exceed the direct costs.* For example, a worker may be injured on the job. In addition to being responsible for the worker's medical expenses and a certain percentage of earnings (direct costs), the firm may incur sizable indirect costs: a machine may be damaged and must be repaired; the assembly line may have to be shut down; costs are incurred in training a new worker to replace the injured worker; and a contract may be canceled because goods are not shipped on time. By preventing the loss from occurring, both indirect costs and direct costs are reduced.

Second, the social costs of losses are reduced. For example, assume that the worker in the preceding example dies from the accident. Society is deprived forever of the goods and services the deceased worker could have produced. The worker's family loses its share of the worker's earnings and may experience considerable grief and financial insecurity. And the worker may personally experience great pain and suffering before dying. In short, these social costs can be reduced through an effective loss-control program.

Retention

Retention is a third method of handling risk. An individual or a business firm retains all or part of a given risk. Risk retention can be either active or passive.

Active Retention Active risk retention means that an individual is consciously aware of the risk and deliberately plans to retain all or part of it. For example, a motorist may wish to retain the risk of a small collision loss by purchasing an auto insurance policy with a $250 or higher deductible. A homeowner may retain a small part of the risk of damage to the home by purchasing a homeowners policy with a substantial deductible. A business firm may deliberately retain the risk of petty thefts by employees, shoplifting, or the spoilage of perishable goods. In these cases, a conscious decision is made to retain part or all of a given risk.

Active risk retention is used for two major reasons. First, it can save money. Insurance may not be purchased at all, or it may be purchased with a deductible; either way, there is often a substantial saving in the cost of insurance. Second, the risk may be deliberately retained because commercial insurance is either unavailable or unaffordable.

Passive Retention Risk can also be retained passively. Certain risks may be unknowingly retained because of ignorance, indifference, or laziness. Passive retention is very dangerous if the risk retained has the potential for destroying you financially. For example, many workers with earned incomes are not insured against the risk of long-term total and permanent disability under either an individual or group disability income plan. However, the adverse financial consequences of total and permanent disability generally are more severe than premature death. Therefore, people who are not insured against this risk are using the technique of risk retention in a most dangerous and inappropriate manner.

In summary, risk retention is an important technique for handling risk, especially in a modern corporate risk management program, which will be discussed in Chapters 3 and 4. Risk retention, however, is appropriate primarily for high-frequency, low-severity risks where potential losses are relatively small. Except under unusual circumstances, risk retention should not be used to retain low-frequency, high-severity risks, such as the risk of catastrophic medical expenses, long-term disability, or a lawsuit.

Noninsurance Transfers

Noninsurance transfers are another technique for handling risk. The risk is transferred to a party other than an insurance company. A risk can be transferred by several methods, among which are the following:

- Transfer of risk by contracts
- Hedging price risks
- Incorporation of a business firm

Transfer of Risk by Contracts Unwanted risks can be transferred by contracts. For example, the risk of a defective television or stereo set can be transferred to the retailer by purchasing a service contract, which makes the retailer responsible for all repairs after the warranty expires. The risk of a rent increase can be transferred to the landlord by a long-term lease. The risk of a price increase in construction costs can be transferred to the builder by having a fixed price in the contract.

Finally, a risk can be transferred by a **hold-harmless clause**. For example, if a manufacturer of scaffolds inserts a hold-harmless clause in a contract with a retailer, the retailer agrees to hold the manufacturer harmless in case a scaffold collapses and someone is injured.

Hedging Price Risks Hedging price risks is another example of risk transfer. **Hedging** is a technique for transferring the risk of unfavorable price fluctuations to a speculator by purchasing and selling futures contracts on an organized exchange, such as the Chicago Board of Trade or New York Stock Exchange.

For example, the portfolio manager of a pension fund may hold a substantial position in long-term U.S. Treasury bonds. If interest rates rise, the value of the Treasury bonds will decline. To hedge that risk, the portfolio manager can sell U.S. Treasury bond futures. Assume that interest rates rise as expected, and bond prices decline. The value of the futures contract will decline, which will enable the portfolio manager to make an offsetting purchase at a lower price. The profit obtained from closing out the futures position will partly or completely offset the decline in the market value of the Treasury bonds. Of course, markets do not always move as expected, and the hedge may not be perfect. Transaction costs also are incurred. However, by hedging, the portfolio manager has reduced the potential loss in bond prices if interest rates rise.

Incorporation of a Business Firm Incorporation is another example of risk transfer. If a firm is a sole proprietorship, the owner's personal assets can be attached by creditors for satisfaction of debts. If a firm incorporates, personal assets cannot be attached by creditors for payment of the firm's debts. In essence, by incorporation, the liability of the stockholders is limited, and the risk of the firm having insufficient assets to pay business debts is shifted to the creditors.

Insurance

For most people, insurance is the most practical method for handling a major risk. Although private insurance has several characteristics, three major characteristics should be emphasized. First, *risk transfer* is used because a pure risk is transferred to the insurer. Second, the *pooling technique* is used to spread the losses of the few over the entire group so that average loss is substituted for actual loss. Finally, the risk may be reduced by application of the *law of large numbers* by which an insurer can predict future loss experience with greater accuracy. Each of these characteristics is treated in greater detail in Chapter 2.

SUMMARY

- There is no single definition of risk. Risk traditionally has been defined as uncertainty concerning the occurrence of a loss.

- Objective risk is the relative variation of actual loss from expected loss. Subjective risk is uncertainty based on an individual's mental condition or state of mind. Chance of loss is defined as the probability that an event will occur; it is not the same thing as risk.

- Peril is defined as the cause of loss. Hazard is any condition that creates or increases the chance of loss. There are three major types of hazards. Physical hazard is a physical condition present that increases the chance of loss. Moral hazard is dishonesty or character defects in an individual that increase the chance of loss. Morale hazard is carelessness or indifference to a loss because of the existence of insurance.

- The basic categories of risk include the following:
    - Pure and speculative risks
    - Fundamental and particular risks

  A pure risk is a risk where there are only the possibilities of loss or no loss. A speculative risk is a risk where either profit or loss is possible.

  A fundamental risk is a risk that affects the entire economy or large numbers of persons or groups within the economy, such as inflation, war, or recession. A particular risk is a risk that affects only the individual and not the entire community or country.

- The following types of pure risk can threaten an individual's financial security:
    - Personal risks
    - Property risks
    - Liability risks

- Personal risks are those risks that directly affect an individual. Major personal risks include the following:
    - Risk of premature death
    - Risk of insufficient income during retirement
    - Risk of poor health
    - Risk of unemployment

- Property risks affect persons who own property. If property is damaged or lost, two principal types of losses may result:
    - Direct loss to property
    - Indirect, or consequential, loss

      A direct loss is a financial loss that results from the physical damage, destruction, or theft of the property.

      An indirect, or consequential, loss is a financial loss that results indirectly from the occurrence of a direct physical damage or theft loss. Examples of indirect losses are the loss of use of the property, loss of profits, loss of rents, and extra expenses.

- Liability risks are extremely important because there is no maximum upper limit on the amount of the loss, and if a person must pay damages, a lien can be placed on income and assets to satisfy a legal judgment; substantial legal defense costs and attorney fees may also be incurred.

- Risk entails three major burdens on society:
    - The size of an emergency fund must be increased.
    - Society is deprived of needed goods and services.
    - Worry and fear are present.

- There are five major methods of handling risk:
    Avoidance
    Loss control
    Retention
    Noninsurance transfers
    Insurance

KEY CONCEPTS AND TERMS

Avoidance	Noninsurance transfers
Chance of loss	Objective probability
Direct loss	Objective risk
Fundamental risk	Particular risk
Hazard	Peril
Hedging	Personal risks
Hold-harmless clause	Physical hazard
Human life value	Premature death
Incorporation	Property risks
Indirect, or consequential, loss	Pure risk
Law of large numbers	Retention
Liability risks	Risk
Loss control	Speculative risk
Moral hazard	Subjective probability
Morale hazard	Subjective risk

REVIEW QUESTIONS

1. Explain briefly the meaning of risk.

2. How does objective risk differ from subjective risk?

3. Define chance of loss.

4. Distinguish between an objective probability and a subjective probability.

5. Define peril, hazard, physical hazard, moral hazard, and morale hazard.

6. Explain the difference between pure and speculative risk and between fundamental and particular risk.

7. Identify the major types of pure risk that are associated with great financial insecurity.

8. Why is pure risk harmful to society?

9. What is the difference between a direct loss and an indirect, or consequential, loss?

10. Describe briefly the five major methods of handling risk. Give an example of each method.

APPLICATION QUESTIONS

1. Union Insurance received an application to provide property insurance on a frame dwelling located near an oil refinery in an industrial section of the city. In considering this property for insurance, the property insurer is concerned with risk, hazard, and chance of loss.
   a. Describe several risks to which the frame dwelling is exposed.
   b. Compare and contrast moral hazard and morale hazard with respect to property insurance on the frame dwelling. Give an example of each.

2. Assume that chance of loss is 3 percent for two different fleets of trucks. Explain how it is possible that objective risk for both fleets can be different even though the chance of loss is identical.

3. Identify the types of financial losses likely to be incurred by each of the following parties.
   a. A person who negligently injures another motorist in an auto accident
   b. A restaurant that is shut down for six months because of a tornado
   c. A family whose family head dies prematurely
   d. An attorney who fails to file a legal brief on time for a client
   e. A tenant whose apartment burns in a fire

4. Several methods are available for handling risk. However, certain techniques are more appropriate than others in a given situation.
   a. (1) Should retention be used in those situations where both loss frequency and loss severity are high? Explain your answer.
      (2) Explain why loss control is a highly desirable method for handling risk.
   b. Explain why chance of loss and risk are not the same thing.

5. Sarah operates a pawn shop in a large city. Her shop is in a high-crime area, and the high cost of burglary insurance is threatening the existence of her business. A trade association points out that several methods other than insurance can be used to handle the burglary exposure. Identify and illustrate three different noninsurance methods that might be used to deal with this exposure.

Case Application

Tyrone is a college senior who is majoring in journalism. He owns a high-mileage 1988 Ford that has a current market value of $900. The current replacement value of his clothes, television set, stereo set, and other personal property in a rented apartment total $5000. He wears disposable contact lenses, which cost $200 for a six-month supply. He also has a waterbed in his rented apartment that has leaked water in the past. An avid runner, Tyrone runs five miles daily in a nearby public park that has the reputation of being extremely dangerous because of drug dealers, numerous assaults and muggings, and drive-by shootings. Tyrone's parents both work to help him pay his tuition.

For each of the following risks or loss exposures, identify an appropriate risk management technique that could be used to deal with the exposure. Explain your answer.

a. Physical damage to the 1988 Ford because of a collision with another motorist
b. Liability lawsuit against Tyrone arising out of the negligent operation of his car
c. Total loss of clothes, television, stereo, and personal property because of a grease fire in the kitchen of his rented apartment
d. Disappearance of one contact lens
e. Waterbed leak that causes property damage to the apartment
f. Physical assault on Tyrone by gang members who are dealing drugs in the park where he runs
g. Loss of tuition from Tyrone's father who is killed by a drunk driver in an auto accident

SELECTED REFERENCES

Bernstein, Peter L. *Against the Gods, The Remarkable Story of Risk*. New York: John Wiley & Son, Inc., 1996.

Crowe, Robert M., and Ronald C. Horn. "The Meaning of Risk," *Journal of Risk and Insurance*, 34 (September 1967): 459–474.

Head, George L. "An Alternative to Defining Risk as Uncertainty," *Journal of Risk and Insurance*, 34 (June 1967): 205–214.

Rejda, George E. *Social Insurance and Economic Security*, 6th ed. Upper Saddle River, NJ: Prentice Hall, 1999, Chapter 1.

Rejda, George E., special ed. "Risk and Its Treatment: Changing Societal Consequences," *Annals of the American Academy of Political and Social Science*, 443 (May 1979): 1–144.

NOTES

1. Risk has also been defined as (1) variability in future outcomes, (2) chance of loss, (3) possibility of an adverse deviation from a desired outcome that is expected or hoped for, (4) the variation in possible outcomes that exist in a given situation, and (5) possibility that a sentient entity can incur a loss.

2. This section is based on George E. Rejda, *Social Insurance and Economic Security*, 6th ed. (Upper Saddle River, NJ: Prentice Hall, 1999), pp. 4–6.

3. U.S. Census Bureau, Current Population Reports, P60-206, *Money Income in the United States, 1998*, U.S. Government Printing Office, Washington, DC, 1999. Data calculated from Table 2, p. 5.

4. Ellen Graham, "Dreams of Cushy Retirement Clash with Meager Savings," *The Wall Street Journal*, December 12, 1997, p. R1.

5. Data based on the 1985 Commissioners Disability Table as cited in Edward E. Graves, ed., *McGill's Life Insurance*, 2nd ed. (Bryn Mawr, PA: The American College, 1998), Table 7-2, p. 168.

Students may take a self-administered test on this chapter at www.awlonline.com/rejda

Chapter 2

Insurance and Risk

Insurance: An ingenious modern game of chance in which the player is permitted to enjoy the comfortable conviction that he is beating the man who keeps the table.

Ambrose Bierce

Learning Objectives

After studying this chapter, you should be able to:

▲ Define insurance and explain the basic characteristics of insurance.

▲ Explain the law of large numbers.

▲ Describe the requirements of an insurable risk from the viewpoint of a private insurer.

▲ Identify the major insurable and uninsurable risks in our society.

▲ Describe the major types of insurance.

▲ Explain the social benefits and social costs of insurance.

▲ Access an Internet site and obtain premium quotes on insurance products that consumers typically purchase.

Internet Resources

- The **American Insurance Association (AIA)** is the leading property and casualty insurance trade association. It represents more than 375 companies writing in excess of $60 billion annually in premiums. The site lists available publications, position papers on important issues in property and casualty insurance, press releases, insurance-related links, and names of state insurance commissioners. Visit this site at:

  http://www.aiadc.org/

- The **Insurance Information Institute (III)** is an excellent site for obtaining information on property and liability insurance. III provides timely consumer information on auto, homeowners, and business insurance, submission of claims and rebuilding after catastrophes, and ways to save money. The site contains background material and information for the news media, including television, newspapers, and radio. Visit this important site at:

  http://www.iii.org/

- **Insurance News Network** provides timely consumer information on new developments in auto, home, life, and health insurance. The site provides information on annuities, insurance company ratings, and state insurance regulations. The site also has a complaint finder, lawsuit library, links to other sites, and reader forums. The insurance News Network is an excellent source for background material. Visit this site at:

http://www.insure.com/

- **InsWeb** operates an online insurance marketplace that enables consumers to get quotes for numerous insurance products, including auto, homeowners, and renters insurance, term insurance, and individual health insurance. The site also provides press releases, stock quotes and other financial information, corporate fact sheets, and testimonials about InsWeb's shopping service. Overall, it is an excellent source of information for consumers. Visit this site at:

http://www.insweb.com

- The **Life and Health Insurance Foundation for Education (LIFE)** is a nonprofit organization that addresses the public's growing need for information on life, health, and disability insurance. LIFE also stresses the important role that agents play in helping individuals, families, and business firms find those insurance products that best meet their needs. The site provides an introduction to insurance concepts and terminology. A life insurance calculator estimates the amount of life insurance needed by asking a number of interactive questions. Visit this site at:

http://life-line.org/

- The **National Association of Mutual Insurance Companies** is a trade association that represents mutual insurance companies involved in property and casualty insurance. Visit this site at:

http://www.namic.org

- **Quicken Insurance** is one of the best insurance information and buying sites on the Internet. The site provides information on life, health, auto, homeowners, disability income, and long-term care insurance, as well as annuities. It offers coverage information and quotes, plus agent referral or direct sign-up data from major insurers. Visit this site at:

http://www.quickeninsurance.com

 ennifer and Mark graduated from a large Midwestern university, married, and moved to Phoenix, Arizona. Like many married couples, they wanted to save money for a down payment on a home. Shortly after they moved into a rented apartment, however, a burglar broke into their home and stole a new television set, stereo, camera, jewelry, silverware, and cash stashed in a jewelry box. The loss totaled $7200. The couple had no insurance. As a result, their goal of accumulating a down payment for a home received a serious setback. What went wrong? The couple made the serious mistake of paying inadequate attention to risk and insurance in their financial plans.

In Chapter 1, we identified major risks that cause financial insecurity. For most people, insurance is the most important technique for handling risk. Consequently, you should understand how insurance works. This chapter discusses the basic characteristics of insurance, requirements of an insurable risk, major type of insurance, and social benefits and social costs of insurance.

DEFINITION OF INSURANCE

There is no single definition of insurance. Insurance can be defined from the viewpoint of several disciplines, including law, economics, history, actuarial science, risk theory, and sociology. But each possible definition will not be examined at this point. Instead, we will examine those common elements that are typically present in any insurance plan. However, before proceeding, a working definition of insurance—one that captures the essential characteristics of a true insurance plan—must be established.

After careful study, the Commission on Insurance Terminology of the American Risk and Insurance Association has defined insurance as follows.[1] **Insurance** *is the pooling of fortuitous losses by transfer of such risks to insurers, who agree to indemnify insureds for such losses, to provide other pecuniary benefits on their occurrence, or to render services connected with the risk.* Although this definition may not be acceptable to all insurance scholars, it is useful for analyzing the common elements of a true insurance plan.

BASIC CHARACTERISTICS OF INSURANCE

Based on the preceding definition, an insurance plan or arrangement typically has certain characteristics. They include the following:

- Pooling of losses
- Payment of fortuitous losses
- Risk transfer
- Indemnification

Pooling of Losses

Pooling or the sharing of losses is the heart of insurance. **Pooling** *is the spreading of losses incurred by the few over the entire group, so that in the process, average loss is substituted for actual loss.* In addition, pooling involves the grouping of a large number of exposure units so that the law of large numbers can operate to provide a substantially accurate prediction of future losses. Ideally, there should be a large number of similar, but not necessarily identical, exposure units that are subject to the same perils. Thus, pool-

ing implies (1) the sharing of losses by the entire group, and (2) prediction of future losses with some accuracy based on the law of large numbers.

With respect to the first concept—loss sharing—consider this simple example. Assume that 1000 farmers in southeastern Kansas agree that if any farmer's home is damaged or destroyed by a fire, the other members of the group will indemnify, or cover, the actual costs of the unlucky farmer who has a loss. Assume also that each home is worth $100,000, and, on average, one home burns each year. In the absence of insurance, the maximum loss to each farmer is $100,000 if the home should burn. However, by pooling the loss, it can be spread over the entire group, and if one farmer has a total loss, the maximum amount that each farmer must pay is only $100 ($100,000/1000). In effect, the pooling technique results in the substitution of an average loss of $100 for the actual loss of $100,000.

In addition, by pooling or combining the loss experience of a large number of exposure units, an insurer may be able to predict future losses with greater accuracy. From the viewpoint of the insurer, if future losses can be predicted, objective risk is reduced. Thus, another characteristic often found in many lines of insurance is risk reduction based on the law of large numbers.

The **law of large numbers** *states that the greater the number of exposures, the more closely will the actual results approach the probable results that are expected from an infinite number of exposures.*[2] For example, if you flip a balanced coin into the air, the *a priori* probability of getting a head is 0.5. If you flip the coin only ten times, you may get a head eight times. Although the observed probability of getting a head is 0.8, the true probability is still 0.5. If the coin were flipped 1 million times, however, the actual number of heads would be approximately 500,000. Thus, as the number of random tosses increases, the actual results approach the expected results.

A practical illustration of the law of large numbers is the National Safety Council's prediction of the number of motor vehicle deaths during a typical holiday weekend. Because millions of vehicles are on the road, the National Safety Council has been able to predict with some accuracy the number of motorists who will die during a typical July 4 holiday weekend. For example, 500 to 700 motorists may be expected to die during a typical July 4 weekend. Although individual motorists cannot be identified, the actual number of deaths for the group of motorists as a whole can be predicted with some accuracy.

However, for most insurance lines, the actuary seldom knows the true probability and severity of loss. Therefore, estimates of both the average frequency and the average severity of loss must be based on previous loss experience. If there are a large number of exposure units, the actual loss experience of the past may be a good approximation of future losses. As noted in Chapter 1, objective risk varies inversely with the square root of the number of cases under observation: as the number of exposures increases, the relative variation of actual loss from expected loss will decline. Thus, the insurer can predict future losses with a greater degree of accuracy as the number of exposures increases. This concept is important because an insurer must charge a premium that will be adequate for paying all losses and expenses during the policy period. The lower the degree of objective risk, the more confidence an insurer has that the actual premium charged will be sufficient to pay all claims and expenses and provide a margin for profit.

A more rigorous statement of the law of large numbers can be found in the Appendix at the end of this chapter.

Payment of Fortuitous Losses

A second characteristic of private insurance is the payment of fortuitous losses. A **fortuitous loss** *is one that is unforeseen and unexpected and occurs as a result of chance*. In other words, the loss must be accidental. The law of large numbers is based on the assumption that losses are accidental and occur randomly. For example, a person may slip on an icy sidewalk and break a leg. The loss would be fortuitous.

Risk Transfer

Risk transfer is another essential element of insurance. With the exception of self-insurance,[3] a true insurance plan always involves risk transfer. **Risk transfer** *means that a pure risk is transferred from the insured to the insurer, who typically is in a stronger financial position to pay the loss than the insured.* From the viewpoint of the individual, pure risks that

are typically transferred to insurers include the risk of premature death, poor health, disability, destruction and theft of property, and liability lawsuits.

Indemnification

A final characteristic of insurance is indemnification for losses. **Indemnification** *means that the insured is restored to his or her approximate financial position prior to the occurrence of the loss.* Thus, if your home burns in a fire, a homeowner's insurance policy will indemnify you or restore you to your previous position. If you are sued because of the negligent operation of an automobile, your auto liability insurance policy will pay those sums that you are legally obligated to pay. Similarly, if you become seriously disabled, a disability-income insurance policy will restore at least part of the lost wages.

REQUIREMENTS OF AN INSURABLE RISK

Insurers normally insure only pure risks. However, not all pure risks are insurable. Certain requirements usually must be fulfilled before a pure risk can be privately insured. From the viewpoint of the insurer, there are ideally six requirements of an insurable risk.

- There must be a large number of exposure units.
- The loss must be accidental and unintentional.
- The loss must be determinable and measurable.
- The loss should not be catastrophic.
- The chance of loss must be calculable.
- The premium must be economically feasible.

Large Number of Exposure Units

The first requirement of an insurable risk is a large number of exposure units. Ideally, there should be a large group of roughly similar, but not necessarily identical, exposure units that are subject to the same peril or group of perils. For example, a large number of frame dwellings in a city can be grouped together for purposes of providing property insurance on the dwellings.

The purpose of this first requirement is to enable the insurer to predict loss based on the law of large numbers. Loss data can be compiled over time, and losses for the group as a whole can be predicted with some accuracy. The loss costs can then be spread over all insureds in the underwriting class.

Accidental and Unintentional Loss

A second requirement is that the loss should be accidental and unintentional; ideally, the loss should be fortuitous and outside the insured's control. Thus, if an individual deliberately causes a loss, he or she should not be indemnified for the loss.

The requirement of an accidental and unintentional loss is necessary for two reasons. First, if intentional losses were paid, moral hazard would be substantially increased, and premiums would rise as a result. The substantial increase in premiums could result in relatively fewer persons purchasing the insurance, and the insurer might not have a sufficient number of exposure units to predict future losses.

Second, the loss should be accidental because the law of large numbers is based on the random occurrence of events. A deliberately caused loss is not a random event because the insured knows when the loss will occur. Thus, prediction of future experience may be highly inaccurate if a large number of intentional or nonrandom losses occur.

Determinable and Measurable Loss

A third requirement is that the loss should be both determinable and measurable. This means the loss should be definite as to cause, time, place, and amount. Life insurance in most cases meets this requirement easily. The cause and time of death can be readily determined in most cases, and if the person is insured, the face amount of the life insurance policy is the amount paid.

Some losses, however, are difficult to determine and measure. For example, under a disability-income policy, the insurer promises to pay a monthly benefit to the disabled person if the definition of disability stated in the policy is satisfied. Some dishonest claimants may deliberately fake sickness or injury to collect from the insurer. Even if the claim is legitimate, the insurer must still determine whether the insured satisfies the definition of disability stated in the policy. Sickness and disability are highly subjective,

and the same event can affect two persons quite differently. For example, two accountants who are insured under separate disability-income contracts may be injured in an auto accident, and both may be classified as totally disabled. One accountant, however, may be stronger willed and more determined to return to work. If that accountant undergoes rehabilitation and returns to work, the disability-income benefits will terminate. Meanwhile, the other accountant would still continue to receive disability-income benefits according to the terms of the policy. In short, it is difficult to determine when a person is actually disabled. However, all losses ideally should be both determinable and measurable.

The basic purpose of this requirement is to enable an insurer to determine if the loss is covered under the policy, and if it is covered, how much should be paid. For example, Shannon has an expensive fur coat that is insured under a homeowners policy. It makes a great deal of difference to the insurer if a thief breaks into her home and steals the coat, or the coat is missing because her husband stored it in a dry-cleaning establishment but forgot to tell her. The loss is covered in the first example but not in the second.

No Catastrophic Loss

The fourth requirement is that ideally the loss should not be catastrophic. This means that a large proportion of exposure units should not incur losses at the same time. As we stated earlier, pooling is the essence of insurance. If most or all of the exposure units in a certain class simultaneously incur a loss, then the pooling technique breaks down and becomes unworkable. Premiums must be increased to prohibitive levels, and the insurance technique is no longer a viable arrangement by which losses of the few are spread over the entire group.

Insurers ideally wish to avoid all catastrophic losses. In the real world, this is impossible, because catastrophic losses periodically result from floods, hurricanes, tornadoes, earthquakes, forest fires, and other natural disasters. Fortunately, several approaches are available for meeting the problem of a catastrophic loss. First, reinsurance can be used by which insurance companies are indemnified by reinsurers for catastrophic losses. **Reinsurance** *is the shifting of part or all of the insurance originally writ-*

ten by one insurer to another insurer. The reinsurer is then responsible for the payment of its share of the loss. Reinsurance is discussed in greater detail in Chapter 26.

Second, insurers can avoid the concentration of risk by *dispersing their coverage over a large geographical area.* The concentration of loss exposures in a geographical area exposed to frequent floods, tornadoes, hurricanes, or other natural disasters can result in periodic catastrophic losses. If the loss exposures are geographically dispersed, the possibility of a catastrophic loss is reduced.

Finally, new financial instruments are now available for dealing with catastrophic losses. These instruments include catastrophe bonds and options sold on the Chicago Board of Trade. These new financial instruments are discussed in Chapter 26.

Calculable Chance of Loss

Another important requirement is that the chance of loss should be calculable. The insurer must be able to calculate both the average frequency and the average severity of future losses with some accuracy. This requirement is necessary so that a proper premium can be charged that is sufficient to pay all claims and expenses and yield a profit during the policy period.

Certain losses, however, are difficult to insure because the chance of loss cannot be accurately estimated, and the potential for a catastrophic loss is present. For example, floods, wars, and cyclical unemployment occur on an irregular basis, and prediction of the average frequency and the severity of losses is difficult. Thus, without government assistance, these losses are difficult for private carriers to insure.

Economically Feasible Premium

A final requirement is that the premium should be economically feasible. The insured must be able to afford to pay the premium. In addition, for the insurance to be an attractive purchase, the premiums paid must be substantially less than the face value, or amount, of the policy.

To have an economically feasible premium, the chance of loss must be relatively low. One view is that if the chance of loss exceeds 40 percent, the cost

of the policy will exceed the amount that the insurer must pay under the contract. For example, an insurer could issue a $1000 life insurance policy on a man age 99, but the pure premium would be about $980, and an additional amount for expenses would have to be added. The total premium would exceed the face amount of the insurance.[4]

Based on these requirements, personal risks, property risks, and liability risks can be privately insured, because the requirements of an insurable risk generally can be met. By contrast, *most market risks, financial risks, production risks, and political risks are usually uninsurable by private insurers.*[5] These risks are uninsurable for several reasons. First, they are speculative and so are difficult to insure privately. Second, the potential of each to produce a catastrophic loss is great; this is particularly true for political risks, such as the risk of war. Finally, calculation of the proper premium for such risks may be difficult because the chance of loss cannot be accurately estimated. For example, insurance that protects a retailer against loss because of a change in consumer tastes, such as a style change, generally is not available. Accurate loss data are not available, and there is no accurate way to calculate a premium. The premium charged may or may not be adequate to pay all losses and expenses. Since private insurers are in business to make a profit, certain risks are uninsurable because of the possibility of substantial losses.

TWO APPLICATIONS: THE RISKS OF FIRE AND UNEMPLOYMENT

You will understand more clearly the requirements of an insurable risk if you can apply these requirements to a specific risk. For example, consider the risk of fire to a private dwelling. This risk can be privately insured because the requirements of an insurable risk are generally fulfilled (see Exhibit 2.1).

Consider next the risk of unemployment, which generally is not privately insurable at the present time. How well does the risk of unemployment meet the requirements of an insurable risk? As is evident in Exhibit 2.2, the risk of unemployment does not completely meet the requirements.

First, predicting unemployment is difficult because of the different types of unemployment and labor. There are professional, highly skilled, semi-

EXHIBIT 2.1
Risk of Fire as an Insurable Risk

Requirements	Does the risk of fire satisfy the requirements?
1. Large number of exposure units	Yes. Numerous exposure units are present.
2. Accidental and unintentional loss	Yes. With the exception of arson, most fire losses are accidental and unintentional.
3. Determinable and measurable loss	Yes. If there is disagreement over the amount paid, a property insurance policy has provisions for resolving disputes.
4. No catastrophic loss	Yes. Although catastrophic fires have occurred, all exposure units normally do not burn at the same time.
5. Calculable chance of loss	Yes. Chance of fire can be calculated, and the average severity of a fire loss can be estimated in advance.
6. Economically feasible premium	Yes. Premium rate per $100 of fire insurance is relatively low.

skilled, unskilled, blue-collar, and white-collar workers. Moreover, unemployment rates vary significantly by occupation, age, gender, education, marital status, city, state, and by a host of other factors, including government programs and economic policies that frequently change. Also, the duration of unemployment varies widely among the different groups. In addition, because a large number of workers can become unemployed at the same time, a potential catastrophic loss is present. And because the different types of unemployment occur irregularly, it is difficult to calculate the chance of loss accurately. For these reasons, the risk of unemployment generally is not privately insurable, but it can be insured by social insurance programs. Social insurance programs are discussed later in the chapter.

ADVERSE SELECTION AND INSURANCE

When insurance is sold, insurers must deal with the problem of adverse selection. **Adverse selection** *is the tendency of persons with a higher-than-average chance of loss to seek insurance at standard (average) rates, which if not controlled by underwriting, results in higher-than-expected loss levels.* For example, adverse selection can result from high-risk drivers who seek auto insurance at standard rates, from

persons with serious health problems who seek life or health insurance at standard rates, and from business firms that have been repeatedly robbed or burglarized and that seek crime insurance at standard rates. If the applicants for insurance with a higher-than-average chance of loss succeed in obtaining the coverage at standard rates, we say that the insurer is "adversely selected against." If not controlled by underwriting, adverse selection can result in higher-than-expected loss levels.

Although adverse selection can never be completely eliminated, it can be controlled by careful underwriting. **Underwriting** *refers to the process of selecting and classifying applicants for insurance.* Applicants who meet the underwriting standards are insured at standard rates. If the underwriting standards are not met, the insurance is denied or an extra premium must be paid. Insurers frequently sell insurance to applicants who have a higher-than-average chance of loss, but such applicants must pay higher premiums. The problem of adverse selection arises when applicants with a higher-than-average chance of loss succeed in obtaining the coverage at standard or average rates.

Policy provisions are also used to control adverse selection. Examples are the suicide clause in life insurance and the preexisting conditions clause in health insurance. These policy provisions are dis-

EXHIBIT 2.2
Risk of Unemployment as an Insurable Risk

Requirements	Does the risk of unemployment satisfy the requirements?
1. Large number of exposure units	Not completely. Although there are a large number of employees, predicting unemployment is difficult because of the different types of unemployment and labor.
2. Accidental and unintentional loss	No. A large proportion of unemployment is due to individuals who voluntarily quit their jobs.
3. Determinable and measurable loss	Not completely. The level of unemployment can be determined, but the measurement of loss is difficult. Some unemployment is involuntary; however, some unemployment is voluntary.
4. No catastrophic loss	No. A severe national recession or depressed local business conditions could result in a catastrophic loss.
5. Calculable chance of loss	No. The different types of unemployment generally are too irregular to estimate the chance of loss accurately.
6. Economically feasible premium	No. Adverse selection, moral hazard, and the potential for a catastrophic loss could make the premium unattractive.

cussed in greater detail later in the text when specific insurance contracts are analyzed.

INSURANCE AND GAMBLING COMPARED

Insurance is often erroneously confused with gambling. There are two important differences between them. *First, gambling creates a new speculative risk, while insurance is a technique for handling an already existing pure risk*. Thus, if you bet $300 on a horse race, a new speculative risk is created, but if you pay $300 to an insurer for fire insurance, the risk of fire is already present and is transferred to the insurer by a contract. No new risk is created by the transaction.

The second difference between insurance and gambling is that gambling is socially unproductive, because the winner's gain comes at the expense of the loser. In contrast, insurance is always socially productive, because neither the insurer nor the insured is placed in a position where the gain of the winner comes at the expense of the loser. The insurer and the insured both have a common interest in the prevention of a loss. Both parties win if the loss does not occur. Moreover, gambling transactions never restore the losers to their former finan-

cial position. In contrast, insurance contracts restore the insureds financially in whole or in part if a loss occurs.

INSURANCE AND HEDGING COMPARED

In Chapter 1, we discussed the concept of hedging, by which risk can be transferred to a speculator through purchase of a futures contract. An insurance contract, however, is not the same thing as hedging. Although both techniques are similar in that risk is transferred by a contract, and no new risk is created, there are some important differences between them. *First, an insurance transaction involves the transfer of insurable risks, because the requirements of an insurable risk generally can be met*. However, hedging is a technique for handling risks that are typically uninsurable, such as protection against a decline in the price of agricultural products and raw materials.

A second difference between insurance and hedging is that insurance can reduce the objective risk of an insurer by application of the law of large numbers. As the number of exposure units increases, the insurer's prediction of future losses improves, because the relative variation of actual loss from expected loss will decline. Thus, many insurance transactions reduce objective risk. In contrast, hedging typically involves only risk transfer, not risk reduction. The risk of adverse price fluctuations is transferred to speculators who believe they can make a profit because of superior knowledge of market conditions. The risk is transferred, not reduced, and prediction of loss generally is not based on the law of large numbers.

TYPES OF INSURANCE

Insurance can be classified as either private or government insurance. Private insurance, in turn, can be classified into life and health insurance and property and liability insurance. Government insurance can be classified into social insurance programs and all other government insurance plans. Thus, the major types of insurance, both private and public, can be classified as follows:

- Private insurance
    Life and health insurance
    Property and liability insurance
- Government insurance
    Social insurance
    Other government insurance

Private Insurance

Life and Health Insurance At the end of 1998, the number of United States life insurers totaled 1563.[6] These insurers are extremely important in providing financial security to individuals and families.

Life insurers pay death benefits to designated beneficiaries when the insured dies. The death benefits are designed to pay for funeral expenses, uninsured medical bills, estate taxes, and other expenses as a result of death. The death proceeds can also be arranged to provide periodic income payments to the deceased's dependents. Life insurers also sell both group and individual retirement plans that pay retirement benefits. In addition, life and health insurers sell individual and group health insurance plans that cover medical expenses from sickness or injury. Finally, both types of insurers sell disability-income coverages that pay income benefits during a period of disability.

Property and Liability Insurance At the end of 1997, 3366 property and liability insurers were operating in the United States.[7] Property and liability insurers can be classified by the types of insurance sold. The major types of insurance sold are listed in Exhibit 2.3 and discussed next.

1. *Fire insurance and allied lines.* Fire insurance covers the loss or damage to real estate and personal property because of fire, lightning, or removal from the premises. Other perils can be added, such as windstorm, hail, tornadoes, and vandalism. Indirect losses can also be covered, including the loss of profits and rents and the extra expenses incurred as a result of a loss from the interruption of business.
2. *Marine insurance.* Marine insurance is often called transportation insurance because it covers goods in transit against most pure risks connected with transportation.

    Marine insurance is divided into ocean marine and inland marine insurance. **Ocean marine insurance** provides protection for all types of ocean-going vessels and their cargoes. Ocean marine insurance is also used to insure vessels and cargo

EXHIBIT 2.3
Property and Liability Insurance

1. Fire insurance and allied lines
2. Marine insurance
   - Ocean marine
   - Inland marine
3. Casualty insurance
   - Automobile insurance
   - General liability insurance
   - Burglary and theft insurance
   - Workers compensation
   - Glass insurance
   - Boiler and machinery insurance
   - Nuclear insurance
   - Crop-hail insurance
   - Health insurance
   - Other miscellaneous lines
4. Multiple-line insurance
5. Fidelity and surety bonds

that sail on the Great Lakes and navigable water-ways in the United States. Contracts can also be written to cover the legal liability of the owners and shippers.

Inland marine insurance provides coverage for goods being shipped on land. This coverage includes imports, exports, domestic shipments, and the means of transportation (for example, bridges, tunnels, and pipelines). In addition, inland marine insurance covers personal property such as fine art, jewelry, and furs.

3. *Casualty insurance.* **Casualty insurance** is a broad field of insurance and covers whatever is not covered by fire, marine, and life insurers.

Automobile insurance covers legal liability arising out of the ownership or operation of an automobile and also provides physical damage insurance on the automobile, medical payments insurance, and protection against uninsured motorists.

General liability insurance covers legal liability arising out of property damage or bodily injury to others. Legal liability may arise out of the ownership of business property, sales or distribution of products, manufacturing or contracting operations, and professional services.

Burglary and theft insurance covers the loss of property, money, and securities because of burglary, robbery, larceny, and other crime perils.

Workers compensation insurance covers workers for a job-related accident or disease. The insurance pays for medical bills, disability-income benefits, and death benefits to dependents of an employee whose death is job related.

Glass insurance provides broad coverage for glass breakage in covered buildings. **Boiler and machinery insurance** is a highly specialized commercial line that covers boilers, turbines, generators, and other power-producing equipment. **Nuclear insurance** provides protection against losses resulting from nuclear accidents. **Crop-hail insurance** covers the loss of crops because of hail storms and other perils. **Health insurance** similar to the coverages provided by life and health insurers is also sold by casualty insurers. Other miscellaneous lines include **title insurance**, which covers a financial loss because of a legal defect in the title to real estate, and **credit insurance**, which covers

manufacturers and wholesalers against loss because an account receivable is not collected.

4. *Multiple-line insurance.* **Multiple-line insurance** combines both property and casualty coverages into one contract. All states have passed multiple-line legislation that permits insurers to write fire and casualty lines in one contract. For example, a homeowners policy combines fire insurance and other perils with liability insurance in one contract.

5. *Fidelity and surety bonds.* **Fidelity bonds** provide protection against loss caused by the dishonest or fraudulent acts of employees, such as embezzlement and theft of money. **Surety bonds** provide for monetary compensation in case of failure by bonded persons to perform certain acts, such as the failure of a contractor to construct a building on time.

Government Insurance

Numerous government insurance programs are in operation at the present time. Government insurance can be divided into social insurance programs and other government insurance programs.

Social Insurance Social insurance programs are government insurance programs with certain characteristics that distinguish them from other government insurance plans. These programs are financed entirely or in large part by mandatory contributions from employers, employees, or both, and not primarily by the general revenues of government. The contributions are usually earmarked for special funds that are kept separate from ordinary government accounts; the benefits, in turn, are paid from these funds. In addition, the right to receive benefits is ordinarily derived from or linked to the recipient's past contributions or coverage under the program; the benefits and contributions generally vary among the beneficiaries according to their prior earnings, but the benefits are heavily weighted in favor of low-income groups. Moreover, most social insurance programs are compulsory; certain covered workers and employers are required by law to pay contributions and participate in the programs. Finally, qualifying conditions and benefit rights are usually prescribed exactly by statute, leaving little room for administrative discretion in the award of benefits.[8]

Major social insurance programs in the United States include the following:

- Old-Age, Survivors, and Disability Insurance (Social Security)
- Medicare
- Unemployment insurance
- Workers compensation
- Compulsory temporary disability insurance
- Railroad Retirement Act
- Railroad Unemployment Insurance Act

Old-Age, Survivors, and Disability Insurance, commonly known as Social Security, is a massive income-maintenance program that provides retirement, survivor, and disability benefits to eligible individuals and families.

Medicare is part of the total Social Security program and covers the medical expenses of most people age 65 and older and certain disabled people younger than age 65.

Unemployment insurance programs provide weekly cash benefits to eligible workers who experience short-term involuntary unemployment. Regular state unemployment benefits are typically paid up to 26 weeks after certain eligibility requirements are met. Extended benefits also may be available to unemployed workers who exhaust their regular benefits.

As noted earlier, *workers compensation insurance* covers workers against a job-related accident or disease. Although workers compensation is a casualty line sold by private insurers, it is also an important form of social insurance. The social insurance aspects of workers compensation are discussed in Chapter 24.

In addition, *compulsory temporary disability insurance*, which exists in five states, Puerto Rico, and the railroad industry, provides for the partial replacement of wages that may be lost because of a temporary nonoccupational disability.[9] The *Railroad Retirement Act* provides retirement benefits, survivor benefits, and disability income benefits to railroad workers who meet certain eligibility requirements. Finally, the *Railroad Unemployment Insurance Act* provides unemployment and sickness benefits to railroad employees.

Other Government Insurance Programs Other government insurance programs exist at both the federal and state level. However, these programs do not have the distinguishing characteristics of social insurance programs. Important federal insurance programs include the Federal Employees Retirement System, the Civil Service Retirement System, various life insurance programs for veterans, pension termination insurance, insurance on checking and savings accounts in commercial banks and saving and loan associations (Federal Deposit Insurance Corporation), federal flood insurance, federal crop insurance, and numerous other programs.

Government insurance programs also exist at the state level. These programs include the Wisconsin State Life Fund, title insurance programs in a few states, and the Maryland Automobile Insurance Fund. In addition, competitive and monopoly workers compensation funds are in operation in several states. Finally, the majority of states have special health insurance pools that make health insurance available to persons who are uninsurable or substandard in health.

BENEFITS OF INSURANCE TO SOCIETY

The major social and economic benefits of insurance include the following:

- Indemnification for loss
- Less worry and fear
- Source of investment funds
- Loss prevention
- Enhancement of credit

Indemnification for Loss

Indemnification permits individuals and families to be restored to their former financial position after a loss occurs. As a result, they can maintain their financial security. Because insureds are restored either in part or in whole after a loss occurs, they are less likely to apply for public assistance or welfare, or to seek financial assistance from relatives and friends.

Indemnification to business firms also permits firms to remain in business and employees to keep their jobs. Suppliers continue to receive orders, and customers can still receive the goods and services they desire. The community also benefits because its tax base is not eroded. In short, the indemnification function contributes greatly to family and business stability and therefore is one of the most important social and economic benefits of insurance.

Less Worry and Fear

A second benefit of insurance is that worry and fear are reduced. This is true both before and after a loss. For example, if family heads have adequate amounts of life insurance, they are less likely to worry about the financial security of their dependents in the event of premature death; persons insured for long-term disability do not have to worry about the loss of earnings if a serious illness or accident occurs; and property owners who are insured enjoy greater peace of mind because they know they are covered if a loss occurs. Worry and fear are also reduced after a loss occurs, because the insureds know that they have insurance that will pay for the loss.

Source of Investment Funds

The insurance industry is an important source of funds for capital investment and accumulation. Premiums are collected in advance of the loss, and funds not needed to pay immediate losses and expenses can be loaned to business firms. These funds typically are invested in shopping centers, hospitals, factories, housing developments, and new machinery and equipment. The investments increase society's stock of capital goods, and promote economic growth and full employment. Insurers also invest in social investments, such as housing, nursing homes, and economic development projects. In addition, because the total supply of loanable funds is increased by the advance payment of insurance premiums, the cost of capital to business firms that borrow is lower than it would be in the absence of insurance.

Loss Prevention

Insurance companies are actively involved in numerous loss-prevention programs and also employ a wide variety of loss-prevention personnel, including safety engineers and specialists in fire prevention, occupational safety and health, and products liability. Some important loss-prevention activities that property and liability insurers strongly support include the following:

- Highway safety and reduction of automobile deaths
- Fire prevention
- Reduction of work-related disabilities
- Prevention of auto thefts
- Prevention and detection of arson losses
- Prevention of defective products that could injure the user
- Prevention of boiler explosions
- Educational programs on loss prevention

The loss-prevention activities reduce both direct and indirect, or consequential, losses. Society benefits, since both types of losses are reduced.

Enhancement of Credit

A final benefit is that insurance enhances a person's credit. Insurance makes a borrower a better credit risk because it guarantees the value of the borrower's collateral or gives greater assurance that the loan will be repaid. For example, when a house is purchased, the lending institution normally requires property insurance on the house before the mortgage loan is granted. The property insurance protects the lender's financial interest if the property is damaged or destroyed. Similarly, a business firm seeking a temporary loan for Christmas or seasonal business may be required to insure its inventories before the loan is made. And if a new car is purchased and financed by a bank or other lending institution, physical damage insurance on the car may be required before the loan is made. Thus, insurance can enhance a person's credit.

COSTS OF INSURANCE TO SOCIETY

Although the insurance industry provides enormous social and economic benefits to society, the social costs of insurance must also be recognized. The major social costs of insurance include the following:

- Cost of doing business
- Fraudulent claims
- Inflated claims

Cost of Doing Business

One important cost is the cost of doing business. Insurers consume scarce economic resources—land, labor, capital, and business enterprise—in providing insurance to society. In financial terms, an expense loading must be added to the pure premium to cover the expenses incurred by companies in their daily operations. An **expense loading** *is the amount needed to pay all expenses, including commissions, general administrative expenses, state premium taxes, acquisition expenses, and an allowance for contingencies and profit.* Sales and administrative expenses of property and liability insurers consume 25 cents of each premium dollar, whereas operating expenses of life insurers account for about 11 percent of total expenditures.[10] As a result, total costs to society are increased. For example, assume that a small country with no property insurance has an average of $100 million of fire losses each year. Also assume that property insurance later becomes available, and the expense loading is 35 percent of losses. Thus, total costs to this country are increased to $135 million.

However, these additional costs can be justified for several reasons. First, from the insured's viewpoint, uncertainty concerning the payment of a covered loss is reduced because of insurance. Second, the costs of doing business are not necessarily wasteful, because insurers engage in a wide variety of loss prevention activities. Finally, the insurance industry provides jobs to millions of workers in the United States. However, because economic resources are used up in providing insurance to society, a real economic cost is incurred.

Fraudulent Claims

A second cost of insurance comes from the submission of fraudulent claims. Examples of fraudulent claims include the following:

- Auto accidents are faked or staged to collect benefits.

- Dishonest claimants fake slip-and-fall accidents.
- Phony burglaries, thefts, or acts of vandalism are reported to insurers.
- False health insurance claims are submitted to collect benefits.
- Dishonest policyowners take out life insurance policies on insureds who are later reported as having died (see Insight 2.1).

Numerous additional fraudulent acts are possible (see Exhibit 2.4, on page 32). The payment of such fraudulent claims results in higher premiums to all insureds. The existence of insurance also prompts some insureds to deliberately cause a loss so as to profit from insurance. These social costs fall directly on society.

Inflated Claims

Another cost of insurance relates to the submission of inflated or "padded" claims. Although the loss is not intentionally caused by the insured, the dollar amount of the claim may exceed the actual financial loss. Examples of inflated claims include the following:

- Attorneys for plaintiffs sue for high liability judgments that exceed the true economic loss of the victim.
- Insureds inflate the amount of damage in automobile collision claims so that the insurance payments will cover the collision deductible.
- Disabled persons often malinger to collect disability-income benefits for a longer duration.

Inflated claims must be recognized as an important social cost of insurance. Premiums must be increased to pay the additional losses. As a result, disposable income and the consumption of other goods and services are reduced.

Cost of Fraudulent and Inflated Claims

Some organizations have attempted to estimate the cost of fraudulent and inflated insurance claims. A 1996 study by Conning and Company estimated that fraud cost the entire insurance industry, including the health and life insurance sectors, $120 billion in 1995. The health insurance sector accounted for al-

Insight 2.1

Woman Sentenced in Insurance Scam

A 60-year-old woman received a two-year prison term for concocting an insurance scheme in which she took out 79 insurance policies, then hoped to collect by claiming that her husband had died.

Bonnie McCaslin of Hastings, Neb., tried to make claims on about 20 of the policies. She would have received $1.86 million if she had succeeded.

The man she claimed was her dead husband was her ex-husband, Timothy, who is an insurance agent in California. He was not involved in his ex-wife's scheme. Court papers indicate that McCaslin or her son, Michael, 31, forged the ex-husband's name on application forms.

The McCaslins made no money from their plan. They tried to obtain a death certificate for Timothy McCaslin from various hospitals and coroners, claiming

that the man had died in natural disasters such as earthquakes and hurricanes.

Bonnie McCaslin and her public defender, Shannon O'Connor, worked out a plea agreement with the U.S. Attorney's Office. O'Connor said the two-year sentence was appropriate considering the odds that the scheme would succeed. "The plan was so ludicrous on its face that they (insurance companies) were never going to lose a dime," O'Connor said after U.S. District Judge Joseph Bataillon sentenced McCaslin.

McCaslin already is serving a state prison sentence for committing perjury and violating her parole with the insurance scheme. The federal and state prison time will be served concurrently.

SOURCE: Adaptation of Rick Ruggles, "Woman Sentenced in Insurance Scam," *Omaha World Herald*, February 27, 1998, p. 13.

most 80 percent of total fraudulent claims ($95 billion). *The Conning study also estimated that 25 percent of workers compensation losses are attributable to fraud; in automobile liability and physical damage insurance, fraud accounted for 10 percent of the losses.*[11]

Another study by the Insurance Research Council showed that one-third of all auto insurance bodily injury claims include some portion of fraud, but only 3 percent are totally fraudulent claims that result from fake auto accidents and injuries. The remaining bodily injury claims included "padding" or exaggeration of injuries from actual accidents. *When translated into dollars, the fraudulent portion of these claims amounted to 17 to 20 cents for each premium dollar paid.*[12]

Public Attitudes Toward Fraud

A recent national survey sponsored by the Insurance Research Council found that many Americans have a lax and permissive attitude toward insurance fraud. *More than one in three Americans (36 percent) be-*

lieve it is acceptable to overstate an insurance claim to make up for the premiums paid in the past, a considerable rise from the 19 percent who held such an attitude in 1993. Forty percent of the respondents believe it is acceptable to pad an insurance claim to offset the deductible that may have to be paid, up from 23 percent in 1993.[13]

Two points help explain these views.[14] First, many Americans seem to have a sense of entitlement toward insurers. Their view is, "I paid my premium, and I am entitled to get as much from the company as I can." Second, deductibles have increased, and many claimants may pad claims when they face the prospect of the payment of a large deductible.

An especially disturbing trend is the lax and permissive attitude of younger Americans. *The Insurance Research Council study found that 63 percent of respondents age 18 to 24 believe it is acceptable to pad an insurance claim to make up for previously paid premiums, and 57 percent of the younger respondents believe it is acceptable to pad a claim to recover the deductible.*[15]

EXHIBIT 2.4

Examples of Insurance Fraud

- *Creating a fraudulent claim.*
  Staged or fake auto accident.
  Staged slip-and-fall accident.
  False claim of foreign object in food or drink.
  Faking a death to collect benefits.
  Murder for profit.
  Phony burglary, theft, or vandalism.
  Arson or intentional water damage.
  Staged theft of auto.
  Staged homeowner accident or burglary.
- *Overstating amount of loss.*
  Inflating bodily injuries in auto accident.
  Inflating value of items taken in burglary or theft.
  Inflating damage claim from minor fender bender.
  Medical providers inflating billing or coding of medical procedures.
- *Misrepresenting facts to receive payment.*
  Claiming preexisting damage occurred in current accident.
  Claiming damages to auto when none occurred.
  Claiming minor injury creates partial or total disability.
  Receiving disability payments and working elsewhere.
- *Misrepresentation to receive payments.*
  Claiming false disability.
  Providing unnecessary medical treatment.
  Charging for medical tests not carried out.
  "Upcoding" for medicine by issuing generic pills and charging for name brands.
  Personal injury mills of doctors, lawyers, and claimants.
- *Misrepresentation to obtain a policy or lower premiums.*
  Misrepresenting health information on life insurance and then submitting a false claim.
  Misrepresenting name, date of birth, or Social Security number and then submitting a
     false claim.
- *Insider and internal fraud.*
  Agent or insurer pocketing premiums, then issuing no policy or a bogus policy.
  Agent or insurer issuing fake policies, certificates, ID cards, or binders.
  Agent or insurer making false entry on document or statement.

SOURCE: Insurance Fraud Prevention Division, Nebraska Department of Insurance.

In summary, the social and economic benefits of insurance generally outweigh the social costs. Insurance reduces worry and fear; the indemnification function contributes greatly to social and economic stability; financial security of individuals and firms is preserved; and from the viewpoint of insurers, objective risk in the economy is reduced. The social costs of insurance can be viewed as the sacrifice that society must make to obtain these benefits.

SUMMARY

- There is no single definition of insurance. However, a typical insurance plan contains four elements:

    Pooling of losses

    Payment of fortuitous losses

    Risk transfer

    Indemnification

    Pooling means that the losses of the few are spread over the group, and average loss is substituted for actual loss. Fortuitous losses are unforeseen and unexpected and occur as a result of chance. Risk transfer involves the transfer of a pure risk to an insurer. Indemnification means that the victim of a loss is restored in whole or in part by payment, repair, or replacement by the insurer.

    The law of large numbers states that the greater the number of exposures, the more likely the actual results will approach the expected results. The law of large numbers permits an insurer to estimate future losses with some accuracy.

- There are several ideal requirements of an insurable risk.

    There must be a large number of exposure units.

    The loss must be accidental and unintentional.

    The loss must be determinable and measurable.

    The loss should not be catastrophic.

    The chance of loss must be calculable.

    The premium must be economically feasible.

- Personal risks, property risks, and liability risks can be privately insured, because the requirements of an insurable risk generally can be met. However, market risks, financial risks, production risks, and political risks generally are uninsurable, because these requirements are difficult to meet.

- Adverse selection is the tendency of persons with a higher-than-average chance of loss to seek insurance at average rates, which, if not controlled by underwriting, results in higher-than-expected loss levels.

- Insurance is not the same as gambling. Gambling creates a new speculative risk, whereas insurance deals with an existing pure risk. Also, gambling is socially unproductive, because the winner's gain comes at the expense of the loser. Insurance is always socially productive because both the insured and insurer win if the loss does not occur.

- Insurance is not the same as hedging. Insurance involves the transfer of a pure risk, whereas hedging involves the transfer of a speculative risk. Also, insurance may reduce objective risk because of the law of large numbers. Hedging typically involves only risk transfer and not risk reduction.

- Insurance can be classified into private and government insurance. Private insurance consists of life and health insurance and property and liability insurance. Government insurance consists of social insurance and other government insurance programs.

- The major benefits of insurance to society are as follows:

    Indemnification for loss

    Less worry and fear

    Source of investment funds

    Loss prevention

    Enhancement of credit

- Insurance entails certain social costs to society, which include the following:

    Cost of doing business

    Fraudulent claims

    Inflated claims

KEY CONCEPTS AND TERMS

Adverse selection	Ocean marine insurance
Casualty insurance	Pooling
Expense loading	Property and liability
Fidelity and surety bonds	insurance
Fortuitous loss	Reinsurance
Indemnification	Requirements of an
Inland marine insurance	insurable risk
Insurance	Risk transfer
Law of large numbers	Social insurance
Life and health insurance	Underwriting
Multiple-line insurance	

REVIEW QUESTIONS

1. Explain the major characteristics of a typical insurance plan.

2. Why is the pooling technique essential to insurance?

3. Explain the law of large numbers and show how the law of large numbers can be used by an insurer to estimate future losses.

4. Explain the major requirements of an insurable risk.

5. Why are most market risks, financial risks, production risks, and political risks considered to be uninsurable by private insurers?

6. How does insurance differ from gambling?

7. How does insurance differ from hedging?

8. Identify the major fields of private and government insurance.

9. How is insurance beneficial to society?

10. Explain the social costs of insurance to society.

APPLICATION QUESTIONS

1. Although no risk completely meets all of the ideal requirements of an insurable risk, some risks come much closer to meeting them than others.
   a. Identify the ideal requirements of an insurable risk.
   b. Compare and contrast automobile collisions and war in terms of how well they meet the requirements of an insurable risk.

2. One author states that "The law of large numbers forms the basis of insurance." Do you agree or disagree with this statement? Explain your answer.

3. a. Private insurers provide numerous benefits to society. Explain how private insurance produces each of the following benefits:
      (1) Indemnification
      (2) Enhancement of credit
      (3) Capital accumulation and investment
   b. One critic of private insurance states that "Private insurance cannot be justified economically because the industry uses scarce economic resources that could be used to provide additional goods and services to society." Do you agree or disagree with this statement? Explain your answer.

4. The potential for adverse selection is present in all forms of insurance. Underwriting is one technique that is used to control adverse selection.
   a. Explain the meaning of "adverse selection."
   b. Why are insurers concerned about adverse selection?
   c. Explain how underwriting can be used to control adverse selection.

SELECTED REFERENCES

Gibbons, Robert J., George E. Rejda, and Michael W. Elliott. *Insurance Perspectives*. Malvern, PA: American Institute for Chartered Property Casualty Underwriters, 1992, Chapters 1 and 2.

Insurance Fraud Prevention Division, Nebraska Department of Insurance. *1998 Annual Report*. Lincoln, NE: Nebraska Department of Insurance, 1998.

Insurance Information Institute. *Insurance Fraud*. New

Case Application

There are numerous definitions of insurance. Based on the definition of insurance stated in the text, indicate whether each of the following guarantees is considered insurance.

a. A television set is guaranteed by the manufacturer against defects for 90 days.

b. A new set of radial tires is guaranteed by the manufacturer against road defects for 50,000 miles.

c. A builder of new homes gives a ten-year guarantee against structural defects in the home.

d. A cosigner of a note agrees to pay the loan balance if the original debtor defaults on the payments.

e. A large group of homeowners agree to pay for losses to homes that burn during the year because of fire.

York: Insurance Information Institute, updated August 1998.

Rejda, George E., Constance M. Luthardt, Cheryl L. Ferguson, and Donald R. Oakes. *Personal Insurance*, 4th ed. Malvern, PA: Insurance Institute of America, 2000, Chapter 1.

Smith, Barry D. and Eric A. Wiening. *How Insurance Works*, 2nd ed. Malvern, PA: Insurance Institute of America, 1994.

NOTES

1. *Bulletin of the Commission on Insurance Terminology of the American Risk and Insurance Association*, (October 1965).

2. Robert I. Mehr and Sandra G. Gustavson, *Life Insurance: Theory and Practice*, 4th ed. (Plano, TX: Business Publications, 1987), p. 31.

3. Self-insurance is discussed in Chapter 3.

4. Robert I. Mehr, Emerson Cammack, and Terry Rose, *Principles of Insurance*, 8th ed. (Homewood, IL: Richard D. Irwin, 1985), pp. 36–37.

5. Market risks include the risks of adverse price changes in raw materials, general price level changes (inflation), changes in consumer tastes, new technology, and increased competition from competitors. Financial risks include the risks of adverse price changes in the price of securities, adverse changes in interest rates, and the inability to borrow on favorable terms. Production risks include shortages of raw materials, depletion of natural resources, and technical problems in production. Political risks include the risks of war, overthrow of government, adverse government regulations, and the nationalization of foreign plants by a hostile government.

6. *ACLI Life Insurance Fact Book 1999* (Washington, DC: American Council of Life Insurance, 1999), p. 78.

7. *The I.I.I. Fact Book 2000* (New York, NY: Insurance Information Institute), p. 1.6.

8. George E. Rejda, *Social Insurance and Economic Security*, 6th ed. (Upper Saddle River, NJ: Prentice Hall, 1999), p. 11.

9. The five states are California, Hawaii, New Jersey, New York, and Rhode Island.

10. *ACLI Fact Book 1999*, Table 7.1, p.100; *The I.I.I. Fact Book 2000*, p. 1.8.

11. *Insurance Fraud*, New York: Insurance Information Institute, updated August 1998.

12. *Ibid.*

13. *Ibid.*

14. Daniel Hays, "Approval of Claim Padding Doubles: Survey," *National Underwriter*, Property & Casualty/Risk & Benefits Management ed., February 2, 1998, p. 8.

15. *Ibid.*

C **Students may take a self-administered test on this chapter at www.awlonline.com/rejda**

Basic Statistics and the Law of Large Numbers

In no industry is the application of probability and statistics more important than in the insurance industry. Insurance actuaries constantly face a trade-off when determining the premium to charge for coverage: the premium must be high enough to cover expected losses and expenses, but low enough to remain competitive with premiums charged by other insurers. Actuaries apply statistical analysis to determine expected loss levels and expected deviations from these loss levels. Through the application of the law of large numbers, insurers reduce their risk of adverse outcomes.

In this appendix we review some statistical concepts that are important to insurers, including probability, central tendency, and dispersion. Next we examine the law of large numbers—its derivation and how insurance companies apply it to reduce risk.

PROBABILITY AND STATISTICS

To determine expected losses, insurance actuaries apply probability and statistical analysis to given loss situations. The probability of an event is simply the long-run relative frequency of the event, given an infinite number of trials with no changes in the underlying conditions. The probability of some events can be determined without experimentation. For example, if a "fair" coin is flipped in the air, the probability the coin will come up "heads" is 50 percent, and the probability it will come up "tails" is also 50 percent. Other probabilities, such as the probability of dying during a specified year or the probability of being involved in an auto accident, can be estimated from past loss data.

A convenient way of summarizing events and probabilities is through a probability distribution. A probability distribution lists events that could occur and the corresponding probability of each event's occurrence. Probability distributions may be discrete, meaning that only distinct outcomes are possible, or continuous, meaning that any outcome over a range of outcomes could occur.[1]

Probability distributions are characterized by two important measures: central tendency and dispersion. Although there are several measures of central tendency, the measure most often employed is the mean (μ) or expected value (EV) of the distribution.[2] The mean or expected value is found by multiplying each outcome by the probability of occurrence, and then summing the resulting products:

$$\mu \text{ or } EV = \Sigma \, X_i \, P_i$$

For example, assume that an actuary estimates the following probabilities of various losses for a certain risk:

Amount of Loss (X_i)		Probability of Loss (P_i)		$X_i P_i$
$ 0	×	.30	=	$ 0
$360	×	.50	=	$180
$600	×	.20	=	$120
		$\Sigma \, X_i \, P_i$	=	$300

Thus, we could say that the mean or expected loss given the probability distribution is $300.

---

*Prepared by Michael J. McNamara, Washington State University.

Although the mean value indicates central tendency, it does not tell us anything about the riskiness or dispersion of the distribution. Consider a second probability-of-loss distribution:

Amount of Loss (X_i)		Probability of Loss (P_i)		$X_i P_i$
$225	×	.40	=	$ 90
$350	×	.60	=	$210
		$\Sigma\ X_i P_i$	=	$300

This distribution also has a mean loss value of $300. However, the first distribution is riskier because the range of possible outcomes is from $0 to $600. With the second distribution, the range of possible outcomes is only $125 ($350 − $225), so we are more certain about the outcome with the second distribution.

Two standard measures of dispersion are employed to characterize the variability or dispersion about the mean value. These measures are the variance (σ^2) and the standard deviation (σ). The variance of a probability distribution is the sum of the squared differences between the possible outcomes and the expected value, weighted by the probability of the outcomes:

$$\sigma^2 = \Sigma\ P_i\,(X_i - EV)^2$$

So the variance is the average squared deviation between the possible outcomes and the mean. Because the variance is in "squared units," it is necessary to take the square root of the variance so that the central tendency and dispersion measures are in the same units. The square root of the variance is the standard deviation. The variance and standard deviation of the first distribution are as follows:

$$\sigma^2 = .30(0 - 300)^2 + .50(360 - 300)^2$$
$$+ .20(600 - 300)^2$$
$$= 27,000 + 1,800 + 18,000$$
$$= 46,800$$
$$\sigma = \sqrt{46,800} = 216.33$$

For the second distribution, the variance and standard deviation are:

$$\sigma^2 = .40(225 - 300)^2 + .60(350 - 300)^2$$
$$= 2,250 + 1,500$$
$$= 3,750$$
$$\sigma = \sqrt{3,750} = 61.24$$

Thus, while the means of the two distributions are the same, the standard deviations are significantly different. *Higher standard deviations, relative to the mean, are associated with greater uncertainty of loss; therefore, the risk is higher. Lower standard deviations, relative to the mean, are associated with less uncertainty of loss; therefore, the risk is lower.*

The two probability distributions used in the discussion of central tendency and dispersion are "odd" in that only 3 and 2 possible outcomes, respectively, could occur. In addition, specific loss levels corresponding to the probabilities are assigned. In practice, estimating the frequency and severity of loss is difficult. Insurers can employ both actual loss data and theoretical loss distributions in estimating losses.[3]

LAW OF LARGE NUMBERS

Even if the characteristics of the population were known with certainty, most insurers do not insure populations. Rather, they select a sample from the population and insure the sample. Obviously, the relationship between population parameters and the characteristics of the sample (mean and standard deviation) is important for insurers, since actual experience may vary significantly from the population parameters. The characteristics of the sampling distribution help to illustrate the law of large numbers, the mathematical foundation of insurance.

It can be shown that the average losses for a random sample of n exposure units will follow a normal distribution because of the Central Limit Theorem. The Central Limit Theorem states:

If you draw random samples of n observations from any population with mean μ_x and standard deviation σ_x, and n is sufficiently large, the distribution of sample means will be approximately normal, with the mean of the distribution equal to the mean of the population ($\mu_{\bar{x}} = \mu_x$), and the standard error of the sample mean ($\sigma_{\bar{x}}$) equal to the standard deviation of the population

(σ_x) divided by the square root of n ($\sigma_{\bar{x}} = \sigma_x/\sqrt{n}$). This approximation becomes increasingly accurate as the sample size, n, increases.

The Central Limit Theorem has two important implications for insurers. First, it is clear that the sample distribution of means does not depend on the population distribution, provided n is sufficiently large. *In other words, regardless of the population distribution (bimodal, unimodal, symmetric, skewed right, skewed left, and so on), the distribution of sample means will approach the normal distribution as the sample size increases.* This result is shown in Exhibit A.1.

The normal distribution is a symmetric, bell-shaped curve. It is defined by the mean and standard deviation of the distribution. About 68 percent of the distribution lies within one standard deviation of the mean, and about 95 percent of the distribution lies within two standard deviations of the mean. The normal curve has many statistical applications (hypothesis testing, confidence intervals, and so on), and is easy to use.

The second important implication of the Central Limit Theorem for insurers is that the standard error of the sample mean distribution declines as the sample size increases. Recall that the standard error is defined as

$$\sigma_{\bar{x}} = \sigma_x/\sqrt{n}$$

In other words, the standard error of the sample mean loss distribution is equal to the standard devia-tion of the population divided by the square root of the sample size. Because the population standard deviation is independent of the sample size, *the standard error of the sampling distribution, $\sigma_{\bar{x}}$, can be reduced by simply increasing the sample size.* For example, an insurer selecting a sample to insure from a population that has a mean loss of \$500 and a standard deviation of \$350 can reduce the standard error of the sampling distribution simply by insuring more units:

n	$\sigma_{\bar{x}}$
10	110.67
100	35.00
1000	11.07
10,000	3.50

This result is shown graphically in Exhibit A.2.

A brief example demonstrates the application of the law of large numbers. Assume, based on previous losses for a certain rating category, that an insurer expects 40 drivers out of a sample of 100 drivers in a rating category to report a physical damage claim during the year. Further assume that the standard deviation of the estimate is 20 drivers.

A second insurer writes coverage on 10,000 drivers in this category. Obviously, the underwriting risk for the second insurer is greater as there are 10,000 units that could report a loss. If the rate of loss does not change, the second insurer should expect 4000 losses (.40 × 10,000) to occur. However, the standard deviation does not increase proportionately. Rather, it increases only by a factor of 10, to 200.[4]

EXHIBIT A.1
Sampling Distribution Versus Sample Size

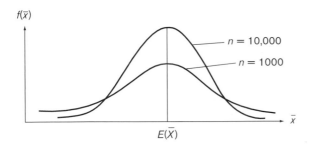

EXHIBIT A.2
Standard Error of the Sampling Distribution Versus Sample Size

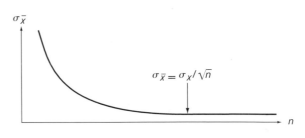

While the second insurer increased its exposure to loss by insuring a larger sample, the predictability of the outcome also increased.

The coefficient of variation (*CV*) is a composite statistic expressing the standard deviation as a percentage of the expected value. For the first insurer, the *CV* is .50 (20/40). For the second insurer, the *CV* is only .05 (200/4000). In the first case, 95 percent of the distribution of expected losses (two standard deviations) lies between 0 and 80 losses, with a mean of 40. For the second insurer, 95 percent of the distribution lies between 3600 and 4400, with a mean of 4000. Obviously, the per-unit risk in the second case is reduced by insuring a larger sample.

Insurance companies are in the loss business—they expect some losses to occur. It is the deviation between actual losses and expected losses that is the major concern. By insuring large samples, insurers reduce their objective risk. There truly is "safety in numbers" for insurers.

NOTES

1. The number of runs scored in a baseball game is a discrete measure as partial runs cannot be scored. Speed and temperature are continuous measures as all values over the range of values can occur.

2. Other measures of central tendency are the median, which is the middle observation in a probability distribution, and the mode, which is the observation that occurs most often.

3. Introductory statistics texts discuss several popular theoretical distributions, such as the binomial and Poisson distributions, that can be used to estimate losses. Another popular distribution, the normal distribution, is discussed in the next section.

4. The underwriting risk for the insurer is equal to the number of units insured, n, multiplied by the standard error of the average loss distribution, $\sigma_{\bar{x}}$. Recalling that $\sigma_{\bar{x}}$ is equal to $\sigma_x / \sqrt{n}$, we can rewrite the expression for underwriting risk as:

$$n \times \sigma_{\bar{x}} = n \times \sigma_x / \sqrt{n} = \sqrt{n} \times \sigma_x$$

Thus, while underwriting risk increases with an increase in a sample size, it does not increase proportionately. Rather it increases by the square root of the increase in the sample size.

Chapter 3

Introduction to Risk Management

> **❝** *The essence of risk management lies in maximizing the areas where we have some control over the outcome while minimizing the areas where we have absolutely no control over the outcome...* **❞**
>
> Peter L. Bernstein
> *Against the Gods, The Remarkable Story of Risk*

Learning Objectives

After studying this chapter, you should be able to:

▲ Define risk management.

▲ Explain the objectives of risk management.

▲ Describe the steps in the risk management process.

▲ Distinguish between risk control and risk financing as major techniques for treating loss exposures.

▲ Access an Internet site and understand topics dealing with commercial risk management.

▲ Apply the principles of risk management to a personal risk management program.

Internet Resources

- The **Captive Insurance Companies Association** is an organization that disseminates information to companies that use captive insurers to solve corporate insurance problems. The organization claims that its Web site enables risk managers, owners of captives, students, and anyone who has an interest in alternative risk transfer techniques to meet with colleagues, ask questions of the finest experts in the field, and find needed resources. Visit the site at:

  http://www.captive.com

- **IFIC RISK WATCH** provides a comprehensive introduction to financial risk management from the International Finance & Commodities Institute. This site educates readers on the most valuable official documents on this subject. Along with a risk management checklist, this site also includes a regulatory documents library, a collection of risk management case studies, and a risk management glossary. Visit the site at:

  http://risk.ifci.ch/index.htm

- The **Nonprofit Risk Management Center** is an organization that conducts research and education on risk management and insurance issues that are of special concern to nonprofit organizations. The organization publishes a newsletter, easy-to-read publications, and informative briefs (called Riskfacts) on frequently asked questions related to risk management and insurance. The organization also offers consulting services and risk audits. Visit the site at:

  http://www.nonprofitrisk.org

- The **Public Risk Management Association** is an organization that represents risk managers of state and local governmental units. The organization provides practical training and education for risk managers in the public sector; publishes a magazine, newsletter, and detailed issue-specific publications; and provides cutting-edge updates on federal regulations and legislation. Visit the site at:

  http://www.primacentral.org

- The **Risk and Insurance Management Society (RIMS)** is the premier professional association in the United States for risk managers and corporate buyers of insurance. RIMS provides a forum for the discussion of common risk management issues, supports loss-prevention activities, and makes known to insurers the insurance needs of its members. RIMS has local chapters in major cities. Visit the site at:

  http://www.rims.org

- The **Self-Insurance Institute of America** is a national association that promotes self-insurance as an alternative method for financing losses. The organization publishes technical articles on self-insurance, holds educational conferences, and promotes the legislative and regulatory interests of the self-insurance industry at both the federal and state levels. Visit the site at:

  http://www.siia.org

ukens Lumber is a medium-sized firm that operates several lumberyards and hardware stores in Seattle, Washington. In recent years, the number of workers injured on the job and employee thefts have increased. A management consultant recommended that the company establish a risk management program to deal with these problems. Risk management is a process that identifies the loss exposures faced by a firm and uses a number of methods, including insurance, to handle those exposures. After implementing the program, Lukens Lumber saw dramatic results. Job-related injuries declined, workers compensation insurance premiums were reduced, and employee thefts decreased. The firm's profitability also improved.

Clearly, Lukens Lumber benefited from its risk management program. Other parties have also recognized the merits of risk management. Today, risk management is widely used by corporations, small employers, farmers, and state and local governments. Even students can benefit from personal risk management programs.

This chapter is the first of two chapters dealing with risk management. This chapter discusses the fundamentals of traditional risk management; the following chapter discusses several advanced topics in risk management. Topics addressed in this chapter include the meaning of risk management, objectives of risk management, steps in the risk management process, and techniques for treating loss exposures. The chapter concludes with a discussion of personal risk management.

MEANING OF RISK MANAGEMENT

Risk management *is a process to identify loss exposures faced by an organization and to select the most appropriate techniques for treating such exposures.* In the past, risk managers generally considered only pure loss exposures faced by the firm. However, newer forms of risk management are emerging that consider certain speculative risks as well. This chapter discusses only the treatment of pure risks or pure loss exposures. Management of speculative risks in a modern risk management program—such as interest rate, currency exchange, and commodity risks—is discussed in Chapter 4.

Risk management should not be confused with insurance management. Risk management is a broader concept and includes all techniques for treating loss exposures, in addition to insurance. In this regard, many risk managers belong to a national professional organization known as the Risk and Insurance Management Society (RIMS). RIMS promotes risk management principles and assists risk managers in the application of alternative techniques for treating loss exposures.

OBJECTIVES OF RISK MANAGEMENT

Risk management has important objectives. These objectives can be classified as either (1) preloss objectives or (2) postloss objectives.[1]

Preloss Objectives

Important objectives before a loss occurs include economy, reduction of anxiety, and meeting legal obligations.

The first objective means that the firm should prepare for potential losses in the most economical way. This preparation involves an analysis of the cost of safety programs, insurance premiums paid, and the costs associated with the different techniques for handling losses.

The second objective is the reduction of anxiety. Certain loss exposures can cause greater worry and fear for the risk manager and key executives. For example, the threat of a catastrophic lawsuit from a defective product can cause greater anxiety than a small loss from a minor fire. The risk manager, however, wants to minimize the anxiety and fear associated with all loss exposures.

The final objective is to meet any legal obligations. For example, government regulations may require a firm to install safety devices to protect workers from harm, to dispose of hazardous waste materials properly, and to label consumer products appropriately. The risk manager must see that these legal obligations are met.

Postloss Objectives

Important objectives after a loss occurs include survival, continued operation, stability of earnings, continued growth, and social responsibility.

The most important postloss objective is survival of the firm. Survival means that after a loss occurs, the firm can resume at least partial operations within some reasonable time period.

The second postloss objective is to continue operating. For some firms, the ability to operate after a loss is extremely important. For example, a public utility firm must continue to provide service. Banks, bakeries, dairies, and other competitive firms must continue to operate after a loss. Otherwise, business will be lost to competitors.

A *third postloss objective is stability of earnings.* Earnings per share can be maintained if the firm continues to operate. However, a firm may incur substantial additional expenses to achieve this goal (such as operating at another location), and perfect stability of earnings may not be attained.

Another postloss objective is continued growth of the firm. A company can grow by developing new products and markets or by acquiring or merging with other companies. The risk manager must therefore consider the effect that a loss will have on the firm's ability to grow.

Finally, the objective of social responsibility is to minimize the effects that a loss will have on other persons and on society. A severe loss can adversely affect employees, suppliers, creditors, and the community in general. For example, a severe loss that shuts down a plant in a small town for an extended period can cause considerable economic distress in the town.

STEPS IN THE RISK MANAGEMENT PROCESS

The risk management process involves four steps: (1) identify potential losses, (2) evaluate potential losses, (3) select the appropriate techniques for treating loss exposures, and (4) implement and administer the program (see Exhibit 3.1). Each of these steps is discussed in some detail in the following section.

IDENTIFYING POTENTIAL LOSSES

The first step in the risk management process is to identify all major and minor loss exposures. This step involves a painstaking analysis of all potential losses. Important loss exposures relate to the following:

1. Property loss exposures
   - Building, plants, other structures
   - Furniture, equipment, supplies
   - Electronic data processing (EDP) equipment; computer software
   - Inventory
   - Accounts receivable, valuable papers and records
   - Company planes, boats, mobile equipment

EXHIBIT 3.1
Steps in the Risk Management Process

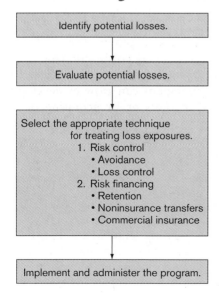

2. Liability loss exposures
   - Defective products
   - Environmental pollution (land, water, air, noise)
   - Sexual harassment of employees, discrimination against employees, wrongful termination
   - Premises and general liability loss exposures
   - Liability arising from company vehicles
   - Misuse of the Internet and e-mail transmissions, transmission of pornographic material
   - Directors' and officers' liability suits
3. Business income loss exposures
   - Loss of income from a covered loss
   - Continuing expenses after a loss
   - Extra expenses
   - Contingent business income losses
4. Human resources loss exposures
   - Death or disability of key employees
   - Retirement or unemployment
   - Job-related injuries or disease experienced by workers
5. Crime loss exposures
   - Holdups, robberies, burglaries
   - Employee theft and dishonesty
   - Fraud and embezzlement
   - Internet and computer crime exposures
6. Employee benefit loss exposures
   - Failure to comply with government regulations
   - Violation of fiduciary responsibilities
   - Group life and health and retirement plan exposures
   - Failure to pay promised benefits
7. Foreign loss exposures
   - Plants, business property, inventory
   - Foreign currency risks
   - Kidnapping of key personnel
   - Political risks

A risk manager has several sources of information that he or she can use to identify the preceding loss exposures. They include the following:

- *Risk analysis questionnaires.* Questionnaires require the risk manager to answer numerous questions that identify major and minor loss exposures.
- *Physical inspection.* A physical inspection of company plants and operations can identify major loss exposures.

- *Flowcharts*. Flowcharts that show the flow of production and delivery can reveal production bottlenecks where a loss can have severe financial consequences for the firm.
- *Financial statements*. Analysis of financial statements can identify the major assets that must be protected.
- *Historical loss data*. Historical and departmental loss data over time can be invaluable in identifying major loss exposures.

In addition, risk managers must keep abreast of industry trends and market changes that can create new loss exposures and cause concern. Major risk management issues include rising workers compensation costs, effects of mergers and consolidations by insurers and brokers, increasing litigation costs, financing risk through the capital markets, increasing repetitive motion injury claims, and numerous other issues (see Insight 3.1).

EVALUATING POTENTIAL LOSSES

The second step in the risk management process is to evaluate and measure the impact of losses on the firm. This step involves an estimation of the potential frequency and severity of loss. **Loss frequency** *refers to the probable number of losses that may occur during some given time period.* **Loss severity** *refers to the probable size of the losses that may occur.*

Once the risk manager estimates the frequency and severity of loss for each type of loss exposure, the various loss exposures can be ranked according to their relative importance. For example, a loss exposure with the potential for bankrupting the firm is much more important in a risk management program than an exposure with a small loss potential.

In addition, the relative frequency and severity of each loss exposure must be estimated so that the risk manager can select the most appropriate technique, or combination of techniques, for handling each exposure. For example, if certain losses occur regularly and are fairly predictable, they can be budgeted out of a firm's income and treated as a normal operating expense. If the annual loss experience of a certain type of exposure fluctuates widely, however, an entirely different approach is required.

Although the risk manager must consider both loss frequency and loss severity, severity is more important, because a single catastrophic loss could wipe out the firm. Therefore, the risk manager must also consider all losses that can result from a single event. Both the maximum possible loss and maximum probable loss must be estimated. The **maximum possible loss** *is the worst loss that could possibly happen to the firm during its lifetime.* The **maximum probable loss** *is the worst loss that is likely to happen.* For example, if a plant is totally destroyed in a flood, the risk manager estimates that replacement cost, debris removal, demolition costs, and other costs will total $10 million. Thus, the maximum possible loss is $10 million. The risk manager also estimates that a flood causing more than $8 million of damage to the plant is so unlikely that such a flood would not occur more than once in 50 years. The risk manager may choose to ignore events that occur so infrequently. Thus, for this risk manager, the maximum probable loss is $8 million.

Catastrophic losses are difficult to predict because they occur infrequently. However, their potential impact on the firm must be given high priority. In contrast, certain losses, such as physical damage losses to cars and trucks, occur with greater frequency, are usually relatively small, and can be predicted with greater accuracy.

SELECTING THE APPROPRIATE TECHNIQUES FOR TREATING LOSS EXPOSURES

The third step in the risk management process is to select the most appropriate techniques for treating loss exposures. These techniques can be classified broadly as either risk control or risk financing.[2] **Risk control** *refers to techniques that reduce the frequency and severity of accidental losses.* **Risk financing** *refers to techniques that provide for the funding of accidental losses after they control.* Many risk managers use a combination of techniques for treating each loss exposure.

Risk Control

As noted above, risk control encompasses techniques that prevent losses from occurring or reduce the

Insight 3.1

What Are the Major Issues Facing Risk Managers?

Risk managers' top concerns reflect industry trends and market changes, according to *Risk & Insurance*'s annual survey of the nation's largest companies.

In fact, issues of little importance in previous years now rank at the top of risk managers' worries. Two top issues are increasing workers compensation costs and the effect of insurer/broker consolidations (see chart).

Workers compensation costs ranked as the risk managers' overall top concern. In fact, 74.2 percent rated this issue as their top concern. The increase in the number of risk managers worried about workers compensation costs reflects concerns about a possible turn in the soft market. Loss costs are at a six-year low, and after four years of continued reduced rates, the experience modification factors are expected to increase, leading to a rise in premiums.

Insurer/broker consolidations also ranked high among risk managers, with 58 percent of respondents indicating that this issue was among their top concerns.

Financing risk through the capital markets was another top concern for 51.6 percent of risk managers. Once again, this concern follows industry trends. The insurance and capital markets are converging, and a tool to convert assets into market securities is becoming more common.

Risk & Insurance asked risk managers at the nation's leading companies to rate the importance of

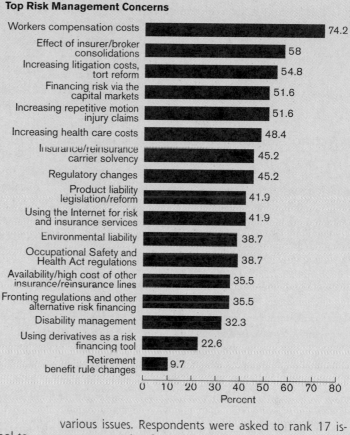

Top Risk Management Concerns

Concern	Percent
Workers compensation costs	74.2
Effect of insurer/broker consolidations	58
Increasing litigation costs, tort reform	54.8
Financing risk via the capital markets	51.6
Increasing repetitive motion injury claims	51.6
Increasing health care costs	48.4
Insurance/reinsurance carrier solvency	45.2
Regulatory changes	45.2
Product liability legislation/reform	41.9
Using the Internet for risk and insurance services	41.9
Environmental liability	38.7
Occupational Safety and Health Act regulations	38.7
Availability/high cost of other insurance/reinsurance lines	35.5
Fronting regulations and other alternative risk financing	35.5
Disability management	32.3
Using derivatives as a risk financing tool	22.6
Retirement benefit rule changes	9.7

various issues. Respondents were asked to rank 17 issues on a scale of 1 to 5, ranging from workers compensation costs to retirement benefit rule changes.

Source: Adaptation of "Building the Global Risk Processor," *Risk & Insurance* (January 1999), p. 16.

---

severity of a loss after it occurs. Major risk-control techniques include the following:

- Avoidance
- Loss control

Avoidance Avoidance *means a certain loss exposure is never acquired, or an existing loss exposure is abandoned.* For example, flood losses can be avoided by not building a new plant in a flood plain. A pharmaceutical firm that markets a drug with dangerous side effects can withdraw the drug from the market.

The major advantage of avoidance is that the chance of loss is reduced to zero if the loss exposure is never acquired. In addition, if an existing loss exposure is abandoned, the chance of loss is reduced or eliminated because the activity or product that could produce a loss has been abandoned.

Abandonment, however, may still leave the firm with a residual liability exposure from the sale of previous products.

Avoidance, however, has two major disadvantages. First, the firm may not be able to avoid all losses. For example, a company may not be able to avoid the premature death of a key executive. Second, it may not be feasible or practical to avoid the exposure. For example, a paint factory can avoid losses arising from the production of paint. Without paint production, however, the firm will not be in business.

Loss Control **Loss control** has two dimensions: loss prevention and loss reduction. **Loss prevention** *refers to measures that reduce the frequency of a particular loss.* For example, measures that reduce truck accidents include driver examinations, zero tolerance for alcohol or drug abuse, and strict enforcement of safety rules. Measures that reduce lawsuits from defective products include installation of safety features on hazardous products, placement of warning labels on dangerous products, and institution of quality-control checks.

Loss reduction *refers to measures that reduce the severity of a loss after it occurs.* Examples include installation of an automatic sprinkler system that promptly extinguishes a fire; segregation of exposure units so that a single loss cannot simultaneously damage all exposure units, such as having warehouses with inventories at different locations; rehabilitation of workers with job-related injuries; and limiting the amount of cash on the premises.

Loss control is especially effective in reducing job-related accidents and disease that can result in costly workers compensation claims. Studies by insurers show that loss-control programs can substantially reduce workers compensation costs (see Insight 3.2).

Risk Financing

As stated earlier, risk financing refers to techniques that provide for the funding of losses after they occur. Major risk-financing techniques include the following:

- Retention
- Noninsurance transfers
- Commercial insurance

Retention Retention *means that the firm retains part or all of the losses that can result from a given loss.* Retention can be either active or passive. Active risk retention means that the firm is aware of the loss exposure and plans to retain part or all of it, such as automobile collision losses to a fleet of company cars. Passive retention, however, is the failure to identify a loss exposure, failure to act, or forgetting to act. For example, a risk manager may fail to identify all company assets that could be damaged in an earthquake.

Retention can be effectively used in a risk management program under the following conditions:[3]

First, no other method of treatment is available. Insurers may be unwilling to write a certain type of coverage, or the coverage may be too expensive. Noninsurance transfers may not be available. In addition, although loss prevention can reduce the frequency of loss, all losses cannot be eliminated. In these cases, retention is a residual method. If the exposure cannot be insured or transferred, then it must be retained.

Second, the worst possible loss is not serious. For example, physical damage losses to automobiles in a large firm's fleet will not bankrupt the firm if the automobiles are separated by wide distances and are not likely to be simultaneously damaged.

Finally, losses are highly predictable. Retention can be effectively used for workers compensation claims, physical damage losses to automobiles, and shoplifting losses. Based on past experience, the risk manager can estimate a probable range of frequency and severity of actual losses. If most losses fall within that range, they can be budgeted out of the firm's income.

Determining Retention Levels If retention is used, the risk manager must determine the firm's **retention level,** *which is the dollar amount of losses that the firm will retain.* A financially strong firm can have a higher retention level than one whose financial position is weak.

Although a number of methods can be used to determine the retention level, only two methods are summarized here. First, a corporation can determine the maximum uninsured loss it can absorb without adversely affecting the company's earnings. One rough rule is that the maximum retention can be set at 5 percent of the company's annual earnings before taxes from current operations.

Insight 3.2

Loss-Control Programs Can Cut Workers Compensation Costs

Loss-control programs can cut a company's overall costs up to 20 percent, according to a study by Wausau Ins. Co.

The Wausau, Wis.-based company said about 40 percent or $1 billion of the business it writes was analyzed for the study. The accounts that were examined were split into those that were serviced by loss control and those that were not.

Wausau said that, for all its workers compensation customers, loss control reduced claim frequency 12 percent, average loss amounts by 9 percent and overall costs by 20 percent.

When only voluntary market customers were included, the overall cost saving was as much as 40 percent, the company said.

Loss-control services for Wausau includes one or more of a variety of techniques including:

- Safety and health services
- Ergonomic assessment
- Safety program design
- Occupational health assessment
- Behavioral management consultation
- Industrial hygiene and air sampling
- Hazard identification and protection and loss analysis

In studying accounts, the company expressed its results on a per-$1 million-of-payroll basis.

The researchers found that for every company with a $1 million payroll (generally about 30 workers), the yearly number of workers compensation claims amounted to about three-and-a-half with loss control. Without loss control the number of claims grew to four.

The figures also increased for the average claim amount, which rose from $1881 for those with loss control to $2062 for firms without it.

Total annual costs for losses were $6627 when loss control was involved and $8234 when it was not.

In making the analysis, nonserviced accounts were limited to those in the same states and industries as the accounts that were serviced.

The researchers said that the impact of policy size was unclear, but some of the differences could be due to policy-size profiles. They noted that the average size for serviced accounts was $5.7 million compared to $1.7 million for nonserviced accounts.

Larger accounts, they said, may have more of their own in-house loss control measures. However, they noted that a $1 million account has a higher probability of having no claims than a $10 million account would.

Nonserviced accounts might be expected to have a downward bias, at least for frequency of claims, the report said.

Bill Mech, Wausau's vice president for loss-analysis and loss-control services, said the research was undertaken because "we want to convince policyholders we've got ways to improve their loss picture."

Prior to doing the study, he said the company had known that loss control makes a difference, but it had only individual success stories and anecdotes.

SOURCE: Adapted from Daniel Hays, "Workers' Comp Loss Control Savings Cited," *National Underwriter*, Property & Casualty/Risk & Benefits Management ed., April 20, 1998, p. 28.

Second, a company can determine the maximum retention as a percentage of the firm's net working capital, such as between 1 and 5 percent. Although this method does not reflect the firm's overall financial position for absorbing a loss, it does measure the firm's ability to fund a loss.

Paying Losses If retention is used, the risk manager must have some method for paying losses. The following methods are typically used:[4]

- *Current net income.* The firm can pay losses out of its current net income and treat losses as expenses for that year. A large number of losses could exceed current income, however, and other assets may then have to be liquidated to pay losses.
- *Unfunded reserve.* An unfunded reserve is a bookkeeping account that is charged with the actual or expected losses from a given exposure.
- *Funded reserve.* A funded reserve is the setting aside of liquid funds to pay losses. Funded

reserves are not widely used by private employers, because the funds may yield a much higher rate of return by being used in the business. Also, contributions to a funded reserve are not income-tax deductible. Losses, however, are tax deductible when paid.

- *Credit line.* A credit line can be established with a bank, and borrowed funds may be used to pay losses as they occur. Interest must be paid on the loan, however, and loan repayments can aggravate any cash-flow problems a firm may have.
- *Captive insurer.* A captive insurer can also be used to pay losses. A **captive insurer** *is an insurer owned and established by a parent firm for the purpose of insuring the parent firm's loss exposures.* If the captive is owned by only one parent, such as a corporation, it is called a **pure captive.** If the captive is owned by several parents, it is called an **association or group captive.** For example, companies that belong to a trade association may own a captive insurer. Many captive insurers are located in the Caribbean because of that region's favorable regulatory climate, low capital requirements, and low taxes. Captive insurers are also domiciled in certain states in the United States.

Captive insurers are formed for several reasons, including the following:

- *Difficulty in obtaining insurance.* The parent firm may have difficulty in obtaining certain types of insurance from commercial insurers, so it forms its own captive insurer to write the coverage. This pattern is especially true for global firms that may be unable to purchase certain coverages from commercial insurers, including liability insurance and political risk insurance. Establishing a captive may also reduce insurance costs because of lower operating expenses, avoidance of an agent's or broker's commission, and interest earned on invested premiums and reserves that otherwise would be received by commercial insurers.
- *Greater stability of earnings.* A captive insurer can provide for greater stability of earnings, because the adverse impact of chance fluctuations on the firm's income is reduced.
- *Easier access to a reinsurer.* A captive insurer has easier access to reinsurance, because many reinsurers will deal only with insurance companies and not with insureds.

- *Profit center.* A captive insurer can become a source of profit if it insures other parties as well as provides insurance to the parent firm and subsidiaries. Exhibit 3.2 gives some examples of the primary business of captive owners and the diverse types of insurance underwritten by captive insurers.
- *Tax treatment of captives.* As a general rule, premiums paid to a single-parent captive are not income-tax deductible. The Internal Revenue Service argues that no substantial transfer of risk to an insurer takes place, and the premiums paid are similar to the contributions to a self-insurance reserve, which are not income-tax deductible. There are certain exceptions, however. In 1991, the courts ruled in a number of cases that premiums paid to a captive are income-tax deductible if the captive also does a significant amount of business with unaffiliated companies or unrelated third parties. In 1992, a federal appeals court ruled that a corporation could deduct premiums paid to a captive insurer if the captive insurer obtains at least 30 percent of its business from unrelated third parties. In 1997, a series of rulings allowed deductions for taxpayers in certain situations involving holding companies; the rulings permitted deductions for unpaid claims to be taken in the year in which the loss occurred.[5] The tax treatment of captives is not completely settled at the present time and is an ongoing issue.

Self-Insurance Our discussion of retention would not be complete without a brief discussion of self-insurance. The term self-insurance is commonly used by risk managers to describe aspects of their risk management programs. However, self-insurance is a misnomer because it is technically not insurance, and a pure risk is not transferred to an insurer. **Self-insurance** *is a special form of planned retention by which part or all of a given loss exposure is retained by the firm.* A better name for self-insurance is self-funding, which expresses more clearly the idea that losses are funded and paid by the firm.

Self-insurance is widely used in workers compensation insurance. Self-insurance is also used by employers to provide group health, dental, vision, and prescription drug benefits to employees. Firms often self-insure their group health insurance benefits be-

EXHIBIT 3.2

Examples of Controlled Third-Party Captive Business

Primary business of captive owner	Type of insurance underwritten
Banks and consumer finance organizations	Credit life, health and disability, mortgage insurance, title insurance, auto and property
Retailers	Credit life, health and disability, extended warranty
Cellular telephone companies	Cell phone coverage
Life insurance companies	Agents' errors and omissions
Auto manufacturers	Personal lines automobile, extended warranty
Franchise organizations	Franchisee property and casualty
Insurance agencies	Participation in client business
Computer manufacturers	Disaster recovery
Manufacturers	Cargo suppliers and distributors, extended warranty
Organizations with significant capital expenditures for building and remodeling	Rolling wrap-ups for casualty and property
Credit card issuers	Credit life, health and disability, automobile for rental cars (collision damage waiver), travel accident, lost baggage, extended warranty
Health care systems	Physician professional liability, affiliate professional liability
Miscellaneous	Joint ventures
Transportation firms	Independent drivers, occupational accident, physical damage, customer cargo coverages
General contractors	Subcontractor coverages

SOURCE: Arthur Koritzinsky, "Enterprise Risk Management Fuels Captive Surge," *National Underwriter, Risk Financing & Insurance Renewal Report*, October 26, 1998, p. S-21.

cause they can save money and control health-care costs. There are other benefits as well (see Insight 3.3).

Finally, self-insured plans are typically protected by some type of stop-loss insurance that limits the employer's out-of-pocket costs once losses exceed certain limits.

Risk Retention Groups Federal legislation enacted in 1981 and 1986 allows employers, trade groups, governmental units, and other parties to form risk retention groups to self-insure products liability and other commercial liability insurance (except workers compensation). A **risk retention group** *is a group captive that writes commercial liability insurance and products liability insurance for employers that have had difficulty in obtaining such insurance.* For example, a group of taxicab drivers may find com-mercial liability insurance too expensive to purchase.

They can self-insure their general liability loss expo-sures by forming a risk retention group.

Risk retention groups are exempt from many state insurance laws that apply to other insurers. Nevertheless, they must be licensed as a liability in-surer in at least one state.

Advantages and Disadvantages of Retention
The retention technique has both advantages and disadvantages in a risk management program.[6] The major advantages are as follows:

- *Save money*. The firm can save money in the long run if its actual losses are less than the loss com-ponent in the insurer's premium.
- *Lower expenses*. The services provided by the insurer may be provided by the firm at a lower cost. Some expenses may be reduced, including loss-adjustment expenses, general administrative

Insight 3.3

Background on Self-Insurance

During the past 25 years, U.S. employers have increasingly turned to alternative means of financing risk when traditional insurance coverage has failed to meet their needs. To provide group health care insurance, workers compensation, and property/casualty insurance, significant numbers of private and public entities cover all or part of their risk themselves; that is, they self-insure or self-fund.

Today, more health care plans are funded directly by employers than by traditional insurance companies. The dramatic rise of self-insurance, or self-funding of health care benefits, is attributable to an awareness by employers that eliminating a third-party insurance carrier for primary coverages allows them to cut costs without reducing benefits. Moreover, by taking an active management role, the employer can be more responsive to their employees' health care needs.

Benefits of Self-Insurance

Some of the benefits of self-insuring are as follows:

- Saves money
- Offers greater flexibility
- Is more responsive to employers' needs
- Is the risk-funding option of choice
- For employer-sponsored benefit plans, offers uniform regulation
- Creates greater claims control
- Reduces or eliminates fraud and abuse
- Helps to control over utilization
- Demands provider quality
- Provides an opportunity to gain meaningful claim statistics
- Offers streamlined administration and creative electronic data claims processing

expenses, commissions and brokerage fees, loss control expenses, taxes and fees, and the insurer's profit.

- *Encourage loss prevention.* Because the exposure is retained, there may be a greater incentive for loss prevention.
- *Increase cash flow.* Cash flow may be increased, because the firm can use the funds that normally would be paid to the insurer at the beginning of the coverage period.

The retention technique, however, has several disadvantages:

- *Possible higher losses.* The losses retained by the firm may be greater than the loss allowance in the insurance premium that is saved by not purchasing the insurance. Also, in the short run, there may be great volatility in the firm's loss experience.
- *Possible higher expenses.* Expenses may actually be higher. Outside experts such as safety engineers may have to be hired. Insurers may be able to provide loss control and claim services less expensively.

- *Possible higher taxes.* Income taxes may also be higher. The premiums paid to an insurer are income-tax deductible. However, if retention is used, only the amounts actually paid out for losses are deductible. Contributions to a funded reserve are not income-tax deductible.

Noninsurance Transfers Noninsurance transfers are another risk financing technique. **Noninsurance transfers** *are methods other than insurance by which a pure risk and its potential financial consequences are transferred to another party.* Examples of noninsurance transfers include contracts, leases, and hold-harmless agreements. For example, a company's contract with a construction firm to build a new plant can specify that the construction firm is responsible for any damage to the plant while it is being built. A firm's computer lease can specify that maintenance, repairs, and any physical damage loss to the computer are the responsibility of the computer firm. Or a firm may insert a hold-harmless clause in a contract, by which one party assumes legal liability on behalf of another party. Thus, a publishing firm may insert a hold-harmless clause in a contract, by which the author, and not the publisher, is held legally liable if the publisher is sued for plagiarism.

In a risk management program, noninsurance transfers have several advantages:[7]

- The risk manager can transfer some potential losses that are not commercially insurable.
- Noninsurance transfers often cost less than insurance.
- The potential loss may be shifted to someone who is in a better position to exercise loss control.

However, noninsurance transfers have several disadvantages. They are summarized as follows:

- The transfer of potential loss may fail because the contract language is ambiguous. Also, there may be no court precedents for the interpretation of a contract that is tailor-made to fit the situation.
- If the party to whom the potential loss is transferred is unable to pay the loss, the firm is still responsible for the claim.
- Noninsurance transfers may not always reduce insurance costs, because an insurer may not give credit for the transfers.

Insurance Commercial insurance is also used in a risk management program. Insurance is appropriate for loss exposures that have a low probability of loss but for which the severity of loss is high.

If the risk manager uses insurance to treat certain loss exposures, five key areas must be emphasized. They are as follows:[8]

- Selection of insurance coverages
- Selection of an insurer
- Negotiation of terms
- Dissemination of information concerning insurance coverages
- Periodic review of the program

First, the risk manager must select the insurance coverages needed. The coverages selected must be appropriate for insuring the major loss exposures identified in step one. To determine the coverages needed, the risk manager must have specialized knowledge of commercial property and liability insurance contracts. Commercial insurance is discussed in Chapters 13–15.

The risk manager must also determine if a deductible is needed and the size of the deductible. A **deductible** is a provision by which a specified amount is subtracted from the loss payment otherwise payable. *A deductible is used to eliminate small claims and the administrative expense of adjusting these claims.* As a result, substantial premium savings are possible. In essence, a deductible is a form of risk retention.

Most risk management programs combine the retention technique discussed earlier with commercial insurance. In determining the size of the deductible, the firm may decide to retain only a relatively small part of the maximum possible loss. The insurer normally adjusts any claims, and only losses in excess of the deductible are paid.

Another approach is to purchase **excess insurance**. A firm may be financially strong and may wish to retain a relatively larger proportion of the maximum possible loss. *Under an excess insurance plan, the insurer does not participate in the loss until the actual loss exceeds the amount a firm has decided to retain.* The retention limit may be set at the maximum probable loss (not maximum possible loss). For example, a retention limit of $1 million may be established for a single fire loss to a plant valued at $25 million. The $1 million would be viewed as the maximum probable loss. In the unlikely event of a total loss, the firm would absorb the first $1 million of loss, and the commercial insurer would pay the remaining $24 million.

Second, the risk manager must select an insurer or several insurers. Several important factors come into play here, including the financial strength of the insurer, risk management services provided by the insurer, and the cost and terms of protection. The insurer's financial strength is determined by the size of policyowners' surplus, underwriting and investment results, adequacy of reserves for outstanding liabilities, types of insurance written, and the quality of management. Several trade publications are available to the risk manager for determining the financial strength of a particular insurer. One of the most important rating agencies is the A. M. Best Company, which rates insurers based on their relative financial strength.

The risk manager must also consider the availability of risk management services in selecting a particular insurer. An insurance agent or broker can provide the desired information concerning the risk management services available from different insurers. These services include loss-control services, assistance in identifying loss exposures, and claim adjustment services.

The cost and terms of insurance protection must be considered as well. All other factors being equal, the risk manager would prefer to purchase insurance at the lowest possible price. Many risk managers will solicit competitive premium bids from several insurers to get the necessary protection and services at the lowest price.

Third, after the insurer or insurers are selected, the terms of the insurance contract must be negotiated. If printed policies, endorsements, and forms are used, the risk manager and insurer must agree on the documents that will form the basis of the contract. If a specially tailored **manuscript policy**[9] is written for the firm, the language and meaning of the contractual provisions must be clear to both parties. In any case, the various risk management services the insurer will provide must be clearly stated in the contract. Finally, if the firm is large, the premiums may be negotiable between the firm and insurer. In many cases, an agent or broker will be involved in the negotiations.

In addition, information concerning insurance coverages must be disseminated to others in the firm. The firm's employees and managers must be informed about the insurance coverages, the various records that must be kept, the risk management services that the insurer will provide, and the changes in hazards that could result in a suspension of insurance. Those persons responsible for reporting a loss must also be informed. The firm must comply with policy provisions concerning how notice of a claim is to be given and how the necessary proofs of loss are to be presented.

Finally, the insurance program must be periodically reviewed. This review is especially important when the firm has a change in business operations or is involved in a merger or acquisition of another firm. The review includes an analysis of agent and broker relationships, coverages needed, quality of loss control services provided, whether claims are paid promptly, and numerous other factors. Even the basic decision—whether to purchase insurance—must be reviewed periodically.

Advantages of Insurance The use of commercial insurance in a risk management program has certain advantages:[10]

- The firm will be indemnified after a loss occurs. The firm can continue to operate and may experience little or no fluctuation in earnings.
- Uncertainty is reduced, which permits the firm to lengthen its planning horizon. Worry and fear are reduced for managers and employees, which should improve their performance and productivity.
- Insurers can provide valuable risk management services, such as loss-control services, exposure analysis to identify loss exposures, and claims adjusting.
- Insurance premiums are income-tax deductible as a business expense.

Disadvantages of Insurance The use of insurance also entails certain disadvantages and costs:

- The payment of premiums is a major cost, because the premium consists of a component to pay losses, an amount for expenses, and an allowance for profit and contingencies. There is also an opportunity cost. Under the retention technique discussed earlier, the premium could be invested or used in the business until needed to pay claims. If insurance is used, premiums must be paid in advance.
- Considerable time and effort must be spent in negotiating the insurance coverages. An insurer or insurers must be selected, policy terms and premiums must be negotiated, the firm must cooperate with the loss-control activities of the insurer, and proof of loss must be filed with the insurer following a loss.
- The risk manager may have less incentive to follow a loss-control program, because the insurer will pay the claim if a loss occurs. Such a lax attitude toward loss control could increase the number of noninsured losses as well.

Which Method Should Be Used?

In determining the appropriate method or methods for handling losses, a matrix can be used that classifies the various loss exposures according to frequency and severity. This matrix can be useful in determining which risk management method should be used (see Exhibit 3.3).

The first loss exposure is characterized by both low frequency and low severity of loss. One example of this type of exposure would be the potential theft of a secretary's dictionary. This type of exposure can be best handled by retention, because the loss occurs infrequently and, when it does occur, it seldom causes financial harm.

The second type of exposure is more serious. Losses occur frequently, but severity is relatively low. Examples of this type of exposure include physical damage losses to automobiles, workers compensation claims, shoplifting, and food spoilage. Loss control should be used here to reduce the frequency of losses. In addition, because losses occur regularly and are predictable, the retention technique can also be used. However, because small losses in the aggregate can reach sizable levels over a one-year period, excess insurance could also be purchased.

The third type of exposure can be met by insurance. As stated earlier, insurance is best suited for low-frequency, high-severity losses. High severity means that a catastrophic potential is present, while a low probability of loss indicates that the purchase of insurance is economically feasible. Examples of this type of exposure include fires, explosions, natural disasters, and liability lawsuits. The risk manager could also use a combination of retention and commercial insurance to deal with these exposures.

The fourth and most serious type of exposure is one characterized by both high frequency and high severity. This type of exposure is best handled by avoidance. For example, a truck driver with several convictions for drunk driving may apply for a job with a trucking company. If the driver is hired and injures or kills someone while under the influence of alcohol, the company would be faced with a catastrophic lawsuit. This exposure can be handled by avoidance. The driver should not be hired.

IMPLEMENTING AND ADMINISTERING THE RISK MANAGEMENT PROGRAM

At this point, we have discussed three of the four steps in the risk management process. The fourth step is implementation and administration of the risk management program. This step begins with a policy statement.

Risk Management Policy Statement

A **risk management policy statement** is necessary to have an effective risk management program. *This statement outlines the risk management objectives of the firm, as well as company policy with respect to treatment of loss exposures.* It also educates top-level executives in regard to the risk management process, gives the risk manager greater authority in the firm, and provides standards for judging the risk manager's performance.

In addition, a **risk management manual** may be developed and used in the program. The manual describes in some detail the risk management program of the firm and can be a very useful tool for training new employees who will be participating in the program. Writing the manual also forces the risk manager to state precisely his or her responsibilities, objectives, and available techniques.

Cooperation with Other Departments

The risk manager does not work alone. Other functional departments within the firm are extremely important in identifying pure loss exposures and methods for treating these exposures. These departments can cooperate in the risk management process in the following ways:

- *Accounting.* Internal accounting controls can reduce employee fraud and theft of cash.

EXHIBIT 3.3
Risk Management Matrix

Type of loss	Loss frequency	Loss severity	Appropriate risk management technique
1	Low	Low	Retention
2	High	Low	Loss control and retention
3	Low	High	Insurance
4	High	High	Avoidance

- *Finance.* Information can be provided showing how losses can disrupt profits and cash flow, and the effect that losses will have on the firm's balance sheet and profit and loss statement.
- *Marketing.* Accurate packaging can prevent liability lawsuits. Safe distribution procedures can prevent accidents.
- *Production.* Quality control can prevent the production of defective goods and liability lawsuits. Effective safety programs in the plant can reduce injuries and accidents.
- *Human resources.* This department may be responsible for employee benefit programs, pension programs, safety programs, and the company's hiring, promotion, and dismissal policies.

This list indicates how the risk management process involves the entire firm. Indeed, without the active cooperation of the other departments, the risk management program will be a failure.

Periodic Review and Evaluation

To be effective, the risk management program must be periodically reviewed and evaluated to determine whether the objectives are being attained. In particular, risk management costs, safety programs, and loss-prevention programs must be carefully monitored. Loss records must also be examined to detect any changes in frequency and severity. Finally, the risk manager must determine whether the firm's overall risk management policies are being carried out, and whether the risk manager is receiving the total cooperation of the other departments in carrying out the risk management functions.

PERSONAL RISK MANAGEMENT

The principles of corporate risk management are also applicable to a personal risk management program. **Personal risk management** *refers to the identification of pure risks faced by an individual or family, and to the selection of the most appropriate technique for treating such risks.* Personal risk management considers other methods for handling risk in addition to insurance.

Steps in Personal Risk Management

A personal risk management program involves four steps: (1) identify potential losses, (2) evaluate potential losses, (3) select the appropriate technique for handling losses, and (4) review the program periodically.

Identify Potential Losses The first step is to identify all potential losses that can cause serious financial problems. Catastrophic financial losses can result from the following:

1. Personal risks
   - Loss of earned income to the family because of the premature death of the family head
   - Insufficient income and financial assets during retirement
   - Catastrophic medical bills and the loss of earnings during an extended period of disability
   - Loss of earned income from unemployment
2. Property risks
   - Direct physical damage to a home and personal property because of fire, lightning, windstorm, flood, earthquake, or other causes
   - Indirect losses resulting from a direct physical damage loss, including extra expenses, moving to another apartment or home during the period of reconstruction, loss of rents, and loss of use of the building or property
   - Theft of valuable personal property, including money and securities, jewelry and furs, paintings and fine art, cameras, computer equipment, coin and stamp collections, and antiques
   - Direct physical damage losses to cars, motorcycles, and other vehicles from a collision and other-than-collision losses
   - Theft of cars, motorcycles, or other vehicles
3. Liability risks
   - Legal liability arising out of personal acts that cause bodily injury or property damage to others
   - Legal liability arising out of libel, slander, defamation of character, and similar exposures
   - Legal liability arising out of the negligent operation of a car, motorcycle, boat, or recreational vehicle

- Legal liability arising out of business or professional activities
- Payment of attorney fees and other legal defense costs

Evaluate Potential Losses The second step is to estimate the frequency and severity of potential losses so that the most appropriate technique can be used to deal with the risk. For example, the chance that your home will be totally destroyed by a fire, tornado, or hurricane is relatively small, but the severity of the loss can be catastrophic. Such losses should be insured because of their catastrophic potential. On the other hand, if loss frequency is high, but loss severity is low, such losses should not be insured (such as minor scratches and dents to your car). Other techniques such as retention are more appropriate for handling these types of small losses. For example, minor physical damage losses to your car can be retained by purchasing collision insurance with a deductible.

Select the Appropriate Technique for Handling Losses The third step is to select the most appropriate technique for handling each potential loss. The major methods for handling potential losses are avoidance, loss control, retention, noninsurance transfers, and insurance.

1. *Avoidance.* Avoidance is one method for handling a potential loss. For example, you can avoid being mugged in a high-crime rate area by staying out of the area, and you can avoid the loss from the sale of a home in a depressed real estate market by renting instead of buying.
2. *Loss control.* Loss control refers to activities that reduce both the frequency and severity of loss. For example, you can reduce your risk of an auto accident by driving within the speed limits, taking a safe driving course, and driving defensively. Car theft can be prevented by locking the car, removing the keys from the ignition, and installing anti-theft devices.

   Loss control also aims to reduce the severity of a loss. For example, wearing a helmet reduces the severity of a head injury in a motorcycle accident. Wearing a seat belt reduces the severity of an injury in an auto accident. Having a fire extin-

guisher on the premises reduces the severity of a fire.

3. *Retention.* Retention means that you retain part or all of a loss if it should occur. As noted earlier, risk retention can be active or passive. Active risk retention means you are aware of the risk and plan to retain part or all of it. For example, you can retain small collision losses to your car by buying a collision insurance policy with a deductible. Likewise, you can retain part of a loss to your home or to personal property by buying a homeowner's policy with a deductible.

   Risk can also be retained passively because of ignorance, indifference, or laziness. This practice can be dangerous if the retained risk could result in a catastrophic loss. For example, many workers are not insured against the risk of long-term disability, even though the adverse financial consequences from a long-term permanent disability generally are more severe than the financial consequences of premature death. Thus, workers who are not insured against this risk are using risk retention in a most dangerous and inappropriate manner.

4. *Noninsurance transfers.* Noninsurance transfers are methods other than insurance by which a pure risk is transferred to a party other than an insurer. For example, the risk of damage to rental property can be transferred to the tenant by requiring a damage deposit and by inserting a provision in the lease holding the tenant responsible for damages. Likewise, the risk of a defective television set can be transferred to the retailer by purchasing an extended-warranty contract that makes the retailer responsible for labor and repairs after the warranty expires.

5. *Insurance.* In a personal risk management program, most people rely heavily on insurance as the major method for dealing with risk. The use of insurance in a personal risk management program is discussed in greater detail later in the text when specific insurance contracts are analyzed.

Review the Program Periodically The final step is to review the personal risk management program periodically. At least every two or three years, you should determine whether all major risks are adequately covered. You should also review your program at major events in your life, such as a divorce, birth of a new child, purchase of a home, change of jobs, or death of a spouse or family member.

SUMMARY

- Risk management is a process to identify loss exposures faced by an organization and to select the most appropriate techniques.

- Risk management has several important objectives. Preloss objectives include the goals of economy, reduction of anxiety, and meeting legal obligations. Postloss objectives include survival of the firm, continued operation, stability of earnings, continued growth, and social responsibility.

- There are four steps in the risk management process.

    Potential losses must be identified.

    Potential losses must be evaluated in terms of loss frequency and loss severity.

    Appropriate methods for treating loss exposures must be selected.

    The risk management program must be implemented and properly administered.

- Risk control refers to techniques that reduce the frequency and severity of accidental losses. Major risk-control techniques include avoidance and loss control.

- Risk financing refers to techniques that provide for the funding of accidental losses after they occur. Major risk-financing techniques include retention, noninsurance transfers, and commercial insurance.

- Avoidance means that a loss exposure is never acquired or an existing loss exposure is abandoned. Loss prevention refers to measures that reduce the frequency of a particular loss. Loss reduction refers to measures that reduce the severity of a loss after it occurs.

- Retention means that the firm retains part or all of the losses that result from a given loss exposure. This technique can be used if no other method of treatment is available, the worst possible loss is not serious, and losses are highly predictable. Losses can be paid out of the firm's current net income; an unfunded or funded reserve can be established to pay losses; a credit line with a bank can provide funds to pay losses; or the firm can form a captive insurer.

- The advantages of retention are the saving of money on insurance premiums, lower expenses, greater incentive for loss prevention, and increased cash flow. Major disadvantages are possible higher losses that exceed the loss component in insurance premiums, possible higher expenses if loss-control and claims personnel must be hired, and possible higher taxes.

- A captive insurer is an insurer that is owned and established by a parent firm for the purpose of insuring the parent firm's loss exposures. Captive insurers are formed because of difficulty in obtaining insurance. They can also provide for greater stability of earnings; access to a reinsurer is easier; and captive insurers can be profit centers.

- Self-insurance or self-funding is a special form of planned retention by which part or all of a given loss exposure is retained by the firm.

- Noninsurance transfers are methods other than insurance by which a pure risk and its financial consequences are transferred to another party.

- Noninsurance transfers offer several advantages. The risk manager may be able to transfer some uninsurable exposures; noninsurance transfers may cost less than insurance; and the potential loss may be shifted to someone who is in a better position to exercise loss control. There are also several disadvantages. The transfer of a potential loss may fail because the contract language is ambiguous; the firm is still responsible for the loss if the party to whom the potential loss is transferred is unable to pay the loss; and an insurer may not give sufficient premium credit for the transfers.

- Commercial insurance can also be used in a risk management program. Use of insurance involves a selection of insurance coverages, selection of an insurer, negotiation of contract terms with the insurer, dissemination of information concerning the insurance coverages, and periodic review of the insurance program.

- The major advantages of insurance include indemnification after a loss occurs, reduction in uncertainty, availability of valuable risk management services, and the income-tax deductibility of the premiums. The major disadvantages of insurance include the cost of insurance, time and effort that must be spent in negotiating for insurance, and a possible lax attitude toward loss control because of the existence of insurance.

- A risk management program must be properly implemented and administered. This effort involves preparation of a risk management policy statement, close cooperation with other individuals and departments, and periodic review of the entire risk management program.

- The principles of corporate risk management can also be applied to a personal risk management program.

KEY CONCEPTS AND TERMS

Association or group captive	Personal risk management
Avoidance	Pure captive
Captive insurer	Retention
Deductible	Retention level
Excess insurance	Risk control
Loss control	Risk financing
Loss frequency	Risk management
Loss severity	Risk management manual
Manuscript policy	Risk management policy statement
Maximum possible loss	Risk retention group
Maximum probable loss	Self-insurance
Noninsurance transfers	

REVIEW QUESTIONS

1. Define risk management. How does risk management differ from insurance management?

2. Explain the objectives of a risk management program both before and after a loss occurs.

3. Explain the steps in the risk management process.

4. How can a risk manager identify potential losses? How does a risk manager evaluate and analyze each potential loss?

5. Distinguish between risk control and risk financing as major techniques for treating loss exposures. Give examples of each.

6. What conditions must be fulfilled before retention is used in a risk management program?

7. Define a captive insurer and explain why captive insurers are formed.

8. Is self-insurance the same as insurance? Explain.

9. Give several examples of noninsurance transfers.

10. Explain the basic factors that a risk manager must consider if commercial insurance is used in a risk management program.

APPLICATION QUESTIONS

1. The High-Rise Corporation manufactures and sells ladders and scaffolds that are used by construction firms. These products are sold to more than 1000 independent retailers in the United States. Management is concerned that the company could be sued if one of its products is defective and someone is injured. Because the cost of products liability insurance has increased, the company is looking for ways to control its loss exposures.
   a. Describe the steps in the risk management process.
   b. For each of the following risk management techniques, describe a specific action using that technique that may be helpful in dealing with the products liability exposure of the High-Rise Corporation.
      (1) Avoidance
      (2) Loss prevention
      (3) Loss reduction
      (4) Noninsurance transfers
   c. Captive insurers are a popular approach that many large corporations use to finance retained loss exposures. Explain the advantages of using a captive insurer in a risk management program.

2. Gem Corporation has 10,000 salespersons and employees in the United States who drive company cars. Ben Kim, risk manager of Gem Corporation, has recommended to the firm's management that the company should implement a partial retention program for collision losses to company cars.
   a. Describe the factors that Gem Corporation should consider in deciding whether it should partially retain the collision loss exposure to company cars.
   b. If the partial retention program is implemented, explain the various methods that Gem Corporation can use to pay for any collision losses to the company's cars.
   c. Explain the advantages and disadvantages of a partial retention program to Gem Corporation.
   d. Give an example of a noninsurance transfer that the company could use in its risk management program.

3. Luis has just been appointed head of the risk management department of Gates Manufacturing. His first ac-

tion as a risk manager is to prepare a formal risk management policy statement.

a. What benefits can the firm expect to receive from a well-prepared risk management policy statement?
b. Describe the different techniques that Luis might use to identify the firm's pure loss exposures.
c. Explain the advantages and disadvantages of using commercial insurance in the company's risk management program.

SELECTED REFERENCES

Harrington, Scott E., and Gregory R. Niehaus. *Risk Management and Insurance.* Boston, MA: Irwin/McGraw-Hill, 1999.

Head, George L., ed. *Essentials of Risk Control*, 3rd ed., vols. 1 and 2. Malvern, PA: Insurance Institute of America, 1995.

Head, George L., Michael W. Elliott, and James D. Blinn.

Case Application 1

City Bus Corporation provides school bus transportation to private and public schools in Lancaster County. City Bus owns 50 buses that are garaged in three different cities within the county. The firm faces competition from two larger bus companies that operate in the same area. Public school boards and private schools generally award contracts to the lowest bidder, but the level of service and overall performance are also considered.

a. Briefly describe the steps in the risk management process that should be followed by the risk manager of City Bus.
b. Identify the major loss exposures faced by City Bus.
c. For each of the loss exposures identified in (b), identify a risk management technique or combination of techniques that could be used to handle the exposure.
d. Describe several sources of funds for paying losses if retention is used in the risk management program.
e. Identify other departments in City Bus that would also be involved in the risk management program.

Case Application 2

Jennifer is a college junior who is majoring in business administration. She resides in a college dorm and has a roommate, Karen. Jennifer has a part-time job to help pay her miscellaneous expenses, but her parents are paying her tuition. Both parents must work to pay her tuition. In addition to an extensive wardrobe, books and supplies for her courses, and personal items, Jennifer owns an expensive stereo, a television set, and a trumpet that she plays as a member of the college band. She also owns a late-model sports car that she drives to and from her part-time job and to the beach and mountains where she loves to surf and ski. Jennifer and Karen frequently visit a local college bar on Friday evening where they drink and relax after a hard week of study and work.

Jennifer sometimes drinks excessively, but she will not allow Karen to drive her back to the dorm.

a. Describe briefly the steps in the personal risk management process.
b. Identify the major pure risks or loss exposures to which Jennifer is exposed with respect to each of the following:
   (1) Personal risks
   (2) Property risks
   (3) Liability risks
c. With respect to each of the pure risks or loss exposures mentioned, identify an appropriate personal risk management technique that could be used to treat the exposure.

Essentials of Risk Financing, 3rd ed. Malvern, PA: Insurance Institute of America, 1996.

Head, George L., and Stephen Horn II. *Essentials of Risk Management*, 3rd ed., vols. 1 and 2. Malvern, PA: Insurance Institute of America, 1997.

Williams, C. Arthur, Jr., Michael L. Smith, and Peter C. Young. *Risk Management and Insurance*, 8th ed. Boston, MA: Irwin/McGraw-Hill, 1998.

Vaughan, Emmett J. *Risk Management*. New York: John Wiley & Sons, Inc., 1997.

NOTES

1. Robert I. Mehr and Bob A. Hedges, *Risk Management: Concepts and Applications* (Homewood, IL: Richard D. Irwin, 1974), Chapters 1 and 2. See also George L. Head and Stephen Horn II, *Essentials of Risk Management*, 3rd ed., Vol. 1 (Malvern, PA: Insurance Institute of America, 1997), pp. 70–79.

2. This section is based on Head and Horn, *Essentials of Risk Management*, pp. 36–44, and C. Arthur Williams, Jr., et al., *Principles of Risk Management and Insurance*, 2nd ed., Vol. I (Malvern, PA: American Institute for Property and Liability Underwriters, 1981), Chapters 2–3.

3. Williams, et al., pp. 125–126.

4. Head and Horn, pp. 40–42.

5. These cases include *Harper v. Commissioner, 1991*; *Sears, Roebuck and Co. v. Commissioner, 1991*; and *Amerco v. Commissioner, 1991*.

6. Williams, et al., pp. 126–133.

7. *Ibid.*, pp. 103–104.

8. *Ibid.*, pp. 107–123, 146–151.

9. A manuscript policy is one specifically designed for a firm to meet its specific needs and requirements.

10. Williams, et al., pp. 108–116.

C Students may take a self-administered test on this chapter at www.awlonline.com/rejda

Chapter 4

Advanced Topics in Risk Management*

> " *The field of Risk Management is undergoing monumental change. Risk Managers must understand financial markets and be able to effectively incorporate quantitative analysis and technology in their risk management programs.* "
>
> Millicent W. Workman, CPCU,
> Risk Manager, Mueller Industries

Learning Objectives

After studying this chapter, you should be able to:

▲ Explain the expanding scope of risk management, including financial risk management and enterprise risk management.

▲ Describe the impact of the underwriting cycle and consolidation in the insurance industry on the practice of risk management.

▲ Explain the methods that a risk manager employs to forecast losses.

▲ Show how financial analysis can be applied to risk management decision making.

▲ Describe how technology is used in risk management programs.

▲ Access an Internet site and obtain information about commercial risk management.

Internet Resources

- The **Captive Insurance Companies Association** is an organization that disseminates information to companies that use captive insurers to solve corporate insurance problems. The organization claims that its Web site enables risk managers, owners of captives, students, and anyone who has an interest in alternative risk transfer techniques to meet with colleagues, ask questions of the finest experts in the field, and find needed resources. Visit the site at:

  http://www.captive.com

- **IFIC RISK WATCH** provides a comprehensive introduction to financial risk management from the International Finance & Commodities Institute. This site educates readers on the most valuable official documents on this subject. Along with a risk management checklist, this site also includes a regulatory documents

*Prepared by Michael J. McNamara, Washington State University.

library, a collection of risk management case studies, and a risk management glossary. Visit the site at:

http://risk.ifci.ch/index.htm

- The **Nonprofit Risk Management Center** is an organization that conducts research and education on risk management and insurance issues that are of special concern to nonprofit organizations. The organization publishes a newsletter, easy-to-read publications, and informative briefs (called Riskfacts) on frequently asked questions related to risk management and insurance. The organization also offers consulting services and risk audits. Visit the site at:

http://www.nonprofitrisk.org

- The **Public Risk Management Association** is an organization that represents risk managers of state and local governmental units. The organization provides practical training and education for risk managers in the public sector; publishes a magazine, newsletter, and detailed issue-specific publications; and provides cutting-edge updates on federal regulations and legislation. Visit the site at:

http://www.primacentral.org

- The **Risk and Insurance Management Society (RIMS)** is the premier professional association in the United States for risk managers and corporate buyers of insurance. RIMS provides a forum for the discussion of common risk management issues, supports loss-prevention activities, and makes known to insurers the insurance needs of its members. RIMS has local chapters in major cities. Visit the site at:

http://www.rims.org

- The **Self-Insurance Institute of America** is a national association that promotes self-insurance as an alternative method for financing losses. The organization publishes technical articles on self-insurance, holds educational conferences, and promotes the legislative and regulatory interests of self-insurance at both the federal and state levels. Visit the site at:

http://www.siia.org

 niversal Holdings (UH) is a conglomerate consisting of 16 separate companies. UH has followed a "growth through acquisition" strategy, purchasing companies that UH executives believe have not yet realized their true potential. Because the companies acquired are large and operate in different sectors of the economy, each company is responsible for its own risk management program.

Northeast Petroleum (NP), UH's latest acquisition, owns and operates a refinery and 78 service stations. The company also sells heating oil to more than 40,000 business and residential customers in four Northeastern states. NP has never employed a "risk manager." Instead, the risk management function has been performed primarily by the company's treasurer, as time permitted. Insurance coverages have been renewed each year, with little attention given to the company's loss exposures, claims, scope of insurance coverages, and cost of insurance. Shortly after NP's purchase by UH, Tom Bryant was hired as the company's first full-time risk manager. Tom has been charged with developing a state-of-the-art risk management program for NP.

As discussed in Chapter 3, Tom's job as risk manager will involve more than simply purchasing insurance. He must identify the loss exposures faced by the company, analyze those exposures, select and implement a combination of risk treatment measures, and monitor the success of the risk management program. The fact that NP has never had a risk manager and the nature of NP's operations combine to provide an excellent opportunity for Tom to apply some advanced risk management methods in the program that he designs.

This chapter builds on the discussion of risk management in Chapter 3 and discusses some advanced topics in risk management. Topics discussed include the changing scope of risk management, insurance market dynamics, loss forecasting, financial analysis in risk management decision making, and application of technology in risk management programs.

THE CHANGING SCOPE OF RISK MANAGEMENT

Traditionally, risk management was limited in scope to pure loss exposures, including property risks, liability risks, and personnel risks. An interesting trend emerged in the 1990s, however, as many businesses began to expand the scope of risk management to include speculative financial risks. Recently, a few businesses have gone a step further, expanding their risk management programs to consider all risks faced by the organization.

Financial Risk Management

Business firms face a number of speculative financial risks. **Financial risk management** *refers to the identification, analysis, and treatment of speculative financial risks.* These risks include the following:

- Commodity price risk
- Interest rate risk
- Currency exchange rate risk

Commodity Price Risk **Commodity price risk** *is the risk of losing money if the price of a commodity changes.* Producers and users of commodities face commodity price risks. For example, consider an agricultural operation that will have thousands of bushels of grain at harvest time. At harvest, the price of the commodity may have increased or decreased, depending on the supply and demand for grain. Because little storage is available for the crop, the grain must be sold at the current market price, even if that price is low. In a similar fashion, users and distributors of commodities face commodity price risks. Consider a cereal company that has promised to deliver 500,000 boxes of cereal at an agreed-upon price in six months. In the meantime, the price of grain—a commodity needed to produce the cereal—may increase or decrease, altering the profitability of the transaction.

Interest Rate Risk Financial institutions are especially susceptible to interest rate risk. **Interest rate risk** *is the risk of loss caused by adverse interest rate movements.* For example, consider a bank that has loaned money at fixed interest rates to home purchasers under 15- and 30-year mortgages. If interest rates increase, the bank must pay higher rates on deposits while the mortgages are locked in at lower rates. Similarly, a corporation might issue bonds at a time when interest rates are high. For the bonds to sell at their face value when issued, the coupon interest rate must equal the investor-required rate of return. If interest rates later decline, the company must still pay the higher coupon interest rate.

Currency Exchange Rate Risk The currency exchange rate is the value for which one nation's currency may be converted to another nation's currency. For example, one Canadian dollar might be worth the equivalent of two-thirds of one U.S. dollar. At this currency exchange rate, one U.S. dollar may be converted to one and one-half Canadian dollars.

U.S. companies that have international operations are susceptible to currency exchange rate risk. **Currency exchange rate risk** *is the risk of loss of value caused by changes in the rate at which one nation's currency may be converted to another nation's currency.* For example, a U.S. company faces currency exchange rate risk when it agrees to accept a specified amount of foreign currency in the future as payment for a commodity or work performed. Likewise, U.S. companies with significant foreign operations face an earnings risk because of fluctuating exchange rates. When a U.S. company generates profits abroad, those gains must be translated back into U.S. dollars. When the U.S. dollar is strong (that is, has a high value relative to a foreign currency), the foreign currency purchases fewer U.S. dollars and the company's earnings therefore are lower. A weak U.S. dollar (that is, having a low value relative to a foreign currency) means that foreign profits can be exchanged for a larger number of U.S. dollars, and consequently the firm's earnings are higher.

Managing Financial Risks The traditional separation of pure and speculative risks meant that different business departments addressed these risks. Pure risks were handled by the risk manager through risk retention, risk transfer, and loss control. Speculative risks were handled by the finance division through contractual provisions and capital market instruments. Examples of contractual provisions that address financial risks include call features on bonds that permit bonds with high coupon rates to be retired early and adjustable interest rate provisions on mortgages through which the interest rate varies with interest rates in the general economy. A variety of capital market approaches are also employed, including options contracts, forward contracts, futures contracts, and interest rate swaps.[1] For example, the grain producer cited earlier could hedge the commodity price risk by using futures contracts (see Exhibit 4.1).

During the 1990s, some businesses began taking a more holistic view of the pure and speculative risks faced by the organization, hoping to achieve cost

---

EXHIBIT 4.1
Hedging a Commodity Price Risk

Steve is a corn grower who estimates in May that his corn production will total 20,000 bushels of corn, with the harvest completed by December. Checking the price of futures contracts, he notices that the price of December corn is $2.90 per bushel. Steve would like to hedge the risk that the price of corn will be lower at harvest time and can do so by the appropriate use of futures contracts. Because corn futures contracts are traded in 5000 bushel units, Steve would sell four contracts in May totaling 20,000 bushels in the futures market. In December, he would buy back four contracts to offset his futures position. As demonstrated below, it doesn't matter whether the price of corn has increased or decreased. By using futures contracts and ignoring transaction expenses, Steve has locked in total revenue of $58,000.

If the market price of corn drops to $2.50 per bushel in December:

Revenue from sale of corn:	20,000 × $2.50	=	$50,000
Sale of four contracts at $2.90 in May	58,000		
Purchase of four contracts at $2.50 in December	50,000		
Gain on futures transaction:			8,000
Total revenue			$58,000

If the market price of corn increases to $3.00 per bushel in December:

Revenue from sale of corn:	20,000 × $3.00	=	$60,000
Sale of four contracts at $2.90 in May	58,000		
Purchase of four contracts at $3.00 in December	60,000		
Loss on futures transaction:			(2,000)
Total revenue			$58,000

SOURCE: Adapted from George E. Rejda and Michael J. McNamara, *Personal Financial Planning* (Addison-Wesley Educational Publishers, 1998), Exhibit 15.3, p. 554.

savings and better risk treatment solutions by combining coverage for both types of risk. In 1997, Honeywell became the first company to enter into an "integrated risk program" with American International Group (AIG).[2] An **integrated risk program** *is a risk treatment technique that combines coverage for pure and speculative risks in the same contract.* At the time, Honeywell was generating more than one-third of its profits abroad. Its integrated risk program provided traditional property and liability insurance, as well as coverage for currency exchange rate risk.

In recognition of the fact that they are treating these risks jointly, some organizations have created a new position. The **chief risk officer (CRO)** *is responsible for treatment of the pure and speculative risks faced by the organization.* Combining responsibilities in one area permits treatment of the risks in a unified, and often more economical way. For example, the risk manager may be concerned about a large self-insured property claim. The financial manager may be concerned about losses caused by adverse changes in the exchange rate. Either loss, by itself, may not harm the organization if the company has a strong balance sheet. The occurrence of both losses, however, may damage the business more severely. An integrated risk management program can be designed to consider both contingencies by including a double-trigger option. A **double-trigger option** *is a provision that provides for payment only if two specified losses occur.* Thus payments would be made only if a large property claim *and* a large exchange rate loss occurred. The cost of such coverage is less than the cost of treating each risk separately.

Enterprise Risk Management

Encouraged by the success of financial risk management, a few organizations are considering the next logical step. **Enterprise risk management** *is a comprehensive risk management program that addresses an organization's pure risks, speculative risks, strategic risks, and operational risks.* Pure and speculative risks were defined previously. *Strategic risk* refers to uncertainty regarding the organization's goals and objectives, and the organization's strengths, weaknesses, opportunities, and threats. *Operational risks*

are risks that develop out of business operations, including such things as manufacturing products and providing services to customers. By packaging all of these risks in a single program, the corporation offsets one risk against another, and in the process reduces its overall risk. As long as the risks combined in the program are not perfectly positively correlated, the combination of exposures reduces risk. Indeed, if some of the risks are negatively correlated, risk can be reduced significantly.

Consider NP's operations, for example. During the summer, the company agrees to deliver heating oil in the fall at a specified price. Between summer and the delivery date, the price of heating oil may increase. Considering this risk only, Tom Bryant may decide to use heating oil futures contracts to hedge the company's price risk. NP's other business operations, which include 78 service stations, provide a natural hedge position, however. If the price of fuel increases during the summer months, NP will make money through its service station operations, but lose money covering the promised heating oil delivery. Likewise, if the price of heating oil and gasoline falls between the summer and the fall, NP will make money delivering heating oil at a price higher than the current market price of heating oil at a time when gasoline sales may not be as profitable.

An enterprise risk program can account for a wide array of risks. Insight 4.1 discusses this exciting innovation in risk management.

INSURANCE MARKET DYNAMICS

Chapter 3 discussed the various methods of dealing with risk. When property and liability loss exposures are not eliminated through risk avoidance, losses that occur must be financed in some other way. The risk manager must choose between two methods of funding losses: *risk retention* and *risk transfer.* Retained losses can be paid out of current earnings, from loss reserves, by borrowing, or by a captive insurance company. Risk transfer shifts the burden of paying for losses to another party, most often a property and liability insurance company. Decisions about whether to retain risks or to transfer them must take into account the current conditions in insurance markets. Two important factors must be considered:

- The underwriting cycle
- Consolidation in the insurance industry

The Underwriting Cycle

For many years, a cyclical pattern has been observed in a number of underwriting results and profitability measures in the property and liability insurance industry. *This cyclical pattern in underwriting stringency, premium levels, and profitability is referred to as the underwriting cycle. Property and liability insurance markets fluctuate between periods of tight underwriting standards and high premiums, called a* "hard" insurance market, *and periods of loose underwriting standards and low premiums, called a* "soft" insurance market.

A number of measures can be used to ascertain the status of the underwriting cycle. Exhibit 4.2 shows the combined ratio for the property and liability insurance industry over time. The **combined ratio** *is the ratio of losses paid plus expenses to premiums.* If the ratio is greater than 1 (or 100 percent), underwriting operations are unprofitable. If the ratio is less than 1 (or 100 percent), insurance companies are making money on underwriting operations.

Risk managers must consider current premium rates and underwriting standards when making their retention and transfer decisions. When the market is "soft," insurance can be purchased at favorable terms (for example, lower premiums, broader coverage, removal of exclusions). In a "hard" market, more retention is used because some insurance coverages are limited in availability or may not be affordable. The continued soft market of the late 1990s, for example, led some risk managers to

EXHIBIT 4.2
Combined Ratio for All Lines of Property and Liability Insurance, 1954–1998

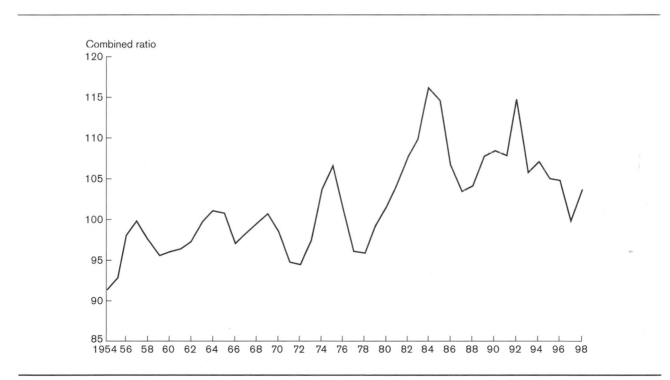

Source: *Best's Aggregates & Averages—Property-Casualty* (Oldwick, NJ: A.M. Best Company, 1999), p. 256.

Insight 4.1

The Final Frontier of Risk

Star Trek's Captain Kirk would appreciate the gesture. A pioneering group of insurers is breaching the new frontier, selling comprehensive insurance policies that cover corporate risk like no other insurance of the past. Paying homage to the star voyager's spaceship, they have named the pioneering strategy, "enterprise risk management."

Half a dozen corporations are said to be in the final stages of buying the new policy, with two—Canada's United Grain Growers and Dayton, Ohio-based Mead Corp.—about to close in the next few weeks. These companies are seeking a more comprehensive system of transferring risks, one that addresses not only their customary property and casualty exposures, but their financial, strategic, and operational risks as well.

Enterprise risk management is the solution, they say. "It's a system of identifying, analyzing, quantifying, and comparing a wide range of risks, and then transferring them in a single block," says Doug Oliver, vice-president of financial engineering at New York-based AIG Risk Finance, a division of American International Group. The exposures can include the weather, the market price of natural gas, the nonpayment of credit, and the fiduciary liabilities of a board of directors, he notes.

Rather than transfer such risks individually via different instruments—the traditional approach—the exposures are grouped together and transferred in a basket to an insurer. By taking this approach, risk-transfer costs are less for buyers, since risks frequently are uncorrelated; that is, the possibility of all of them causing losses in a given calendar period is rare. "As long as you can put risks together that are not perfectly correlated, like the risk of a fire occurring at the same time there is an adverse movement in a foreign currency and a drop in the equity market, you reduce overall risk and, thus, risk transfer costs," Oliver explains.

Take the case of Mead Corp. The company plans to close a deal with AIG for a single insurance policy that baskets a wide array of its exposures, including property/casualty, foreign-exchange translation, interest rate, and various commodity price risks. Mead anticipates saving 20 percent less the cost of its previous, traditional risk transfer program.

Holistic Healers

Enterprise risk management is the logical conclusion of a voyage toward a new kind of risk-transfer system. Academics had long touted the natural offsetting positions that accrue when risks are combined in a single-transfer vehicle. Insurers took this theory and tested it, developing multiline property and casualty insurance policies in the early 1990s.

Coming out of the hard market of the previous decade, corporate customers of insurance were on the prowl for more economical ways to transfer risk, and the new multiline policies, written on a three- to five-year contract basis, were just the ticket.

In mid-1997, Honeywell took the next pioneering step, adding foreign-exchange exposures to its multiline policy, thereby marking the first time a financial exposure was transferred via a basket of insured risk. The Minneapolis-based Global Controls Company said it is considering adding other corporate exposures to its integrated risk portfolio, including interest-rate fluctuations and adverse weather events.

Mead and United Grain Growers (UGG) are two of six corporations taking the final step—a basket covering virtually every risk facing the companies. Winnipeg-based UGG, for example, worked with its broker, London-based Willis Corroon, to identify 32 risks outside of its customary hazard (insurable) risks. "The process involved about 20 of UGG's key people from various parts of the firm," says Carl Groth, a Willis Corroon senior vice-president and director of its New York-based alternative risk transfer division.

"We prioritized the risks and then selected six for the portfolio. These included credit, weather, environmental, counterparty exposures (a default from a noncredit event), inventory, and various grain commodities, such as barley and wheat. We blended these risks with the company's customary property/casualty risks."

The offsetting positions offered by basketing uncorrelated risks seem to be the main reason why enterprise risk transfer is attracting corporate adherents.

The Process

Due to the fact that a plethora of completely different exposures are bundled together in an enterprise risk basket, no two policies are alike. The level of self-insured retention also varies, geared to the particular risk-taking appetite of each buyer. In short, the strategy is custom-tailored—a far cry from off-the-shelf insurance policies or generic derivatives.

The first part of an enterprise risk management process involves detailed discussions with various corporate department heads, since, in most traditionally structured companies, different departments oversee different risks. A company's assistant treasurer monitors foreign-exchange risk, its commodity traders manage commodity risks, and the risk manager supervises property exposures.

After sharing information on the different strategic, financial, operational, and hazard risks facing the company, the next step is to pick those risks that would benefit most from a portfolio approach. "The key here is to select the risks that are least correlated," Groth says.

Part of this process involves risk quantification. Brokers and insurers use so-called value-at-risk (VAR) techniques developed by the banking industry to calculate the amount of risk in each area. *All the risks are mathematically reduced to a common denominator, called a unit of risk, which permits comparison with each other. The exercise helps determine the most advantageous portfolio of risk to take to market.*

For the most part, brokers seek a single source of transfer, preferably an insurance company, according

to Groth. Nevertheless, the portfolio could be taken to the capital markets or broken into different layers spread among several insurers and investment banks. Most programs, including Mead's and UGG's, sit on top of a significant layer of corporate self-insurance, which is determined by the risk-quantification process.

The complex nature of enterprise risk management explains, in part why only half a dozen companies are said to be in the process of buying such policies. Another reason for the slow acceptance is the protracted soft insurance market and vibrant derivatives market. A final one is corporate cold feet. "Why should we tinker with something new when what we're already doing is working just fine," says one risk manager.

Earnings Stability

At the heart of enterprise risk management is a pronounced corporate desire to maintain or increase shareholder value. Wall Street analysts tend to punish the valuations of companies that fail to meet quarterly earnings estimates. By transferring the risks that create volatility for corporate earnings, share values are stabilized.

Will other insurers and reinsurers jump onto the enterprise bandwagon? "You need wide expertise, ranging from knowledge about property and casualty risks to capital-market strategies," says AIG's Oliver.

Markets also must be of substantial size to take on such broad-based risk. "You want an AAA-rated carrier with a big enough balance sheet to put out hundreds of millions of dollars of capacity if the insured's plant burns down, oil prices rise, and the equity market turns downward—in the same breath," Oliver adds. "Although it's unlikely, the planets can all line up against you." Captain Kirk would understand.

SOURCE: Russ Banham, "The Final Frontier of Risk," *Reactions* (May 1999), pp. 20–22.

purchase multiple-year insurance contracts in an effort to lock in favorable terms.

What causes these price fluctuations in property and liability insurance markets? Although a number of explanations have been offered,[3] two obvious factors affect property and liability insurance pricing and underwriting decisions:

- Insurance industry capacity
- Investment returns

Insurance Industry Capacity In the insurance industry, **capacity** *refers to the relative level of surplus. Surplus is the difference between an insurer's assets and its liabilities.* When the property and liability insurance industry is in a strong surplus position, insurers can reduce premiums and loosen underwriting standards, because they have a cushion to draw on if underwriting results prove unfavorable. Given the flexibility of financial capital and the competitive nature of the insurance industry, other insurers often follow suit if one insurer takes this step. As competition intensifies, premiums are reduced further, and underwriting standards are applied less stringently. Underwriting losses begin to mount for insurers, because inadequate premiums have been charged to inferior risks. External factors (such as earthquakes, hurricanes, and large liability awards) may increase the level of claims, exacerbating the problem. The underwriting losses reduce insurers' surplus positions; and at some point, premiums must be raised and underwriting standards tightened to restore the depleted surplus. These actions will lead to a return to profitable underwriting, which helps to replenish the surplus position. When adequate surplus is restored, insurers once again become able to reduce premiums and loosen underwriting standards, causing the cycle to repeat.

Investment Returns Would you sell insurance if, for every dollar you collected in premiums, you expected to pay 78 cents in losses and 26 cents in expenses? That payout rate would lead to a loss of 4 cents per dollar of premiums collected. Property and liability insurance companies can, and often do, sell coverages at an expected loss, hoping to offset underwriting losses with investment income. In reality, insurance companies are in two businesses: underwriting risks and investing premiums. If insurers expect favorable investment results, they can sell their insurance coverages at lower premium rates, hoping to offset underwriting losses with investment income. Many people cite the high rates of return on the equity portion of insurers' investment portfolios as a major factor contributing to the prolonged soft market in the 1990s.

Consolidation in the Insurance Industry

The 1990s constituted a period of great consolidation in the financial services industry. **Consolidation** *means the combining of business organizations through mergers and acquisitions.* A number of consolidation trends have changed the insurance marketplace for risk managers:

- Insurance company mergers and acquisitions
- Insurance brokerage mergers and acquisitions
- Cross-industry consolidations

Insurance Company Mergers and Acquisitions
Given the market structure of the property and liability insurance industry (many companies, relatively low barriers to entry given the flexibility of financial capital, and relatively homogenous products), the greater number of insurance company consolidations in the 1990s may not have severe effects on risk managers' operations. Risk managers may notice, however, that the marketplace is populated by fewer large, independent insurance organizations as a result of consolidation. Mergers and acquisitions are discussed in greater detail later in the text.

Insurance Brokerage Mergers and Acquisitions
Consolidation of insurance brokerages has had profound consequences for risk managers. **Insurance brokers** *are intermediaries who represent insurance purchasers. Insurance brokers attempt to place their clients' business with insurers.* Clearly, a risk manager wants to obtain insurance coverages and related services under the most favorable financial terms available. Periodically, risk managers contact several insurance agents and insurance brokers in an effort to obtain competitive insurance coverage bids. The number of large, national insurance brokerages has declined significantly in recent years because of consolidation. For example, before the consolidation of recent years, a risk manager could obtain

coverage bids through Sedgwick Group, Johnson & Higgins, and Marsh & McLennan. As a result of consolidation, these three large, independent brokerages are now a single entity—Marsh and McLennon Companies, Inc. Other large insurance brokerages have merged with or been acquired by other insurance brokerages as well.[4]

Cross-Industry Consolidation Consolidation in the financial services arena is not limited to insurance companies and insurance brokerages. The boundaries separating institutions with depository functions and institutions that underwrite risks are blurring. Citigroup provides the best example of this cross-industry consolidation. Citigroup includes Citibank, Travelers Insurance Group, Smith Barney, and several other financial services operations. Recently, the U.S. Office of Thrift Supervision granted some insurance companies authority to engage in banking activities.[5] In the future, it may become commonplace for insurers to offer a broad array of financial services to their policyowners, including lending, banking, and investment services.

LOSS FORECASTING

The risk manager must have some indication of the organization's loss frequency and severity when selecting a risk treatment method. Although loss history provides valuable information, there is no guarantee that future losses will follow past loss trends. Risk managers can employ a number of techniques to assist in predicting loss levels, including the following:

- Probability analysis
- Regression analysis
- Forecasting using loss distributions

Probability Analysis

Chance of loss is the probability that an adverse event will occur. The probability (P) of such an event is equal to the number of events likely to occur (X) divided by the number of exposure units (N). Thus, if the vehicle fleet has 500 vehicles and on average 100 vehicles suffer physical damage each year, the probability that a fleet vehicle will be damaged in any given year is:

$$P(\text{physical damage}) = 100/500 = .20 \text{ or } 20\%$$

Some probabilities of events can be easily deduced (for example, the probability that a fair coin will come up "heads" or "tails"). Other probabilities (for example, the probability that a male age 50 will die before reaching age 60) may be estimated from prior loss data.

The risk manager must also be concerned with the characteristics of the event being analyzed. Some events are independent. *An event is* **independent** *if its occurrence does not affect the occurrence of another event.* For example, assume that a business has production facilities in Louisiana and Virginia, and that the probability of a fire at the Louisiana plant is 5 percent and that the probability of a fire at the Virginia plant is 4 percent. Obviously, the occurrence of one of these events does not influence the occurrence of the other event. If events are independent, the probability that they will occur together is the product of the individual probabilities. Thus, the probability that both production facilities will be damaged by fire is:

$$P(\text{fire at Louisiana plant}) \times P(\text{fire at Virginia plant}) = P(\text{fire at both plants})$$
$$.04 \times .05 = .002 \text{ or } .2\%$$

Other events are dependent. *If two or more events are* **dependent**, *the occurrence of one event affects the occurrence of the other.* If two buildings are located close together, and one building catches on fire, the probability that the other building will burn is increased. For example, suppose that the individual probability of a fire loss at either building is 3 percent. The probability that the second building will have a fire given that the first building has a fire, however, may be 40 percent. Then what is the probability of two fires? This is a conditional probability that is equal to the probability of the first event multiplied by the probability of the second event given that the first event has occurred:

$$P(\text{fire at one bldg}) \times P\left(\begin{array}{c}\text{fire at second bldg}\\\text{given fire at first bldg}\end{array}\right) = P(\text{both burn})$$
$$.03 \times .40 = .012 \text{ or } 1.20\%$$

Events may also be mutually exclusive. *Events are* **mutually exclusive** *if the occurrence of one event precludes the occurrence of the second event.* For example, if a building is destroyed by fire, it cannot also be destroyed by flood. Mutually exclusive probabilities are additive. If the probability that a building will be destroyed by fire is 2 percent and the probability that the building will be destroyed by flood is 1 percent, then the probability the building will be destroyed by either fire or flood is:

$$P(\text{fire destroys bldg}) + P(\text{flood destroys bldg})$$
$$= P(\text{fire or flood destroys bldg})$$
$$.02 + .01 = .03 \text{ or } 3\%$$

If the independent events are not mutually exclusive, then more than one event could occur. Care must be taken not to "double-count" when determining the probability that at least one event will occur. For example, if the probability of minor fire damage is 4 percent and the probability of minor flood damage is 3 percent, then the probability of at least one of these events occurring is:

$$P(\text{minor fire}) + P(\text{minor flood})$$
$$- P(\text{minor fire and flood}) = P(\text{at least one event})$$
$$.04 + .03 - (.04) \times (.03) = .0688 \text{ or } 6.88\%$$

Assigning probabilities to individual and joint events and analyzing the probabilities can assist the risk manager in formulating a risk treatment plan.

Regression Analysis

Regression analysis *is a method of characterizing the relationship between two or more variables and then using this characterization as a predictor.* One variable—the dependent variable—is hypothesized to be a function of one or more independent variables. It is not difficult to envision relationships that would be of interest to risk managers in which one variable is dependent upon another variable. Consider workers compensation claims. It is logical to hypothesize that the number of workers compensation claims should be positively related to some variable representing employment (for example, the number of employees, payroll, or hours worked). Likewise, we

would expect the number of physical damage claims for a fleet of vehicles to increase as the size of the fleet increases or as the number of miles driven each year by fleet vehicles increases.

The first panel in Exhibit 4.3 provides data for a company's annual payroll in thousands of dollars and the corresponding number of workers compensation claims during the year. In the second panel of Exhibit 4.3, the number of claims is plotted against payroll. Regression analysis provides the coordinates of the line that best fits the points in the chart. This line will minimize the sum of the squared deviations of the points from the line. Our hypothesized relationship is as follows:

$$\text{Number of workers compensation claims}$$
$$= B_0 + (B_1 \times \text{Payroll [in thousands]})$$

where B_0 is a constant and B_1 is the coefficient of the independent variable.

The regression results provided at the bottom of Exhibit 4.3 were obtained using spreadsheet software. The coefficient of determination, R-square, ranges from 0 to 1 and measures the model fit. An R-square value close to 1 indicates that the model does a good job of predicting Y values. By substituting the estimated payroll for next year (in thousands), the risk manager estimates that 509 workers compensation claims will occur in the next year.

Forecasting Using Loss Distributions

Another useful tool for the risk manager is loss forecasting based on loss distributions. A **loss distribution** *is a probability distribution of losses that could occur.* Forecasting by using loss distributions works well if the history of losses tends to follow a specified distribution and the sample size is large. Knowing the parameters that specify the loss distribution (for example, mean, standard deviation, and frequency of occurrence) enables the risk manager to estimate the number of events, severity, and confidence intervals. Many loss distributions can be employed, depending on the pattern of losses. The Appendix at the end of this chapter discusses loss forecasting based on the normal distribution, a widely used measure.

EXHIBIT 4.3
Relationship Between Payroll and Number of Workers Compensation Claims

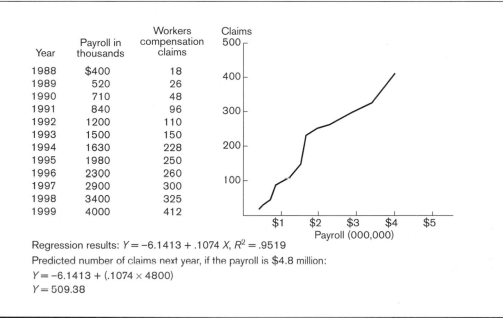

Year	Payroll in thousands	Workers compensation claims
1988	$400	18
1989	520	26
1990	710	48
1991	840	96
1992	1200	110
1993	1500	150
1994	1630	228
1995	1980	250
1996	2300	260
1997	2900	300
1998	3400	325
1999	4000	412

Regression results: $Y = -6.1413 + .1074\ X$, $R^2 = .9519$

Predicted number of claims next year, if the payroll is $4.8 million:

$Y = -6.1413 + (.1074 \times 4800)$
$Y = 509.38$

FINANCIAL ANALYSIS IN RISK MANAGEMENT DECISION MAKING

Risk managers must make a number of important decisions, including whether to retain or transfer loss exposures, which insurance coverage bid is best, and whether to invest in loss control projects. Underlying a risk manager's decisions is simple economics—weighing the costs and benefits of a course of action to see whether it is in the economic interests of the company and its claimholders. Financial analysis can be applied to assist in risk management decision making. To make decisions involving cash flows in different time periods, the risk manager must employ time value of money analysis.

The Time Value of Money

Because risk management decisions will likely involve cash flows in different time periods, the time value of money must be considered. The **time value** of money *means that when valuing cash flows in different time periods, the interest-earning capacity of money must be taken into account.* A dollar received today is worth more than a dollar received one year from today, because the dollar received today can be invested immediately to earn interest. Therefore, when evaluating cash flows in different time periods, it is important to adjust dollar values to reflect the earning of interest.

A lengthy discourse on the time value of money is beyond the scope of this text.[6] Instead, we will limit our treatment to the valuation of single cash flows.

Suppose you open a bank account today and deposit $100. The value of the account today—the present value—is $100. Further assume that the bank is willing to pay 5 percent interest, compounded annually, on your account. What is the account balance one year from today? At that time, you would have your original $100, plus an additional 5 percent of $100, or $5 in interest:

$$100 + (\$100 \times .05) = \$105$$

Factoring, you would have

$$\$100 \times (1 + .05) = \$105$$

Thus, if you multiply the starting amount (the present value, or PV) by 1 plus the interest rate (i), it will give you the amount one year from today (the future value, or FV):

$$PV \times (1 + i) = FV$$

If you want to know the account balance after two years, simply multiply the balance at the end of the first year by 1 plus the interest rate. In this way, we arrive at the simple formula for the future value of a present amount:

$$PV (1 + i)^n = FV, \text{ where } "n" \text{ is the number}$$
$$\text{of time periods}$$

In the second year, not only will you earn interest on the original deposit, but you will also earn interest on the $5 in interest you earned in the first period. *Because you are earning interest on interest (compound interest), the operation through which a present value is converted to a future value is called* **compounding**.

Compounding also works in reverse. Assume that you know the value of a future cash flow, but you want to know what the cash flow is worth today, adjusting for the time value of money. Dividing both sides of our compounding equation by $(1 + i)^n$ yields the following expression:

$$PV = \frac{FV}{(1+i)^n}$$

Thus, if you want to know the present value of any future amount, divide the future amount by 1 plus the interest rate, raised to the number of periods. *This operation—bringing a future value back to present value—is called* **discounting**.

Financial Analysis Applications

In many instances, the time value of money can be applied in risk management decision making. We will consider two applications:

- Analyzing insurance coverage bids
- Loss-control investment decisions

Analyzing Insurance Coverage Bids Assume that Tom Bryant would like to purchase property insurance on a building. He is analyzing two insurance coverage bids. The bids are from comparable insurance companies, and the coverage amounts are the same. The premiums and deductibles, however, differ. Insurer A's coverage requires an annual premium of $90,000 with a $5000 per claim deductible. Insurer B's coverage requires an annual premium of $35,000 with a $10,000 per claim deductible. Tom is wondering whether the additional $55,000 in premiums is warranted to obtain the lower deductible. Using some of the loss forecasting methods just described, Tom predicts the following losses will occur:

Expected Number of Losses	Expected Size of Losses
12	$5000
6	$10,000
2	over $10,000
$n = 20$	

Which coverage bid should Tom select, based on the number of expected claims and the magnitude of these claims? For simplicity, assume that premiums are paid at the start of the year, losses and deductibles are paid at the end of the year, and 5 percent is the interest (discount) rate.

With Insurer A's bid, Tom's expected cash outflows in one year would be the first $5000 of 20 losses that are each $5000 or more, for a total of $100,000 in deductibles. The present value of these payments is:

$$PV = \frac{100,000}{(1+.05)^1} = \$95,238$$

The present value of the total expected payments ($90,000 insurance premium at the start of the year plus the present value of the deductibles) would be $185,238.

With Insurer B's bid, Tom's expected cash outflows for deductibles at the end of the year would be:

($5000 \times 12) + ($10,000 \times 6)
$$+ ($10,000 \times 2) = $140,000$$

The present value of these deductible payments is:

$$PV = \frac{140,000}{(1+.05)^1} = $133,333$$

The present value of the total expected payments ($35,000 insurance premium at the start of the year plus the present value of the deductibles) would be $168,333. Because the present values calculated represent the present values of cash outflows, Tom should select the bid from Insurer B, because it minimizes the present value of the cash outflows.

Loss-Control Investment Decisions Loss-control investments are undertaken in an effort to reduce the frequency and severity of losses. Such investments can be analyzed from a capital budgeting perspective by employing time value of money analysis. **Capital budgeting** *is a method of determining which capital investment projects a company should undertake.* Only those projects that benefit the organization financially should be accepted. If not enough capital is available to undertake all of the acceptable projects, then capital budgeting can assist the risk manager in determining the optimal set of projects to consider.

A number of capital budgeting techniques are available.[7] Methods that take into account time value of money, such as net present value (*NPV*), should be employed. The **net present value** *of a project is the sum of the present values of the future cash flows minus the cost of the project.*[8] Cash flows are generated by increased revenues and reduced expenses. The cash flows are discounted at an interest rate that considers the rate of return required by the organization's capital suppliers and the riskiness of the project. A positive net present value represents an increase in value for the firm; a negative net present value would decrease the value of the firm if the investment were made.

For example, Tom Bryant has noticed a distressing trend in premises-related liability claims from several of NP's service stations. Patrons claim to have been injured on the premises (for example, slip-and-fall injuries near gas pumps), and they have sued

NP for their injuries. Tom has decided to install camera surveillance systems at several of the "problem" service stations at a cost of $85,000 per system. He expects each surveillance system to generate an after-tax net cash flow of $40,000 per year for three years. The present value of $40,000 per year for three years discounted at the appropriate interest rate (we assume 8 percent) is $103,084. Therefore, the *NPV* of this project is:

$$NPV = PV \text{ of future cash flows} - \text{cost of project}$$
$$= $103,084 - $85,000$$
$$= $18,084$$

As the project has a positive net present value, the investment is acceptable.

Although the cost of a project is usually known with some certainty, the future cash flows are merely estimates of the benefits that will be obtained by investing in the project. These benefits may come in the form of increased revenues, decreased expenses, or a combination of the two. Although some revenues and expenses associated with the project are easy to quantify, other values—such as employee morale, reduced pain and suffering, public perceptions of the company, and lost productivity when a new worker is hired to replace an injured experienced worker—can prove difficult to measure.

USE OF TECHNOLOGY IN RISK MANAGEMENT PROGRAMS

Our discussion of advanced risk management topics would not be complete without a brief discussion of the application of technology to risk management programs. We will break our discussion into two parts:

- Risk management information systems
- Other technology applications

Risk Management Information Systems

A key concern for risk managers is accurate and accessible risk management data. A **risk management information system (RMIS)** *is a computerized data base that permits the risk manager to store and analyze risk management data and to use such data to*

Insight 4.2

Risk Maps: Tools of the Trade

A risk management tool that is garnering great interest among risk managers these days is the risk map. Risk maps are graphs that let the risk manager chart an accidental loss exposure's probability and loss characteristics.

The construction of risk maps is a process that has great intrinsic value. The risks facing the organization must be carefully assessed and inventoried. To come up with credible probability and loss estimates, the risk manager often needs to get a better understanding of how loss processes work. A range of informational sources, both internal and external to the organization, needs to be queried. All these efforts give the risk manager a fuller appreciation of the risks facing his or her organization.

Knowing how the risks facing the organization behave is key to understanding how to manage them. These behavioral characteristics are determined by the probability and financial consequences of loss. The risk map makes these characteristics plain. To fully appreciate the behavior of the exposures facing the organization and how we can best deal with them, we have to make risk maps dynamic. Once we identify this dynamic behavior, we can come up with and test alternative management strategies. The modeling of the behavior of accidental losses through time based on the probability/loss characteristics of these losses is known as simulation. By using the risk mapping exercise to provide direct inputs into the simulation exercise, we have transformed the risk map into a useful source of data for risk management program construction.

A simple risk map is shown in the diagram. Annual probability of loss is shown on one axis, and the monetary consequences of loss shown on the other. For example, the annual probability of a $100,000 transportation loss is assessed at .1 (one loss every 10 years). Estimates of probability and consequences for the various exposures facing the organization are usually com-

bined on the map, giving the viewer the full perspective on the risks facing the organization, as well as their relativity. The probability and loss estimates associated with each exposure come from a variety of sources, including actuarial data, engineering studies, and expert opinion.

Simulating Risk

Simulation is the process of modeling real-world phenomena in a controlled setting. The output of the risk management simulation is a picture of how we might expect the accidental loss exposures facing the organization to develop over time.

The inputs to the simulation model are the probability and consequences of accidental losses facing the organization. This information is provided by the risk map. Random numbers are then used to recreate the loss picture for any given number of years into the future. For each exposure probability, a random number is generated that corresponds to that probability.

Given the amount of numerical calculations involved, it is obvious that simulations are best carried out using computers. The widespread availability of desktop spreadsheet programs can put the power of simulation in the hands of virtually any risk manager. The risk mapping and simulation environments can in this way be integrated into one.

Program Planning

How does this get us closer to the utilization of risk maps for constructing real risk management programs? Using the simulation, we can now put alternate risk management programs to the test. To do so, we apply potential risk management structures to the simulated losses and observe their long-term effects.

Alternative risk management plans are touted by a variety of interests, including insurance brokers, consultants, insurers, and a variety of financial intermediaries.

The combined risk map/simulation approach allows us to sort through the many claims of superiority, often conflicting, among the many proposals.

By creating the simulation in a portable environment, like a popular spreadsheet computer program, we can provide a detailed model of the organization's risk structure to those parties that might offer superior risk management structures. Side-by-side comparisons of alternate plans can also be made using this approach. All proposals can, in this way, be made to compete under common criteria.

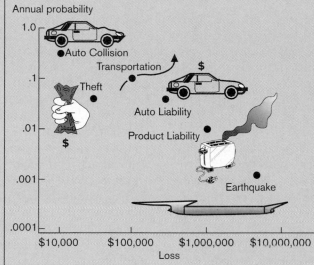

Better Risk Maps

A useful by-product of the combination of risk mapping and simulation based on this mapping is that we are able in the process to construct more reliable risk maps. Risk maps are often based on expert opinion. These opinions may not always reconcile with real life. To assess how well they do, we could run a simulation based on these inputs and match it to actual experience. Does the simulation look right? If it does, we may have a pretty good fit between opinion and reality. If not, we may want to reevaluate our opinions.

Due to the complex nature of loss exposures and the lack of reliable statistical data, what appear as points on the map are usually better specified as ranges or intervals. These interval estimates recognize that in creating risk maps using expert opinion, the opinions may themselves be very uncertain.

Simulations allow us to assess the outcomes of various *possibilities* in these estimates. Alternate program structures could be appraised in the face of this uncertainty. Risk maps can in this way be made to more accurately reflect the uncertainties involved in their construction and application.

Theory into Practice

The risk map is a great theoretical tool for the risk manager. Combined with simulation, this theoretical tool can be easily transformed into a practical decision aid. The combination of risk maps and simulation provides an infinitely richer framework for risk management program construction than simplistic summary measures. Risk mapping combined with simulation lets us see what's behind these summary measures, thus enabling us to deal with the true manifestations and effects of risk.

In effect, the risk map/simulation combination provides a virtual laboratory for the working risk manager, allowing him or her to create better programs for dealing with risk. It provides a simple platform for experimentation and the testing of ideas, as well as a vehicle for the dissemination of these ideas. With the help of readily available tools, like the desktop computer and spreadsheet programs, we obtain, at last, a useful marriage of theory and practical application.

Source: Adapted from Mark Jablonski, "Risk Maps: Tools of the Trade," *Risk & Insurance*, October 15, 1999, pp. 33–36.

predict future loss levels. Risk management information systems may be of great assistance to risk managers in decision making. Such systems are marketed by a number of vendors, or they may be developed in-house.

Risk management information systems have multiple uses. With regard to property exposures, the database may include a listing of a corporation's properties and the characteristics of those properties (construction, occupancy, protection, and exposure), property insurance policies, coverage terms, loss records, a log of fleet vehicles (including purchase dates, claims history, and maintenance records), and other data. On the liability side, the database may contain a listing of claims, the status of individual claims (pending, filed, in litigation, being appealed, or closed), historic claims, exposure bases (payroll, number of fleet vehicles, number of employees, and so on), and liability insurance coverages and coverage terms.

Organizations with many employees often find risk management information systems of great assistance in tracking employees, especially in the area of workers compensation claims. For example, a business with production facilities across the country may self-insure its workers compensation program but hire a third party to administer the program. In addition to settling claims, the third party may provide detailed claims records to the company that became part of the company's database. Armed with these data, the risk manager can perform a number of analyses, such as examining the number of injuries incurred by geographic region, by type of injury or body part (for example, laceration or lower back injury), by job classification, and by employee identification number. Such an analysis may reveal, for example, that the injury rate is greater in the Southwest or that a small number of employees account for a disproportionately high number of claims. In turn, the risk manager may use the results in measuring the effectiveness of loss-control investments and in targeting additional loss control efforts. Accurate workers compensation records are also important if the business decides to purchase private insurance, because past performance must be documented to obtain lower premiums from insurers.

Other Technology Applications

Three other technological applications warrant discussion: risk management Web sites, risk management intranets, and risk mapping. Some risk management departments have established their own Web sites, which include answers to "frequently asked questions" (FAQs) and a wealth of other information. In addition, some organizations have expanded the traditional risk management Web site into a risk management intranet. An **intranet** *is a Web site with search capabilities designed for a limited, internal audience.*[9] For example, a software company that sponsors trade shows at numerous venues each year might use a risk management intranet to make information available to interested parties within the company. Through the intranet, employees can obtain a list of procedures to follow (formulated by the risk management department) along with a set of forms that must be signed and filed before the event can be held (such as hold-harmless agreements).

Some organizations have developed or are developing sophisticated "risk maps." **Risk maps** *are grids detailing the potential frequency and severity of risks faced by the organization.* Construction of these maps requires risk managers to analyze each risk that the organization faces before plotting it on the map. Use of risk maps varies from simply graphing the exposures to employing simulation analysis to estimate likely loss scenarios. In addition to property, liability, and personnel exposures, financial risks and other risks that fall under the broad umbrella of "enterprise risk" may be included on the risk map.

Risk mapping is a logical step on the road to establishing an enterprise risk management program. Insight 4.2 describes the benefits and uses of risk maps.

SUMMARY

■ Financial risk management is the identification, analysis, and treatment of speculative financial risks. Such risks include commodity price risk, interest rate risk, and currency exchange rate risk.

- An integrated risk program is a risk treatment technique that combines coverage for pure and speculative risks within the same contract.

- Enterprise risk management is a comprehensive risk management program that addresses an organization's pure, speculative, strategic, and operational risks.

- A cyclical pattern—called the underwriting cycle—has been observed in underwriting stringency, premium levels, and profitability in the property and liability insurance industry. In a "hard" insurance market, premiums are high and underwriting standards are tight. In a "soft" insurance market, premiums are low and underwriting standards are loose.

- Two important factors that affect property and liability insurance company pricing and underwriting decisions are the level of capacity in the insurance industry and investment returns.

- The insurance industry has been experiencing consolidation through insurance company mergers and acquisitions, insurance brokerage mergers and acquisitions, and cross-industry consolidation.

- Risk managers can use a number of techniques to improve loss prediction. These techniques include probability analysis, regression analysis, and forecasting by using loss distributions.

- When analyzing events, the characteristics of the events must be considered. Events may be independent, dependent, or mutually exclusive.

- Regression analysis is a method of characterizing the relationship that exists between two or more variables and then using the characterization as a predictor.

- In analyzing cash flows in different periods, the risk manager must consider the time value of money.

- Changing a present value into a future value is called compounding; determining the present value of a future amount is called discounting.

- Risk managers can apply time value of money analysis in many situations, including insurance coverage bid analysis and loss control investment analysis.

- A risk management information system (RMIS) is a computerized database that permits risk managers to store and analyze risk management data and to use such data to predict future losses.

- Risk managers may use Web sites, intranets, and risk maps in their risk management programs.

KEY CONCEPTS AND TERMS

Capacity
Capital budgeting
Chief risk officer (CRO)
Combined ratio
Commodity price risk
Compounding
Consolidation
Currency exchange rate risk
Dependent event
Discounting
Double-trigger option
Enterprise risk management
Financial risk management
"Hard" insurance market
Independent event
Insurance brokers
Integrated risk program
Interest rate risk
Intranet
Loss distribution
Mutually exclusive events
Net present value (NPV)
Regression analysis
Risk management information system (RMIS)
Risk maps
"Soft" insurance market
Surplus
Time value of money
Underwriting cycle

REVIEW QUESTIONS

1. Name three speculative financial risks that may be considered by a risk manager.

2. How does enterprise risk management differ from traditional risk management?

3. What is the underwriting cycle? Differentiate between a "hard" insurance market and a "soft" insurance market.

4. What is meant by "consolidation" in the insurance industry?

5. Why is loss forecasting necessary when making a decision about whether to retain or transfer loss exposures? What techniques can a risk manager use to predict future losses?

6. What is the danger of simply using past losses to estimate future losses?

7. Why is time value of money analysis used in risk management decision making?

8. What variables are difficult to quantify when analyzing investments in loss-control projects?

9. What is a risk management information system (RMIS)? How does a risk management Web site differ from a risk management intranet?

10. What types of information can be obtained from a claims management database?

APPLICATION QUESTIONS

1. Integrated risk management programs are new to many risk managers and the insurance companies that offer such programs. What additional expertise, aside from knowledge of property and liability insurance, must an insurance company possess to offer integrated risk management products?

2. A risk manager self-insured a property risk for one year. The following year, even though no losses had occurred, the risk manager purchased property insurance to address the risk. What is the best explanation for the change in how the risk was handled, even though no losses had occurred?

3. Why do insurance brokerage mergers and acquisitions have a greater influence on corporate risk managers than do property and liability insurance company mergers and acquisitions?

4. What would be the effect of ignoring the time value of money when making risk management decisions? What does the net present value of a loss control investment really represent to the owners of the organization?

5. During a "hard" insurance market, a manufacturing company decided to self-insure its workers compensation loss exposure. The company hired a third party to administer the workers compensation claims. Even though the risk was being self-insured, the risk manager insisted that the third-party administrator maintain meticulous records. When asked why such detailed records were necessary, the risk manager replied, "For story time with an insurance company next year." What did the risk manager mean?

SELECTED REFERENCES

Banhan, Russ. "Kit and Caboodle—Understanding the Skepticism about Enterprise Risk Management," *CFO—The Magazine for Senior Financial Executives*, April 1999, pp. 63–70.

Harrington, Scott E., and Gregory R. Niehaus. *Risk Management and Insurance*, Boston, MA: Irwin/McGraw-Hill, 1999.

Thornhill, Wil, and Amy Derksen. "A United Approach: Creating Integrated Risk Plans," *Risk Management*, August 1998, pp. 36–40.

Vaughan, Emmett J. *Risk Management*, New York, NY: John Wiley & Sons, 1997.

Williams, C. Arthur, Jr., Michael L. Smith, and Peter C. Young. *Risk Management and Insurance*, 8th ed., Boston, MA: Irwin/McGraw-Hill, 1998.

NOTES

1. See an investments text for a detailed explanation of these capital market instruments.

2. As reported in "Who Needs Derivatives?" by Carolyn T. Geer, *Forbes Magazine*, April 21, 1997.

3. For a recent review of the literature on the causes of underwriting cycles, see Renbao Chen, Kie Ann Wong, and Hong Chew Lee, "Underwriting Cycles in Asia," *Journal of Risk and Insurance*, 1999, Vol. 66, No. 1, pp. 29–47.

4. For a listing of "Representative Mergers or Acquisitions of Insurance Brokers during the 19th Century," see "Broker Consolidation—Where Is It Heading?" by Peter Godfrey, *Risk Management*, August 1998, pp. 10–22.

5. "Four Insurers Gain Federal Bank Charter," by Alex Maurice, *National Underwriter, Property & Casualty/ Risk & Benefits Management*, May 17, 1999, pp. 19, 50.

6. Introductory business finance textbooks discuss the time value of money in greater detail.

7. Some other methods include internal rate of return, accounting rate of return, and the payback method. Net present value is preferred by many because it employs the time value of money, uses the appropriate cash-flow measure, and provides a dollars and cents answer that is easily interpreted.

8. The relevant cash-flow measure considers cash inflows and cash outflows. Capital investments decrease in value over time, and businesses are permitted to allocate a portion of the reduction in value each year as a depreciation expense. Because depreciation is a non-cash expense, it is not considered a cash outflow. Depreciation must be considered, however, when determining the annual tax liability.

9. For a discussion of risk management intranets, see "Net Working," by Mark Dorn, *Risk Management*, June 1999, pp. 41–44.

Case Application 1

Great West States (GWS) is a railroad company operating in the Western region of the United States. Juanita Salazar is risk manager of GWS. At the direction of the company's chief executive officer, she is searching for ways to handle the company's risks in a more economical way. The CEO stressed that Juanita should consider not only pure risks, but also financial risks. Juanita discovered that the only significant financial risk facing the organization is a commodity price risk—the risk of a significant increase in the price of fuel oil for the company's locomotives. A review of the company's income and expense statement showed that last year about 16 percent of its expenses were related to fuel oil.

Juanita was also asked to determine whether the installation of a new sprinkler system at the corporate headquarters building would be justified. The cost of the project would be $40,000. She estimates the project would provide an after-tax net cash flow of $25,000 per year for three years, with the first of these cash flows coming one year from today.

GWS is considering expanding its routes to include Colorado, New Mexico, Texas, and Oklahoma. The company is concerned about the number of derailments that might occur. Juanita ran a regression with "thousands of miles GWS locomotives traveled" as the independent variable and "number of derailments" as the dependent variable. Results of the regression are as follows:

$$Y = 2.31 + .022X$$

With the expansion, GWS trains will travel an estimated 640,000 miles next year.

a. With regard to the fuel oil price risk:
   (1) Discuss how Juanita could use futures contracts to hedge the price risk.
   (2) Discuss how a double-trigger, integrated risk management plan could be employed.
b. What is the net present value (NPV) of the sprinkler system project, assuming the rate of return required by GWS investors is 10 percent?
c. How many derailments should Juanita expect next year, assuming the regression results are reliable and GWS goes ahead with the expansion plan? (Hint: Be careful of scale factors when considering the independent variable.)

Case Application 2

Terry Smith is risk manager of Gotham City. One building that is of great concern to him is The Hexagon—a new arena located in a flood plain near a river. "The Hex" took three years to construct at a cost of $60 million. Terry has assigned the following probabilities to some events that could occur during the coming year:

Major fire destroys The Hex	.50%
Minor fire damages The Hex	4.00%
Theft of property from The Hex given that a minor fire has occurred	30.00%
Major flood destroys The Hex	.25%
Minor flood damages The Hex	2.00%

What is the probability of the following events occurring this year?

a. A major fire or a major flood will destroy The Hex.
b. A minor fire will damage The Hex and, after The Hex is damaged by the fire, theft of property will occur.
c. A minor fire and a minor flood will both damage The Hex.
d. A minor fire, a minor flood, or both will damage The Hex.

Loss Forecasting Using the Normal Distribution

Risk managers may employ probability distributions to assist in measuring loss exposures. Several distributions are available, including the normal, binomial, exponential, and Poisson distributions. Selection of the distribution is often based upon prior loss history, especially when the number of losses, n, is large. We will examine application of the normal distribution, which may be used in many situations.

The normal distribution is a symmetric bell curve summarized by two parameters: the expected value and the standard deviation (m and s, respectively, in the discussion that follows). The area under a normal curve is equal to 1, with 50 percent of the distribution on either side of the expected value. Based on values of m and s, and an "area under a normal curve" table, the probability of an event (x) can be estimated based on the standard variate, z:

$$z = \frac{x - m}{s}$$

Several examples will demonstrate how probability distributions can be employed by a risk manager in estimating loss levels.

EXAMPLE 1

Assume that the number of weather-related property losses is normally distributed with the mean (m) equal to 16 and standard deviation (s) equal to 4.

What is the probability that the number of losses will be between 16 and 21?

$$z = \frac{21 - 16}{4} = 1.25$$

Referring to Exhibit A.1, the corresponding probability for a standard variate of 1.25 is 39.44 percent. Therefore, the probability of between 16 and 21 weather-related property losses occurring is almost 40 percent.

EXAMPLE 2

Assume that the number of vehicle physical damage claims is normally distributed with a mean of 400 and a standard deviation of 75. What is the probability that the number of vehicle physical damage losses will be between 425 and 475?

$$z = \frac{475 - 400}{75} = 1.00;$$ the corresponding probability from the table is .3413, and

$$z = \frac{425 - 400}{75} = 0.33;$$ the corresponding probability from the table is .1293

P(number of losses between 425 and 475)
$$= .3413 - .1293 = .2120$$

EXAMPLE 2   81

EXHIBIT A.1
Areas Under the Normal Curve (One Tail)

z	.00	.01	.02	.03	.04	.05	.06	.07	.08	.09
0.0	.0000	.0040	.0080	.0120	.0160	.0199	.0239	.0279	.0319	.0359
0.1	.0398	.0438	.0478	.0517	.0557	.0596	.0636	.0675	.0714	.0753
0.2	.0793	.0832	.0871	.0910	.0948	.0987	.1026	.1064	.1103	.1141
0.3	.1179	.1217	.1255	.1293	.1331	.1368	.1406	.1443	.1480	.1517
0.4	.1554	.1591	.1628	.1664	.1700	.1736	.1772	.1808	.1844	.1879
0.5	.1915	.1950	.1985	.2019	.2054	.2088	.2123	.2157	.2190	.2224
0.6	.2257	.2291	.2324	.2357	.2389	.2422	.2454	.2486	.2517	.2549
0.7	.2580	.2611	.2642	.2673	.2704	.2734	.2764	.2794	.2823	.2852
0.8	.2881	.2910	.2939	.2967	.2995	.3023	.3051	.3078	.3106	.3133
0.9	.3159	.3186	.3212	.3238	.3264	.3289	.3315	.3340	.3365	.3389
1.0	.3413	.3438	.3461	.3485	.3508	.3531	.3554	.3577	.3599	.3621
1.1	.3643	.3665	.3686	.3708	.3729	.3749	.3770	.3790	.3810	.3830
1.2	.3849	.3869	.3888	.3907	.3925	.3944	.3962	.3980	.3997	.4015
1.3	.4032	.4049	.4066	.4082	.4099	.4115	.4131	.4147	.4162	.4177
1.4	.4192	.4207	.4222	.4236	.4251	.4265	.4279	.4292	.4306	.4319
1.5	.4332	.4345	.4357	.4370	.4382	.4394	.4406	.4418	.4429	.4441
1.6	.4452	.4463	.4474	.4484	.4495	.4505	.4515	.4525	.4535	.4545
1.7	.4554	.4564	.4573	.4582	.4591	.4599	.4608	.4616	.4625	.4633
1.8	.4641	.4649	.4656	.4664	.4671	.4678	.4686	.4693	.4699	.4706
1.9	.4713	.4719	.4726	.4732	.4738	.4744	.4750	.4756	.4761	.4767
2.0	.4772	.4778	.4783	.4788	.4793	.4798	.4803	.4808	.4812	.4817
2.1	.4821	.4826	.4830	.4834	.4838	.4842	.4846	.4850	.4854	.4857
2.2	.4861	.4864	.4868	.4871	.4875	.4878	.4881	.4884	.4887	.4890
2.3	.4893	.4896	.4898	.4901	.4904	.4906	.4909	.4911	.4913	.4916
2.4	.4918	.4920	.4922	.4925	.4927	.4929	.4931	.4932	.4934	.4936
2.5	.4938	.4940	.4941	.4943	.4945	.4946	.4948	.4949	.4951	.4952
2.6	.4953	.4955	.4956	.4957	.4959	.4960	.4961	.4962	.4963	.4964
2.7	.4965	.4966	.4967	.4968	.4969	.4970	.4971	.4972	.4973	.4974
2.8	.4974	.4975	.4976	.4977	.4977	.4978	.4979	.4979	.4980	.4981
2.9	.4981	.4982	.4982	.4983	.4984	.4984	.4985	.4985	.4986	.4986
3.0	.4987	.4987	.4987	.4988	.4988	.4989	.4989	.4989	.4990	.4990

EXAMPLE 3

Assume that the number of losses is normally distributed with $m = 33$ and $s = 8$. What is the probability that fewer than 21 losses will occur?

$$z = \frac{21 - 33}{8} = -1.50;$$ the corresponding probability from the normal curve table is .4332

Subtracting this value from .50 (half the normal curve), the probability is .0668.

EXAMPLE 4

An interesting and related application using the normal curve involves determining x based on an as-sumed probability. For example, assume that losses are normally distributed with $m = 500$ and $s = 100$. Above what value of x do the highest 10 percent of all x values fall?

We know that the area to the right of the value of x is .10. As the exhibit shows probabilities between the expected value and x, we need to look in the body of the exhibit for the z value corresponding to .40. This z value for this area is approximately 1.28. By substituting all of the known values back into our expression for z, we can solve for x:

$$1.28 = \frac{x - 500}{100}, \; x = 500 + (1.28 \times 100), \; x = 628$$

The upper 10 percent of all claims are higher than 628.

Part Two

Legal Principles in Risk and Insurance

Chapter 5

Fundamental Legal Principles

" The education of those engaged in the important functions of the insurance business calls for an understanding of the essentials of insurance law. "

Edwin W. Patterson,
Essentials of Insurance Law, 2nd ed.

Learning Objectives

After studying this chapter, you should be able to:

▲ Explain the fundamental legal principles that are reflected in insurance contracts, including the
  principle of indemnity,
  principle of insurable interest,
  principle of subrogation, and
  principle of utmost good faith.

▲ Explain how the legal concepts of representations, concealment, and warranty support the principle of utmost good faith.

▲ Describe the basic requirements for the formation of a valid insurance contract.

▲ Show how insurance contracts differ from other contracts.

▲ Explain the law of agency and how it affects the actions of insurance agents.

▲ Access an Internet site and obtain consumer information on insurance law.

Internet Resources

- **America's LAW∗LINKS** is a comprehensive legal resource guide for both attorneys and consumers. The site has a "Legal Subjects Index." Click on "Insurance Law" for a variety of legal topics relevant to insurance consumers. Visit the site at:
  http://www.lawlinks.com/

- The **Legal Information Institute** of Cornell Law School provides detailed information on legal topics, including insurance law. Legal topics are listed alphabetically under "Law About . . ." Click on to "Insurance" for federal and state insurance statutes, recent court decisions on insurance, and related links. Visit the site at:
  http://www.law.cornell.edu/

■ **Nolo.com** is a leading source of self-help legal information for consumers, including topics on insurance law. In the "Legal Encyclopedia" section, click "Insurance" for consumer topics on insurance. Visit the site at:

http://www.nolo.com/

 ichard, age 26, has a serious drinking problem. He recently moved to another state and applied for auto insurance in that state. In the application, he stated that he did not use alcohol, had never been fined for a moving vehicle violation, and had no offenses other than traffic tickets. In fact, Richard had three convictions for drunk driving and had been involved in several auto accidents. The policy was issued. Shortly thereafter, Richard had another accident in which the other driver was killed. The deceased driver's family sued Richard for wrongful death. After investigating the claim, Richard's insurer discovered his earlier drunk driving convictions. The insurer denied liability because Richard had made several material misrepresentations. Richard's introduction to insurance law was costly and painful.

As Richard found out, insurance law can have substantial consequences for you after a loss occurs. When you buy insurance, you expect to be paid for a covered loss. Insurance law and contractual provisions determine whether you can collect and how much will be paid. Insurance contracts are complex legal documents that reflect both general rules of law and insurance law. Thus, you should have a clear understanding of the basic legal principles that underlie insurance contracts.

This chapter discusses the fundamental legal principles on which insurance contracts are based, legal requirements for a valid insurance contract, and legal characteristics of insurance contracts that distinguish them from other types of contracts. The chapter concludes with a discussion of the law of agency and its application to insurance agents.

PRINCIPLE OF INDEMNITY

The principle of indemnity is one of the most important legal principles in insurance. The **principle of indemnity** *states that the insurer agrees to pay no more than the actual amount of the loss; stated differently, the insured should not profit from a loss.* Most property and liability insurance contracts are contracts of indemnity. If a covered loss occurs, the insurer should not pay more than the actual amount of the loss. Nevertheless, a contract of indemnity does not mean that all covered losses are always paid in full. Because of deductibles, dollar limits on the amount paid, and other contractual provisions, the amount paid may be less than the actual loss.

The principle of indemnity has two fundamental purposes. *The first purpose is to prevent the insured from profiting from a loss.* For example, if Kristin's home is insured for $100,000, and a partial loss of $20,000 occurs, the principle of indemnity would be violated if $100,000 were paid to her. She would be profiting from insurance.

The second purpose is to reduce moral hazard. If dishonest insureds could profit from a loss, they might deliberately cause losses with the intention of collecting the insurance. If the loss payment does not exceed the actual amount of the loss, the temptation to be dishonest is reduced.

Actual Cash Value

The concept of *actual cash value* underlies the principle of indemnity. In property insurance, the basic method for indemnifying the insured is based on the actual cash value of the damaged property at the time of loss. The courts have used three major methods to determine actual cash value:

- Replacement cost less depreciation
- Fair market value
- Broad evidence rule

Replacement Cost Less Depreciation

Under this rule, **actual cash value** *is defined as replacement cost less depreciation.* This rule has been used traditionally to determine the actual cash value of property in property insurance. It takes into consideration both inflation and depreciation of property values over time. Replacement cost is the current cost of restoring the damaged property with new materials of like kind and quality. Depreciation is a deduction for physical wear and tear, age, and economic obsolescence.

For example, Shannon has a favorite couch that burns in a fire. Assume she bought the couch five years ago, the couch is 50 percent depreciated, and a similar couch today would cost $1000. Under the actual cash value rule, Shannon will collect $500 for the loss because the replacement cost is $1000, and depreciation is $500, or 50 percent. If she were paid the full replacement value of $1000, the principle of indemnity would be violated, because she would be receiving the value of a new couch instead of one that was five years old. In short, the $500 payment represents indemnification for the loss of a five-year-old couch. This idea can be summarized as follows:

$$Replacement\ cost = \$1000$$
$$Depreciation = \$500\ (couch\ is\ 50\ percent$$
$$depreciated)$$
$$Actual\ cash\ value = Replacement\ cost$$
$$- Depreciation$$
$$\$500 = \$1000 - \$500$$

Fair Market Value

Some courts have ruled that fair market value should be used to determine actual cash value of a loss. **Fair market value** *is the price a willing buyer would pay a willing seller in a free market.*

The fair market value of a building may be below its actual cash value based on replacement cost less depreciation. This difference is due to several reasons, including a poor location, deteriorating neighborhood, or economic obsolescence of the building. For example, in major cities, large homes in older residential areas often have a market value well below replacement cost less depreciation. If a loss occurs, the fair market value may reflect more accurately the value of the loss. In one case, a building valued at $170,000 based on the actual cash value rule had a market value of only $65,000 when a loss occurred. The court ruled that the actual cash value of the property should be based on the fair market value of $65,000 rather than on $170,000.[1]

Broad Evidence Rule

Many states now use the broad evidence rule to determine the actual cash value of a loss. The **broad evidence rule** *means that the determination of actual cash value should include all relevant factors an expert would use to determine the value of the property.* Relevant factors include replacement cost less depreciation, fair market value, present value of expected income from the property, comparison sales of similar property, opinions of appraisers, and numerous other factors.

Although the actual cash value rule is used in property insurance, different methods are employed in other types of insurance. In liability insurance, the insurer pays up to the policy limit the amount of damages that the insured is legally obligated to pay because of bodily injury or property damage to another. In life insurance, the amount paid when the insured dies is the face value of the policy. In business income insurance, the amount paid is usually based on the loss of profits plus continuing expenses when the business is shut down because of a loss from a covered peril.

Exceptions to the Principle of Indemnity

There are several important exceptions to the principle of indemnity. They include the following:

- Valued policy
- Valued policy laws
- Replacement cost insurance
- Life insurance

Valued Policy A **valued policy** *is one that pays the face amount of insurance if a total loss occurs.* Valued policies typically are used to insure antiques, fine arts, rare paintings, and family heirlooms. Because of the difficulty of determining the actual value of the property at the time of loss, the insured and insurer both agree on the value of the property when the policy is first issued. For example, you may have a valuable antique clock that was owned by your great-grandmother. Assume that the clock is worth $10,000 today and is insured for that amount. If the clock is totally destroyed in a fire, you would be paid $10,000 and not the actual cash value. Because the amount paid may exceed the actual cash value, the principle of indemnity is violated.

Valued Policy Laws Valued **policy laws** are another exception to the principle of indemnity.[2] The specified perils to which a valued policy law applies vary among the states. Laws in some states cover only fire; other states cover fire, lightning, windstorm, and tornado; and some states include all insured perils. In addition, the laws generally apply only to real property, and the loss must be total. For example, a building insured for $200,000 may have an actual cash value of $175,000. If a total loss from a fire occurs, the face amount of $200,000 would be paid. Because the insured would be paid more than the actual cash value, the principle of indemnity would be violated.

The original purpose of a valued policy law was to protect the insured from an argument with the insurer if an agent had deliberately overinsured property so as to receive a higher commission. After a total loss, the insurer might offer less than the face amount for which the policyowner had paid premiums on the grounds that the building was overinsured. However, the importance of a valued policy law has declined over time because inflation in property values has made overinsurance less of a problem. Underinsurance is now the greater problem, because it results in both inadequate premiums for the insurer and inadequate protection for the insured.

Despite their reduced importance, valued policy laws can lead to overinsurance and an increase in moral hazard. Most buildings are not physically inspected before they are insured. If an insurer fails to inspect a building for valuation purposes, overinsurance and possible moral hazard may result. The in-

sured may not be concerned about loss prevention, or may even deliberately cause a loss to collect the insurance proceeds. Although valued policy laws provide a defense for the insurer when fraud is suspected, the burden of proof is on the insurer to prove fraudulent intent. Proving fraud is often difficult. For example, in an older case, a house advertised for sale at $1800 was insured for $10,000 under a fire insurance policy. About six months later, the house was totally destroyed by a fire. The insurer denied liability on the grounds of misrepresentation and fraud. An appeals court ordered the face amount of insurance to be paid, holding that nothing prevented the company from inspecting the property to determine its value, and the insured's statement concerning the value of the house was an expression of opinion, not a representation of fact.[3]

Replacement Cost Insurance Replacement cost insurance is a third exception to the principle of indemnity. **Replacement cost insurance** *means there is no deduction for depreciation in determining the amount paid for a loss.* For example, assume the roof on your home is 5 years old and has a useful life of 20 years. The roof is damaged by a tornado, and the current cost of replacement is $10,000. Under the actual cash value rule, you would receive only $7500 ($10,000 − $2500 = $7500). Under a replacement cost policy, you would receive the full $10,000 (less any applicable deductible). Because you receive the value of a brand new roof instead of one that is 5 years old, the principle of indemnity is technically violated.

Replacement cost insurance is based on the recognition that payment of the actual cash value can still result in a substantial loss to the insured, because few persons budget for depreciation. In our example, you would have had to pay $2500 to restore the damaged roof, since it was one-fourth depreciated. To deal with this problem, replacement cost insurance can be purchased to insure homes, buildings, and business and personal property.

Life Insurance Life insurance is another exception to the principle of indemnity. A life insurance contract is not a contract of indemnity but is a valued policy that pays a stated sum to the beneficiary upon the insured's death. The indemnity principle is difficult to apply to life insurance for the obvious reason that the actual cash value rule (replacement cost less depreciation) is meaningless in determining the value of a human life. Moreover, to plan for personal and business purposes, such as the need to provide a specific amount of monthly income to the deceased's dependents, a certain amount of life insurance must be purchased before death occurs. For these reasons, a life insurance policy is another exception to the principle of indemnity.

PRINCIPLE OF INSURABLE INTEREST

The principle of insurable interest is another important legal principle. The **principle of insurable interest** *states that the insured must be in a position to lose financially if a loss occurs, or to incur some other kind of harm if the loss takes place.* For example, you have an insurable interest in your car because you may lose financially if the car is damaged or stolen. You have an insurable interest in your personal property, such as a television set or VCR, because you may lose financially if the property is damaged or destroyed.

Purposes of an Insurable Interest

To be legally enforceable, all insurance contracts must be supported by an insurable interest. Insurance contracts must be supported by an insurable interest for the following reasons.[4]

- To prevent gambling
- To reduce moral hazard
- To measure the amount of the insured's loss in property insurance

First, an insurable interest is necessary to prevent gambling. If an insurable interest were not required, the contract would be a gambling contract and would be against the public interest. For example, you could insure the property of another and hope for an early loss. You could similarly insure the life of another person and hope for an early death. These contracts clearly would be gambling contracts and would be against the public interest.

Second, an insurable interest reduces moral hazard. If an insurable interest were not required, a dishonest person could purchase a property insurance contract on someone else's property and then deliberately cause a loss to receive the proceeds. But if the

insured stands to lose financially, nothing is gained by causing the loss. Thus, moral hazard is reduced. In life insurance, an insurable interest requirement reduces the incentive to murder the insured for the purpose of collecting the proceeds.

Finally, in property insurance, an insurable interest measures the amount of the insured's loss. Most property contracts are contracts of indemnity, and one measure of recovery is the insurable interest of the insured. If the loss payment cannot exceed the amount of one's insurable interest, the principle of indemnity is supported.

Examples of an Insurable Interest

Several situations that satisfy the insurable interest requirement are discussed in this section. However, it is helpful at this point to distinguish between an insurable interest in property and liability insurance and in life insurance.

Property and Liability Insurance *Ownership of property* can support an insurable interest, because owners of property will lose financially if their property is damaged or destroyed.

Potential legal liability can also support an insurable interest. For example, a dry-cleaning firm has an insurable interest in the property of the customers, because the firm may be legally liable for damage to the customer's goods caused by the firm's negligence.

Secured creditors have an insurable interest as well. A commercial bank or savings and loan institution that lends money to buy a house has an insurable interest in the property pledged. The property serves as collateral for the mortgage, so if the building is damaged, the collateral behind the loan is impaired. A bank that makes an inventory loan to a business firm has an insurable interest in the stock of goods, because the goods are collateral for the loan. However, the courts have ruled that unsecured, or general, creditors normally do not have an insurable interest in the debtor's property.[5]

Finally, a *contractual right* can support an insurable interest. Thus, a business firm that contracts to purchase goods from abroad on the condition that they arrive safely in the United States has an insurable interest in the goods because of the loss of profits if the merchandise does not arrive.

Life Insurance The question of an insurable interest does not arise when you purchase life insurance on your own life. The law considers the insurable interest requirement to be met whenever a person voluntarily purchases life insurance on his or her life. Thus, you can purchase as much life insurance as you can afford, subject of course to the insurer's underwriting rules concerning the maximum amount of insurance that can be written on any single life. Also, when you apply for life insurance on your own life, you can name anyone as beneficiary. The beneficiary is not required to have an insurable interest in your life.[6]

If you wish to purchase a life insurance policy on the life of another person, however, you must have an insurable interest in that person's life. Close ties of blood or marriage will satisfy the insurable interest requirement in life insurance. For example, a husband can purchase a life insurance policy on his wife's life and be named as beneficiary. Likewise, a wife can insure her husband and be named as beneficiary. A grandparent can purchase a life insurance policy on the life of a grandchild. However, remote family relationships will not support an insurable interest. For example, cousins cannot insure each other unless a pecuniary relationship is present.

If there is a **pecuniary interest**, the insurable interest requirement in life insurance can be met. Even when there is no relationship by blood or marriage, one person may be financially harmed by the death of another. For example, a corporation can insure the life of an outstanding salesperson, because the firm's profit may decline if the salesperson dies. One business partner can insure the life of the other partner to have the cash to purchase the deceased partner's interest if he or she dies.

When Must an Insurable Interest Exist?

In property insurance, the insurable interest must exist at the time of the loss. There are two reasons for this requirement. First, most property insurance contracts are contracts of indemnity. If an insurable interest did not exist at the time of loss, financial loss would not occur. Hence, the principle of indemnity would be violated if payment were made. For example, if Mark sells his home to Susan, and a fire occurs before the insurance on the home is canceled, Mark cannot collect because he no longer has an insurable interest in the property. Susan cannot collect either because she is not named as an insured under the policy.

Second, you may not have an insurable interest in the property when the contract is first written, but may expect to have an insurable interest in the future, at the time of possible loss. For example, in ocean marine insurance, it is common to insure a return cargo by a contract entered into prior to the ship's departure. However, the policy may not cover the goods until they are on board the ship as the insured's property. Although an insurable interest does not exist when the contract is first written, you can still collect if you have an insurable interest in the goods at the time of loss.

In contrast, in life insurance, the insurable interest requirement must be met only at the inception of the policy, not at the time of death. Life insurance is not a contract of indemnity but is a valued policy that pays a stated sum upon the insured's death. Because the beneficiary has only a legal claim to receive the policy proceeds, the beneficiary does not have to show that a loss has been incurred by the insured's death. For example, if Michelle takes out a policy on her husband's life and later gets a divorce, she is entitled to the policy proceeds upon the death of her former husband if she has kept the insurance in force. The insurable interest requirement must be met only at the inception of the contract (see Insight 5.1).

PRINCIPLE OF SUBROGATION

The principle of subrogation strongly supports the principle of indemnity. **Subrogation** *means substitution of the insurer in place of the insured for the purpose of claiming indemnity from a third person for a loss covered by insurance.*[7] The insurer is therefore entitled to recover from a negligent third party any loss payments made to the insured. For example, assume that a negligent motorist fails to stop at a red light and smashes into Megan's car, causing damage in the amount of $5000. If she has collision insurance on her car, her company will pay the physical damage loss to the car (less any deductible) and then attempt to collect from the negligent motorist who caused the accident. Alternatively, Megan could attempt to collect directly from the negligent motorist for the damage to her car. Subrogation does not apply if a loss payment is not made. However, to the extent that a loss payment is made, the insured gives

Insight 5.1

No Insurable Interest at the Time of Death: Is a Corporation Entitled to the Life Insurance Proceeds?

Legal Facts

A corporation purchased a $1 million life insurance policy on an officer who was a 20 percent stockholder in the company. Shortly thereafter, the officer sold his stock and resigned. Two years later he died. The insurer paid the death proceeds to the corporation. The personal representative of the deceased insured's estate claimed the insurable interest was only temporary and must continue until death. Is the corporation entitled to the policy proceeds even though it had no insurable interest at the time of death?

Court Decision

The court rejected the argument that the corporation's insurable interest must continue until death.* Its decision reflects the principle that termination of an insurable interest before the policy matures does not affect the policyholder's right of recovery under a policy valid at its inception. The insurable interest requirement must be met only at the inception of the policy.

In re Al Zuni Trading, 947 F.2d 1402 (1991).
SOURCE: Adaptation of Buist M. Anderson, *Anderson on Life Insurance, 1992 Supplement* (Boston, MA: Little, Brown and Company, 1992), p. 29. ©1992, Little, Brown and Company.

---

to the insurer legal rights to collect damages from the negligent third party.

Purposes of Subrogation

Subrogation has three basic purposes. *First, subrogation prevents the insured from collecting twice for the same loss.* In the absence of subrogation, the insured could collect from the insurer and from the person who caused the loss. The principle of indemnity would be violated because the insured would be profiting from a loss.

Second, subrogation is used to hold the guilty person responsible for the loss. By exercising its subrogation rights, the insurer can collect from the negligent person who caused the loss.

Finally, subrogation helps to hold down insurance rates. Subrogation recoveries can be reflected in the rate-making process, which tends to hold rates below where they would be in the absence of subrogation.

Importance of Subrogation

You should keep in mind five important corollaries of the principle of subrogation.

1. *The general rule is that by exercising its subrogation rights, the insurer is entitled only to the amount it has paid under the policy.*[8] Some insureds may not be fully indemnified after a loss because of insufficient insurance, satisfaction of a deductible, or legal expenses in trying to recover from a negligent third party. Many policies currently have a provision stating how a subrogation recovery is to be shared between the insured and insurer.

In the absence of any policy provision, the courts have used different rules in determining how a subrogation recovery is to be shared. *One commonly held view is that the insured must be reimbursed in full for the loss; the insurer is then entitled to any remaining balance up to the insurer's interest, with any remainder going to the insured.*[9] For example, Andrew has a $100,000 home insured for only $80,000 under a homeowners policy. Assume that the house is totally destroyed in a fire because of faulty wiring by an electrician. The insurer would pay $80,000 to Andrew and then attempt to collect from the negligent electrician. After exercising its subrogation rights against the negligent electrician, assume that the insurer has a net recovery of $50,000 (after deduction of legal expenses). Andrew would receive $20,000, and the insurer can retain the balance of $30,000.

2. *The insured cannot impair the insurer's subrogation rights.* The insured cannot do anything after a

loss that prejudices the insurer's right to proceed against a negligent third party. For example, if the insured waives the right to sue the negligent party, the right to collect from the insurer for the loss is also waived. This case could happen if the insured admits fault in an automobile accident or attempts to settle a collision loss with the negligent driver without the insurer's consent. If the insurer's right to subrogate against the negligent motorist is adversely affected, the insured's right to collect from the insurer is forfeited.[10]

3. *The insurer can waive its subrogation rights in the contract.* To meet the special needs of some insureds, the insurance company may waive its subrogation rights by a contractual provision for losses that have not yet occurred. For example, to rent an apartment house, a landlord may agree to release the tenants from potential liability if the building is damaged. If the landlord's insurer waives its subrogation rights, and if a tenant negligently starts a fire, the insurer would have to reimburse the landlord for the loss, but could not recover from the tenant because the subrogation rights were waived.

The insurer may decide not to exercise its subrogation rights after a loss occurs. The legal expenses may exceed the possible recovery; a counterclaim against the insured or insurer may be filed by the alleged wrongdoer; the insurer may wish to avoid embarrassment of the insured; or the insurer company may wish to maintain good public relations.[11]

4. *Subrogation does not apply to life insurance and to most individual health insurance contracts.* Life insurance is not a contract of indemnity, and subrogation has relevance only for contracts of indemnity. Individual health insurance contracts usually do not contain subrogation clauses.[12]

5. *The insurer cannot subrogate against its own insureds.* If the insurer could recover a loss payment for a covered loss from an insured, the basic purpose of purchasing the insurance would be defeated.

PRINCIPLE OF UTMOST GOOD FAITH

An insurance contract is based on the principle of **utmost good faith.** *That is, a higher degree of honesty is imposed on both parties to an insurance contract than is imposed on parties to other contracts.* This principle has its historical roots in ocean marine insurance. The marine underwriter had to place great faith in statements made by the applicant for insurance concerning the cargo to be shipped. The property to be insured may not have been visually inspected, and the contract may have been formed in a location far removed from the cargo and ship. Thus, the principle of utmost good faith imposed a high degree of honesty on the applicant for insurance.

The principle of utmost good faith is supported by three important legal doctrines: representations, concealment, and warranty.

Representations

Representations *are statements made by the applicant for insurance.* For example, if you apply for life insurance, you may be asked questions concerning your age, weight, height, occupation, state of health, family history, and other relevant questions. Your answers to these questions are called representations.

The legal significance of a representation is that the insurance contract is voidable at the insurer's option if the representation is (1) material, (2) false, and (3) relied on by the insurer.[13] **Material** *means that if the insurer knew the true facts, the policy would not have been issued, or would have been issued on different terms. False* means that the statement is not true or is misleading. *Reliance* means that the insurer relies on the misrepresentation in issuing the policy at a specified premium.

For example, Scott applies for life insurance and states in the application that he has not visited a doctor within the last five years. However, six months earlier, he had surgery for lung cancer. In this case, he has made a statement that is both false and material, and the policy is voidable at the insurer's option. If Scott dies shortly after the policy is issued, say three months, the company could contest the death claim on the basis of a material misrepresentation. Insight 5.2 provides an additional application of this legal principle.

If an applicant for insurance states an opinion or belief that later turns out to be wrong, the insurer must prove that the applicant spoke fraudulently and intended to deceive the company before it can deny

Insight 5.2

Misrepresentation of Material Facts Allows Life Insurer to Deny Liability

Legal Facts

Kirk applied for a life insurance policy. He stated in the application he had never smoked cigarettes. In fact, he had smoked for 13 years, and during the month before he applied for insurance, he was smoking approximately 10 cigarettes daily. About 10 months later, Kirk died of reasons unrelated to smoking. The beneficiary filed a claim for the death proceeds. While investigating the claim, the insurer discovered that Kirk smoked and denied payment because of a material misrepresentation. The insurer sought to cancel the policy and refunded the premiums paid. Based on the preceding facts, can Kirk's insurer deny liability because of Kirk's false statements?

Court Decision

An appellate court ruled that a policy is void when the insured knowingly makes false statements that are material. Because smoking habits are clearly material, the policy was void. The insurer did not have to pay the claim.*

*New York Life Insurance Co. v. Johnson, United States Court of Appeals, Third Circuit, 1991. 923 F.2d 279.
SOURCE: Adapted from Gaylord A. Jentz et al., West's Business Law, Alternate Edition, 6th ed. (Minneapolis/St. Paul, MN: West Publishing Company, 1994), p. 1021.

---

payment of a claim. For example, assume that you are asked if you have high blood pressure when you apply for health insurance, and you answer no to the question. If the insurer later discovers you have high blood pressure, to deny payment of a claim, it must prove that you intended to deceive the company. Thus, a statement of opinion or belief must also be fraudulent before the insurer can refuse to pay a claim.

Finally, an **innocent** (unintentional) **misrepresentation** of a material fact, if relied on by the insurer, also makes the contract voidable. A majority of court opinions have ruled that an innocent misrepresentation of a material fact makes the contract voidable.

Concealment

The doctrine of concealment also supports the principle of utmost good faith. A **concealment** *is intentional failure of the applicant for insurance to reveal a material fact to the insurer.* Concealment is the same thing as nondisclosure; that is, the applicant for insurance deliberately withholds material information from the insurer. The legal effect of a material concealment is the same as a misrepresentation—the contract is voidable at the insurer's option.

To deny a claim based on concealment, a nonmarine insurer must prove two things: (1) the concealed

fact was known by the insured to be material, and (2) the insured intended to defraud the insurer.[14] For example, Joseph DeBellis applied for a life insurance policy on his life. Five months after the policy was issued, he was murdered. The death certificate named the deceased as Joseph DeLuca, his true name. The insurer denied payment on the grounds that Joseph had concealed a material fact by not revealing his true identity and that he had an extensive criminal record. In finding for the insurer, the court held that intentional concealment of his true identity was material and breached the obligation of good faith.[15]

The doctrine of concealment is applied in a harsher manner in ocean marine insurance. An ocean marine insurer is not required to prove that the concealment is intentional. Applicants are required to reveal all material facts that pertain to the property to be insured. The applicant's lack of awareness of the materiality of the fact is of no consequence. Thus, an ocean marine insurer can successfully deny payment of a claim if it can show that the concealed fact is material.

Warranty

The doctrine of warranty also reflects the principle of utmost good faith. A **warranty** *is a statement of fact* *or a promise made by the insured, which is part of the insurance contract and must be true if the insurer is to be liable under the contract.*[16] For example, in exchange for a reduced premium, the owner of a liquor store may warrant that an approved burglary and robbery alarm system will be operational at all times. The clause describing the warranty becomes part of the contract.

In its strictest form based on the common law, a warranty is a harsh legal doctrine. Any breach of the warranty, even if minor or not material, allows the insurer to deny payment of a claim. However, the courts and legislation have softened and modified the harsh common law doctrine of warranty. Some modifications of the doctrine of warranty are summarized as follows:

- Statements made by the applicant for insurance are considered to be representations and not warranties. Thus, the insurer cannot deny liability for a loss if a misrepresentation is not material.
- Most courts will interpret a breach of warranty liberally in those cases where a minor breach affects the risk only temporarily or insignificantly.
- "Increase in hazard" statutes have been passed that state that the company cannot deny a claim unless the breach of warranty increases the hazard.
- Statutes have been passed that allow the insured to recover unless the breach of warranty actually contributed to the loss.

REQUIREMENTS OF AN INSURANCE CONTRACT

An insurance policy is based on the law of contracts. To be legally enforceable, an insurance contract must meet four basic requirements: offer and acceptance, consideration, competent parties, and legal purpose.

Offer and Acceptance

The first requirement of a binding insurance contract is that there must be **an offer and an acceptance** of its terms. In most cases, the applicant for insurance makes the offer, and the company accepts or rejects the offer. An agent merely solicits or invites the prospective insured to make an offer. The require-

ment of offer and acceptance can be examined in greater detail by making a careful distinction between property and liability insurance, and life insurance.

In property and liability insurance, the offer and acceptance can be oral or written. In the absence of specific legislation to the contrary, oral insurance contracts are valid. As a practical matter, most property and liability insurance contracts are in written form. The applicant for insurance fills out the application and pays the first premium (or promises to pay the first premium). This step constitutes the offer. The agent then accepts the offer on behalf of the insurance company. In property and liability insurance, agents typically have the power to bind their companies through use of a binder. A **binder** *is a temporary contract for insurance and can be either written or oral.* The binder obligates the company immediately prior to receipt of the application and issuance of the policy. Thus, the insurance contract can be effective immediately, because the agent accepts the offer on behalf of the company. This procedure is usually followed in personal lines of property and liability insurance, including homeowners policies and auto insurance. However, in some cases, the agent is not authorized to bind the company, and the application must be sent to the company for approval. The company may then accept the offer and issue the policy or reject the application.

In life insurance, the procedures followed are different. A life insurance agent does not have the power to bind the insurer. Therefore, the application for life insurance is always in writing, and the applicant must be approved by the insurer before the life insurance is in force. The usual procedure is for the applicant to fill out the application and pay the first premium. A **conditional premium receipt** is then given to the applicant. The most common conditional receipt is the "insurability premium receipt." If the applicant is found insurable according to the insurer's normal underwriting standards, the life insurance becomes effective as of the date of the application. Some insurability receipts make the life insurance effective on the date of the application or the date of the medical exam, whichever is later.

For example, assume that Aaron applies for a $100,000 life insurance policy on Monday. He fills out the application, pays the first premium, and receives a conditional premium receipt from the agent. On Tuesday morning, he takes a physical examination, and on Tuesday afternoon, he is killed in a boating accident. The application and premium will still be forwarded to the insurer, as if he were still alive. If he is found insurable according to the insurer's underwriting rules, the life insurance is in force, and $100,000 will be paid to his beneficiary.

However, if the applicant for life insurance does not pay the first premium when the application is filled out, a different set of rules applies. Before the life insurance is in force, the policy must be issued and delivered to the applicant, the first premium must be paid, and the applicant must be in good health when the policy is delivered. Some insurers also require that there must be no interim medical treatment between submission of the application and delivery of the policy. These requirements are considered to be "conditions precedent"—in other words, they must be fulfilled before the life insurance is in force.[17]

Consideration

The second requirement of a valid insurance contract is **consideration**. Consideration refers to the value that each party gives to the other. The insured's consideration is payment of the first premium (or a promise to pay the first premium) plus an agreement to abide by the conditions specified in the policy. The insurer's consideration is the promise to do certain things as specified in the contract. This promise can include paying for a loss from an insured peril, providing certain services, such as loss prevention and safety services, or defending the insured in a liability lawsuit.

Competent Parties

The third requirement of a valid insurance contract is that each party must be **legally competent**. This means the parties must have legal capacity to enter into a binding contract. Most adults are legally competent to enter into insurance contracts, but there are some exceptions. Insane persons, intoxicated persons, and corporations that act outside the scope of their authority cannot enter into enforceable insurance contracts. Minors normally are not legally competent to enter into binding insurance contracts; but most states have enacted laws that permit minors, such as a teenager age 15, to enter into a valid life or health insurance contract.

Legal Purpose

A final requirement is that the contract must be for a **legal purpose**. An insurance contract that encourages or promotes something illegal or immoral is contrary to the public interest and cannot be enforced. For example, a street pusher of heroin and other illegal drugs cannot purchase a property insurance policy that would cover seizure of the drugs by the police. This type of contract obviously is not enforceable because it would promote illegal activities that are contrary to the public interest.

DISTINCT LEGAL CHARACTERISTICS OF INSURANCE CONTRACTS

Insurance contracts have distinct legal characteristics that make them different from other legal contracts. Several distinctive legal characteristics have already been discussed. As we noted earlier, most property and liability insurance contracts are contracts of indemnity; all insurance contracts must be supported by an insurable interest; and insurance contracts are based on utmost good faith. Other distinct legal characteristics are as follows:

- Aleatory contract
- Unilateral contract
- Conditional contract
- Personal contract
- Contract of adhesion

Aleatory Contract

An insurance contract is aleatory rather than commutative. An **aleatory contract** *is one in which the values exchanged may not be equal but depend on an uncertain event.* Depending on chance, one party may receive a value out of proportion to the value that is given. For example, assume that Lorri pays a premium of $500 for $100,000 of homeowners insurance on her home. If the home were totally destroyed by fire shortly thereafter, she would collect an amount that greatly exceeds the premium paid. On the other hand, a homeowner may faithfully pay premiums for many years and never have a loss.

In contrast, other commercial contracts are commutative. A **commutative contract** *is one in which the values exchanged by both parties are theoreti-*

cally even. For example, the purchaser of real estate normally pays a price that is viewed to be equal to the value of the property.

Although the essence of an aleatory contract is chance, or the occurrence of some fortuitous event, an insurance contract is not a gambling contract. Gambling creates a new speculative risk that did not exist before the transaction. Insurance, however, is a technique for handling an already existing pure risk. Thus, although both gambling and insurance are aleatory in nature, an insurance contract is not a gambling contract because no new risk is created.

Unilateral Contract

An insurance contract is a unilateral contract. A **unilateral contract** *means that only one party makes a legally enforceable promise.* In this case, only the insurer makes a legally enforceable promise to pay a claim or provide other services to the insured. After the first premium is paid, and the insurance is in force, the insured cannot be legally forced to pay the premiums or to comply with the policy provisions. Although the insured must continue to pay the premiums to receive payment for a loss, he or she cannot be legally forced to do so. However, if the premiums are paid, the insurer must accept them and must continue to provide the protection promised under the contract.

In contrast, most commercial contracts are *bilateral* in nature. Each party makes a legally enforceable promise to the other party. If one party fails to perform, the other party can insist on performance or can sue for damages because of the breach of contract.

Conditional Contract

An insurance contract is a **conditional contract.** That is, the insurer's obligation to pay a claim depends on whether the insured or the beneficiary has complied with all policy conditions. *Conditions are provisions inserted in the policy that qualify or place limitations on the insurer's promise to perform.* The conditions section imposes certain duties on the insured if he or she wishes to collect for a loss. Although the insured is not compelled to abide by the policy conditions, he or she must do so to collect for a loss. The insurer is

not obligated to pay a claim if the policy conditions are not met. For example, under a homeowners policy, the insured must give immediate notice of a loss. If the insured delays for an unreasonable period in reporting the loss, the insurer can refuse to pay the claim on the grounds that a policy condition has been violated.

Personal Contract

In property insurance, insurance is a **personal contract,** *which means the contract is between the insured and the insurer.* Strictly speaking, a property insurance contract does not insure property, but insures the owner of property against loss. The owner of the insured property is indemnified if the property is damaged or destroyed. Because the contract is personal, the applicant for insurance must be acceptable to the insurer and must meet certain underwriting standards regarding character, morals, and credit.

A property insurance contract normally cannot be assigned to another party without the insurer's consent. If property is sold to another person, the new owner may not be acceptable to the insurer. *Thus, the insurer's consent is normally required before a property insurance policy can be validly assigned to another party.* In contrast, a life insurance policy can be freely assigned to anyone without the insurer's consent because the assignment does not usually alter the risk and increase the probability of death.

Conversely, a payment for a property loss can be assigned to another party without the insurer's consent. Although the insurer's consent is not required, the contract may require that the insurer be notified of the assignment of the proceeds to another party.

Contract of Adhesion

A **contract of adhesion** *means the insured must accept the entire contract, with all of its terms and conditions.* The insurer drafts and prints the policy, and the insured generally must accept the entire document and cannot insist that certain provisions be added or deleted or the contract rewritten to suit the insured. Although the contract can be altered by the addition of endorsements or forms, the endorsements and forms are drafted by the insurer. To redress the imbalance that exists in such a situation, *the courts have ruled that any ambiguities or uncertainties in the contract are construed against the insurer.* If the policy is ambiguous, the insured gets the benefit of the doubt.

The general rule that ambiguities in insurance contracts are construed against the insurer is reinforced by the principle of reasonable expectations. The **principle of reasonable expectations** *states that an insured is entitled to coverage under a policy that he or she reasonably expects it to provide, and that to be effective, exclusions or qualifications must be conspicuous, plain, and clear.*[18] Some courts have ruled that insureds are entitled to the protection that they reasonably expect to have, and that technical restrictions in the contract should not be a hidden pitfall. For example, in one case, a liability insurer refused to defend the insured on the grounds that the policy excluded intentional acts. The court ruled that the insurer was responsible for the defense costs. The insured had a reasonable expectation that defense costs were covered under the policy because the policy covered other types of intentional acts.[19]

LAW AND THE INSURANCE AGENT

An insurance contract normally is sold by an agent who represents the principal. An agent is someone who has the authority to act on behalf of someone else. The principal (insurer) is the party for whom action is to be taken. Thus, if Patrick has the authority to solicit, create, or terminate an insurance contract on behalf of Apex Fire Insurance, he would be the agent and Apex Fire Insurance would be the principal.

General Rules of Agency

Three important rules of law govern the actions of agents and their relationship to insureds:[20]

- There is no presumption of an agency relationship.
- An agent must have authority to represent the principal.
- A principal is responsible for the acts of agents acting within the scope of their authority.

No Presumption of an Agency Relationship There is no presumption that one person legally can act as an agent for another. Some visible evidence of any agency relationship must exist. For example, a person who claims to be an agent for an auto insurer may collect premiums and then abscond with the funds. The auto insurer is not legally responsible for the person's actions if it has done nothing to create the impression that an agency relationship is in existence. However, if the person has a calling card, rate book, and application blanks supplied by the insurer, then it can be presumed that a legitimate agent is acting on behalf of that insurer.

Authority to Represent the Principal An agent must be authorized to represent the principal. An agent's authority is derived from three sources: (1) express powers, (2) implied powers, and (3) apparent authority.

Express powers are powers specifically conferred on the agent. These powers are normally stated in the *agency agreement* between the agent and the principal. The agency agreement may also withhold certain powers. For example, a life insurance agent may be given the power to solicit applicants and arrange for physical examinations. Certain powers, such as the right to extend the time for payment of premiums or the right to alter contractual provisions in the policy, may be denied.

Agents also have **implied powers**. Implied powers refer to the authority of the agent to perform all incidental acts necessary to fulfill the purposes of the agency agreement. For example, an agent may have the express authority to deliver a life insurance policy to the client. It follows that the agent also has the implied power to collect the first premium.

Finally, an agent may bind the principal by **apparent authority**. If an agent acts with apparent authority to do certain things, and a third party is led to believe that the agent is acting within the scope of reasonable and appropriate authority, the principal can be bound by the agent's actions. Third parties have to show only that they have exercised due diligence in determining the agent's authority based on the agent's actual authority or conduct of the principal. For example, an agent for an auto insurer may frequently grant his or her clients an extension of time to pay overdue premiums. If the insurer has not expressly granted this right to the agent and has not taken any action to deal with the violation of company policy, it could not later deny liability for a loss on the grounds that the agent lacked authority to grant the time extension. The insurer first would have to notify all policyowners of the limitations on the agent's powers.

Principal Responsible for Acts of Agents A final rule of agency law is that the principal is responsible for all acts of agents when they are acting within the scope of their authority. This responsibility also includes fraudulent acts, omissions, and misrepresentations.

In addition, knowledge of the agent is presumed to be knowledge of the principal with respect to matters within the scope of the agency relationship. For example, if a life insurance agent knows that an applicant for life insurance is addicted to alcohol, this knowledge is imputed to the insurer even though the agent deliberately omits this information from the application. Thus, if the insurer issues the policy, it cannot later attack the validity of the policy on the grounds of alcohol addiction and the concealment of a material fact.

Waiver and Estoppel

The doctrines of waiver and estoppel have direct relevance to the law of agency and to the powers of insurance agents. The practical significance of these concepts is that an insurer legally may be required to pay a claim that it ordinarily would not have to pay.

Waiver *is defined as the voluntary relinquishment of a known legal right.* If the insurer voluntarily waives a legal right under the contract, it cannot later deny payment of a claim by the insured on the grounds that such a legal right was violated. For example, assume that an insurer receives an application for insurance at its home office, and that the application contains an incomplete or missing answer. The insurer does not contact the applicant for additional information, and the policy is issued. The insurer later could not deny payment of a claim on the basis of an incomplete application. In effect, the insurer has waived its requirement that the application be complete.

The legal term *estoppel* was derived centuries ago from the English common law. **Estoppel** *occurs when a representation of fact made by one person to another person is reasonably relied on by that person to such an extent that it would be inequitable to allow the first person to deny the truth of the representation.*[21] Stated simply, if one person makes a statement to another person who then reasonably relies on the statement to his or her detriment, the first person cannot later deny the statement was made. The law of estoppel is designed to prevent persons from changing their minds to the detriment of another party. For example, assume that Richard's auto insurance premium is due. He calls his agent and asks for an extension of time. The agent states, "Don't worry. There is a ten-day grace period for overdue premiums." If Richard has an accident during the so-called grace period, the insurer cannot deny liability for the loss on the grounds that the premium was not paid on time. In effect, the insurer would be estopped, or prevented, from denying payment of the claim. Richard has reasonably relied on the statement by his agent, and the insurer cannot later change its mind to Richard's detriment.

SUMMARY

- The principle of indemnity states that the insurer should not pay more than the actual amount of the loss; in other words, the insured should not profit from a covered loss.

- There are several exceptions to the principle of indemnity. These exceptions include a valued policy, valued policy laws, replacement cost insurance, and life insurance.

- The principle of insurable interest means that the insured must stand to lose financially if a loss occurs, or must incur some other kind of harm if the loss takes place. All insurance contracts must be supported by an insurable interest to be legally enforceable. There are three purposes of the insurable interest requirement:

    To prevent gambling

    To reduce moral hazard

    To measure the amount of loss in property insurance

■ In property and liability insurance, the ownership of property, potential legal liability, secured creditors, and contractual rights can support the insurable interest requirement. In life insurance, the question of an insurable interest does not arise when a person purchases life insurance on his or her own life. However, if life insurance is purchased on the life of another person, there must be an insurable interest in that person's life. Close ties of love, affection, blood, and marriage or a pecuniary interest will satisfy the insurable interest requirement in life insurance.

■ In property insurance, the insurable interest requirement must be met at the time of loss. In life insurance, the insurable interest requirement must be met only at the inception of the policy.

■ The principle of subrogation means that the insurer is entitled to recover from a negligent third party any loss payments made to the insured. The purposes of subrogation are to prevent the insured from collecting twice for the same loss, to hold the negligent person responsible for the loss, and to hold down insurance rates. If the insurer exercises its subrogation rights, the insured generally must be fully restored before the insurer can retain any sums collected from the negligent third party. Also, the insured cannot do anything that might impair the insurer's subrogation rights. However, the insurer can waive its subrogation rights in the contract either before or after the loss. Finally, subrogation does not apply to life insurance contracts and to most individual health insurance contracts.

■ The principle of utmost good faith means that a higher degree of honesty is imposed on both parties to an insurance contract than is imposed on parties to other contracts.

■ The legal doctrines of representations, concealment, and warranty support the principle of utmost good faith. Representations are statements made by the applicant for insurance. The insurer can deny payment for a claim if the representation is material, false, and is relied on by the insurer in issuing the policy at a specified premium. In the case of statements of belief or opinion, the misrepresentation must also be fraudulent before the insurer can deny a claim. Concealment of a material fact has the same legal effect as a misrepresentation: the contract is voidable at the insurer's option.

■ A warranty is a statement of fact or a promise made by the insured, which is part of the insurance contract and must be true if the insurer is to be liable under the contract. Based on common law, any breach of the warranty, even if slight, allows the insurer to deny payment of a claim. The harsh, common law doctrine of a warranty, however, has been modified and softened by court decisions and statutes.

■ To have a valid insurance contract, four requirements must be met:

There must be an offer and acceptance.

Consideration must be exchanged.

The parties to the contract must be legally competent.

The contract must be for a legal purpose.

■ Insurance contracts have distinct legal characteristics. An insurance contract is an *aleatory contract* in which the values exchanged may not be equal and depend on the occurrence of an uncertain event. An insurance contract is *unilateral* because only the insurer makes a legally enforceable promise. An insurance contract is *conditional* because the insurer's obligation to pay a claim depends on whether the insured or beneficiary has complied with all policy provisions. A property insurance contract is a *personal contract* between the insured and insurer and cannot be validly assigned to another party without the insurer's consent. A life insurance policy is freely assignable without the insurer's consent. Finally, insurance is a *contract of adhesion*, which means the insured must accept the entire contract, with all of its terms and conditions; if there is an ambiguity in the contract, it will be construed against the insurer.

■ Three general rules of agency govern the actions of agents and their relationship to insureds:

There is no presumption of an agency relationship.

An agent must have the authority to represent the principal.

A principal is responsible for the actions of agents acting within the scope of their authority.

■ An agent can bind the principal based on express powers, implied powers, and apparent authority.

■ Based on the legal doctrines of waiver and estoppel, an insurer may be required to pay a claim that it ordinarily would not have to pay.

KEY CONCEPTS AND TERMS

Actual cash value
Aleatory contract
Apparent authority
Binder
Broad evidence rule
Commutative contract
Concealment
Conditional contract
Conditional premium receipt
Consideration
Contract of adhesion
Estoppel
Express powers
Fair market value
Implied powers
Innocent misrepresentation
Legal purpose
Legally competent parties

Material fact
Offer and acceptance
Pecuniary interest
Personal contract
Principle of indemnity
Principle of insurable interest
Principle of reasonable expectations
Principle of utmost good faith
Replacement cost insurance
Representations
Subrogation
Unilateral contract
Valued policy
Valued policy laws
Waiver
Warranty

REVIEW QUESTIONS

1. Explain the principle of indemnity. How does the concept of actual cash value support the principle of indemnity?

2. Show how a valued policy, valued policy laws, replacement cost insurance, and life insurance are exceptions to the principle of indemnity.

3. What is an insurable interest? Why is an insurable interest required in every insurance contract?

4. Explain the principle of subrogation. Why is subrogation used?

5. Explain the principle of utmost good faith. How do the legal doctrines of representations, concealment, and warranty support the principle of utmost good faith?

6. Identify the four requirements that must be met to have a valid insurance contract.

7. Insurance contracts have distinct legal characteristics that distinguish them from other contracts. Explain these characteristics.

8. Explain the three general rules of agency that govern the actions of agents and their relationship to insureds.

9. What are the various sources of authority that enable an agent to bind the principal?

10. What is the meaning of waiver and estoppel?

APPLICATION QUESTIONS

1. Scott borrowed $500,000 from the Gateway Bank to purchase a fishing boat. He keeps the boat at a dock owned by the Marina Company. He uses the boat to earn income by fishing. Scott also has a contract with the Blue Fin Fishing Company to transport shrimp from one port to another.
   a. Do any of the following parties have an insurable interest in Scott or his property? If an insurable interest exists, explain the extent of the interest.
      (1) Gateway Bank
      (2) Marina Company
      (3) Blue Fin Fishing Company
   b. If Scott did not own the boat but operated it on behalf of the Blue Fin Fishing Company, would he have an insurable interest in the boat? Explain.

2. A drunk driver ran a red light and smashed into Kristen's car. The cost to repair the car is $5000. She has collision insurance on her car with a $250 deductible.
   a. Can Kristen collect from both the negligent driver's insurer and her own insurer? Explain your answer.
   b. Explain how subrogation supports the principle of indemnity.

3. a. Representations and warranties exist in many contracts, but they are particularly important in insurance contracts. Explain the difference between representations and warranties that are found in insurance contracts, and give an example of each.
   b. Insurance is a *conditional contract*. Explain the meaning of the term.
   c. Explain some additional characteristics of insurance contracts that distinguish them from other contracts.

4. One requirement for the formation of a valid insurance contract is that the contract must be for a legal purpose.
   a. Identify three factors, other than the legal purpose requirement, that are essential to the formation of a binding insurance contract.
   b. Show how each of the three requirements in part (a) is fulfilled when the applicant applies for an auto insurance policy.
   c. In each of the following cases, indicate whether a

person is legally competent to enter into a valid insurance contract.

(1) A male, age 15, who applies for insurance on his life

(2) A married woman, age 21, who applies for an auto policy and is the named insured

(3) A female, age 21, who signs an application for life insurance when she is intoxicated

(4) A male, age 21, who has been convicted of drunk driving and has been canceled by an insurer

5. Nicole is applying for a health insurance policy. She has a chronic liver ailment and other health problems. She honestly disclosed the true facts concerning her medical history to the insurance agent. However, the agent did not include all the facts in the application. Instead, the agent stated that he was going to cover the material facts in a separate letter to the insurance company's underwriting department, but the agent did not furnish the material facts to the insurer, and the contract was issued as standard. A claim occurred shortly thereafter. After investigating the claim, the insurer denied payment. Nicole contends that the company should pay the claim because she answered honestly all questions that the agent asked.

a. On what basis can the insurance company deny payment of the claim?

b. What legal doctrines can Nicole use to support her argument that the claim should be paid?

SELECTED REFERENCES

Anderson, Buist M. *Anderson on Life Insurance*. Boston: Little, Brown, 1991. See also *Anderson on Life Insurance, 1996 Supplement*.

Crawford, Muriel L., *Life and Health Insurance Law*, 8th ed. Boston: Irwin/McGraw-Hill, 1998.

Dobbyn, John F. *Insurance Law in a Nutshell*, 2nd ed. St. Paul, MN: West Publishing Company, 1989.

Fire Casualty & Surety Bulletins. Fire and Marine Volume. Cincinnati: National Underwriter Company. These bulletins contain interesting cases concerning the meaning of actual cash value, insurable interest, and other legal concepts.

Case Application

Carmine purchased an automobile service station from Ben. The purchase price included the building, equipment, and other assets. The business was financed by a loan from National Bank, which held a mortgage on the building. Carmine also converted a one-car repair bay into a short-order restaurant. When Carmine applied for property insurance on the business, he did not tell the insurance company about the restaurant because his premiums would have been substantially increased. Six months after the business opened, a car caught fire and damaged the roof over a bay in the service station area.

a. Do any of the following parties have an insurable interest in the business at the time of the fire?
  1. Ben
  2. Carmine
  3. National Bank

b. Ben told Carmine he could save money by taking over Ben's insurance instead of buying a new policy. Would it be appropriate for Carmine to take over Ben's insurance without notifying Ben's insurer? Explain.

c. Investigation of the fire revealed that the car owner knew the gas tank had a leak, but this information was not disclosed to Carmine when the car was brought in for service. Explain how subrogation might apply in this case.

d. Did Carmine show utmost good faith when he applied for property insurance on the business? Explain.

e. Could Carmine's insurer deny coverage for the fire on the basis of a material concealment? Explain.

Graves, Edward E., and Burke A. Christensen, eds. *McGill's Legal Aspects of Life Insurance*. Bryn Mawr, PA: The American College, 1997.

Keeton, Robert E., and Alan I. Widiss. *Insurance Law: A Guide to Fundamental Principles, Legal Doctrines, and Commercial Practices*. Student edition. St. Paul, MN: West Publishing Company, 1988.

Lorimer, James J., et al. *The Legal Environment of Insurance*. 4th ed., vols. 1 and 2. Malvern, PA: American Institute for Property and Liability Underwriters, 1993.

Wiening, Eric A., and Donald S. Malecki. *Insurance Contract Analysis*. Malvern, PA: American Institute for Chartered Property Casualty Underwriters, 1992.

NOTES

1. *Jefferson Insurance Company of New York v. Superior Court of Alameda County*, 475 P. 2d 880 (1970).

2. Valued policy laws are in force in Arkansas, Florida, Georgia, Kansas, Louisiana, Minnesota, Mississippi, Missouri, Montana, Nebraska, New Hampshire, North Dakota, Ohio, South Carolina, South Dakota, Tennessee, Texas, West Virginia, and Wisconsin.

3. *Gamel v. Continental Ins. Co.*, 463 S.W. 2d 590 (1971). For additional information concerning valued policy laws, the interested student should consult the *Fire Casualty & Surety Bulletins*, Fire and Marine Volume, Misc. Property section (Cincinnati: National Underwriter Company).

4. Edwin W. Patterson, *Essentials of Insurance Law*, 2nd ed. (New York: McGraw-Hill, 1957), pp. 109–111, 154–159.

5. Patterson, p. 114.

6. Buist M. Anderson, *Anderson on Life Insurance* (Boston: Little, Brown, 1991), p. 361.

7. Patterson, pp. 147–148.

8. James J. Lorimer et al., *The Legal Environment of Insurance*, 3rd ed., vol. 1 (Malvern, PA: American Institute for Property and Liability Underwriters, 1987), p. 376.

9. Lorimer et al., p. 377.

10. Patterson, p. 149.

11. C. Arthur Williams, Jr., George L. Head, Ronald C. Horn, and G. William Glendenning, *Principles of Risk Management and Insurance*, 2nd ed., vol. 2 (Malvern, PA: American Institute for Property and Liability Underwriters, 1981), p. 228.

12. Group health insurance contracts may contain subrogation clauses.

13. John F. Dobbyn, *Insurance Law*, 2nd ed. (St. Paul, MN: West Publishing Company, 1989), p. 157.

14. James J. Lorimer et al., *The Legal Environment of Insurance*, 4th ed., vol. I (Malvern, PA: American Institute for Chartered Property Casualty Underwriters, 1993), pp. 112–114.

15. *Ibid.*, pp. 115–116.

16. Joseph L. Frascona, *Business Law, The Legal Environment, Text and Cases*, 3rd ed. (Dubuque, Iowa: William C. Brown, 1987), p. 1006.

17. Edward E. Graves, ed., *McGill's Life Insurance* (Bryn Mawr, PA: The American College, 1994), p. 789.

18. Lorimer et al., *The Legal Environment of Insurance*, 3rd ed., vol. I, pp. 402–403.

19. *Ibid.*, p. 403.

20. Graves, pp. 805–808.

21. Patterson, pp. 495–496.

Chapter 6

Analysis of Insurance Contracts

"The insurance contract is one of the most important inventions of the human mind in modern times."

Edwin W. Patterson,
Essentials of Insurance Law, 2nd ed.

Learning Objectives

After studying this chapter, you should be able to:

▲ Identify the basic parts of any insurance contract.

▲ Explain the meaning of an "insured" in an insurance contract.

▲ Describe the common types of deductibles that appear in insurance contracts.

▲ Explain how coinsurance works in a property insurance contract.

▲ Show how coinsurance works in a health insurance contract.

▲ Explain what happens when more than one insurance contract covers the same loss.

▲ Access an Internet site and obtain consumer information on specific types of insurance products.

Internet Resources

■ The **New York State Insurance Department** publishes a number of consumer publications on basic insurance contracts that can be ordered online. The publications are helpful in understanding the various contractual provisions and coverages that appear in homeowners and auto insurance and other insurance coverages. Visit the site at:

http://www.ins.state.ny.us/

■ The **State of Wisconsin Office of the Commissioner of Insurance** also makes available a number of consumer guides and publications on specific insurance contracts. These guides and publications are helpful in understanding the contractual provisions and coverages that appear in life, health, auto, and homeowners insurance. Visit the site at:

http://badger.state.wi.us/agencies/oci/oci_home.htm

■ The **Insurance Information Institute** publishes consumer materials dealing with property and liability insurance. The publications can help you understand the contractual provisions and coverages that appear in homeowners, auto, personal liability, and flood insurance, and other property and liability insurance coverages. Visit the site at:

http://www.iii.org/

elsi, age 25, recently graduated from college and accepted a job as a marketing analyst with a large national firm in Orlando, Florida. She purchased a homeowners policy that covered her personal property in a rented apartment. The policy contained a number of limits on certain types of property. Later, a thief broke into Kelsi's apartment and stole a coin collection worth $5000. Kelsi was upset when her agent told her the homeowners policy would pay only $200 for the loss. She made the common mistake of not reading her homeowners policy and understanding the limits on certain types of property.

Kelsi is not alone. Most people do not read or understand the contractual provisions that appear in their insurance policies. Individuals typically own several insurance policies, including auto and homeowners insurance as well as life and health insurance. These policies are complex legal documents that reflect the legal principles discussed in Chapter 5.

Although insurance contracts are not identical, they contain similar contractual provisions. This chapter discusses the basic parts of an insurance policy, the meaning of an "insured," exclusions, deductibles, coinsurance, and other-insurance provisions. Grasping these topics will provide you with a foundation for a better understanding of specific insurance contracts discussed later in the text.

BASIC PARTS OF AN INSURANCE CONTRACT

Despite their complexities, insurance contracts generally can be divided into the following parts:

- Declarations
- Definitions
- Insuring agreement
- Exclusions
- Conditions
- Miscellaneous provisions

Although all insurance contracts do not necessarily contain all six parts in the order given here, such a classification provides a simple and convenient framework for analyzing most insurance contracts.

Declarations

The declarations section is the first part of an insurance contract. **Declarations** *are statements that provide information about the property or activity to be insured.* Information contained in the declarations section is used for underwriting and rating purposes and for identification of the property or activity to be insured. The declarations section usually can be found on the first page of the policy or on a policy insert.

In property insurance, the declarations page typically contains information concerning the identification of the insurer, name of the insured, location of the property, period of protection, amount of insurance, amount of the premium, size of the deductible (if any), and other relevant information. In life insurance, although the first page of the policy technically is not called a declarations page, it contains the insured's name, age, premium amount, issue date, and policy number.

Definitions

Insurance contracts typically contain a page or section of definitions. Key words or phrases have quotation marks (". . .") around them or are in **boldface** type. For example, the insurer is frequently referred to as "we," "our," or "us." The insured is referred to as "you" and "your." The purpose of the various definitions is to define clearly the meaning of key words or phrases so that coverage under the policy can be determined more easily.

Insuring Agreement

The insuring agreement is the heart of an insurance contract. The **insuring agreement** *summarizes the major promises of the insurer.* The insurer, in other words, agrees to do certain things, such as paying losses from insured perils, providing certain services (such as loss-prevention services), or agreeing to defend the insured in a liability lawsuit. The promises of the insurer and the conditions under which losses are paid are described in the insuring agreement.

There are two basic forms of an insuring agreement in property and liability insurance: (1) named-perils coverage and (2) "all-risks" coverage. *Under a* **named-perils policy,** *only those perils specifically named in the policy are covered.* If the peril is not named, it is not covered. For example, in the homeowners policy, personal property is covered for fire, lightning, windstorm, and certain other named perils. Only losses caused by these perils are covered. Flood damage is not covered because flood is not a listed peril.

Under an **"all-risks" policy** *(also called an open perils policy), all losses are covered except those losses specifically excluded.* If the loss is not excluded, then it is covered. For example, the physical damage section of the personal auto policy covers losses to a covered auto. Thus, if a smoker burns a hole in the upholstery, or a bear in a national park damages the vinyl top of a covered auto, the losses would be covered because they are not excluded.

"All-risks" coverage is generally preferable to named-perils coverage, because the protection is broader with fewer gaps in coverage. If the loss is not excluded, then it is covered. In addition, a greater burden of proof is placed on the insurer to deny a claim. *To deny payment, the insurer must prove that the loss is excluded. In contrast, under a named-perils contract, the burden of proof is on the insured to show that the loss was caused by a named peril.*

Many insurers and rating organizations have deleted the word *all* in their "all-risks" policy forms or are using special terminology. In the homeowners policy drafted by the Insurance Services Office, the phrase *risk of direct loss to property* is now used instead of the term *"all-risks."* However, this term is interpreted to mean that all losses are covered except those losses specifically excluded. Likewise, the Insurance Services Office has drafted a *special-causes-of-loss form* that is used in commercial property insurance. Once again, this terminology is interpreted to mean that all losses are covered except those losses excluded. The deletion of any reference to "all-risks" is intended to avoid creating unreasonable expectations among policyowners that the policy covers all losses, even those losses that are specifically excluded.

Life insurance is another example of an "all-risks" policy. Most life insurance contracts cover all causes of death whether by accident or by disease. The major exclusions are suicide during the first two years of the contract; certain aviation hazard exclusions, such as military flying, crop dusting, or sports piloting; and in some contracts, death caused by war.

Exclusions

Exclusions are another basic part of any insurance contract. There are three major types of exclusions: excluded perils, excluded losses, and excluded property.

Excluded Perils   The contract may exclude certain perils, or causes of loss. Under a homeowners policy, the perils of flood, earth movement, and nuclear radiation or radioactive contamination are specifically excluded. In the physical damage section of the personal auto policy, collision is specifically excluded if the car is used as a public taxicab. In disability income policies, the peril of war may be excluded.

Excluded Losses   Certain types of losses may be excluded. For example, in a homeowners policy, failure of an insured to protect the property after a loss occurs is excluded. In the personal liability section of a homeowners policy, a liability lawsuit arising out of the operation of an automobile is excluded. Professional liability losses are also excluded; a specific professional liability policy is needed to cover this exposure.

Excluded Property   The contract may exclude or place limitations on the coverage of certain property. For example, in a homeowners policy, certain types of personal property are excluded, such as cars, planes, animals, birds, and fish. In a liability insurance policy, property of others in the care, control, and custody of the insured is usually excluded.

Reasons for Exclusions Exclusions are necessary for the following reasons:[1]

- Some perils considered uninsurable
- Presence of extraordinary hazards
- Coverage provided by other contracts
- Moral hazard problems
- Coverage not needed by typical insureds

Exclusions are necessary because the peril may be considered uninsurable by commercial insurers. A given peril may depart substantially from the requirements of an insurable risk, as discussed in Chapter 2. For example, most property and liability insurance contracts exclude losses for potential catastrophic events such as war or exposure to nuclear radiation. A health insurance contract may exclude losses within the direct control of the insured, such as an intentional, self-inflicted injury. Finally, predictable declines in the value of property, such as wear and tear and inherent vice, are not insurable. "Inherent vice" refers to the destruction or damage of property without any tangible external force, such as the tendency of fruit to rot and the tendency of diamonds to crack.

Exclusions are also used because extraordinary hazards are present. A hazard is a condition that increases the chance of loss or severity of loss. Because of an extraordinary increase in hazard, a loss may be excluded. For example, the premium for liability insurance under a personal auto policy is based on the assumption that the car is normally used for personal and recreational use and not as a taxicab. The chance of an accident, and a resulting liability lawsuit, is much higher if the car is used as a taxicab for hire. Therefore, to provide coverage for a taxicab at the same premium rate for a family car could result in inadequate premiums for the insurer and unfair rate discrimination against other insureds who are not using their vehicles as taxicabs.

Exclusions are also necessary because coverage can be better provided by other contracts. Exclusions are used to avoid duplication of coverage and to limit coverage to the policy best designed to provide it. For example, a car is excluded under a homeowners policy because it is covered under the personal auto policy and other auto insurance contracts. If both policies covered the loss, there would be unnecessary duplication.

In addition, certain property is excluded because of moral hazard or difficulty in determining and measuring the amount of loss. For example, homeowner contracts typically limit the coverage of money to $200. If unlimited amounts of money were covered, fraudulent claims could increase. Also, loss-adjustment problems in determining the exact amount of the loss could increase. Thus, because of moral hazard, exclusions are used.

Finally, exclusions are used because the coverage is not needed by the typical insured. For example, most homeowners do not own private planes. To cover aircraft as personal property under the homeowners policy would be grossly unfair to the vast majority of insureds who do not own planes because premiums would be substantially higher.

Conditions

The conditions section is another important part of an insurance contract. **Conditions** *are provisions in the policy that qualify or place limitations on the insurer's promise to perform.* In effect, the conditions section imposes certain duties on the insured. If the policy conditions are not met, the insurer can refuse to pay the claim. Common policy conditions include notifying the insurer if a loss occurs, protecting the property after a loss, filing a proof of loss with the insurer, and cooperating with the insurer in the event of a liability suit.

Miscellaneous Provisions

Insurance contracts also contain a number of miscellaneous provisions. In property and liability insurance, some miscellaneous provisions refer to cancellation, subrogation, requirements if a loss occurs, assignment of the policy, and other-insurance provisions. In life and health insurance, typical provisions include the grace period, reinstatement of a lapsed policy, and misstatement of age. Details of these provisions are discussed later in the text when specific insurance contracts are analyzed.

DEFINITION OF THE "INSURED"

Insurance contracts typically contain a definition of the "insured" under the policy. The contract must indicate the person or persons for whom the protection is provided. Several possibilities exist concerning the persons who are insured under the policy. First, some policies insure only *one person*. For example, in many life and health insurance contracts, only one person is specifically named as insured under the policy.

Second, the policy may contain a formal definition of the named insured. The **named insured** *is the person or persons named in the declarations section of the policy*. For example, the named insured under a homeowners policy includes the person named in the declarations page and his or her spouse if a resident of the same household. Thus, Kathy may be the named insured under a homeowners policy. Her husband is also included in the definition of the named insured as long as he resides in the same household.

The policy may also cover other parties even though they are not specifically named in the policy. For example, in addition to the named insured, a homeowners policy covers resident relatives of the named insured or spouse and any person under age 21 who is in the care of an insured, such as a child in a foster home. The homeowners policy also covers resident relatives who are attending college and are away from home. The personal auto policy covers the named insured and spouse, resident relatives, and any other person using the automobile with the permission of the named insured (see Insight 6.1). In short, a contract may provide broad coverage with respect to the number of persons who are insured under the policy.

ENDORSEMENTS AND RIDERS

Insurance contracts frequently contain **endorsements and riders**. The terms *endorsements* and *riders* are often used interchangeably and mean the same thing. *In property and liability insurance, an endorsement is a written provision that adds to, deletes from, or modifies the provisions in the original contract. In life and health insurance, a rider is a document that amends or changes the original policy.*

There are numerous endorsements in property and liability insurance that modify, extend, or delete provisions found in the original policy. For example, a homeowners policy excludes coverage for earthquakes. However, an earthquake endorsement can be added that covers damage from an earthquake or from earth movement.

In life and health insurance, numerous riders can be added that increase or decrease benefits, waive a condition of coverage present in the original policy, or amend the basic policy. For example, a waiver-of-premium rider can be added to a life insurance policy. If the insured should become disabled, all future premiums are waived after an elimination period of six months, for as long as the insured remains disabled according to the terms of the rider.

An endorsement attached to a contract normally has precedence over any conflicting terms in the contract, unless a law or regulation requires that a standard policy be used or that a policy contain certain provisions. An endorsement cannot be used to circumvent the purpose of legislation by modifying the terms of a standard policy or by changing the wording of a required provision. If an endorsement is contrary to a law or regulation, the policy is read and applied as if that endorsement did not exist.[2]

DEDUCTIBLES

A deductible is another common policy provision. A **deductible** *is a provision by which a specified amount is subtracted from the total loss payment that otherwise would be payable.* Deductibles typically are found in property, health, and auto insurance contracts. A deductible is not used in life insurance because the insured's death is always a total loss, and a deductible would simply reduce the face amount of insurance. Also, a deductible generally is not used in personal liability insurance because the insurer must provide a legal defense, even for a small claim. The insurer wants to be involved from the first dollar of loss so as to minimize its ultimate liability for a claim. Also, the premium reduction that would result from a small deductible in personal types of third-party liability coverages would be relatively small.[3]

Purposes of Deductibles

Deductibles have several important purposes. They include the following:

Insight 6.1

Are You Insured When You Drive Another Person's Car?

College students frequently drive cars owned by friends or roommates. Are you insured when you drive another person's car? To answer that question, we must examine the definition of an insured that appears in the personal auto policy, which reads as follows:

"Insured" as used in this Part means:

1. You or any "family member" for the ownership, maintenance, or use of any auto or "trailer."
2. Any person using "your covered auto."
3. For "your covered auto," any person or organization but only with respect to legal responsibility for acts or omissions of a person for whom coverage is afforded under this Part.
4. For any auto or "trailer" other than "your covered auto," any other person or organization but only with respect to legal responsibility for acts or omissions of you or any "family member" for whom coverage is afforded under this Part. This provision applies only if the person or organization does not own or hire the auto or "trailer."

Mike is the named insured under the personal auto policy that contains the above provision. His daughter, Patti, lives in a dormitory during the school year while she attends college away from home. Although she does not presently live at home, she generally would qualify as a family member because her college stay is temporary, and she regards her parents'

home as her permanent residence address.

Patti drives a Ford titled in Mike's name and listed on the declarations page in Mike's policy. Because she is a family member, she is an insured while driving the Ford because of the policy definition of an "insured." What happens if Patti allows her boyfriend to drive the Ford? Although the boyfriend is not a family member, he nevertheless qualifies as "any person using your covered auto." The boyfriend is an insured.

What if Patti occasionally drives her roommate's car? Assuming she is a family member under her father's policy, Patti is insured while driving any car, including her roommate's.

Suppose Patti is involved in an auto accident while using her car on a field trip sponsored by the college as part of her college studies. The injured party sues both Patti and the college. Patti clearly is an insured and is covered. Is the college also an "insured" under Patti's policy? Yes. The definition of an insured extends coverage to any person or organization who is legally responsible for any acts or omissions by an insured. Thus, the college is considered an insured. Patti's insurer is obligated to defend the college in the suit.

Source: Adapted from Eric A. Wiening and Donald S. Malecki, *Insurance Contract Analysis* (Malvern, PA: American Institute for Chartered Property Casualty Underwriters, 1992), pp. 175–176.

- To eliminate small claims
- To reduce premiums
- To reduce moral and morale hazard

A deductible eliminates small claims that are expensive to handle and process. For example, an insurer can easily incur expenses of $100 or more in processing a $50 claim. Because a deductible eliminates small claims, the insurer's loss-adjustment expenses are reduced.

Deductibles are also used to reduce premiums paid by the insured. Because deductibles eliminate small claims, premiums can be substantially reduced. Insurance is not an appropriate technique for paying

small losses that can be better budgeted out of personal or business income. Insurance should be used to cover large catastrophic events, such as medical expenses of $250,000 or more from a terminal illness. Insurance that protects against a catastrophic loss can be purchased more economically if deductibles are used. This concept of using insurance premiums to pay for large losses rather than for small losses is often called the **large-loss principle**. The objective is to cover large losses that can financially ruin an individual and exclude small losses that can be budgeted out of the person's income.

Other factors being equal, a large deductible is preferable to a small one. For example, many motorists with auto insurance have policies that contain a $250 deductible for collision losses instead of a $500 or larger deductible. They may not be aware of how expensive the extra insurance really is. For example, assume you can purchase collision insurance on your car with a $250 deductible at an annual premium of $600, while a policy with a $500 deductible has an annual premium of $525. If you select the $250 deductible over the $500 deductible, you have an additional $250 of collision insurance, but you must pay an additional $75 in annual premiums. Using a simple benefit-cost analysis, you are paying an additional $75 for an additional $250 of insurance, which is a relatively expensive increment of insurance. When analyzed in this manner, larger deductibles are preferable to smaller deductibles.

Finally, deductibles are used by insurers to reduce both moral and morale hazard. Some dishonest insureds may deliberately cause a loss to profit from insurance. Deductibles reduce moral hazard because the insured may not profit if a loss occurs.

Deductibles are also used to reduce morale hazard. Morale hazard is carelessness because of insurance, which increases the chance of loss. Deductibles encourage people to be more careful with respect to the protection of their property and prevention of a loss.

Deductibles in Property Insurance

The following deductibles are commonly found in property insurance contracts:

- Straight deductible
- Aggregate deductible

Straight Deductible With a **straight deductible**, *the insured must pay a certain number of dollars of loss before the insurer is required to make a payment.* Such a deductible typically applies to each loss. An example can be found in automobile collision insurance. For instance, assume that Tanya has collision insurance on her new Toyota, with a $500 deductible. If a collision loss is $7000, she would receive only $6500.

Aggregate Deductible An **aggregate deductible** *is sometimes used in commercial property insurance,* *by which all covered losses during the year are added together until they reach a certain level.* If total covered losses are below the aggregate deductible, the insurer pays nothing. Once the deductible is satisfied, all losses thereafter are paid in full. For example, assume that a property insurance contract contains a $1000 aggregate deductible for the calendar year. If a loss of $500 occurs in January, the insurer pays nothing. If a $2000 loss occurs in February, the insurer would pay $1500. At this point, the aggregate deductible of $1000 has now been satisfied for the year. If a $5000 loss occurs in March, the loss is paid in full. Any other covered losses occurring during the year would also be paid in full.

Deductibles in Health Insurance

In health insurance, the deductible can be stated in terms of dollars or time. Some commonly used deductibles in health insurance are the following:

- Calendar-year deductible
- Corridor deductible
- Elimination (waiting) period

Calendar-year Deductible A **calendar-year deductible** is a type of aggregate deductible that is found in basic medical expense and major medical insurance contracts. Eligible medical expenses are accumulated during the calendar year, and once they exceed the deductible amount, the insurer must then pay the benefits promised under the contract. Once the deductible is satisfied during the calendar year, no additional deductibles are imposed on the insured.

Corridor Deductible Employers with basic medical expense plans often wish to supplement the basic benefits with major medical benefits. A **corridor deductible** is a deductible that can be used to integrate a basic medical expense plan with a supplemental major medical expense plan. The corridor deductible must be satisfied before the major medical plan pays any benefits.

The corridor deductible applies only to eligible medical expenses that are not covered by the basic medical expense plan. For example, assume that Janet has $10,000 of covered medical expenses, of which $8000 is paid by the basic medical expense plan. If the supplemental major medical plan has a $200 corridor deductible, the supplemental plan will cover the remaining $1800 of expenses, subject to any limitations or coinsurance provisions that may apply.

Elimination (Waiting) Period A deductible can also be expressed as an elimination period. An **elimination period** *is a stated period of time at the beginning of a loss during which no insurance benefits are paid.* An elimination period is appropriate for a single loss that occurs over some time period, such as the loss of work earnings. Elimination periods are commonly used in disability-income contracts. For example, disability-income insurance contracts that replace part of a disabled worker's earnings typically have elimination periods of 30, 60, or 90 days, or even longer.

COINSURANCE

Coinsurance is a contractual provision that often appears in property insurance contracts. This is especially true of commercial property insurance contracts.

Nature of Coinsurance

A **coinsurance clause** *in a property insurance contract requires the insured to insure the property for a stated percentage of its insurable value. If the coinsurance requirement is not met at the time of loss, the insured must share in the loss as a coinsurer.* The insurable value of the property is the actual cash value, replacement cost, or some other value described in the valuation clause of the policy.[4] If the insured wants to collect in full for a partial loss, the coinsurance requirement must be satisfied. Otherwise, the insured will be penalized if a partial loss occurs.

A coinsurance formula is used to determine the amount paid for a covered loss. The coinsurance formula is as follows:

$$\frac{\text{Amount of insurance carried}}{\text{Amount of insurance required}} \times \text{Loss} = \frac{\text{Amount}}{\text{of recovery}}$$

For example, assume that a commercial building has an actual cash value of $500,000, and that the

owner has insured it for only $300,000. If an 80 percent coinsurance clause is present in the policy, the required amount of insurance based on actual cash value is $400,000 (80% × $500,000). If a replacement cost policy is used, the required amount of insurance would be based on replacement cost. Thus, if a $10,000 loss occurs, only $7500 will be paid by the insurer. This situation can be illustrated as follows:

$$\frac{\$300,000}{\$400,000} \times \$10,000 = \$7500$$

As the insured has only three-fourths of the required amount of insurance at the time of loss, only three-fourths of the loss, or $7500, will be paid. Because the coinsurance requirement is not met, the insured must absorb the remaining amount of the loss.

Finally, in applying the coinsurance formula, two additional points should be kept in mind. First, the amount paid can never exceed the amount of the actual loss even though the coinsurance formula produces such a result. This case could happen if the amount of insurance carried is greater than the required amount of insurance. Second, the maximum amount paid for any loss is limited to the face amount of insurance.

Purpose of Coinsurance

The fundamental purpose of coinsurance is to achieve **equity in rating**. Most property insurance losses are partial rather than total losses. But if everyone insures only for the partial loss rather than for the total loss, the premium rate for each $100 of insurance would be higher. This rate would be inequitable to insureds who wish to insure their property to full value. For example, if everyone insures to full value, assume that the pure premium rate for fire insurance is 6 cents for each $100 of insurance, ignoring expenses and the profit allowance of the insurer (see Exhibit 6.1).

However, if each property owner insures only for a partial loss, the pure premium rate will increase from 6 cents per $100 of fire insurance to 10 cents per $100 (see Exhibit 6.2). This rate would be inequitable to property owners who want to insure

---

EXHIBIT 6.1
Insurance to Full Value

Assume that 10,000 buildings are valued at $75,000 each and are insured to full value for a total of $750 million of fire insurance. The following fire losses occur:

2 total losses	$150,000
30 partial losses at $10,000 each	300,000
Total fire losses paid by insurer	$= $450,000$

$$\text{Pure premium rate} = \frac{\$450,000}{\$750,000,000}$$

$$= 6 \text{ cents per } \$100 \text{ of insurance}$$

EXHIBIT 6.2
Insurance to Half Value

Assume that 10,000 buildings are valued at $75,000 each and are insured to half value for a total of $375 million of fire insurance. The following fire losses occur:

2 total losses ($150,000) Insurer pays only $75,000	
30 partial losses at $10,000 each	300,000
Total fire losses paid by insurer	$= $375,000$

$$\text{Pure premium rate} = \frac{\$375,000}{\$375,000,000}$$

$$= 10 \text{ cents per } \$100 \text{ of insurance}$$

---

their buildings to full value. If full coverage is desired, the insured would have to pay a higher rate of 10 cents, which we calculated earlier to be worth only 6 cents. This rate would be inequitable. *So, if the coinsurance requirement is met, the insured receives a rate discount, and the policyowner who is underinsured is penalized through application of the coinsurance formula.*

As an alternative to coinsurance, *graded rates* could be used, by which rate discounts would be given as the amount of insurance to value is increased. However, this system would require an accurate appraisal of each property to determine the required amount of insurance, which would be extremely expensive for the insurer. In addition, the appraisal method is unsatisfactory if property values fluctuate widely during the policy period. For these reasons, the coinsurance formula, rather than a table of graded rates, is used to achieve equity in rating.

Coinsurance Problems

Some practical problems arise when a coinsurance clause is present in a contract. First, inflation can result in a serious coinsurance penalty if the amount of insurance is not periodically increased for inflation. The insured may be in compliance with the coinsurance clause when the policy first goes into effect; however, price inflation could increase the replacement cost of the property. The result is that the insured may not be carrying the required amount of insurance at the time of loss, and he or she will then be penalized if a loss occurs. Thus, if a coinsurance clause is present, the amount of insurance carried should be periodically evaluated to determine whether the coinsurance requirement is being met.

Second, the insured may incur a coinsurance penalty if property values fluctuate widely during the policy period. For example, there may be a substantial increase in inventory values because of an unexpected arrival of a shipment of goods. If a loss occurs, the insured may not be carrying sufficient insurance to avoid a coinsurance penalty. One solution to this problem is an *agreed value optional coverage*, by which the insurer agrees in advance that the amount of insurance carried meets the coinsurance requirement. Another solution is a *reporting form*, by which property values are periodically reported to the insurer.

Third, if a small loss occurs, the insured may incur a financial hardship if he or she is required to take a physical inventory of the undamaged and damaged goods for purposes of determining whether the coinsurance requirement has been met. Under a *waiver of inventory clause*, the insured is relieved of the obligation of taking a physical inventory of the undamaged goods if the loss is less than 2 percent of the amount of insurance.

COINSURANCE IN HEALTH INSURANCE

Health insurance contracts frequently contain a coinsurance clause, which is technically called a **percent-**

age participation clause. In particular, major medical policies typically have a coinsurance provision that requires the insured to pay a certain percentage of covered medical expenses in excess of the deductible. A typical plan requires the insured to pay 20 or 25 percent of covered expenses in excess of the deductible. For example, assume that Megan has covered medical expenses in the amount of $50,500, and that she has a major medical policy with a $500 deductible and an 80–20 coinsurance clause. The insurer pays 80 percent of the bill in excess of the deductible, or $40,000, and Megan pays 20 percent, or $10,000 (plus the deductible).

The purposes of coinsurance in health insurance are (1) to reduce premiums and (2) to prevent overutilization of policy benefits. Because the insured pays part of the cost, premiums are reduced. In addition, the patient will not demand the most expensive medical services if he or she pays part of the cost.

OTHER-INSURANCE PROVISIONS

Other-insurance provisions typically are present in property and liability insurance and health insurance contracts. These provisions apply when more than one contract covers the same loss. *The purpose of these provisions is to prevent profiting from insurance and violation of the principle of indemnity.* If the insured could collect the full amount of the loss from each insurer, there would be profiting from insurance and a substantial increase in moral hazard. Some dishonest insureds would deliberately cause a loss so as to collect multiple benefits.

Some important other-insurance provisions in property and liability insurance include (1) the pro rata liability clause, (2) contribution by equal shares, and (3) primary and excess insurance.

Pro Rata Liability

Pro rata liability is a generic term for a provision that applies when two or more policies of the same type cover the same insurable interest in the property. *Each insurer's share of the loss is based on the proportion that its insurance bears to the total amount of insurance on the property.* For example, assume that Luis owns a building and wishes to insure it

for $200,000. For underwriting reasons, insurers may limit the amount of insurance they will write on a given property. Assume that an agent places $100,000 of insurance with Company A, $50,000 with Company B, and $50,000 with Company C, for a total of $200,000. If a $10,000 loss occurs, each company will pay only its pro rata share of the loss (see Exhibit 6.3). Thus, Luis would collect $10,000 for the loss and not $30,000.

The basic purpose of the pro rata liability clause is to preserve the principle of indemnity and to prevent profiting from insurance. In the preceding example, if the pro rata liability clause were not present, the insured would collect $10,000 from each insurer, or a total of $30,000 for a $10,000 loss.

Contribution by Equal Shares

Contribution by equal shares is another type of other-insurance provision that is frequently found in liability insurance contracts. Each insurer shares equally in the loss until the share paid by each insurer equals the lowest limit of liability under any policy, or until the full amount of the loss is paid. For example, assume that the amount of insurance provided by Companies A, B, and C is $100,000, $200,000, and $300,000 respectively. If the loss is $150,000 each insurer pays an equal share, or $50,000 (see Exhibit 6.4).

However, if the loss were $500,000, how much would each insurer pay? In this case, each insurer would pay equal amounts until its policy limits are exhausted. The remaining insurers then continue to

---

EXHIBIT 6.3
Pro Rata Liability Example

Company A	$\dfrac{\$100,000}{\$200,000}$ or $\frac{1}{2} \times \$10,000 = \$5000$
Company B	$\dfrac{\$50,000}{\$200,000}$ or $\frac{1}{4} \times \$10,000 = \$2500$
Company C	$\dfrac{\$50,000}{\$200,000}$ or $\frac{1}{4} \times \$10,000 = \underline{\$2500}$

Total loss payment = $10,000

share equally in the remaining amount of the loss until each insurer has paid its policy limit in full, or until the full amount of the loss is paid. Thus, Company A would pay $100,000, Company B would pay $200,000, and Company C would pay $200,000 (see Exhibit 6.5). If the loss were $600,000, Company C would pay the remaining $100,000.

Primary and Excess Insurance

Primary and excess insurance is another type of other-insurance provision. *The primary insurer pays first, and the excess insurer pays only after the policy limits under the primary policy are exhausted.*

Auto insurance is an excellent example of primary and excess insurance. For example, assume that Bob occasionally drives Jill's car. Bob's policy has a liability insurance limit of $100,000 per person for bodily injury liability. Jill's policy has a limit of $50,000 per person for bodily injury liability. If Bob negligently injures another motorist while driving

Jill's car, both policies will cover the loss. *The normal rule is that liability insurance on the borrowed car is primary and any other insurance is considered excess.* Thus if a court orders Bob to pay damages of $75,000, Jill's policy is primary and pays the first $50,000. Bob's policy is excess and pays the remaining $25,000.

The **coordination-of-benefits provision** in group health insurance is another example of primary and excess coverage. This provision is designed to prevent overinsurance and the duplication of benefits if one person is covered under more than one group health insurance plan.

The majority of states have adopted part or all of the coordination-of-benefits provisions developed by the National Association of Insurance Commissioners (NAIC). The rules are complex, and only two of them are discussed here. *First, coverage as an employee is usually primary to coverage as a dependent.* For example, assume that Jack and Kelly McVay both work, and that each is insured as a dependent under the other's group health insurance plan. If

---

EXHIBIT 6.4
Contribution by Equal Shares (Example 1)

Amount of loss = $150,000

	Amount of insurance	Contribution by equal shares	Total paid
Company A	$100,000	$50,000	$50,000
Company B	$200,000	$50,000	$50,000
Company C	$300,000	$50,000	$50,000

EXHIBIT 6.5
Contribution by Equal Shares (Example 2)

Amount of loss = $500,000

	Amount of insurance	Contribution by equal shares	Total paid
Company A	$100,000	$100,000	$100,000
Company B	$200,000	$100,000 + $100,000	$200,000
Company C	$300,000	$100,000 + $100,000	$200,000

Jack incurs covered medical expenses, his policy pays first as primary coverage. He then submits his unreimbursed expenses (such as the deductible and coinsurance payments) to Kelly's insurer. Kelly's coverage then applies as excess insurance. No more than 100 percent of the eligible medical expenses are paid under both plans.

Second, the birthday rule applies to dependents in families where the parents are married or are not separated. Under this rule, *the plan of the parent whose birthday occurs first during the year is primary.* For example, assume that Kelly's birthday is in January, and Jack's birthday is in July. If their daughter is hospitalized, Kelly's plan is primary. Jack's plan would be excess. The purpose of the birthday rule is to eliminate gender discrimination with respect to coverage of dependents.

SUMMARY

- Insurance contracts generally can be divided into the following parts:

  Declarations

  Definitions

  Insuring agreement

  Exclusions

  Conditions

  Miscellaneous provisions

- Declarations are statements concerning the property or activity to be insured.

- The definitions page or section defines the key words or phrases so that coverage under the policy can be determined more easily.

- The insuring agreement summarizes the promises of the insurer. There are two basic types of insuring agreements:

  Named-perils coverage

  "All-risks" coverage

- All policies contain one or more exclusions. There are three major types of exclusions:

  Excluded perils

  Excluded losses

  Excluded property

- Exclusions are necessary for several reasons. The peril may be considered uninsurable by private insurers; ex-

traordinary hazards may be present; coverage is provided by other contracts; moral hazard is present to a high degree; and coverage is not needed by the typical insured.

- Conditions are provisions that qualify or place limitations on the insurer's promise to perform. The conditions section imposes certain duties on the insured if he or she wishes to collect for a loss.

- Miscellaneous provisions in property and liability insurance include cancellation, subrogation, requirements if a loss occurs, assignment of the policy, and other insurance provisions.

- The contract also contains a definition of the "insured." The contract may cover only one person, or it may cover other persons as well even though they are not specifically named in the policy.

- An endorsement, or rider, is a written provision that adds to, deletes from, or modifies the provisions in the original contract. An endorsement normally has precedence over any conflicting terms in the contract to which the endorsement is attached.

- A deductible is a provision by which a specified amount is subtracted from the total loss payment that otherwise would be payable. Deductibles are used to eliminate small claims, to reduce premiums, and to reduce moral and morale hazard. Examples of deductibles include a straight deductible, aggregate deductible, calendar-year deductible, corridor deductible, and elimination (waiting) period.

- A coinsurance clause in property insurance requires the insured to insure the property for a stated percentage of its actual cash value at the time of loss. If the coinsurance requirement is not met at the time of loss, the insured must share in the loss as a coinsurer. The fundamental purpose of coinsurance is to achieve equity in rating.

- A coinsurance clause (percentage participation clause) is typically found in major medical policies. A typical provision requires the insurer to pay 80 percent of covered expenses in excess of the deductible and the insured to pay 20 percent.

- Other-insurance provisions are present in many insurance contracts. These provisions apply when more than one policy covers the same loss. The purpose of these provisions is to prevent profiting from insurance and violation of the principle of indemnity. Some important other-insurance provisions include the pro rata liability clause, contribution by equal shares, and primary and excess insurance.

KEY CONCEPTS AND TERMS

Aggregate deductible
"All-risks" policy
Calendar-year deductible
Coinsurance clause
Conditions
Contribution by equal
  shares
Coordination-of-benefits
  provision
Corridor deductible
Declarations
Deductible
Elimination (waiting)
  period

Endorsements and riders
Equity in rating
Exclusions
Insuring agreement
Large-loss principle
Named insured
Named-perils policy
Other-insurance provisions
Percentage participation
  clause (coinsurance)
Primary and excess
  insurance
Pro rata liability
Straight deductible

REVIEW QUESTIONS

1. Describe the basic parts of an insurance contract.

2. Identify the major types of exclusions typically found in insurance contracts. Why are exclusions used by insurers?

3. Define the term *conditions*. What is the significance of the conditions section to the insured?

4. How can an insurance contract cover other persons even though they are not specifically named in the policy?

5. What is an endorsement or rider? If an endorsement conflicts with a policy provision, how is the problem resolved?

6. Why do deductibles appear in insurance contracts? Identify some common deductibles that are found in insurance contracts.

7. Explain how a coinsurance clause in property insurance works. Why is coinsurance used?

8. Describe a typical coinsurance clause (percentage participation clause) in a major medical policy.

9. What is the purpose of other-insurance provisions? Give an example of the pro rata liability clause and contributions by equal shares.

10. Show how a statement in a policy concerning primary and excess insurance can prevent the duplication of policy benefits.

APPLICATION QUESTIONS

1. Jason owns a light plane that he flies on weekends. He is upset when you inform him that aircraft are excluded as personal property under the homeowners policy. As an insured, he feels that his plane should be covered just like any other personal property he owns.
   a. Explain to Jason the rationale for excluding certain types of property such as aircraft under the homeowners policy.
   b. Explain some additional reasons why exclusions are present in insurance contracts.

2. a. A manufacturing firm incurred the following insured losses, in the order given, during the current policy year.

Loss	Amount of loss
A	$ 2500
B	3500
C	10,000

   How much would the company's insurer pay for each loss if the policy contained the following type of deductible?
   (1) $1000 straight deductible
   (2) $15,000 annual aggregate deductible
   b. Explain the coordination-of-benefits provision that is typically found in group medical expense plans.

3. Karen owns a small warehouse that is insured for $200,000 under a commercial property insurance policy. The policy contains an 80 percent coinsurance clause. The warehouse is damaged by fire to the extent of $50,000. The actual cash value of the warehouse at the time of loss is $500,000.
   a. What is the insurer's liability, if any, for this loss? Show your calculations.
   b. Assume that Karen carried $500,000 of fire insurance on the warehouse at the time of loss. If the amount of loss is $10,000, how much will she collect?
   c. Explain the theory or rationale of coinsurance in a property insurance contract.

4. Alex owns a commercial office building that is insured under three property insurance contracts. He has $100,000 of insurance from Company A, $200,000

from Company B, and $200,000 from Company C.

a. If a $100,000 loss occurs, how much will Alex collect from each insurer? Explain your answer.

b. What is the purpose of the other-insurance provisions that are frequently found in insurance contracts?

5. a. Assume that a $60,000 liability claim is covered under two liability insurance contracts. Policy A has a $100,000 limit of liability for the claim, while Policy B has a $25,000 limit of liability. Both contracts provide for *contribution by equal shares*.

   (1) How much will each insurer contribute toward this claim? Explain your answer.

   (2) If the claim were only $10,000, how much would each insurer pay?

   b. Assume that Mike drives Donna's car with her permission and negligently injures another person while driving her car. Mike has an auto insurance contract with a liability insurance limit of $100,000 per per-

---

Case Application

Joshua owns a motorboat that struck and damaged another boat anchored at a marina. When the accident occurred, Joshua's friend, Zoe, was operating the motorboat. The owner of the damaged boat has asked Zoe to pay for the damage. Joshua is listed as the named insured on the declarations page of a boatowners liability policy. Joshua's policy included the following provisions:

What Is Covered

"We" will pay all sums which an "insured" becomes legally obligated to pay as damages due to bodily injury or property damage arising out of the ownership, maintenance, or use of the described vessel.

What Is Not Covered

"We" do not cover liability arising from the ownership, maintenance, or use of the described vessel:

1. that results from an intentional act of an insured . . .
2. to persons while they are being towed by the described vessel as water skiers, aquaplaners, or similar water sports.

Definitions

1. The words "you" and "your" mean the persons named on the Declarations.
2. The words "we," "us," and "our" mean the company providing this insurance.
3. "Bodily Injury" means bodily harm, sickness, or disease to a person.
4. "Insured" means "you" and:

   - "your" spouse;
   - "your" relatives if residents of your household;
   - persons under the age of 21 in "your" care;
   - a person who operates a covered vessel with "your" permission.
   - "Property damage" means an injury to or the destruction of property. This includes the loss of use.

a. The above provisions refer to a described vessel. Identify the section of the policy that would describe Joshua's motorboat.

b. Explain whether Joshua's policy would provide coverage for the claim against Zoe. Identify the policy provisions that would be relevant in this situation.

c. The owner of the damaged boat uses the boat to transport customers for deep-sea fishing. The owner is also holding Zoe responsible for the loss of revenues while the boat is being repaired. Explain whether Joshua's policy would pay for the lost revenues.

d. Assume that a skier towed by Joshua's motorboat is injured because of Joshua's negligence. If the injured skier sued Joshua for the injury, would Joshua be covered under the policy? Explain.

son for bodily injury liability. Donna has a similar policy with a liability limit of $50,000 per person.

(1) If a court awards a liability judgment of $75,000 against Mike, how much will each insurer pay?

(2) If the liability judgment is $200,000, how much will each insurer pay?

SELECTED REFERENCES

Anderson, Buist M. *Anderson on Life Insurance*. Boston: Little, Brown, 1991, Chapters 6–14. See also *Anderson on Life Insurance—1996 Supplement*.

Crawford, Muriel L. *Life and Health Insurance Law*, 8th ed. Boston: Irwin/McGraw-Hill, 1998.

Dobbyn, John F. *Insurance Law in a Nutshell*, 2nd ed. St. Paul, MN: West Publishing Company, 1989.

Keeton, Robert E., and Alan I. Widiss. *Insurance Law: A Guide to Fundamental Principles, Legal Doctrines, and Commercial Practices*, Student edition. St. Paul, MN: West Publishing Company, 1988.

Lorimer, James J., et al. *The Legal Environment of Insurance*, 4th ed., vols. 1 and 2. Malvern, PA: American Institute for Property and Liability Underwriters, 1993.

Wiening, Eric A. "Reading an Insurance Policy." *The CPCU Handbook of Insurance Policies*, 3rd ed. Malvern, PA: American Institute for CPCU/Insurance Institute of America, 1998, pp. 1–39.

Wiening, Eric A., and Donald S. Malecki. *Insurance Contract Analysis*. Malvern, PA: American Institute for Chartered Property Casualty Underwriters, 1992.

NOTES

1. C. Arthur Williams, Jr., George L. Head, Ronald C. Horn, and G. William Glendenning, *Principles of Risk Management and Insurance*, 2nd ed., vol. 2 (Malvern, PA: American Institute for Chartered Property Casualty Underwriters, 1981), pp. 52–56.

2. Williams et al., pp. 60–61.

3. *Ibid.*, p. 201.

4. Eric A. Wiening and Donald S. Malecki, *Insurance Contract Analysis* (Malvern, PA: American Institute for Chartered Property Casualty Underwriters, 1992), p. 294.

Students may take a self-administered test on this chapter at www.awlonline.com/rejda

Part Three

Personal Property and Liability Risks

Chapter 7

The Liability Risk

> "I'm not an ambulance chaser. I'm usually there before the ambulance."
>
> Melvin Belli

Learning Objectives

After studying this chapter, you should be able to:

▲ Explain the law of negligence and the elements of a negligent act.

▲ Identify several legal defenses that can be used in a lawsuit.

▲ Apply the law of negligence to specific liability situations.

▲ Discuss the special problems of product liability and professional liability.

▲ Explain the defects in the civil justice system and proposals for reform.

▲ Access an Internet site and obtain consumer information on the law of negligence.

Internet Resources

- **America's LAW✶LINKS** is a comprehensive legal resource guide for both attorneys and consumers. The site has a "Legal Subjects Index." Click on "Accident and Personal Injury Law" for introductory articles on accidents and personal injury. Visit the site at:

  http://www.lawlinks.com/

- **FREEADVICE.com** is a leading legal site for consumers and small businesses. The site provides general legal information to help people understand their legal rights on 100 legal topics but is not a substitute for an attorney. Check out "Accident Law" and "Insurance Law." Visit the site at:

  http://www.freeadvice.com/index.htm

- **Nolo.com** is a leading source of self-help legal information for consumers, including topics dealing with personal injury law. Visit the site at:

  http://www.nolo.com/

- The **Legal Information Institute** of Cornell Law School provides detailed information on torts, personal injury, and products liability law. Legal topics are listed alphabetically under "Law About . . ." Click on "Torts and Personal Injury" and "Products Liability" for general information and court decisions dealing with these subjects. Related links are also given. Visit the site at:

  http://www.law.cornell.edu/

uis, age 35, owns three large Rottweiler dogs in Miami, Florida. He was fined earlier by the city because the dogs often ran free without a lease and frightened the neighbors. One afternoon, the dogs escaped from a fenced yard because Luis carelessly left the gate open.

Without provocation, the dogs viciously attacked a six-year-old girl, who later died from the mauling. The parents of the deceased child sued Luis for a wrongful death and were awarded damages of $300,000. Luis could not pay and was forced to declare bankruptcy.

Luis experienced the legal effects of being negligent in a financially painful manner. Like Luis, other people often face similar liability situations. Motorists are sued for the negligent operation of their vehicles; business firms are sued because of defective products that injure others; physicians, attorneys, accountants, engineers, teachers, and other professionals are sued for malpractice, negligence, and incompetence. Even government and charitable institutions are often sued today because they no longer enjoy complete immunity from lawsuits. Thus, the liability risk is extremely important to people who wish to avoid or minimize potential losses.

This chapter discusses the law of negligence and the civil justice system in the United States. This knowledge is important because it forms the foundation for an understanding of liability insurance discussed later in the text. Specific topics discussed include the law of negligence, elements of a negligent act, application of the law of negligence to specific liability situations, and current tort liability problems. The chapter concludes with a discussion of defects in the U.S. legal system and proposals for reform.

BASIS OF LEGAL LIABILITY

Each person has certain legal rights. A **legal wrong** *is a violation of a person's legal rights, or a failure to perform a legal duty owed to a certain person or to society as a whole.*

There are three broad classes of legal wrongs. A *crime* is a legal wrong against society that is punishable by fines, imprisonment, or death. A *breach of contract* is another class of legal wrongs. Finally, a *tort* is a legal wrong for which the law allows a remedy in the form of money damages. The person who is injured or harmed (called the *plaintiff* or *claimant*) by the actions of another person (called the *defendant* or *tortfeasor*) can sue for damages.

Torts generally can be classified into three categories:

- Intentional torts
- Absolute liability
- Negligence

Intentional Torts

Legal liability can arise from an intentional act or omission that results in harm or injury to another person or damage to the person's property. Examples of intentional torts include assault, battery, trespass, false imprisonment, fraud, libel, slander, and patent or copyright infringement.

Absolute Liability

Because the potential harm to an individual or society is so great, some people may be held liable for the harm or injury done to others even though negligence cannot be proven. **Absolute liability** *means that liability is imposed regardless of negligence or fault.* Absolute liability is also referred to as **strict liability.** Some common situations of absolute liability include the following:

- Occupational injury and disease of employees under a workers compensation law
- Blasting operations that injure another person
- Manufacturing of explosives, medicines, and food products
- Owning wild or dangerous animals
- Crop spraying by airplanes

Negligence

Negligence is another type of tort that can result in substantial liability. Because negligence is so important in liability insurance, it merits special attention.

LAW OF NEGLIGENCE

Negligence *typically is defined as the failure to exercise the standard of care required by law to protect others from an unreasonable risk of harm.* The meaning of the term *standard of care* is based on the care required of a reasonably prudent person. In other words, your actions are compared with the actions of a reasonably prudent person under the same circumstances. If your conduct and behavior are below the standard of care required of a reasonably prudent person, you may be found negligent.

The standard of care required by law is not the same for each wrongful act. Its meaning is complex and depends on the age and knowledge of the parties involved; court interpretations over time; skill, knowledge, and judgment of the claimant and tortfeasor; seriousness of the harm; and a host of additional factors.

Elements of a Negligent Act

To collect damages, the injured person must show that the tortfeasor is guilty of negligence. There are four essential elements of a negligent act:

- Existence of a legal duty
- Failure to perform that duty
- Damage or injury to the claimant
- Proximate cause relationship between the negligent act and the infliction of damages

Existence of a Legal Duty *The first requirement is the existence of a legal duty to protect others from*

harm. For example, a motorist has a legal duty to stop at a red light and to drive an automobile safely within the speed limits. A manufacturer has a legal duty to produce a safe product. A physician has a legal duty to inquire about allergies before prescribing a drug.

If there is no legal duty imposed by law, you cannot be held liable. For example, you may be a champion swimmer, but you have no legal obligation to dive into a swimming pool to save a two-year-old child from drowning. Nor do you have a legal obligation to stop and pick up a hitchhiker at night when the temperature is 30 degrees below zero. To be guilty of negligence, there must first be a legal duty or obligation to protect others from harm.

Failure to Perform That Duty *The second requirement is the failure to perform the legal duty required by law*: that is, you fail to comply with the standard of care to protect others from harm. Your actions would be compared with the actions of a reasonably prudent person under similar circumstances. If your conduct falls short of this standard, the second requirement would be satisfied.

The defendant's conduct can be either a positive or negative act. A driver who speeds in a residential area or runs a red light is an example of a positive act that a reasonably prudent person would not do. A negative act is simply the failure to act: you fail to do something that a reasonably prudent person would have done. For example, if you injure someone because you failed to repair the faulty brakes on your automobile, you could be found guilty of negligence.

Damage or Injury *The third requirement is damage or injury to the claimant.* The injured person must show damage or injury as a result of the actions of the alleged tortfeasor. For example, a speeding motorist may run a red light, smash into your car, and seriously injure you. Because you are injured and your car is damaged, the third requirement of a negligent act has been satisfied.

The dollar amount of damages awarded in a judgment depends on several factors. There are three types of damage awards:

- Special damages
- General damages
- Punitive damages

Special damages are paid for losses that can be determined and documented, such as medical expenses, loss of earnings, or property damage. *General damages* are paid for losses that cannot be specifically measured or itemized, such as compensation for pain and suffering, disfigurement, or loss of companionship of a spouse. Finally, *punitive damages* are paid to punish people and organizations so that others are deterred from committing the same wrongful act.

Proximate Cause Relationship The final requirement of a negligent act is that a proximate cause relationship must exist. A **proximate cause** *is a cause unbroken by any new and independent cause, which produces an event that otherwise would not have occurred.* That is, there must be an unbroken chain of events between the negligent act and the infliction of damages. For example, a drunk driver who runs a red light and kills another motorist would meet the proximate cause requirement.

Defenses Against Negligence

Certain legal defenses can defeat a claim for damages. Some important legal defenses include the following.

- Contributory negligence
- Comparative negligence
- Last clear chance rule
- Assumption of risk

Contributory Negligence A few states have contributory negligence laws. **Contributory negligence** *means that if the injured person's conduct falls below the standard of care required for his or her protection, and such conduct contributed to the injury, the injured person cannot collect damages.* Thus, under the strict common law, if you contributed in any way to your own injury, you cannot collect damages. For example, if a motorist on an expressway suddenly slows down without signaling and is rear-ended by another driver, the failure to signal could constitute contributory negligence. The first motorist cannot collect damages for injuries if contributory negligence is established.

Comparative Negligence Because of the harshness of contributory negligence laws if strictly applied, most states have enacted some type of comparative negligence law. Such laws allow an injured person to recover damages even though he or she has contributed to the injury. Under a **comparative negligence law**, if both the plaintiff (injured person) and the defendant contribute to the plaintiff's injury, the financial burden of the injury is shared by both parties according to their respective degrees of fault.

Comparative negligence laws are not uniform among the states. The major types of comparative negligence laws can be classified as follows:[1]

- Pure rule
- 49 percent rule
- 50 percent rule

Under the *pure rule*, you can collect damages for your injury even if you are negligent, but your damage award is reduced proportionately. For example, if you are 60 percent responsible for an auto accident and your actual damages are $10,000, your damage award is reduced to $4000.

Under the *49 percent rule*, you can recover reduced damages only if your negligence is less than the negligence of the other party. This rule means you can recover from the other party only if you are 49 percent or less at fault.

Under the *50 percent rule*, you can recover reduced damages only if your negligence is not greater than the negligence of the other party. This rule means you can recover only if you are not more than 50 percent at fault. You should not confuse the 50 percent law with the 49 percent law discussed earlier. Unlike the 49 percent law, the 50 percent law allows each party to recover damages when both parties are equally at fault. However, each party's recovery would be limited to 50 percent of the actual damages.

Last Clear Chance Rule The doctrine of last clear chance is another statutory modification of the contributory negligence doctrine. Under the **last clear chance rule**, *a plaintiff who is endangered by his or her own negligence can still recover damages from the defendant if the defendant has a last clear chance to avoid the accident but fails to do so.* For example, a jaywalker who walks against a red light is breaking the law. But if a motorist has a last clear chance to avoid hitting the jaywalker and fails to do so, the injured jaywalker can recover damages for the injury.

Assumption of Risk The **assumption of risk** doctrine is another defense that can be used to defeat a claim for damages. *Under this doctrine, a person who understands and recognizes the danger inherent in a particular activity cannot recover damages in the event of an injury.* In effect, the assumption of risk bars recovery for damages even though another person's negligence causes the injury. For example, assume you are teaching a friend with a severe vision impairment to drive a car, and he negligently crashes into a telephone post and injures you. He could use the assumption of risk doctrine as a legal defense if you sue for damages.

IMPUTED NEGLIGENCE

Imputed negligence *means that under certain conditions, the negligence of one person can be attributed to another.* Several examples can illustrate this principle. First, an *employer–employee relationship* may exist where the employee is acting on behalf of the employer. The negligent act of an employee can be imputed to the employer. Therefore, if you are driving a car to deliver a package for your employer and negligently injure another motorist, your employer could be held liable for your actions.

Second, many states have some type of **vicarious liability law,** by which an automobile driver's negligence is imputed to the vehicle's owner. For example, if the driver is acting as an agent for the owner of the vehicle, the owner can be held legally liable. Thus, if Jeff drives Lisa's car to a dry cleaner to pick up a garment, Lisa could be held legally liable if Jeff should injure someone while driving the car.

Third, under the **family purpose doctrine,** the owner of an automobile can be held liable for the negligent acts committed by immediate family members while they are operating the family car. Thus, if Shannon, age 16, negligently injures another motorist while driving her father's car and is sued for $100,000, her father could be held liable.

In addition, imputed negligence may arise out of a *joint business venture.* For example, two brothers may be partners in a business. One brother may negligently injure a customer with a company car, and the injured person sues for damages. Both partners could be held liable for the injury.

A **dram shop law** is a final example of imputed negligence. Under such a law, a business that sells liquor can be held liable for damages that may result from the sale of liquor. For example, assume that a bar owner continues to serve a customer who is drunk, and that after the bar closes, the customer injures three people while driving home. The bar owner could be held legally liable for the injuries.

RES IPSA LOQUITUR

An important modification of the law of negligence is the doctrine of *res ipsa loquitur*, meaning "the thing speaks for itself." *Under this doctrine, the very fact that the injury or damage occurs establishes a presumption of negligence on behalf of the defendant. It is then up to the defendant to refute the presumption of negligence.* That is, the accident or injury normally would not have occurred if the defendant had not been careless. Examples of the doctrine of *res ipsa loquitur* include the following:

- A dentist extracts the wrong tooth.
- A surgeon leaves a surgical sponge in the patient's abdomen.
- A surgical operation is performed on the wrong patient.

To apply the doctrine of *res ipsa loquitur*, the following requirements must be met:

- The event is one that normally does not occur in the absence of negligence.
- The defendant has exclusive control over the instrumentality causing the accident.
- The injured party has not contributed to the accident in any way.

SPECIFIC APPLICATIONS OF THE LAW OF NEGLIGENCE

Property Owners

Property owners have a legal obligation to protect others from harm. However, the standard of care owed to others depends upon the situation. Three groups traditionally have been recognized: (1) trespasser, (2) licensee, and (3) invitee.[2] However, as will be discussed later, a number of jurisdictions have abolished or modified these common law classifications.

Trespasser A **trespasser** *is a person who enters or remains on the owner's property without the owner's consent.* In general, the trespasser takes the property as he or she finds it. The property owner does not have any obligation to the trespasser to keep the land in reasonably safe condition. However, the property owner cannot deliberately injure the trespasser or set a trap that would injure the trespasser. The duty to refrain from injuring the trespasser or from setting a trap to injure that person is sometimes referred to as the duty of slight care.

Licensee A **licensee** *is someone who enters or remains on the premises with the occupant's expressed or implied permission.* Examples of licensees include door-to-door salespersons, solicitors for charitable or religious organizations, police officers and fire fighters when they are on the property to perform their duties, and social guests in almost all jurisdictions. A licensee takes the premises as he or she finds them. However, the property owner or occupant is required to warn the licensee of any unsafe condition or activity on the premises, which is not apparent or open, but there is no obligation to inspect the premises for the benefit of the licensee.

Invitee An **invitee** *is someone who is invited onto the premises for the benefit of the occupant.* Examples of invitees include business customers in a store, mail carriers, and garbage collectors. In addition to warning the invitee of any dangerous condition, the occupant has an obligation to inspect the premises and to eliminate any dangerous condition revealed by the inspection. For example, a store escalator may be faulty. The customers must be warned about the unsafe escalator (perhaps by a sign) and prevented from using it. The faulty escalator must be repaired; otherwise, customers in the store could be injured, and the owner would be liable.

Many jurisdictions have abolished either partly or completely the preceding common law classifications with respect to the degree of care owed to visitors. According to the Nebraska Supreme Court, 36 states and the District of Columbia have reconsidered the traditional common law classification scheme. Of the 37 jurisdictions, 23 have abolished either some or all or the categories.[3]

Attractive Nuisance Doctrine

An **attractive nuisance** *is a condition that can attract and injure children.* Under the attractive nuisance doctrine, the occupants of land are liable for the injuries of children who may be attracted by some dangerous condition, feature, or article. This doctrine is based on the principles that children may not be able to recognize the danger involved and may be injured, and that it is in the best interest of society to protect them rather than protect the owner's right to the land. Thus, the possessor of the land must keep the premises in a safe condition and use ordinary care to protect the trespassing children from harm.[4]

Several examples can illustrate the attractive nuisance doctrine, by which the occupant or owner can be held liable:

- The gate to a swimming pool is left unlocked, and a three-year-old child drowns.
- A homeowner has a miniature house for the children. A neighbor's child attempts to enter through an unlocked window, which falls on her neck and strangles her.
- A building contractor carelessly leaves the keys in a tractor. While driving the tractor, two small boys are seriously injured when the tractor overturns.

Owners and Operators of Automobiles

The owner of an automobile who drives in a careless and irresponsible manner can be held liable for property damage or bodily injury sustained by another person. There is no single rule of law that can be applied in this situation. The legal liability of the owner who is also the operator has been modified over time by court decisions, comparative negligence laws, the last clear chance rule, no-fault automobile insurance laws (see Chapter 11), and a host of additional factors. However, the laws in all states clearly require the owner of an automobile to exercise reasonable care while operating the automobile.

With respect to the liability of the owner who is not the operator, the general rule is that the owner is not liable for the negligent acts of operators. But there are exceptions to this general principle. In all states the owner can be held liable for an operator's negligence if an *agency relationship* exists. As stated earlier, if your friend drives your car on a business errand for you and injures someone, you can be held liable. In addition, under the *family purpose doctrine* discussed earlier, the owner of an automobile can be held liable for the negligent operation of the vehicle by an immediate family member.

Governmental Liability

Based on the common law, federal, state, and local governments could not be sued unless the government gave its consent. The immunity from lawsuits was based on the doctrine of **sovereign immunity**, meaning that the king or queen can do no wrong. This doctrine, however, has been significantly modified over time by both statutory law and court decisions.

At present, government can be held liable if it is negligent in the performance of a **proprietary function**. Proprietary functions of government typically include the operation of water plants; electrical, transportation, and telephone systems; municipal auditoriums; and similar money-making activities. Thus, if some seats collapse at a rock concert in a city auditorium, the city can be sued and held liable for injuries to spectators. With respect to *governmental functions*—for example, the planning of a sewer system—the general rule is that a municipality can be sued only with its consent. Even this immunity has been eroded, however. Because the distinction between a proprietary and governmental function is often a fine line, some courts have eliminated the distinction entirely.[5]

Charitable Institutions

At one time, charitable institutions were generally immune from lawsuits. This immunity has gradually been eliminated by state law and court decisions. The trend today is to hold charities responsible for acts of negligence. This is particularly true with respect to commercial activities. For example, a hospital operated by a religious order can be sued for malpractice, and a church sponsoring a dance, carnival, or bingo game can be held liable for injuries to participants.

Employer and Employee Relationships

Under the doctrine of **respondant superior**, an employer can be held liable for the negligent acts of employees while they are acting on the employer's behalf. Thus, if a sales clerk in a sporting goods store carelessly drops a barbell set on a customer's toe, the owner of the store can be held liable.

For an employer to be held liable for the negligent acts of the employees, two requirements must be fulfilled. First, the worker's legal status must be that of an employee. A person typically is considered an employee if he or she is given detailed instructions on how to do a job, is furnished tools or supplies by the employer, and is paid a wage or salary at regular intervals. Second, the employee must be acting within the scope of employment. That is, the employee must be engaged in the type of work that he or she is employed to perform. There is no simple test to determine whether the tort is committed within the scope of employment. Numerous factors are considered, including whether the act is authorized by the employer, whether the act is one commonly performed by the employee, and whether the act is intended to advance the employer's interests.[6]

Parents and Children

Under the common law, parents usually are not responsible for their children's torts. Children who reach the age of reason are responsible for their own wrongful acts. However, there are several exceptions to this general principle. *First, a parent can be held liable if a child uses a dangerous weapon, such as a gun or knife, to injure someone.* For example, if a ten-year-old child is permitted to play with a loaded revolver, and someone is thereby injured or killed, the parents can be held responsible. *Second, the parent can be legally liable if the child is acting as an agent for the parent.* For example, if a son or daughter is employed in the family business, the parents can be held liable for any injury to a customer caused by the child's actions. *Third, if a family car is operated by a minor child, the parents can be held liable under the family purpose doctrine discussed earlier.* In addition, property damage and vandalism by children have increased over time, especially by teenagers. *Most states have passed laws that hold the parents liable for the willful and malicious acts of children that result in property damage to others.* For example, Nebraska has a parental liability law that holds the parents liable for the willful and intentional destruction of property by minor children.

In recent years, some troubled teenagers have killed or injured other students in shooting incidents. Elementary and high school students have been killed or injured in Kentucky, Mississippi, Arkansas, Georgia, and Colorado. Parents of the victims have sued the parents of the shooters on the grounds that parents have a legal duty to supervise their children and prevent them from committing violent acts. However, the victims' parents often face daunting legal obstacles in their efforts to recover damages (see Insight 7.1).

Animals

Owners of wild animals are held absolutely liable (strict liability) for the injuries of others even if the animals are domesticated. For example, an owner of an exotic pet such as a tiger is absolutely liable if the pet escapes and injures someone even if the owner uses due care in keeping the animal restrained.

In addition, depending on the state, strict liability may also be imposed on the owners of ordinary house dogs. Until recently, dog owners were liable for dog bites and other injuries only if the injured person could prove that the owner knew the dog was dangerous. If the dog had never bitten anyone, the dog owner usually was not liable. *However, in about 30 states and the District of Columbia, the injured person has to show only that the dog caused the injury; in such cases, the dog owner is liable based on the doctrine of strict liability.*[7]

SPECIAL TORT LIABILITY PROBLEMS

Certain tort liability problems have emerged that have caused serious problems for risk managers, business firms, physicians and other professionals, government officials, liability insurers, and taxpayers.

Products Liability

Products liability *refers to the legal liability of manufacturers, wholesalers, or retailers of products to persons who incur bodily injuries or property damage from a defective product.* A manufacturer or seller of a product can be held liable as a result of improper product design, improper assembly of the product, failure to test and inspect the product, failure to warn of inherently dangerous characteristics, deceptive advertising, and failure to foresee possible abuse or misuse of the product.

Consumers injured by defective products are often willing to sue manufacturers because of certain legal and economic trends that have emerged over time. *First, the courts have gradually rejected the older* **privity of contract** *doctrine.*[8] Under this doctrine, the original seller of the goods was not liable to anyone for a defective product except to the immediate buyer or one in privity with the original seller. Thus, only the person who was a party to the contract could bring action against the manufacturer of a defective product. Because a manufacturer sells to wholesalers and retailers, the injured person had recourse only against the retailer. However, as a result of adverse court decisions, injured persons in most states can now directly sue the manufacturer of a defective product. *In addition, emphasis on consumerism and consumer legislation have encouraged individuals to sue because of injuries from defective products.* In particular, the Consumer Product and Safety Act of 1972 has been credited with stimulating an increase in products liability lawsuits. *Finally, the substantial number of new products has resulted in an increase in defective products that cause injury.*

Solutions to the Problem Several solutions have been proposed or enacted to reduce the magnitude of the products liability problem. They include the following:

- *Shorter statute-of-limitations period.* The manufacturer or seller's liability for a defective product would be subject to a shorter statute of limitations after the product is purchased.

Insight 7.1

Assigning Blame in School Deaths Faces Obstacles

Who can be held legally accountable when troubled teens turn into schoolyard gunmen?

Parents of victims have sued parents of shooters after school shooting sprees in Kentucky, Mississippi, Arkansas, and Colorado. Two of the lawsuits also name teachers and other school officials as defendants.

The civil suits are based on the theory that parents have a duty to supervise their children and prevent violence, and school employees have a duty to keep the buildings safe. Each suit alleges that adults knew enough about the attacks beforehand to have acted to prevent tragedy.

Parents of several victims in the 1997 high-school shooting in West Paducah, Kentucky, also have filed a federal lawsuit against 25 media and entertainment companies for marketing violent movies, Internet games, and pornographic Web sites. The plaintiffs, who claim that such materials are "unreasonably dangerous" when used by minors, are seeking more than $100 million in damages.

It isn't clear what litigation, if any, will be filed in the wake of the Littleton, Colorado, shootings. But lawyers are already involved.

Plaintiffs seeking to recover civil damages in such cases face formidable legal hurdles. "The burden is very high," says Richard Schwartz, a Jackson, Mississippi, attorney who represents the parents of a victim in the Pearl, Mississippi, high-school shooting in 1997. He says his clients decided against filing a civil lawsuit and instead lobbied successfully for a new state law allowing the death penalty to be imposed in cases involving killings on school grounds.

While many state statutes specifically authorize civil damages against parents of kids who do harm, juries often disagree about what is appropriate parental behavior. And even when plaintiffs prevail in court, it can be difficult for them to collect damages from middle-class parents. Homeowner's insurance policies often cover damages at relatively modest sums. And school districts are typically insulated from substantial damage awards under the legal doctrine of sovereign immunity, which limits suits against police and other government operations.

After 16-year-old Luke Woodham killed his mother and then shot nine students, two of them fatally, in Pearl, Mississippi, the mother of one of the dead teens sued the school district; Luke's father, John P. Woodham Jr.; and the parents of five other students who were allegedly part of a satanic cult known as the Kroth. Luke Woodham has been convicted of murder and sentenced to life in prison.

In her lawsuit, Kaye Long, the mother of the 17-year-old Lydia Kaye Dew, alleges that the Pearl Public

---

- *State-of-the-art defense.* If the product conformed to the prevailing state of the art at the time it was manufactured, it would not be considered a defective product today.
- *Alteration of the product defense.* The manufacturer would have a defense if the injury were caused by alteration, modification, or misuse of the product by the defendant.
- *Limitation on attorney's fees.* This step would discourage some attorneys from attempting to persuade injured persons to bring suit.
- *Elimination of punitive damages.* This measure would reduce the amount of damages awarded.
- *Proposed product liability legislation.* Proposals for a federal products liability law have been in-

troduced in each session of Congress since the early 1980s. One recent federal proposal would place a cap on punitive damages; eliminate the joint and several liability rule for noneconomic damages; establish an 18-year statute of repose, which would prevent a person from suing over a defective product that has been in continuous use; and hold liable barkeepers who sell alcohol to already intoxicated customers and people who sell firearms to felons.

Professional Liability

Professional liability is another important liability problem that merits discussion.

School District was aware of Mr. Woodham's violent nature and negligently failed to control him. Her suit also alleges the elder Mr. Woodham and the other parents "knew or should have known that their children were members of a satanic cult." According to Michael Hartung, Ms. Long's attorney, a member of the Kroth had been arrested a few months before the attack and gave police a detailed account of the secret society and plans to attack the high school.

The school district claims it isn't liable under the sovereign immunity doctrine. Mr. Woodham, Luke's father, who isn't represented by counsel, couldn't be located for comment. Of the parents, only one has counsel. That attorney declined to comment. The others either couldn't be reached or didn't return calls seeking comment.

Mississippi is one of the few states with a law making it easier to prove parents are negligent if their children act violently or deface property. But even there, plaintiffs can't collect more than $250,000 under the statute. "You don't bring this type of case to make millions," says Mr. Hartung.

The West Paducah shooting, two months after the Pearl incident, also spawned lawsuits against school officials. After 14-year-old Michael Carneal killed three students and wounded five more at his high school, parents of three victims sued his par-

ents, 30 school board members, principals, and some teachers. Mr. Carneal has been sentenced to life in prison after pleading guilty but mentally ill to murder charges.

A trial-court judge dismissed the parents' lawsuit against the school officials. "They were overreaching," says Bowling Green, Kentucky, lawyer Michael Owsley, who represents the school personnel. The plaintiffs plan to file an appeal in state Supreme Court.

The judge did allow the lawsuit to proceed against Mr. Carneals's parents and several students who allegedly conspired with their son. "There were a litany of warning signals that should have alerted the parents," says Michael Breen, the Bowling Green, Kentucky, lawyer who represents the plaintiffs. According to court papers, Mr. Carneal's grades had plummeted and his mother had found knives and pictures of dead pigs in his room. Several students said he brought guns to school repeatedly. In addition, he had written two disturbing stories, including one called "Halloween Surprise," in which he and a fictitious brother gunned down preppies and then detonated a nuclear device.

SOURCE: Adapted from Margaret A. Jacobs, "Assigning Blame in School Deaths Faces Obstacles," *The Wall Street Journal*, May 3, 1999, pp. B1, B4.

Medical Malpractice Medical malpractice *is improper or negligent treatment in the eyes of the law.* It is an act that a reasonable physician would not have done under the same circumstances, or a failure to do something that a physician should have done. For example, a surgeon who performs a surgical procedure incorrectly causing paralysis of the patient could be held legally liable.

The medical malpractice problem for physicians reached a critical point in the 1970s. Because of inflation, increasing claims, and soaring jury awards, malpractice insurers experienced huge underwriting losses, which resulted in higher malpractice insurance rates and withdrawal of some insurers from the market. By 1989, however, the malpractice situation

had improved significantly. The number of claims peaked in 1985 and declined through 1989. Since then, the underwriting results have fluctuated. Insurers earned underwriting profits for 1994–1995, for example, but had underwriting losses for 1996–1998.

Although the medical malpractice claim situation has improved, the average settlement award is still relatively high. Jury Verdict Research data show that the average medical malpractice settlement in 1995 was slightly less than $700,000, up from $677,000 in 1994, but below the high of $1.4 million in 1991.[9]

The medical malpractice problem produces several undesirable economic effects. First, because of the fear of a malpractice suit, many physicians practice defensive medicine, which results in unnecessary diagnostic tests and medical procedures and higher total health care costs.

Second, as a result of high medical malpractice premiums and fear of being sued, many physicians avoid or abandon certain high-risk areas, such as obstetrics. Some physicians no longer provide prenatal care and deliver babies. The result is a reduction in the availability of obstetrical care in many parts of the country, but especially in rural areas.

Third, patients are more willing to sue their physicians than in the past. This is true for several reasons.[10] According to experts who have studied the problem, *some physicians provide improper or negligent care*. In many cases, physicians make errors in judgment or attempt medical procedures beyond their normal skills. As a result, the patient is harmed, and the physician is sued.

Many patients also sue their physicians because of unrealistic expectations. Advances in medical technology often result in high medical expectations. A failure of a physician to meet such expectations often results in a lawsuit.

Some patients sue their physicians because of the philosophy of entitlement. Many Americans believe that if people are harmed, they are entitled to receive damages. Juries occasionally leave the impression that the key question is not whether negligence was present, but who is better able to bear the burden of loss. The attitude often is "someone was injured, and therefore, someone should compensate that person."

Finally, there has been a deterioration in the physician–patient relationship. The medical profession as a group no longer commands the prestige it once enjoyed in the past. Moreover, physicians are now more willing to testify in court against other physicians than they were in the past.

Several approaches have been taken to solve the medical malpractice problem. They include the following:

- *Limit on damages.* Many states have enacted laws that limit the amount of damages awarded.
- *Arbitration panels.* Many states have formed arbitration panels to resolve disputes between physicians and patients.
- *Attorneys' fees.* Limitations would be placed on contingent fees charged by attorneys.

- *Statute of limitations.* The statute of limitations for filing lawsuits against physicians would be shortened.
- *More effective state medical review boards.* Monitoring activities of state review boards would be upgraded so that problem physicians could be identified more easily. In some cases, state medical review boards have not taken prompt action to revoke the licenses of problem physicians.
- *Retraining problem physicians.* Physicians cited by review boards would have to undergo retraining.
- *Joint underwriting associations.* Professional liability joint underwriting associations (JUA) have been formed that require liability insurers in the state to write their share of professional liability insurance.

Errors and Omissions by Attorneys Lawsuits against attorneys for errors and omissions have also increased for several reasons. *First, the standards for judging legal negligence have been broadened.* In the past, only a blatant legal error or omission could produce a suit. Today, because of adverse court decisions, attorneys are held to a higher standard of care than in the past.

Second, the old rule of privity, which made an attorney responsible only to his or her clients, has lost its former force. An attorney today may be held liable by a party who may be harmed by the attorney's performance but is not a client.

Third, there has been an increased willingness on the part of attorneys to testify against each other and even to sue each other. Testimony by one attorney against another was uncommon until recently.

Finally, because of an increase in the scope of government, there are more complex laws, rules, and regulations. New laws with respect to pollution, ecology, consumerism, and privacy have produced an entirely new bundle of individual rights. Thus, the margin for legal errors or omissions has increased, which has resulted in additional lawsuits.

Several solutions to the legal malpractice problem have been offered. They include the following:

- *Defensive practice of law.* Attorneys are now specializing in limited areas of law. Questionable matters of law in other areas are referred to other legal specialists.
- *Educational seminars.* Local bar associations are

conducting seminars on complex government regulations. Classes are also held on how an attorney can avoid a legal malpractice lawsuit. Also, attorneys may be required to meet certain continuing education requirements to keep their state license.

■ *Waiver of rights.* In some cases, clients are asked to waive certain rights if the attorney's legal work or advice is in error.

Liability of Architects and Engineers The number of lawsuits against architects and engineers has also increased over time. The increased number of lawsuits in this professional area can be explained by several factors. First, the courts have broadened their interpretation of professional liability. Architects and engineers are now held legally liable for injuries to the general public as well as to the building owners, and to workers injured by a hazardous condition on the construction site. Second, new building materials and techniques have increased the risk of a lawsuit. Third, in some jurisdictions, the courts have interpreted the statute of limitations as starting when a construction defect is discovered, rather than when the building was first designed. The overall result is a substantial increase in the architect's or engineer's potential liability exposure. Finally, the substantial increase in building costs has also increased the size of claims. Multimillion-dollar judgments in the construction industry are not uncommon.

Two approaches are now used to control this enormous liability exposure. First, professional architectural and engineering societies have sponsored loss-control seminars through which loss frequency and loss severity can be reduced. Second, many architects and engineers are analyzing the financial feasibility of proposed projects more carefully, so as to avoid those projects where lawsuits may be brought for the purpose of eliminating or reducing their professional fees.

Professional Liability in Other Fields Other professional groups are experiencing similar liability problems. Public accounting firms have experienced a substantial increase in both the number and size of claims. Pharmacists have been sued in large numbers. Insurance agents have experienced a substantial

increase in lawsuits because of errors and omissions. Even education has come under the malpractice attack. In one case, a young woman sued a university for a tuition refund on the grounds that she learned nothing in a particular course because of poor teaching. In some states, parents have sued the school district because their children can barely read, even though they have received diplomas.

Directors and Officers

Directors and officers of corporations have also experienced an increase in liability lawsuits. Because average claim settlements are high, many corporations have experienced a substantial increase in liability insurance premiums for directors and officers, higher deductibles, and reductions in the amount of available insurance. The majority of suits against directors and officers are filed by disgruntled stockholders because of financial losses. Lawsuits often result if the market price of the stock drops sharply because earnings expectations were not realized.

Other Problem Areas

Certain other problems exist. Elementary schools are being sued because of an unsafe learning environment and alleged acts of sexual harassment of students by teachers; the threat of legal proceedings can be emotionally draining and time consuming (see Insight 7.2).

Employers are also being sued because of sexual harassment of employees. Police departments are being sued because of brutality, wrongful death, or civil rights violation. Fraternities are being sued because of "keg parties" in which someone is injured or dies because of the excessive consumption of alcohol. Finally, new novel suits are constantly emerging; one recent case involved a suit by a son against his father (see Insight 7.3).

REFORMING THE CIVIL JUSTICE SYSTEM

Many legal experts believe the civil justice system is seriously flawed and must be reformed.

Insight 7.2

Lawsuits Threaten Schools

The threat of litigation hovers over every American public school, taking professional time from teaching and learning, costing the taxpayers dearly and affecting our students' achievement.

Furthermore, there is a growing and critical shortage of applicants for principals' jobs across the country. Why aren't more people applying?

Stress is a major factor. When a principal spends up to 20 percent of his or her time on the job keeping up with the legal decisions, negotiating with parents, students, and staff and documenting nearly every action, that's stress.

A recent survey of more than 500 school principals showed that nearly 65 percent reported that litigation in schools increased in the last 10 years.

Recent Supreme Court decisions—holding schools directly accountable for student-to-student sexual harassment (Davis vs. Monroe County Board of Education) and making them physically and financially responsible for full-time nurses for all students who need them (Cedar Rapids Community School District vs. Garret F.)—have exacerbated the situation.

School principals often find themselves "darned if they do" and "darned if they don't."

For example, a school board sets up a zero-tolerance policy for weapons. It states clearly that any student who brings a weapon to school—whether it's a plastic butter knife or a loaded handgun—must be suspended. Then a child accidentally brings a Boy Scout knife to school—it's been left in his backpack from the meeting the night before.

The principal, acting on orders from the school board, suspends the child. The newspapers make a laughingstock of the school. The parents are outraged. However, if that child had taken the knife out on the school bus and poked it in another child's eye, the school would be in legal trouble.

Principals honestly lament the freedom they've lost to simply hug a child. As the American Tort Reform Association points out, physical contact has either been terminated or modified in more than half the schools surveyed.

A Kentucky principal told me how very concerned she and her staff are about touching students. Even when offering sympathy or calming a child down, she said, "a lot of thought is given in every situation before you can react."

Principals say the only time they will hug a child is in the hallway.

However, perhaps the most troubling part of the litigation dilemma is time away from the work of running the school. Let me give you some examples.

A principal in Washington state spent more than 100 hours one year working with the parents of one learning-disabled student when they differed with the school's educational approach. This is a lot of time for someone who oversees the education of 500 students and manages a staff of 40.

A Missouri middle school principal explained what principals actually do to protect themselves and their systems from lawsuit.

She keeps a log of every phone call; writes up every parent meeting; asks staff involved in meetings to submit reports as well; interviews witnesses involved in any injury; reads back the witnesses' statements to them; fills out state and federal forms for any weapon brought to school; reports any fights to the police; and completes accident reports for every scraped knee.

More recently, this principal has spent an inordinate amount of time getting to the bottom of a rising tide of sexual harassment allegations from students reporting on their peers.

Most of these never meet the tough new federal definition of harassment, but all are taken very seriously and use many hours of administrators' and students' time.

The National Association of Elementary School Principals found in a survey of its membership last year that few principals were actually named in civil suits. Of those that were, nearly a third saw the case dropped, about a quarter had out-of-court settlements and the rest were resolved in the principal's favor.

Virtually no judgments were found against principals. This leads us to believe that most of the suits shouldn't have been brought in the first place.

SOURCE: Adaptation of Vincent L. Ferrandino, "Lawsuits Threaten Schools," *Sunday World-Herald*, September 19, 1999, p. 27-A.

Defects in the Civil Justice System

Critics argue that the present civil justice system has the following defects:[11]

- Costly and inefficient
- Uncertainty of legal outcomes
- Increased compensation awards
- Long delay in settling lawsuits

Costly and Inefficient System Critics argue that the present system is costly and inefficient. The number of new lawsuits has increased substantially over time. The number of civil cases filed in U.S. District Courts alone increased from 168,800 in 1980 to 239,000 in 1995.[12] The legal costs in settling these and other claims are enormous. *One study by Tillinghast-Towers Perrin showed that the American civil liability system cost $161 billion in 1995, or 2.3 percent of the nation's gross domestic product. This cost is more than double the average for other industrialized countries.*[13]

Critics also argue that the present system is inefficient because injured claimants receive only a relatively small fraction of the amounts paid on liability claims. *Out of each dollar spent on liability claims, the Tillinghast study estimates that injured persons receive only 24 cents for their actual (economic) losses and another 22 cents for pain and suffering. The remainder (54 cents) goes to claimants' lawyers, defense costs, and administrative costs.*[14]

Uncertainty of Legal Outcomes Critics also argue that because of changing legal doctrines, there is considerable uncertainty in predicting legal outcomes. The result is considerable confusion for insurers, employers, professionals, government officials, and taxpayers.

For example, an injured party at one time had to prove that the other party was at fault in order to collect damages. Today, emphasis is on providing an injured party with some form of legal redress, regardless of blame. Thus, critics of the legal system argue that the ability to pay is more important today than determining who is at fault, and that the burden of paying injured persons falls heavily on insurers, wealthy persons, corporations, and others with "deep pockets."

As a result of the uncertainty in legal outcomes, property and liability insurers maintain they often must pay tort liability claims that they did not envision paying when the insurance was first written.

Increased Compensation Awards Critics also argue that awards for damages in certain types of lawsuits have increased substantially over time. For example, according to Jury Verdict Research, the median amount awarded to plaintiffs for injuries in 1995 was $62,000, up 17 percent from the median award of $53,000 in 1994. Median medical malpractice awards increased 40 percent from $356,000 in 1994 to $500,000 in 1995. Median awards to paraplegics more than doubled from $2.4 million in 1994 to 6.5 million in 1995. And median sexual harassment awards increased 40 percent from $131,140 in 1994 to $183,984 in 1995.[15]

Long Delay in Settling Lawsuits The civil justice system is also marred by long delays in settling lawsuits. Cases often take months or even years to settle. In 1950, only 20 civil trials in the federal courts lasted longer than 20 days. By 1981, the number of comparable lengthy trials increased ninefold. In addition, the National Center for State Courts found that the median processing time in 1989 for all tort cases in 25 urban trial courts was 441 days. The median time varied greatly, ranging from 215 days in Wichita, Kansas, to 953 days in Boston, Massachusetts. More recent data show that lengthy delays are still a problem. Jury Verdict Research data show that for 1996, it took about 30 months from the time of the incident for a trial to begin.[16]

A considerable amount of time involves a pretrial examination of the facts, such as interviews, depositions, and requests for documents. Repeated requests for documents can be time consuming and expensive during the discovery state of a suit. Moreover, attorneys frequently use delaying tactics during the discovery stage as an economic weapon against opponents. The overall result is a substantial increase in costs.

Tort Reform

In view of the preceding defects, most states have enacted some type of tort-reform legislation in recent

Insight 7.3

Man Sues Father, but It's Nothing Personal

Steve Jakopovic Jr.and his father, Steve Sr., were driving home to North Platte, Neb., after spending the weekend in Lincoln, where they had watched Steve Jr.'s teen-age son compete at the state wrestling meet.

The night before the trip home, Jakopovic Jr. had helped out at a Lincoln saloon where his girlfriend tends bar.

It had been a long night, so Jakopovic Jr., 41, agreed to let his father drive while he caught some shut-eye.

About 2:30 P.M., more than two hours later and with both men dozing off, the car slammed into a guardrail three miles west of Odessa and landed in the median of Interstate 80.

"I yelled, 'Dad, you're in the median,'" said Jakopovic Jr.

Jakopovic Sr., 78, cranked the wheel to the right in an attempt to get the car out. But it veered back across the roadway, taking a chunk out of another guardrail.

Jakopovic Jr. escaped with whiplash and an injured left shoulder.

His father was left with a totaled 1989 Chrysler New Yorker, bruised ribs, a sore hip—and a $5,000 to $10,000 lawsuit filed by his son.

"It's not a unique case but certainly an unusual case," said Lincoln County District Court Judge Don Rowlands, who during his 13 years on the bench has never ruled in a lawsuit involving a son suing his father.

A jury in Lincoln County District Court on May 12 awarded Jakopovic Jr. $5,000.

"Me and my father never had any hard feelings over this," Jakopovic Jr. said. "It wasn't him I was after. I was trying to get compensated" for medical bills and work time he lost.

He said a claims representative from his father's insurance company, Allied Insurance, told him he didn't have a claim because he is related to the driver.

"They told me they wouldn't do a darn thing," the younger Jakopovic said. "I kind of thought that was baloney."

The insurance company's attorney, Martin Troshynski of North Platte, did not return calls placed to his law firm.

The son argued that since he hasn't lived with his dad for nearly 25 years, he should not be considered a family member.

"I love my son," said the elder Jakopovic. "I told him, 'You might as well as sue me.'"

More than a year after the accident, Jakopovic Jr. consulted an attorney who agreed to represent him in a lawsuit against his dad.

"It was the only way we could force the issue," said attorney Jim Paloucek of North Platte.

Paloucek said that instead of paying the son's $700 for medical bills and $1,700 in lost wages, the insurance company now has to pay double that amount.

"They didn't think a jury would hit them with a verdict." Paloucek said. "The sad thing is that the insurance company put the father and son through this."

Judge Rowlands said there has been no mention of an appeal. He said he wasn't surprised that the jury awarded the son $5,000, which may not be a large verdict but shows that jurors believed the son was entitled to some compensation.

Jakopovic Jr. is back at work as a self-employed mechanic but says he still has trouble lifting his left arm above his shoulder.

Jakopovic Sr. now has a 1992 Buick LeSabre and a new insurance company after his former company— which paid him $3,500 for damages to his car and $100 for medical bills—sent him a cancellation notice along with the check.

"They dropped me like a rock after the accident," he *said.*

SOURCE: Niz Proskocil, "Man Sues Father, but It's Nothing Personal," *Sunday World-Herald*, May 23, 1999, p. 4-B.

years. Some important tort reforms include the following:

- *Regulation of attorney fees*
- *Limits on the maximum amounts paid as damages*
- *Penalties to deter frivolous suits and defenses*
- *Limiting or restricting punitive damage awards*
- *Caps on noneconomic damages, such as pain and suffering*
- *Modifying the collateral source rule*
- *Modifying the joint and several liability rule*

The first five reforms are self-explanatory, but the latter two proposals require a brief explanation. Under the **collateral source rule,** *the defendant cannot introduce any evidence that shows the injured party has received compensation from other collateral sources.* For example, a delivery driver who is injured in a rear-end collision may be able to collect medical expenses from the negligent driver. However, job-related medical expenses are also covered under a state's workers compensation law. Therefore, the injured delivery driver might "double dip" and receive a total amount that exceeds the medical bills. The collateral source rule would be modified to allow recovery from other sources to be considered in determining the amount of damages.

Under the **joint and several liability rule,** *several people may be responsible for the injury, but a defendant who is only slightly responsible may be required to pay the full amount of damages.* This would be true if such a defendant had substantial financial assets ("deep pockets") to pay damages to the injured party, and the other defendants had little or no assets. Under tort reform, the joint and several liability rule would be modified. For example, many states now prohibit application of the joint and several liability rule to noneconomic damages, such as pain and suffering.

In addition, **alternative dispute resolution (ADR) techniques** are also used to resolve legal disputes. *An ADR is a technique for resolving a legal dispute without litigation.* For example, *arbitration* can be used by which parties in the dispute agree to be bound by the decision of an independent third party. *Mediation* can also be used by which a neutral third party tries to arrange a settlement between the contending parties without resorting to litigation. To re-

duce lawsuits between insurers and consumers over claims, many states now use binding arbitration or formal mediation to resolve disputes between disgruntled consumers and insurers.

Obstacles to Tort Reform by State Courts
Although the states have enacted hundreds of tort reforms since the mid-1980s, state courts frequently nullify such reforms. In the past decade alone, state courts have nullified 73 tort-reform laws.[17] In 1996, the South Dakota Supreme Court declared unconstitutional a cap on total compensatory damages of $1 million in medical malpractice lawsuits. In 1997, the Illinois Supreme Court struck down the Omnibus Tort Reform Act enacted in 1995. The court declared unconstitutional a legislative decision to abolish the joint and several liability doctrine by which one party only 1 percent responsible for a defective product or negligent act could be held responsible for 100 percent of the damage award. However, although only one part of the law was found to be unconstitutional, the court struck down the entire act. In 1998, Kentucky struck down a punitive-damages reform measure that had been enacted in 1988. Finally, a number of states have thrown out statutes that place caps on pain and suffering. As a result of adverse court decisions, the liability laws now vary widely among the states.

SUMMARY

- A tort is a legal wrong for which the law allows a remedy in the form of money damages. There are three categories of torts: intentional torts, absolute or strict liability, and negligence.

- Negligence is defined as the failure to exercise the standard of care required by law to protect others from an unreasonable risk of harm. There are four elements of a negligent act:

    Existence of a legal duty

    Failure to perform that duty

    Damages or injury to the claimant

    Proximate cause relationship

- *Contributory negligence* means that if the injured person's conduct falls below the standard of care required for his or her protection, and such conduct contributed to the injury, the injured person cannot collect damages. Under a *comparative negligence law*, the injured person can collect, but the award for damages would be reduced. Under the *last clear chance rule*, the plaintiff who is endangered by his or her own negligence can still recover damages from the defendant if the defendant has a last clear chance to avoid the accident but fails to do so. Under the *assumption of risk doctrine*, a person who understands and recognizes the danger inherent in a particular activity cannot recover damages in the event of injury.

■ Under certain conditions, the negligence of one person can be imputed to another. Imputed negligence may arise from an employer-employee relationship, vicarious liability law, family-purpose doctrine, joint business venture, or a dram shop law.

■ Under the doctrine of *res ipsa loquitur* (the thing speaks for itself), the very fact that the injury or damage occurs establishes a presumption of negligence on behalf of the defendant.

■ The standard of care required by law varies with the situation. Specific liability situations can involve property owners, an attractive nuisance, owners and operators of automobiles, governmental units and charitable institutions, employers and employees, parents and children, and the owners of animals.

■ Certain legal and economic trends have emerged over time that often encourage consumers who are injured by defective products to sue for damages. These trends include rejection of the privity of contract doctrine by the courts, increased emphasis on consumerism, new consumer protection laws, and the substantial number of new products produced each year, some of which can cause injury.

■ Large numbers of physicians have been sued for medical malpractice. Physicians are often sued because of improper or negligent care, unrealistic patient expectations, the philosophy of entitlement, and a deterioration in the physician-patient relationship.

■ Other professionals have been sued in large numbers, including attorneys, accountants, architects, engineers, and insurance agents.

■ Many legal experts believe the civil justice system in the United States must be reformed because of the following defects:

Costly and inefficient

Uncertainty of legal outcomes

Increased compensation awards

Long delay in settling lawsuits

■ Tort-reform provisions include regulating attorney fees, placing limits on the maximum amount paid as damages, penalizing frivolous lawsuits and defenses, limiting or restricting punitive damage awards, placing caps on noneconomic damages, modifying the collateral source rule, and modifying the joint and several liability rule.

KEY CONCEPTS AND TERMS

Absolute (strict) liability
Alternative dispute
  resolution (ADR)
  techniques
Arbitration
Assumption of risk
Attractive nuisance
Collateral source rule
Comparative negligence
  law
Contributory negligence
  law
Dram shop law
Elements of negligent act
Family purpose doctrine
General damages
Governmental function
Imputed negligence
Invitee
Joint and several liability
  rule

Joint underwriting
  association (JUA)
Last clear chance rule
Licensee
Mediation
Negligence
Philosophy of entitlement
Plaintiff
Privity of contract
Products liability
Proprietary function
Proximate cause
Punitive damages
Res ipsa loquitur
Respondeat superior
Sovereign immunity
Special damages
Tort
Tortfeasor
Trespasser
Vicarious liability

REVIEW QUESTIONS

1. Define the meaning of a tort and list the three broad classes of torts.

2. Define negligence. What are the essential elements of a negligent act?

3. Describe some legal defenses that can be used if a person is sued.

4. How does comparative negligence differ from contributory negligence?

5. Explain the meaning of imputed negligence.

6. What is a vicarious liability law?

7. Explain the meaning of *res ipsa loquitur*.

8. Briefly describe the standard of care to protect others from harm for each of the following liability situations:
   a. Property owners
   b. An attractive nuisance
   c. Owners and operators of automobiles
   d. Governmental units and charitable institutions
   e. Employers and employees
   f. Parents and children
   g. Owners of animals

9. Identify the factors that have encouraged purchaser of defective products to sue for damages.

10. Explain some defects in the civil justice system in the United States.

APPLICATION QUESTIONS

1. Smith Construction is building a warehouse for Ramon. The construction firm routinely leaves certain construction machinery at the building site overnight and on weekends. Late one night, Fred, age 10, began playing on some of Smith's construction equipment. Fred accidentally released the brakes of a tractor on which he was playing, and the tractor rolled down a hill and smashed into the building under construction. Fred was severely injured in the accident. Fred's parents sue both Smith Construction and Ramon for the injury.
   a. Based on the elements of a negligent act, describe the requirements that must be met for Smith Construction to be held liable for negligence.
   b. Describe the various classes of persons that are recognized by the law with respect to entering upon the property of another. In which class of persons would Fred belong?
   c. What other legal doctrine is applicable in this case because of Fred's age? Explain your answer.

2. a. Parkway Distributors is a wholesale firm that employs several outside salespersons. Alma, a salesperson employed by Parkway Distributors, was involved in an accident with another motorist while she was using her car to make regular sales calls for Parkway Distributors. Alma and the motorist are seriously injured in the accident. The motorist sues both Alma and Parkway Distributors for the injury based on negligence.
      (1) Describe the requirements that the motorist must establish to show that Alma is guilty of negligence.
      (2) On what legal basis might Parkway Distributors be held legally liable for the injury to the motorist? Explain your answer.
   b. Tom asks his girlfriend, LaToya, to go to a supermarket and purchase some steaks for dinner. While driving Tom's car to the supermarket, LaToya runs a stop sign and seriously injures a pedestrian. Does Tom have any legal liability for the injury? Explain your answer.

3. Whirlwind Mowers manufactures and sells power lawn mowers to the public and distributes the products through its own dealers. Uri is a homeowner who has purchased a power mower from an authorized dealer on the basis of the dealer's recommendation that "the mower is the best one available to do the job." Uri was cutting his lawn when the mower blade flew off and seriously injured his leg.
   a. Uri sues Whirlwind Mowers and asks damages based on negligence in producing the power motor. Is Whirlwind Mowers guilty of negligence? Explain your answer.
   b. The doctrine of *res ipsa loquitur* can often be applied to cases of this type. Show how this doctrine can be applied to this case. Your answer must include a discussion of *res ipsa loquitur*.
   c. Explain the various types of damage awards that Uri might receive if Whirlwind Mowers is found guilty of negligence.

4. a. The number of products liability lawsuits has increased over time, and the dollar amount of the damage awards has also increased.
      (1) Explain the factors that have caused products liability lawsuits to increase over time.
      (2) Discuss some possible solutions for reducing the magnitude of this problem.
   b. Medical malpractice lawsuits have increased over time. How do you explain the increase in the number of malpractice lawsuits against physicians?
   c. Explain the various types of tort-reform legislation to correct the deficiencies in the civil justice system.

Case Application

Raphael went deer hunting with Ed. After seeing bushes move, Raphael quickly fired his rifle at what he thought to be a deer. However, Ed caused the movement in the bushes and was seriously injured by the bullet. Ed survived and later sued Raphael on the grounds that "Raphael's negligence was the proximate cause of the injury."

a. Based on the above facts, is Raphael guilty of negligence? Your answer must include a definition of negligence and the essential elements of a negligent act.

b. Raphael's attorney believes that if contributory negligence could be established, it would greatly influence the outcome of the case. Do you agree with Raphael's attorney? Your answer must include a definition of contributory negligence.

c. If Raphael can establish comparative negligence on the part of Ed, would the outcome of the case be changed? Explain your answer.

d. Assume that Raphael and Ed are hunting on farmland without obtaining permission from the owner. If Raphael fell into a marshy pond covered by weeds and injured his back, would the property owner be liable for damages? Explain your answer.

SELECTED REFERENCES

Felsenthal, Edward. "Increase in Size of Jury Awards May Spur Efforts to Alter System." *The Wall Street Journal*, January 5, 1996.

Hirsch, Donald J. *Casualty Claim Practice*, 6th ed. Burr Ridge, IL: Richard D. Irwin, 1996, Chapters 3–5.

Lorimer, James J., et al. *The Legal Environment of Insurance*, 4th ed., Vol. II. Malvern, PA: American Institute for Property and Liability Underwriters, 1993.

Northeast Louisiana Chapter, The Society of CPCU. "Liability Concerns of Dog Owners and Their Insurers." *CPCU Journal*, Vol. 45, No. 3 (September 1992), pp. 183–188.

"The Liability System," *The Fact Book, 1999, Property/ Casualty Insurance Facts*. Insurance Information Institute: New York, NY, pp. 57–62.

President's Council on Competitiveness. *A Report from the President's Council on Competitiveness, Agenda for Civil Justice Reform in America*. Washington, DC: U.S. Government Printing Office, 1991.

United States Congress, Joint Economic Committee. *Improving the American Legal System: The Economic Benefits of Tort Reform*. Joint Economic Committee Study, Washington, DC, March 1996.

NOTES

1. James J. Lorimer et al. *The Legal Environment of Insurance*, 4th ed., vol. 2 (Malvern, PA: America Institute for Property and Liability Underwriters, 1993), pp. 18–19.

2. This section is based on Donald J. Hirsch, *Casualty Claim Practice*, 6th ed. (Burr Ridge, IL: Richard D. Irwin, 1996), pp. 58–62.

3. *Opinion of the Supreme Court of Nebraska, Case Title, Roger W. Heins, Appellant, v. Webster County, Nebraska, doing business as Webster County Hospital, Appellee.* Filed August 23, 1996, No. S-94-713.

4. Lorimer et al., p. 30.

5. *Ibid.*, p. 23.

6. Lorimer et al., p. 132.

7. Northeast Louisiana Chapter of the Society of CPCU, "Liability Concerns of Dog Owners and Their Insurers," *CPCU Journal*, Vol. 45, No. 3 (September 1992), p. 184.

8. For a detailed analysis of this issue, see Hirsch, pp. 187–190.

9. *The Fact Book, 1999 Property Casualty Insurance Facts* (New York: Insurance Information Institute), p. 55.

10. Charles P. Hall, Jr., "Medical Malpractice Problem," *Annals of the American Academy of Political and Social Science*, 443 (May 1979), pp. 82–93.

11. President's Council on Competitiveness, *Agenda for Civil Justice Reform in America* (Washington, DC: U.S. Government Printing Office, 1991); *Insurance Facts, 1986–87 Property/Casualty Fact Book* (New York: Insurance Information Institute), pp. 55–59.

12. U.S. Bureau of the Census, *Statistical Abstract of the United States: 1996* (116th edition), Washington, DC, 1996.

13. *The Fact Book, 1999 Property/Casualty Insurance Facts*, p. 57.

14. *Ibid.*

15. Edward Felsenthal, "Increase in Size of Jury Awards May Spur Efforts to Alter System," *The Wall Street Journal*, January 5, 1996, p. B2.

16. Data cited in this section are from *The Liability System*, Latest Facts, Updated August 1998, Insurance Information Institute: New York, NY (August 1998).

17. Dick Thornburgh, "A New Judicial Imperialism," *The Wall Street Journal*, May 18, 1998, p. A23.

Students may take a self-administered test on this chapter at www.awlonline.com/rejda

Chapter 8

Homeowners Insurance, Section I

> *" There's no place like home, after the other places close. "*
>
> English Proverb

Learning Objectives

After studying this chapter, you should be able to:

▲ Identify the major homeowners policies for homeowners, condominium owners, and renters.

▲ Explain the major provisions in the Homeowners 3 policy, including:

    Section I property coverages

    Section I perils insured against

    Section I exclusions.

▲ Given a specific loss situation, explain whether the Homeowners 3 policy would cover the loss.

▲ Explain the insured's duties after a loss occurs.

▲ Explain and give an illustration of the replacement cost provision in the Homeowners 3 policy.

▲ Access an Internet site to obtain consumer information about homeowners insurance.

Internet Resources

- The **Insurance Information Institute** provides timely information on homeowners insurance and other personal property insurance coverages. Numerous consumer brochures and articles on homeowners insurance and other property and liability coverages can be accessed directly online. Visit the site at:

  http://www.iii.org/

- The **Insurance News Network** provides up-to-date information, premium quotes, and other consumer information on homeowners insurance. In addition, the site includes timely information and news releases about events that affect the insurance industry. Visit the site at:

  http://www.insure.com/

- **INSWEB** provides premium quotes on homeowners, auto, and other insurance products. You can comparison shop with ease from your computer. Quotes are also available from an agent of your choice. The site includes a page for insurance professionals as well. Visit the site at:

  http://www.insweb.com/

- **MoneyCentral** is designed primarily for investors, but also provides important consumer information on various insurance coverages. Click on "Insurance" for information on homeowners insurance and other insurance coverages. Visit the site at:

  http://moneycentral.msn.com/home.asp

teve, age 34, and Brenda, age 33, are married with two preschool children. The couple purchased a new home in Albany, New York. One week before Christmas, the home burned because their children were playing with matches. The home sustained severe property damage. Most of the family's personal possessions were destroyed, including Christmas gifts, furniture, clothes, and other personal property. While the home was being rebuilt, the family had to rent a furnished apartment for five months. The entire loss exceeded $90,000. The couple owned a homeowners policy, which paid most of the covered losses. Instead of being financially ruined, Steve and Brenda resumed their careers and moved on with their lives.

Insurers pay similar homeowners claims daily. As a result, homeowners and renters are protected against the financial devastation that can result from an uninsured loss. This chapter discusses the popular homeowner policies that are widely used to insure homes, condominiums, and personal property.

Each homeowners policy is divided into two major sections. Section I covers the property of the insured, which can include a home or condominium, other structures, and personal property. Section II provides coverage for personal liability insurance and medical payments to others. This chapter discusses only the Section I provisions. The Section II provisions are discussed in Chapter 9.

HOMEOWNERS 2000 PROGRAM

Homeowners insurance contracts were first introduced in the 1950s. Since that time, they have been revised several times. The following discussion is based on the new Homeowners 2000 Program by the Insurance Service Office (ISO).[1] The new program became effective in Colorado in December 2000 and will be gradually introduced in the remaining states in 2001.

The ISO forms are widely used throughout the United States. Some insurers, however, use the homeowners forms designed by the American Association of Insurance Services (AAIS), which is an advisory organization similar to ISO. Other insurers use their own forms, which differ slightly from the ISO forms.

Package Policy

Homeowners insurance is a **package policy** *that combines two or more separate coverages into one policy.* Prior to the introduction of homeowners insurance in the 1950s, property insurance on a private dwelling and personal property, theft coverage, and personal liability insurance could not be obtained in one policy. With the enactment of multiple-line laws, insurers were allowed to combine these coverages into one policy. As a result, the total premium is less than if separate policies had been purchased; there are fewer gaps in coverage; the major insurance needs of property owners are more easily met in one contract; and the insured deals with only one insurer. The majority of eligible private dwellings are now insured under some type of homeowners policy.

Eligible Dwellings

The eligibility requirements for a homeowners policy are fairly strict. A homeowners policy on a private dwelling is designed for the owner-occupants of a one-, two-, three-, or four- family dwelling used exclusively for private residential purposes (although certain business occupancies are permitted, such as a home day care business and offices for business or professional purposes). A one family dwelling may not be occupied by more than one additional family or two roomers or boarders. Separate homeowners forms are written for renters and condominium owners.

Overview of Homeowners Policies

The following forms are now used in the new ISO homeowners program:

- HO-2 (broad form)
- HO-3 (special form)
- HO-4 (contents broad form)
- HO-5 (comprehensive form)
- HO-6 (unit-owners form)
- HO-8 (modified coverage form)

Homeowners 2 (Broad Form) Homeowners 2 *is a named-perils policy that insures the dwelling, other structures, and personal property against loss from certain listed perils.* Covered perils include fire, lightning, windstorm, hail, explosion, and other perils. A complete list of covered perils can be found in Exhibit 8.1 on pages 142–143. HO-2 also covers the addi-

tional living expenses or fair rental value in the event a covered loss makes the dwelling uninhabitable.

Homeowners 3 (Special Form) Homeowners 3 *insures the dwelling and other structures against risk of direct physical loss to property.* This means that all direct physical losses to the dwelling and other structures are covered, except certain losses specifically excluded. Losses to the dwelling and other structures are paid on the basis of full replacement cost with no deduction for depreciation if certain conditions are met (discussed later).

Personal property is covered for the same *broad form perils* listed in HO-2. Homeowners 3 is a popular and widely used form that is discussed in greater detail later in this chapter.

Homeowners 4 (Contents Broad Form) Homeowners 4 *is designed for tenants who rent apartments, houses, or rooms.* Homeowners 4 covers the tenant's personal property against loss or damage and also provides personal liability insurance. Personal property is covered for the same named perils listed in Homeowners 2. In addition, as much as 10 percent of the insurance on personal property can be applied to cover any additions or alterations to the building made by the insured. Most renters need a homeowners policy (see Insight 8.1).

Homeowners 5 (Comprehensive Form) The Homeowners 2000 Program reintroduces a new policy form (HO-5) that provides open perils coverage ("all-risks coverage") on both the buildings and personal property. HO-5 was withdrawn from use when the 1984 homeowners program was introduced. After that time, similar coverage was obtained by endorsing the HO-3 policy with a specific endorsement.

The new HO-5 form insures the dwelling, other structures, and personal property against the risk of direct physical loss to property. This provision means that all direct physical losses are covered except those losses specifically excluded. Unlike the other homeowners forms that cover personal property only for certain named perils, HO-5 insures personal property for all direct physical losses except certain losses specifically excluded. HO-5 also provides personal liability insurance.

Insight 8.1

Renters Insurance Is a Must if You Rent an Apartment or House

The majority of tenants do not own a renters insurance policy. Replacing your property, however, may cost more than you think if a loss occurs. An average two-bedroom apartment can easily contain personal property that may cost more than $20,000 to replace. For example, Lori and Mark graduated from college, married, and moved to San Francisco. Like most married couples, they wanted to save money for a down payment on a home. Unfortunately, a burglar broke into their apartment and stole a new wide-screen television set, VCR, camcorder, stereo, diamond ring, camera, silverware, and cash hidden in a jewelry box. The loss totaled $9000. The couple had no insurance. When the couple sued the landlord on the grounds of inadequate security, a judge ruled the landlord was not liable. In short, Lori and Mark had to eat the loss.

Thousands of renters experience similar uninsured losses each year. HO-4 (contents broad form) is designed for renters and covers furniture, clothes, and most other personal property. The policy also provides a limited amount of insurance for building additions and alterations, such as wallpaper in the kitchen.

Personal property is covered both on and off the premises for numerous perils, including fire and lightning, windstorm or hail, explosion, vandalism or malicious mischief, and theft. Even loss from a volcanic eruption is covered. HO-4 does not cover the building, however, because the owner is responsible for insurance on the building.

If the tenant cannot live in the apartment because of a covered loss, such as a fire, the policy pays the additional living expenses of temporarily living in another apartment or house. It also provides at least $100,000 of personal liability insurance that covers the tenant and spouse if either is sued because of property damage or bodily injury to another person. Even fire legal liability is covered. For example, if a malfunctioning barbecue set on the patio causes a fire and damages the apartment, legal liability arising out of the incident would be covered.

Renters insurance is moderately priced. In most cases, an HO-4 policy costs less than $250 annually. For example, one insurer charges only $180 annually for a $25,000 renters policy in San Antonio, Texas.

Homeowners 6 (Unit-Owners Form)

Homeowners 6 *is designed for the owners of condominium units and cooperative apartments.* The condominium association carries insurance on the building and other property owned in common by the owners of the different units. Homeowners 6 covers the personal property of the unit owner for the same named perils listed in Homeowners 2. In addition, there is a minimum of $5000 of insurance on the condominium unit that covers certain property, such as built-in appliances, carpets, additional kitchen cabinets, and wallpaper. Finally, the policy pays a loss assessment charge of up to $1000 if the insured is assessed for a loss not covered by the condominium association's insurance.

Homeowners 8 (Modified Coverage Form)

Homeowners 8 *is a modified coverage form that covers loss to the dwelling and other structures based on the amount required to repair or replace using common construction materials and methods.* Payment is not based on replacement cost.

The policy provides limited coverage for the theft of personal property. Theft coverage is limited to a maximum of $1000 per occurrence and applies only to losses that occur on the residence premises or in a bank or public warehouse.

The HO-8 form is designed for an older home whose replacement cost exceeds its market value. For example, under an HO-2 or HO-3 policy, a home with a market value of $100,000 may have a replacement cost of $150,000. To be indemnified on the basis of replacement cost, the homeowner must carry insurance equal to at least 80 percent of the replacement cost. However, a homeowner may be reluctant to insure a house for $120,000 (80% × $150,000) when its current market value is only

EXHIBIT 8.1

Comparison of ISO Homeowners Coverages

Coverage	HO-2 (broad form)	HO-3 (special form)	HO-4 (contents broad form)
	Section I Coverages		
A. Dwelling	Minimum varies by company.	Minimum varies by company.	Not applicable
B. Other structures	10% of A	10% of A	Not applicable
C. Personal property	50% of A	50% of A	Minimum amount varies.
D. Loss of use	30% of A	30% of A	30% of C
Covered perils	Fire or lightning Windstorm or hail Explosion Riot or civil commotion Aircraft Vehicles Smoke Vandalism or malicious mischief Theft Falling objects Weight of ice, snow, or sleet Accidental discharge or overflow of water or steam Sudden and accidental tearing apart, cracking, burning, or bulging of a steam, hot water, air conditioning, or automatic fire protective sprinkler system, or from within a household appliance Freezing of a plumbing, heating, air conditioning, or automatic fire sprinkler system, or of a household appliance Sudden and accidental damage from artificially generated electrical current Volcanic eruption	Dwelling and other structures are covered against risk of direct loss to property. All losses are covered except certain losses specifically excluded. Personal property is covered for the same perils as HO-2.	Same perils as HO-2 for personal property
	Section II Coverages[a]		
E. Personal liability	$100,000	$100,000	$100,000
F. Medical payments to others	$1000 per person	$1000 per person	$1000 per person

[a]Minimum amounts can be increased.

HO-5 (comprehensive form)	HO-6 (unit-owners form)	HO-8 (modified coverage form)
	Section I Coverages	
Minimum varies by company.	$5000 minimum.	Minimum varies by company.
10% of A	Included in Coverage A	10% of A
50% of A	Minimum amount varies.	50% of A
30% of A	50% of C	10% of A
Dwelling and other structures are covered against risk of direct physical loss to property. All direct physical losses are covered except those losses specifically excluded.	Same perils as HO-2 for personal property	Fire or lightning
		Windstorm or hail
		Explosion
		Riot or civil commotion
		Aircraft
		Vehicles
		Smoke
Personal property is covered against risk of direct physical loss to property. All direct physical losses are covered except those losses specifically excluded.		Vandalism or malicious mischief
		Theft (applies only to loss on the residence premises or in a bank or public warehouse up to a maximum of $1000)
		Volcanic eruption

	Section II Coverages[a]	
$100,000	$100,000	$100,000
$1000 per person	$1000 per person	$1000 per person

$100,000. Likewise, an insurer will not insure a house for $120,000 under a homeowners policy when its current market value is substantially lower. Thus, to make homeowners coverage available for older homes and to reduce moral hazard, the HO-8 form has been developed.

Exhibit 8.1 compares the various homeowners forms, basic coverages, and insured perils.

ANALYSIS OF HOMEOWNERS 3 POLICY (SPECIAL FORM)

In the remainder of this chapter, we examine the major provisions that appear in Section I in the Homeowners 3 policy (special form). As you study this section, you may find it helpful to refer to the Homeowners 3 policy in Appendix A at the end of the text.

Persons Insured

The definitions page in the homeowners policy defines the meaning of an "insured." The following persons are insured under the Section I coverages:

- *Named insured and spouse.* The named insured and spouse if a resident of the named insured's household are both covered.
- *Family members.* Relatives residing in the named insured's household are also covered.
- *Other persons under age 21.* Other persons under age 21 who are in the care of an insured are covered. This definition can include a foster child, a ward of the court, or a foreign exchange student.
- *Full time student away from home.* A full time student who was a resident of the named insured's household before moving out to attend school is also covered, provided the student is under age 24 and a relative of the named insured, or is under age 21 and in the care of an insured.

In addition to these people, the following persons are insured under the Section II coverages:

- *Any person legally responsible for covered animals or watercraft.* For example, if you leave your dog with a neighbor, the neighbor is covered if the dog bites someone. However, the policy excludes coverage for a person or organization having custody of animals or watercraft for business purposes, such as an operator of a dog kennel or boat marina.
- *With respect to a motor vehicle to which the insurance applies, employees of the insured while working for the insured.* For example, if a hired gardener injures someone while operating a riding mower, the gardener is covered under the insured's policy.

SECTION I COVERAGES

There are four basic coverages and several additional coverages in Section I of the Homeowners 3 policy:

- Coverage A: Dwelling
- Coverage B: Other structures
- Coverage C: Personal property
- Coverage D: Loss of use
- Additional coverages

Coverage A: Dwelling

Coverage A covers the dwelling on the residence premises as well as any structure attached to the dwelling. Thus, the home and an attached garage or carport would be insured under this section. Materials and supplies intended for construction or repair of the dwelling or other structures are also covered here.

Coverage A specifically excludes land. Thus, if the land on which the dwelling is located is damaged from an insured peril—such as from an airplane crash—the land is not covered.

Coverage B: Other Structures

Coverage B insures other structures on the residence premises that are separated from the dwelling by clear space. This coverage includes a detached garage, tool shed, or horse stable. Structures connected to the dwelling only by a fence, utility line, or other similar connection are considered to be other structures.

The amount of insurance under Coverage B is based on the amount of insurance on the dwelling (Coverage A). Under the HO-3 policy, 10 percent of the insurance on the dwelling applies as additional insurance to the other structures. For example, if the home is insured for $100,000, the other structures are covered for $10,000.

Coverage B has several important exclusions. First, with the exception of a private garage, there is no coverage if the other structure is rented to someone who is not a tenant of the dwelling. For example, assume that Sam owns and occupies a home that has a horse stable on the premises. If Sam rents the horse stable to another person, he would have no coverage if the stable burns in a fire.

Second, other structures from which a business is conducted are not covered. Thus, if Charles operates an auto repair business in a detached garage, the garage is not covered if it is damaged in a tornado.

Third, other structures used to store business property are excluded. However, the new form will cover a structure that contains business property owned by the insured or tenant of the dwelling provided such property does not include gaseous or liquid fuel, other than fuel in a permanently installed fuel tank in a vehicle parked in the structure. For example, if a professional painter stores ladders in a storage shed on the premises, the shed would be covered as long as it does not contain gaseous or liquid fuel (other than fuel in a parked vehicle).

Coverage C: Personal Property

Personal property owned or used by an insured is covered anywhere in the world. This provision also includes borrowed property. In addition, after a loss and at the named insured's request, the insurance can be extended to cover the personal property of a guest or resident employee while the property is in any residence occupied by an insured. For example, if you invite a guest to dinner and the guest's coat burns in a fire, the loss can be covered under your policy.

The amount of insurance on personal property is equal to 50 percent of the insurance on the dwelling. That amount can be increased. For example, if Eric's home is insured for $100,000, an additional $50,000 of insurance applies to personal property. The full amount of insurance on personal property applies both on and off the premises anywhere in the world. *One exception is that if personal property is usually located at another residence, such as a cabin or vacation home, the off-premises coverage is limited to 10 percent of Coverage C, or $1000, whichever is greater.* For example, assume that Eric has $50,000 of insurance on his personal property. He could take that prop-

erty on an extended trip to Europe and have coverage up to a maximum of $50,000 while it is off the premises. Assume by contrast that Eric owns a cabin or summer home on a river, and that furniture and fishing gear are normally kept there the entire year. In this case, a maximum of $5000 (10% x $50,000) would apply to the loss of personal property at that location.

The preceding 10 percent limitation does not apply to personal property that is moved from the residence premises because the residence premises is being repaired or remodeled and is not a fit place in which to live or store property. For example, the limitation does not apply to personal property located at a residence temporarily occupied by an insured while the residence premises is undergoing repair or remodeling and is not a fit place in which to live.

In addition, if the insured moves personal property to a newly acquired principal residence, the property is not subject to the preceding limitation for 30 days after the move begins. Thus, the insured's personal property is covered for the perils insured against while the property is being moved to the new location, as well as at the new principal residence itself. The insurer must be notified within 30 days for full protection to continue.

Special Limits of Liability Because of moral hazard and loss-adjustment problems, and a desire by the insurer to limit its liability, certain types of property have maximum dollar limits on the amount paid for any loss (see Exhibit 8.2). The special limits can be increased by an endorsement or by scheduling.

The $200 limit on money includes coin collections. If you have a valuable coin collection, it should be scheduled and insured for a specific amount of insurance. A **schedule** *is a list of covered property with specific amounts of insurance.* A valuable stamp collection should also be specifically insured because there is a $1500 limit on stamps.

Coverage on watercraft of all types is limited to $1500, including trailers, furnishings, equipment, and outboard motors. A boat with a value in excess of this limit should be specifically insured.

The theft of jewelry and furs is limited to a maximum of $1500. Expensive jewelry and furs should be scheduled and specifically insured. In addition, there is a $2500 limit on the theft of firearms and a $2500 limit on the theft of silverware, goldware,

EXHIBIT 8.2
Special Limits of Liability

Type of Property	Amount
1. Money, bank notes, bullion, gold, silver, platinum, coins, medals, stored value cards, and smart cards	$200
2. Securities, valuable papers, manuscripts, personal records, passports, tickets, and stamps	$1500
3. Watercraft of all types	$1500
4. Trailers not used with watercraft of all types	$1500
5. Theft of jewelry, watches, furs, and precious and semiprecious stones	$1500
6. Theft of firearms and related equipment	$2500
7. Theft of silverware, goldware, platinumware, and pewterware	$2500
8. Property on the residence premises used primarily for business purposes	$2500
9. Property away from the residence premises used primarily for business purposes (except adaptable electronic equipment described in 10 and 11 below)	$500
10. Electronic apparatus, while in or upon a motor vehicle, but only if the apparatus is equipped to be operated by power from the motor vehicle's electrical system while still capable of being operated by other power sources	$1500
11. Electronic apparatus used primarily for business while away from the premises and not in or upon a motor vehicle. The apparatus must be equipped to be operated by power from the motor vehicle's electrical system while still capable of being operated by other power sources.	$1500

platinumware, and pewterware. Thus, a valuable gun or silverware collection should be specifically insured based on the current value of the collection. Note that the limits on jewelry and furs, guns, silverware, and goldware apply only to the theft peril. The full amount of insurance applies to losses from other covered perils.

Property used primarily for business purposes is limited to $2500 on the premises and $500 away from the premises. However, the $500 limit does not apply to adaptable electronic apparatus.

The homeowners policy provides $1500 of coverage on portable electronic apparatus used in motor vehicles that can also be operated independently from other power sources, such as certain portable televisions, cellular phones, fax machines, and CD players.

The coverage applies to electronic apparatus while in or upon a motor vehicle but only if the apparatus is equipped to be operated by power from the motor vehicle's electrical system while still capable of being operated by other power sources. The limit applies to electronic equipment used either for personal or business use while in or upon a motor vehicle. For example, the theft of a portable cellular phone from a locked car is covered up to $1500. Higher limits can be obtained by an endorsement.

Finally, there is a $1500 limit on electronic apparatus used primarily for business while away from the residence premises and not in or upon a motor vehicle. The apparatus must be equipped to be operated by power from the motor vehicle's electrical system while still capable of being operated by other power sources. For example, a laptop computer used primarily for business purposes is covered up to $1500 if it is stolen while you are on a business trip.

Property Not Covered Certain types of property are excluded under Coverage C. The following property is not covered.

1. *Articles separately described and specifically insured.* Coverage C does not cover articles separately described and specifically insured under either the homeowners policy or some other policy. The intent here is to avoid duplicate coverage. Thus, if jewelry or furs are specifically insured, the homeowners policy will not contribute toward the loss.

2. *Animals, birds, and fish.* Pets are excluded because they are difficult to value. Specialized coverages can be used to insure valuable animals, such as thoroughbred horses and pedigreed dogs.

3. *Motor vehicles.* Motor vehicles and their accessories and equipment are specifically excluded. Thus, cars, motorcycles, and motorscooters are excluded under the policy. Likewise, the theft of a car battery or hubcaps from the car would not be covered.

The exclusion also applies to electronic equipment and accessories designed to be operated solely by power from the electrical system of a motor vehicle, but only while the property is in or upon the motor vehicle. Accessories include antennas, tapes, wires, records, discs, and similar property that can be used with the electronic equipment while in or upon the vehicle. Thus, the theft of stereo tape players, stereo tapes, CB radios, and similar property is excluded from coverage. You should remember that the exclusion of electronic equipment and accessories applies only while the property is in or upon the vehicle. A stereo tape or CB radio that is removed from the vehicle and taken into the house would be covered under the homeowners policy.

Finally, motor vehicles not required to be registered for use on public roads that are used to service the insured residence or designed to assist the handicapped are exempt from the exclusion. Thus, a garden tractor, riding lawn mower, or electric wheelchair would be covered under the policy.

4. *Aircraft and parts.* Aircraft and parts are specifically excluded. However, the policy does cover hobby or model aircraft not used or designed to carry people or cargo.

5. *Hovercraft and parts.* The Homeowners 2000 Program added a new exclusion of hovercraft and parts. Hovercraft is defined as a self-propelled motorized ground effect vehicle and includes, but is not limited to, flarecraft and air cushion vehicles.

6. *Property of roomers, boarders, and other tenants.* Property of roomers and boarders who are not related to an insured is excluded. Thus, if the insured rents a room to a student, the student's property is not covered under the insured's homeowners policy. However, the property of roomers, boarders, and tenants related to an insured is covered.

7. *Property in a regularly rented apartment.* Property in an apartment regularly rented or being held for rental to others by an insured is specifically excluded. However, as discussed later, the homeowners policy provides some coverage for landlord's furnishings in an apartment on the residence premises that is regularly rented or held for rental.

8. *Property rented or held for rental to others off the residence premises.* Property away from the residence premises that is rented to others is specifically excluded. For example, if Jennifer owns a bike rental business, the bicycles are not covered under Jennifer's homeowners policy.

9. *Business records.* The homeowners policy excludes books of account, drawings or other paper records, and electronic data processing tapes, wires, records, discs, or other software media that contain business data. The overall effect of this exclusion is to eliminate coverage for the expense of reproducing business records.

10. *Credit cards, electronic fund transfer cards, or access devices.* Coverage of personal property does not include credit cards, electronic fund transfer cards, or access devices. There is some coverage for the unauthorized use of such cards under Additional Coverages (discussed later).

11. *Water or steam.* The Homeowners 2000 Program excludes coverage of water or steam as personal property. Thus, water or steam delivered through a public water main or in bulk is now excluded.

Coverage D: Loss of Use

Coverage D provides protection when the residence premises cannot be used because of a covered loss. The amount of additional insurance under this coverage is 30 percent of the amount of insurance on the dwelling (Coverage A). Three benefits are provided: *additional living expense, fair rental value,* and *prohibited use.*

Additional Living Expense If a covered loss makes the residence premises not fit to live in, the company pays the additional living expenses that the insured may incur as a result of the loss. **Additional living expense** *is the increase in living expenses actually incurred by the insured to maintain the family's normal standard of living.* For example, assume that Heather's home is damaged by a fire. If she rents a furnished apartment for three months at $800 per month, the additional living expense of $2400 would be covered.

Fair Rental Value The fair rental value is also paid when part of the premises is rented to others. **Fair rental value** *means the rental value of that part of the residence premises rented to others or held for rental less any expenses that do not continue while the premises are not fit to live in.* For example, Heather may rent a room to a student for a monthly rent of $200. If the home is uninhabitable after a fire, and it takes three months to rebuild, Heather would receive $600 for the loss of rents (less any expenses that do not continue). This payment would be in addition to the payment under the additional living expense coverage described earlier.

Prohibited Use Loss-of-use coverage also includes prohibited use losses. Even if the covered home is not damaged, a civil authority may prohibit the insured from using the premises because of direct damage to neighboring premises from an insured peril. The additional living expenses and fair rental value can be paid for up to two weeks. For example, Heather may be ordered out of her home by a fire marshal because the house next door is unstable after an explosion occurred. Her additional living expenses and fair rental value loss would be covered for up to two weeks.

Additional Coverages

In addition to basic Coverages A, B, C, and D, the HO-3 policy provides several additional coverages.

Debris Removal The homeowners policy pays the reasonable expense of removing the debris of covered property damaged by an insured peril. Debris removal also pays the cost of removing volcanic ash, dust, or particles from a volcanic eruption that causes a direct loss to a building or property inside a building.

The cost of removing debris is included in the policy limit that applies to the damaged property. However, if the actual damage plus the cost of removal exceeds the policy limit, an additional 5 percent of the amount of insurance is available for debris removal. For example, assume that a detached garage is covered for $20,000, and a total loss from a fire occurs. If the entire $20,000 is needed to rebuild the garage, up to $1000 is available for debris removal.

In addition, the Homeowners 2000 Program broadens the coverage for the removal of fallen trees from the premises. The policy covers the removal of trees owned by the named insured felled by windstorm or hail, or by the weight of ice, snow, or sleet. Coverage also applies to the removal of a neighbor's tree felled by a Coverage C peril. Coverage applies provided the tree (1) damages a covered structure, or (2) blocks a driveway and prevents a motor vehicle required to be registered for road use from entering or leaving the residence premises, or (3) blocks and prevents use of a ramp or access fixture designed to assist a handicapped person to enter and leave the dwelling. The maximum paid is limited to $1000 regardless of the number of fallen trees. No more than $500 of that limit is paid for the removal of any one tree.

Reasonable Repairs The policy pays the reasonable cost of necessary repairs incurred by the insured to protect the property from further damage after a covered loss occurs. For example, a broken picture window may have to be temporarily boarded up immediately after a severe windstorm to protect personal property from further damage.

Trees, Shrubs, and Other Plants The homeowners policy covers trees, shrubs, plants, or lawns on the residence premises against loss from a limited number of perils. *Coverage is provided only for fire, lightning, explosion, riot, civil commotion, aircraft, vehicles not owned or operated by a resident of the premises, vandalism, malicious mischief, or theft.* Note that *windstorm* is not listed. Therefore, wind damage is not covered. If an expensive tree is blown over in a severe windstorm, the cost of replacing the tree is not covered.

The maximum limit for a loss under this coverage is 5 percent of the insurance that covers the dwelling. However, no more than $500 of that limit can be applied to any single tree, plant, or shrub (but not lawns).

Fire Department Service Charge The policy pays up to $500 if the named insured is liable by a contract or agreement for a fire department charge when firefighters are called to protect covered property from an insured peril. No deductible applies to the coverage.

Property Removal If property is removed from the premises because it is endangered by an insured peril, direct loss from any cause is covered for a maximum of 30 days while the property is removed. Thus, furniture being moved and stored in a public warehouse because of a fire in the home is covered for a direct loss from any cause for a maximum of 30 days. For example, if an earthquake occurred and damaged the furniture stored in a warehouse after the fire, the loss caused by this otherwise excluded peril would be covered.

Credit Card, Electronic Fund Transfer Card or Access Device, Forgery and Counterfeit Money If credit cards are stolen or lost and used in an unauthorized manner, any loss to the insured is covered up to a maximum of $500. Likewise, loss that results from the theft or unauthorized use of an insured's electronic fund transfer card or access device is covered. If a forged or altered check results in a loss to the insured, it is also covered. If the insured accepts counterfeit money in good faith, that loss is covered, too.

Loss Assessment The insurer pays up to $1000 for any loss assessment charged against the named insured by a corporation or association of property owners because of the direct loss to property collectively owned by all members. For example, property owners in a subdivision may belong to a homeowners association that collectively owns a neighborhood swimming pool with a small storage shed. Assume that lightning destroys the storage shed. If the homeowners association subsequently assesses each property owner his or her share of the loss, the insurer will pay the loss assessment charge that otherwise the property owner would have to pay.

Collapse Collapse of a building (or any part of a building) is covered only if the loss is caused by any of the following:

1. Perils insured against in Coverage C
2. Hidden decay, unless known to the insured prior to collapse
3. Hidden insects or vermin damage, unless known to the insured prior to collapse
4. Weight of contents, equipment, animals, or people
5. Weight of rain that collects on a roof
6. Use of defective materials or methods in construction, remodeling, or renovation if the collapse occurs during the course of construction, remodeling, or renovation

Glass or Safety Glazing Material The policy covers the breakage of glass or safety glazing material that is part of a covered building, storm door, or storm window. Damage to covered property from the glass or safety glazing material is also covered. For example, if a baseball breaks a storm window, the glass damage is covered. If the shattering of glass also causes damage to a lamp near the window, the lamp damage would be covered.

Landlord's Furnishings The homeowners policy will pay up to $2500 for loss to the named insured's appliances, carpets, and other household furnishings in each apartment on the residence premises that is regularly rented out or held for rental by an insured. The coverage applies to all losses caused by the perils insured against (Coverage C perils), with the exception of theft. For example, Susan has a furnished apartment on the second floor of her house that is rented to students. The appliances, carpets, and furniture inside the apartment are covered up to $2500.

Ordinance or Law Many communities have building codes that may increase the cost of repairing or reconstructing a damaged building. For example, a new ordinance may require the use of copper pipes rather than galvanized or plastic pipes when the pipes must be replaced after a loss.

The named insured can now apply up to 10 percent of the amount of insurance on Coverage A to cover the increased costs of construction or repair because of some ordinance or law. If higher amounts of insurance are desired, an endorsement can be added to the policy. The coverage provided is additional insurance.

Grave Markers The Homeowners 2000 Program added a new additional coverage for grave markers. Grave markers, including mausoleums, are covered for up to $5000 for loss caused by a peril insured against under Coverage C.

Deductible A deductible of $250 applies to each covered loss. However, for an additional premium, the insured can reduce the deductible amount to $100. The deductible can be increased to reduce premiums. The deductible does not apply to a fire department service charge or to losses involving credit cards, ATM cards, forgery, or counterfeit money.

SECTION I PERILS INSURED AGAINST

In this section, we discuss the various perils, or causes of loss, to covered property.

Dwelling and Other Structures

The dwelling and other structures are insured against "risk of direct physical loss to property." *This means that all direct physical losses are covered except cer-*

tain losses specifically excluded. If a loss to the dwelling or other structure is not excluded, the loss is covered under the policy.

Excluded Losses Certain types of losses to the dwelling and other structures, however, are specifically excluded. They include the following:

1. *Collapse.* Losses involving collapse are specifically excluded, except those collapse losses covered under "additional coverages."
2. *Freezing.* Freezing of a plumbing, heating, air conditioning, or automatic fire protection sprinkler system, or household appliance, or the discharge, leakage, or overflow from within the system or appliance is not covered unless heat is maintained in the building, or the water supply is shut off and drained.

   However, if the building has an automatic fire protective sprinkler system, the insured is required to continue the water supply and maintain heat in the building for the coverage to apply.
3. *Fences, pavement, patio, and similar structures.* Damage to a fence, pavement, patio, swimming pool, foundation, and similar structures is not covered if the damage is caused by freezing and thawing, or from the pressure of weight or water or ice.
4. *Dwelling under construction.* Theft in or to a dwelling under construction, or of materials and supplies used in construction, is not covered until the dwelling is both completed and occupied.
5. *Vandalism and malicious mischief.* Damage from vandalism, malicious mischief, or the breakage of glass and safety-glazing materials is not covered if the dwelling is vacant for more than 60 consecutive days immediately before the loss.
6. *Mold, fungus, or dry rot.* However, the policy will cover a loss that results from the accidental discharge or overflow of water from a storm drain, water, or sewer pipe off the residence permises, or from a plumbing, heating, or air conditioning, fire protective sprinkler system, or household appliance on the premises.
7. *Other exclusions.* The following losses are also excluded:
   - Wear and tear, marring, deterioration
   - Mechanical breakdown, latent defect, inherent vice (tendency of property to decompose)

- Smog, rust or other corrosion, or dry rot
- Smoke from agricultural smudging or industrial operations
- Discharge, seepage, or release or escape of pollutants unless the discharge or release is caused by a Coverage C peril
- Settling, cracking, shrinking, bulging, or expansion of pavements, patios, foundations, walls, floors, roofs, or ceilings
- Birds, vermin, rodents, or insects
- Animals owned or kept by an insured

Personal Property

Personal property (Coverage C) is covered on a named-perils basis. The policy pays for a direct physical loss to personal property from the perils discussed in the following section.

Fire or Lightning The homeowners policy covers a direct physical loss to property from fire or lightning. A direct physical loss means that fire or lightning is the proximate cause of the loss. **Proximate cause** *means there is an unbroken chain of events between the occurrence of a covered peril and damage or destruction of the property.* For example, assume a fire starts in the bedroom of your home. Firefighters spray the other rooms to keep the fire from spreading, and the water causes considerable damage to your books, furniture, and drapes. The entire loss is covered, including the water damage, because the fire is the proximate cause of loss.

What is a fire? The homeowners policy does not define a fire; however, various court decisions have clarified its meaning. Two requirements must be met. *First, there must be combustion or rapid oxidation that causes a flame or at least a glow.* Thus, scorching, heating, and charring that occur without a flame or glow are not covered. For example, a garment accidentally scorched by an iron is not covered because there is no flame or glow.

Second, the fire must be hostile or unfriendly. A hostile fire is outside its normal confines. A friendly fire is intentionally started and is exactly where it is supposed to be. For example, the glow at the end of a lit cigar would be a friendly fire. However, if the burning ashes fell on a couch causing a fire, the fire would be hostile, and the loss would be covered.

The homeowners policy also covers the peril of lightning. For example, the cost of rebuilding a chimney damaged by lightning would be covered, even if no fire occurs.

Windstorm or Hail Windstorm or hail damage is also covered. However, damage to the interior of the building and its contents because of rain, snow, sand, or dust is not covered unless there is an opening in the roof or wall caused by wind or hail that then allows the elements to enter. For example, if a window is left open, rain damage to a sofa is not covered. But if the wind or hail should break the window, allowing rain to enter through the opening, the water damage to personal property inside the room would be covered.

An important exclusion applies to boats. Boats and related equipment are covered only while inside a fully enclosed building. For example, if a boat is stored in the driveway of the home and is damaged by a windstorm, the loss is not covered.

Explosion Broad coverage is provided for damage caused by an explosion. Any type of explosion loss is covered, such as a furnace explosion that damages personal property.

Riot or Civil Commotion Damage to personal property from a riot or civil commotion is covered. Each state defines the meaning of a riot. It is usually defined as an assembly of three or more persons who commit a lawful or unlawful act in a violent or tumultuous manner, to the terror or disturbance of others. Civil commotion is a large or sustained riot that involves an uprising of the citizens.

Aircraft Aircraft damage, including damage from self-propelled missiles and spacecraft, is covered. For example, if a commercial jet crashes into your residential area, damage to your personal property is covered. Likewise, if a self-propelled missile from a nearby military base goes astray, the property is covered against loss.

Vehicles Property damage from vehicles is covered. For example, if your suitcase, clothes, and camera are damaged in an auto accident, the loss is covered. Likewise, if you carelessly back out of the garage and run over your bicycle, the loss is covered.

Smoke Sudden and accidental damage from smoke is covered, including emissions of smoke or fumes from a furnace or related equipment. For example, if the fireplace malfunctions and smoke pours into the family room, any smoke damage to the furniture, rugs, or drapes is covered. However, smoke damage from agricultural smudging or industrial operations is specifically excluded.

Vandalism or Malicious Mischief If someone enters your home and damages your personal property, the loss is covered.

Theft Theft losses are covered, including the attempted theft and the loss of property when it is likely that the property has been stolen.

Although coverage of theft is fairly broad, there are several exclusions. They include the following:

1. *Theft by an insured is excluded.* For example, if Brandi, age 16, steals $100 from her mother's purse before running away from home, the theft is not covered.
2. *Theft in or to a dwelling under construction*, or of materials and supplies used in the construction of a dwelling, is not covered until the dwelling is completed and occupied.
3. *Theft from any part of the premises rented to someone other than an insured is not covered.* For example, if the insured rents a room to a student, the theft of a radio owned by the insured and located inside the room would not be covered.

Several important exclusions also apply when the theft occurs away from the residence premises. They include the following:

1. *Temporary residence.* If property is located at any other residence owned, rented to, or occupied by an insured, the loss is not covered unless an insured is temporarily residing there. For example, Brian owns a cabin on the river. Theft of property inside the cabin is not covered unless Brian is temporarily residing there. He is not required to be physically present in the residence at the time of loss, but he must be temporarily living or residing there. For example, if he is fishing at the river when the theft occurs, the loss would be covered.

In addition, *theft of personal property of a student while at a residence away from home is covered if the student has been there any time during the 45 days immediately preceding the loss.* For example, assume you are attending college and are temporarily living away from home. If your television set is stolen from your college residence, the loss is covered by your parent's HO-3 policy if you have been there any time during the 45-day period preceding the loss.
2. *Watercraft.* Theft of a boat, its furnishings, equipment, and outboard motor is excluded if the theft occurs away from the premises.
3. *Trailers and campers.* Theft of trailers or campers away from the premises is not covered. Trailers and campers can be covered under the personal auto policy, which is discussed in Chapter 10.

Falling Objects Damage to personal property from falling objects is covered. However, loss to property inside the building is not covered unless the roof or outside wall of the building is first damaged by the falling object. For example, if a hand mirror falls off its stand and breaks, the loss is not covered. But if the mirror falls and breaks because the exterior of the dwelling is first damaged by a falling tree, the loss would be covered.

Weight of Ice, Snow, or Sleet Damage to indoor personal property resulting from the weight of ice, snow, or sleet is covered. For example, if the weight of snow causes the roof to collapse, damage to the personal property inside the dwelling would be covered.

Accidental Discharge or Overflow of Water or Steam If loss results from an accidental discharge or overflow of water or steam from a plumbing, heating, air conditioning, or automatic fire protective sprinkler system, or from a household appliance, the property damage is covered. For example, if an automatic dishwasher malfunctions and floods the kitchen, water damage to personal property, such as an area rug, would be covered. However, the cost of repairing the system or appliance from which the water or steam escapes is not covered.

Sudden and Accidental Tearing Apart, Cracking, Burning, or Bulging of a Steam, Hot Water, Air Conditioning, or Automatic Fire Protective Sprinkler System, or Appliance for Heating Water If any of these perils cause damage to personal property, the loss is covered. For example, damage to personal property from a hot water heater that suddenly cracks is covered.

Freezing of a Plumbing, Heating, Air Conditioning, or Automatic Fire Protective Sprinkler System, or Household Appliance Freezing is not covered unless the insured used reasonable care to maintain heat in the building, or shuts off the water supply and drains the system.

Sudden and Accidental Damage from an Artificially Generated Electrical Current For example, an electrical power surge that causes an electric clothes dryer to burn out would be covered. However, loss to tubes, transistors, or electronic components that are part of appliances, computers, or home entertainment units specifically excluded. Thus, a television picture tube that burns out is not covered.

Volcanic Eruption Loss resulting from a volcanic eruption is also covered. However, losses caused by earthquakes, land shock waves, or tremors are excluded.

SECTION I EXCLUSIONS

In addition to the specific exclusions previously discussed, several general exclusions appear in the policy.

Ordinance or Law

With the exception of the ordinance or law coverage described earlier under the additional coverages section, and glass replacement as required by law, the policy excludes loss due to any ordinance or law. However, as we noted earlier, if the amount of insurance provided under the additional coverages section is inadequate, higher amounts can be obtained by an endorsement to the policy.

Earth Movement

Property damage from earth movement is excluded. This includes damage from an earthquake, shock waves from a volcanic eruption, landslide, mudslide or mudflow, subsidence or sinkholes, or earth sinking or shifting. However, an ensuing loss caused by fire or explosion is covered. An earthquake endorsement can be added to the policy.

Water Damage

Property damage from certain water losses is specifically excluded. The following types of water damage losses are not covered:

- Floods, surface water, waves, tidal water, and overflow or spray from a body of water
- Water or water-borne material that backs up through sewers or drains or overflows from a sump
- Water or water-borne material below the surface of the ground that exerts pressure on or seeps through a building, sidewalk, driveway, foundation, swimming pool, or other structure

Power Failure

There is no coverage for loss caused by the failure of power or other utility service if the failure takes place off the residence premises. For example, if the contents of a freezer thaw and spoil because of the failure of an electrical power plant ten miles away, the loss is not covered. However, if the power failure is caused by an insured peril on the residence premises, any resulting loss is covered. Thus, if lightning strikes the home and power is interrupted on the premises, the spoilage of food in a freezer is covered.

Neglect

If the insured neglects to use all reasonable means to save and preserve the property at or after the time of loss, the loss is not covered. For example, a broken picture window may have to be boarded up after a windstorm to protect personal property in the room from further damage.

War

Property damage from war is specifically excluded. War is commonly excluded in property insurance contracts.

Nuclear Hazard

Nuclear hazard losses are excluded, including nuclear reaction, radiation, or radioactive contamination. For example, if a radiation leak from a nuclear power plant contaminates your property, the loss is not covered.

Intentional Loss

An intentional loss is excluded. An intentional loss is a loss arising out of any act the insured commits or conspires to commit with the intent to cause a loss. For example, if the insured arranges to have his home burned to collect the insurance payment, the loss is not covered.

Governmental Action

Loss due to governmental action is also excluded. Governmental action refers to the destruction, confiscation, or seizure of property by any governmental or public authority. For example, the house and cash of a drug dealer that is seized by drug enforcement officials would not be covered. However, the exclusion does not apply to acts ordered by a government or public authority to prevent the spread of a fire.

Weather Conditions

This exclusion applies only to weather conditions that contribute to a loss that would otherwise be excluded. For example, landslide damage caused by excessive rain and heavy winds is excluded under this provision. Likewise, flooding or earth movement caused by excessive rain is excluded. However, damage to a house caused solely by windstorm or hail would be covered.

Acts or Decisions

This exclusion applies to losses that result from the failure to act by any person, group, organization, or government body. For example, if a governmental unit fails to develop a plan to control flood losses, property damage from a flood that resulted from failure to develop a plan would not be covered.

Faulty, Inadequate, or Defective Planning and Design

Also excluded are losses that result from faulty or defective planning, zoning, design, workmanship, materials, or maintenance. For example, a completed house that pulls away from the foundation because of faulty design or poor construction would not be covered.

In summary, the Section I coverages provide broad coverage on the home and more limited coverage on personal property. Most homeowners do not bother to read the policy, however, and often have questions concerning the coverages provided. Insight 8.2 discusses several questions that homeowners frequently ask concerning coverage.

SECTION I CONDITIONS

Section I in the homeowners policy contains numerous conditions. The most important are discussed here.

Insurable Interest and Limit of Liability

If more than one person has an insurable interest in the property, the insurer's liability for any one loss is limited to the insured's insurable interest at the time of loss but not to exceed the maximum amount of insurance.

Duties After a Loss

The insured must perform certain duties after a loss occurs. The insurer has the right to deny coverage for a loss if the insured does not comply with his or her duties, and such failure is prejudicial to the insurer. The following duties are required:

- *Give prompt notice.* The insured must give prompt notice to the insurer or an agent of the insurer. In case of a theft, the police must be notified as well. The credit card company must also be notified in case of loss or theft of a credit or ATM card.

Insight 8.2

Frequently Asked Questions About Homeowners Insurance

Homeowners frequently ask questions about homeowners insurance. The following questions apply to the HO-3 policy.

1. Are you covered for direct losses due to fire, lightning, tornadoes, windstorms, hail, explosion, vandalism, and theft?

Yes. HO-3 provides broad coverage for numerous perils, including those mentioned above.

2. Your house is totally destroyed in a fire. You have $150,000 of insurance on the structure. Will this amount be enough to rebuild?

If the cost of the rebuilding is $150,000 or less, you have enough coverage. HO-3 pays for damage on a replacement cost basis. If the replacement cost is $120,000, that is all the insurance you need. If the cost of rebuilding is $180,000, you will be short $30,000. If you elect not to replace your home, you will receive replacement cost less depreciation, or actual cash value.

3. Are you covered for flood?

No. Flood insurance is provided by the federal government under a program run by the Federal Insurance Administration.

4. A pipe bursts and water flows all over your floors. Are you covered?

Yes. HO-3 covers the accidental discharge of water from a plumbing system.

5. Water seeps into your basement from the ground. Are you covered?

No. HO-3 excludes water seepage. Also, if water seepage is not due to a flood, you will not be covered under a flood insurance policy.

6. Are you covered for earthquake damage?

No. Earthquake coverage is sold as an additional coverage to the policy. In earthquake-prone areas, the cost is relatively high. In other areas, it is cheap.

7. A neighbor slips on your sidewalk and threatens to take you to court for damages. Does your policy protect you?

Yes. If the accident is a result of your negligence, the policy will pay damages up to the policy limit as well as your legal defense costs (see Chapter 9).

8. During a storm, a tree falls and damages your roof. Are you covered?

Yes. the roof damage is covered. You are also covered for the removal of the tree, up to a $500 limit.

9. During a storm, a tree is damaged by heavy winds. Are you covered for the cost of replacing the tree?

No. Trees and shrubs are covered for certain losses such as vandalism, theft, and fire, but not wind damage.

10. During a storm, the power from the electric utility company is lost. Food in the refrigerator spoils and must be thrown out. Can you make a claim?

The general answer is no, with some exceptions. In some states, food spoilage is covered under the homeowners policy. Also, if the power loss is due to a break in a power line on or close to your property, you may be covered.

11. Your golf clubs are stolen from the trunk of your car. Can you recover?

Yes. HO-3 covers personal property anywhere in the world.

12. You have a power boat with a 50-horsepower engine. If it is stolen, are you covered?

If the boat is stolen from your residence, in most cases you can recover only $1500. If the boat is stolen elsewhere, you are not covered.

13. Are you covered for an "Act of God"?

Yes, you are normally covered for "Acts of God" with the notable exceptions of floods and earthquakes. The term "Acts of God" refers to natural disasters like hurricanes and tornadoes, as opposed to human acts like thefts or auto accidents.

Source: Adapted from "Frequently Asked Questions About Homeowners Insurance," Insurance Information Institute.

- *Protect the property.* The insured must protect the property from further damage, make reasonable and necessary repairs to protect the property, and keep an accurate record of the repair expenses.
- *Prepare an inventory of damaged personal property.* The inventory must show in detail the quantity, description, actual cash value, and the amount of loss. Taking an inventory of your property before a loss occurs is highly advisable.
- *Exhibit the damaged property.* The insured may be required to show the damaged property to the insurer as often as is reasonably required. The insured may also be required to submit to questions under oath without any other insured being present and sign a sworn statement.
- *File a proof of loss within 60 days after the insurer's request.* The proof of loss must include the time and cause of loss, interest of the insured and all others in the property, all liens on the property, other insurance covering the loss, and other relevant information.

Loss Settlement

Covered losses to *personal property* are paid on the basis of *actual cash value* at the time of loss, but not to exceed the amount necessary to repair or replace the property. Carpets, domestic appliances, awnings, outdoor antennas, and outdoor equipment, whether attached to the dwelling or not, are also indemnified on the basis of actual cash value.

Covered losses to the *dwelling and other structures* are paid on the basis of *replacement cost* with no deduction for depreciation. Replacement cost insurance on the dwelling is one of the most valuable features of the homeowner policies. If the amount of insurance carried is equal to at least 80 percent of the replacement cost of the damaged building at the time of loss, full replacement cost is paid with no deduction for depreciation up to the limits of the policy. **Replacement cost** *is the amount necessary to repair or replace the dwelling with material of like kind and quality at current prices.* For example, assume that a home has a current replacement value of $100,000 and is insured for $80,000. If the home is damaged by a tornado, and repairs cost $20,000, the full $20,000 is paid with no deduction for depreciation. If the home is totally destroyed, however,

the maximum amount paid for the damage to the building is the face amount of the policy—in this case, $80,000.

A different set of rules applies if the amount of insurance is less than 80 percent of the replacement cost at the time of loss. Stated simply, if the insurance carried is less than 80 percent of the replacement cost, the insured receives the *larger* of the following two amounts:

(1) Actual cash value of that part of the building damaged

or

$$(2) \quad \frac{\text{Amount of insurance carried}}{80\% \times \text{Replacement cost}} \times \text{Loss}$$

For example, assume that a dwelling has a replacement cost of $100,000, but is insured for only $60,000. The roof of the house is 10 years old and has a useful life of 20 years, so it is 50 percent depreciated. Assume that the roof is severely damaged by a tornado, and the replacement cost of a new roof is $20,000. Ignoring the deductible, the insured receives the larger of:

$$\begin{aligned}(1) \quad \text{Actual cash value} &= \$20,000 - \$10,000 \\ &= \$10,000\end{aligned}$$

$$(2) \quad \frac{\$60,000}{80\% \times \$100,000} \times \$20,000 = \$15,000$$

The insured receives $15,000 for the loss. The entire loss would have been paid if the insured had carried at least $80,000 of insurance.

With the exception of losses that are both less than 5 percent of the amount of insurance and less than $2500, the insured must actually repair or replace the property to receive full replacement cost. Otherwise, the loss is paid on the basis of actual cash value. However, the insured can submit a claim for the actual cash value and then collect an additional amount when the actual repair or replacement is completed, provided the additional claim is made within 180 days after the loss.

Many insurers now offer a **guaranteed replacement cost** endorsement by which the insured agrees to insure the home to 100 percent of its estimated replacement cost rather than 80 percent. *In the event of a total loss, the insurer agrees to replace the home exactly as it was before the loss even though the replacement cost exceeds the amount of insurance stated in the policy.* For example, if your policy limits are $100,000 and it costs $120,000 to rebuild your house, the insurer will pay $120,000.

Many insurers now limit the maximum amounts paid under the guaranteed replacement cost endorsement. Maximum limits typically range from 120 percent to 150 percent of insured value. This limitation was established because of the combined effects of underappraising the value of the home by some insurance agents, price gouging by some contractors because of a shortage of building materials, inflation, and fraud in some cases. Because of these problems, replacement cost guarantees are quickly disappearing (see Insight 8.3).

Loss to a Pair or Set

In the event of **loss to a pair or set,** *the insurer can elect either to repair or replace any part of the pair or set or to pay the difference between the actual cash value of the property before and after the loss.* For example, assume that Kathy has a set of three matching wall decorations hanging on the wall in her living room, and one of the decorations is badly damaged in a fire. The insurer can elect either to replace or repair the damaged wall decoration or to pay the difference in the actual cash value of the set before and after the loss.

Appraisal Clause

An **appraisal clause** *is used when the insured and insurer agree that the loss is covered, but the amount of the loss is in dispute.* Either party can demand that the dispute be resolved by an appraisal. Each party selects a competent and impartial appraiser. The appraisers then select an umpire. If they cannot agree on an umpire after 15 days, a judge in a court of record will appoint one. If the appraisers fail to agree on the amount of the loss, only their differences are submitted to the umpire. An agreement in writing by any two of the three is then binding on both parties. Each party pays the fee of his or her appraiser, and the umpire's fee is shared equally by both parties.

Other Insurance and Service Agreement

If other insurance covers a Section I loss, the insurer will pay only the proportion of the loss that its limit of liability bears to the total amount of insurance covering the loss. The pro rata liability clause was explained in Chapter 6.

The Homeowners 2000 Program added a new provision when a home warranty or service agreement covers the loss. Many homeowners purchase home warranty contracts or appliance service agreements that guarantee the repair or replacement of defective parts if certain conditions are met. The homeowners policy is excess over any amount payable under a home warranty or service agreement.

Suit Against the Insurer

No legal action can be brought against the insurer unless all policy provisions have been complied with, and legal action is started within two years after the loss occurs.

Insurer's Option

After giving written notice to the insured, the insurer has the right to repair or replace any part of the damaged property with like property. For example, assume that a television set is stolen. By giving written notice, the insurer can replace the stolen TV with a similar item rather than paying cash. Insurers often can purchase television sets, stereos, and other types of property from wholesale distributors at a lower cost than the insured would pay in the retail market. By exercising the replacement option, an insurer can meet its contractual obligation for a covered loss, but its loss settlement costs can be reduced.

Loss Payment

The insurer is required to make a loss payment directly to the insured unless some other person is named in the policy or is legally entitled to receive the loss payment. In many homeowners contracts, a mortgagee (lender) is named in the policy, which allows the mortgagee to receive a loss payment to the

Insight 8.3

Home Insurance Loses Its Safety Net

How To Be Sure You Can Rebuild Your Home

Read any good insurance policies lately? You might be surprised by a plot twist in the fine print: Major homeowners insurance companies, including State Farm and Allstate, no longer promise to pay whatever it takes to rebuild your home if disaster strikes. Instead, the burden is on you to make sure that the stated coverage would provide enough to rebuild—although some insurers will agree to add in a buffer of 20 percent or so.

For example, State Farm offers a 20 percent cushion, known as "Option ID—Increased Dwelling Limit," to homeowners whose policies cover 100 percent of State Farm's estimate of the home's replacement value. The buffer does not cost extra, but you have to make sure it's included in your policy. Allstate caps its payout at 120 percent of a policy's stated coverage amount, too, but you don't have to request the extra protection to get it.

Companies say they have jettisoned the guarantee-replacement promise because some homeowners were deliberately understating the value of their homes (often by neglecting to report improvements and additions) and counting on the guarantee to bail them out in case of a catastrophic loss.

It's Your Problem

Now that guarantees are history, any miscalculation will be your problem, not the insurance company's. And when you consider that the common wisdom is to build a cushion of at least 10 percent into any remodeling budget for unexpected expenses, a 20 percent buffer doesn't leave much room for error.

Your insurer will estimate how much coverage you need, but how do you know if that estimate is correct?

It might not be, but it's bound to be closer if you take these precautions:

- Tell your insurance agent about any remodeling that you've done, even if you only upgraded your kitchen appliances.
- Ask your agent to make sure that your policy includes an automatic annual adjustment for inflation.
- Get policy quotes from a couple of competitors—and compare the coverage amounts they recommend.
- Get your own estimate of rebuilding costs, and compare that with the insurance company's figure. For a rough idea, start by figuring the total square footage of your home, upstairs and downstairs. (You may find those numbers on your copy of the survey filed away with your mortgage papers.) Then multiply the square footage by the local cost of construction per square foot. Contractors should be able to give you a ballpark figure.

Or use this method, suggested by William Young, director of consumer affairs for the National Association of Home Builders: Check the price of new houses similar to yours. Take away one-fourth of the new-home price to account for the value of the land; the rest of the price typically represents the actual cost of building the house itself.

To be really safe, you may want to hire a local contractor or appraiser to estimate the cost of rebuilding. Alan Hummel, a Des Moines appraiser, says such an appraisal typically costs $200 to $700, depending on the complexity of evaluating the property.

SOURCE: Elizabeth Razzi, "Home Insurance Loses Its Safety Net," *Kiplinger's Personal Finance Magazine* (December 1999), p. 64.

extent of its insurable interest. A legal representative of the insured is also entitled to receive a loss payment. For example, if Angela dies before receiving payment for a covered loss, the loss payment is made to the executor of her estate.

Abandonment of Property

The insurer is not obligated to accept any property abandoned by the insured after a loss occurs. The insurer has the option of paying for the damaged property in full and then taking the damaged property as salvage, or the insurer can elect to have the property repaired. However, the decision to exercise these options belongs to the insurer. For example, assume your personal property is insured for $50,000. A fire occurs, and the salvage value of the property after the loss is $10,000. The insurer can pay you $40,000, or it can take all the damaged property and pay you $50,000. However, you cannot abandon the property to the insurer and demand payment of $50,000.

Mortgage Clause

The **mortgage clause** is designed to protect the mortgagee's insurable interest. The mortgagee usually is a savings and loan institution, commercial bank, or other lending institution that makes a loan to the mortgagor (home buyer) so that the property can be purchased. The property serves as collateral for the mortgage loan. If the property is damaged or destroyed, the collateral securing the loan is impaired, and the loan may not be repaid.

The mortgagee's insurable interest in the property can be protected by the mortgage clause that is part of the homeowner policy. *Under this provision, if the mortgagee is named in the policy, the mortgagee is entitled to receive a loss payment from the insurer to the extent of its interest, regardless of any policy violation by the insured.* For example, if Troy intentionally sets fire to his house, his loss is not covered because the fire is intentional. However, the mortgagee's insurable interest in the property is still protected. The loss payment would be paid to the mortgagee to the extent of the mortgagee's interest. The mortgagee is also entitled to a 10-day cancellation notice if the insurer decides to cancel.

In exchange for the guarantee of payment, the mortgage clause imposes certain obligations on the mortgagee. They are as follows:

- To notify the insurer of any change in ownership, occupancy, or substantial change in risk of which the mortgagee is aware
- To pay any premium due if the insured neglects to pay the premium
- To provide a proof-of-loss form if the insured fails to do so
- To give subrogation rights to the insurer in those cases where the insurer denies liability to the in-

sured but must make a loss payment to the mortgagee

Policy Period

The policy period begins and ends at 12:01 a.m. on the dates specified in the policy period. Only losses that occur during the policy period are covered.

Concealment or Fraud

There is no coverage if an insured intentionally conceals or misrepresents any material fact, engages in fraudulent conduct, or makes false statements relating to the insurance. The provision applies both before and after a loss.

SECTION I AND II CONDITIONS

The homeowners policy contains several common conditions that apply to both Section I and Section II. They are summarized as follows:

- *Liberalization Clause.* If the insurer broadens the coverage it offers without charging a higher premium within 60 days before inception of the policy or during the policy period, the broadened coverage applies immediately to the present policy. However, the liberalization clause does not apply to changes that are implemented with a general program revision that includes both a broadening and restriction of coverage.
- *Waiver or Change of Policy Provisions.* A waiver or change in any policy provision must be approved in writing by the insurer to be valid. For example, an agent cannot orally waive any policy provision in the homeowners policy.
- *Cancellation.* The insured can cancel at any time by returning the policy or by notifying the insurer in writing when the cancellation is to become effective.

    The insurer can cancel under the following conditions:

    1. The premium is not paid. The insured must be given at least 10 days' written notice of cancellation.
    2. A new policy can be canceled for any reason if

it has been in force for less than 60 days and is not a renewal policy. The insured must be given at least 10 days' notice of cancellation.

3. If the policy has been in force for 60 or more days or is a renewal policy, the insurer can cancel if there is a material misrepresentation of fact that would have caused the insurer not to issue the policy, or if the risk has increased substantially after the policy was issued.

4. If the policy is written for a period longer than one year, it can be canceled for any reason on the anniversary date by giving the insured at least 30 days' notice of cancellation.

- *Nonrenewal of the Policy.* The insurer has the right not to renew the policy when it expires. The insured must be given at least 30 days' notice before the expiration date if the policy is not renewed.

- *Assignment of the Policy.* The homeowners policy cannot be assigned to another party without the insurer's written consent. Thus, if Richard sells his home to Michelle, he cannot validly assign his homeowners policy to Michelle. The homeowners policy is a personal contract between the insured and insurer. The assignment provision allows the insurer to select its own insureds and provides some protection against moral hazard and adverse selection. However, after a loss occurs, the loss payment can be freely assigned to another party without the insurer's consent. The party who receives the payment does not become a new insured, and the risk to the insurer is not increased.

- *Subrogation.* A general principle is that an insured cannot unilaterally waive the insurer's right of subrogation against a third party who caused the loss without jeopardizing coverage under the policy. However, the homeowners policy contains an important exception to this general principle. The subrogation clause allows the insured to waive in writing, before a loss occurs, all rights of recovery against any person. For example, assume that Jerome lives in one unit of a duplex and rents out the other unit. The lease may state that Jerome as landlord waives his right of recovery against the tenant if the tenant should negligently cause a loss (such as a fire). The waiver would protect the tenant against a subrogation recovery by Jerome's insurer if the tenant should cause a loss. To be effective, however, the waiver must be in writing before a loss occurs.

If the right of recovery is not waived, the insurer may require the insured to assign all rights of recovery against a third party to the extent of the loss payment. This provision allows the insurer to exercise its subrogation rights against a negligent third party who caused the loss.

- *Death of Named Insured or Spouse.* If the named insured or resident spouse dies, coverage is extended to the legal representative of the deceased but only with respect to the premises and property of the deceased. Coverage also continues for resident relatives who are insured under the policy at the time of the named insured or spouse's death.

SUMMARY

- The homeowners policy is a package policy that can be used to cover the dwelling, other structures, personal property, additional living expenses, and personal liability claims.

- Section I provides coverage on the dwelling, other structures, personal property, loss-of-use benefits, and additional coverages. Section II provides personal liability insurance to the insured and also covers the medical expenses of others who may be injured while on the insured premises or by some act of the insured or by an animal owned by the insured.

- The HO-2 policy (broad form) covers the dwelling, other structures, and personal property against loss on a named-perils basis.

- The HO-3 policy (special form) covers the dwelling and other structures against risk of direct physical loss to the described property. All losses to the dwelling and other structures are covered except those losses specifically excluded. Personal property is covered only on a named-perils basis.

- The HO-4 policy (contents broad form) is designed for renters. HO-4 covers the personal property of tenants on a named-perils basis and also provides personal liability insurance.

- The HO-5 policy (comprehensive form) provides open perils coverage ("all-risks coverage") on both the buildings and personal property. HO-5 insures the dwelling, other structures, and personal property against the risk of direct physical loss to property. All direct physical losses are covered except those losses specifically excluded.

- The HO-6 policy (unit-owners form) is designed for condominium owners. HO-6 covers the personal property of the insured on a named-perils basis. There is also a minimum of $5000 insurance on the condominium unit that covers certain property, such as alterations, fixtures, and improvements.

- The HO-8 policy (modified coverage form) is designed for older homes. Losses to the dwelling and other structures are paid on the basis of the amount required to repair or replace the property using common construction materials and methods. Losses are not paid based on replacement cost.

- The conditions section imposes certain duties on the insured after a loss to covered property occurs. The insured must give immediate notice of the loss; the property must be protected from further damage; the insured must prepare an inventory of the damaged personal property and may be required to show the damaged property to the insurer as often as is reasonably required; and proof of loss must be filed within 60 days after the insurer's request.

- The replacement cost provision is one of the most valuable features of the homeowners policy. Losses to the dwelling and other structures are paid on the basis of replacement cost if the insured carries insurance at least equal to 80 percent of the replacement cost at the time of loss. Losses to personal property are paid on the basis of actual cash value. However, an endorsement can be added that covers personal property on a replacement cost basis.

- The appraisal provision is designed to resolve disputes over the amount paid. Each party selects its own appraiser. The appraisers then select an umpire. An agreement by any two is binding on all parties.

- The mortgage clause provides protection to the mortgagee. The mortgagee is entitled to receive a loss payment from the insurer regardless of any policy violation by the insured.

KEY CONCEPTS AND TERMS

Additional living expense
Appraisal clause
Fair rental value
Guaranteed replacement cost
Homeowners 2 (broad form)
Homeowners 3 (special form)
Homeowners 4 (contents broad form)
Homeowners 5 (comprehensive form)
Homeowners 6 (unit-owners form)
Homeowners 8 (modified coverage form)
Loss to a pair or set
Mortgage clause
Package policy
Proximate cause
Replacement cost
Schedule

REVIEW QUESTIONS

1. What are the advantages of a package policy to the insured?
2. Identify the basic types of homeowner policies and indicate the groups for which each form is designed.
3. List the basic coverages that are provided in Section I of the homeowners policy.
4. What additional coverages are provided in Section I of the homeowners policy?
5. Explain the special limits of liability that apply to certain types of property. Why are these limits used?
6. List the various exclusions that are found in Section I of the Homeowners 3 policy.
7. What duties are imposed on the insured after a loss occurs?
8. Describe the replacement cost provisions of the homeowners policy and give an example.
9. Show how the appraisal clause can be used to resolve disputes.
10. Explain briefly how the mortgage clause protects the mortgagee's insurable interest.

APPLICATION QUESTIONS

1. Amber has her home and personal property insured under a Homeowners 3 (special form) policy. Indicate whether each of the following losses is covered. If the loss is not covered, explain why it is not covered.

a. Amber carelessly spills a can of paint while painting a bedroom. A wall-to-wall carpet that is part of the bedroom is badly damaged and must be replaced.

b. Water backs up from a clogged drainpipe, floods the basement, and damages some books stored in a box.

c. Amber's house is totally destroyed in a tornado. Her valuable Doberman pinscher dog is killed in the tornado.

d. Smoke from a nearby industrial plant damages Amber's freshly painted house.

e. Amber is on vacation, and a thief breaks into her hotel and steals a suitcase containing jewelry, money, clothes, and an airline ticket.

f. Amber's son is playing baseball in the yard. A line drive breaks the living room window.

g. A garbage truck accidentally backs into the garage door and shatters it.

h. Defective wiring causes a fire in the attic. Damage to the house is extensive. Amber is forced to move into a furnished apartment for three months while the house is being rebuilt.

i. Amber's son is attending college but is home for Christmas. A stereo set is stolen from his dormitory room during his absence.

j. During the winter, heavy snow damages part of the front lawn, and the sod must be replaced.

k. During a windstorm, a picket fence and an elm tree are blown over.

l. Carpeting is damaged from the overflow of water from a bathtub because the insured left the water running while answering the telephone.

m. The home is badly damaged in a severe earthquake. As a result of the earthquake, the front lawn has a three-foot crack and is now uneven.

n. An icemaker in the refrigerator breaks and water seeps into the flooring and carpets, causing considerable damage to the dwelling.

2. James has his home and personal property insured under a Homeowners 3 (special form) policy. The dwelling is insured for $60,000. The replacement cost of the home is $100,000. Indicate the extent to which each of the following losses would be covered under James's Homeowners 3 policy. (Ignore the deductible.)

a. Lightning strikes the roof of the house and severely damages it. The actual cash value of the damaged roof is $10,000, and it will cost $16,000 to replace the damaged portion.

b. A living room window is broken in a hailstorm. The drapes are water stained and must be replaced. The actual cash value of the damaged drapes is $200. Replacement cost is $300.

c. The hot water heater explodes and damages some household contents. The actual cash value of the damaged property is $1000, and the cost of replacing the property is $1600.

3. Sarah owns a valuable diamond ring that has been in her family for generations. She is told by an appraiser that the ring has a current market value of $20,000. She feels that the ring is adequately insured because she owns a Homeowners 3 (special form) policy. Is Sarah correct in her thinking? If not, how would you advise her concerning proper protection of the ring?

4. Paul has his home and its contents insured under a Homeowners 3 (special form) policy. He carries $80,000 of insurance on the home, which has a replacement cost of $100,000. Explain the extent to which each of the following losses is covered. (Ignore the deductible.) If Paul's policy does not cover the loss or inadequately covers any of these losses, show how full coverage can be obtained.

a. Paul's coin collection, which is valued at $5000, is stolen from his home.

b. Teenage vandals break into Paul's home and rip up a painting owned by Paul's wife. The painting is valued at $1000.

c. A motorboat stored in the driveway of Paul's home is badly damaged during a hailstorm. The actual cash value of the damaged portion is $2000, and its replacement cost is $5000.

5. Pierre owns a home with an actual cash value of $200,000 that is subject to a $100,000 mortgage held by First Federal as the mortgagee. Pierre has the home insured for $160,000 under the HO-3 policy, and First Federal is named as mortgagee under the Mortgage Clause. Assume there is a covered fire loss to the dwelling in the amount of $50,000. To whom would the loss be paid? Explain your answer.

SELECTED REFERENCES

Fire, Casualty & Surety Bulletins, Personal Lines Volume. Dwelling Section. Cincinnati: National Underwriter Company. The bulletins are updated monthly.

Hamilton, Karen L., and Donald S. Malecki. *Personal Insurance: Property and Liability*, 1st ed. Malvern, PA: American Institute for Chartered Property Casualty Underwriters, 1994, Chapter 2.

Rejda, George E., Constance M. Luthardt, Cheryl L. Ferguson, and Donald R. Oakes. *Personal Insurance*, Fourth ed. Malvern, PA: Insurance Institute of America, 2000.

NOTE

1. The discussion of homeowners insurance in this chapter is based on the *Fire, Casualty & Surety Bulletins*, Personal Lines Volume, Dwelling Section (Cincinnati: National Underwriter Company); and the copyrighted homeowners forms drafted by the Insurance Services Office (ISO). The ISO forms and various policy provisions are used with the permission of ISO.

Case Application

Arturo and Phoebe are married and own a home insured for $150,000 under the HO-3 policy. The replacement cost of the home is $250,000. Personal property is insured for $75,000. Phoebe has jewelry and furs valued at $10,000. Arturo has a coin collection valued at $15,000 and a high-speed motorboat valued at $20,000.

a. Assume you are a financial planner who is asked to evaluate the couple's HO-3 policy. Based on the above facts, do you believe that their present coverages are adequate? If not, make several recommendations for improving the coverage.

b. A fire damaged one bedroom. The actual cash value of the loss is $10,000. The cost of repairs is $16,000. How much will the insurer pay for the loss?

c. A burglar broke into the home and stole a new television set, a VCR, and several paintings. The actual cash value of the stolen property is $4000. The cost of replacing the property is $9000. In addition, the coin collection was also taken. Indicate the extent, if any, to which an unendorsed HO-3 policy will cover the preceding losses.

d. Assume that Arturo and Phoebe have a disagreement with their insurer concerning the value of the above losses. How would the dispute be resolved under their HO-3 policy?

e. Assume that Phoebe operates an accounting business from her home. Her home business office contains a computer used solely for business, office furniture, file cabinets, and other business personal property. Explain whether her HO-3 policy would cover business personal property used in a home business.

Students may take a self-administered test on this chapter at www.awlonline.com/rejda

Chapter 9

Homeowners Insurance, Section II

" How to win in court: If the law is on your side, pound on the law; if the facts are on your side, pound on the facts; if neither is on your side, pound on the table. "

Unknown

Learning Objectives

After studying this chapter, you should be able to:

▲ Explain the personal liability coverage found in Section II of the homeowners policy.

▲ Describe the medical payments to others coverage found in Section II of the homeowners policy.

▲ Identify the major exclusions that apply to the Section II coverages in the homeowners policy.

▲ Identify several endorsements that can be added to a homeowners policy.

▲ Explain the important rules that consumers should follow when shopping for a homeowners policy.

▲ Access an Internet site and obtain a premium quote for a homeowners policy.

Internet Resources

■ The **Insurance Information Institute** provides timely information on homeowners insurance and other personal property insurance coverages. Numerous consumer brochures and articles on homeowners insurance and other property and liability coverages can be accessed directly online. Visit the site at:

http://www.iii.org/

■ The **Insurance News Network** provides news, premium quotes, and other consumer information on homeowners insurance. The site also provides news releases about events that affect the insurance industry. Visit the site at:

http://www.insure.com/

■ INSWEB provides premium quotes on homeowners, auto, and other insurance products. You can comparison shop with ease from your computer. Quotes are also available from an agent of your choice. In addition, the site includes a page for insurance professionals. Visit the site at:

http://www.insweb.com/

- **MoneyCentral** is designed primarily for investors, but also provides important consumer information on various insurance coverages. Click on "Insurance" for information about homeowners insurance and other insurance coverages. Visit the site at:

  http://moneycentral.msn.com/home.asp

- **Quicken Insurance** is considered to be one of the best consumer sites for obtaining timely information on homeowners, condominium, renters, and auto insurance. The site provides premium quotes for homeowners, auto, and life insurance, as well as other personal insurance lines. It offers agent referral or direct signup data from major insurance companies. Visit the site at:

  http://www.quickeninsurance.com

 ason, age 28, is a self-employed carpenter who lives in Tulsa, Oklahoma. He rented an apartment and carelessly started a fire when he was grilling hamburgers on the patio to his apartment. The apartment owner sued Jason for the property damage and was awarded damages of $90,000. Like most renters, Jason did not own a homeowners policy, which would have paid the loss. As a result, he experienced a serious financial setback and later declared bankruptcy.

Jason learned in a painful way the value of personal liability insurance. This chapter discusses the important provisions that appear in Section II of a homeowners policy. Section II provides personal liability insurance to the names insured and his or her family members and also covers the medical expenses of others who are injured by personal acts of the insured or by an animal owned by the insured.

In addition, the chapter discusses several endorsements that can be added to a homeowners policy to broaden the coverages. It concludes with a discussion of important rules to follow when you shop for a homeowners policy.

PERSONAL LIABILITY INSURANCE

Personal liability insurance protects the named insured and his or her family members against legal liability arising out of their personal acts. The insurer will provide a legal defense and pay out those sums that the insured is legally obligated to pay up to the policy limit.[1] With the major exceptions of legal liability arising out of the negligent operation of an automobile, and business and professional liability, most personal acts are covered.

The Homeowners 2000 Program by the Insurance Services Office (ISO) made several changes to the Section II coverages. The following section discusses the latest edition of the Section II coverages in the homeowners policy.

Insuring Agreements

The Section II liability coverages in the homeowners policy provide the following two coverages:

- Coverage E: Personal liability, $100,000 per occurrence
- Coverage F: Medical payments to others, $1000 per person

Higher limits are available for a small additional premium.

Coverage E: Personal Liability Personal liability *insurance protects the insured when a claim or suit for damages is brought because of bodily injury or property damage caused by the insured's negligence.*

165

Thus, if you are liable for damages, the insurer will pay up to the policy limits those sums that you are legally obligated to pay. Damages also include any prejudgment interest awarded against you.

The minimum amount of liability insurance is at least $100,000 for each occurrence. The insurance amount is a single limit that applies to both bodily injury and property damage liability on a per-occurrence basis. **Occurrence** *is defined as an accident, including continuous or repeated exposure to substantially the same general harmful conditions, which results in bodily injury or property damage during the policy period.* An occurrence can be a sudden accident, or it can be a gradual series of incidents that occur over time.

The insurer also agrees to provide a legal defense even if the suit is groundless, false, or fraudulent. The insurer has the right to investigate and settle the claim or suit either by defending you in a court of law or by settling out of court. As a practical matter, most personal liability suits are settled out of court. The insurer's obligation to defend you ends when the amount paid for damages equals the limit of liability. The insurer must defend you and cannot offer or tender its policy limits to be relieved of its duty to defend. Defense coverage continues until the policy limits are exhausted by payment of a judgment or settlement.

Personal liability coverage is broad. The following examples illustrate the types of losses covered:

- While burning leaves in the yard, you accidentally set fire to your neighbor's house.
- You are playing golf and accidentally hit another golfer in the head with a golf ball.
- You are riding a bicycle and carelessly run into and injure another student.
- A guest in your home trips on a torn carpet and sues you for bodily injury.
- You are shopping and carelessly break an expensive Chinese vase.

Personal liability insurance is based on legal liability. Before the insurer will pay any sums for damages, you must be legally liable. In contrast, medical payments to others, discussed next, is not based on negligence or legal liability.

Coverage F: Medical Payments to Others This coverage is a mini-accident policy that is part of a homeowners policy. **Medical payments to others** *pays the reasonable medical expenses of another person who is accidentally injured on an insured location, or by the activities of an insured, resident employee, or animal owned by or in the care of an insured.* This coverage can be illustrated by the following examples:

- A guest slips in your home and breaks an arm. Reasonable medical expenses are paid up to the policy limits.
- A neighbor's child falls off a swing in your backyard and is injured. The child's medical expenses are covered up to the policy limits.
- Your dog bites a neighbor. The neighbor's medical expenses are paid up to the policy limits.

The insurer will pay all necessary medical expenses incurred or medically ascertained within three years from the date of the accident. The medical expenses covered are the reasonable charges for medical and surgical procedures, X rays, dental care, ambulances, hospital stays, professional nursing, prosthetic devices, and funeral services.

Medical payments coverage does not apply to you or to regular residents of your household, other than a residence employee. For example, a swing set in your backyard may collapse, and your daughter and a neighbor's child are injured. Only the medical expenses of the neighbor's child are covered. An exception is a **residence employee** who is injured on the premises. For example, a baby-sitter may burn her hand while cooking lunch for the children. Her medical expenses would be covered under the policy.

With respect to the medical expenses of others, the policy states the situations under which the benefits are paid. Coverage F applies only to the following persons and situations:

- To a person on the insured location with the permission of an insured
- To a person off the insured location, if the bodily injury (a) arises out of a condition on the insured location or the ways immediately adjoining; (b) is caused by the activities of an insured; (c) is caused by a residence employee in the course of the residence employee's employment by an insured; or (d) is caused by an animal owned by or in the care of an insured

Medical payments to others covers the medical expenses of a person who is accidentally injured while on an insured location with the permission of an insured. Insured locations are defined in the policy and include the following:

- Residence premises shown in the declarations
- Any other residence acquired during the policy period, such as a summer home
- Rental of a garage or storage unit
- Nonowned premises where the insured is temporarily residing, such as a motel room
- Vacant land other than farmland
- Land owned or rented to an insured on which a residence is being built for an insured
- Cemetery plots or burial vaults
- Part of a premises occasionally rented to an insured for nonbusiness purposes, such as a hall rented for a wedding reception

Several important points are worth noting. *First, medical payments to others is not based on negligence or legal liability.* However, the insured is still protected if a lawsuit arises out of the injury. Thus, if your dog bites a child and $1000 of medical expenses are paid by your insurer, you are still insured under Coverage E if a lawsuit later results from the injury.

Second, medical payments to others covers injuries away from an insured location if the injury is caused by the activities of an insured, by a residence employee in the course of employment by an insured, or by an animal owned by or in the care of an insured. Thus, if you are playing recreational basketball and accidentally injure another player, the injured person's medical expenses would be paid by your policy up to the policy limit.

Finally, liability loss exposures arising out of the personal activities of an insured are covered anywhere in the world under Coverage E and not just at an insured location. The meaning of an "insured location" becomes significant in determining whether medical payments to others are payable under Coverage F, and also in defining excluded activities at an insured location.

SECTION II EXCLUSIONS

The Section II coverages contain numerous exclusions. The Homeowners 2000 program revised the definitions, exclusions, and related exceptions for motor vehicles, watercraft, and aircraft, and added a new exclusion for hovercraft liability (discussed later).

Motor Vehicle Liability Coverages E and F exclude liability arising out of motor vehicles if the involved vehicle is:

- Registered for use on public roads or property
- Not registered for use on public roads or property but such registration is required by law or government regulation
- Used in an organized race or speed contest
- Rented to others
- Used to carry persons or cargo for a charge
- Used for any business purpose, except for a motorized golf cart while on a golfing facility

Thus, liability arising out of cars, trucks, motorcycles, mopeds, and motorbikes is not covered. In addition, if you are towing a boat trailer, horse trailer, or rental trailer, coverage does not apply. Coverage can be obtained by purchasing an auto insurance policy.

Certain vehicles, however, are exceptions to the preceding exclusion, and therefore, coverage applies. The preceding exclusion of motor vehicles does not apply to the following:

- *The vehicle is in dead storage on a insured location.* For example, a car may be on blocks in the insured's garage. A liability claim arising out of dead storage of the car is covered if the car is not subject to motor vehicle registration.
- *The vehicle is used solely to service an insured's residence.* For example, if you injure someone with a riding lawn mower while cutting the lawn, coverage applies.
- *The vehicle is designed to assist the handicapped or is parked on an insured location.* For example, if a handicapped person injures someone while operating a motorized wheelchair, coverage applies.
- *The vehicle is designed for recreational use off public roads and is not owned by the insured, or is owned by the insured, and the occurrence takes place on an insured location.* For example, property damage caused by the insured while operating a rented snowmobile would be covered. Also,

an owned snowmobile used on an insured location would be covered.

- *A nonowned motorized golf cart used to play golf on a golf course is covered.* Thus, if you accidentally injure a golfer on a golf course, coverage applies.

    The Homeowners 2000 Program also includes coverage for a motorized golf cart owned by the insured that has a maximum speed limit of 25 miles per hour. Coverage applies to an owned golf cart if the occurrence takes place on a golfing facility when the cart is used (1) to play golf or for other recreational or leisure activity allowed by the facility, or (2) to travel to and from an area where motor vehicles or golf carts are parked or stored, or (3) to cross public roads at designated points to access the golfing facility. An owned golf cart is also covered on a private residential community, including its roads upon which a motorized golf cart can legally travel, which is subject to a property owner's association and contains an insured's residence.

Watercraft Liability The Section II coverages exclude watercraft liability if the involved watercraft is used in an organized race or speed contest (except sailing vessels or a predicted log cruise), rented to others, used to carry people or cargo for a fee, or used for any business purpose.

Certain watercraft are exceptions to the exclusion, and therefore, coverage applies. The watercraft exclusion does not apply to the following:

- The watercraft is stored.
- The watercraft is a sailing vessel less than 26 feet in length, or is 26 feet or more in length and is not owned by or rented to an insured.

In addition, if not a sailing vessel, the following watercraft are covered:

- Boats not owned by an insured, with an inboard or inboard-outdrive engine or motor of 50 horsepower or less
- Boats not owned or rented by an insured, with an inboard-outdrive engine or motor of more than 50 horsepower
- Boats with outboard engines or motors of 25 total horsepower or less
- Boats with outboard engines or motors of more than 25 horsepower, if the outboard engine or

motor is not owned by an insured
- Boats with outboard engines or motors of more than 25 total horsepower if the insured (a) acquires them before the policy period and declares them at the policy inception, or (b) reports to the insurer within 45 days after acquiring them

Aircraft Liability The Section II coverages exclude aircraft liability. An aircraft is any device used or designed to carry people or cargo in flight, such as an airplane, helicopter, glider, or balloon. However, the exclusion does not apply to model or hobby aircraft not used or designed to carry people or cargo.

Hovercraft Liability The Homeowners 2000 Program added a new exclusion for hovercraft liability. Hovercraft is defined as a self-propelled motorized ground effect vehicle and includes flarecraft and air cushion vehicles.

Expected or Intentional Injury The Section II coverages do not apply to bodily injury or property damage that is expected or intended by an insured. For example, if a softball player intentionally hits the umpire with a bat, it is clear that the player intended to injure the umpire. Thus, any claim or suit for damages would not be covered.

The exclusion does not apply to bodily injury that results from the use of reasonable force by an insured to protect persons or property. Thus, if Mark injures a mugger who is trying to rob him, any resulting suit for damages would be covered.

Business Activities Liability arising out of or in connection with a business activity engaged in by the insured is also excluded. For example, if you operate a beauty shop in your home and carelessly burn a customer with a hair dryer, a lawsuit by the customer is not covered. However, garage sales not conducted as a regular business are covered. Business activities, however, are clearly excluded.

Legal liability arising out of the rental of any part of the premises is also excluded. For example, if you own a twelveplex apartment house that is rented to students, liability claims arising out of ownership of the apartment building are not covered.

There are several exceptions to the preceding exclusion. First, if a house is occasionally rented and used only as a residence, coverage applies. For example, if a professor rents his or her home while on sabbatical leave, coverage will still apply.

Coverage also applies if part of the residence is rented to others. For example, assume that you live in a duplex and rent the other unit to a single family. Liability coverage still applies if the renting family does not take in more than two roomers or boarders.

Coverage also applies if part of the insured residence is rented and used as an office, school, studio, or private garage. For example, if a room above a garage is rented to an artist who uses the room as a studio, the insured still has coverage for claims arising out of the rental.

Finally, coverage also applies to minors under age 21 who are involved in a part-time or occasional self-employed business with no employees. For example, minors are covered while delivering newspapers, washing cars, cutting lawns, or baby-sitting.

Professional Services Legal liability arising out of professional services is excluded. Physicians and dentists are not covered for malpractice claims under the homeowners policy. Also, attorneys, accountants, nurses, architects, engineers, and other professionals are not covered for legal liability for rendering or failing to render professional services. The loss exposures involving professional activities are substantially different from those faced by the typical homeowner. For this reason, a professional liability policy is necessary to cover professional activities. Professional liability insurance is examined in greater detail in Chapter 14.

Uninsured Locations Liability arising out of the ownership or rental of a premises that is not an "insured location" is also excluded. The meaning of "insured location" has already been explained. Examples of uninsured locations would be farmland owned or rented by an insured, a principal or secondary residence owned by an insured other than the named insured or spouse, and land owned by the insured on which a fourplex is being built.

War Section II coverages exclude war, undeclared war, civil war, insurrection, rebellion, and other hostile military acts. The homeowners contracts also exclude liability arising out of the discharge of a nuclear weapon even if accidental.

Communicable Disease Exclusion Liability arising out of the transmission of a communicable disease by an insured is excluded under both personal liability insurance and medical payments to others. This exclusion is in response to the increased number of lawsuits by persons who claim they were infected with the AIDS or herpes virus as a result of sexual relations with an insured. The exclusion applies to all communicable diseases and is not limited only to sexually transmitted diseases.

Sexual Molestation, Corporal Punishment, or Physical or Mental Abuse The homeowners policy excludes bodily injury or property damage liability arising out of sexual molestation, corporal punishment, or physical or mental abuse. For example, if an insured is sued because of bodily injury to a neighbor's child allegedly caused by sexual molestation, the suit would not be covered.

Controlled Substance Exclusion Liability arising out of the use, sale, manufacture, delivery, transfer, or possession of a controlled substance is specifically excluded. Controlled substances include cocaine, LSD, marijuana, and all narcotic drugs. The exclusion does not apply to the legitimate use of prescription drugs by a person who is following the orders of a licensed physician.

Personal Liability Exclusions

Another set of exclusions applies only to personal liability (Coverage E).

Contractual Liability Contractual liability *means that you agree to assume the legal liability of another party by a written or oral contract.* The policy excludes the following contractual liability exposures:

■ *Liability of an insured for any loss assessment* charged against the insured as a member of any association, corporation, or community of property owners. However, an additional coverage (discussed later) provides $1000 of coverage for a loss assessment if certain conditions are met.

■ *Liability under any contract or agreement is excluded.* However, the exclusion does not apply to written contracts (a) that directly relate to the ownership, maintenance, or use of an insured location, or (b) where the liability of others is assumed by the insured prior to an occurrence. Thus, there would be coverage for liability assumed under a written lease, an equipment rental agreement if the equipment is used to maintain the residence premises, an easement, and other written contracts where legal liability of a non-business nature is assumed by an insured prior to an occurrence.

Property Owned by the Insured *Property damage to property owned by the insured is also excluded.* Thus, if a teenage son accidentally breaks some furniture, the parents' claim for damages against their son would not be covered.

Property in the Care of the Insured *Damage to property rented to, occupied or used by, or in the care of the insured is not covered.* For example, if you rent a boat and damage it, personal liability insurance does not apply.

The exclusion does not apply to property damage caused by fire, smoke, or explosion. For example, if you rent an apartment and carelessly start a fire, you can be held liable for the damage. In such a case, the homeowners policy would cover the property damage to the apartment up to the policy limit.

Workers Compensation *There is no coverage for bodily injury to any person who is eligible to receive benefits provided by the named insured under a workers compensation, nonoccupational disability, or occupational disease law.* This is true if the workers compensation benefits are either mandatory or voluntary. In some states, domestic workers must be covered for workers compensation benefits by their employers; in other states, the coverage is voluntary.

Nuclear Energy *The homeowners policy excludes liability arising out of nuclear energy.* If any insured is involved in a nuclear incident, any resulting liability is not covered by the homeowners policy.

Bodily Injury to an Insured *There is no coverage for bodily injury to the named insured or to any resident of the household who is a relative or under age 21 and in the care of an insured.* For example, if one spouse accidentally trips and injures the other spouse, the injured spouse cannot collect damages.

Medical Payments Exclusions

Another set of exclusions under Section II applies only to medical payments to others (Coverage F).

Injury to a Resident Employee Off an Insured Location *If an injury to a resident employee occurs off an insured location and does not arise out of or in the course of employment by an insured, medical payments coverage does not apply.* For example, if Tanya is employed by the insured as a baby-sitter and is injured on her way home, her medical expenses are not covered.

Workers Compensation This exclusion is similar to the workers compensation exclusion discussed earlier under personal liability insurance. *Medical payments coverage does not apply to any person who is eligible to receive benefits provided by the named insured under a workers compensation, nonoccupational disability, or occupational disease law.* The injured employee's medical expenses should be covered by workers compensation insurance.

Nuclear Energy *Medical payments coverage does not cover any person for bodily injury that results from nuclear reaction, radiation, or radioactive contamination.*

Persons Regularly Residing on the Insured Location *Medical payments coverage does not cover injury to any person (other than a residence employee of an insured) who regularly resides on any part of the insured location.* Thus, a tenant injured in a household accident cannot receive payment for medical expenses. The intent here is to minimize collusion among household members.

SECTION II ADDITIONAL COVERAGES

A homeowners policy provides several additional coverages, including coverage for claim expenses, first-aid expenses, damage to the property of others, and loss-assessment charges.

Claim Expenses

Claim expenses are paid as an additional coverage. The insurer pays the court costs, attorney fees, and other legal expenses incurred in providing a legal defense. The claim expenses are paid in addition to the policy limits for liability damages.

The insurer also pays the premiums on bonds required in a suit defended by the insurer. For example, a judgment may be appealed, and if an appeal bond is required, the insurer pays the premium.

Reasonable expenses incurred by the insured at the insurer's request to assist in the investigation and defense of a claim or suit are also paid. This obligation includes payment for the actual loss of earnings up to $250 per day. Finally, interest on a judgment that accrues after the judgment is awarded, but before payment is made, is also paid by the insurer.

First-Aid Expenses

The insurer pays any **first-aid expenses** incurred by the insured for bodily injury covered under the policy. For example, a guest may slip in your home and break a leg. If you call an ambulance to take the injured person to the hospital and are later billed for $400 by the ambulance company, this amount would be paid as a first-aid expense.

Damage to Property of Others

Damage to property of others *pays up to $1000 per occurrence for property damage caused by an insured.* The damaged property is valued on the basis of replacement cost. This coverage can be illustrated by the following examples:

- A son, age 10, accidentally breaks a neighbor's window while playing softball.
- At a party, you carelessly burn a hole in the owner's carpet with your cigarette.

- You borrow your neighbor's lawn mower and accidentally damage the blade by striking a rock.

Legal liability does not apply to this coverage. Payment is made even though there is no legal obligation to do so. The purpose of this coverage is to preserve personal friendships and keep peace in the neighborhood. Also, in many states, the parents are held responsible for the property damage caused by a young child. If this coverage were not provided, the person whose property is damaged would have to file a claim for damages against the insured who caused the damage. A maximum of $1000 is paid under this coverage. Amounts in excess of this limit are paid only by proving negligence and legal liability by the person who caused the damage.

Damage to property of others also contains a unique set of exclusions. The major exclusions are summarized as follows:

- *Property Covered Under Section I.* Property damage is excluded to the extent of any amount recoverable under Section I of the policy.
- *Intentional Property Damage by an Insured, Age 13 or Older.* If the property damage is intentionally caused by an insured, age 13 or older, coverage does not apply. This exclusion is extremely relevant to teenage vandalism, which is a serious national problem. Thus, if a teenager damages a plate-glass window with a sling shot, deliberately knocks over a mailbox, or maliciously damages a tree, the parents' policy will not cover the property damage.
- *Property Owned by an Insured.* Property damage to property owned by an insured is also excluded. For example, if a son damages some power tools owned by his parents, the damage would not be covered. However, coverage does apply if the property is rented. Thus, if you rent a portable television set and accidentally drop it, the damage is covered.
- *Property Owned by or Rented to a Tenant.* Coverage does not apply to property owned by or rented to a tenant of an insured or to a resident in the named insured's household.
- *Business Liability.* Property damage arising out of a business engaged in by an insured is excluded. Thus, if you operate a lawn-maintenance business and accidentally cut down a shrub while

mowing a customer's lawn, the damage is not covered.

- *Act or Omission in Connection with the Premises.* Property damage caused by an act or omission in connection with a premises owned, rented, or controlled by the insured, other than an insured location, is not covered. For example, without an endorsement, farmland owned by the insured is not covered under the homeowners policy. Thus, if the insured should accidentally damage the tractor of the tenant who is farming the land, coverage does not apply.

- *Motor Vehicles, Aircraft, Watercraft, or Hovercraft.* Property damage that results from the ownership, maintenance, or use of a motor vehicle, aircraft, watercraft, or hovercraft is not covered. For example, if you run over a neighbor's ten-speed bicycle with your automobile, the loss is not covered.

Loss Assessment

The homeowners policy provides coverage of $1000 for certain loss assessments. Higher limits are available by endorsement. For example, assume that you belong to a homeowners association that rents a hall for a monthly meeting. Someone is injured at one of the meetings and is awarded a judgment of $110,000. If the association's liability policy has policy limits of only $100,000, the $10,000 balance will be split among the association members and each member would be assessed a portion of the $10,000 balance. The homeowners policy would pay your loss-assessment charge up to $1000.

ENDORSEMENTS TO A HOMEOWNERS POLICY

Some property owners have special needs or desire broader coverage than that provided by a standard homeowners policy. Numerous endorsements can be added to a homeowners policy to meet individual needs, including the following:

- Inflation guard endorsement
- Earthquake endorsement
- Personal property replacement cost endorsement
- Scheduled personal property endorsement

- Personal injury
- Watercraft and recreational vehicles
- Home business insurance coverage

Inflation Guard Endorsement

Some homeowners are underinsured because of inflation, which increases the replacement cost of a home. If a loss occurs and you do not carry insurance at least equal to 80 percent of the replacement cost of the dwelling, you will be penalized because the full replacement cost will not be paid.

To deal with inflation, you should add an **inflation guard endorsement** to your homeowners policy if it is not included by your insurer. The inflation guard endorsement is designed for use with the ISO homeowner forms and provides for an annual pro rata increase in the limits of liability under Coverages A, B, C, and D. The percentage increase is selected by the insured, such as 4 percent or 6 percent. For example, if the policyowner selects a 6 percent inflation guard endorsement, the various limits are increased by 6 percent annually. This specified annual percentage increase is prorated throughout the policy year. Thus, a house originally insured for $100,000 would be covered for $103,000 at the end of six months.

Earthquake Endorsement

An **earthquake endorsement** can be added that covers earthquakes, landslides, volcanic eruption, and earth movement. A single earthquake is defined as all earthquake shocks that occur within a 72-hour period. A deductible must be satisfied. The base deductible is 5 percent of the limit that applies *either* to the dwelling (Coverage A) or to personal property (Coverage C), whichever is greater. There is a minimum deductible of $250. The deductible can be increased with a reduction in premiums. There is no other deductible that applies to an earthquake loss. The deductible does not apply to Coverage D (loss of use) and to additional coverages.

Although earthquakes can cause catastrophic losses, a high percentage of property owners in earthquake zones do not have earthquake insurance. Insurers in California selling homeowners insurance must offer earthquake insurance on new policies; however, a majority of homeowners are not insured against earthquakes. The major reasons for their reluctance are cost, high deductibles, a mistaken belief that earthquakes will not occur, and the belief that the federal government will provide disaster relief.

After the earthquake in Northridge, California in 1994, property insurers were reluctant to offer earthquake insurance because of the fear of bankruptcy. Over a 25-year period prior to the Northridge earthquake, California insurers collected only $3.4 billion in earthquake premiums, but they paid out more than three times that amount on Northridge claims alone ($12.5 billion).

As a result of the crisis in the homeowners insurance market, California enacted legislation in 1995 that allows insurers to offer a new earthquake policy with a maximum deductible of 15 percent.[2] A privately funded, state-run earthquake pool was also created to deal with the problem.

Personal Property Replacement Cost Loss Settlement

An unendorsed homeowner policy pays losses to personal property on the basis of actual cash value. However, a **personal property replacement cost loss settlement endorsement** can be added to the policy. *Covered losses are settled at replacement cost with no deduction for depreciation.* The endorsement applies to personal property, awnings, carpets, domestic appliances, and outdoor equipment. Claims are paid on the basis of replacement cost with no deduction for depreciation.

The replacement cost endorsement for personal property has several important limitations. The amount paid is limited to the *smallest* of the following amounts:

- Replacement cost at the time of loss
- Full repair cost
- Coverage C amount, if applicable
- Any special dollar limits in the policy (such as limits on jewelry, furs, and silverware)
- For loss to any item, the limit of liability that applies to the item

If the cost to repair or replace exceeds $500, the property must actually be repaired or replaced to re-

ceive replacement cost. Otherwise, only the cash value is paid.

The replacement cost endorsement excludes certain types of property, such as antiques, fine arts, and similar property; collector's items and souvenirs; property that is not in good or workable condition; and obsolete property stored or not used.

As a general rule, you should consider adding the replacement cost endorsement for personal property to your homeowners policy. Because of depreciation, the amount paid for a loss based on actual cash value policy is substantially less than that payable based on replacement cost. Most insureds typically are unaware of the big gap between replacement cost and actual cash value (see Insight 9.1).

Scheduled Personal Property Endorsement

If you have valuable jewelry, furs, silverware, cameras, musical instruments, fine arts, antiques, or stamp or coin collections, the **scheduled personal property endorsement** can be added to the policy to provide broader coverage. All direct physical losses to the scheduled items are covered except certain losses specifically excluded.

Personal Injury

The homeowners policy only covers legal liability arising out of bodily injury or property damage to someone else. Personal injury coverage, which should not be confused with bodily injury, can be added to the homeowners policy as an endorsement.

Personal injury means legal liability arising out of the following:

- False arrest, detention, or imprisonment
- Malicious prosection
- Wrongful eviction, wrongful entry, or invasion of the right of private occupancy of a room, dwelling, or premises
- Oral or written publication of material that slanders a person or organization, or an organization's products or services
- Oral or written publication of material that violates a person's right to privacy

For example, if you have a person arrested who is later found innocent, or if you make false state-

Insight 9.1

You Should Consider the Big Gap Between Replacement Cost and Actual Cash Value

If you own personal property, you should consider the big gap between replacement cost and actual cash value. You stand to pay a large amount out of pocket because of depreciation if the loss payment is based on actual cash value. The following table, based on the depreciation schedule of a large property and liability insurer, shows that the insured would receive $7790 (less the deductible) based on *replacement cost* compared with only $3967 based on *actual cash value*. Actual cash value is replacement cost less depreciation.

Item	Age	Replacement Cost	Depreciation	Actual Cash Value
Television set	5 years	$ 900	$ 450	$ 450
Sofa	4 years	1500	600	900
Draperies	2 years	2000	400	1600
Five women's dresses	4 years	500	400	100
Three men's shoes	2 years	200	133	67
Three end tables	15 years	1200	900	300
Refrigerator	10 years	800	560	240
Area rug	New	200	0	200
Cosmetics	6 months	200	180	20
Kitchen dishes	4 years	250	200	50
Thirty cans of food	New	40	0	40
Totals		**$7790**	**$3823**	**$3967**

NOTE: The above hypothetical losses show the effect of depreciation, which is based on age and condition of the property; the older the item, the greater the amount of depreciation.

ments that damage a person's reputation, you may be liable for damages. These losses are not covered under the homeowners policy but would be covered by the personal injury endorsement.

Watercraft and Recreational Vehicles

As noted earlier, boats and recreational vehicles such as snowmobiles have specific limitations and exclusions under Section II of the homeowners policy. Separate endorsements can be added to provide additional liability coverages on boats and recreational vehicles.

- *Watercraft.* The **watercraft endorsement** covers watercraft otherwise excluded under the homeowners policy. The endorsement provides liability and medical payments coverage on any inboard or inboard-outdrive powered watercraft; sailing vessels 26 feet or more in length; and watercraft powered by one or more outboard motors exceeding 25 total horsepower.
- *Snowmobiles.* Snowmobiles owned by an insured are covered only while they are on an insured location. The **snowmobile endorsement** provides personal liability coverage and medical payments to owned snowmobiles away from an insured location. For example, if your snowmobile strikes

and injures another person on a snowmobile trail in a public park, the loss would be covered.

Home Business Insurance Coverage

A growing number of business owners operate a business out of their homes. A standard homeowners policy provides only limited coverage on business property, and legal liability arising out of a business operation is excluded. A **home business insurance coverage** endorsement can be added that covers both business property and legal liability arising out of a home-based business. This type of endorsement increases the coverage on business property on the residence premises from $2500 to the Coverage C limit on personal property. Coverage on business property away from the premises is increased from $500 to $5000. The endorsement also provides coverage for accounts receivable, valuable papers and records, and the loss of business income and extra expenses when loss from an insured peril causes the business to be suspended.

The home business insurance endorsement covers business liability loss exposures that are normally found in a commercial package policy for a business firm. Personal liability coverage includes (1) advertising injury, (2) personal injury, and (3) products and completed operations exposures associated with the home business. These coverages are discussed in more detail in Chapter 14.

Some insurers now offer an in-home business policy that is specifically designed for a home-based business (see Insight 9.2).

SHOPPING FOR A HOMEOWNERS POLICY

As an informed consumer, you should understand how the cost of a homeowners policy is determined. In addition, certain suggestions should be followed to make you a better-informed insurance consumer.

Cost of Homeowners Insurance

Homeowners insurance premiums are based on a number of factors, which include the following:

- Construction
- Location
- Fire-protection class
- Construction costs
- Age of home
- Type of policy
- Deductible amount
- Insurer

First, *construction* of the home is extremely important in determining the rate paid. The more fire-resistant the home is, the lower the rate. Thus wooden homes cost more to insure than brick homes. However, earthquake insurance costs are substantially less for wooden homes.

Second, *location* of the home is another important rating factor. For rating purposes, the loss experience of each territory is determined. Insureds who reside in territories with high losses from fires, crime, or natural disasters must pay higher rates than insureds who reside in low-loss territories.

Third, the *fire-protection class* affects the rates charged. The Insurance Services Office rates the quality of public fire departments from one to ten. The lower the number, the better the fire department and the lower the rate. Accessibility of the home to the fire department and water supply and hydrants are also important. Homes in rural areas generally have higher rates than homes in large cities.

In addition, *construction costs* have a significant effect on rates. The costs of labor and materials vary widely in the United States. The higher the cost of repairing or rebuilding your home, the higher your premium is likely to be.

The *age of the home* also affects the rates charged. Insurers charge less to insure newer homes than older ones, which are more susceptible to damage from fire and storms. Also, old wiring and outdated building code standards can make older homes more susceptible to loss.

The preceding rating factors deal with the home itself and generally are outside of the insured's control. However, the remaining three factors—type of policy, deductible amount, and insurer—are important cost factors within the insured's control.

The *type of policy* is extremely important in determining the total premium. The Homeowners 3 policy (special form) is more expensive than the

Insight 9.2

Is Your Home Business Covered Under a Homeowners Policy?

Are you one of the millions of home-based business owners who thinks your homeowners insurance has you covered? Think again. Most homeowners policies usually cover only up to $2500 for loss of property in your home office and a piddling $500 if the loss occurs away from home. There is no liability coverage if a client falls down your steps and sues you. And don't expect compensation for lost income if a fire shuts you down.

In most states, depending on the type and size of your business, you can buy an endorsement to your homeowners policy. But "you are not buying much insurance," says Nancy James, an independent agent and technology-risk specialist in Concord, Massachusetts. An endorsement normally gives you limited business-liability protection and higher property-loss limits.

You might be better off with a so-called in-home business policy, which typically includes liability coverage for injury at home or away from your office, on-and off-premises property loss, and lost-income recovery. These policies, which are not available in all states, typically merge business coverage limits with the limits on an underlying homeowners policy. For example, with the Business at Home Endorsement—available in about 20 states from Fireman's Fund—if your property-liability limit is $300,000, your home and

business share that amount in the event of a loss. Other companies that offer in-home business policies in some states include CNA and Kemper.

The Hartford sells a policy to AARP members and through independent agents in 46 states and the District of Columbia for an average annual premium for the business portion of about $200.

If you live in a state where in-home policies are not available, look for a business-owners policy (BOP). BOPs are usually as broad as regular commercial policies but cost less. For example, the annual premium for a basic BOP from RLI insurance runs from $150 to $280, depending on where you live and the type of business you run. Many companies offer BOPs, including CNA, Fireman's Fund, the Hartford, Kemper, and State Farm.

"Certain kinds of insurance might be overkill for some home-based business," says David Hanania, president of the Home Business Institute, in White Plains, New York. For help assessing your business's risks and finding the right policy, contact an independent insurance agent.

Homeowners 2 policy (broad form) because it provides broader coverage.

The *deductible amount* has an important effect on cost. The higher the deductible, the lower the premium. A flat $250 deductible now applies to all covered losses. The deductible can be increased with a reduction in premiums. It does not apply to a fire department service charge, coverage for credit or ATM cards, scheduled property that is specifically insured, and the personal liability coverages under Section II.

Finally, the *choice of the homeowner's insurer* has significant consequences for the total premium. There is considerable price variation among insurers, depending on loss experience, underwriting standards, and geographical area.

Suggestions for Buying a Homeowners Policy

As a careful insurance consumer, you should remember certain suggestions when purchasing a homeowners policy (see Exhibit 9.1).

Carry Adequate Insurance The first suggestion is to carry adequate amounts of property insurance on both your home and personal property. This consideration is particularly important if a room is added or home improvements are made because the value of the home may be substantially increased. The home must be insured for at least 80 percent of its replacement cost to avoid a penalty if a loss occurs. *However, you should seriously consider insuring*

EXHIBIT 9.1
Tips for Buying a Homeowners Policy

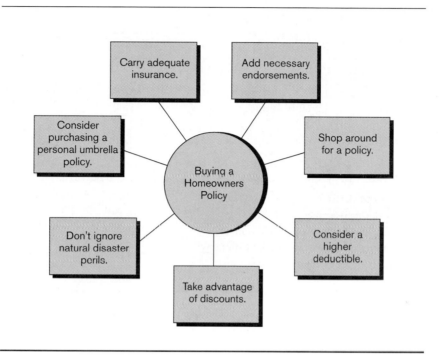

your home for 100 percent of replacement cost. Few homeowners can afford an additional 20 percent payment out of pocket if a total loss occurs. When you add the guaranteed replacement cost endorsement to the policy, full replacement cost is paid even if the actual cost exceeds the policy limit.

Add Necessary Endorsements Certain endorsements may be necessary depending on your needs, local property conditions, or high values for certain types of personal property. To deal with inflation, you should add an *inflation guard endorsement* to your homeowners policy if your insurer does not include it. An *earthquake endorsement* is desirable if you live in an earthquake zone. The *personal property replacement cost endorsement* is also desirable because you are indemnified on the basis of replacement cost with no deduction for depreciation; the replacement cost endorsement provides for a more adequate loss payment if your personal property is damaged or stolen. In addition, if you own valuable

property, such as jewelry, furs, fine art, or a valuable coin or stamp collection, you should add the *scheduled personal property endorsement* to your policy. Each item is listed and specifically insured for a certain amount.

Shop Around for a Homeowners Policy Another important suggestion is to shop around for a homeowners policy. Because considerable price variation occurs among insurers, you can reduce your homeowners premium by shopping around. Consequently, it pays to get a premium quote from several insurers before you buy a homeowners policy. Several Internet sites provide premium quotes (see Internet Resources). Some states also publish shoppers' guides to assist consumers who purchase homeowners policies. These guides indicate the wide variation in premiums charged by insurers. For example, Exhibit 9.2 shows the five lowest- and five highest-cost policies in Phoenix, Arizona as a result of a survey of 81 insurers by the Arizona Depart-

EXHIBIT 9.2
Annual Premiums for HO-3 in Phoenix, Arizona, 1999

Five lowest-cost policies

Rank	Name of Insurer	Masonry	Frame
1	Electric Insurance Company	$369.00	$369.00
2	United Services Auto Association	388.13	431.25
3	Pharmacists Mutual Insurance Company	395.00	483.00
4	Sentry Insurance	402.00	414.00
5	Armed Forces Insurance Exchange	408.00	447.00

Five highest-cost policies

Rank	Name of Insurer	Masonry	Frame
77	Ohio Casualty Insurance Company	$945	$945
78	Southern Insurance Company	1049	1049
79	American Spirit Insurance Company	1106	1106
80	American Security Insurance Company	1340	1400
81	American Bankers Insurance Company of Florida	1583	1583

Coverages: Dwelling Coverage: $150,000; Other Structures Coverage: $15,000; Contents Coverage: $112,500; Additional Living Expense Coverage: $15,000; Personal Liability Coverage: $100,000; Medical Payments Coverage: $1,000; $250 Flat Deductible.

Characteristics: A two-story, single-family dwelling containing single-cylinder dead-bolt locks, one fire extinguisher, and two smoke detectors. Above-average condition, masonry or frame (composition roof), built in October 1998.

Source: Arizona Department of Insurance, *1999 Homeowner Premium Comparison Survey* (July 1999).

ment of Insurance. *The cost difference between the lowest- and highest-cost policy is about 329 percent.* Clearly, it pays to shop around.

Consider a Higher Deductible Another suggestion for reducing premiums is to purchase a policy with a higher deductible. The standard homeowners deductible is $250. *A higher deductible can substantially reduce your premiums.* You can usually get a discount of 10 percent with a $500 deductible and a 20 to 30 percent discount with a $1000 deductible. For example, Patrick has a $1000 deductible in his homeowners policy instead of the standard $250, which saves him $180 annually. In other words, Patrick saves $180 each year but loses only $750 in coverage. That additional $750 is very expensive coverage.

Take Advantage of Discounts When you shop for a homeowners policy, you should inquire whether you are eligible for any discounts or credits, which can further reduce your premiums. Insurers offer a wide variety of discounts based on numerous factors, including age of the home, fire and smoke alarms, sprinkler system, deadbolt locks, and fire extinguishers.

The Appendix to this chapter provides additional suggestions for reducing the cost of a homeowners policy.

Don't Ignore Natural Disaster Perils The homeowners policy covers hurricanes, tornadoes, windstorms, and fire losses. However, earthquakes and floods are specifically excluded. Although federal flood insurance is available, and an earthquake endorsement can be added to the homeowners policy, most property owners are not insured against these two perils. If you reside in a flood or earthquake zone, you should seriously consider covering such perils in your personal risk management program.

Consider Purchasing a Personal Umbrella Policy A basic homeowners policy provides only $100,000 of personal liability insurance, which is insufficient in the event of a catastrophic liability loss. A **personal umbrella policy** provides an additional $1 million to $10 million of liability insurance after the underlying coverage is exhausted. It also covers liability arising out of personal injury, including coverage for libel, slander, and defamation of character. The homeowners policy does not cover personal injury without an endorsement. Finally, in addition to coverage on your home and personal activities, the personal umbrella policy provides excess liability insurance on your cars, boats, and recreational vehicles. The personal umbrella policy is explained in greater detail in Chapter 12.

Finally, most homeowners think about their policies only when they are filing a claim, refinancing their mortgage, or buying a new home. Ideally, you should periodically review your homeowners policy to determine whether the present coverages are adequate. When you review the policy, don't overlook the details (see Insight 9.3 on pp. 180–181).

SUMMARY

- Section II of the homeowners policy protects the named insured, resident relatives, and other persons for legal liability arising out of their personal acts.

- Insured locations include the residence premises described in the declarations, other residences acquired during the policy period, a residence where the insured is temporarily residing, vacant land other than farmland, cemetery or burial plots, land on which a residence is being built, and occasional rental of a premise for other than business purposes.

- Personal liability insurance (Coverage E) protects the insured against a claim or suit for damages because of bodily injury or property damage caused by the insured's negligence. The company will defend the insured and pay out those sums that the insured is legally obligated to pay up to the policy limits.

- Medical payments to others (Coverage F) pays the reasonable medical expenses of another person who may be accidentally injured on the premises, or by the activities of an insured, resident employee, or animal owned by or in the care of an insured. It is not necessary to prove negligence and establish legal liability before the medical expenses are paid. The coverage does not apply to injuries of the named insured and regular residents of the household, other than residence employees.

- Section II also provides four additional coverages: (1) claim expenses, (2) first-aid expenses, (3) damage to property of others, and (4) coverage for a loss assessment charge.

- Numerous endorsements can be added to a homeowners policy to meet individual needs, including the following:

  Inflation-guard endorsement

  Earthquake endorsement

  Personal property replacement cost loss settlement endorsement

  Scheduled personal property endorsement

  Personal injury

  Watercraft and recreational vehicles

  Home business insurance coverage endorsement

- The cost of a homeowners policy depends on numerous factors. These factors include construction, location, fire-protection class, construction costs, age of the home, type of policy, deductible amount, and insurer.

- Certain suggestions should be followed when shopping for a homeowners policy:

  Carry adequate insurance.

  Add necessary endorsements.

  Shop around for a homeowners policy.

  Consider a higher deductible.

  Take advantage of discounts.

  Don't ignore natural disaster perils.

  Consider purchasing a personal umbrella policy.

Insight 9.3

Homeowners Insurance: Don't Overlook the Details

If you have thought about your homeowners insurance in the past few months, it is probably because you are refinancing your mortgage, buying a new home, or filing a claim.

But unless you're in the last category, you probably didn't pay too much attention to the details. And that could be a mistake.

Just ask Pamela Rogers-Amy or Sara Harrington. Both had big losses from fires. Both were sure they would be fully covered by their insurance. Both now say they will never shop for homeowners insurance in the same way again.

"People don't know what they've bought," says Ms. Harrington, whose Lexington, Massachusetts, house was struck by lightning in 1995 and reduced to a shell by the resulting fire. "It is a cliché to say you have to read the fine print, but you do."

Homeowners insurance policies are complex documents full of legalese and exclusions, which often can conceal big gaps in coverage. Because the policies can be so daunting, many people opt simply to shop for the best price. Too often, homeowners don't pay enough attention to coverage and service.

True, price is an important element. But the difference in cost between "bare-bones coverage and a policy that will cover everything is not usually large," says Judith W. Lau, a Wilmington, Delaware, financial adviser.

Each insurer offers its own mix of coverage and pricing, depending on the market it is targeting, and each has its own personality when it comes to claims.

"Some companies seem to try to help you. Other companies play hardball," says Robert Hunter, director of insurance for the Consumer Federation of America in Washington.

Sara Harrington and her husband, for example, say they spent months haggling with their insurer about what dollar figure to put on their loss. In the end, the settlement left them exhausted, frustrated, and $40,000 to $50,000 short of the cost of rebuilding their one-year-old house.

The first step is figuring out the amount of insurance you need. This is typically done by using insurance-company estimates based on square-footage, building material, and other criteria. The value of your land isn't included.

Many people protect themselves on this critical issue by buying a policy with "guaranteed replacement cost." Under this provision, an insurer agrees to pay the entire cost of replacing a home even if that exceeds the insured amount of the policy.

Some insurers, however, are backing away from guaranteed replacement, saying it has become too expensive. State Farm Fire & Casualty Co., Bloomington, Illinois, for example, is phasing out its program, replacing it with a maximum payout of 120 percent of the policy amount. "That means homeowners have to pay more attention when reviewing their replacement-cost estimates," says Judith Mintel, associate general counsel for State Farm.

Relying solely on insurers' guidelines for replacement value can leave you underinsured. Talking to a local contractor can probably give you a better idea what it would cost to rebuild, but even then you need to factor in special features like fancy moldings or custom hardwood floors.

Still, having a high enough replacement value, or even a guaranteed replacement policy, won't protect you if you run afoul of policy exclusions.

Pamela Rogers-Amy of White Lake, Michigan, thought she was completely covered when she and her husband bought an insurance policy that provided guaranteed replacement for their 1950s house. But they didn't buy something called an "ordinance-and-law" rider, which Ms. Rogers-Amy says their agent said they didn't need.

"I was told whatever it costs to rebuild your home, we will pay for it," she says.

But when the house was severely damaged by a fire in 1994, the insurance didn't cover building-code upgrades that White Lake required before the couple could move back into their home. *Without ordinance-and-law coverage, the insurer would pay only to rebuild what was there.* It made no difference, she says, that the original structure could no longer be legally built in White Lake.

With the insurance company agreeing to pay $93,000, Ms. Rogers-Amy and her husband were $125,000 short of what their contractor said it would cost to rebuild, because their home failed to meet code requirements in everything from the wiring and plumbing to the foundation and the roof structure. The couple is now suing their insurer.

If ordinance-and-law seems an esoteric detail, consider all the people hit by Hurricane Andrew who found their insurance coverage wouldn't pay to raise their homes out of the flood plain, as now required by law. "The only thing we promise is to put you back the way you were before the loss occurred," explains State Farm's Ms. Mintel.

Who needs ordinance-and-law coverage? Insurance experts say people with new houses probably don't need to worry. But Ms. Rogers-Amy says everyone should buy this relatively inexpensive coverage, making sure the rider is for 100 percent of the policy value, paid at replacement cost and covering both the damaged and undamaged portions of a house.

Searching out such details about your homeowners policy can take work. Each insurer can handle an issue differently and policies are being revised constantly. That means it may take repeated phone calls to get information from your insurer.

For example, some companies don't sell ordinance-and-law coverage at all. High-end insurers may automatically include 100 percent coverage in the policy. And others limit the amount you can buy.

Moreover, ordinance-and-law isn't the only exclusion people need be wary of. Many policies exclude damage from backup of sewers and drains.

Philip L. Ladd, president of Dwight Rudd & Company, an independent insurance broker in Boston, cites the case of a homeowner who found he wasn't covered when a guest at an at-home business dinner fell, suffered a cut lip, and sued. He hadn't purchased a $20-a-year rider for incidental business coverage, which was excluded in his policy.

Once you've figured out how much coverage you need, the bill may look daunting. *If so, consider cutting the premium cost by raising your deductible.* "Self-insure the smaller losses to make sure you have the coverage you need," says Mr. Ladd, noting people should consider deductibles of $1000, $2500 or higher if the savings are significant. "Most people can afford to cover the loss of a bicycle."

And don't turn down coverage that adds to your bill just because it seems unlikely. Noting that Boston is in an earthquake zone, Mr. Ladd says he now recommends *earthquake insurance* to all his clients and buys it for his own house. "The purpose of insurance is to cover a disaster," he says, adding that his peace of mind is well worth the extra $100 he pays each year.

Flood insurance is another type of coverage that may be worth considering, although it isn't something you can get as part of your homeowner's policy. This insurance is available only through the national flood-insurance program, although your homeowners insurance company can write a policy through the federal program, explains Consumer Federation of America's Mr. Hunter.

SOURCE: Adapted from Lynn Asinof, "Homeowner's Insurance: Don't Overlook the Details," *The Wall Street Journal*, February 13, 1998, pp. C1, C11.

KEY CONCEPTS AND TERMS

Claim expenses
Contractual liability
Damage to property of
  others
Earthquake endorsement
First-aid expenses
Home business insurance
  coverage
Inflation guard
  endorsement
Medical payments to others

Occurrence
Personal injury
Personal liability
Personal property
  replacement cost loss
  settlement endorsement
Personal umbrella policy
Scheduled personal
  property endorsement
Snowmobile endorsement
Watercraft endorsement

REVIEW QUESTIONS

1. Explain the meaning of an occurrence under Section II of the homeowners policy.

2. Does the homeowners policy provide personal liability coverage only at the residence described in the declarations? Explain.

3. Describe the coverage for personal liability (Coverage E) in Section II of the homeowners policy.

4. Describe the coverage for medical payments to others (Coverage F) in Section II of the homeowners policy.

5. Who are the persons covered for medical payments to others (Coverage F) in the homeowners policy?

6. List the exclusions that apply to the Section II coverages in the homeowners policy.

7. In addition to coverage for personal liability (Coverage E) and medical payments to others (Coverage F), several additional coverages are provided in Section II of the homeowners policy. Identify the additional coverages that are found in Section II.

8. Describe several endorsements that can be added to a homeowners policy.

9. Identify the major factors that determine the cost of a homeowners policy.

10. Explain briefly the suggestions that consumers should follow when shopping for a homeowners policy.

APPLICATION QUESTIONS

1. Indicate whether the following losses are covered under Section II in the homeowners policy. Assume there are no special endorsements. Give reasons for your answers.
   a. The insured's dog bites a neighbor's child and also chews up the neighbor's coat.
   b. The insured accidentally injures another player while playing softball.
   c. A guest slips on a waxed kitchen floor and breaks an arm.
   d. A neighbor's child falls off a swing in the insured's yard and breaks an arm.
   e. The insured accidentally falls on an icy sidewalk and breaks a leg.
   f. While driving to the supermarket, the insured injures another motorist with the automobile.
   g. A ward of the court, age 10, in the care of the insured, deliberately breaks a neighbor's window.
   h. The insured paints houses for a living. A can of paint accidentally falls on a customer's roof and discolors it.
   i. The insured falls asleep while smoking a cigarette in a rented hotel room, and the room is badly damaged by the fire.
   j. The insured borrows a camera, and it is stolen from a motel room while the insured is on vacation.

2. Joseph is the named insured under a Homeowners 3 policy (special form) with a liability limit of $100,000 per occurrence and a $1000 limit for medical payments to others. For each of the following situations, explain whether the loss is covered under Section II of Joseph's homeowners policy.
   a. Joseph is a self-employed accountant who works in his home. One of Joseph's clients sues him for negligence in the preparation of a financial statement and recovers a $3000 judgment against him.
   b. A maid who works for Joseph's wife falls from a ladder in the home and is injured. The maid incurs medical expenses of $1000. The maid sues Joseph for $10,000 alleging that his wife is negligent. The employer does not have workers compensation insurance.
   c. Joseph's 25-year-old son, who recently married and now lives in his own apartment, negligently kills another hunter in a hunting accident. The son is sued for $1 million in a wrongful-death accident.

3. Martha rents an apartment and is the named insured under a Homeowners 4 policy (contents broad form) with a liability limit of $100,000 per occurrence and $1000 medical payments. For each of the following sit-

Case Application

Lucia and her husband, Geraldo, recently purchased a new home for $250,000. The home is insured under an HO-3 policy for $250,000 with no endorsements attached. The home is located in an area where property values have increased steadily over the years. Lucia collects antiques for a hobby. Geraldo has a stamp collection that contains several rare stamps. The couple also owns a 30-foot sailboat that they use on weekends.

a. Assume you are a risk management consultant who has been asked to evaluate the couple's HO-3 policy. Identify three endorsements that Lucia and Geraldo may wish to purchase to modify their HO-3 policy.
b. Explain how the above HO-3 policy would be modified by each endorsement identified in your answer to (a) above.
c. For each of the following losses, indicate whether Section II of the homeowners policy would provide full coverage for the loss. If

full coverage would not be provided, explain why.

(1) Lucia entertains members of a local garden club in her home and serves the guests a buffet luncheon. Two guests become seriously ill and sue Lucia, alleging she had served them contaminated food. The court awards each guest damages of $60,000.
(2) Geraldo is an architect. The roof of a new addition to a client's home collapses. The client alleges that the roof collapsed because of Geraldo's faulty design. The cost of rebuilding is $40,000. The client seeks to recover that amount from Geraldo.
(3) During a visit to a friend's home, Lucia accidentally breaks a figurine that she picked up to admire. The figurine has a value of $475. The friend is seeking payment from Lucia.

uations, indicate to what extent, if any, the loss is covered under Section II of Martha's homeowners policy. Assume there are no special endorsements, and each situation is an independent event.

a. Martha is at a party at a friend's house. She accidentally burns a hole in the living room couch with her cigarette. It will cost $500 to repair the damaged couch.
b. Martha rents a snowmobile at a ski resort and accidentally collides with a skier. Martha is sued for $200,000 by the injured skier.

4. Personal liability insurance in a homeowners policy is written on an occurrence basis. Explain the meaning of an occurrence and give an illustration in your answer.

5. Explain whether each of the following losses would be covered under Section II in the homeowners policy. If the exposure is not covered, explain how coverage can be obtained.
a. The insured owns a restaurant in a large city. The insured is sued by several customers who allege they

became seriously ill from a contaminated banana cream pie.
b. While operating a 30-foot sailboat, the insured injures a swimmer.
c. The insured is sued by his ex-wife, who alleges her reputation has been ruined because the insured lied about her relationship with another man.

SELECTED REFERENCES

Fire, Casualty & Surety Bulletins. Personal Lines volume. Dwelling section. Cincinnati, OH: National Under-writer Company. The bulletins are updated monthly.

Hamilton, Karen L., and Donald S. Malecki. *Personal Insurance: Property and Liability*, first edition. Malvern, PA: American Institute for Chartered Property Casualty Underwriters, 1994, Chapter 3.

"Homeowners Insurance." *The CPCU Handbook of Insurance Policies*, third edition. Malvern, PA: American Institute for CPCU, 1998, pp. 41–62.

Rejda, George E., Constance M. Luthardt, Cheryl L. Ferguson, and Donald R. Oakes. *Personal Insurance*, fourth edition. Malvern, PA: Insurance Institute of America, 2000.

NOTES

1. The discussion of Section II liability coverages in this chapter is based largely on the *Fire, Casualty & Surety Bulletins*, Personal Lines volume, Dwelling section (Cincinnati: National Underwriter Company); and the copyrighted HO-3 policy and subsequent coverage modifications drafted by the Insurance Services Office (ISO). The HO-3 policy and various policy provisions are used with the permission of ISO.

2. Insurance Information Institute data.

 Students may take a self-administered test on this chapter at www.awlonline.com/rejda

Twelve Ways to Save Money on Your Homeowners Insurance

The price you pay for your homeowners insurance can vary by hundreds of dollars depending on the company. Companies offer several types of discounts, but they don't offer the same discount or the same amount of discount in all states. That's why you should ask your agent or company representative about any discounts available to you.

Here are 12 steps you can take to help you save money:

1. SHOP AROUND

Friends, family, the phone book, and Internet are some of the sources you can use to find homeowners insurers. Get quotes from several companies.

But don't consider price alone. The insurer you select should offer both a fair price and excellent service. Quality service may cost a bit more, but you buy insurance in case you need to make a claim, so it's important to get a company with a good reputation. Talk to a number of companies to get a feeling for the type of service they give. Ask them what they would do to lower your costs.

Check the financial ratings of the companies with *AM Best or Standard and Poor's.*

2. RAISE YOUR DEDUCTIBLE

Deductibles are the amount of money you must pay for a loss before the company starts to pay. Deductibles on homeowners policies typically start at $250.

Increase your deductible to:

$ 500—save up to 12 percent
$1000—save up to 24 percent
$2500—save up to 30 percent
$5000—save up to 37 percent

3. BUY YOUR HOME AND AUTO POLICIES FROM THE SAME COMPANY

Some companies that sell homeowners and auto insurance will take 5 to 15 percent off your premium if you buy two or more policies from them.

4. WHEN YOU BUY A HOME

Consider how much insuring it will cost.

This Appendix is adapted from "Twelve Ways to Save Money on your Homeowners Insurance," Insurance Information Institute.

A new home's electrical, heating, and plumbing systems and overall structure are likely to be in better shape than those of an older house. Companies may offer you a discount of 8 to 15 percent if your house is new.

Check the home's construction. Brick, because of its resistance to wind damage, is better in the East. Frame, because of its resistance to earthquake damage, is better in the West. Choosing wisely could cut your premium by 5 to 15 percent.

The closer your house is to firefighters and their equipment, the lower your premium will be.

5. INSURE YOUR HOUSE, NOT THE LAND

The land under your house isn't at risk for fire, theft, and other perils covered in your homeowners policy. So don't include its value in deciding how much insurance to buy. If you do, you'll pay a higher premium than you should.

6. IMPROVE YOUR HOME SECURITY AND SAFETY

You can usually get discounts of at least 5 percent for a smoke detector, burglar alarm, or dead-bolt locks. Some companies will reduce premiums by as much as 15 or 20 percent if you install a sophisticated sprinkler system and a fire and burglar alarm that rings at the police station or other monitoring facility. These systems aren't cheap, and not every system qualifies for the discount. Before you buy such a system, find out what kind your company recommends, how much the device costs, and how much you will save on premiums.

7. STOP SMOKING

Smoking accounts for more than 23,000 residential fires each year. That's why some companies reduce premiums if none of the residents in a house smokes.

8. SEEK OUT DISCOUNTS FOR SENIORS

Retired people stay at home more and spot fires sooner than working people and have more time for maintaining their homes. If you're at least 55 years old and retired, you may qualify for a discount of as much as 10 percent at some companies.

9. SEE IF YOU CAN GET GROUP COVERAGE

Alumni and business associations often work out insurance packages with an insurance company that include discounts for association members. Ask your association's director if an insurer is offering a discount on homeowners insurance to you and your fellow graduates or colleagues.

10. STAY WITH AN INSURER

If you've kept your coverage with a company for several years, you may receive special consideration. Several companies will reduce their premiums by 5 percent if you stay with them for 3 to 5 years, and by 10 percent if you remain a policyholder for 6 years or more.

11. COMPARE THE LIMITS IN YOUR POLICY TO THE VALUE OF YOUR POSSESSIONS AT LEAST ONCE A YEAR

You want your policy to cover any *major purchases* or *additions to your home*. But you don't want to spend money for coverage you don't need.

12. LOOK FOR PRIVATE INSURANCE FIRST

If you live in a high-risk area—one that is especially vulnerable to coastal storms, fires, or crime—and have been buying your homeowners insurance through a government plan, you should check with an insurance agent or company representative. You may find that you can take steps that would allow you to buy insurance at a lower price in the private market.

Chapter 10

Automobile Insurance

"A careful driver is one who honks his horn when he goes through a red light."

Henry Morgan

Learning Objectives

After studying this chapter, you should be able to:

▲ Identify the persons who are insured for liability coverage under the Personal Auto Policy (PAP).

▲ Describe the liability coverage in the PAP.

▲ Explain the medical payments coverage in the PAP.

▲ Describe the uninsured motorists coverage in the PAP.

▲ Explain the coverage for damage to your auto in the PAP.

▲ Explain the duties imposed on the insured after an accident or loss.

▲ Access an Internet site to obtain consumer information about auto insurance.

Internet Resources

- **Geico Direct** sells auto insurance directly over the phone (800-624-8341). The company claims that a 15-minute call can save you 15 percent or more on auto insurance rates. Geico Direct also has a Web site that provides similar premium quotes online. Visit the site at:

  http://www.geico.com

- The **Insurance Information Institute** provides timely information on auto insurance and other personal property insurance coverages. Numerous consumer brochures and articles on auto insurance and other property and liability coverages can be accessed directly online. Visit the site at:

  http://www.iii.org/

- The **Insurance News Network** provides premium quotes for auto insurance, homeowners insurance, and other insurance products. The site also provides timely information and news releases about auto insurance and events that affect the insurance industry. Visit the site at:

  http://www.insure.com/

- **INSWEB** provides premium quotes for auto, homeowners, and other insurance products. You can comparison shop from your computer. Quotes are also available from an agent of your choice. In addition, the site includes a page for insurance professionals. Visit the site at:

  http://www.insweb.com/

- **MoneyCentral** is designed primarily for investors, but it also provides important consumer information on various insurance coverages. Premium quotes can be obtained for auto insurance and other insurance coverages. Click on "Insurance" to obtain information on auto insurance. Visit the site at:

  http://moneycentral.msn.com/home.asp

- **Quicken Insurance** is an excellent source of consumer information about auto insurance. The site provides premium quotes for auto insurance, homeowners insurance, and other insurance products. It offers agent referral or direct signup data from major insurance companies. Visit the site at:

  http://www.quickeninsurance.com

- **State insurance departments** provide a considerable amount of consumer information on auto insurance, including coverage questions, premium comparison, and other information. For starters, check out the following sites:

  New York   **www.ins.state.ny.us**

  Wisconsin   **badger.state.wi.us/agencies/oci/oci_home.htm**

  California   **www.insurance.ca.gov**

randon, age 22, overslept and was rushing to an 8:00 A.M. class at a local college. While driving at a high rate of speed on a crowded expressway, he lost control of his car and smashed into another motorist. The driver was seriously injured, and her car was wrecked beyond repair. Although Brandon was unhurt, his car sustained severe body damage. He received a citation from the police for reckless driving. Brandon reported the accident to his insurer, who subsequently settled the bodily injury and physical damage claim with the injured driver. His insurer also paid for the damage to his car less a modest deductible.

Brandon's policy protected him against the financial consequences of his negligent act. Auto insurance provides similar protection to millions of motorists. It is one of the most important coverages to emphasize in a personal risk management program. Legal liability arising out of an auto accident can reach catastrophic levels. Medical expenses, pain and suffering, the unexpected death of a family member, and physical damage to an expensive car are additional costs that must also be recognized.

*This chapter discusses the major provisions of the **Personal Auto Policy** (PAP) drafted by the Insurance Services Office (ISO). The PAP policy is widely used throughout the United States. Some insurers, such as State Farm and Allstate, have designed their own forms that differ somewhat from the PAP form, but the differences are relatively minor.*

OVERVIEW OF PERSONAL AUTO POLICY

The PAP was introduced in 1977 and has been revised several times. The following discussion is based on the latest 1998 edition of the PAP.[1]

Eligible Vehicles

Only certain types of vehicles are eligible for coverage under the PAP. An eligible vehicle is a four-wheel motor vehicle owned by the insured or leased by the insured for at least six continuous months. Thus, a private passenger auto, station wagon, or sport utility vehicle owned by the insured is eligible for coverage.

A pickup or van is eligible for coverage if the vehicle has a gross vehicle weight of less than 10,000 pounds and is not used for the delivery and transportation of goods and materials. The limitation on use does not apply if (1) such use is incidental to the named insured's business of installing, maintaining, or repairing furnishings or equipment (such as a plumber who transports work tools and supplies in a van) or (2) the vehicle is used in ranching or farming.

Your Covered Auto

An extremely important provision is the definition of **your covered auto**. Four classes of vehicles are considered to be covered autos:

- Any vehicle shown in the declarations
- A newly acquired auto
- A trailer owned by the named insured
- A temporary substitute vehicle

First, any vehicle shown in the declarations is a covered auto. Covered autos include a private passenger auto, station wagon, sport utility vehicle, pickup, or van owned by the named insured. A private passenger auto, pickup, or van leased for at least six months is also a covered auto.

Second, a newly acquired private passenger auto, pickup, or van is a covered auto if it is acquired by the named insured during the policy period. As noted earlier, a pickup or van must have a gross vehicle weight of less than 10,000 pounds and must not be used to transport business materials unless the materials are incidental to the named insured's business,

and that business is installing, maintaining, or repairing furnishings and equipment, or is farming or ranching.

With respect to any coverage provided in the policy (except Coverage for Damage To Your Auto), a newly acquired auto has the broadest coverage provided for any vehicle shown in the declarations. Coverage begins on the date that you become the owner. However, if the newly acquired auto is an *additional vehicle*, you must notify the insurer within 14 days after you become the owner for the coverage to be effective from the purchase date. If the newly acquired auto *replaces* a vehicle shown in the declarations, coverage is provided on the replacement vehicle without having to ask the company to insure it. As a result, liability coverage, medical payments coverage, and the uninsured motorists coverage apply automatically to the replacement vehicle without the insured having to first notify the insurer.

However, with respect to physical damage coverage on a newly acquired auto, the 1998 edition of the PAP now contains notification provisions that apply separately to collision losses and to other-than-collision losses. Collision coverage on a newly acquired auto becomes effective on the date that you become the owner. *However, you must ask the insurer to insure the vehicle within 14 days after you become the owner if the declarations page indicates that at least one auto is insured for collision coverage.* In such a case, the newly acquired auto has the broadest coverage provided for any auto shown in the declarations. The older 1994 PAP contained a 30-day notification period. A similar provision applies to coverage for other-than-collision losses.

If the declarations page does not indicate collision coverage for at least one auto, a newly acquired auto is automatically insured for collision coverage for four days after you become the owner. You must notify the insurer within the four-day period. However, if loss occurs before you notify the insurer, a $500 collision deductible must be met. A similar provision applies to coverage for other-than-collision losses. The 1994 PAP did not contain this provision.

Third, a trailer owned by the named insured is a covered auto. A trailer is a vehicle designed to be pulled by a private passenger auto, pickup, or van and also includes a farm wagon or farm implement while being towed by such vehicles. For example, you may be pulling a boat trailer that overturns and injures another motorist. The liability section of the PAP would cover the loss.

Finally, a **temporary substitute vehicle** *is a covered auto.* A temporary substitute auto is a non-owned auto or trailer you are temporarily using because of mechanical breakdown, repair, servicing, loss, or destruction of a covered vehicle. Thus, if you drive a loaner car while your car is in the garage for repairs, your PAP covers the vehicle.

Summary of PAP Coverages

The PAP consists of a declarations page, a definitions page, and the following six parts:

Part A: Liability Coverage
Part B: Medical Payments Coverage
Part C: Uninsured Motorists Coverage
Part D: Coverage for Damage to Your Auto
Part E: Duties after an Accident or Loss
Part F: General Provisions

PART A: LIABILITY COVERAGE

Liability coverage (Part A) is the most important part of the PAP. It protects a covered person against a suit or claim arising out of the negligent ownership or operation of a covered vehicle.

Insuring Agreement

In the insuring agreement, the insurer agrees to pay any damages for bodily injury or property damage for which an insured is legally responsible because of an auto accident. The 1998 PAP is typically written with split limits. **Split limits** *means that the amounts of insurance for bodily injury liability and property damage liability are stated separately.* For example, split limits of $250,000/$500,000/$100,000 means that you have bodily injury liability coverage of $250,000 for each person and $500,000 for each accident. You also have $100,000 of property damage liability coverage. (Practitioners frequently refer to such limits as 250/500/100.)

Liability coverage can also be written with a single limit by adding an appropriate endorsement to the policy. A **single limit** *applies to both bodily injury and property damage liability: the total amount of insurance applies to the entire accident without a separate limit for each person.* For example, a single limit of $500,000 would apply to both bodily injury and property damage liability.

The amount paid as damages includes any prejudgment interest awarded against the insured. Many states now allow plaintiffs (injured persons) to receive interest on the judgment from the time the suit is entered to the time the judgment is determined. Any prejudgment interest is considered part of the damage award and is subject to the policy limit of liability.

In addition to the payment for damages, the insurer agrees to defend you and pays all legal defense costs. The defense costs are paid in addition to the policy limits. *However, the insurer's duty to settle or defend the claim ends when the limit of liability has been exhausted by payment of judgments or settlements.* This provision means that the insurer cannot deposit the policy limits into an escrow account and walk away from defending the insured. The obligation to defend ends only when the policy limits are exhausted by payment of a judgment against the insured or settlement with a claimant

In addition, the insurer has no obligation to defend any claim not covered by the policy. For example, if you intentionally cause bodily injury or property damage and are sued, the insurer has no obligation to defend you because intentional acts are specifically excluded.

Finally, all states have financial responsibility or compulsory insurance laws that require motorists to carry a minimum amount of liability insurance or to post a bond at the time of an accident. The minimum liability limits per person for bodily injury range from $10,000 to $50,000 and are woefully inadequate in view of the high damage awards in recent years.

Insured Persons

The following four groups are insured under the liability section of the PAP:

- The named insured and any resident family member
- Any person using the named insured's covered auto
- Any person or organization, but only for liability

arising out of an insured person's use of a covered auto on behalf of that person or organization

- Any person or organization legally responsible for the named insured's or family members' use of any auto or trailer (other than a covered auto or one owned by that person or organization)

First, the named insured and resident family members are insured for liability coverage. The named insured also includes a spouse if a resident of the same household. In recognition of the widespread divorce and separation found today, the 1998 policy broadens the definition of "you" and "your" to extend coverage for up to 90 days to a spouse who no longer resides in the named insured's household and is not listed as a named insured in the PAP. If a spouse ceases to be a resident of the same household and is not listed as a named insured, the spouse is covered for 90 days following the change in residency, or until the spouse obtains a separate PAP or the policy period ends, whichever occurs first. If both spouses are named in the declarations as named insureds in the same PAP, the policy covers both spouses even though one spouse no longer resides in the same residence.

For example, Jennifer and James are married and live in the same residence. Jennifer is the named insured under her PAP policy. Assume that James is not listed as a named insured in her policy. He is still considered a named insured because he is Jennifer's husband. If the couple separates and James moves into an apartment, he is covered for 90 days under Jennifer's policy, or until he purchases his own policy if earlier. However, if both were named insureds under the same PAP, James would be covered as a named insured until the policy expires, or until he purchases his own policy, if earlier.

A family member is a person related to the named insured by blood, marriage, or adoption who resides in the same household, including a ward or foster child. Thus, the husband, wife, and children are covered while using any auto, owned or nonowned. If the children are attending college and are temporarily away from home, they are still insured under their parents' policy.

Second, any other person using the named insured's covered auto is also insured provided that person can establish a reasonable belief that permission to use the covered auto exists. For example,

Roger may have permitted his girlfriend, Tina, to drive his car several times over the past six months. If Tina takes Roger's car without his express permission, she is covered under his policy as long as she can show a reasonable belief that Roger would have given her permission to use the car.

Third, any person or organization legally responsible for the acts of a covered person while using a covered auto is also insured. For example, if Claude drives his car on an errand for his employer and injures someone, the employer is covered for any suit or claim.

Finally, coverage applies to any person or organization legally responsible for the named insured's or family members' use of any auto or trailer (other than a covered auto or one owned by the person or organization). For example, Claude may borrow the car of a fellow worker to mail a package for his employer. If Claude injures someone while driving that car, the employer is also covered for any suit or claim. However, the PAP does not extend coverage to the employer when the named insured is using an auto owned by the employer. So if Claude is driving to the post office in a company car, the employer is not insured under Claude's PAP.

Supplementary Payments

In addition to the policy limits and a legal defense, certain supplementary payments can be paid.

- Up to $250 for the cost of a bail bond
- Premiums on appeal bonds and bonds to release attachments
- Interest accruing after a judgment
- Up to $200 daily for the loss of earnings
- Other reasonable expenses

Premiums on a bail bond can be paid up to $250 because of an auto accident that results in property damage or bodily injury. However, payment is not made for a traffic violation such as a speeding ticket except if an accident occurs. For example, assume Richard is drunk and injures another motorist in an auto accident. If he is arrested, and bail is set at $2500, the insurer will pay the bail bond premium up to a maximum of $250.

Premiums on an appeal bond and a bond to release an attachment of property in any suit defended by the insurer are also paid as supplementary payments. If interest accrues after a judgment is awarded, the interest is also paid as a supplementary payment. Any prejudgment interest, however, is part of the liability limits.

The insurer will also pay up to $200 daily for the loss of earnings (but not other income) due to attendance at a hearing or trial at the company's request.

Finally, other reasonable expenses incurred at the insurer's request are paid. For example, you may be a defendant in a trial and be requested to testify. If you have meal or transportation expenses, they would be paid as a supplemental payment.

Exclusions

A lengthy list of exclusions applies to the liability coverage under the PAP. They are summarized as follows:

1. *Intentional injury or damage.* Intentional bodily injury or property damage is specifically excluded.

2. *Property owned or transported.* Liability coverage is not provided to any person for damage to property owned or being transported by that person. For example, the suitcase and camera belonging to a friend may be damaged in an auto accident while you and your friend are on vacation together. The damage would not be covered.

3. *Property rented, used, or in the insured's care.* Damage to property rented to, used by, or in the care of the insured is not covered. For example, if you rent some skis that are damaged in an auto accident, the property damage is not covered. The exclusion, however, does not apply to property damage to a residence or private garage. For example, if you rent a house and carelessly back into a partly opened garage door, the property damage to the door would be covered.

4. *Bodily injury to an employee.* Bodily injury to an employee of the insured who is injured during the course of employment is also excluded. The intent here is to cover the employee's injury under a workers compensation law. However, a domestic employee injured during the course of employment would be covered if workers compensation benefits are not required or available.

5. *Use as a public or livery conveyance.* There is no liability coverage on a vehicle while it is being used as a public or livery conveyance. The intent here is to exclude coverage if the insured makes the vehicle available for hire to the general public. However, the exclusion does not apply to share-the-expense carpools.

6. *Vehicles used in the automobile business.* If a person is employed or engaged in the automobile business, liability arising out of the operation of vehicles in the automobile business is excluded. The automobile business refers to the selling, repairing, servicing, storing, or parking of vehicles designed for use mainly on public highways. It also includes road testing and delivery. For example, assume you take your car to a garage for repairs. If an automobile mechanic has an accident and injures someone while road testing your car, your PAP liability coverage does not protect the mechanic. (However, if you are sued because you are the car owner, you are covered.) The intent of this exclusion is to exclude loss exposures that should be covered under the auto repair firm's liability policy, such as a garage policy.

The preceding exclusion does not apply to the operation, ownership, or use of a covered auto by the named insured, any resident family member, or any partner, agent, or employee of the named insured or family member. For example, if an auto mechanic has an accident while driving his or her car to pick up a part, the mechanic's PAP would cover the loss.

7. *Other business vehicles.* Liability coverage does not apply to any vehicle maintained or used in any other business (other than farming or ranching). This exclusion is similar to the preceding automobile business exclusion except it applies to all other business use with certain exceptions. The intent here is to exclude liability coverage for commercial vehicles and trucks that are used in a business. For example, if you drive a city bus or operate a large cement truck, your PAP liability coverage does not apply.

The exclusion does not apply to an owned or nonowned private passenger auto, pickup, or van.

Thus, you are covered if you drive your car on company business.

8. *Using a vehicle without reasonable belief of permission.* If a person uses a vehicle without a reasonable belief that he or she has permission to do so, the liability coverage does not apply. The exclusion does not apply to a family member who is using a covered auto owned by the named insured.

9. *Nuclear energy exclusion.* Liability of insureds who are covered under special nuclear energy contracts is also excluded.

10. *Vehicle with fewer than four wheels.* Liability coverage does not apply to any vehicle that has fewer than four wheels or is designed for use mainly off public roads. Thus, motorcycles, mopeds, motorscooters, minibikes, and trail bikes are excluded. However, the 1998 PAP now provides liability coverage arising out of the use of a *nonowned* golf cart.

11. *Vehicle furnished or made available for the named insured's regular use.* Liability coverage excludes a vehicle other than a covered auto that is owned by, furnished, or made available for the named insured's regular use. You can occasionally drive another person's car and still have coverage under your policy. *However, if the nonowned auto is driven regularly or is furnished or made available for your regular use, your PAP liability coverage does not apply.* For example, if your employer furnishes you with a car, or if a car is available for your regular use in a company carpool, the liability coverage does not apply. The key point is not how frequently you drive someone else's car, but whether it is furnished or made available for your regular use.

For an additional premium, the *extended nonowned coverage endorsement* can be added to the PAP that covers the insured while operating a nonowned auto on a regular basis.

12. *Vehicle owned by, furnished, or made available for the regular use of any family member.* This exclusion is similar to the preceding exclusion. However, it does not apply to the named insured and spouse. For example, if Mary borrows a car owned and insured by her son who lives with her, the liability coverage under Mary's PAP would cover her while driving the son's car.

13. *Racing vehicle.* Liability coverage does not apply to any vehicle while it is located inside a racing facility for the purpose of competing in or preparing for a prearranged racing or speed contest.

Limit of Liability

As noted earlier, the 1998 PAP is typically written with split limits. That is, the amounts of insurance for bodily injury liability and property damage liability are stated separately. The maximum amount paid for bodily injury to each person is the amount shown in the declarations. Subject to this limit for each person, the maximum amount paid for bodily injury to all persons resulting from any one auto accident is the amount shown in the declarations. The maximum amount paid for property damage resulting from any one auto accident is also shown in the declarations.

Out-of-State Coverage

An important feature applies if the accident occurs in a state other than where the covered auto is principally garaged. If the accident occurs in a state that has a financial responsibility law with higher liability limits than the limits shown in the declarations, the PAP automatically provides the higher specified limits.

In addition, if the state has a compulsory insurance or similar law that requires a nonresident to have insurance whenever he or she uses a vehicle in that state, the PAP provides the required minimum amounts and types of coverage. This provision insures compliance with an out-of-state no-fault law and the payment of required benefits. No-fault auto insurance laws are discussed in Chapter 11.

Other Insurance

In some cases, more than one auto liability policy covers a loss. The PAP has a provision for determining the amount and priority of payments. If other applicable liability insurance applies to an *owned vehicle*, the insurer pays only its pro rata share of the loss. The insurer's share is the proportion that its limit of liability bears to the total applicable limits of liability under all policies. However, if the insurance applies to a *nonowned vehicle*, the insurer's insurance is excess over any other collectible insurance (see Exhibit 10.1).

PART B: MEDICAL PAYMENTS COVERAGE

Medical payments coverage is frequently included in the PAP. Benefits are paid without regard to fault.

Insuring Agreement

Under this provision, the company will pay all reasonable medical and funeral expenses incurred by an insured for services rendered within three years from the date of the accident. Covered expenses include medical, surgical, X-ray, dental, and funeral expenses. The benefit limits typically range from $1000 to $10,000 per person and apply to each insured who is injured in the accident.

Medical payments coverage is not based on fault. Thus, if you are injured in an auto accident and you are at fault, medical payments can still be paid to you and to other injured passengers in the car.

Insured Persons

Two groups are insured for medical payments coverage:

- Named insured and family members
- Other persons while occupying a covered auto

The named insured and family members are covered if they are injured while occupying any motor vehicle or are injured as pedestrians when struck by a motor vehicle designed for use mainly on public roads. For example, if the parents and children are hurt in an auto accident while on vacation, their medical expenses are covered up to the policy limits. If the named insured or any family member is struck by a motor vehicle or trailer while walking, his or her medical expenses are also paid. However, if you are injured by a farm tractor, snowmobile, or bull-

EXHIBIT 10.1
Examples of Other Insurance

Example 1

Maria carelessly injures another motorist while driving her own car and must pay damages of $30,000. If two auto liability policies cover the loss, each insurer pays its pro rata share of the loss. Assume that Maria is insured for $50,000 in Company A and $100,000 in Company B. Company A pays $10,000 and Company B pays $20,000. This can be illustrated by the following.

Comany A
$$\frac{\$50,000}{\$150,000} \times \$30,000 = \$10,000$$

Company B
$$\frac{\$100,000}{\$150,000} \times \$30,000 = \underline{\$20,000}$$
$$\text{Total} \qquad \$30,000$$

Example 2

Ben is the named insured and borrows Susan's car with her permission. Both policies will cover any loss. Ben has $50,000 of liability insurance and Susan has $100,000. Ben negligently injures another motorist and must pay damages of $125,000. *The rule is that insurance on the borrowed car is primary, and other insurance is excess.* Each company pays as follows:

Susan's insurer (primary)	$100,000
Ben's insurer (excess)	25,000
Total	$125,000

Susan's insurer pays $100,000 while Ben's insurer pays the remaining $25,000.

dozer, your injury is not covered, because these vehicles are not designed for use mainly on public roads.

Other persons are also covered for their medical expenses while occupying a covered auto. For example, if you own your car and are the named insured, all passengers in your car are covered for their medical expenses under your policy. However, if you are operating a *nonowned vehicle*, other passengers in the car (other than family members) are not covered for their medical expenses under your policy. The intent here is to have other passengers in the nonowned vehicle seek protection under their own insurance or under the medical expense coverage that applies to the nonowned vehicle.

Exclusions

Medical payments coverage has numerous exclusions. They are summarized as follows:

1. *Motorized vehicle with fewer than four wheels.* Bodily injury while occupying a motorized vehicle with fewer than four wheels is excluded.
2. *Public or livery conveyance.* If a covered auto is used as a public or livery conveyance, the medical payments coverage does not apply. The exclusion does not apply to a share-the-expense carpool.
3. *Using the vehicle as a residence.* Coverage does not apply if the injury occurs while the vehicle is being used as a residence or premises. For example, if you own and occupy a camper trailer as a residence in a campground while on vacation, medical expense coverage does not apply if you burn yourself while cooking on a stove in the trailer.
4. *Injury occurring during course of employment.* Coverage does not apply if the injury occurs during the course of employment, and workers compensation benefits are required or available.
5. *Vehicle furnished or made available for the named insured's regular use.* Coverage does not apply to any injury sustained while occupying or when struck by a vehicle (other than a covered auto) that is owned by the named insured or is furnished or made available for the named insured's regular use. The intent here is to avoid providing "free" medical payments coverage on an owned or regularly used car not described in the policy.
6. *Vehicle furnished or made available for the regular use of any family member.* A similar exclusion applies to any vehicle (other than a covered auto) that is owned by any family member or is furnished or made available for the regular use of any family member. The exclusion does not apply to the named insured and spouse. For example, if a son living at home owns a car that is not insured for medical payments coverage, and the parents are injured while occupying the son's car, the parent's medical expenses would be covered under their policy.
7. *Using a vehicle without a reasonable belief of permission.* Coverage does not apply if the injury occurs while occupying a vehicle without a reasonable belief of being entitled to do so. The exclusion does not apply to a family member who is using a covered auto owned by the named insured.
8. *Vehicle used in the business of an insured.* Coverage does not apply to any injury sustained while occupying a vehicle when it is being used in the business of an insured. The intent here is to exclude medical payments coverage for nonowned trucks and commercial vehicles used in the business of an insured person. The exclusion does not apply to a private passenger auto (owned or nonowned), an owned pickup or van, or trailer used with any of the preceding vehicles.
9. *Nuclear weapon, radiation, or war.* Bodily injury from a nuclear weapon, nuclear radiation, or war is not covered.
10. *Racing vehicle.* Coverage does not apply to a bodily injury sustained while occupying a vehicle located inside a racing facility for the purpose of competing in or preparing for a prearranged racing or speed contest.

Other Insurance

If other automobile medical payments insurance applies to an *owned vehicle*, the insurer pays its pro rata share of the loss based on the proportion that its limits bear to the total applicable limits.

However, medical payments coverage is excess with respect to a *nonowned vehicle*. For example, assume that Kim is driving her car and picks up Sydney for lunch. Kim loses control of the car and hits a tree, and Sydney is injured. Sydney's medical bills are $6000. Kim has $2000 of medical expenses coverage, and Sydney has $5000. Kim's insurer pays the first $2000 as primary insurer, and Sydney's insurer pays the remaining $4000 as excess insurance.

PART C: UNINSURED MOTORISTS COVERAGE

Some persons are irresponsible and drive without liability insurance. The **uninsured motorists coverage** pays for the bodily injury (and property damage in some states) caused by an uninsured motorist, by a hit-and-run driver, or by a negligent driver whose insurance company is insolvent.

Insuring Agreement

The insurer agrees to pay compensatory damages that an insured is legally entitled to receive from the owner or operator of an uninsured motor vehicle because of bodily injury caused by an accident. Damages include medical bills, lost wages, and compensation for a permanent disfigurement resulting from the accident. Several important points must be emphasized with respect to this coverage.

1. *The coverage applies only if the uninsured motorist is legally liable.* If the uninsured motorist is not liable, the insurer will not pay for the bodily injury.
2. *The insurer's maximum limit of liability for any single accident is the amount shown in the declarations.* You cannot receive duplicate payments for the same elements of loss under the uninsured motorists coverage and Part A (liability coverage) or Part B (medical payments coverage) of the policy, or any underinsured motorists coverage provided by the policy. Also, you cannot receive a duplicate payment for any element of loss for which payment has been made by or on behalf of persons or organizations legally responsible for the accident. Finally, the insurer will not pay you for any part of a loss if you are entitled to be paid for that part of the loss under a workers compensation or disability benefits law.
3. *The claim is subject to arbitration if the insured and insurer disagree over the amount of damages or whether the insured is entitled to receive any damages.* Under this provision, each party selects an arbitrator. The two arbitrators select a third arbitrator. A decision by two of the three arbitrators is binding on all parties. However, the decision is binding only if the damage award does not exceed the state's minimum financial responsibility law limits.
4. *Some states also include coverage for property damage from an uninsured motorist in their uninsured motorists law.* In these states, if an uninsured driver runs a red light and smashes into your car, the property damage to the car would be covered under the uninsured motorists coverage, subject to any applicable deductible.

There is considerable variation among the states that include property damage coverage in their uninsured motorists law. In some states, property damage coverage is an optional coverage that is purchased separately from the regular uninsured motorists coverage. In other states, both bodily injury and property damage coverages are included together in the uninsured motorists coverage; however, the insured may have the option of waiving the coverage if it is not desired. In some states, both bodily injury and property damage coverage are mandatory under the state's uninsured motorists law. Finally, the property damage is subject to a deductible.

Insured Persons

Three groups are insured under the uninsured motorists coverage:

- The named insured and his or her family members
- Any other person while occupying a covered auto
- Any person legally entitled to recover damages

First, the named insured and his or her family members are covered if they are injured by an uninsured motorist. Second, any other person who is injured while occupying a covered auto is also insured; the coverage applies only if the individual is occupying a covered auto. Finally, any person legally entitled to recover damages is insured. An individual may not be physically involved in the accident but may be entitled to recover damages from the person or organization legally responsible for the bodily injury of the insured person. For example, if the named insured is killed by an uninsured motorist, the surviving spouse could still collect damages under the uninsured motorists coverage.

Uninsured Vehicles

An extremely important provision defines an uninsured motor vehicle. Four groups of vehicles are considered to be uninsured vehicles:

1. An uninsured vehicle is a motor vehicle or trailer for which no bodily injury liability insurance policy or bond applies at the time of the accident.

2. A bodily injury liability policy or bond may be in force on a vehicle. However, the amount of insurance on that vehicle may be less than the amount required by the state's financial responsibility law in the state where the named insured's covered auto is principally garaged. This vehicle is also considered to be an uninsured motor vehicle.

3. A hit-and-run vehicle is also considered to be an uninsured vehicle. Thus, if the named insured or any family member is struck by a hit-and-run driver while occupying a covered auto or a nonowned auto, or while walking, the uninsured motorists coverage will pay for the injury.

4. Another uninsured vehicle is one to which a bodily injury liability policy applies at the time of the accident, but the insurer or bonding company denies coverage or becomes insolvent. For example, if you have a valid claim against a negligent driver, but his or her insurer becomes insolvent before the claim is paid, your uninsured motorists coverage would pay the claim.

Certain vehicles are not considered to be uninsured motor vehicles. An uninsured motor vehicle does not include any of the following:

1. Any vehicle owned by or furnished for the regular use of the named insured or any family member

2. Any vehicle owned or operated by a qualified self-insurer (except a self-insurer that is or becomes insolvent)

3. Any vehicle owned by a governmental unit or agency

4. Any vehicle operated on rails or crawler treads

5. Any vehicle designed mainly for use off public roads, while not on a public road

6. Any vehicle used as a residence or premises

Exclusions

The uninsured motorists coverage has several general exclusions, summarized as follows:

1. *No uninsured motorists coverage on vehicle.* Coverage does not apply to an insured while occupying or when struck by a motor vehicle, owned by that insured, which is not insured for coverage under this policy.

2. *Family members.* Family members are not covered while they are occupying a vehicle owned by the named insured that is insured for uninsured motorists coverage on a primary basis under any other policy. The intent is to have such family members seek protection under the policy insuring the vehicle that they are occupying.

3. *Settling without the insurer's consent.* If an insured or legal representative settles a bodily injury claim without the insurer's consent, coverage does not apply. The purpose of this exclusion is to protect the insurer's interest in the claim.

4. *Using the vehicle as a public or livery conveyance.* If an insured occupies a covered auto when it is being used as a public or livery conveyance, coverage does not apply. The exclusion does not apply to a share-the-expense carpool.

5. *No reasonable belief of permission.* Coverage does not apply to any insured who is using a vehicle without a reasonable belief that he or she is entitled to do so. This exclusion does not apply to a family member who is using a covered auto owned by the named insured.

6. *No benefit to workers compensation insurer.* The uninsured motorists coverage cannot directly or indirectly benefit a workers compensation insurer or self-insurer. A workers compensation insurer may have a legal right of action against a third party who has injured an employee. If an uninsured driver injures an employee who receives workers compensation benefits, the workers compensation insurer could sue the uninsured driver or attempt to make a claim under the injured employee's uninsured motorists coverage. This exclusion prevents the uninsured motorists coverage from providing benefits to the workers compensation insurer.

7. *No punitive damages.* The PAP excludes payment for punitive or exemplary damages under the uninsured motorists coverage.

Other Insurance

If other insurance applies to the loss, recovery for damages under all such policies may equal but not exceed the highest applicable limit on any one vehicle under any policy providing protection on either a primary or excess basis. Thus, you can collect in total an amount equal to the highest limit of all policies that apply to you.

In addition, if the insurer provides uninsured motorists coverage on a *vehicle not owned by the named insured*, the insurance provided is excess over any collectible insurance providing coverage on a primary basis.

Finally, if one or more policies provide uninsured motorists coverage, the insured's policy will pay only its pro rata share of the loss, which is the proportion that the insurer's limit of liability bears to the total of all applicable limits provided. The pro rata rule applies regardless of whether the coverage is on a primary basis or excess basis.

Underinsured Motorists Coverage

The **underinsured motorists coverage** can be added to the PAP to provide more complete protection. The underinsured motorists coverage applies when a negligent driver carries liability insurance, but the limits carried are less than the insured's actual damages for bodily injury.

An underinsured vehicle is defined as a vehicle to which a liability policy or bond applies at the time of the accident, but the liability limits carried are less than the limits provided by the insured's underinsured motorists coverage. The maximum amount paid for the bodily injury under the coverage varies among the states. *In general, the maximum amount paid is the underinsured motorist's limit less the amount paid by the negligent driver's insurer.* For example, assume that Nadia adds the underinsured motorists coverage to her policy in the amount of $100,000. She is injured by a negligent driver who has liability limits of $25,000/$50,000, which satisfy the state's minimum required limits. If her bodily injury damages are $100,000, she would receive only $25,000 from the negligent driver's insurer, because that amount is the applicable limit of liability. However, she would receive another $75,000 from her insurer under the underinsured motorists coverage.

However, assume that Nadia's bodily injury damages are $125,000. The maximum amount she would collect under the underinsured motorists coverage is still only $75,000, which is the difference between the $100,000 limit under her underinsured

motorists coverage and the $25,000 collected from the negligent driver's insurer (see preceding rule). To collect the full amount of her injury, Nadia should have carried limits of at least $125,000.

You should not confuse the underinsured motorists coverage with the uninsured motorists coverage. The two coverages are mutually exclusive. You can collect under one coverage or the other, depending on the situation, but not both. The uninsured motorists coverage applies when the bodily injury (or property damage in some states) is caused by an uninsured motorist, by a hit-and-run driver, or by a driver whose insurer is insolvent. In contrast, the underinsured motorists coverage is applicable only when the other driver has auto liability insurance, but the liability limits carried are less than the limit provided by the underinsured motorists coverage.

PART D: COVERAGE FOR DAMAGE TO YOUR AUTO

Part D (**coverage for damage to your auto**) provides coverage for the damage or theft of an automobile.

Insuring Agreement

The insurer agrees to pay for any direct and accidental loss to a covered auto or nonowned auto, including its equipment, less any deductible. If two autos insured under the same policy are damaged in the same accident, only one deductible must be met. If the deductible amounts are different, the higher deductible will apply. *Two optional coverages are available: (1) collision and (2) other than collision (also called comprehensive).* A collision loss is covered only if the declarations page indicates that collision coverage is provided for that auto. Likewise, coverage for an other-than-collision loss is in force only if the declarations page indicates that other-than-collision coverage is provided for that auto.

The physical damage coverages under Part D also apply to a newly acquired private passenger auto, pickup, van, camper body, or trailer provided that the named insured requests coverage within 14 days after becoming the owner. *In addition, the Part D coverages apply to a nonowned auto and tempo-*

rary substitute auto on an excess basis. For example, if you rent a car on a vacation, your Part D coverages apply to that car. However, if an accident occurs, you will be responsible for paying the deductible just as if the loss had occurred to your own car.

As mentioned earlier, the Part D coverages on your car also apply to rental cars. However, there may be some restrictions on the Part D coverages when a car is rented, such as a limit on the number of days of coverage in a year when a car is rented. In addition, many insurers have discontinued providing liability and collision coverage on rental cars used for business purposes without payment of an extra premium. Thus, before you rent a car, you should check with your agent to determine the extent to which your present coverages apply to a rental car. This information is especially important in determining whether you should purchase the "collision damage waiver," which covers physical damage to the rental car if you have an accident.

Collision Loss Collision *is defined as the upset of your covered auto or nonowned auto or its impact with another vehicle or object.* The following are examples of a collision loss:

- Your car hits another car, a telephone pole, a tree, or a building.
- Your car is parked, and you find the rear fender dented when you return.
- You open the car door in a parking lot, and the door is damaged when it hits the vehicle parked next to you.

Collision losses are paid regardless of fault. If you cause the accident, your insurer will pay for the damage to your car, less any deductible. If some other driver damages your car, you can either collect from the negligent driver (or from his or her insurer), or look to your insurer to pay the claim. If you collect from your own insurer, you must give up subrogation rights to your insurer, who will then attempt to collect from the negligent driver who caused the accident. If the entire amount of the loss is recovered, your insurer will refund the deductible.

Other-Than-Collision Loss The PAP can be written to cover an **other-than-collision loss**. The PAP distin-

guishes between a collision and an other-than-collision loss. This distinction is important because some car owners do not desire collision coverage on their cars. Also, the deductibles under the two coverages may be different. Other-than-collision coverage is frequently written with a lower deductible.

Loss from any of the following perils is considered to be an other-than-collision loss:

- Missiles or falling objects
- Fire
- Theft or larceny
- Explosion or earthquake
- Windstorm
- Hail, water, or flood
- Malicious mischief or vandalism
- Riot or civil commotion
- Contact with a bird or animal
- Glass breakage

These losses are self-explanatory, but a few comments are in order. Theft of the vehicle is covered, including the theft of equipment, such as hub caps, tires, or a stereo set. Theft of an air bag from a covered vehicle parked on the street is also covered. In recent years, the number of stolen air bags has increased substantially, with the bags subsequently being used by dishonest repair shops to defraud insurers (see Insight 10.1).

In addition, colliding with a bird or animal is not a collision loss. Thus, if you hit a bird or deer with your car, the physical damage to the car is considered to be an other-than-collision loss.

Finally, if glass breakage is caused by a collision, you can elect to have it covered as a collision loss. This distinction is important because both coverages (collision loss and other-than-collision loss) are written with deductibles. Without this qualification, you would have to pay two deductibles if the car has both body damage and glass breakage in the same accident (assuming both coverages are elected). By treating glass breakage as part of the collision loss, only one deductible must be satisfied.

Nonowned Auto The Part D coverages also apply to a nonowned auto. A **nonowned auto** *is a private passenger auto, pickup, van, or trailer not owned by or furnished or made available for the regular use of the named insured or family member, while it is in*

Insight 10.1

Latest Repair Fraud Sees Stolen Air Bags

When Kathy Myers' 17-year-old daughter crashed the family's 1997 Honda Accord earlier this summer and walked away unhurt, Myers was deeply impressed with the value of air bags. So she was furious to learn that although her insurance company paid a body shop to have new air bags installed in her car, she got used bags.

The standard Honda factory identification numbers had been removed from the bags, raising questions about their source—which could include theft or salvage from another wrecked Accord.

It meant there was no guarantee the replacement bags would function, according to safety researchers. For an air bag to work properly, it must exactly match the year and model of the vehicle for which it was designed.

"I don't understand how anyone in good conscience could do that," says Myers, a nurse from Munroe Falls, Ohio. "What scares me the most is that if he did it with me . . . how many more people have the same problem?"

Unfortunately, Myers' problem probably isn't unique. There appears to be a small but thriving business in air bag thefts and fraudulent repairs, says Brian O'Neill, president of the Insurance Institute for Highway Safety, a research firm supported by the insurance industry and based in Arlington, Virginia.

About 50,000 air bags were stolen in 1996, apparently to be used in fraudulent repairs, says Ed Sparkman, a senior manager at the National Insurance Crime Bureau in Chicago.

A study by State Farm Insurance Cos. has found that since 1993, the number of stolen air bags per 10,000 vehicles equipped with air bags almost tripled.

The government has required dual air bags in new cars since the 1998 model year.

The incentive for stealing air bags is simple and ancient: profit.

"I can buy one off the street for $200 and charge the insurance company $1000, so I just made $800," Sparkman says.

Myers learned of the problem because she was unhappy with the paint and bodywork done by Green Auto Collision of Uniontown, Ohio. She took the Honda to Sanzone Body & Paint in nearby Tallmadge. Sanzone is affiliated with WreckCheck, a national organization that specializes in checking the quality of such repairs and representing consumers in disputes with either a body shop or insurance firm.

Owner Mark Sanzone noticed the driver's side air bag felt soft, and he got Myers' permission to remove the bag and check it. That's when he found the factory tags had been removed.

Sanzone checked with Park Honda in Akron, Ohio, and learned that Green Auto Collision purchased two air bags for a 1997 Accord on August 3 and returned them September 17.

Linda Kifer, chief operating officer at Park Honda, confirms Green Auto Collision purchased the bags for $1518 and then returned them for a refund.

Jim Spencer, of Green Auto Collision, declines to discuss the matter other than to say he did "quality repairs."

Myers remains furious: "Poor workmanship is one thing . . . but he basically let my family drive off without any regard to our safety."

Myers' problems highlight the importance of using well-known, well-established body shops with good reputations, experts say.

One way to check for a functioning air bag is to watch the instrument panel when the car is turned on, says Sparkman of the crime bureau. The air bag light should flicker.

However, the insurance institute's O'Neill says some repair shops use a small resistor to fool the car into believing the air bag is functioning.

The best way to tell if the air bag is new is to ask the body shop to pull the air bag and show it has the manufacturer's markings, says Brian Maze, a spokesman for State Farm.

Source: Adapted from "Latest Repair Fraud Sees Stolen Air Bags," *Omaha World Herald,* October 16, 1999, p. 37. Reprinted with permission from Newhouse News Service.

the custody of or is being operated by the named insured or family member. In addition, a nonowned auto includes a temporary substitute vehicle. For example, if Megan borrows Mike's car, Megan's collision coverage and other-than-collision coverage on her car apply to the borrowed car. However, Megan's insurance is excess over any physical damage insurance on the borrowed car.

The Part D coverages apply only if the nonowned auto is not furnished or made available for the regular use of the named insured or family member. You can occasionally drive a borrowed automobile, and your physical damage insurance will cover the borrowed vehicle. *However, if the vehicle is driven on a regular basis or is furnished or made available for your regular use, the Part D coverages do not apply.* The key point here is not how frequently you drive a nonowned auto, but whether the vehicle is furnished or made available for your regular use.

A temporary substitute vehicle is also considered to be a nonowned auto. A temporary substitute vehicle is a nonowned auto or trailer that is used as a temporary replacement for a covered auto that is out of normal use because of its breakdown, repair, servicing, loss, or destruction. *Thus, the Part D coverages that apply to a covered auto also apply to a temporary substitute vehicle for that auto.* Hence, if your car is in the shop for repairs, and you are furnished a loaner car, your physical damage insurance also applies to the loaner car.

If you have an accident while operating a nonowned auto, the PAP provides the broadest coverage applicable to any covered auto shown in the declarations. For example, assume that you own two cars. One vehicle is insured for both a collision loss and an other-than-collision loss, and the other is insured only for an other-than-collision loss. If you drive a nonowned auto, the borrowed vehicle is covered for both collision and other-than-collision losses.

Deductible The collision coverage is typically written with a straight deductible of $250, or some higher amount. Coverage for other-than-collision losses is also normally written with a deductible. Deductibles are designed to reduce small claims, hold down premiums, and encourage the insured to be careful in protecting the car from damage or theft.

Transportation Expenses

Part D also provides a supplementary payment for temporary transportation expenses. The insurer will pay, without application of a deductible, up to $20 daily to a maximum of $600 for temporary transportation expenses incurred by the insured because of loss to a covered auto. Payments can be made for a train, bus, taxi, rental car, or other transportation expense. *Payments are made for other-than-collision losses only if the declarations indicate that other-than-collision coverage is provided on that auto. Likewise, payments are made for collision losses only if the declarations indicate that collision coverage is provided for that auto.*

The coverage also includes payment of any expenses for which the insured is legally responsible because of loss to a nonowned auto, such as the loss of daily rents on a rental car. However, such expenses are paid for other-than-collision losses or for collision losses only if the declarations indicate that these coverages are in effect.

Finally, if the loss is caused by the total theft of a covered auto or nonowned auto, expenses incurred during the first 48 hours after the theft occurred are not covered. If the loss is caused by other than theft, expenses incurred during the first 24 hours after the auto has been withdrawn from use are not covered.

Coverage for *towing and labor costs* can be added by an endorsement. This coverage pays for towing and labor costs if a covered auto or nonowned auto breaks down, provided the labor is performed at the place of breakdown. The maximum amount paid is $25, $50, or $75 for each breakdown depending on the amount of insurance purchased. For example, if you call a repair truck because your car fails to start, the labor costs and any tow-in costs will be paid up to the policy limits. Labor costs, however, are covered only for work done at the place of the breakdown. The cost of repairs at a service station or garage is not covered.

Exclusions

Numerous exclusions apply to the Part D coverages, summarized as follows:

1. *Use as a public or livery conveyance.* Loss to a covered auto or any nonowned auto is excluded if the vehicle is being used as a public or livery conveyance. Again, the exclusion does not apply to a share-the-expense carpool.

2. *Damage from wear and tear, freezing, and mechanical or electrical breakdown.* There is no coverage for any damage due to wear and tear, freezing, mechanical or electrical breakdown, or road damages to tires. The intent is to exclude the normal maintenance cost of operating an automobile and to cover tire defects under the tire manufacturer's warranty. However, the exclusion does not apply to the total theft of a covered auto or any nonowned auto. For example, if a stolen car is recovered but the electrical system is damaged by a thief who hot-wired the car, the loss is covered.

3. *Radioactive contamination or war.* Damage from radioactive contamination or war is excluded.

4. *Electronic equipment designed for the reproduction of sound.* The PAP excludes electronic equipment and accessories designed for the reproduction of sound, such as radios, stereos, tape decks, or compact disc players. This exclusion does not apply to equipment and accessories permanently installed in a covered auto or nonowned auto. For example, the theft of a permanently installed radio would be covered.

Likewise, the exclusion does not apply if the equipment is removable from a permanently installed housing unit, is operated solely by power from the auto's electrical system, and is in or upon the auto at the time of loss. For example, a removable stereo that is stolen from the trunk of your car would be covered.

5. *Other electronic equipment.* The PAP excludes electronic equipment that receives or transmits audio, visual, or data signals. Such equipment includes citizens band radios, telephones, two-way mobile radios, scanning monitor receivers, television monitor receivers, video cassette recorders, audio cassette recorders, and personal computers. This exclusion does not apply to electronic equipment necessary for the operation of the auto or to a permanently installed telephone. Note that the telephone must be permanently installed. Consequently, a cell phone that many motorists use while driving would not be covered.

Some safety experts consider use of a cell phone while driving to be extremely dangerous. *Research studies show the risk of having a crash while using a cell phone is four times higher than when a cell phone is not used.*[2] Also, the growing use of cell phones and laptop computers by drivers is creating a whole new array of potentially hazardous distractions that can result in auto accidents (see Insight 10.2).

6. *Tapes, records, and discs.* Loss to stereo tapes, records, discs, or other media designed for use with the electronic equipment described previously is also excluded. An endorsement can be added to the PAP to cover excluded tapes and electronic equipment.

7. *Government destruction or confiscation.* The PAP excludes the total loss to a covered auto or nonowned auto due to destruction or confiscation by a governmental or civil authority. For example, if a federal drug agency confiscates a drug dealer's car, the loss would not be covered.

8. *Trailer, camper body, or motor home.* The PAP excludes loss to a trailer, camper body, or motor home not shown in the declarations. This exclusion also applies to facilities and equipment, such as cooking, dining, plumbing or refrigeration equipment, and awnings or cabanas. For example, damage to a stove or refrigerator is not covered.

The exclusion does not apply to a nonowned trailer. Likewise, it does not apply to a trailer or camper body acquired during the policy period provided that you notify the insurer within 14 days after you become the owner.

9. *Loss to a nonowned auto used without reasonable belief of permission.* Loss to a nonowned auto is not covered when it is used by the named insured or his or her family member without a reasonable belief of permission.

10. *Radar detection equipment.* Equipment for the detection or location of radar or laser is excluded. This exclusion is justified because radar detection equipment is designed to circumvent state and federal speed laws.

Insight 10.2

Cell Phones Again Tied to Crashes: New Report Indicts Distracting Devices

Cellular phones and other popular new devices—even laptop computers—are increasingly distracting drivers on America's streets and highways.

Driver inattention already is a factor in half of all auto accidents, officials say, and things can only be expected to get worse.

"As cars more and more become an extension of the home and office, we are creating a whole new array of potentially hazardous distractions," said Dr. Ricardo Martinez, head of the National Highway Traffic Safety Administration.

"We are beginning to see crashes . . . where drivers were using laptop computers while driving, and third-party suppliers are now providing hardware for mounting laptop computers adjacent to the driver or, in some cases, right on the steering wheel."

Martinez, a former emergency-room doctor, recalled treating a driver who crashed into a tree while changing a tape. In another case, several bicyclists were struck by a car when the driver reached into the glove compartment for a compact disc.

"We're adding so many distractions, we're creating part-time drivers," he said.

But the government stopped short of calling for restrictions, saying additional research is needed and noting that the wireless equipment also has benefits.

The biggest problem is lack of solid information on how many crashes involve cellular phones and other equipment, the new report said.

But a review of accident reports from several states found "trends which show that cellular telephone use is a growing factor in crashes."

"Contrary to expectations, the majority of drivers were talking on their telephones rather than dialing at the time of the crash," the report said. "A few drivers also were startled when their cellular phones rang, and as they reached for their phones they ran off the road."

The "overwhelming majority" of cellular phone users were in the striking vehicle in an accident, the report added.

With cellular phone use growing rapidly, the report concluded, an increasing number of drivers will be exposed to this distraction. And previous government studies have cited driver inattention as a primary or contributing cause in up to half of all highway crashes.

Jeffrey Nelson of the Cellular Telecommunications Industry Association called the study "very balanced."

"Common sense tells us that when people are in their vehicles they have an opportunity to do an increasing number of different things," he observed. Making sure they use the technology safely, he said, is "educational opportunity that the industry takes very seriously."

There are 50 million cellular phones in use today and their number is expected to double by the turn of the century. That's up from just 345,000 cell phones in use in 1985, according to the new government study.

The Australian state of Victoria banned use of cell phones by drivers in 1988. Since then similar bans have been imposed in Spain, Israel, Portugal, Italy, Brazil, and Chile. In addition, driver use of hand-held phones is banned in Switzerland and Britain.

Source: Adapted from "Cell Phones Again Tied to Crashes," *Omaha World-Herald*, January 8, 1998, p. 9. Reprinted with permission from the Associated Press.

11. *Custom furnishings or equipment.* Loss to customized furnishings or equipment in or upon a pickup or van is not covered. Such furnishings or equipment include special carpeting, furniture or bars, height-extending roofs, and custom murals or paintings. However, an endorsement can be added that covers the excluded furnishings or equipment.

12. *Nonowned auto used in the automobile business.* Loss to a nonowned auto maintained or used by

someone engaged in the business of selling, repairing, servicing, storing, or parking vehicles designed for use on public highways is specifically excluded. For example, if a mechanic damages a customer's car while road testing it, the loss is not covered under the mechanic's PAP. Instead, this business loss exposure should be covered under a commercial garage policy.

13. *Racing vehicle.* Loss to a covered auto or nonowned auto is not covered while it is located in-

Insight 10.3

Totaled! Now What Do You Do?

I was tooling along downtown, driving my trusty Toyota and chatting with a colleague. Suddenly, out of nowhere, a 16-year-old girl ran a red light and smashed into me. My car careered across the road, rear-ending another.

The wreck was only my first shock; the second hit me when the auto-body shop declared that my nine-year-old car was totaled. Then the adjuster called to offer me just $2800. That's when I moved from shock to anger. I believed my car was worth more than that. By doing some homework, I channeled my anger and eventually won $1000 more from the adjuster.

"Many people don't realize that the adjuster's offer is negotiable," says Mike Erwin, spokesperson for the Insurance Information Institute based in Washington, D.C.

An adjuster can take anywhere from two days to two weeks to develop a settlement offer. While you're waiting, research your car's value. If the adjuster calls with an offer you don't like, just say no. Tell him you'll mail or fax your research within a few days. Here's how to get the best settlement possible.

1. *Call your bank or credit union and get the Kelley Blue Book prices for your car.* You'll want the Blue Book's wholesale price—the amount a dealer would pay at an auction or might offer on a trade-in car. Get the retail value, too—it's a higher figure that assumes the costs the dealer might incur on the car. If you're online, you can get the figures on the Kelley Blue Book Web site at www.kbb.com.

   The market price—what you'd likely pay if you bought the car from a car dealer or individual seller—will be somewhere in between wholesale and retail. That's the price you want to present to the adjuster to show your car's worth.

2. *When you talk to your bank, ask how much they'd loan on your car if you were buying it today.* On my 1988 Toyota Corolla, First Technology Credit Union in Portland, Oregon, would have loaned me 85 percent ($3961) of the Kelley Blue Book retail value ($4625). Wholesale value on my car was $2200.

   This is an excellent piece of information, because it reveals the value of your car to the financial community.

3. *Call your state insurance commission to see what information you're entitled to have.* "Some states require the adjuster to give you a copy of the information used to determine your car's value," says Russel

---

side a racing facility for the purpose of competing in or preparing for a prearranged racing or speed contest.

14. *Rental car.* Loss to, or loss of use of, a vehicle rented by the named insured or family member is not covered if a state law or rental agreement precludes the car rental agency from recovering from the named insured or family member.

Limit of Liability

The amount paid for a physical damage loss is the lower of the actual cash value of the damaged or stolen property or the amount necessary to repair or replace the property with other property of like kind and quality. If the cost of repairs exceeds the vehicle's actual cash value, the vehicle may be declared a total loss, and the amount paid is the actual cash value less any deductible (see Insight 10.3). For a partial loss (such as a smashed fender), only the amount necessary to repair or replace the damaged property with property of like kind and quality will be paid. If the value of the vehicle is increased after the repairs are completed (such as repainting the entire car when only one fender is damaged), the insurer will not pay for the betterment or increase in value.

The policy also has limits on the amount paid for certain losses. For example, loss to a nonowned trailer is limited to $500. Loss to equipment designed

Kennel, a compliance officer for the Oregon State Insurance Division in Salem, Oregon.

Typically, the adjuster uses a database service that finds advertisements for cars similar to yours. If you can get this information, call the telephone number listed with each ad to find out if the car being sold is truly representative of your car. Your car might be more valuable if it has fewer miles or more features, for example.

4. *Scan newspaper and Internet advertisements for vehicles similar to yours.* These vehicles don't have to be identical, but they should be close enough to ensure a fair comparison. Call the phone number listed with each ad and talk to the seller. Ask if the car has been sold and, if so, what the selling price was. This is critical information to the adjuster, who doesn't put much stock in the "asking prices" because sellers can get less—or more—than what they ask.

5. *Check the Internet for car sales in your area.* Here are three good sites used by sellers to post car advertisements: www.traderonline.com, www.carprices.com, and www.own-a-car.com. Give them a try.

6. *Visit used-car lots to learn the retail price for vehicles similar to yours.* Ask how much the sales agent might discount the car. Again, remember that the discounted or actual selling price will be more credible

to the adjuster than the retail sticker price.

7. *Ask the car dealer if he would talk to your adjuster about the price of similar vehicles in your market.* The car dealer has a stake in making sure you get the best settlement for your vehicle—the more money you get, the more you'll have available to spend on your next car.

8. *Now, write your letter to the adjuster.* List the price you expect, cite three to five of the best sources that support the higher value for your car, and, if possible, include telephone numbers for verification. Don't inflate the price; just list the amount you think is fair.

Make note of your car's positive features, such as new tires under warranty, low mileage, or an excellent maintenance record. Be sure to mention if you were the car's sole owner, if the car was completely paid for, and any other factors that contribute to the value of the car to you.

Using these steps, I was able to persuade the adjuster on my claim to raise her offer by a substantial amount: 36 percent.

SOURCE: Adapted from Erin Maclellan, "Totaled! Now What Do You Do?," *Family Money* (November/December, 1999), pp. 50–53. Reprinted with permission

for the reproduction of sound, which is installed in locations not used by the auto manufacturer for such equipment, is limited to $1000.

Payment of Loss

The insurer has the option of paying for a physical damage loss in money (including any sales tax) or repairing or replacing the damaged or stolen property. If the car or its equipment is stolen, the insurer will pay the expense of returning the stolen car to the named insured and will also pay for any damage resulting from the theft. The insurer also has the right to keep all or part of the recovered stolen property at an agreed or appraised value.

Other Sources of Recovery

If other insurance covers a physical damage loss, the insurer pays only its pro rata share. The insurer's share is the proportion that its limit of liability bears to the total of all applicable limits.

With respect to a nonowned auto (including a temporary substitute), the Part D coverages are excess over any other collectible source of recovery. *Thus, any physical damage insurance on the borrowed car is primary, and your physical damage insurance is excess.* If you borrow a car and damage it, the owner's physical damage insurance (if any) applies first, and your collision insurance is excess, subject to any deductible. For example, assume that you borrow a friend's car and damage it in an accident. The owner's collision deductible is $500, and your collision deductible is $250. If damages to the borrowed car are $2000, the owner's PAP pays $1500 ($2000 – $500), and your PAP pays $250 ($500 – $250). The remaining $250 of loss would have to be paid either by the owner or by you. In short, if the owner's collision deductible is larger than your deductible, your insurer pays the difference between the two deductibles.

Appraisal Provision

The PAP contains an appraisal provision for handling disputes over the amount of a physical damage loss. This provision is particularly important in the case of damage to a low-mileage car or to a car in above-average condition. The insured may claim that the car is worth more than the amount stated in the various publications of car prices that auto dealers use. To resolve the dispute, either party can demand an appraisal of the loss. Each party selects an appraiser. The two appraisers then select an umpire. Each appraiser states separately the actual cash value of the car and the amount of the loss. If the appraisers fail to agree, they submit their differences to the umpire. A decision by any two parties is binding on all. Each party pays his or her appraiser, and the umpire's expenses are shared equally. Finally, by agreeing to an appraisal, the insurer does not waive any rights under the policy.

PART E: DUTIES AFTER AN ACCIDENT OR LOSS

You should know what to do if you have an accident or loss. Some obligations are based on common sense, while others are required by law and by the provisions of the PAP. You should first determine if anyone is hurt. If someone is injured, an ambulance should be called. If there are bodily injuries, or the property damage exceeds a certain amount (such as $200), you must notify the police in most jurisdictions. You should give the other driver your name, address, and the name of your agent and insurer and request the same information from him or her.

Your insurance agent should be promptly notified of the accident, even if there are no injuries or property damage. Failure to report the accident

promptly to your insurer could jeopardize your coverage if you are later sued by the other driver.

After the accident occurs, a number of duties are imposed on you. You must cooperate with the insurer in the investigation and settlement of a claim. You must send to the insurer copies of any legal papers or notices received in connection with the accident. If you are claiming benefits under the uninsured motorists, underinsured motorists, or medical payments coverages, you may be required to take a physical examination at the insurer's expense. You must also authorize your insurer to obtain medical reports and other pertinent records. Finally, you must submit a proof of loss at the insurer's request.

Some additional duties are imposed on you if you are seeking benefits under the uninsured motorists coverage. The police must be notified if a hit-and-run driver is involved. Also, if you bring a lawsuit against the uninsured driver, you must send copies of the legal papers to your insurer.

If your car is damaged, and you are seeking indemnification under Coverage D, other duties are imposed on you. You must take reasonable steps to protect the vehicle from further damage; your insurer will pay for any expense involved. You must also permit the insurer to inspect and appraise the car before it is repaired. If you and the insurer cannot agree on the amount of the physical damage loss, you can demand an appraisal.

PART F: GENERAL PROVISIONS

This section contains a number of general provisions. Only two of them are discussed here.

Policy Period and Territory

The PAP provides coverage only in the United States, its territories or possessions, Puerto Rico, and Canada. The policy also provides coverage while a covered auto is being transported between the ports of the United States, Puerto Rico, or Canada. For example, if you rent a car while vacationing in England, Germany, or Mexico, you are not covered. Additional auto insurance must be purchased to be covered while driving in foreign countries. If you intend to drive in Mexico, you should first obtain liability insurance from a Mexican insurer. A motorist from the United States who has not purchased insurance from a Mexican insurer could be detained in jail after an accident, have his or her automobile impounded, and be subject to other penalties as well.

Termination

An important provision applies to termination of the insurance by either the insured or insurer. There are four parts to this provision:

- Cancellation
- Nonrenewal
- Automatic termination
- Other termination provisions

Cancellation The named insured normally can cancel at any time by returning the policy to the insurer or by giving advance written notice of the effective date of **cancellation**.

The insurer also has the right of cancellation. If the policy has been in force for *less than 60 days*, the insurer can cancel by sending a cancellation notice to the named insured. At least 10 days' notice must be given if the cancellation is for nonpayment of premiums and at least 20 days' notice in all other cases. Thus, the insurer has 60 days to investigate a new insured to determine whether he or she is acceptable.

After the policy has been in force for 60 days, or if it is a renewal or continuation policy, the insurer can cancel for only three reasons: (1) the premium has not been paid, (2) the driver's license of any insured has been suspended or revoked during the policy period, or (3) the policy was obtained through material misrepresentation.

Nonrenewal The insurer may decide not to renew the policy when it comes up for renewal. If the insurer decides not to renew the policy, the named insured must be given at least 20 days' notice of its intention not to renew.

Automatic Termination If the insurer decides to renew the policy, an automatic termination provision becomes effective. This means that if the named insured does not accept the insurer's offer to renew, the policy automatically terminates at the end of the current policy period. Thus, once the insurer bills the named insured for another period, the insured must

pay the premium, or the policy automatically terminates on its expiration date. However, some insurers may provide a short grace period to pay the renewal premium.

Finally, if other insurance is obtained on a covered auto, the PAP insurance on that auto automatically terminates on the day the other insurance becomes effective.

Other Termination Provisions Many states place additional restrictions on the insurer's right to cancel or not renew. If state law requires a longer period of advance notice to the named insured or modifies any termination provision, the PAP is modified to comply with those requirements. Also, if the policy is canceled, the named insured is entitled to any premium refund; however, making or offering to make a premium refund is not a condition for cancellation. Finally, the effective date of cancellation stated in the cancellation notice is the end of the policy period.

The Appendix that appears at the end of this chapter summarizes in convenient outline form the major coverages that appear in the 1998 PAP.

INSURING MOTORCYCLES AND OTHER VEHICLES

The PAP excludes coverage for motorcycles, mopeds, and similar vehicles. However, a **miscellaneous-type vehicle endorsement** can be added to the PAP to insure motorcycles, mopeds, motorscooters, golf carts, motor homes, dune buggies, and similar vehicles. One exception is a snowmobile, which requires a separate endorsement to the PAP. The miscellaneous-type vehicle endorsement can be used to provide the same coverages found in the PAP.

You should be aware of several points if the miscellaneous-type vehicle endorsement is added to the PAP. First, the liability coverage does not apply to a nonowned vehicle. Although other persons are covered while operating your motorcycle with your permission, the liability coverage does not apply if you operate a nonowned motorcycle (other than as a temporary substitute vehicle).

Second, a passenger hazard exclusion can be elected, which excludes liability for bodily injury to any passenger on the motorcycle. When the exclusion is used, the insured pays a lower premium. For example, if a passenger on your motorcycle is thrown off and is injured, the liability coverage on the motorcycle does not apply.

Finally, the amount paid for any physical damage losses to the motorcycle is limited to the lowest of (1) the stated amount shown in the endorsement, (2) the actual cash value, or (3) the amount necessary to repair or replace the property (less any deductible).

SUMMARY

- The Personal Auto Policy (PAP) consists of a declarations page, a definitions page, and six major parts:

  Part A: Liability Coverage

  Part B: Medical Payments Coverage

  Part C: Uninsured Motorists Coverage

  Part D: Coverage for Damage to Your Auto

  Part E: Duties After an Accident or Loss

  Part F: General Provisions

- Liability coverage protects the insured from bodily injury and property damage liability arising out of the negligent operation of an automobile or trailer.

- A covered auto includes any vehicle shown in the declarations; newly acquired vehicles; a trailer owned by the insured; and a temporary substitute auto.

- Insured persons include the named insured and spouse, resident family members, other persons using a covered auto if a reasonable belief that permission to use the vehicle exists, and any person or organization legally responsible for the acts of a covered person.

- Medical payments coverage pays all reasonable medical, dental, and funeral expenses incurred by an insured person for services rendered within three years from the date of the accident.

- Uninsured motorists coverage pays for the bodily injury of a covered person caused by an uninsured motorist, a hit-and-run driver, or a negligent driver whose insurer is insolvent.

- Underinsured motorists coverage can be added as an endorsement to the PAP. The coverage applies when a negligent driver carries liability insurance, but the liability limits carried are less than the limit provided by the underinsured motorists coverage.

- Coverage for damage to your auto pays for any direct physical loss to a covered auto or nonowned auto less any deductible. A collision loss or other-than-collision loss is covered only if the declarations page indicates that such coverages are in effect.

- Certain duties are imposed on the insured after an accident occurs. A person seeking coverage must cooperate with the insurer in the investigation and settlement of a claim and send to the insurer copies of any legal papers or notices received in connection with the accident.

- After the policy has been in force for 60 days, or it is a renewal or continuation policy, the insurer can cancel the policy only if the premium has not been paid, the driver's license of an insured has been suspended or revoked during the policy period, or the policy was obtained through material misrepresentation. If the insurer decides not to renew the policy when it comes up for renewal, the named insured must be given at least 20 days' notice of its intention not to renew.

- Motorcycles and mopeds can be insured by adding the miscellaneous-type vehicle endorsement to the personal auto policy.

KEY CONCEPTS AND TERMS

Cancellation	Other-than-collision loss
Collision	Personal Auto Policy (PAP)
Coverage for damage to your auto	Single limit
	Split limits
Extended nonowned coverage endorsement	Supplementary payments
Liability coverage	Temporary substitute vehicle
Medical payments coverage	Underinsured motorists coverage
Miscellaneous-type vehicle endorsement	Uninsured motorists coverage
Nonowned auto	Your covered auto
Nonrenewal	

REVIEW QUESTIONS

1. Describe the major coverages that are found in the PAP.

2. Indicate the types of vehicles that are eligible for coverage under the PAP.

3. Who are the persons insured for liability coverage under the PAP?

4. Describe the supplementary payments that can be paid under the liability section of the PAP.

5. If you drive a nonowned auto and damage it, will your PAP pay for the damage? Explain.

6. Who are the persons insured for medical payments coverage under the PAP?

7. Explain the major features of the uninsured motorists coverage in the PAP.

8. Describe the insuring agreement under coverage for damage to your auto in the PAP.

9. Explain the duties imposed on the insured after an accident or loss occurs.

10. How can motorcycles and mopeds be insured under the PAP?

APPLICATION QUESTIONS

1. Fred has a PAP with the following coverages:

   Liability coverages: $100,000/$300,000/$50,000
   Medical payments coverage: $5000 each person
   Uninsured motorists coverage: $25,000 each person
   Collision loss: $250 deductible
   Other-than-collision loss: $100 deductible

   With respect to each of the following situations, indicate whether the loss is covered. Assume that each situation is a separate event.

   a. Fred's son, age 16, is driving a family car and kills a pedestrian in a drag racing contest. The heirs of the deceased pedestrian sue for $100,000.

   b. Fred borrows a friend's car to go to the supermarket. He fails to stop at a red light and negligently smashes into another motorist. The other driver's car, valued at $5000, is totally destroyed. In addition, damages to the friend's car are $1000.

   c. Fred's daughter, Myra, attends college in another state and drives a family auto. Fred tells her that no other person is to drive the family car. Myra lets her boyfriend drive the car, and he negligently injures another motorist. The boyfriend is sued for $10,000.

   d. Fred's wife is driving a family car in a snowstorm. She loses control of the car on an icy street and smashes into the foundation of a house. The property damage to the house is $20,000. Damages to the family car are $5000. Fred's wife has medical expenses of $3000.

   e. Fred is walking across a street and is struck by a motorist who fails to stop. He has bodily injuries in the amount of $15,000.

   f. Fred's car is being repaired for faulty brakes. While road testing the car, a mechanic injures another motorist and is sued for $50,000.

   g. Fred's car hits a cow crossing a highway. The cost of repairing the car is $700.

   h. A thief breaks a car window and steals a camera and golf clubs locked in the car. It will cost $200 to replace the damaged window. The stolen property is valued at $500.

   i. Fred's wife goes shopping at a supermarket. When she returns, she finds that the left rear fender has been damaged by another driver who did not leave a name. The cost of repairing the car is $500.

   j. Fred works for a construction company. While driving a large cement truck, he negligently injures another motorist. The injured motorist sues Fred for $20,000.

   k. Fred's son drives a family car on a date. He gets drunk, and his girlfriend drives him home. The girlfriend negligently injures another motorist who has bodily injuries in the amount of $10,000.

   l. Several stereo tapes valued at $200 are stolen from Fred's car. The car was locked when the theft occurred.

   m. A video cassette recorder (VCR) and personal laptop computer are stolen from Fred's car. The value of the stolen property is $2500.

   n. While driving a rented golf cart, Fred accidentally injures another golfer with the cart.

2. Louise is the named insured under a PAP that provides coverage for bodily injury and property damage liability, medical payments, and the uninsured motorists coverage. For each of the following situations, briefly explain whether the claim is covered by Louise's PAP.

   a. Louise ran into a telephone pole and submitted a medical expense claim for Jason, a passenger in Louise's car at the time of the accident.

   b. Louise loaned her car to Bianca. While operating Louise's car, Bianca damaged Gray's car in an accident caused by Bianca's negligence. Bianca is sued by Gray for damages.

   c. Louise's husband ran over a bicycle while driving the car of a friend. The owner of the bicycle demands that Louise's husband pay for the damage.

   d. In a fit of anger, Louise deliberately ran over the

wagon of a neighbor's child that had been left in Louise's driveway after repeated requests that the wagon be left elsewhere. The child's parents seek reimbursement.

3. Clarice has a PAP with the following coverages:

Liability coverages: $100,000/$300,000/$50,000
Medical payment coverage: $5000 each person
Uninsured motorists coverage: $25,000 each person
Collision loss: $250 deductible
Other-than-collision loss: $100 deductible
Towing and labor cost coverage: $25 each disablement

To what extent, if any, is each of the following losses covered under Clarice's PAP? Treat each event separately.

a. Clarice rents a car while on vacation. She is involved in an accident with another motorist when she fails to yield the right of way. The injured motorist is awarded a judgment of $100,000. The rental agency carries only liability limits of $30,000 on the rental car. The rental agency carries no collision insurance on its cars and is seeking $15,000 from Clarice for repairs to the rental car.

b. Clarice borrows her friend's car with permission. She is in an accident with another motorist in which she is at fault. The cost of repairing the friend's car is $2000. The friend has a $500 deductible for collision losses and $100 for other-than-collision losses.

c. Clarice is employed as a salesperson and is furnished a company car. She is involved in an accident with another motorist while driving the company car during business hours. The injured motorist claims Clarice is at fault and sues her for $10,000. Damages to the company car are $2500.

d. Clarice's car will not start because of a defective battery. A wrecker tows the car to a service station where the battery is replaced. Towing charges are $60. The cost of replacing the battery is $100.

4. Gilbert was driving a neighbor's pickup truck to get a load of firewood. A child darted out between two parked cars and ran into the street in front of the truck. In an unsuccessful attempt to avoid hitting the child, Gilbert lost control of the vehicle and hit a telephone pole. The child was critically injured, the pickup truck was badly damaged, and the telephone pole collapsed. Gilbert has liability coverage and collision coverage under his PAP. The neighbor also has a PAP with liability coverage and collision coverage on the pickup.

a. If Gilbert is found guilty of negligence, which insurer will pay first for the bodily injuries to the child and the property damage to the telephone pole? Explain.

b. Which insurer will pay for the physical damage to the neighbor's pickup? Explain.

5. Pablo traded in his 1995 Ford for a new Ford. One week later, he hit an oily spot in the road on his way to work and skidded into a parked car. The 1995 Ford was insured under the PAP with full coverage, including a $250 deductible for a collision loss. At the time of the accident, Pablo had not notified his insurer of the trade-in. The physical damage to the parked car was $5000. Damage to Pablo's car was $3000. Will Pablo's PAP cover either or both of these losses? Explain.

SELECTED REFERENCES

Fire, Casualty & Surety Bulletins. Personal Lines volume, Personal Auto section. Cincinnati: National Underwriter Company. The bulletins are updated monthly. Up-to-date information on the personal auto policy can be found in the Personal Lines volume, Personal Auto section.

Hamilton, Karen L., and Donald S. Malecki. *Personal Insurance: Property and Liability,* first edition. Malvern, PA: American Institute for CPCU, 1994, Chapter 4.

"Personal Auto Policy." *The CPCU Handbook of Insurance Policies*, third edition. Malvern, PA: American Institute for CPCU/Insurance Institute of America, 1998, pp. 67–80.

Rejda, George E., Constance M. Luthardt, Cheryl L. Ferguson, and Donald R. Oakes. *Personal Insurance,* fourth edition. Malvern, PA: Insurance Institute of America, 2000.

NOTES

1. The material in this chapter is based on *Fire, Casualty & Surety Bulletins*, Personal Lines volume, Personal Auto section (Cincinnati, OH: National Underwriter Company); and the 1998 edition of the Personal Auto Policy (copyrighted) by the Insurance Services Office. The Personal Auto Policy is used with the permission of the Insurance Services Office.

2. Insurance Research Council, News Release, *Cell Phone Owners Prefer to Ignore Risks: Use Phones While Driving, Says New Survey*, December 23, 1997.

Case Application

Kim, age 20, is a college student who recently purchased her first car from a friend who had financial problems. The vehicle is a high-mileage 1988 Toyota Tercel with a current market value of $1000. Assume you are a financial planner and Kim asks your advice concerning the various coverages in the PAP.

a. Briefly describe the major coverages that are available in the PAP.

b. Which of the available coverages in (a) should Kim purchase? Justify your answer.

c. Which of the available coverages in (a) should Kim not purchase? Justify your answer.

d. Assume that Kim purchases the PAP coverages that you have recommended. To what extent, if any, would Kim's insurance cover the following situations?

   (1) Danielle, Kim's roommate, borrows Kim's car with her permission and injures another motorist. Danielle is at fault.

   (2) Kim is driving under the influence of alcohol and is involved in an accident where another motorist is seriously injured.

   (3) During the football season, Kim charges a fee to transport fans from a local bar to the football stadium. Several passengers are injured when Kim suddenly changes lanes without signaling.

   (4) Kim drives her boyfriend's car on a regular basis. While driving the boyfriend's car, she is involved in an accident in which another motorist is injured. Kim is at fault.

   (5) Kim rents a car in England where she is participating in a summer study program. The car is stolen from a dormitory parking lot.

e. Kim also owns a motorcycle. To what extent, if any, does Kim's PAP cover the motorcycle?

 Students may take a self-administered test on this chapter at www.awlonline.com/rejda

Summary of 1998 Personal Auto Policy Coverages

Part A—Liability Coverage

Insuring Agreement	Persons Insured	Exclusions
Pays damages for bodily injury and property damage for which the insured is legally liable because of an auto accident	Named insured and resident family members[a]	Intentional bodily injury or property damage
Legal defense costs paid	Any person using a covered auto with permission	Damage to property owned or transported by an insured
Supplemental payments:	Any person or organization legally responsible for acts or omissions of an insured while using a covered auto on behalf of that person or organization	Property rented to, used by, or in the insured's care (except a residence or private garage)
Up to $250 for the cost of a bail bond; interest accruing after a judgment; up to $200 daily for the loss of earnings due to attendance at a hearing or trial; and other reasonable expenses incurred at the company's request	Any person or organization legally responsible for acts or omissions of an insured while using any auto or trailer on behalf of that person or organization (other than a covered auto or auto owned or hired by that person or organization)	Injury to an employee during the course of employment
		Using a vehicle as a public or livery conveyance (exclusion does not apply to a share-the-expense carpool)
		Vehicles used in the automobile business (exclusion does not apply to the operation, ownership, or use of covered autos)
		Other business vehicles used in any business other than farming or ranching (exclusion does not apply to an owned or nonowned private passenger auto, pickup, or van, or a trailer used with the preceding vehicles)
		Nuclear energy exclusion
		Vehicle with fewer than four wheels, or one designed for use off public roads[b]
		Any vehicle, other than a covered auto, owned by, furnished, or made available for the named insured's regular use
		Any vehicle, other than a covered auto, owned by, furnished, or made available for a family member's regular use (exclusion does not apply to the named insured's use of a vehicle owned by a family member, or a vehicle made available for a family member's regular use)
		Vehicle located inside a racing facility to complete, practice, or prepare for a prearranged racing contest

[a] The 1998 PAP extends coverage for 90 days to a spouse who is no longer a resident of the named insured's household.

[b] Exclusion does not apply to use of the vehicle in a medical emergency, to a trailer, or to a nonowned golf cart.

Part B—Medical Payments Coverage

Insuring Agreement	Persons Insured	Exclusions
Pays reasonable medical and funeral expenses incurred by an insured for services rendered within three years of the accident	Named insured and resident family members while occupying a motor vehicle, or if injured as a pedestrian by a motor vehicle designed for use mainly on public roads Other persons while occupying a covered auto	Occupying a motorized vehicle with fewer than four wheels Using a covered auto as a public or livery conveyance (exclusion does not apply to a share-the-expense carpool) Using the vehicle as a residence or premises Injury occurring during the course of employment if workers compensation benefits are required or available Vehicle furnished or made available for the named insured's regular use Vehicle furnished or made available for the regular use of any family member Occupying a vehicle without a reasonable belief of being entitled to do so Vehicle used in the business of an insured (exclusion does not apply to a private passenger auto, an owned pickup or van, or a trailer used with any of the preceding vehicles) Nuclear weapons, war, nuclear reaction, or radiation Occupying a vehicle located inside a racing facility for the purpose of competing in or preparing for a prearranged racing contest

Part C—Uninsured Motorist Coverage

Insuring Agreement	Persons Insured	Exclusions
Pays compensatory damages that an insured is legally entitled to recover from the owner or operator of an uninsured motor vehicle because of bodily injury sustained by an insured caused by an accident	Named insured and resident family members Any other person while occupying a covered auto Any person legally entitled to recover damages because of bodily injury to a person described above	No uninsured motorist coverage on a motor vehicle owned by an insured No coverage for a family member who occupies, or is struck by, a motor vehicle owned by the named insured that is insured for uninsured motorists coverage on a primary basis by another policy Settling a claim without the insurer's consent Using a covered auto as a public or livery conveyance (exclusion does not apply to a share-the-expense carpool) Using a vehicle without a reasonable belief that the insured is entitled to do so No benefit to workers compensation insurer No punitive damages paid

Part D—Coverage for Damage to Your Auto

Insuring Agreement	Persons Insured	Exclusions

Pays for direct and accidental loss to a covered auto or to a nonowned auto, including their equipment, minus any deductible, caused by a collision or other than collision. Declarations must indicate such coverage is provided for each vehicle.
 	
Loss caused by the following is considered other-than-collision:
  Missiles or falling objects
  Fire
  Theft or larceny
  Explosion or earthquake
  Windstorm
  Hail, water, or flood
  Malicious mischief or vandalism
  Riot or civil commotion
  Contact with a bird or animal
  Breakage of glass
 	
Transportation expenses:
  Pays up to $20 daily, to a maximum of $600, for transportation expenses because of loss to a covered auto caused by collision or other than collision. Declarations must indicate such coverage is provided for each vehicle.
 	
Also pays expenses for which the insured is legally liable because of loss to a nonowned auto
	Part D does not specifically mention the persons insured. However, coverage applies to the named insured and spouse, resident family members, and any person using a covered auto with permission.	Loss to a covered auto or nonowned auto while being used as a public or livery conveyance (exclusion does not apply to share-the-expense carpool)
		
		Damage from wear and tear, freezing, and mechanical or electrical breakdown
		
		Radioactive contamination or war
		
		Electronic equipment and accessories designed for the reproduction of sound—including radios, stereos, tape decks, or compact disc players—unless permanently installed in the auto. Certain other exceptions apply.
		
		Other electronic equipment, including citizens band radios, telephones, two-way mobile radios, scanning monitor receivers, television monitor receivers, video cassette recorders, and personal computers[c]
		
		Tapes, records, and discs used with the preceding equipment
		
		Government destruction or confiscation
		
		Loss to a trailer, camper body, or motor home not shown in the declarations (except if newly acquired and reported within 14 days)
		
		Loss to nonowned auto used without a reasonable belief of permission to do so
		
		Radar or laser detection equipment
		
		Custom furnishings or equipment in a pickup or van
		
		Nonowned auto maintained or used in the automobile business
		
		Vehicle located inside a racing facility for the purpose of competing in or preparing for a prearranged racing contest
		
		Loss to a rental car if a state law or rental agreement precludes the rental company from recovering from the insured

[c] Exclusion does not apply to electronic equipment for the normal operation of the auto or to a permanently installed car telephone.

Chapter 11

Automobile Insurance and Society

"The current system of paying for auto injuries suffers from two fundamental problems: premiums are too high and victims with serious injuries rarely receive full compensation."

Joint Economic Committee, 105th Congress

Learning Objectives

After studying this chapter, you should be able to:

▲ Describe the various approaches for compensating auto accident victims.

▲ Explain the meaning of no-fault auto insurance and the rationale for no-fault insurance laws.

▲ Identify the methods for providing auto insurance to high-risk drivers.

▲ Identify the major factors that determine the cost of auto insurance to consumers.

▲ Explain the rules that should be followed in shopping for auto insurance.

▲ Access an Internet site and obtain a premium quote for auto insurance.

Internet Resources

- **Geico Direct** sells auto insurance directly over the phone (800-624-8341). The company claims that a 15-minute call can save you 15 percent or more on auto insurance rates. Geico Direct's Web site provides similar premium quotes on-line. Visit the site at:

  http://www.geico.com

- The **Insurance Information Institute** provides timely information on auto insurance and other personal property insurance coverages. Numerous consumer brochures and articles on auto insurance and other property and liability coverages can be accessed directly online. Visit the site at:

  http://www.iii.org/

- The **Insurance News Network** provides premium quotes for auto insurance, homeowners insurance, and other insurance products. The site also provides timely information and news releases about auto insurance and events that affect the insurance industry. Visit the site at:

  http://www.insure.com/

- **INSWEB** provides premium quotes for auto, homeowners, and other insurance products. You can comparison shop from your computer. In addition, the site includes a page for insurance professionals. Visit the site at:

  http://www.insweb.com/

- **MoneyCentral** is designed primarily for investors, but the site also provides important consumer information on various insurance coverages. Premium quotes can be obtained for auto insurance and other insurance coverages. Click on "Insurance" to obtain information about auto insurance. Visit the site at:

  http://moneycentral.msn.com/home.asp

- **Quicken Insurance** is an excellent site for obtaining consumer information about auto insurance. It provides premium quotes for auto insurance, homeowners insurance, and other insurance products. It offers agent referral or direct signup data from major insurance companies. Visit the site at:

  http://www.quickeninsurance.com

*K*aren, age 23, graduated from a Northeastern university and accepted a teaching position at an elementary school in Miami Beach, Florida. Just before the fall term began, a speeding motorist ran a red light at a busy intersection and smashed into her car. It will cost $2200 to repair the car. Karen did not carry collision insurance. When she attempted to collect damages from the negligent driver, she discovered that the driver was unemployed and had no auto insurance. In short, Karen had to eat the loss.

Karen's introduction to the auto insurance reparations system was costly. She was fortunate to experience only a physical damage loss to her car. Each year, millions of motorists are injured or killed in auto accidents. Society then has the problem of compensating these victims for the bodily injuries and property damage caused by negligent drivers. Society also has the burden of providing auto insurance to irresponsible drivers, including drunk drivers, high-risk drivers, and drivers who habitually break traffic laws. In addition, it must deal with the problem of compensating innocent accident victims who are injured by uninsured drivers. Some critics argue that the present system for compensating auto accident victims is severely flawed and should be replaced by an alternative system called no-fault insurance. Likewise, some consumer groups believe that auto insurance rates are too high, which has led to cries for legislative reform.

This chapter discusses the preceding problems in depth. Four areas are emphasized: (1) the various approaches for compensating auto accident victims, (2) no-fault auto insurance as an alternative to the present system, (3) methods for providing auto insurance to high-risk drivers, and (4) suggestions for buying auto insurance.

APPROACHES FOR COMPENSATING AUTOMOBILE ACCIDENT VICTIMS

In many cases, innocent persons who are injured in auto accidents are unable to recover financial damages from the negligent motorists. Although accident victims may have bodily injuries or suffer property damage, they may recover nothing or receive less than full indemnification. To deal with this problem, the states use a number of approaches to provide some protection to accident victims from irresponsible and reckless drivers. They include the following:[1]

- Financial responsibility laws
- Compulsory insurance laws
- Unsatisfied judgment funds
- Uninsured motorists coverage
- No-fault auto insurance

Financial Responsibility Laws

All states have enacted some type of financial responsibility law or compulsory insurance law requiring motorists to furnish proof of financial responsibility up to certain minimum dollar limits that vary by state. A **financial responsibility law** *does not require proof of financial responsibility until after the driver has his or her first accident or until after conviction for certain offenses, such as driving under the influence of alcohol.* Proof of financial responsibility is typically required under the following circumstances:

- After an accident involving bodily injury or property damage over a certain amount
- Failure to pay a final judgment resulting from an auto accident
- Conviction for certain offenses, such as drunk driving or reckless driving

Under these conditions, if a motorist does not meet the state's financial responsibility law requirements, the state can revoke or suspend the motorist's driving privileges.

Evidence of financial responsibility can be provided by producing an auto liability insurance policy with at least certain minimum limits, such as $25,000/$50,000/$25,000.[2] Other ways in which the financial responsibility law can be satisfied are by posting a bond, by depositing securities or money in

the amount required by law, or by showing that the person is a qualified self-insurer. Exhibit 11.1 shows the minimum liability insurance requirements in the various states.

Although financial responsibility laws provide some protection against irresponsible motorists, they have two major defects:

- *There is no guarantee that all accident victims will be paid.* Financial responsibility laws normally have no penalties other than the loss of driving privileges. Thus, the accident victim may not be paid if he or she is injured by an uninsured driver, hit-and-run driver, or driver of a stolen car. An irresponsible motorist often drives without a license, so the law fails to achieve the objective of getting the irresponsible driver off the road.
- *Accident victims may not be fully indemnified for their injuries.* Most financial responsibility laws require only minimum liability insurance limits, which are relatively low. If the bodily injury exceeds the minimum limit, the accident victim may not be fully compensated.

Compulsory Insurance Laws

Most jurisdictions have enacted some type of compulsory automobile liability insurance law as a condition for driving within the state. A **compulsory insurance law** *requires motorists to carry at least a minimum amount of liability insurance before the vehicle can be licensed or registered.*

Some people believe that compulsory insurance laws are superior to financial responsibility laws because motorists must provide evidence of financial responsibility before an accident occurs. However, a recent study by the National Association of Independent Insurers (NAII) casts doubt on the effectiveness of these laws. The study concludes that compulsory liability insurance laws do not reduce the number of uninsured drivers, auto losses, or insurance premiums. More specifically, the study notes the following defects:[3]

- *Compulsory insurance laws do not compel drivers to buy and keep insurance over the long term.* Uninsured motorist populations continue to increase in states with compulsory laws.
- *Substantial numbers of motorists continue to op-*

EXHIBIT 11.1

Financial Responsibility and Compulsory Auto Insurance Limits by State

State	Liability Limits[1]	State	Liability Limits[1]	State	Liability Limits[1]
Alabama*	20/40/10	Kentucky	25/50/10	North Dakota	25/50/25
Alaska	50/100/25	Louisiana	10/20/10	Ohio	12.5/25/7.5
Arizona	15/30/10	Maine	50/100/25	Oklahoma	10/20/10
Arkansas	25/50/15	Maryland	20/40/10	Oregon	25/50/10
California	15/30/5[2]	Massachusetts	20/40/5	Pennsylvania	15/30/5
Colorado	25/50/15	Michigan	20/40/10	Rhode Island	25/50/25
Connecticut	20/40/10	Minnesota	30/60/10	South Carolina	15/30/10
Delaware	15/30/5	Mississippi***	10/20/5	South Dakota	25/50/25
D.C.	25/50/10	Missouri	25/50/10	Tennessee***	25/50/10
Florida**	10/20/10	Montana	25/50/10	Texas	20/40/15
Georgia	15/30/10	Nebraska	25/50/25	Utah	25/50/15
Hawaii	20/4010	Nevada	15/30/10	Vermont	25/50/10
Idaho	25/50/15	New Hampshire***	25/50/25	Virginia	25/50/20
Illinois	20/40/15	New Jersey	15/30/5[3]	Washington	25/50/10
Indiana	25/50/10	New Mexico	25/50/10	West Virginia	20/40/10
Iowa	20/40/15	New York	25/50/10[4]	Wisconsin***	25/50/10
Kansas	25/50/10	North Carolina	25/50/15	Wyoming	25/50/20

[1]The first two figures refer to bodily injury liability and the third figure to property damage liability. For example, 20/40/10 means coverage up to $40,000 for all persons injured in an accident, subject to a limit of $20,000 for one individual, and $10,000 coverage for property damage.

[2]Low-cost policy limits for Los Angeles and San Francisco low income drivers in the California Automobile Assigned Risk Plan are 10/20/3; pilot program; effective January 1, 2000 until January 1, 2004.

[3]Drivers may choose a Standard or Basic Policy. Basic Policy limits are 10/10/5.

[4]50/100 if injury results in death.

*Effective June, 2000.

**Property damage liability only is compulsory.

***Liability insurance not compulsory; limits are for financial responsibility.

NOTE: Data are from Alliance of American Insurers, American Insurance Association, National Association of Independent Insurers, Insurance Information Institute.

SOURCE: *The I.I.I. Insurance Fact Book 2000* (New York, NY: Insurance Information Institute), p. 2.10.

erate vehicles without insurance. In 1995, about 15 percent of the entire driver population in the nation had no liability insurance. However, of the 43 states that required drivers to buy such insurance, 13 states had estimated uninsured motorist populations higher than the countrywide norm. In five of these jurisdictions, more than 20 percent of the drivers were uninsured.

■ *Despite compulsory insurance laws, claim frequency and loss costs associated with financially irresponsible drivers continue to increase in those states requiring such insurance.*

■ *The injury loss experience connected to drivers without liability insurance is on average worse in compulsory states than in noncompulsory states.* Drivers with insurance in the compulsory states are 21 percent more likely to file an injury claim in an accident caused by someone without coverage. In addition, it costs 27 percent more to provide uninsured motorists coverage for injury claims in states with compulsory insurance laws.

■ *The combined average liability insurance premium in seven states without compulsory laws is 26 percent less than the nationwide average.* Conversely, policyowners in compulsory states must pay higher-than-average premiums. From 1992 to

1996, the average combined liability premium in the noncompulsory states rose $37 overall, whereas the increase in the compulsory states was $46.

Unsatisfied Judgment Funds

Five states—Maryland, Michigan, New Jersey, New York and North Dakota—have established unsatisfied judgment funds for compensating innocent accident victims. An **unsatisfied judgment fund** *is a state fund for compensating auto accident victims who have exhausted all other means of recovery.* These funds have certain common characteristics:[4]

- The accident victim must obtain a judgment against the negligent motorist and must show that the judgment cannot be collected.
- The maximum amount paid generally is limited to the state's compulsory insurance law. The amount paid may also be reduced by collateral sources of recovery, such as workers compensation benefits.
- The negligent driver is not relieved of legal responsibility when the fund makes a payment to the accident victim. Negligent drivers must repay the fund or lose their driver's license until the fund is reimbursed for the payments.

The method of financing benefits varies from state to state. Funds can be obtained by charging a fee to each motorist, by assessing insurers based on the amount of auto liability insurance written in the sate, by assessing the uninsured motorists in the state, and by surcharging drivers with convictions for moving vehicle violations.

Uninsured Motorists Coverage

Uninsured motorists coverage is another approach for compensating injured auto accident victims. The injured person's insurer agrees to pay the accident victim who has a bodily injury (or property damage in some states) caused by an uninsured motorist, by a hit-and-run driver, or by a negligent driver whose insurer is insolvent.

Uninsured motorists coverage has the following advantages.

- *Motorists have some protection against an uninsured driver.* Many states require the coverage to

be mandatorily included in all auto liability insurance policies sold within the state. In other states, coverage is included in the policy unless the insured voluntarily declines the protection by signing a written waiver.

- *Claim settlement is faster and more efficient than a tort liability lawsuit.* Although the accident victim must establish negligence by the uninsured driver, it is not necessary to sue the negligent driver and win a judgment.

Uninsured motorist's coverage, however, has several defects as a technique for compensating injured auto accident victims. They include the following:

- *Unless higher limits are purchased, the maximum amount paid is limited to the state's financial responsibility or compulsory insurance law requirement.* The minimum limits are relatively low. Thus, the accident victim may not be fully compensated for his or her loss.
- *The injured person must establish that the uninsured motorist is legally liable for the accident.* This task may be difficult in some cases and expensive if an attorney must be hired.
- *Property damage is not covered in many states.* Unless you have collision coverage, you would collect nothing for any property damage caused by an uninsured motorist in those states.

No-Fault Auto Insurance

No-fault auto insurance is another method for compensating injured accident victims. Because of dissatisfaction and defects in the traditional tort liability system, about half of the states, the District of Columbia, and Puerto Rico currently have no-fault laws in effect. Although no-fault laws vary among the states, certain common characteristics are present.

Definition of No-Fault Insurance
No-fault auto insurance *means that after an auto accident involving a bodily injury, each party collects from his or her insurer regardless of fault.* It is not necessary to determine who is at fault and prove negligence before a loss payment is made. Regardless of who caused the accident, each party collects from his or her insurer.

In addition, a true no-fault law places some restriction on the right to sue the negligent driver who caused the accident. If a bodily injury claim is below a certain **monetary threshold** (such as $2000), an injured motorist would not be permitted to sue but instead would collect from his or her insurer. However, if the bodily injury claim exceeds the threshold amount, the injured person has the right to sue the negligent driver for damages. In some states, a verbal rather than monetary threshold is used. A **verbal threshold** *means that a suit for damages is allowed only in serious cases, such as those involving death, dismemberment, disfigurement, or permanent loss of a bodily member or function.* Thus, if the injured person has a less severe injury than those listed, the injured person would not be permitted to sue but instead would collect from his or her insurer.

Basic Characteristics of No-Fault Plans No-fault plans vary widely among the states with respect to the type of law, benefits provided, and restrictions on the right to sue.[5] Proposals for new types of no-fault plans are continually emerging.

1. *Types of no-fault plans.* Several types of no-fault plans and proposals exist. They include the following:

- Pure no-fault plan
- Modified no-fault plan
- Add-on plan
- Choice no-fault plan

Under a **pure no-fault plan**, *accident victims cannot sue at all, regardless of the amount of the claim, and no payments are made for pain and suffering.* In effect, the tort liability system is abolished, because accident victims cannot sue for damages. Instead, injured persons would receive unlimited medical benefits and lost wages from their insurers. No state has enacted a pure no-fault plan at this time, but Michigan's law comes closest to this concept.

Under a **modified no-fault plan**, *an injured person has the right to sue a negligent driver only if the bodily injury claim exceeds the dollar or verbal threshold.* Otherwise, the accident victim collects from his or her insurer. Thus, modified no-fault plans only partially restrict the right to sue.

An **add-on plan** *pays benefits to an accident victim without regard to fault, but the injured person*

still has the right to sue the negligent driver who caused the accident. This plan also includes the right to sue for pain and suffering (general damages). Hence the name: the law adds benefits but takes nothing away. Because the injured person retains the right to sue, add-on plans are not true no-fault laws.

Three states (Kentucky, New Jersey, and Pennsylvania) have **choice no-fault plans.** Under such laws, motorists can elect to be covered under the state's no-fault law with lower premiums or can retain the right to sue under the tort liability system with higher premiums.

Slightly more than half of the jurisdictions with no-fault laws have enacted modified plans where restrictions are placed on the right to sue. The remainder have add-on plans or choice no-fault laws. As noted earlier, no state has enacted a pure no-fault plan, and three states have choice no-fault laws.

2. *No-fault benefits.* No-fault benefits are provided by adding an endorsement to the auto insurance policy. The endorsement is typically called "basic reparations benefits coverage" or "personal injury protection coverage," which describes the no-fault benefits. Benefits are restricted to the injured person's *economic loss,* such as medical expenses, a percentage of lost wages, and certain other expenses. The injured person can sue for *noneconomic loss* (such as pain and suffering and inconvenience) only if the dollar threshold is exceeded or the verbal threshold is met.

The following benefits are typically provided:

- Medical expenses
- Loss of earnings
- Essential services expenses
- Funeral expenses
- Survivors' loss benefits

Medical expenses are paid usually up to some maximum limit. Rehabilitation expenses incurred by an injured accident victim are also paid.

Payments are made for the loss of earnings. The no-fault benefits are typically limited to a stated percentage of the disabled person's weekly or monthly earnings, with a maximum limit in terms of dollar amount and duration.

Benefits are paid for **essential services expenses** *ordinarily performed by the injured person.* Examples include housework, cooking, lawn mowing, and house repairs.

Funeral expenses are paid up to some dollar limit. In some states, funeral expenses are included as part of the medical expense limit. In other states, funeral expenses are a separate benefit.

Survivors' loss benefits *are payable to eligible survivors, such as a surviving spouse and dependent children.* The survivors typically receive periodic income payments or a lump sum to compensate them for the death of a covered person.

A number of states also require that **optional no-fault benefits** above the prescribed minimums be made available. Likewise, many states require insurers to offer **optional deductibles** that may be used to restrict or eliminate certain no-fault coverages.

3. *Right to sue.* In those states with add-on plans, there are no restrictions on the right to sue. The accident victim can receive first-party no-fault benefits from his or her insurer and still sue the negligent driver for damages.

All states permit a lawsuit in the event of a serious injury. A serious injury typically is a personal injury that results in death, dismemberment, disfigurement, bone fracture, permanent loss of a bodily function or organ, or permanent disability. Under these circumstances, the injured person can sue for damages, including payment for pain and suffering.

In those states with modified no-fault laws, the right to sue is restricted. In general, the accident victim can sue the negligent driver for general damages, including pain and suffering, only if a dollar or verbal threshold is met.

Finally, the three states with choice no-fault laws allow motorists to elect coverage under the state's no-fault law with lower premiums and restrictions on lawsuits or, alternatively, to retain the right to sue under the tort liability system with higher premiums.

4. *Exclusion of property damage.* With the exception of Michigan, no-fault laws cover only bodily injury and exclude property damage. Thus, if a negligent driver smashed into your car, you would still be permitted to sue for the property damage to your car. It is argued that the defects inherent in the tort liability system with respect to bodily injuries

are not normally present to the same degree in property damage claims; thus, a lawsuit for property damage does not normally result in long court delays, expensive legal fees, and defects similar to those now found in bodily injury lawsuits.

Arguments for No-Fault Laws Proponents of no-fault laws argue that an alternative system is needed because of defects in the present tort liability system. These defects include the following:

- *Difficulty in determining fault.* Critics argue that auto accidents occur suddenly and unexpectedly, and determination of fault is often difficult. In contrast, under a no-fault law, it is not necessary to determine fault. Each party collects from his or her insurer if the bodily injury claim is below a certain dollar threshold or does not meet the description of a verbal threshold.

- *Inequity in claim payments.* Under the present system, small claims are often overpaid, whereas serious claims may be underpaid. A 1991 study by the Rand Institute for Civil Justice, for example, showed that accident victims with relatively minor injuries and medical expenses of less than $2000 recovered, on average, about two and one-half times their economic loss. *In contrast, claimants with damages of more than $100,000 recouped, on average, just 9 percent of their economic losses.*[6]

- *High transactions costs and attorney fees.* Critics also argue that the present tort system incurs high transactions costs and attorney fees. A Joint Economic Committee Study showed that for each premium dollar paid for bodily injury liability, attorneys (both plaintiffs and defendants) receive more than 28 cents of the premium dollar. Overhead expenses, state taxes and fees, and commissions and selling expenses eat up another 28 cents. Fraudulent and excessive claims account for another 13 cents out of each premium dollar. *Only 31 cents of each premium dollar is paid to injured claimants for medical bills, lost wages, and pain and suffering related to actual economic loss* (see Exhibit 11.2).

- *Fraudulent and excessive claims.* The Joint Economic Committee Study showed that the present system is flawed because of fraudulent and

EXHIBIT 11.2
Distribution of Bodily Injury Premiums

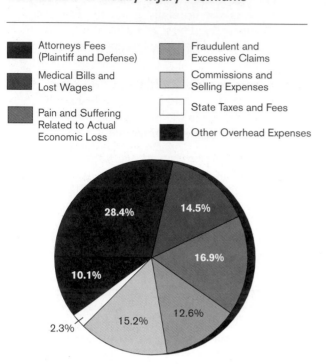

- Attorneys Fees (Plaintiff and Defense)
- Medical Bills and Lost Wages
- Pain and Suffering Related to Actual Economic Loss
- Fraudulent and Excessive Claims
- Commissions and Selling Expenses
- State Taxes and Fees
- Other Overhead Expenses

28.4%
14.5%
16.9%
10.1%
12.6%
15.2%
2.3%

Source: "Auto Choice: Impact on Cities and the Poor," *Joint Economic Committee Study*, 105th Congress, Washington, DC (March 1998), Figure 3.

excessive claims. Two types of abuse are observed. First, explicit fraud occurs, including staged auto accidents, fake claims, and collusion among doctors, attorneys, and chiropractors. Second, the present system encourages injured victims to inflate their claims above their actual losses to increase their damage awards. Because payments for noneconomic losses (pain and suffering) are difficult to calculate, one rule of thumb currently followed is to calculate such losses as two to three times the claimant's economic losses (medical bills and lost wages). *Because pain and suffering awards are based on a multiple of medical expenses and wage loss, claimants have a powerful incentive to inflate their claims.* According to one estimate, fraudulent and excessive auto insurance claims cost each American household $200 annually in additional premiums.[7]

- *High cost of auto insurance.* Critics of the present system argue that auto insurance premiums are excessively high in certain parts of the country. According to the Joint Economic Committee, excessive and unnecessary fraud, litigation, and injury claims pushed the average insurance premium to more than $774 in 1996.[8]

  The high cost of auto insurance has severe financial effects for some urban drivers. In particular, auto insurance in the inner cities is prohibitively expensive. The Joint Economic Committee estimates that the average premium for a female, age 38, in central Los Angeles with a clean driving record is almost $3500 annually. Also, the high cost of auto insurance increases the proportion of uninsured drivers. For example, a 1995 survey by the California Department of Insurance found that 28 percent of the drivers in that state were uninsured; in Los Angeles County, the figure was 37 percent; in San Francisco, it was nearly 33 percent.[9] Finally, the high cost of auto insurance has severe financial consequences for low-income families. For households with auto insurance, the poorest fifth of those households spends more than 16 percent of household income on auto insurance, or more than seven times the amount spent by the wealthiest fifth (see Exhibit 11.3).

- *Delay in payments.* Under the present system, many claims are not paid promptly because of the time consumed by investigation, negotiation, and waiting for a court date. Moreover, hiring an attorney does not necessarily speed up payment. An Insurance Research Council (IRC) study of closed claims in 1997 showed that claimants without attorneys received payments significantly more quickly than claimants with attorneys. *Thirty-one percent of bodily injury claimants without an attorney received a final payment from their insurers within 30 days of the injury report, compared with only 1 percent of claimants represented by attorneys.*[10]

  In addition, hiring an attorney does not necessarily mean that injured claimants will be better off financially than claimants without attorneys. *According to the IRC study, claimants represented by attorneys received lower net payments than claimants without attorneys after deducting*

EXHIBIT 11.3
Vehicle Insurance as a Share of Household Income

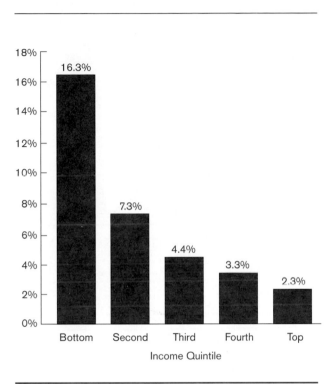

SOURCE: "Auto Choice: Impact on Cities and the Poor," *Joint Economic Committee Study*, 105th Congress, Washington, DC (March 1998), Figure 10.

legal fees and economic losses (such as medical expenses and lost wages). On average, claimants with attorneys received net payments of $708, whereas claimants without attorneys received net payments of $1449 (see Exhibit 11.4). Although claimants with attorneys received substantially higher gross payments, they incurred average legal fees of 32 percent of the award. This group also incurred higher economic losses (primarily medical expenses) to be paid out of their claim settlement.[11]

Arguments Against No-Fault Laws Supporters of the present system argue that no-fault laws are also defective. Major arguments against no-fault laws include the following:

- *Defects of the negligence system are exaggerated.* Generations of judges, lawyers, and juries have successfully applied negligence concepts to auto accidents. A large proportion of fatal crashes and serious accidents involve alcohol where fault can usually be determined without difficulty. Also, the fact that most claims are settled out of court suggests that the present system is working fairly well.
- *Claims of efficiency and premium savings are exaggerated.* Predictions of greater efficiency and premium savings from no-fault laws are exaggerated and unreliable. In many states with no-fault laws, premiums have increased more rapidly than in tort liability states.
- *Court delays are not universal.* Court delays because of congestion are a problem only in certain large metropolitan areas, and this delay can be reduced by providing for more adequate courts and improved procedures. Also, court delays are a separate problem and should be attacked as such rather than used as an argument for a no-fault system. The courts are burdened because of an increase in the number of divorce cases, drug and other criminal cases, and other types of civil suits.
- *Safe drivers may be penalized.* A no-fault plan can penalize safe drivers and provide a bonus for irresponsible motorists who cause the accidents. The rating system may inequitably allocate the accident costs to the drivers who are not at fault, and their premiums may go up as a result.
- *There is no payment for pain and suffering.* Plaintiff attorneys argue that the true cost to the accident victim cannot be measured only by the actual dollar amount of medical expenses and loss of wages. Pain and suffering should also be considered in determining the amount of damages.
- *The present system just needs to be reformed.* This reform could be accomplished by increasing the number of judges and courtrooms, limiting the fees of attorneys, and using arbitration rather than the courts to settle small cases. Rather than replacing the old system with a new system of no-fault, the present system needs only to be reformed, not abandoned.

Evaluation of No-Fault Laws? A few states have repealed their no-fault laws because of low dollar

EXHIBIT 11.4

Net Payment to Bodily Injury Claimants by Attorney Representation

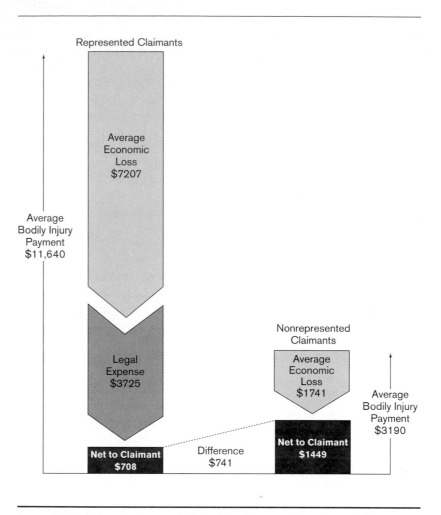

SOURCE: *Injuries in Auto Accidents, an Analysis of Auto Insurance Claims, Executive Summary* (Malvern, PA: Insurance Research Council, 1999), Figure 1-6, p. 9.

thresholds that resulted in additional lawsuits. Other states have changed their plans over time. A study of no-fault plans by the Institute for Civil Justice provides valuable information concerning the effectiveness of no-fault plans. The major conclusions are as follows:[12]

■ *No-fault plans reduce transaction costs (attorney fees and claim processing costs).* All no-fault plans

reduce transaction costs. However, a no-fault plan that absolutely banned compensation for noneconomic loss would eliminate about three-fourths of the transaction costs. Alternative plans that allow some access to the liability system would reduce transaction costs by 20 to 40 percent, depending on the plan design.

■ *No-fault plans match the compensation received for an injury more closely with the economic loss sustained.* No-fault plans increase the fraction of economic loss that is compensated and reduce the amount paid for noneconomic loss. Economic loss includes medical bills, lost wages, and other losses measured in monetary terms. Injured people with smaller claims tend to recover amounts that approximate their medical costs and lost wages. However, seriously injured people recover a larger share of their losses because they can collect both no-fault benefits and liability compensation.

- *No-fault plans eliminate compensation for noneconomic loss, such as pain and suffering, for injured people below the threshold.* Noneconomic losses include pain and suffering, disfigurement, and other losses not measured in monetary terms.
- *No-fault plans generally pay benefits more quickly.* On average, no-fault plans pay benefits to injured people about two months faster than under the traditional system.
- *No-fault plans can yield substantial savings over the traditional system, or such plans can increase costs depending on the plan design.* Under different no-fault alternatives, total injury coverage costs may decrease. Such costs, however, may be higher under no-fault plans, depending on the threshold and level of no-fault benefits. This is especially true in states that have relatively low dollar thresholds. Whether a particular no-fault plan will reduce total injury coverage costs will depend on the provisions in the plan and plan design.

Proposed Federal No-Fault Legislation

Several federal no-fault proposals have been introduced in Congress over the years. A recent proposal is the *Auto Choice Reform Act of 1997.* Under this plan, drivers would have two choices: (1) remain in the present tort liability system based on existing state law, or (2) choose a new system called personal protection insurance (PPI).

Drivers who elect the tort liability system would retain the same basic rights that they currently have under existing state law by purchasing "tort maintenance" coverage. In a collision involving two tort liability drivers, the injured party could sue the negligent driver for economic losses (medical bills and lost wages), as well as for noneconomic losses (pain and suffering), as under the present tort system.

However, in a collision between a tort liability driver and a PPI driver, the tort driver would recover economic and noneconomic losses, including pain and suffering, up to the policy limits from his or her own insurer. If losses exceed the tort maintenance coverage limit, the tort liability driver could sue the negligent PPI driver for any remaining economic loss (but not for any noneconomic losses).

Drivers who elect the PPI system would recover only their economic losses up to the policy limits from their own insurers, regardless of fault. Damages would not be paid for pain and suffering. However, PPI drivers would retain the right to sue under existing state negligence laws for economic losses in excess of their policy limits. Because PPI provides insurance coverage only for economic losses, PPI drivers could neither sue nor be sued for noneconomic losses, with the exceptions of intentional injury or an accident caused by a drunk or drug-impaired driver.

Proponents believe the auto choice plan will reduce fraud, inflated claims, and litigation, and substantially lower premiums. According to a 1998 Joint Economic Committee Study, this plan could reduce private passenger auto insurance premiums by 23 percent for 1998, or an average of $184 per car.[13]

AUTO INSURANCE FOR HIGH-RISK DRIVERS

Some drivers have difficulty obtaining auto insurance through normal market channels. This is especially true of younger drivers, who account for a disproportionate number of auto accidents, drivers who have poor driving records, and drivers with one or more convictions for drunk driving. These drivers can obtain automobile insurance in the **shared market** (also called the **residual market**). The shared market refers to plans in which auto insurers participate to make insurance available to drivers who are unable to obtain coverage in the standard markets.

High-risk drivers who have difficulty in obtaining auto insurance in the standard markets can purchase the insurance from a number of sources. They include the following:

- Auto insurance plans
- Joint underwriting associations (JUAs)
- Reinsurance facility

- Maryland Automobile Insurance Fund
- Specialty automobile insurers

Auto Insurance Plans

Most states have an auto insurance plan (also called an assigned risk plan) that makes auto insurance available to motorists who are unable to obtain protection in the voluntary market. Under an **auto insurance plan,** all auto insurers in the state are assigned their proportionate share of high-risk drivers based on the total volume of auto insurance written in the state. The premiums charged, however, are substantially higher than those charged in the voluntary markets. It is not uncommon for high-risk drivers to pay two or three times the standard premium.

The major advantage of automobile insurance plans is that a high-risk driver generally has at least one source for obtaining liability insurance. Thus, the social objective of protecting innocent accident victims is at least partially met. Nevertheless, such plans have several disadvantages, which include the following:

- *Despite higher premiums paid by high-risk drivers, auto insurance plans have incurred substantial underwriting losses.* Thus, good drivers in the voluntary markets are subsidizing the substandard drivers.
- *High premiums may cause many high-risk drivers to go uninsured.* This effect is the exact opposite of what the plans are intended to accomplish.
- *Many drivers who are "clean risks" with no driving convictions are arbitrarily placed in the plans.* This can happen when poor territorial loss experience or inadequate rate increases granted by regulatory officials cause insurers to restrict the writing of auto insurance in a given territory in the voluntary market.
- *The driver does not have a choice of insurers.* Thus, freedom of choice is reduced.

Joint Underwriting Associations

A few states have established joint underwriting associations to make auto insurance available to high-risk drivers. A **joint underwriting association (JUA)** is an organization of auto insurers operating in the state in which high-risk business is placed in a common pool, and each company pays its pro rata share of pool losses and expenses. The JUA influences the design of the high-risk auto policy and sets the rates that are charged. All underwriting losses are proportionately shared by the companies on the basis of premiums written in the state.

A limited number of insurance companies are designated as servicing insurers to service the high-risk JUA business. Each agent or broker is assigned a company that provides claim services and other services to the policyowners. Although only a limited number of large insurers are servicing insurers, all insurers share in the underwriting losses, as noted earlier.

Reinsurance Facility

A few states have established a **reinsurance facility (** or **pool)** for placing high-risk drivers. Under this arrangement, the insurance company must accept all applicants for insurance, both good and bad drivers. If the applicant is considered a high-risk driver, the insurer has the option of placing the driver in the reinsurance pool. Although the high-risk driver is in the reinsurance pool, the original insurer services the policy. Underwriting losses in the reinsurance facility are shared by all auto insurers in the state.

Maryland Automobile Insurance Fund

The **Maryland Automobile Insurance Fund** is a state fund that makes auto insurance available to motorists in Maryland who are unable to obtain insurance in the voluntary markets. The state fund came into existence because of high rates charged by private insurers, large numbers of motorists who had been placed in the assigned risk plan, and difficulties experienced by high-risk drivers in obtaining insurance. The fund limits the insurance to drivers who have been canceled or refused insurance by private insurers.

Specialty Auto Insurers

Specialty auto insurers are insurers that specialize in insuring motorists with poor driving records. These insurers typically insure drivers who have been canceled or refused insurance, teenage drivers, and drivers convicted of drunk driving. The premiums are substantially higher than those paid in the normal or standard markets. The actual premium paid is based on the individual's driving record, typically over the past three years. The higher the number of chargeable accidents or moving vehicle traffic violations, the higher the premium charged. The liability insurance limits are at least equal to the financial responsibility law requirement in the state, and many insurers offer higher limits on an optional basis. In addition, because the drivers have a high probability of being involved in an accident, medical payments coverage often has relatively low limits, and collision insurance may require a high deductible.

Some insurers have driver incentive plans to encourage safe driving; premiums are periodically reduced if the insured has had no chargeable offenses during the policy period. However, if another accident or traffic violation occurs during the policy period, the driver typically is surcharged and must pay higher premiums.

COST OF AUTO INSURANCE

Auto insurance is a costly and necessary coverage. Payment of auto insurance premiums can quickly deplete a modest checking account. Depending on the area in which you live, your age, driving experience, and other factors, the annual cost of insuring your car can range from several hundred dollars to several thousand dollars. You should have some knowledge of the factors that determine your auto insurance premiums and what you can do to reduce the premiums. This section discusses the major factors that determine the cost of auto insurance. Discussion is limited to liability insurance and physical damage insurance on the car, as these two coverages account for a large proportion of the total annual premium.

The major rating factors for determining private passenger auto premiums are as follows:

- Territory
- Age, gender, and marital status
- Use of the auto
- Driver education
- Good student discount

- Number and types of cars
- Individual driving record

Territory

A base rate for liability insurance is first established, determined largely by the territory where the auto is principally used and garaged. Each state is divided into rating territories—for example, a large city, a part of a city, a suburb, or a rural area. Claims data are compiled for each territory in determining the basic rate. Thus, a city driver normally pays a higher rate than a rural driver because of the higher number of auto accidents in congested cities. In addition, because of increased litigation, higher claim costs, large numbers of vehicles, and traffic congestion, average annual auto insurance premiums are substantially higher in certain states, such as New Jersey and New York (see Exhibit 11.5).

Age, Gender, and Marital Status

Age, gender, and marital status are important in determining the total premium. Most states permit these factors to be used in determining premiums.

Age is an extremely important rating factor because young drivers account for a disproportionate number of auto accidents. In 1998, drivers under age 25 accounted for about 14 percent of all licensed drivers; however this group accounted for about 27 percent of the drivers in all accidents and 24 percent of all fatal accidents (see Exhibit 11.6, on page 229. Older drivers over age 65 are also involved in a high percentage of fatal accidents (see Exhibit 11.7, on page 230).

Gender is also important. In recent years, female drivers have experienced higher accident rates than male drivers. However, male drivers are involved in a higher proportion of accidents where someone is killed.[14] Although insurers generally charge female drivers lower rates than males, the rate gap is narrowing, especially at the younger ages.

Marital status is also important for some age groups, because young married male drivers tend to have relatively fewer accidents than unmarried male drivers in the same age category.

Certain credits and rate discounts may be allowed with respect to the rating factor of age. A premium credit may be given if a youthful driver of a

EXHIBIT 11.5

Auto Insurance Average Expenditures by State, 1997

State	Average Expenditure[a]	Rank	Liability	Collision	Comprehensive
Alabama	$615.99	29	$331.08	$266.97	$105.38
Alaska	776.38	12	482.62	308.71	131.41
Arizona	818.51	10	513.41	231.28	156.96
Arkansas	565.86	38	326.03	228.19	115.45
California[b]	776.22	13	503.86	249.64	122.09
Colorado	774.12	14	487.57	213.93	178.58
Connecticut	909.12	5	604.05	261.26	177.35
Delaware	827.79	9	575.79	227.40	89.00
D.C.[c]	1,039.34	2	597.84	376.02	206.45
Florida	759.19	16	488.98	214.41	110.78
Georgia	652.71	25	348.17	305.32	134.04
Hawaii	912.36	4	695.95	240.65	97.16
Idaho	479.37	46	289.52	183.36	104.19
Illinois	665.74	24	374.97	237.27	114.33
Indiana	571.14	36	346.12	220.04	97.32
Iowa	456.02	50	259.92	160.16	100.69
Kansas	516.18	43	275.04	186.56	170.25
Kentucky	597.36	33	390.97	229.40	96.07
Louisiana	841.07	8	548.65	268.21	148.29
Maine	477.59	47	284.13	179.83	78.86
Maryland	771.59	15	480.98	241.36	113.03
Massachusetts[d]	802.94	11	563.33	200.43	110.54
Michigan	736.28	18	326.76	382.45	146.09
Minnesota	671.26	23	438.01	167.46	125.46
Mississippi	648.25	26	347.17	262.31	143.73
Missouri	613.94	31	355.25	226.37	118.89
Montana	501.00	45	283.88	185.82	160.71
Nebraska	504.54	44	277.17	173.83	157.11
Nevada	848.15	7	586.83	251.84	117.40
New Hampshire	615.54	30	366.45	236.92	84.17
New Jersey	1,125.89	1	738.08	377.23	177.44
New Mexico	689.87	22	441.33	234.73	158.49
New York	952.89	3	640.84	277.98	194.73
North Carolina	555.85	40	341.79	218.13	92.54
North Dakota	436.23	51	228.36	164.38	152.76
Ohio	572.34	35	349.20	202.23	79.28
Oklahoma	565.70	39	337.45	203.36	156.71
Oregon	621.12	28	395.43	202.07	99.99
Pennsylvania	718.26	19	452.45	235.54	109.79
Rhode Island	865.67	6	602.69	279.95	117.81
South Carolina	629.06	27	401.11	227.01	104.80

EXHIBIT 11.5
Auto Insurance Average Expenditures by State, 1997 (continued)

State	Average expenditure[a]	Rank	Liability	Collision	Comprehensive
South Dakota	$470.26	49	$270.39	$163.55	$161.47
Tennessee	585.72	34	325.04	246.63	96.54
Texas[e]	740.09	17	506.76	180.79	137.13
Utah	609.70	32	377.36	217.08	108.19
Vermont	519.27	42	287.38	217.23	88.36
Virginia	565.93	37	359.03	186.99	82.56
Washington	693.07	21	467.59	190.19	105.01
West Virginia	706.60	20	446.41	250.43	124.59
Wisconsin	548.30	41	318.53	177.77	107.55
Wyoming	477.48	48	250.61	191.05	178.45
Countrywide	$705.87		$439.99	$235.76	$122.34

[a]Average Expenditure = Total premiums written/Liability Car-Years. A car-year is equal to 365 days of insured coverage for a single vehicle and is the standard measurement for automobile insurance.

[b]Preliminary.

[c] The District of Columbia is entirely urban and its results may not be directly compared to states with rural areas.

[d]Data incorporate Safe Driver Plan credits and surcharges.

[e]Due to the absence of county mutual data, Texas results are not comparable to results from other states.

NOTE: Reprinted from State Average Expenditures and Premiums for Personal Automobile Insurance in 1997, published by the National Association of Insurance Commissioners in March 1999.

SOURCE: Insurance Information Institute, *The I.I.I. Insurance Fact Book 2000*, pp. 2.5, 2.6.

EXHIBIT 11.6
Accidents by Age of Drivers, 1998

Age Group	Number of Drivers	Percent of Total	Drivers in Fatal Accidents	Percent of Total	Drivers in All Accidents	Percent of Total
Under 20	9,984,000	5.4%	6400	11.4%	2,940,000	13.8%
20–24	15,529,000	8.4	7100	12.7	2,800,000	13.1
25–34	37,265,000	20.1	11,900	21.2	4,900,000	23.0
35–44	41,859,000	22.6	11,300	20.1	4,400,000	20.8
45–54	33,662,000	18.2	7700	13.7	2,940,000	13.8
55–64	21,337,000	11.5	4600	8.2	1,570,000	7.4
65–74	15,244,000	8.2	3600	6.4	1,010,000	4.7
Over 74	10,570,000	5.7	3500	6.2	710,000	3.3
Total	185,450,000	100.0[a]	56,100	100.0[a]	21,300,000	100.0[a]

[a] Percent of total columns may not add due to rounding.

NOTE: Data are from National Safety Council.

SOURCE: Insurance Inforamation Institute, *The I.I.I. Fact Book 2000*, p. 3.19.

EXHIBIT 11.7

Motor Vehicle Deaths per 100,000 Persons by Age, 1998

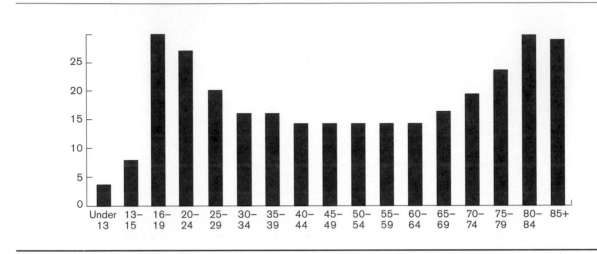

NOTE: Insurance Institute for Highway Safety data.

SOURCE: *The I.I.I. Insurance Fact Book 2000*, p. 3.19.

family car is attending a school or college more than 100 miles away from home and does not have a car at school. Also, female drivers ages 30 through 64 may be eligible for a rate discount if they are the only drivers in their households. Older drivers are also eligible for rate discounts from many insurers.

Use of the Auto

Use of the auto is another important rating factor. Insurers classify vehicles on the basis of how the car is driven, such as the following:

- Pleasure use—not used in business or customarily driven to work, unless the one-way mileage to work is under 3 miles.
- Drive to work—not used in business, but is driven 3 to 15 miles to work each day.
- Drive to work—not used in business, but is driven 15 or more miles each way.
- Business use—customarily used in business or professional pursuits.
- Farm use—principally garaged on a farm or ranch, and not used in any other business or driven to school or work.

A car classified for farm use has the lowest rating factor, followed next by pleasure use of the car. Driving the car to work or using it for business purposes requires a higher rating factor.

Driver Education

If a youthful operator successfully completes an approved driver education course, he or she can receive a driver training credit, such as 10 or 15 percent. The rate credit is based on the premise that driver education courses for teenage drivers can reduce accidents and hold down insurance rates.

Good Student Discount

A **good student discount** is available in many states. The cost reduction is based on the premise that good students are better drivers. The psychological makeup and intellectual capacity of the superior student also contribute to the safer operation of an automobile. Also, a superior student will probably spend more time studying and less time driving the family car.

To qualify for the discount, the individual must be a full-time student in high school or college, be at least age 16, and meet one of the following:

- Rank in the upper 20 percent of the class
- Have a B average, or the equivalent
- Have at least a 3.0 average
- Be on the Dean's List or honor roll

A school official must sign a form indicating that the student has met one of the scholastic requirements.

Number and Types of Cars

A **multicar discount** is available if the insured owns two or more cars. This discount is based on the assumption that two cars owned by the same person will not be driven as frequently as only one car owned by that person or family.

The year, make, and model also affect the cost of physical damage insurance on the car. Premiums on a new car will be considerably higher than premiums on a car that is several years old. As the car gets older, the collision premiums decline.

Also, the damageability and repairability of the car are important rating factors for physical damage insurance. New cars are now rated based on susceptibility to damage and cost of repairs. Cars that are damage-resistant and relatively easy to repair generally have lower rates.

In the past, auto insurers have often used generic car parts instead of original parts to repair damaged autos. Purchasing such generic parts has enabled insurers to hold down the cost of auto insurance. Recently, however, the use of generic auto parts has resulted in class action lawsuits by disgruntled motorists who claim that generic parts are of lower quality, and that an auto policy promises to repair or replace the car with materials of "like kind and quality." As a result of a judgment against a large auto insurer on this issue, some observers believe that auto insurance premiums will likely increase in the future (see Insight 11.1).

Individual Driving Record

Many insurers have **safe driver plans** where the premiums paid are based in large part on the individual driving record of the insured and operators who live with the insured. The insured who has a clean driving record qualifies for a lower rate than drivers who have poor records. A clean driving record means that the driver has not been involved in any accident where he or she is at fault and has not been convicted of a serious traffic violation in the last three years. A driver without a clean record must pay higher premiums.

Points are assessed for accidents and traffic violations, and rate surcharges are applied accordingly. Points are charged for a conviction of drunk driving, failure to stop and report an accident, homicide or assault involving an automobile, driving on a suspended or revoked driver's license, and other offenses. The actual premium paid is based on the total number of accumulated points.

Most insurers impose a surcharge for a chargeable accident that exceeds a given amount, such as $500. The surcharge generally lasts three years. For example, the base premium may be surcharged 10 percent for the first accident and 25 percent for the second.

In addition to these rating factors, many insurers are now using *credit scores* based on an applicant's credit record for purposes of underwriting or rating. If the credit score is below a certain level, an applicant may be denied insurance or placed in a higher rating class. Such use of credit scores in underwriting or rating is highly controversial, however (see Insight 11.2).

SHOPPING FOR AUTO INSURANCE

As a careful insurance consumer, you should remember certain suggestions when you buy an auto insurance policy (see Exhibit 11.8).

Carry Adequate Liability Insurance

The most important rule in purchasing auto insurance is to carry adequate liability insurance. If you carry minimum limits to satisfy the state's financial or compulsory insurance law, such as $25,000/$50,000/$25,000, you are seriously underinsured. Even if you carry higher limits of $100,000/$300,000/$50,000, you are still underinsured in most states. A negligent driver who is underinsured could have a deficiency judgment filed against him or

Insight 11.1

Parts Case May Hike Premiums:
Auto Insurers Say Generic Parts Have Helped to Keep Costs Down

A court in Marion, Illinois, has imposed a record $1.2 billion judgment against State Farm for ordering some collision damage to be repaired with generic car parts. Three groups—insurers, auto body shops, and trial lawyers—are arguing over what it means.

Its ultimate effect may be rising insurance rates, not a triumph for consumers.

State Farm, the nation's largest auto insurer, and some other insurers say that if they have to stop buying generic sheet-metal parts—generally knock-offs from Taiwan—and rely only on the auto makers, policyholders could pay additional billions of dollars. However, State Farm says it can cover the direct costs of the verdict without raising rates.

It is not only that Ford charges $400 for the hood on a 1995 Taurus while the generic part costs $202, or that Pontiac wants $216 for the fender on a 1995 Grand Am that a Taiwanese manufacturer will sell for $59. *If the generic parts disappear, insurers say, the car makers will have a monopoly, abandoning all restraint.*

The insurance industry's poster car is the 1997 Taurus GL, which sold for $19,000 new, but would cost $72,000 if assembled from spare Ford parts today, a trade group estimated. And that is with the restraining influence of competition from generic parts.

The lawyers who brought the suit against State Farm dismiss the insurers' arguments and say the decision will give policyholders what they were promised in their policies: replacement parts of "like kind and quality."

Nobody can make a bumper or a headlight assembly for a Toyota that is as good as Toyota's, and sell it for less than Toyota does, the lawyers contend, pointing to economies of scale and competitors' need to reverse-engineer. Imitation parts cannot "transcend their destiny," one lawyer said, and become genuine.

The auto body shops say that not having to deal with generic parts means that their work will go faster and easier, leaving fewer grounds for consumer complaints.

But the shops, the insurers say, have a history of billing for genuine parts, installing the generic ones and pocketing the difference—sometimes to satisfy customers who want the shop to absorb the deductible.

The dispute over repair parts applies only to sheet metal, since other parts are not generally seen as threats to automotive purity.

"There is a whole world of after-market parts that people are very accustomed to using," said Michael J. Donoghue, vice president of claims at Allstate, the second-largest auto insurer.

He cited Midas mufflers, Monroe shock absorbers, and NAPA parts. "People don't seem to question those things," he said.

Many consumers, however, have learned that they can end up with poor repairs no matter the source of the parts.

Good body work, like good house painting, can require an assertive consumer, willing to reject shoddy jobs. In auto body repairs, the paint, the most visible part of the project, is applied by the body shop, regardless of where the parts are made.

Disputes over collision damage probably go back to the creation of the second car, providing a target for the first one to collide with. After an accident, many people feel dissatisfied with their insurance companies. In their defense, the insurers point out that drivers deal with them mostly during times of trauma, hardly the best circumstances for getting to like someone with power over you.

The immediate stakes in the current dispute are highest for the State Farm customers who filed 4.7 million accident claims in the last 12 years, and whose cars were repaired with generic parts. Those customers are in line for payments averaging $250, unless an appeals court intervenes.

State Farm says that if its appeal fails and it must pay the $1.2 billion, the verdict will cost customers nothing.

It is not clear how the verdict will make any of the parties happier. The sum is huge by historical standards but perhaps not for State Farm, which has $16 billion salted away for catastrophes. Spread among the 37 million policies issued by the company, the cost of the judgment comes to about $32 a car.

SOURCE: Adapted from "Parts Case May Hike Premiums," *Sunday World-Herald*, October 17, 1999, pp. 1-M, 3-M. Reprinted with permission from *The New York Times*.

Insight 11.2

What Your Auto Insurer Knows About You

When you apply for auto insurance or submit a claim, you are probably unaware of the streams of information about you that flow among insurers and private businesses. Companies that make money by selling information about you include Fair Isaac and ChoicePoint.

Fair Isaac, based in California, calculates the credit scores for auto insurance applicants. Fair Isaac says a credit score is a snapshot of a person's level of risk. The company uses statistical models and mathematical tables that assign points for factors indicative of repayment, such as bankruptcy, liens, and history of bill payments. Fair Isaac will not reveal the methods it uses, but the company maintains its scoring system is objective.

ChoicePoint, which is an offshoot of the Equifax credit reporting company, maintains a database called CLUE (comprehensive loss underwriting exchange). The company uses the information it gathers for credit reporting, claims history reporting, and driving-record reporting. When a consumer fills out a new auto insurance application, the potential insurer may query ChoicePoint for a credit score and claims history. "If you've got a car that's been in 35 accidents, that's something the insurance company is going to want to know," says Mark Wheeler, spokesperson for ChoicePoint.

The use of credit scores for purposes of underwriting or rating in auto insurance is controversial. *Critics claim credit scores are flawed; the correlation between credit history and driving records is weak; and credit scores don't accurately reflect your driving behavior.* Credit scores generally are based on credit activity. If you have some unusual activity within the month before you buy auto insurance, your credit score may be downgraded. As a result, you may not be able to get the best rate.

Despite the flaws in using credit scores, many insurers continue to use applicants' credit scores in their underwriting decisions. For example, the Travelers Group will not write coverage if an applicant's credit report has what is called the "big five"—foreclosure, repossession, lien, claims judgment against you, and bankruptcy. Actuaries for Travelers have determined that applicants with any of the "big five" on their credit report file 30 percent more claims than people who do not have credit problems.

Source: Adapted from Joe Frey, "What Your Auto Insurer Knows About You," *Insurance News Network*, February 1, 1999.

her, under which both present and future income and assets could be attached to satisfy the judgment. You can avoid this problem by carrying adequate liability limits.

You should also consider purchasing a personal umbrella policy, which will provide another $1 million to $10 million of liability insurance on your car on an excess basis after the underlying insurance is exhausted. The personal umbrella policy is discussed in Chapter 12.

Carry Higher Deductibles

Another important suggestion is to carry higher deductibles for collision and other-than-collision losses (also called comprehensive). Some insureds carry deductibles as low as $100, which is too low in view of the rapid inflation in car prices over time. Many insureds have $250 deductibles. Increasing the deductible from $250 to $500, however, will reduce your collision and comprehensive cost by 15 to 30 percent.

If you own an expensive car with a market value of $20,000 or more, you might even consider a $1000 collision deductible. For example, assume that a male driver, age 40, owns a 1999 Cadillac DeVille that he drives to work less than 30 miles weekly in a small Midwestern city. Based on the rates of one insurer, a $250 deductible requires an annual premium of about $767 for collision coverage. If the deductible is increased to $1000, the annual premium is reduced to about $601, or a drop of about 22 percent. Stated differently, the insured would give up $750 of coverage for a premium re-

EXHIBIT 11.8
Tips for Buying Auto Insurance

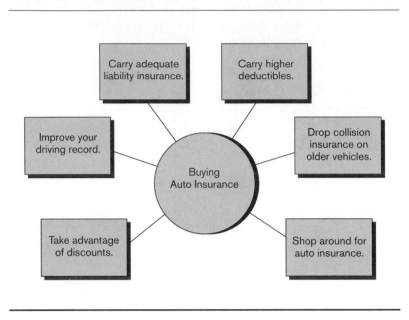

duction of $166. *That $750 is an expensive increment of insurance.*

Drop Collision Insurance on an Older Vehicle

You should consider dropping collision insurance on your car if it is an older model with a low market value. The cost of repairs after an accident will often exceed the value of an older car, but the insurer will pay no more than its current market value (less the deductible). One rough rule of thumb is that when a standard auto (such as a Chevrolet, Ford, or Dodge) is more than six years old, you should drop the physical damage insurance on the car.

Shop Around for Auto Insurance

Another important suggestion is to shop carefully for auto insurance. There is intense price competition among insurers. Contact several insurers and compare premiums. Many state insurance departments publish shoppers' guides to help insurance con-

sumers make better purchase decisions. State insurance departments also have Web sites that provide information on auto insurance rates in different cities within the state. For example, Exhibit 11.9 compares the rates of 15 insurers that write 72 percent of the coverage in Nebraska for six different classes of drivers in southeast and southwest Omaha. As you can see, rates among insurers vary widely for the same coverages.

Take Advantage of Discounts

When shopping for auto insurance, you should determine whether you are eligible for one or more discounts. All insurers do not offer the same discounts, and certain discounts are not available in all states. Common discounts include the following:

- *Multicar discount*—10 to 15 percent
- *No accidents in three years*—5 to 10 percent
- *Drivers over age 50*—5 to 15 percent
- *Defensive driving course*—5 to 10 percent
- *Antitheft device*—5 to 50 percent discount for comprehensive (other-than-collision)

- *Automatic seat belt and air bag*—20 to 60 percent for medical payments
- *Antilock brakes*—5 to 10 percent
- *Good student discount*—5 to 25 percent
- *Auto and homeowners policy with same insurer*—5 to 15 percent
- *College student away from home without a car*—10 to 40 percent

Improve Your Driving Record

If you are a high-risk driver and are paying exorbitant premiums, having a clean driving record over the past three years will substantially reduce your premiums. In the meantime, you should consider other alternatives. Although physical damage insurance on a new or late-model car can easily double the premiums for a high-risk driver, an older car can

be driven without collision insurance. You might also consider riding a motorcycle or bicycle or using mass transit. Nevertheless, there is no substitute for a good driving record.

To maintain a good driving record, you should not drive after you have been drinking alcohol. Drunk drivers account for a relatively high proportion of auto accidents in which someone is seriously injured or killed. A conviction for driving under the influence (DUI) can have a devastating effect on the premiums you are charged. Premiums can easily double or triple after a DUI conviction.

Finally, in the past two years, auto insurance rates have declined. Many auto insurers have reduced rates because of improved claim experience. If your premiums have not gone down, consumer experts recommend that you request a reduction or change insurers (see Insight 11.3).

EXHIBIT 11.9
Auto Insurance Premiums for Omaha, Nebraska (Six-Month Premiums)

Type of Car and Coverage Limits

1997 Ford Taurus GL Sedan 4 Door

Liability Limits of:

$25,000/$50,000	Bodily Injury
$25,000	Property Damage
$1000	Medical Payments
$25,000/$50,000	Underinsured Motorist
$25,000/$50,000	Uninsured Motorist
$250	Collision Deductible
$100	Comprehensive Deductible

Hypothetical Drivers

Example 1: 17-Year-Old Male, Principal driver, pleasure use, driving fewer than 12,000 miles annually. No violations or accidents in the last three years.
Example 2: 17-Year-Old Female, Principal driver, pleasure use, driving fewer than 12,000 miles annually. No violations or accidents in the last three years.
Example 3: 21-Year-Old Male, Principal driver, pleasure use, driving fewer than 12,000 miles annually. No violations or accidents in the last three years.
Example 4: 21-Year-Old Female, Principal driver, pleasure use, driving fewer than 12,000 miles annually. No violations or accidents in the last three years.
Example 5: 44-Year-Old Married Male or Female, Principal driver, pleasure use, driving fewer than 12,000 miles annually. No violations or accidents in the last three years.
Example 6: 65-Year-Old Married Male or Female, Principal driver, pleasure use, driving fewer than 12,000 miles annually. No violations or accidents in the last three years.

EXHIBIT 11.9

Auto Insurance Premiums for Omaha, Nebraska (Six-Month Premiums) (continued)

	Premiums: Southeast Omaha					
	Example 1	*Example 2*	*Example 3*	*Example 4*	*Example 5*	*Example 6*
Company	*17-yr-old Male*	*17-yr-old Female*	*21-yr-old Male*	*21-yr-old Female*	*44-yr-old Married Male or Female*	*65-yr-old Married Male or Female*
Allied Property & Casualty Ins. Co.	$1286	$ 845	$ 961	$ 706	$318	$272
Allstate Indemnity Co.	2102	1376	1493	1028	730	730
Allstate Insurance Co.	1613	998	869	656	459	415
Amco Insurance Co.	1365	896	1020	749	338	288
American Family Mutual Ins. Co.	1555	989	989	668	442	400
American Standard Ins. Co. of Wisconsin	1504	1306	1412	956	636	574
Dairyland Ins. Co.	1926	1422	1524	1032	798	876
Farm Bureau Ins. Co. of Nebraska	1147	823	623	473	276	276
Farmers Insurance Exchange[a]	N/A	N/A	1354	1048	441	428
Farmers Mutual Ins. Co. of Nebraska	905	654	565	437	302	256
Mid-Century Ins. Co.[b]	2346	1719	1452	1356	978	948
Motor Club Ins. Assoc.	1201	672	744	427	308	279
Progressive Northern Ins. Co.	2008	1436	1179	892	618	657
Shelter Mutual Ins. Co.	1559	982	878	637	367	325
State Farm Mutual Auto Ins. Co.	1302	891	717	559	385	338

	Premiums: Southwest Omaha					
Allied Property & Casualty Ins. Co.	$1145	$ 753	$ 856	$ 629	$284	$243
Allstate Indemnity Co.	1968	1279	1423	962	687	687
Allstate Insurance Co.	1357	840	721	545	378	342
Amco Insurance Co.	1216	799	909	668	302	258
American Family Mutual Ins. Co.	1555	989	989	668	442	400
American Standard Ins. Co. of Wisconsin	1504	1306	1412	956	636	574
Dairyland Ins. Co.	1926	1422	1524	1032	798	276
Farm Bureau Ins. Co. of Nebraska	1147	823	623	473	276	276
Farmers Insurance Exchange[a]	N/A	N/A	969	757	312	303
Farmers Mutual Ins. Co. of Nebraska	905	654	565	437	302	256
Mid-Century Ins. Co.[b]	1730	1262	1049	989	705	683
Motor Club Ins. Assoc.	1201	672	744	427	308	279
Progressive Northern Ins. Co.	1854	1325	1095	826	570	603
Shelter Mutual Ins. Co.	1425	897	802	582	335	297
State Farm Mutual Auto Ins. Co.	1143	783	630	491	339	297

[a]The collision deductible for Examples 3 and 4 were changed from $250 to $200 because the company does not offer a $250 deductible. For Examples 5 and 6 the following coverages apply: Bodily Injury/Property Damage—30/60/25, Medical—$2000, Uninsured/Underinsured Motorist—30/60, Comprehensive deductible—$120, and Collision deductible $240.

[b]The collision deductible was changed from $250 to $200 because the company does not offer a $250 deductible.

NOTE: The premiums shown are for six months based on the rates in effect as of August 1, 1999.

SOURCE: Nebraska Department of Insurance, *1999 Auto Rate Guide.*

Insight 11.3

> ### Driving a Bargain: Car Insurance Is Getting Cheaper Amid Heated Competition. Go Ahead, Demand a Better Rate.
>
> After some fat years for insurance companies, motorists are finally sharing in the benefits of a safer driving climate. The average rate for auto coverage fell 2.8 percent last year—the first decline in 25 years. Premiums should fall an additional 4.5 percent this year, and motorists with good driving records may save even more. The best part is that you may get a rate reduction without having to ask. Competition is that intense. But don't count on it. Review your policy to make sure that you're not overpaying.
>
> The lower rates have been a long time coming, given the powerful trends that have helped insurers to powerful profits. Start with safer cars: most vehicles now have air bags and antilock brakes. Autos are harder to steal too—newer models have security systems that disable the engine when you take the key out. Stiffened penalties have curbed drunk driving. And baby boomers have moved into the demographic sweet spot for cautious driving. Motorists ages 40 to 59 have a lower rate of traffic deaths than any other group.
>
> Warren Buffett, the investor and head of Berkshire Hathaway, noted some of these trends two years ago, when his Geico insurance subsidiary doubled its projected 4 percent profit margin because the number of claims was decreasing. Last year margins were well over the target again. Buffett warned that such stellar results would not persist because they would soon invite competition. That's what has happened, and now he expects the industry's margins to contract as insurers cut prices to battle for market share—bad news if you own the stocks but not if you're a policyholder.
>
> Geico and State Farm have been among the leaders cutting prices, and others will be forced to match them. So pull out your policy and see if your insurer is following suit. If not, play hardball. As when asking for a lower credit-card or mortgage rate, if you make it clear that you're ready to shop around, you'll probably get the best results. Don't think it's worth your time? Fair enough. A 3 percent-to-5 percent reduction may not amount to much, and many companies will give it to you automatically when you renew. But chances are, it's time to revisit your policy anyway. You should do that every few years to make sure your policy fits your constantly changing insurance needs. That car you covered three years ago has depreciated. It may not be worth the price of collision insurance. And if $500 doesn't seem like the mountain of money it once was, raise your deductible to cut your premium as much as 30 percent. If you've moved to a rural location or drive much less than before, you can get a lower rate. You can also get discounts by bundling several cars on one policy or by earning good grades in school or by having a spotless driving record in the past three years. And, of course, if your teenager has moved out, your heart may hurt but your pocketbook will enjoy a lower insurance tab.
>
> While reviewing your auto insurance, look at your homeowners policy, too. With housing values going up, you may need to increase your coverage. If your net worth has risen, you should consider raising the limit on your umbrella policy. For home or auto, the best way to shop for insurance is to look at your current policy and make sure it's right—then get quotes on identical coverage from three insurers. Now that you're part of the safe-driving crowd, there's no reason to get careless with your money.
>
> SOURCE: Daniel Kadlec, "Driving a Bargain," *Time* (May 24, 1999), p. 93. Reprinted with permission.

SUMMARY

- Financial responsibility laws require motorists to show proof of financial responsibility at the time of an accident involving bodily injury or property damage over a certain amount, for conviction of certain offenses, and for failure to pay a final judgment resulting from an auto accident. Most motorists meet the financial responsibility law requirements by carrying auto liability insurance limits of a certain amount.

- Compulsory insurance laws require motorists to carry auto liability insurance at least equal to a certain amount before the vehicle can be licensed or registered.

- Five states have unsatisfied judgment funds to compensate accident victims who have exhausted all other means of recovery. The accident victim must obtain a judgment against the negligent driver who caused the accident and show that the judgment cannot be collected.

- Uninsured motorists coverage is another approach for compensating auto accident victims. Uninsured motorists coverage compensates the accident victim who has bodily injuries caused by an uninsured motorist, by a hit-and-run driver, or by a negligent driver whose company is insolvent.

- No-fault auto insurance means that after an auto accident involving a bodily injury, each party collects from his or her own insurer, regardless of fault. There are several types of no-fault plans:

  Pure no-fault plan
  Modified no-fault plan
  Add-on plan
  Choice no-fault plan

- The arguments for no-fault auto insurance laws are summarized as follows:

  Difficulty in determining fault
  Inequity in claim payments
  High transaction costs and attorney fees
  Fraudulent and excessive claims
  High cost of auto insurance
  Delay in payments

- The arguments against no-fault auto insurance laws are summarized as follows:

  The defects of the negligence system are exaggerated.
  Claims of efficiency and premium savings are exaggerated.
  Court delays are not universal.
  Safe drivers may be penalized.
  There is no payment for pain and suffering.
  The present system needs only to be reformed.

- Several approaches are used to provide auto insurance to high-risk drivers:

  Automobile insurance plans
  Joint underwriting association (JUA)
  Reinsurance facility

  Maryland Automobile Insurance Fund
  Specialty automobile insurers

- The premium charged for auto insurance is a function of numerous variables, including territory; age, gender, and marital status; use of the auto; driver education; good student discount; number and types of autos; and the insured's driving record.

- Consumer experts suggest several rules to follow when shopping for auto insurance:

  Carry adequate liability insurance.
  Carry higher deductibles.
  Drop collision insurance on an older vehicle.
  Shop around for insurance.
  Take advantage of discounts.
  Improve your driving record.

KEY CONCEPTS AND TERMS

Add-on plan
Automobile insurance plan
Choice no-fault plan
Compulsory insurance law
Essential services expenses
Financial responsibility law
Good student discount
Joint underwriting associations (JUAs)
Maryland Automobile Insurance Fund
Modified no-fault plan
Monetary threshold
Multicar discount
No-fault auto insurance
Optional deductibles
Optional no-fault benefits
Pure no-fault plan
Reinsurance facility (or pool)
Safe driver plans
Shared market (residual market)
Specialty auto insurers
Survivors' loss benefits
Uninsured motorists coverage
Unsatisfied judgment fund
Verbal threshold

REVIEW QUESTIONS

1. What is a financial responsibility law?
2. Explain the meaning of a compulsory insurance law.
3. What is an unsatisfied judgment fund? How do these funds work?
4. Explain the meaning of no-fault auto insurance. Describe the major types of no-fault laws.
5. List the arguments for and against no-fault auto insurance.
6. Explain the purpose of an automobile insurance plan.

7. What is a joint underwriting association (JUA)?

8. How does a reinsurance facility work?

9. What factors determine the premium charged for auto insurance?

10. Explain the suggestions that a person should follow when shopping for auto insurance.

APPLICATION QUESTIONS

1. All states have passed some type of financial responsibility or compulsory insurance law to compensate accident victims.

   a. Describe how a financial responsibility law functions. In your answer, indicate the various ways in which proof of financial responsibility can be satisfied.

   b. Does a compulsory auto liability insurance law adequately protect innocent accident victims? In your answer, state the arguments for and against compulsory insurance laws.

2. Unsatisfied judgment funds are used in some states to compensate accident victims.

   a. Describe the major features of an unsatisfied judgment fund.

   b. How effective are unsatisfied judgment funds in meeting the problem of compensating innocent accident victims?

3. Many states have passed some type of no-fault auto insurance law to compensate accident victims.

   a. Describe the benefits that are typically paid under a no-fault law.

   b. Explain the rationale for enactment of a no-fault auto insurance law.

   c. What is a "threshold" in a no-fault automobile insurance law?

   d. How well have no-fault auto insurance laws worked? Explain your answer.

Case Application

Paige, age 22, recently graduated from college and has purchased a new Neon sedan. She has a clean driving record. Collision coverage on the car in the small Southern city where she lives would cost approximately $315 annually with a $100 deductible, $283 with a $250 deductible, $246 with a $500 deductible, and $184 with a $1000 deductible. The state has a compulsory insurance law that requires minimum liability limits of $25,000/$50,000/$10,000. Paige would like to purchase collision insurance with a $100 deductible because the out-of-pocket cost to repair her car in an accident where she is at fault would be relatively small. She also would like to purchase only minimum liability limits, because she has few financial assets to protect. Paige is also concerned that she might be seriously injured by a driver who has no insurance.

Assume that you are a risk management consultant and that Paige asks your advice concerning her auto insurance coverages. Based on the above facts, answer the following questions.

a. Paige wants to know why auto insurance costs so much. Explain to her the factors that determine auto insurance rates.

b. Do you recommend that Paige purchase collision insurance with a $100 deductible? Explain your answer.

c. Do you agree with Paige that only minimum liability limits should be purchased because she has few financial assets to protect? Explain your answer.

d. Assume that Paige adds the uninsured motorist coverage to her policy. Would she be completely protected against the financial consequences of a bodily injury caused by an uninsured driver? Explain your answer.

e. Paige would like to reduce her auto premiums because her monthly car payments are high. Explain to Paige the various methods for reducing or holding down auto insurance premiums.

4. Automobile insurance plans (assigned risk plans) are used in most states to meet the problem of providing auto insurance to high-risk drivers.
   a. Describe the eligibility requirements for obtaining insurance from an automobile insurance plan.
   b. Explain the process for assigning high-risk drivers to individual insurers.
   c. Are the automobile insurance plans financially self-supporting? Explain your answer.

5. Several states have established a reinsurance facility or a joint underwriting association (JUA) for providing auto insurance to high-risk drivers.
   a. Describe how a reinsurance facility works.
   b. Describe how a joint underwriting association (JUA) functions.
   c. Is the problem of providing auto insurance to high-risk drivers adequately met by these approaches? Explain your answer.

SELECTED REFERENCES

Abrahamse, Allan, and Stephen Carroll. "The Effects of a Choice Auto Insurance Plan on Insurance Costs and Compensation." *CPCU Journal*, Vol. 51, No. 1 (Spring 1998), pp. 19–39.

"Are You Paying Too Much for Auto Insurance?" *Consumer Reports*, Vol. 62, No. 1 (January 1997), pp. 10–17.

"Auto Insurance, Hidden Costs." *Consumer Reports*, Vol. 63, No. 5 (May 1998), p. 9.

Barth, Michael M. "Another Look at the Use of Credit Reports in Underwriting Personal Auto Insurance." *CPCU Journal*, Vol. 51, No. 1 (Spring 1998), pp. 49–58.

Carrol, Stephen J., and James S. Kakalik. "No-Fault Approaches to Compensating Auto Accident Victims." *The Journal of Risk and Insurance*, Vol. 60, No. 2 (June 1993), pp. 265–287.

———. *No-Fault Automobile Insurance: A Policy Perspective*. Santa Monica, CA: RAND, Institute for Civil Justice, 1991.

Carrol, Stephen J., James S. Kakalik, Nicholas M. Pace, and John L. Adams. *No-Fault Approaches to Compensating People Injured in Automobile Accidents*. Santa Monica, CA: RAND, Institute for Civil Justice, 1991.

Fire, Casualty & Surety Bulletins. Cincinnati, OH: National Underwriter Company. The bulletins are updated monthly. Detailed information on the material discussed in this chapter can be found in the Personal Lines volume.

Maroney, Patrick, Kevin Eastman, and Ann Butler. "An Analysis of the Auto Choice Reform Act of 1997." *Risk Management and Insurance Review*, Vol. 2, No. 2 (Winter 1999), pp. 60–71.

Rejda, George E., Constance M. Luthardt, Cheryl L. Ferguson, and Donald R. Oakes. *Personal Insurance*, fourth edition. Malvern, PA: Insurance Institute of America, 2000, Chapter 2.

The I.I.I. Insurance Fact Book 2000. New York, NY: Insurance Information Institute.

United States Congress, Joint Economic Committee. "Auto Choice: Impact on Cities and the Poor." *Joint Economic Committee Study*, 105th Congress, Washington, DC, March 1998.

———. "Auto Choice: Relief for Businesses & Consumers." *Joint Economic Committee Study*, 105th Congress, Washington, DC, July 1998.

———. "The Benefits and Savings of Auto-Choice." *Joint Economic Committee Study*, April 1997.

NOTES

1. A complete discussion of these laws can be found in *Fire, Casualty & Surety Bulletins*, Personal Lines volume, Personal Auto section (Cincinnati, OH: National Underwriter Company). Discussion of financial responsibility laws is based on this source.

2. The first two figures refer to bodily injury liability limits, and the third figure refers to property damage liability.

3. NAII data as cited in Tony Attrino, "Compulsory Auto Laws Blasted," *National Underwriter*, Property & Casualty/Risk & Benefits Management ed., September 7, 1998, pp. 2, 65.

4. George E. Rejda, Constance M. Luthardt, Cheryl L. Ferguson, and Donald R. Oakes, *Personal Insurance*, third edition (Malvern, PA: Insurance Institute of America, 1997), pp. 26–27.

5. This discussion is based on "No-Fault Automobile Insurance," in *Fire, Casualty & Surety Bulletins*, Personal Lines volume, Personal Auto section (Cincinnati, OH: The National Underwriter Company). The bulletins are updated monthly.

6. Stephen J. Carrol et al., *No-Fault Approaches to Compensating People Injured in Automobile*

Accidents (Santa Monica, CA: RAND, Institute for Civil Justice, 1991), p. 22.

7. "Auto Choice: Relief for Businesses & Consumers," *Joint Economic Committee Study*, 105th Congress, Washington, DC, July 1998.

8. "Auto Choice: Impact on Cities and the Poor," *Joint Economic Committee Study*, 105th Congress, Washington, DC, March 1998.

9. *Ibid.*

10. *Injuries in Auto Accidents, an Analysis of Auto Insurance Claims, Executive Summary* (Malvern, PA: Insurance Research Council, 1999), p. 9.

11. *Ibid*, p. 8.

12. Carrol et al., pp. xvi, 43.

13. "Auto Choice: Relief for Businesses & Consumers," *Joint Economic Committee Study*, 105th Congress, Washington, DC, July 1998.

14. *The I.I.I. Insurance Fact Book 2000* (New York, NY: Insurance Information Institute), p. 3.20.

 Students may take a self-administered test on this chapter at www.awlonline.com/rejda

Chapter 12 Other Property and Liability Insurance Coverages

"Variety is the very spice of life."

William Cowper,
Olney Hymns (1779)

Learning Objectives

After studying this chapter, you should be able to:

▲ Describe the major forms that are used in the ISO dwelling program.

▲ Explain how a mobilehome can be insured.

▲ Identify the types of property that can be insured under the personal articles floater.

▲ Explain how recreational boats can be insured.

▲ Explain the basic provisions of the federal flood insurance programs.

▲ Describe the basic characteristics of title insurance.

▲ Explain the major characteristics of a personal umbrella policy.

▲ Access an Internet site and obtain consumer information about property and liability insurance.

Internet Resources

■ The **Federal Emergency Management Agency (FEMA)** provides valuable consumer information about the National Flood Insurance Program. Check out this site at:

http://www.fema.gov

■ The **Insurance Information Institute (III)** provides valuable consumer information on a number of property and liability insurance contracts for individuals and families. Useful features include "Consumer Alerts," a widely requested brochure. The III sponsors a site at:

http://www.iii.org/

■ Another site with lots of useful information about home, auto, and other property and liability insurance coverages is the **Independent Insurance Network** sponsored by the Independent Insurance Agents of America. You can find this site at

http://www.independentagent.com

hania, age 28, is an account executive for an investment management firm. She recently received a one-karat diamond engagement ring valued at $10,000 from her boyfriend. Although Shania has a homeowners policy, an insurance agent suggested that she insure the ring because of its value and because of certain limits on jewelry under a homeowners policy. Shania insured the ring under a personal articles floater for $10,000. Without such coverage, the maximum paid in the event of theft would be only $1500.

Shania had a specialized need for insurance that required a certain coverage. Likewise, some property owners have special needs that require special insurance coverages. This chapter discusses several property and liability insurance coverages designed to meet specific needs. Topics discussed include the Insurance Services Office (ISO) dwelling program, mobilehome insurance, inland marine floaters, insurance on boats, title insurance, and federal flood insurance. The chapter concludes with a discussion of the personal umbrella policy.

ISO DWELLING PROGRAM

Although the majority of homeowners are insured under a homeowners policy, certain dwellings are ineligible for coverage under a homeowners policy. For example, if the home is not occupied by the owner but is rented to a tenant, the property owner is ineligible for a homeowners policy. Also, some property owners do not need a homeowners policy, or they may want a less costly policy. Most of these homes can be insured under a dwelling policy drafted by the Insurance Services Office (ISO).

The ISO dwelling forms are narrower in coverage than the current homeowners forms. One major difference is that the dwelling forms do not include coverage for theft or for personal liability insurance without appropriate endorsements. In contrast, the homeowners forms automatically include theft coverage and personal liability insurance as part of a package policy.

Three major dwelling forms are now used in the ISO dwelling program:[1]

- Dwelling Property 1 (basic form)
- Dwelling Property 2 (broad form)
- Dwelling Property 3 (special form)

Dwelling Property 1 (Basic Form)

Dwelling Property 1 (basic form) provides coverages similar to the homeowners policies discussed in

Chapter 8. Coverage A insures the *dwelling* and structures attached to the dwelling. Loss to the dwelling is indemnified on a replacement cost basis.

Coverage B provides insurance on *other structures*, such as a detached garage or tool shed.

Coverage C insures *personal property* owned or used by the insured and residing family members; up to 10 percent of the insurance can be applied to cover personal property anywhere in the world.

Coverage D covers the *fair rental value* if a loss makes part of the dwelling rented to others or held for rental unfit for normal use. A maximum of 10 percent of the insurance on the dwelling can be applied to cover the loss of rents, subject to a maximum monthly limit of 1/12 of that 10 percent. For example, if the dwelling is insured for $60,000, a total of $6000 can be applied to cover the loss of rents, with a maximum monthly limit of $500.

Finally, Coverage E provides *additional living expense* coverage, which pays for the necessary increase in living expenses incurred by the named insured so that the household can maintain its normal standard of living.

The basic form provides coverage only for a limited number of perils that apply to both the dwelling and personal property. Coverage for the perils of fire, lightning, and internal explosion can be purchased separately. Coverage for vandalism and malicious mischief and the extended coverage perils can be added by payment of an additional premium. The *extended coverage perils* are windstorm or hail, explosion, riot or civil commotion, aircraft, vehicles, smoke, and volcanic eruption.

Dwelling Property 2 (Broad Form)

Dwelling Property 2 (**broad form**) provides broader coverage than the basic form. The broad form includes all of the perils listed in the basic form plus several additional perils. The additional perils are damage from burglars; falling objects; weight of ice, snow, or sleet; accidental discharge or overflow of water or steam; explosion of a steam or hot water heating system, air conditioning or automatic fire protective sprinkler system, or appliance for heating water; freezing of a plumbing, heating, air conditioning, or automatic fire protective system or household appliance; and sudden and accidental

damage from an artificially generated electrical current.

Dwelling Property 3 (Special Form)

Dwelling Property 3 (**special form**) insures the dwelling and other structures against "risk of direct loss to property." All direct physical losses are covered except certain losses specifically excluded. However, personal property is covered for the same named perils found in the broad form discussed earlier.

Endorsements to the Dwelling Program

Several endorsements can be added to a dwelling form, depending on the needs and desires of the property owner. They include *theft coverage*, which can be written on a limited or broad basis by an endorsement. Personal liability insurance is also available by adding a *personal liability supplement* to the policy, which provides personal liability insurance similar to the liability coverages found in the homeowners policy.

MOBILEHOME INSURANCE

Many low-income and middle-income families cannot afford conventional housing. Thus, there is considerable interest in less expensive forms of housing, such as mobilehomes.

Under the ISO program, **mobilehome insurance** is written by adding an endorsement to either a Homeowners 2 or Homeowners 3 policy, which tailors the homeowners policy to meet the special characteristics of mobilehomes. A number of specialty insurers also write a mobilehome insurance based on their own forms tailored to the mobilehome exposures. The following discussion of mobilehome insurance is based on the ISO program.[2]

Eligibility

The mobilehome must be at least 10 feet wide and 40 feet long, must be capable of being towed on its own chassis, and must be designed for year-round living. These requirements are imposed to eliminate coverage for camper trailers pulled by automobiles and insured under an auto insurance policy.

Coverages

Coverages on a mobilehome are similar to those found in a homeowners policy. Coverage A insures mobilehomes on a *replacement cost basis*. It also insures floor coverings, household appliances, dressers, cabinets, and other built-in furniture when installed on a permanent basis. In addition, the policy covers utility tanks and other structures attached to the mobilehome such as a carport or small storage shed.

Some mobilehomes have depreciated to the point where replacement cost coverage is inappropriate. In such cases, an optional actual cash value endorsement can be added. Under this endorsement, the insurer has the option of (1) paying the cost of repairs, (2) replacing the damaged property with similar property, but not necessarily from the same manufacturer, or (3) paying the amount in money. If paid in money, the insurer pays the lower of the difference in actual cash value before and after the loss or the cost to replace the property with similar property.

Coverage B insures other structures and is 10 percent of Coverage A, with a minimum limit of $2000. Coverage C insures unscheduled personal property and is limited to 40 percent of Coverage A. Coverage D provides for loss-of-use coverage and is 20 percent of the Coverage A limit.

An additional coverage pays up to $500 for the cost incurred in transporting the mobilehome to a safe place to avoid damage when it is endangered by a covered peril, such as a forest fire. No deductible applies to this coverage. The $500 limit can be increased to a higher limit by an endorsement.

Finally, Coverages E and F provide for comprehensive personal liability insurance and medical payments to others. This coverage is similar to the coverage provided in the homeowner contracts.

INLAND MARINE FLOATERS

Many people own certain types of valuable personal property—such as jewelry, furs, and cameras—that are frequently moved from one location to another. This property can be insured by an appropriate inland marine floater. An **inland marine floater** *is a policy that provides broad and comprehensive protection on property frequently moved from one location to another.*

Basic Characteristics of Inland Marine Floaters

Although inland marine floaters are not uniform, they have certain common characteristics:[3]

- *Coverage can be tailored to the specific type of personal property to be insured.* For example, under the personal articles floater, several types of property can be insured, such as jewelry, coins, or stamps. The insured can select the appropriate coverage needed.
- *Desired amounts of insurance can be selected.* The homeowners policy has several limits on personal property. For example, there is a $200 limit on money and coins, a $1500 limit on stamp collections, and a $2500 limit for the theft of silverware or goldware. Higher limits are available through a floater policy.
- *Broader and more comprehensive coverage can be obtained.* For example, the personal articles floater insures against risks of direct physical loss to covered property. Consequently, all direct physical losses are covered except those losses specifically excluded.
- *Most floaters cover insured property anywhere in the world.* This protection is especially valuable for global travelers.

Personal Articles Floater

The **personal articles floater (PAF)** is another contract that provides comprehensive protection on valuable personal property.[4] The coverage also can be added as an endorsement to a homeowners policy. When written as a separate contract, the PAF insures certain optional classes of personal property on an "all-risks" basis. *All direct physical losses are covered except certain losses specifically excluded.*

The classes of personal property that can be covered include the following:

- *Jewelry.* Because of moral hazard, insurance on jewelry is underwritten carefully. Each item is described with a specific amount of insurance.
- *Furs.* Each item is listed separately with a specific amount of insurance.
- *Cameras.* Most photographic equipment can be covered under the PAF. Each item must be individually described and valued.
- *Musical instruments.* Musical instruments, cases, amplifying equipment, and similar articles can also be covered. Instruments played for pay are not covered unless an endorsement is added to the policy.
- *Silverware.* The PAF can also be written to cover silverware and goldware.
- *Golfer's equipment.* Golf clubs and equipment are covered anywhere in the world. Golfer's clothes in a locker are also covered when the insured is playing golf.
- *Fine arts.* Fine arts include paintings, etchings, lithographs, antique furniture, rare books, rare glass, bric-a-brac, and manuscripts. Coverage of fine arts is on a valued basis. The amount of insurance listed in the schedule for that item is the amount paid for a total loss.
- *Stamp and coin collections.* Stamp and coin collections can be insured on a *blanket basis*; the stamps or coins are not described, and the insurance applies to the entire collection. The amount paid is the cash market value at the time of loss, with a $1000 maximum limit on any unscheduled coin collection and a $250 maximum limit on any single stamp or coin. However, if the stamps or coins are valuable, they can be individually *scheduled*. In case of loss to a scheduled item, the amount paid is the lowest of actual cash value, reasonable cost of repairs, replacement cost, or amount of insurance.

Scheduled Personal Property Endorsement

Coverage provided by a **personal articles floater (PAF)** can be added to a homeowners policy by use of the **scheduled personal property endorsement (HO-61)**. The endorsement provides essentially the same coverages provided by the free-standing personal articles floater.

INSURANCE ON PLEASURE BOATS

Millions of Americans own or operate boats for pleasure and recreation. The homeowners policy, however, provides only limited coverage of boats. Coverage on a boat, its equipment, and boat trailer is limited to $1500. Direct loss from windstorm or hail is covered only if the boat is inside a fully enclosed building. Theft of the boat or its equipment away from the premises is excluded. Also, boats are covered only against a limited number of named perils (broad form perils), and more comprehensive protection may be desired. Finally, legal liability arising out of the operation or ownership of larger boats is not covered under the homeowners policy. For these reasons, boat owners often purchase separate insurance contracts that provide broader protection.[5]

Insurance on recreational boats generally can be classified into two categories:

- Boat owners package policy
- Yacht insurance

Boat Owners Package Policy

Many insurers have designed a **boat owners package policy** that combines physical damage insurance on the boat, medical expense insurance, liability insurance, and other coverages into one policy. Although the package policies are not uniform, they have certain common characteristics.

Physical Damage Coverage A boat owners policy provides physical damage insurance on the boat on an "all-risks" basis. All direct physical losses are covered except certain losses specifically excluded. Thus, if the boat collides with another boat, is stranded on a reef, or is damaged by heavy winds, the loss is covered. Certain exclusions apply, including wear and tear, gradual deterioration, mechanical breakdown, use of the boat for commercial purposes, and use of the boat (except sailboats in some policies) in any race or speed contest.

Liability Coverage The insured is covered for property damage and bodily injury liability arising out of the negligent ownership or operation of the boat. For example, if an operator carelessly damages another boat, swamps another boat, or accidentally injures some swimmers, the loss is covered. Certain exclusions apply, including intentional injury, use of the boat for commercial purposes, and use of the boat (sailboats sometimes excepted) in any race or speed test.

Medical Expense Coverage This coverage is similar to that found in auto insurance contracts. The coverage pays the reasonable and necessary medical expenses of a covered person who is injured while in the boat or while boarding or leaving the boat. Most policies impose a limit of one to three years during which time the medical expenses must be incurred. In addition, many boat owners policies cover the medical expenses of waterskiers who are injured while being towed. If not covered, coverage can be obtained by an endorsement to the policy.

Uninsured Boaters Coverage Some boat owners policies have an optional uninsured boaters coverage for bodily injury caused by an uninsured boater, which is similar to the uninsured motorists coverage in auto insurance.

Yacht Insurance

Yacht insurance is designed for larger boats, such as cabin cruisers, inboard motorboats, and sailboats over 26 feet in length. Yacht policies are not standard, but certain coverages typically appear in all policies. The following section summarizes the major provisions of a yacht policy of one insurer.

Property Damage This coverage insures the yacht and its equipment for property damage on an "all-risks" basis. The policy covers accidental direct physical loss or damage to the yacht except certain losses specifically excluded. Coverage applies to the yacht, spars, sails, machinery, furniture, dinghies, outboard motors, and other equipment. Thus, if the yacht is damaged or sinks because of heavy seas, high winds, or collision with another vessel, the loss is covered. Exclusions include wear and tear; weathering; damage from insects, mold, animals, and marine life; marring, scratching, denting, and blistering; and manufacturer's defects. A deductible applies to property damage losses.

Liability Coverage Liability coverage insures the legal liability of an insured arising out of the ownership, operation, or maintenance of the yacht. For example, collision with another boat or damage to a dock or marina would be covered. The coverage also includes the cost of raising, removing, or destroying a sunken or wrecked yacht.

Medical Payments Coverage This coverage pays for necessary and reasonable medical expenses because of accidental bodily injury. Covered expenses include medical, hospital, ambulance, professional nursing, and funeral costs incurred within one year of the accident. Coverage applies only to people who are injured while in or upon the yacht or while boarding or leaving the yacht. Employees are not covered.

Uninsured Boater This coverage pays the bodily injury damages up to the policy limit that the insured is legally entitled to recover from an uninsured owner or operator of another yacht.

Other Coverages Other coverages include coverage for legal liability incurred by the insured to maritime workers who are injured in the course of employment and who are covered under the U.S. Longshoremen's and Harbors Workers Compensation Act; physical damage insurance on a vessel trailor listed in the declarations; and coverage for personal property while aboard the yacht. Personal property includes clothing, personal effects, fishing gear, and sports equipment, but not money, jewelry, traveler's checks, or other valuables.

In recent years, the number of boating accidents has increased. Insight 12.1 discusses the growing problem of boating accidents caused by inexperienced boaters, soaring boat sales, drunken operators, and disregard of safety rules by some boaters.

FEDERAL PROPERTY INSURANCE PROGRAMS

Federal insurance programs are often necessary because certain perils are difficult to insure privately, and coverage may not be available at affordable premiums from private insurers. Three government insurance programs merit a brief discussion:

Insight 12.1

Accidents Are on the Rise as Inexperienced Skippers Crowd the Waterways

On a beautiful clear day a few months ago, Todd Hoffman was steering his $50,000 power boat into the Gulf of Mexico when he heard a noise behind him. Looking back, he watched in horror as a small boat jumped off a wave and landed squarely on the back of his boat.

"It missed taking my head off by nearly a foot," says Patrick Welsh, one of Mr. Hoffman's passengers, who dived into the hull as soon as he saw the boat coming. "It was a very close call."

In their case, no one got hurt. But boating accidents have picked up at an alarming rate in recent years. In all, about 8000 accidents are expected this year [1999], up about 33 percent from six years ago, and safety experts are blaming everything from soaring boat sales to cutbacks in Coast Guard monitoring to an onslaught of new, inexperienced skippers. In Michigan, which has the greatest number of registered U.S. boaters, there were 514 accidents last year [1998], up 21 percent from a year earlier; 58 fatalities were reported in California last year [1998], up 35 percent from 1997.

Crowded waters carry the same troubles as packed roads, except there's drunken boating instead of drunken driving, water rage as opposed to road rage, and boating without life jackets rather than driving without seat belts. Just like the advent of sport-utility vechiles on the road, boats are getting bigger and more powerful, making accidents more lethal and parking spaces, or "slips" harder to find.

As for Mr. Hoffman's accident, it cost the financial planner $8000 in repairs and changed his whole view about his favorite pastime. And the driver of the boat? "I won't be going out on a boat again for a while," says Chris Kallas, a 28-year-old medical technician. Mr. Kallas is selling his boat, which he had only had for a couple of months before the accident.

No License Required

Indeed, safety experts say the number of inexperienced boaters is getting out of hand. Unlike cars, almost anyone can hop behind the wheel of a boat. The federal government only sets the operating rules for federally controlled waters, which include navigable rivers and some ocean coastlines. *Most states don't require boating licenses, boating education, or even liability insurance.* It's perfectly legal to have alcohol on boats (though not to

- Federal flood insurance
- FAIR plans
- Federal crop insurance

Federal Flood Insurance

Buildings in flood zones are difficult to insure privately because the ideal requirements of an insurable risk discussed in Chapter 2 are not easily met. The exposure units in flood zones are not independent of each other, and the potential for a catastrophic loss is present. Thus, premiums for flood insurance in flood-prone areas would be too high for most insureds to pay. Also, adverse selection is a problem because only property owners in flood zones are likely to seek protection. For these reasons, financial assistance from the federal government is needed.

The **National Flood Insurance Program (NFIP)** was created by the National Flood Insurance Act of 1968.[6] *The purpose of the act is to provide flood insurance at subsidized rates to persons in flood zones.* It is now available in all states, the District of Columbia, Puerto Rico, and the Virgin Islands. It can be purchased from agents and brokers who represent private insurers. Agents or brokers who are not affiliated with private insurers can write federal flood insurance directly with the NFIP.

Federal law requires individuals to purchase flood insurance if they have federal guaranteed financing to build, buy, refinance, or repair structures located in special flood zones in the participating community. This financing requirement includes FHA and VA loans as well as most conventional mortgage loans.

drive drunk), children can drive boats without an adult in many states, and most waterways have no marked traffic-control patterns or speed limits.

Some say the growing traffic of jet skis in the same waterways used by bigger and faster boats has contributed to the problem. Sixteen-year-old Adam Herford had only been skiing a few times before he was in a collision with a speed boat last month in the Lake of the Ozarks in Missouri. The impact of the crash blew a hole in the rented speed boat, piloted by Andy Nicols, causing it to sink. A police report blamed both Messrs. Herford and Nicols, who had less than 10 hours boating experience before the accident, for going too fast and not watching for other boats.

A Boating Boom

Adding to the chaos: the sheer number of boats out there now. Thanks to a strong economy, loose regulation, and a 1993 repeal of a 10 percent tax on boats costing more than $100,000, there's been a boom in recreational boating. Last year [1998], consumers spent an estimated $19 billion on boats and marine equipment—the most ever—up 70 percent since 1993. And the boats are getting bigger too—so much so that

the Oakland Yacht Club in Alameda, California, for example, had to refigure its slips, converting eight small spaces into larger ones to accommodate the increase in demand from people with bigger boats.

In the meantime, some harbors are doing their part to reduce accidents by increasing patrol staff, drunk-boating check points, and speeding citations. The Nahant Harbor in Massachusetts, for instance, added two to its staff of eight. But harbormaster Bill Waters says problems are still "overwhelming," especially when the newer, inexperienced boaters call in emergencies when their boats have only run aground or run out of gas. "They're in over their heads and they panic," he says. "It gets hard to sort out the real emergencies from plain stupidity."

States are also jumping in, trying to reduce mishaps by requiring more regulation. Boaters in Arkansas must now carry proof of at least $50,000 in liability insurance before they can register or renew a registration. Alabama, Connecticut, Indiana, and New Jersey all require some type of boating license or certificate now, while 22 other states require boating education.

SOURCE: Adapted from Nancy Keates, "No Smooth Sailing," *The Wall Street Journal*, August 27, 1999, p. W5. Reprinted with permission.

Write-Your-Own Program In 1983, the federal government enacted a *write-your-own program* to encourage private insurers to write flood insurance with financial assistance from the federal government. Under the write-your-own program, private insurers sell federal flood insurance under their own names, collect the premiums, retain a specified percentage for operating expenses and commissions, and invest the remainder. The insurers service the policies and pay all claims. The federal government is responsible for any underwriting losses.

Eligibility Requirements Most buildings and their contents can be covered by flood insurance if the community agrees to adopt and enforce sound flood control and land use measures.

When a community joins the program, it is provided with a flood hazard boundary map that shows the general area of flood losses, and residents are allowed to purchase limited amounts of insurance at subsidized rates under the emergency portion of the program.

A flood insurance rate map is then prepared that divides the community into specific zones to determine the probability of flooding in each zone. When this map is prepared, and the community agrees to adopt more stringent flood control and land use measures, the community enters the regular phase of the program. Higher amounts of flood insurance can then be purchased.

Definition of Flood Flood is defined as a general and temporary condition of partial or complete inundation of normally dry areas from (1) the overflow of inland or tidal waters, (2) the unusual and rapid accumulation of runoff or surface waters from any source, and (3) mudslides that are proximately caused by flooding. Thus, flood damage caused by an overflow of rivers, streams, or other bodies of water, by abnormally high waves, or by severe storms is covered. Mudslide damage is also covered if the mudslide is caused by the accumulation of water on the earth's surface or under the ground.

Amounts of Insurance Under the *emergency program*, maximum coverage on single-family dwellings is limited to $35,000 on the building and $10,000 on the contents. For other residential and nonresidential buildings, maximum coverage is limited to $100,000 on the building and $100,000 on the contents (see Exhibit 12.1).

Under the *regular* program, maximum coverage on single-family dwellings is limited to $250,000 on the building and $100,000 on the contents. Commercial structures can be insured up to a limit of $500,000 on the building and $500,000 on the contents (see Exhibit 12.2).

The insured is required to carry insurance equal to 80 percent of the replacement cost of the dwelling or the maximum amount of insurance available, whichever is less. If this requirement is met, the cost to replace or repair the property is paid up to the policy limit with no deduction for depreciation.

Waiting Period With certain exceptions, there is a 30-day waiting period for new applications and for endorsements to increase the amount of insurance on existing policies. The purpose is to reduce adverse selection. Without a waiting period, property owners in flood zones could delay purchasing insurance until an imminent flood threatens their property.

Deductible A $500 deductible applies separately to both the building and contents. The deductible is $750 for property insured under the emergency program or property located in certain flood zones. A $250 deductible applies to claims involving sewer backup, land subsidence, or water seepage. Higher deductibles—up to $5000—are available with a saving in premiums.

There are numerous misconceptions and myths about the federal flood insurance program. Insight 12.2 discusses some common misunderstandings about the program.

Premiums Because the rates are subsidized, the cost of the protection is relatively low. In low- to moderate-risk areas, coverage is available for as little as $100 per year. In high-risk areas, the average premium is slightly more than $300 per year.

FAIR Plans

During the 1960s, major riots occurred in many cities in the United States, resulting in millions of dollars in property damage. Subsequently, many property owners in riot-prone areas were unable to obtain property insurance at affordable premiums. This problem resulted in the creation of **FAIR plans** (Fair Access to Insurance Requirements), which were enacted into law as a result of the Urban Property and Reinsurance Act of 1968. *The basic purpose of a FAIR plan is to make property insurance available to urban property owners who are unable to obtain coverage in the normal markets.* FAIR plans typically provide coverage for fire and extended-coverage insurance, vandalism, malicious mischief, and, in a few states, crime insurance and sprinkler leakage. FAIR plans have been established in 31 states and the District of Columbia. In addition, beach and windstorm plans operate in seven states along the Atlantic and Gulf Coast seaboard, where property is highly vulnerable to damage from severe windstorms and hurricanes.[7]

EXHIBIT 12.1
Emergency Program Flood Insurance Coverages

Buildings	
Single Family dwelling	$ 35,000
2–4 Family Dwelling	35,000
Other Residential	100,000
Nonresidential	100,000
Contents	
Residential	$ 10,000
Nonresidential	100,000

SOURCE: Federal Emergency Management Agency.

EXHIBIT 12.2
Regular Program Flood Insurance Coverages

	Basic insurance limits	Additional insurance limits	Total insurance available
Building Coverage			
Single Family Dwelling	$ 50,000 /	$200,000	$250,000
2–4 Family Dwelling	$ 50,000 /	$200,000	$250,000
Other Residential	$135,000 /	$115,000	$250,000
Nonresidential	$135,000 /	$365,000	$500,000
Contents Coverage			
Residential	$ 15,000 /	$ 85,000	$100,000
Nonresidential	$115,000 /	$385,000	$500,000

SOURCE: Federal Emergency Management Agency.

Each state with a FAIR plan has a pool or syndicate that provides basic property insurance to persons who cannot obtain insurance in the regular markets. The pools or syndicates are operated by private insurers. Each insurer in the pool or syndicate is assessed its proportionate share of losses and expenses based on the proportion of property insurance premiums written in the state.

Before a building can be insured, it must first be inspected. If it meets certain underwriting standards, a policy is issued. If the building is substandard, it may still be insurable at substantially higher premiums. In some cases, certain improvements to the building must be made before the policy is issued. Finally, insurance may be denied if the condition of the building makes it uninsurable. If the insurance is denied, the applicant must be informed of the reasons the property cannot be insured.

FAIR plans are controversial. Critics argue that they are no longer needed and should be phased out, because the social threat of widespread riot losses has subsided. Also, some critics charge that property insurers have used the FAIR plans to rid themselves of undesirable businesses, such as bowling alleys, bars, restaurants, and property subject to brush fires in certain areas, such as California. Critics also argue that the subsidized rates under California's FAIR

plan encourage property owners to buy expensive homes in areas where brush fires frequently occur. As a result, the taxpayers must pay the cost of bailing out wealthy people whose homes are damaged or destroyed by brush fires. In rebuttal, property insurers maintain that FAIR plan premiums are inadequate, that sizable underwriting losses have been incurred since the plans began operating, and that arson-for-profit claims have increased.

Federal Crop Insurance

Many farmers desire crop insurance that provides protection against adverse weather conditions and other perils that damage crops. Federal crop insurance provides coverage for unavoidable crop losses, such as hail, wind, excessive rain, drought, and plant disease. The Federal Agricultural Improvement and Reform (ACT), also known as "Freedom to Farm," requires farm producers to purchase multiple-peril crop insurance or to sign a statement waiving eligibility for disaster payments for any losses.

Several federal crop insurance programs are in existence, and producers have a choice of coverages. Only the catastrophic coverage plan (CAT) is discussed here. The CAT plan provides producers with

Insight 12.2

Myths and Facts About the National Flood Insurance Program

To clear up misconceptions about the National Flood Insurance Program (NFIP), the NFIP has compiled the following list of common myths about the program.

1. **Myth: You can't buy flood insurance if you are located in a high-flood-risk area.**
   Fact: You can buy federal flood insurance no matter where you live if your community belongs to the NFIP, except in Coastal Barrier Resource System (CBRS) areas. The program was created in 1968 to provide affordable flood insurance to people who live in areas with the greatest risk of flooding, called Special Flood Hazard Areas (SFHAs). In fact, under the National Flood Insurance Act, lenders must require borrowers whose property is located within an SFHA to purchase flood insurance as a condition of receiving a federally backed mortgage loan. There is an exemption for conventional loans on properties within CBRS areas.

2. **Myth: You can't buy flood insurance immediately before or during a flood.**
   Fact: You can purchase flood coverage at any time. There is a 30-day waiting period after you've applied and paid the premium before the policy becomes effective, with the following exception: (1) If the initial purchase of flood insurance is in connection with the making, increasing, extending, or renewing of a loan, there is no waiting period. The coverage becomes effective at the time of the loan, provided that application and payment of premium are made at or prior to loan closing. (2) If the initial purchase of flood insurance is made during the 13-month period following the effective date of a revised flood map for a community, there is a one-day waiting period.

   The policy does not cover a "loss in progress," defined by the NFIP as a loss occurring as of 12:01 A.M. on the first day of the policy term. In addition, you cannot increase the amount of insurance coverage you have during a loss in progress.

3. **Myth: Homeowners insurance policies cover flooding.**
   Fact: Unfortunately, many homeowners do not find out until it is too late that their homeowners policies do not cover flooding. NFIP protects your most valuable assets—your home and belongings.

4. **Myth: Flood insurance is only available for homeowners.**
   Fact: Flood insurance is available to protect homes, condominiums, apartments, and nonresidential buildings, including commercial structures. A maximum of $250,000 of building coverage is available for single-family residential buildings, and $250,000 per unit for multifamily residences. The limit for contents coverage on all residential buildings is $100,000, which is also available to renters.

   Commercial structures can be insured to a limit of $500,000 for the building and $500,000 for the contents.

5. **Myth: You can't buy flood insurance if your property has been flooded.**
   Fact: It doesn't matter how many times your home, apartment or business has flooded. You are still eligible to purchase flood insurance, provided that your community is participating in the NFIP.

6. **Myth: Only residents of high-risk flood zones need to insure their property.**
   Fact: Even if you live in an area that is not flood-prone, it's advisable to have flood insurance. Between 25 percent and 30 percent of the NFIP's claims come from outside high-flood-risk areas. The NFIP's Preferred Risk, available for just over $100 per year, is designed for residential properties located in low- to moderate-flood-risk zones.

7. **Myth: Federal flood insurance can only be purchased through the NFIP directly.**
   Fact: NFIP flood insurance is sold through private insurance companies and agents, and is backed by the federal government.

8. **Myth: The NFIP does not offer any type of basement coverage.**
   Fact: Yes, it does. The NFIP defines a basement as any area of a building with a floor that is below ground level on all sides. While flood insurance does not cover basement improvements, such as finished walls, floors, or ceilings, or personal belongings that may be kept in a basement, such as furniture and other contents, it does cover structural elements, essential equipment, and other basic items normally located in a basement. Many of these items are covered under building coverage, and some are covered under contents coverage.

   The following items are covered under building coverage, as long as they are connected to a power source and installed in their functioning location:

   - Sump pumps
   - Well water tanks and pumps, cisterns and the water in them

- Oil tanks and the oil in them, natural gas tanks and the gas in them
- Pumps and/or tanks used in conjuction with solar energy
- Furnaces, hot water heaters, air conditioners, and heat pumps
- Electrical junction and circuit breaker boxes, and required utility connections
- Foundation elements
- Stairways, staircases, elevators, and dumbwaiters
- Unpainted drywalls and sheet rock walls and ceilings, including fiberglass insulation
- Cleanup

The following items are covered under contents coverage:

- Clothes washers
- Clothes dryers
- Food freezers and the food in them

9. **Myth: Federal disaster assistance will pay for flood damage.**
Fact: Before a community is eligible for disaster assistance, it must be declared a federal disaster area. Federal disaster declarations are issued in less than 50 percent of flooding incidents. The premium for an NFIP policy, averaging a little more than $300 a year, is less expensive than interest on federal disaster loans.

Furthermore, if you are uninsured and receive federal disaster assistance after a flood, you must purchase flood insurance to remain eligible for future disaster relief.

10. **Myth: The NFIP encourages coastal development.**
Fact: One of the NFIP's primary objectives is to guide development away from high-flood-risk areas. NFIP regulations minimize the impact of structures that are built in SFHAs by requiring them not to cause obstructions to the natural flow of floodwaters. Also, as a condition of community participation in the NFIP, those structures built within SFHAs must adhere to strict floodplain management regulations.

In addition, the Coastal Barrier Resources Act (CBRA) of 1982 relies on the NFIP to discourage building in fragile coastal areas by prohibiting the sale of flood insurance in designated CBRA areas. These laws do not prohibit property owners from building along coastal areas; however, they do transfer the financial risk of such construction from federal taxpayers to those who choose to live or invest in these areas.

11. **Myth: The NFIP does not cover flooding resulting from hurricanes of the overflow of rivers or tidal waters.**
Fact: The NFIP defines covered flooding as a general and temporary condition during which the surface of normally dry land is partially or completely inundated. Two adjacent properties or two or more acres must be affected. Flooding can be caused by any one of the following:

- The overflow of inland or tidal waters
- The unusual and rapid accumulation or runoff of surface waters from any source, such as heavy rainfall
- Mudslides or mudflows, caused by flooding, that could be described as a river of liquid mud
- The collapse or destabilization of land along the shore of a lake or other body of water, resulting from erosion or the effect of waves, or water currents exceeding normal, cyclical levels

12. **Myth: Wind-driven rain is considered flooding.**
Fact: No, it isn't. Rain entering through wind-damaged windows, doors, or a hole in a wall or roof, resulting in standing water or puddles, is considered windstorm, rather than flood damage. Federal flood insurance covers only damage caused by the general condition of flooding (defined above), typically caused by storm surge, wave wash, tidal waves, or the overflow of any body of water above normal, cyclical levels. Buildings that sustain this type of damage usually have a watermark, showing how high the water rose before it subsided. Although the Standard Flood Insurance Policy (SFIP) specifically excludes wind and hail damage, most homeowners policies provide such coverage.

Source: Adapted from "Myths and Facts About the National Flood Insurance Program," Federal Emergency Management Agency, February 1998.

a financial safety net against the risk of a major crop loss.

The CAT plan for grain sorghum in Nebraska in 1999 can be used as an illustration. *The CAT plan provides coverage equal to 55 percent of the actual production history. Insurance payments are equal to 60 percent of the Federal Crop Insurance Corporation (FCIC) price.* For example, assume that the actual production history is an average of 100 bushels per acre. The yield guarantee is 55 bushels per acre, and the FCIC price is $1.95 per bushel. If the actual yield is 45 bushels per acre, the indemnity payment for the loss of 10 bushels per acre is $11.70 per acre (60% × $1.95 × 10).

TITLE INSURANCE

Any discussion of property insurance coverages would not be complete without a brief description of title insurance on the home. **Title insurance** *protects the owner of property or the lender of money for the purchase of property against any unknown defects in the title to the property under consideration.* Defects to a clear title can result from an invalid will, incorrect description of the property, defective probate of a will, undisclosed liens, easements, and numerous other legal defects that occurred sometime in the past. In particular, the problem of a forged title has increased in recent years. Without a clear title, the owner could lose the property to someone with a superior claim or incur other losses because of an unknown lien, unmarketability of the title, and attorney expenses. Title insurance is designed to provide protection against these losses.

Any liens, encumbrances, or easements against real estate are normally recorded in a courthouse in the area where the property is located. This information is recorded in a legal document known as an abstract, which is a history of ownership and title to the property. When real estate is purchased, the purchaser may hire an attorney to search the abstract to determine whether there are any defects to a clear title to the property. However, the purchaser is not fully protected by this method, because there may be an unknown lien, encumbrance, or other title defect not recorded in the abstract. The owner could still incur a loss despite a diligent and careful title search. Thus, the owner needs a stronger guarantee that he

or she will be indemnified if a loss occurs. Title insurance can provide that guarantee.

Title insurance policies have certain characteristics that distinguish them from other contracts:

- *The policy provides protection against title defects that have occurred in the past, prior to the effective date of the policy.*
- *The policy is written by the insurer based on the assumption that no losses will occur.* Any known title defects or facts that have a bearing on the title are listed in the policy and excluded from coverage.
- *The premium is paid only once when the policy is issued.* No additional premiums are required even though the policy term runs indefinitely into the future.
- *The policy term runs indefinitely into the future.* As long as the title defect occurred before the issue date of the policy, any insured loss is covered, no matter when it is discovered in the future.
- *If a loss occurs, the insured is indemnified in dollar amounts up to the policy limits.* The policy does not guarantee possession by the owner, removal of any title defects, or a legal remedy against known defects.

The policy limit is usually the purchase price of the house. If the house appreciates in value over the years, the homeowner could be underinsured at the time of loss. This consideration is especially important in those areas where inflation in housing prices is occurring.

PERSONAL UMBRELLA POLICY

Personal liability claims occasionally reach catastrophic levels and can exceed the liability limits of a homeowners or auto insurance policy. For example, catastrophic losses can result from a chain-reaction accident on an icy highway where cars collide and several people are killed or injured; a boating accident in which a boat is swamped by another boat and several people are injured or drown; or a defamation-of-character lawsuit by someone who claims that his or her reputation is ruined.

The **personal umbrella policy** *provides protection against a catastrophic lawsuit or judgement.* Most insurers write this coverage in amounts ranging from $1 million to $10 million. Coverage is broad and covers catastrophic liability loss exposures arising out of the home, cars, boats, recreational vehicles, sports, and other personal activities.

Basic Characteristics

Although personal umbrella policies differ among insurers, they share several common characteristics, including the following:[8]

- Excess liability insurance
- Broad coverage
- Self-insured retention or deductible
- Reasonable cost

Excess Liability Insurance *The personal umbrella policy provides excess liability insurance over underlying insurance contracts that apply.* The umbrella policy pays only after the basic limits of the underlying contracts are exhausted. The insured is required to carry certain minimum amounts of liability insurance on the underlying contracts. Although the required amounts vary among insurers, the amounts shown in Exhibit 12.3 are typical.

If the required amounts of underlying insurance are not maintained, the umbrella insurer pays only the amount that it would have paid had the underlying insurance been kept in force.

Broad Coverage *The umbrella policy provides broad coverage of personal liability loss exposures.* The policy covers bodily injury and property damage liability, as well as personal injury. Personal injury typically includes false arrest, detention, or imprisonment; malicious prosecution; wrongful eviction or wrongful entry; libel, slander, and defamation of character; and oral or written publication of material that violates a person's right to privacy.

In addition, the umbrella policy covers certain losses not covered by any underlying contract after a self-insured retention or deductible is met. In addition to the policy limits, most umbrella policies pay legal defense costs as well.

Self-insured Retention The umbrella policy typically contains a self-insured retention or deductible. The **self-insured retention**, or **deductible**, *applies only to losses covered by the umbrella policy but not by any underlying contract.* The self-insured retention is typically $250 but can be higher. Examples of claims not covered by the underlying contracts but insured under an umbrella policy include libel, slander, defamation of character, and a wide variety of additional claims (see Insight 12.3).

To illustrate, assume that Andrea has a $1 million personal umbrella policy and an auto insurance policy with limits of $250,000 per person and $500,000 per accident for bodily injury liability. If she negligently injures another motorist and must pay damages of $650,000, the auto policy pays the first $250,000. The umbrella policy then pays the remaining $400,000, because the underlying limit of $250,000 per person under the auto policy has been exhausted. The self-insured retention does not apply here.

Now assume that Andrea is sued by her ex-husband for defamation of character and must pay damages of $50,000. If there is no underlying coverage and the self-insured retention is $250, her umbrella policy would pay $49,750. The self-insured retention must be met in this case.

EXHIBIT 12.3
Typical Underlying Coverage Amounts Required to Qualify for a Personal Umbrella Policy

Auto liability insurance	$250,000 / $500,000 / $50,000 or $500,000 single limit
Personal liability insurance (separate contract or homeowners policy)	$100,000 or $300,000
Large watercraft	$500,000

Insight 12.3

The Perils an Umbrella Policy Can Protect Against

Auto accidents cause most of the personal injuries that result in huge monetary settlements paid by umbrella liability insurance. But there are plenty of other calamities that can put your assets at serious risk. Consider these recent real-life cases:

- You know the game: One person kneels behind another and a third person pushes the "victim" over. In a case settled last year, three 10-year-olds were the players. One child broke his arm and the other two were sued. The case cost the kneeling boy $100,000 and the one who did the pushing $195,000.
- A 40-year-old window washer broke his heel in a fall after a downspout he was holding onto broke away from the house on which he was working. Although the worker was found partially responsible, the fall cost the homeowner $1.2 million.
- A 22-year-old suffered permanent eye damage when he was struck by a golf ball. He sued, claiming that the golfer who hit the ball had failed to look out for other players. The errant shot cost the golfer $160,000.

- A professional dancer suffered permanent knee damage—and an end to her career—when she was knocked down on a beginner's ski slope. She offered to settle for the $300,000 covered by the defendant's insurance, but was rebuffed. The case went to trial, where it cost the defendant $2.2 million.
- A woman suffered severe cuts when her leg was hit by the propeller of a boat she was attempting to board. She sued, claiming that the boat began to move before she was safely aboard. The injury cost the boat owner $175,000.
- At an end-of-school swim party, a 16-year-old dove and hit his head on the bottom of the pool. He became a quadriplegic, and the case resulted in a $1.5-million settlement against the homeowner.
- A 5-year-old suffered brain damage when a dinner bell at his grandfather's house fell and struck him in the head. A lawsuit against the grandfather led to a $500,000 settlement.

Source: *Kiplinger's Personal Finance Magazine,* Vol. 49, No. 7 (July 1995), p. 82. Reprinted with permission.

Reasonable Cost An umbrella policy is also reasonable in cost. The actual cost depends on several variables, including the number of cars, boats, and motorcycles to be covered. For most families, the annual premium for a $1 million umbrella policy is less than $250.

ISO Personal Umbrella Policy

Until recently, a standard personal umbrella policy did not exist. In 1998, however, the Insurance Services Office (ISO) introduced a standard personal umbrella policy. Member companies can use the ISO policy or their own umbrella policy. The following discussion summarizes the basic characteristics of the 1998 ISO policy.

Persons Insured The ISO umbrella policy covers the named insured and spouse, if a resident of the same household, resident family members, and household residents younger than age 21 in the care of an insured aged 21 or older. Also insured is any person using an auto, recreational motor vehicle, or watercraft owned by the named insured and covered under the umbrella policy. In addition, the policy covers any other person or organization who is legally responsible for acts or omissions of the named insured or family member while using an auto or recreational motor vehicle covered under the policy. For example, if James does volunteer work and negligently injures another motorist while delivering food baskets for a local church, the church is covered under the umbrella policy.

Coverages The umbrella policy pays for damages in excess of the retained limit for bodily injury, property damage, or personal injury for which the insured is legally liable because of a covered loss. The **retained limit** is (1) the total limits of the underlying insurance or any other insurance available to an insured, or (2) the deductible stated in the declarations if the loss is covered by the umbrella policy but not by any underlying insurance or other insurance.

In addition to the liability limit, the policy pays legal defense costs; expenses incurred by the insurer while defending the suit; premiums on any required bonds; reasonable expenses incurred by an insured at the insurer's request, including the loss of earnings up to $250 daily; and interest on any unpaid judgment.

Exclusions The ISO policy contains numerous exclusions. Major exclusions include the following:

- *Expected or intentional injury.* Expected or intention injury is excluded. However, the policy does cover intentional bodily injury resulting from reasonable force to protect people or property, such as firing a gun at an intruder who is breaking into the home.
- *Certain personal injury losses.* The policy excludes coverage for certain personal injury losses, such as libel and slander that the insured knows to be false or which occurred prior to the policy's inception. It also excludes criminal acts and acts committed against an employee, such as discrimination in hiring, firing, or promotion.
- *Rental of the premises.* With certain exceptions, the ISO policy excludes liability arising out of rental of the residence premises to someone else. This exclusion does not apply to the occasional rental of the residence premises, such as a professor who goes on a sabbatical leave and rents out his or her home for six months. The exclusion also does not apply if part of the residence premises is rented as an office, school, studio, or private garage.
- *Business liability.* The policy excludes liability arising out of business activities by the insured. This exclusion does not apply to an insured who performs civic or public activities without compensation other than reimbursement for expenses, such as a Girl or Boy Scout leader. Likewise, it does not apply to minors younger than age 18 (21 if a full-time student) who are self-employed, such as in delivering newspapers, mowing lawns, baby sitting, or removing snow.
- *Professional services.* The policy excludes liability arising out of the rendering of or failure to render professional services.

- *Aircraft, watercraft, and recreational vehicles.* The policy excludes liability arising out of the ownership or use of aircraft, except model or hobby aircraft. Also excluded are activities involving watercraft or recreational motor vehicles unless coverage is provided by underlying insurance.
- *No reasonable belief.* The ISO personal umbrella policy excludes coverage for a person using an auto, recreational motor vehicle, or watercraft without a reasonable belief that he or she is entitled to do so. This exclusion does not apply to a family member who uses a vehicle owned by the named insured, such as a teenager who drives a family car without first getting permission.
- *Vehicles used in racing.* The policy excludes the use of autos, recreational motor vehicles, or watercraft in a prearranged race or speed contest. The exclusion does not apply to sailboats or to watercraft involved in predicted log cruises.
- *Communicable disease, sexual molestation, or use of a controlled substance.* The policy excludes liability arising out of the transmission of a communicable disease; sexual molestation; corporal punishment; physical or mental abuse; or the use or sale of a controlled substance, such as cocaine, marijuana, and narcotic drugs (except prescription drugs).
- *Board of directors.* The ISO policy excludes acts or omissions of an insured as an officer or member of a board of directors. This exclusion does not apply to nonprofit organizations in which the insured receives no compensation other than reimbursement for expenses.
- *Care, custody, and control.* The policy excludes coverage for property damage to property rented to, used by, or in the care, custody, and control of the insured to the extent that the insured is required by contract to provide insurance for such property. The exclusion does not apply to property damage caused by fire, smoke, or explosion.

In addition, the ISO personal umbrella policy excludes liability arising out of bodily injury to the named insured or any family member; damage to property owned by an insured; bodily injury to any person eligible to receive workers compensation benefits; and liability arising out of the escape of fuel from a fuel system, absorption or inhalation of lead, or lead contamination.

SUMMARY

- The ISO dwelling program is designed for dwellings that are ineligible for coverage under the homeowner contracts and for persons who do not want or need a homeowners policy.

- The *Dwelling Property 1 policy* is a basic form that provides fire and extended-coverage insurance and coverage for vandalism or malicious mischief. The *Dwelling Property 2 policy* is a broad form that includes all perils covered under the basic form and some additional perils. The *Dwelling Property 3 policy* is a special form that covers the dwelling and other structures against risks of direct loss to property. All direct physical losses are covered except for those losses specifically excluded; personal property is covered on a named-perils basis.

- A mobilehome can be insured by an endorsement to a Homeowners 2 or Homeowners 3 policy. Thus, the coverages on a mobilehome are similar to those found in homeowner contracts.

- An *inland marine floater* provides broad and comprehensive protection on personal property that is frequently moved from one location to another. Although inland marine floaters are not uniform, they share certain common characteristics. Insurance can be tailored to the specific types of personal property to be insured; desired amounts of insurance and type of coverage can be selected; broader and more comprehensive coverage can be obtained; and most floaters cover insured property anywhere in the world.

- The *personal articles floater (PAF)* insures certain optional classes of personal property on an "all-risks" basis. All direct physical losses are covered except certain losses specifically excluded. The classes are jewelry, furs, cameras, musical instruments, silverware, golfer's equipment, fine arts, postage stamps, and rare and current coins. Individual items are listed and insured for specific amounts.

- The *scheduled personal property endorsement* is an endorsement that can be added to the homeowners policy that provides essentially the same coverages provided by the personal articles floater.

- Insurance on pleasure or recreational boats generally can be divided into two categories. A *boat owners package policy* combines physical damage insurance, medical expense insurance, liability insurance, and other coverages into one contract. A *yacht policy* is designed for larger boats such as cabin cruisers and inboard motorboats. The yacht policy provides physical damage insurance on the boat and equipment, liability insurance, medical payments insurance, and other coverages on a broad and comprehensive basis.

- The flood peril is difficult to insure privately because of the problems of a catastrophic loss, prohibitively high premiums, and adverse selection. Federal flood insurance is available at subsidized rates to cover buildings and personal property in flood zones.

- Under the *write-your-own program*, private insurers write flood insurance, collect premiums, and pay claims. They are then reimbursed for any losses by the federal government.

- *FAIR plans* provide basic property insurance to individuals who are unable to obtain coverage in the normal markets. The property must be inspected before the policy is issued. If the property meets certain underwriting standards, it can be insured at standard or surcharged rates. In some cases, the owner may be required to make certain improvements in the property before the policy is issued. If the insurance is denied, the applicant must be informed of the reasons why the property cannot be insured.

- Federal crop insurance programs provide coverage for unavaoidable crop losses, such as those caused by hail, wind, drought, and plant disease.

- *Title insurance* protects the owner of property or lender of money against any unknown defects in the title to the property.

- The *personal umbrella policy* is designed to provide protection against a catastrophic lawsuit or judgment. The major features of the personal umbrella policy are as follows:

    The policy provides excess liability insurance over basic underlying insurance contracts.

    Coverage is broad and includes protection against certain losses not covered by the underlying contracts.

    A self-insured retention must be met for certain losses covered by the umbrella policy but not by any underlying contract.

    The umbrella policy is reasonable in cost.

KEY CONCEPTS AND TERMS

Boat owners package
    policy
Dwelling Property 1
    (basic form)
Dwelling Property 2
    (broad form)
Dwelling Property 3
    (special form)
FAIR plan
Flood
Inland marine floater
Mobilehome insurance
National Flood Insurance
    Program

Personal articles floater
    (PAF)
Personal umbrella
    policy
Retained limit or
    deductible
Scheduled personal
    property endorsement
    (HO-61)
Self-insured retention
Title insurance
Yacht insurance

REVIEW QUESTIONS

1. Describe briefly the major forms that are now used in the dwelling program.

2. Identify the basic coverages in a policy covering mobilehomes.

3. Show how the personal articles floater can be used to cover a valuable silverware, coin, or stamp collection.

4. Identify the coverages found in a typical boat owners package policy.

5. Describe the major coverages in a yacht policy.

6. Why is the flood peril difficult to insure privately?

7. Describe briefly the major provisions of the federal flood insurance program.

8. What is the purpose of a FAIR plan?

9. Describe the basic characteristics of title insurance.

10. Explain the major characteristics of the personal umbrella policy.

APPLICATION QUESTIONS

1. Fernando owns a fourplex and lives in one unit. The building is insured under the Dwelling Property 1 (basic form) policy for $160,000. The replacement cost of the building is $200,000. Explain to what extent, if any, Fernando will recover for the following losses:

   a. A fire occurs in one of the apartments because of defective wiring. The actual cash value of the damage is $10,000, and the replacement cost is $12,000.

   b. The tenants move out because the apartment is unfit for normal living. It will take three months to restore the apartment to its former condition. The apartment is rented for $600 monthly.

   c. A tenant's personal property is damaged in the fire. The actual cash value of the damaged property is $5000, and its replacement cost is $7000.

2. Marcie owns a mobilehome that is insured by an endorsement to a Homeowners 3 policy. Explain to what extent, if at all, this policy would pay for each of the following losses:

   a. A severe windstorm damages the roof of the mobilehome.

   b. A built-in range and oven are also damaged in the storm.

   c. A window air conditioner is badly damaged in the storm.

   d. Marcie must move to a furnished apartment for three months while the mobilehome is being repaired.

3. Morgan has an outboard motorboat insured under a boat owners package policy. Indicate whether each of the following losses would be covered under Morgan's policy. If the loss is not covered, or not completely covered, explain why.

   a. Morgan's boat was badly damaged when it struck a log floating in the water.

   b. An occupant in Morgan's boat was injured and incurred medical expenses when the boat struck a concrete abutment.

   c. The motor was stolen when the boat was docked at a marina.

   d. A small child in Morgan's boat was not wearing a life jacket. The child fell overboard and drowned. The child's parents have sued Morgan.

4. Jann has a personal umbrella policy in the amount of $1 million. The self-insured retention is $250. Jann has the following liability limits under his homeowners and automobile insurance contracts:

Homeowners policy: $100,000

Personal auto policy: $250,000/$500,000/$50,000

Indicate whether each of the following losses would be covered under Jann's personal umbrella policy. If the loss is not covered, or not covered fully, explain why.

a. Jann coaches a Little League baseball team. A team member sitting behind third base was struck in the face by a line drive and lost the sight in one eye. Jann is sued by the parents, who allege that Jann's coaching is inadequate. The team member is awarded damages of $1 million.

b. Jann is a member of the board of directors for the local Young Men's Christian Association (YMCA). Jann is sued by a YMCA member who was seriously injured when a trampoline collapsed. The injured member is awarded damages of $500,000.

c. Jann accuses a male teenager, age 14, of stealing his racing bike valued at $2000. The police arrest the youth and book him. The police later arrest the actual thief and recover the bicycle. Jann is sued by the youth's parents for the false arrest. The teenager is awarded damages of $100,000.

d. Jann fails to stop at a red light, and his car struck another motorist. The injured motorist is awarded damages of $200,000.

SELECTED REFERENCES

Chesebrough, John R., and George E. Rejda. "Personal Umbrella Liability Insurance—A Critical Analysis," *CPCU Journal*, Vol. 48, No. 2 (June 1995), pp. 98–104.

Fire, Casualty & Surety Bulletins. Fire and Marine volume and Casualty and Surety volume. Cincinnati, OH: National Underwriter Company. See also the Personal Lines volume. The bulletins are published monthly.

"Personal Umbrella Liability Policy," *The CPCU Handbook of Insurance Policies*, third edition. Malvern, PA: American Institute for CPCU/Insurance Institute of America, 1998, pp. 119–125.

Rejda, George E., Constance M. Luthardt, Cheryl L. Ferguson, and Donald R. Oakes. *Personal Insurance*, fourth edition. Malvern, PA: Insurance Institute of America, 2000.

NOTES

1. The ISO dwelling program is described in detail in *Fire, Casualty & Surety Bulletins*, Personal Lines volume, Dwelling section. The dwelling property forms by the Insurance Services Office were also used by the author in preparing this section.

2. For a detailed explanation of mobilehomes, see "Mobilehome Insurance," *Fire, Casualty & Surety Bulletins*, Personal Lines volume, Dwelling section.

3. George E. Rejda, Constance M. Luthardt, Cheryl L. Ferguson, and Donald R. Oakes, *Personal Insurance*, third edition (Malvern, PA: Insurance Institute of America, 1997), pp. 226–227.

4. Discussion of the personal articles floater is based on *Fire, Casualty & Surety Bulletins*, Personal Lines volume, Misc. Personal section.

5. Insurance on pleasure boats is based on *Fire, Casualty & Surety Bulletins*, Companies and Coverages volume, Aircraft-Marine section; and the boatowners policy discussed in the *CPCU Handbook of Insurance Policies*, third edition (Malvern, PA: American Institute for CPCU and Insurance Institute of America, 1998), pp. 92–100.

6. Current details of the federal flood insurance program can be found in the *Fire, Casualty & Surety Bulletins*, Fire and Marine volume, Catastrophe section.

7. FAIR plans exist in Arkansas (rural), California, Connecticut, Delaware, District of Columbia, Florida (joint underwriting association), Georgia, Hawaii, Illinois, Indiana, Iowa, Kansas, Kentucky, Louisiana, Maryland, Massachusetts, Michigan, Minnesota, Mississippi (rural), Missouri, New Jersey, New Mexico, New York, North Carolina, Ohio, Oregon, Pennsylvania, Rhode Island, Virginia, Washington, West Virginia, and Wisconsin. Beach and windstorm plans exist in Alabama, Florida, Louisiana, Mississippi, North Carolina, South Carolina, and Texas.

8. Discussion of the personal umbrella policy is based on John R. Chesebrough and George E. Rejda, "Personal Umbrella Liability Insurance—A Critical Analysis," *CPCU Journal*, Vol. 48, No. 2 (June 1995), pp. 98–104; "Personal Umbrella Liability Insurance," in *Fire, Casualty & Surety Bulletins*, Companies and Coverage volume, Personal Packages section (Cincinnati, OH: National Underwriter Company); and "Personal Umbrella Liability Policy," *The CPCU Handbook of Insurance Policies*, third edition (Malvern, PA: American Institute for CPCU/Insur-

Case Application

Jesse is a former zookeeper who retired early because of poor health. He recently purchased a small cottage near a river for $60,000 that will be his major residence. The river occasionally overflows during heavy rainstorms, which has caused damage to several homes in the area. Jesse lives alone. However, he has two dogs, a cat, a parrot, and a domesticated wild tiger as pets. He also owns a small 15-horsepower runabout boat that is used to cross the river to buy groceries and supplies from a convenience store.

An insurance agent has informed Jesse that an HO-3 policy cannot be obtained on the cottage because the underwriter would not approve the application. The agent stated that he would try to get the underwriter to approve Dwelling Property 3 policy (DP-3). If that policy cannot be obtained, the agent would try to get a Dwelling Property 1 policy (DP-1). As a last resort, the agent stated

that coverage could be obtained through the state's FAIR plan.

a. Assume you are a personal insurance advisor. Identify the major loss exposures that Jesse faces.

b. Explain the major differences among the HO-3, DP-3, and DP-1 policies discussed by the agent.

c. To what extent will each of the coverage alternatives discussed by the agent cover the loss exposures identified in (a)?

d. Assume that Jesse obtains a DP-3 policy. Do you recommend that he also purchase the personal liability supplement? Explain.

e. Assume that Jesse obtains a DP-1 policy. Do you recommend that he also purchase flood insurance through the federal flood insurance program? Explain.

 Students may take a self-administered test on this chapter at www.awlonline.com/rejda

Part Four

Commercial Property and Liability Risks

Chapter 13

Commercial Property Insurance

"Knowledge of commercial property insurance is absolutely essential to a successful risk management program."

Connie Luthardt, CPCU
American Institute for CPCU

Learning Objectives

After studying this chapter, you should be able to:

▲ Identify the major documents that form a commercial package policy.

▲ Explain the major provisions of the building and personal property coverage form.

▲ Describe the major coverages for insuring a business income loss, including the business income coverage form and extra expense insurance.

▲ Explain the major provisions of builders risk insurance, glass insurance, and boiler and machinery insurance.

▲ Identity the major types of ocean marine and inland marine insurance.

▲ Describe the basic characteristics of the businessowners policy for small- to medium-sized business firms.

▲ Access an Internet site to obtain information about commercial property insurance.

Internet Resources

- The **Alliance of American Insurers** is a trade association of property and liability insurers that provides educational, legislative, promotional, and safety services to its members. Visit the site at:

  http://www.allianceai.org

- **A. M. Best Company** is a rating organization that publishes books and periodicals relating to the insurance industry, including some on property and liability insurance. Visit the site at:

  http://www.ambest.com

- The **American Insurance Association** is a trade and service organization for property and liability insurers that provides a forum for discussing problems as well as safety, promotional, and legislative services. Visit the site at:

  http://www.aiadc.org

- The **Highway Loss Data Institute** is a nonprofit organization that compiles, processes, and provides the public with insurance data on human and economic losses resulting from highway accidents. Visit the site at:
  http://www.hwysafety.org

- The **Insurance Information Institute** is a primary source of information, analysis, and referral on subjects dealing with property and liability insurance. Visit the site at:
  http://www.iii.org

- The **Inland Marine Underwriters Association** provides a forum for discussing common problems encountered by inland marine insurers. Visit the site at:
  http://www.imua.org

- The **Insurance Services Office (ISO)** provides statistical information, actuarial analysis, policy language, and technical information to participants in property and liability insurance markets. ISO has drafted a considerable number of commercial property forms, as discussed in this chapter. Visit the site at:
  http://www.iso.com

- The **Insurance Research Council** is a division of the American Institute for CPCU. It provides the public and the insurance industry with timely research information relating to property and liability insurance. Visit the site at:
  http://www.ircweb.org

- The **National Association of Independent Insurers** is a trade association that provides information to fire, casualty, and surety insurers. Visit the site at:
  http://www.naii.org

- The **Risk and Insurance Management Society (RIMS)** is an organization of corporate buyers of insurance that makes known to insurers the insurance needs of business and industry, supports loss prevention, and provides a forum for discussing common objectives and problems. Visit the site at:
  http://www.rims.org

 al, age 45, is the owner and manager of Sal's Pizza, which is located near the campus of a large Eastern University. The restaurant is known for its high-quality pizza and is a popular hangout for college students. Recently, a baking oven overheated and caused a severe fire, which resulted in extensive property damage. The restaurant was expected to be closed for at least four months. When Sal called his agent to report the fire, the agent stated that the property damage to the building was fully covered except for a small deductible. Sal was relieved to hear that the insurance on the business would also cover most of profits lost during the four-month shutdown period.

Like Sal's Pizza, business firms own valuable commercial real estate; business personal property, such as office furniture, computers, supplies, and machinery; and inventories of finished products. This property can be damaged or destroyed by a direct physical damage loss to covered property. In addition, firms may have in their possession the property of customers, which can be damaged or destroyed if a loss occurs. Moreover, like Sal's Pizza, firms may experience a substantial loss of business income or incur sizable extra expenses in the event of a loss.

This chapter discusses commercial property insurance, with special emphasis on the commercial property insurance program developed by the Insurance Services Office (ISO). More specifically, it focuses on the commercial package policy, the building and personal property coverage form, business income insurance, and other property coverages. The chapter also discusses ocean marine and inland marine insurance, which covers transportation and other commercial risks. It concludes with an examination of the businessowners policy, which is designed for owners of small- to medium-sized business firms.

OVERVIEW OF COMMERCIAL PACKAGE POLICY

A **package policy** *is one that combines two or more ISO coverages into a single policy.* If both property and liability insurance lines are combined into a single policy, it is also known as a *multiple-line policy.* The following section discusses the general format and structure of the **commercial package policy (CPP)**, which is widely used by business firms.

The CPP can be used to insure motels, hotels, apartment houses, office buildings, retail stores, institutions such as churches and schools, processing firms such as dry cleaners, manufacturing firms, and a wide variety of other commercial firms. It can also be tailored to cover most commercial property and liability loss exposures in a single policy, with the major exceptions of workers compensation and surety bonds.

With a package policy, the firm has fewer gaps in protection, relatively lower premiums because individual policies are not purchased, and the convenience of a single policy.

Under the ISO program, each commercial package policy contains (1) *a common policy declarations page*, (2) *a common policy conditions page*, and (3) *two or more coverage parts.*[1] Exhibit 13.1 shows in greater detail the various parts of a commercial package policy.

Common Policy Declarations

Each commercial package policy contains a *common policy declarations page* that shows the name and address of the insured, policy period, description of the insured property, coverage parts that apply, and the premium paid.

Common Policy Conditions

Each commercial package policy also contains a *common policy conditions page* that applies to all commercial lines of insurance. The common conditions are summarized as follows:

- *Cancellation.* Either party can cancel by giving the other party advance notice. The insurer can cancel by giving notice of cancellation for nonpayment of premiums at least 10 days in advance and 30 days in advance for any other reason. If the insurer cancels, a pro rata refund of the premium is made. If the insured cancels, the refund may be less than pro rata.
- *Changes.* Any changes in the policy can be made only by an endorsement issued by the insurer.
- *Examination of books and records.* The insurer has the right to audit the insured's books and records any time during the policy period and up to three years after the policy period ends.
- *Inspections and surveys.* The insurer has the right to make inspections and surveys that relate to insurability of the property and premiums to be charged.
- *Premiums.* More than one party may be named as an insured in the declarations page. The first named insured in the declarations is the party responsible for the payment of premiums.
- *Transfer of rights and duties.* The insured's rights and duties under the policy cannot be transferred without the insurer's written consent. One exception is that the rights and duties can be trans-

EXHIBIT 13.1
Components of the Commercial Package Policy (CPP)

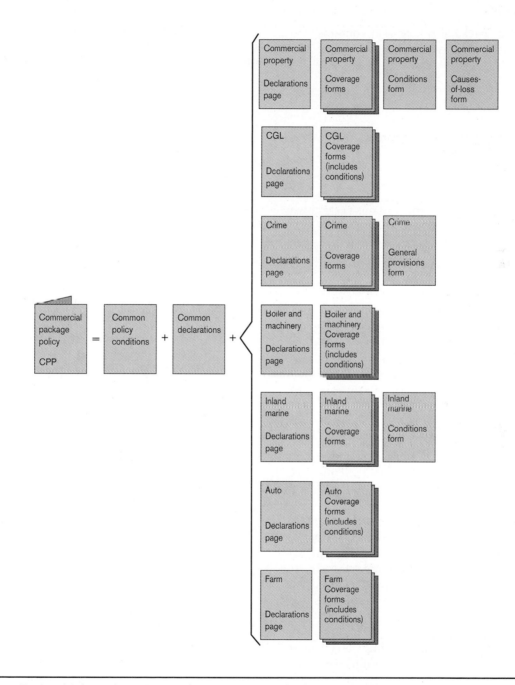

SOURCE: Jerome Trupin and Arthur L. Flitner, *Commercial Property Insurance and Risk Management*, fifth edition, Vol. 1 (Malvern, PA: American Institute for CPCU, 1998), Exhibit 3.2, p. 105.

ferred to a legal representative if an individual named insured should die.

Coverage Parts

Each commercial package policy also contains two or more *coverage parts*, which can include the following:

- Commercial property coverage forms
- Commercial general liability coverage forms
- Commercial crime coverage forms
- Boiler and machinery coverage forms
- Inland marine coverage forms
- Commercial auto coverage forms
- Farm coverage forms

Each coverage part, in turn, contains (1) its own declarations page that applies to that coverage, (2) the specific conditions that apply to that coverage part, (3) coverage forms that describe the various coverages provided, and (4) a causes-of-loss form that describes the various perils that are covered.

BUILDING AND PERSONAL PROPERTY COVERAGE FORM

The building and personal property coverage form is one of several property forms that are included in the ISO program. This form is widely used to cover a direct physical damage loss to commercial buildings and business personal property.

Covered Property

The insured can select the property to be covered. Covered property can include (1) the building, (2) business personal property of the insured, and (3) personal property of others in the care, custody, or control of the insured. Depending on its needs, a business firm can elect one or all three coverages (see Insight 13.1).

Building The form covers the building described in the declarations and includes any completed additions and fixtures, machinery, and equipment that are permanently installed. Certain outdoor fixtures are also covered, such as light poles, flag poles, and mailboxes. Finally, equipment used to maintain or service the building (such as fire-extinguishing equipment, appliances for cooking and dishwashing, floor buffers, and vacuum cleaners) is covered.

Business Personal Property of the Insured Business personal property of the insured inside or on the building or within 100 feet of the premises is also covered. It includes furniture and fixtures; machinery and equipment; stock or inventory; and all other personal property owned by the insured and used in the insured's business. In addition, the insured's interest in the personal property of others is covered to the extent of labor, materials, and other charges. For example, a machine shop may repair a piece of machinery owned by a customer. If parts and labor are $1000 and the machinery is damaged from an insured peril before it is delivered to the customer, the insured's interest of $1000 is covered.

The insured's use interest in improvements and betterments as a tenant is also covered as business personal property. Improvements and betterments include fixtures, alterations, installations, or additions that are made part of the building at the insured's expense and cannot be removed legally. An example of an improvement is the installation of a new air conditioning unit by an insured who leases a building to open a new bar and restaurant.

Finally, business personal property includes leased personal property for which the insured has a contractual obligation to insure. An example would be leased computer equipment, for which the insured is required to provide insurance.

Personal Property of Others Personal property of others in the care, custody, or control of the insured is also covered. For example, if a tornado destroys a machine shop and equipment belonging to customers is damaged, the loss would be covered.

Additional Coverages Four additional coverages are provided, summarized as follows:

1. *Debris removal.* The cost of debris removal is limited to 25 percent of the sum of the direct physical damage loss plus the deductible. For example, for a $4000 physical damage loss and a $500 deductible, the policy would pay a maximum of

Insight 13.1

Examples of Coverage Under the Building and Personal Property Coverage Form

The building and personal property coverage form can be used to cover a building, business personal property, and personal property of others. Most business firms do not require coverage in all three categories. Depending on its needs, a firm can elect only those coverages desired.

Examples

1. Worldwide Realty, Inc., is the owner of a building rented to others. It has purchased coverage for the building only.
2. Sue Brown, doing business as Sue's Leather Restoring, operates in Worldwide Realty's building. Sue has no need for building insurance because she is only a tenant. She has purchased coverage for her own business personal property and for the per-

sonal property of others in her care, custody, or control.
3. Smith and Jones, LLP, a law firm operating in Worldwide Realty's building, has purchased coverage only for its own business personal property because it does not have an insurable interest in the building and does not have any personal property of others in its possession.
4. City Laundry, Inc., a commercial laundry, owns and occupies the building adjacent to Worldwide Realty's building. City Laundry has purchased coverage for the building, its business personal property, and the personal property of others in its care, custody, or control.

Source: Adapted from Jerome Trupin and Arthur L. Flitner, *Commercial Property Risk Management and Insurance*, fifth edition, Vol. 1 (Malvern, PA: American Institute for CPCU, 1998), p 109.

$1125 [.25 × ($4000 + $500)]. For debris removal costs that exceed this limit, an additional $10,000 is available under the "limits of insurance" provision in the policy.

The additional coverage does not apply to the cost of extracting pollutants from land or water or to the cost of removing, restoring, or replacing polluted land or water.

2. *Preservation of property.* If property is moved to another location for safekeeping because of a covered loss, any direct physical loss or damage to the property while being moved or while stored at the other location is covered. Coverage applies only if the loss or damage occurs within 30 days after the property is first moved.
3. *Fire department service charge.* A maximum of $1000 can be paid for a fire department service charge. No deductible applies to this coverage.
4. *Pollutant cleanup and removal.* The insurer also pays the cost to clean up and remove pollutants from land or water at the described premises if the release or discharge of the pollutants results from a covered cause of loss. The maximum paid is lim-

ited to $10,000 during each separate 12-month policy period.

Extensions of Coverage If a coinsurance requirement of 80 percent or higher is shown in the declarations, or a value-reporting period symbol is shown on the declarations page, the insurance can be extended to cover other property. Each extension is an additional amount of insurance. The extensions of coverage are summarized as follows:

1. *Newly acquired or constructed property.* Insurance on the building is extended to cover new buildings while being built on the described premises and to newly acquired buildings at other locations. The insurance applies for a maximum period of 30 days and is limited to a maximum of $250,000 for each building. In addition, the insurance on business personal property ($100,000 maximum) can be applied to business personal property at newly acquired locations. This insurance also applies for a maximum period of 30 days.

2. *Personal effects and property of others.* Insurance on business personal property can be extended to cover the personal effects of the named insured, officers, partners, or employees. However, the extension does not apply to theft. The extension also applies to personal property of others in the named insured's care, custody, or control. The maximum paid is limited to $2500.

3. *Valuable papers and records.* Insurance on business personal property can also be extended to cover the costs of researching, replacing, or restoring lost information on lost or damaged valuable papers and records. The maximum paid is limited to $2500.

4. *Property off the premises.* Covered property (other than stock) that is temporarily at a location not owned, leased, or operated by the insured is covered up to $10,000. The extension does not apply to covered property in or on a vehicle, property in the care, custody, or control of salespersons, or property at a fair or exhibition. Coverage does apply, however, to property off the premises for repair, tools and equipment on a job site, and property loaned to others by the insured.

5. *Outdoor property.* Outdoor fences, radio and television antennas, detached signs, and trees, plants, and shrubs are covered up to a maximum of $1000, but not more than $250 for any single tree, shrub, or plant. The insurance applies only to losses caused by fire, lightning, explosion, riot or civil commotion, or aircraft.

Other Provisions

Numerous additional provisions are included in the building and personal property coverage form, but it is beyond the scope of this text to discuss each of them. Several important provisions, however, are summarized here.

Deductible A standard deductible of $250 applies to each occurrence. Higher deductible amounts are available. Only one deductible must be satisfied if several buildings or different types of business personal property are damaged in the same occurrence.

Coinsurance If a coinsurance percentage is stated in the declarations, the coinsurance requirement must be met to avoid a coinsurance penalty. To reduce misunderstanding and confusion, the form contains several excellent examples of how coinsurance works.

Valuation Provision A valuation provision states the rules for establishing the value of covered property at the time of loss. Except for certain losses (see Exhibit 13.2), insured property is valued at its actual cash value. Actual cash value is interpreted to mean replacement cost less depreciation.

Optional Coverages Three optional coverages are available, which eliminates the need for separate endorsements.

1. *Agreed value.* This option suspends the coinsurance clause and substitutes a new agreement that covers any loss in the same proportion that the limit of insurance bears to the agreed value shown in the declarations. For example, if the agreed value for an item is $100,000, and the limit of insurance is $100,000, then any loss is covered at a rate of 100 percent.

2. *Inflation guard.* This option automatically increases the amount of insurance by an annual percentage shown in the declarations.

3. *Replacement cost.* Under the replacement cost option, there is no deduction for depreciation if a loss occurs. However, this option does not apply to the property of others; contents of a residence; manuscripts; works of art, antiques, and similar property; and stock (unless designated in the declarations). Replacement cost insurance generally is recommended when buildings and their contents are insured. Otherwise, the loss is paid on an actual cash value basis.

CAUSES-OF-LOSS FORMS

A *causes-of-loss form* must be added to the policy to have a complete contract. There are four causes-of-loss forms:

- Causes-of-loss basic form
- Causes-of-loss broad form
- Causes-of-loss special form
- Causes-of-loss earthquake form

EXHIBIT 13.2
Valuation of Property—Building and Personal Property Coverage Form

Property Type	Valuation Basis
Property other than that specifically listed	Actual cash value
Building damage of $2500 or less	Replacement cost except for some personal property items considered part of a building
Stock sold but not delivered	Selling price less discounts and unincurred costs
Glass	Replacement cost for safety glazing if required by law
Improvements and betterments:	
(a) replaced by other than the insured	Not covered
(b) replaced by the insured	Actual cash value
(c) not replaced	Percentage of cost based on remaining life of lease
Valuable papers and records	Cost of blank media plus cost of transaction or copying ($2500 research cost as coverage extension)

SOURCE: Bernard L. Webb, Arthur L. Flitner, and Jerome Trupin, *Commercial Insurance*, third edition (Malvern, PA: Insurance Institute of America, 1996), Exhibit 2-4, p. 36.

The earthquake form can be used with any of the three causes-of-loss forms, or it can be used separately to provide earthquake and volcanic eruption insurance.

Causes-of-Loss Basic Form

The **causes-of-loss basic form** provides coverage for the following perils: fire, lightning, explosion, windstorm or hail, smoke, aircraft or vehicles, riot or civil commotion, vandalism, sprinkler leakage, sinkhole collapse, and volcanic action.

These perils are self-explanatory, but two comments are in order. *Sprinkler leakage* provides coverage for the accidental leakage or discharge of any substance from an automatic sprinkler system. For example, if the sprinkler system in a department store accidentally leaks water that damages the stock, the loss is covered.

Sinkhole collapse means the sinking or collapse in underground empty spaces created by the action of water on limestone or dolomite rock formations. Although damage caused by the sinkhole collapse is

covered, the cost of filling the sinkhole is specifically excluded.

Causes-of-Loss Broad Form

The **causes-of-loss broad form** includes all causes of loss covered by the basic form plus several additional causes:

- Falling objects
- Weight of snow, ice, or sleet
- Water damage

The broad form also covers collapse and the breakage of glass as additional coverages. Collapse is covered only if caused by the following:

- Any broad form peril
- Hidden decay
- Hidden insect or vermin damage
- Weight of people or personal property
- Weight of rain that collects on a roof
- Use of defective materials or methods in construction or remodeling if collapse occurs during the course of construction or remodeling

As noted earlier, the broad form covers the breakage of glass as an additional coverage. There is a maximum limit of $100 per glass pane or glass plate and $500 for any occurrence.

Exhibit 13.3 summarizes the covered causes of loss under both the basic form and broad form.

Causes-of-Loss Special Form

The **causes-of-loss special form** insures against "risks of direct physical loss" (formerly called "all-risks"). That is, all direct physical damage losses to insured property are covered unless specifically excluded or limited in the form itself. The burden of proof falls on the insurer to show that the loss is not covered because of a specific exclusion or limitation that applies. In addition, collapse is included as an additional coverage.

The special form provides for two other extensions of coverage. First, property in transit is covered for certain perils up to $1000 while the property is in or on a motor vehicle owned, leased, or operated by the insured. Second, if a covered water damage loss occurs, the cost of tearing out and replacing part of

the building or structure to repair the leaking water system or appliance is covered.

Because of its advantages, most risk managers prefer the special form (see Insight 13.2).

Causes-of-Loss Earthquake Form

Damage from earthquakes can be covered by adding the **causes-of-loss earthquake form** to a commercial property policy. All earthquake shocks or volcanic eruptions that occur within a 168-hour period are considered to be a single event. Consequently, the policy limit applies to all damage that occurs during this period.

A percentage deductible is stated in the declarations and is usually 2 to 5 percent of the value of the insured property. In some areas where earthquakes are more likely to occur, the percentage deductible can be as high as 10 percent.

REPORTING FORMS

A firm may have sharp fluctuations in its inventories throughout the year. A **reporting form** requires the

---

EXHIBIT 13.3
Comparison of Basic Form and Broad Form

Both forms cover:	*Broad form also covers:*
1. Fire	12. Falling objects
2. Lightning	13. Weight of snow, ice, or sleet
3. Explosion	14. Water damage
4. Windstorm or hail	15. Glass breakage*
5. Smoke	16. Collapse*
6. Aircraft or vehicles	
7. Riot or civil commotion	
8. Vandalism	
9. Sprinkler leakage	
10. Sinkhole collapse	
11. Volcanic action	

*Glass breakage and collapse are provided as additional coverages.

SOURCE: Jerome Trupin and Arthur L. Flitner, *Commercial Property Insurance and Risk Management*, fifth edition, Vol. 1 (Malvern, PA: American Institute for CPCU, 1998), Exhibit 5-1, p. 191.

Insight 13.2

Advantages of the Special Causes-of-Loss Form

The special form insurance provides coverage for risks of direct physical loss to covered property. *The burden of proof as to coverage falls on the insurer—not the insured.* As long as the insured can demonstrate that a direct physical loss has occurred to covered property, the cause of loss is presumed to be covered unless the *insurer* can prove that an exclusion applies.

In contrast, the basic and broad forms place the burden of proof on the insured. Unless the *insured* can prove that one of the named perils caused the loss, the insurer has no obligation to pay. Which party has the burden of proof can make a major difference when the cause of loss is not entirely clear.

Insured and students of insurance sometimes ask for examples of "all-risks" type losses that would not be covered under a broad form. Some examples include the following:

- *Theft.* Because many types of theft are not excluded, those that are not excluded are covered.
- *Friendly fire.* The named peril "fire" is generally held to mean only *hostile fire.* No such limitation applies to the special form and most other "all-risks" forms because they do not exclude damage by friendly fire. Although court decisions are eroding the doctrine of friendly fire, an insured that has suffered a loss caused by a friendly fire might have to institute a lawsuit to prevail under a named perils policy.

- *Vehicle damage.* The aircraft or vehicles peril of the basic and broad forms contains a contact requirement. However, vehicles can harm property without making contact with the damaged property. The special form covers damage by vehicles whether or not direct physical contact occurs. It also covers damage caused by vehicles regardless of whether the insured owns or operates the damage-causing vehicle. The basic and broad forms exclude coverage when the vehicle is owned by the insured or operated in the course of the insured's business.
- *Water damage caused by ice dam.* When melting snow or ice backs up under roof shingles (usually because gutters are clogged with ice, a phenomenon referred to as "ice damming"), the resulting water damage is covered by the special form but not by the basic form or the broad form.

These examples help to illustrate the breadth of "all-risks" coverage. *The key point is this: a cause of loss that is not specifically excluded is covered.*

Another advantage is the relatively small additional premium charged for special form coverage instead of broad form coverage. The vast majority of risk managers and experienced insurance producers therefore prefer the special form.

Source: Adapted from Jerome Trupin and Arthur L. Flitner, *Commercial Property Risk Management and Insurance,* fifth edition, Vol. 1 (Malvern, PA: American Institute for CPCU, 1998), pp. 210–211.

---

insured to report periodically the value of the insured inventory. As long as the report is accurate, the amount of insurance on the inventory is automatically adjusted based on the amount of insured values.

Under the ISO commercial property program, the *value reporting form* is used to insure fluctuations in inventory. A provisional premium is paid at the inception of the policy based on the limit of insurance. The final premium is determined at the end of the policy period based on the values reported. The insured has the option of reporting daily, weekly, monthly, quarterly, or at the end of the policy year. As long as the insured reports the correct values, the full amount of the loss is covered up to the policy limits. For example, assume that the insured correctly reports an inventory of $1 million at the last reporting date, and the inventory is increased to $5 million before the next reporting date. If a total loss occurs, the entire inventory of $5 million would be covered (less the deductible).

However, the value reporting form contains a *full reporting clause* (honesty clause) that requires the insured to report the values honestly. If the insured is dishonest or careless and underreports, he or she will be penalized if a loss occurs. *If the insured underreports the property values at a location, and a loss occurs at that location, recovery is limited to the proportion that the last value reported bears to the correct value that should have been reported.* For example, if the actual inventory on hand is $500,000, and the insured reports only $400,000, only four-fifths of any loss will be paid (less the deductible).

BUSINESS INCOME INSURANCE

Business firms often experience a consequential, or indirect, loss as a result of a direct physical damage loss to covered property, such as the loss of profits, rents, or extra expenses. **Business income insurance** (formerly called business interruption insurance) is designed to cover the loss of business income, expenses that continue during the shutdown period, and extra expenses because of a direct physical loss to insured property.

Two basic ISO forms are used to insure business income losses: (1) business income and extra expense coverage form and (2) extra expense coverage form.[2]

Business Income Coverage Form

The **business income and extra expense coverage form** is used to cover the loss of business income regardless of whether the income is derived from retail or service operations, manufacturing, or rents. When a firm has a business income loss, profits are lost, and certain expenses may still continue, such as rent, interest, insurance premiums, and some salaries. The present form covers both the loss of business income and extra expenses that result from a physical damage loss to covered property.

Loss of Business Income The business income and extra expense coverage form covers the loss of business income due to the suspension of operations during the period of restoration. The suspension of operations must result from the direct physical loss or damage to property caused by an insured peril at the described premises. The insured perils are listed in the causes-of-loss form attached to the policy. *Business income is defined as the net profit or loss (before income taxes) that would have been earned plus continuing normal operating expenses, includ-*

ing payroll. In effect, the amount paid represents the profit (or loss) that would have occurred if the suspension of operations had not occurred, plus expenses that continue during the period of suspension. For example, assume that a retail shoe store has a fire and must suspend operations for six months. All regular employees are laid off during the shutdown period. Assume also that the firm's estimated sales and expenses for the 12 months of the policy period are as shown in Exhibit 13.4.

Assuming that income is earned equally over the period, the store's normal net income for 12 months is estimated to be $100,000. Thus, if the store is shut down for only six months, it will lose net income of $50,000. During the shutdown period, the firm also had continuing expenses of $20,000, such as the payment of rent, interest, utilities, and other expenses. Thus, the total loss payment would be $70,000. This can be summarized as follows.

Net income lost during the period of suspension	$50,000
Continuing expenses during the period of suspension	+20,000
Amount paid	$70,000

The loss payment of $70,000 represents the loss of net income plus an amount for continuing expenses.

Additional Coverages The business income form automatically provides several additional coverages, summarized as follows:

1. *Extra expenses.* Extra expenses are the necessary expenses incurred by the firm during a period of

---

EXHIBIT 13.4
Estimated Sales and Expenses for the 12 Months of the Policy Period

Sales	$800,000
Less cost of goods sold	– 400,000
Gross income	$400,000
Less expenses	– 300,000
Net income before taxes	$100,000

restoration that would not have been incurred if the loss had not taken place. Examples of covered extra expenses are the cost of relocating temporarily, increased rent at another location, and the rental of substitute equipment.

2. *Action of civil authority.* Loss of business income and extra expenses caused by action of a civil authority that prohibits access to the described premises because of a covered cause of loss are also paid. The coverage for business income begins 72 hours after the time of that action and continues for up to three consecutive weeks after the coverage begins.

3. *Alterations and new buildings.* The loss of business income as a result of a direct physical damage loss to a new building on the premises (whether completed or under construction) is covered. The loss of business income because of alterations or additions to existing buildings is covered as well.

4. *Extended business income.* A business that reopens may experience reduced earnings after the repairs are completed, and additional time may be needed to recapture old customers. For example, a restaurant that reopens after a fire may need time to attract former customers. The extended business income provision covers the reduction in earnings for a limited period after the business reopens. The extended period begins on the date the property is repaired and operations are resumed and ends after 30 consecutive days or when business income returns to normal, whichever occurs first.

Coinsurance The business income coverage form can be purchased with a coinsurance requirement of 50, 60, 70, 80, 90, 100, or 125 percent. The last percentage can be used if the business expects to be shut down for more than one year. *The basis for coinsurance is the sum of net income that would have been earned plus continuing normal operating expenses, including payroll, for the 12 months following the inception of the policy or the last anniversary date, whichever is later.* This sum is then multiplied by the coinsurance percentage to determine the required amount of insurance. For example, assume that net income and operating expenses for the 12 months of the current policy term are $400,000, and that the coinsurance percentage is 50 percent; the required amount of insurance would be $200,000.

The actual coinsurance percentage selected depends on the length of time it takes to resume operations, and on the period of time during which most of the business is done. If the firm expects to be shut down for more than one year, the 125 percent option should be selected. If the firm expects to be shut down for no more than six months and business is uniform throughout the year, a coinsurance percentage of 50 percent should be selected. However, when seasonal peak periods are considered, this percentage may be inadequate, because 50 percent of the firm's business may not occur within a consecutive six-month period. Thus, when business income is seasonal or has peak periods, a coinsurance percentage higher than 50 percent is advisable to provide greater protection during a prolonged shutdown period that continues during the peak period.

Ordinary payroll is covered under the business income coverage form unless it is excluded by an endorsement to the policy. The endorsement can exclude ordinary payroll, or it can be covered for a limited period, such as 90 days. Limiting or excluding ordinary payroll reduces the premium.

Optional Coverages The business income form also has coverages that can be activated by an appropriate entry on the declarations page. The optional coverages are summarized as follows:

1. *Maximum period of indemnity.* This optional coverage eliminates coinsurance and pays for the loss of business income for a maximum period of 120 days. The amount paid cannot exceed the policy limit. This option can be used by smaller firms that will not be shut down for more than 120 days if a loss occurs.

2. *Monthly limit of indemnity.* This optional coverage eliminates coinsurance and limits the maximum monthly amount that will be paid for each consecutive 30-day period to a fraction of the policy limit. The fractions are one-third, one-fourth, and one-sixth. For example, if the fraction selected is one-third, and the policy limit is $120,000, the maximum paid for each consecutive 30-day period is $40,000.

3. *Agreed value.* This option suspends the coinsurance clause and places no limit on the monthly amount paid, provided that the agreed amount of business income insurance is carried. The agreed

amount is the coinsurance percentage (50 percent or higher) multiplied by an estimate of net income and operating expenses for the 12 months of the policy period.

4. *Extended period of indemnity.* This option extends the recovery period following completion of repairs from 30 days to a longer period stated in the declarations. The extended period of indemnity can be 60, 90, 120, 150, 180, 270, or 360 days. This option is advantageous for those firms that need a longer recovery period to recapture old business and resume normal operations.

Extra Expense Coverage Form

Certain firms such as banks, newspapers, and bakeries must continue to operate after a loss occurs; otherwise, customers will be lost to competitors. The **extra expense coverage form** is a separate form that can be used to cover the extra expenses incurred by the firm in continuing operations during a period of restoration. Loss of profits is not covered, because the firm will still be operating. However, the additional expenses to continue operating are covered, subject to certain limits stated in the declarations on the amount of insurance that can be used. A common limitation is that up to 40 percent of the insurance can be used during the first month following the loss, up to 80 percent for two months, and up to 100 percent when the restoration period exceeds two months.

Business Income from Dependent Properties

Some firms depend on a single supplier for raw materials and supplies or on a single customer to purchase most or all of the firm's products. The insured's business may incur a loss because of property damage incurred by the sole supplier or customer. An appropriate endorsement can be added to a business income policy that covers loss of income at the insured's location that results from direct damage to property at other locations.

There are four types of dependent properties situations for which this coverage may be needed.[3]

- *Contributing location.* A contributing location is a location that furnishes materials or services to

the insured. For example, the insured may depend on one supplier for raw materials. If the supplier's factory is damaged, the insured's business may be forced to shut down.

- *Recipient location.* A recipient location is a location that purchases the insured's products or services. For example, a specialized cheese manufacturer may sell most of its cheese production to a resort hotel. If the hotel is closed because of fire, the cheese factory may have to shut down.
- *Manufacturing location.* A manufacturing location is a location that manufactures products for delivery to the insured's customers. If the manufacturer's plant is damaged, the products cannot be delivered, and the insured would incur a loss.
- *Leader location.* A leader location is a location that attracts customers to the insured's place of business. For example, a major department store in a shopping center may have a fire. As a result, smaller stores in the shopping center may experience a decline in sales.

Miscellaneous Business Income Coverages

Several specialized business income coverages are available that cover the loss of certain types of business income or extra expenses. The *leasehold interest coverage form* covers the loss that may result from the cancellation of a valuable lease when the building is damaged by a covered cause of loss. *Tuition fees insurance* covers the loss of tuition if a school or college has a covered loss. *Weather insurance* covers losses due to weather conditions, such as the loss of business because of excessive rain or snow.

OTHER COMMERCIAL COVERAGES

The building and personal property coverage form discussed earlier is designed to meet the commercial property and liability insurance needs of most business firms. However, many firms have certain needs that require the use of specialized coverages, which include the following:

- Builders risk insurance
- Condominium insurance
- Glass insurance

- Boiler and machinery insurance
- Credit insurance
- Difference in conditions (DIC) insurance

Builders Risk Insurance

A new building under construction is exposed to numerous perils, especially the peril of fire. Under the simplified commercial property program by ISO, the **builders risk coverage form** can be used to insure buildings under construction. This form can be used to cover the insurable interest of a general contractor, subcontractor, or building owner.

Under the builders risk coverage form, insurance is purchased equal to the *full value* of the completed building. Because the building is substantially overinsured during the initial stages of construction, the rate charged is adjusted to reflect the average value exposed.

If desired, a *builders risk reporting form* can be attached as an endorsement, which requires the builder to report monthly the value of the building under construction. The initial premium reflects the value of the building at the inception of the policy period and not the completed value of the building. As construction progresses, the amount of insurance on the building is increased based on the reported values. The final premium paid is based on the actual values reported.

The reporting form is used to cover high-value buildings under construction (such as a high-rise office building), where the value of the building is relatively low during the initial period of construction when the foundation is being built. The value of the building then accelerates as additional stories are added.

Condominium Association Coverage Form

Owners of individual condominium units have a common interest in the building, which includes the exterior walls, the roof, and the plumbing, heating, and air conditioning systems. However, property insurance on the building and other condominium property is purchased in the name of the condominium owners association.

The **condominium association coverage form** provides insurance on the building and equipment to maintain or service the building. If required by the condominium association agreement, the form also covers fixtures, improvements, alterations that are part of the building, and appliances within the individual units (such as a refrigerator, stove, or dishwasher). In addition, the association form covers business personal property, such as outdoor furniture and a riding lawn mower. However, personal property of the individual unit-owners is specifically excluded. The unit-owner's personal property (such as furniture, clothes, and household contents) is normally insured under the Homeowners 6 policy (unit-owners form).

Condominium Commercial Unit-Owners Coverage Form

Business or professional firms may own individual units in a commercial condominium. For example, a physician or business firm may own individual office space in a commercial office building that is legally organized as a condominium.

The **condominium commercial unit-owners coverage form** covers the unit-owner's business personal property, which includes furniture; fixtures and improvements that are part of the building and owned by the unit-owner, machinery and equipment, stock, personal property used in the business; and personal property of others in the care, control, and custody of the insured.

The commercial form does not cover the building, because insurance on the building is purchased by the condominium owners association. In addition, the commercial form excludes fixtures and improvements that are part of the building and appliances within a unit (such as a refrigerator, stove, or dishwasher) if the association agreement requires the association to insure such property.

Glass Insurance

Because of architectural and decorative considerations, the use of glass in building construction has increased. Building owners may desire broader coverage for glass breakage than that provided by the broad and special causes-of-loss forms discussed earlier. Under the ISO commercial property insurance program, the **glass coverage form** is the basic form for writing glass insurance.[4] It can be used with other coverages, or it can be used to create a separate glass insurance policy.

To be covered, the glass must be scheduled either in the declarations or in a glass coverage schedule. Coverage is broad and comprehensive. Glass breakage from most causes is covered (except from fire, nuclear hazard, or war and military action). Glass damage from the accidental or malicious application of chemicals is covered as well.

The insurer has four options for paying a glass claim:

- Pay the actual value of the lost or damaged property.
- Pay the cost of repairing or replacing the property.
- Take the property at an agreed or appraised value.
- Repair or replace the property with property of like kind and quality.

The insurer must let the insured know of its settlement intention within 30 days after a sworn statement of loss.

Certain other items are also paid, including the expense of (1) debris removal, (2) installing temporary plates or boarding up openings, (3) repairing or replacing frames, and (4) removing or repairing any obstructions to repair the broken glass.

Finally, the glass insurance is suspended if the building is vacant for 60 consecutive days unless the insurer is notified and an additional premium is paid.

Boiler and Machinery Insurance

A boiler explosion can cause substantial property damage to the firm and may damage the property of others. Boiler and machinery insurance can be used to insure boilers, machinery, and other equipment for both direct and indirect loss. Business firms often purchase boiler and machinery insurance for the extensive loss-prevention services that insurers provide. Safety engineers will periodically inspect the boiler and other machinery for structural defects and other weaknesses that can cause a loss. Thus, there is great emphasis on loss prevention in the interest of safety.

The **boiler and machinery coverage form** is used to insure boilers and machinery against loss from an explosion or from other covered causes. Boiler and machinery insurance can be written separately as a monoline policy, or it can be part of a commercial package policy.

Coverage Provided The insurer agrees to pay for direct damage to covered property from a covered cause of loss. *Covered property* is property owned by the insured or property in the insured's care, custody, or control for which the insured is legally liable. A *covered cause of loss* is defined as an accident to an object listed in the declarations. An *object* refers to the boiler, machinery, or equipment described in the declarations. An *accident* is a sudden and accidental breakdown of an object or part of an object, such as an explosion, bursting flywheel, or electrical short circuit. At the time the breakdown occurs, there must be physical damage to the object that requires repair or replacement.

Legal Defense The policy provides a legal defense if the insured is sued because of a covered accident that causes damage to the property of another in the insured's care, custody, or control. The insurer either settles the suit or claim or defends the insured. The insurer reserves the right to settle the suit or claim at any point.

Extension of Coverage The boiler and machinery coverage form has several extensions of coverage, summarized as follows:

1. *Expediting expenses.* The insurance can be applied to cover the reasonable extra cost of making temporary repairs, expediting permanent repairs, or expediting permanent replacement of damaged property. For example, overtime wages and extra transportation charges to speed up delivery of a replacement part are examples of covered expenses. The maximum amount paid for expediting expenses is the lower of $25,000 or what is left of the limit of insurance after the insurer pays for a loss to covered property.
2. *Automatic coverage for newly acquired property.* Newly acquired objects similar to the boiler and machinery described in the declarations are automatically covered. The insured must notify the insurer within 90 days and pay an additional premium.

3. *Supplementary payments.* Certain supplementary payments are also made. They include expenses incurred by the insurer in defending a suit; the cost of bonds to release attachments; reasonable expenses incurred by the named insured, including loss of earnings up to $100 daily because of time off from work; court costs assessed against the insured; prejudgment interest; and interest on the original judgment.

Indirect Losses Indirect, or consequential, losses can be covered by an appropriate endorsement, including the following:

1. *Business income insurance* can be added to cover the loss of business income from an insured loss. Under a *valued form*, a specified daily amount is paid for each day of total shutdown regardless of the firm's actual loss of earnings. If the firm is partially shut down, a proportionate part of the daily indemnity is paid. Under an *actual loss sustained form*, the amount paid for a loss is the loss of net profits that would have been earned plus continuing expenses.
2. *Extra expense insurance* covers the extra expense of maintaining operations after an accident to an insured object until the firm can resume its normal operations. The extra expense endorsement excludes the loss of income. For example, a firm may have its own power plant to produce electricity and have an emergency standby connection with an outside public utility firm in case power is interrupted. If an accident occurs and the power is interrupted, the extra costs of the outside power would be covered.
3. *Consequential damage insurance* covers the spoilage of specified property from the lack of power, light, heat, steam, or refrigeration if an accident occurs to an insured object. For example, the loss of refrigeration in a meat packing plant results in the spoilage of meat. The spoilage loss would be covered by this endorsement.

Credit Insurance

Credit insurance protects a firm against abnormal credit losses because of customer insolvency or past due accounts when they are filed for collection within a specified time stated in the policy. Credit insurance is written only for manufacturers, wholesalers, and service organizations. Retail firms are ineligible for coverage. Only abnormal credit losses are covered; normal credit losses (called the primary loss) are seldom covered. Credit insurance is designed to cover only those losses that exceed the firm's normal credit losses in the regular course of business. There usually is a limit on the amount paid on any one account, which is based on the debtor's credit rating. There is also a maximum limit on total losses paid during the policy term.

Credit losses generally are subject to two deductibles. First, credit losses are reduced by the *primary loss amount*, which reflects the firm's normal credit losses. The primary loss amount for a firm is a percentage of the firm's net annual sales based on the bad-debt experience of similar firms, or the firm's actual loss experience. If normal credit losses were covered, the premiums for credit insurance would be considerably higher.

Second, the insured is expected to bear a portion of any credit loss by a *coinsurance percentage* that acts as a deductible. The coinsurance percentage typically is 10 to 20 percent and applies to each covered loss. The purpose of this deductible is to encourage the insured to be careful in granting credit, especially to firms with marginal credit ratings.

Difference in Conditions Insurance

Difference in conditions (DIC) insurance is an "all-risks" policy that covers other perils not insured by basic property insurance contracts.[5] DIC insurance is written as a separate contract to supplement the coverage provided by the underlying contracts. As such, it excludes perils covered by the underlying contracts (such as fire and extended coverage perils, vandalism and malicious mischief, and sprinkler leakage). However, most other insurable perils are covered. The policy can also be written to cover flood, earthquake, and building collapse. A substantial deductible must be satisfied for losses not covered by the underlying contracts.

DIC insurance has two major advantages. First, it can be used to fill gaps in coverage. Many large multinational corporations use a DIC policy to insure their overseas property. Many foreign countries require property insurance to be purchased locally; if the local coverage is inadequate, a DIC policy can fill the gap in coverage.

Second, DIC insurance can be used to insure unusual and catastrophic exposures that are not covered by the underlying contracts. Some unusual losses that have been paid include the following:

- An accident caused molasses to spill into a machine. The cost to clean the machine was $38,000.
- Dust collection on a roof solidified and the weight caused the roof to collapse.
- A city water main broke, which flooded the basement of an industrial plant, causing hundreds of thousands of dollars of damage.

Finally, DIC is less expensive than the purchase of separate contracts for flood and earthquake. It costs less because it is excess over the underlying coverages, and it does not require either coinsurance or insurance to full value.

TRANSPORTATION INSURANCE

Billions of dollars of goods are shipped by business firms each year. These goods are exposed to damage or loss from numerous transportation perils. The goods can be protected by ocean marine and inland marine contracts. **Ocean marine insurance** *provides protection for goods transported over water.* All types of ocean-going vessels and their cargo can be insured by ocean marine contracts; the legal liability of ship owners and cargo owners can also be insured.

Inland marine insurance *provides protection for goods shipped on land.* It includes insurance on imports and exports, domestic shipments, and means of transportation such as bridges and tunnels. In addition, inland marine insurance can be used to insure fine art, jewelry, furs, and other property.[6]

Ocean Marine Insurance

Ocean marine insurance is one of the oldest forms of transportation insurance. The ocean marine contracts are incredibly complex, reflecting basic marine law, trade, customs, and court interpretations of the various policy provisions.

Ocean marine insurance can be divided into four major classes to reflect the various insurable interests:

- **Hull insurance** *covers physical damage to the ship or vessel.* It is similar to collision insurance that covers physical damage to an automobile caused by a collision. Hull insurance is always written with a deductible. In addition, it contains a **collision liability clause** (also called a **running down clause**) that covers the owner's legal liability if the ship collides with another vessel or damages its cargo. However, the running down clause does not cover legal liability on that vessel arising out of injury or death to other persons, damage to piers and docks, and personal injury and death of crew members.
- **Cargo insurance** *covers the shipper of the goods if the goods are damaged or lost.* The policy can be written to cover a single shipment. If regular shipments are made, an *open-cargo policy* can be used that insures the goods automatically when a shipment is made. The shipper is required to report periodically the number of shipments that are made. The open-cargo policy has no expiration date and remains in force until it is canceled.
- **Protection and indemnity (P&I) insurance** *is usually written as a separate contract that provides comprehensive liability insurance for property damage or bodily injury to third parties.* P&I insurance protects the ship owner for damage caused by the ship to piers, docks, and harbor installations, damage to the ship's cargo, illness or injury to the passengers or crew, and fines and penalties.
- **Freight insurance** *indemnifies the ship owner for the loss of earnings if the goods are damaged or lost and are not delivered.*

Basic Concepts in Ocean Marine Insurance

Ocean marine insurance is based on certain fundamental concepts. The following section discusses these concepts and related contractual provisions.

Implied Warranties Ocean marine contracts contain three **implied warranties**: (1) seaworthy vessel,

(2) no deviation from course, and (3) legal purpose. The ship owner implicitly warrants that the vessel is *seaworthy*, which means that the ship is properly constructed, maintained, and equipped for the voyage to be undertaken. The warranty of *no deviation* means that the ship cannot deviate from its original course, no matter how slight the deviation. However, an intentional deviation is permitted in the event of an unavoidable accident, to avoid bad weather, to save the life of an individual on board, or to rescue persons from some other vessel. The warranty of *legal purpose* means that the voyage should not be for some illegal venture, such as smuggling drugs into a country.

The implied warranties are based on court decisions, and they are just as binding as any expressed warranty stated in the contract. A violation of an implied warranty, such as an unexcused deviation, permits the insurer to deny liability for the loss. The implied warranties are strictly enforced, because a breach of them would cause an increase in hazard to the insurer.

Covered Perils An ocean marine policy provides broad coverage for certain specified perils, including **perils of the sea**, such as damage or loss from bad weather, high waves, collision, sinking, and stranding. Other covered perils include loss from fire, enemies, pirates, thieves, jettison (throwing goods overboard to save the ship), barratry (fraud by the master or crew at the expense of the ship or cargo owners), and similar perils.

Ocean marine insurance can also be written on an "all-risks" basis. All unexpected and fortuitous losses are covered except those losses specifically excluded. Common exclusions are losses due to delay, war, inherent vice (tendency of certain types of property to decompose), and strikes, riots, or civil commotion.

Particular Average In marine insurance, the word *average* refers to a partial loss. A **particular average** *is a loss that falls entirely on a particular interest*, as contrasted with a general average, a loss that falls on all parties to the voyage. Under the *free-of-particular-average clause* (FPA), partial losses are not covered unless the loss is caused by certain perils, such as stranding, sinking, burning, or collision of the vessel.

The FPA clause can be written with a franchise deductible, where the franchise amount is stated as a percentage of the insured property. Thus, an FPA clause of 3 percent means that a covered loss under 3 percent falls entirely on the insured; if the loss is 3 percent or more, the insurer pays the loss in full.

General Average A **general average** *is a loss incurred for the common good and consequently is shared by all parties to the venture.* For example, if a ship damaged by heavy waves is in danger of sinking, part of the cargo may be jettisoned to save the ship. The loss falls on all parties to the voyage: the ship owner, cargo owners, and freight interests. In this context, *freight* refers to the revenue that a cargo ship earns. Each party must pay its share of the loss based on the proportion that its interest bears to the total value in the venture. For example, assume that the captain must jettison $1 million of steel to save the ship. Also assume that the various interests are as follows:

Value of steel	$ 2 million
Value of other cargo	3 million
Value of ship and freight	+15 million
Total	$20 million

The owner of the steel would absorb 2/20 of the loss, or $100,000. The owners of the other cargo would pay 3/20 of the loss, or $150,000. Finally, the ship and freight interests would pay 15/20 of the loss, or $750,000.

Four conditions must be satisfied to have a general average loss.[7]

- *Necessary.* The sacrifice is necessary to protect all interests in the venture—ship, cargo, and freight.
- *Voluntary.* The sacrifice must be voluntary.
- *Successful.* The effort must be successful. At least part of the value must be saved.
- *Free from fault.* Any party that claims a general average contribution from other interests in the voyage must be free from fault with respect to the risk that threatens the venture.

Coinsurance Although an ocean marine policy does not contain a specific coinsurance clause, losses are settled as if there is a 100 percent coinsurance clause.

An ocean marine policy is a valued contract, by which the face amount is paid if a total loss occurs. If the insurance carried does not equal the full value of the goods at the time of loss, the insured must share in the loss. Thus, if $50,000 of cargo insurance is carried on goods worth $100,000, only one-half of any partial loss will be paid. The policy face is paid in the event of a total loss.

Inland Marine Insurance

Inland marine insurance grew out of ocean marine insurance. Ocean marine insurance first covered property from the point of embarkation to the place where the goods landed. As commerce and trade developed, the goods had to be shipped over land as well. Inland marine insurance developed in the 1920s to cover property being transported over land, means of transportation such as bridges and tunnels, and property of a mobile nature.

Nationwide Marine Definition

As inland marine insurance developed, conflicts arose between fire insurers and marine insurers. To resolve the confusion and conflict, the companies drafted a **nationwide marine definition** in 1933 to define the property that marine insurers could write. The definition was approved by the National Association of Insurance Commissioners (NAIC) and was later revised and broadened in 1953. In 1976, the NAIC drafted a new definition of marine insurance that has been adopted by most states. At present, marine insurers can write insurance on the following types of property:

- Imports
- Exports
- Domestic shipments
- Means of transportation and communication
- Personal property floater risks
- Commercial property floater risks

Major Classes of Inland Marine Insurance

Commercial property that can be insured by inland marine contracts can be conveniently classified into five categories:[8]

- Domestic goods in transit
- Property held by bailees
- Mobile equipment and property
- Property of certain dealers
- Means of transportation and communication

Domestic Goods in Transit   Domestic goods may be shipped by a common carrier, such as a trucking company, railroad, or airline, or by the company's own trucks. The goods can be damaged because of fire, lightning, flood, earthquake, or other perils. They can also be damaged from the collision, derailment, or overturn of the transportation vehicle. These losses can be insured by an inland marine policy.

Although a common carrier is legally liable for safe delivery of the goods, liability does not extend to all losses. For example, a common carrier is not responsible for losses due to acts of God (such as lightning), acts of public authority, acts of public enemies (war), improper packaging by the shipper, and inherent vice.

In addition, shipping charges are reduced if the shipper agrees to limit the carrier's liability for the goods at less than their full value (called a released bill of lading). Consequently, the shipper can save money by agreeing to a released bill of lading and then purchase insurance to cover the shipment.

Property Held by Bailees   Inland marine insurance can be used to insure property held by a bailee. A **bailee** *is someone who has temporary possession of property that belongs to another.* Examples of bailees are dry cleaners, laundries, and television repair shops. Under common law, bailees are legally liable for damage to customers' property only if they or their employees are negligent. However, to ensure customer goodwill, many bailees purchase bailee's customer insurance that covers the damage or loss to customers' property while in the bailee's possession regardless of fault, normally from certain named perils.

Mobile Equipment and Property   Inland marine property floaters can be used to cover property that is frequently moved from one location to another, such as a tractor, crane, or bulldozer. Also, plumbing, heating, or air conditioning equipment can be covered while being transported to a job site or while being installed.

In addition, a property floater policy can be used to insure certain other types of property, such as fine art, livestock, theatrical property, computers, and signs.

Property of Certain Dealers Inland marine insurance is also used to insure the property of certain dealers. Specialized inland marine policies or inland marine "block" policies are used to insure the property of jewelers, furriers, and dealers in diamonds, fine art, cameras, and musical instruments, and other dealers. Most policies provide coverage on an "all-risks" basis.

Means of Transportation and Communication

Means of transportation and communication *refer to property at a fixed location that is used in transportation or communication.* Inland marine insurance can be used to cover bridges, tunnels, piers, docks, wharves, pipelines, power transmission lines, radio and television towers, outdoor cranes, and similar equipment for loading, unloading, or transporting. For example, a bridge may be damaged by a flood, ice jam, or a ship that collides with it; a television tower or power line may be blown over in a windstorm; or a fire may start in a tunnel when a gasoline truck overturns and explodes. These losses can be insured under inland marine contracts.

The commercial property loss exposures just described can be insured by a wide variety of inland marine contracts. For purposes of regulation, inland marine contracts are classified into two categories: (1) filed forms and (2) nonfiled forms. With filed forms, the policy forms and rates are filed with the state insurance department. Filed forms are typically used in situations where there are a large number of potential insureds and the loss exposures are reasonably homogeneous.

In contrast, nonfiled forms refer to policy forms and rates that are not filed with the state insurance department. Nonfiled forms are used in situations where the insured has specialized or unique needs, the number of potential insureds is relatively small, and the loss exposures are diverse.[9]

Filed Inland Marine Forms

Under the ISO simplified commercial inland marine program, the various policy forms and rates are filed with the state insurance department.

Numerous forms can be used in the ISO commercial inland marine insurance program. The major forms are summarized here:

- The **accounts receivable coverage form** indemnifies the firm if it is unable to collect outstanding customer balances because of damage or destruction of the records. A firm may incur a sizable loss if its accounts receivable records are destroyed by a fire, theft, or other peril, and the amount owned by customers cannot be collected.
- The **camera and musical instrument dealers coverage form** is used to cover stock in trade consisting principally of cameras or musical instruments and related equipment and accessories. The property of others in the insured's care, custody, or control is also covered.
- The **commercial articles coverage form** covers photographic equipment and musical instruments that are used commercially by photographers, professional musicians, motion picture producers, production companies, and other persons.
- The **equipment dealers coverage form** covers the stock in trade of dealers in agricultural implements and construction equipment. The form can also be extended to cover furniture, fixtures, office supplies, and machinery used in the business.
- The **film coverage form** covers exposed motion picture film as well as magnetic or video tapes.
- The **floor plan coverage form** refers to a financing plan in which the dealer borrows money to buy merchandise to display and sell, but the title is held by the lending institution or manufacturer. For example, a firm selling television sets, refrigerators, and home appliances could insure merchandise under this form.
- The **jewelers block coverage form** covers jewelry, watches, and precious stones of retail and wholesale jewelers, jewelry manufacturers, and diamond wholesalers.
- The **mail coverage form** covers securities in transit by first-class mail, registered or certified mail, or express mail. It is designed for stock brokerage firms, banks, and other financial institutions that ship securities by mail.
- The **physicians and surgeons equipment coverage form** covers the medical, surgical, or dental equipment of physicians and dentists, including furniture, fixtures, and improvements.

- The **signs coverage form** covers neon, mechanical, and electrical signs. Each covered sign must be scheduled.
- The **theatrical property coverage form** covers costumes, stage scenery, and similar property used in theatrical productions. For example, a New York play may be presented in another city, which requires the shipment of stage props and scenery to that city. The theatrical property can be covered under this form.
- The **valuable papers and records coverage form** covers loss to valuable papers and records, such as student transcripts in a university, plans and blueprints of an architectural firm, and prescription records in a drugstore. The form covers the cost of reconstructing the damaged or destroyed records. It can also be used to insure the loss of irreplaceable records, such as a rare manuscript. Each item must be scheduled with a specified amount of insurance.

Nonfiled Inland Marine Forms

A wide variety of nonfiled forms are available to meet the specialized or unique needs of commercial firms. Only a few of them are discussed here.

Shipment of Goods We noted earlier that inland marine insurance can be used to cover the domestic shipment of goods. An **annual transit policy** can be used by manufacturers, wholesalers, and retailers to cover the shipment of goods on public trucks, railroads, and coastal vessels. Both outgoing and incoming shipments can be insured. Although these forms are not standardized, they have similar characteristics. They can be written either on an "all-risks" or a named-perils basis.

Although a transit policy provides broad coverage, it contains certain exclusions. The policy can be written to cover the theft of an entire shipment, but pilferage of the goods generally is not covered. Other common exclusions are losses from strikes, riots or civil commotion, leakage and breakage (unless caused by an insured peril), marring, scratching, dampness, molding, and rotting.

A **trip transit policy** is used by firms and individuals to cover a single shipment. For example, an electrical transformer worth several thousand dollars that is shipped from an Eastern factory to the West Coast or the household goods of executives who are transferred can be insured under a variation of the trip transit policy.

Bailee Forms As stated earlier, a bailee is someone who has temporary possession of property that belongs to others. A *bailee's liability policy* can be used to cover the firm's liability for the property of customers, such as clothes in a laundry. A bailee's liability policy, however, covers the loss only if the firm is legally liable. In contrast, a *bailee's customers policy* can be used to cover the loss or damage to the property of others regardless of legal liability. A bailee's customers policy generally is designed for firms that hold the property of others that have high value, such as fur coats. A covered loss is paid regardless of legal liability, and the goodwill of customers is maintained.

Business Floaters A **business floater** is an inland marine policy that covers property that frequently moves (floats) from one location to another. Numerous business floaters are available. For example, a *contractors equipment floater* can be used to insure the property of contractors, such as bulldozers, tractors, cranes, earth movers, and scaffolding equipment. A *garment contractors floater* covers garments and parts of garments that are sent by a garment manufacturer to outside firms for processing, such as buttonhole makers, pleaters, or embroiderers.

Means of Transportation and Communication Inland marine contracts can be used to cover bridges, tunnels, towers, pipelines, power lines, and similar property. This type of property can be insured either on a risk-of-direct-physical-loss basis or on a named-perils basis, depending on the specific needs of the insured. For example, a toll bridge can lose revenues because a ship ran into a bridge pylon, forcing the bridge to close. A business income policy can be written to cover the loss of income.

BUSINESSOWNERS POLICY (BOP)

The **businessowners policy** (BOP) is a package policy specifically designed for small- to medium-sized retail stores, office buildings, apartment buildings, and similar firms. The following discussion is based on the businessowners policy drafted by the ISO.[10]

Eligible Firms

The BOP can be written to cover buildings and business personal property of the owners of apartments and residential condominium associations; office and office condominium associations; retail establishments; and eligible mercantile, service, or processing firms such as appliance firms, beauty parlors, and photocopy services.

Apartment buildings cannot exceed six stories in height and are limited to a maximum of 60 dwelling units. Office buildings are limited to a maximum of six stories or a maximum area of 100,000 square feet in total floor area. Buildings used primarily for certain eligible mercantile, service, or processing occupancies cannot exceed 25,000 square feet in total floor area, and annual gross sales for eligible classes cannot exceed $3 million at any insured location.

In 1997, ISO continued its practice of gradually broadening the eligibility requirements for the BOP program. BOP coverage is now available for certain contractors, "limited-cooking" and fast-food restaurants, and convenience stores.

Certain business firms are ineligible for a BOP because the loss exposures are outside those contemplated for the average small- to medium-sized firm. They include automobile repair or service stations; dealers in automobiles, motorcycles, or mobile homes; parking lots; bars; places of amusement such as a bowling alley; and banks and financial institutions.

BOP Coverages

The BOP is designed to meet the property insurance needs of most small- to medium-sized firms in one contract. The following is a summary of the basic characteristics of the BOP.

1. *Buildings.* The BOP covers the buildings described in the declarations, including completed additions, fixtures, and outdoor fixtures. The building coverage also includes personal property in apartments or rooms furnished by the named insured as a landlord, and personal property owned by the named insured to maintain or service the premises, such as fire-extinguishing equipment and refrigerating and dishwashing appliances. The limit of insurance on the building is automatically increased by a stated percentage each year to keep pace with inflation.

2. *Business personal property.* Business personal property is also covered. It includes property owned by the named insured used in the business; property of others in the insured's care, custody, and control for which the insured is legally liable; tenant's improvements and betterments; and leased personal property for which the named insured has a contractual responsibility to insure. A peak season provision provides for a temporary increase of 25 percent of the amount of insurance when inventory values are at their peak.

In addition, business personal property at newly acquired locations is covered for a maximum of $100,000 for 30 days. This provision provides automatic protection until the BOP can be endorsed to cover the new location. Business personal property in transit or temporarily away from the insured location is covered up to a maximum of $5000.

3. *Covered perils.* Two property forms are used under the BOP. The *standard property coverage form* provides coverage on a named-perils basis. Covered perils are fire, lightning, explosion, windstorm or hail, smoke, aircraft or vehicles, riot or civil commotion, vandalism, sprinkler leakage, sinkhole collapse, volcanic action, and certain transportation perils. The *special property coverage form* insures against "risks of direct physical loss." All direct physical losses are covered unless specifically excluded or limited in the form itself.

4. *Additional coverages.* The BOP provides several additional coverages needed by the typical businessowner:

- Debris removal
- Preservation of property coverage after a loss occurs
- Fire department service charge
- Collapse
- Water damage, other liquids, or molten material damage

- Business income, extended business income, and extra expense
- Pollutant cleanup and removal
- Loss of business income because of action by a civil authority
- Money order and counterfeit paper currency losses ($1000 maximum)
- Forgery and alteration losses ($2500 maximum)
- Increased cost of construction
- Exterior building glass

5. *Optional coverages.* The BOP provides several optional coverages to meet the specialized needs of businessowners by payment of an additional premium:

- Outdoor signs
- Interior glass
- Money and securities
- Employee dishonesty
- Mechanical breakdown

6. *Deductible.* A standard deductible of $500 per occurrence applies to all property coverages. Higher deductibles are available if desired. The deductible does not apply, however, to the fire department service charge, business income losses, extra expenses, and action by a civil authority.

7. *Business liability insurance.* The businessowner is insured for bodily injury and property damage liability and advertising and personal injury liability. Medical expense coverage is also provided. These liability loss exposures are discussed in Chapter 14.

SUMMARY

- Under the ISO commercial property insurance program, a commercial package policy contains a common declarations page, a common policy conditions page, and two or more coverage parts. Each coverage part, in turn, has its own declarations page, policy conditions, coverage forms, and a causes-of-loss form.

- A *commercial package policy* combines two or more ISO coverage parts into a single policy. A package policy has fewer gaps in coverage, relatively lower premiums because individual policies are not purchased, and the convenience of a single policy.

- The coverage parts under the ISO commercial insurance program include the following:

    Commercial property coverage

    Commercial general liability coverage

    Crime coverage

    Boiler and machinery coverage

    Inland marine coverage

    Commercial auto coverage

    Farm coverage

- The *building and personal property coverage form* can be used to insure the commercial building, business personal property, and personal property of others in the care and custody of the insured.

- Under the ISO commercial property insurance program, a causes-of-loss form must be added to a commercial policy to form a complete contract. There are four causes-of-loss forms:

    Causes-of-loss basic form

    Causes-of-loss broad form

    Causes-of-loss special form

    Causes-of-loss earthquake form

- The *business income and extra expense coverage form* covers the loss of business income due to the suspension of business operations because of a covered loss. Business income is the net profit or loss before income taxes that would have been earned if the loss had not occurred, plus normal operating expenses, including payroll. Extra expenses incurred as a result of a loss are also covered.

- The *extra expense coverage form* covers only the extra expenses incurred by the firm in continuing operations during the period of restoration. Loss of profits is not covered, because the firm will still be operating.

- Certain miscellaneous commercial coverages are important to business firms that have unique or specialized needs, including builders risk insurance, condominium insurance, glass insurance, boiler and machinery insurance, and difference in conditions insurance.

- Ocean marine insurance can be classified into four categories that reflect the various insurable interests:

    Hull insurance

    Cargo insurance

    Protection and indemnity insurance

    Freight insurance

- A particular average loss in marine insurance is a loss that falls entirely on a particular interest, as contrasted with a general average loss that falls on all parties to the voyage.

- Inland marine contracts are used to insure the following classes of commercial property:

  Domestic goods in transit

  Property held by bailees

  Mobile equipment and property

  Property of certain dealers

  Means of transportation and communication

- For purposes of regulation, inland marine contracts are classified into filed forms and nonfiled firms. Filed forms are policy forms and rates that are filed with the state insurance department. Nonfiled forms are not filed with the state insurance department.

- Filed inland marine forms include the following:

  Accounts receivable coverage form

  Camera and musical instrument dealers coverage form

  Commercial articles coverage form

  Equipment dealers coverage form

  Film coverage form

  Floor plan coverage form

  Jewelers block coverage form

  Mail coverage form

  Physicians and surgeons equipment coverage form

  Signs coverage form

  Theatrical property coverage form

  Valuable papers and records coverage form

- Nonfiled inland marine forms include the following:

  Annual transit policy

  Trip transit policy

  Bailee forms

  Business floaters

  Insurance on means of transportation and communication

- The *businessowners policy* is a package policy for small- to medium-sized business firms. It covers the building, business personal property, loss of business income, extra expenses, and business liability exposures. Optional coverages are available for outdoor signs, interior glass, money and securities, employee dishonesty, and mechanical breakdown.

KEY CONCEPTS AND TERMS

Annual transit policy
Bailee
Boiler and machinery coverage form
Builders risk coverage form
Building and personal property coverage form
Business floater
Business income and extra expense coverage form
Business income insurance
Businessowners policy (BOP)
Cargo insurance
Causes-of-loss forms (basic, broad, special, earthquake)
Collision liability clause (running down clause)
Commercial package policy (CPP)
Condominium association coverage form
Condominium commercial unit-owners coverage form
Credit insurance
Difference in conditions insurance
Extra expense coverage form
Freight insurance
Garment contractors floater
General average
Glass coverage form
Hull insurance
Implied warranties
Inland marine insurance
Means of transportation and communication
Nationwide marine definition
Ocean marine insurance
Package policy
Particular average
Perils of the sea
Protection and indemnity (P&I) insurance
Reporting form
Trip transit policy

REVIEW QUESTIONS

1. Identify the major documents that are used to form a commercial package policy.

2. Briefly explain the advantages of a package policy to the insured.

3. Describe the major provisions of the building and personal property coverage form.

4. Explain the major provisions in the business income and extra expense coverage form.

5. Identify the major coverages under a boiler and machinery insurance policy.

6. Describe each of the major classes of ocean marine insurance.

7. What is the difference between a particular average loss and a general average loss in ocean marine

insurance? What conditions must be fulfilled to have a general average loss?

8. Identify the major classes of commercial property that can be insured under an inland marine insurance policy.

9. Briefly describe several inland marine forms that are filed with state insurance departments.

10. Identify the major coverages under the businessowners policy.

APPLICATION QUESTIONS

1. a. Describe briefly how the causes-of-loss broad form differs from the causes-of-loss special form.
   b. Alicia owns a television repair shop that is insured under a commercial property insurance policy. The policy includes the building and personal property coverage form and the causes-of-loss broad form. Indicate whether the following losses would be covered under her policy. If not, why not?
      (1) A fire occurs on the premises, and the building is badly damaged.
      (2) Television sets owned by customers are damaged by vandals who break into the shop after business hours.
      (3) A burglar steals some money and securities from an unlocked safe.

2. Issac owns a retail shoe store. The store is insured for $90,000 under the business income coverage form with a 50 percent coinsurance provision. Because of an explosion, Issac was forced to close the store for one month before it could be reopened. If the explosion had not occurred, Issac's estimated net profits and operating expenses for the 12-month period after the policy's inception date would have been $180,000. However, for the one-month period that the store was closed, Issac had a business income loss of $12,000 (loss of net income plus continuing operating expenses).
   a. How much will Issac recover for the business income loss? Show your calculations.
   b. How does the business income coverage form differ from the extra expense coverage form?

3. a. The *Mary Queen*, an ocean-going oil tanker, negligently collided with a large freighter. The *Mary*

Queen is insured by an ocean marine hull insurance policy with a running down clause. For each of the following losses, explain whether the ocean marine coverage would apply to the loss.
   (1) Damage to the *Mary Queen*
   (2) Damage to the freighter
   (3) Death or injury to the crew members on the freighter
   b. Briefly explain each of the following ocean marine terms or provisions.
      (1) Free-of-particular average
      (2) General average
      (3) Open cargo policy

SELECTED REFERENCES

Fire, Casualty & Surety Bulletins, Fire and Marine volume. Cincinnati, OH: National Underwriter Company. The various commercial coverages are discussed in the Commercial Property section, Business Income section, Inland Marine section, and Boiler & Machinery section.

Gordis, Philip. *Property and Casualty Insurance*, thirty-third edition, revised. Indianapolis, IN: The Rough Notes Co., 1995.

Rodda, William H., et al. *Commercial Property Risk Management and Insurance*, second edition, Vol. 1. Malvern, PA: American Institute for Property and Liability Underwriters, 1983.

The CPCU Handbook of Insurance Policies, third edition. Malvern, PA: American Institute for CPCU/Insurance Institute of America, 1998.

Trieschmann, James S., et al. *Commercial Property Insurance and Risk Management*, fourth edition, Vol. 2. Malvern, PA: American Institute for CPCU, 1994.

Trupin, Jerome, and Arthur L. Flitner. *Commercial Property Insurance and Risk Management*, fifth edition, Vol. 1. Malvern, PA: American Institute for CPCU, 1998.

Webb, Bernard L., Arthur L. Flitner, and Jerome Trupin. *Commercial Insurance*, third edition. Malvern, PA: Insurance Institute of America, 1996.

NOTES

1. This chapter is based on *Fire, Casualty & Surety Bulletins*, Fire and Marine volume, Commercial Property section (Cincinnati, OH: National Under-

writer Company); Jerome Trupin and Arthur L. Flitner, *Commercial Property Insurance and Risk Management*, fifth edition, Vol. 1 (Malvern, PA: American Institute for CPCU, 1998); and Bernard L. Webb, Arthur L. Flitner, and Jerome Trupin, *Commercial Insurance*, third edition (Malvern, PA: Insurance Institute of America, 1996). The author also drew on the various commercial property forms that appeared in *The CPCU Handbook of Insurance Policies*, third edition (Malvern, PA: American Institute for CPCU/Insurance Institute of America, 1998).

2. This section is based on *Fire, Casualty & Surety Bulletins*, Fire and Marine volume, Business Income section; and Trupin and Flitner, Chapters 7–8.

3. *Ibid.*, p. 372.

4. This section is based on *Fire, Casualty & Surety Bulletins*, Fire and Marine volume, Commercial Property section.

5. Material in this section is based on James S. Trieschmann et al., *Commercial Property Insurance and Risk Management*, fourth edition, Vol. 2 (Malvern, PA: American Institute for CPCU, 1994), pp. 198–202; and William H. Rodda et al., *Commercial Property Risk Management and Insurance*, second edition, Vol. I (Malvern, PA: American Institute for Property and Liability Underwriters, 1983), pp. 216–223.

6. Transportation insurance is discussed in detail in *Fire, Casualty & Surety Bulletins*, Fire and Marine volume, Inland Marine section; Trieschmann et al., Chapter 11; Rodda et al., Chapters 8–9; and Philip Gordis,

Case Application

a. Kimberly owns and operates a tennis shop in a resort area. The business is seasonal. A large part of the annual revenues are due to sales in June, July, and August. Kimberly keeps the shop open during the remaining months of the year, but the inventory carried during those months is reduced. During the summer months, the amount of inventory on hand is substantially increased. Kimberly has the business insured under the standard businessowners policy (BOP) with no special endorsements attached.

(1) Assume you are a risk management consultant. Identify the major loss exposures that Kimberly faces.

(2) Assume that a covered loss occurs in July, which damages part of the inventory. Does the BOP provide any protection for the increase in inventory during the summer months? Explain your answer.

(3) Kimberly plans to hire an additional employee during the summer months when sales are increasing. She is concerned about possible employee theft and dishonesty. Explain to Kimberly how this loss exposure can be handled under the BOP.

b. Assume you are a risk management consultant. Identify the type of inland marine policy that could be purchased to protect the following types of property. Indicate whether the policy form would be filed or nonfiled.

(1) Property of customers in a dry cleaning establishment

(2) Scenery, props, and costumes used by a local theatrical group

(3) Cameras and equipment owned by a professional photographer

Property and Casualty Insurance, thirty-third edition, revised (Indianapolis, IN: The Rough Notes Co., 1995), Chapters 16 and 20. The author drew on these sources in preparing this section.

7. Gordis, pp. 336–337.

8. Webb et al., pp. 156–160.

9. *Ibid.*, p. 162.

10. A detailed explanation of the businessowners policy can be found in *Fire, Casualty & Surety Bulletins*, Fire and Marine volume, Commercial Property section (Cincinnati, OH: National Underwriter Company); and Webb et al., Chapter 11.

Students may take a self-administered test on this chapter at www.awlonline.com/rejda

Chapter 14

Commercial Liability Insurance

> *" The litigious nature of American society results in risk that is difficult to quantify, but which can directly impact a company's bottom line. Liability insurance is a key tool for managing such risk. "*

William B. Hedrick,
Liability Risk Manager,
The Boeing Co.

Learning Objectives

After studying this chapter, you should be able to:

▲ Identify the major liability loss exposures of business firms.

▲ Describe the basic coverages provided by the commercial general liability policy (CGL).

▲ Explain the coverage provided by a workers compensation policy.

▲ Describe the important provisions of the commercial umbrella policy.

▲ Identify the liability coverages provided by the businessowners policy (BOP).

▲ Describe the basic characteristics of a medical malpractice liability policy.

▲ Access an Internet site and obtain information about commercial liability insurance.

Internet Resources

- **Associated Aviation Underwriters** is a pool of property and liability insurers that writes all classes of aviation insurance. Visit the site at:
  http://www.aau.com

- The **Defense Research Institute** is a service organization created to improve the administration of justice and the skills of defense attorneys. Visit the site at:
  http://www.dri.org

- The **Institute for Civil Justice** is an organization within the Rand Corporation that conducts independent, objective research of the civil justice system. Visit the site at:
  http://www.rand.org

- The **Insurance Information Institute** is a primary source of information, analysis, and referral on subjects dealing with property and liability insurance. Visit the site at:

  http://www.iii.org

- The **Insurance Services Office (ISO)** provides statistical information, actuarial analyses, policy language, and technical information to participants in property and liability insurance markets. ISO drafted the commercial general liability policy discussed in this chapter. Visit the site at:

  http://www.iso.com

- The **National Council on Compensation Insurance** develops and administers rating plans and systems for workers compensation insurance. Visit the site at:

  http://www.ncci.com

- The **National Safety Council** provides national support and leadership in the field of safety; publishes safety materials of all kinds; and conducts a public information and publicity program to support safety. Visit the site at:

  http://www.nsc.org

- The **Risk and Insurance Management Society (RIMS)** is an organization of corporate buyers of insurance that makes known to insurers the insurance needs of business and industry, supports loss prevention, and provides a forum for discussing common objectives and problems. Visit the site at:

  http://www.rims.org

 ichael, age 48, is the general manager of a large meat packing plant in Chicago, Illinois. During a recent one-week period, the plant processed several batches of contaminated hamburger. More than 20 people who consumed the hamburger became seriously ill from bacteria poisoning. As a result, several lawsuits were filed against the company. Michael was concerned about how the suits would affect the company's profits. He was relieved when the company's risk manager stated that the firm's general liability insurance policy would cover the claims.

Like this meat packing plant, many business firms operate in an intensely competitive environment where liability lawsuits are routine. The suits range from small nuisance claims to multimillion-dollar demands. Firms are sued because of defective products, injuries to customers, property damage, pollution of the environment, sexual harassment, discrimination against employees, and numerous other reasons. Commercial liability insurance can provide firms with the protection needed to deal with these loss exposures.

This chapter discusses major liability loss exposures of business firms and the commercial liability coverages available for insuring these exposures. Topics covered include the commercial general liability policy (CGL), the employment practices liability policy, workers compensation and employers liability insurance, commercial auto liability insurance, aviation insurance, bailee's liability insurance, and the commercial umbrella liability policy. The chapter concludes with a discussion of professional liability insurance.

GENERAL LIABILITY LOSS EXPOSURES

General liability refers to the legal liability arising out of business operations other than automobile or aviation accidents and employee injuries. The major general liability loss exposures of business firms include the following:

- Premises and operations
- Products liability
- Completed operations
- Contractual liability
- Contingent liability

Premises and Operations

Legal liability can arise out of the *ownership and maintenance of the premises* where the firm does business. Firms are legally required to maintain the premises in a safe condition and are responsible for the actions of their employees. Customers in a store fall into the legal category of *invitees*, and the highest degree of care is owed to them. The customers must be warned and protected against any dangerous condition on the premises. For example, a firm can be held liable if a customer trips on a torn carpet and breaks a leg, or if a ceiling collapses and injures a customer.

Legal liability can also arise out of the firm's operations, either on or off the premises. For example, employees unloading lumber in a lumberyard may accidentally damage a customer's truck, or a construction worker on a high-rise building may carelessly drop a tool that injures a pedestrian.

Products Liability

Products liability *refers to the legal liability of manufacturers, wholesalers, and retailers to persons who are injured or incur property damage from defective products.* As noted in Chapter 7, the number of products liability lawsuits and the size of the damage awards have increased substantially over time. Firms can be successfully sued on the basis of negligence, breach of warranty, and strict liability. These topics were discussed earlier in Chapter 7, and additional treatment is not needed here.

Completed Operations

Completed operations *refers to liability arising out of faulty work performed away from the premises after the work or operation is completed.* Contractors, plumbers, electricians, repair shops, and similar firms are liable for bodily injuries and property damage to others after their work is completed. When the work is in progress, it is part of the operations exposure. However, after the work is completed, it is a completed-operations exposure. For example, a hot water tank may explode if it is improperly installed, or ductwork in a supermarket may collapse and injure a customer because of improper installation.

A general liability policy provides coverage for both products liability and completed operations. Both products liability and completed-operations loss exposures are now included in a definition called **products-completed operations hazard**. *The policy covers liability losses that occur away from the premises and arise out of the insured's product or work after the insured has relinquished possession of the product or the work has been completed.* For example, assume that a gas furnace is improperly installed and explodes one month later. The installer's liability is insured under the products-completed operations coverage.

Contractual Liability

Contractual liability *means that the business firm agrees to assume the legal liability of another party by a written or oral contract.* For example, a manufacturing firm rents a building, and the lease specifies that the building owner is to be held harmless for any liability arising out of use of the building. Thus, by a written lease, the manufacturing firm assumes some potential legal liability that ordinarily would be the owner's responsibility.

Contingent Liability

Contingent liability *refers to liability arising out of work done by independent contractors.* As a general rule, business firms are not legally liable for work done by independent contractors. However, under certain conditions, a firm can be held liable for work performed by independent contractors. A firm can be held liable if (1) the activity is illegal, (2) the situation or type of work does not permit delegation of authority, or (3) the work done by the independent contractor is inherently dangerous.[1] For example, a general contractor may hire a subcontractor to perform a blasting operation. If someone is injured by the blast, the general contractor can be held liable even though the subcontractor is primarily responsible.

Other General Liability Loss Exposures

Business firms are often exposed to other important general liability loss exposures, as summarized here.

- *Environmental pollution.* Chemical, manufacturing, and other firms may pollute the environment with smoke, fumes, acids, toxic chemicals, waste materials, and other pollutants. In addition, leaking underground storage tanks are a major liability exposure for many firms.
- *Fire legal liability.* Another important loss exposure is **fire legal liability**. A firm may rent or use property such as a building that belongs to another party. If a fire occurs because of the negligence of the firm or its employees, the firm can be held legally liable for the loss.
- *Liquor liability.* Under a **liquor liability law** (also called a **dramshop law**), bars, restaurants, taverns, and other establishments that sell liquor can be held legally liable for injuries caused by intoxicated customers. However, general liability policies typically exclude liquor liability coverage for firms in the business of manufacturing, selling, distributing, or serving of alcoholic beverages.
- *Directors and officers liability.* An increasing number of officers and directors of business firms have been sued in recent years by employees, stockholders, competing firms, government agencies, and other parties. Numerous lawsuits have been initiated by angry stockholders who claimed that they incurred financial loss because of mismanagement by officers and directors. A **directors and officers liability policy** can be used to cover the legal liability of directors and officers.
- *Personal injury.* In addition to bodily injury and property damage liability, a business firm may be sued for personal injury. **Personal injury** *refers to false arrest, detention or imprisonment, malicious prosecution, libel, slander, defamation of character, violation of the right of privacy, and unlawful entry or eviction.* For example, a department store may be successfully sued by an innocent customer who is erroneously arrested for shoplifting.
- *Property in the insured's care, custody, or control.* Liability can also arise out of damage to property in the insured's care, custody, or control. General liability policies usually exclude coverage for this exposure. This exclusion can be a problem for firms that work on the property of others, such as an automobile repair garage or a television repair shop. In some cases, a bailee's liability policy can be used to cover liability for damage to personal property in the care, custody, or control of the insured.
- *Sexual harassment.* Employers increasingly are being sued by employees on the grounds of sexual harassment. Such suits are expensive to defend. To reduce the possibility of a sexual harassment suit, many employers have adopted strict policies that prohibit certain actions, such as lewd or suggestive language.
- *Employment practices.* Employers increasingly are being sued by employees because of discrimination, failure to hire or promote, wrongful termination, and other employment-related practices.

In addition to these exposures, new commercial liability loss exposures are continually emerging. One new exposure is the legal liability of stock brokerage firms arising out of the breakdown of an electronic trading network when online investors and traders are unable to execute their trades (see Insight 14.1).

COMMERCIAL GENERAL LIABILITY (CGL) POLICY

The **commercial general liability (CGL) policy** is widely used by business firms to cover their general liability loss exposures. The CGL policy has two coverage forms: an occurrence form and a claim-made form. The following section discusses both forms of the CGL policy drafted by the Insurance Services Office (ISO).[2]

Insight 14.1

Online Crashes Raise Liability Issue

The question of who—if anyone—is liable when electronic trading networks break down resurfaced last week when Charles Schwab Group's online system crashed three times.

"Liability for failure of electronic services is an area of increasing importance as more and more commerce is conducted over the Internet," said David Leebron, dean of the Columbia University Law School.

That said, Leebron and other legal experts predicted that investors will face a number of difficult challenges trying to prove not only that they lost money as a direct result of a computer crash, but also that their online brokerage firm was somehow negligent.

Securities lawyers say there's no legal precedent to turn to because online trading is so young.

"We're treading on new ground," said Ivo Caytas, a securities lawyer in New York.

ETrade Group Inc. was hit with two class-action lawsuits filed by investors in February after software problems caused ETrade's computers to shut down on three separate occasions. But those cases are far from being resolved.

Schwab, which also experienced technical problems that shut down its trading network last February, has not yet been targeted by lawsuits. The company has an estimated 2.2 million online customers.

Any case against an online brokerage firm would be hard to win, the experts argue, because prior to opening an online trading account, investors sign disclaimers that acknowledge the risks associated with Internet investing.

"By signing the disclaimer you're acknowledging that online systems aren't guaranteed 100 percent of the time and that breakdowns and problems may occur," said Frank Lallos, a senior analyst at Gomez Advisors Inc., a Lincoln, Massachusetts, Internet research firm.

That means a case against an online brokerage firm would have to prove that the company was negligent in some fashion not covered in the disclaimer.

For example, an investor claiming damages in the wake of a computer crash would have to prove that the brokerage firm failed to maintain its systems according to standards that would have prevented the shutdown.

Evidence that a firm failed to maintain a proper backup system, or that the company cut important corners in order to reduce system overlap might be grounds for damages, according to Caytas.

But taking on a huge brokerage firm such as Charles Schwab would be a lengthy and expensive battle, Caytas said.

"As a lawyer, you'd be fighting a major institution at every step. You don't do that for a single client unless the amount is huge," he said. "Charles Schwab is one of the largest brokerage firms in the country and they have very deep pockets."

So the only cost-effective method to wage such a battle is a class-action lawsuit involving possible hundreds of people claiming damages.

A class-action lawsuit raises its own problems, however, said Columbia Law School's Leebron.

Once a disclaimer is signed acknowledging that electronic systems can break down, an investor seeking damages would have to make a very specific case to prove that he or she lost money due to the negligence of the brokerage firm.

And the more specific the charges, the less likely the case can be applied to enough people to justify a class-action suit, Leebron said.

SOURCE: "Online Crashes Raise Liability Issue," *Sunday World-Herald*, October 24, 1999, p. 2-M.

Overview of the CGL Occurrence Policy

The CGL occurrence policy can be written alone or as part of a commercial package policy. The complete contract consists of a common policy declarations page, common policy conditions page, CGL declarations page, CGL coverage form, and applicable endorsements.

The occurrence form contains five major sections:

- Section I—Coverages
  Coverage A: Bodily injury and property damage liability
  Coverage B: Personal and advertising injury liability
  Coverage C: Medical payments
  Supplementary payments: Coverages A and B
- Section II—Who Is an Insured?
- Section III—Limits of Insurance
- Section IV—Commercial General Liability Conditions
- Section V—Definitions

Section I—Coverages

Section I provides coverage for bodily injury and property damage liability, personal and advertising injury liability, medical payments, and certain supplementary payments.

Coverage A: Bodily Injury and Property Damage Liability The insurer agrees to pay on behalf of the insured all sums up to the policy limits that the insured is legally obligated to pay because of **bodily injury and property damage** to which the insurance applies. The bodily injury or property damage must be caused by an occurrence. An **occurrence** *is defined as an accident, including continuous or repeated exposure to substantially the same general harmful conditions.* For example, an explosion occurs in a store, and several customers are injured, or a drug company manufactures a defective batch of flu vaccine, and over a period of time several persons become violently ill. These incidents would be considered occurrences and would be covered by the CGL.

Defense Costs The insurer also pays the legal defense costs. The insurer has the right to investigate a claim or suit and settle it at its discretion. The insurer's duty to defend ends when the applicable limits of insurance are paid out. The legal defense costs are paid in addition to the policy limits.

Exclusions A lengthy list of exclusions applies to both bodily injury and property damage liability. Major exclusions include the following:

- *Expected or intended injury.* Bodily injury or property damage that is expected or intended by the insured is not covered. However, the exclusion does not apply to bodily injury that results from the use of reasonable force to protect persons or property.
- *Contractual liability.* The policy excludes liability assumed by a contract or agreement. However, the exclusion does not apply to liability assumed by an *insured contract* or to liability that the insured would have in the absence of the contract or agreement. An insured contract refers to a lease of the premises, a sidetrack agreement, an easement agreement required by a municipality, an elevator maintenance agreement, or tort liability assumption (liability imposed by law in the absence of any contract or agreement).
- *Liquor liability.* The exclusion applies only to firms in the business of manufacturing, distributing, selling, serving, or furnishing alcohol. For example, if a bartender continues to serve a drunken customer who injures another person, the bar owner is not covered for any claim or suit. However, the liquor exclusion does not apply to firms that are not in the liquor business. For example, an insured that serves drinks at a company-sponsored party would be covered. Coverage can be obtained by firms in the liquor manufacturing and distribution business by adding the liquor liability coverage form to the policy.
- *Workers compensation.* Any legal obligation of the insured to pay benefits under a workers compensation law or similar law is excluded.
- *Employers liability.* The policy excludes liability for bodily injury to an employee arising out of and in the course of employment. It also excludes a claim by a spouse or close relative who is seeking damages as a result of a job-related injury to an employee of the insured. For example, a suit by a spouse who seeks damages for the loss of consortium (loss of companionship, affection, and comfort) following a work-related injury is not covered.
- *Pollution exclusion.* Pollution and contamination claims are excluded. This exclusion also applies to cleanup costs that are incurred as a result of a government order. Coverage can be obtained by a pollution endorsement or by the addition of adding a separate pollution liability coverage form to the policy.

- *Aircraft, auto, and watercraft exclusion.* Liability arising out of the ownership or operation of aircraft, autos, and watercraft is specifically excluded. The intent here is to exclude legal liability covered by other policies. The exclusion does not apply to watercraft while ashore on premises owned or rented by the insured and to nonowned watercraft less than 26 feet in length and not used to carry people or property for a fee. In addition, the exclusion does not apply to bodily injury to customers resulting from parking automobiles on the premises or next to the premises, which is important for firms that park the cars of customers. However, physical damage to the car being parked is not covered because of the care, custody, or control exclusion (discussed later).
- *Mobile equipment.* Mobile equipment is not covered when the equipment is (a) being transported by an auto or (b) used in or in preparation for any racing, speed, or demolition contest, or in any stunting activity. For example, a bulldozer is excluded while being transported to a job site by an auto. However, coverage can be added by an endorsement to the policy.
- *War.* Bodily injury or property damage due to war is specifically excluded. War is defined to include civil war, insurrection, rebellion, or revolution. The exclusion applies only to liability assumed by a contract or agreement.
- *Damage to property.* The CGL policy excludes property owned, rented, or occupied by the insured, premises that the insured sells or abandons, property loaned to the named insured, and personal property in the insured's care, custody, or control. Other excluded losses are property damage to that particular part of real property on which the insured, contractors, or subcontractors are working and part of any property that must be restored, repaired, or replaced because the insured's work is performed incorrectly.
- *Property damage to the insured's product.* The policy excludes **property damage to the insured's product** if the damage results from a defect in the product. For example, a defective hot water tank may explode. The damage to the tank itself is not covered. However, property damage from the explosion would be covered under the manufacturer's liability policy.

- *Property damage to the insured's work.* The policy also excludes **property damage to the insured's work** that is included in the "products-completed operations hazard." The insured's work refers to the work or operations of the insured as well as material, parts, and equipment used in the work. For example, an employee of a heating contractor may improperly install a gas furnace that later explodes after it was installed. Although the property damage to the customer's building is covered, the value of the employee's work is specifically excluded. The exclusion does not apply if the work is performed by a subcontractor on behalf of the insured.
- *Property damage to impaired property.* The policy also excludes **property damage to impaired property** that is not physically damaged. If property is impaired because of a defect in the insured's product or work, or failure to perform, the loss is not covered. Impaired property is tangible property that cannot be used or is less useful because (1) it incorporates the insured's product or work, or (2) the insured fails to perform the terms of a contract or agreement, and (3) the property can be restored to use by correction of the insured's product or work or fulfillment of the contract. For example, assume that the insured manufactures airplane parts, and a faulty part causes several jets to be grounded. The planes are considered impaired property. The loss of use of the jets is not covered by the insured's CGL policy.
- *Recall of products.* Damages and expenses arising out of the recall of defective products are also excluded. In recent years, firms have incurred substantial losses in recalling defective products such as automobiles, drugs, or food products. Th CGL specifically excludes such losses. Coverage can be obtained, however, by an endorsement to the policy.

In addition to the preceding exclusions, CGL policies typically include an endorsement that excludes suits by aggrieved employees against their employers because of sexual harassment, wrongful discharge, failure to promote, and similar employment practices. Specific coverage for these loss exposures must be purchased (discussed later).

Coverage B: Personal and Advertising Injury Liability Under this coverage, the insurer agrees to pay those sums that the insured is legally obligated to pay because of personal injury or advertising injury. Personal injury includes the following:

- False arrest, detention, or imprisonment
- Malicious prosecution
- Wrongful eviction or entry
- Libel or slander
- Publication of material that violates a person's right to privacy

For example, if a customer is falsely arrested for shoplifting, the firm is covered if the customer sues.

The policy also covers **advertising injury**, which is an injury due to the following:

- Oral statement or written publication of material that slanders or libels
- Publication of material that results in a violation of a person's right to privacy
- Misappropriation of advertising ideas
- Infringement of a copyright, title, or slogan

For example, if a retail furniture store uses copyrighted material in an ad without permission and is sued, the CGL would cover the suit.

Coverage C: Medical Payments
Medical payments cover the medical expenses of persons who are injured in an accident on the premises or on ways next to the premises, or as a result of the insured's operations. The medical expenses must be incurred within one year of the accident and are paid without regard to legal liability. For example, if a customer falls on a slippery floor in a supermarket, the medical expenses are covered up to the policy limits.

Supplementary Payments: Coverages A and B
Certain supplementary payments are included under Coverages A and B in addition to the policy limits:

- All expenses incurred by the insurer
- Up to $250 for the cost of a bail bond because of an accident or traffic violation arising out of the use of a vehicle to which the insurance applies
- Cost of bonds to release attachments
- Actual loss of earnings by the insured up to $250 a day because of time off from work
- All costs taxed against the insured in the suit
- Prejudgment interest and interest that accrues after entry of the judgment

Section II—Who Is an Insured?

The named insured stated in the declarations includes the owner and spouse if a sole proprietorship; partners, members, and their spouses if a partnership or joint venture; members and managers if a limited liability company; and officers, directors, and stockholders if a corporation.

In addition, the following are insureds: employees acting within the scope of their employment, any real estate managers of the insured, a temporary representative if the insured should die, a legal representative if the insured should die, drivers of mobile equipment owned by the insured, and newly acquired or formed organizations.

Section III—Limits of Insurance

The limits of insurance state the maximum amount that the insurer will pay regardless of the number of insureds, claims made or suits brought, or persons or organization making such claims or bringing suits. Six limits apply (see Exhibit 14.1).

1. *General aggregate limit.* The **general aggregate limit** is the maximum amount that the insurer will pay for the sum of the following: damages under Coverage A, except bodily injury and property damage included in the "products-completed operations hazard;" damages under Coverage B; and medical expenses under Coverage C.
2. *Products-completed operations aggregate limit.* The **products-completed operations aggregate limit** is the maximum amount that the insurer will pay under Coverage A because of bodily injury and property damage included in the "products-completed operations hazard."
3. *Personal and advertising injury limit.* This limit is the maximum amount that the insurer will pay under Coverage B for personal injury and advertising injury.
4. *Each-occurrence limit.* The **each-occurrence limit** is the maximum amount that the insurer will pay for the sum of all damages under Coverage A and the medical expenses under Coverage C arising out of any one occurrence.
5. *Fire damage limit.* This limit is the maximum amount that the insurer will pay under Coverage

EXHIBIT 14.1
Illustration of the CGL Limits of Insurance

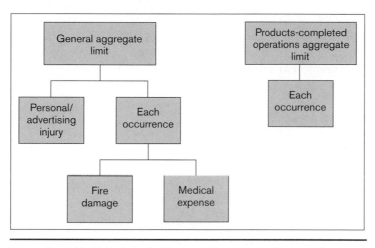

SOURCE: Bernard L. Webb, Arthur L. Flitner, and Jerome Trupin, *Commercial Insurance*, third edition (Malvern, PA: Insurance Institute of America, 1996); Exhibit 9-1, p. 215.

A for property damage to rented premises from a single fire.
6. *Medical expense limit.* This limit is the maximum amount that the insurer will pay under medical expenses because of a bodily injury sustained by any one person.

Section IV—Commercial General Liability Conditions

This section states the various conditions that apply to the general liability coverage form. The conditions include provisions dealing with bankruptcy; duties in the event of an occurrence, claim, or suit; legal action against the insurer; other insurance; premium audit; and numerous additional conditions.

Section V—Definitions

This section in the CGL policy defines more precisely the various terms used in the policy. Numerous definitions are stated in some detail. However, space limitations preclude a discussion of these definitions here.

Overview of the CGL Claims-Made Policy

The Insurance Services Office (ISO) also offers a claims-made policy, which is similar to the occurrence policy with the major exceptions of payment of claims on a claims-made basis, inclusion of an extended reporting period (Section V), and moving of the definitions to Section VI.

Meaning of "Claims Made" An occurrence policy is one that covers claims arising out of occurrences that take place during the policy period, regardless of when the claim is made. In contrast, the **claims-made policy** *covers only claims that are first reported during the policy period, provided the event occurred after the retroactive date (if any) stated in the policy.* The retroactive date is an extremely important concept that is discussed later.

To illustrate the difference between the two concepts, assume that a building contractor replaces an occurrence policy with a claims-made policy. If the contractor is sued because of a defect in a building constructed five years earlier, the occurrence policy would defend the claim. However, assuming no retroactive coverage, the claims-made policy would not cover the loss because it occurred before the inception date of the policy.

Rationale for Claims-Made Policies Insurers have resorted to claims-made policies because of the problem of **long-tail** claims. The long-tail refers to a relatively small number of claims that are reported years after the policy was first written. Under an occurrence policy, the insurer that provided coverage when the incident occurred is responsible for the claim. Consequently, insurers found themselves paying claims on policies that had expired years earlier. As a result, they found it extremely difficult to estimate accurately the correct premiums to charge and the correct loss reserve to establish for incurred but not yet reported (IBNR) claims. Under a claims-made policy, premiums, losses, and loss reserves can be estimated with greater accuracy.

Retroactive Date A claims-made policy can be written to cover events that occur prior to the inception of the policy. Coverage will depend on the retroactive date, if any, inserted in the policy. To be covered, the occurrence must take place after the retroactive date, and the claim must be reported during the current policy term. If the occurrence takes place before the retroactive date, the claims-made policy will not respond.

For example, assume that the retroactive date is the date of the original claims-made policy. The issue date of the original claims-made policy is January 1, 1998. The most recent claims-made policy is issued on January 1, 2000. The insured would be covered for all occurrences that take place after January 1, 1998, and are reported during the current policy period.

Extended Reporting Periods The claims-made policy also contains a provision that extends the period for reporting claims. *The purpose of the extended reporting period is to provide coverage under an expired claims-made policy when the claim is first reported after the policy expires.*

The **basic extended reporting period** is automatically provided without an extra charge whenever one of the following occurs:

- The policy is canceled or not renewed.

- The insurer renews or replaces the policy with a retroactive date that is later than the retroactive date in the original policy.
- The claims-made policy is replaced with an occurrence policy.

The basic extended reporting period provides for two separate reporting periods or "tails." The first tail is a five-year period after the policy expires, and the second tail is a 60-day period after the expiration date. For example, assume that a customer in a supermarket slips and falls on a wet floor during the policy period. The insured reports the occurrence promptly to the company, but no actual claim is made against the insured during the policy period. Any resulting claim arising out of that reported occurrence is covered by the expired policy if the claim is made before the end of the five-year period.

The second tail of 60 days applies to all other claims; these claims result from occurrences that take place during the policy period (or after the retroactive date), but are not reported to the insurer during the policy period. Coverage applies if the occurrence is reported to the insurer within 60 days after the policy expires. For example, referring back to our illustrative example, the insured may have been unaware that the customer fell, so the incident was not reported to the company. However, if a claim is made against the insured after the policy expires, coverage applies if the occurrence is reported to the insurer within 60 days after the expiration date.

If the insured wants a longer reporting period after the policy expires, the supplemental extended reporting period can be added by an endorsement and payment of an additional premium. The insured must request the endorsement in writing within 60 days after the policy expires.

EMPLOYMENT PRACTICES LIABILITY INSURANCE

Employers are frequently sued by employees because of wrongful termination, discrimination, sexual harassment, failure to promote, and other employment-related practices. In recent years, the number of such suits has increased substantially. General liability insurance policies generally exclude or offer limited protection against liability arising out of the employment practices of employers. Many insurers now offer a separate policy or have specific endorsements to deal with these exposures.

ISO has recently introduced an employment-related practices liability coverage form that deals with employment practices loss exposures. The following discussion is based on the ISO form.

Insuring Agreement

The ISO form is a claims-made policy. The insurer agrees to pay damages arising out of an injury if a claim is first made during the policy period or during a 30-day grace period after the policy period ends. An *injury*, as defined in the policy, includes any of the following:

- Refusal to employ, termination of employment, demotion or failure to promote, reassignment, negative evaluation, and defamation or humiliation
- Coercing a person to commit an unlawful act or omission within the scope of employment
- Work-related sexual harassment
- Other work-related verbal, physical, mental, or emotional abuse, such as discrimination based on race, age, and gender

Co-payment

The ISO form includes a co-payment provision that requires the insured to pay part of the damages and legal defense costs up to some maximum limit. For example, assume that the co-payment percentage is 20 percent, and the maximum co-payment charge is $25,000. If actual damages and legal defense costs amount to $100,000, the insured would pay $20,000. If the actual claim is $200,000, the insured would pay a maximum of $25,000.

Legal Defense

The ISO form also provides for a legal defense, although legal defense costs are included as part of the policy limit. Payment of legal defense costs reduces the limit of insurance available to the insured.

Note that a claim cannot be settled without the insured's consent. This provision is designed to pro-
tect the employer's image and reputation. However, if the insurer works out a settlement with a claimant but the employer refuses to settle, any final settlement above the initial settlement is the employer's responsibility.

Exclusions

The ISO form contains a number of exclusions. Liability arising out of the following is excluded:

- Criminal, fraudulent, or malicious acts
- Contractual liability
- Workers compensation and similar laws
- Failure to comply with the Americans with Disabilities Act
- Violation of laws applicable to employers, such as the Age Discrimination in Employment Act, and the Family and Medical Leave Act of 1993
- Strikes and lockouts
- Liability of an insured who commits a sexual harassment offense (For example, an employer but not the supervisor would be covered if an immediate supervisor sexually harasses an employee.)
- Termination of employment, job relocation, or assignment due to business decisions
- Intentional discrimination or coercion
- Retaliatory actions (such as actions taken against an employee who files a complaint with a governmental authority)

Because of the growing number of sexual harassment suits filed in recent years, interest in employment practices liability insurance is increasing. Most insurers will check an employer's policy and program on sexual harassment very carefully before writing such insurance (see Insight 14.2).

WORKERS COMPENSATION AND EMPLOYERS LIABILITY INSURANCE

All states have workers compensation laws that require most employers to provide workers compensation benefits to employees who have a job-related injury or an occupational disease. Employers can meet their legal obligation to injured employees by buying workers compensation insurance.

Insight 14.2

Insurance Covers Harassment Claims: As Settlements Rise, Firms Buy Policies

Astra USA recently agreed to pay a record $10 million to settle a harassment lawsuit, restructured its personnel department, and implemented sexual harassment training. But the case highlights serious questions raised by the recent corporate drive to buy harassment insurance.

Are insurers looking closely enough at the companies they sell to? Will companies—which spend up to $500,000 a year on the insurance—relax once their coffers are protected?

"There's a danger that sexual harassment can become just a cost of doing business for those who've invested in insurance coverage," said Jonathan Turley, a law professor at George Washington University.

Companies insured against sexual harassment claims will have less incentive to avoid lawsuits because their legal costs won't come out of their own pockets, he said. "Corporate cultures respond to the bottom line."

Insurer David Sterling, meanwhile, says the industry is lowering its standards of risk assessment in order to sell more policies. "There are so many insurance companies competing, those (presale) demands have dropped," he said. Other insurers disagree.

Michael Furgueson, vice president of Chubb Insurance, said most insurers check a company's programs carefully. But he said he "can't say every underwriting process is flawless in uncovering what goes on in a company."

Before selling a policy, insurers typically check company rules on sexual harassment, financial statements, and past lawsuits or allegations. After a policy is sold, some insurers offer more in-depth advice on a company's risk of being sued.

At Chubb, underwriters study handbooks, finances, programs, and litigation trends before making a sale, although they don't audit company procedures out of concern that results could be used against the company in potential lawsuits. Chubb also offers companies lists of law firms that provide seminars in harassment-prevention.

It's not hard to see why companies are shopping for coverage. The number of sexual harassment charges filed with the Equal Employment Opportunity Commission rose from 6883 in 1991 to 15,889 last year. Monetary settlements paid to victims leaped from $7 million seven years ago to nearly $50 million last year.

Companies don't buy a specific harassment policy. Rather, they purchase what the industry calls employment practices liability insurance, created in the early 1990s to cover harassment, wrongful termination, and discrimination. Still, insurers say fears of harassment suits are driving sales—and the increasing size of the coverage.

Midsize companies that wanted $2.5 million in coverage last year now are asking for $10 million lim-

---

This section discusses the current version of the workers compensation and employers liability policy drafted by the National Council on Compensation Insurance.[3] The historical development of workers compensation as a form of social insurance is treated in Chapter 24.

The workers compensation and employers liability policy provides the following coverages:

- Part One: Workers Compensation Insurance
- Part Two: Employers Liability Insurance
- Part Three: Other-States Insurance

Part One: Workers Compensation Insurance

Part One refers to **workers compensation insurance**. Under this section, the insurer agrees to pay all workers compensation benefits and other benefits that the employer must legally provide to covered employees who have a job-related injury or an occupational disease. There are no policy limits for Part One. The insurer instead pays all benefits required by the workers compensation law of any state listed in the declarations. In recent years, occupational dis-

its, said Lisa DeSimone, vice president of employment practices liability at Reliance National Insurers. Companies pay up to $500,000 for $25 million in coverage, she said.

For Vincam, a company that provides employees as a longer-term version of temps, the decision to buy the insurance meant boosting its prices, but clients supported the move, said Jeff Lamb, vice president of marketing and business development. "Businesses want to know there's something in back of them should the unknown occur."

At Astra, harassment of women began at least as far back as 1993, according to the Equal Employment Opportunity Commission. A year later, the Westborough, Massachusetts, company purchased employment practices liability insurance. The EEOC began investigating complaints from female employees in 1996.

"Our insurance brokers advised us that this was a trend in the industry, and it was an investment we would want to consider," said Astra spokeswoman Ann Gillespie, who refused to name the insurer or the size of the policy.

Despite the insurance's popularity, some companies choose to go it alone, believing that good anti-harassment programs are their best protection.

"We have nothing of the sort. There's been no need," said IBM spokeswoman Kendra Collins. "We've been very fortunate. We rely on our programs, and we believe in them."

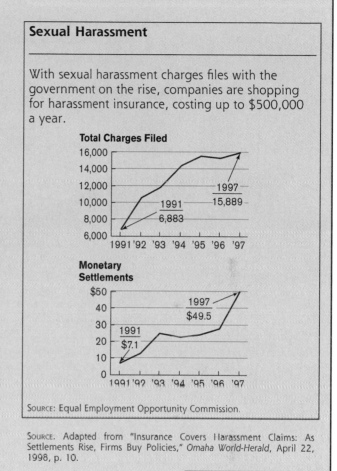

Sexual Harassment

With sexual harassment charges files with the government on the rise, companies are shopping for harassment insurance, costing up to $500,000 a year.

Total Charges Filed

1991 — 6,883

1997 — 15,889

Monetary Settlements

1991 — $7.1

1997 — $49.5

SOURCE: Equal Employment Opportunity Commission.

SOURCE: Adapted from "Insurance Covers Harassment Claims: As Settlements Rise, Firms Buy Policies," *Omaha World-Herald*, April 22, 1998, p. 10.

ease has become increasingly more important in the payment of workers compensation claims. Claims due to workplace violence and workplace homicides have also increased (see Insight 14.3).

Under certain conditions, the employer can be held responsible for payments made by the insurer that exceed regular workers compensation benefits. The employer is responsible for any payments in excess of the benefits regularly provided by the workers compensation law because of serious and willful misconduct; knowingly employing workers in violation of the law; failure to comply with a health or safety regulation; or discharge, coercion, or discrimination against any employee in violation of the workers compensation law. The employer must reimburse the insurer for any payments that exceed regular workers compensation benefits.

Part Two: Employers Liability Insurance

Part Two refers to **employers liability insurance**, which covers employers against lawsuits by employees who are injured in the course of employment, but whose injuries (or disease) are not compensable

Insight 14.3

Workplace Violence and Workplace Homicides Are Serious National Problems

The scene is familiar. An angry employee fired from his job returns to the workplace and shoots and kills his former supervisor and five former coworkers. The public is shocked; television networks carry the story as a major event; and talk-show hosts speak psycho babble to determine why the event occurred.

Each year, thousands of workers are the victims of workplace violence and homicide. There are four categories of workplace acts that can result in death or injury to employees: (1) anger by employees toward employers, (2) robbery and other business crimes, (3) domestic quarrels that spill over into the workplace, and (4) terrorism or hate crimes. Workers most likely to be killed or assaulted include cab drivers; employees of fast-food stores, liquor stores, gas stations, hotels, and motels; bartenders; police officers; nurses; and teachers.

Workplace homicide paints a serious problem. *Homicide is now the second leading cause of death on the job, next to motor vehicle crashes. In 1996, 912 workplace homicides occurred. For women workers, homicide is the number one cause of workplace death.*[*]

Other statistics tell a harrowing tale:[†]

- An employee is almost twice as likely to be killed by coworkers, former coworkers, or clients as a police officer is in the line of duty.
- One million individuals are victims of violent crime at work each year.
- Six million employees are threatened at the work site each year.
- The chance of being attacked threatened, or harassed on the job is one in four.

These perturbing figures may be the tip of the iceberg. Studies conducted by the Department of Justice estimate that more than half the incidents of workplace violence go unreported.

[*]Beth Lindamood, "Prevention Program Targets Workplace Violence," *Workers' Compensation Monitor* (May 1998), p. 12.
[†]Russ Banham, "Defusing Workplace Violence," *1997 Issues Report, Vital Workers Compensation Information* (Boca Raton, FL: National Council on Compensation Insurance, 1997), p. 75.

SOURCE: *Social Insurance and Economic Security*, sixth edition by George E. Rejda, ©1998. Adapted by permission of Prentice-Hall, Inc. Upper Saddle River, NJ.

under the state's workers compensation law. This part is similar to other liability insurance policies where negligence must be established before the insurer is legally obligated to pay.

Employers liability insurance is needed for several reasons. First, a few states do not require workers compensation insurance for smaller employers with fewer than a certain number of employees, such as three or fewer. In such cases, an employer is covered under the employers liability section if an employee with a work-related injury or disease sues for damages.

Second, an injury or disease that occurs on the job may not be considered to be work related, and, therefore, would not be covered under the state's workers compensation law. However, the injured employee may still believe that the employer should be held accountable, and the employer would be covered if sued.

Third, some state workers compensation laws permit lawsuits by spouses and dependents for the *loss of consortium*. The employer would be covered under Part Two in such a case.

Finally, in a growing number of cases, employers are confronted with lawsuits because of *third-party over cases*. An injured employee may sue a negligent third party, and the third party, in turn, sues the employer for contributory negligence. The lawsuit would be covered under Part Two (unless the employer assumed the liability of the third party). For example, assume that a machine is defective, and its operator is injured. In addition to the payment of workers compensation benefits, the state may allow the injured employee to sue the negligent third party. If the injured employee sues the manufacturer of the defective machine, the manufacturer, in turn, could sue the employer for failure to provide proper operating instructions or failure to enforce safety rules. The employer would be covered in such cases.

The employers liability section of the ISO policy also contains several exclusions. Major exclusions include liability assumed under contract, punitive damages, bodily injury to an employee employed in violation of the law, workers compensation claims (covered under Part One), intentional injury, bodily injury outside the United States or Canada, and damages arising out of coercion, demotion, evaluation, reassignment, harassment, discrimination, or termination of any employee.

Part Three: Other-States Insurance

Part Three of the workers compensation and employers liability policy provides **other-states insurance**. Workers compensation coverage (Part One) applies only to those states listed on the information page (declarations page) of the policy. However, the employer may face a workers compensation claim under the law of another state. This possibility could arise if an employee is injured while on a business trip in a state that was not considered when the workers compensation policy was first written, or if the law of a particular state is broadened so that employees are now covered under that state's workers compensation law. Also, the employer's operations may be expanded in a particular state, which brings the employees under the state's workers compensation law.

Other-states insurance applies only if one or more states are shown on the information page of the policy. The information page is the equivalent of a declarations page. *In such cases, if the employer begins work in any of the states listed, the policy applies as if that state were listed in the policy for workers compensation purposes.* Thus, the employer has coverage for any workers compensation benefits that it may have to make under that state's workers compensation law.

Voluntary Compensation Coverage

Some employers wish to provide workers compensation benefits to employees even though they are not required by law to do so. A **voluntary compensation endorsement** can be added to the policy by which the insurer agrees to pay workers compensation benefits to employees not covered under the law.

COMMERCIAL AUTO INSURANCE

Legal liability arising out of the ownership and use of cars, trucks, and trailers is another important loss exposure for many firms. This section examines several commercial auto coverages that can be used to meet this exposure.[4]

Business Auto Coverage Form

The ISO business auto coverage form is widely used by business firms to insure their commercial auto exposures. Firms have considerable flexibility with respect to the autos that can be covered. There are nine numerical classifications, each of which has a numbered symbol:

1. Any auto
2. Owned autos only
3. Owned private passenger autos only
4. Owned autos other than private passenger autos only
5. Owned autos subject to no-fault plans
6. Owned autos subject to a compulsory uninsured motorists law
7. Specifically described autos
8. Hired autos only
9. Nonowned autos only

If one or more of the symbols 1 through 6 are selected, there is automatic coverage on any new owned autos that the firm acquires during the policy period. If symbol 7 is used, new cars are covered only if two conditions are met: (1) the insurer must already cover all autos that the insured owns for the coverage provided, or the new auto must replace one that the insured previously owned that had such coverage, and (2) the firm informs the insurer within 30 days after acquisition that it wants the auto insured for that coverage.

Liability Insurance Coverage The insured is covered for a bodily injury or property damage claim arising out of an accident caused by the ownership, maintenance, or use of a covered auto. The insurer also agrees to defend the insured and pay all legal defense costs.

When liability insurance is provided, there is also automatic coverage on all trailers that have a load capacity of 2000 pounds or less and are designed primarily for travel on public roads. Also, mobile equipment, such as a bulldozer, grader, or scraper, is covered while being carried or towed by a covered auto. Liability coverage also applies to a temporary substitute auto that is used because a covered auto is out of service because of breakdown, service, or damage.

Physical Damage Insurance The insured has a choice of physical damage coverages that can be used to insure covered autos against damage or loss. Several physical damage coverages are available, summarized as follows:

- *Comprehensive coverage.* The insurer will pay for loss to a covered auto or its equipment from any cause except the covered auto's collision with another object or its overturn.
- *Specified causes-of-loss coverage.* Only losses from specified perils are covered: fire, lightning, or explosion; theft; windstorm, hail, or earthquake; flood; mischief or vandalism; and the sinking, burning, collision, or derailment of any conveyance transporting the covered auto.
- *Collision coverage.* Loss caused by the covered auto's collision with another object or its overturn is covered under this provision.

Coverage for towing and labor costs can be added if desired. The company will pay up to the limit shown in the declarations for towing and labor costs incurred each time a covered auto of the private passenger type is disabled. However, the labor must be performed at the place of disablement.

In addition, the insurer will pay up to $15 per day (after 48 hours) up to a maximum of $450 for transportation expenses incurred by the insured because of the theft of a covered auto of the private passenger type. The coverage applies only to covered autos that are insured for either comprehensive or specified causes-of-loss coverage.

Nonownership Liability Coverage

Salespersons, repair and maintenance employees, employees who make deliveries, inspection personnel, and other employees frequently drive their automobiles on company business. A business firm can be held legally liable for damages caused by employees while they are using their own cars on company business. If the employee carries liability insurance on his or her car, the firm is protected as an additional insured. The liability limits may be inadequate, however, or the policy may have lapsed. The firm may also be exposed to liability claims arising from the operation of other nonowned automobiles—for example, a restaurant or hotel that parks cars for the guests. These nonownership exposures can also be insured by selecting the appropriate covered auto designation symbol or combination of symbols.

Garage Coverage Form

The **garage coverage form** is a specialized form designed to meet the insurance needs of "garages," which include service stations, parking garages, automobile dealerships, repair shops, and similar businesses. The major coverages include liability coverage, garagekeepers coverage, and physical damage coverage.

Liability Coverage The liability section of the garage coverage form is broad and comprehensive. The company agrees to pay all sums that the insured must legally pay as damages because of bodily injury or property damage caused by an accident in the course of garage operations. *Garage operations* are defined to include automobiles, business premises, and business activities. As such, the liability section automatically includes premises and operations liability coverage, products and completed operations coverage, and incidental contractual liability, as well as automobile liability insurance.

The insured has a choice of autos that can be covered, and numerical symbols are used to denote the covered autos, an approach similar to the business auto policy.

The liability section of the garage policy contains numerous exclusions. Only two of them are discussed here. *First, damage to the property of others in the insured's care, custody, or control is excluded.* Thus, damage to a customer's car on an automobile servicing hoist, or damage to a customer's car while it is being road tested by a mechanic, would not be covered. These common exposures can be covered by adding garagekeepers coverage to the policy.

Second, there is no coverage for property damage to any of the insured's products if the product is defective at the time it is sold. This exclusion is important for firms that sell automobiles, gasoline, parts, tires, batteries, or other products. For example, assume that a tire dealer sells a tire that has a hidden defect. The defective tire later blows out, and the car is damaged in a collision. This exclusion eliminates coverage for the defective tire, but the property damage caused by the defective tire would be covered. The intent of this exclusion is to cover property damage or bodily injury caused by a defective product but not any damage to the product itself.

Garagekeepers Coverage The owner of a parking lot, auto repair shop, or storage garage who keeps a customer's car for storage or repair and receives compensation is legally considered a bailee for hire. Regardless of signs to the contrary posted on the premises, the garage owner can be held legally liable for the loss or damage to a customer's car because of the failure to exercise ordinary care. As noted earlier, the garage coverage form excludes coverage for property of others in the care, custody, or control of the insured. This exclusion can be eliminated by adding garagekeepers coverage to the policy. Under this coverage, the insurer agrees to pay all sums that the insured legally must pay as damages for loss to customers' autos while in the garage owner's care for service, repairs, parking, or storage. Three coverages are available: (1) comprehensive coverage, (2) specified causes-of-loss coverage, and (3) collision coverage. These coverages are based on the legal liability of the insured. For example, if a customer's car is stolen because the garage owner carelessly left the garage door unlocked, the loss would be covered. It is possible, however, to broaden the coverage on customers' automobiles without regard to legal liability by the payment of an additional premium.

Physical Damage Coverage Physical damage insurance on covered autos can also be included in the garage policy. The following three coverages are available:

- *Comprehensive coverage.* The company will pay for a loss from any cause except for the covered auto's collision with another object or its overturn.
- *Specified causes-of-loss coverage.* Covered perils are fire, lightning, explosion, theft, windstorm,

hail, earthquake, flood, mischief, vandalism, and the sinking, burning, collision, or derailment of any conveyance transporting the covered auto.
- *Collision coverage.* Loss caused by the covered auto's collision with another object or its overturn is covered under this provision.

AVIATION INSURANCE

Major commercial airlines own fleets of expensive jets, and the liability exposure is enormous. Occasionally, a commercial jet will crash, killing hundreds of passengers and causing extensive property damage to surrounding buildings. Legal liability arising out of the crash of a fully loaded jet airliner can be catastrophic. In addition, some firms own aircraft used on company business. Company planes sometimes crash, resulting in death or bodily injury to the passengers, as well as death or injury to people on the ground and substantial property damage to surrounding buildings where the crash occurs. Finally, thousands of Americans own or operate small planes, which may crash because of pilot error or inexperience.

Most states apply the common-law rules of negligence to aviation accidents. However, some states have absolute or strict liability laws that hold the owners or operators of aircraft absolutely liable for certain aviation accidents. As a result of international treaties and agreements among countries, absolute liability is also imposed on commercial airlines for aviation accidents that occur during international flights.

Aviation Insurers

Aviation insurance is a highly specialized market that is underwritten by a relatively small number of insurer organizations. Most of the domestic aviation market is accounted for by two multicompany aviation pools: United States Aircraft Insurance Group (USAIG) and Associated Aviation Underwriters (AAU). Both pools underwrite and manage aviation insurance on behalf of the individual insurers that belong to the pool. The two pools account for most of the aviation insurance that is written for commercial airlines, aircraft manufacturers, and large domestic airports.

Aviation Insurance for Private Business and Pleasure Aircraft

AAU offers a policy designed for the owners and operators of private business and pleasure aircraft. The policy provides physical damage coverage for damage to the aircraft, liability coverage for injury to passengers and people on the ground, and medical expense coverage for passengers.[5]

Physical Damage Coverage A plane on the ground can be damaged from fire, collapse, theft, vandalism, or other perils. While taxiing, the plane can collide with vehicles, buildings, or other aircraft. The most severe exposure is present when the plane is in flight. A plane can collide with another aircraft; it can be struck by lightning or damaged by turbulent winds; it can experience mechanical difficulties from a fire or explosion.

Physical damage insurance provides coverage for direct damage to the aircraft. The insured has a choice of physical damage coverages. There are three insuring agreements for physical damage to the aircraft:

- *"All-risks" basis.* All physical damage losses to the aircraft, including disappearance, are covered except those losses excluded.
- *"All-risks" basis, not in flight.* The aircraft is covered on an "all-risks" basis only when it is on the ground and not in flight. Fire or explosion following a crash is not covered.
- *"All-risks" basis, not in motion.* The aircraft is covered on an "all-risks" basis only when it is standing still. Fire or explosion after a crash is not covered.

Although aircraft can be covered on an "all-risks" basis, certain exclusions apply. Excluded losses include damage to tires (unless caused by fire, theft, or vandalism), wear and tear, deterioration, mechanical or electrical breakdown, and failure of installed equipment. However, these exclusions do not apply if a covered loss occurs.

Liability Coverage Liability coverage pays for bodily injury or property damage arising out of the insured's ownership, maintenance, or use of the insured aircraft. Coverage also applies to bodily injury arising out of the premises where the aircraft is stored.

Liability coverage contains several important exclusions. Excluded losses are liability assumed in a contract, workers compensation, and damage to property in the insured's care, custody, and control (except personal effects of passengers up to $250 and damage to an aircraft hangar or its contents up to $5000). Also excluded are damage or injury from noise, such as sonic boom, interference with the quiet enjoyment of property, and pollution losses.

Medical Payments to Passengers The policy provides medical payments coverage to passengers, which includes hospital, ambulance, nursing, and funeral services. Crew members can be covered for an additional premium.

BAILEE'S CUSTOMER INSURANCE

A bailee is someone who has temporary possession of property that belongs to another party. Bailees—such as a laundry or dry cleaner, for example—are legally liable for damage to the customers' goods only if they or their employees are guilty of negligence. However, the customers expect to be paid for the loss or damage to their goods regardless of who is at fault. If the customers are not reimbursed, the bailee may lose future business. In the case of a destructive fire or tornado, the business may be financially ruined if customers are not reimbursed for their damaged property.

A bailee's customer policy is a generic name for a policy that covers loss or damage to the property of customers regardless of the bailee's legal liability. Although the policies are not standard, they can be written to meet the needs of a particular bailee, including laundries and dry cleaners, tailors, television repair shops, and upholsterers.

A bailee's customer policy can be illustrated by an analysis of the **bailee coverage named-perils policy** drafted by the American Association of Insurance Services (AAIS).[6] The policy is written on a named-perils basis. The perils covered are fire; lightning; windstorm; hail; explosion; strike; riot or civil commotion; damage from aircraft, spacecraft, or self-propelled missiles; damage from physical contact with vehicles; collision, derailment, upset, or overturn of a transporting land vehicle; vandalism; and theft. For example, if a suit or dress is damaged in a fire or tornado, or if the garment is damaged when a delivery truck overturns in a collision, the loss would be covered.

This policy contains numerous exclusions. Excluded are those losses that result from dishonest or illegal acts; voluntary parting with the title or possession of covered property if the insured is induced to do so by trickery or fraud; mysterious disappearance; any cause when the only proof is an inventory shortage; theft of property left overnight in or on delivery vehicles (unless the vehicle is locked in a private garage or building occupied by the insured); breaking of fragile items or marring, scratching, tearing, or ripping (unless caused by a covered peril); a process performed on the covered property (except if a fire or explosion results); explosion or implosion inside a boiler; and misdelivery. For example, if a garment is damaged by cleaning fluid or shrinks in the cleaning process, the loss is not covered.

COMMERCIAL UMBRELLA POLICY

Because firms are often sued for large amounts, they may seek protection against catastrophic loss exposures not adequately insured under standard liability policies. The **commercial umbrella policy** can provide protection against catastrophic liability judgments that might otherwise bankrupt a firm.

Although commercial umbrella contracts are not totally uniform, they do share certain common provisions. The following discussion briefly summarizes the major provisions of a typical commercial umbrella policy.[7]

Coverages

The commercial umbrella policy pays for damages in excess of the retained limit for bodily injury, property damage, personal injury, or advertising injury for which the insured is legally liable because of a covered loss. The **retained limit** *is the greater of (1) the total amount of the applicable limits of the underlying insurance contracts and the applicable limits of any other insurance providing coverage to the insured or (2) a self-insured retention (SIR) if the loss is not covered by any underlying insurance or other insurance contract, but is covered by the umbrella policy.*

If the loss is covered by both an underlying insurance contract (or other insurance) and the umbrella policy, the umbrella policy pays only after the underlying limits are exhausted. For example, assume that the underlying limit under a commercial general liability policy (CGL) is $1 million for each occurrence, and a judgment against the insured amounts to $3 million. The underlying insurance would pay $1 million, and the umbrella policy would pay the remaining $2 million.

If the loss is not covered by any underlying insurance or other insurance but is covered by the umbrella policy, the insured must satisfy a self-insurance retention (SIR). The SIR can range from $500 for small firms to $1 million or more for large corporations. For example, assume that a firm's SIR amount is $25,000. A customer in the firm's store who is falsely accused and arrested for shoplifting wins a judgment against the insured in the amount of $100,000. If the loss is not covered by any underlying or other insurance contract, the insured would pay $25,000. The umbrella policy would pay the remaining $75,000.

Legal defense costs are also paid after the underlying insurance limits or any other insurance limits providing coverage to the insured are exhausted. In addition, legal defense costs are paid if the loss is covered by the umbrella policy but not by any underlying insurance or any other insurance.

Required Underlying Coverages

Insureds are required to carry certain minimum amounts of liability insurance before the umbrella insurer will pay any claims. The following underlying coverages and limits are typically required:

Commercial general liability insurance

$1,000,000 (each occurrence)
$2,000,000 (general aggregate)
$2,000,000 (completed-operations aggregate)

Business auto liability insurance

$1,000,000 (combined single limit)

Employer liability insurance

$500,000 (bodily injury per accident)
$500,000 (bodily injury by disease per
    employee)
$500,000 (disease aggregate)

The commercial umbrella liability applies when the loss exceeds the underlying limits.

Exclusions

A commercial umbrella policy contains numerous exclusions. Typical exclusions include the following:

- Bodily injury or property damage expected or intended by the insured
- Obligations of the insured under a workers compensation or similar law
- Obligations of the insured under the Employee Retirement Income Security Act of 1974 (ERISA)
- Property damage to impaired property
- Property damage to the insured's products
- Property damage arising out of the insured's work
- Expenses incurred in recalling defective products
- Property damage to the insured's property
- Certain personal injury or advertising injury losses, such as libel and slander that the insured knows to be false or that occurred before the beginning of the policy period
- Under advertising injury, breach of contract, incorrect description of an item, mistake in an advertised price, and offenses committed by an insured in the advertising, broadcasting, publishing, or telecasting business
- Pollution losses
- Liability arising out of asbestos products or materials
- Liability arising out of refusal to hire or promote, termination of employment, and various acts against employees, including harassment, molestation, and discrimination
- Liability arising out of watercraft or aircraft unless provided by underlying insurance

LIABILITY INSURANCE, BUSINESSOWNERS POLICY

The businessowners policy (BOP) discussed in Chapter 13 also contains a **business liability cover-**age form that provides general liability insurance to business firms. The liability coverage is written only on an occurrence basis, and with some minor exceptions, it is similar to the commercial general liability coverage form discussed earlier.[8]

Basic Coverages

The BOP liability form contains two basic coverages: (1) business liability coverage and (2) medical expenses coverage. Business liability includes coverage for bodily injury, property damage, personal injury, and advertising liability. Coverage for medical expenses is also provided. Thus, if a customer in a retail shoe store falls and breaks an arm, the customer's medical expenses would be paid without regard to legal liability.

Amount of Insurance

The minimum amount of insurance provided for liability and medical expenses is $300,000 for each occurrence, which can be increased to $500,000, $1 million, or $2 million. This limit is the maximum that the insurer will pay for both liability and medical expense losses.

The BOP has a medical expense limit of $5000 per person and a fire legal liability limit of $50,000. Higher fire legal liability limits are available.

In addition, the BOP has two aggregate limits on the total amounts of covered claims that can be paid during the policy period. *The first aggregate limit applies to products and completed operations losses and is equal to the liability and medical expense limit discussed earlier. The second aggregate limit applies to all other covered losses (including medical expenses) and is equal to twice the liability and medical expense limit.* Fire legal liability is an exception. Fire legal liability losses are subject only to the fire legal liability limit and do not reduce the aggregate limit.

Legal Defense

The insurer pays the legal costs of defending the insured. The legal costs are in addition to the amount that the insurer is legally obligated to pay because of the insured's negligence.

The definition of an insured also includes employees while they are acting within the scope of their activities. This feature protects a negligent employee who might be named in the lawsuit along with the employer.

Exclusions

In general, the liability form excludes claims involving pollution, automobiles, aircraft, watercraft, workers compensation, and professional services. However, druggists liability insurance is included in the current form if the insured is a retail druggist or drugstore. In addition, liability coverage for hired and nonowned autos can be added as an endorsement to the policy. The latter coverage is especially important if the firm has employees who park the cars of customers. Finally, the policy contains the usual liquor liability exclusion discussed earlier, with an important exception. *Liability coverage* is provided if alcohol is served at functions incidental to the insured's business. Thus, if the company has a Christmas party, and an intoxicated employee injures someone, the firm is covered if a lawsuit ensues.

PROFESSIONAL LIABILITY INSURANCE

Chapter 7 examined the problem of professional liability and the increased number of lawsuits against physicians, surgeons, attorneys, accountants, professors, and other professionals. This section briefly discusses some professional liability insurance coverages that provide protection against a malpractice lawsuit or lawsuit involving a substantial error or omission.

Physicians Liability Insurance

Physicians, surgeons, and dentists require substantial amounts of **physicians liability insurance** that covers acts of malpractice or omission resulting in harm or injury to patients. The *physicians, surgeons, and dentists professional liability coverage part* drafted by the ISO covers acts of malpractice by physicians and surgeons. This policy has the following characteristics:[9]

- Broad coverage is provided.
- Liability is not restricted to accidental acts.

- The insured's liability for the negligent acts of employees is covered.
- There is a maximum limit per medical incident and an aggregate limit for each coverage.
- Professional liability insurance is not a substitute for general liability insurance.
- The current forms may permit the insurer to settle a claim without the insured physician's or surgeon's consent.
- An extended reporting period can be added.

The insuring agreement provides broad coverage. The insurer agrees to pay all sums that the insured is legally obligated to pay as damages because of injury caused by a medical incident. A *medical incident* is any act or omission in the furnishing of professional medical or dental services by the insured, an employee of the insured, or any person acting under the personal direction or supervision of the insured. For example, if Dr. Jones operates on a patient and the patient is paralyzed after the operation, Dr. Jones would be covered for a malpractice lawsuit.

Liability is not restricted to accidental acts of the physician or surgeon. In many cases, the physician or surgeon deliberately intends to do a certain act; however, the professional diagnosis or the performance of the act may be faulty, and the patient is injured. For example, Dr. Jones may intend to operate on a patient by using a certain surgical procedure. If the patient is harmed or injured by the operation, Dr. Jones would still be covered for his willful, intentional act to operate in a certain way.

The policy covers the physician for liability arising out of the negligent acts of an employee; however, a nurse typically is not included as an insured under the physician's policy but must secure his or her own professional liability policy. For example, if the office nurse gives a wrong shot to a patient, and the patient is harmed, the physician has liability coverage for the incident. However, the nurse is not covered under the physician's policy for the incident.

There is a maximum limit per medical incident and an aggregate limit for each coverage. For example, a patient and the patient's family may file separate claims against a physician for damages arising out of the same medical incident. Under current forms, the per-medical-incident limit is the maximum that would be paid for both claims. The aggregate limit is the maximum amount that would be paid as damages during any policy year.

Professional liability insurance is not a substitute for other necessary forms of liability insurance. General liability insurance is also needed to cover liability arising out of a hazardous condition on the premises or acts of the insured that are not professional in nature. For example, a patient may trip on a torn carpet in the doctor's office and break an arm. The professional liability policy would not cover this event.

Current forms permit the insurer to settle the claim without the physician's or surgeon's consent. Payment of a claim could be viewed as an admission of guilt. Older forms required the insurer to obtain the physician's consent before a claim could be settled. However, current forms permit the insurer to settle without the physician's consent because an occasional claim against a physician in certain high-risk categories is not viewed as being overly detrimental to his or her character.

Finally, an extended reporting period endorsement can be added. A physician with a claims-made policy may retire, change insurers, or drop the malpractice insurance. To protect the physician, an extended reporting period endorsement can be added, which covers future claims arising out of incidents that occurred during the period in which the claims-made policy was in force.

In summary, a professional liability policy for physicians and surgeons provides considerable protection. The insurance is expensive, however. Malpractice insurance covering certain high-risk specialties can cost $75,000 or more each year in certain parts of the country. Physicians have responded to the medical malpractice problem by practicing defensive medicine, by abandoning high-risk specialties such as obstetrics and neurosurgery, and by pushing for legislation to limit malpractice awards. Despite these efforts to reduce lawsuits, medical mistakes by physicians and hospitals remain high (see Insight 14.4).

Errors and Omissions Insurance

Errors and omissions insurance provides protection against loss incurred by a client because of negligent acts, errors, or omissions by the insured. Professionals who need errors and omissions insurance include insurance agents and brokers, travel agents, real estate agents, stockbrokers, attorneys, consultants, engineers, architects, and other individuals who give advice to clients. The errors and omissions coverage is designed to meet the needs of each profession.

This type of coverage can be illustrated by the *insurance agents and brokers errors and omissions policy.* The policy has a number of provisions. First, the insurer agrees to pay all sums that the insured is legally obligated to pay because of any negligent act, error, or omission by the insured (or by any other person for whose acts the insured is legally liable) in the conduct of business as general agents, insurance agents, or insurance brokers. For example, assume that Mark is an independent agent who fails to renew a property insurance policy for a client. The policy lapses, and a subsequent loss is not covered. If the client sues for damages, Mark would be covered for the omission. The policy is normally sold with a sizable deductible so that the agent has an incentive to minimize mistakes and errors.

Errors and omissions policies are generally issued on a claims-made basis covering claims made against the agent or broker only because of errors during the current policy period (or after the retroactive date).

Finally, the policy contains relatively few exclusions. However, claims that result from dishonest, fraudulent, criminal, or malicious acts by the insured, libel and slander, bodily injury, and destruction of tangible property are specifically excluded.

SUMMARY

- General liability refers to the legal liability of business firms arising out of business operations other than liability for automobile or aviation accidents or employee injuries. The most important general liability loss exposures are as follows:

    Premises and operations

    Products liability

    Completed operations

    Contractual liability

    Contingent liability

- Legal liability can arise out of the *ownership and maintenance of the premises* where the firm does business.

Insight 14.4

Report Says Mistakes In Medicine Too Frequent

Medical mistakes kill anywhere from 44,000 to 98,000 hospitalized Americans a year, says a new report that calls the errors stunning and demands major changes in the nation's health care system to protect patients.

The groundbreaking report by the Institute of Medicine says there are ways to prevent many of the mistakes and sets as a minimum goal a 50 percent reduction in medical errors within five years.

The problem is less a case of recklessness by individual doctors or nurses than it is the result of basic flaws in the way hospitals, clinics and pharmacies operate, the report says. The institute cited two studies that estimate hospital errors cost at least 44,000, and perhaps as many as 98,000, lives, but research on the topic is unable to pinpoint fatalities more precisely.

Doctors' notoriously poor handwriting too often leaves pharmacists squinting at tiny paper prescriptions. Did the doctor order 10 milligrams or 10 micrograms? Does the prescription call for the hormone replacement Premarin or the antibiotic Primaxin?

Too many drug names sound alike, causing confusion for doctor, nurse, pharmacist and patient alike. Consider the painkiller Celebrex and the anti-seizure drug Cerebyx, or Narcan, which treats morphine overdoses, and Norcuron, which can paralyze breathing muscles.

Medical knowledge grows so rapidly that it is difficult for health care workers to keep up with the latest treatment or newly discovered danger. Technology poses a hazard when device models change from year to year or model to model, leaving doctors fumbling for the right switch.

And most health professionals do not have their competence regularly retested after they are licensed to practice, the report said.

Indeed, health care is a decade or more behind other high-risk industries in improving safety, the report said. It pointed to the transportation industry as a model: Just as engineers designed cars so they cannot start in reverse and airlines limit pilots' flying time so they're rested and alert, so can health care be improved.

"These stunningly high rates of medical errors . . . are simply unacceptable in a medical system that promises first to 'do no harm,'" wrote William Richardson, president of the W.K. Kellogg Foundation and chairman of the institute panel that compiled the report.

But "errors can be prevented by designing systems that make it hard for people to do the wrong thing and easy for people to do the right thing," Richardson concluded. Unfortunately, he continued, medical mistakes usually are "discussed only behind closed doors."

In recent years, however, researchers have begun coming up with ways to avert medical mistakes. Some hospitals now use computerized prescriptions, avoiding the handwriting problem and using software that warns if a particular patient should not use the prescribed drug. Many hospitals now mark patients' arms or legs—while they're awake and watching—to prevent removal of the wrong limb. Anesthesiologists made their field safer by getting manufacturers to standardize anesthesia equipment from one model to the next. The Food and Drug Administration is trying to prevent new drugs from hitting the market with sound-alike names.

But the Institute of Medicine concluded that reducing medical mistakes requires a bigger commitment and recommended some immediate stops:

- Establish a federal Center for Patient Safety in the Department of Health and Human Services. Congress would have to spend some $35 million to set it up, and it should eventually spend $100 million a year in safety research, even building prototypes of safety systems. Still, that represents just a fraction of the estimated $8.8 billion spent each year as a result of medical mistakes, the report calculated.
- The government should require that hospitals, and eventually other health organizations, report all serious mistakes to state agencies so experts can detect patterns of problems and take action.

Source: Adapted from Lauran Neergaard, "Report Says Mistakes In Medicine Too Frequent," *Lincoln Journal Star*, November 30, 1999, p. 2A. Reprinted with permission from the Associated Press.

Products liability means that the firm can be held liable for property damage or bodily injury arising out of a defective product. *Completed operations* refers to liability arising out of faulty work performed away from the premises after the work is completed. *Contractual liability* means that the business firm agrees to assume the legal liability of another party by a written or oral contract. *Contingent liability* means that the firm can be held liable for work by independent contractors.

■ Other important general liability loss exposures include environmental pollution; property in the insured's care, custody, or control; fire legal liability; liability arising out of a liquor or dramshop law; directors and officers liability; and personal injury.

■ The *commercial general liability policy (CGL)* can be used to cover most general liability loss exposures of business firms. The CGL provides coverage for the following:

> Bodily injury and property damage liability
> Personal and advertising injury liability
> Medical payments
> Supplementary payments

■ An *occurrence policy* covers liability claims arising out of occurrences that take place during the policy period, regardless of when the claim is made.

■ A *claims-made policy* covers only claims that are first reported during the policy period or extended reporting period, provided that the event occurred after the retroactive date, if any, stated in the policy.

■ Insurers have resorted to claims-made policies because of the problem of the *long-tail*. The long-tail refers to the relatively small number of claims that are reported years after the policy is first written. As a result of these claims, it is difficult to estimate premiums, losses, and loss reserves accurately. A claims-made policy enables an insurer to estimate premiums and losses more accurately.

■ *Employment-practices liability insurance* covers employers against suits arising out of wrongful termination, discrimination against employees, sexual harassment, and other employment-related practices.

■ All states have workers compensation laws that require covered employers to provide workers compensation benefits to employees who become disabled because of work-related accidents or occupational disease. The workers compensation insurer pays all benefits that the employer must legally provide to employees who are occupationally disabled.

■ The *business auto coverage form* can be used by business firms to insure their liability exposures from automobiles. The employer can select those autos to be covered under the policy.

■ The *garage coverage form* is designed to meet the insurance needs of service stations, parking garages, repair shops, and similar firms. The major coverages include liability insurance, garagekeepers insurance, and physical damage insurance. *Garagekeepers insurance* covers the garage owner's liability for damage to customers' automobiles while the autos are in the garage owner's care for service or repairs.

■ Aviation insurance covering private business and pleasure aircraft provides physical damage coverage on the aircraft, liability coverage for injury to passengers and people on the ground, and medical expense coverage for passengers.

■ The *bailee coverage named-perils policy* can be used to cover the loss or damage to the property of customers regardless of the bailee's legal liability.

■ The *commercial umbrella policy* provides protection to firms against a catastrophic judgment that may bankrupt the firm. The umbrella policy is excess insurance over the underlying coverages.

■ Section II of the businessowners policy provides business liability coverage and medical expense coverage to small- to medium-sized business firms. The insured's employees are also covered for their negligent acts while acting within the scope of their employment.

■ Physicians liability insurance is designed to cover professional liability arising out of a medical incident. The policy has several important features:

> Coverage is broad.
> Liability is not restricted to accidental acts.
> The insured is protected against the negligent acts of employees.
> There is a maximum limit for each medical incident and an aggregate limit for each coverage.
> Current forms permit the company to settle a claim without the physician's or surgeon's consent.

KEY CONCEPTS AND TERMS

Advertising injury

Aviation insurance

Bailee coverage named-
perils policy

Basic extended reporting
period

Bodily injury and property
damage

Business auto coverage
form

Business liability coverage
form

Claims-made policy

Commercial general
liability (CGL) policy

Commercial umbrella
policy

Completed operations

Contingent liability

Contractual liability

Directors and officers
liability policy

Each-occurrence limit

Employers liability
insurance

Employment practices
liability insurance

Errors and omissions
insurance

Fire legal liability

Garage coverage form

General aggregate limit

Liquor liability law
(dramshop law)

Long-tail

Medical payments

Occurrence

Occurrence policy

Other-states insurance

Personal injury

Physicians liability
insurance

Products-completed
operations aggregate limit

Products-completed
operations hazard

Products liability

Property damage to
impaired property

Property damage to the
insured's product

Property damage to the
insured's work

Retained limit

Voluntary compensation
endorsement

Workers compensation and
employer liability
insurance

REVIEW QUESTIONS

1. Identify the major general liability loss exposures of business firms.

2. Define each of the following:

   a. Products liability

   b. Completed operations liability

   c. Contractual liability

   d. Contingent liability

3. Briefly describe the meaning of "products and completed operations hazard."

4. Briefly explain the major coverages in the commercial general liability policy.

5. Explain the difference between an occurrence policy and a claims-made policy.

6. Describe the three coverages in the insuring agreements of a workers compensation policy. Why is coverage for employers liability (Part Two) needed?

7. Describe the major features of the business auto coverage form and the garage coverage form.

8. Briefly explain the major coverages that are used to insure aircraft.

9. Why is liability insurance needed by a bailee? In your answer, give a brief description of the bailee coverage named-perils policy.

10. Briefly describe the major features of the commercial umbrella policy.

11. Explain the major characteristics of a professional liability policy.

APPLICATION QUESTIONS

1. Mario owns an appliance and furniture store and is insured under a commercial general liability policy written on an occurrence basis. Explain whether Mario's CGL policy would provide coverage for each of the following situations:

   a. Mario forcibly detained a customer whom he erroneously accused of shoplifting. Eight months later, after the policy had expired, the customer sued Mario for defamation of character.

   b. Mario's employees were delivering a large desk to a customer's house. The customer's front door and the desk were scratched and damaged when the desk hit the door. The customer immediately filed a claim for the damage to the door and the desk.

   c. An advertising firm sues Mario for using copyrighted material without permission when the material first appears in a special holiday ad. Mario maintains that the ad material is original and belongs to him.

   d. Unknown to Mario, an automatic dishwasher had a defective part. One week after the dishwasher was installed in a customer's house, it malfunctioned and caused considerable water damage to the kitchen carpet. The homeowner holds Mario responsible for the damage.

e. An employee accidentally knocked over a heavy lamp that injured a customer's foot. The customer later presents a bill for medical expenses to Mario for payment.

2. Carla operates a sporting goods store in a rented location at a shopping mall. She is insured under a CGL policy with the following limits:

General aggregate limit $1,000,000

Products-completed operations aggregate limit 1,000,000

Personal and advertising injury limit   250,000

Each-occurrence limit   300,000

Fire damage limit (any one fire)   100,000

Medical expense limit (any one person)   5000

The propane tank that Carla kept in the store exploded. Indicate the dollar amount, if any, that Carla's insurer will pay for each of the following losses:

a. Three customers were injured by flying debris with medical expenses of $6000, $7500, and $5000, respectively.

b. A fire resulted from the explosion. Damages are $50,000.

c. The store had to suspend operations for three months. Carla's lost profits are estimated to total $20,000. She also had continuing expenses of $10,000 during the period of suspension.

3. Joanna owns and operates a small retail food store in a suburban shopping center. The store is insured for liability coverage under a businessowners policy. Indicate with reasons whether the following situations are covered under Joanna's businessowners policy. Treat each situation separately.

a. A clerk accidentally injures a customer with a shopping cart. Both Joanna and the clerk are sued.

b. A customer slips on a wet floor and breaks a leg.

c. Joanna has a customer arrested for shoplifting. The customer is innocent and sues for damages.

d. A woman returns a spoiled package of gourmet cheese and demands her money back.

e. Joanna has a Christmas party for her employees after the store closes. One employee gets drunk and injures another motorist while driving home. The injured motorist sues both Joanna and the employee.

4. A surgeon is insured under a physicians, surgeons, and dentists professional liability policy. Indicate with reasons whether the following situations are covered by the professional liability policy. Treat each situation separately.

a. An office nurse gives a patient a wrong drug. Both the physician and the nurse are sued.

b. The surgeon sets the broken arm of a patient. The patient sues because the arm becomes deformed and crooked.

c. A patient waiting to see the doctor is injured when the legs of an office chair collapse.

SELECTED REFERENCES

Fire, Casualty & Surety Bulletins. Fire and Marine volume. Cincinnati, OH: National Underwriter Company. Casualty & Surety volume. The bulletins are published monthly. Detailed information on all forms of commercial liability insurance can be found in this volume.

Malecki, Donald S., and Arthur L. Flitner. *Commercial Liability Insurance and Risk Management*, fourth edition, Vol. 1. Malvern, PA: American Institute for CPCU, 1998.

Malecki, Donald S., et al. *Commercial Liability Insurance and Risk Management*, third edition, Vol. 2. Malvern, PA: American Institute for CPCU, 1996.

The CPCU Handbook of Insurance Policies, third edition. Malvern, PA: American Institute for CPCU/Insurance Institute of America, 1998.

Webb, Bernard L., Arthur L. Flitner, and Jerome Trupin, *Commercial Insurance*, third edition. Malvern, PA: Insurance Institute of America, 1996.

NOTES

1. Emmett J. Vaughan, and Therese M. Vaughan, *Fundamentals of Risk and Insurance,* eighth edition. (New York, NY: Wiley, 1999), p. 613.

2. This section is based on *Fire, Casualty & Surety Bulletins*, Casualty and Surety volume, Public Liability section (Cincinnati, OH: National Underwriter Company); and Bernard L. Webb, Arthur L. Flitner, and Jerome Trupin, *Commercial Insurance*, third edition (Malvern, PA: Insurance Institute of America, 1996). The author also drew on the various commercial general liability forms of the Insurance Services Office (copyrighted) that appeared in *The CPCU Handbook of Insurance Policies*, third edition (Malvern, PA: American Institute for CPCU/Insurance Institute of America, 1998). The author drew heavily on these sources in the preparation of this chapter.

Case Application

a. Lastovica Construction is insured under a commercial general liability (CGL) policy. The firm agreed to build a new plant for the Smith Corporation. A heavy machine used by Lastovica Construction accidentally fell from the roof of the partially completed plant. Mike, an employee of the firm, was severely injured when the falling machine crushed his foot. Tara, a pedestrian, was also injured by the machine while walking on a public sidewalk in front of the building.

 (1) Tara sued both Lastovica Construction and the Smith Corporation for her injury. Indicate the extent, if any, of the CGL insurer's obligation to provide a legal defense for Lastovica Construction.

 (2) What legal defense could the Smith Corporation use to counter Tara's claim based on the nature of its relationship with Lastovica Construction? Explain your answer.

 (3) Does Lastovica Construction have any responsibility for Mike's medical expenses and lost wages? Explain.

b. Jacques owns a restaurant that is insured under a claims-made CGL policy. The policy term is January 1, 1999, through December 31, 1999. On December 15, 1999, a customer became violently ill from eating a piece of banana cream pie that had become contaminated. On February 1, 2000, the customer made a claim against Jacques for the illness. Jacques had no prior notice that the customer had become ill. Explain with reasons whether Jacques's policy will cover the loss.

---

3. The workers compensation and employers liability policy is discussed in detail in *Fire, Casualty & Surety Bulletins*, Casualty and Surety volume, Workers Compensation section (Cincinnati, OH: National Underwriter Company).

4. This section is based on the *Fire, Casualty & Surety Bulletins*, Casualty and Surety volume, Auto section (Cincinnati, OH: National Underwriter Company), and the business auto coverage form and garage coverage form found in *The CPCU Handbook of Insurance Policies*, pp. 347–377.

5. Aviation insurance is discussed in *Fire, Casualty & Surety Bulletins*, Companies & Coverages volume, Aircraft-Marine Section (Cincinnati, OH: National Underwriter Company).

6. *1993–1994 Policy Kit for Insurance Professionals* (Schaumburg, IL: Alliance of American Insurers, 1993–94), pp. 356–358.

7. A detailed discussion of the commercial umbrella policy can be found in Webb et al., pp. 341–350. See also *The CPCU Handbook of Insurance Policies*, third edition, pp. 451–466.

8. A detailed discussion of the businessowners policy can be found in *Fire, Casualty & Surety Bulletins*, Fire and Marine volume, Commercial Property section (Cincinnati, OH: National Underwriter Company).

9. Professional liability insurance for physicians is discussed in *Fire, Casualty & Surety Bulletins*, Casualty and Surety volume, Public Liability section (Cincinnati, OH: National Underwriter Company).

C Students may take a self-administered test on this chapter at **www.awlonline.com/rejda**

Chapter 15

Crime Insurance and Surety Bonds

" Organized crime in America takes in over forty billion dollars a year and spends very little on office supplies. "

Woody Allen

Learning Objectives

After studying this chapter, you should be able to:

▲ Define burglary, robbery, and theft.

▲ Explain the coverage provided under the employee dishonesty coverage form.

▲ For a given crime coverage form, describe the coverage provided with respect to the property covered and the insured perils.

▲ Identify the three parties to a bond and show how surety bonds differ from insurance.

▲ Identify the major types of surety bonds and give an example where each can be used.

▲ Access an Internet site and obtain information about commercial crime insurance.

Internet Resources

- The **Coalition Against Insurance Fraud** is an alliance of consumer, law enforcement, and insurance industry groups that attempts to reduce all types of insurance fraud by public advocacy and education. Visit the site at:
  http://www.insurancefraud.org

- The **National Association of Surety Bond Producers** is a trade association of surety bond producers. Visit the site at:
  http://www.nasbp.org

- The **National Insurance Crime Bureau** is a nonprofit organization dedicated to combating crime and vehicle theft. Visit the site at:
  http://www.nicb.com

- The **Surety Association of America** is a statistical, rating, development, and advisory organization for surety companies. Visit the site at:
  http://www.surety.org

- The **Surety Information Office** is a source of information about contract surety bonds. Visit the site at:
  http://www.sio.org

Bill, age 42, is the president and major stockholder of a small bank in Waco, Texas. Bank examiners revealed that $25,000 had been recently withdrawn by a wire transfer from an account with no name or documentation. An investigation pointed to a computer programmer in a consulting firm that the bank hired three years earlier to update its computer system. The computer had been programmed to round down any fractional interest credits and to deposit the fractional cents into a special account. When the balance reached $25,000, the computer was programmed to wire the funds to a Swiss bank. The bank lost more than $100,000. Fortunately for Bill and the bank, a commercial crime insurance policy was in force that covered most of the computer fraud loss.

As this example shows, most firms need protection against crime loss exposures. In addition to losses through computer fraud, business firms incur billions of dollars of losses annually because of robbery, burglary, larceny, motor vehicle theft, and employee dishonesty. "White-collar" crimes such as embezzlement, fraud, and illegal activities are also widespread.

This chapter discusses the Insurance Services Office (ISO) commercial crime insurance program that protects business firms against robbery, burglary, theft, employee dishonesty, and other crime losses. It concludes with a discussion of surety bonds that provide indemnification to an injured party if the bonded party fails to perform.

COMMERCIAL CRIME INSURANCE PROGRAM

In 1986, ISO introduced a simplified-language commercial crime program to replace the older commercial crime insurance forms. Since then, the commercial crime program has been modified several times. The general format is similar to the commercial package policy discussed in Chapter 13.

Basic Definitions

Most property crimes against business firms are due to burglary, robbery, or theft. For purposes of insurance, **burglary** is defined as the taking of property from inside the premises by someone who unlawfully enters or exits the premises, leaving behind marks of forcible entry or exit. **Robbery** is defined as the taking of property from a person by someone who (1) has caused or threatens to cause bodily harm to that person, or (2) has committed an obviously unlawful act that is witnessed by that person. **Theft** is a much broader term and is defined as any act of stealing. It includes burglary and robbery, as well as shoplifting and employee theft.

Common Crime Insurance Provisions

Under the ISO program, a *crime general provisions form* is included in most crime policies. The general provisions form contains common crime insurance provisions that apply to most crime coverages. It is beyond the scope of this text to discuss each provision in detail. However, certain common provisions are extremely important in understanding commercial crime insurance. They include the following:

- Dishonest acts committed by the insured
- Indirect loss
- Discovery period for a loss
- Loss sustained during prior insurance
- Noncumulation of limit of insurance

Dishonest Acts Committed by the Insured Loss that results from any dishonest or criminal act committed by the insured or by any partners of the insured is specifically excluded.

Indirect Loss Any indirect loss that results from a covered loss is specifically excluded. For example, if the business is temporarily closed because of property damage by a burglar, the business income loss is not covered.

Discovery Period for a Loss The **discovery period** means that the insurer will pay for a covered loss that occurs during the policy period if the loss is discovered no later than one year after the policy period ends. *The purpose of this provision is to provide coverage for a loss that occurs during the policy period but is not discovered until after the policy expires.* For example, if a $10,000 loss is discovered during the discovery period and traced to an employee who stole the money before the policy expired, the loss would be covered up to the limit of insurance.

Loss Sustained During Prior Insurance Another important provision is titled **loss sustained during prior insurance**. *Under this provision, the current policy provides coverage for a loss that occurred during the term of the prior policy but was discovered only after the discovery period under the prior policy had expired.*

The purpose of this provision is to enable an employer to change insurers without penalty. This provision applies only if there is no break in the continuity of coverage under both policies. The current policy must become effective at the time of cancellation or termination of the previous policy. In addition, the loss must have been covered by the current policy had it been in effect when the prior loss occurred.

The maximum recovery under this provision is limited to the policy limit under the previous policy, or the limit of insurance under the current policy, whichever is less.

Noncumulation of Insurance Limits Another common provision is referred to as **noncumulation of limit of insurance**. The limit of insurance stated in the policy is not cumulative. Thus, regardless of the number of years the insurance is in force, the limit of insurance is not cumulative from year to year. For example, if the limit of insurance is $10,000, and a dishonest treasurer embezzles $50,000 over a five-year period, the maximum amount paid for the loss is $10,000, not $50,000.

Commercial Crime Coverage Forms

Numerous crime coverage forms are currently used.[1] Each form is designated by a letter (see Exhibit 15.1). Forms A, B, O, and P have been developed by the Surety Association of America. The remaining forms are designed by ISO. The crime coverage forms can be issued separately as a monoline policy or as part of a commercial package policy.

Form A. Employee Dishonesty Form A covers the loss of money, securities, and property other than money and securities that result from the dishonest acts of employees. **Employee dishonesty** *is defined to mean dishonest acts committed by an employee alone, or in collusion with others, that result in loss to the insured or financial benefit to the employee.* Examples of covered losses include embezzlement of funds by the company's treasurer; stealing by a cashier; theft of goods by a factory worker; and even unauthorized discounts to friends by a salesperson.

There are two employee dishonesty coverage forms. One form provides **blanket coverage** that covers all employees for their dishonest acts. The other form provides **scheduled coverage** in which individual employees or positions are identified. Scheduled coverage, in turn, is written on a **name schedule** or **position schedule** basis. Under a name schedule, the names of covered employees are listed in a schedule, and the limit of insurance that applies to each employee is also stated. Under a position schedule, the schedule identifies the covered positions, location of the positions, and the number of employees occupying each position.

The blanket form provides coverage on a *per-loss basis*, which means that the maximum amount paid for any one occurrence is the limit of insurance stated in the declarations. *An occurrence is a loss involving one or more employees, whether the result of a single act or series of acts.* Thus, the maximum insurance limit applies in the event of collusion by two

EXHIBIT 15.1
Crime Coverage Forms

Form A	Employee Dishonesty (Blanket)
Form A	Employee Dishonesty (Schedule)
Form B	Forgery or Alteration
Form C	Theft, Disappearance, and Destruction
Form D	Robbery and Safe Burglary—Property Other Than Money and Securities
Form E	Premises Burglary
Form F	Computer Fraud
Form G	Extortion
Form H	Premises Theft and Robbery Outside the Premises—Property Other Than Money and Securities
Form I	Lessees of Safe Deposit Boxes
Form J	Securities Depostied with Others
Form K	Liability for Guests' Property—Safe Deposit Box
Form L	Liability for Guests' Property—Premises
Form M	Safe Depository Liability
Form N	Safe Depository Direct Loss
Form O	Public Employee Dishonesty (Per Loss)
Form P	Public Employee Dishonesty (Per Employee)
Form Q	Robbery and Safe Burglary—Money and Securities
Form R	Money Orders and Counterfeit Paper Currency

SOURCE: Bernard L. Webb, Arthur L. Flitner, and Jerome Trupin, *Commercial Insurance*, third edition (Malvern, PA: Insurance Institute of America, 1996), Exhibit 5-1, p. 119.

or more employees. For example, assume that the limit of insurance is $20,000 and that two cashiers acting together over a period of months have embezzled $40,000. This loss is considered one occurrence, and only $20,000 will be paid.

In contrast, under the scheduled form, coverage applies on a *per-employee basis. In this form, an occurrence is defined as loss caused by each employee, whether the result of a single act or series of acts.* The most the insurer is obligated to pay for any loss is the limit of insurance shown in the schedule for each employee. Referring back to our earlier example, if both employees who are parties to the theft are named in the schedule or occupy a covered position, there would be two occurrences. Assuming the limit of insurance on each employee is $20,000, the maximum paid would be $40,000.

Employee dishonesty insurance also contains several important exclusions and limitations, including the following:

- *Employee canceled under prior insurance.* There is no coverage for any loss caused by an employee for whom coverage has been canceled under a previous policy and not reinstated since the last cancellation.
- *Inventory shortages.* There is no coverage for any loss if proof of loss depends on an inventory computation or on a profit and loss computation. The intent here is to exclude inventory losses, such as errors in record keeping, that may not be due to employee dishonesty.
- *Cancellation as to any employee.* The insured must notify the insurer of any dishonest act even though the loss does not exceed the deductible. The insurance coverage ceases immediately on that employee involved in the dishonest act. The firm could encounter some serious coverage problems if a minor loss by a dishonest employee is not reported. If that employee later became involved in another loss, and the insurer became

aware of the earlier loss, the insured would have no coverage.

Employee thefts are widespread and cause billions of dollars of losses each year to business firms. Many employees steal from their employers because they believe they are not being paid their true worth. Therefore, the employees "settle the score" by stealing (see Insight 15.1).

Form B. Forgery or Alteration

Form B provides coverage against loss that results from the forgery or alteration of checks, drafts, bills of exchange, promissory notes, and similar instruments. For example, a cashier in a supermarket may cash a forged $500 payroll check for a customer. This loss would be covered. Loss caused by the insured's employees, officers, and directors is specifically excluded. These groups are covered for dishonest acts under Form A, as discussed earlier.

Form C. Theft, Disappearance, and Destruction

Form C covers the theft, disappearance, or destruction of money and securities **inside the premises**. Containers of covered property such as a cash register, safe, vault, or cash box are also covered. For example, a bank may be held up; money may be destroyed in a fire or a tornado; or a cash register or safe may be damaged in a burglary. These losses would be covered.

The form also provides coverage **outside the premises** while the property is in the care and custody of a messenger. A messenger is defined as the named insured, any partner, or any employee who has custody of the money or securities outside the premises. For example, the owner of a retail store may be robbed of the day's receipts while taking the money to a bank. In addition, the loss of money or securities in the custody of an armored-car company is covered. The amount payable is limited only to the amount of loss that cannot be recovered from the armored-car company.

Form D. Robbery and Safe Burglary—Property Other Than Money and Securities

Form D covers the robbery of property inside the premises other than money and securities while in the care of a custodian. A custodian is defined as the named insured, any partner, or any employee who has custody of the property inside the premises, with the exception of a watchperson or janitor. For example, if the owner of an art shop is robbed of several valuable paintings, the loss would be covered.

The form also covers the loss of property other than money and securities from **safe burglary inside the premises**. Damage to the premises, safe, or vault is covered if the insured owns the property or is legally liable for damages. For example, a burglar may break into a safe inside the premises. The loss of property inside the safe, other than money and securities, and damage to the building and safe are all covered.

The form also covers **robbery outside the premises** if the property is in the care of a messenger. A messenger is defined as the named insured, any partner, or any employee who has custody of the property outside the premises. For example, a garment shop employee may be pushing a cart of clothes to a parking lot for a special sale. If someone grabs an expensive coat and runs away, the loss is covered even though no threats are made. (Remember the definition of robbery also includes the witnessing of an unlawful act.)

Form E. Premises Burglary

Form E provides coverage for premises burglary and robbery of a watchperson. Covered property is property inside the premises other than money or securities. For example, if a retail television store is burglarized and several sets are stolen, the loss would be covered. *To be a covered burglary loss, there must be marks of forcible entry or exit.* Damage to the premises is also covered. For example, if a thief cuts a hole in the roof to gain entry, the damage to the roof is covered if the insured owns the building or is legally liable for damages.

Robbery of a watchperson is covered as well. If property inside the premises is stolen by violence or threat of violence to a security guard on duty, the loss would be covered.

Form F. Computer Fraud

Form F covers the theft of money, securities, and property by computer fraud. For example, a personal computer may be used to gain access to a business computer. The business computer may be instructed to issue a check to a fictitious person. If the check is issued and cashed, the theft loss would be covered.

Insight 15.1

Settling the Score: Pilfering at Work Is Not Uncommon

Connecticut Bob (not his real name) is in Virginia on business—he travels a lot for his company—when he spots a great toolbox at Sears.

A perfect Father's Day gift, he decides, as he fishes out his credit card.

But as he lugs the purchase to his rental car, he wonders: "how in the heck am I going to get this huge thing home?"

His solution was simple: Ship it by Federal Express and charge the $100 or so fee to his company's business account.

"I rationalized that if the company wants me to do this much traveling, I don't have the time at home to shop," Connecticut Bob said.

His story is not unusual: *Recent studies show that nearly half of American workers surveyed admit to stealing something from their employers, whether it was cash, envelopes, long-distance phone time, laptop computers, food. Even toilet paper.*

The numbers are even higher, closer to 60 percent, when researchers factor in what's called "time theft"—coming in late to work, leaving early, abusing sick days, or simply not showing up.

"Major taking or stealing is, obviously, very rare," said Roy Lewicki, a management professor at Ohio State University's Fisher College of Business and an employee theft expert.

"But minor taking is not uncommon—a dozen pencils here, a handful of paper there," Lewicki said. "And doing less than a full day's work for full day's pay? That's rampant."

Workers, most of whom consider themselves generally honest, have been pilfering from their employers forever—slipping batteries into their pockets for Junior's train set, tossing an unstamped Mother's Day card or a handful of bills into the office mail bin, copying and faxing cartoons to friends or resumes to prospective employers.

While hard statistics are scarce, some sociologists theorize that the nation's shift from manufacturing to a service-driven economy may be leading to an upswing in employee theft. If the recent rise in firms offering workplace surveillance and investigation services is any indication, they could be right.

Why do generally honest employees take from the hand that feeds them? And how do they convince themselves that it's OK?

Lewicki said employees who steal generally have a score to settle—a sense that "what they are getting back from the organization is worth less than what they're giving to the organization."

His studies have shown that while employees acknowledge that their behavior may be dishonest, they have moved the line between what's wrong and what's acceptable.

"They say to themselves that it's only a little bit, that it's not going to hurt anybody, and no one is going to miss it," Lewicki said. "In their mind, this wasn't taking."

Feelings of being owed something beyond what they find in their paycheck are magnified by the disintegrating relationship between companies and workers, some experts say.

"In this era of downsizing, and with a movement toward more marginal work, more part-time, more temporary, and more low-paying jobs, the bonds between employee and employer may be weakened," said Douglas Eichar, a sociology professor at the University of Hartford.

One-third of workers surveyed in a national study on workplace pressure cited the effects of downsizing as contributing to their tendency to act unethically or dishonestly.

So, as the implicit contract between employee and employer shifts to something more tenuous than it has been, workers seem more willing to take a little here, a little there.

Connecticut Bob put it this way: "I considered it one of the benefits the company should be able to extend for the sacrifices we make. Maybe it wasn't the most honest thing to do, but it hasn't come back to haunt me."

SOURCE: Adapted from "Settling the Score: Pilfering at Work Is Not Uncommon," *Omaha World-Herald*, August 9, 1997, p. 7. Copyright The Hartford Courant. Reprinted with permission.

Computer crimes are widespread, and most major corporations are victims of computer-related crimes. These crimes include credit card fraud, unauthorized access to confidential files, telecommunication fraud, and unlawful copying of computer software programs.

Form G. Extortion Form G covers extortion losses. Extortion *is the surrender of property away from the premises as a result of a threat to do bodily harm to the named insured, relative, or invitee who is being held captive.* For example, if Fred arrives at work and receives a phone call that his wife is being held captive and will be harmed unless $100,000 is delivered to a location away from the premises, the loss is potentially recoverable. However, the loss is excluded if the property is surrendered before making a reasonable effort to report the extortionist's demands to the FBI, local authorities, or an associate of the named insured.

Form H. Premises Theft and Robbery Outside the Premises—Property Other Than Money and Securities Form H covers the theft of property, other than money and securities, inside the premises and robbery outside the premises while in the care and custody of a custodian. The property is covered against actual or attempted theft, which is defined as any act of stealing. This form can be used by a firm that wants the broader coverage provided by the theft peril rather than the narrower perils of burglary and robbery.

Form I. Lessees of Safe Deposit Boxes Form I covers the theft of securities, and burglary and robbery of property other than money and securities, while inside a safe deposit box or during the course of deposit or removal from the box. Section 1 of the form covers securities against loss by theft, disappearance, or destruction. Section 2 of the form covers property other than money and securities against loss by burglary, robbery, and vandalism. For example, if a burglar breaks into a safe deposit box and steals some securities and jewelry, the loss is covered.

Form J. Securities Deposited with Others Form J covers the theft, disappearance, or destruction of securities deposited with others, such as with a bank or stock brokerage firm. For example, if shares of common stock are deposited in a bank as collateral for a loan, and the securities disappear or are stolen, the loss would be covered.

Form K. Liability for Guests' Property—Safe Deposit Box Form K covers the legal liability of the insured for loss or damage to the property of guests while in a safe deposit box on the premises. The policy is based on legal liability. Loss to the property of guests is not covered unless the insured is legally liable. For example, if a guest's jewelry is deposited in a hotel's safe deposit box and is stolen, the loss would be covered.

Form L. Liability for Guests' Property—Premises Form L covers the legal liability of the insured arising out of the property of guests inside the premises and in the insured's possession. The form excludes coverage for loss to vehicles and their equipment, property inside the vehicle, and samples or articles held for sale or delivery. For example, if a motel carelessly damages the luggage of a guest, the loss would be covered.

Form M. Safe Depository Liability Form M covers the insured's legal liability arising out of loss or damage to the property of customers while inside a safe deposit box or vault, or temporarily elsewhere on the premises while in the course of deposit or removal from the box or vault. Customers' property is defined as money, securities, and property other than money and securities.

This form is designed for insureds, other than financial institutions, that provide safe deposit facilities. There are hundreds of private safe deposit companies operating in the United States at the present time. Financial institutions, however, such as banks and savings and loans institutions, are ineligible for coverage. Financial institutions can obtain coverage under a bankers blanket bond or other financial institution bond.

Form N. Safe Depository Direct Loss Form N provides coverage for direct damage to the property of customers while inside a safe deposit box or vault, or temporarily elsewhere on the premises in the course of deposit or removal from the safe or vault. The covered causes of loss are actual or attempted robbery or burglary, destruction, and damage.

Form O. Public Employee Dishonesty—Per Loss

Form O is designed to cover employee dishonesty for government entities. The form covers the loss of money, securities, and property other than money and securities against dishonest acts by employees. The limit of insurance applies to each loss. In Form O, an occurrence is defined to mean all loss caused by one or more employees in a single act or series of acts.

Form P. Public Employee Dishonesty—Per Employee

Form P is similar to Form O except that the limit of insurance applies to each employee. An occurrence is defined to mean all losses caused by each employee in a single act or series of acts.

Form Q. Robbery and Safe Burglary—Money and Securities

Form Q covers the robbery of a custodian inside the premises, safe burglary inside the premises, and robbery of a messenger outside the premises. The form covers only money and securities.

Form R. Money Orders and Counterfeit Paper Currency

Form R covers losses due to money orders that are not paid upon presentation and counterfeit paper currency. For example, if a supermarket accepts a stolen American Express money order in the amount of $250, the loss would be covered.

ISO Crime Coverage Plans

The various commercial crime coverage forms just discussed can be combined to meet the specialized needs of business firms and to approximate the protection provided under the previous crime insurance program. ISO has numerous crime coverage plans, which describe the different ways in which the crime coverage forms can be combined to obtain the desired protection.

It is beyond the scope of this text to discuss each crime coverage plan in detail. However, *Plan 1, Commercial Crime*, can be used as an illustration. Plan 1 permits the use of any combination of coverage forms A through J, as well as Q, to meet the crime insurance needs of a particular firm. For example, Heavenly Hamburgers, a fast-food chain, may want protection against employee dishonesty (Form A), robbery and safe burglary (Form D), and coverage for the theft, disappearance, and destruction of money and securities (Form C). This combination will meet most commercial crime exposures faced by the firm.

Finally, in addition to the crime coverages just discussed, a few insurers offer highly specialized coverages for certain loss exposures such as the kidnap and ransom of wealthy individuals and celebrities (see Insight 15.2).

SURETY BONDS

A **surety bond** *is a bond that provides monetary compensation if the bonded party fails to perform certain promised acts.* For example, a contractor may be financially overextended and unable to complete a building project. A public official may embezzle public funds, or the executor of an estate may illegally convert part of the estate assets to his or her own use. Surety bonds can be used to meet these loss exposures.[2]

Parties to a Surety Bond

There are always three parties to a surety bond:

- Principal
- Obligee
- Surety

The **principal** *is the party who agrees to perform certain acts or fulfill certain obligations.* For example, Lastovica Construction may agree to build an office building for the city of Omaha. If the company is required to obtain a performance bond before the contract is awarded, Lastovica Construction would be known as the principal.

The **obligee** *is the party who is reimbursed for damages if the principal fails to perform.* In the previous example, the city of Omaha would be reimbursed for damages if Lastovica Construction failed to complete the building on time or according to contract specifications.

Insight 15.2

Kidnapping Insurance Is Growth Business

Overseas business travelers have so many things to remember: passport, briefcase, that Berlitz pocket dictionary, and, oh yeah, the kidnapping insurance policy.

Kidnap-and-ransom insurance is becoming increasingly popular as a means of protecting one's assets against blackmail, extortion, and hijacking.

One of the fastest-growing markets is Mexico, where hundreds of people have become victims of ransom kidnapping during the past decade.

"Wealthy people down there buy these policies like you would buy homeowner's insurance," said Bill Harrison, assistant vice president with American International Underwriters, the international arm of insurance company American International Group.

Premiums vary, but some brokers offer $1 million worth of coverage for as little as $500 or $1000 per year.

The price includes a policy, professional advice from a security firm, access to highly trained negotiators, and even a 30-day paid vacation for policy holders and their families after a kidnap ordeal.

Sales have risen steadily through the decade, according to AIG. Companies say the upsurge may be due to increased kidnap risk, or it could be that more small insurance brokers are advertising the product.

And kidnapping insurance also includes other coverages.

Extortion coverage appeals to many small companies, since even a dairy farmer could fall victim to a worker's threat to contaminate the milk supply, companies said.

But for multinational corporations, ransom coverage is the big draw. Just last month, eight armed men swept into one of Mexico City's main Chrysler dealerships and scooped up an executive. He was freed a month later.

Insurance companies declined to say how much they were willing to pay policyholders so as not to inspire would-be kidnappers or extortionists.

Policyholders are also mum. If they say how much coverage they have, the policy is voided.

Source: "Kidnapping Insurance Is Growth Business," *Lincoln Journal Star*, June 27, 1998, p. 5B. Reprinted with permission from the Associated Press.

The surety is the final party to a bond. The **surety (obligor)** *is the party who agrees to answer for the debt, default, or obligation of another.* For example, Lastovica Construction may purchase a performance bond from United Fidelity. If Lastovica Construction (principal) fails to perform, the city of Omaha (obligee) would be reimbursed for any loss by United Fidelity (surety).

Comparison of Surety Bonds and Insurance

Surety bonds are similar to insurance contracts in that both provide protection against specified losses. However, there are some important differences between them, as listed in Exhibit 15.2.

Types of Surety Bonds

Different types of surety bonds can be used to meet specific needs and situations. Although surety bonds are not uniform and have different characteristics, they can generally be grouped into the following categories:

- Contract bonds
    Bid bond
    Performance bond
    Payment bond
    Maintenance bond
- License and permit bonds
- Public official bonds
- Judicial bonds
    Fiduciary bond
    Court bond

EXHIBIT 15.2
Comparison of Insurance and Surety Bonds

Insurance

1. There are two parties to an insurance contract.
2. The insurer expects to pay losses. The premium reflects expected loss costs.
3. The insurer normally does not have the right to recover a loss payment from the insured.
4. Insurance is designed to cover unintentional losses that ideally are outside of the insured's control.

Surety bonds

1. There are three parties to a bond.
2. The surety theoretically expects no losses to occur. The premium is viewed as a service fee, by which the surety's credit is substituted for that of the principal.
3. The surety has the legal right to recover a loss payment from the defaulting principal.
4. The surety guarantees the principal's character, honesty, integrity, and ability to perform. These qualities are within the principal's control.

- Federal surety bonds
- Miscellaneous surety bonds

Contract Bonds A **contract bond** *guarantees that the principal will fulfill all contractual obligations.* There are several types of contract bonds. Under a *bid bond*, the owner (obligee) is guaranteed that the party awarded a bid on a project will sign a contract and furnish a performance bond. Under a *performance bond*, the owner is guaranteed that work will be completed according to the contract specifications. For example, if a building is not completed, the surety is responsible for completion of the project and the extra expense in hiring another contractor.

A *payment bond* guarantees that the bills for labor and materials used in building the project will be paid by the contractor when the bills are due. A *maintenance bond* guarantees that poor workmanship by the principal will be corrected, or defective materials will be replaced. This maintenance guarantee is often included in a performance bond for one year without additional charge.

Exhibit 15.3 compares the various types of contract bonds.

License and Permit Bonds These types of bonds are commonly required of persons who must obtain a license or permit from a city or town before they can engage in certain activities. A **license and permit bond** *guarantees that the person bonded will comply with all laws and regulations that govern his or her activities.* For example, a liquor store owner may post a bond guaranteeing that liquor will be sold according to the law. A plumber or electrician may post a bond guaranteeing that the work performed will comply with the local building code.

Public Official Bonds This type of bond is usually required by law for public officials who are elected or appointed to public office. A **public official bond** *guarantees that public officials will faithfully perform their duties for the protection of the public.* For example, a state treasurer must comply with state law governing the deposit of public funds.

Judicial Bonds Judicial bonds *guarantee that the party bonded will fulfill certain obligations specified by law.* There are two classes of judicial bonds. The first type, a *fiduciary bond,* guarantees that the person responsible for the property of another will faithfully exercise his or her duties, give an accounting of all property received, and make up any deficiency for which the courts hold the fiduciary liable. For example, administrators of estates, receivers or

EXHIBIT 15.3

Comparison of Contract Bonds

	Obligee	*Principal*	*Guarantee*
Bid bond	The owner or the party calling for the bid	The bidder	The bidder will enter into the contract and provide a performance bond if the bid is accepted.
Performance bond	The property owner or the party having the work done	The contractor	The contract will be performed by the contractor according to plans and specifications.
Payment bond	Same as performance bond	The contractor	The project will be free of liens—that is, certain bills for labor and materials will be paid.
Maintenance bond	Same as performance bond	The contractor	The work will be free from defects in materials and workmanship for a specified period.

SOURCE: Donald S. Malecki, et al., *Commercial Liability Insurance and Risk Management*, third edition, Vol. 2 (Malvern, PA: American Institute for CPCU, 1996), p. 209.

liquidators, or guardians of minor children may be required to post a bond guaranteeing their performance.

The second type of judicial bond, a *court bond*, is designed to protect one person (obligee) against loss in the event that the person bonded does not prove that he or she is legally entitled to the remedy sought against the obligee. For example, *an attachment bond* guarantees that if the court rules against the plaintiff who has attached the property of the defendant in a lawsuit, the defendant will be reimbursed for damages as a result of having the property attached.

Finally, a *bail bond* is another type of court bond. If the bonded person fails to appear in court at the appointed time, the entire bond may be forfeited.

Federal Surety Bonds These bonds are required by federal agencies that regulate the actions of business firms such as manufacturers, wholesalers, and large import firms. A **federal surety bond** *guarantees that the bonded party will comply with federal standards.*

The bond also guarantees the payment of taxes or duties that accrue if the bonded party fails to pay.

Miscellaneous Surety Bonds This category consists of bonds that cannot be classified in any other group. For example, an *auctioneer's bond* guarantees the faithful accounting of sales proceeds by an auctioneer; a *lost-instrument bond* guarantees the obligee against loss if the original instrument (such as a lost stock certificate) turns up in the possession of another party; and an *insurance agent bond* indemnifies an insurer for any penalties that may result from the unlawful acts of agents.

SUMMARY

- *Burglary* is the taking of property from inside the premises by someone who unlawfully enters or leaves the premises, and there are marks of forcible entry or exit.

- *Robbery* is the taking of property from a person by

someone who has caused or threatens to cause bodily harm to that person or who has committed an obviously unlawful act that is witnessed by that person.

- *Theft* is any act of stealing.

- There are a wide variety of crime coverage forms in the commercial crime program developed by the Insurance Services Office. The coverage forms are designed to meet the commercial crime exposures of business firms.

- The *employee dishonesty coverage form (Form A)* covers the loss of money, securities, and property other than money and securities that results from the dishonest acts of employees.

- Several exclusions and limitations apply to the employee dishonesty coverage form, including the following:

  Loss caused by an employee who has been canceled under a previous policy and has not been reinstated is specifically excluded.

  There is no coverage for an inventory shortage if proof of loss depends on an inventory computation or on a profit or loss computation.

  The insured is required to notify the insurer of any dishonest act. Coverage ceases immediately on the employee involved in the dishonest act.

- The various crime coverage forms can be combined to meet the specialized needs of business firms. The Insurance Services Office has a number of plans that combine the various crime coverage forms and endorsements.

- There are three parties to a surety bond. The *principal* is the party who agrees to perform certain obligations. The *obligee* is the party who is reimbursed for damages if the principal fails to perform. The *surety* is the party who agrees to answer for the debt, default, or obligation of another.

- Surety bonds are similar to insurance contracts in that losses are expected. However, there are several major differences between surety bonds and insurance.

  There are two parties to an insurance contract; there are three parties to a bond.

  The insurer expects to pay losses; the surety theoretically expects no losses to occur.

  The insurer normally does not have the right to recover a loss payment from the insured; the surety has the right to recover from a defaulting principal.

  Insurance covers unintentional losses outside of the insured's control; the surety guarantees the princi-

pal's character and ability to perform, which are within the principal's control.

- Surety bonds guarantee the performance of the principal. They include various contract bonds, license and permit bonds, public official bonds, judicial bonds, federal surety bonds, and miscellaneous surety bonds.

KEY CONCEPTS AND TERMS

Blanket coverage
Burglary
Commercial crime coverage forms
Contract bond
Discovery period
Employee dishonesty
Employee dishonesty coverage form (Form A)
Extortion
Federal surety bond
Forgery or alteration coverage form (Form B)
Inside the premises
ISO crime coverage plans
Judicial bond
License and permit bond
Loss sustained during prior insurance
Name schedule
Noncumulation of limit of insurance

Obligee
Outside the premises
Position schedule
Premises burglary coverage form (Form E)
Principal
Public official bond
Robbery
Robbery and safe burglary coverage form (Form D)
Robbery outside the premises
Safe burglary inside the premises
Scheduled coverage
Surety (obligor)
Surety bond
Theft
Theft, disappearance, and destruction coverage form (Form C)

REVIEW QUESTIONS

1. Define burglary, robbery, and theft.

2. Briefly describe some common policy provisions that apply to most commercial crime coverages.

3. Briefly describe the various documents that form a complete commercial crime policy under the crime insurance program developed by the Insurance Services Office.

4. Briefly describe the coverage provided by the employee dishonesty coverage form.

5. Briefly explain the exclusions and limitations under the employee dishonesty coverage form.

6. Identify three other crime coverage forms and give an example where each can be used.

7. Describe the three parties to a surety bond.

8. How do surety bonds differ from insurance contracts?

9. Identify three surety bonds and give an example where each can be used.

APPLICATION QUESTIONS

1. Southeast Community College is insured under a theft, disappearance, and destruction coverage form with an insurance limit of $25,000. What dollar amount, if any, will the insurer pay for the following losses that resulted from a single theft in the business office? If the loss is not covered, or not fully covered, explain why not.
   a. $2000 damage to the building when a thief broke into the business office
   b. $3000 to replace student records taken from a file cabinet
   c. $15,000 in cash taken from a locked cash box that was pried open
   d. $10,000 in negotiable bonds that were stolen from a safe in the business office

2. Carmine owns several retail stores. The employees are insured under the employee dishonesty coverage form with an insurance limit of $10,000. Carmine discovered that Iris, a long-time accountant, had embezzled $3000 from the firm to pay the gambling debts of her son, who had been threatened with bodily harm. Iris agreed to repay the firm, and the embezzlement was not reported to the insurer. Several months later, Iris stole $2000 from the company's cash receipts and then disappeared. What is the liability of the insurer, if any, for the loss? Explain your answer.

3. Clocktower Super Market is insured under an employee dishonesty coverage form that was issued on January 1, 1999. The coverage is written on a *blanket basis*, and the limit of insurance is $10,000. The coverage terminated on January 1, 2000, and was replaced with a new policy by another insurer on the same date with a policy term of one year. What dollar amount, if any, will each insurer pay for the following losses?
   a. An embezzlement of $5000 by a single employee occurred in 1999. The loss is not discovered until July 2000.
   b. Three cashiers acting together stole $15,000 in early 2000. The loss is discovered in December 2000.
   c. Would your answer to part (b) be the same or different if this coverage is written on a name schedule basis with a limit of insurance of $10,000 on each named employee? Explain your answer.

4. Vasquez Construction has been awarded a contract by a school board to build a new public school and must provide a performance bond.

Case Application

Numerous crime coverage forms can be used to insure specific crime exposures. Assume that you are a risk management consultant. For each of the following losses, identify an appropriate crime coverage form that could be used to insure the loss.

a. Camille owns a liquor store and is taking the day's receipts to the bank. She is confronted by a person with a gun and is told to hand over the money. Fearing for her life, she surrenders the money.

b. Travis owns a supermarket. When the store was closed, a burglar broke into a locked safe, and stole several thousand dollars.

c. Isabel is a bank teller. Just before the bank closed, a customer she was waiting on pulled out a gun and held up the bank. The robber ordered her to put the cash in her register into a brown paper bag. An undisclosed amount of cash was stolen.

d. Barry is the president of a stock brokerage firm. He received a phone call telling him that his wife was being held hostage and would not be released until he placed a sum of money under a bush in the city park.

e. Elliott owns a sporting goods store. A thief hid in the store until closing and removed merchandise from the store shelves. The thief then broke a window to get out and escaped with the merchandise.

a. With respect to the performance bond, identify the principal, surety, and obligee.
b. If Vasquez Construction fails to complete the building according to the terms of the contract, what would be the surety's obligation?
c. Does the surety have any recourse against Vasquez Construction in this example? Explain your answer.

SELECTED REFERENCES

The CPCU Handbook of Insurance Policies, third edition. Malvern, PA: American Institute for CPCU/Insurance Institute of America, 1998.

Fire, Casualty & Surety Bulletins. Casualty and Surety volume, Crime section and Surety section. Cincinnati, OH: National Underwriter Company. The bulletins are updated monthly. Detailed information on commercial crime insurance and surety bonds can be found in this volume.

Malecki, Donald S., et al. *Commercial Liability Insurance and Risk Management*, third edition, Vol. 2. Malvern, PA: American Institute for CPCU, 1996, Chapter 14.

Trieschmann, James S., et al. *Commercial Property Insurance and Risk Management*, fourth edition, Vol. 2. Malvern, PA: American Institute for CPCU, 1994, Chapter 10.

Webb, Bernard L., Arthur L. Flitner, and Jerome Trupin. *Commercial Insurance*, third edition. Malvern, PA: Insurance Institute of America, 1996, Chapter 5.

NOTES

1. The commercial crime coverage forms discussed in this section are based on *Fire, Casualty & Surety Bulletins*, Casualty and Surety volume, Crime section (Cincinnati, OH: National Underwriter Company); and Bernard L. Webb, Arthur L. Flitner, and Jerome Trupin, *Commercial Insurance*, third edition (Malvern, PA: Insurance Institute of America, 1996), Chapter 5. The author also drew on the various (copyrighted) commercial crime coverage forms and documents of the Insurance Services Office that appeared in *The CPCU Handbook of Insurance Policies*, third edition (Malvern, PA: American Institute for CPCU/Insurance Institute of America, 1998). The author drew heavily on these sources in the preparation of this chapter.

2. The discussion of surety bonds is based on *Fire, Casualty & Surety Bulletins*, Casualty and Surety volume, Surety section (Cincinnati, OH: National Underwriter Company).

 Students may take a self-administered test on this chapter at www.awlonline.com/rejda

Part Five

Life and Health Risks

Chapter 16

Fundamentals of Life Insurance

> *"I'm not afraid to die. I just don't want to be there when it happens."*
>
> Woody Allen

Learning Objectives

After studying this chapter, you should be able to:

▲ Explain the meaning of premature death.

▲ Describe the financial impact of premature death on the different types of families.

▲ Explain the needs approach for estimating the amount of life insurance to own.

▲ Explain the yearly renewable term method for providing life insurance protection to an individual.

▲ Show how the level-premium method can provide lifetime insurance protection.

▲ Access an Internet site and obtain consumer information about life insurance.

Internet Resources

■ **A. M. Best Company** is a ratings organization that publishes books and periodicals relating to the insurance industry, including life insurance. The company publishes *Best's Review*, Life & Health edition, which provides considerable information about life insurance products and the life insurance industry. Visit the site at:

http://www.ambest.com

■ The **American Council of Life Insurance** represents the life insurance industry on issues dealing with legislation and regulation at the federal and state level. The site provides consumer information on the purposes and types of life insurance. Visit the site at:

http://www.acli.com/

■ The **Life Office Management Association** provides extensive information dealing with the management and operations of life insurers and financial services companies. Visit the site at:

http://www.loma.org/

- **LIMRA International, Inc.** is the principal source of life insurance sales and marketing statistics. The organization provides news and information about the financial services field, conducts research, and publishes a wide range of publications. Visit the site at:

  http://www.limra.com

- The **National Association of Insurance and Financial Advisors** represents sales professionals in life and health insurance and the financial services industry. The organization promotes ethical standards, supports legislation in the interest of policyowners and agents, and provides agent education seminars. Visit the site at:

  http://www.naifa.org/index.html

- **National Underwriter Company** publishes books and periodicals about life insurance products. The company publishes the *National Underwriter*, Life & Health/Financial Services edition, a weekly trade publication, which provides timely news about the life insurance industry. Visit the site at:

  www.nunews.com

- The **Society of Financial Service Professionals** represents individuals who have earned the professional Chartered Life Underwriter (CLU) and Chartered Financial Consultant (ChFC) designations. The site provides timely information on life insurance products. Visit the site at:

  www.financialpro.org

- The **American College** offers professional certification and graduate degree programs in the financial services industry. It offers numerous programs and courses leading to the award of professional designation (CLU, ChFC, and others). Visit the site at:

  http://www.amercoll.edu

Rebecca, age 35, is the sole support for her disabled husband and two small children. She earns $28,000 annually and has $40,000 of life insurance and $10,000 in savings. If Rebecca dies suddenly, could her family survive on the $50,000 left to them? Probably not. Although Social Security survivor benefits may be available, other financial factors must be considered, such as payment of the mortgage, the children's college education, and financial support for her disabled husband. Clearly, $50,000 will not go far. Rebecca's premature death will create financial insecurity for the surviving family members because the family's share of her earnings is lost forever. She can, however, purchase life insurance to restore the lost earnings.

This chapter discusses the risk of premature death and how life insurance can alleviate the financial consequences of premature death. Topics discussed include the meaning of premature death, the financial impact of premature death on the different types of families, and an analysis of the various methods of estimating the amount of life insurance to own. The chapter concludes with a discussion of the basic methods for providing life insurance to an individual, which include the yearly renewable term method and the level-premium method.

PREMATURE DEATH

Meaning of Premature Death

Premature death *can be defined as the death of a family head with outstanding unfulfilled financial obligations*, such as dependents to support, children to educate, and a mortgage to pay off. Premature death can cause serious financial problems for the surviving family members because their share of the deceased breadwinner's earnings is lost forever. If replacement income from other sources is inadequate, or if the accumulated financial assets available to the family are also inadequate, the surviving family members will be exposed to great financial insecurity.

Costs of Premature Death

As stated in Chapter 1, certain costs are associated with premature death. These costs are worth repeating. First, the family's share of the deceased breadwinner's earnings is lost forever. Second, additional expenses are incurred because of funeral expenses, uninsured medical bills, estate settlement costs, and federal estate taxes for large estates. Third, because of insufficient income, some families will experience a reduction in their standard of living (see Insight 16.1). Finally, certain noneconomic costs are incurred, such as emotional grief, loss of a role model, and counseling and guidance for the children.

Chances of Dying Prematurely

The problem of premature death has declined over time due to significant breakthroughs in medical science, improvements in health because of economic growth and higher real incomes, and improvements in public health and sanitation. In 2000, estimated life expectancy at birth based on the intermediate set of demographic assumptions was 73.8 years for males and 79.6 years for females.[1] Although life expectancy has increased over time, large numbers of Americans still die each year from three major causes of death—heart disease, cancer, and stroke.

Although heart disease is a leading cause of death, cardiovascular death rates have plummeted in recent years. This decline is due largely to a reduction in cigarette smoking, better control of blood pressure, decreases in cholesterol levels, and improved medical treatments for heart attacks and strokes (see Insight 16.2).

Exhibit 16.1 indicates the chances of dying *before age 65* for selected ages. Roughly one in five people now age 20 will die prior to age 65.

Economic Justification of Life Insurance

The purchase of life insurance is economically justified if the insured earns an income, and others are dependent on that earning capacity for at least part of their financial support. If the breadwinner dies prematurely, life insurance can be used to restore the

EXHIBIT 16.1
Probability of Death Prior to Age 65

Age	Within a year	Prior to age 65	Age	Within a year	Prior to age 65
0	0.0100	0.21	35	0.0017	0.18
5	0.0003	0.20	40	0.0022	0.17
10	0.0002	0.20	45	0.0032	0.16
15	0.0006	0.20	50	0.0050	0.14
20	0.0011	0.19	55	0.0081	0.12
25	0.0012	0.19	60	0.0126	0.07
30	0.0014	0.18			

SOURCE: Kenneth Black, Jr., and Harold D. Skipper, Jr., *Life Insurance*, twelfth edition (Englewood Cliffs, NJ: Prentice-Hall, 1994), Table 1-1, p. 7.

Insight 16.1

Get Life Insurance—Before It's Too Late

Dear Ann Landers: I am a 43-year-old widow with two children, 10 and 11 years of age. My husband passed away due to a sudden seizure. He was only 37. Although "Tom" made a good living, we were just getting by and never managed to save anything. The only life insurance Tom had was through his work and that wasn't much. When he died, I received benefits for one year. After paying the funeral expenses and outstanding debts, there was nothing left.

Tom and I had discussed life insurance and decided it was something we could not afford at the time, so we waited. Now, it is too late. And it isn't only life insurance. If only we had paid out an extra $15 a month for insurance on our mortgage, it would have paid off the house. A few extra dollars on our auto loan would have paid off our car.

My children and I get by on Social Security benefits, which is a lot less than what Tom was earning. I wish I could be a stay-at-home mom, but that's not possible. I have to work. Because of the Social Security benefits, I am allowed to make only a specified amount of money per year. *Our total income is less than half of what it was. It is difficult to explain to two young children why we have to cut back on so many things.* I am doing everything I can to hold on to our home so that when the children are ready for college, I can sell it and pay their tuition.

My message to your readers is, HAVE LIFE INSURANCE. All the "if onlys" in the world won't help if you don't. My Tom was 37 years old. It can happen anytime, anywhere to anyone.

—Finding My Way in Tampa, Fla.

SOURCE: Adapted from Ann Landers, "Get Life Insurance—Before It's Too Late," *Lincoln Journal Star*, October 1, 1999.

family's share of the deceased breadwinner's earnings.

It should also be noted that a life insurance policy is a *valued policy* that pays a stated sum to a named beneficiary and is not a contract of indemnity. *The insured event is the uncertainty of the time of death.* We must all die, but the time of death is uncertain.

As stated earlier, a family head may die with outstanding financial obligations and dependents to support, which may result in financial insecurity for the surviving dependents. However, the financial impact of premature death of the breadwinner is not uniform but depends on the type of family in which the breadwinner dies.

FINANCIAL IMPACT OF PREMATURE DEATH ON DIFFERENT TYPES OF FAMILIES

The composition of the family has changed significantly over time. As a result, premature death has a more severe financial impact on certain types of families than on others. The major types of families in the United States can be classified as follows:[2]

- Single people
- Single-parent families
- Two-income earners
- Traditional families
- Blended families
- Sandwiched families

Single People

The number of single people has increased in recent years. Younger adults are postponing marriage, often beyond age 30, and many young and middle-aged adults are single because of divorce.

Premature death of a single person who has no dependents to support or outstanding financial obligations is not likely to create a financial problem for others. Other than needing a modest amount of life insurance for burial purposes and uninsured medical bills, this group does not need large amounts of life insurance.

Insight 16.2

Cardiovascular Death Rate Plummets

Death rates from cardiovascular diseases have fallen by 60 percent since 1950, a federal agency announced, indicating that the advance against the leading killer of Americans has been one of the major public health achievements of the 20th century.

It has been known for years that death rates from heart attacks and strokes have been falling. But the new report, in summarizing trends over a century, dramatically illustrated what has been accomplished, experts said.

The national Centers for Disease Control and Prevention [reported] that deaths from strokes have declined steadily since the beginning of the century. Deaths from heart disease peaked in the 1960s and have been falling ever since.

If the heart attack death rate from 1963 had prevailed in 1996, the report said, an additional 621,000 Americans would have died in 1996 alone.

In 1950, the death rate from heart disease was 307.4 per 100,000 people. In 1996, it was 134.6 per 100,000. In 1950, the stroke death rate per 100,000 people was 88.8. In 1996, it was 26.5.

The decline "is stunning," said Dr. Gilbert Omenn, a public health expert who is executive vice president for medical affairs at the University of Michigan. "It is a true success story of grand proportions."

Dr. David Jacobs, a professor of epidemiology at the University of Minnesota's School of Public Health, said the decline in the death rate is "surely one of the great accomplishments of the century."

The CDC said no one factor was responsible for the decline. Instead, the centers noted, the contributing factors constitute an almost humdrum list inspired by public health campaigns and clinical trials that showed the benefits of controlling risks.

One major factor was a decline in cigarette smoking over the past 30 years, with 25 percent of adults smoking today, down from 42 percent. Other factors included better control of blood pressure, decreases in cholesterol levels, and improved treatments for heart attacks and strokes.

The cardiovascular disease story is a model for all the remaining common diseases, Omenn said. He predicted that diseases such as cancer, arthritis, and Alzheimer's disease will be controlled not by a wonder drug like a penicillin but by a mixture of preventive measures and treatments.

SOURCE: Adapted from "Cardiovascular Death Rate Plummets," *Omaha World Herald*, August 6, 1999, p. 1. Reprinted with permission from *The New York Times*.

Single-Parent Families

The number of single-parent families with children under age 18 has increased sharply in recent years because of the large number of children born outside marriage, divorce, legal separation, and death. Premature death of a family head in a single-parent family can cause great financial insecurity for the surviving children. *The need for large amounts of life insurance on the family head is great.* However, many single-parent families are living in poverty, and their ability to purchase large amounts of life insurance is limited. In 1996, 42 percent of female-headed families with children and no husband present were poor, compared to about 9 percent of the families with a male present.[3] These families are simply too poor to purchase large amounts of life insurance.

Two-Income Earners

Families in which both spouses work have largely replaced the traditional family in which only one spouse works. The number of women in the labor force with children has increased dramatically over time, especially for married women with children. *In two-income families with children, the death of one income earner can cause considerable financial insecurity for the surviving family members because both incomes are normally needed to maintain the family's standard of living.* The need for life insurance is great because it can replace the lost earnings, and the family can maintain its previous standard of living.

In contrast, in the case of a married working couple without children, premature death of one income earner is not as likely to cause serious financial problems for the surviving spouse. The surviving spouse is already in the workforce and is supporting herself or himself. Moreover, career couples without children do not have to pay child-care costs or college education costs for the children. Thus, the need for large amounts of life insurance by income earners within this group is considerably less.

Traditional Families

Traditional families are families in which only one parent is in the labor force, and the other parent stays at home to take care of dependent children. *Premature death can cause great financial insecurity in families with children in which only one parent works outside the home. The need for life insurance on family heads in this group is great.* If the working spouse dies with an insufficient amount of life insurance, the family may have to adjust its standard of living downward.

Blended Families

A blended family is one in which a divorced or widowed spouse with children remarries, and the new spouse also has children. *Premature death of a working spouse in a blended family can cause great financial insecurity. The need for life insurance on both family heads within this group is great.* Both spouses may be in the labor force at the time of remarriage, and the death of one spouse may result in a reduction in the family's standard of living since the family's share of that income is lost.

Sandwiched Families

A sandwiched family is one in which a son or daughter with children is also supporting one or both parents. Thus, the son or daughter is "sandwiched" between the younger and older generation. *Premature death of a working spouse in a sandwiched family can cause considerable financial insecurity to*

the surviving family members, and the need for life insurance is great. Premature death can result in the loss of financial support to both the surviving children and the aged parent(s). These families need to be protected by life insurance to replace the loss of income to the surviving family members.

AMOUNT OF LIFE INSURANCE TO OWN

Once you determine that you need life insurance, the next step is to calculate the correct amount of life insurance to own. In 1998, the average amount of life insurance coverage per insured household was only $178,600, which represents only 32 months of disposable personal income per insured household.[4] The correct amount of life insurance to own, however, is an individual matter, because family needs and financial goals vary widely. In the past, some life insurers and financial planners have proposed certain arbitrary rules for determining the amount of life insurance to own, such as six to ten times annual earnings. These rules are meaningless, however, because they do not take into account that family size, income, financial goals, and needs vary from family to family.

Three approaches can be used to estimate the amount of life insurance to own:

- Human life value approach
- Needs approach
- Capital retention approach

Human Life Value Approach

As noted earlier, the family's share of the deceased breadwinner's earnings is lost forever if the family head dies prematurely. This loss is called the human life value. **Human life value** *can be defined as the present value of the family's share of the deceased breadwinner's future earnings.* It can be calculated by the following steps:

1. Estimate the individual's average annual earnings over his or her productive lifetime.
2. Deduct federal and state income taxes, Social Security taxes, life and health insurance premiums, and the costs of self-maintenance. The remaining amount is used to support the family.
3. Determine the number of years from the person's present age to the contemplated age of retirement.

4. Using a reasonable discount rate, determine the present value of the family's share of earnings for the period determined in step 3.

For example, assume that Francisco, age 25, is married and has two children. He earns $25,000 annually and plans to retire at age 65. (For the sake of simplicity, assume that his earnings remain constant.) Of this amount, $10,000 is used for federal and state taxes, life and health insurance, and Francisco's personal needs. The remaining $15,000 is used to support his family. This stream of future income is then discounted back to the present to determine Francisco's human life value. Using a reasonable discount rate of 6 percent, the present value of $1 payable annually for 40 years is $15.05. Therefore, Francisco has a human life value of $225,750 ($15,000 × $15.05 = $225,750). This sum represents the present value of the family's share of Francisco's earnings that would be lost if he should die prematurely. As you can see, the human life has an enormous economic value when earning capacity is considered. The major advantage of the human life value concept is that it crudely measures the economic value of a human life.

However, the human life value approach has several defects that limit its usefulness in trying to measure accurately the correct amount of life insurance to own. *First, other sources of income are not considered*, such as Social Security survivor benefits.

Second, in its simplest form, work earnings and expenses are assumed to remain constant. This assumption is clearly unrealistic. Moreover, it is difficult to estimate accurately the future increase in earnings.

Third, the amount of income allocated to the family is a critical factor in determining the human life value. This amount can change quickly depending on several factors, such as divorce, birth, or death in the family.

Fourth, the long-run discount rate is critical. The human life value can be substantially increased merely by assuming a lower discount rate.

Finally, the effects of inflation on earnings and expenses are ignored. Inflation can quickly erode the real purchasing power of the policy proceeds.

Needs Approach

The second method for estimating the amount of life insurance to own is the **needs approach**. Under this method, the various family needs that must be met if the family head should die are analyzed, and the amount of money needed to meet these needs is determined. The amount of existing life insurance and financial assets is then subtracted from the total amount needed. The difference, if any, is the amount of new life insurance that should be purchased. The most important family needs are the following:

- Estate clearance fund
- Income during the readjustment period
- Income during the dependency period
- Life income to the surviving spouse
- Special needs
  Mortgage redemption fund
  Educational fund
  Emergency fund
- Retirement needs

Estate Clearance Fund An **estate clearance fund** or cleanup fund is needed immediately when the family head dies. Immediate cash is needed for burial expenses; uninsured medical bills; installment debts; estate administration expenses; and estate, inheritance, and income taxes.

Income During the Readjustment Period The **readjustment period** is a one- or two-year period following the breadwinner's death. During this period, the family should receive approximately the same amount of income received while the family head was alive. The purpose of the readjustment period is to give the family time to adjust its living standard to a different level.

Income During the Dependency Period The **dependency period** follows the readjustment period; it is the period until the youngest child reaches age 18. The family should receive income during this period so that the surviving spouse can remain at home, if necessary, to care for the children. The income needed during the dependency period is substantially reduced if the surviving spouse is already in the labor force and plans to continue working.

Life Income to the Surviving Spouse Another important need is to provide life income to the surviving spouse, especially if he or she is older and has been out of the labor force for many years. Two income periods must be considered: (1) income during the blackout period, and (2) income to supplement Social Security benefits after the blackout period. The **blackout period** refers to the period from the time that Social Security survivor benefits terminate to the time the benefits are resumed. Social Security benefits to a surviving spouse terminate when the youngest child reaches age 16 and start again when the spouse attains age 60.

If a surviving spouse has a career and is already in the labor force, the need for life income is greatly reduced or eliminated. However, this conclusion is not true for an older spouse under age 60 who has been out of the labor force for years, and for whom Social Security survivor benefits have temporarily terminated. The need for income during the blackout period is especially important for this group.

Special Needs Families should also consider certain special needs, including a mortgage redemption fund, an educational fund, and an emergency fund.

1. *Mortgage redemption fund.* It is often desirable to provide the family with a mortgage-free home. The amount of monthly income needed by surviving family members is greatly reduced when monthly mortgage payments or rent payments are not required.
2. *Educational fund.* The family head may wish to provide an educational fund for the children. If the children plan to attend a private college or university, the cost will be considerably higher than at a public institution.
3. *Emergency fund.* A family should also have an emergency fund. An unexpected event may occur that requires large amounts of cash, such as major dental work, home repairs, or a new car.

Retirement Needs Because the family head may survive to retirement, a family should consider the need for adequate retirement income. Most retired workers are eligible for Social Security retirement benefits and may also be eligible for retirement benefits from an employer. If retirement income from these sources is inadequate, you can obtain additional income from cash-value life insurance, individual investments, a retirement annuity, or an individual retirement account (IRA). We will discuss these retirement products in Chapter 20.

An Illustration of the Needs Approach

Exhibit 16.2 contains a worksheet that you can use to determine the amount of life insurance you need. The first part of the worksheet shows the amount needed to meet your various cash needs, income needs, and special needs. The second part analyzes your present financial assets for meeting these needs. The final part determines the amount of additional life insurance needed, which is calculated by subtracting total assets from total needs. For example, Jennifer and Scott Smith are married and have a son, age 1. Jennifer, age 33, earns $40,000 annually as a marketing analyst for a large oil company. Scott, age 35, earns $30,000 as an elementary school teacher. Jennifer would like her family to be financially secure if she dies prematurely.

Cash Needs Jennifer estimates that her family will need at least $10,000 for funeral expenses. Although she is currently insured under a group health insurance plan, certain medical services are excluded, and she must pay an annual deductible and coinsurance charges. Thus, she estimates that the family will need $3000 for uninsured medical expenses. She is also making monthly payments on a new car loan and credit card debts. Installment debts currently total $12,000. In addition, she estimates that the cost of probating her will and attorney fees will be $3000, and no federal estate taxes will be payable.

Income Needs Jennifer also wants to provide monthly income to her family during the readjustment and dependency periods until her son reaches age 18. Jennifer and Scott's net take-home pay is approximately $4000 each month. Jennifer believes that her family can maintain its present standard of living if it receives 75 percent of that amount, or $3000 monthly. Thus, she wants the family to receive $3000 monthly for 17 years during the readjustment and dependency periods.

EXHIBIT 16.2
How Much Life Insurance Do You Need?

What you will need	Jennifer Smith		Your needs	
Cash needs				
Funeral costs	$ 10,000		$ _____	
Uninsured medical bills	3,000		_____	
Installment debts	12,000		_____	
Probate costs	3,000		_____	
Federal estate taxes	0		_____	
State inheritance taxes	0		_____	
Total estate clearance fund		$ 28,000		$ _____
Income needs				
Readjustment period	14,400		_____	
Dependency period	108,000		_____	
Blackout period	0		_____	
Retirement income	0		_____	
Total income needs		$ 122,400		$ _____
Special needs				
Mortgage redemption fund	110,000		_____	
Emergency fund	25,000		_____	
College education fund	100,000		_____	
Total special needs		$ 235,000		$ _____
Total needs		$ 385,400		$ _____

What you have today	Jennifer Smith		Your assets	
Checking account and savings	$ 10,000		$ _____	
Mutual funds and securities	25,000		_____	
IRAs and Keogh plan	4,200		_____	
Section 401(k) plan and employer savings plan	4,500		_____	
Private pension death benefit	10,000		_____	
Current life insurance	50,000		_____	
Other financial assets	0		_____	
Total assets		$ 103,700		$ _____
Additional life insurance needed				
Total needs		$ 385,400		$ _____
Less total assets		103,700		_____
Additional life insurance needed		$ 281,700		$ _____

The family's need for $3000 per month is reduced if other sources of income are available. Scott's net take-home pay is about $1800 monthly. In addition, Scott and his son are eligible for Social Security survivor benefits. Scott's benefits are payable until his son reaches age 16, whereas his son's benefits are payable until age 18. In this example, we assume that only the son will receive Social

Security survivor benefits. Because Scott's earnings substantially exceed the maximum annual limit allowed under the Social Security earnings test, he will lose all of his Social Security survivor benefits. However, his son will continue to receive benefits until age 18. The Social Security Administration has prepared a simplified form that will give you an accurate estimate of the Social Security survivor benefits payable if you should die. (Call 800-772-1213 for a form to determine your estimated benefits.) Jennifer's son will receive an estimated $600 each month from Social Security until age 18. Thus, the family would receive a total of $2400 monthly from Scott's take-home pay and the son's Social Security benefit. Because their income goal is $3000 monthly, there is a monthly shortfall of $600. Jennifer's family needs an additional $14,000 to provide monthly income of $600 during the two-year readjustment period, and another $108,000 to provide monthly income for an additional 15 years during the dependency period. Thus, the family needs a total of $122,400 to meet the monthly goal of $3000 during the readjustment and dependency periods.

If Jennifer considers the time value of money, it will take less than $122,400 of life insurance to accomplished the desired income goal. Likewise, if she takes inflation into account, she must increase the amount of life insurance just to maintain the real purchasing power of the benefits. *However, she can ignore both present value and future inflation if she assumes that one offsets the other. Thus, in our example, we assume that the life insurance proceeds are invested at an interest rate equal to the rate of inflation.* Such an assumption builds into the program an automatic hedge against inflation that preserves the real purchasing power of the death benefit. In addition, the calculations are simplified, and the use of present value tables and assumptions concerning future inflation rates are unnecessary.

In addition, Scott is currently in the labor force and plans to continue working if Jennifer should die. Thus, there is no need to provide additional income during the blackout period.

A final need to consider is retirement income. Scott will receive Social Security retirement benefits and a lifetime pension from the school district's retirement plan. He also has an individual retirement account (IRA) that will provide additional retirement income. Jennifer believes that Scott's total retirement income will be sufficient to meet his needs, so he does not need additional retirement income.

In summary, after considering Scott's take-home pay and Social Security survivor benefits, Jennifer determines that she will need an additional $122,400 to meet the income goal of $3000 monthly during the readjustment and dependency periods. Additional income during the blackout period is not needed.

Special Needs Jennifer would like the mortgage paid off if she should die; the current mortgage balance is $110,000. She also wants to establish an emergency fund of $25,000 for the family and an educational fund of $100,000 for her son. Thus, her special needs total $235,000.

Determining the Amount of New Life Insurance Needed After determining total family needs, the next step is to add up all financial assets that can be used to satisfy these needs. Jennifer has a checking account and personal savings in the amount of $10,000. She owns several mutual funds and individual stocks with a current market value of $25,000. She has an individual retirement account with a current balance of $4200, and $4500 in a Section 401(k) plan sponsored by her employer; a lump-sum pension benefit of $10,000 is also payable when she dies. She is insured for $40,000 under her employer's group life insurance plan, and she has an individual policy in the amount of $10,000. Total financial assets available upon her death are $103,700.

Total family needs are $385,400, but her current financial assets are only $103,700. Thus, Jennifer needs an additional $281,700 of life insurance to protect her family.

Insight 16.3 shows additional applications of the needs approach for families and individuals with different financial goals and objectives.

Advantages and Disadvantages of the Needs Approach The major advantage of the needs approach is that it is a reasonably accurate method for determining the amount of life insurance to own when specific family needs are recognized. The needs

Insight 16.3

Life Insurance: Three Families' Needs

Life insurance needs vary depending on individual and family situations. The amount of life insurance needed can be determined by the needs approach. First, you estimate what your future financial needs would be less any Social Security benefits you expect. (Contact your local Social Security office for more information.) Second, you determine what current assets you have, including your present life insurance, to meet these needs. (Omit assets like automobiles and your personal residence that would not likely be sold by your family.)

Third, subtract your assets from your needs to determine the amount of additional life insurance you should have, if any. (While certain assets will generate investment income, it has been assumed that all such income will be offset by the effects of inflation.)

The needs approach tailors your life insurance protection to your individual needs. Three hypothetical family situations are described below to illustrate how the needs approach identifies the type and amount of financial security different members require.

Chris Swift

Chris Swift is 39 and earns $60,000 a year. He has a wife and two children, ages 12 and 6. He has four primary financial needs: (1) to provide income to support his family for 12 years until the younger child is 18, (b) to build a 20-year retirement fund for his wife, (c) to establish a college education fund for his children, and (d) to provide for other miscellaneous

expenses (for example, emergencies, funeral, and so on). He calculated his total financial needs, taking into account the Social Security benefits his family would receive if he died. In spite of these benefits and his current assets, his present insurance provides only part of what he needs. He needs an additional $606,000 of insurance.

1. Financial needs			
a. Family living expenses	$360,000		
b. Retirement fund for wife	200,000		
c. College education	200,000		
d. Other (emergency, final expenses)	32,000		
Total financial needs		$792,000	
2. Current assets			
a. Cash and savings	$ 26,000		
b. Mutual funds	50,000		
c. Life insurance	110,000		
Less: Current assets		−$186,000	
3. Additional life insurance needed		$606,000	

Kim Lukens

Kim Lukens is married, 51 years old, and earns $75,000 a year. She has two grown children who are

out of college, so she has no education or family living expense needs. (She assumes her husband could sup-

approach also considers other sources of income and financial assets. Finally, it can be used to recognize needs during a period of disability or retirement.

The needs approach, however, has several disadvantages. First, future projections over the insured's

lifetime require numerous assumptions and the use of a computer. Dynamic programming models with changing assumptions can be complex and usually are not needed by the typical insured.

Second, family needs must be periodically evalu-

port himself until age 62 if she died.) Kim has two primary financial needs: (a) to establish a 20-year retirement fund beyond what Social Security will provide, and (b) to provide an estate clearance fund. She needs an additional $102,000 of insurance.

1. Financial needs		
a. Retirement fund	$400,000	
b. Estate clearance fund	32,000	
Total financial needs		$432,000
2. Current assets		
a. Cash and savings	$ 55,000	
b. Mutual funds and securities	125,000	
c. Life insurance	150,000	
Less: Current assets		−$330,000
3. Additional life insurance needed		$102,000

Stephanie Hauser

Stephanie Hauser is a single 29-year-old who earns $28,000 per year. She rents an apartment but has investment real estate holdings. She provides a modest amount of financial support for her 62-year-old disabled mother. If Stephanie should die, she would like to provide $7500 per year to support her mother for the rest of her life. Stephanie has two primary financial needs: (a) to provide income to support her mother, and (b) to provide for other miscellaneous expenses that might occur. Stephanie can insure her mother's financial support for life by purchasing $90,000 of additional life insurance with her mother as beneficiary.

1. Financial needs		
a. Dependent support	$165,000	
b. Other (emergency, final expenses)	17,000	
Total financial needs		$182,000
2. Current assets		
a. Cash, savings, and securities	$ 6,000	
b. Equity in real estate, excluding home	36,000	
c. Life insurance	50,000	
Less: Current assets		−$ 92,000
3. Additional life insurance needed		$ 90,000

ated to determine whether they are still appropriate as circumstances change. The need for life insurance can change quickly if there is a divorce, birth, or death of a family member.

In addition, in its simplest form, the needs approach ignores inflation, which can result in a substantial understatement of the amount of life insurance to own. However, the effects of inflation can be incorporated in a dynamic programming model, which requires the use of a computer.

Finally, the needs approach ignores the preservation of estate assets for the heirs, such as the children.

Capital Retention Approach

The **capital retention approach** (also called capital needs analysis) is another method for estimating the amount of life insurance to own. Unlike the needs approach, which assumes liquidation of the life insurance proceeds, the capital retention approach preserves the capital needed to provide income to the family. The income-producing assets are then available for distribution later to the heirs.

The amount of life insurance needed based on the capital retention approach can be determined by the following steps:

- Prepare a personal balance sheet.
- Determine the amount of income-producing capital.
- Determine the amount of additional capital needed (if any).

Prepare a Personal Balance Sheet The first step is to prepare a personal balance sheet that lists all assets and liabilities. The balance sheet should include all death benefits from life insurance and from other sources. For example, Enrique, age 35, has a wife and two children, ages 3 and 5. Enrique earns $60,000 annually. If he should die, he wants his family to receive $30,000 annually. He also wants to establish an emergency fund and educational fund, and pay off the mortgage, auto loan, and charge accounts. Enrique's personal balance sheet, including death benefits from life insurance and his pension plan, is as follows:

Assets

House	$125,000
Automobiles	15,000
Personal and household property	45,000
Securities and investments	28,000
Checking account	2,000
Individual and group life insurance	200,000
Private pension death benefit	20,000
Total	$435,000

Liabilities

Mortgage	$100,000
Auto loan	10,000
Charge accounts and other bills	5,000
Total	$115,000

Determine the Amount of Income-Producing Capital The next step is to determine the amount of income-producing assets that can provide income to the family. This step is performed by subtracting the liabilities, cash needs, and non-income-producing capital from total assets. Enrique has $55,000 of capital that can produce income for the family. This situation is illustrated as follows:

Total assets		$435,000
Less:		
Mortgage payoff	$100,000	
Other liabilities	15,000	
Final expenses	10,000	
Emergency fund	10,000	
Educational fund	60,000	
Non-income-producing capital (automobiles, personal and household property, value of home)	185,000	
Total deductions		−380,000
Capital now available for income		$ 55,000

In the preceding illustration, the home is not an income-producing asset. Unless the home is sold or rented, it ordinarily does not produce cash income for the family. Thus, the home is considered to be part of *non-income-producing capital* that is subtracted from total assets to arrive at the amount of liquid assets that can produce income for the family.

Determine the Amount of Additional Capital Needed The final step is to determine the amount of additional capital (if any) that is needed. This step involves a comparison of the income objective with other sources of income, such as Social Security survivor benefits. In Enrique's case, his family would have an income shortage of $14,700 annually based on his present financial situation. Assuming the liquid assets and life insurance proceeds can be invested to earn 6 percent annually, Enrique needs an additional $245,000 of life insurance to meet his financial goals. This situation is illustrated as follows:

Income objective for family	$ 30,000
Less:	
Capital now available for income ($55,000 × 6%)	–3,300
Social Security survivor benefits	–12,000
Income shortage	$ 14,700
Total new capital required ($14,700/0.06)	$245,000

The capital retention approach has the advantages of simplicity, ease of understanding, and preservation of capital. In addition, investment income on the emergency and educational funds can be used as a partial hedge against inflation, or it can be accumulated to offset rising educational costs. The major disadvantage, however, is that a larger amount of life insurance is required to produce a given amount of income.

Summary As the preceding discussion showed, many families need substantial amounts of life insurance. Unfortunately, many families are seriously underinsured, and a recent survey shows that 26 percent of American households own no life insurance at all (see Insight 16.4). What happens when one spouse dies prematurely? *In most cases, a widow's financial situation is more likely than a widower's to deteriorate when the spouse dies.* A recent study of beneficiaries by LIMRA International showed that although widows received a median death benefit almost double the amount paid to widowers ($100,300 versus $50,300), the amount paid was not considered adequate. *The study reported that 45 percent of the widows and 37 percent of the widowers said that the life insurance on their spouse was inadequate. In addition, half of the widows and one-third of the widowers were just getting by financially one to two years after the death occurred.*[5] Widows were much less likely to work part- or full-time, so that the insurance proceeds must be stretched out and were not considered sufficient for maintaining their previous lifestyle. It is clear that greater consumer education on the correct amount of life insurance to own is necessary.

METHODS FOR PROVIDING LIFE INSURANCE PROTECTION

Two basic methods can be used to provide life insurance to individuals: the yearly renewable term method and the level-premium method.[6]

Yearly Renewable Term Method

Yearly renewable term insurance *provides life insurance protection for only one year.* The insured is permitted to renew the policy for successive one-year periods with no evidence of insurability. That is, evidence of good health or a physical examination is not required when the policy is renewed.

The pure premium for yearly renewable term insurance is determined by the death rate at each attained age. For the sake of simplicity, interest and operating expenses of the insurer are ignored in this discussion. The insurance protection is for one year only, and individuals within the group must pay their pro rata share of death claims. Based on the Commissioners 1980 Standard Ordinary Table of Mortality, the death rate for males at age 30 is 1.73 for each 1000 lives. If 100,000 males, age 30, are insured for $1000 for one year, the insurance company must pay 173 death claims, or $173,000. If interest and expenses are ignored, each insured must pay a premium of $1.73 ($173,000/100,000 = $1.73). You will notice that the $1.73 in premiums is the same as the death rate at age 30. At age 31, the male death rate is 1.78 per 1000 lives. If the 99,827 survivors want the protection for another year, the insurer must pay 178 death claims, or $178,000. Each of the 99,827 insureds must pay their pro rata share of the death claims, or $1.78 ($178,000/99,827 = $1.78). Finally, if the 99,649 survivors wish to insure their lives for another year, the insurer must pay $183,000 in death claims. Each insured's share of the total death claims would be $1.83 ($183,000/99,649 = 1.83).

You can see that the yearly renewable term insurance premium increases as the individual gets older. *The premium increase is gradual during the early years, but it rises sharply during the later years.* The following illustration shows the pure premiums for $1000 of yearly renewable term insurance for males at various attained ages. (Interest and expenses are again ignored.)

Insight 16.4

New LIFE Study Reveals Crisis of Underinsurance

A study conducted by Roper Starch Worldwide and commissioned by the Life and Health Insurance Foundation for Education (LIFE) reveals that more than 25 million American households have no life insurance coverage. *Today, only 74 percent of all households own some form of life insurance, down from 83 percent in 1976.* Much of the drop is due to the continued decline in ownership of individual life insurance. For the first time, the proportion of households with group coverage now surpasses the percentage with individual coverage.

In addition, many households that have coverage appear to be underinsured. For instance, married people with a single income say that most households need five times the primary wage earner's income in life insurance, but they personally have only three times their income. Yet, even five times one's income may not be enough. While individual needs vary, most insurance professionals recommend life insurance coverage equal to seven to ten times a person's income.

"There's a real crisis of underinsurance in this country," said David F. Woods, president of *LIFE*. "This study underscores the fact that millions of people are exposing their families to potential financial hardship. If a parent or spouse were to die unexpectedly, how would these families continue to pay their mortgages and daily expenses, or put their children through college?"

According to the study, people who feel that their households are inadequately insured cite several reasons for not owning more life insurance.

The top reason is cost. "What a lot of consumers don't realize is that the cost of life insurance has actually gone down," said Woods. "With the variety of insurance products on the market today, price shouldn't be an obstacle when obtaining adequate coverage."

The second most commonly cited reason for not having more insurance is a lack of knowledge. Almost 60 percent of people say that not knowing enough about insurance is a reason they haven't secured additional coverage for their households. Nearly half the public haven't purchased more insurance because they are worried about making a wrong decision, and 43 percent say they simply haven't gotten around to it.

One in Four U.S. Households Now Has No Life Insurance

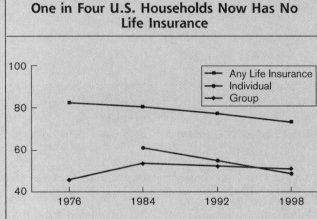

Reasons Why People Don't Have More Insurance (of People Who Say Their Household Needs More Life Insurance)

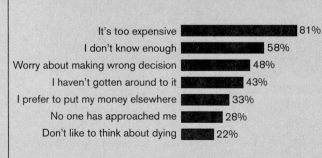

SOURCE: Adapted from Society of Financial Service Professionals, "New LIFE Study Reveals Crisis of Underinsurance," *Society Page* (April 1999), pp. 22–23.

Age 30	$1.73
Age 40	$3.02
Age 50	$6.71
Age 60	$16.08
Age 70	$39.51
Age 80	$98.84
Age 90	$221.77
Age 98	$657.98
Age 99	$1000.00

Because premiums increase with age, yearly renewable term insurance premiums eventually become prohibitive in cost, so some insureds may drop their insurance. The healthier members may drop their life insurance as the premiums increase, but the unhealthy persons will continue to renew their policies despite the premium increase. This situation leads to adverse selection against the insurer. The insurer may then have a disproportionate number of impaired lives in the group, which drives the death rate up even more.

You can see that under the yearly renewable method, the premiums are substantial at the older ages. Therefore, if the insured wants lifetime protection, the yearly renewable term method is impractical because the premiums are prohibitive in cost at the older ages. Some other method must be used to provide lifetime protection. This method is called the level-premium method.

Level-Premium Method

Under the **level-premium method**, premiums do not increase from year to year but remain level throughout the premium paying period, and the insured has lifetime protection to age 100. Under this method, premiums paid during the early years of the policy are higher than is necessary to pay current death claims, while those paid in the later years are inadequate for paying death claims. The redundant or excess premiums paid during the early years are invested at compound interest, and the accumulated funds are then used to supplement the inadequate premiums paid during the later years of the policy. Because the method of investing and accumulating the fund is regulated by state law, it is referred to as a **legal reserve**. The legal reserve technically is a composite liability account of the insurer and should not be allocated to individual contracts. However, for our purposes, we can view the legal reserve as the aggregate of the individual accounts established for the individual policyowners.[7]

As stated earlier, under the level-premium method, premiums do not increase with age. *A level premium is possible because the excess premiums are invested at compound interest and are used to supplement the deficiency in premiums during the later years.* In contrast, under the yearly renewable term method, the premiums are very low during the early years but gradually increase to a point where they become prohibitive in cost. For this reason, lifetime protection cannot be provided to most insureds under the yearly renewable term method.

Fundamental Purpose of the Legal Reserve

The excess premiums paid during the early years are reflected in a legal reserve. The concept of a legal reserve can be illustrated in greater detail by Exhibit 16.3, which represents the legal reserve under an ordinary life policy. The legal reserve steadily increases over time and is equal to the face amount of the policy at age 100. If the insured is still alive at age 100, the face amount of the policy is paid at that time. *The difference between the face amount of the policy and the legal reserve is called the net* **amount at risk**. The net amount at risk represents the pure insurance

---

EXHIBIT 16.3

Relationship between the Net Amount at Risk and Legal Reserve

portion of the policy. It declines over time as the legal reserve increases. Thus, from a conceptual standpoint, the death claim can be viewed as consisting of two elements: a legal reserve (saving element) and the net amount at risk (protection element).[8] As the legal reserve increases, the net amount at risk declines. *It follows that the fundamental purpose of the legal reserve is to provide lifetime protection.* As the death rate increases with age, the legal reserve also increases, and the net amount at risk declines, which produces a cost of insurance within practical limits.[9] Therefore, by the level-premium method, the insurer can provide the insured with lifetime protection.

Cash Values Cash values should not be confused with the legal reserve. Under the level-premium method, a legal reserve results. Because of the legal reserve, cash values become available. The policyowner may no longer want the insurance, and the policy can be surrendered for its cash surrender value. However, cash values and the legal reserve are not the same thing and are computed separately. The cash values are below the legal reserve for several years, but after the policy has been in force over an extended period, such as 15 years, the cash surrender value will equal the full reserve. The various cash surrender options are examined in Chapter 18.

You should also remember that cash values are the by-product of the level-premium method, not the purpose of it. The fundamental purpose of the level-premium method is to provide lifetime protection and not to build up a savings account in the form of cash values. This is not to say that an individual cannot save by purchasing cash-value life insurance. Indeed, in the aggregate, large amounts are annually saved by policyowners in the form of accumulated cash values. However, the savings feature is incidental to the fundamental goal of lifetime protection.

SUMMARY

- Premature death means that a family head dies with outstanding unfulfilled financial obligations, such as dependents to support, children to educate, or a mortgage to be paid off. Great financial insecurity may result if a family head dies prematurely.
- At least four costs are associated with premature death:

  There is the loss of the human life value. The family's share of the deceased breadwinner's earned income is lost forever.

  Additional expenses may be incurred, such as burial costs, expenses of the last illness, and probate and estate settlement costs.

  Because of insufficient income, some families may experience a reduction in their standard of living.

  Noneconomic costs are incurred, such as the emotional grief of the surviving dependents and the loss of a role model and guidance for the children.

- The purpose of life insurance can be economically justified if a person has an earning capacity, and someone is dependent on those earnings for at least part of his or her financial support.

- The financial impact of premature death on the family varies by family type. Premature death can cause considerable economic insecurity if a family head dies in a single-parent family, in a family with two-income earners with children, or in a traditional, blended, or sandwich family. In contrast, if a single person without dependents or an income earner in a two-income family without children dies, financial problems for others are unlikely.

- The human life value is defined as the present value of the family's share of the deceased breadwinner's earnings. This approach crudely measures the economic value of a human life.

- The needs approach can be used to determine the amount of life insurance to own. After considering other sources of income and financial assets, the various family needs are converted into specific amounts of life insurance. The most important family needs are as follows:

  Estate clearance fund

  Income during the readjustment period

  Income during the dependency period

  Life income to the surviving spouse

  Special needs: mortgage redemption fund, education fund, emergency fund

  Retirement needs

- The capital retention approach for estimating the amount of life insurance to own is based on the assumption that income-producing capital will be preserved and not liquidated.

- Under the yearly renewable term method, life insurance protection is provided for one year only. The policy can be renewed for successive one-year periods with no evidence of insurability. The method is not suitable for lifetime protection because premiums increase with age until they reach prohibitively high levels.

- Under the level-premium method, premiums do not increase from year to year but remain level throughout the premium-paying period. The insured has lifetime protection to age 100. Under this method, premiums paid during the early years are higher than are necessary to pay current death claims. The excess premiums paid during the early years are invested and used to supplement the inadequate premiums paid during the later years.

- The legal reserve is a liability item that reflects the excess premiums paid during the early years of the policy. It steadily increases until it reaches the face amount of the policy by age 100. The fundamental purpose of the legal reserve is to provide lifetime protection.

- Because a legal reserve is necessary for lifetime protection, cash values become available. However, cash values are the by-product of the level-premium method, not the purpose of it. Because the insured has paid more than is actuarially necessary during the early years of the policy, he or she should receive something back if the policy is surrendered.

KEY CONCEPTS AND TERMS

Blackout period	Level-premium method
Capital retention approach	Needs approach
Cash values	Net amount at risk
Dependency period	Premature death
Estate clearance fund	Readjustment period
Human life value	Yearly renewable term
Legal reserve	insurance

REVIEW QUESTIONS

1. Explain the meaning of premature death and identify the costs associated with premature death.

2. Explain the economic justification for the purchase of life insurance.

3. Define the human life value. How is the human life value measured?

4. Describe the needs approach for determining the amount of life insurance to own.

5. Describe the capital retention approach for determining the amount of life insurance to own.

6. Explain the yearly renewable term method for providing life insurance to individuals.

7. Is the yearly renewable term method suitable for lifetime protection?

8. Explain the level-premium method for providing life insurance to individuals.

9. Describe the purpose of the legal reserve in cash value life insurance.

10. Why does a level-premium whole life policy provide cash values?

APPLICATION QUESTIONS

1. "The financial impact of premature death is uniform for all families." Do you agree or disagree with this statement? Explain your answer.

2. The human life value concept provides a method for estimating the amount of life insurance to own.
   a. Describe the steps in the calculation of an individual's human life value.
   b. Keeping all other factors unchanged, explain the effect, if any, of a reduction in the interest rate used to calculate the individual's human life value.
   c. Explain the defects in the human life value approach as a technique for determining the amount of life insurance to own.

3. José, age 30, is married and has one child. He has been told that he should purchase life insurance to protect his family.
   a. Describe each of the basic family needs for which José may need life insurance.
   b. Explain the limitations in the needs approach as a method for determining the amount of life insurance to own.

4. A significant aspect of the level-premium method is the fact that the net amount at risk decreases over the duration of the contract.
   a. What is the net amount at risk?
   b. Explain why the net amount at risk decreases over the duration of the contract.

Case Application 1

Scott, age 28, and Brenda, age 25, are married and have a daughter, age 3. Scott has the following cash and income needs:

Cash needs

Estate clearance	$20,000
Mortgage redemption	90,000
Emergency fund	20,000
Education fund	50,000

Income needs

Readjustment period	$2000 monthly
Dependency period	2000 monthly
Blackout period	1000 monthly

Brenda is employed outside the home. Her monthly net take-home pay is $1500 after taxes and other deductions. She plans to continue working if Scott should die. Based on the assumption that the life insurance proceeds can be invested at a rate of interest equal to the rate of inflation, answer the following questions:

a. How much additional life insurance, if any, is needed to meet Scott's cash needs if his present life insurance and financial assets total $100,000?

b. Ignoring the availability of Social Security survivor benefits, how much additional life insurance, if any, is needed to provide the desired amount of income during the readjustment and dependency periods?

c. In the above example, how much additional life insurance, if any, is needed if Social Security survivor benefits of $500 monthly are paid to the child until age 18?

d. How much additional life insurance, if any, is needed to provide the desired amount of income during the blackout period if Brenda does not work outside the home?

---

c. What is the actuarial significance of a decreasing net amount at risk?

5. An agent remarked that "the fundamental purpose of the legal reserve is to accumulate cash values and provide a means of saving money." Do you agree or disagree with this statement? Explain your answer.

SELECTED REFERENCES

Belth, Joseph M. *Life Insurance: A Consumer's Handbook*, second edition. Bloomington, IN: Indiana University Press, 1985.

Black, Kenneth, Jr., and Harold D. Skipper, Jr. *Life Insurance*, thirteenth edition. Upper Saddle River, NJ: Prentice-Hall, 2000.

Dorfman, Mark S., and Saul W. Adelman. *Life Insurance: A Financial Planning Approach*, second edition. Chicago, IL: Dearborn Financial Publishing, 1992.

Graves, Edward E., ed. *McGill's Life Insurance*, second edition. Bryn Mawr, PA: The American College, 1998.

LIMRA International, Inc. *1998 Survivor Study, Fulfilling the Promise: The Role of the Life Insurance Company and Agent*. Windsor, CT: LIMRA International, 1998.

LIMRA International, Inc. *1998 Survivor Study—The Financial Impact of Death*. Windsor, CT: LIMRA International, 1999.

Rejda, George E., Constance M. Luthardt, Cheryl L. Ferguson, and Donald R. Oakes. *Personal Insurance*, fourth edition. Malvern, PA: Insurance Institute of America, 2000.

NOTES

1. *The 1999 Annual Report, Communication from the Board of Trustees, the Federal Old-Age and Survivors Insurance and Disability Insurance Trust Funds* (Washington, DC: U.S. Government Printing Office, 1999), Table II.D2, p. 62.

2. This section is based on George E. Rejda, *Social Insurance and Economic Security*, sixth edition (Upper Saddle River, NJ: 1999), pp. 42–47.

3. *Ibid.*, p. 43.

Case Application 2

Althea, age 35, is a registered nurse who earns $40,000 annually. She is married and has two children, ages 2 and 5. If she should die, she wants her family to receive $20,000 annually. She also wants to set up a final expense fund of $10,000, establish an educational fund of $100,000, and pay off the mortgage, automobile loan, and outstanding credit card balances. Her husband, Nicholas, is capable of supporting himself if she should die. Althea's personal balance sheet, including life insurance and a pension death benefit, is as follows:

Assets

Condominium	$150,000
Personal property	40,000
Two automobiles	18,000
Mutual funds	55,000
Checking account	2,000
Individual and group life insurance	180,000
Pension death benefit	15,000
Total	$460,000

Liabilities

Mortgage	$125,000
Auto loan	8,000
Credit card balance	2,000
Total	$135,000

Estimated Social Security survivor benefits are $12,080 annually. Assume that the life insurance proceeds and liquid funds can earn 6 percent annually. Using the capital retention method, calculate the amount of additional life insurance that Althea should purchase to attain her financial goals.

4. *ACLI Life Insurance Fact Book 1999* (Washington, DC: American Council of Life Insurance, 1999), Table 1.7, p. 12.

5. *1998 Survivor Study—The Financial Impact of Death* (Windsor, CT: LIMRA International, 1999), pp. 5, 27.

6. Edward E. Graves, ed., *McGill's Life Insurance*. second edition (Bryn Mawr, PA: The American College, 1998), pp. 21–34.

7. *Ibid.*, p. 28. The legal reserve technically is a liability item that must be offset by sufficient assets. Otherwise, regulatory authorities may declare the insurer to be insolvent.

8. This separation is only a theoretical concept. In practice, the death claim paid by the insurer does not consist of two separate benefits that equal the face value of the policy. An ordinary life insurance policy is an undivided contract, and the death benefit is the face amount of insurance.

9. The *cost of insurance* is a technical term that is obtained by multiplying the net amount at risk by the death rate at the insured's attained age. Under the level-premium method, the cost of insurance can be kept within reasonable bounds at all ages.

Students may take a self-administered test on this chapter at www.awlonline.com/rejda

Chapter 17

Types of Life Insurance

"There are worse things in life than death. Have you ever spent an evening with an insurance salesman?"

Woody Allen

Learning Objectives

After studying this chapter, you should be able to:

▲ Describe the major characteristics of term insurance.

▲ Explain the major features of ordinary life insurance.

▲ Identify the basic characteristics of variable life insurance.

▲ Explain the major characteristics of universal life insurance.

▲ Show how variable universal life insurance differs from universal life insurance.

▲ Describe the basic characteristics of current assumption whole life insurance.

▲ Access an Internet site to obtain and evaluate consumer information about life insurance.

Internet Resources

- The **American Council of Life Insurance** represents the life insurance industry on issues dealing with legislation and regulation at the federal and state levels. The site provides consumer information on the purposes and types of life insurance. Visit the site at:

  http://www.acli.com/

- **INSWEB** provides timely information and premium quotes for life insurance as well as homeowners, auto, and other insurance products. Visit the site at:

  http://www.insweb.com/

- The **Insurance News Network** provides up-to-date information, premium quotes, and other consumer information on life insurance. The site also provides news releases about events that affect the insurance industry. Visit the site at:

  http://www.insure.com/

ichael, age 28, is a single parent with two children, ages 2 and 4. His wife was killed in an auto accident one year ago by a drunk driver. Michael earns $23,000 annually as a maintenance worker for a cleaning service, and money is tight. He is trying to assess his life insurance needs and the type of life insurance to buy to protect his family. A life insurance agent met with him and presented several proposals. Michael is thoroughly confused and does not understand the various life insurance plans presented to him.

The material in this chapter will help Michael answer questions concerning the various types of life insurance that can be purchased today. Three principal areas are emphasized. The chapter begins with a discussion of the traditional forms of life insurance—term, whole life, and endowment insurance. Next, several variations of whole life insurance are examined, including variable life insurance, universal life insurance, and variable universal life insurance. The chapter concludes with a discussion of other types of life insurance that have unique features or are designed to meet special needs.

TYPES OF LIFE INSURANCE

From a generic viewpoint, life insurance policies can be classified as either **term insurance** or **cash-value life insurance**. Term insurance provides temporary protection, while cash-value life insurance has a savings component and builds cash values. Numerous variations and combinations of these two types of life insurance are available today.

Term Insurance

Term insurance has several basic characteristics.[1] First, the period of protection is temporary, such as 1, 5, 10, or 20 years. Unless the policy is renewed, the protection expires at the end of the period.

Most term insurance policies are **renewable**, which means that the policy can be renewed for additional periods without evidence of insurability.

The premium is increased at each renewal and is based on the insured's attained age. The purpose of the renewal provision is to protect the insurability of the insured. However, it results in adverse selection against the insurer. Because premiums increase with age, insureds in good health tend to drop their insurance, while those in poor health will continue to renew, regardless of the premium increase. To minimize adverse selection, many insurers have an age limitation beyond which renewal is not allowed, such as age 70 or 80. Some insurers, however, permit term policies to be renewed to age 95 or 99.

Most term insurance policies are also **convertible**, which means the term policy can be exchanged for a cash-value policy without evidence of insurability. There are two methods for converting a term policy. Under the *attained-age method*, the premium charged is based on the insured's attained age at the time of conversion. Under the *original-age method*, the premium charged is based on the insured's original age when the term insurance was first purchased. Most insurers offering the original-age method require the conversion to take place within five years of the issue date of the term policy. The policyowner must also pay the difference between the premiums paid on the term policy and those that would have been paid on the new policy, with interest on the difference at a specified rate.[2] The purpose of the financial adjustment is to place the insurer in the same financial position it would have achieved if the policy had been issued at the original age. Because of the financial adjustment required, few term insurance policies are converted based on the original-age method.

Finally, term insurance policies have no cash-value or savings element. Although some long-term policies develop a small reserve, it is used up by the contract expiration date.

Types of Term Insurance A wide variety of term insurance products are sold today. They include the following:

- Yearly renewable term
- 5-, 10-, 15-, or 20-year term
- Term to age 65
- Decreasing term
- Reentry term

Yearly renewable term insurance is issued for a one-year period, and the policyowner can renew for successive one-year periods to some stated age without evidence of insurability. Premiums increase with age at each renewal date. Most yearly renewable term policies also allow the policyowner to convert to a cash-value policy.

Term insurance can also be issued for *5, 10, 15, or 20 years, or for longer periods*. The premiums paid during the term period are level, but they increase when the policy is renewed.

A *term to age 65 policy* provides protection to age 65, at which time the policy expires. The policy can be converted to a permanent plan of insurance, but the decision to convert must be exercised before age 65. For example, the insurer may require conversion to a permanent policy before age 60. Because premiums are level, the policy develops a small reserve that is used up by the end of the period.

Decreasing term insurance is a form of term insurance where the face amount gradually declines each year. Although the face amount declines over time, the premium is level throughout the period. In some policies, the premiums are structured so that the policy is fully paid for a few years before the coverage expires. For example, a 20-year decreasing term policy may require premium payments for 17 years. This method avoids paying a relatively large premium for only a small amount of insurance near the end of the term period. Finally, decreasing term insurance can be written as a separate policy, or it can be added as a rider to an existing contract.

Reentry term (also called *revertible term*) is another important term insurance product. Under a reentry term policy, renewal premiums are based on select (lower) mortality rates if the insured can periodically demonstrate acceptable evidence of insurability. Select mortality rates are based on the mortality experience of recently insured lives. However, to remain on the low-rate schedule, the insured must periodically show that he or she is in good health and is still insurable. The rates are substantially increased if the insured cannot provide satisfactory evidence of insurability.

Uses of Term Insurance Term insurance is appropriate in three situations. *First, if the amount of income that can be spent on life insurance is limited, term insurance can be effectively used.* Because of mortality improvements and keen price competition, term insurance rates have declined sharply in recent years. Substantial amounts of life insurance can be purchased for a relatively modest annual premium outlay (see Exhibit 17.1). However, term insurance premiums for longer term periods are expected to increase in the future (see Insight 17.1).

Second term insurance is appropriate if the need for protection is temporary. For example, decreasing term insurance can be effectively used to pay off the mortgage if the family head dies prematurely.

Finally, term insurance can be used to guarantee future insurability. A person may desire large amounts of permanent insurance, but may be financially unable to purchase the needed protection today. Inexpensive term insurance can be purchased, which can be converted later into a permanent insurance policy without evidence of insurability.

Limitations of Term Insurance Term insurance has two major limitations. *First, term insurance premiums increase with age and eventually reach prohibitive levels.* Thus, term insurance is not suitable for individuals who need large amounts of life insurance beyond age 65 or 70. For example, based on the rates of one insurer, the premium for a $500,000 annually renewable term policy for a male nonsmoker, age 25, is $353. The premium increases to $2914 at age 65 and $9805 at age 75.

Second, term insurance is inappropriate if you wish to save money for a specific need. Term insurance policies do not accumulate cash values. Thus, if you wish to save money for a child's college education or accumulate a fund for retirement, term insurance is inappropriate unless it is supplemented with an investment plan.

Decreasing term insurance also has several disadvantages and should not be used to meet all of your insurance needs. If you become uninsurable, you must convert the remaining insurance to a permanent plan to freeze the insurance at its present level. If the policy is not converted, the insurance protection continues to decline even though you are uninsurable. Moreover, decreasing term insurance does not provide for changing needs, such as a birth or adoption of a child. Nor does it provide an effective hedge against inflation. Because of inflation, the amount of life insurance in most families should be periodically increased just to maintain the real purchasing power of the original policy.

Whole Life Insurance

In contrast to term insurance, which provides short-term protection, **whole life insurance** *is a cash-value policy that provides lifetime protection.* From a

EXHIBIT 17.1
Best Buys in Term Life Insurance, $250,000

Age	Female premiums 10 year	15 year	20 year	25 year	30 year	Age	Male premiums 10 year	15 year	20 year	25 year	30 year
35	$ 103	$ 125	$ 145	$ 183	$ 205	35	$ 123	$ 138	$ 165	$ 223	$ 253
40	$ 123	$ 158	$ 185	$ 238	$ 260	40	$ 148	$ 183	$ 225	$ 288	$ 335
45	$ 190	$ 215	$ 253	$ 330	$ 385	45	$ 225	$ 300	$ 360	$ 450	$ 513
50	$ 253	$ 290	$ 363	$ 490	$ 495	50	$ 338	$ 455	$ 525	$ 743	$ 828
55	$ 365	$ 413	$ 550	$ 835	$ 1,015	55	$ 500	$ 670	$ 768	$ 1,640	$ 2,330
60	$ 503	$ 615	$ 845	$ 2,135	$ 2,400	60	$ 783	$ 990	$1,335	$ 3,630	$ 3,630
65	$ 775	$ 975	$1,593	$ 3,900	$ 3,900	65	$1,330	$1,650	$2,693	$ 5,250	$ 5,250
70	$1,338	$1,600	$2,970	$ 7,220	$ 7,220	70	$2,473	$3,175	$4,860	$ 8,790	$ 8,790
75	$2,275	$4,870	$5,820	$10,370	$12,420	75	$4,400	$7,443	$9,600	$13,260	$15,030

Note: The premiums are guaranteed annual premiums for a nonsmoker based on a market survey of life insurers in late 1999. Final premiums and coverage availability will vary depending on age, sex, state availability, hazardous activities, and personal and family health history.

SOURCE: Quotesmith.com, Inc. (December 1999).

Insight 17.1

Look for Term Insurance Rates to Rise in the Future

In recent years, the cost of term life insurance has dropped dramatically. But the era of low-cost, long-term policies with guaranteed premiums may be ending.

In an effort to assure that life insurance companies are able to pay future claims, the National Association of Insurance Commissioners (NAIC) has adopted Regulation XXX ("Triple X"), *which increases the reserves that life insurance companies must maintain for term life insurance products.* These additional reserves are designed to provide consumers with a higher level of safety and confidence.

However, Triple X may impact consumers in other, less positive, ways as well. By raising reserve requirements, adoption of this regulation by states is likely to increase costs for many insurance companies. *Two important effects of these cost increases are expected to be:*

1) *Increased premiums for new term life policies—particularly those with 15- to 30-year terms.*
2) *Elimination of premium-guarantee periods of more than five years for new term life policies,* which means the premiums you pay could increase after the first five years.

In New York, where a similar regulation has been in effect for several years, premium-guarantee periods on many term policies have been reduced to five years to hold down premiums.

How soon—and if—Triple X could impact you will depend on where you live. Adoption of the regulation is voluntary for states. However, some are expected to adopt it as early as January 1, 2000, with many others expected to sign on by midyear.

Triple X will not affect the rates or premium guarantees of policies issued before the regulation takes effect. So now may be a good time to consider your insurance needs. If term life insurance makes sense for you, and particularly if a 20- or 30-year policy provides the right coverage for your situation, you may want to purchase a policy soon. Current term life premiums are attractive, and by acting now you can lock in those premiums for the term of the policy you select.

SOURCE: "XXX Marks the Spot, Look for Term-Insurance Rates to Rise in 2000," *On Investing* (Fall 1999), p. 56.

---

historical or traditional perspective, the following two types of whole life insurance merit some discussion:

- Ordinary life insurance
- Limited-payment life insurance

Ordinary Life Insurance Ordinary life insurance (also called straight life and continuous premium whole life) provides lifetime protection to age 100, and the death claim is a certainty.[3] If the insured is still alive at age 100, the face amount of insurance is paid to the policyowner at that time.

In addition, premiums do not increase from year to year but remain level throughout the premium paying period. Under an ordinary life policy, the policyowner is overcharged for the insurance protection during the early years and undercharged during the later years when premiums are inadequate to pay death claims. As stated in Chapter 16, the excess premiums are reflected in a liability item known as a legal reserve. The legal reserve makes it possible to provide lifetime protection.

Ordinary life insurance also has an investment or saving element called a **cash surrender value**. The cash values are due to the overpayment of insurance premiums during the early years. As a result, the policyowner builds a cash equity in the policy. The policy may be surrendered for its cash value, or the cash value may be borrowed under a loan provision. The cash values are relatively small during the early years, but increase over time. For example, in many ordinary life policies, a $100,000 policy issued at age 20 would have at least $50,000 of cash value at age 65.

Finally, ordinary life insurance contains cash surrender or nonforfeiture options, dividend options (if participating), and settlement options that can be used to meet a wide variety of financial needs and objectives. These options are discussed in Chapter 18.

Uses of Ordinary Life Insurance Ordinary life insurance is appropriate in two general situations: (1) when lifetime protection is needed, and (2) when additional savings are desired.

An ordinary life policy is appropriate when lifetime protection is needed. This means that the need for life insurance will continue beyond age 65 or 70. Some financial planners and consumer experts point out that the average person does not need large amounts of life insurance beyond age 65, because the need for life insurance declines with age. This view is an oversimplification of a complex issue and can be misleading. Some persons may need substantial amounts of life insurance beyond age 65. For example, an estate clearance fund is still needed at the older ages; there may be a sizable federal estate tax problem if the estate is large, so substantial amounts of life insurance may be needed for estate liquidity; a divorce settlement may require the purchase and maintenance of a life insurance policy on a divorced spouse, regardless of age; and the policyowner may wish to leave a sizable bequest to a surviving spouse, children, or charity, regardless of when death occurs. Because an ordinary life policy can provide lifetime protection, these objectives can be realized even though the insured dies at an advanced age.

Ordinary life insurance can also be used to save money. Some insureds wish to meet their protection and savings needs by an ordinary life policy. As stated earlier, ordinary life insurance builds cash values that can be obtained by surrendering the policy or by borrowing the cash value.

Insight 17.2 discusses other situations that justify the use of cash-value life insurance.

Limitation of Ordinary Life Insurance *The major limitation of ordinary life insurance is that some persons are still underinsured after the policy is purchased.* Because of the savings feature, some persons may voluntarily purchase or else be persuaded by a life insurance agent to purchase an ordinary life policy when term insurance would be a better choice. For example, assume that Mark, age 30, is a married graduate student with two dependents to support. He estimates that he can spend only $500 annually on life insurance. This premium would purchase about $56,000 of ordinary life insurance. The same premium would purchase about $500,000 of yearly renewable term insurance from many insurers. It is

difficult to justify the purchase of an ordinary life insurance policy if it leaves the insured inadequately covered.

Limited-Payment Life Insurance A **limited-payment policy** is another type of traditional whole life insurance. The insurance is permanent, and the insured has lifetime protection. The premiums are level, but they are paid only for a certain period. For example, Shannon, age 35, may purchase a 20-year limited payment policy in the amount of $25,000. After 20 years, the policy is completely paid up, and no additional premiums are required. A paid-up policy should not be confused with one that *matures*. A policy matures when the face amount is paid as a death claim or as an endowment. A policy is *paid up* when no additional premium payments are required.

The most common limited-payment policies are for 10, 20, 25, or 30 years. A policy paid up at age 65 or 70 is another form of limited-payment insurance. An extreme form of limited-payment life insurance is **single-premium whole life insurance**, which provides lifetime protection with a single premium. Because the premiums under a limited-payment policy are higher than those paid under an ordinary life policy, the cash values are also higher.

A limited-payment policy should be used with caution. It is extremely difficult for a person with a modest income to insure his or her life adequately with a limited-payment policy. Because of the relatively high premiums, the amount of permanent life insurance that can be purchased is substantially lower than if an ordinary life policy were purchased. If permanent life insurance is desired, most persons will find that their need for permanent protection can be better met by an ordinary life policy.

Endowment Insurance

Endowment insurance is another traditional form of life insurance. An endowment policy pays the face amount of insurance if the insured dies within a specified period; if the insured survives to the end of the endowment period, the face amount is paid to the policyowner at that time. For example, if Stephanie, age 35, purchased a 20-year endowment policy and died any time within the 20-year period, the face amount would be paid to her beneficiary. If

Insight 17.2

When Cash-Value Life Insurance Makes Sense

The key reason to buy cash-value insurance is to guarantee coverage for the rest of your life at a predictable cost. Many people don't need insurance that long—most need it to provide support for their kids until they graduate college or to cover their spouse until their pension kicks in. But some people in some circumstances may want lifelong protection:

■ *You'll owe estate taxes.* If your estate is large enough to create an estate-tax bill when you die (that is, if it's above $625,000 now [1998], a ceiling that will rise to $1 million in 2006), your heirs can use the death benefit to pay the IRS. Because you don't know when you will die, you need to hold on to your life insurance indefinitely.

■ *You don't know how long you'll need insurance.* Few companies offer term policies with level premiums for more than 30 years, and the price jumps after the term is over. If there's any chance that your need for insurance will run longer than that, buy a cash-value policy or a term policy that converts. For example, if you don't know how long you'll be supporting dependents, you might want a cash-value policy.

■ *You want to leave a legacy.* Even if no one will suffer financially when you die, you might want to leave

money to your grandchildren or to a charity—which may mean you have to keep the policy in force for the rest of your life.

■ *You need another tax shelter.* If you've invested as much as you can in your IRA, 401(k) plan, and other tax-deferred savings options, and if you need insurance for more than 10 to 15 years (the surrender period for many agent-sold policies), then cash-value insurance can give you another tax-deferred option. You may come out ahead if you trade frequently or are in a high tax bracket and tend to have large tax bills on your long-term savings.

How to Buy

Find an agent or financial planner who knows several companies' performance and limitations from experience—then get a few recommendations. Also contact a few low-load companies, which work directly with customers or through fee-only financial planners, such as USAA (800-531-4440), and Ameritas (direct sales through Veritas; 800-552-3553).

SOURCE: Adapted from "When Cash-Value Life Insurance Makes Sense," *Kiplinger's Personal Finance Magazine* (May 1998), p. 100.

she survives to the end of the period, the face amount is paid to her.

At the present time, endowment insurance is relatively unimportant in terms of total life insurance in force. Endowment insurance accounts for less than 1 percent of the life insurance in force. Because of the Deficit Reduction Act of 1984 (DEFRA), most new endowment policies cannot meet the tax definition of life insurance. If this definition is not met, the investment income credited to the cash surrender value is subject to current taxation. Thus, adverse tax consequences have discouraged the purchase of new endowment policies, and most life insurers have discontinued the sale of new endowment policies. Even so, many older endowment policies are still in force, and some contracts are still used in tax-qualified retirement plans. Although endowment policies are

no longer readily available in the United States, they remain popular in many foreign countries.

VARIATIONS OF WHOLE LIFE INSURANCE

Traditional whole life policies have been criticized because the rate of return on the savings component is relatively low and is not disclosed to the policyowner. As a result, many policyowners have replaced their older life insurance policies with life insurance products that offer higher returns. Also, life insurers have experienced keen competition in recent years from mutual funds, commercial banks, and other financial institutions. To become more competitive and to overcome the criticisms of traditional cash-value policies, insurers have developed a wide variety of whole life products that combine insurance protection with an investment element. Some important variations of whole life insurance include the following:

- Variable life insurance
- Universal life insurance
- Variable universal life insurance
- Current assumption whole life insurance
- Indeterminate-premium whole life insurance

Variable Life Insurance

Variable life insurance *can be defined as a fixed-premium policy in which the death benefit and cash surrender values vary according to the investment experience of a separate account maintained by the insurer*. The amount of life insurance and the cash surrender value may increase or decrease with the investment experience of the separate account.

Although there are different policy designs, variable life policies have certain common features. *First, a variable life policy is a permanent whole life contract with a fixed premium.* The premium is level and is guaranteed not to increase.

Second, the entire reserve is held in a separate account and is invested in equities or other investments. The policyowner generally has the option of investing the cash values in a variety of investments, such as a common stock fund, bond fund, balanced fund, money market fund, or international fund. If the investment experience is favorable, the face amount of insurance is increased. If the investment experience is poor, the amount of insurance could be reduced, but it can never fall below the original face amount.

Finally, cash surrender values are not guaranteed, and there are no minimum guaranteed cash values. The actual cash values depend on the investment experience. Thus, although the risk of excessive mortality and expenses is borne by the insurer, the investment risk is retained entirely by the policyowner.

Universal Life Insurance

Universal life insurance is another important variation of whole life insurance. A considerable amount of universal life is sold today as an investment rather than as protection.

Basic Characteristics Universal life insurance *can be defined as a flexible premium policy that provides lifetime protection under a contract that unbundles the protection and saving components.* The policyowner determines the amount and frequency of the premium payments, which can be monthly, quarterly, semiannually, annually, or a single payment. The premiums, less any explicit expense charges, are credited to a cash-value account from which monthly mortality charges are deducted and to which monthly interest is credited based on current rates that may change over time. In addition, many universal life policies have a monthly deduction for administrative expenses.

Universal life insurance has certain characteristics, which include the following:[4]

- Unbundling of component parts
- Two forms of universal life
- Considerable flexibility
- Cash withdrawals permitted
- Favorable income tax treatment

Unbundling of Component Parts A distinct characteristic of universal life insurance is the separation or unbundling of three components: protection component, saving component, and expense component. The separation of these parts is reported annually to the policyowner in a disclosure statement covering the previous year. The annual disclosure statement shows the premiums paid, death benefit, and cash surrender value. The statement also shows the mortality charge for the cost of insurance, expense charge for sales and administrative expenses, and interest credited to the cash-value account.

1. *Mortality charge.* A monthly mortality charge is deducted from the cash-value account for the cost of the insurance protection. The cost of insurance is determined by multiplying the applicable monthly rate by the net amount at risk (difference between the current death benefit and cash value).

The policy contains a table that shows the maximum rate per $1000 of insurance that the company can charge for the cost of the insurance protection. The maximum guaranteed rate is based either on the 1958 CSO mortality table or, for policies issued after 1989, on the 1980 CSO tables for male and female lives. These tables are conservative and overstate the actual death rates. Most insurers charge less than the contractually guaranteed maximum rate. However, the insurer has the right to increase the current mortality charge up to the maximum guaranteed rate stated in the policy.

In addition, the monthly rate for the cost of insurance is usually lower if the insured is a nonsmoker and meets certain other requirements that relate to smoking habits.

2. *Expense charges.* When a life insurance policy is sold, the insurer incurs relatively high first-year acquisition expenses because of commissions, sales, and administrative expenses. Thus, the premium charged must include a loading for expenses.

The expense charges in a universal life policy can be in the form of a (1) front-end load, (2) back-end load, or (3) both. If the policy has a *front-end load*, insurers typically deduct 5 to 10 percent of each premium for expenses. Some insurers also charge a first-year policy fee, such as $250. Many insurers also charge a monthly fee for administrative expenses, such as $4 or $5 monthly. There may be a special fee for each partial cash withdrawal, such as $25.

If the policy has only a *back-end load*, the entire premium is credited to the cash-value account and earns interest at the quoted rate. In such a case, how does the insurer recover its acquisition and renewal expenses? There are at least three sources of income available for expenses. *First, the insurer can credit the cash-value account with a lower interest rate than is actually earned on the invested assets.* The difference is available for expenses.

Second, the mortality charge may include a margin for expenses. The actual mortality charge assessed against the policy may be increased, which provides additional income for expenses.

Third, a back-end loaded policy typically has a relatively high back-end surrender charge that applies if the policy is surrendered during the early years. As a result, the policyowner can lose a substantial amount of money if the policy is surrendered during the early years. The surrender charge is reduced annually and usually disappears after a period of time, such as 10, 15, or 20 years.

3. *Interest rate.* The saving component or cash value is also shown separately. The interest earnings on the cash value depend on the interest rate. Two rates of interest are stated. The guaranteed cash value is based on a contractually *guaranteed minimum interest rate*, such as 4 or 4½ percent. The projected cash value is based on a higher *current interest rate* declared by the company, such as 6 percent. The current interest rate is not guaranteed but changes periodically depending on market conditions and company experience.

If the policyowner borrows the cash value, the amount borrowed is normally credited with a lower rate of interest. The cash value representing the amount borrowed is credited with either the guaranteed minimum interest rate or a rate 1 or 2 percent below the policy loan rate.

To illustrate the interaction of the three components, consider a simple example. Assume that Jacob, age 25, buys a universal life policy with a face amount of $100,000. The planned annual premium is $497, which can be changed. For sake of simplicity, assume that the mortality charge, expense charge, and the crediting of interest are made annually. (However, in practice, universal life policies have a monthly mortality and expense charge and monthly crediting of interest.)

Each premium is subject to a 5 percent expense charge. The policy also has a monthly administrative charge of $2.50. The policy provides for a maximum mortality charge, but the current mortality charge is only about two-thirds of the maximum rate. The policy has a guaranteed interest rate of 4 percent and a current interest rate of 6½ percent that is not guaranteed.

When Jacob pays the first premium of $497, there is an expense charge of approximately $25 (5 percent of $497). There is also an administrative charge of $30 ($2.50 monthly). The first-year mortality charge is $119 ($1.19 per $1000 of the specified $100,000 death benefit). The remaining $323 is credited with $21 of interest (6.5 percent on $323). Thus, the cash-value account at the end of the first year is $344. This calculation can be summarized as follows:

Annual premium ($497) −
  Expense and administrative charges ($55) −
  Mortality charge ($119) + Interest ($21)
    = Cash-value account at end of year ($344)

However, if Jacob surrenders the policy at the end of the first year, the surrender value is zero because of the surrender charge. A declining surrender

EXHIBIT 17.2

$100,000 Universal Life Policy, Male Age 25, Nonsmoker, 6½ Percent Assumed Interest

| | | End of year | | | | | | |
| | | Guaranteed[a] | | | Projected[b] | | | |
Year	Planned annual premium	Death benefit	Cash value	Surrender value	Death benefit	Cash value	Surrender value	Age
1	$497.00	$100,000	$ 291	$ 0	$100,000	$ 344	$ 0	26
2	497.00	100,000	595	0	100,000	723	21	27
3	497.00	100,000	912	210	100,000	1,122	420	28
4	497.00	100,000	1,242	540	100,000	1,546	844	29
5	497.00	100,000	1,585	930	100,000	1,999	1,344	30
6	497.00	100,000	1,943	1,335	100,000	2,481	1,873	31
7	497.00	100,000	2,315	1,753	100,000	2,995	2,433	32
8	497.00	100,000	2,703	2,188	100,000	3,531	3,016	33
9	497.00	100,000	3,095	2,627	100,000	4,103	3,635	34
10	497.00	100,000	3,504	3,083	100,000	4,712	4,291	35
11	497.00	100,000	3,942	3,568	100,000	5,387	5,013	36
12	497.00	100,000	4,387	4,059	100,000	6,095	5,767	37
13	497.00	100,000	4,839	4,558	100,000	6,849	6,568	38
14	497.00	100,000	5,298	5,064	100,000	7,642	7,408	39
15	497.00	100,000	5,765	5,578	100,000	8,508	8,321	40
16	497.00	100,000	6,241	6,101	100,000	9,423	9,283	41
17	497.00	100,000	6,714	6,620	100,000	10,389	10,295	42
18	497.00	100,000	7,195	7,148	100,000	11,411	11,364	43
19	497.00	100,000	7,675	7,675	100,000	12,493	12,493	44
20	497.00	100,000	8,153	8,153	100,000	13,672	13,672	45

[a] The guaranteed values are based on a 4 percent guaranteed interest rate.
[b] The projected values are based on an assumed interest rate of 6½ percent and are not guaranteed.

charge applies if the policy is terminated within 19 years after the issue date. Exhibit 17.2 shows in greater detail the cash-value accumulation based on the guaranteed and current interest rates.

Two Forms of Universal Life Insurance Another characteristic is that universal life insurance is available in two forms, as illustrated by Exhibit 17.3. *Option A pays a level death benefit during the early policy years.* As the cash value increases over time, the amount of pure insurance protection declines. However, the death benefit increases during the later years of the policy. If the death benefit did not increase, the policy would effectively become an endowment contract and would not meet the current

definition of life insurance by the Internal Revenue Service. Thus, the policy would not qualify for favorable income tax treatment.

Option B provides for an increasing death benefit. The death benefit is equal to a specified amount of insurance plus the accumulated cash value. Thus, as the cash value increases over time, the death benefit also increases. Option B is more expensive because the insurer must pay a higher death benefit.

Considerable Flexibility Universal life insurance also has several desirable features that provide considerable flexibility. They include the following:

■ Premiums can be increased or decreased, and the frequency of payments can be varied.

EXHIBIT 17.3
Universal Life Insurance Death Benefits

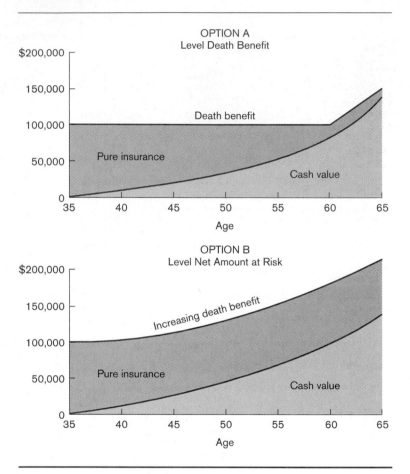

OPTION A
Level Death Benefit

OPTION B
Level Net Amount at Risk

SOURCE: Kenneth Black, Jr. and Harold D. Skipper, Jr., *Life Insurance*, thirteenth edition, 2000, p. 118. Reprinted by permission of Prentice-Hall, Inc., Upper Saddle River, NJ.

■ Premium payments can be any amount as long as there is sufficient cash value to cover mortality costs and expenses.

■ The death benefit can be increased or decreased. (Evidence of insurability is required to increase the amount of insurance.)

■ The policy can be changed from a level death benefit to a death benefit equal to a specified face amount plus the policy cash value (with evidence of insurability).

■ The policyowner can add to the cash value at any time, subject to maximum guideline limits that govern the relationship of the cash value to the death benefit.

■ A partial cash withdrawal (not a loan) can be made without terminating the policy.

■ Policy loans are permitted at competitive interest rates.

■ If the policy permits, additional insureds can be added to the policy.

Cash Withdrawals Permitted Part or all of the cash value can also be withdrawn. Interest is not charged on the amounts withdrawn, but the death benefit is reduced by the amount of the withdrawal. Most insurers also charge a surrender fee for each cash withdrawal.

Policy loans are also permitted. As stated earlier, the cash value borrowed is usually credited with only the lower guaranteed rate of interest or is credited with a rate that is below the current rate paid on nonborrowed funds.

Favorable Income-Tax Treatment At present, universal life insurance enjoys the same favorable federal income-tax advantages as traditional cash-value policies. The death benefit paid to a named beneficiary is normally received income-tax free. Interest credited to the cash value is not taxable to the policyowner in the year credited.

Limitations of Universal Life Insurance Although universal life insurance is superior to traditional cash-value policies in many respects, it has several limitations. Financial planners and consumer experts point out the following defects in present universal life insurance contracts.[5]

1. *Misleading rates of return.* Advertised rates of return on most universal life insurance contracts typically range from about 5 to 6½ percent, depending on the insurer. *However, the rates advertised are gross rates of return and not net rates.* The advertised rates do not reflect sales commissions, expenses, and the cost of the insurance protection. After these deductions, the effective yearly returns are substantially lower than the advertised rates and are often negative for several years after the policy is purchased. For example, an earlier study by the National Insurance Consumer Organization of four universal life policies for a 40-year-old nonsmoking male, based on a $250,000 death benefit and $2,500 annual premium, showed the following annual rates of return.[6]

Company	Quoted interest rate on saving portion	Net Rate of Return		
		5 years	10 years	20 years
Jefferson Standard	10.75%	−19.1%	5.0%	9.0%
Life of Virginia	10.25	8.9	9.4	9.9
Massachusetts Mutual	9.70	−11.7	2.9	7.5
USAA	10.25	6.8	8.6	9.8

The above calculations were based on the insurers' current interest rates and expense charges but assumed insurance rates for the least costly term policies available. As you can see, the advertised gross rates overstate the net rate of return on the saving component because they do not reflect charges for sales commissions, expenses, and the cost of insurance.

2. *Incomplete disclosure.* As stated earlier, the protection, saving, and expense components in a universal life policy are unbundled or separated. *However, this disclosure is incomplete and not rigorous, because the policyowner is not given information on how the expenses are allocated between the protection and saving components in the policy.* Professor Joseph Belth, a widely respected consumer insurance expert, maintains that the cost of the insurance protection and the yearly rate of return on the saving component cannot be accurately determined without making some assumptions concerning the allocation of expenses between the protection and saving components.[7] The yearly rates of return will vary widely depending on how the expenses are allocated between the protection and saving components. Belth argues that the advertising of universal life insurance policies is often misleading and deceptive because the ads quote a high gross return on the saving component and may quote a low cost for the protection component, but neither figure includes an allocation of the expense charges. Thus, he argues, net rates of return rather than gross rates should be disclosed to the policyowners.

3. *Decline in interest rates.* Many earlier sales presentations showed sizable cash values at some future date based on relatively high interest rates. The sales illustrations also showed that premium payments would vanish after a relatively short period, such as ten years. *However, interest rates have declined sharply in recent years. As a result, the cash-value and premium-payment projections based on higher interest rates are misleading and invalid.* Because of the sharp decline in interest rates, many policyowners have become disenchanted with universal life insurance and have surrendered or lapsed their policies. In particular, policyowners who expected premium payments to vanish after a relatively short period are angry because the premiums have not vanished according to the schedule furnished them when the policy was first purchased.

4. *Right to increase mortality charge.* Another limitation is that the insurer has the right to increase the current mortality charge up to the maximum limit. Thus, other expenses can be hidden in the mortality charge. If the insurer's expenses increase, the mortality charge could be increased to recoup these costs. The increase may not be noticed or questioned because the insured may believe that the increase is justified because he or she is getting older.

5. *Lack of firm commitment to pay premiums.* Another limitation is that the policyowner often lacks a firm commitment to pay premiums. As a result, the policy may lapse because of nonpayment of premiums. As stated earlier, under a universal life policy, premiums can be reduced or skipped. However, at some point, money may have to be added to the account, or the policy may lapse. Many insurers have experienced a substantial increase in lapsed universal life policies, which is partly due to the lack of a firm commitment by policyowners to make fixed and regular premium payments.

Variable Universal Life Insurance

Variable universal life insurance is another interest-sensitive product. This policy is similar to the universal life policy but with two major exceptions:

- The policyowner has a variety of investment options for investment of the cash values.
- There is no minimum guaranteed rate of interest.

A variable universal life policy allows the policyowner to invest the cash values in a wide variety of investments. For example, the insurer may have an aggressive stock fund, bond fund, balanced fund, global fund, real estate fund, and money market fund. Depending on the policyowner's investment goals and objectives and tolerance for risk, the funds can be invested accordingly.

In addition, a variable universal life policy has no minimum guaranteed rate of interest, and the cash value is not guaranteed. If the investment experience is poor, cash values can decline to zero. Thus, the investment risk falls entirely on the policyowner. There is wide variation in investment returns, depending on how the funds are invested. For this reason, financial planners recommend caution in the purchase of a variable universal life policy.

Current Assumption Whole Life Insurance

Current assumption whole life insurance (also called interest-sensitive whole life) is a nonparticipating whole life policy in which the cash values are based on the insurer's current mortality, investment, and expense experience. A nonparticipating policy is a policy that does not pay dividends.

Common Features Although current assumption whole life products vary among insurers, they share some common features, summarized as follows:[8]

1. *An accumulation account is used to reflect the cash value under the policy.* The accumulation account is credited with the premiums paid less expenses and mortality charges plus interest based on current rates.
2. *If the policy is surrendered, a surrender charge is deducted from the accumulation account.* A surrender charge that declines over time, such as 10 to 20 years, is deducted from the accumulation account to determine the net cash surrender value.
3. *A guaranteed interest rate and current interest rate are used to determine cash values.* The minimum cash values are based on the guaranteed interest rate, such as 4 or $4\frac{1}{2}$ percent. However, the accumulation account is credited with a higher interest rate based on current market conditions and company experience.
4. *A fixed death benefit and maximum premium level at the time of issue are stated in the policy.* (However, under the low-premium version discussed next, both are subject to change.)

In addition to having the preceding characteristics, current assumption whole life products generally can be classified into two categories: (1) low-premium products and (2) high-premium products.

Low-Premium Products Under the low-premium version, the initial premium is substantially lower than the premium paid for a regular, nonparticipating whole life policy. The low premium is initially guaranteed only for a certain period, such as two years. However, after the initial guaranteed period expires, a *redetermination provision* allows the insurer to recalculate the premium based on the same or different actuarial assumptions with respect to mortality, interest, and expenses (hence, the name "current assumption whole life"). If the new premium is higher than the initial premium, the policyowner generally has the option of paying the higher premium and maintaining the same death benefit. Alternatively, the policyowner can continue to pay the lower premium, but the death benefit is reduced.

High-Premium Products Although premiums are higher under the second category, these policies typically contain a *vanishing premium provision* in which the premiums vanish after a certain time period, such as ten years. The premium vanishes when the accumulation account exceeds the net single premium needed to pay up the contract based on current interest and mortality costs.[9] *However, the policy remains paid up only if current interest and mortality experience remain unchanged or are more favorable than initially assumed.* If the accumulation account falls below the minimum cash surrender value, additional premiums are required, or the standard nonforfeiture options apply.

Indeterminate-Premium Whole Life Insurance

An **indeterminate-premium whole life policy** *is a generic name for a nonparticipating policy that permits the insurer to adjust premiums based on anticipated future experience.* The maximum premium that can be charged is stated in the policy. The actual premium paid when the policy is issued is considerably lower and may be guaranteed for some initial period, such as two to three years. The intent is to have the actual premium paid reflect current market conditions. After the initial guaranteed period expires, the insurer can increase premiums up to the maximum limit if future anticipated experience with respect to mortality, investments, and expenses is expected to worsen. However, the premiums may not change if future experience is expected to be similar to past experience. Conversely, if future experience is expected to improve, then the insurer can further reduce the premiums if it desires to do so.

Exhibit 17.4 summarizes the basic characteristics of the major forms of life insurance. This chart helps to clarify the major types of life insurance and how they differ.

OTHER TYPES OF LIFE INSURANCE

A wide variety of additional life insurance products are sold today. Some policies are designed to meet special needs or have unique features. Others combine term insurance and cash-value life insurance to meet these needs.

Modified Life Insurance

A **modified life policy** is a whole life policy in which premiums are lower for the first three to five years and higher thereafter. The initial premium is slightly higher than for term insurance, but considerably lower than for an ordinary life policy issued at the same age.

There are several variations of the modified life policy. Under one version, the premium increases only once at the end of three or five years, and a dividend is paid that can be used to offset most or all of the premium increase. Under another version, the premiums gradually increase each year for five years and remain level thereafter. Finally, term insurance can be used for the first three to five years, which automatically converts into an ordinary life policy at a slightly higher premium than for a regular ordinary life policy issued at the same age.

The major advantage of a modified life policy is that insureds can purchase permanent insurance immediately even though they cannot afford the higher premiums for a regular policy. Modified life insurance is particularly attractive to persons who expect that their incomes will increase in the future and that higher premiums will not be financially burdensome.

Preferred Risks

Many life insurers sell policies at lower rates to individuals known as **preferred risks**. These people are individuals whose mortality experience is expected to be lower than average. The policy is carefully underwritten and is sold only to individuals whose health history, weight, occupation, and habits indicate more favorable mortality than the average. The insurer may also require the purchase of a minimum amount of insurance, such as $100,000. If an individual qualifies for a preferred rate, substantial savings are possible.

EXHIBIT 17.4
Life Insurance Comparison Chart

	Term	Ordinary life	Variable life	Universal life	Variable universal life	Current assumption whole life
Death benefit	Level or decreasing	Fixed level	Guaranteed minimum death benefit + increases from investments	Either level or increasing amount	Either level or increasing amount	Fixed level
Cash value	None	Guaranteed cash values	Depends on investment performance (not guaranteed)	Guaranteed minimum cash value + excess interest	Depends on investment performance (not guaranteed)	Guaranteed minimum cash value + excess interest
Premium	Increases at each renewal	Level premiums	Fixed level	Flexible premiums	Flexible premiums	May vary based on experience; guaranteed maximum premium
Policy loans	No	Yes	Yes	Yes Loans affect interest rate credited to cash value	Yes	Yes
Partial withdrawal of cash value	No	No	No	Yes	Yes	Yes
Surrender charge	No	No	Yes	Yes	Yes	Yes

SOURCE: Adapted from Glenn L. Wood, Claude C. Lilly III, Donald S. Malecki, Edward E. Graves, and Jerry S. Rosenbloom, *Personal Risk Management and Insurance*, fourth edition, Vol. 2 (Malvern, PA: American Institute for Property and Liability Underwriters, 1989), p. 259. Copyright © 1989 by the American Institute for Property and Liability Underwriters. Reprinted by permission of the American Institute for Property and Liability Underwriters.

A discount for nonsmokers is a current example of a preferred risk policy. Most insurers offer substantially lower rates to nonsmokers in recognition of the more favorable mortality that can be expected of this group.

Second-to-Die Life Insurance

Second-to-die life insurance (also called survivorship life) is a form of life insurance that insures two or more lives and pays the death benefit upon the death of the second or last insured. The insurance usually is whole life, but it can be term. Because the death proceeds are paid only upon the death of the second or last insured, the premiums are substantially lower than if two individual policies were issued.

Second-to-die life insurance is widely used at the present time in estate planning. As a result of an unlimited marital deduction, the deceased's entire estate can be left to a surviving spouse free of any federal estate tax. However, when the surviving spouse dies, a sizable federal estate tax may be payable. A second-to-die policy would provide the cash to pay the estate taxes.

Juvenile Insurance

Juvenile insurance refers to life insurance purchased by a parent or adult on the lives of children younger than a certain age, such as age 14 or 15. Insurers generally require the child to be at least one month old before he or she can be insured. Some insurers, however, will insure a child as young as one day old.

The major disadvantage in insuring children is that the family head may be inadequately insured. Scarce premium dollars that could be used to increase the life insurance on the family head are instead diverted to the children.

Other arguments for life insurance on children are not convincing. One argument is that insurance on children is less expensive because it is purchased at a younger age. This argument is deceptive. Although insurance premiums on children are lower, they are paid over a much longer time period. Premiums at the older ages are higher, but they are paid for shorter periods of time. Moreover, when present values are taken into account, the child's

policy can be more expensive. One study indicated that the present value of the premiums for a $20,000 life-paid-up-at-age-65 policy issued by one insurer on a child at age 15 is $5584 at a 4 percent discount rate. However, the present value of the premiums for the same type of policy issued by the same insurer at age 35 is only $3905.[10] In short, a juvenile insurance policy may be no bargain when it comes to cost.

Another argument is that life insurance should be purchased to guarantee the future insurability of the children. This argument has slightly greater validity, but only if the husband and wife are adequately insured. Unfortunately, a guaranteed insurability option cannot be purchased separately but must be added to the permanent life insurance policy. Even if future insurability cannot be guaranteed, the odds are that the children will still be able to purchase insurance in the future. More than 90 percent of all new policies sold are issued at standard rates.

Savings Bank Life Insurance

Savings bank life insurance (SBLI) is a type of life insurance that was sold originally by mutual savings banks in three states—Massachusetts, New York, and Connecticut. More recently, however, SBLI is also sold directly to consumers over the phone or through Internet Web sites in those states and in additional states as well. To be eligible, the applicant must either reside or work in the state where the insurance is sold. The objective is to avoid the substantial acquisition expenses incurred by commercial insurers when life insurance is initially sold.

SBLI sells a number of insurance products, including term and while life insurance, insurance for children and seniors, and tax-deferred annuities.

Maximum limits on the amount of life insurance on an individual's life have been raised. Applicants can now purchase a substantial amount of life insurance in those states where SBLI is sold. In Massachusetts, the amount of term insurance on a single life ranges from $100,000 to $5 million. In addition, SBLI products in Massachusetts are sold directly to consumers in a number of surrounding states, including Maine, New Hampshire, and Rhode Island.

In Connecticut, substantial amounts of SBLI life insurance can also be purchased. Applicants can purchase individual term insurance up to a maximum of $1 million; whole life insurance is also available up to a maximum of $1 million. Higher limits are available, but any amount over $1 million requires a separate underwriting decision.

In New York, SBLI is no longer sold through savings banks, except in a limited number of banks where agents are still available. The insurance is sold directly to consumers over the phone or through other sources. The amount of life insurance individuals can purchase is substantial. In early 2000, individual term insurance could be purchased in amounts up to $1 million. Whole life insurance is also available up to a maximum of $1 million.

The objective of SBLI is to provide low-cost insurance to consumers by holding down operating costs and the payment of high sales commissions. The cost of life insurance to consumers is an important topic that will be discussed in Chapter 19.

Industrial Life Insurance

Industrial life insurance (sometimes called *debit insurance*) is a class of life insurance that is issued in small amounts, and the premiums are payable weekly or monthly. In the past, the premiums were collected at the insured's home by an agent of the company. More than nine out of ten such policies were cash-value policies.

In recent years, industrial life insurance has also been called **home service life insurance**, reflecting the fact that individual policies are serviced by agents who call at the policyowner's home to collect the premiums. The amount of life insurance per policy generally ranges from $5000 to $25,000. Home service life insurance is relatively unimportant and accounts for less than 1 percent of all life insurance in force.

Group Life Insurance

Group life insurance is a type of insurance that provides life insurance on a group of people in a single master contract. Physical examinations are not required, and certificates of insurance are issued as evidence of insurance.

Group life insurance is important in terms of total life insurance in force. Most group life contracts provide term insurance coverage. In 1998, group life insurance accounted for 40 percent of all life insurance in force in the United States.[11] It is an important employee benefit provided by employers and will be discussed in greater detail in Chapter 22.

SUMMARY

- *Term insurance* provides temporary protection and is typically renewable and convertible without evidence of insurability. Term insurance is appropriate when income is limited, or there are temporary needs. Because term insurance usually has no cash values, it cannot be used for retirement or savings purposes.

- There are several traditional forms of whole life insurance. *Ordinary life insurance* is a form of whole life insurance that provides lifetime protection to age 100. The premiums are level and are payable for life. The policy develops an investment or saving element called a cash surrender value, which results from the overpayment of premiums during the early years. An ordinary life policy is appropriate when lifetime protection is desired or additional savings are desired.

- A *limited-payment policy* is another traditional form of whole life insurance. The insured also has lifetime protection, but the premiums are paid only for a limited period, such as 10, 20, or 30 years, or until age 65.

- An *endowment policy* pays the face amount of insurance if the insured dies within a specified period. If the insured survives to the end of the endowment period, the face amount of insurance is paid to the policyowner at that time.

- *Variable life insurance* is a fixed-premium policy in which the death benefit and cash surrender value vary according to the investment experience of a separate account maintained by the insurer. The entire reserve is held in a separate account and is invested in equities or other investments. The cash surrender values are not guaranteed.

- *Universal life insurance* is another variation of whole life insurance. Conceptually, universal life can be viewed as a flexible-premium policy that provides lifetime protection under a contract that separates the protection and saving components. Universal life insurance has the following features:

Unbundling of protection, savings, and expense components

Two forms of universal life insurance

Considerable flexibility

Cash withdrawals permitted

Favorable income-tax treatment

- *Variable universal life insurance* is similar to universal life insurance with two major exceptions. First, the cash values can be invested in a wide variety of investments. Second, there is no minimum guaranteed interest rate, and the investment risk falls entirely on the policyowner.

- *Current assumption whole life insurance* is a nonparticipating whole life policy in which the cash values are based on the insurer's current mortality, investment, and expense experience. An accumulation account is credited with a current interest rate that changes over time.

- An *indeterminate-premium whole life policy* is a nonparticipating policy that permits the insurer to adjust premiums based on anticipated future experience. The initial premiums are guaranteed for a certain time period and can then be increased up to some maximum limit.

- A *modified life policy* is a whole life policy in which premiums are lower for the first three to five years and are higher thereafter.

- Many insurers sell policies with lower rates to preferred risks. The policies are carefully underwritten and sold only to individuals whose health history, weight, occupation, and habits indicate more favorable mortality than average. Minimum amounts of insurance must be purchased.

- *Second-to-die life insurance* (*survivorship life*) insures two or more lives and pays the death benefit upon the death of the second or last insured.

- *Juvenile insurance* refers to life insurance purchased by a parent or other adult on the lives of children younger than a certain age, such as age 15 or 16.

- *Savings bank life insurance* is sold in mutual savings banks of three states—Massachusetts, New York, and Connecticut—and in surrounding states as well. It is also sold directly to consumers.

- *Industrial life insurance* is a type of insurance in which the policies are sold in small amounts, and the premiums are paid to an agent at the policyowner's home.

- *Group life insurance* provides life insurance on people in a group under a single master contract.

KEY CONCEPTS AND TERMS

Cash surrender value
Cash-value life insurance
Convertible
Current assumption whole life insurance
Endowment insurance
Group life insurance
Home service life insurance
Indeterminate-premium whole life policy
Industrial life insurance
Juvenile insurance
Limited-payment policy
Modified life policy
Ordinary life insurance
Preferred risks
Reentry term
Renewable
Savings bank life insurance
Second-to-die life insurance
Single-premium whole life insurance
Term insurance
Universal life insurance
Variable life insurance
Variable universal life insurance
Whole life insurance

REVIEW QUESTIONS

1. Describe the basic characteristics of term insurance.
2. When is the use of term insurance appropriate?
3. Describe the basic characteristics of ordinary life insurance.
4. Under what situations can an ordinary life policy be used?
5. Describe the basic features of a variable life insurance policy.
6. Explain the major characteristics of universal life insurance.
7. Explain the limitations of universal life insurance.
8. Describe the basic characteristics of variable universal life insurance.
9. Describe the major characteristics of a preferred risk policy.
10. Should life insurance be purchased on the lives of children? Explain.

APPLICATION QUESTIONS

1. Mark, age 32, wants to purchase a five-year term insurance policy in the amount of $100,000. The policy is both renewable and convertible.

a. Describe the situations under which term insurance can be used.

b. What rights does Mark have because the policy is renewable and convertible? Explain your answer.

c. If Mark wishes to save money for retirement purposes, do you recommend purchase of this contract?

d. Explain to Mark the advantages and disadvantages of a reentry term policy.

2. Kelly, age 35, is considering the purchase of the following individual life insurance policies with a face amount of $100,000.

(1) Five-year renewable and convertible term policy (renewable until age 65)

(2) Ordinary life policy

(3) Twenty-payment life policy

(4) Life-paid-up-at-age-65 policy

a. Which of these contracts require the highest and lowest current annual premium outlays?

b. If Kelly intends to keep the insurance until age 65, under which of these contracts will the annual premium increase?

c. Which of these contracts will allow Kelly to continue her life insurance beyond age 65? Explain your answer.

3. For each of the following situations, describe a life insurance policy that can be used to meet the situation. Treat each item separately.

a. An increasing face amount of life insurance to offset inflation

b. Insuring the human life value of an individual, age 30, at the lowest possible annual premium

c. Life insurance that is paid up when the insured retires at age 65

d. A policy that permits the cash value to be invested in stocks, bonds, or other investments

e. A policy that provides flexibility as financial circumstances change

f. Insurance that is sold over the counter at a depository institution

g. A policy designed to pay estate taxes upon the death of a surviving spouse

4. a. How is universal life insurance similar to traditional cash-value policies?

b. How does universal life insurance differ from traditional cash-value policies?

c. Explain the major differences between universal life and variable universal life insurance.

d. Describe the major features of each of the following:

(1) Current assumption whole life insurance

(2) Indeterminate premium whole life insurance

SELECTED REFERENCES

Belth, Joseph M. *Life Insurance: A Consumer's Handbook*, second edition. Bloomington, IN: Indiana University Press, 1985.

Black, Kenneth, Jr., and Harold D. Skipper, Jr. *Life Insurance*, thirteenth edition. Upper Saddle River, NJ: Prentice-Hall, 2000.

Dorfman, Mark S., and Saul W. Adelman. *Life Insurance: A Financial Planning Approach*, second edition. Chicago, IL: Dearborn Financial Publishing, 1992.

Graves, Edward E., ed. *McGill's Life Insurance*, second edition. Bryn Mawr, PA: The American College, 1998.

Mehr, Robert I., and Sandra G. Gustavson. *Life Insurance: Theory and Practice*, fourth edition. Plano, TX: Business Publications, 1987.

Rejda, George E., Constance M. Luthardt, Cheryl L. Ferguson, and Donald R. Oakes. *Personal Insurance*, fourth edition. Malvern, PA: Insurance Institute of America, 2000.

NOTES

1. These characteristics are discussed in greater detail in Edward E. Graves, ed., *McGill's Life Insurance*, second edition (Bryn Mawr, PA: The American College, 1998), Chapter 3; and Kenneth Black, Jr., and Harold D. Skipper, Jr., *Life Insurance*, twelfth edition (Englewood Cliffs, NJ: Prentice-Hall, 1994) Chapter 4.

2. Black and Skipper, pp. 86–87.

3. Because of increases in longevity, some insurers are now extending the period of protection to some later age, such as 103.

4. This section is based on Graves, pp. 77–89; Black and Skipper, pp. 126–142; and Joseph M. Belth, ed., "The War Over Universal Life—Part 1," *Insurance Forum*, Vol. 8, No. 11 (November 1981).

5. Limitations of universal life are discussed in detail in Belth, ed., "The War Over Universal Life—Part 1," *Insurance Forum*, Vol. 8, No. 11 (November 1981); "The War Over Universal Life—Part 2," *Insurance Forum*, Vol. 8, No. 12 (December 1981); and "Universal Life Insurance," *Consumer Reports* (August 1986).

Case Application

Sharon, age 28, is a single parent who earns $22,000 annually as a secretary at a local university. She is the sole support of her son, age 3. Sharon is concerned about the financial well-being of her son if she should die. Although she finds it difficult to save, she would like to start a savings program to send her son to college. She is presently renting an apartment but would like to own her home someday. A friend has informed her that life insurance might be useful in her present situation. Sharon knows nothing about life insurance, and the amount of income available for life insurance is limited. Assume you are a financial planner who is asked to make recommendations concerning the type of life insurance that Sharon should buy. The following types of life insurance policies are available:

- Five-year renewable and convertible term
- Life paid up at age 65
- Ordinary life insurance
- Universal life insurance

a. Which of these policies would best meet the need for protection of Sharon's son if she should die prematurely? Explain your answer.
b. Which of these policies best meets the need to accumulate a college retirement fund for Sharon's son? Explain your answer.
c. Which of these policies best meets the need to accumulate money for a down payment on a home? Explain your answer.
d. What major obstacle does Sharon face if she tries to meet all of her financial needs by purchasing cash-value life insurance?
e. Sharon decides to purchase the five-year term policy in the amount of $300,000. The policy has no cash value. Identify a basic characteristic of a typical term insurance policy that would help Sharon accumulate a fund for retirement.

6. Karen Slater, "Return on Universal Life Insurance Can Be a Lot Less Than Expected," *Wall Street Journal*, February 11, 1986.

7. See Belth, ed., "The War Over Universal Life—Part 1."

8. This section is based on Black and Skipper, pp. 109–113.

9. *Ibid.*, p. 112.

10. Glenn L. Wood, et al., *Personal Risk Management and Insurance*, fourth edition, Vol. II (Malvern, PA: American Institute for Property and Liability Underwriters, 1989), p. 29.

11. *ACLI Life Insurance Fact Book 1999* (Washington, DC: American Council of Life Insurance, 1999), p. 18.

 Students may take a self-administered test on this chapter at www.awlonline.com/rejda

Chapter 18

Life Insurance Contractual Provisions

> *"Nearly every family buys life insurance; yet few policyholders ever read a life contract with any effort to understand its provisions."*
>
> Mehr and Gustavson,
> *Life Insurance: Theory and Practice,* 4th ed.

Learning Objectives

After studying this chapter, you should be able to:

▲ Describe the incontestable clause, suicide clause, and grace period provision.

▲ Identify the dividend options that are found in participating policies.

▲ Explain the nonforfeiture options that are found in cash-value policies.

▲ Describe the various settlement options for the payment of life insurance proceeds.

▲ Describe the waiver of premium benefit and accelerated death benefits rider that can be added to a life insurance policy.

▲ Access an Internet site and evaluate consumer information about life insurance contracts.

Internet Resources

- **A. M. Best Company** is a rating organization that publishes books and periodicals relating to the insurance industry, including life insurance. The company publishes *Best's Review,* Life & Health edition, which provides considerable information about life insurance and the topics discussed in this chapter. Visit the site at:

  http://www.ambest.com

- The **American Council of Life Insurance** represents the life insurance industry on issues dealing with legislation and regulation at the federal and state levels. The site provides consumer information on the purposes and types of life insurance. Visit the site at:

  http://www.acli.com/

- **INSWEB** provides timely information and premium quotes for life insurance as well as for homeowners, auto, and other insurance products. Visit the site at:

  http://www.insweb.com/

- The **Insurance News Network** provides up-to-date information, premium quotes, and other consumer information on life insurance. The site also provides news releases about events that affect the insurance industry. Visit the site at:

  http://www.insure.com/

- The **National Underwriter Company** publishes books and other documents on life insurance products. The company publishes the *National Underwriter*, Life & Health/Financial Services edition, weekly trade publication that provides news about the life insurance industry. Visit the site at:

  www.nunews.com

- **Quicken Insurance** is considered to be one of the best consumer sites for obtaining timely information on life insurance and other insurance products. The site provides premium quotes for life insurance. Visit the site at:

  http://www.quickeninsurance.com

- **State insurance departments** provide consumer information on the various coverages discussed in this chapter. For starters, check out the following sites:

  New York   **www.ins.state.ny.us**

  Wisconsin   **badger.state.wi.us/agencies/oci/oci_home.htm**

  California   **www.insurance.ca.gov**

- The **Viatical Association of America** is a trade association that represents viatical settlement brokers and funding companies. A viatical settlement enables terminally ill individuals to obtain cash from their life insurance policies. Visit the site at:

  http://www.viatical.org/

ndrew, age 36, and Michelle, age 34, are married and have two small children. Michelle is the owner and beneficiary of a $300,000 life insurance policy on Andrew's life. Three years after the policy was purchased, Andrew committed suicide because of chronic depression and the bankruptcy of his business. Because Andrew deliberately caused his own death, Michelle was concerned that the insurer might deny payment of the claim. Michelle's life insurance agent, however, assured her that the claim would be paid in full.

In the preceding case, Michelle's financial security was affected by a contractual provision in a life insurance policy dealing with suicide. Life insurance contracts contain dozens of contractual provisions that affect the insured and beneficiary and payment of the death proceeds. Some contractual provisions are mandatory and must be included in every life insurance policy. Other provisions are optional.

This chapter discusses some common life insurance contractual provisions. It is divided into three major parts. The first part discusses life insurance contractual provisions that can have important financial consequences for consumers. The second part analyzes the basic options that frequently appear in life insurance policies, including dividend options, nonforfeiture options, and settlement options. The final part discusses additional benefits and riders that can be added to a life insurance policy.

LIFE INSURANCE CONTRACTUAL PROVISIONS

Life insurance policies contain numerous contractual provisions. This section discusses the major contractual provisions that life insurance consumers should understand.

Ownership Clause

The owner of a life insurance policy can be the insured, the beneficiary, a trust, or another party. In most cases, the applicant, insured, and owner are the same person. Under the **ownership clause**, *the policy-owner possesses all contractual rights in the policy while the insured is living.* These rights include naming and changing the beneficiary, surrendering the policy for its cash value, borrowing the cash value, receiving dividends, and electing settlement options. These rights generally can be exercised without the beneficiary's consent.

The policy also provides for a change of ownership. The policyowner can designate a new owner by filing an appropriate form with the company. The insurer may require the policy to be endorsed to show the new owner.

Entire-Contract Clause

The **entire-contract clause** *states that the life insurance policy and attached application constitute the entire contract between the parties.* All statements in the application are considered to be representations rather than warranties. No statement can be used by the insurer to void the policy unless it is a material misrepresentation and is part of the application. In addition, no officer of the insurer can change the policy terms unless the policyowner consents to the change.

There are two basic purposes of the entire-contract clause. It prevents the insurer from amending the policy without the knowledge or consent of the owner by changing its charter or bylaws. It also protects the beneficiary, because a statement made in connection with the application cannot be used by the insurer to deny a claim unless the statement is a material misrepresentation and is part of the application.

Incontestable Clause

The **incontestable clause** *states that the insurer cannot contest the policy after it has been in force two years during the insured's lifetime.* That is, after the policy has been in force for two years during the insured's lifetime, the insurer cannot later contest a death claim on the basis of material misrepresentation, concealment, or fraud when the policy was first issued. The insurer has two years in which to discover any irregularities in the contract. With few exceptions, if the insured dies, the death claim must be paid after the contestable period expires. For example, if Charles, age 40, applies for a life insurance policy, conceals the fact that he has high blood pressure, and dies within the two-year period, the insurer could contest the claim on the basis of a material concealment. But if he dies *after* expiration of the period, the insurer must pay the claim.

The purpose of the incontestable clause is to protect the beneficiary from financial hardship if the insurer tries to deny payment of the claim years after the policy was first issued. Because the insured is dead, he or she cannot refute the insurer's allegations. As a result, the beneficiary could be financially harmed if the claim is denied on the grounds of a material misrepresentation or concealment.

The incontestable clause is normally effective against fraud. If the insured makes a fraudulent misstatement to obtain the insurance, the company has two years to detect the fraud. Otherwise, the death claim must be paid. However, there are certain situations where the fraud is so outrageous that payment of the death claim would be against the public interest. In these cases, the insurer can contest the claim after the contestable period runs out. They include the following:[1]

- The beneficiary takes out a policy with the intent of murdering the insured.
- The applicant for insurance has someone else take a medical examination.
- An insurable interest does not exist at the inception of the policy.

Suicide Clause

Most life insurance policies contain a suicide clause. The **suicide clause** *states that if the insured commits* *suicide within two years after the policy is issued, the face amount of insurance will not be paid; there is only a refund of the premiums paid.* In some life insurance policies, suicide is excluded for only one year. If the insured commits suicide after the period expires, the policy proceeds are paid just like any other claim.

In legal terms, death is normally considered an unintentional act because of the strong instinct of self-preservation. Thus, there is a presumption against suicide. Consequently, the burden of proving suicide always rests on the insurer. To deny payment of the claim, the insurer must prove conclusively that the insured has committed suicide.

The purpose of the suicide clause is to reduce adverse selection against the insurer. By having a suicide clause, the insurer has some protection against the individual who wishes to purchase life insurance with the intention of committing suicide.

Grace Period

A life insurance policy also contains a **grace period** *during which the policyowner has a period of 31 days to pay an overdue premium.* Universal life and other flexible-premium policies usually have longer grace periods, such as 61 days. The insurance remains in force during the grace period. If the insured dies within the grace period, the overdue premium is deducted from the policy proceeds.

The purpose of the grace period is to prevent the policy from lapsing by giving the policyowner additional time to pay an overdue premium. The policyowner may be temporarily short of funds or may have forgotten to pay the premium. In such cases, the grace period provides considerable financial flexibility.

Reinstatement Clause

A policy may lapse if the premium has not been paid by the end of the grace period, or if an automatic premium loan provision is not in effect. The **reinstatement provision** *permits the owner to reinstate a lapsed policy.* The following requirements must be fulfilled to reinstate a lapsed policy:

- Evidence of insurability is required.
- All overdue premiums plus interest must be paid from their respective due dates.

- Any policy loan must be repaid or reinstated, with interest from the due date of the overdue premium.
- The policy must not have been surrendered for its cash value.
- The policy must be reinstated within a certain period, typically three or five years from the date of lapse.

It may be advantageous for a policyowner to reinstate a lapsed policy rather than purchase a new one. First, the premium is lower because the reinstated policy was issued at an earlier age. Second, the acquisition expenses incurred in issuing the policy must be paid again under a new policy. Third, cash values and dividends are usually higher under the reinstated policy; the new policy may not develop any cash values until the end of the third year. Fourth, the incontestable period and suicide period under the old policy may have expired. Reinstatement of a lapsed policy does not reopen the suicide period, and a new incontestable period generally applies only to statements contained in the application for reinstatement. Statements contained in the original application cannot be contested after the original contestable period expires. Finally, the reinstated policy may contain more favorable policy provisions, such as a 6 percent interest rate on policy loans.

A major disadvantage of reinstating a lapsed policy is that a substantial cash outlay is required if the policy lapsed several years earlier. Also, most life insurers have reduced their rates over time and have developed new products. As a result, it may be less expensive to purchase a new policy rather than reinstate a lapsed policy even though the insured is older when the new purchase is made. As a practical matter, most lapsed policies are not reinstated because of the required cash outlay.

Misstatement of Age or Sex Clause

Under the **misstatement of age or sex clause,** *if the insured's age or sex is misstated, the amount payable is the amount that the premiums paid would have purchased at the correct age and sex.* For example, assume that Troy, age 35, applies for a $20,000 ordinary life policy, but his age is incorrectly stated as age 34. If the premium is $20 per $1000 at age 35 and $19 per $1000 at age 34, the insurer will pay only 19/20 of the death proceeds. Thus, only $19,000 would be paid (19/20 × $20,000 = $19,000).

Beneficiary Designation

The beneficiary is the party named in the policy to receive the policy proceeds. The principal types of beneficiary designations are as follows:

- Primary and contingent beneficiary
- Revocable and irrevocable beneficiary
- Specific and class beneficiary

Primary and Contingent Beneficiary A **primary beneficiary** *is the beneficiary who is first entitled to receive the policy proceeds on the insured's death.* A **contingent beneficiary** *is entitled to the proceeds if the primary beneficiary dies before the insured.* If the primary beneficiary dies before receiving the guaranteed number of payments under an installment settlement option, the remaining payments are paid to the contingent beneficiary.

In many families, the husband will name his wife primary beneficiary (and vice versa), and the children will be named as contingent beneficiaries. The legal problem in naming *minor children* as beneficiaries is that they lack the legal capacity to receive the policy proceeds directly. Most insurers will not pay the death proceeds directly to minor children.[2] Instead, they will require a guardian to receive the proceeds on the minor's behalf. If a court of law appoints a *guardian*, payment of the proceeds may be delayed and legal expenses will be incurred. One solution is to have a *guardian* named in the will who can legally receive the proceeds on the children's behalf. Another approach is to pay the proceeds to a *trustee* (such as a commercial bank with a trust department), which has the discretion and authority to use the funds for the children's welfare.

The insured's estate can be named as primary or contingent beneficiary. However, many financial planners do not recommend designation of the estate as beneficiary. The death proceeds may be subject to attorney fees and other probate expenses, federal estate taxes, state inheritance taxes, and claims of creditors. Payment of the proceeds may also be delayed until the estate is settled.

Revocable and Irrevocable Beneficiary Most beneficiary designations are revocable. A **revocable beneficiary** *means that the policyowner reserves the right to change the beneficiary designation without the beneficiary's consent.* The revocable beneficiary has only the expectation of benefits, and the policyowner can change the beneficiary whenever desired. All policy rights under the contract can be exercised without the consent of the revocable beneficiary.

In contrast, an **irrevocable beneficiary** *is one that cannot be changed without the beneficiary's consent.* If the policyowner wishes to change the beneficiary designation, the irrevocable beneficiary must consent to the change. However, most policies today provide that the interest of a beneficiary, even an irrevocable beneficiary, terminates if the beneficiary dies before the insured. Thus, if the irrevocable beneficiary dies before the insured, all rights to the policy proceeds revert to the policyowner, who can then name a new beneficiary.[3]

Specific and Class Beneficiary A **specific beneficiary** means the beneficiary is specifically named and identified. In contrast, under a **class beneficiary**, a specific person is not named but is a member of a group designated as beneficiary, such as "children of the insured." A class designation is appropriate whenever the insured wishes to divide the policy proceeds equally among members of a particular group.

Most insurers restrict the use of a class designation because of the problem of identifying members of the class. Although all insurers permit the designation of children as a class, they will not permit this designation to be used when the class members cannot be identified, or the relationship to the insured is remote. For example, the class designation "my children" means that all children of the insured share in the policy proceeds, whether legitimate, illegitimate, or adopted. But if "children of the insured" is used as the designation, the insured's children by any marriage would be included, but the spouse's children by a former marriage would be excluded. Thus, a class designation must be used with great care.

Change-of-Plan Provision

Life insurance policies usually contain a **change-of-plan provision** that allows policyowners to exchange their present policies for different contracts. The purpose of this provision is to provide flexibility to the policyowner. The original policy may no longer be appropriate if family needs and financial objectives change.

If the change is to a *higher-premium policy*, such as changing from an ordinary life to a limited-payment policy, the policyowner must pay the difference in the policy reserve under the new policy and the policy reserve under the original policy. Evidence of insurability is not required, because the pure insurance protection (net amount at risk) is reduced.

In addition, based on company practice, the policyowner may be allowed to change to a *lower-premium policy*, such as changing from a limited-payment policy to an ordinary life policy. In such a case, the insurer refunds the difference in cash values under the two policies to the policyowner. Evidence of insurability is required in this type of change, because the pure insurance protection is increased (higher net amount at risk).

Exclusions and Restrictions

A life insurance policy contains remarkably few exclusions and restrictions. *Suicide* is excluded only for the first two years. During a period of war, some insurers may insert a **war clause** in their policies, which excludes payment if the insured dies as a direct result of war. The purpose of the war clause is to reduce adverse selection against the insurer when large numbers of new insureds may be exposed to death during war time.

In addition, **aviation exclusions** may be present in some policies. Most newly issued policies do not contain any exclusions with respect to aviation deaths, and aviation death claims are paid like any other claim. However, some insurers exclude aviation deaths other than as a fare-paying passenger on a regularly scheduled airline. Military aviation may also be excluded or be covered only by payment of an extra premium. In addition, a private pilot who does not meet certain flight standards may have an aviation exclusion rider inserted in the policy, or be charged a higher premium.

During the initial underwriting of the policy, the insurer may discover *certain undesirable activities or hobbies* of the insured. These activities may be excluded or covered only by payment of an extra premium. Some excluded activities are automobile racing, sky diving, scuba diving, flying a hang glider, and travel or residence in a dangerous country.

Payment of Premiums

Life insurance premiums can be paid annually, semiannually, quarterly, or monthly. If the premium is paid other than annually, the policyowner must pay a carrying charge, which can be relatively expensive when the true rate of interest is calculated. For example, the semiannual premium may be 52 percent of the annual premium and so could be viewed as a carrying charge of only 4 percent. However, the actual charge is 16.7 percent. Assume that your annual premium is $1000. You pay the semiannual premium of $520 and defer payment of $480. Six months later, the $480 and $40 carrying charge are due. This means that you are paying $40 for the use of $480 for six months, which is the equivalent of an annual percentage rate of 16.7 percent.[3]

Assignment Clause

A life insurance policy is freely assignable to another party. There are two types of assignments. *Under an* **absolute assignment,** *all ownership rights in the policy are transferred to a new owner.* For example, the policyowner may wish to donate a life insurance policy to a church, charity, or educational institution. This goal can be accomplished by an absolute assignment. The new owner can then exercise the ownership rights in the policy.

Under a **collateral assignment,** *the policyowner assigns a life insurance policy as collateral for a loan.* The assignment form used is typically the American Bankers Association's assignment form. *Under this form, only certain rights are transferred to the creditor to protect its interest, and the policyowner retains the remaining rights.* The party to whom the policy is assigned can receive the policy proceeds only to the extent of the loan; the balance of the proceeds is paid to the beneficiary.

The purpose of the assignment clause is to protect the insurer from paying the policy proceeds twice if an unrecorded assignment is presented to the insurer after the death claim is paid to the beneficiary. If the insurer is not notified of the assignment, the proceeds are paid to the named beneficiary when the policy matures as a death claim or endowment. Under general rules of law, the insurer is relieved of any further obligation under the policy, even though a valid assignment is in existence at the insured's death. However, if the insurer is notified of the assignment, a new contract exists between the insurer and assignee (one who receives the assignment, such as a bank), and the insurer then recognizes the assignee's rights as being superior to the beneficiary's rights.

Policy Loan Provision

Cash-value life insurance contains a **policy loan provision** that allows the policyowner to borrow the cash value. The interest rate is stated in the policy. Older policies typically have a 5 or 6 percent loan rate. Newer policies typically have an 8 percent loan rate. However, all states permit insurers to charge a variable policy loan interest rate based on the National Association of Insurance Commissioner's model bill. If a variable rate is used, limits exist on the maximum rate that can be charged. The maximum interest rate is the greater of Moody's Composite Yield on seasoned corporate bonds two months prior to the determination date or the interest rate credited to the cash value plus 1 percent.[4] The policy loan rate can be revised as often as every three months. Many insurers pay higher dividends to policyholders who have their old policies endorsed to provide for a flexible loan rate.

On newly issued participating contracts, many insurers will reduce the dividend based on the amount of cash value borrowed. This step has the effect of indirectly increasing the effective interest rate on the policy loan. Under interest-sensitive policies, such as universal life and variable universal life, the current interest rate credited to the cash values that are borrowed is typically reduced, which again increases the effective interest rate on the loan.

Interest on a policy loan must either be paid annually or added to the outstanding loan if not paid. If the loan is not repaid by the time the policy matures as a death claim or endowment, the face amount of the policy is reduced by the amount of indebtedness. With the exception of a policy loan to pay a premium, the insurer can defer granting the loan for up to six months, but this is rarely done.

Persons who borrow their cash values often believe that they are paying interest on their own money. *This view is clearly incorrect. The cash legally belongs to the insurer.* Although you have the contractual right to surrender or borrow the cash value, the cash legally belongs to the insurer. Interest must be paid on the loan because the insurer assumes a certain interest rate when premiums, legal reserves, dividends, and surrender values are calculated. The insurer's assets must be invested in interest-bearing securities and other investments so that the contractual obligations can be met. *A policyowner must pay interest on the loan to offset the loss of interest to the insurer.* If the loan had not been granted, the insurer could have earned interest on the funds.

Notice, too, that policy loan provisions make it necessary for the insurer to keep some assets in lower-yielding, liquid investments to meet the demand for policy loans. Because these funds could have been invested in higher-yielding investments, policyowners who borrow should pay interest because higher yields must be forsaken to maintain liquidity.

Advantages of Policy Loans The major advantage of a policy loan is the relatively low rate of interest that is paid. This is especially true for older contracts. The low policy loan rates of 5, 6, or 8 percent are substantially lower than the rates charged by banks. There is also no credit check on the policyowner's ability to repay the loan; there is no fixed repayment schedule; and the policyowner has complete financial flexibility in determining the amount and frequency of loan repayments.

Disadvantages of Policy Loans The major disadvantage is that the policyowner is not legally required to repay the loan, and the policy could lapse if the total indebtedness exceeds the available cash value. Rather than repay the loan, the policyowner may let the policy lapse or may surrender the policy for any remaining cash value. Finally, if the loan has not been repaid by the time the policy matures, the face amount of insurance is reduced by the amount of the debt.

Automatic Premium Loan

The automatic premium loan provision can be added to most cash-value policies. *Under the* **automatic premium loan provision,** *an overdue premium is automatically borrowed from the cash value after the grace period expires, provided the policy has a loan value sufficient to pay the premium.* The policy continues in force just as before, but a premium loan is now outstanding. Interest is charged on the premium loan at the stated contractual rate. Premium payments can be resumed at any time without evidence of insurability.

The basic purpose of an automatic premium loan is to prevent the policy from lapsing because of nonpayment of premiums. The policyowner may be temporarily short of funds or may forget to pay the premium. Thus, the automatic premium loan provides considerable financial flexibility to the policyowner.

The automatic premium loan provision, however, has two major disadvantages. First, it may be overused. The policyowner may get into the habit of using the automatic premium loan provision too frequently. If the cash values are relatively modest and are habitually borrowed over an extended period, they could eventually be exhausted, and the contract would terminate. Second, the policy proceeds will be reduced if the premium loans are not repaid by the time the policy matures.

DIVIDEND OPTIONS

Life insurance policies frequently contain dividend options. If the policy pays dividends, it is known as a **participating policy.** Both stock and mutual insurers issue participating policies; the policyowner has the right to share in the divisible surplus of the insurer. The dividend represents largely a refund of part of the gross premium if the insurer has favorable experience with respect to mortality, interest, and expenses. In contrast, a policy that does not pay dividends is known as a **nonparticipating policy.**

Policy dividends are generally derived from three sources: (1) the difference between expected and actual mortality experience; (2) excess interest earnings on the assets required to maintain legal reserves; and (3) the difference between expected and actual operating expenses. Because the dividends paid are determined by the insurer's actual operating experience, they cannot be guaranteed.

There are several ways in which dividends can be taken:

- Cash
- Reduction of premiums
- Accumulate at interest
- Paid-up additions
- Term insurance (fifth dividend option)

Cash

A dividend is usually payable after the policy has been in force for a stated period, typically one or two years. The policyowner receives a check equal to the dividend, usually on the anniversary date of the policy.

Reduction of Premiums

The dividend can be used to reduce the next premium coming due. The dividend notice will indicate the amount of the dividend, and the policyowner must then remit the difference between the premium and actual dividend paid. This option is appropriate whenever premium payments become financially burdensome. It can also be used if the policyowner has a substantial reduction in income and expenses must be reduced.

Accumulate at Interest

The dividend can be retained by the insurer and accumulated at interest. The policy guarantees a minimum interest rate such as 3 percent, but a higher rate may be paid based on current market conditions. The accumulated dividends generally can be withdrawn at any time. If not withdrawn, they are added to the amount paid when the policy matures, or the contract is surrendered for its cash value. The dividend itself is not taxable for income-tax purposes. However, the interest income on the accumulated dividends is taxable income and must be reported annually for federal and state income-tax purposes. Thus, the interest option may be undesirable for policyowners who wish to minimize income taxes.

Paid-up Additions

Under the paid-up additions option, the dividend is used to purchase a small amount of paid-up whole life insurance. For example, assume that Paige, age 20, owns an ordinary life policy. If a dividend of $50 were paid, about $200 of paid-up whole life insurance could be purchased.

The paid-up additions option has some favorable features. *First, the paid-up additions are purchased at net rates, not gross rates*; there is no loading for expenses. *Second, evidence of insurability is not required.* Thus, if the insured is substandard in health or is uninsurable, this option may be appealing, because additional amounts of life insurance can be purchased without demonstrating insurability.

The paid-up additions option also has some unfavorable features. *First, in some policies, the paid-up increments of insurance may be overpriced.* The frequently advanced argument that paid-up additions are relatively inexpensive because they are purchased at net rates is somewhat misleading. In a careful price analysis of paid-up additions, Professor Joseph Belth found that the paid-up additions purchased in some policies were indeed low-priced, but in other policies, they were high-priced increments of life insurance.[5]

A second disadvantage is that paid-up additions are a form of single-premium whole life insurance. Consumer experts point out that rarely is a single-premium policy appropriate for most insureds. For example, if $100,000 of ordinary life insurance is desired, the insured normally does not pay a single premium of $40,000 to obtain the protection. Why, then, should a $40 dividend be used to buy a $100 paid-up addition? Because most persons are underinsured, a better approach would be to use the dividends to purchase another policy, assuming, of course, that the person is insurable.[6]

Term Insurance (Fifth Dividend Option)

Some insurers have a fifth dividend option by which the dividend is used to purchase term insurance. Two forms of this option are typically used. *The dividend can be used to purchase one-year term insurance equal to the cash value of the basic policy, and the remainder of the dividend is then used to buy paid-up additions or is accumulated at interest.* This option may be appropriate if the policyowner regularly borrows the cash value. The face amount of the policy would not be reduced by the amount of any outstanding loans at the time of death.

A second form of this option is to use the dividend to purchase yearly renewable term insurance. The actual amount of term insurance purchased depends on the amount of the dividend, the insured's attained age, and the insurer's term insurance rates. However, it is not uncommon for a $40 dividend to purchase $10,000 or more yearly renewable term insurance under this option. Unfortunately, this desirable option is offered by only a small proportion of companies.

Other Uses of Dividends

The dividends can also be used to convert a policy into a *paid-up contract*. If the paid-up option is used, the policy becomes paid-up whenever the reserve value under the basic contract plus the reserve value of the paid-up additions or deposits equal the net single premium for a paid-up policy at the insured's attained age. For example, an ordinary life policy issued at age 25 could be paid up by age 48 by using this option.

The dividend can also be used to *mature a policy as an endowment.* When the reserve value under the basic policy plus the reserve value of the paid-up additions or deposits equal the face amount of insurance, the policy matures as an endowment. For example, a $50,000 ordinary life policy issued at age 25 would mature as an endowment at age 58 by using this option.[7]

Finally, keep in mind that the use of dividend options will vary among policyowners. There is no best dividend option. The best option to use is the one that best meets your financial goals and objectives (see Insight 18.1).

NONFORFEITURE OPTIONS

If a cash-value policy is purchased, the policyowner pays more than is actuarially necessary for the life insurance protection. Thus, the policyowner should get

Insight 18.1

something back if the policy is surrendered. The payment to a withdrawing policyowner is known as a nonforfeiture value or cash surrender value.

All states have standard **nonforfeiture laws** that require insurers to provide at least a minimum nonforfeiture value to policyowners who surrender their policies. There are three **nonforfeiture options** or cash surrender options:

- Cash value
- Reduced paid-up insurance
- Extended term insurance

Cash Value

The policy can be surrendered for its cash value, at which time all benefits under the policy cease. A policy normally does not build any cash value until the end of the second or third year, although some policies have a small cash value at the end of the first year. The cash values are small during the early years because the relatively high first-year acquisition expenses incurred by the insurer in selling the policy have not yet been recovered. However, over a long period, the cash values accumulate to substantial amounts.

The insurer can delay payment of the cash value for six months if the policy is surrendered. This provision is required by law and is a carryover from the Great Depression of the 1930s, when cash demands on life insurers were excessive. Insurers generally do not delay payment of the cash value because of fear that confidence in the company will be undermined.

The cash surrender option can be used if the insured no longer needs life insurance. Although it is usually not advisable to surrender a policy for cash because other options may be more appropriate, there are circumstances where the cash surrender option can be used. For example, if an insured is retired and no longer has any dependents to support, the need for substantial amounts of life insurance may be reduced. In such a case, the cash surrender option could be used (see Insight 18.2)

Reduced Paid-up Insurance

*Under the **reduced paid-up insurance** option, the cash surrender value is applied as a net single premium to purchase a reduced paid-up policy.* The amount of insurance purchased depends on the insured's attained age, the cash surrender value, and the mortality and interest assumptions stated in the original contract. The reduced paid-up policy is the same as the original policy, but the face amount of insurance is reduced. An ordinary life or limited-payment policy would be converted to a reduced paid-up policy. An endowment policy would mature at the same date but for a reduced amount. If the original policy is participating, the reduced paid-up policy also pays dividends.

The reduced paid-up insurance option is appropriate if life insurance is still needed, but the policy-

Insight 18.2

How to Cash in Life Insurance: To Wring Money from a Policy You Don't Need, Try These Strategies

Take this pop quiz to see if you're in line for some serious dough: 1. Does anyone else depend on your income? 2. Do you expect to have an estate-tax bill? 3. Do you own a cash-value life insurance policy?

If you answered no to the first two questions and yes to the third, you may want to know the answer to this question: What's the best way to get the cash from the policy?

You have a slew of complicated options that can help you avoid taxes on your payout: borrowing from the policy, making a tax-free exchange into an annuity, withdrawing a little at a time. But in most cases, the simplest method is best: Cash out the policy.

If you cash out your life insurance policy, you'll owe income tax on any amount you receive above what you paid in premiums. But "it's unusual to see someone owe taxes," says John Hixson, a financial planner from Lake Charles, Louisiana. Because most policies are loaded with front-end fees, it can take 12 to 15 years before the cash value is greater than the premiums paid, says Hixson.

With a universal or variable universal life insurance policy, you can withdraw up to the amount of premiums paid without owing taxes. And with whole life—for which you have to cash in the entire policy—your tax bill may not be as steep as you think because, as with any life insurance policy, you're taxed only on the earnings, not the entire cash value.

Other Options

If the potential tax bill seems daunting, you could borrow against most (but not all) of your cash value. If you die before repaying the loan, the amount will be subtracted from the death benefit and never taxed. But this strategy has some drawbacks: You'll owe interest on the loan and you'll still be paying for insurance you no longer need. "I can't think of a situation where the tax deferral is going to overcome the cost of the insurance" says Hixson.

Some policies let you pay interest and any premiums from your remaining cash value—eliminating out-of-pocket costs—but your policy would be in danger of "self-destructing," says Ed Graves, a professor of insurance at the American College in Bryn Mawr, Pennsylvania. If those costs nibble away at the cash value for too long, the policy may run out of money and eventually lapse—leaving you with just as large a tax bill as if you'd withdrawn the money.

You can also defer taxes and cut insurance costs by making a tax-free exchange into a variable annuity. But this strategy rarely helps if you need the money soon, says Joe Harper, a financial planner from Columbus, Ohio. You'll usually begin a new surrender period—during which you may be charged up to 9 percent of your principal if you withdraw money in the first seven years—and you'll have to pay a new set of annual fees. If you die with an annuity, your heirs will be taxed on the gains; they won't with stocks or mutual funds. Life-insurance death benefits are also income-tax-free.

Source: Kimberly Lankford, "How to Cash in Life Insurance," *Kiplinger's Personal Finance Magazine* (May 1999), p. 52. Reprinted with permission.

owner does not wish to pay premiums. For example, assume that Mark has a $100,000 ordinary life policy that he purchased at age 21. He is now age 65 and wants to retire, but he does not want to pay premiums after retirement. The cash surrender value can be used to purchase a reduced paid-up policy of about $83,000.

Extended Term Insurance

Under the **extended term insurance option,** *the net cash surrender value is used as a net single premium to extend the full face amount of the policy (less any indebtedness) into the future as term insurance for a certain number of years and days.* In effect, the cash value is used to purchase a paid-up term insurance policy equal to the original face amount (less any indebtedness) for a limited period. The length of the term insurance protection is determined by the insured's attained age when the option is exercised, the net cash surrender value, and the premium rates for extended term insurance. For example, in our earlier illustration, if Mark stopped paying premiums at age 65, the cash value would be sufficient to keep the $100,000 policy in force for another 15 years and 272 days. If he is still alive after that time, the policy is no longer in force.

If the policy lapses for nonpayment of premiums, and the policyowner has not elected another option, the extended term option automatically goes into effect in most policies. This means that many policies are still in force even though the policyowners mistakenly believe the policy is not in force because of nonpayment of premiums. However, if the automatic premium loan provision has been added to the policy, it has priority over the extended term option.

A whole life or endowment policy contains a table of nonforfeiture values that indicates the benefits under the three options at various ages. Exhibit 18.1 illustrates the nonforfeiture values for an ordinary life policy issued at age 21.

SETTLEMENT OPTIONS

Settlement options, or *optional methods of settlement,* refer to the various ways that the policy proceeds can be paid other than in a lump sum. The policyowner may elect the settlement option prior to the insured's death, or the beneficiary may be granted the right. In addition, most policies permit the cash surrender value to be paid under the settlement options if the policy is surrendered. The most common settlement options are as follows:

- Interest option
- Fixed-period option
- Fixed-amount option
- Life income options

Interest Option

Under the **interest option,** *the policy proceeds are retained by the insurer, and interest is periodically paid*

EXHIBIT 18.1
Nonforfeiture Options (Dollar Amount for Each $1000 of Ordinary Life Insurance Issued at Age 21)

End of policy year	Cash or loan value	Paid-up insurance	Extended term insurance Years	Days
1	$ 0.00	$ 0	0	0
2	0.00	0	0	0
3	4.79	15	1	315
4	16.21	48	6	161
5	27.91	81	11	15
6	39.91	113	14	275
7	52.20	145	17	158
8	64.78	176	19	157
9	77.66	206	20	342
10	90.84	236	22	29
11	104.33	265	22	351
12	118.13	294	23	231
13	132.25	322	24	54
14	146.69	350	24	191
15	161.43	377	24	290
16	176.47	403	24	356
17	191.79	429	25	28
18	207.38	454	25	42
19	223.22	478	25	36
20	239.29	502	25	13
Age 60	563.42	806	17	26
Age 65	608.49	833	15	272

to the beneficiary. The interest can be paid monthly, quarterly, semiannually, or annually. Most insurers guarantee a minimum interest rate on the policy proceeds retained under the interest option. If the policy is participating, a higher rate of interest is paid based on excess interest earnings. For example, an insurer may pay 5 percent on the proceeds even though the contractual rate is only 3 percent.

The beneficiary can be given withdrawal rights, by which part or all of the proceeds can be withdrawn. The beneficiary may also be given the right to change to another settlement option.

The interest option provides considerable flexibility, and it can be used in a wide variety of circum-

EXHIBIT 18.2

Fixed-Period Option (Minimum Monthly Income Payments per $1000 Proceeds, 3 Percent Interest)

Period (years)	Monthly payment	Period (years)	Monthly payment	Period (years)	Monthly payment
1	$84.50	11	$8.86	21	$5.32
2	42.87	12	8.24	22	5.15
3	29.00	13	7.71	23	4.99
4	22.07	14	7.26	24	4.84
5	17.91	15	6.87	25	4.71
6	15.14	16	6.53	26	4.59
7	13.17	17	6.23	27	4.48
8	11.69	18	5.96	28	4.37
9	10.54	19	5.73	29	4.27
10	9.62	20	5.51	30	4.18

stances. In particular, it can be effectively used if the funds will not be needed until some later date. For example, educational funds could be retained at interest until the children are ready for college. Meanwhile, the interest income can supplement the family's income.

Fixed-Period Option

Under the **fixed-period (installment-time) option,** *the policy proceeds are paid to a beneficiary over some fixed period of time.* Payments can be made monthly, quarterly, semiannually, or annually. Both principal and interest are systematically liquidated under this option. If the primary beneficiary dies before receiving all payments, the remaining payments will be paid to a contingent beneficiary or to the primary beneficiary's estate.

Exhibit 18.2 illustrates the fixed-period option of one insurer for each $1000 of proceeds at a guaranteed interest rate of 3 percent. The length of the period determines the amount of each payment. If the fixed period is five years, a $100,000 policy would provide a monthly income of $1791. However, the monthly benefit would be only $962 if a ten-year period is elected.

The fixed-period option can be used in those situations where income is needed for a definite time period, such as during the readjustment, dependency, and blackout periods. The fixed-period option, however, should be used with caution. It is extremely inflexible. Partial withdrawals by the beneficiary normally are not allowed because of the administrative expense of recomputing the amount of the payment during the fixed period. However, many insurers will permit the beneficiary to withdraw the commuted value of the remaining payments in a lump sum.

Fixed-Amount Option

Under the **fixed-amount (installment-amount) option,** *a fixed amount is periodically paid to the beneficiary.* The payments are made until both the principal and interest are exhausted. If excess interest is paid, the period is lengthened, but the amount of each payment is unchanged.

For example, assume that the death benefit is $50,000, the credited interest rate is 4 percent annually, and the desired monthly benefit is $3000. The actual monthly payout schedule would be calculated by the insurer. In this case, the beneficiary would receive $3000 monthly for 18 months. At that time, the principal and interest would be exhausted.

The fixed-amount option provides considerable flexibility. The beneficiary can be given limited or unlimited withdrawal right and the right to switch the unpaid proceeds to another option. The beneficiary may also be allowed to increase or decrease the fixed amount. It is also possible to arrange a settlement agreement, by which the periodic payments can be increased at certain times, such as when grown children start college. Unless there is some compelling reason for using the fixed-period option, the fixed-amount option is recommended because of its greater flexibility.

Life Income Options

Death benefits can also be paid to the beneficiary under a **life income option**. The cash surrender value can also be disbursed under a life income option. The major life income options are as follows.

Life Income *Under this option, installment payments are paid only while the beneficiary is alive and cease on the beneficiary's death.* Although this option provides the highest amount of installment income, there may be a substantial forfeiture of the proceeds if the beneficiary dies shortly after the payments start. Because there is no refund feature or guarantee of payments, other life income options are usually more desirable.

Life Income with Period Certain *Under this option, a life income is paid to the beneficiary with a certain number of guaranteed payments.* If the primary beneficiary dies before receiving the guaranteed number of payments, the remaining payments are paid to a contingent beneficiary. For example, assume that Karen is receiving $1000 monthly under a life income option with 10 years certain. If she dies after receiving only one year of payments, the remaining nine years of payments will be paid to a contingent beneficiary or to her estate.

Life Income with Refund Under this option, a lifetime income is paid to the beneficiary. *If the beneficiary dies before receiving payments equal to the amount of insurance, the difference is refunded in installments or in a lump sum to another beneficiary.* For example, assume Paige has $100,000 of life insurance paid to her under the refund option. If she dies after receiving payments of only $10,000, the re-

maining $90,000 is paid to another beneficiary or to her estate.

Joint-and-Survivor Income *Under this option, income payments are paid to two persons during their lifetimes, such as a husband and wife.* For example, Richard and Margo may be receiving $1200 monthly under a joint-and-survivor income annuity. If Richard dies, Margo continues to receive $1200 monthly during her lifetime. There are also variations of this option, such as a joint-and-two-thirds annuity or joint-and-one-half annuity. Thus, the monthly income of $1200 would be reduced to $800 or $600 on the death of the first person.

Various life income options for single lives are illustrated in Exhibit 18.3, which shows the amount of monthly income paid by one insurer for each $1000 of insurance, and the guaranteed interest rate is 3 percent.

Females usually receive lower periodic payments under the life income options than males because of a longer life expectancy. For example, if the proceeds are $100,000, a female beneficiary, age 65, would receive $570 monthly under the life income option with ten years certain, while the male beneficiary the same age would receive $645.

Exhibit 18.4 illustrates the monthly payments under the joint-and-survivor income option of one insurer for each $1000 of insurance and a guaranteed interest rate of 3½ percent. If the insurance proceeds are $200,000 and the male and female beneficiary are both age 65, a monthly payment of $996 would be paid during the lifetimes of both persons.

Advantages of Settlement Options

The major advantages of settlement options are summarized as follows:

1. *Periodic income is paid to the family.* Settlement options can restore part or all of the family's share of the deceased breadwinner's earnings. The financial security of the family can then be maintained.
2. *Principal and interest are guaranteed.* The insurance company guarantees both principal and interest. There are no investment worries and administrative problems, because the funds are invested by the insurer.

EXHIBIT 18.3

Life Income Options (Minimum Monthly Income Payments per $1000 Proceeds, 3 Percent Interest)

Adjusted age		Period certain			
Male	Female	None	10 Years	20 Years	Refund
50	55	$ 4.62	$4.56	$4.34	$4.36
51	56	4.72	4.65	4.40	4.44
52	57	4.83	4.75	4.46	4.52
53	58	4.94	4.85	4.53	4.61
54	59	5.07	4.96	4.59	4.69
55	60	5.20	5.07	4.66	4.79
56	61	5.33	5.19	4.72	4.88
57	62	5.48	5.31	4.78	4.99
58	63	5.64	5.43	4.84	5.09
59	64	5.80	5.57	4.90	5.20
60	65	5.98	5.70	4.96	5.32
61	66	6.16	5.85	5.02	5.44
62	67	6.36	5.99	5.07	5.57
63	68	6.57	6.14	5.13	5.71
64	69	6.79	6.30	5.17	5.85
65	70	7.03	6.45	5.22	6.00
66	71	7.28	6.62	5.26	6.15
67	72	7.54	6.78	5.30	6.31
68	73	7.83	6.95	5.33	6.48
69	74	8.13	7.11	5.36	6.66
70	75	8.45	7.28	5.39	6.85
71	76	8.79	7.45	5.41	7.05
72	77	9.16	7.62	5.43	7.26
73	78	9.55	7.79	5.45	7.48
74	79	9.96	7.95	5.46	7.71
75	80	10.41	8.11	5.48	7.95

3. *Settlement options can be used in life insurance planning.* Life insurance can be programmed to meet the policyowner's needs and objectives.

4. *An insurance windfall can create problems for the beneficiary.* The funds may be spent unwisely; bad investments may be made; and others may try to get the funds. Many insurers now offer money market accounts for investment of the death proceeds so that beneficiaries are not forced to make immediate decisions concerning disposition of the funds.

Disadvantages of Settlement Options

The major disadvantages of settlement options are summarized as follows:

1. *Higher yields often can be obtained elsewhere.* Interest rates offered by other financial institutions may be considerably higher.

2. *The settlement agreement may be inflexible and restrictive.* The policyowner may have a settlement agreement that is too restrictive. The beneficiary may not have withdrawal rights or the right

EXHIBIT 18.4
Joint-and-Survivor Life Income Option (Minimum Monthly Income Payments per $1000 Proceeds, 3½ Percent Interest)

Male adjusted age	Female adjusted age						
	55	60	65	70	75	80	85 and over
55	$4.16	$4.34	$4.51	$4.65	$4.76	$4.84	$4.88
60	4.26	4.51	4.75	4.98	5.16	5.29	5.37
65	4.35	4.65	4.98	5.31	5.61	5.84	5.98
70	4.41	4.76	5.17	5.62	6.07	6.44	6.68
75	4.46	4.84	5.32	5.88	6.48	7.03	7.42
80	4.48	4.89	5.41	6.05	6.79	7.52	8.07
85 and over	4.50	4.92	5.46	6.15	6.99	7.85	8.53

to change options. For example, the funds may be paid over a 20-year period under the fixed-period option with no right of withdrawal. An emergency may arise, but the beneficiary could not withdraw the funds.

3. *Life income options have limited usefulness at the younger ages.* Life income options should rarely be used before age 65 or 70, which restricts their usefulness at the younger ages. If a life income option is elected at a young age, the income payments are substantially reduced. Also, using a life income option is the equivalent of purchasing a single-premium life annuity, which may be purchased at a lower cost from another insurer.

Use of a Trust

The policy proceeds can also be paid to a trustee, such as the trust department of a commercial bank. Under certain circumstances, it may be desirable to have the policy proceeds paid to a trustee rather than disbursed under the settlement options. This would be the case if the amount of insurance is substantial; if considerable flexibility and discretion in the amount and timing of payments are needed; if there are minor children or mentally handicapped adults who cannot manage their own financial affairs; or if the amounts paid must be periodically changed as the beneficiary's needs and desires change. These advantages are partly offset by the payment of a trustee's fee, and the investment results cannot be guaranteed.

ADDITIONAL LIFE INSURANCE BENEFITS

Other benefits can often be added to a life insurance policy by the payment of an additional premium. These benefits provide valuable protection to the policyowner.

Waiver-of-Premium Provision

A **waiver-of-premium provision** can be added to a life insurance policy. In some policies, the waiver-of-premium provision is automatically included. Under this provision, if the insured becomes totally disabled from bodily injury or disease before some stated age, all premiums coming due during the period of disability are waived. During the period of disability, death benefits, cash values, and dividends continue as if the premiums had been paid.

Before any premiums are waived, the insured must meet the following requirements:

- Become disabled before some stated age, such as before age 60 or 65
- Be continuously disabled for six months (Some insurers have a waiting period of four months.)
- Satisfy the definition of total disability
- Furnish proof of disability satisfactory to the insurer

There is a retroactive refund of premiums paid by the policyowner during the first six months of disability if all premiums are being waived under the contract. Newer waiver-of-premium provisions, however, may not provide a retroactive refund.

The insured must also satisfy the definition of disability stated in the policy. Some common definitions of disability are as follows:

- The insured cannot engage in *any occupation* for which he or she is reasonably fitted by education, training, and experience.
- During the first two years, total disability means that the insured cannot perform all duties of *his or her occupation*. After the initial period, total disability means that the insured cannot engage in any occupation reasonably fitted by education, training, and experience.
- Total disability is the entire and irrecoverable loss of sight of both eyes, or the use of both hands or both feet, or one hand and one foot.

The first definition of total disability appears in many older life insurance policies. *Under this definition, the insured is considered totally disabled if he or she cannot work in any occupation reasonably fitted by education, training, and experience.* For example, assume that Dr. Brown is a chemistry professor who has throat cancer and cannot teach. If he can find some other job for which he is reasonably fitted by training and education, such as a research scientist for a chemical firm, he would not be considered disabled. However, if he cannot work in any occupation reasonably fitted by his education, training, and experience, then he would be considered totally disabled.

The second definition of total disability is more liberal and is found in many newer life insurance policies. *For the first two years of disability (in some companies, five years), total disability means the insured cannot perform all the duties of his or her own occupation.* After the initial period expires, the definition becomes stricter. *The insured is considered totally disabled only if he or she cannot engage in any occupation reasonably fitted by education, training, and experience.* For example, assume that Dr. Pudwill is a dentist whose hand is severely injured in a hunting accident. For the first two years, he would be considered totally disabled, because he is unable to perform all duties of his occupation. Premiums during this initial period would be waived. However, after the initial period expires, if he could work in any occupation for which he is reasonably fitted by

his education and training, he would not be considered totally disabled. Thus, if he could get a job as a research scientist or as a professor in a dental school, he would not be considered disabled. He would then have to resume premium payments.

Total disability can also be defined in terms of the loss of use of bodily members. For example, if Geoffrey loses his eyesight in an explosion, or if both legs are paralyzed from some crippling disease, he would be considered totally disabled.

Before any premiums are waived, the insured must furnish satisfactory proof of disability to the insurer. The insurer may also require continuing proof of disability once each year. If satisfactory proof of disability is not furnished, no further premiums will be waived.

If you have adequate amounts of disability-income insurance, the waiver-of-premium rider is not needed. If you become disabled, the life insurance premiums could be treated like any other type of monthly expense that must be paid, such as housing, utilities, and food. However, most breadwinners are underinsured against the risk of long-term disability. Thus, many financial planners recommend adding this provision to a life insurance policy, especially if the face amount of life insurance is large. During a period of long-term disability, premium payments can be financially burdensome. Because most persons are underinsured for disability-income benefits, waiver of premiums during a period in which income is reduced is highly desirable.

Guaranteed Purchase Option

The **guaranteed purchase option** *permits the insured to purchase additional amounts of life insurance at specified times in the future without evidence of insurability.* The purpose of the option is to guarantee the insured's future insurability. Additional amounts of life insurance may be needed in the future, or the insured may be unable to afford additional amounts of life insurance today. The guaranteed purchase option guarantees the ability to purchase additional amounts of life insurance at standard rates, even though the insured may be substandard in health or be uninsurable.

Amount of Insurance The typical option permits additional amounts of life insurance to be purchased with no evidence of insurability when the insured attains ages 25, 28, 31, 34, 37, and 40. The option usually is not available after age 40. However, some insurers permit an option to be exercised beyond age 40 up to age 65.

The amount of life insurance that can be purchased at each option date is limited to the face amount of the basic policy subject to some minimum and maximum amount. The minimum amount of each additional policy is $5000 or $10,000, and the maximum amount is stated in the rider. With some insurers, the additional policy is limited to a maximum of $25,000. For example, assume that Saul, age 22, purchases a $25,000 ordinary life policy with a guaranteed purchase option and becomes uninsurable after the policy is issued. Assuming that he elects to exercise each option, he would have the following amount of insurance:

Age 22	$25,000 (basic policy)
	+
Age 25	$25,000
Age 28	25,000
Age 31	25,000
Age 34	25,000
Age 37	25,000
Age 40	25,000
Total insurance at age 40	$175,000

Although uninsurable, Saul has increased his insurance coverage from $25,000 to $175,000.

Advanced Purchase Privilege Most insurers have some type of advance purchase privilege, by which an option can be immediately exercised on the occurrence of some event. If the insured marries, has a birth in the family, or legally adopts a child, an option can be immediately exercised prior to the next option due date. Some insurers will provide automatic term insurance for 90 days if the insured marries or a child is born. The insurance expires after 90 days unless the guaranteed insurability option is exercised.

If an option is exercised under the advance purchase privilege, the number of total options is not increased. If an option is exercised early, each new purchase eliminates the next regular option date. Finally, the policyowner typically has only 30 to 60 days to exercise an option. If the option expires without being used, it cannot be exercised at some later date. In some insurers, failure to exercise an option may terminate all subsequent options. This provision protects the insurer from adverse selection.

Other Considerations Four additional points should be noted concerning the guaranteed purchase option. One important consideration is whether the waiver-of-premium rider can be added to the new policy without furnishing evidence of insurability. Insurer practices vary in this regard. The most liberal provision permits the waiver-of-premium rider to be added to the new policy if the original policy contains such a provision. If the premiums are waived under the basic policy, they are also waived under the new policy. Thus, in our earlier example, if premiums are being waived under Saul's original policy of $25,000 because he is totally disabled, the premiums for each new policy will also be waived as long as he remains disabled. A less liberal approach is to permit the disabled insured to purchase a new policy with no evidence of insurability, but not to waive the new premiums under the waiver-of-premium rider.

Second, the guaranteed purchase option usually cannot be added to a term insurance policy. It is restricted to cash-value policies.

Third, when an option is exercised, the premium is based on the insured's attained age. As each option is exercised, the premium rate increases because the insured is older. However, even though the insured may be substandard in health or uninsurable, the premium rate is a standard rate based on the insured's attained age.

Finally, the incontestable clause in each additional policy is effective from the date of issue of the basic policy. If the two-year contestable period under the basic policy has expired, a new incontestable clause does not apply to each additional policy. However, suicide is treated differently. The suicide provision in each additional policy is effective from the date of issue of the additional policy.

Accidental Death Benefit Rider

The **accidental death benefit rider** (also known as **double indemnity**) *doubles the face amount of life insurance if death occurs as a result of an accident.* In some policies, the face amount is tripled. The cost of the rider is relatively low. For example, at one insurer, the rider costs $69 annually when added to a $100,000 policy issued to a male age 35. Thus, if the insured dies as a result of an accident, $200,000 will be paid.

Requirements for Collecting Benefits Before a double indemnity benefit is paid, several requirements must be satisfied:

- Death must be caused directly and independently of any other cause by accidental bodily injury.
- Death must occur within 90 days of the accident.
- Death must occur before some specified age, such as age 60, 65, or 70.

The first requirement is that accidental injury must be the direct cause of death. If death occurs from some other cause, such as disease, the double indemnity benefit is not paid. For example, assume that Sam is painting his two-story house. If the scaffold collapses and Sam is killed, a double indemnity benefit would be paid because the direct cause of death is an accidental bodily injury. However, if Sam died from a heart attack and fell from the scaffold, the double payment would not be made. In this case, heart disease is the direct cause of death, not accidental bodily injury.

The second requirement is that death must occur within 90 days of the accident. The purpose of this requirement is to establish the fact that accidental bodily injury is the proximate cause of death. However, because modern medical technology can prolong life for extended periods, many insurers are using longer time periods, such as 120 or 180 days.

Finally, the accidental death must occur before some specified age. To limit their liability, insurers typically impose some age limitation. Although some policies provide lifetime accidental death benefits, coverage usually terminates on the policy anniversary date just after the insured reaches a certain age, such as age 70.

Financial planners generally do not recommend purchase of the double indemnity rider. Although the cost is relatively low, there are three major objections to the rider. *First, the economic value of a human life is not doubled or tripled if death occurs from an accident.* Therefore, it is economically un-

sound to insure an accidental death more heavily than death from disease. *Second, most persons will die as a result of a disease and not from an accident.* Because most persons are underinsured, the premiums for the double indemnity rider could be better used to purchase an additional amount of life insurance, which would cover both accidental death and death from disease. *Finally, the insured may be deceived and believe that he or she has more insurance than is actually the case.* For example, a person with a $50,000 policy and a double indemnity rider may believe that he or she has $100,000 of life insurance.

Cost-of-Living Rider

The **cost-of-living rider** *allows the policyowner to purchase one-year term insurance equal to the percentage change in the consumer price index with no evidence of insurability.* The amount of term insurance changes each year and reflects the cumulative change in the consumer price index (CPI) from the issue date of the policy. However, insurers may limit the amount of insurance that can be purchased each year, such as a maximum of 10 percent of the policy face value. The policyowner pays the entire premium for the term insurance.

For example, assume that Luis, age 28, buys a $100,000 ordinary life insurance policy and that the CPI increases 5 percent during the first year. He would be allowed to purchase $5000 of one-year term insurance, and the total amount of insurance in force would be $105,000. The term insurance can be converted to a cash-value policy with no evidence of insurability.

Accelerated Death Benefits Rider

Many insurers now make available a living benefits rider that can be added to a life insurance policy. The **accelerated death benefits rider** *allows insureds who are terminally ill or who suffer from certain catastrophic diseases to collect part or all of their life insurance benefits before they die, primarily to pay for the medical care they require.* Benefits may also be payable if the insured is receiving long-term care in a nursing home or hospital.

Although accelerated death benefits riders are not uniform, they generally can be classified as follows:

- Terminal illness rider
- Catastrophic illness rider
- Long-term care rider

The *terminal illness rider* allows terminally ill insureds with a limited life expectancy (24 months or less) to receive part or all of the policy proceeds. Insurers generally allow the rider to be added without an extra premium, but any lump sums advanced are discounted for interest to reflect the time value of money. The face amount of insurance, cash values if any, and premiums are reduced after the payment is made. For example, based on the rider of one insurer, Dr. Harry Crockett, age 59, who is terminally ill with cancer, requests 50 percent of his $100,000 term insurance policy. After the benefit is discounted for interest, he receives $46,296. After the payment is made, premiums are reduced 50 percent, and the face amount is reduced to $50,000.

The *catastrophic illness rider* allows insureds who have certain catastrophic diseases to collect part or all of the policy face amount. Covered diseases typically include AIDS, life-threatening cancer, coronary artery disease, kidney failure, and similar types of catastrophic diseases.

The *long-term care rider* allows insureds who require long-term care to collect part of their life insurance prior to death. The rider may cover care in a skilled nursing facility, intermediate care facility, or custodial care facility. Some riders also cover certain types of home care. To illustrate, based on the rider of one insurer, a monthly benefit can be paid equal to 2 percent of the face amount of insurance up to a maximum of 50 percent of the face amount. Thus, if the face amount is $200,000, a monthly benefit of $4000 could be paid up to 25 months.

As an alternative, terminally ill insureds may be able to sell their policies to private firms. A number of firms will buy the life insurance policies of terminally ill insureds at a discount (called a viatical settlement), especially policies owned by AIDS patients. The cash enables AIDS victims to pay their medical bills and other expenses. However, critics argue that the states do not adequately regulate such purchases, and that there is potential for abuse (see Insight 18.3).

SUMMARY

- The *incontestable clause* states that the company cannot contest the policy after it has been in force two years during the insured's lifetime.

- The *suicide clause* states that if the insured commits suicide within two years after the policy is issued, the face amount is not paid. There is only a refund of the premiums paid.

- The *grace period* allows the policyowner a period of 31 days to pay an overdue premium. Universal life and other flexible premium policies usually have longer grace periods, such as 61 days. The insurance remains in force during the grace period.

- There are several types of beneficiary designations. A *primary beneficiary* is the party who is first entitled to receive the policy proceeds upon the insured's death. A *contingent beneficiary* is entitled to the proceeds if the primary beneficiary dies before the insured or dies before receiving the guaranteed number of payments under an installment settlement option. A *revocable beneficiary* designation means that the policyowner can change the beneficiary without the beneficiary's consent. An *irrevocable beneficiary* designation is one that cannot be changed without the beneficiary's consent.

- A *dividend* represents a refund of part of the gross premium if the experience of the company is favorable. Dividends paid to policyowners are not taxable and can be taken in several ways:
  Cash
  Reduction of premiums
  Accumulate at interest
  Paid-up additions
  Term insurance (in some companies)

- There are three *nonforfeiture* or cash surrender options:
  Cash value
  Reduced paid-up insurance
  Extended term insurance

- The cash value can be borrowed under the policy loan provision. An automatic premium loan provision can also be added to the policy, by which an overdue premium is automatically borrowed from the cash value.

- *Settlement options* are the various ways that the policy proceeds can be paid other than in a lump sum. The

Insight 18.3

Playing the Death Pool

A highly entrepreneurial secondary market for life insurance policies that has taken shape in the past two years is causing uncertainty and concern among regulators and insurers. With the help of brokers, healthy insureds are selling their life policies for cash. Other individuals are investing into pools of cash created and maintained by brokers to make the purchases. *The business is largely unregulated.*

Secondary Market

The secondary market for life policies grabbed a foothold 10 years ago with the advent of viaticals—the buying and selling of policies owned by the terminally ill. The justification for viaticals was—and is—that some terminally ill people and their families need money to help them through their last difficult months. The new market is based on the proposition that some insureds no longer want, need, or can afford their coverage. These deals are known in the business as "senior settlements" or "high-net-worth transactions" [see box].

Critics see many problems with the budding industry.

"It sets up the situation in which people are gaining when other folk are dying," said Thomas Foley, former life and health actuary in the North Dakota Department of Insurance. "To my mind, that's inappropriate activity."

Assuming they sell their policies to reputable parties initially, insureds still have no assurances about who ultimately will come to own them. "I think it gets back to the most fundamental question of all—the transfer of a policy to a person without an insurable interest," said Joseph M. Belth, a semi-retired insurance professor at Indiana University. "That's creating a powerful incentive for homicide."

Investors face dangers to their financial health. "I would be skeptical about investing without knowing the basis of the scheme intending to make money," said James Hunt, a life insurance actuary in Concord, New Hampshire, who consults with the Consumer Federation of America. In some brokered deals, the investor faces odds about as good "as going to Las Vegas," he said.

"*It's a totally unregulated market,*" said Belth, who also publishes a monthly newsletter, *The Insurance Forum.* "There are no standards, no rules, and they [brokers] can do anything they want. You talk about your cowboys out there; this is a totally unregulated market, and it's open season."

In extreme cases known as "wet-ink" transactions, the sick and elderly are offered financial incentives to secure life policies for immediate resale. The transactions may involve deceptive applications or misleading answers to health questions. The buyers receive a payoff, usually 5 percent or so of the face amount of the policies, the intermediaries get a slice of the action, and the investors hope the insureds die soon enough that they can make a healthy profit.

Help on the Way?

Some states have laws that provide safeguards for sellers of policies, known as "viators." A model act passed

---

most common settlement options are as follows:

  Interest option

  Fixed-period option

  Fixed-amount option

  Life income options

■ A *waiver-of-premium provision* can be added to a life insurance policy, by which all premiums coming due during a period of total disability are waived. Before

any premiums are waived, the insured must meet the following requirements:

  Become disabled before some stated age, such as age 60 or 65

  Be continuously disabled for six months

  Satisfy the definition of total disability

  Furnish proof of disability satisfactory to the insurer

■ The *guaranteed purchase option* permits the policy-

A Look at the Secondary Market

Life insurance transactions in the secondary market fall into four general categories.

Traditional viaticals	The insured's life expectancy is two years or less. This segment makes up the bulk of viatical purchases.
Chronically ill	The insured's life expectancy is shorter than normal but more than two years.
Senior settlements and high-net-worth settlements	The insured's life expectancy is normal. Targets people over 65. Often involves transactions for policies with high face values.
Wet-ink transactions	Transfers of newly issued policies. Individuals may be recruited to buy policies and sell them immediately. Raises the most alarms for regulators and insurers.

by the National Association of Insurance Commissioners in 1993 outlined licensing requirements for brokers and viatical companies as well as disclosures that must be provided to viators. This year [1999], the NAIC is likely to extend the disclosure protections to the chronically ill.

The Viatical Settlements Working Group is charged with taking up issues associated with healthy people selling their policies.

The NAIC doesn't address the protection of investors in viatical settlements. Belth says many of those are also seniors who are lured by advertisements promising high returns and guarantees. *"These investors are getting scammed,"* he said. *"There are situations in which investors put in their money and nothing's happening. The insureds are not dying, and these investors are getting wiped out financially."*

Investors don't get much protection because viatical settlement transactions currently fall through regulatory cracks. In 1995, the U.S. Securities and Exchange Commission alleged that Life Partners Inc., a large viatical firm in Waco, Texas, was selling unregistered securities. A federal district court judge sided with the SEC, but Life Partners appealed and won. The appeals court ruled in July 1996 that a viatical transaction is not a security.

Though the Life Partners case was not binding on the states, the company was able to use the verdict to fend off regulatory efforts, said Roger Walter, general counsel for the Kansas securities commissioner and chairman of a viatical task force with the North American Securities Administrators Association.

Source: Adapted from Ron Panko, "Playing the Death Pool," *Best's Review*, Life & Health edition (April 1999), pp. 21–25. Copyrighted by A. M. Best Company. Used with permission.

owner to purchase additional amounts of life insurance at specified times in the future without evidence of insurability. The purpose of the option is to guarantee the insured's future insurability.

- The *accidental death benefit rider (double indemnity rider)* doubles the face amount of life insurance if death occurs as a result of an accident. Consumer experts generally do not recommend purchase of the double indemnity rider.

- The *cost-of-living rider* allows the policyowner to purchase one-year term insurance equal to the percentage change in the consumer price index with no evidence of insurability.

- The *accelerated death benefits rider* pays part of the life insurance death benefit to a terminally ill insured before death occurs to help pay for medical and other expenses.

KEY CONCEPTS AND TERMS

Absolute assignment
Accelerated death benefits
  rider
Accidental death benefit
  rider (double indemnity)
Automatic premium loan
  provision
Aviation exclusions
Change-of-plan provision
Class beneficiary
Collateral assignment
Contingent beneficiary
Cost-of-living rider
Entire-contract clause
Extended term insurance
Fixed-amount (installment-
  amount) option
Fixed-period (installment-
  time) option
Grace period
Guaranteed purchase
  option

Incontestable clause
Interest option
Irrevocable beneficiary
Life income option
Misstatement of age or sex
  clause
Nonforfeiture laws
Nonforfeiture options
Nonparticipating policy
Ownership clause
Participating policy
Policy loan provision
Primary beneficiary
Reduced paid-up insurance
Reinstatement provision
Revocable beneficiary
Settlement options
Specific beneficiary
Suicide clause
Waiver-of-premium
  provision
War clause

REVIEW QUESTIONS

1. Briefly explain the ownership clause and entire-contract clause in a life insurance contract.

2. Describe the incontestable clause and explain why it appears in a life insurance policy.

3. Explain the requirements for reinstating a lapsed life insurance policy.

4. If the insured's age is misstated, can the company refuse to pay the policy proceeds? Explain.

5. Describe the various beneficiary designations in life insurance.

6. Can a life insurance policy be assigned to another party? Explain.

7. Are dividends to policyowners guaranteed? Explain.

8. Explain the nonforfeiture or cash surrender options that are found in cash-value life insurance.

9. Identify the various settlement options for the payment of life insurance proceeds.

10. Explain the definition of total disability that is found in a typical waiver-of-premium provision.

APPLICATION QUESTIONS

1. A policy that pays dividends is known as a participating policy. The dividends can be paid several ways.
   a. Explain the nature of a life insurance dividend.
   b. Describe the dividend options that are typically found in participating life insurance policies.
   c. For each option described in part (b), indicate an appropriate situation where it can be used.

2. Life insurance proceeds can be paid under the fixed-period or fixed-amount settlement options. Compare the fixed-period option and the fixed-amount option with respect to the degree of flexibility that can be obtained if they are used in a settlement plan or agreement.

3. Jim, age 32, purchased a $300,000 five-year renewable and convertible term insurance policy. In answering the health questions, Jim told the agent that he had not visited a doctor within the last five years. However, he had visited the doctor two months earlier. The doctor told Jim that he had a serious heart disease. Jim did not reveal this information to the agent when he applied for life insurance. Jim died three years after the policy was purchased. At that time, the life insurer discovered the heart ailment. Explain the extent of the insurer's obligation, if any, with respect to payment of the death claim.

4. Additional riders and benefits often can be added to a life insurance policy to provide greater protection to the insured. Describe each of the following riders and options:
   a. Waiver-of-premium rider
   b. Guaranteed purchase option
   c. Double indemnity rider
   d. Cost-of-living rider
   e. Accelerated death benefits rider

SELECTED REFERENCES

Anderson, Buist M. *Anderson on Life Insurance.* Boston, MA: Little, Brown and Company, 1991. See also the *September 1996 Supplement to Anderson on Life Insurance.*

Case Application

Sonja, age 25, recently purchased a $50,000 ordinary life insurance policy on her life. The waiver-of-premium rider and guaranteed purchase option are attached to the policy. For each of the following situations, indicate the extent of the insurer's obligation, if any, to Sonja or to Sonja's beneficiary. Identify the appropriate policy provision or rider that applies in each case. Treat each event separately.

a. Sonja fails to pay the second annual premium due on January 1. She dies 15 days later.

b. Sonja commits suicide three years after the policy was purchased.

c. At Sonja's death, the life insurer discovers that Sonja deliberately lied about her age. Instead of being 25 years old, as she indicated, she was actually 26 years old at the time the policy was purchased.

d. Two years after the policy was purchased, Sonja is told that she has leukemia. She is uninsurable but would like to obtain additional life insurance.

e. Sonja is seriously injured in an automobile accident. After six months, she is still unable to return to work. She has no income from her job, and the insurance premium payments are financially burdensome.

f. Sonja has a mentally disabled son. She wants to make certain that her son will have a continuous income after her death.

g. Sonja lets her policy lapse. After four years, she wants to get the policy reinstated. Her health is fine. Point out to Sonja how she can get her life insurance back.

h. Sonja wants to retire and does not wish to pay the premiums on her policy. Indicate the various options that are available to her.

i. Ten years after the policy was purchased, Sonja is fired from her job. She is unemployed and is in desperate need of cash.

j. When Sonja applied for life insurance, she concealed the fact that she had high blood pressure. She dies five years later.

Belth, Joseph M. *Life Insurance: A Consumer's Handbook*, second edition. Bloomington, IN: Indiana University Press, 1985.

Black, Kenneth, Jr., and Harold D. Skipper, Jr. *Life Insurance*, thirteenth edition. Upper Saddle River, NJ: Prentice-Hall, 2000.

Crawford, Muriel L. *Life and Health Insurance Law*, eighth edition. Boston, MA: Irwin/McGraw-Hill, 1998.

Graves, Edward E., ed. *McGill's Life Insurance*, second edition. Bryn Mawr, PA: The American College, 1998, Chapters 34–35.

Graves, Edward E., and Burke A. Christensen, eds. *McGill's Legal Aspects of Life Insurance*, Bryn Mawr, PA: The American College, 1997.

Rejda, George E., Constance M. Luthardt, Cheryl L. Ferguson, and Donald R. Oakes. *Personal Insurance*, fourth edition. Malvern, PA: Insurance Institute of America, 2000.

Thornton, John H., and Kennes C. Huntley. "A Survey of Life Insurance Policy Provisions." *Journal of the American Society of CLU & ChFC*, Vol. XLIV, No. 3 (May 1990), pp. 32–84.

NOTES

1. Edward E. Graves, ed., *McGill's Life Insurance,* second edition (Bryn Mawr, PA: The American College, 1998), p. 872.

2. There are some exceptions. In some states, minors can receive a limited amount of proceeds.

3. Joseph M. Belth, editor, "Special Issue on Fractional Premiums," *The Insurance Forum*, Vol. 25, No. 12 (December 1998), Appendix C, pp. 151–152.

4. Black, Kenneth, Jr., and Harold D. Skipper, Jr. *Life Insurance*, twelfth edition (Englewood Cliffs, NJ: Prentice-Hall, 1994), p. 225.

5. Joseph M. Belth, *Life Insurance: A Consumer's Handbook*, second edition. (Bloomington, IN: Indiana University Press, 1985).

6. If a person is insurable, a reasonable approach would be to accumulate the dividends either at interest or under the paid-up additions option for several years. The accumulated cash could then be used to purchase a new policy.

7. Robert I. Mehr and Sandra G. Gustavson, *Life Insurance, Theory and Practice*, fourth edition (Plano, TX: Business Publications, Inc., 1987), p. 206.

Students may take a self-administered test on this chapter at www.awlonline.com/rejda

Chapter 19

Buying Life Insurance

“ When you buy life insurance, it's relatively easy to compare first-year premium costs. But that figure tells you nothing about what the policy will cost over the long run. ”

Consumers Union

Learning Objectives

After studying this chapter, you should be able to:

▲ Explain the defects in the traditional net cost method for determining the cost of life insurance.

▲ Explain the use of the interest-adjusted surrender cost index and net payment cost index for determining the cost of life insurance

▲ Explain the yearly-rate-of return method for determining the annual rate of return on the saving component in a life insurance policy.

▲ Describe the rules to follow when purchasing life insurance.

▲ Access an Internet site to obtain premium quotes on a life insurance policy.

Internet Resources

- **Ameritas Direct** sells life insurance and annuities directly to consumers without traditional agents. Visit the site at:
  www.ameritasdirect.com

- **InstantQuote** provides term life insurance quotes on the Internet without resorting to agents. Visit the site at:
  www.instantquote.com

- The **Insurance News Network** provides premium quotes on life insurance and news releases about events that affect the insurance industry. Visit the site at:
  http://www.insure.com/

- **INSWEB** provides timely information and premium quotes for life insurance and other insurance products. Visit the site at:
  http://www.insweb.com/

- **MasterQuote of America** provides instant quotes on term life insurance. Visit the site at:

  http://www.masterquote.com

- **Quicken Insurance** is considered to be one of the best consumer sites for obtaining premium quotes on life insurance and other insurance products. Visit the site at:

  http://www.quickeninsurance.com

- **QuoteNavigator.Com** provides affordable term insurance quotes from numerous insurance carriers. Visit the site at:

  www.quotenavigator.com

- **Quotesmith.com** provides instant insurance quotes from more than 300 top-rated companies. Visit the site at:

  www.quotesmith.com

 ichelle, age 28, is divorced and has a son, age 2. She earns $55,000 as a sales representative for a national oil company. Michelle wants to update her life insurance program. Recently, a life insurance agent presented her with several proposals. Although Michelle is a careful shopper, she does not know how to evaluate the plans offered to her. Moreover, like most insurance consumers, she is unaware of the importance of performing a cost comparison of the different policies.

This chapter is designed to answer the questions that Michelle may have concerning the purchase of life insurance. Most consumers buy life insurance without much thought. They are often unaware of the huge cost variations among insurers and frequently purchase life insurance from the first agent who persuades them to buy. As a result, they may pay more than is necessary for their insurance protection. Purchase of a high-cost policy rather than a low-cost policy can cost thousands of dollars over your lifetime.

This chapter discusses the fundamentals of buying life insurance. Specific topics covered include the various methods for determining the cost of life insurance, the rate of return earned on the saving component of a cash-value policy, taxation of life insurance, and suggested guidelines for buying life insurance.

DETERMINING THE COST OF LIFE INSURANCE

The cost of life insurance is a complex subject. In general, cost can be viewed as the difference between what you pay for a life insurance policy and what you get back. If you pay premiums and get nothing back, the cost of the insurance equals the premiums paid. However, if you pay premiums and later get something back, such as cash values and dividends, your cost will be reduced. Thus, in determining the cost of life insurance, four major cost factors must be considered: (1) annual premiums, (2) cash values, (3) dividends, and (4) time value of money. Two widely used cost methods that consider some or all of the preceding factors are the *traditional net cost method* and the *interest-adjusted cost method*. Although the following discussion is based on cash-value life insurance, the same cost methods can be used to determine the cost of term insurance.

Traditional Net Cost Method

From a historical perspective, life insurers earlier used the **traditional net cost method** to illustrate the net cost of life insurance. Under this method, the annual premiums for some time period are added together. Total expected dividends to be received during the same period and the cash value at the end of the period are then subtracted from the total premiums to determine the net cost of life insurance. For example, assume that the annual premium for a $10,000 ordinary life insurance policy issued to a female, age 20, is $132.10. Estimated dividends over a 20-year period are $599, and the cash surrender value at the end of the twentieth year is $2294 (see Exhibit 19.1). The average cost per year is minus $12.55 (−$1.26 per $1000).

The traditional net cost method has several defects and is misleading. The most glaring defects are as follows:

■ *The time value of money is ignored.* Interest that the policyowner could have earned on the premiums by investing them elsewhere is ignored.

EXHIBIT 19.1
Traditional Net Cost Method

Total premiums for 20 years	$2642
Subtract dividends for 20 years	−599
Net premiums for 20 years	$2043
Subtract the cash value at the end of 20 years	−2294
Insurance cost for 20 years	−$251
Net cost per year (−$251 ÷ 20)	−$12.55
Net cost per $1000 per year (−$12.55 ÷ 10)	−$1.26

■ *The insurance is often shown to be free.* This is contrary to common sense, because no life insurer can provide free life insurance to the public and remain in business.
■ *The steepness of the dividend scale is ignored.* Some insurers pay small dividends at first and then pay ballooning dividends in later years. The timing and amount of each dividend are ignored.
■ *The dividend scale is assumed to remain unchanged.* In most insurers, dividends will change over time.
■ *The net cost is based on the assumption that the policy will be surrendered.* The assumption that the policyowner will keep the insurance exactly 20 years (or some other period) and then surrender the policy is questionable.

Interest-Adjusted Method

The **interest-adjusted method** developed by the National Association of Insurance Commissioners is a more accurate measure of life insurance costs. *Under this method, the time value of money is taken into consideration by applying an interest factor to each element of cost.*

There are two principal types of interest-adjusted cost indexes, the *surrender cost index* and the *net payment cost index*. The surrender cost index is useful if you believe that you may surrender the policy at the end of 10 or 20 years, or some other time period. The net payment cost index is useful if you intend to keep your policy in force, and cash values are of secondary importance to you.

Surrender Cost Index The **surrender cost index** *measures the cost of life insurance if you surrender the policy at the end of some time period, such as 10 or 20 years* (see Exhibit 19.2).

The annual premiums are accumulated at 5 percent interest, which recognizes the fact that the policyowner could have invested the premiums elsewhere. Dividends are also accumulated at 5 percent interest, which considers interest earnings on the dividends as well as the amount and timing of each dividend. Using the same policy as before, the accumulated net premiums for 20 years are $3762.

The next step is to subtract the cash value at the end of 20 years from the net premiums, which results

EXHIBIT 19.2
Surrender Cost Index

Total premiums for 20 years, each accumulated at 5%	$4586
Subtract dividends for 20 years, each accumulated at 5%	−824
Net premiums for 20 years	$3762
Subtract the cash value at the end of 20 years	−2294
Insurance cost for 20 years	$1468
Amount to which $1 deposited annually at the beginning of each year will accumulate to in 20 years at 5%	$34.719
Interest-adjusted cost per year ($1468 ÷ $34.719)	$42.28
Cost per $1000 per year ($42.28 ÷ 10)	$4.23

in a total insurance cost of $1468. The policyowner pays this amount for the insurance protection for 20 years, after considering the time value of money.

The final step is to convert the total interest-adjusted cost for 20 years into an annual cost. This is done by dividing the total interest-adjusted cost by an *annuity due* factor of 34.719. This factor means that a $1 deposit at the *beginning* of each year at 5 percent interest will accumulate to $34.719 at the end of 20 years. By dividing the total interest-adjusted cost of $1468 by $34.719, you end up with an annual interest-adjusted cost of $42.28, or $4.23 for each $1000 of insurance. As you can see, the interest-adjusted cost is positive, which means that it costs something to own life insurance when foregone interest is considered. In this case, the average annual cost is $42.28 if the policy is surrendered after 20 years.

Net Payment Cost Index The **net payment cost index** *measures the relative cost of a policy if death occurs at the end of some specified time period, such as 10 or 20 years.* It is based on the assumption that you will not surrender the policy. Therefore, it is the appropriate cost index to use if you intend to keep your life insurance in force.

The net payment cost index is calculated in a manner similar to the surrender cost index except

that the cash value is not subtracted (see Exhibit 19.3).

If the policy is kept in force for 20 years, the policy has an annual cost of $108.36 ($10.84 per $1000) after interest is considered.

Substantial Cost Variation Among Insurers

There are enormous cost variations in cash-value life insurance based on the interest-adjusted cost indexes. Exhibit 19.4 shows the 10-year interest-adjusted costs for selected insurers for a $100,000 participating whole life policy issued to a male, age 35.

In the interpretation of these indexes, the lower the index number, the less costly is the policy. As shown in Exhibit 19.4, the surrender cost index ranged from a low of $1.24 per $1000 for USAA Life to a high of $2.97 per $1000 for Massachusetts Mutual Life. The net payment cost index ranged from a low of $8.24 per $1000 for Manufacturers Life to a high of $10.47 for General American. *This wide variation in cost highlights the point stated earlier—you can save thousands of dollars over a long period by paying careful attention to the cost index when you shop for life insurance.*

Unfortunately, most consumers do not consider interest-adjusted cost data when they buy life insurance. Instead, they use premiums as a basis for comparing costs. However, using premiums alone provides an incomplete comparison. Interest-adjusted

EXHIBIT 19.3
Net Payment Cost Index

Total premiums for 20 years, each accumulated at 5%	$4586
Subtract dividends for 20 years, each accumulated at 5%	−824
Insurance cost for 20 years	$3762
Amount to which $1 deposited annually at the beginning of each year will accumulate to in 20 years at 5%	$34.719
Interest-adjusted cost per year ($3762 ÷ $34.719)	$108.36
Cost per $1000 per year ($108.36 ÷ 10)	$10.84

EXHIBIT 19.4

Comparison of Life Insurance Costs for Selected Companies

	Surrender cost index			Net payment index	
1	USAA Life	1.24	1	Manufacturers	8.24
2	Government Personnel Mut. Life	1.59	2	United Heritage Life	8.32
3	Country Life	1.74	3	John Hancock Mutual Life	8.71
4	Phoenix Home Life Mutual	1.92	4	Phoenix Home Life Mutual	9.08
5	Mutual Life of New York	2.10	5	Columbus Life	9.16
6	Columbian Mutual Life	2.35	6	State Farm	9.29
7	National Life Vermont	2.39	7	American Family Life	9.43
8	AmerUs Life	2.40	8	Country Life	9.55
9	John Hancock Mutual Life	2.47	8	Security Mutual of New York	9.55
10	Western-Southern Life	2.49	9	United Farm Family Life	9.57
11	Ohio National Life	2.51	10	Phoenix Home Life Mut. (Home Life)	9.65
12	Mutual Trust Life	2.54	11	Farm Family Life	9.66
12	Security Mutual of New York	2.54	12	Mutual Life of New York	9.82
13	Farm Family Life	2.56	13	Ohio National Life	9.83
13	Manufactures Life	2.56	14	Berkshire Life	10.17
14	United Farm Family Life	2.60	15	New York Life	10.19
15	Penn Mutual Life	2.64	16	USAA Life	10.24
16	American Family Life	2.84	17	Farmers & Traders Life	10.28
17	State Farm	2.87	18	Knights of Columbus	10.40
18	Massachusetts Mutual Life	2.97	19	General American	10.47

Note: The indexes shown are the annual costs over a ten-year period for a $100,000 participating whole life policy issued to a male, age 35.

SOURCE: Adapted from Kim Kelleher, "Looking at Whole Life," *Best's Review*, Life/Health edition (July 1998), p. 53. Copyrighted by A. M. Best Company. Used with permission.

cost data will give you more accurate information about the expected cost of a policy.

Obtaining Cost Information

If you are solicited to buy life insurance, you can ask the agent to give you interest-adjusted cost data on the policy. Cost data can also be obtained by calling certain price quoting services at their toll-free numbers. In addition, cost data are available on the Internet (see Exhibit 19.5). Finally, most policy illustrations include interest-adjusted cost data.

If you use interest-adjusted cost data, keep in mind the following points:

- *Shop for a policy and not an insurer.* Some insurers have excellent low-cost policies at certain ages and amounts, but they are not as competitive when other ages and amounts are considered.

- *Compare only similar plans of insurance.* You should compare policies of the same type with the same benefits. Otherwise, the comparison can be misleading.

- *Ignore small variations in the cost index numbers.* Small cost differences can be offset by other policy features or by services that you can expect to get from an agent or insurer.

- *Cost indexes apply only to a new policy.* The cost data should not be used to determine whether to *replace* an existing policy with a new one. Other factors should be considered as well (see Insight 19.1).

- *The type of policy you buy should not be based solely on a cost index.* You should buy the type of policy that best meets your needs, such as term, whole life, or some combination. Once you have decided on the type of policy, then compare costs.

EXHIBIT 19.5
Obtaining Life Insurance Premium Quotes Online

Premium quotes for life insurance and other insurance products are available from numerous online sources. The following is a sample of the sources available:

Name	Web address	Toll-free telephone
Ameritas Direct	www.ameritasdirect.com	800-689-6830
Direct Quote	www.directquote.com	800-845-3853
InstantQuote	www.instantquote.com	888-223-2220
MasterQuote of America	http://www.masterquote.com	800-337-LIFE
Quicken Insurance	http://www.quickeninsurance.com	800-695-0011
QuoteNavigator.Com	www.quotenavigator.com	888-428-2200
Quotesmith.com	www.quotesmith.com	800-431-1147
Select Quote	www.selectquote.com	800-311-6498
Zurich Direct	www.zurichdirect.com	800-517-2336

NAIC Policy Illustration Model Regulation

Our discussion of life insurance costs would not be complete without a brief discussion of the Life Insurance Policy Illustration Model Regulation drafted by the National Association of Insurance Commissioners (NAIC). The model act applies to new policies sold on or after January 1, 1997, or later, if changed by an adopting state.

If adopted by the states, the model act will have a dramatic and sweeping impact on the way policy illustrations are calculated and presented. Certain deceptive sales practices are prohibited in the illustration of policy values. Insurers are prohibited from using anticipated gains from improvements in mortality in the sales illustration; the term "vanishing premium" cannot be used; the applicant and agent must sign the illustration and indicate they have discussed and understand that the "nonguaranteed elements" in the policy are subject to change and can be lower or higher; and the values shown in the illustration must be justified by a self-support test. For example, lapse-supported pricing cannot be used. The self-support test requires that assumptions concerning lapses must be limited to actual experience for the first five years and zero lapses for the remaining life of the block of policies.

Finally, the insurer must provide an annual report on the policy and notify the policyowners when a change occurs in the dividend scale or individual pricing elements that would negatively affect the policy values. When fully implemented, the model regulation should reduce misunderstanding of policy values by policyowners and reduce deceptive sales practices by agents.

RATE OF RETURN ON SAVING COMPONENT

Another important consideration is the rate of return earned on the saving component of a traditional whole life insurance policy. Consumers normally do not know the annual rate of return they earn on the saving component in their policies. A consumer who buys a traditional cash-value policy with a low return can lose a considerable amount of money over the life of the policy. Thus, the annual rate of return you earn on the saving component is critical if you intend to invest money in a life insurance policy over a long period of time.

Linton Yield

The **Linton yield** is one method that can be used to determine the rate of return on the saving portion of a cash-value policy. It was developed by M. Albert Linton, a well-known life insurance actuary. In

Insight 19.1

Factors to Consider in Replacing a Life Insurance Policy

If you already own a life insurance policy, a health insurance policy, or an annuity contract, you should be careful if you consider replacing it. Although the relative financial strength of the original company and the replacing company is an important factor in your decision, you should consider other factors as well. Some of those additional factors are described briefly in the following paragraphs.

If you consider replacing life or health insurance, *your state of health and other items affecting your eligibility should be reviewed.* You may not qualify for new insurance, or you may qualify only at high rates.

You should determine the cost of getting out of the original policy. Many policies contain substantial surrender charges.

You should determine the cost of getting into the replacement policy. Many policies involve substantial front-end expenses.

You should determine whether the cost of continuing the original policy is reasonable. If the cost is reasonable, there may be little if any advantage in replacing it. [A procedure for making such a determination is described in the Appendix to this chapter.]

You should consider the tax implications of a replacement. In some situations, the termination of a life insurance policy or an annuity contract may trigger an income tax liability. You may be able to defer the tax, but you should consult your tax adviser.

You should consider the incontestability clause. For example, if a life insurance policy is more than two years old, the company usually is barred from alleging that the policy is void because of false statements you made in the application. Thus the original policy may not be contestable, while the replacement policy may be contestable for two years.

You should also be aware of the suicide clause. Suicide usually is excluded during the first two years of a life insurance policy. Thus the original policy may currently cover suicide, while the replacement policy may not cover suicide for two years.

If someone recommends replacement, you should try to determine the amount of compensation the person making the recommendation will receive if you follow the advice. Some who recommend replacement are motivated by a genuine desire to help you reduce your expenses or avoid the problems that may arise if your original company gets into financial trouble. However, in the current environment of public concern about the financial strength of insurance companies, some persons may descend on the policyowners of a troubled company like sharks who detect blood in the water. The fact that a person receives a commission does not necessarily mean he or she is giving bad advice, but you should be on guard.

Source: Adapted from Joseph M. Belth, ed., "The Replacement Problem," *The Insurance Forum,* Vol. 26, No. 9 (September 1999), p. 256.

essence, the Linton yield is the average annual rate of return on a cash-value policy if it is held for a specified number of years. It is based on the assumption that a cash-value policy can be viewed as a combination of insurance protection and a savings fund. To determine the average annual rate of return for a given period, it is first necessary to determine that part of the annual premium that is deposited in the savings fund. This amount can be determined by subtracting the cost of the insurance protection for that year from the annual premium (less any dividend). The balance of the premium is the amount that can be deposited into the savings fund. Thus, the average annual rate of return is the compound interest rate that is required to make the savings deposits equal the guaranteed cash value in the policy at the end of a specified period.

Calculation of the Linton yield is complex and requires certain information. Unfortunately, current rates of return based on the Linton yield are not readily available to consumers. An earlier study by Consumers Union showed that as of 1985, the annual rates of return for a $50,000 *participating* whole life policy issued to a male age 25 ranged from 4.47 percent to 11.91 percent at the end of 20 years. For *nonparticipating* policies, the annual rates of return ranged from −3.26 percent to 10.97 percent at the end of 20 years.[1] Because interest rates have declined sharply since 1985, Linton yields today would be substantially lower.

Annual rates of return based on the Linton yield are often negative during the early years of the policy. These negative returns reflect the heavy first-year acquisition and administrative expenses when the policy is first sold. An agent receives a commission, and there may be a medical examiner's fee, an inspection report, and other expenses involved in issuing the policy. As a result of these expenses, most cash-value policies have little or no cash value at the end of the first year, and the cash values remain relatively low during the early years. Thus, if you surrender the policy or allow it to lapse during the early years, you will lose a substantial amount of money.

Because current information is not readily available, the Linton yield has limited usefulness as a consumer tool. We must therefore consider other methods. The yearly rate-of-return method discussed next is a simple, but valuable methodology that can enable you to calculate the annual rate of return on the saving component in your policy.

Yearly Rate-of-Return Method

Professor Joseph M. Belth has developed a simple method for calculating the **yearly rate of return** on the saving component of a cash value policy.[2] The yearly rate of return is based on the following formula:

$$i = \frac{(CV + D) + (YPT)(DB - CV)(.001)}{(P + CVP)} - 1$$

where

i = yearly rate of return on the saving component, expressed as a decimal
CV = cash value at end of policy year
D = annual dividend
YPT = assumed yearly price per $1000 of protection (see benchmark prices in Exhibit 19.6)
DB = death benefit
P = annual premium
CVP = cash value at end of preceding policy year

The first expression in the numerator of the formula is the amount available in the policy at the end of the policy year. The second expression in the numerator is the assumed price of the protection component, which is determined by multiplying the amount of protection by an assumed price per $1000 of protection. Assumed prices per $1000 of protection for various ages are benchmarks derived from certain U.S. population death rates (see Exhibit 19.6). Finally, the expression in the denominator of the formula is the amount available in the policy at the beginning of the policy year.

For example, assume that Mark purchased a $100,000 participating ordinary life policy at age 35. He is now age 42 and at the beginning of the eighth policy year. He would like to know the yearly rate of return on the saving component for the eighth year of the policy. The annual premium is $1500. The cash value in the policy is $7800 at the end of the seventh policy year and $9200 at the end of the eighth policy year. The eighth-year dividend is $400. Because Mark is age 42 at the beginning of the eighth policy year, the benchmark price is $4.00 (see Exhibit 19.6).

Based on the preceding information, the yearly rate of return for the eighth policy year is calculated as follows:

$$i = \frac{(9200 + 400) + (4)(100{,}000 - 9200)(.001)}{(1500 + 7800)} - 1$$

$$= \frac{(9600) + (4)(90{,}800)(.001)}{(9300)} - 1$$

$$= \frac{9600 + 363}{9300} - 1$$

$$= \frac{9963}{9300} - 1 = 1.071 - 1 = .071 = 7.1\%$$

The yearly rate of return for the eighth policy year is 7.1 percent, assuming that the yearly price per $1000 of protection is $4.

The major advantage of Belth's method is simplicity—you do not need a computer. The information needed can be obtained by referring to your policy and premium notice, or by contacting your agent or insurer. The same methodology can be used to evaluate an existing life insurance policy. (See the Appendix at the end of the chapter.)

EXHIBIT 19.6
Benchmark Prices

Age	Benchmark price
Under 30	$ 1.50
30–34	2.00
35–39	3.00
40–44	4.00
45–49	6.50
50–54	10.00
55–59	15.00
60–64	25.00
65–69	35.00
70–74	50.00
75–79	80.00
80–84	125.00

Note: The benchmark prices were derived from certain U. S. population death rates. The benchmark figure for each five-year age bracket is close to the death rate per $1000 at the highest age in that bracket.

SOURCE: Adapted from Joseph M. Belth, *Life Insurance: A Consumer's Handbook*, second edition (Bloomington, IN: Indiana University Press, 1985), Table 9, p. 84. Reprinted by permission of the author.

TAXATION OF LIFE INSURANCE

Treatment of life insurance buying would be incomplete without a discussion of the taxation of life insurance. This section discusses briefly the taxation of life insurance.

Federal Income Tax

Life insurance proceeds paid in a lump sum to a designated beneficiary are generally received income-tax free by the beneficiary. If the proceeds are periodically liquidated under the settlement options, the payments consist of both principal and interest. The principal is received income-tax free, but the interest is taxable as ordinary income.

Premiums paid for individual life insurance policies generally are not deductible for income-tax purposes. Dividends on life insurance policies are received income-tax free. However, interest on dividends retained under the interest option is taxable to the policyowner. If the dividends are used to buy paid-up additions to the policy, the cash value of the paid-up additions accumulates income-tax free.

Thus, compared with the interest option, the paid-up additions option provides a small tax advantage.

In addition, the annual increase in cash value under a permanent life insurance policy is presently income-tax free. However, if the policy is surrendered for its cash value, any gain is taxable as ordinary income. If the cash value exceeds the premiums paid less any dividends, the excess is taxable as ordinary income.

Federal Estate Tax

If the insured has any *incidents of ownership* in the policy at the time of death, the entire proceeds are included in the gross estate of the insured for federal estate-tax purposes. Incidents of ownership include the right to change the beneficiary, the right to borrow the cash value or surrender the policy, and the right to elect a settlement option. The proceeds are also included in the insured's gross estate if they are payable to the estate. They can be removed from the gross estate if the policyowner makes an *absolute assignment* of the policy to someone else and has no incidents of ownership in the policy at the time of death. However, if the assignment is made within three years of death, the proceeds will be included in the deceased's gross estate for federal estate-tax purposes.

A federal estate tax is payable if the decedent's taxable estate exceeds certain thresholds. The tax starts at a stiff 37 percent and rises to 55 percent for estates of $3 million or more. For individuals dying before 1998, a *unified tax credit* of $192,800 was available, which eliminated the federal estate tax completely on taxable estates of $600,000 or less. However, as a result of the Taxpayer Relief Act of 1997, the amount of property excluded from federal estate taxes will gradually increase to $1 million according to the following schedule:

Year of death	Unified tax credit	Excluded amount
1998	$202,050	$ 625,000
1999	211,300	650,000
2000–2001	220,550	675,000
2002–2003	229,800	700,000
2004	287,300	850,000
2005	326,300	950,000
2006 and later	345,800	1,000,000

To determine whether a federal estate tax is payable, the gross estate must first be calculated. The *gross estate* includes the value of the property you own when you die, one-half of the value of the property owned jointly with your spouse, life insurance death proceeds in which the insured has any incidents of ownership, and certain other items. The gross estate can be reduced by certain deductions in determining the *taxable estate*. Allowable deductions include funeral and administrative expenses, claims against the estate, estate settlement and probate costs, charitable contributions, and certain other deductions.

In addition, the gross estate can be reduced by the *marital deduction*, which is a deduction of the value of the property included in the gross estate but passed on to the surviving spouse. This property is taxed later, when the surviving spouse dies. For example, assume that Richard dies in 2001 and has a gross estate of $1,400,000. He leaves $600,000 of property outright to his spouse. Thus, the marital deduction is $600,000. Assume that debts, funeral expenses, and administrative costs total $125,000. The taxable estate is $675,000, and the tentative federal tax is $220,550. However, as a result of the unified tax credit of $220,550, the federal estate tax is zero (see Exhibit 19.7).

SHOPPING FOR LIFE INSURANCE

Developing a sound life insurance program involves seven steps, as illustrated in Exhibit 19.8 and discussed next.

Determine Whether You Need Life Insurance

The first step is to determine whether you need life insurance. If you are married or single with one or more dependents to support, you may need a substantial amount of life insurance. You may also need life insurance if you have a temporary need, such as paying off the mortgage on your home. In addition, if you have accumulated substantial assets, large amounts of life insurance may be needed to provide estate liquidity and to pay federal estate taxes that are due within nine months of your death.

EXHIBIT 19.7
Calculating Federal Estate Taxes*

Gross estate		$1,400,000
Less:		
Debts	$75,000	
Administrative costs	40,000	
Funeral expenses	10,000	
		−125,000
Adjusted gross estate		$1,275,000
Less:		
Marital deduction		−600,000
Taxable estate		$ 675,000
Tentative tax		$ 220,550
Less:		
Unified credit		−220,550
Federal estate tax		$ 0

*Individual dies in 2001.

However, if you are single and no one is presently dependent on you for financial support, you do not need life insurance, other than a modest amount for burial purposes. The arguments for buying life insurance when you are young and insurable are not compelling. Even if your situation should change and you need life insurance in the future, more than nine out of ten applicants for life insurance are accepted at standard rates. Thus, it is a waste of money to buy life insurance when it is not needed.

Estimate the Amount of Life Insurance You Need

The needs approach and capital retention approach are practical methods for determining the amount of life insurance needed. Persons with dependents often need surprisingly large amounts of life insurance. In determining the amount needed, you must consider your family's present and future financial needs, potential survivor benefits from Social Security, and the financial assets currently owned.

If you carry a sufficient amount of life insurance, it is unnecessary to purchase additional life insurance

EXHIBIT 19.8
Shopping for Life Insurance

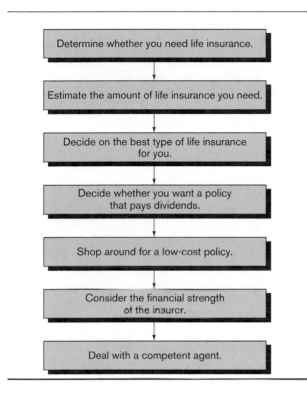

Determine whether you need life insurance.

Estimate the amount of life insurance you need.

Decide on the best type of life insurance for you.

Decide whether you want a policy that pays dividends.

Shop around for a low-cost policy.

Consider the financial strength of the insurer.

Deal with a competent agent.

as supplemental coverage. These coverages include accidental death insurance from life insurers, accidental death and dismemberment insurance offered by commercial banks, credit life insurance on consumer loans, and life insurance sold by mail. In addition, flight insurance sold at airports is a bad buy for most consumers because commercial jets rarely crash (see Insight 19.2).

Decide on the Best Type of Life Insurance for You

The next step is to select the best type of life insurance policy for you. *The best policy is the one that best meets your financial needs.* If the amount of money you can spend on life insurance is limited, or if you have a temporary need, consider only term insurance. If you need lifetime protection, consider or-

dinary life insurance or universal life insurance. If you believe that you cannot save money without being forced to do so, also consider ordinary life insurance or universal life insurance as a savings vehicle. However, remember that the annual rates of return on cash-value policies can vary enormously.

Also, avoid purchasing a policy that you cannot afford. A large percentage of new life insurance policies lapse for nonpayment of premiums during the first two years. The lapse rate for policies in force for less than two years was about 15 percent in 1998.[3] *If you drop the policy after a few months or years, you will lose a substantial sum of money. Be sure you can afford the premium.*

Decide Whether You Want a Policy That Pays Dividends

In recent decades, participating life insurance policies that pay dividends generally have been better buys than nonparticipating policies because of high interest rates that permitted insurers to raise their dividends. However, interest rates have declined in recent years, and many insurers have reduced their dividends because excess interest earnings have declined. Thus, if you believe that interest rates will be higher in the future, you should consider a participating policy because excess interest has a powerful impact on dividends. However, if you believe that interest rates will continue to fall and will remain at lower levels in the future, then consider a nonparticipating policy. Policies that do not pay dividends generally require a lower premium outlay.

Shop Around for a Low-Cost Policy

One of the most important suggestions is to shop carefully for a low-cost policy. There is enormous variation in the cost of life insurance. You should not purchase a life insurance policy from the first agent who approaches you. *Instead, you should compare the interest-adjusted cost of similar policies from several insurers before you buy* (see Exhibit 19.5). Otherwise, you may be overpaying for the insurance protection. If you make a mistake and purchase a high-cost policy, this mistake can cost you thousands of dollars over your lifetime.

Insight 19.2

Skip the Flight Insurance at Airports

Flight insurance. This hardy perennial pays off if you die in a plane crash. American Express, for example, sells cardholders $1 million of coverage for $14 per trip. Sure, plane crashes are high-impact news events that get people worried about safety. But think a minute. You already have adequate comprehensive life insurance, right? Why would your family need more money if you died in a crash than if you were run over by a cab at the airport? And don't forget that American Express automatically gives you $100,000 of coverage free when you charge your ticket on Amex's green and gold cards.

Finally, your chances of dying in a crash are wildly improbable. If every passenger on every scheduled U.S. commercial flight had paid $14 for a $1 million policy in 1995, and a $1 million claim was paid for every victim that year, the result would be a $7.4 billion profit to the insurer.

Suggestion: Skip the insurance and the airplane food, and buy a good lunch.

SOURCE: Excerpted from William Giese, "Insurance You Can Do Without," *Kiplinger's Personal Finance Magazine* (February 1997), p. 72. Reprinted with permission.

When you shop for a low-cost policy, you should also consider **low-load life insurance.** Some life insurers sell insurance directly to the public by using telephone representatives or fee-only financial planners. The major advantage is that marketing expenses account for only 10 to 25 percent of the first year's premium rather than 90 to 125 percent on policies sold by agents. Two major low-load insurers that sell policies by phone are Ameritas Direct (800-689-6830) and USAA Life (800-531-8000).

Consider the Financial Strength of the Insurer

In addition to cost, you should consider the financial strength of the insurer issuing the policy. Some life insurers have become insolvent and have gone out of business. Although all states have state guaranty funds that pay the claims of insolvent life insurers, there are limits on the amount guaranteed. Although death claims are paid promptly, you may have to wait years before you can borrow or withdraw your cash value. Thus, it is important to buy life insurance only from financially sound insurers.

A number of rating organizations periodically grade and rate life insurers on their financial strength (see Exhibit 19.9). The companies are rated based on the amount of their capital and surplus, legal reserves, quality of investments, past profitability, com-

petency of management, and numerous other factors. However, the various ratings are not always a reliable guide for consumers and can be confusing. There are wide variations in the grades given by the different rating agencies. Joseph M. Belth, a nationally known consumer expert in life insurance, recommends that an insurer should receive a high rating from at least two of the following four rating agencies before a policy is purchased. The following are considered high ratings for someone who is conservative:[4]

Standard & Poor's: AAA, AA+, AA, AA –
Moody's: Aaa, Aa1, Aa2, Aa3, A1
Duff & Phelps: AAA, AA+, AA
Weiss: A+, A, A–, B+, B, B–

Deal with a Competent Agent

You should also deal with a competent agent when you buy life insurance. Selling life insurance is a tough job, and only a relatively small proportion of new life insurance agents are successful.

Most new agents receive only a minimum amount of training before they are licensed to sell life insurance. New agents also are often placed under intense pressure to sell life insurance. Even mature agents are expected to sell a certain amount of insurance. As a result, some agents have engaged in deceptive sales practices by misrepresenting the insurance to clients or by recommending policies that maxi-

EXHIBIT 19.9
Rating Categories of Major Rating Agencies*

Rank number	Ratings				
	Standard & Poor's	Moody's	Duff & Phelps	Weiss	A.M. Best
1	AAA	Aaa	AAA	A+	A++
2	AA+	Aa1	AA+	A	A+
3	AA	Aa2	AA	A−	A
4	AA−	Aa3	AA−	B+	A−
5	A+	A1	A+	B	B++
6	A	A2	A	B−	B+
7	A−	A3	A−	C+	B
8	BBB+	Baa1	BBB+	C	B−
9	BBB	Baa2	BBB	C−	C++
10	BBB−	Baa3	BBB−	D+	C+
11	BB+	Ba1	BB+	D	C
12	BB	Ba2	BB	D−	C−
13	BB−	Ba3	BB−	E+	D
14	B+	B1	B+	E	E
15	B	B2	B	E−	F
16	B−	B3	B−	F	
17	CCC	Caa1	CCC		
18	CC	Caa2	DD		
19	R	Caa3	SR		
20		Ca			
21		C			

*The ratings in a given rank are not necessarily equivalent to one another.

SOURCE: Joseph M. Belth, ed., "Rating Categories," *The Insurance Forum*, Vol. 26, No. 9 (September 1999), p. 250.

mize commissions rather than meeting the client's needs. Because of deceptive sales practices by agents, several major life insurers have been subject to heavy fines by state insurance departments and class action litigation by angry policyowners.

To reduce the possibility of receiving bad advice or being sold the wrong policy, you should consider the professional qualifications of the agent. An agent who is a **Chartered Life Underwriter (CLU)**, **Chartered Financial Consultant (ChFC)**, or **Certified Financial Planner (CFP)** should be technically competent to give proper advice. More importantly, agents who hold the preceding professional designations are expected to abide by a code of ethics that places their clients' interests ahead of their own.

Agents who are currently studying for these professional designations should also be considered.

SUMMARY

- There are enormous cost variations among similar life insurance policies. Purchase of a high-cost policy can cost thousands of dollars over the insured's lifetime for the same amount of insurance protection.

- The traditional net cost method to illustrate the cost of life insurance has several defects:

    The time value of money is ignored.

    The insurance is often shown to be free.

> The steepness of the dividend scale is ignored.
>
> The dividend scale is assumed to remain unchanged.
>
> The net cost is based on the assumption that the policy will be surrendered.

■ The interest-adjusted method is a more accurate measure of life insurance costs. The time value of money is taken into consideration by applying an interest factor to each element of cost. If you are interested in surrendering the policy at the end of a certain period, the surrender cost index is the appropriate cost index to use. If you intend to keep your policy in force, the net payment cost index should be used.

■ Annual rates-of-return data on the saving component in traditional cash-value life insurance policies are not readily available to consumers. However, the yearly rate-of-return method can be helpful in this regard.

■ Life insurance experts typically recommend several rules to follow when shopping for life insurance:

> Determine whether you need life insurance.
>
> Estimate the amount of life insurance you need.
>
> Decide on the best type of insurance for you.
>
> Decide whether you want a policy that pays dividends.
>
> Shop around for a low-cost policy.
>
> Consider the financial strength of the insurer.
>
> Deal with a competent agent.

KEY CONCEPTS AND TERMS

Certified Financial Planner (CFP)
Chartered Financial Consultant (ChFC)
Chartered Life Underwriter (CLU)
Interest-adjusted method
Linton yield

Low-load life insurance
Net payment cost index
Surrender cost index
Traditional net cost method
Yearly rate-of-return method

REVIEW QUESTIONS

1. Describe the traditional net cost method for determining the cost of life insurance.

2. Explain the defects of the traditional net cost method.

3. Explain the surrender cost index and net payment cost index. How are these indexes an improvement over the traditional net cost method?

4. Where can you obtain interest-adjusted cost information?

5. List the rules that should be followed if interest-adjusted data are used.

6. Why are the rates of return on the saving element in most cash-value policies negative during the early years?

7. Briefly explain the yearly rate-of-return method that can be used to determine the rate of return on the saving component of a cash-value policy.

8. Describe the rules that should be followed when shopping for life insurance.

9. Is it desirable to replace an older life insurance policy with a new policy? Explain.

10. Should cost be the only factor to consider when a life insurance policy is purchased? Explain.

APPLICATION QUESTIONS

1. A life insurance agent remarked that "most life insurance policies cost about the same, and it really is not necessary to be concerned about cost." Do you agree or disagree with the agent's remarks? Explain.

2. A friend remarked that "cash-value life insurance is a good place to save money, because the annual return is reasonable and the money is safe." Do you agree or disagree with this statement? Explain your answer.

3. You have been asked for some advice on how to buy life insurance. What suggestions can you give?

4. Contrast the Linton yield and the yearly rate-of-return method as techniques for determining the rates of return on the saving component of a cash-value policy.

SELECTED REFERENCES

Belth, Joseph M. *Life Insurance: A Consumer's Handbook*, second edition. Bloomington, IN: Indiana University Press, 1985.

Black, Kenneth, Jr., and Harold D. Skipper, Jr. *Life Insurance*, thirteenth edition. Upper Saddle River, NJ: Prentice-Hall, 2000.

Case Application

A participating ordinary life policy in the amount of $10,000 is issued to an individual, age 35. The following cost data are given:

Annual premium	$230
Total dividends for 20 years	$1613
Cash value at end of 20 years	$3620
Accumulated value of the annual premiums at 5 percent for 20 years	$7985
Accumulated value of the dividends at 5 percent for 20 years	$2352
Amount to which $1 deposited annually at the beginning of each year will accumulate in 20 years at 5 percent	$34.719

a. Based on the above information, compute the annual net cost for each $1000 of life insurance at the end of 20 years using the *traditional net cost method*.

b. Compute the annual *surrender cost index* for each $1000 life insurance at the end of 20 years.

c. Compute the annual *net payment cost index* for each $1000 of life insurance at the end of 20 years.

Dorfman, Mark S., and Saul W. Adelman. *Life Insurance: A Financial Planning Approach*, second edition. Chicago, IL: Dearborn Financial Publishing, 1992.

Graves, Edward E., ed. *McGill's Life Insurance*, second edition. Bryn Mawr, PA: The American College, 1998.

Mehr, Robert I., and Sandra G. Gustavson. *Life Insurance: Theory and Practice*, fourth edition. Plano, TX: Business Publications, 1987.

Rejda, George E., Constance M. Luthardt, Cheryl L. Ferguson, and Donald R. Oakes. *Personal Insurance*, fourth edition. Malvern, PA: Insurance Institute of America, 2000.

2. This section is based on Joseph M. Belth, *Life Insurance: A Consumer's Handbook*, second edition. (Bloomington, IL: Indiana University Press, 1985), pp. 89–91, 208–209.

3. *ACLI Life Insurance Fact Book 1999* (Washington, DC: American Council of Life Insurance, 1999), Table 1.6, p. 11.

4. Joseph M. Belth, ed., "The Financial Strength of Life-Health Insurance Companies," *The Insurance Forum*, Vol. 26, No. 9 (September 1999), p. 253.

NOTES

1. "Life Insurance: How to Protect Your Family: Whole Life Insurance," *Consumer Reports*, 51 (July 1986): 458.

Is Your Life Insurance Reasonably Priced? (How to Evaluate an Existing Life Insurance Policy)*

If you own a life insurance policy on which you have paid premiums for some years, and if you are wondering whether you are receiving fair value for your money, this Appendix is aimed at you.

THE PLAYERS

Many of those in the life insurance business are legitimate and ethical salespeople; however, the business is plagued by a significant number of replacement artists and conservation artists. A replacement artist is a person who uses dubious methods to convince you—the owner of an existing life insurance policy—to replace your policy with a new one. Some replacement artists attempt to discredit the agent and the company from which you bought your existing policy. Some of what replacement artists say may be accurate, but some of it may be deceptive or even false. The problem is that most policyowners cannot determine what is accurate and what is not.

A conservation artist, on the other hand, is a person who uses dubious methods to convince you—the owner of an existing life insurance policy—that your policy should not be replaced. Some conservation artists attempt to discredit the replacement artist. Some of what conservation artists say may be accurate, but some of it may be deceptive or even false. The problem is that most policyowners cannot determine what is accurate and what is not.

In short, a war is going on between replacement artists and conservation artists. As the owner of an existing life insurance policy, you are caught in the middle. You probably do not know enough about life insurance to be able to distinguish accurate information from inaccurate information, and you probably do not know whom to believe. The purpose of this Appendix is to arm you with the ability to find out for yourself whether the life insurance protection you own is reasonably priced.

THE GENERAL APPROACH

This Appendix describes three steps you must follow to determine whether the life insurance protec-

---

*The material in this appendix was written by Joseph M. Belth, Ph.D., professor emeritus of insurance in the Kelley School of Business at Indiana University (Bloomington), and author of *Life Insurance: A Consumer's Handbook* (1985). It was first published in the June 1982 issue of *Insurance Forum*, of which Professor Belth is the editor, and was modified slightly in 1999 for purposes of this Appendix. Copyright © 1982 by Insurance Forum, Inc., P.O. Box 245, Ellettsville, IN 47429. Used by permission.

tion you own is reasonably priced: (1) gather certain information about each policy you wish to evaluate; (2) perform certain calculations using the information gathered in the first step; and (3) compare the results of your calculations with certain benchmarks.

Gathering Information

The most difficult step is not the arithmetic, but rather assembling the necessary information. Some of what you need is in the policy itself, but you may find the information difficult to extract. And some of what you need may not be in the policy. It is suggested that you obtain the information by writing a carefully worded letter to the president of the life insurance company that issued the policy. A suggested letter is shown after the explanatory appendix.

You may find the address of the company on the policy itself, on a recent premium notice, or by calling your local library. You may find the policy number on the policy itself or on a recent premium notice. Your letter should request the following items of information:

1. The amount that the insurance company would have paid to your beneficiary if you had died at the end of the most recently completed policy year. This is the death benefit (*DB*) of your policy.
2. The amount that the insurance company would have paid to you if you had surrendered your policy at the end of the most recently completed policy year. This is the cash value (*CV*) of your policy. (Some policies do not have cash values, so the amount here could be zero.)
3. The amount that the insurance company would have paid to you if you had surrendered your policy at the end of the year preceding the most recently completed policy year. This (*CVP*) corresponds to item 2, but for one year earlier.
4. The annual premium (*P*) for the most recently completed policy year. (Policies that are "paid up" require no further premiums, so the amount here could be zero.)
5. The dividend (*D*) for the most recently completed policy year. (Some policies do not pay dividends,

so the amount here could be zero.)
6. The date on which the most recently completed policy year began.
7. Your insurance age, in accordance with the company's method of determining age, on the date referred to in item 6.

It is recommended that you word the letter exactly as illustrated, and that you keep a copy of the letter. If you receive no response, or if you receive an inadequate response, you should file a written complaint with your state insurance commissioner. You may obtain the address of your state insurance commissioner from your local library.

The Calculations

Once you have acquired the information listed in the preceding section, you are ready to perform certain calculations, except for the choice of an interest rate (*i*). It is suggested that you use an interest rate of 6 percent (0.06) in your calculations. (For comments concerning the interest rate, see the explanatory appendix.)

Now you are ready to perform certain calculations to arrive at a yearly price per $1000 of protection for the most recently completed policy year. The formula is as follows:

$$\frac{(P + CVP)(1 + i) - (CV + D)}{(DB - CV)(0.001)}$$

To illustrate, suppose the response to your letter provided the following information:

1. Death benefit (*DB*): $25,000
2. Cash value at end of most recently completed policy year (*CV*): $10,450
3. Cash value at end of year preceding most recently completed policy year (*CVP*): $10,000
4. Annual premium (*P*): $550
5. Dividend (*D*): $400
6. Date on which most recently completed policy year began: March 10, 2000
7. Your insurance age on March 10, 2000: 56

Your next step is to plug these figures into the formula. The calculations are as follows.

$$\frac{(550 + 10{,}000)(1 + 0.06) - (10{,}450 + 400)}{(25{,}000 - 10{,}450)(0.001)}$$

$$= \frac{(10{,}550)(1.06) - 10{,}850}{(14{,}550)(0.001)}$$

$$= \frac{11{,}183 - 10{,}850}{14.550}$$

$$= \frac{333}{14.550} = 22.89$$

In other words, the yearly price per $1000 of protection in the most recently completed policy year (which began on March 10, 2000) is $22.89, assuming 6 percent interest.

The Comparison

The benchmarks against which to compare yearly prices per $1000 of protection are shown in the table below.

Benchmarks

Age	Price
Under 30	$ 1.50
30–34	2.00
35–39	3.00
40–44	4.00
45–49	6.50
50–54	10.00
55–59	15.00
60–64	25.00
65–69	35.00
70–74	50.00
75–79	80.00
80–84	125.00

The suggested interpretations of the benchmark figures are as follows:

1. If the yearly price per $1000 of protection is less than the benchmark figure, the price of your protection is low, and you should not consider replacing your policy.
2. If the yearly price per $1000 of protection is more than the benchmark figure but less than double that figure, the price of your protection is moderate, and again you should not consider replacing your policy.
3. If the yearly price per $1000 of protection is more than double the benchmark figure, the price of your protection is high, and you should consider replacing your policy.

To illustrate, the benchmark figure for age 56 is $15, and the yearly price per $1000 of protection that came out of your calculations is $22.89. Because the latter is more than the benchmark figure but less than double that figure, the price of your protection is moderate, and you should not consider replacing your policy.

SEVERAL WARNINGS

Life insurance policies are complex financial instruments. In this Appendix, we have tried to simplify the subject so that you can find out for yourself whether your life insurance protection is reasonably priced. The simplification process, however, makes it necessary to voice warnings in several areas.

1. If your policy carries an extra premium because of a health impairment or other problem, the analysis of such a policy is beyond the scope of this Appendix.
2. If your policy covers more than one life, the analysis of such a policy is also beyond the scope of this Appendix. Examples are family policies (in which husband, wife, and children are covered in one policy) and second-to-die policies (which cover two lives and pay the face amount on the second death).
3. It is possible that the year for which you perform the calculations—the most recently completed policy year—is not representative of other policy years. For example, the price of the protection in the first one or two policy years is often quite high, reflecting sales commissions and other ex-

penses associated with the issuance of a life insurance policy. As another example, the price in a single isolated year may be quite low or quite high because of certain structural characteristics of the policy. For these reasons, you might wish to gather the information and perform the calculations for a few other years, especially if the figure for the most recently completed policy year is either very low or very high. The postscript of the suggested letter is optional; it is designed to help you obtain the information for a few other years, should you wish to perform the calculations.

4. You may obtain a negative result. This may arise because of an unusual year, as mentioned in the preceding paragraph, or because the price of the protection in your policy is extremely low. A negative figure does not mean the company is crazy— remember that you are using a modest interest rate of 6 percent in your calculations.

5. If the amount payable on surrender of your policy is equal to the amount payable on death, you have no life insurance protection, and the yearly price per $1000 of protection is without meaning. Under these circumstances, you should view your policy as a savings account. Calculate the yearly rate of return (expressed as a decimal) with the following formula:

$$\frac{CV + D}{P + CVP} - 1$$

You can then judge your policy by comparing the yearly rate of return with what you can earn on a savings account. In making such a comparison, however, you should consider the income-tax situation, as discussed in the explanatory appendix below.

6. If the amount payable on surrender of your policy is only slightly smaller than the amount payable on death (less than, say, 5 percent below the amount payable on death), you have very little life insurance protection, and the yearly price per $1000 of protection has very little meaning. Under these circumstances, you should view your policy as essentially a savings account. Use the above formula to approximate the yearly rate of return.

7. If yours is a small policy—less than, say, $3000 in face amount—the yearly price per $1000 of protection may be high because of the expenses associated with the maintenance of a small policy. It may not be worth the bother to replace a small policy; indeed, a small policy may not be worth keeping unless you have some emotional attachment to it.

8. We were careful to say that, if the price of the protection in your policy is high, you should *consider* replacing your policy. We did *not* say you should necessarily replace your policy. There are several reasons for you to proceed with caution: a replacement necessarily involves the purchase of a new policy, and the purchase of a new policy requires care if you wish to acquire low-priced protection; surrendering an existing policy may involve the sacrifice of certain valuable policy provisions; surrendering an existing policy may involve certain income-tax considerations; purchasing a new policy may involve significant expenses in the first one or two years, as mentioned earlier; and because of a health impairment or other problem, you may find it difficult to qualify for a new policy.

AN EXPLANATORY APPENDIX

Instead of following the suggestions in this Appendix blindly, you may prefer to acquire some understanding of the formula and the benchmarks. The purpose of this section is to provide a brief explanation.

Let's consider the numerator of the formula. The first parenthetical expression $(P + CVP)$ is the amount that you would have had available to put into some other savings vehicle if you had decided to surrender the policy at the end of the year preceding the most recently completed policy year. You would have received the cash value (CVP) and you would have been relieved of the annual premium (P).

Multiplying this expression by $(1 + i)$ tells you what you would have had in that other savings vehicle by the end of the most recently completed policy year if you had invested the $(P + CVP)$ at an annual interest rate of i. This leads us to a discussion of the interest rate.

The interest rate you choose is not important if your policy has little or no cash value. However, the interest rate you choose is quite important if your policy has a substantial cash value. If your policy has a cash value, it probably has a loan clause that permits you to borrow against the policy up to approximately the cash value at a fixed interest rate of 5 to 8 percent or at a variable interest rate. If you believe you could put the money in some other savings vehicle at a much higher interest rate and with a high degree of safety, and if the amount available is substantial, you should consider borrowing against your policy and investing the proceeds of the loan. Bear in mind, however, that the savings vehicle you are thinking about may produce interest income that is subject to current income tax, and that the interest you pay on the policy loan is not deductible. The interest earnings built into cash-value life insurance, on the other hand, are income-tax deferred and eventually will be either partially or fully income-tax exempt. For simplicity, we suggested you use an interest rate of 6 percent in the calculations.

The last parenthetical expression in the numerator of the formula $(CV + D)$ is the amount that you had available at the end of the most recently completed policy year, having continued the policy for that year. The difference between the product of the first two expressions ($11,183 in the example) and the last expression ($10,850) is the price you paid ($333) for the life insurance protection in that year (assuming 6 percent interest).

Now let's consider the denominator of the formula. The cash value is the saving component of the policy, and is an asset from your point of view. Therefore, the life insurance protection you had ($14,550) is the difference between the death benefit ($25,000) and the cash value ($10,450). The other expression in the denominator moves the decimal point three places to the left, so that the denominator represents the amount of life insurance protection in thousands of dollars (14.550).

Since the price you paid for the protection (assuming 6 percent) was $333, and since the amount of protection in thousands of dollars was 14.550, the yearly price per $1000 of protection (assuming 6 percent) was $22.89.

Finally, the benchmarks were derived from certain United States population death rates. The benchmark figure for each five-year age bracket is slightly above the death rate per 1000 at the highest age in that bracket. What we are saying is that, if the price of your life insurance protection per $1000 is in the vicinity of the "raw material cost" (that is, the amount needed just to pay death claims based on population death rates), your life insurance protection is reasonably priced.

SUGGESTED LETTER

President
XYZ Life Insurance Company
Post Office Box 245
Ellettsville, IN 47429

Dear President:

Please furnish me with the following information concerning my policy number 1 234 567.

1. The amount that you would have paid in a single sum to my beneficiary if I had died at the end of the most recently completed policy year, including any supplemental term life insurance benefits. Please disregard any accidental death benefits, any dividends, and any loan against the policy.
2. The amount that you would have paid in a single sum to me if I had surrendered the policy at the end of the most recently completed policy year. Please disregard any dividends and any loan against the policy.
3. The amount that you would have paid in a single sum to me if I had surrendered the policy at the end of the year preceding the most recently completed policy year. Please disregard any dividends and any loan against the policy.
4. The premium for the most recently completed policy year, including the premiums for any supplemental term life insurance benefits. Please exclude the premiums for any accidental death benefits, disability benefits, or guaranteed insurability benefits. Please exclude the interest on any loan against the policy, and assume I paid the year's premium in full at the beginning of the year.
5. The dividend for the most recently completed policy year, including the dividends for any sup-

plemental term life insurance benefits. Please exclude any dividends for any accidental death benefits or disability benefits. Please exclude any dividends credited to dividend accumulations or additions.

6. The date on which the most recently completed policy year began.
7. My age, according to your records, when the most recently completed policy year began.

Thank you for providing the information that I have requested.

Sincerely yours,

[*Editor's note*: The following postscript is optional. See the third point in the section entitled "Several Warnings."]

P.S.: Please furnish the above information for the two policy years preceding the most recently completed policy year, and for the two policy years following the most recently completed policy year. In the case of amounts payable in future years, please identify any nonguaranteed amounts and base the figures on your company's current scale.

Chapter 20 | Annuities and Individual Retirement Accounts

> ❝ *Buy an annuity cheap, and make your life interesting to yourself and everybody else that watches the speculation.* ❞
>
> Charles Dickens

Learning Objectives

After studying this chapter, you should be able to:

▲ Show how an annuity differs from life insurance.

▲ Describe the basic characteristics of a fixed annuity and a variable annuity.

▲ Explain the major characteristics of an equity-indexed annuity.

▲ Describe the basic characteristics of a traditional tax-deductible individual retirement account (IRA).

▲ Explain the basic characteristics of a Roth IRA.

▲ Explain the income tax treatment of a traditional IRA and a Roth IRA.

▲ Access an Internet site and obtain consumer information about IRAs.

Internet Resources

- **Annuity.com** provides annuity quotes online and timely information about fixed, equity indexed, variable, and other tax-deferred annuities. Visit the site at:
  www.annuity.com

- **Annuityshopper.com** provides online annuity rates for immediate annuities from major insurers. The site claims consumers can save thousands of dollars by shopping for immediate annuities through its service. Visit the site at:
  www.annuityshopper.com

- **Charles Schwab** provides informative articles and information on retirement planning, annuities, and individual retirement accounts (IRAs). Visit the site at:
  www.schwab.com

- **Fidelity Investments** offers timely information on retirement planning, annuities, and IRAs, including interactive calculators for making IRA decisions. Visit the site at:
  www.fidelity.com

- **Insure.com** provides timely information on annuities, IRAs, and other insurance products. A quarterly survey of top-ranked variable annuities based on the VARDS Report is also available. Visit the site at:

  www.insure.com

- **InsWeb** is one of the most complete insurance marketplace sources on the Internet. Premium quotes on a variety of insurance products can be obtained. The site also provides information on annuities and IRAs. Visit it at:

  www.insweb.com

- **Quicken Insurance** provides information on all types of insurance products including annuities and IRAs. Visit the site at:

  www.quickeninsurance.com

- The **Roth IRA Web** site is devoted to Roth IRAs and provides a considerable amount of consumer information on this type of IRA. The site provides links to articles, books, tapes, calculators, IRS documents, and a message board on Roth IRAs. Visit the site at:

  www.rothira.com

- **TIAA-CREF** is an excellent source of accurate information on retirement planning, annuities, and IRAs. Visit the site at:

  www.tiaa-cref.org

- The **Vanguard Group** provides timely information on variable annuities, IRAs, and retirement planning. Visit the site at:

  www.vanguard.com

ennifer, age 25, graduated from college and accepted a job as a marketing analyst for an international oil company with an annual salary of $32,000. She wants to save money to provide for a comfortable retirement. Unfortunately, Jennifer is ineligible to participate in the company's Section 401(k) retirement plan for one year. A financial planner recommended an individual retirement account (Roth IRA). Jennifer could start saving immediately for retirement; the investment income would accumulate income-tax-free; and the retirement fund would grow to a sizable amount. The planner pointed out that if Jennifer saved $2000 annually for 40 years, and the IRA account earned an average annual return of 10 percent, she would have more than $970,000 in her account at age 65. If her contributions were invested in a Roth IRA, she could withdraw the finds free of current income taxes.

Like Jennifer, millions of workers dream of achieving financial independence and a comfortable retirement. Planning for a comfortable retirement should receive high priority in a personal risk management program. Retirement planning is especially important today because the proportion of older people in the population is increasing; the period of retirement for many workers is growing longer because of increased life expectancy and early retirement; and studies show that many workers are not saving enough for a comfortable retirement.[1]

This chapter discusses the timely topic of retirement planning and shows how annuities and IRAs can assure a comfortable retirement. Two major areas are emphasized. The first part discusses the annuity concept and the different types of annuities sold today. The second part discusses the characteristics of IRAs, including the traditional tax-deductible IRA, the Roth IRA, and the educational IRA.

INDIVIDUAL ANNUITIES

Workers retiring today typically receive Social Security retirement benefits and benefits from their employers' retirement plans. Individual annuities can also be purchased to provide additional retirement income. Although the premiums are paid with after-tax dollars, the investment income is free of current income taxes. The investment income accumulates on a tax-deferred basis and is not taxed until actually paid out. The investment returns of tax-deferred compounding over long periods can be impressive (see Exhibit 20.1).

Annuity Principle

An **annuity** *can be defined as a periodic payment that continues for a fixed period or for the duration of a*

EXHIBIT 20.1
Tax-deferred Compounding Builds Wealth Faster

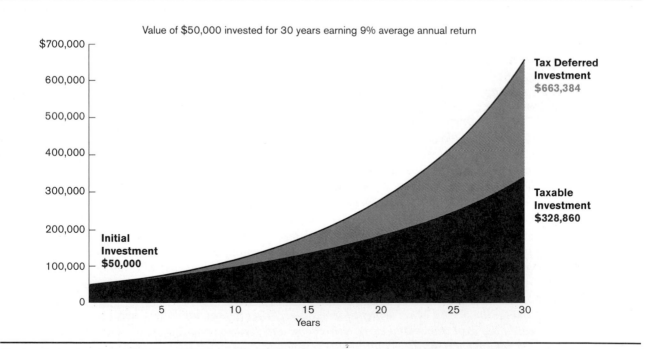

Value of $50,000 invested for 30 years earning 9% average annual return

The chart shows a hypothetical $50,000 taxable and tax deferred investment. Fees and expenses are not included, which would lower the performance shown. The taxable investment is taxed at a combined federal and state tax rate of 28 percent per year on the investment returns.

SOURCE: *Understanding Annuities* (Newark, NJ: Prudential Investments, 1998), p. 7.

designated life or lives. The person who receives the periodic payments or whose life governs the duration of payment is known as the **annuitant**.

An annuity is the opposite of life insurance. Life insurance creates an immediate estate and provides protection against dying too soon before financial assets can be accumulated. In contrast, an annuity provides protection against living too long and exhausting one's savings while the individual is still alive. Thus, *the fundamental purpose of an annuity is to provide a lifetime income that cannot be outlived.* It protects against the loss of income because of excessive longevity and the exhaustion of savings.

Annuities are possible because the risk of excessive longevity is pooled by the group. Individuals acting alone cannot be certain that their savings will be sufficient during retirement. Some will die early before exhausting their savings, whereas others will still be alive after exhausting their principal. Although the insurance company cannot predict how long any particular member of the group will live, it can determine the approximate number of annuitants who will be alive at the end of each successive year. Thus, the company can calculate the amount that each person must contribute to the pool. Interest can be earned on the funds before they are paid out to the annuitants. Also, some annuitants will die early, and their unliquidated principal can be used to provide additional payments to annuitants who survive beyond their life expectancy. Thus, annuity payments consist of three sources: (1) premium payments, (2) interest earnings, and (3) the unliquidated principal of annuitants who die early. By pooling the risk of excessive longevity, insurers can pay a lifetime income to annuitants that cannot be outlived.

Annuitants tend to be healthy individuals who live longer than most persons. Because of the higher life expectancy of annuitants, actuaries use special annuity tables to calculate annuity premiums.

TYPES OF ANNUITIES

Insurers sell a wide variety of individual annuities. For sake of convenience and understanding, the major annuities sold today can be classified as follows:

- Fixed annuity
- Variable annuity
- Equity-indexed annuity

Fixed Annuity

A **fixed annuity** pays periodic income payments that are guaranteed and fixed in amount. During the **accumulation period** prior to retirement, premiums are credited with a fixed rate of interest. There are typically two interest rates: a guaranteed rate and a current rate. The *guaranteed rate* is the minimum interest rate that will be credited to the funds in the fixed annuity contract, such as 3 or 4 percent. The *current rate* is higher and is based on market conditions; current rates are not guaranteed or are guaranteed only for a limited period. For example, the guaranteed rate may be 4 percent, but the current rate may be 6 percent for only one year.

During the **liquidation period**, the accumulated funds can be *annuitized* or paid to the annuitant in the form of guaranteed lifetime income; however, the periodic income payments are fixed in amount, and generally do not change. As such, fixed annuities provide limited protection against inflation.

Payment of Benefits A fixed annuity can be purchased so that the income payments start immediately. This type of fixed annuity is called an immediate annuity. An **immediate annuity** *is one where the first payment is due one payment interval from the date of purchase.* For example, if the income is paid monthly, the first payment starts one month from the purchase date, or one year from the purchase date if the income is paid annually. Immediate annuities are typically purchased in a lump sum by people near retirement. Because of the wide variation in monthly payments, financial planners recommend that consumers shop around before purchasing an immediate annuity.

A fixed annuity can also be purchased that defers the income payments until some later date. A **deferred annuity** *provides income payments at some future date.* This type of annuity is essentially a plan for accumulating a sum of money prior to retirement on a tax-deferred basis. If the annuitant dies during the accumulation period prior to retirement, a death benefit is typically paid equal to the sum of the gross premiums paid or the cash value if higher. At the maturity date of the contract, the annuitant can receive the funds in a lump sum or have them paid out under one of the settlement options (discussed later).

A fixed annuity that defers the income payments until a future date can be purchased with a lump sum, or the contract may permit flexible premium payments. A deferred annuity purchased with a lump sum is called a **single-premium deferred annuity**. In contrast, a **flexible-premium annuity** allows the annuity owner to vary the premium payments; there is no requirement that the owner must deposit a specified amount each year. Thus, the annuity owner has considerable flexibility in the payment of premiums.

Annuity Settlement Options The annuity owner has a choice of **annuity settlement options**. Cash can be withdrawn in a lump sum or in installments, or the funds can be annuitized or paid out as life income. As a practical matter, relatively few annuities are annuitized.

The following settlement options are typically available:

- *Cash option.* The funds can be withdrawn in a lump sum or in installments. The taxable portion of the distribution (discussed later) is subject to federal and state income taxes. The cash option also leads to adverse selection against the insurer because those in poor health will take cash rather than annuitize the funds.
- *Life annuity (no refund).* A **life annuity** (**no refund**) provides a life income to the annuitant only while the annuitant remains alive. *No additional payments are made after the annuitant dies.* This type of settlement option pays the highest amount of periodic income payments because it has no refund features. It is suitable for someone who needs maximum lifetime income and has no dependents or has provided for them through other means. However, because of the risk of forfeiting the unpaid principal if death occurs early, relatively few annuity owners elect this option.
- *Life annuity with guaranteed payments.* A **life annuity with guaranteed payments** pays a life income to the annuitant with a certain number of guaranteed payments, such as for 5, 10, 15, or 20 years. If the annuitant dies before receiving the guaranteed number of payments, the remaining payments are paid to a designated beneficiary. This option can be used by someone who needs lifetime income but who also wishes to provide income to the beneficiary in the event of an early

death. Because of the guaranteed payments, the periodic income payments are less than the income paid by a life annuity with no refund.

- *Installment refund annuity.* An **installment refund annuity** pays a life income to the annuitant. If the annuitant dies before receiving total income payments equal to the purchase price of the annuity, the payments continue to the beneficiary until they equal the purchase price. A **cash refund annuity** is another version of this option. If the annuitant dies before receiving total payments equal to the purchase price of the annuity, the balance is paid in a lump sum to the beneficiary.
- *Joint-and-survivor annuity.* A **joint-and-survivor annuity** option pays benefits based on the lives of two or more annuitants, such as a husband and wife or a brother and sister. The annuity income is paid until the last annuitant dies. Some contracts pay the full amount of the original income payments until the last survivor dies. Other plans pay only two-thirds or one-half of the original income after the first annuitant dies.

In summary, a fixed annuity provides periodic income payments to an annuitant that cannot be outlived. In particular, an immediate annuity can be especially attractive for retired people who want a guaranteed amount of income during the period of retirement regardless of how long they live (see Insight 20.1).

Variable Annuity

A second type of annuity is a variable annuity. A **variable annuity** pays a lifetime income, but the income payments vary depending on common stock prices. *The fundamental purpose of a variable annuity is to provide an inflation hedge by maintaining the real purchasing power of the periodic payments during retirement.* It is based on the assumption of a correlation between the cost of living and common stock prices over the long run.

Basic Characteristics of a Variable Annuity Premiums are invested in a portfolio of common stocks or other investments that presumably will increase in value during a period of inflation. The premiums are used to purchase **accumulation units** during the period prior to retirement, and the value of each accumulation unit varies depending on common stock prices. For example, assume that the accumulation unit is initially valued at $1, and the annuitant makes a monthly premium payment of $100. During the first month, 100 accumulation units are purchased.[2] If common stock prices increase during the second month, and the accumulation unit rises to $1.10, about 91 accumulation units can be purchased. If the stock market declines during the third month, and the accumulation unit declines to $0.90, about 111 accumulation units can be purchased. Thus, accumulation units are purchased over a long period of time in both rising and falling markets.

At retirement, the accumulation units are converted into **annuity units**. The number of annuity units remains constant during the liquidation period, but the value of each unit will change each month or year depending on the level of common stock prices. For example, at retirement, assume that the annuitant has 10,000 accumulation units. Assume that the accumulation units are converted into 100 annuity units.[3] As stated earlier, the number of annuity units remains constant, but the value of each unit will change over time. Assume that the annuity unit is initially valued at $10 when the annuitant retires. A monthly income of $1000 will be paid. During the second month, if the annuity unit increases in value to $10.10, the monthly income also increases to $1010. During the third month, if the annuity units decline in value to $9.90 because of a stock market decline, the monthly income is reduced to $990. Thus, the monthly income depends on the level of common stock prices.

To illustrate, assume a male investor, age 35, invests $50,000 in a variable annuity that earns 9 percent annually. During the accumulation period of 30 years, the annuity grows in value to $663,384 before taxes. The annuity owner could receive an after-tax lump-sum cash distribution of $460,967, or withdraw $5000 monthly for 14 years, or receive a life income of $3090 monthly under the installment refund option (see Exhibit 20.2).

Guaranteed Death Benefit Variable annuities typically provide a guaranteed death benefit that protects the principal against loss due to market declines. *The typical death benefit states that if the annuitant dies before retirement, the amount paid to the beneficiary will be the higher of two amounts:* *the amount invested in the contract or the value of the account at the time of death.* Thus, if the annuitant dies during a market decline, the beneficiary receives an amount at least equal to the total amount invested in the contract.

Some variable annuities go one step further and pay enhanced death benefits. Enhanced benefits either (1) guarantee the principal (contributions made) plus interest or (2) periodically adjust the value of the account to lock in investment gains. For example, the annuity may contain a *rising-floor* death benefit by which the death benefit is periodically reset. Thus, a 5 percent rising-floor benefit may be periodically reset so that the beneficiary will receive the principal plus 5 percent interest.

A second example is the *stepped-up benefit* by which the contract periodically locks in investment gains, such as every five years. For example, assume that $10,000 is invested in year 1, and the account is now worth $15,000 in year 5. The new death benefit is $15,000, even though the annuity owner has invested only $10,000.

Fees and Expenses Variable annuity owners pay a number of fees and expenses. Some fees consist of investment management and administrative fees; other fees are insurance charges that pay for the guarantees and other services provided. In addition, most variable annuities have surrender charges.

Specifically, variable annuities typically contain the following fees and expenses:

- *Investment management charge.* This charge is a payment to the investment manager and asset-management company for the brokerage services and investment advice provided in the management of the investment portfolio.
- *Administrative charge.* This charge covers the paperwork, record keeping, and periodic reports to the annuity owner.
- *Management and expense risk charge.* This fee, called the "M&E" fee, pays for (1) the mortality risk associated with the guaranteed death benefit and excessive longevity; (2) a guarantee that annual expenses will not exceed a certain percentage of assets after the contract is issued; and (3) an allowance for profit.
- *Surrender charge.* Most annuities have a surrender charge if the annuity is surrendered during the

Insight 20.1

Ensuring Your Nest Egg Doesn't Crack

Retirement is the great financial riddle.

Think of the uncertainties. You don't know how long you will live. You don't know what investment returns you will earn. You have only a limited sum of money. And there are no second chances.

One possible solution: Immediate fixed annuities. When you purchase an immediate fixed annuity, you hand over a wad of money and, in return, get a check a month for the rest of your life. The payment's size depends on a host of factors, including your age, sex, prevailing interest rates and type of annuity purchased.

"Sometimes, you just want to sit there and know the checks are in the mail," says Richard Van Der Noord, a financial planner in Macon, GA. "I like immediate annuities. But I liked them a lot more when rates were higher."

Immediate annuities are a way of getting somebody else to shoulder risks you would rather not take. Could you afford the cost of retirement if you lived well into your 90s? Could you weather a sharp downturn in the stock and bond markets?

If your nest egg is skimpy and thus these risks loom large, an immediate annuity could be a smart purchase. But if you have saved ample money for retirement, you can probably safely skip annuities and stick with stocks and bonds.

As 401(k) plans and their ilk replace traditional company pensions, worries about living too long and suffering rotten markets have become more pressing. With traditional pension plans, employers assume these risks, often without much difficulty. After all, employers can take a much longer view of market returns, and they know that if one ex-employee lives surprisingly long, another may die shortly after quitting the work force.

By contrast, with a 401(k) plan and the subsequent management of that money in retirement, employees have to grapple with all the uncertainty created by their own longevity and the returns earned in their lifetime.

"The immediate annuity is for people who want the absolute security that they can't outlive their nest egg," says Peter Katt, a fee-only life-insurance adviser in Mattawan, Mich. "The problem is there's nothing left over for your heirs."

Indeed, there seems to be some knee-jerk distaste for immediate annuities, because the income stream typically dies when you do. If you fork over $100,000 for an annuity and drop dead a few years later, your $100,000 is gone.

To overcome these objections, insurance companies offer all kinds of wrinkles. You can, for instance, lock in payments for, say, 10 or 15 years, which ensures that your beneficiaries will get some money, even if you die

---

early years of the contract. This charge helps to pay agents and brokers who sell variable annuities. It is usually a percentage of the account value and declines over time. The surrender charge is typically 7 percent of the account value for the first year, declining one percentage point for each year until it reaches zero for the eighth and later years. Most variable annuities permit partial withdrawals each year of as much as 10 percent of the account value without imposition of a surrender charge.

In addition to these charges, some annuities have a front-end load of 4 or 5 percent; the annuity may have an annual contract fee, such as $25 or $50; and

there may be a charge if finds are transferred from one subaccount to another. *In the aggregate, total fees and expenses in most variable annuities are high and can easily exceed 2 percent of assets. As a result, long-run total returns may be significantly reduced in high-cost annuities.*

Some annuities, however, have relatively low annual expenses, and a small number do not have a surrender charge. Exhibit 20.3 shows the names and telephone numbers for a selected group of low-cost variable annuities.

Investment Performance of Variable Annuities
Variable annuities give the annuity owner several investment choices, similar to mutual funds. The pre-

shortly after purchasing the annuity. But opting for these wrinkles reduces the size of your monthly checks.

To get a handle on annuity pricing, call a fistful of insurers and visit Web sites such as www.annuityshopper .com and www.annuity.com. "With an immediate fixed annuity, you go out and find who is going to give you the most income, and then you try to make some judgment about whether they'll stay in business," Mr. Katt says.

Of course, even the insurer offering the highest payout is charging something for its services. How much? For an answer, I turned to Mark Warshawsky, director of research at the TIAA-CREF Institute, the economic research arm of TIAA-CREF, the New York money manger and insurer. If you think of an immediate annuity's costs as comparable to the annual expenses on a mutual fund, "we come up with an average of 0.7% a year," he says.

But Mr. Warshawsky notes that there can be a big difference in the payout from insurers, so get a bunch of quotes. And don't compromise on safety. Mr. Warshawsky says annuity buyers don't seem to give up any income by sticking with the top-rated insurance companies.

Clearly, you should avoid immediate annuities if your life expectancy is poor. You also probably shouldn't buy if you are in your 50s, because the income may not be much more than you could get by buying bonds.

Annuities can, however, help elderly couples where one spouse is trying to qualify for Medicaid-financed care at a nursing home. If the healthy spouse purchases an annuity, that will provide income for the healthy spouse while reducing the couple's assets and thus enhancing Medicaid eligibility, Mr. Van Der Noord says.

But in most cases, if you decide to buy an immediate annuity, don't invest your entire nest egg. "If you annuitize all your assets, you're giving up a lot of flexibility," says David Bugen, a financial planner in Chatham, NJ. He notes you still need an investment stash to cover items like home repairs and medical emergencies.

Also, immediate annuities offer fixed monthly payments, which will dwindle in spending power thanks to inflation. "That could be catastrophic," says Bill Bengen, a financial planner in El Cajon, Calif. He suggests using a portion of your retirement nest egg to build a balanced portfolio of stocks and bonds, "and then use that to augment the annuity."

SOURCE: Adapted from Jonathan Clements, "Ensuring Your Nest Egg Doesn't Crack," *The Wall Street Journal*, February 8, 2000, p. C1.

miums are invested in investment portfolios called "subaccounts," such as a growth stock fund, corporate bond fund, international stock fund, or money market fund. The funds can be transferred from one account to another without triggering unfavorable income-tax consequences.

The investment performance of variable annuities varies widely depending on the insurer, type of investment, and total expense rate. Exhibit 20.4 shows average annual total returns and average expense rates for various subaccounts for the five-year period ending December 31, 1999. The five-year average annual total return ranged from 3.88 percent for money market accounts to 25.19 percent for growth accounts.

Equity-Indexed Annuity

An equity-indexed annuity is a newer type of annuity that offers the guarantees of a fixed annuity and limited participation in stock market gains. An **equity-indexed annuity** *is a fixed, deferred annuity that allows the annuity owner to participate in the growth of the stock market and also provides downside protection against the loss of principal and prior interest earnings if the annuity is held to term.* Term periods typically range from one to ten years. The annuity value is linked to the performance of a stock market index, typically Standard and Poor's 500 Composite Stock Index. If the stock market rises, the annuity is credited with part of the gain in the index,

EXHIBIT 20.2

Illustration of the Accumulation Period and the Liquidation Period

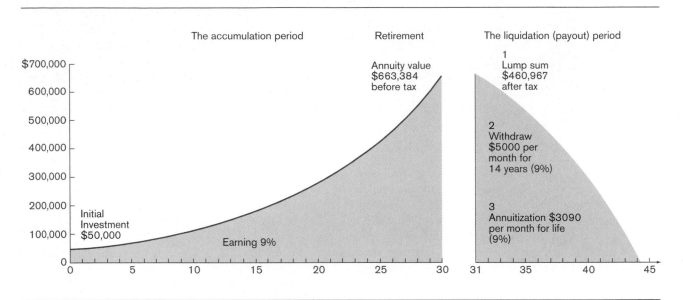

Notes: This chart illustrates the effect of long-term performance on the value of an annuity, using a hypothetical $50,000 tax-deferred investment earning 9 percent annually over a 30-year period. After 30 years, an investment earning 9 percent would grow to $663,384 before taxes.

With a lump sum withdrawal, an investor would receive $460,967 after taxes, assuming a 33 percent marginal tax bracket.

For an investor choosing a systematic withdrawal at $5000 per month after taxes, assuming a 28 percent tax rate, the contract value would fund payments through the fourteenth year, based on the following assumptions: Withdrawals begin after the investor has reached age 59 ½, and are assumed to occur at the beginning of each month. Earnings on the remaining balance of the contract continue to grow at 9 percent for the entire month.

The annuitization example is based on a single life with an installment refund option for a 65-year-old male and a 28 percent tax rate. A contract that earns 9 percent during the accumulation phase would result in a monthly after-tax payment of $3090 for life.

These rates of return are hypothetical and are not intended to project the investment results of any specific annuity. This example doesn't include the effect of charges and expenses. If charges and expenses had been included, the results would have been lower.

Source: Adaptation of *Understanding Annuities* (Newark, NJ: Prudential Investments, 1998), pp. 10–11.

which does not include the reinvestment of dividends. If the stock market declines, the annuity earns at least a minimum return, which typically is 3 percent on 90 percent of the principal invested.

The key elements of an equity-indexed annuity are as follows: (1) the participation rate, (2) the cap on the maximum percentage of gain credited to the contract, (3) the indexing method used, and (4) the guaranteed minimum value.

Participation Rate The *participation rate* is the percentage of growth in the stock index that is credited to the contract. The insurer periodically determines the participation rate, which is subject to change. Participation rates generally range from 25 percent to 90 percent of the gain in the stock index.

A few insurers have participation rates of 100 percent. Investors usually receive only part of the increase in the stock index (excluding the reinvestment of dividends). For example, if the participation rate is 80 percent and the stock index rises 10 percent during the measuring period, the annuity value increases by 8 percent.

Cap on the Maximum Percentage of Gain The *cap* is the maximum percentage of gain that is credited to the contract. For example, assume the annuity has a participation rate of 80 percent and a 10 percent cap. If the index rises 10 percent, the annuity has an 8 percent return. However, if the stock market soars and the index rises 20 percent, the maximum gain is capped at 10 percent (instead of 16

EXHIBIT 20.3
Five Low-Cost Variable Annuities

Name	Total Annual Expenses	Sales Load	Surrender Charge	Minimum Investment	Telephone Number
Personal Annuity Select (TIAA-CREF)	0.37%	None	None	$ 250	800-223-1200
Vanguard Variable Annuity Plan	0.57%[a]	None	None	5000	800-522-5555
USAA Variable Annuity	1.05%[b]	None	None	1000	800-531-4440
Fidelity Retirement Reserves	1.08%[c]	None	None	2500	800-544-2442
Schwab Select Annuity	1.13%[d]	None	None	5000	800-838-0650

[a]Equity Index Portfolio. An annual contract maintenance fee of $25 applies to contracts valued at less than $25,000.
[b]Bankers Trust Equity 500 Index Portfolio. An annual contract fee of $30 is also charged.
[c]Index 500 Portfolio. The separate account fee is .80 percent. Management fees and other expenses are 0.28 percent.
[d]Schwab S&P 500 Fund.

EXHIBIT 20.4
Annuity Funds' Performance and Fees

Averages and returns for periods ended Dec. 31, 1999

Type of Fund	Average Fund Expense	Average Total Expense	Fourth-Quarter Total Return	One-Year Total Return	Three-Year Annualized Return	Five-Year Annualized Return
Aggressive Growth	0.90%	2.16%	+34.63%	+50.10%	+23.34%	+22.62%
Balanced	0.77	2.05	+ 8.21	+10.04	+13.92	+15.50
Corporate Bond	0.69	1.95	+ 0.20	− 1.63	+ 3.76	+ 6.12
Government Bond General	0.65	1.90	− 0.39	− 2.56	+ 3.96	+ 5.84
Growth	0.84	2.11	+22.08	+29.80	+25.06	+25.19
Growth and Income	0.69	1.96	+ 9.79	+12.55	+18.20	+20.93
High-Yield Bond	0.80	2.10	+ 2.22	+ 3.44	+ 4.51	+ 8.49
International Bond	1.06	2.34	+ 0.82	− 0.76	+ 1.35	+ 4.97
International Stock	1.14	2.41	+30.74	+49.70	+19.19	+18.21
Money Market	0.52	1.78	+ 0.95	+ 3.49	+ 3.77	+ 3.88
Specialty Fund	1.01	2.28	+ 8.48	+19.82	+ 9.05	+11.39
U.S. Diversified Equity Average	0.81	2.08	+20.97	+28.55	+22.70	+23.32
Fixed Income Average	0.74	2.00	+ 0.18	− 1.68	+ 3.40	+ 5.87

SOURCE: Excerpted from Bridget O'Brian, "The Web's for Everthing, Right? Not for Selling Variable Annuities," *The Wall Street Journal*, January 10, 2000, p. R26.

percent). Thus, investors should seek annuities with no caps, which will allow larger gains to be realized during periods when stock prices increase rapidly.

Indexing Method The *indexing method* refers to the method for crediting excess interest to the annuity. Insurers use several indexing methods for crediting interest, only one of which is discussed here. Under the *annual reset* method (also known as the *ratchet* method), interest earnings are calculated based on the annual change in the stock index; the index value starting point is also reset annually. Thus, if the stock index decreases during any contract year, the decrease does not have to be recovered before any additional growth in the index will be credited to the contract.

Guaranteed Minimum Value Equity-indexed annuities with terms longer than one year have a guaranteed minimum value that provides downside protection against the loss of principal if the annuity is held to term. This minimum value typically is 90 percent of the single premium (less partial withdrawals) accumulated at 3 percent interest. *The result is a guaranteed minimum value at the end of the term.* For example, an annuity with a seven-year term would have a guaranteed minimum value of 110.69 percent of the single premium at the end of the term (assuming no withdrawals). However, because the minimum guarantee applies to only 90 percent of the single premium, an investor who surrenders the contract during the first three or four policy years may experience a loss of principal. If it is held to term, the principal is guaranteed against loss.

The fact that equity-indexed annuities participate in stock market gains only to a limited extent has created some confusion among annuity owners. Many investors erroneously believe that they are getting stock market returns. Insight 20.2 highlights the problem of determining the annual return on an equity-indexed annuity.

TAXATION OF INDIVIDUAL ANNUITIES

An individual annuity purchased from a commercial insurer is a nonqualified annuity. A *nonqualified annuity* is an annuity that does not meet the Internal Revenue Code requirements. As such, it does not qualify for most income-tax benefits that qualified employer retirement plans receive.

Premiums for individual annuities are not income-tax deductible and are paid with after-tax dollars. However, the investment income is tax deferred and accumulates free of current income taxes until the funds are actually distributed.

The taxable portion of any distribution is taxable as ordinary income. In addition, the taxable portion of a premature distribution before age 59½ is subject to a 10 percent penalty tax, with certain exceptions.[4]

The periodic annuity payments from an individual annuity are taxed according to the General Rule. Under this rule, the *net cost* of the annuity payments is recovered income-tax free over the payment period. The amount of each payment that exceeds the net cost is taxable as ordinary income.

An exclusion ratio must be calculated to determine the nontaxable and taxable portions of the annuity payments. The **exclusion ratio** is determined by dividing the investment in the contract by the expected return:

$$\frac{\text{Investment in the contract}}{\text{Expected return}} = \text{Exclusion ratio}$$

The *investment in the contract (basis)* is the total cost of the annuity, which generally is the total amount of the premiums or other consideration paid for the annuity less any nontaxable distributions previously received.[5] The *expected return* is the total amount that the annuitant can expect to receive under the contract. It is determined by multiplying the annual payments the annuitant will receive by the life expectancy of the annuitant, which is obtained from actuarial tables provided by the IRS.

As an example, assume that Ben, age 65, purchased an immediate annuity for $108,000 that pays a lifetime monthly income of $1000. The annuity has no refund features. Investment in the contract is $108,000. Based on the IRS actuarial table, Ben has a life expectancy of 20 years. Expected return is $240,000 (20 × 12 × $1000). The exclusion ratio is 0.45 ($108,000/$240,000). Each year, until the net cost is recovered, Ben receives $5400 tax free (45% × $12,000), and $6600 is taxable. After the net cost is recovered, the total payment would be taxable.

Insight 20.2

These Investments Are Less Than Meets the Eye

Equity-indexed annuities are sold as the best of both worlds: Their returns are pegged to Standard & Poor's 500-stock index, but your principal is guaranteed if the market falls. So why did some of these annuities return only 8 percent in 1998, when the S&P 500 gained 28.6 percent?

These are fixed annuities, not regulated by the SEC. Insurers hold investors' money in their general accounts, buy bonds and options on the S&P 500, and pay interest based on a percentage of the index's return. Sometimes that percentage is small.

Equity-indexed annuities that report gains each year returned between 8 percent and 17 percent in 1998, says Jack Marrion of the Advantage Group, a research firm. *The range was so large because contracts credit interest differently (Marrion counts 26 variations).*

Some companies, such as Conseco, average the monthly values of the S&P 500 for the year, then multiply the difference from the previous year by 90 percent. Products such as these returned 11 percent to 12 percent in 1998. Some then subtracted an asset fee, which lowered returns to the single digits. Others, such as

Lincoln Benefit, take the index's annual return (not counting dividends), then credit 50 percent to 65 percent of the result. These returned 13 percent to 17 percent in 1998.

The future looks even bleaker. Because last summer's volatile market boosted costs for annuity companies, many of those that were multiplying their S&P 500 calculations by 90 percent lowered their "participation rates" to 60 percent to 70 percent, says Marrion.

Confused? Join the club. Tom Batterman, a financial planner in Wausau, Wisconsin, was called to rescue a couple who "thought they'd get stock-market returns," he says. Instead, their equity-indexed annuity returned just 13 percent. Batterman, who didn't sell them the annuity, concluded they would probably be better off in the long run to pay surrender fees, income tax on their gains, and a 10 percent tax penalty for withdrawing before age 59½, and invest what was left in a real index fund.

SOURCE: Kimberly Lankford, "These Investments Are Less Than Meets the Eye," *Kiplinger's Personal Finance Magazine* (April 1999), p. 44. Reprinted with permission.

In summary, annuities can be attractive to investors who have made maximum contributions to other tax-advantaged plans and who wish to save additional amounts on a tax-deferred basis. Also, because of the surrender charge, the investor should expect to remain invested for 10 or more years.

However, annuities are not for everyone. An annuity should not be purchased if the funds will be needed before age 59½; the worker has not made maximum contributions to other tax-advantaged plans, such as a Section 401(k) plan and an IRA; and the funds will not be invested for at least 10 years (see Insight 20.3)

INDIVIDUAL RETIREMENT ACCOUNTS

An **individual retirement account (IRA)** allows workers with taxable compensation to make annual contributions to a retirement plan up to certain limits and receive favorable income-tax treatment.

The Taxpayer Relief Act of 1997 substantially increased the tax advantages of IRAs. The law now provides for the following types of IRAs:

- Traditional IRA
- Roth IRA
- Education IRA

Traditional IRA

A **traditional IRA** is an IRA that allows workers to deduct part or all of their IRA contributions. The investment income accumulates income-tax free on a tax-deferred basis, and the distributions are taxed as ordinary income.

Eligibility Requirements There are two eligibility requirements for establishing a traditional tax-deductible IRA. *First, the participant must have taxable compensation during the year.* Taxable compensation includes wages and salaries, bonuses,

Insight 20.3

When Annuities Can Work

Variable annuities make sense only if you can answer yes to all of the following questions:

- *Are you contributing the maximum to your IRA, 401(k), or other retirement plan?* These plans provide tax deferral without many of the fees. Some offer an employer match and let you invest pretax money. If you use a Roth IRA, earnings are tax-free in retirement, not just tax-deferred.
- *Can you live without the money until you reach age 59½?* If not, you'll be hit with a 10 percent tax penalty and may have to pay a surrender charge. Make sure you have enough money available for emergencies and preretirement needs, such as paying for your children's education, buying a house, and supporting aging parents. "When you're in your thirties and forties, age 59½ is a long way away," says Lambert.
- *Are you in the 28 percent tax bracket or higher?* If you're in the 15 percent bracket, the benefits of tax deferral may never make up for the fees. You'll do best if you defer taxes while in a high tax bracket and withdraw the money when you drop into a lower bracket in retirement.

  "If you're in the 36 percent to 39.6 percent tax bracket, tax deferral looks good now. But if your in-

come-tax bracket doesn't bump down, you're going to wish you had capital gains instead of ordinary income," says Dee Lee, a financial planner in Harvard, Massachusetts.
- *Do you think you'll need the money before you die?* "Variable annuities are problematic in terms of estate planning," says Lambert. Your heirs will owe income tax on earnings just as you would. Mutual funds, on the other hand, pass to heirs income-tax-free.
- *Have you found a low-fee variable annuity?* Annual insurance fees range from less than $400 to nearly $2000 on a $100,000 account. There's little reason to invest in higher-fee annuities. "The only difference I can see is the salesman comes to your kitchen," says Lee.

  The salesperson usually receives about 6 percent in commission, and the ongoing insurance costs eat into performance. "What you spend on insurance expenses lowers your return," says Patrick Reinkemeyer, publisher of *Morningstar Variable Annuities/Life*. The publication covers about 50 annuities that offer a version of Fidelity Equity Income fund, he says.

Source: Excerpted from Kimberly Lankford, "Boy, Have They Got a Deal for You," *Kiplinger's Personal Finance Magazine* (April 1999), p. 112. Reprinted with permission.

commissions, self-employment income, and taxable alimony and separate maintenance payments. Investment income, pension or annuity income, Social Security, and rental income do not qualify.

Second, the participant must be under age 70½. No IRA contributions are allowed for the tax year in which the participant attains age 70½ or any later year.

Annual Contribution Limits The maximum annual IRA contribution is limited to $2000 or 100 percent of taxable compensation, whichever is less. If the participant has a nonworking or low-earning spouse, the maximum annual IRA contribution is increased to $4000 (**spousal IRA**). However, the maximum annual contribution to each account is limited to $2000.

Traditional IRA contributions may be (1) fully income-tax deductible, (2) partly deductible, or (3) not deductible at all. A full deduction is allowed in two general situations. *First, a worker who is not an active participant in an employer-sponsored retirement plan can make a fully deductible IRA contribution up to the maximum annual limit of $2000 ($4000 for a spousal IRA).* The worker is considered an active participant in a retirement plan if his or her employer or union has a retirement plan in which money is added to the worker's account, or if the worker is eligible for retirement credits. The worker is considered an active participant even if vesting has not been attained.

Second, even if the worker is a participant in the employer's retirement plan, a full deduction is al-

lowed if the worker's modified adjusted gross income is below certain thresholds. Modified adjusted gross income generally is the adjusted gross income figure shown on your tax return without taking into account the IRA deduction and certain other items.[6] For 2001, a full deduction is allowed if the taxpayer's modified adjusted gross income is $33,000 or less ($53,000 or less for married couples filing jointly). As discussed later, the income limits for a full deduction will rise gradually in the future.

The full IRA deduction is gradually phased out as a person's modified adjusted gross income increases. For 2001, the phase-out range is $33,000–$43,000 for single taxpayers and $53,000–$63,000 for married taxpayers filing jointly. For example, in 2001, a single taxpayer with a modified adjusted gross income of $38,000 could contribute $2000 to an IRA but could deduct only $1000.

The phase-out limits will gradually increase in the future according to the following schedule:

Year	Single Taxpayer
2001	$33,000–$43,000
2002	$34,000–$44,000
2003	$40,000–$50,000
2004	$45,000–$55,000
2005 or later	$50,000–$60,000

Year	Married Taxpayer Filing Jointly
2001	$53,000–$63,000
2002	$54,000–$64,000
2003	$60,000–$70,000
2004	$65,000–$75,000
2005	$70,000–$80,000
2006	$75,000–$85,000
2007 and later	$80,000–$100,000

Taxpayers with incomes that exceed the phase-out limits can contribute to a traditional IRA but cannot deduct their contributions. This type of IRA is called a **nondeductible IRA**. In such cases, a Roth IRA (discussed later) should be considered.

Special Phase-Out Rule for Spouses

A special phase-out rule applies to married couples in situations where one spouse is not an active participant in an employer-sponsored retirement plan, but the other spouse is an active participant. *As a result, most homemakers can make a fully deductible contribution to a traditional IRA even though the other spouse is covered under a retirement plan at work.* In such cases, the maximum annual IRA deduction for a spouse who is not an active participant is $2000, even if the other spouse is covered under a retirement plan at work. Eligibility for a full deduction is limited to married couples with modified adjusted gross incomes of $150,000 or less. The deduction is phased out for married couples with modified adjusted gross incomes between $150,000 and $160,000.

For example, Josh is covered under a Section 401(k) retirement plan at work. His wife, Ashley, is a full-time homemaker. For 2001, their modified adjusted gross income is $125,000. Ashley can make a tax-deductible IRA contribution of $2000 because she is not considered an active participant, and the couple's combined modified adjusted gross income is less than $150,000. However, Josh cannot make a tax-deductible contribution because his income exceeds the income threshold for active participants.

Withdrawal of Funds With certain exceptions, distributions from a traditional IRA before age 59½ are considered to be premature distributions. A 10 percent tax penalty must be paid on the amount of the distribution included in gross income. However, the penalty tax does not apply to distributions that result from any of the following:

- Death of the individual
- Disability of the individual
- Substantially equal payments paid over the life expectancy of the individual or the individual and his or her beneficiary
- Portions of any distributions treated as a return of nondeductible contributions
- Distributions used to pay for unreimbursed medical expenses in excess of 7½ percent of adjusted gross income
- Distributions used to pay medical insurance premiums for the worker, spouse, and dependents if the worker has received unemployment compensation benefits for 12 consecutive weeks
- Distributions to pay for qualified higher education expenses

- Qualified acquisition costs for a first-time home buyer (maximum of $10,000)

Distributions from a traditional IRA must start no later than April 1 of the year following the calendar year in which the individual attains age 70½. The funds can be withdrawn in a lump sum or in installments. If taken as installments, a minimum annual distribution requirement must be met. The minimum annual payments are based on the life expectancy of the individual or the joint life expectancy of the individual and his or her beneficiary. If the distributions are less than the amount required by law, a 50 percent excise tax is imposed on the excess accumulation. The purpose of this requirement is to force participants in traditional IRAs to have the funds paid out over a reasonable period so that the federal government can collect taxes on the tax-deferred amounts.

Taxation of Distributions Distributions from a traditional IRA are taxed as ordinary income, except for any nondeductible IRA contributions, which are received income-tax free. Part of the distribution is not taxable if nondeductible contributions are made. The other part is taxable and must be included in the taxpayer's income. A complex formula and an IRS worksheet must be used to compute the nontaxable and taxable portions of each distribution.

In addition, as noted earlier, a 10 percent tax penalty applies to premature distribution taken before age 59½.

Establishing a Traditional IRA Traditional IRAs can be established with a variety of financial organizations. You can set up an IRA with a bank, mutual fund, stock brokerage firm, or life insurer. Contributions to a traditional IRA can be made anytime during the year or up to the due date for filing a tax return, not including extensions.

There are two types of traditional IRAs: (1) an individual retirement account, and (2) an individual retirement annuity.

- *Individual Retirement Account.* An individual retirement account is a trust or custodial account set up for the exclusive benefit of the account holder or beneficiaries. The trustee or custodian must be a bank, a federally insured credit union, a savings and loan institution, or an entity approved by the IRS to act as trustee or custodian. Contributions must be in cash, except for rollover contributions (discussed later) that can be in the form of property other than cash. No part of the contributions can be used to purchase a life insurance policy. Likewise, IRA assets cannot be pledged as collateral for a loan.

- *Individual Retirement Annuity.* A traditional IRA can also be established by purchasing an individual retirement annuity from a life insurer. The annuity must meet certain requirements. The annuity owner's interest in the contract must be nonforfeitable. The contract must be nontransferable by the owner. In addition, the annuity must permit flexible premiums so that if earnings change, the IRA contributions can be changed as well. Contributions cannot exceed $2000 in any year, and the distributions must begin by April 1 of the year following the year in which the annuity owner reaches age 70½.

IRA Investments IRA contributions can be invested in a variety of investments, including certificates of deposit, mutual funds, and individual stocks and bonds in a self-directed brokerage account. Contributions can also be invested in U.S. gold and silver coins, certain platinum coins, or gold, silver, palladium, or platinum bullion. However, the contributions cannot be invested in insurance contracts or collectibles, such as baseball cards or antiques.

IRA Rollover Account A *rollover* is a tax-free distribution of cash or other property from one retirement plan, which is then deposited into another retirement plan. The amount you roll over is tax free but generally becomes taxable when the new plan pays out that amount to you or to your beneficiary. For example, if you quit your job and receive a lump-sum distribution from your employer's qualified retirement plan, the funds can be rolled over or deposited into a special **IRA rollover account**. If you receive the funds directly, the employer must deduct 20 percent for federal income taxes. The tax can be deferred, however, if the employer transfers the funds directly into the IRA rollover account.

The assets in the IRA rollover account can be paid out as income when the worker retires. Exhibit 20.5 shows how long the payments will last given selected rates of return and withdrawal rates.

Roth IRA

The Taxpayer Relief Act of 1997 created a new type of IRA known as a **Roth IRA** that provides substantial tax advantages relative to a traditional tax-deductible IRA. The maximum annual contribution that an individual can make to all IRA accounts (both traditional and Roth) is $2000, not counting rollover contributions. *Unlike a traditional IRA, the annual contributions to a Roth IRA are not tax deductible. However, the investment income accumulates income-tax free, and qualified distributions are not taxable if certain requirements are met.* A qualified distribution is any distribution from a Roth IRA that (1) is made after a five-year period beginning with the first tax year for which a Roth contribution is made, and (2) is made for any of the following reasons:

- The individual is age 59½ or older.
- The individual is disabled.
- The distribution is paid to a beneficiary or to the estate after the individual's death.
- The distribution is used to pay qualified first-time home buyer expenses (maximum of $10,000).

EXHIBIT 20.5

How Long Will Your Retirement Assets Last?

Annual Withdrawal Rate	Average Annual Total Return						
	4%	5%	6%	7%	8%	9%	10%
15%	7	8	8	9	9	10	11
14	8	9	9	10	11	11	13
13	9	9	10	11	12	13	15
12	10	11	11	12	14	16	18
11	11	12	13	14	16	19	25
10	13	14	15	17	20	26	
9	14	16	18	22	28		
8	17	20	23	30			
7	21	25	33				
6	28	36					

Years Your Assets Will Last

Example: If you have saved $100,000 for retirement and withdraw 10 percent of the money each year, your money will last 20 years if you earn an average annual total return of 8 percent.

Source: Adaptation of "How Much Can You Take from Your Retirement Assets," *In The Vanguard* (Winter 1997).

Unlike a traditional IRA, contributions to a Roth IRA can be made after age 70½, and the minimum distribution rules after attainment of age 70½ do not apply to Roth IRAs.

Income Limits Roth IRAs have generous income limits. The maximum annual IRA contribution can be made by single taxpayers with modified adjusted gross incomes of $95,000 or less, and by married couples filing jointly with modified adjusted gross incomes of $150,000 or less. Maximum annual IRA contributions are phased out for single taxpayers with modified adjusted gross incomes between $95,000 and $110,000, and for married couples filing jointly with modified adjusted gross incomes between $150,000 and $160,000.

Conversion to a Roth IRA A traditional IRA can be converted into a Roth IRA. The right to convert is limited to taxpayers with annual adjusted gross incomes of $100,000 or less Although the amount converted is taxed as ordinary income, qualified distributions from the Roth IRA are received income-tax free. Many investment firms, including Fidelity Investments and Charles Schwab, provide interactive calculators on their Web sites that investors can use to determine if conversion to a Roth IRA is financially desirable.

Insight 20.4 compares the investment results of a Roth IRA with those of a traditional IRA and nondeductible IRA for a couple at three different ages. When the tax-free withdrawals are considered during the retirement period, the Roth IRA is a clear winner. However, if you expect to be in a lower tax bracket at retirement, you may be better off in a traditional IRA because of its immediate tax deduction and tax-deferred earnings.

Education IRA

The Taxpayer Relief Act of 1997 also established an **education IRA** to help taxpayers save for the higher-education expenses of their children. Taxpayers can make maximum nondeductible contributions of $500 annually to help pay for qualified higher-educational expenses of the children. The IRA contributions are not income-tax deductible, but the investment income accumulates income-tax free.

Insight 20.4

When Roth IRAs Pay Off

The table below shows how annual contributions of $4000 by a husband and wife the same age would grow in three different IRAs started at three different ages. IRA contributions are made until retirement at age 65. To simplify the example, each account is assumed to return 8 percent a year before retirement and 7 percent after, and the effective federal and state tax rate is 31.6 percent before and after retirement.

During the buildup period, the traditional deductible IRA grows faster than either the Roth IRA or the nondeductible IRA. If the couple withdraws the account over a 20-year period starting at age 65, however, the tax-free Roth IRA is the clear winner regardless when it was started.

For those retiring into a lower tax bracket, the story is quite different. In the example, a couple starting a Roth IRA at age 40 and retiring at age 65 would receive retirement income of some $557,000 over 20 years versus $413,000 from a deductible IRA. A calculation not shown indicates that if their federal tax bracket dropped from 28 percent to 15 percent at retirement, a deductible IRA would provide nearly $559,000 after taxes over the 20-year period.

	Pretax Accumulation			After-Tax Withdrawals[b]		
IRA Started at Age	30	40	55	30	40	55
Roth IRA	$744,409	$315,818	$62,582	$1,313,400	$557,214	$110,417
Deductible IRA[a]	877,277	383,747	79,724	1,098,214	483,308	101,309
Nondeductible IRA	744,409	315,818	62,582	942,606	412,734	88,165
Taxable Account[c]	420,469	214,966	54,248	632,432	323,334	81,596

Data: T. Rowe Price.
[a] Includes return from an amount equal to the deduction invested in a regular taxable account.
[b] Total of annual withdrawals made over a 20-year period starting at age 65.
[c] All values are after-tax.

SOURCE: Adapted from "When Roth IRAs Pay Off," Standard & Poor's, *The Outlook*, January 28, 1998, p. 9. Reprinted by permission of Standard & Poor's, a division of the McGraw-Hill Companies.

Qualified distributions to pay for qualified higher-education expenses are not taxable unless the distributions exceed the actual higher-education expenses made during the year. Qualified higher-education expenses generally include tuition, room and board, books, fees, supplies, and equipment.

The education IRA has certain income limits. The full $500 annual IRA contribution can be made by single filers with modified adjusted gross incomes of $95,000 or less, and by married couples filing jointly with modified adjusted gross incomes of $150,000 or less. The maximum contribution is phased out for single filers with modified adjusted gross incomes between $95,000 and $110,000, and for married couples filing jointly with modified adjusted gross incomes between $150,000 and $160,000.

Exhibit 20.6 compares the basic characteristics of a traditional IRA, Roth IRA, and education IRA.

In summary, an IRA can provide substantial tax advantages, and regular contributions to one can substantially increase a person's retirement income. IRA contributions can accumulate to sizable amounts, especially if the plan is started at an early age. Even high school students with part-time jobs can benefit from an IRA.

SUMMARY

- An annuity provides periodic payments to an annuitant, which continue for either a fixed period or for the duration of a designated life or lives. The fundamental purpose of a life annuity is to provide lifetime income that cannot be outlived.

- A *fixed annuity* pays periodic income payments to an annuitant that are guaranteed and fixed in amount. A fixed annuity can be purchased so that the income payments start immediately or can be deferred to some later date. Deferred annuities typically provide for flexible premiums.

- Annuity settlement options typically include the following:

  Cash

  Life annuity (no refund)

  Life annuity with guaranteed payments

  Installment refund annuity

  Joint-and-survivor annuity

- A *variable annuity* pays a lifetime income, but the income payments will vary depending on the investment experience of the subaccount in which the premiums are invested. The purpose of this type of annuity is to provide an inflation hedge by maintaining the real purchasing power of the periodic payments.

- During the *accumulation period*, variable annuity premiums purchase accumulation units, which are then converted into *annuity units* at retirement. The number of annuity units remains constant during retirement, but the value of the annuity units changes periodically so that the income payments will change over time.

- Variable annuities typically pay a guaranteed death benefit if the annuitant dies before retirement. The typical death benefit is the higher of two amounts: the amount invested in the contract or the value of the account at the time of death.

- Variable annuities have numerous fees and charges. These charges include an investment management fee, a charge for administrative expenses, a management and expense risk charge for the guaranteed death benefit and other guarantees, and a surrender charge that declines over time. In the aggregate, total fees and expenses can be substantial.

- An *equity-indexed annuity* is a fixed, deferred annuity that allows the annuity owner to participate in the growth of the stock market and also provides downside protection against the loss of principal and prior interest earnings if the annuity is held to term.

- The key elements of an equity-indexed annuity are (1) the participation rate, (2) the cap on the maximum percentage of gain credited to the contract, (3) the indexing method used, and (4) the guaranteed minimum value.

- An *exclusion ratio* is used to determine the nontaxable and taxable portions of the periodic annuity payments.

The exclusion ratio is determined by dividing the investment in the contract by the expected return.

- The major types of IRAs are (1) a traditional IRA, (2) Roth IRA, and (3) education IRA.

- A *traditional IRA* allows workers to deduct part or all of their IRA contributions. The investment income accumulates income-tax free on a tax-deferred basis, and the distributions are taxed as ordinary income.

- To be eligible for a traditional IRA, the participant must have taxable compensation and be younger than age 70½.

- The maximum annual IRA contribution is limited to $2000 or 100 percent of taxable compensation, whichever is less. If the participant has a nonworking or low-earning spouse, the maximum annual IRA contribution is increased to $4000 (*spousal IRA*).

- IRA contributions to a traditional IRA are income-tax deductible if the participant (1) is not an active participant in an employer-sponsored retirement plan or (2) has taxable compensation below certain income thresholds.

- Distributions from a traditional IRA are taxed as ordinary income, except for any nondeductible IRA contributions, which are received income-tax free.

- With certain exceptions, distributions from a traditional IRA before age 59½ are considered to be a premature distribution. A 10 percent tax penalty must be paid on the amount of the distribution included in gross income.

- Distributions from a traditional IRA must start no later than April 1 of the year following the calendar year in which the individual attains age 70½.

- IRA contributions to a *Roth IRA* are not income-tax deductible. However, the income accumulates free of taxation, and qualified distributions are received income-tax free if certain requirements are met.

- A qualified distribution from a Roth IRA is any distribution that (1) is made after a five-year period beginning with the first tax year for which a Roth contribution is made, and (2) is paid when the individual attains age 59½, becomes disabled, dies, or is used to pay qualified first-time home buyer expenses. Unlike a traditional IRA, contributions to a Roth IRA can be made after age 59½, and the minimum distribution rules after attainment of age 70½ do not apply.

- An *education IRA* allows taxpayers to make nondeductible IRA contributions up to $500 annually to help

EXHIBIT 20.6

Comparison of Individual Retirement Accounts

Who Can Contribute?	How Much Can I Contribute?	Who Can Make Deductible Contributions?
Traditional IRA Anyone under age 70½ with income from compensation	Total combined contributions to Roth and traditional IRAs limited to $2000 annually or 100% of compensation, whichever is less	■ A single person who does not participate in an employer retirement plan can deduct all contributions, regardless of income. ■ A single person who participates in an employer retirement plan and has MAGI of $33,000 or less for 2001 can deduct all contributions. The $2000 maximum deduction is phased out for MAGI between $33,000 and $43,000 for 2001. ■ A married couple where neither person participates in an employer retirement plan can deduct all contributions, regardless of income. ■ A married person who participates in an employer retirement plan can deduct all IRA contributions if the couple files a joint tax return showing MAGI of $53,000 or less for 2001. The $2000 maximum deduction is phased out if joint MAGI is between $53,000 and $63,000 for 2001. ■ A married person who does not participate in an employer retirement plan and is married to someone who is in an employer retirement plan can deduct all IRA contributions if the person files a tax return showing MAGI of $150,000 or less. The $2000 maximum deduction is phased out between $150,000 and $160,000 of MAGI.
Roth IRA Married couples filing a joint tax return with MAGI of $150,000 or less Single tax filers with MAGI of $95,000 or less Couples and single tax filers with higher incomes may be eligible for reduced contributions	Total combined contributions to Roth and traditional IRAs limited to $2000 annually or 100% of compensation, whichever is less	Contributions are not deductible.

Education IRA
Contributions to benefit a child under age 18 may be made by:
    Couples who file a joint tax return and have joint MAGI of $150,000 or less
    Persons filing an individual tax return with MAGI of $95,000 or less
    Reduced contributions for incomes exceeding these amounts
    Contributions not allowed in any year that a contribution is made to a state tuition program for the child
	No more than $500 total each year for all accounts opened on the child's behalf	Contributions are not deductible.

Note: MAGI is modified adjusted gross income from the federal tax form.

Source: Adapted from CUNA Service Group, Inc. Reprinted with permission.

What Are the Tax Advantages?	Can I Withdraw From the Account?
Earnings compound without tax until withdrawn, usually outearning taxable, non-IRA investments. Contributions may be tax deductible.	Withdraw funds free of 10% tax penalty for: ■ Qualified educational expenses ■ First-time home purchase (maximum $10,000) ■ At age 59½ ■ If you become disabled ■ Qualifying medical expenses (withdrawal of earnings and deductible contributions result in taxable income) ■ Payments to beneficiaries at owner's death ■ Health insurance premiums while unemployed
■ Contributions can be withdrawn tax and penalty free anytime. ■ Earnings can be withdrawn tax and penalty free for any of these reasons after the account has been open five tax years: after age 59½, if you become disabled or die, or for first-time home purchase (maximum $10,000). ■ Withdraw earnings penalty free for the same reasons as those for penalty free withdrawals from traditional IRAs (withdrawal is subject to taxes).	■ Earnings are tax free if account is open for five tax years and funds are withdrawn for a qualified reason. ■ Not required to start withdrawals at age 70½ ■ Taxable income if funds from a traditional IRA are converted to a Roth IRA
Withdrawals for qualified higher-education expenses are tax free.	■ Tax- and penalty-free withdrawals only for qualified expenses (other withdrawal of earnings subject to tax and penalty) ■ Funds can be transferred from one child's account to another child in the family.

pay for qualified higher-education expenses of the children. IRA contributions are not tax deductible. However, the investment income accumulates income-tax free, and qualified distributions to pay for qualified higher-education expenses are not taxable.

KEY CONCEPTS AND TERMS

Accumulation period
Accumulation unit
Annuitant
Annuity
Annuity settlement options
Annuity unit
Cash refund annuity
Deferred annuity
Education IRA
Equity-indexed annuity
Exclusion ratio
Fixed annuity
Flexible-premium annuity
Immediate annuity
Individual retirement account (IRA)

Installment refund annuity
IRA rollover account
Joint-and-survivor annuity
Life annuity (no refund)
Life annuity with guaranteed payments
Liquidation period
Nondeductible IRA
Roth IRA
Single-premium deferred annuity
Spousal IRA
Traditional IRA
Variable annuity

REVIEW QUESTIONS

1. How does an annuity differ from life insurance?

2. Describe the major characteristics of a fixed annuity.

3. Identify the annuity settlement options that are typically found in a fixed annuity.

4. Describe the basic characteristics of a variable annuity.

5. Explain the major characteristics of an equity-indexed annuity.

6. Explain the eligibility requirements for a traditional IRA.

7. What are the annual contribution limits to an IRA?

8. Explain the basic characteristics of a traditional IRA.

9. Describe the major characteristics of a Roth IRA.

10. What is an education IRA?

APPLICATION QUESTIONS

1. Although both fixed and variable annuities can provide lifetime income to annuitants, they differ in important ways.
   a. Compare and contrast (i) a fixed annuity with (ii) a variable annuity with respect to each of the following:
      (1) Determining how the premiums are invested
      (2) Stability of income payments after retirement
      (3) Death benefits if the annuitant dies before retirement
   b. Explain the method for determining the nontaxable and taxable portions of the periodic income payments from an individual annuity.

2. An equity-indexed annuity and a variable annuity are both similar and different in many respects.
   a. Explain the major similarities between an equity-indexed annuity and a variable annuity.
   b. Identify the major differences between an equity-indexed annuity and a variable annuity.

3. Travis, age 25, graduated from college and obtained a position as a tax accountant. He is ineligible to participate in his employer's retirement plan for one year.
   a. Assume that Travis has a beginning salary of $45,000 for 2001 and does not participate in the employer's retirement plan. Is Travis eligible to establish a traditional tax-deductible IRA? Explain your answer.
   b. Assume the same facts in (a). Is Travis eligible to establish a Roth IRA? Explain your answer.

4. A traditional IRA and a Roth IRA have both similarities and differences. Compare and contrast (i) a traditional IRA with (ii) a Roth IRA with respect to each of the following:
   a. Income-tax treatment of IRA contributions and distributions
   b. Income limits for eligibility
   c. Determining how the IRA contributions are invested
   d. Eligibility, if any, of a nonworking spouse in the home to make an IRA contribution

SELECTED REFERENCES

Chandler, Darlene K. *The Annuity Handbook, A Guide to Nonqualified Annuities*, second edition. Cincinnati,

Case Application

Richard and Nicole are married and file a joint tax return. Richard is a graduate student who works part-time and earned $10,000 in 2001. He is not eligible to participate in his employer's retirement plan because he is a part-time worker. Nicole is a high school teacher who earned $42,000 in 2001 and is an active participant in the school district's retirement plan. Assume you are a financial planner and the couple asks for your advice. Based on the preceding facts, answer each of the following questions.

a. Is Richard eligible to set up and deduct contributions to a traditional IRA? Explain your answer.

b. Is Nicole eligible to set up and deduct contributions to a traditional IRA? Explain your answer.

c. Assume that Richard graduates and the couple's modified adjusted gross income is $120,000. Both Richard and Nicole participate in their employers' retirement plans. Can either Richard or Nicole, or both, establish a Roth IRA? Explain your answer.

d. Nicole has a baby and withdraws from the paid labor force to raise the couple's child. She is not an active participant in the school district's retirement plan. Richard receives a promotion and continues to participate in his employer's retirement plan. His annual salary is $110,000. Can Nicole make a tax-deductible contribution to a traditional IRA? Explain your answer.

e. Explain to Richard and Nicole the advantages of a Roth IRA over a traditional IRA.

OH: The National Underwriter Company, 1998.

Cordell, David M., ed. *Fundamentals of Financial Planning*, fourth edition. Bryn Mawr, PA: The American College, 1999, pp. 602–605.

Del Prete, Dom. "IRAs for Retirement Savings," *Fidelity Focus* (Winter 1998), pp. 16–20.

Graves, Edward E., ed. *McGill's Life Insurance*, second edition. Bryn Mawr, PA: The American College, 1998, Chapter 6.

Mitchell, Olivia S. and James F. Moore. "Can Americans Afford to Retire? New Evidence on Retirement Saving Adequacy," *The Journal of Risk and Insurance*, Vol. 65, No. 3 (September 1998), pp. 371–400.

Prudential Investments. *Understanding Annuities*. Newark, NJ: Prudential Investments, 1998.

"The Right Way to Invest in Annuities," *Mutual Funds* (May 1999), pp. 52–55.

Charles Schwab. *Schwab IRA Answers*. San Francisco, CA: Charles Schwab & Co., 1998.

"When Roths Are a Bad Idea," *Mutual Funds* (June 1999), pp. 73–76.

NOTES

1. An annual survey of saving rates by Merrill Lynch shows that the "baby boomers" born after World War II are not saving enough for a comfortable retirement. The 1997 *Merrill Lynch Baby Boom Retirement Index* showed that baby boomers as a group are saving only 38.5 percent of the funds they will need to maintain the same standard of living in retirement that they enjoy today. See *News*, Merrill Lynch & Co., June 5, 1997.

2. A deduction for administrative expenses and sales expenses is ignored. Some individual variable annuity contracts have a front-end load.

3. The actual number of annuity units will depend on the market value of the account, the attained age of the annuitant, the number of guaranteed payments, the conversation rates, the assumed investment return, and other factors.

4. The 10 percent penalty tax does not apply to individuals who attain age $59^{1/2}$ or become totally disabled; when the distribution is received by a beneficiary or estate after the individual dies; when the distribution is part of substantially equal payments paid over the life expectancy of the individual or individual and beneficiary; or when the distribution is from an annuity contract under a qualified personal injury settlement. Certain other exceptions also apply.

5. The procedure for determining the total cost of an annuity is complex. Total cost must be reduced by (1) any refunded premiums, rebates, dividends, or unpaid loans that you received by the later of the annuity starting date or the date on which you received your first payment; (2) any additional premiums paid for double indemnity or disability payments; and (3) any other tax-free amounts you received under the contract or plan before the later of the dates specified in item 1. In addition, an adjustment must be made for any refund features in the annuity. The IRS provides worksheets for making these calculations.

6. Modified adjusted gross income is essentially the adjusted gross income figure shown on your tax return without taking into account any IRA deductions, student loan interest deduction, foreign earned income exclusion, foreign housing exclusion or deduction, exclusion of qualified bond interest, and exclusion of employer-paid adoption expenses.

 Students may take a self-administered test on this chapter at www.awlonline.com/rejda

Chapter 21 | Individual Health and Disability-Income Insurance

" They had me on the operating table all day. They looked into my stomach, my gallbladder, they examined everything inside of me. Know what they decided? I need glasses. "

Joe E. Lewis

Learning Objectives

After studying this chapter, you should be able to:

▲ Explain the major health care problems in the United States.

▲ Identify the basic coverages provided by individual hospital-surgical plans.

▲ Explain the basic characteristics of major medical insurance.

▲ Describe the major characteristics of disability-income contracts.

▲ Explain the rules to follow when purchasing individual health insurance.

▲ Access an Internet site to obtain consumer information about individual health insurance plans.

Internet Resources

- **EHealthInsurance.com** offers online applications for major medical insurance from several leading insurers. It allows you to shop privately for health insurance without sales pressure.
  www.ehealthinsurance.com

- **HealthAxis.com** sells major medical, short-term medical, and individual health insurance to college and graduate students. The company claims to serve as a bridge between the Internet and the insurance industry. Visit the site at:
  www.healthaxis.com

- The **Health Insurance Association of America** is a major source of health insurance information for consumers. The organization is responsible for public relations, government relations, and research on behalf of the private health insurance industry. Visit the site at:
  http://www.hiaa.org/

- **INSWEB** provides timely information and premium quotes for individual health insurance and Medicare policies. Applicants fill out health forms, and the site provides quotes from multiple insurers. The insurers then contact the applicants by phone or e-mail. Visit the site at:

  http://www.insweb.com/

- The **Insurance News Network** provides up-to-date information, premium quotes, and other consumer information on health insurance and other insurance products. It also provides news releases about events that affect the insurance industry.

  http://www.insure.com/

- The **National Association of Health Underwriters** is a professional association of people who sell and service medical expense, major medical, and disability-income insurance. Visit the site at:

  http://www.nahu.org/

- **Quicken Insurance** is an excellent consumer site for obtaining timely information on health insurance, disability-income insurance, long-term care insurance, and other insurance products. Visit the site at:

  http://www.quickeninsurance.com

- **State insurance departments** often provide consumer information on the various coverages discussed in this chapter. For starters, check out the following sites:

New York	**www.ins.state.ny.us**
Wisconsin	**badger.state.wi.us/agencies/oci/oci_home.htm**
California	**www.insurance.ca.gov**

im, age 32, is a self-employed carpenter who was diagnosed as having a brain tumor that required immediate surgery. His surgeon's fee, hospital expenses, and other medical bills totaled $125,000. Tim had no health insurance. In addition, he was out of work for more than one year and did not have an individual or group disability-income policy to restore his lost earnings. In short, because of the lack of health insurance, Tim was exposed to serious financial insecurity as result of the unexpected surgery. He eventually had to declare bankruptcy.

As Tim's experience demonstrates, health insurance should be given high priority in any personal risk management program. If you become seriously ill or are injured, you face two major financial problems: payment of your medical bills and the loss of earned income. A serious illness can produce catastrophic medical bills. Without proper protection, you may have to pay thousands of dollars out of your own pocket. In addition, an extended disability can result in the loss of thousands of dollars of earned income.

This chapter is the first of two chapters dealing with private health insurance. The discussion in Chapter 21 is limited to individual health and disability income insurance coverages. Chapter 22 discusses the various group health insurance plans *provided by employers. Although group health insurance accounts for more than 90 percent of the total medical expense premiums paid, a considerable amount of individual insurance is still sold. Individual plans are especially important for individuals and families who are not covered by group insurance.*

This chapter discusses the problems of health care in the United States, individual hospital-surgical plans, major medical insurance, long-term care insurance, and disability-income insurance. It concludes with a discussion of the important rules to follow when purchasing individual health insurance.

HEALTH CARE PROBLEMS IN THE UNITED STATES

Although the United States provides the highest-quality health care in the world and the health of Americans has improved remarkably, the present health care delivery system is a source of considerable frustration. The system has four major problems:[1]

- Rising health care expenditures
- Inadequate access to medical care
- Uneven quality of medical care
- Waste and inefficiency

Rising Health Care Expenditures

Total health care spending has increased substantially over time. *Projected national health care expenditures for the United States for 2000 totaled $1.3 trillion, or 14.3 percent of the nation's gross domestic product, up from 8.9 percent in 1980.*[2] Thus, roughly one in seven dollars of the nation's income is now spent on health care. If present trends continue, health care spending will reach 16.2 percent of the gross domestic product by 2008.[3]

Numerous factors explain the rise in health care expenditures. They include population growth that increases the demand for medical care, general price inflation and medical care inflation, new and expensive technology, aging of the population, cost shifting by Medicare and Medicaid to private health insurers, and state-mandated health insurance benefits. The growth in private health insurance has also contributed to the problem, because health insurance removes a financial barrier to care and increases the demand for medical care. Finally, the tax subsidy of health insurance has contributed to the problem. Health insurance contributions by employers are income-tax deductible and are not taxable to employees. As a result, the tax subsidy has encouraged the growth of expensive group health insurance plans that are more likely to be used.

Inadequate Access to Medical Care

Another problem is that certain groups have inadequate access to medical care. *First, millions of Americans have no health insurance.* The March 1999, Current Population Survey shows that despite low unemployment, the percentage of the nonelderly population without health insurance remains stubbornly high. *In 1998, an estimated 44.3 million people, or 16.3 percent of the population, were not covered by health insurance. This number was up by about 1 million from the previous year.*[4] People likely to be uninsured include employees working for smaller employers that cannot afford health insurance, low-income families who cannot qualify for government health insurance programs, individuals of Hispanic origin, illegal and legal immigrants, part-time workers, and single people younger than age 25. Some states have a high proportion of uninsured residents, including Arizona, California, New Mexico, and Texas.

Second, some welfare recipients find it difficult to find a physician who will treat them promptly because of inadequate reimbursement rates. This limited access to health care is especially detrimental to women with high-risk pregnancies who delay receiving prenatal care.

Finally, residents of small rural communities often have an access problem because of the shortage of physicians in many rural areas.

Uneven Quality of Medical Care

In addition, the quality of medical care is uneven and varies widely, depending on physician specialty and geographic location. Research studies show that many patients are dissatisfied with the care provided by hospitals; some surgical operations are unnecessary; medical treatment for the same condition varies widely depending on geographic location; and some medical care provided by physicians is inappropriate or of low quality.[5] The large number of medical malpractice suits over time is another indication that some physicians at times provide low-quality medical care.

Waste and Inefficiency

A final problem is the waste and inefficiency in the present system. The administrative costs of delivering health insurance benefits are excessively high; there is excessive paperwork by both health care providers and insurers; claim forms are not uniform nationally; a considerable amount of medical care provided by physicians is considered inappropriate; defensive medicine by physicians often results in unnecessary tests and procedures; there is duplication of expensive technology in many cities; and fraud and abuse by health care providers are widespread.

TYPES OF INDIVIDUAL HEALTH INSURANCE COVERAGES

Health insurers sell a wide variety of individual health insurance coverages. The quality of the coverage varies widely. Some plans provide broad and comprehensive protection, while others are limited with numerous exclusions.

Important individual coverages include the following:

- Hospital-surgical insurance
- Major medical insurance
- Long-term care insurance
- Disability-income insurance

HOSPITAL-SURGICAL INSURANCE

Insurers sell a variety of individual **hospital-surgical insurance plans**. These plans are also called basic plans because they cover routine medical expenses and generally are not designed to cover catastrophic losses. The types of covered medical expenses vary widely among insurers. The most complete plans cover the following:

- Hospital expenses
- Surgical expenses
- Outpatient diagnostic X rays and lab expenses
- Physician's in-hospital expense benefit
- Maternity expenses

Hospital Expenses

An individual hospital-surgical policy covers medical expenses incurred while the insured is in a hospital. A typical policy provides benefits for (1) daily room and board charges and (2) miscellaneous hospital expenses incurred during the hospital stay.

There are two basic approaches for paying *daily room and board charges*. Under an **indemnity plan**, actual room and board charges are paid up to some maximum daily limit, such as up to $400 daily for 120 days. Under a plan that provides **service benefits**, the full cost of a semi-private room is paid subject to any deductible or coinsurance requirements. Newer plans typically provide service benefits for hospital care.

Individual hospital-surgical plans also cover *miscellaneous hospital expenses*, such as X rays, drugs, laboratory fees, and other ancillary charges. Depending on the plan, part or all of the miscellaneous expenses are paid up to some maximum limit. For example, the plan may pay a maximum benefit for miscellaneous expenses that is some multiple of the daily room and board benefit, such as 10, 15, or 20 times the daily benefit.

Surgical Expenses

Individual hospital-surgical plans also include coverage for surgical expenses. Several methods are used to compensate surgeons. Older plans use a **schedule approach** by which the various surgical operations are listed in a schedule, and a maximum dollar amount is paid for each procedure, such as $400 for an appendectomy and $2000 for a valve replacement in the heart.

A **relative-value schedule** is a variation of the schedule approach in which units or points are attached to each operation based on the degree of difficulty. A conversion factor is then used to convert the relative value of the operation into a dollar amount that is paid to the physician. One advantage of a relative-value schedule is that it can be adapted to differences in the cost of living and in surgeons' fees in different geographical areas.

Newer plans typically reimburse surgeons on the basis of their **reasonable and customary charges**. Under this approach, surgeons are reimbursed based on their normal fees as long as the fee is reasonable and customary. Many insurers consider a fee to be reasonable and customary if it does not exceed the 80th or 90th percentile for a similar medical procedure performed by other surgeons in the same area. The policy pays the reasonable and customary fee, subject to any deductible or coinsurance requirements. The insured must pay that portion of the fee that exceeds the upper limit. Because insurers differ in how usual and customary fees are calculated, some insureds may have to pay substantial amounts out-of-pocket for that portion of the fee that exceeds the allowable upper limit.

Outpatient Diagnostic X Rays and Lab Expenses

Many hospital-surgical plans cover *outpatient diagnostic X rays and lab expenses*. Many physicians have well-equipped offices for routine X rays and laboratory tests for diagnosing the medical problems of patients. The maximum amount paid is limited to a stated dollar amount, such as $200 or $500 for any single illness or injury. However, some plans provide for maximum higher limits of several thousands of dollars.

Physician's In-Hospital Benefit

Many plans provide a *physician's in-hospital benefit*. This benefit pays for *nonsurgical treatment* provided by a physician to a patient while in the hospital. The

policies limit the maximum amount paid for each visit and also usually limit the number of visits during any single hospital stay.

Maternity Expenses

Individual hospital-surgical policies may cover part of the insured's maternity expenses. Some policies include maternity benefits, whereas others offer the coverage as an optional benefit. A maternity benefits rider can be added to the policy by payment of an additional premium. The rider is relatively expensive, and the amount paid is limited and below the actual cost of childbirth.

The maternity rider results in strong adverse selection because women who are likely to become pregnant will add the rider to their individual policies. Adverse selection is controlled by high premiums, by limits on the amount paid, and by a lengthy elimination period of ten months. Because of its cost, many financial planners do not recommend purchase of the rider.

MAJOR MEDICAL INSURANCE

Insureds often desire broader coverage than that provided by the basic coverages just discussed. **Major medical insurance** is designed to pay a high proportion of the covered expenses of a catastrophic illness or injury. A typical individual major medical policy has the following characteristics:

- Broad coverage
- High maximum limits
- Benefit period
- Deductible
- Coinsurance
- Exclusions

Broad Coverage

Major medical insurance provides broad coverage of all reasonable and necessary medical expenses and other related expenses from a covered illness or injury. The policy covers eligible expenses incurred while in the hospital, in the doctor's office, or at home. Eligible medical expenses include hospital room and board charges, miscellaneous hospital services and supplies, treatment by licensed physicians and surgeons, prescription drugs, durable medical equipment, and numerous other expenses.

High Maximum Limits

Major medical policies are also written with high lifetime limits of $500,000, $1 million, $2 million, or some higher amount. Some plans have no maximum limits. High limits are necessary to meet the crushing financial burden of a major catastrophic illness or injury.

Benefit Period

The maximum amount paid under a major medical policy depends partly on the length of the benefit period. A **benefit period**, *such as three years, refers to the length of time that major medical benefits will be paid after the deductible is satisfied*. When the benefit period ends, the insured must then satisfy a new deductible to establish a new benefit period. For example, assume that Jennifer has a $1 million major medical expense policy with a $500 deductible and a three-year benefit period. Assume that she is severely injured in an auto accident and satisfies the deductible on the first day of her injury. A three-year benefit period for that illness is then established. At the end of three years, Jennifer must again satisfy a new deductible if the maximum amount of $1 million has not been paid.

The purpose of the benefit period is to provide a definite time period within which eligible medical expenses for a specific disease or injury must be incurred in order to be reimbursed under the policy.

Deductible

A major medical policy usually contains a deductible that must be satisfied before benefits are paid. The purpose of the deductible is to eliminate payment of small claims and the relatively high administrative expenses of processing small claims. By eliminating small claims, the insurer can provide high policy limits and still keep the premiums reasonable.

The following types of deductible provisions are commonly found in individual major medical policies:

- Calendar-year deductible
- Family deductible
- Common-accident provision

Most major medical policies have a calendar-year deductible. A **calendar-year deductible** *means the deductible has to be satisfied only once during the calendar year*. All covered medical expenses incurred by the insured during the calendar year can be applied toward the deductible. Once the deductible is met, no additional deductible has to be satisfied during the calendar year. To avoid paying for two deductibles in a short period, most plans have a carryover provision. This provision means that unreimbursed medical expenses incurred during the last three months of the calendar year that are applied to this year's deductible can also be carried over and applied to next year's deductible.

The **family deductible** *specifies that medical expenses for all family members are accumulated for purposes of satisfying the deductible*. The accumulation period typically is one month, but a longer period could be used. For example, a $100 monthly deductible may be used. If medical expenses for the entire family exceed $100 during the month, the major medical policy starts to pay.

Individual major medical policies also contain a **common-accident provision**. *Only one deductible has to be satisfied if two or more family members are injured in a common accident, such as an automobile accident.*

Coinsurance

Major medical policies contain a **coinsurance provision** *that requires the insured to pay a certain percentage of eligible medical expenses in excess of the deductible*. (Coinsurance is also called a percentage participation clause.) A typical plan requires the insured to pay 20 percent or 25 percent of covered expenses in excess of the deductible. For example, assume that Megan has covered medical expenses in the amount of $10,500. She has a $1 million major medical policy with a $500 deductible and an 80-20 coinsurance provision. The insurer will pay $8000 of the total bill, and Megan will pay $2000 (plus the deductible). This is summarized as follows:

Covered expenses	$10,500
Less the deductible	−500
Remaining expenses	$10,000
80% paid by insurer	8000
20% paid by Megan	$ 2000

The purposes of the coinsurance clause are to reduce premiums and to prevent overutilization of policy benefits. Because the insured pays part of the cost, premiums are reduced. It is also argued that the patient will not demand the most expensive medical services if he or she pays part of the cost, and that physicians and other health care providers will be more restrained in setting their fees if the patient pays part of the cost.

Major medical policies also contain a **stop-loss limit** by which 100 percent of the eligible medical expenses are paid after the insured incurs a certain amount of out-of-pocket expenses, such as $2000. *The purpose of the stop-loss limit is to reduce the financial burden of a catastrophic loss.* For example, if Megan's covered medical expenses in excess of the deductible are $100,000 and the stop-limit is $2000, her major medical policy would pay $98,000. She would pay only $2000 (plus the deductible). Without the stop-limit, Megan would have to pay $20,000 (plus the deductible).

Exclusions

All major medical policies contain exclusions. Some common exclusions include the following:

- Expenses caused by war or military conflict
- Elective cosmetic surgery
- Dental care, except as a result of an accident
- Eye and hearing examinations, eyeglasses, and hearing aids
- Pregnancy and childbirth, except complications of pregnancy (Maternity can be covered with a rider.)
- Expenses covered by workers compensation and similar laws
- Services furnished by governmental agencies unless the patient has an obligation to pay
- Experimental surgery

In addition, major medical plans typically contain **internal limits** for certain types of expenses, to control cost. There may be annual or lifetime limits on the amount paid for certain diseases, such as alcoholism and drug addiction. For example, one plan limits inpatient coverage for alcoholism and drug addiction to no more than 45 days of treatment during any successive 12-month period.

Although major medical insurance is effective in dealing with the crushing financial burden of a critical illness, nonmedical expenses are not covered. These expenses include child-care costs, alterations to your home or car to accommodate your medical condition, reduction in your spouse's wages from time as a caregiver, and travel for treatment at a distant location. Some insurers have designed a new *critical illness policy* that pays a lump sum for nonmedical expenses upon the diagnosis of certain disease (see Insight 21.1).

LONG-TERM CARE INSURANCE

Long-term care insurance is another coverage that is rapidly growing in popularity. **Long-term care insurance** pays a daily or monthly benefit for medical or custodial care received in a nursing facility, in a hospital, or at home.

Chance of Entering a Nursing Home

Many older Americans will spend some time in a nursing home. *One national study projects that 43 percent of the people who attained age 65 in 1990 will enter a nursing home sometime during their lifetime.* About one in three will spend three months or longer in a nursing home; and about one in 11 will spend five years or longer in a nursing home. Stated differently, two out of three people who attained age 65 in 1990 will never enter a nursing home or will be there for less than three months.[6]

The cost of long-term care in a nursing home is staggering. Most long-term facilities charge $40,000 to $65,000 or even more for each year of care. Medicare does not cover long-term care in a nursing facility, and custodial care is excluded altogether. In addition, most elderly are not initially eligible for long-term care under the Medicaid program, which

Insight 21.1

Critical Illness Insurance Pays Extra Costs That Accompany Serious Illnesses

Medical care these days can help you survive heart attacks, cancers, organ failures, strokes, and other serious illnesses that used to kill you.

But a medical crisis can add living expenses that eat away your finances, even if you have good health insurance. Nonmedical expenses such as child care, travel for treatment, or home renovations can drain your cash, the equity in your home and even your retirement account.

Now there's a new type of insurance that covers the risk of surviving serious medical problems: critical illness insurance. *A critical illness policy pays you a lump sum if you are diagnosed as having specific serious illnesses—heart attack, stroke, cancer, or others. The payment isn't related to medical costs and you don't have to die or be hospitalized to collect.*

While some experts warn against buying such specialized insurance, critical illness coverage has become popular in parts of Europe and Asia and arrived in the United States in the past year.

Mutual of Omaha is joining what may be a rush of U.S. companies into the new market. So far there are fewer than a half-dozen, but one executive expects as many as 25 to join in by the end of the year.

Not everyone agrees that critical illness insurance is necessary.

Gail Shearer, director of health policy and analysis for Consumers Union in Washington, which publishes *Consumer Reports* magazine, said she thinks critical illness insurance amounts to a sort of gambling.

"The issue is, 'How should the country spend its health care dollars?'" Shearer said. There's a danger that people will buy only critical illness insurance and not standard medical coverage or that they may buy

more coverage than they need—especially the elderly who are fearful of medical costs.

People also could be misled about when the policy pays off, she said.

"It sounds to me like it's gambling," Shearer said, because the policies pay off only for a narrow set of medical conditions. "If you're talking about health care costs, this is not how you would design health care coverage. It's going to have lots of holes in it."

People would be better off banking the money they would spend on premiums for critical illness coverage, she said, and first should get comprehensive health insurance.

Mutual of Omaha said critical illness insurance is intended to supplement standard health insurance, not replace it. But critical illness coverage can provide added peace of mind even if you never suffer from such an illness, said Carl Scott, senior vice president for individual marketing at Mutual.

Critical illness insurance is intended to cover the gaps between health insurance, disability insurance, life insurance, and regular income. A critical-care policy pays when an insured person receives a doctor's diagnosis of one of 13 covered medical conditions, such as a heart attack or cancer [see box].

There is no continuing series of medical-related claims, although some of the illnesses trigger only a partial payment of the policy amount.

Scott said the insurance supplies a healthy dose of cash to cover expenses such as a second opinion outside your medical policy; co-payments for prescription drugs; home or car alteration; child care; travel to treatment; home nursing care; housekeeping; rehabilitation; a drop in your income; your spouse's lost wages

---

is a welfare program that imposes strict eligibility requirements and a stringent means test. As a result, many older Americans have purchased long-term care policies to meet the crushing financial burden of an extended stay in a nursing facility.

Basic Characteristics

Numerous insurers sell long-term care policies. The policies sold currently usually have certain generic characteristics.[7]

Critical Care Insurance

- **Payment**: With a medical diagnosis of a covered condition. Once the policy amount is paid out, coverage ends.

- **Qualifying**: Applicants talk to a Mutual underwriter over the telephone and send a "mouth fluid" swab to a laboratory. Dishonest answers negate the policy.

- **Premiums**: For a nonsmoker's $50,000 policy, between $302 per year for a 25-year-old man and $872 for a 55-year-old man.

- **Early cancer**: If cancer is detected within the first 30 days after the policy is issued, Mutual terminates the policy and returns the premiums paid.

- **Age**: Between 20 and 64. After 64, coverage amounts drop by 50 percent.

- **Policy amounts**: $25,000 to $75,000, with upper amounts aimed at business owners or partners.

- **Covered diagnoses** (and the percentages of policy amount paid):

  — Heart attack, 100 percent.

  — First coronary artery bypass surgery, 25 percent.

  — First coronary angioplasty, 25 percent.

  — Life-threatening cancer, meaning it is malignant and growing uncontrollably outside its original area and invading normal tissue, 100 percent.

  — First malignant tumor that has not spread, 25 percent.

  — Stroke when a blood vessel ruptures in the brain or a clot blocks blood flow through the brain and the effects of the neurological injury last at least 30 days, 100 percent.

  — Advanced stages of Alzheimer's disease, requiring permanent daily supervision and the inability to perform at least three daily living activities by yourself, 100 percent.

  — Clinical evidence of a major organ failure, organs or tissue must be replaced, and you are registered with the organ-sharing network, 100 percent.

  — Multiple sclerosis, paralysis, kidney failure, blindness, deafness, 100 percent.

  The policies also offer riders for other physical conditions, charging added premiums.

from time as a caregiver; and short-term home health care.

The premium amounts are determined by the age of the purchaser and other factors. The company doesn't guarantee that premiums won't increase. Scott said, but they should remain fairly stable because the payout amounts won't change.

SOURCE: Adapted from Steve Jordan, "Policy Targets Extra Costs," *Sunday World-Herald*, May 23, 1999, p. 1-M.

Type of Care Provided The policies typically cover skilled nursing care, intermediate nursing care, and custodial care. *Skilled nursing care* is medical care provided by skilled medical personnel 24 hours a day under the supervision of a physician, such as care provided by a registered nurse or physical therapist. *Intermediate nursing care* is medical care for a stable condition that requires daily but not continuous 24-hour nursing supervision. The care is ordered by a physician and supervised by registered nurses. It is less specialized than skilled nursing care and often involves more personal care. *Custodial care* is care that helps the patient with daily living activities, such as assistance in bathing, eating, dressing, and using the toilet; this type of care is also called personal care.

Many policies also cover *home health care*. Some plans cover only skilled nursing care provided in the home by registered nurses, licensed practical nurses, and physical, occupational, or speech therapists. Other policies are broader and also cover the services of home health aides from licensed agencies who provide patients with personal or custodial care. However, few policies pay for someone to come into your home and cook meals or run errands.

Aggregate Benefits Purchasers have a choice of benefits, such as daily benefits of $100, $120, or $150, which are paid over a maximum period of two, three, or four years, or over the insured's lifetime. Other plans have a choice of lifetime maximum benefits, such as $120 daily and a $250,000 lifetime limit.

Elimination Period An **elimination period** is a waiting period during which time benefits are not paid. Elimination periods can range from zero to 365 days. Common elimination periods are 30, 60, 100, or 180 days. A longer elimination period can substantially reduce premiums.

Eligibility for Benefits All policies include one or more **gatekeeper provisions**, which determine whether the insured is eligible to receive benefits. One common gatekeeper provision requires the insured to be unable to perform a certain number of **activities of daily living**, commonly called **ADLs**. Examples include walking, bathing, dressing, eating, getting into and out of bed, and using the toilet. Benefits are paid if the insured cannot perform a certain number of ADLs listed in the policy without assistance from another person, such as two out of six ADLs.

Inflation Protection Protection against inflation is usually made available as an optional benefit. For example, based on an inflation rate of 5 percent annually, a daily charge of $86 will increase to $228 in 20 years.[8] Protection against inflation is especially important if the policy is purchased at a younger age.

Two methods are used to provide protection against inflation. One method allows the insured to purchase additional amounts of insurance in the future without evidence of insurability. For example, one insurer allows the insured to exercise four options, one every five years, to increase his or her coverage 20 percent each time an option is exercised.

A second method provides for an automatic benefit increase by which the daily benefit is increased by a fixed percentage, such as 5 percent for the next 10 or 20 years. The dollar amount of the annual increase will depend on whether the inflation adjustment is based on simple or compound interest. A daily benefit of $80 will increase to $160 in 20 years based on 5 percent simple interest; however, if the benefit is compounded, it will increase to $212. Adding an automatic benefit increase to the policy is expensive and could double the amount of the annual premium in some cases.

Guaranteed Renewable The policies sold currently are **guaranteed renewable**. Once issued, the policy cannot be canceled. However, rates can be increased for the underwriting class in which the insured is placed.

Premiums Coverage is expensive. For example, one insurer charges $830 annually for a policy sold in Nebraska to a person age 60 with a $100 daily benefit, five-year maximum limit, and a thirty-day elimination period. That same policy sold to a person at age 79 would cost $4,450 annually.

Taxation of Long-Term Care Insurance Long-term care insurance now receives favorable income tax treatment as a result of the Health Insurance Portability and Accountability Act of 1996. A long-term care policy that meets certain requirements is treated as an accident and health insurance contract. The coverage can be an individual or group plan. Premiums are deductible by the employer under a group plan and are not taxable to the employee.

Annual premiums are deductible as medical expenses under an individual plan if the premiums plus other unreimbursed medical expenses exceed 7½ percent of the individual's adjusted gross income. However, certain annual limits apply. For 1999, the maximum annual deduction for long-term care premiums ranged from $210 for people age 40 or below to $2660 for people over age 70. These limits are indexed for inflation.

For 1999, if the policy is a *per diem policy* that pays a specific daily amount, the maximum daily benefit excludable from income is limited to $190 (indexed for inflation). Finally, long-term care insurance cannot be made available to employees in a cafeteria plan or flexible spending account.

DISABILITY-INCOME INSURANCE

Disability-income insurance is another important form of individual health insurance. A serious disability can result in a substantial loss of work earnings. Unless you have replacement income from disability-income insurance, or income from other sources, you may be financially insecure. Many workers seldom think about the financial consequences of a long-term disability. However, the probability of becoming disabled before age 65 is much higher than is commonly believed, especially at the younger ages. For example, *the probability that a person age 25 will be totally disabled for at least 90 days prior to age 65 is 54 percent* (see Exhibit 21.1).

The financial loss to the family from long-term total and permanent disability can be substantially greater than the financial loss that results from premature death at the same age. In the case of prema-

ture death, the family loses its share of the deceased family head's future earnings, and funeral expenses are also incurred. However, in the case of long-term total and permanent disability, earned income is lost; medical bills are being incurred; savings are reduced or depleted; employee benefits may be lost; and additional expenses are incurred, such as getting someone to care for the disabled person. It is clear that disability-income insurance should be a high priority in a personal risk management program.

Disability-income insurance provides income payments when the insured is unable to work because of sickness or injury. An individual policy pays monthly income benefits to an insured who becomes totally disabled from a sickness or accident. The amount of disability insurance you can buy is related to your earnings. To prevent overinsurance and to reduce moral hazard and malingering, most insurers limit the amount of disability income sold to no more than 60 to 80 percent of your gross earnings.

Meaning of Total Disability

The most important policy provision in a disability income policy is the meaning of "total disability." Most policies require the worker to be totally disabled to receive benefits.

Definitions of Total Disability There are several definitions of total disability. The most important include the following:

- Inability to perform all duties of the insured's own occupation
- Inability to perform the duties of any occupation for which the insured is reasonably fitted by education, training, and experience
- Inability to perform the duties of any gainful occupation
- Loss-of-income test

The most liberal definition defines total disability in terms of your own occupation. **Total disability** *is the complete inability of the insured to perform each and every duty of his or her own occupation.* An example would be a surgeon whose hand is blown off in a hunting accident. The surgeon could no longer perform surgery and would be totally disabled under this definition.

EXHIBIT 21.1
Probability of Becoming Disabled for at Least 90 Days Before Age 65

Age	
25	54%
30	52
35	50
40	48
45	44
50	39
55	32
60	9

Based on 1985 Commissioners Disability Table.

SOURCE: Adapted with permission from Edward E. Graves, ed., *McGill's Life Insurance* 2nd ed. (Bryn Mawr, PA: The American College, 1998), Table 7-2, p. 168. Copyright © 1998 by the American College. All Rights Reserved.

The second definition is more restrictive. In this case, *total disability is the complete inability to perform the duties of any occupation for which the insured is reasonably fitted by education, training, and experience.* Thus, if the surgeon who lost a hand in a hunting accident could get a job as a professor in a medical school or as a research scientist, he or she would not be considered disabled because these occupations are consistent with the surgeon's training and experience.

The third definition is the most restrictive and is commonly used for hazardous occupations where a disability is likely to occur. *Total disability is defined as the inability to perform the duties of any gainful occupation.* The courts generally have interpreted this definition to mean that the person is totally disabled if he or she cannot work in any gainful occupation reasonably fitted by education, training, and experience.

Finally, some insurers use a loss-of-income test to determine if the insured is disabled. *You are considered disabled if your income is reduced as a result of a sickness or accident.* A disability-income policy containing this definition typically pays a percentage of the maximum monthly benefit equal to the percentage of earned income that is lost. For example, assume that Stanley earns $5000 monthly and has a disability-income contract with a maximum monthly benefit of $3000. If Stanley's work earnings are reduced to $2500 monthly because of the disability (50 percent), the policy pays $1500 monthly (50 percent of $3000).

Most insurers now combine the first two definitions. *For the initial period of disability—typically two years—total disability is defined in terms of the insured's own occupation. After the initial period of disability expires, the second definition is applied.* For example, Dr. Myron Pudwill is a dentist who can no longer practice because of arthritis in his hands. For the first two years, he would be considered totally disabled. However, after two years, if he could work as a dental supply representative or as a professor in a dental school, he would no longer be considered disabled because he is reasonably fitted for these occupations by his education and training.

Finally, the policy may also contain a definition of *presumptive disability*. A total disability is presumed to exist if the insured suffers the total and irrecoverable loss of sight in both eyes, or the total loss or use of both hands, both feet, or one hand and one foot.

Partial Disability Some disability-income policies also pay partial disability benefits. **Partial disability** *is defined as the inability of the insured to perform one or more important duties of his or her occupation.* Partial disability benefits are paid at a reduced rate for a shorter period. For example, a person may be totally disabled from an automobile accident. If the person recovers and goes back to work on a part-time basis to see if recovery is complete, partial disability benefits may be paid.

Residual Disability Newer policies frequently include a residual disability benefit, or this provision can be added as an additional benefit. **Residual disability** *means that a pro rata disability benefit is paid to an insured whose earned income is reduced because of an accident or sickness.* The typical residual disability provision has a time and duties test that considers both income and occupation. One common residual disability provision is as follows:[9]

1. You are not able to do one or more of your important daily business duties, or you are not able to do your usual daily business duties for as much time as it would normally take for you to do them.
2. Your loss of monthly income is at least 25 percent of your prior monthly income.
3. You are under the care and attendance of a physician.

However, some insurers use an alternative definition of residual disability that considers only the loss of earned income. In this definition, **residual disability** *means that you are engaged in your regular or another occupation, and your income is reduced because of an accident or sickness by at least 20 percent of your prior income.*

Finally, most insurers consider a loss of earned income in excess of 75 or 80 percent to be a loss of 100 percent, in which case the full monthly benefit for total disability is paid.

One major advantage of the residual disability definition is the payment of a partial benefit if the insured returns to work but earnings are reduced. For example, Chris is a salesperson who earns $4000 monthly. He is seriously injured in an auto accident. When he returns to work, his earnings are only $3000 monthly, or a reduction of 25 percent. If his disability-income policy pays a monthly benefit of $2000 for total disability, a residual benefit of $500 is paid, and his total monthly income is $3500.

Benefit Period

The benefit period is the length of time that disability benefits are payable after the elimination period is met. The insured has a choice of benefit periods, such as 2, 5, 10 years, or up to age 65 or 70 (provided the insured is still performing his or her occupation).

Most disabilities are relatively short. In fact, the majority of disabilities have durations of less than two years.[10] However, this fact does not mean that a two-year benefit period is adequate. The longer the disability lasts, the less likely the disabled person will recover. For example, a person who became disabled at age 22 and remains disabled for two years has a 41 percent chance of remaining disabled for at least five more years.[11] Thus, because of uncertainty concerning the duration of disability, you should elect a longer benefit period—ideally, one that pays benefits to age 65.

Exhibit 21.2 contains a convenient worksheet that can help you estimate the amount of disability-income insurance needed. The worksheet takes into consideration other sources of income, such as investment income and disability benefits from your employer.

Elimination Period

Individual policies normally contain an elimination period (waiting period), during which time benefits are not paid. Insurers offer a range of elimination periods, such as 30, 60, 90, 180, or 365 days. Most insurers have stopped offering elimination periods that are shorter than 14 days, and elimination periods of 30 or more days are now the rule.

High-quality disability-income policies are expensive and can cost as much as 2 to 3 percent of your annual earnings. Increasing the elimination period from 30 to 90 days can substantially reduce the premiums. For example, in one plan, a male accountant who purchases a monthly benefit of $4250 to age 65 will pay $4036 annually for a policy with a 30-day elimination period. However, if he elects a 90-day elimination period, the annual premium would be about $1888, or 53 percent less. The majority of employers have sick leave or short-term disability plans that would provide some income during the longer elimination period. One disadvantage, however, is that a group disability-income plan is usually not convertible into an individual policy if the worker becomes unemployed. Thus, group insurance is not a satisfactory substitute for a high-quality disability-income policy.

Finally, to make disability-income insurance more affordable, *some insurers sell policies with initially lower rates that gradually increase with age*. This approach is similar to term life insurance rates that increase as the insured gets older.

Waiver of Premium

A **waiver-of-premium** provision is built into the policy, which states that if the insured is totally disabled for 90 days, future premiums will be waived as long as the insured remains disabled. In addition, there may be a refund of the premiums paid during the initial 90-day period. If the insured recovers from the disability, premium payments must be resumed.

Rehabilitation Provision

Disability-income policies typically include a rehabilitation provision. The insurer and insured may agree on a vocational rehabilitation program. To encourage rehabilitation, part or all of the disability-income benefits are paid during the training period. At the end of training, if the insured is still totally disabled, the benefits continue as before. But if the individual is fully rehabilitated and is capable of returning to work, the benefits will terminate. The costs of rehabilitation are usually paid by the company.

EXHIBIT 21.2
How Much Disability-Income Insurance Do You Need?

1. ESTIMATED MONTHLY EXPENSES

   Mortgage/rent _____

   Utilities _____

   Miscellaneous home expenses _____

   Loan payments _____

   Food _____

   Clothing _____

   Insurance payments/expenses _____

   Medical and dental expenses _____

   Miscellaneous (vacation, entertainment, and so on) _____

   Education _____

   Transportation _____

   TOTAL _____

2. Estimated Monthly Income

   If you are single:

   Current monthly take-home pay _____

   Subtract investment income _____

   TOTAL _____

   If you are married[a]

   Current monthly take-home pay _____

   Subtract investment income _____

   Subtract spouse's pay _____

   TOTAL _____

3. EXISTING BENEFITS

   Social Security/workers compensation _____

   Other government insurance _____

   Group disability-income insurance _____

   Individual disability-income insurance _____

   Total _____

4. THE AMOUNT OF DISABILITY INCOME INSURANCE
   YOU NEED _____

   If the total from 3 is greater than the total from 2, you probably have adequate coverage. But if the total from 3 is less than the total in 2, subtract total 3 from total 2. This is the amount of additional monthly coverage you need.

5. HOW MANY MONTHS CAN YOU AFFORD TO LIVE WITHOUT
   YOUR SALARY? _____

$$\frac{\text{Amount from savings accounts that you would feel comfortable spending}}{\text{Total expenses − Short-term disability benefits provided by your employe}} = \begin{array}{l}\text{The number of months}\\\text{you can get by without}\\\text{long-term disability}\\\text{coverage.}\end{array}$$

[a]This worksheet should be completed for each spouse.

Accidental Death, Dismemberment, and Loss-of-Sight Benefits

Some disability-income policies pay accidental death, dismemberment, and loss-of-sight benefits in the event of an accident. The maximum amount paid, known as the principal sum, is based on a schedule. For example, the principal sum is paid for loss of both hands or both feet or sight of both eyes.

Optional Disability-Income Benefits

Several optional benefits can be added to a disability-income policy. They include the following:

1. *Cost-of-living rider.* Under this option, the disability benefits are periodically adjusted for increases in the cost of living, usually measured by the Consumer Price Index. Two limitations generally apply to the cost-of-living adjustment. First, the annual increase in benefits may be limited to a certain maximum percentage (such as 5 percent per year). Second, there may be a maximum limit on the overall increase in benefits (such as a 100 percent maximum increase in benefits). The rider is expensive and can increase the basic premium by 25 to 40 percent.
2. *Option to purchase additional insurance.* Your income may increase, and you may need additional disability-income benefits. Under this option, the insured has the right to purchase additional disability-income benefits at specified times in the future with no evidence of insurability. The premium is generally based on the insured's age at the time the additional benefits are purchased.
3. *Social Security rider.* Social Security disability benefits are difficult to obtain because of a strict definition of disability and stringent eligibility requirements. The Social Security rider pays you an additional amount if you are turned down for Social Security disability benefits.
4. *Return of premium.* This rider pays back some of the premiums paid into the policy. For example, after 10 years, you would receive 80 percent of the premiums paid, less any claims. The option is controversial and has little to recommend it. Disability-income insurance is designed to provide income protection and should not be viewed as being similar to cash-value life insurance. The op-tion is also expensive and can increase the already high cost of a policy by 30 to 100 percent.

Tighter Disability-Income Market

Although disability-income insurance is important, it is becoming more difficult to obtain. Disability-income insurers have experienced an explosion of claims and high underwriting losses in recent years. As a result, the market for disability-income insurance has tightened and becomes more restrictive. The underwriting losses are due to several factors, including an excessive number of claims by physicians with noncancellable policies that could not be repriced; a substantial increase in claims for alcohol and drug abuse and emotional disorders; liberal policy provisions; inadequate rates; payment of lifetime benefits; and liberal claims treatment of physicians and attorneys.

Some insurers have withdrawn from the disability-income market, while others have redesigned their policies. Disability insurers have also reduced the maximum benefit period available under the own-occupation definition of disability to two years; the amount of insurance has been cut back from a maximum of 80 percent of income to 60 or 65 percent; new policies sold to physicians do not pay lifetime benefits, and monthly payments are capped; elimination periods have been increased; and underwriting standards have tightened.

INDIVIDUAL MEDICAL EXPENSE CONTRACTUAL PROVISIONS

All states have laws that require certain contractual provisions to appear in individual medical expense insurance contracts, while other provisions are optional. It is beyond the scope of this text to analyze in detail all contractual provisions. Instead, attention is focused on those provisions that are commonly found in newly issued contracts and are relevant to insurance consumers.

Renewal Provisions

A renewal provision refers to the length of time that an individual policy can remain in force. Renewal provisions include the following:[12]

- Optionally renewable
- Guaranteed renewable
- Noncancellable

Optionally Renewable This provision gives the insured the least protection with respect to continuation of coverage. Under an **optionally renewable policy,** *the insurer has the right to terminate a policy on any anniversary date, or in some cases, on a premium date.* The policy is renewable only with the consent of the insurer. Instead of nonrenewal, the insurer may specify the conditions that must be met before the policy is renewed. These conditions could include a policy amendment that excludes certain types of losses or injuries to certain parts of the body, or coverage for certain occurrences may be limited.

Guaranteed Renewable Most individual medical expense policies are guaranteed renewable. This type of renewal provision provides considerable protection to the insured. A **guaranteed renewable policy** *is one in which the insurer guarantees to renew the policy to some stated age. However, the insurer has the right to increase premium rates for the underwriting class in which the insured is placed.* The policy cannot be canceled, and renewal of the policy is at the insured's sole discretion.

Noncancellable A noncancellable policy provides the greatest protection to the insured. A **noncancellable policy** *is one that cannot be canceled. The insurer guarantees renewal of the policy to some stated age, and the premiums are guaranteed and cannot be increased during that period.* A noncancellable medical expense policy allows the insured to keep the insurance in force by the timely payment of premiums until at least age 50, or if the policy is issued after age 44, for at least five years from the issue date. Provided the insured pays the premiums on time, the insurer cannot cancel, refuse to renew, or increase premium rates stated in the policy, or unilaterally make any changes in the policy provisions.

Preexisting-Conditions Clause

To control adverse selection, individual medical expense policies usually contain some type of **preexisting conditions clause.** A preexisting condition is a physical or mental condition for which the insured received treatment or that existed during some specified time period—such as five years—prior to the effective date of the policy. Preexisting conditions are not covered until the policy has been in force for a specified period, such as two years, unless the condition is disclosed in the application and not excluded by a rider.

The preexisting-conditions exclusion usually applies to health conditions not disclosed in the application. If the condition is disclosed in the application, it usually would be covered unless the insurer excludes the condition by attaching an exclusionary rider.

Many states have placed restrictions on the types of preexisting-conditions clauses that insurers can use. For example, a state may limit exclusions for a preexisting condition to 12 months, with a six-month look-back period (how far back the insurer can go to see whether the condition existed before the policy inception date).

In addition, the Health Insurance Portability and Accountability Act (HIPPA) of 1996 guarantees the availability of individual health insurance coverage with no preexisting-conditions limitations to certain individuals who have lost their group health insurance coverage. HIPPA is discussed in Chapter 22.

Notice of Ten-Day Right to Examine Policy

If you are not satisfied with the policy, you have 10 days to send it back after receiving it. The entire premium will be refunded, and the policy will be void.

Claims

A number of important provisions in an individual medical expense policy deal with claims. Under the *notice of claim provision*, you are required to give written notice to the insurer within 20 days after a covered loss occurs or as soon as is reasonably possible. Under the *claim forms provision*, the insurer is required to send you a claim form within 15 days after notice is received. Finally, under the *proof-of-loss provision*, you must send written proof of loss to the insurer within 90 days after a covered loss occurs. If it is not reasonably possible to provide proof of loss within 90 days, your claim will not be affected if the proof is sent as soon as possible. However, in any event, you must provide proof of loss within one year unless you are legally incapable of doing so.

Grace Period

A grace period is a required provision. The **grace period** *is a 31-day period after the premium due date to pay an overdue premium.* If the premium is paid after the due date but within the grace period, coverage is still in force.

Reinstatement

If the premium is not paid within the grace period, the health insurance policy lapses. The **reinstatement provision** *permits the insured to reinstate a lapsed policy.* If the insured pays the premium to the insurance company or agent, and an application is not required, the policy is reinstated. However, if an application for reinstatement is required, the policy is reinstated only when the insurer approves the application. If the insurer has not previously notified the insured that the application for reinstatement has been denied, the policy is then automatically reinstated on the forty-fifth day following the date of the conditional receipt. The reinstated policy is subject to a ten-day waiting period for sickness, but accidents are covered immediately.

Time Limit on Certain Defenses

The time limit on certain defenses is a required provision and has the same effect as the incontestable clause in life insurance. The **time limit on certain defenses** *states that after the policy has been in force for two years, the insurer cannot void the policy or deny a claim on the basis of misstatements in the application, except for fraudulent misstatements.* After two years, the insurer could deny a claim if it could prove that the insured made a fraudulent misstatement when the policy was first issued.

SHOPPING FOR HEALTH INSURANCE

High-quality individual health insurance plans are expensive. You should not waste money by buying

healthier insurance coverages that do not provide meaningful protection. Certain guidelines should be followed when you are purchasing health insurance (see Exhibit 21.3). They include the following:

- Insure for the catastrophic loss.
- Consider group health insurance first.
- Use preferred providers whenever possible.
- Don't ignore disability-income insurance.
- Avoid limited policies.
- Watch out for restrictive policy provisions and exclusions.
- Use deductibles and elimination periods to reduce premiums.

Insure for the Catastrophic Loss

The most important rule is to purchase health insurance that provides protection against a catastrophic loss that can destroy you financially. The cost of a serious illness or injury can prove ruinous. Open-heart surgery can cost more than $100,000; a kidney or heart transplant can cost more than $400,000; and the cost of a crippling auto accident requiring several major operations, plastic surgery, and rehabilitation can exceed $200,000. Unless you have adequate health insurance or financial assets to meet these expenditures, you will be financially insecure. The inability to pay for catastrophic medical bills is a major cause of personal bankruptcy. *Thus, you should purchase a high-quality individual major medical policy or be covered under a group major medical plan.* To limit your out-of-pocket expenses, make certain that the major medical policy has a stop-loss limit that requires the insurer to pay 100 percent of all covered expenses in excess of the stop-loss limit.

Consider Group Health Insurance First

In dealing with the risk of poor health, you should first consider whether group health insurance is available. You may be eligible to participate in a group health insurance plan sponsored by your employer.

Group health insurance is preferable to individual coverage for several reasons. First, employers frequently make available a number of group health insurance plans to their employees, ranging from tra-

EXHIBIT 21.3
Guidelines for Health Insurance Shoppers

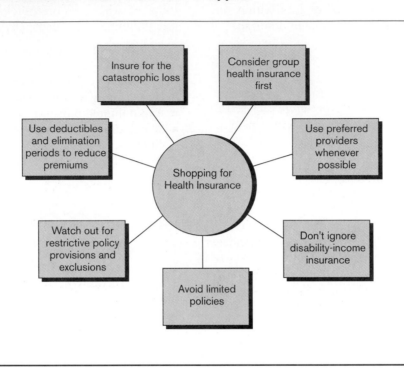

ditional group indemnity plans to managed care plans, such as those involving health maintenance organizations (HMOs) and preferred provider organizations (PPOs). The various group indemnity plans have different deductible amounts, coinsurance requirements, and stop-loss limits. Managed care plans typically have no deductible or coinsurance requirements, or the amounts paid out-of-pocket are relatively low. Depending on your financial circumstances and need for protection, you can select the plan that best meets your needs and ability to pay. Managed care plans are discussed in greater detail in Chapter 22.

Second, group health insurance is typically broader in coverage than individual protection and has fewer exclusions and restrictions.

Third, employers usually pay a large part of the monthly premiums, which makes the plan financially attractive to the employees and their families. Some employers pay the entire cost.

Finally, group health insurance plans provide substantial tax advantages to employees. The employer's contributions do not result in taxable income to the employee, and the employee's contributions can often be made with *before-tax dollars*. These tax advantages should not be ignored.

Use Preferred Providers Whenever Possible

Another important suggestion is to use **preferred providers** whenever possible. Insurers frequently establish networks of caregivers who agree to provide medical services to the insureds at discounted fee. Preferred providers include physicians, dentists, hospitals, pharmaceutical firms, and other health care providers who are part of the network. If you see a preferred provider, your out-of-pocket cost will be substantially less than if you see a provider outside the network.

Don't Ignore Disability-Income Insurance

You should not ignore the importance of disability-income insurance in your health insurance program. A substantial amount of earned income is lost each year because of sickness and injury, but not replaced by disability-income and sick-leave benefits. Data show clearly that many workers are paying insufficient attention to the risk of disability in their personal insurance programs. For example, employees lost $81.1 billion in earnings from short-term nonoccupational sickness in 1994. *Of that amount, only about 46 percent was restored by individual insurance, group benefits to workers in private employment, and sick leave for government employees.*[13] The proportion of income replaced during a long-term disability would be even less. Thus, it is clear that most workers are underinsured with respect to both short-term and long-term disability.

You should consider purchasing an individual guaranteed renewable or noncancellable disability-income policy that will pay at least two-thirds of your earnings up to age 65 with an elimination period of 30 to 90 days. Even if you are covered under a group short-term or long-term disability-income plan, you should still consider an individual policy. If you lose your job, group disability-income benefits generally cannot be converted into an individual policy.

Avoid Limited Policies

A **limited policy** covers only certain diseases or accidents, pays limited benefits, or places serious restrictions on the right to receive the benefits. A **hospital indemnity policy** is one example of a limited policy. It pays a fixed daily or monthly benefit if you are confined to a hospital. For example, the plan may pay $3000 monthly ($100 daily) for a maximum of five years if you are hospitalized, ask no health questions, and charge a first month's premium of only $1. It sounds like a good deal, but in health insurance, there is no such thing as a "free lunch." The policy is limited. Most people will never collect benefits for an extended period. The average hospital stay for people younger than age 65 is less than seven days. Even if you are confined for only seven days, the benefit paid would be only $700. During that time, you may have incurred several thousands of dollars of medical expenses, but only a small amount would be paid by the hospital indemnity benefit. In addition, the policy covers you only while you remain in the hospital. If you recover at home, no payment is made. Finally, the application contains a preexisting-conditions clause that excludes a preexisting condition for one or two years after the policy is purchased.

A **cancer policy** is another example of a limited policy. If you are insured under a high-quality individual or group major medical policy, you do not need a cancer policy. Many consumer experts recommend that a cancer policy should not be purchased (see Insight 21.2). They argue that it is illogical to insure yourself more heavily against only one disease because you do not know how you will become disabled.

Accident-only policies should be avoided because they are limited in coverage and benefits. A list of these policies is endless, but includes accident insurance offered by sponsors of credit cards, travel accident policies to cover you while on vacation, and airline accident policies sold over the counter or from vending machines in airports.

Watch Out for Restrictive Policy Provisions and Exclusions

If you are shopping for an individual policy, you should be aware of any restrictions on coverage that might apply. Two common restrictions are a preexisting-conditions clause and an **exclusionary rider**. An individual policy with a preexisting-conditions clause longer than one year should not be purchased. If possible, you should also avoid buying an individual policy in which an exclusionary rider appears. If you have been treated for certain diseases, such as cancer or heart disease, the insurer may add a rider to the policy that excludes the condition.

As a last resort, if you are uninsurable and cannot obtain either individual or group coverage, you may be eligible for coverage from a state high-risk pool for the uninsurable (see Insight 21.3). The majority of states operate such high-risk pools. Information on enrolling is available from your state insurance department.

Insight 21.2

Cancer Insurance a Controversial Sell

Cancer can strike anyone, regardless of gender, age, or lifestyle. Even athletes in top physical condition can get cancer: Darryl Strawberry and Mario Lemieux, for example. If cancer runs in your family, you might be especially concerned about your risk.

Is Cancer Insurance Right for You?

Here are a few points to keep in mind:

- **What does the policy pay for?** A good policy will pay for such items as hospital stays, medicine, surgery, doctors' visits, radiation treatment, and chemotherapy.
- **Increased benefits after extended hospital stay.** Some policies might promise increased benefits after a lengthy hospital stay (longer than 90 days). [However,] according to the Wisconsin Office of Insurance, the average hospital stay in relation to cancer is 13 days.
- **Are cancer-related illnesses covered?** Cancer, along with its treatments, can lead to other physical problems, such as infections, diabetes, and pneumonia. Most cancer policies do *not* cover treatment for these illnesses.
- **Will travel expenses be covered?** Often, cancer treatments require travel to a hospital hundreds of miles away. Many cancer policies will cover these travel expenses. Some policies will cover not only the travel of the patient, but of others as well.
- **Will your medical policy pay duplicate benefits?** While most cancer insurance policies will pay out even if you're already getting coverage under another policy, the reverse may not be true. Some major medical policies *won't* pay out if you hold other coverage, such as cancer insurance.

Opinions differ on whether or not cancer insurance is a "good buy." "What people need is major medical coverage that protects them against cancer, getting hit by a truck, and everything else," says Bob Hunter, a spokesperson for the Consumer Federation of America. "They also need disability insurance coverage which covers them when they are out of work because they're sick."

Hunter explains that cancer insurance fails one of his two basic tests—tests he feels every consumer should apply to a prospective policy. *The first test: Does the policy cover a major financial catastrophe?* Contracting cancer certainly falls into the category of major financial disaster. With multiple doctor visits, the potential for chemotherapy, and the possibility of extended hospital stays, cancer can be very expensive.

The second test: Does the policy provide comprehensive coverage? Cancer insurance fails Hunter's second test. Cancer insurance is just that: for cancer only. It will not cover you for anything else, such as heart disease, stroke, diabetes, or high blood pressure. One in two men and one in three women may contract cancer during the course of their lives, according to the American Cancer Society. This means one in two men and two in three women *don't* contract cancer.

"Nobody should buy cancer insurance," Hunter concludes. *"It is a totally inappropriate way to buy insurance."*

The Health Insurance Association of America (HIAA) emphasizes that cancer insurance, if purchased, should be viewed as extra coverage on top of what a consumer needs. "Any specialized coverage [such as cancer insurance] is intended to supplement comprehensive health coverage," [says] HIAA spokesperson Richard Coorsh.

The American Cancer Society concurs. In its official statement on cancer insurance, it say, "Cancer insurance is supplemental, not a substitute for comprehensive coverage."

Source: Adapted from "Cancer Insurance a Controversial Sell," *insure.com, The Consumer Insurance Guide,* December 15, 1998.

Insight 21.3

The Last Resort: State High-Risk Pools for the Uninsurable

The majority of states have special high-risk pools that provide health insurance to people who are medically uninsurable. Applicants must show they have been refused health insurance elsewhere before they are accepted. Two eligibility requirements are commonly imposed. First, the applicant must be a resident of the state. Second, the applicant must provide proof of one or more of the following: (1) be rejected by at least one insurer, (2) be presently insured under a plan with a higher premium than the pool premium, (3) be presently insured with a restrictive rider or rated policy, or (4) be offered a policy with a restrictive waiver or rider.

Major medical benefits are typically provided. A calendar-year deductible and 80 to 20 percent coinsurance are common. The plans typically have an annual stop-loss limit that caps annual out-of-pocket expenses.

The insurance is expensive, with maximum rates generally ranging from 125 to 400 percent of individual standard rates. Despite the high premiums, the pools have incurred substantial underwriting losses. Health insurers doing business in a particular state are assessed their pro rata share of excess losses. In many states, the insurers can deduct all or part of the assessments from the state premium taxes paid. General revenue appropriations and taxes on tobacco and cigarettes are also used to fund excess losses in some states.

The major advantage of these pools is that they provide health insurance coverage to the medically uninsurable. The pools, however, are not a viable solution to the national problems of health insurance affordability and accessibility. They have incurred substantial underwriting deficits; the assessment method of funding such deficits is defective since the true cost is hidden and is shifted indirectly to taxpayers through premium tax offsets or to policyowners through higher premiums; only a small fraction of the medically uninsurable have obtained insurance through the pools; and high premiums make the insurance unaffordable to may applicants.

SOURCE: George E. Rejda and Michael J. McNamara, *Personal Financial Planning* (Reading, MA: Addison-Wesley Educational Publishers, 1998), p. 365.

Use Deductibles and Elimination Periods to Reduce Premiums

High-quality individual health insurance coverages are expensive. A comprehensive major medical policy that covers the entire family can cost $6000 to $8000 annually. You can reduce your premiums by purchasing a policy with a substantial deductible. If you can afford it, an annual deductible of $500 or $1000 will substantially reduce your premiums. Likewise, premiums for a disability-income policy can be substantially reduced by buying the policy with a 90-day elimination period.

Finally, you should contact more than one insurer before purchasing a policy. Although price is important, it should not be the only consideration. A low-premium policy may contain restrictive provisions, pay limited benefits, or reflect a restrictive claims policy. Exhibit 21.4 contains a worksheet that will enable you to compare policies. Premium quotes can be conveniently obtained from various Internet sites (see the Internet Resources listings).

SUMMARY

- Individual health insurance policies can generally be classified into the following categories:

  Hospital-surgical insurance

  Major medical insurance

  Long-term care insurance

  Disability-income insurance

- Individual hospital-surgical policies typically cover hospital expenses, surgical expenses, outpatient diagnostic X rays and lab expenses, and physician's in-hospital

EXHIBIT 21.4

Have You Chosen the Best Health Plan? Use This Checklist to Compare

	Plan A	Plan B	Plan C
What it costs:			
Premium (your cost)	_____	_____	_____
Deductible (what you pay before your health plan pays)	_____	_____	_____
Doctor Visit (% you pay)	_____	_____	_____
Pharmacy (per prescription)	_____	_____	_____
Vision	_____	_____	_____
Emergency (% you pay)	_____	_____	_____
Out-of-Area (% you pay or if covered at all)	_____	_____	_____
What it covers:			
Doctor Visits	_____	_____	_____
Outpatient Tests and Procedures	_____	_____	_____
Preventive Care (help control blood pressure, cholesterol, and so on)	_____	_____	_____
Women's Preventive Care (Pap smear, mammography)	_____	_____	_____
Maternity.	_____	_____	_____
Well Baby Care	_____	_____	_____
Physicals (annual)	_____	_____	_____
Hospitalization	_____	_____	_____
Emergency or Urgent Care	_____	_____	_____
Mental Health	_____	_____	_____
Is it convenient?			
Do I have to file claim forms?	_____	_____	_____
Is there toll-free access to a customer service representative?	_____	_____	_____
Does the plan limit access to specialists?	_____	_____	_____
Can I use a specialist as a primary care physician (that is, an OB/GYN)?. . .	_____	_____	_____

SOURCE: Clarkson Hospital. Reprinted with permission from NHS Clarkson Hospital, Omaha, Nebraska.

expenses. Some policies also cover the partial cost of a pregnancy, or maternity benefits can be added as an optional benefit.

- Major medical insurance is designed to cover the expenses of a catastrophic illness or injury. A typical major medical plan has certain characteristics:

> Broad coverage
>
> High maximum limits
>
> Benefit period
>
> Deductible
>
> Coinsurance
>
> Exclusions

- Long-term care insurance pays a daily or monthly benefit for medical or custodial care in a nursing facility or at home.

- Disability-income policies provide for the periodic payment of income to an individual who is totally disabled. The benefits are paid after an elimination period is satisfied. The insured generally has a choice of benefit periods. In addition, after 90 days, all premiums are waived if the insured is totally disabled.

- The definition of disability is stated in a disability-income policy. For the first two years, total disability is typically defined as the inability to perform all duties of the insured's own occupation. After that time, total disability is defined as the inability to perform the duties of any occupation for which the insured is reasonably fitted by education, training, and experience.

- A renewal provision refers to the length of time that an individual medical expense policy can remain in force. Renewal provisions include the following:

    Optionally renewable

    Guaranteed renewable

    Noncancellable

- Health insurance policies contain certain contractual provisions. Some provisions are required by state law, while others are optional.

- Consumer experts recommend certain rules to follow when health insurance is purchased:

    Insure for the catastrophic loss.

    Consider group insurance first.

    Use preferred providers whenever possible.

    Don't ignore disability-income insurance.

    Avoid limited policies.

    Watch out for restrictive policy provisions and exclusions.

    Use deductibles and elimination periods to reduce premiums.

KEY CONCEPTS AND TERMS

Accident-only policy
Activities of daily living (ADLs)
Benefit period
Calendar-year deductible
Cancer policy
Coinsurance provision
Common-accident provision
Disability-income insurance
Elimination (waiting) period
Exclusionary rider
Family deductible
Gatekeeper provisions
Grace period
Guaranteed renewable policy
Hospital indemnity policy
Hospital-surgical insurance plan
Indemnity plan
Internal limits
Limited policy
Long-term care insurance
Major medical insurance
Noncancellable policy
Optionally renewable policy
Partial disability
Preexisting-conditions clause
Preferred provider
Reasonable and customary charges
Reinstatement provision
Relative-value schedule
Residual disability
Schedule approach
Service benefits
Stop-loss limit
Time limit on certain defenses
Total disability
Waiver of premium

REVIEW QUESTIONS

1. Describe the benefits that are typically included in a hospital-surgical insurance policy.

2. Explain the basic characteristics of a major medical policy. Why are deductibles and coinsurance used in a major medical policy?

3. Describe the various types of deductibles that may be found in major medical policies.

4. Briefly describe the characteristics of long-term care insurance.

5. Explain the major features of a disability-income policy.

6. Explain the various definitions of total disability that are found in individual disability-income contracts.

7. Explain the meaning of partial disability and residual disability in a disability-income policy.

8. Identify the options that can be added to a disability-income policy.

9. Describe the basic types of renewal provisions in individual health insurance policies.

10. Briefly describe the following clauses:
    a. Preexisting conditions
    b. Time limit on certain defenses

APPLICATION QUESTIONS

1. Explain the major differences between a typical individual hospital-surgical insurance policy and an individual major medical policy with respect to each of the following:
    a. Use of a surgical schedule
    b. Use of deductibles
    c. Benefit limits

2. George and Lu and their two daughters, Kelly and Karen, are insured under an individual major medical policy. The policy contains a $500 deductible that applies to each covered person, a common accident provision, and an 80 percent coinsurance provision.

   a. Lu had gallbladder surgery and incurred covered medical expenses of $9300. How much of the loss will be paid by the insurance company? Show your calculations.

   b. George, Kelly, and Karen were injured in the same bobsledding accident. Covered medical expenses were $1500 for George, $900 for Kelly, and $600 for Karen. How much of the total loss will be paid by the insurance company? Show your calculations.

3. Mark is insured under an individual major medical insurance policy. The plan has a calendar-year deductible of $300, 80-20 percent coinsurance, and a stop-limit of $2000. Mark recently had an appendectomy operation and incurred the following medical expenses:

Outpatient diagnostic tests	$ 700
Hospital expenses	18,000

Surgeon's fee	1500
Prescription drugs outside of the hospital	100

In addition, Mark could not work for four weeks and lost $2000 in earnings.

   a. Based on the above information, how much of the loss will be paid by the insurance company? Show your calculations.

   b. If Mark's policy did not have a stop-loss limit, how much would the insurance company pay? Show your calculations.

4. If you are shopping for an individual health insurance policy, what important factors should you consider? Explain your answer.

SELECTED REFERENCES

Black, Kenneth, Jr., and Harold D. Skipper, Jr. *Life Insurance*, thirteenth edition. Upper Saddle River, NJ: Prentice-Hall, 2000, Chapters 7, 9, 10.

Case Application

Lorri, age 28, is a registered nurse who earns $3000 monthly in a hospital. She is seriously injured in an automobile accident in which she is at fault and is expected to be off work for at least one year. She has a guaranteed renewable disability-income policy that pays $1800 monthly up to age 65 for accidents and sickness after a 90-day elimination period. A residual disability benefit is included in the policy. Lorri's policy contains the following provisions:

Total disability means: (a) your inability during the first 24 months to perform substantially all of the important duties of your occupation; and you are not working at any gainful occupation; (b) after the first 24 months that benefits are payable, it means your inability to engage in any gainful occupation.

Gainful occupation means: Any occupation or employment for wage or profit that is reasonably consistent with your education, training, and experience.

   a. If Lorri is off work for one year because of the accident, indicate the extent, if any, of the insurer's obligation to pay disability benefits.

   b. Assume that Lorri is disabled for one year, recovers, and returns to work part-time. If she earns $1500 monthly after returning to work, indicate the extent, if any, of the insurer's obligation to pay her disability benefits.

   c. Assume that after two years, Lorri is unable to return to work as a full-time hospital nurse. A drug manufacturer offers her a job as a lab technician, which she accepts. Indicate the extent, if any, of the insurer's obligation to pay her disability benefits.

   d. Following the accident, could Lorri's insurer cancel her policy or increase her premiums? Explain your answer.

Graves, Edward E., ed. *McGill's Life Insurance*, second editon. Bryn Mawr, PA: The American College, 1998, Chapters 7, 8.

Health Insurance Association of America. *Fundamentals of Health Insurance*, Part A and Part B. Washington, DC: Health Insurance Association of America, 1997.

Health Insurance Association of America. *Guide to Disability Income Insurance*. Washington, DC: Health Insurance Association of America, April 1997.

Health Insurance Association of America. *Guide to Health Insurance*. Washington, DC: Health Insurance Association of America, April 1997.

Health Insurance Association of America. *Source Book of Health Insurance Data, 1999–2000*. Washington, DC: Health Insurance Association of America, 2000.

Rejda, George E., Constance M. Luthardt, Cheryl L. Ferguson, and Donald P. Oakes. *Personal Insurance*. fourth edition. Malvern, PA: Insurance Institute of America, 2000.

Rejda, George E. "Problem of Poor Health," in *Social Insurance and Economic Security*, sixth edition. Upper Saddle River, NJ: Prentice-Hall, 1999, Chapter 8.

Sadler, Jeff. *Disability Income: The Sale, the Product, the Market*, second edition. Cincinnati, OH: National Underwriter Company, 1995.

NOTES

1. This section is based on George E. Rejda, *Social Insurance and Economic Security*, sixth edition. (Upper Saddle River, NJ: Prentice-Hall, 1999), pp. 170–181.

2. Health Care Financing Administration, *National Health Expenditures Projections: 1998–2008*, July 12, 1999.

3. *Ibid.*

4. U.S. Bureau of the Census, *Health Insurance Coverage 1998, Current Population Reports*, P60-208, Washington, DC (October 1999), p. 1.

5. George E. Rejda, *Social Insurance and Economic Security*, pp. 180–181.

6. *A Shopper's Guide to Long-Term Care Insurance* (Kansas City, MO: National Association of Insurance Commissioners, 1996), p. 6.

7. *Ibid.*

8. *Ibid.*, p. 11.

9. Kenneth Black, Jr., and Harold D. Skipper, Jr., *Life Insurance*, thirteenth edition (Upper Saddle River, NJ: Prentice-Hall, 2000), pp. 157–158.

10. Edward E. Graves, *McGill's Life Insurance*, p. 181.

11. *Ibid.*, Table 7-4, p. 170.

12. *Fundamentals of Health Insurance*, Part A (Washington, DC: Health Insurance Association of America, 1997), pp. 111–112.

13. George E. Rejda, *Social Insurance and Economic Security*, p. 169.

Chapter 22

Employee Benefits: Group Life and Health Insurance

> *" Employee benefits constitute a major part of every individual's financial and economic security. "*
>
> Jerry S. Rosenbloom
> *The Handbook of Employee Benefits*, 4th ed.

Learning Objectives

After studying this chapter, you should be able to:

▲ Explain the underwriting principles followed in group insurance.

▲ Describe the basic characteristics of group term life insurance.

▲ Explain the major characteristics of the following group health insurance coverages:
   Basic medical expense insurance
   Major medical insurance
   Dental insurance
   Short-term disability-income insurance
   Long-term disability-income insurance

▲ Explain the meaning of "managed care" and describe the characteristics of the following managed care plans:
   Health maintenance organizations (HMOs)
   Preferred provider organizations (PPOs)

▲ Describe the characteristics of cafeteria plans.

▲ Access an Internet site and obtain consumer information about HMOs and other managed care plans.

Internet Resources

- **Blue Cross and Blue Shield** plans are nonprofit corporations that provide medical, hospital, and surgical benefits to plan members in specific geographical areas. The various plans account for a substantial portion of the group health insurance market. Visit the site at:

  http://www.bluecares.com/

- The **Employee Benefit Research Institute (EBRI)** is a nonprofit organization devoted exclusively to the dissemination of data, policy research, and education on economic security and employee benefits. Visit the site at:

  http://www.ebri.org/

- The **International Foundation of Employee Benefit Plans** is a nonprofit educational organization that provides programs, publications, and research studies to individuals in the employee benefits field. The organization cosponsors the professional Certified Employee Benefit Specialist (CEBS) program. Visit the site at:

  http://www.ifebp.org/

- The **Health Care Financing Administration (HCFA)**, which is part of the U.S. Department of Health and Human Service, administers the Medicare program. HCFA provides timely information on Medicare, Medicaid, health care expenditures, and medical expenses incurred by the elderly. Visit the site at:

  http://www.hcfa.gov/

- The **Health Insurance Association of America** is a major source of health insurance information for consumers. The organization is responsible for public relations, government relations, and research on behalf of the private health insurance industry. Visit the site at:

  http://www.hiaa.org/

- The **National Center for Health Statistics (NCHS)** is part of the Centers for Disease Control and Prevention, U.S. Department of Health and Human Services. NCHS provides data on health status, lifestyles and exposure to unhealthy influences, the onset and diagnosis of illness and disability, and the use of health care. Visit the site at:

  http://www.cdc.gov/nchs/

*E*mployee benefits are very important in a personal risk management program. Employee benefits are employer-sponsored plans that pay benefits if a worker dies, becomes sick or disabled, or retires. The various benefits provide considerable financial security to employees and their families. They are also important in calculating total employee compensation. Although the starting salaries in many companies may be relatively low, generous employee benefits can substantially increase employees' total compensation packages. For example, Amy, age 22, is an English major who graduated from college and accepted an entry-level job with a national book publisher at an annual salary of $23,000. However, when employer contributions for life insurance, health and dental insurance, retirement, vacation, and other benefits are factored in, Amy's total annual compensation increases substantially to $28,000—an increase of about 22 percent.*

This chapter is the first of two chapters dealing with employee benefit plans. Chapter 22 is limited to employer-sponsored group life and health insurance plans. Retirement plans are discussed in Chapter 23. Topics discussed in this chapter include group life insurance, medical expense plans, dental insurance, disability-income plans, and the Health Insurance Portability and Accountability Act. The chapter concludes with a discussion of cafeteria plans.

GROUP INSURANCE

Group insurance differs from individual insurance in several respects. A distinctive characteristic is the coverage of many persons under one contract. A **master contract** is formed between the insurer and the group policyowner for the benefit of the individual members. In most plans, the group policyowner is the employer. Employees receive a certificate of insurance that shows they are insured.

A second characteristic is that group insurance usually costs less than comparable insurance purchased individually. Employers usually pay part or all of the cost, which reduces or eliminates premium payments by the employees. In addition, administrative and marketing expenses are reduced as a result of mass distribution methods.

Another characteristic is that individual evidence of insurability is usually not required. Group selection of risks is used, not individual selection. The insurer is concerned with the insurability of the group as a whole rather than with the insurability of any single member within the group.

Finally, **experience rating** is used in group insurance plans. If the group is sufficiently large, the actual loss experience of the group is a major factor in determining the premiums charged.

Basic Underwriting Principles

Because individual evidence of insurability is usually not required, group insurers must observe certain underwriting principles so that the loss experience of the group is favorable. These principles are as follows:[1]

- Insurance incidental to the group
- Flow of persons through the group
- Automatic determination of benefits
- Minimum participation requirements
- Third-party sharing of cost
- Simple and efficient administration

Insurance Incidental to the Group Insurance must be incidental to the group; that is, the group should not be formed for the sole purpose of obtaining insurance. This requirement is necessary to reduce adverse selection against the insurer. If the group is formed for the specific purpose of obtaining insurance, a disproportionate number of unhealthy persons would join the group to obtain low-cost insurance, and the loss experience would be unfavorable.

Flow of Persons Through the Group Ideally, there should be a flow of younger persons into the group and a flow of older persons out of the group. Without a flow of younger persons into the group, the average age of the group will increase, and premium rates will likewise increase. Higher premiums may cause some younger and healthier members to drop out of the plan, while the older and unhealthy members will still remain, which would lead to still higher losses and increased rates. However, turnover of employees should not be so significant that administrative costs are high.

Automatic Determination of Benefits Benefits should be automatically determined by some formula that precludes individual selection of insurance amounts. The amount of insurance can be based on earnings, position, length of service, or some combination of these factors. *The purpose of this requirement is to reduce adverse selection against the insurer.* If individual members were permitted to select the amount of insurance, unhealthy persons would select larger amounts, while healthier persons would be likely to select smaller amounts. The result would be a disproportionate amount of insurance on the impaired lives. However, many group insurance plans allow employees to select their own benefit levels up to certain maximum limits. If additional amounts of insurance are desired above the maximum allowed, evidence of insurability is usually required.

Minimum Participation Requirements A minimum percentage of the eligible employees must participate in the plan. If the plan is a **noncontributory plan**, the premiums are paid entirely by the employer, and 100 percent of the eligible employees must be covered. If the plan is a **contributory plan**, the employee pays part of the cost and a large proportion of the eligible employees must elect to participate in the plan. In a contributory plan, it may be difficult to get 100 percent participation, so a lower percentage such as 50 to 75 percent is typically required.

There are two reasons for the minimum participation requirement. First, if a large proportion of eligible employees participate, adverse selection is reduced, because the possibility of insuring a large proportion of unhealthy lives is reduced. Second, if a high proportion of eligible members participate, the expense rate per insured member or per unit of insurance can be reduced.

Third-Party Sharing of Cost Ideally, individual members should not pay the entire cost of their protection. In most groups, the employer pays part of the cost. A third-party sharing of cost avoids the problem of a substantial increase in premiums for older members. In a plan in which the members pay the entire cost, younger persons help pay for the insurance provided to older persons. Once they become aware of this fact, some younger persons may drop out of the plan and obtain their insurance more cheaply elsewhere. Older unhealthy members will still remain, causing premiums to increase even more. However, if the employer absorbs any increase in premiums because of adverse mortality experience, premiums paid by the employees can be kept fairly stable. In addition, a third-party sharing of cost makes the plan more attractive to individual members and encourages greater participation in the plan.

Simple and Efficient Administration The group plan should be simple and efficiently administered. Premiums are collected from the employees by payroll deduction, which reduces the insurer's administrative expenses and keeps participation in the plan high.

Eligibility Requirements in Group Insurance

Insurers typically require that certain eligibility requirements must be satisfied before the insurance is in force. The eligibility requirements generally are designed to reduce adverse selection against the insurer.

Eligible Groups Types of groups eligible for group insurance are determined by insurance company policy and state law. Eligible groups include individual employer groups, multiple-employer groups, labor unions, creditor-debtor groups, and miscellaneous groups, such as fraternities and sororities.

Group insurers usually require the group to be a certain size before the group is insured. Traditionally, this size was ten lives, but some insurers now insure groups with as few as two or three members. There are two reasons for a minimum-size requirement. First, the insurer has some protection against insuring a group that consists largely of substandard individuals, so that the financial impact of one impaired life on the loss experience of the group is reduced. Second, certain fixed expenses must be met regardless of the size of the group. The larger the group, the broader the base over which these expenses can be spread, and the lower the expense rate per unit of insurance.

Eligibility Requirements Before employees can participate in a group insurance plan, they must meet certain eligibility requirements, including the following:

- Be full-time employees
- Satisfy a probationary period
- Apply for insurance during the eligibility period
- Be actively at work

Employers generally require the workers to be employed full-time before they can participate in the plan. A **full-time worker** is one who works the required number of hours established by the employer as a normal work week, which must be at least 30 hours. However, some group plans today permit part-time workers to be covered. In some group insurance plans, new employees may have to satisfy a **probationary period**, which is a period of one to six months, before he or she can participate in the plan. The purpose of the probationary period is to eliminate transient workers who will be with the firm for only a short period. It is administratively expensive to maintain records and insure workers who will not be working permanently for the firm.

After the probationary period (if any) expires, the employee is eligible to participate in the plan. However, if the plan is contributory, the employee must request coverage either before or during the eligibility period. The **eligibility period** is a period of time—typically 31 days—during which the employee can sign up for the insurance without furnishing evidence of insurability.

Finally, the employee must be **actively at work** on the day the insurance becomes effective. The employee who is actively at work is presumably meeting certain minimum health standards, which also gives the insurer some protection against adverse selection.

GROUP LIFE INSURANCE PLANS

Group life insurance is a popular and relatively inexpensive employee benefit. At the end of 1998, $5.7 trillion of group life insurance was in force, which accounted for 40 percent of the total life insurance in force in the United States.[2]

The major types of group life insurance plans are the following:

- Group term life insurance
- Group accidental death and dismemberment insurance (AD&D)
- Group universal life insurance

Group Term Life Insurance

Group term life insurance is the most important form of group life insurance. More than 90 percent of the group life insurance in force is group term life insurance. The insurance provided is **yearly renewable term insurance**, which provides low-cost protection to the employees during their working careers.

The amount of term insurance on an employee's life is typically one to five times the annual salary or earnings. The term insurance remains in force as long as the employee is part of the group. If the employee quits or is laid off, he or she has the right to convert the group term insurance to an individual cash-value policy within 31 days without evidence of insurability. However, the group term insurance normally cannot be converted into an individual term insurance policy.[3] As a practical matter, relatively few employees convert their group insurance because of the problem of cost and because group insurance will probably be provided by another employer. Those employees who do convert are usually substandard in health or uninsurable, which results in strong adverse selection against the insurer.

Most group plans allow a modest amount of life insurance to be written on the employee's spouse and dependent children. Because of state law and tax considerations, the amount of dependent life insurance is relatively low. The insurance on the spouse's life can be converted to an individual cash-value policy. Some states require that the conversion option should also apply to the insurance on the children.

Most employers provide a reduced amount of term insurance on retired employees. The amount of insurance may be a flat amount, such as $10,000, or it may be a percentage of the amount of insurance at the date of retirement, such as 50 percent.

Group term insurance has the major advantage of providing low-cost protection to employees that can be used to supplement individual life insurance policies. However, it has two major disadvantages. First, the insurance is temporary and terminates when the individual is no longer part of the group. Second, it is expensive for an older worker to convert to an individual policy after retirement.

Finally, group term life insurance is used by commercial banks and other lending institutions to insure the lives of debtors. Credit life insurance provides for the cancellation of any outstanding debt if the borrower dies. The lending institution is both the policyowner and beneficiary. The unpaid balance of the loan is paid to the creditor at the debtor's death. Many financial planners do not recommend the purchase of credit life insurance because of excessive rates. Although the rates are regulated by the states, some debtors are overcharged for their protection, because term insurance can often be purchased more cheaply on an individual basis.

Group Accidental Death and Dismemberment Insurance

Many group life insurance plans also provide **group accidental death and dismemberment (AD&D) insurance** that pays additional benefits if the employee dies in an accident or incurs certain types of bodily injury. The AD&D benefit is some multiple of the group life insurance benefit, such as one or two times the insurance on the employee's life. The full AD&D benefit, called the **principal sum**, is paid if the employee dies in an accident. In addition, a percentage of the principal sum is paid for certain types of dismemberments, such as one-half the principal sum for the loss of a hand, foot, or eye because of accidental bodily injury.

Many plans also make available **voluntary accidental death and dismemberment insurance** in which employees can voluntarily purchase additional amounts of AD&D insurance. The employees normally pay the entire cost of the voluntary coverage.

Group Universal Life Insurance

In addition to group term life insurance, some employers make available **group universal life insurance** for their employees. These plans are similar to individual universal life insurance policies, but have some important differences. The major characteristics of group universal life plans are summarized as follows:[4]

1. *Plan design.* Two approaches are used in the plan design. Under the first approach, there is only one plan. The employee who wants only term insurance pays only the mortality and expense charges. The employee who wants to accumulate cash values must pay higher premiums. Under the second approach, two plans are used—term insurance and universal life insurance. The employee who wants only term insurance pays into the term insurance plan. The employee who wants universal life insurance must pay higher premiums so that cash values are accumulated. The employee may be required to pay initial premiums equal to two or three times the cost of the pure insurance protection.

2. *Amount of insurance.* Universal life insurance is issued on a guaranteed basis up to certain limits with no evidence of insurability. Employees generally select the amount of guaranteed coverage equal to some multiple of their salaries, such as one to five times their annual salary. Higher amounts of insurance require evidence of insurability, usually based on a simplified medical questionnaire.

3. *Mortality and expense charges.* Most group universal life plans have guaranteed mortality charges for three years; after that time, the group is experience-rated. Expense charges must also be paid. These charges are generally lower than the expenses assessed against individual policies. Finally, there is a minimum interest rate guarantee on the cash values, such as 4 or 4½ percent; higher current rates are paid that change over time, such as 5½ or 6 percent.

4. *Premium flexibility.* Premiums can be reduced, increased, or even eliminated if the cash value is sufficient to pay current mortality and expense charges.

5. *Loans and withdrawals.* Employees can make policy loans and withdrawals. The loan or withdrawal amount must be at least equal to a certain minimum amount, such as $250 or $500. The policy loan rate usually is based on some index, such as Moody's composite bond yield. Interest credited to the cash values on the amounts borrowed is also reduced, such as 2 percent less than Moody's composite bond yield.

6. *Options at retirement.* The retired employee has the option of continuing the universal life coverage, and the insurer bills the retired employee directly. The employee also has the option of terminating the coverage and withdrawing the cash value; electing a settlement option for liquidation of the cash value in the form of annuity income; or decreasing the amount of pure insurance so that the cash value is sufficient to keep the policy in force with no additional premiums required.

7. *Dependent coverage.* A term insurance rider can be added to cover dependents, such as $10,000 to $50,000 on the spouse and $5000 to $10,000 on each child.

GROUP MEDICAL EXPENSE INSURANCE

Group medical expense insurance is an employee benefit that pays the cost of hospital care, physicians' and surgeons' fees, and related medical expenses. These plans are extremely important in providing financial security to employees and their families. Group plans currently account for more than 90 percent of the total premiums paid for medical expense insurance.

Group medical expense insurance is available from a number of sources. Major sources include the following:

- Commercial insurers
- Blue Cross and Blue Shield plans
- Health maintenance organizations
- Self-insured plans by employers

Commercial Insurers

Commercial life and health insurers sell both individual and group medical expense plans. Some property and casualty insurers also sell medical expense coverages. Most individuals and families insured by commercial insurers are covered under group plans. The business is highly concentrated. Most of the business is written by a small number of insurers

Commercial insurers also sponsor managed care plans that provide benefits to members in a cost-effective manner, including health maintenance organizations (HMOs) and preferred provider organizations (PPOs). Managed care plans are discussed in greater detail later in the chapter.

Blue Cross and Blue Shield Plans

Blue Cross and Blue Shield plans are medical expense plans that cover hospital expenses, physician's and surgeon's fees, ancillary charges, and other medical expenses. Major medical insurance is also available. The various plans sell individual, family, and group coverages. Most insureds are covered by group plans.

Blue Cross plans cover hospital expenses and other related expenses. The plans typically provide **service benefits** rather than cash benefits to the insured. Blue Cross plans usually pay the full cost of a semiprivate room, and payment is made directly to the hospital rather than to the insured.

Blue Shield plans cover physicians' and surgeons' fees and related medical expenses. Most plans today write both Blue Cross and Blue Shield coverages. In early 1997, 49 joint plans were in existence that wrote both Blue Cross and Blue Shield coverages. Six separate Blue Cross plans and four separate Blue Shield plans were also in existence. The joint plans offer both basic medical expense benefits and major medical insurance. Finally, like commercial insurers, Blue Cross and Blue Shield plans also sponsor managed care plans, including HMOs and PPOs.

In the majority of states, Blue Cross and Blue Shield plans are nonprofit organizations that receive favorable tax treatment and are regulated under special legislation. However, to raise capital and become more competitive, a few Blue Cross and Blue Shield plans have recently converted to a for-profit status with stockholders and a board of directors. In addition, many nonprofit plans own profit-seeking affiliates. Blue Cross and Blue Shield plans are discussed in greater detail in Chapter 25.

Health Maintenance Organizations

Health maintenance organizations (HMOs) are managed care plans that provide broad, comprehensive health care services to the members for a fixed, prepaid fee. There is heavy emphasis on controlling costs, and the care provided by physicians is carefully monitored. HMOs are discussed in greater detail later in the chapter.

Self-insured Plans by Employers

Many employers self-insure part or all of the health insurance benefits provided to their employees. **Self-insurance** (also called **self-funding**) *means that the employer pays part or all of the cost of providing health insurance to the employees.*

Self-insured plans are usually established with stop-loss insurance and an administrative services only (ASO) contract. **Stop-loss insurance** *means that a commercial insurer will pay claims that exceed a certain dollar amount up to some maximum limit.* This arrangement protects employees when claims exceed a center level.

An **ASO contract** *is a contract between an employer and a commercial insurer (or other third party) in which the insurer provides only administrative services.* These services can include plan design, claims processing, actuarial support, and record keeping.

Employers self-insure their medical expense plans for several reasons, including the following:

- Under the Employee Retirement Income Security Act of 1974 (ERISA), self-insured plans generally are not subject to state regulation. Thus, a national employer does not have to comply with separate state laws.
- Costs may be reduced or increase less rapidly because of savings in state premium taxes, commissions, and the insurer's profit.
- The employer retains part or all of the funds needed to pay claims and earns interest until the claims are paid.
- Self-insured plans are exempt from state laws that require insured plans to offer certain state-mandated benefits.

TYPES OF GROUP MEDICAL EXPENSE PLANS

Group medical expense plans have changed rapidly over time. Older plans were often called **traditional** group indemnity plans or fee-for-service plans. These plans permitted insureds considerable freedom in selecting their own physicians and other health care providers; the plans paid cash indemnity benefits for covered services up to certain maximum limits; and cost containment was not heavily stressed. It should be noted, however, that newer group indemnity plans have several cost-containment provisions, such as preadmission certification by which a covered person must be approved for admission into a hospital and second surgical opinions.

Two types of traditional group indemnity plans that merit some discussion are (1) basic medical expense insurance and (2) major medical insurance.

Basic Medical Expense Insurance

Basic medical expense insurance *is a generic name for group plans that provide only basic benefits.* The benefits are sufficient to pay routine medical expenses but generally are not designed to cover a catastrophic loss. Group basic medical expense plans typically provide the following benefits:

- Hospital expense insurance
- Surgical expense insurance
- Physicians' visits
- Miscellaneous benefits

Hospital expense insurance covers medical expenses incurred while in a hospital. Some older indemnity plans pay actual room and board charges up to some stated maximum, such as $500 per day. Newer plans typically pay service benefits in which the full cost of a semiprivate room is paid if the employee is hospitalized. In addition to daily room and board benefits, most new plans provide full payment (generally up to some maximum dollar amount) for miscellaneous hospital charges, such as drugs, X rays, and operating room charges.

Surgical expense insurance is usually included in a basic plan to help pay surgeons' and physicians' fees for surgical operations. Several methods are used to compensate surgeons. Older plans may use a schedule approach in which the various surgical operations are listed in a schedule, and a maximum dollar amount is specified for each procedure. A variation of the schedule approach is a relative-value schedule in which units or points are assigned to each operation based on the degree of difficulty. A

conversion factor is then used to convert the relative value of the operation into a specific dollar amount paid to the physician.

Newer plans typically reimburse physicians on the basis of their reasonable and customary charges. A physician is paid his or her usual fee as long as it is considered reasonable and customary. Many insurers consider a fee to be reasonable and customary if it does not exceed the 85th or 90th percentile amount for a similar medical procedure performed by other physicians in the same area. However, insurers differ in how usual and customary fees are calculated. As a result, patients often must pay substantial amounts out-of-pocket because of "balance billing" by physicians for the remainder of the fee not paid by insurance.

Group basic medical expense plans also provide benefits for physicians' visits other than for surgery. Most plans cover physicians' visits only while the employee is hospitalized, but some plans cover office or home visits as well. The amount paid can be a fixed amount, or it can be based on the physician's reasonable and customary charges.

Finally, basic plans provide a wide variety of miscellaneous benefits. Depending on the plan, basic benefits may cover home health care visits by medical specialists, extended-care facility benefits, radiation therapy, diagnostic X rays, CAT scans and magnetic resonance imaging (MRI), and supplemental accident benefits.

Major Medical Insurance

Many employers also provide major medical insurance for their employees. Major medical insurance can be written as a supplement to a basic medical expense plan, or it can be combined with a basic plan to form a comprehensive major medical policy.

Supplemental Major Medical Insurance Supplemental major medical insurance *is designed to supplement the benefits provided by a basic plan.* Some medical expenses are not covered under a basic plan, or the benefits paid may be exhausted under the basic plan. Medical expenses not covered under a basic plan may be eligible for reimbursement under the supplemental major medical plan.

Supplemental major medical insurance plans have characteristics similar to the individual major medical policies described in Chapter 21, but the benefits have much higher limits and are more comprehensive.

Most supplemental major medical plans have high lifetime limits that typically range from $250,000 to $2 million. A few plans have no limits. These high limits reflect the rapid increase in medical costs over time.

A **coinsurance provision** of 80 percent is typically found in supplemental major medical plans. However, the coinsurance provision is modified by a **stop-loss limit**, which places a dollar limit on the maximum amount that an individual must pay. Under a stop-loss provision, once the individual's out-of-pocket expenses exceed a certain amount, such as $2000, all remaining eligible medical expenses are paid in full.

A corridor deductible may be used to integrate a basic medical expense plan with a supplemental major medical plan. Before the supplemental major medical plan pays any benefits, a corridor deductible must be met. A **corridor deductible** *applies only to eligible medical expenses not covered by the basic medical expense plan.* As noted earlier, some medical expenses are not covered under a basic plan, or the expenses may be covered but the benefits paid by the basic plan are exhausted. These expenses may be eligible for reimbursement under the supplemental major medical plan, subject to a corridor deductible. This type of deductible can be illustrated by the following example:

Total medical expenses	$30,000
Paid by basic medical expense plan	20,000
Remaining medical expenses	$10,000
Corridor deductible paid by the insured	200
Balance of medical expenses to be paid	$9800
80 percent paid by supplemental major medical plan	7840
20 percent paid by the insured	$1960

Comprehensive Major Medical Insurance Many employers have comprehensive major medical plans for their employees. **Comprehensive major medical insurance** *is a combination of basic benefits and major medical insurance in one policy.* This type of plan is widely used by employers who want both basic benefits and major medical protection in a single policy. This type of plan is characterized by a deductible, such as $200 or $300 per year, by high maximum limits of $250,000 to $2 million or higher limits, and by coinsurance. In addition, the deductible and coinsurance provisions may not be applied to certain medical expenses. For example, in one plan, the deductible does not apply to hospital expenses. The first $3000 of covered hospital expenses are paid in full, and a coinsurance rate of 80 percent is applied to the remaining hospital expenses.

A **calendar-year deductible** is widely used in comprehensive major medical plans. The deductible has to be met only once during the calendar year. All covered medical expenses incurred by the insured during the year can be used to satisfy the deductible.

The deductible applies separately to the employee and each family member. However, to minimize the financial impact on the family, the major medical plan may contain a **family deductible provision.** Under this provision, additional deductibles for family members are waived if two or three separate deductibles have been satisfied by individual family members during the year.

MANAGED CARE PLANS

Traditional group indemnity plans have declined in importance because of the rapid growth in managed care plans. Employers and insurers have designed new types of managed care plans to hold down the escalation in health care costs. **Managed care** *is a generic name for medical expense plans that provide covered services to the members in a cost-effective manner.* Under such plans, the employees' choice of physicians and hospitals may be limited to certain health care providers; cost control and cost reduction are heavily emphasized; utilization review is done at all levels; the quality of the care provided by physicians is carefully monitored and evaluated; health care providers share in the financial results through various risk-sharing techniques; and preventive care and healthy lifestyles are emphasized. Managed care plans have grown rapidly over time. The proportion of workers covered by some type of managed care plan increased from 58 percent in 1993 to over 85 percent at the beginning of 1998.[5]

There are several types of managed care plans. The most important include the following:

- Health maintenance organizations (HMOs)
- Preferred provider organizations (PPOs)
- Exclusive provider organizations (EPOs)
- Point-of-service (POS) plans

Health Maintenance Organizations

A **health maintenance organization (HMO)** *is an organized system of health care that provides comprehensive services to its members for a fixed, prepaid fee.* HMOs account for a significant share of the group health insurance market. In 1999, enrollments in HMOs accounted for 30 percent of all employee enrollments in health insurance (see Exhibit 22.1).

Basic Characteristics HMOs have a number of basic characteristics. *First, the HMO has the responsibility for organizing and delivering comprehensive health services to its members.* The HMO owns or leases medical facilities, enters into agreements with hospitals and physicians to provide medical services, hires ancillary personnel, and has general managerial control over the various services provided.

Second, an HMO provides broad, comprehensive health services to the members. Most services are covered in full, with relatively few maximum limits on individual services. However, many HMOs will limit the amount paid for the treatment of alcoholism and drug addiction. Covered services typically include the full cost of hospital care, surgeons' and physicians' fees, maternity care, laboratory and X ray services, outpatient services, special-duty nursing, and numerous other services. Office visits to HMO physicians are also covered, either in full or at a nominal charge for each visit.

Third, selection of a physician is usually limited to physicians who are affiliated with the HMO. However, as will be discussed later, some newer HMOs allow insureds to select any physician at higher out-of-pocket costs. In addition, because HMOs operate in a limited geographical area, there may be limited coverage for treatment received

EXHIBIT 22.1

National Employee Enrollment in Health Insurance Plans, 1993–1999

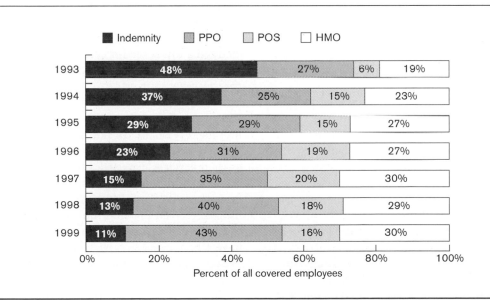

SOURCE: William M. Mercer, Incorporated.

outside of the area. HMOs typically cover only emergency medical treatment received outside of the geographical area of the HMO.

Fourth, HMO members pay a fixed, prepaid fee (usually paid monthly) for the medical services provided. High deductibles and coinsurance requirements are usually not emphasized. However, many HMOs now require co-payments for certain diseases, such as alcoholism or drug addiction. There may also be a nominal fee for certain services, such as $10 for an office visit or $10 for a prescription drug.

In addition, there is heavy emphasis on controlling costs. HMOs typically pay network physicians or medical groups a **capitation fee**, which is a fixed annual amount for each plan member regardless of the number of services provided. Some HMOs pay physicians a salary, which holds down costs because the provider has no financial incentive to provide unnecessary services. HMOs also enter into contracts with specialists and other providers to provide certain services at negotiated fees. In addition, access to an expensive specialist is controlled by a gatekeeper physician. A **gatekeeper physician** is a primary care physician whether medical care from a specialist is necessary. However, some HMOs now allow patients to bypass the primary care physician and see a specialist directly. Finally, HMOs emphasize preventive care and healthy lifestyles, which also hold down costs.

Types of HMOs There are several types of HMOs. Under a **staff model**, physicians are employees of the HMO and are paid a salary and possibly an incentive bonus to hold down costs.

Under a **group model**, physicians are employees of another group that has a contract with the HMO to provide medical services to its members. The HMO pays the group of physicians a monthly or annual capitation fee for each member. As stated earlier, a capitation fee is a fixed amount for each member regardless of the number of services provided. In return, the group agrees to provide all covered services to the members during the year. The group model typically has a closed panel of physicians that requires members to select physicians affiliated with the HMO.

Under a **network model**, the HMO contracts with two or more independent group practices to provide medical services to covered members. The HMO pays a fixed monthly fee for each member to the medical group. The medical group then decides how the fees will be distributed among the individual physicians.

A final type of HMO is an **individual practice association plan (IPA)**. An IPA is an open panel of physicians who work out of their own offices and treat patients on a fee-for-service basis. However, the individual physicians agree to treat HMO members at reduced fees. Physicians may be paid a capitation fee for each member or may be paid a reduced fee. For example, they may be paid only 90 percent of their usual fee for an office visit. In addition, to encourage cost containment, most IPAs have risk-sharing agreements with the participating physicians. Payments may be reduced if the plan experience is poor. A bonus is paid if the plan experience is better than expected.

Preferred Provider Organizations

A **preferred provider organization (PPO)** is a plan that contracts with health care providers to provide medical services to the members at reduced fees. The employer, insurer, or other group negotiates contracts with physicians, hospitals, and other providers of care to provide certain medical services to the plan members at discounted fees. To encourage patients to use PPO providers, deductibles and co-payment charges are reduced. In addition, the patient may be charged a lower fee for certain routine treatments, or offered increased benefits such as preventive health care services.

PPOs should not be confused with HMOs. There are two important differences.[6] First, PPO providers typically do not provide medical care on a prepaid basis, but are paid on a fee-for-service basis as their services are used. However, as stated earlier, the fees charged are below the provider's regular fee. Second, unlike an HMO, patients are not required to use a preferred provider but have freedom of choice every time they need care. However, the patients have a financial incentive to use a preferred provider because the deductible and co-payment charges are reduced.

PPOs offer the major advantage of controlling health care costs because provider fees are negotiated at a discount. PPOs also help physicians to build up their practice. Patients benefit because they pay less for their medical care. Enrollments in PPOs have increased rapidly over time and accounted for 43 percent of all employee enrollments in 1999 (see Exhibit 22.1).

Exclusive Provider Organizations

An **exclusive provider organization (EPO)** is a plan that does not cover medical care received outside a network of preferred providers. If patients receive medical care outside the network, they must pay the entire cost themselves. The preferred providers who are in the network are reimbursed on a fee-for-service basis based on a schedule of negotiated fees.

Point-of-Service Plans

A point-of-service (POS) plan is another important type of managed care plan. A **point-of-service (POS) plan** offers a full range of health services through a combination of HMO and PPO features. Members can elect to receive services under the defined managed care program or can go outside the network for care. *If patients see providers who are in the network, they pay little or nothing out of pocket, which is similar to an HMO. However, if the patients receive care from providers outside the network, the care is covered, but the patients must pay substantially higher deductibles and co-payments.* For example, a patient who sees a physician outside the network may be required to pay a $500 annual deductible and a coinsurance charge of 30 percent. If the patient sees a participating physician within the network, there is no additional charge.

The POS plan has the major advantage of preserving freedom of choice for plan members; it also eliminates the fear that plan members will not be able to see a physician or specialist of their choice. The major disadvantage is the substantially higher cost that a member must pay to see a provider outside the network.

Advantages of Managed Care Plans

Managed care plans have a number of advantages for employers, employees, and health insurers. One major advantage is that the rate of increase in health insurance premiums has been reduced over time because of the heavy emphasis on cost control. However, HMO rates are beginning to rise because of rising medical costs, reduced earnings by HMO chains, and pressure on profit margins.

Other advantages are that managed care plans generally have lower hospital and surgical utilization rates than traditional group indemnity plans; plan members pay little or nothing out of pocket if they utilize network providers; and employees do not have to file claim forms.

Disadvantages of Managed Care Plans

According to many critics, the major disadvantage of managed care plans is that the quality of care is being reduced because of the heavy emphasis on cost control. Critics argue that access to specialists may be delayed because some gatekeeper physicians do not promptly refer sick patients to specialists because of the additional cost to the plan; some patients who should be hospitalized are not admitted into a hospital; and certain diagnostic tests are not performed. In addition, critics agree that for-profit HMOs skimp on preventive care to maximize profits (see Insight 22.1).

Many physicians criticize managed care plans because of the restrictions placed on their freedom to treat patients. HMO physicians must often obtain approval from plan administrators or insurers before certain diagnostic tests or procedures can be given; they may have to argue for additional days of hospital coverage for patients who are too sick to be released; referral to a specialist may be denied or delayed; and prescription drugs may be limited only to certain drugs on an approved list. In addition, physicians argue that some HMOs impose a "gag rule" on the right of the doctor to discuss with patients alternative methods of treatment not approved by the HMO. Thus, many plan physicians believe the traditional doctor–patient relationship is being seriously compromised by outside third parties. As a result, a rising number of doctors are cutting their links to HMOs (see Insight 22.2).

In addition, managed care plans commonly provide financial incentives to health care providers to hold down costs, such as an incentive bonus based

Insight 22.1

For-Profit HMOs Score Lower on Care

For-profit health maintenance organizations are more likely than nonprofit HMOs to skimp on preventive care to maximize profits, Harvard University researchers have concluded.

For-profit plans scored lower on each of 14 measures of medical quality, including rates of such routine services as mammograms, immunizations, and eye exams for diabetics, according to a report published in the *Journal of the American Medical Association.*

"The differences are large enough to be significant clinically," said Dr. Stephanie Woolhandler of Cambridge (Massachusetts) Hospital and Harvard Medical School, who wrote the report with Dr. David Himmelstein and others.

The study results come amid the debate in Congress over proposed new regulation of the managed care industry.

A health-plan industry group said that the *JAMA* study, whose authors advocate a national health plan, "confuses ideology and analysis." In fact, the spokeswoman for the American Association of Health Plans applied an opposite spin to the report.

"The clear conclusion (of the study) is that managed care is improving the quality of health care," said Susan

Pisano in Washington. She said that HMOs as a whole—nonprofit and for-profit alike—had rates of preventive services that were higher than those of fee-for-service (nonmanaged care) providers in previous studies.

The study used health care data reported voluntarily by HMOs in 1996 to the National Committee for Quality Assurance in Washington. The data represent 329 HMOs, 248 of them investor-owned and 81 nonprofit, making up 56 percent of the total U.S. enrollment in HMOs.

The HMOs were rated on 14 quality-of-care measures that included rates of completed immunizations for 2- and 13-year-olds; mammography and Pap smears; prenatal care in the first trimester; postpartum checkups for women delivering babies; prescription of beta-blockers for patients discharged from the hospital following a heart attack; eye exams in the past year for diabetics receiving insulin; and outpatient follow-up for patients discharged from mental hospitals.

SOURCE: Adapted from "For-Project HMOs Score Lower on Care," *Omaha World-Herald,* July 14, 1999, p. 2.

on the profitability of the plan. Critics argue that network physicians often have a financial conflict of interest between providing the highest-quality medical care to their patients and holding down costs to increase plan profits and the amount of their bonus.

Finally, many workers are unaware of the various restrictions and limitations in managed care plans, and state regulation of HMOs varies widely.

Patients' Bill of Rights

At the time of this writing, federal legislation had been introduced that would protect the rights of patients in managed care plans. Legislation is considered necessary because of the denial of care and widespread dissatisfaction with managed care plans voiced by both patients and physicians.

Several proposals have been introduced. One includes the following provisions:

- Allows patients harmed by the denial of care the right to sue the managed care plan.
- Requires health plans to pay for emergency-room care even if the hospital is outside the network.
- Allows women to see obstetricians and gynecologists without prior approval and to designate them as primary-care physicians.
- Requires health plans to pay routine health care costs associated with clinical trials.
- Defines "medical necessity" and prohibits plans from interfering with a doctor's care if the services provided are medically necessary.
- Requires health plans to pay for an overnight hospital stay for a patient who has a mastectomy if the doctor and patient want it.

Insight 22.2

Rising Number of Doctors Cut Links to HMOs

Now is the winter of doctors' discontent. And judging from the grumbling in physicians' lounges and examination rooms, summer may never come again.

Across the United States, doctors are complaining that the era of managed health care has robbed them of autonomy, quality, income, time, prestige—even self-respect.

For this, they wonder aloud, they spent their youths in laboratories and libraries?

"This is life in hell," said Dr. Rex Greene, a Pasadena, California, oncologist and president of the Los Angeles County Medical Association—and he describes himself as an optimist.

Increasingly, physicians are going far beyond grumbling.

A growing minority are rebelling outright—dropping health maintenance organization contracts, seeking clout and redress in professional alliances or unions, filing lawsuits, retiring early, going out on disability, or moving out of markets colonized by managed care.

Consider the San Diego gastroenterologist who slapped his physician group with a lawsuit after he was fired for supposedly spending too much time or money on patients. Or the cardiothoracic surgeon from the same city who yanked down his shingle and moved to South Dakota, where managed care is nearly nonexistent. Or the 33-year-old Pasadena internist whose frustration forced him two years ago to cut all ties to HMOs.

"I have been un-neutered, restored to my vigorous self," said the internist, Dr. Andre Ettinger. "I can finally take care of patients rather than having to punt the ball all the time."

Nine in 10 physicians have at least one managed care contract, but recently, hundreds of physicians en masse have rejected contracts in California, Texas, Florida, Georgia, and Colorado. Patients have been left to scramble for substitute doctors.

A survey of 900 doctors, aged 40 and younger, published by *California Physician* magazine last August, found seven in ten were dissatisfied with their relationships with managed care organizations. *Just more than half identified "denial of care" by health plans as their greatest ethical concern. More than half also reported they are making less money than they had expected.*

Doctors' frustration is surfacing in ways ranging from individual resistance to organized action:

■ *The traditionally conservative American Medical Association is pushing a broad patients' rights agenda in Washington*—including the right to sue HMOs—that has rankled some leading Republicans who prefer a more moderate approach.

■ *San Diego pediatric gastroenterologist Thomas W. Self drew national attention last year when he sued his medical group*, charging it had fired him for spending too much time and money on his young patients. He won a $2.5 million settlement.

■ *Labor unions, though still anathema to many doctors, are stepping up their organizing efforts and seeing remarkable success.* Even the AMA has started a collective bargaining unit, though it draws the line at strikes.

■ *Doctors, once in the work-till-they-drop category, increasingly are filing disability claims, delaying their return to work after injury or simply not going back.* Insurers say the overwhelming reason is dismay with managed care.

■ *Physicians are becoming more outspoken in their critiques of HMOs.* One physicians' network on Long Island, New York, drew scrutiny from federal regulators after it went so far as to put out advertisements warning Medicare patients against joining HMOs.

Source: Adapted from "Doctors who Lose Patience," by Julie Marquis, *Los Angeles Times*, March 3, 1999. Copyright 1999 Los Angeles Times. Reprinted by Permission.

■ Allows patients who are pregnant or undergoing a plan of treatment the right to keep their doctors for 90 days even if the doctor leaves the network.

■ Allows patients to appeal denials first through an internal process and then to outside experts.

GROUP MEDICAL EXPENSE CONTRACTUAL PROVISIONS

Group medical expense insurance plans contain numerous contractual provisions that can have a significant financial impact on the insured. Three important provisions deal with (1) preexisting conditions, (2) coordination of benefits, and (3) continuation of group health insurance.

Preexisting Conditions

Group medical expense plans typically contain a **preexisting-conditions provision** that excludes coverage for a medical condition for a limited period after the worker enters the plan. The purposes of this provision are to reduce adverse selection against the insurer and to control employer costs.

In 1996, Congress enacted the **Health Insurance Portability and Accountability Act,** which places limits on the right of insurers and employers to deny or limit coverage for preexisting conditions.

Most employees who change or lose jobs now have access to group health insurance coverage. Employers and insurers that offer health insurance plans are prohibited from dropping people because they are sick, or from imposing waiting periods for preexisting conditions for more than 12 months (18 months for late enrollees). Employers and health insurers must also give credit for previous coverage so that workers who maintain continuous health insurance coverage (without a gap of 63 days) can never be excluded because of a preexisting condition.

The following discussion summarizes the major provisions of the law dealing with preexisting conditions:

- Employer-sponsored group health insurance plans cannot exclude or limit coverage for a preexisting condition for more than 12 months (18 months for late enrollees). A **preexisting condition** *is defined as a medical condition diagnosed or treated during the previous six months.* A preexisting condition exclusion cannot be applied to pregnancy, newly born children, or adopted children.
- After the initial 12-month period expires, no new preexisting condition period may ever be imposed on workers who maintain continuous coverage, with no more than a 63-day gap in coverage, even if the workers should change jobs or health plans.
- *Insurers and employers must give credit for previous coverage of less than 12 months with respect to any preexisting condition exclusion found in the new health plan.* For example, a worker with

a preexisting condition who was previously insured for eight months under a group plan when he or she changes jobs or health plans would face a maximum additional exclusion of four months for a preexisting condition, rather than the normal 12 months.

- Discrimination based on health status is prohibited. Employers that offer health insurance to employees and dependents cannot exclude, drop from coverage, or charge higher premiums based on health status. Health status is broadly defined to include the individual's medical condition; physical and mental illness; medical history; claims experience; evidence of insurability, including conditions arising out of acts of domestic violence; genetic information; and disability.
- The law also guarantees the availability of group health insurance to small employers. Commercial insurers, HMOs, and other groups issuing health insurance coverages are prohibited from denying coverage to firms that employ between 2 and 50 employees.

Because of limits on preexisting conditions and credit for previous and continuous coverage, employees will no longer be afraid to change jobs for fear of losing their group health insurance protection. As a result, they can change jobs and still be assured of health insurance coverage. Thus, the new law makes the health insurance protection "portable."

However, portability does not mean that employees can take their present group health insurance benefits with them when they change jobs. **Portability** *means that when employees change jobs, the new employer or health plan must give them credit for previous and continuous health insurance coverage.* When the employees leave their present job, the insurer or employer must provide information showing how long they were covered while working at that job. The worker then presents this documentation to the new employer or health plan. If a worker has been covered for 12 months or more by a previous employer or health plan and does not have a gap in coverage of more than 63 days, the worker is eligible for coverage under the new employer's plan even though he or she has a preexisting condition.

The legislation also includes a demonstration project to evaluate the effectiveness of medical savings accounts (MSAs). **A medical savings account** *is a* *high-deductible major medical policy that allows the insured to pay premiums with before-tax dollars.* Participants must be self-employed or must be employed in a business with 50 or fewer employees. The insured or employer buys an approved MSA policy with a high deductible, ranging from $1550 to $2300 annually for individuals and $3050 to $4600 for families. The insured then deposits 65 percent to 75 percent of the deductible amount into the MSA. The deposits earn interest income-tax free; the contributions are excluded from taxable income; and funds withdrawn to pay medical bills are not taxed unless they are used for nonmedical purposes.

MSAs are controversial. Proponents argue that insureds with MSAs will be more sensitive to the cost of medical care and will shop around for low-cost providers. Opponents argue that only healthy insureds will elect MSAs to save money, which will drive up costs for other insureds who are covered under group indemnity or managed care plans.

Coordination of Benefits

Group medical insurance plans typically contain a **coordination-of-benefits provision**, which specifies the order of payment when an insured is covered under two or more group health insurance plans. Total recovery under all plans is limited to 100 percent of covered expenses. The purpose is to prevent overinsurance and duplication of benefits if an insured is covered by more than one plan.

The coordination-of-benefit provisions in most group plans are based on rules developed by the National Association of Insurance Commissioners (NAIC). These rules are complex and are beyond the scope of this text to discuss in detail. The following summarizes the major provisions based on the latest NAIC rules.

1. *Coverage as an employee is usually primary to coverage as a dependent.* For example, Karen and Chris Swift both work, and each is insured as a dependent under the other's group medical insurance plan. If Karen incurs covered medical expenses, her plan pays first. She then submits any unreimbursed expenses (such as the deductible and coinsurance payments) to Chris's insurer for payment. No more than 100 percent of the eligible medical expenses are paid under both plans.

2. With respect to dependent children, if the parents are married or are not separated (regardless of whether they have ever been married), *the plan or the parent whose birthday occurs first during the year is primary; the plan of the parent with the later birthday is secondary.* For example, if Karen's birthday is in January and Chris's birthday is in July, Karen's plan would pay first if her son is hospitalized. Chris's plan would be secondary.

3. If the parents of dependent children are not married, or are separated (regardless of whether they have ever been married), or are divorced, and if there is no court decree specifying who is responsible for the child's health care expenses, the following rules apply:

   - The plan of the parent who is awarded custody pays first.
   - The plan of the step-parent who is the spouse of the parent awarded custody pays second.
   - The plan of the parent without custody pays third.
   - The plan of the step-parent who is the spouse of the parent without custody pays last.

Continuation of Group Health Insurance

Employees often quit their jobs, are laid off, or are fired. If a qualifying event occurs that results in a loss of coverage, employees and covered dependents can elect to remain in the employer's plan for a limited period under the Consolidated Omnibus Budget Reconciliation Act of 1985 (also known as COBRA). The COBRA law applies to firms with 20 or more employees. *A qualifying event includes termination of employment for any reason (except gross misconduct), divorce or legal separation, death of the employee, and attainment of a maximum age by dependent children.* If the worker loses his or her job or no longer works the required number of hours, the terminated worker and his or her covered dependents can elect to remain in the employer's plan for as long as 18 months. However, the worker must pay 102 percent of the group insurance rate. If the worker dies or is divorced or legally separated or has a child who is no longer eligible for coverage, covered dependents have the right to remain in the group plan for up to three years (see Insight 22.3).

After the period of protection under COBRA expires, some workers with preexisting conditions may be unable to obtain individual health insurance. The Health Insurance Portability and Accountability Act guarantees individual health insurance to eligible persons with no evidence of insurability if certain conditions are met. Eligible persons with health problems are guaranteed individual health insurance if they can meet the following requirements: (1) have employment-based health insurance for at least 18 months, (2) are ineligible for COBRA or have exhausted their COBRA coverage, and (3) are ineligible for coverage under any other employment-based health plan. The insurance provided is a guaranteed renewable policy.

GROUP DENTAL INSURANCE

Group dental insurance helps pay the cost of normal dental care and also covers damage to teeth from an accident. Dental insurance has the principal advantage of helping employees meet the costs of regular dental care. It also encourages insureds to see their dentists on a regular basis, thereby preventing or detecting dental problems before they become serious.

Types of Plans

There are two basic types of group dental insurance plans.[7] Under a **scheduled dental insurance plan**, the various dental services are listed in a schedule, and a flat dollar amount is paid for each service. If the dentist charges more than the specified amount, the patient must pay the difference.

Under a **nonscheduled dental insurance plan** (also called **comprehensive dental insurance**), most dental services are covered, including oral examinations, X rays, cleaning, fillings, extractions, inlays, bridgework and dentures, oral surgery, root canals, and orthodontia. Dentists are reimbursed on the basis of their reasonable and customary charges subject to any limitations on benefits stated in the plan.

Cost Controls

To control costs and reduce adverse selection against the insurer when the plan is initially installed, several cost controls are used. They include the following:

- Deductibles and coinsurance
- Maximum limit on benefits
- Waiting periods
- Exclusions
- Predetermination-of-benefits provision

Most dental insurance plans use **deductibles** and **coinsurance** to control costs. The coinsurance percentage may vary depending on the type of service. To encourage regular visits to a dentist, many plans do not impose any coinsurance requirements for one or two routine dental examinations each year. However, fillings and oral surgery may be paid only at a rate of 80 percent, while the cost of orthodontia or dentures is typically paid at a lower rate of 50 percent.

Maximum limits on benefits are also used to control costs. There may be a maximum annual limit on the amount paid, such as $2000 during the calendar year. Another approach is to impose a lifetime maximum on certain types of dental services, such as a lifetime maximum of $2000 for dentures.

Waiting periods for certain types of services are used to control costs as well. For example, some plans do not cover dentures until the employee is insured for at least one year, and there may be only one replacement of dentures for each five-year period.

Certain **exclusions** are used to reduce costs. Common exclusions include cosmetic dental work, such as capping a tooth; replacement of lost or stolen dental devices, such as dentures or a space retainer; and benefits provided under a workers compensation or similar law.

A **predetermination-of-benefits provision** is also used to control costs. Under this provision, if the cost of dental treatment exceeds a certain amount, such as $200, the dentist submits a plan of treatment to the insurer. The insurer then specifies the services covered and how much the plan will pay. The employee is informed of the amount the plan will pay and then makes a decision on whether to proceed with the proposed plan of treatment.

Finally, it should be pointed out that, just as in medical expense insurance, there are dental HMOs, PPOs, and self-funded plans by employers that provide dental insurance to employees.

Insight 22.3

What Happens to My Health Insurance If I Lose My Job?

If you have had health coverage as an employee benefit and you leave your job, voluntarily or otherwise, one of your first concerns will be maintaining protection against the costs of health care. You can do this in one of several ways:

- First, you should know that under a federal law (the Consolidated Omnibus Budget Reconciliation Act of 1985, commonly known as COBRA), group health plans sponsored by employers with 20 or more employees are required to offer continued coverage for you and your dependents for 18 months after you leave your job. (Under the same law, following an employee's death or divorce, the worker's family has the right to continue coverage for up to three years.) If you wish to continue your group coverage under this option, you must notify your employer within 60 days. You must also pay the entire premium, up to 102 percent of the cost of the coverage.
- If COBRA does not apply in your case—perhaps because you work for an employer with fewer than 20 employees—you may be able to convert your group policy to individual coverage. The advantage of that option is that you may not have to pass a medical exam, although an exclusion based on a preexisting condition may apply, depending on your medical history and your insurance history.

- If COBRA doesn't apply and converting your group coverage is not for you, then, if you are healthy, not yet eligible for Medicare, and expect to take another job, you might consider an interim or short-term policy. These policies are designed to provide medical insurance for people with a short-term need, such as those temporarily between jobs or those making the transition between college and a job. These policies, typically written for two to six months and renewable once, cover hospitalization, intensive care, and surgical and doctors' care provided in the hospital, as well as expenses for related services performed outside the hospital, such as X rays or laboratory tests.
- Another possibility is obtaining coverage through an association. Many trade and professional associations offer their members health coverage—often HMOs—as well as basic hospital-surgical policies, and disability and long-term care insurance. If you are self-employed, you may find association membership an attractive route.

SOURCE: *Guide to Health Insurance* (Washington, DC: Health Insurance Association of America, April 1997).

GROUP DISABILITY-INCOME INSURANCE

Group disability-income insurance pays weekly or monthly cash payments to employees who are disabled from accidents or illness. There are two basic types of plans: (1) short-term plans and (2) long-term plans.

Short-Term Plans

Many employers have short-term plans that pay disability benefits for relatively short periods ranging from 13 weeks to two years. The majority of short-term plans sold today pay benefits for a maximum period of 26 weeks. In addition, most plans have a short elimination period of one to seven days for sickness, while accidents are typically covered from the first day of disability. The elimination period reduces nuisance claims, holds down costs, and discourages malingering and excessive absenteeism.

More short-term plans cover only **nonoccupational disability**, which means that an accident or illness must occur off the job. *Disability is usually defined in terms of the worker's own occupation. You are considered totally disabled if you are unable to perform all of the duties of your own occupation.* Partial disability is seldom covered under a group short-term plan; you must be totally disabled to qualify.

The amount of disability-income benefits is related to the worker's normal earnings and is typically equal to some percentage of weekly earnings, such as 50 to 70 percent. Thus, if Amy's weekly earnings are $600, she could collect a maximum weekly benefit of $420 if she becomes disabled.

In addition, short-term plans have relatively few exclusions. As noted earlier, a disability that occurs on the job is usually not covered, because occupational disability is covered under a workers compensation law. Also, except for very small groups, pre-existing conditions are covered immediately. Most plans also cover alcoholism, drug addiction, and nervous and mental disorders.

Long-Term Plans

Many employers also have long-term plans that pay benefits for longer periods, typically ranging from two years to age 65. However, if the disability occurs beyond age 65, benefits are paid for a limited period. For example, under the plan of one disability insurer, if the worker is younger than 60 at the time of disability, the maximum benefit period is to age 65. However, if a worker age 66 becomes disabled, the maximum benefit period is only 21 months.

A dual definition of disability is typically used to determine whether a worker is totally disabled. *For the first two years, you are considered disabled if you are unable to perform all of the duties of your own occupation. After two years, you are still considered disabled if you are unable to work in any occupation for which you are reasonably fitted by education, training, and experience.* In addition, in contrast to short-term plans, long-term plans typically cover both occupational and nonoccupational disability.

The disability-income benefits are usually paid monthly, and the maximum monthly benefits are substantially higher than the benefits paid by short-term plans. The maximum monthly benefit is generally limited to 50 to 65 percent of the employee's normal earnings. Most plans commonly pay maximum monthly benefits of $2000, $3000, $4000, or even higher amounts. A waiting period of three to six months is typically required before the benefits are payable.

To reduce malingering and moral hazard, other disability-income benefits paid by the employer are taken into consideration. If the disabled worker is also receiving Social Security or workers compensa-

tion benefits, the long-term disability benefit is reduced accordingly. However, many plans limit the reduction only to the amount of the initial Social Security disability benefit. Thus, if Social Security disability benefits are increased because of increases in the cost of living, the long-term disability-income benefit is not reduced further.

Some long-term plans have additional supplemental benefits. Under the **cost-of-living adjustment**, benefits paid to disabled employees are adjusted annually for increases in the cost of living. However, there may be a maximum limit on the percentage increase in benefits.

Under the **pension accrual benefit**, the plan makes a pension contribution so that the disabled employee's pension benefit remains intact. For example, if both Carlos and his employer contribute 6 percent of his salary into a pension plan, and Carlos becomes disabled, the plan would pay an amount equal to 12 percent of his monthly salary into the company's pension plan for as long as he remains disabled. Thus, Carlos would still receive his pension at the normal retirement age.

Finally, if the disabled worker dies, the plan may pay monthly **survivor income benefits** to an eligible surviving spouse or children for a limited period following the disabled worker's death, such as two years.

CAFETERIA PLANS

The final part of this chapter deals with cafeteria plans. **Cafeteria plans** *allow employees to select those employee benefits that best meet their specific needs.* Instead of a single benefits package that applies to all employees, cafeteria plans allow employees to select among the various group life, medical expense, disability, dental, and other plans that are offered. Cafeteria plans also allow employers to introduce new benefits to meet the specific needs of certain employees.

Although cafeteria plans vary among employers, they share certain common characteristics. First, in many plans, the employer gives each employee a certain number of dollars or credits that can be spent on the different benefits or taken as cash. If taken as cash, the employer's credits are taxed as income to the employee.

Second, cafeteria plans typically allow employees to establish a flexible spending account. A **flexible spending account** *is an arrangement by which the employee agrees to a salary reduction, which can be used to pay for unreimbursed medical and dental expenses, dependent care expenses, and other expenses permitted by the Internal Revenue Code.* In effect, the worker pays for the benefits with before-tax dollars.

Finally, if the cafeteria plan meets certain requirements specified in the Internal Revenue Code, the employer's credits are not currently taxable to the employee. Also, any additional amounts spent by the employee on the various benefits are generally paid with before-tax dollars, which provides a significant tax advantage.

Cafeteria plans have certain advantages, including the following:

- Employees can select those benefits that best meet their specific needs.
- Employee appreciation of the benefit package may increase, because employees have a greater awareness of the cost of the benefits selected.
- Employees generally pay their share of the cost of benefits with before-tax dollars, which reduces taxes and increases take-home pay.
- Employers can more easily control rising employee benefit costs. For example, an employer may limit the number of benefit dollars or credits given to each employee or offer the employees a medical expense plan with a higher deductible.

Cafeteria plans also have certain disadvantages, including the following:

- The employer may incur higher initial development and administrative costs in establishing a cafeteria plan rather than a traditional benefits plan.
- Labor union attitudes may be negative. The labor union may believe that a cafeteria plan is contrary to the practice of bargaining for the best benefits package for all employees.
- Administrative complexity is increased. The employee benefits manager must have knowledge of the details of a large number of plans and must be able to answer the specific questions of employees concerning these plans.

SUMMARY

- Group insurance provides benefits to a number of persons under a single master contract. Low-cost protection is provided, because the employer pays part or all of the premiums. Evidence of insurability is usually not required. Larger groups are subject to experience rating, by which the group's loss experience determines the premiums charged.

- Certain underwriting principles are followed in group insurance to obtain favorable loss experience:

    Insurance must be incidental to the group.

    There should be a flow of persons through the group.

    The benefits should be determined by some formula that precludes individual selection of insurance amounts.

    A minimum percentage of eligible employees must participate in the plan.

    There should be a third-party sharing of costs.

    There should be simple and efficient administration.

- Most groups today are eligible for group insurance benefits. However, employees must meet certain eligibility requirements:

    Be full-time employees.

    Satisfy a probationary period in some plans.

    Apply for insurance during the eligibility period.

    Be actively at work.

- There are several types of group life insurance plans:

    Group term life insurance

    Group accidental death and dismemberment (AD&D) insurance

    Group universal life insurance

- Group medical expense plans are available from a number of sources, including:

    Commercial insurers

    Blue Cross and Blue Shield

    Health maintenance organizations (HMOs)

    Self-insured plans by employers

- Group basic medical expense insurance provides only basic benefits, which typically include:

    Hospital expense insurance

    Surgical expense insurance

Physicians' visits insurance

Coverage for miscellaneous benefits

- Group major medical insurance is designed to cover catastrophic losses. There are two basic types of group major medical plans:

    Supplemental major medical insurance

    Comprehensive major medical insurance

- Managed care is a generic name for a medical expense plan that provides necessary medical care in a cost-effective manner.

- A health maintenance organization (HMO) is a managed care plan that provides broad, comprehensive services to its members for a fixed, prepaid fee. A typical HMO has the following characteristics:

    Organized plan to deliver health services to the members

    Broad, comprehensive health services

    Fixed, prepaid fee

    Emphasis on cost containment

- A preferred provider organization (PPO) is a plan that contracts with health care providers to provide certain medical services to its members at discounted fees. Members pay lower deductibles and coinsurance charges if preferred providers are used.

- An exclusive provider organization (EPO) is a managed care plan that does not cover medical care received outside the network of preferred providers.

- A point-of-service (POS) plan is a managed care plan that allows members to receive medical care outside the network of preferred providers. However, the patient must pay higher deductible and co-payment charges.

- Group medical expense plans contain certain contractual provisions that may have a financial impact on the insured. Major provisions include:

    Preexisting-conditions provision

    Coordination-of-benefits provision

    Continuation of group health insurance under the COBRA law

- There are two basic types of group dental insurance plans:

    Scheduled plans

    Nonscheduled plans (comprehensive plans)

- Many employers provide disability-income benefits to covered employees. There are two basic types of plans:

Short-term disability-income plans

Long-term disability-income plans

- Cafeteria plans allow employees to select those benefits that best meet their specific needs. Flexible spending accounts in a cafeteria plan allow employees to pay for the benefits with before-tax dollars.

KEY CONCEPTS AND TERMS

ASO contract

Basic medical expense insurance

Blue Cross and Blue Shield plans

Cafeteria plans

Calendar-year deductible

Coinsurance provision

Comprehensive major medical insurance

Contributory plan

Coordination-of-benefits provision

Corridor deductible

Cost-of-living adjustment

Eligibility period

Exclusive provider organization (EPO)

Experience rating

Family deductible provision

Flexible spending account

Group accidental death and dismemberment (AD&D) insurance

Group dental insurance

Group disability-income insurance

Group medical expense insurance

Group term life insurance

Group universal life insurance

Health Insurance Portability and Accountability Act

Health maintenance organization (HMO)

Hospital expense insurance

Managed care

Master contract

Medical savings account

Noncontributory plan

Nonoccupational disability

Nonscheduled dental insurance plan (comprehensive dental insurance)

Pension accrual benefit

Point-of-service (POS) plan

Portability

Predetermination-of-benefits provision

Preexisting condition

Preferred provider organization (PPO)

Principal sum

Probationary period

Reasonable and customary changes

Relative-value schedule

Scheduled dental insurance plan

Self-insurance (self-funding)

Service benefits

Stop-loss insurance

Stop-loss limit

Supplemental major medical insurance

Surgical expense insurance

Survivor income benefits

Traditional group indemnity plan

Voluntary accidental death and dismemberment insurance

Yearly renewable term insurance

REVIEW QUESTIONS

1. Describe the nature of group insurance plans and show how group insurance differs from individual insurance.

2. Describe the underwriting principles that are followed in group insurance.

3. Explain the eligibility requirements that are commonly required in group insurance plans.

4. Describe the major forms of group life insurance.

5. Identify the benefits commonly found in group basic medical expense plans.

6. Explain the two basic types of group major medical insurance.

7. What is a managed care plan? Identify the major types of managed care plans.

8. Briefly explain each of the following group provisions:
   a. Preexisting conditions
   b. Coordination of benefits
   c. Continuation of group health insurance under the COBRA law

9. Describe the two types of group dental insurance plans.

10. Explain the characteristics of group short-term and long-term disability-income plans.

11. Explain the characteristics of cafeteria plans.

APPLICATION QUESTIONS

1. Although individual underwriting and evidence of insurability are not usually required in group life insurance, there are several factors inherent in the group approach that result in favorable plan experience. Explain these factors.

2. Compare group term life insurance with group universal life insurance with respect to the following:
   a. Continuation of coverage after leaving this group
   b. Use of employer contributions
   c. Right to convert the coverage

3. Compare group short-term disability-income plans with group long-term disability-income plans with respect to each of the following:
   a. Benefit period
   b. Definition of disability
   c. Consideration of other benefits

4. Compare a supplemental group major medical plan with a comprehensive group major medical plan with respect to each of the following:
   a. Use of deductibles
   b. Use of coinsurance
   c. Use of a stop-loss limit

5. When group dental insurance plans are initially installed, the insurer is exposed to a high degree of adverse selection. Describe several features that are incorporated into group dental insurance plans to make this coverage feasible despite the possibility of adverse selection.

6. HMOs can be viewed as an acceptable alternative to the traditional group indemnity plans for consumers.
   a. Describe the basic characteristics of HMOs.
   b. Explain the major characteristics of PPOs.
   c. How does a PPO differ from an HMO?
   d. What are the advantages and disadvantages of managed care plans?

SELECTED REFERENCES

Beam, Burton T., Jr., and John J. McFadden. *Employee Benefits*, fifth edition. Chicago, IL: Dearborn Financial Publishing, 1998.

Black, Kenneth, Jr., and Harold D. Skipper, Jr. *Life and Health Insurance*, thirteenth edition. Upper Saddle River, NJ: Prentice-Hall, 2000, Chapters 19–20.

Health Insurance Association of America. *Fundamentals of Health Insurance, Part A* and *Part B*. Washington, DC: Health Insurance Association of America, 1997.

Health Insurance Association of America. *Guide to Managed Care*. Washington, DC: Health Insurance Association of America, March 1997.

Rosenbloom, Jerry S., ed., *The Handbook of Employee Benefits: Design, Funding, and Administration*, fourth edition. Burr Ridge, IL: Irwin Professional Publishing, 1996.

Source Book of Health Insurance Data, 1999–2000. Washington, DC: Health Insurance Association of America, 1999.

NOTES

1. Burton Beam, Jr., and John J. McFadden, *Employee Benefits*, fifth edition (Chicago, IL: Dearborn Financial Publishing, 1998), pp. 90–97.

2. *ACLI Life Insurance Fact Book 1999* (Washington, DC: American Council of Life Insurance, 1999), p. 18.

Case Application

Nancy Olson is president of a consulting firm that has ten employees. The only employee benefit provided by the firm is a paid two-week vacation for employees with one or more years of service. The firm's profits have substantially increased, and Nancy would like to provide some additional benefits to the employees. Nancy would like advice concerning the types of benefits to provide. Assume you are an employee benefits consultant. Based on the following considerations, answer the following questions:

a. Nancy would like to provide life insurance for the employees equal to two times their salaries. What type of life insurance do you recommend?

b. Several employees have expressed an interest in having some life insurance in force on their lives after retirement. Explain to Nancy how employees can keep life insurance on their lives after retirement.

c. Nancy would also like to provide health insurance benefits to the employees. Identify the major types of group health insurance plans that she might consider.

d. Assume that Nancy decides to offer both a traditional group indemnity health insurance plan and a point-of-service HMO option to the employees. Explain the major differences between these two plans to Nancy.

e. Are there any other group insurance benefits that Nancy should consider? Explain your answer.

f. Nancy would like to give the employees a choice of benefit plans. Explain to Nancy how this goal can be accomplished.

3. In a few states, the terminating employee is allowed to purchase term insurance for a limited period (such as one year), after which he or she must convert to some form of cash-value life insurance.

4. Beam and McFadden, pp. 156–163.

5. *Source Book of Health Insurance Data, 1999–2000.* (Washington, DC: Health Insurance Association of America, 1999), p. 58.

6. Beam and McFadden, p. 295.

7. *Ibid.*, pp. 332–335.

Students may take a self-administered test on this chapter at www.awlonline.com/rejda

Chapter 23

Employee Benefits: Retirement Plans

" Retirement at age 65 is ridiculous. When I was sixty-five, I still had pimples. "

George Burns

" When some fellers decide to retire, nobody knows the difference. "

Kin Hubbard

Learning Objectives

After studying this chapter, you should be able to:

▲ Explain the basic features of private retirement plans, including:
- Minimum age and service requirements
- Retirement ages
- Vesting rules

▲ Distinguish between defined-contribution and defined-benefit retirement plans.

▲ Describe the basic characteristics of Section 401(k) plans.

▲ Explain the major features of profit-sharing plans and thrift plans.

▲ Describe the basic characteristics of Keogh plans for the self-employed.

▲ Identify the major features of SIMPLE retirement plans for small employers.

▲ Access an Internet site and obtain consumer information about Section 401(k) plans.

Internet Resources

- The **Association of Private Pension and Welfare Plans** is an organization that represents plan sponsors and technical professionals in the employee benefits field. The site provides an analysis of proposed legislation affecting private pension plans and other employee benefits. Visit the site at:

  http://www.appwp.org

- The **Employee Benefit Research Institute (EBRI)** is a nonprofit organization that makes available research studies and notes on qualified retirement plans. Visit the site at:

  http://www.ebri.org/

- **Fidelity Investments** provides a substantial amount of timely information on retirement planning and qualified retirement plans, including 401(k) plans. Visit its 401(k) site at:

  http://www.401k.com

- **Pension Benefit Guaranty Corporation** is a federal corporation that protects the retirement benefits of workers in defined-benefit pension plans. The site provides timely information on these types of pension plans. Visit the site at:

  http://www.pbgc.gov

- The **Pension and Welfare Benefits Administration** (**PWBA**) is an agency of the U.S. Department of Labor that provides information and statistics on qualified retirement plans. Visit the site at:

  http://www.dol.gov/dol/pwba

- **Charles Schwab** provides informative articles and information on retirement planning, annuities, and individual retirement accounts (IRAs). Visit the site at:

  www.schwab.com

- The **Vanguard Group** provides timely information on retirement planning, variable annuities, and IRAs. Visit the site at:

  www.vanguard.com

- **TIAA-CREF** has an excellent site that provides a considerable amount of information on retirement planning and retirement options. Visit the site at:

  www.tiaa-cref.org

icole, age 26, is a computer programmer for a large national money-center bank. She earns $35,000 annually and recently became eligible to participate in the bank's retirement plan. The bank has a Section 401(k) retirement plan for eligible employees. Nicole has a number of questions about the plan, including the amount she can contribute, the amount contributed by the bank, investment options, and the retirement age. She also wants to know whether she will receive anything if she should quit her job prior to retirement.

Like Nicole, many employees are bewildered by the complexities of private retirement plans. This chapter deals with the questions that Nicole and others may have concerning the basic features of private retirement plans. Although they may seem complicated, private retirement plans are extremely important in maintaining the worker's economic security during retirement. When added to Social Security retirement benefits, their benefits enable retired workers to attain a higher standard of living during retirement.

This chapter discusses the fundamentals of private retirement plans. It is divided into two major parts. The first part discusses the fundamentals of private retirement plans, including minimum age and service requirements, retirement ages, and vesting rules. The second part describes the major types of private retirement plans, including defined-contribution and defined-benefit plans, Section 401(k) plans, profit-sharing plans, and retirement plans for the self-employed.

FUNDAMENTALS OF PRIVATE RETIREMENT PLANS

Millions of workers participate in private retirement plans. These plans have an enormous social and economic impact on the nation. Retirement benefits increase the economic security of both individuals and families during retirement. Retirement contributions are also an important source of capital funds to the financial markets. These funds are invested in new plants, machinery, equipment, housing developments, shopping centers, and other worthwhile economic investments.

Federal legislation and the Internal Revenue Code have had a great influence on the design and growth of private retirement plans. The **Employee Retirement Income Security Act of 1974 (ERISA)** established minimum pension standards to protect the rights of covered workers. More recently, the **Small Business Job Protection Act of 1996** and the **Taxpayer Relief Act of 1997** increased the tax advantages of private retirement plans for both employees and employers. The Internal Revenue Service (IRS) also exerts a significant influence on private retirement plans. The IRS continuously issues new rules and regulations that affect the design and growth of private retirement plans. The following discussion is based on current IRS requirements at the time of this writing.[1]

Favorable Income Tax Treatment

Private retirement plans that meet certain IRS requirements are called **qualified plans** and receive favorable income tax treatment. The employer's contributions are tax deductible up to certain limits as an ordinary business expense; the employer's contributions are not considered taxable income to the employees; the investment earnings on plan assets accumulate on a tax-deferred basis; and the pension benefits attributable to the employer's contributions are not taxed until the employee retires or receives the funds. The tax advantages to employees are substantial (see Exhibit 23.1).

EXHIBIT 23.1

Tax Advantage of a Tax-Deferred Retirement Plan

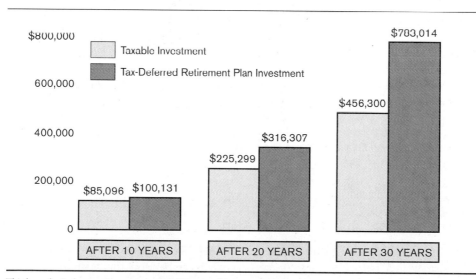

This hypothetical example assumes a $10,000 annual investment, an 8 percent annual rate of return, and a 36 percent combined federal and state tax bracket. The taxable investments are invested on an after-tax basis; their earnings are taxed every year, and the tax liability is deducted from the balance. The tax-deferred retirement plan investments are invested on a pre-tax basis, and their earnings grow tax-deferred until they are withdrawn at the end of each specified period, when they are each taxed at a rate of 36 percent.

SOURCE: Fidelity Investments.

Minimum Coverage Requirements

A qualified plan must benefit workers in general and not only **highly compensated employees**.[2] Certain **minimum coverage requirements** must be satisfied to receive favorable tax treatment. The coverage rules are complex and beyond the scope of the text to discuss in detail. However, to reduce discrimination in favor of highly compensated employees, a qualified retirement plan must meet one of the following tests:

1. **Ratio percentage test.** The plan must benefit a percentage of nonhighly compensated employees that is at least 70 percent of the highly compensated employees covered by the plan. Thus, if a plan covers 100 percent of the highly compensated employees, it must also cover at least 70 percent of the nonhighly compensated employees. Likewise, if the plan covers only 50 percent of the highly compensated employees, it must also cover at least 35 percent (50% × 70%) of the nonhighly compensated employees.

   For example, Ajax Manufacturing has 1000 eligible employees, and 100 employees are highly compensated. Assume that 100 percent of the highly compensated employees (100) are covered by the plan. The ratio percentage test is satisfied if at least 70 percent of the nonhighly compensated employees, or 630 employees, are also covered by the plan.

2. **Average benefits test.** Under this test, two requirements must be met: (1) the plan must benefit a reasonable classification of employees and must not discriminate in favor of highly compensated employees, and (2) the average benefit for the nonhighly compensated employees must be at least 70 percent of the average benefit provided to all highly compensated employees.

Minimum Age and Service Requirements

Most pension plans have a **minimum age and service requirement** that must be met before employees can participate in the plan. *Under present law, all eligible employees who have attained age 21 and have completed one year of service must be allowed to participate in the plan.* One exception is that the plan can require two years of service if there is 100 percent immediate vesting (discussed later) upon entry into the plan.

For purposes of determining eligibility, a year of service is a 12-month period during which the employee works at least 1000 hours. An hour of service is any hour for which the employee works or is entitled to be paid.

Retirement Ages

A typical pension plan has three retirement ages:

- Normal retirement age
- Early retirement age
- Late retirement age

Normal Retirement Age The **normal retirement age** is the age that a worker can retire and receive a full, unreduced benefit. Age 65 is the normal retirement age in most plans. However, as a result of an amendment to the Age Discrimination Act, most employees cannot be forced to retire at some stated mandatory retirement age. To remain qualified, a private pension plan cannot impose a mandatory retirement age.

Early Retirement Age An **early retirement age** is the earliest age that workers can retire and receive a retirement benefit. The majority of employees currently retire before age 65. For example, a typical plan may permit a worker with 10 years of service to retire at age 55.

In a defined benefit plan (discussed later), the retirement benefit is actuarially reduced for early retirement. The actuarial reduction is necessary for three reasons: (1) the worker's full benefit will not have accrued by the early retirement date; (2) the retirement benefit is paid over a longer period of time; and (3) early retirement benefits are paid to some workers who would have died before reaching the normal retirement age.

Late Retirement Age The **late retirement age** is any age beyond the normal retirement age. A relatively small number of older employees continue working beyond the normal retirement age. However, under current law with certain exceptions, workers can defer retiring with no maximum age limit as long as they can do their jobs. Employees who continue working beyond the normal retirement age continue to accrue benefits under the plan.

Benefit Formulas

Qualified retirement plans are designed to pay retirement benefits, which, together with Social Security benefits, will generally restore about 50 to 60 percent of the worker's gross earnings prior to retirement. A benefit formula is used to determine contributions or benefits.

Defined-Contribution Formulas In a **defined-contribution formula**, *the contribution rate is fixed, but the retirement benefit is variable.* For example, both the employer and employee may contribute 6 percent of pay into the plan. Although the contribution rate is known, the retirement benefit will vary depending on the worker's age, earnings, investment returns, and normal retirement age.

In a defined-contribution plan, a fixed percentage of salary is typically used to determine the retirement contributions. For example, both the employee and employer may contribute 6 percent of salary into the plan. Each employee has an individual account, and the actual retirement benefit will depend on the value of the employee's account at retirement.

Defined-Benefit Formulas In a **defined-benefit plan,** *the retirement benefit is known, but the contributions will vary depending on the amount needed to fund the desired benefit.* For example, assume a worker, age 50, is entitled to a retirement benefit at the normal retirement age equal to 50 percent of average pay for the highest three consecutive years of earnings. An actuary then determines the amount that must be contributed to produce the desired benefit.

In a defined-benefit plan, the benefit amount can be based on **career-average earnings**, which is an average of the worker's earnings while participating in the plan, or it can be based on an average of **final pay**, which generally is an average of the worker's earnings over a three- to five-year period prior to retirement.

When a new defined-benefit pension plan is installed, some older workers may be close to retirement. To pay more adequate retirement benefits, defined-benefit plans may give credit for service with the firm prior to the installation of the plan. The **past-service credits** provide additional pension benefits. The actual amount paid, however, will depend on the benefit formula used to determine benefits.

In a defined-benefit plan, numerous formulas can be used to determine the retirement benefit. They include the following:

1. *Flat dollar amount for all employees.* This formula is sometimes used in collective bargaining plans by which a flat dollar amount is paid to all employees regardless of their earnings or years of service. Thus, the plan may pay $500 monthly to each worker who retires.
2. *Flat percentage of annual earnings.* Under this formula, the retirement benefit is a fixed percentage of the worker's earnings, such as 25 to 50 percent. The benefit may be based on career-average earnings or on an average of final pay.
3. *Flat dollar amount for each year of service.* Under this formula, a flat dollar amount is paid for each year of credited service. For example, the plan may pay $30 monthly at the normal retirement age for each year of credited service. If the employee has 30 years of credited service, the monthly pension is $900.

   Years of service are extremely important in determining the total pension benefit. Frequent job changes and withdrawal from the labor force for extended periods can significantly reduce the size of the pension benefit. This is especially true for women who may have prolonged breaks in employment due to family considerations.
4. *Unit-credit formula.* The unit-credit formula is widely used at the present time. Under this formula, both earnings and years of service are considered. For example, the plan may pay a retirement benefit equal to 1 percent of the worker's final average pay multiplied by the number of years of service. Thus, a worker with a final average monthly salary of $3000 and 30 years of service would receive a monthly retirement benefit of $900.

The preceding discussion shows that the calculation of pension benefits can be complex, which can result in errors in the calculation of benefits. Unfortunately, plan administrators often commit errors that shortchange plan recipients. Some experts esti-

changed in 2002

mate that 5 to 25 percent of the nation's retirees are not getting the benefits they deserve because of errors in calculating benefits. An audit by the Pension Benefit Guaranty Corporation, for example, found that 8 percent of the participants did not receive the correct benefits when they accepted lump-sum payments.[3] Errors occur because of complex pension laws, mergers and layoffs, downsizing, and recording errors. Consequently, you should periodically check to see whether your pension contributions and records are accurate (see Insight 23.1).

Vesting Provisions

Vesting *refers to the employee's right to the benefits attributable to the employer's contributions if employment terminates prior to retirement.* The employee is always entitled to a refund of his or her contributions plus any investment earnings on the contributions upon termination of employment. However, the right to the employer's contribution, or benefits attributable to the contributions, depends on the extent to which vesting has been attained.

A qualified plan must meet one of the following **minimum vesting standards:**

- *Cliff vesting.* Under this rule, the worker must be 100 percent vested after five years of service.
- *Graded vesting.* Under this rule, the rate of vesting must meet the following minimum standard:

Years of service	Percentage vested
3	20%
4	40
5	60
6	80
7	100

From the employer's viewpoint, the basic purpose of vesting is to reduce labor turnover. Employees have an incentive to remain with the firm until a vested status has been attained. In a defined-benefit plan, if employees terminate their employment before full vesting is attained, the forfeitures generally are used to reduce the employer's future pension contributions. However, in a defined-contribution plan, forfeitures can either be reallocated to the accounts of the remaining participants or used to reduce future employer contributions.

Limits on Contributions and Benefits

For 2000, under a *defined-contribution plan,* the maximum annual addition that can be made to an employee's account is limited to 25 percent of compensation, or $30,000, whichever is lower. This figure is indexed for inflation.

For 2000, *under a defined-benefit plan,* the maximum annual benefit is limited to 100 percent of the worker's average compensation for the three highest consecutive years of compensation, or $135,000, whichever is lower. This latter figure is indexed for inflation.

There is also a maximum limit on the annual compensation that can be counted when determining benefits and contributions under all plans. For 2000, the maximum annual compensation that can be counted in the contribution or benefit formula is $170,000 (indexed for inflation).

Participants in defined-benefit plans are protected against the loss of pension benefits up to certain limits if the pension plan should terminate. The **Pension Benefit Guaranty Corporation (PBGC)** is a federal corporation that guarantees the payment of vested or nonforfeitable benefits up to certain limits if a private pension plan is terminated. For 2000, the maximum monthly guarantee is $3221.59 ($38,659.08 annually).

Early Distribution Penalty

A 10 percent tax penalty applies to funds withdrawn before age 59½. The 10 percent tax applies to the amount included in gross income. However, the early distribution penalty does not apply to distributions that are:

- Made after age 59½
- Made after the death or total and permanent disability of the employee
- Made after attaining age 55 and separation from service
- Made as part of a series of substantially equal payments paid over the worker's life expectancy or joint life expectancy of the worker and beneficiary after separation from service
- Distributions to pay for qualified higher education expenses
- Distributions to pay for a first-time home puchase

Insight 23.1

Ten Common Causes of Errors in Pension Calculation: Consumer Tips for Safeguarding Your Pension

Ten Common Causes of Errors in Pension Calculations

- All relevant compensation, such as commissions, overtime, and bonuses (if these were to be included in your plan), was not included in calculating your benefits.
- The calculation was not based on all of your years of service with the company, or all of your work within different divisions.
- The plan administrator used an incorrect benefit formula, such as the wrong interest rate.
- The plan used wrong Social Security data in calculating your benefits.
- Basic information such as your birth date and/or Social Security number was incorrect.
- Your company merged with another company or went out of business, and there is confusion over which pension benefits should be paid.
- Assets in your account were improperly valued.
- Your employer failed to make required contributions on your behalf.
- Basic mistakes were made in the mathematical calculations.
- You failed to update your personnel office with changes (marriage, divorce, death of spouse) that may affect your benefits.

Consumer Tips for Safeguarding Your Pension

- Know your pension plan. Obtain and review your **Summary Plan Description (SPD)**, the rulebook for your pension.
- Review your individual benefit statement and individual account information. Know what your accrued and vested benefits are.
- Maintain a pension file. Keep records of where you've worked, dates you've worked there, your salary, and any plan documents or benefit statements you've received.
- Notify your plan administrator of any changes that may affect your benefit payments (such as marriage, divorce, or the death of a spouse).
- Know the person in your company who has information about your pension plan and can give you plan documents.
- Know how the merger or acquisition of your company will affect your pension benefit.
- Know your pension rights. Request information on your pension rights and how to protect your pension. Call 1-800-998-7542 for publications.
- Contact the Department of Labor's Pension and Welfare Benefits Administration if you have any additional questions about your rights under the law.

Source: U.S. Department of Labor, Pension and Welfare Benefits Administration.

- Distributions that do not exceed deductible medical expenses under the Internal Revenue Code (medical expenses that exceed 7½ percent of adjusted gross income)
- Payments to an alternate payee as a result of a qualified domestic relations order
- Payments made in connection with certain employee stock ownership plans (ESOPs)

The pension contributions, however, cannot remain in the plan indefinitely. Plan distributions must start no later than April 1 of the calendar year following the year in which the individual attains age 70½. However, participants older than 70½ who are still working can delay receiving minimum distributions from a qualified retirement plan. The required beginning date of a participant who is still employed after age 70½ is April 1 of the calendar year that follows the calendar year in which he or she retires. *The preceding rule does not apply to individual retirement acounts (IRAs).*

Funding of Pension Benefits

Qualified private pension plans use advance funding

to fund the pension benefits. **Advance funding** *means the employer systematically and periodically sets aside funds prior to the employee's retirement.* This type of funding increases the security of benefits for the active employees because funds are periodically set aside prior to retirement, and the contributions and investment income receive favorable income-tax treatment.

A qualified plan must also meet certain minimum funding standards. In a defined-benefit plan, the employer must make an annual contribution at least equal to the normal cost of the plan, plus an amount sufficient to amortize any unfunded liabilities over a period of years, which can range from 5 to 40 years depending on the liability and when it occurred.[4] **Normal cost** is the amount necessary to fund the pension costs attributable to the current year's operation of the plan. Liabilities under the plan may arise because of an unfunded initial past-service liability, changes in actuarial assumptions, and plan experience. If the employer fails to meet the minimum funding standard, a tax penalty is imposed.

The minimum funding standard technically applies to defined-contribution pension plans. However, because there is no past-service liability, the minimum funding standard is met provided the employer makes the required contribution each year based on the plan's contribution formula.[5]

Integration with Social Security

The majority of qualified private pension plans are integrated with Social Security. Because employers pay half of the total Old-Age, Survivors, and Disability Insurance (OASDI) payroll tax, they argue that OASDI retirement benefits should be considered in the calculation of private pension benefits. As a result, pension costs can be reduced. Also, integration provides a method for increasing pension benefits for highly compensated employees without increasing the cost of providing benefits to lower-paid employees.

The Internal Revenue Service has prescribed complex integration rules (called permitted disparity rules) that must be followed when a qualified retirement plan is integrated with OASDI. Only one of them—an *excess plan*—is discussed here. In a defined-contribution plan, the pension contribution rate can be higher for employees with earnings above a specified integration level than for employees with earnings below that level. The maximum integration level is the OASDI wage base. Thus, if the integration level is set at the OASDI wage base ($76,200 for 2000), highly compensated employees can receive an additional 5.7 percent of compensation in excess of the wage base, provided that the employer makes contributions at least equal to 5.7 percent of total compensation for all employees.

For example, the Smith Corporation has a defined-contribution pension plan that has a contribution rate of 6 percent of compensation, plus 5.7 percent of compensation in excess of the taxable OASDI wage base ($76,200 in 2000). The rule described above is met. Thus, if Kristin earns $100,000, the contribution made on her behalf will be $7357. This amount is 6 percent of $100,000 ($6000) plus 5.7 percent of $23,800 ($100,000 minus $76,200), or $1357.

If the employer cannot afford to contribute at least 5.7 percent of total compensation for all employees, the maximum disparity must be reduced. For example, if the contribution rate for all employees is 4 percent of total compensation, then an additional contribution of 4 percent of compensation in excess of the integration level can be made.

Finally, as noted earlier, the maximum integration level is the OASDI wage base. The integration level can be set lower, but this approach generally reduces the maximum disparity allowed.

Top-Heavy Plans

Special rules apply to top-heavy plans. A **top-heavy plan** generally is a retirement plan in which more than 60 percent of the benefits or contributions are designated for key employees. A plan is considered top-heavy if the present value of the cumulative accrued benefits for the key employees exceeds 60 percent of the present value of the cumulative accrued benefits under the plan for all covered employees. (Accrued benefits are measured in terms of benefits for defined-benefit plans and account balances for defined-contribution plans.)

A top-heavy plan must meet certain additional requirements to retain its qualified status. These requirements include the following:

- A special rapid vesting schedule must be used for nonkey employees (100 percent vesting after three years, or 20 percent after two years and 20 percent for each year thereafter).
- Certain minimum benefits or contributions must be provided for nonkey employees.

TYPES OF QUALIFIED RETIREMENT PLANS

A wide variety of qualified retirement plans are available today to meet the specific needs of employers. The most important include the following:

- Defined-contribution plans
- Defined-benefit plans
- Section 401(k) plans
- Profit-sharing plans
- Keogh plans
- Simplified employee pension (SEP) plans
- SIMPLE retirement plans

The following sections discuss the basic characteristics of these plans.

DEFINED-CONTRIBUTION PLANS

As noted earlier, a **defined-contribution plan** is a retirement plan in which the contribution rate is fixed, but the actual retirement benefit varies, depending on the worker's age of entry into the plan, contribution rate, investment returns, and the age of normal retirement.

One type of defined-contribution plan is a **money purchase plan**, which specifies the amount of annual contributions to a participant's account. For example, the plan may specify a contribution rate of 4½ percent of salary by the employee and 6 percent by the employer.

Defined-contribution plans are widely used by business firms today. One financial advantage to the firm is that past-service credits are typically not granted for service prior to the plan's inception date, which reduces the employer's cost. Defined-contribution plans are also widely used by nonprofit organizations and state and local governments, where pension costs must be budgeted as a percentage of payroll.

In this type of pension plan, each employee has an individual account, and the retirement contributions and investment income are credited to the account. The employee receives periodic statements that show the account value and investment returns. Amounts forfeited by employees who terminate their employment before they attain full vesting are used to reduce future employer contributions or are reallocated to the accounts of the remaining employees.

However, from the employee's perspective, a defined-contribution plan has several disadvantages. Retirement benefits can only be estimated; the benefit formula may produce an inadequate benefit if the worker enters the plan at an advanced age; and any investment losses must be borne by the employee. Also, some employees do not understand the factors to consider in choosing a particular investment, such as a stock fund, bond fund, money market fund, and other investment options.

In addition, because of fear and the desire to protect principal, some employees invest a large proportion of their retirement contributions in a **stable value fund.** This type of fund is a fixed-income fund that credits the contributions with a specified rate of interest but offers limited opportunities for the growth of principal. As a result, the retirement benefits may be inadequate.

DEFINED-BENEFIT PLANS

Traditional Defined-Benefit Plans

From a historical perspective, employers typically established defined-benefit plans that paid guaranteed benefits to retired workers. As we noted earlier, a **defined-benefit plan** is a retirement plan in which the retirement benefit is know in advance, but the contributions vary depending on the amount needed to fund the desired benefit. Such plans typically pay benefits based on a *unit-benefit formula* that considers both earnings and years of participation in the plan. For example, the plan may provide a retirement benefit payable at the normal retirement age equal to 1 percent of final pay for each year of credited service. Assume Jennifer retires at age 65 and has 25 years of credited service and final pay of $30,000 based on an average of her three highest consecutive years of earnings. She would receive an annual lifetime pension of $7500.

Defined-benefit retirement plans have the major advantages of guaranteeing the worker's retirement benefit; the retirement benefits reflect more accurately the effects of inflation because the benefits are usually based on a final-pay formula; the plans are usually noncontributory, which means that only the employer contributes to the plan; and the investment risk falls directly on the employer, not the employee. In addition, defined-benefit plans favor workers who enter the plan at older ages because the employer must contribute a relatively larger amount for older workers than for younger workers.

Defined-benefit plans have declined in relative importance over the years (see Exhibit 23.2). Because of actuarial considerations, they are more complicated and expensive to administer and fund than defined-contribution plans. Also, these plans initially have large unfunded past-service liabilities because of past-service credits that are expensive to fund. In contrast, defined-contribution plans do not provide past-service credits for service prior to the plan's inception. For these reasons, defined-benefit plans have declined in importance over time.

Cash-Balance Plans

Many employers have converted their traditional defined-benefit plans to a newer type of plan called a cash-balance plan. A **cash-balance plan** *is a defined-benefit plan in which the benefits are defined in terms of a hypothetical account balance; actual retirement benefits will depend on the value of the participant's account at retirement.*

In a typical cash-balance plan, the employer establishes "hypothetical accounts" for plan participants. The accounts are hypothetical because the contributions and interest credits are bookkeeping credits. Actual contributions are not allocated to the participants' accounts, and the accounts do not reflect actual investment gains or losses. The investment credits are also hypothetical and are based on an interest rate stated in the plan or on some external index.

Each year, the participants' accounts are credited with (1) a *pay credit*, such as 4 percent of compensation, and (2) an *interest credit*, such as 5 percent of the account balance. The interest credit can be based on a fixed rate or on a variable rate pegged to some index, such as a one-year Treasury bill rate. Investment gains and losses on the plan's

EXHIBIT 23.2
Number of Private-Sector Defined-Benefit and Defined-Contribution Plans, 1975–1997

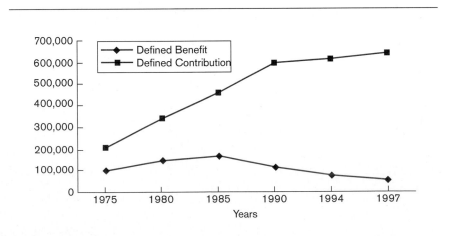

SOURCE: *Facts from EBRI* (Washington, DC: Employee Benefit Research Institute, December 1998).

assets do not directly affect the benefits promised to the participants. Thus, the employer bears the investment risks and realizes any investment gains. For example, assume that the employer makes a contribution of 4 percent of pay each year to the participants' accounts. If James earns $50,000 annually, his "account" is credited with $2000. Each year, his account balance will be credited with a stated interest rate, such as 5 percent. At retirement, James can elect to receive a life annuity that will pay him a life income. Instead of an annuity, the cash-balance plan may allow him to elect a lump-sum payment equal to the account balance, which can then be rolled over into an IRA.

Many employers have converted traditional defined-benefit plans into cash-balance plans in an effort to hold down pension costs. Also, younger workers benefit because they can understand the plan better; benefits accrue at a faster pace than under a traditional defined-benefit plan; and the benefits are portable for workers who leave before retirement age.

However, critics argue that the switch to a cash-balance plan can reduce expected pension benefits for older workers by 20 percent to 50 percent. Here's why. The benefits earned under the traditional defined-benefit formula may exceed the benefit amount earned under the new cash-balance formula. *In this situation, older participants may not earn any additional benefits until their benefits under the new cash-balance plan formula exceed the benefits earned under the old formula. It may take several years before additional benefits accrue under the new plan.* Actuaries call this effect a "wear away," because you wear away the old benefit before earning a new benefit. As a result, many older workers believe cash-balance plans are discriminatory (see Insight 23.2).

SECTION 401(K) PLANS

Section 401(k) plans are becoming increasingly popular among employees as a tax-deferred saving plan. A **Section 401(k) plan** *is a qualified cash or deferred arrangement (CODA) that allows eligible employees the option of putting money into the plan or receiving the funds as cash.* A Section 401(k) plan can be a qualified profit-sharing plan, saving or thrift plan, or stock bonus plan. A plan can be established that includes both employer and employee contributions, or the employee contributions alone.

In a typical plan, both the employer and employees contribute, and the employer matches part or all of the employee's contributions. For example, for each dollar contributed by the employee, the employer may contribute 25 or 50 cents, or some higher amount.

Most plans allow the employees to determine how the funds are invested. Employees typically have a choice of investments, such as a common stock fund, bond fund, fixed-income fund, and other funds. Many plans also allow the contributions to be invested in company stock. However, it is risky to invest a large proportion of the funds in the company's stock.

Annual Limit on Elective Deferrals

Eligible employees can voluntarily elect to have their salaries reduced if they participate in a Section 401(k) plan. For 2000, the maximum salary reduction is $10,500 (indexed for inflation). The amount of salary deferred is then invested in the employer's Section 401(k) plan. The amounts deferred are not subject to the federal income tax until the funds are withdrawn. However, Social Security taxes must be paid on the contributions to the plan.

Actual Deferral Percentage Test

To prevent discrimination in favor of highly compensated employees in a Section 401(k) plan, an **actual deferral percentage (ADP) test** must be satisfied. That is, the actual percentage of salary deferred for highly compensated employees is subject to certain limitations. In general, the eligible employees are divided into two groups: (1) highly compensated employees, and (2) other eligible employees. The percentage of salary deferred for each employee is totaled and then averaged to get an ADP for each group. The ADPs of both groups are then compared. The rules for calculating the ADPs are complex and beyond the scope of this text to discuss in detail. However, Exhibit 23.3 shows the permissible ADPs for highly compensated employees based on these rules. For example, if the nonhighly compensated group has an ADP of 6 percent, the ADP for the

Insight 23.2

Some Workers Facing Pension Hit

Some employees work for employers converting traditional pension plans to new "cash balance" retirement plans, under which an employer creates hypothetical employee accounts to which the employer contributes a percentage of the employee's pay each year, as well as interest.

But the pain of conversion to these little-understood hybrid plans won't be shared across the board: Younger employees and recently hired workers will earn pension benefits right away.

All this will come as a surprise to many people, even at the hundreds of companies that already have made this pension shift. Cash-balance plans are growing popular with employers who see drawbacks to traditional pension plans, which pay retiring employees designated monthly amounts. Upon eliminating a so-called defined-benefit plan and adopting a cash-balance one, an employer determines the value of benefits built up by his employees under the traditional plan, and places some, or all, of that value into individual employee accounts. Those individual accounts then grow, courtesy of pay and interest credits made by the employer, over the years.

While these individual accounts can be taken with an employee when changing jobs, what is riling some who've looked closely at this newfangled plan is that employers have a lot of leeway in how they credit workers for the value of their built-up pension benefits. *Older workers, in particular, often aren't credited for the full value of what they've already earned, and the result is that they can work years before earning pension benefits above and beyond what they had under the traditional plan.*

"It would be nice if they told people they will work a number of years" without benefit of improving their pension standing, says an employee at Empire Blue Cross Blue Shield, in Albany, New York, which adopts a cash-balance plan in January. The 25-year Empire veteran, who doesn't wish to be identified, calculated she must work seven years before earning new pension benefits. An Empire spokeswoman says employees will receive detailed information soon about their status.

Employers aren't eager to tell employees that their pension accrual might cease for a while, because they figure workers will get pretty mad if they find out. Which is true.

When Ispat Inland Inc., a steel company in East Chicago, Indiana, announced last month it would shift to a cash-balance plan Jan. 1, Paul Schroeder, a 44-year-old engineer with 19 years at the company, calculated it would take 9 to 13 years before he acquired additional pension benefits. After some Ispat employees confronted management last week, employees received a communication from the human-resources department confirming "the vast majority would experience a plateau in the growth of their pension benefit."

What's the size of this plateau? Five to 13 years for some, according to an Ispat spokesman. Facing a 13-year plateau, for example, would be a 40-year-old with 22 years of service, earning $45,000.

Here are answers to commonly asked questions about opening-account balances:

What happens when an employer converts to a cash-balance plan?

Employers generally determine a value of each employee's existing pension and put this into an individual "account." Then, each year, the employer credits the account with a percentage of pay (often 4%) and interest, often 5%.

Is the starting account balance the equivalent of the old pension benefit?

In many cases, no. The actual value of your old pension benefit might be $50,000, but your opening balance might be, say, $35,000. As a result, you wouldn't actually earn a new pension benefit until the pay and interest credits bring the account to $50,000. (The ranges vary.)

Some employers call this a "plateauing" of your pension; actuaries call it "wear away," because you wear away the old benefit before earning a fresh one.

Is this legal?

By law, an earned pension can't be taken away or reduced. But a low opening balance doesn't violate this law, because, if you quit your job before your pension benefit started growing again, you would receive the full $50,000 in the above example.

It is legal for employers to establish opening balances using whatever criteria they deem appropriate. In a session in March held by the Conference of Consulting Actuaries in Washington, a panel of pension experts joked that the starting balance could be based on shoe size or license plate numbers.

Of course, employers use more rational factors when calculating opening balances. One with a big punch: excluding the value of early-retirement subsidies. "It effectively means [affected employees] aren't getting an accrual, and they're angry, legitimately an-

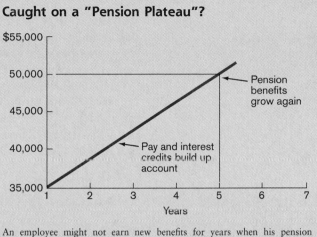

Caught on a "Pension Plateau"?

An employee might not earn new benefits for years when his pension converts to a "cash balance" plan. Consider this hypothetical: If an employee's old pension benefit has a lump-sum value of $50,000, but the employee is given a $35,000 opening balance, it could take five years for the account to grow to $50,000.

gry," says William Sohn, a cash-balance expert with Buck Consultants in New York. But, from an employer's perspective, such subsidies aid only early retirees, so removing them seems fair, he adds.

Don't employers have to tell you that your opening balance is lower?

Good question. Most employers aren't very clear. The information given by Empire Blue Cross Blue Shield to employees says: "Your starting account balance represents the current value of the benefit you have earned as of Dec. 31, 1998." In fact, balances will be lower for employees like the one quoted above.

The Empire employee complains she and a colleague haven't been able to obtain the information needed to calculate exactly how long their wear-away period is. Among other things, they'd like to figure out if it makes sense to look for jobs elsewhere with better benefits.

An Empire spokeswoman says the company will tell employees what old benefits are worth and what opening balances will be. She points out that the company has increased its matching contribution to the 401(k) plan to help employees save more.

SOURCE: Adapted from Ellen E. Schultz, "Some Workers Facing Pension Hit," *The Wall Street Journal*, December 18, 1998, pp. C1, C21.

EXHIBIT 23.3
**Permissible Actual Deferral Percentages (ADPs)
for Highly Compensated Employees**

ADP for Non-HCE	ADP for HCE
1%	2%
2	4
3	5
4	6
5	7
6	8
7	9
8	10
9	11.25
10	12.50
11	13.75
12	15

Source: Nicholas Kaster, et al., *1999 U.S Master Pension Guide* (Chicago, IL: CCH Incorporated, 1999), p. 786.

highly compensated group is limited to 8 percent for favorable tax treatment.

Limitations on Distributions

A 10 percent penalty tax applies to an early distribution of funds before age $59\frac{1}{2}$ with certain exceptions. Exceptions include death or disability of the employee, payments that are part of a life or joint life annuity payout, separation from service after age 55, payments for medical expenses deductible under the Internal Revenue Code, and payments to a qualified payee under a qualified domestic relations order.

The plan may permit the withdrawal of funds for a hardship withdrawal. The IRS recognizes four reasons for a hardship withdrawal:

- Certain unreimbursable medical expenses
- Purchase of a primary residence
- Payments for post-secondary education expenses
- Payments to prevent eviction or foreclosure on your home

The 10 percent penalty still applies to a hardship withdrawal. However, 401(k) plans typically have a **loan provision** that allows funds to be borrowed without a tax penalty.

Despite the substantial tax penalties for a premature distribution, many employees often use their 401(k) funds and other retirement funds for purposes other than retirement, such as spending the funds outright, paying off debts, or buying a home. Employees who take money out of their retirement plans early will receive a substantially lower amount of income during retirement. As a result, they may be exposed to serious financial insecurity during retirement.

In summary, a 401(k) plan can play an important role in your retirement plans. In addition to saving money on a tax-deferred basis, your take-home pay will increase. There are other advantages as well (see Insight 23.3).

PROFIT-SHARING PLANS

Many employers have profit-sharing plans to provide retirement income to eligible employees. A **profit-sharing plan** *is a defined-contribution plan in which the employer's contributions are typically based on the firm's profits.* However, there is no requirement that the employer must actually earn a profit to contribute to the plan.

Employers establish profit-sharing plans for several reasons. Eligible employees are encouraged to work more efficiently; the employer's cost is not affected by the age or number of employees; and there is greater flexibility in employer contributions. If there are no profits, there are no contributions.

The profit-sharing contributions can be discretionary—based on an amount determined annually by the board of directors—or they can be based on a formula, such as a certain percentage of profits above a certain level. There are annual limits, however, on the amount that can be contributed into an employee's account. *For 2000, the maximum annual employer contribution is limited to 15 percent of employee compensation or $25,500, whichever is lower (13.04 percent if self-employed).*

The profit-sharing funds are typically distributed to the employees at retirement, death, disability, or termination of employment (only the vested portion), or after a fixed number of years (at least two years). Amounts forfeited by employees who leave the company before they attain full vesting are reallocated to the accounts of the remaining participants.

A 10 percent tax penalty applies to a distribution to a participant younger than age 59½. To avoid the tax penalty, many plans have loan provisions that permit employees to borrow from their accounts.

RETIREMENT PLANS FOR THE SELF-EMPLOYED

Sole proprietors and partners can establish qualified retirement plans and enjoy most of the favorable tax advantages now available to participants in qualified corporate pension plans. Retirement plans for the owners of unincorporated business firms are commonly called **Keogh plans** or **HR-10 plans**. The contributions to the plan are income-tax deductible up to certain limits, and the investment income accumulates on a tax-deferred basis. The amounts deposited and the investment earnings are not taxed until the funds are distributed.

With certain exceptions, the same rules that apply to qualified corporate pension plans now apply to retirement plans for the self-employed.

Limits on Contributions and Benefits

For 2000, if the Keogh plan is a defined-contribution plan, the maximum annual contribution is limited to 25 percent of compensation or $30,000, whichever is lower. However, for purposes of determining the amount that can be contributed, self-employment net earnings must be reduced by (1) one-half of the Social Security self-employment tax and (2) the actual contributions into the plan. This latter adjustment presents a problem because the amount of the Keogh deduction and the amount of net earnings are dependent on each other. Fortunately, the IRS has prepared a worksheet to help you make the correct calculation. *However, for our purposes here, the maximum annual contribution into a defined-contribution Keogh plan is limited to 20 percent of net earnings after subtracting one-half of the Social Security self-employment tax.* If the 20 percent figure is used, the resulting amount is exactly equal to 25 percent of compensation after the two adjustments are made.

For example, after deducting one-half of the Social Security payroll tax, Shannon has net self-employment earnings of $50,000. She can make a maximum tax-deductible contribution of $10,000

into the plan, which reduces her taxable earnings to $40,000. This amount is exactly equal to 25 percent of her net income after the contribution is made ($10,000/$40,000 = 25%).

For 2000, if the Keogh plan is a *defined-benefit plan*, a self-employed individual can fund for a maximum annual benefit equal to 100 percent of average compensation for the three highest consecutive years of compensation, or $135,000, whichever is lower. This latter figure is indexed for inflation.

For example, assume that Nancy, age 50, establishes a defined-benefit plan that will provide a retirement benefit equal to 50 percent of her net income at age 65. If average net income for the three highest consecutive years is $50,000, she can fund for a maximum annual benefit of $25,000. An actuary then determines the amount that she can contribute annually into the plan to reach that goal. In this case, based on 7 percent interest and certain actuarial assumptions, Nancy could contribute $10,847 annually into the plan.

Other Requirements

Certain other requirements must also be met, including the following:

- All employees at least age 21 and with one year of service must be included in the plan. A two-year waiting period can be required if the plan provides for full and immediate vesting upon entry.
- Certain annual reports must be filed with the IRS.
- A 10 percent tax penalty applies to the withdrawal of funds prior to age 59½ (except for certain distributions as noted earlier).
- Plan distributions must start no later than April 1 of the year following the calendar year in which the self-employed person attains age 70½.
- If the plan is top-heavy, the special top-heavy rules discussed earlier must also be met.

SIMPLIFIED EMPLOYEE PENSION (SEP)

A **simplified employee pension (SEP)** is a retirement plan in which the employer contributes to an IRA established for each eligible employee; however, the annual contribution limits are substantially higher. SEP plans are popular with smaller employers because the amount of required paperwork is minimal.

Insight 23.3

Eight Reasons Why 401(k)s Are a Smart Idea

There's lots of talk about Social Security. Even if you do receive Social Security payments later in life, *they were never meant to be your only means of income during retirement*. In fact, in 1998 the Social Security Administration estimated that Social Security will provide less than a quarter of what you'll need to pay for housing, food, and other living expenses—not to mention an occasional golf game.

It's up to you to save and invest for your own future. That's just one of the reasons why it's a great idea to participate in your company's 401(k) retirement plan. Here are seven more reasons.

- **You can increase your take-home pay.**
  Investing money through your 401(k) plan gives you the benefit of "tax-deferred saving." This lets you *increase* your talk-home pay and *decrease* your current income tax bill. Take a look at a hypothetical chart to see how contributing to the plan compares with saving outside the plan.
- **A "company match" can help your investments grow.**
  Some companies offer a "match" as an incentive to join the company retirement plan. It means that the company will contribute a certain amount to your

Contributing to Your 401(k) on a Pre-tax Basis Helps You Increase Your Take-Home Pay

	Pre-tax savings in the plan	Saving in a taxable account outside of the plan
Annual gross salary	$50,000	$50,000
6 percent of pay before-tax contribution	−3,000	0
Taxable pay	47,000	50,000
Less 28 percent federal income tax	−13,160	−14,000
6 percent regular savings in a taxable account outside the plan (from gross salary)	0	−3,000
Take-home pay	$33,840	$33,000
Annual difference in take-home pay	**$840**	

Actual results may vary, and taxes will be due when you withdraw from the plan.

In one type of plan, called a **SEP-IRA,** the employer contributes to an IRA owned by each employee. The SEP-IRA must cover all qualifying employees who are at least age 21, have worked for the employer in at least three of the immediately preceding five years, and have received at least $450 (indexed for inflation) from the employer in compensation during the tax year.

For 2000, the maximum annual tax-deductible employer contribution to a SEP-IRA is limited to 15 percent of the employee's compensation, or $25,500, *whichever is less.* There is full and immediate vesting of all employer contributions under the plan.

SIMPLE RETIREMENT PLANS

Smaller employers are eligible to establish a Savings Incentive Match Plan for Employees, or SIMPLE for short. The **SIMPLE retirement plan** is limited to employers that employ 100 or fewer eligible employees and do not maintain another qualified plan. Under a

account (usually between $0.25 and $1.00) for every dollar that you contribute, up to a certain limit. The match formula can vary.

- **Automatic payroll deduction makes it easy to save.**
Saving is ultra convenient with your 401(k) because the money comes right out of your pay before you get your paycheck. This automatic payroll deduction helps make saving your number one priority. You don't see the money, so you're not tempted to spend it!
- **Most of your plan's investment choices are managed by professionals.**
Many of the investment options in your company's 401(k) plan are mutual funds. By investing in mutual funds, you place your money in the hands of a highly experienced team of investment professionals.
- **Most plans allow access to money in an emergency.**
The money you invest in your company's 401(k) plan is designed to help you when you need it most: at retirement. But for those unexpected circumstances that can arise, many plans allow employees to dip into their account balances before retirement.
- **Account services keep you informed.**
Account services provide frequent and up-to-date information about your account, so you can always be informed about how your investments are performing.

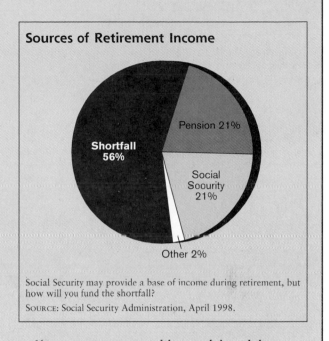

Sources of Retirement Income

Shortfall 56%

Pension 21%

Social Security 21%

Other 2%

Social Security may provide a base of income during retirement, but how will you fund the shortfall?

SOURCE: Social Security Administration, April 1998.

- **Your money can go with you, job to job.**
One reason why plans like 401(k)s have become so popular is that they are portable: generally speaking, you can take them from job to job (with some exceptions).

SOURCE: Adaptation of *Eight Reasons Why 401(k)s Are a Smart Idea,* Fidelity Investments.

SIMPLE plan, employers are exempt from most nondiscrimination and administrative rules that apply to qualified plans. By simplifying the pension rules, Congress believes that smaller employers will be encouraged to establish pension plans for their employees.

A SIMPLE plan can be structured either as an IRA or as a 401(k) plan. Only the IRA arrangement is discussed here. Under a SIMPLE plan, eligible employees can elect to contribute a percentage of salary up to $6000 annually. *The employer has the option of either (1) matching the employee's contributions on a dollar-for-dollar basis up to 3 percent of salary, or (2) making a nonelective contribution of 2 percent of salary for all eligible employees.* If employers are strapped for cash during lean years, they can reduce the matching contribution to 1 percent of salary provided that the employees are notified and that the employer has made a 3 percent matching contribution for three out of the last five years. The $6000 annual contribution is indexed for inflation in increments of $500. Exhibit 23.4

EXHIBIT 23.4
SIMPLE Retirement Plan Contribution Methods

Comparing Employer Contribution Methods

To illustrate the differences between these two contribution methods, let's look at hypothetical funding requirements for an employee making $30,000 per year.

	If the employer chooses the 3% matching contribution	If the employer chooses the 2% nonelective contribution
Example A *The employee contributes 5% of salary ($30,000) or $1500.*		
	Employer matches employee's contribution on a dollar-for-dollar basis, up to 3% of the employee's compensation (**3% × $30,000 = $900**). Of course, in any two years in a five-year period, the employer has the flexibility to reduce its match to 1% of the employee's compensation (**1% × $30,000 = $300**).	Employer contributes 2% of the employee's compensation (**2% × $30,000 = $600**).
Example B *The employee contributes 2.5% of salary ($30,000) or $750.*		
	Employer matches the employee's contribution on a dollar-for-dollar basis, up to 3% of his compensation. Since the employee chose to contribute only 2.5% of his compensation, which is $750, the employer would have to match only $750. In any two years in a five-year period, the employer could reduce its match to **1% or $300**.	Employer contributes 2% of the employee's compensation (**2% × $30,000 = $600**).
Example C *The employee decides not to contribute anything.*		
	The employer is not required to contribute anything because there's no salary reduction contribution for the employer to match.	The employer is required to contribute 2% of the employee's compensation (**2% × $30,000 = $600**).

SOURCE: Fidelity Investments.

---

illustrates the difference between the two contribution methods.

All employees who have received at least $5000 from the employer during any two previous years and are reasonably expected to receive at least $5000 in compensation during the current year must be allowed to participate in a SIMPLE plan. Self-employed individuals can also participate. All contributions go into an IRA account and are fully and immediately vested. Withdrawal of funds by SIMPLE participants who are younger than age 59½ are subject to a 10 percent tax penalty; however, withdrawals during the first two years of participation are subject to a stiff 25 percent tax penalty.

FUNDING AGENCY AND FUNDING INSTRUMENTS

An employer must also select a funding agency when a pension plan is established. A **funding agency** *is a financial institution that provides for the accumulation or administration of the funds that will be used to pay pension benefits.* If the funding agency is a commercial bank or individual trustee, the plan is called a *trust-fund plan*. If the funding agency is a life insurer, the plan is called an *insured plan*. If both funding agencies are used, the plan is called a *combination plan*.

The employer must select a funding instrument to fund the pension plan. A **funding instrument** *is a* *trust agreement or insurance contract that states the terms under which the funding agency will accumulate, administer, and disburse the pension funds.* The major funding instruments are as follows:[6]

- Trust-fund plan
- Deposit-administration plan
- Immediate-participation guarantee (IPG) plan
- Group deferred annuity
- Guaranteed investment contract (GIC)

Trust-Fund Plan

The majority of pension assets are in trust-fund plans. Under a **trust-fund plan**, all contributions are deposited with a trustee, who invests the funds according to the trust agreement between the employer and trustee. The trustee can be a commercial bank or an individual trustee. Annuities are not usually purchased when the employees retire, and the pension benefits are paid directly out of the fund. The trustee does not guarantee the adequacy of the fund, nor are there any guarantees of principal and interest rates. A consulting actuary periodically determines the adequacy of the fund.

Deposit-Administration Plan

A **deposit-administration plan** is an insured plan. All pension contributions are deposited in an unallocated fund. When the worker retires, an immediate annuity is purchased out of the plan's assets.

A **separate account** is a variation of the deposit-administration plan. Under a separate account, the pension funds are segregated, so that the account assets are not commingled with the insurer's general assets. The pension funds can be invested in an equity account or fixed-income account.

Immediate-Participation Guarantee Plan

An **immediate-participation guarantee (IPG) plan** is another insured plan. All pension contributions are deposited in an unallocated fund. The fund immediately reflects any unfavorable plan experience with respect to mortality, investments, and expenses. Annuities generally are not purchased when the workers retire; the pension benefits are paid directly

out of the plan's assets. The insurer does not guarantee the adequacy of the fund. However, the insurer periodically evaluates the fund to determine whether it is sufficient to continue paying the promised benefits to the retired workers. If the fund declines to a level that is inadequate for paying full benefits to the retired workers, annuities would then be purchased for them.

Group Deferred Annuity

A group deferred annuity is an insured plan that has declined in importance in recent years. Under a **group deferred annuity**, a single-premium deferred annuity is purchased each year equal to the retirement benefit earned for that year. For example, under a defined-benefit pension plan, the worker may earn for the current year a monthly retirement benefit of $25 starting at age 65. A benefit equal to that amount would be purchased for that year. The benefit amount paid at retirement is the sum of the benefits payable under all deferred-annuity contracts that have been purchased on the worker's behalf.

Group deferred annuities are not widely used today because newer and more flexible pension products have been developed. Most plans have changed to other methods of funding, but older deferred annuities purchased before the change still remain in force.

Guaranteed Investment Contract

A **guaranteed investment contract (GIC)** is an arrangement in which the insurer guarantees a relatively high interest rate for a number of years on a lump-sum deposit. Guaranteed investment contracts have been popular with employers in recent years because of the interest rate guarantee by the insurer. In addition, the principal is guaranteed against loss. Finally, most guaranteed investment contracts make annuity options or other payment options available, but the employer is not required to use these options.

SUMMARY

- Under the tax law, qualified pension plans must meet certain minimum coverage requirements, which are de-

Establishing Individual Accounts Under this approach, each worker would have an individual retirement account. The OASDI payroll tax would be reduced by 2 percentage points (or by some other amount), which would be used to fund the worker's retirement benefits. If the worker died before retirement, the deceased worker's spouse or beneficiary would inherit the assets.

A major criticism of the present program is the relatively low return that younger workers will receive on the OASDI taxes paid. The Advisory Council on Social Security estimates that the *internal real rate of return* on OASDI payroll taxes paid by average and upper-income single workers in the future will be less than 2 percent.[12] The projected rates of return are relatively low compared with those available from other investments in the economy. Proponents believe that individual accounts will allow younger workers to earn substantially higher real rates of return, especially if the funds are invested in common stocks.

The establishment of individual accounts is a controversial issue. Critics argue that the risk to the workers will increase. Workers would have to bear any investment losses, and the present program with its safety net and income guarantees would be dramatically altered.

Using the Projected Budget Surplus to Save Social Security Thanks to the robust economy and low unemployment, the federal budget is projected to incur a surplus in excess of $1.9 trillion over the next ten years. As discussed earlier, part of this surplus could be used to fund the OASDI program. Thus, general revenue financing would help fund the program under this proposal. At present, the OASDI program is funded largely by earmarked payroll taxes, and general revenue financing is not the major source of revenue.

Using the surplus to save Social Security is controversial. Although the long-range solvency of the OASDI trust funds would be substantially improved, at least two objections to this proposal have been made. First, the expected surplus may not materialize if the nation experiences a recession, and federal tax revenues decline. Second, general revenue financing represents a dramatic departure from the present principle of a financially self-supporting program based largely on payroll taxes. The present financing system encourages a more responsible attitude on the part of elected representatives, which could be lost by relying on general revenue financing.

Medicare Financial Crisis

Part A of Medicare will also experience a serious financial crisis in the future. *The 2000 Board of Trustees report showed that the Hospital Insurance (HI) trust fund will be exhausted in 2023.*

This unsatisfactory financial condition is due to several factors, including an increase in the number of Medicare beneficiaries, inflation in hospital costs exceeding the overall rate of inflation, fraud and abuse by health care providers, substantial increases in home health care costs, and an inefficient and inflationary fee-for-service method of reimbursement.

To hold down Medicare costs, Congress has reduced payments to hospitals and physicians, placed spending limits on specified services, limited fees paid to physicians, implemented the diagnosis-related group method in which flat amounts are paid to hospitals for each specific case, and enacted other cost-reduction measurers. Despite these efforts, Medicare costs continue to increase.

More recently, the National Bipartisan Commission on the Future of Medicare has made several recommendations to improve the solvency of Medicare and modernize the program.[14] Major recommendations include the following: (1) increasing gradually the Medicare eligibility age from age 65 to 67 to match the scheduled increase for OASDI; (2) increasing competition by allowing beneficiaries to enroll in private health insurance plans that would compete with the traditional fee-for-service Medicare plan; (3) combining the Part A and Part B trust funds into a single Medicare trust fund. These recommendations remain controversial. At the time of this writing, Congress had not enacted any of these recommendations into law.

Outpatient Prescription Drugs Under Medicare

Another important issue is coverage of outpatient prescription drugs under the Medicare program.

Defined-benefit plan

Defined-contribution formula

Defined-contribution plan

Deposit-administration plan

Early retirement age

Employee Retirement Income Security Act of 1974 (ERISA)

Final pay

Funding agency

Funding instrument

Group deferred annuity

Guaranteed investment contract (GIC)

Highly compensated employees

Immediate-participation guarantee (IPG) plan

Keogh plans (HR-10 plans)

Late retirement age

Minimum age and service requirement

Minimum coverage requirements

Minimum vesting standards

Money purchase plan

Normal cost

Normal retirement age

Past-service credits

Pension Benefit Guaranty Corporation (PBGC)

Profit-sharing plan

Qualified plan

Ratio percentage test

Section 401(k) plan

Separate account

SEP-IRA

SIMPLE retirement plan

Simplified employee pension (SEP)

Stable value fund

Taxpayer Relief Act of 1997

Top-heavy plan

Trust-fund plans

Vesting

REVIEW QUESTIONS

1. Describe the federal income-tax advantages to employers and employees in a qualified retirement plan.

2. Explain the minimum coverage requirements that an employer must meet to have a qualified retirement plan.

3. Identify the three retirement ages normally found in private retirement plans.

4. Describe the basic characteristics of a defined-contribution retirement plan.

5. Describe the basic features of a defined-benefit retirement plan. What is a cash-balance plan?

6. Identify the basic characteristics of a Section 401(k) plan.

7. Identify the key characteristics of a profit-sharing plan.

8. Describe the basic features of a Keogh plan for the self-employed (HR-10 plan).

9. What is a simplified employee pension (SEP)? Explain your answer.

10. Describe the major characteristics of a SIMPLE retirement plan.

APPLICATION QUESTIONS

1. Qualified *defined-contribution* and *defined-benefit* retirement plans must meet certain requirements to receive favorable income-tax treatment. Explain briefly each of the following:
   a. Minimum age and service requirements
   b. Vesting provisions
   c. Limitations on contributions and benefits
   d. Early distribution tax penalty

2. Employers frequently establish Section 401(k) plans to provide retirement benefits to their employees.
   a. What is the purpose of the actual deferral percentage (ADP) rules in a Section 401(k) plan?
   b. When can Section 401(k) funds be withdrawn? Explain your answer.
   c. Explain the federal income-tax consequence of taking an early distribution under a Section 401(k) plan.

3. Self-employed persons can establish a qualified retirement plan (Keogh plan) and receive favorable income-tax treatment. Briefly explain each of the following:
   a. Income-tax advantages of a qualified Keogh plan
   b. Employees who must be included in the plan
   c. Limitations on annual contributions and benefits

4. Eligible employers can establish a SIMPLE retirement plan for their employees and receive favorable income-tax treatment.
   a. Explain the type of employer for which a SIMPLE retirement plan is designed.
   b. What is the maximum annual contribution that an eligible employee can make to a SIMPLE retirement plan?
   c. Explain the contribution methods available to employers under a SIMPLE retirement plan.

5. An employer must select a *funding agency* and a *funding instrument* when a pension plan is established.
   a. What is a funding agency?
   b. Briefly describe each of the following funding instruments:

    (1) Trust-fund plan

    (2) Deposit-administration plan

    (3) Immediate participation guarantee (IPG) plan

  c. What is a guaranteed investment contract (GIC)?

SELECTED REFERENCES

Allen, Everett T. Jr., et al. *Pension Planning: Pension, Profit Sharing, and Other Deferred Compensation Plans*, eighth edition. Burr Ridge, IL: McGraw-Hill Companies, 1997.

Beam, Burton T. Jr., and John J. McFadden. *Employee Benefits*, fifth edition. Chicago, IL: Dearborn Financial Publishing, 1998.

Commerce Clearing House. *1999 U.S. Master Tax Guide*. Chicago, IL: CCH Incorporated, 1999.

Kaster, Nicholas, et al. *2000 U.S. Master Pension Guide*. Chicago, IL: CCH Incorporated, 2000.

McGill, Dan M., et al. *Fundamentals of Private Pensions*, seventh edition. Philadelphia, PA: University of Pennsylvania Press, 1996.

Rosenbloom, Jerry S., ed. *The Handbook of Employee Benefits, Design, Funding, Administration*. Burr Ridge, IL: Irwin Professional Publishing, 1996.

Tacchino, Kenn Beam, and David A. Littell. *Planning for Retirement Needs*, second edition. Bryn Mawr, PA: The American College, 1998.

NOTES

1. This chapter is based on Nicholas Kaster et al, *1999 U.S. Master Pension Guide* (Chicago, IL: CCH Incorporated, 1999); *1999 U.S. Master Tax Guide* (Chicago, IL: CCH Incorporated, 1999); Burton T. Beam, Jr., and John J. McFadden, *Employee Benefits*, fifth edition (Chicago, IL: Dearborn Financial Publishing, 1998). IRS tax documents for taxpayers are also used.

2. For 2000, highly compensated employees are employees who (1) owned 5 percent of the company at any time during the year or preceding year or (2) had compensation from the employer in excess of $85,000 (indexed for inflation) during the preceding year, and if the employer so elects, were in the top-paid group of employees for the preceding year (that is, the highest 20 percent of employees based on compensation).

Case Application

Richard, age 40, is the owner of Auto Repair, Inc. Because of a tight labor market, he wants to establish a retirement plan for his employees. He is considering several retirement plans, including (i) a *defined-contribution plan*, (ii) a *Section 401(k) plan*, and (iii) a *SEP-IRA*. Assume you are a financial planner and Richard asks for your advice. Answer the following questions.

a. Explain to Richard the advantages and disadvantages of each of the three retirement plans.

b. Richard's salary is $100,000 for the current tax year. If he elects to set up a defined-contribution plan, what is the maximum tax-deductible contribution Richard can make to the plan?

c. Susan, the company's office manager, is 28 years old, and earns $35,000. She has worked for the company for three years. Can Richard exclude her from participating in the defined-contribution plan to hold down pension costs? Explain your answer.

d. Assume Auto Repair selects a Section 401(k) plan. The plan allows participants to defer 6 percent of their salary up to annual maximum limit ($10,500 for 2000). The employer makes a matching contribution of 50 cents for each dollar contributed. James, age 25, is a mechanic who has decided to defer only 3 percent of his salary because of substantial personal debts. What advice would you give to James?

e. Richard's wife, Maria, age 35, is self-employed as a freelance writer. After deducting half of the Social Security self-employment payroll tax, she has a net income of $50,000 for the current tax year. What is the maximum tax-deductible contribution Maria can make to a defined-contribution Keogh plan?

3. Linda Abbott, "Coming Up Short: Pension Errors Cost a Bundle," *Everybody's Money* (Winter 1997), p. 9.

4. Vincent Amoroso, "Costing and Funding Retirement Benefits," in Jerry S. Rosenbloom, ed., *The Handbook of Employee Benefits, Design, Funding, Administra-* *tion* (Burr Ridge, IL: Irwin Professional Publishing, 1996), p. 987.

5. Beam and McFadden, p. 552.

6. Amoroso, pp. 959–966.

 Students may take a self-administered test on this chapter at www.awlonline.com/rejda

Chapter 24

Social Insurance

"Economic security is one of the unfulfilled needs of humans. Social security programs have been designed to aid people in their quest for economic security."

Robert J. Myers
Social Security, 4th ed.

Learning Objectives

After studying this chapter, you should be able to:

▲ Explain the reasons why social insurance programs are established.

▲ Describe the basic characteristics of social insurance programs.

▲ Identify the major benefits provided by the Old-Age, Survivors, and Disability Insurance (OASDI) program.

▲ Identify the major benefits under the Medicare program.

▲ Describe the basic objectives and important provisions of state unemployment insurance programs.

▲ Explain the basic objectives and major provisions of workers compensation insurance.

▲ Access the Social Security Administration's Web site and obtain information about the Social Security (OASDI) program.

Internet Resources

- The **Employment and Training Administration (ETA)** is a federal agency in the U.S. Department of Labor that provides detailed information and data on state unemployment compensation programs. Visit the site at:

  http://www.doleta.gov/

- The **Health Care Financing Administration (HCFA)**, which is part of the U.S. Department of Health and Human Services, administers the Medicare program. HCFA provides timely information and data on the Medicare program. Visit the site at:

  http://www.hcfa.gov/

- The **National Academy of Social Insurance** is a professional organization that attempts to improve public understanding of social insurance programs. It published timely and important research studies on Social Security and Medicare. Visit the site at:

  www.nasi.org

- The **National Council on Compensation Insurance** develops and administers rating plans and systems for workers compensation insurance. Visit the site at:

  http://www.ncci.com

- The **Office of the Chief Actuary** in the Social Security Administration provides actuarial cost estimates of the OASDI and Medicare programs and determines the annual cost-of-living adjustments in benefits. The site provides a number of timely publications. Visit the site at:

  http://www.ssa.gov/OACT/index.html

- The **Social Security Administration (SSA)** is an independent federal agency that administers the Social Security program. Its Web site provides current information on OASDI retirement, survivor, and disability benefits and recent changes in the program. Visit the site at:

  www.ssa.gov

- The **Social Security Advisory Board** is an independent, bipartisan board that advises the President and members of Congress on matters relating to Social Security. Its Web site provides timely and relevant reports dealing with Social Security. Visit the site at:

  http://www.ssab.gov/

ocial insurance programs are compulsory government insurance programs with certain characteristics that distinguish them from private insurance and other government insurance programs. The various programs provide a safety net against the financial insecurity that can result from premature death, unemployment, poor health, job-related disabilities, and old age. Social insurance programs are especially valuable to individuals and families with limited incomes. For example, Jennifer is a single parent, age 30, who became totally and permanently disabled in an auto accident in 2000. She is the sole support of her son, age 3. Assume that she is eligible for Social Security disability benefits. If her annual earnings are $20,000 in 2000, Jennifer and her son would receive monthly disability benefits of approximately $1218,[1] which would enable her to maintain at least a minimum standard of living.

This chapter discusses the major social insurance programs in the United States. The programs discussed include the Social Security program (OASDI), Medicare, state unemployment insurance programs, and workers compensation programs.

SOCIAL INSURANCE

Reasons for Social Insurance

Although the United States has a highly developed system of private insurance, social insurance pro-

grams are necessary for three reasons. *First, social insurance programs are enacted to solve complex social problems.* A social problem affects most or all of society and is so serious that direct government intervention is necessary. For example, the Social Security program came into existence because of the Great Depression of the 1930s, when massive unemployment required a direct government attack on economic insecurity.

Second, social insurance programs are necessary because certain risks are difficult to insure privately. For example, unemployment is difficult to insure privately because it does not completely meet the requirements of an insurable risk. However, the risk of unemployment can be insured by state unemployment insurance programs.

Third, social insurance programs provide a base of economic security to the population. Social insurance programs provide a layer of financial protection to most persons against the long-term financial consequences of premature death, old age, occupational and nonoccupational disability, and unemployment.

Basic Characteristics of Social Insurance

Social insurance programs in the United States have certain characteristics that distinguish them from other government insurance programs:[2]

- Compulsory programs
- Floor of income
- Emphasis on social adequacy rather than individual equity
- Benefits loosely related to earnings
- Benefits prescribed by law
- No means test
- Full funding unnecessary
- Financially self-supporting

Compulsory Programs With few exceptions, social insurance programs are compulsory. A compulsory program has two major advantages. First, the goal of providing a floor of income to the population can be achieved more easily. Second, adverse selection is reduced, because both healthy and unhealthy lives are covered.

Floor of Income Social insurance programs are generally designed to provide only a floor of income with respect to the risks that are covered. Most persons are expected to supplement social insurance benefits with their own personal program of savings, investments, and private insurance.

The concept of a floor of income is difficult to define precisely. One extreme view is that the floor of

income should be so low as to be virtually nonexistent. Another extreme view is that the social insurance benefit by itself should be high enough to provide a comfortable standard of living, so that private insurance benefits would be unnecessary. A more realistic view is that social insurance benefits, when combined with other income and financial assets, should be sufficient for most persons to maintain a reasonable standard of living. Any group whose basic needs are still unmet would be provided for by supplemental public assistance (welfare) benefits.

Social Adequacy Rather Than Individual Equity Social insurance programs pay benefits based largely on social adequacy rather than on individual equity. **Social adequacy** *means that the benefits paid should provide a certain standard of living to all contributors. This means that the benefits paid are heavily weighted in favor of certain groups, such as low-income persons, large families, and the presently retired aged.* In technical terms, the actuarial value of the benefits received by these groups exceeds the actuarial value of their contributions. In contrast, the individual equity principle is followed in private insurance. **Individual equity** *means that contributors receive benefits directly related to their contributions; the actuarial value of the benefits is closely related to the actuarial value of the contributions.*

The basic purpose of the social adequacy principle is to provide a floor of income to all covered persons. If low-income persons received social insurance benefits actuarially equal to the value of their tax contributions (individual equity principle), the benefits paid would be so low that the basic objective of providing a floor of income to everyone would not be achieved.

Benefits Loosely Related to Earnings Social insurance benefits are related to the worker's earnings. The higher the worker's covered earnings, the greater will be the benefits. The relationship between higher earnings and higher benefits is loose and disproportionate, but it does exist. Thus, some consideration is given to individual equity.

Benefits Prescribed by Law Social insurance programs are prescribed by law. The benefits or benefit formulas, as well as the eligibility requirements, are established by law. In addition, the administration or supervision of the program is performed by government.

No Means Test Social insurance benefits are paid as a matter of right without any demonstration of need. A formal means test is not required. A **means test** is used in public assistance—welfare applicants must show that their income and financial assets are below certain levels. By contrast, applicants for social insurance benefits have a statutory right to the benefits if they fulfill certain eligibility requirements.

Full Funding Unnecessary It is unnecessary for social insurance programs to be fully funded. For example, a **fully funded program** under Social Security means that the accumulated assets plus the present value of future contributions payable over the next 75 years will be sufficient to discharge all liabilities for benefits payable over the next 75 years. The OASDI trust-fund balance totaled $631 billion on September 30, 1997. To be fully funded, a trust-fund balance of $3553 trillion would have been required.[3]

A fully funded Social Security program is unnecessary for several reasons. First, because the program will operate indefinitely and not terminate in the predictable future, full funding is unnecessary. Second, because the Social Security program is compulsory, new workers will always enter the program and pay taxes to support it. Third, the federal government can use its taxing and borrowing powers to raise additional revenues if the program has financial problems. Finally, from an economic viewpoint, full funding would require substantially higher Social Security taxes, which would be deflationary and cause substantial unemployment. In contrast, private pension plans must emphasize full funding, because private pension plans can terminate.

Financially Self-supporting Social insurance programs in the United States are designed to be financially self-supporting. This means the programs should be almost completely financed from the earmarked contributions of covered employees, employers, and the self-employed, and interest on the trust-fund investments.

Although the present OASDI program has sufficient funds to pay benefits and expenses for many years, it is expected to develop a long-range actuarial deficit. The Clinton administration and others have proposed using general revenues of the federal government to help finance the program. The federal budget is currently experiencing a substantial surplus. Under the proposals, part of the surplus would be used to reduce the long-range actuarial deficit. However, use of general revenues would violate the principle of a financially self-supporting program.

OLD-AGE, SURVIVORS, AND DISABILITY INSURANCE (OASDI)

The Old-Age, Survivors, and Disability Insurance (OASDI) program, commonly known as **Social Security**, is the most important social insurance program in the United States. Social Security was enacted into law as a result of the Social Security Act of 1935. More than nine out of ten workers are working in occupations covered by Social Security, and about one in six persons receives a monthly cash benefit.[4]

Covered Occupations

The following groups are covered under the Social Security program:

1. *Employees in private firms.* Virtually all private-sector employees are covered under the program at the present time.
2. *Federal civilian employees.* Federal civilian employees hired after 1983 are covered on a compulsory basis. However, federal civilian employees hired before 1984 are covered only for Hospital Insurance under Medicare but not for OASDI.
3. *State and local government employees.* State and local government employees can be covered by a voluntary agreement between the state and the federal government. About 70 percent are now covered. However, state and local government employees hired after March 1986 are covered for Hospital Insurance under the Medicare program and must pay the Hospital Insurance tax.

After July 1, 1991, all state and local government employees who are not participating in a public retirement system are covered on a compulsory basis. However, students employed in public schools, colleges, and universities can be excluded.

4. *Employees of nonprofit organizations.* All employees of nonprofit charitable, educational, and religious organizations are covered if they are paid at least $100 during the year.

5. *Self-employment.* Self-employed persons are covered if their net annual earnings are $400 or more.

6. *Other groups.* Ministers are covered on a self-employment basis unless they elect out because of conscience or religious principles. U.S. military personnel are covered on a compulsory basis. Finally, railroad workers subject to the Railroad Retirement Act are not required to pay OASDI taxes directly. However, because of certain coordinating provisions, railroad employees are, in reality, covered compulsorily for OASDI and Hospital Insurance (HI).

Determination of Insured Status

Before you or your family can receive benefits, you must have credit for a certain amount of work in covered employment. For 2000, you receive one **credit** (also called a **quarter of coverage**) for each $780 of covered earnings. A maximum of four credits can be earned each year. The amount of covered earnings required to earn one credit will automatically increase each year as average wages in the national economy rise.

To become eligible for the various benefits, you must attain an insured status. There are three types of insured status: (1) fully insured, (2) currently insured, and (3) disability insured. Retirement benefits require a fully insured status. Survivor benefits require either a fully insured or currently insured status, although certain survivor benefits require a fully insured status. Disability benefits require a disability-insured status.

Fully Insured To be eligible for retirement benefits, you must be fully insured. You are **fully insured** for retirement benefits if you have 40 credits. However, for people born before 1929, fewer credits are required as shown by the following:

Year of birth	Credits needed
1929 or later	40
1928	39
1927	38
1926	37
1925	36
1924	35

Currently Insured You are **currently insured** if you have earned at least 6 credits during the last 13 calendar quarters ending with the quarter of death, disability, or entitlement to retirement benefits.

Disability Insured The number of credits required to be **disability insured** depends on your age when you become disabled. If you are *age 31 or older*, you must have earned a certain number of credits as shown by the following:

Disabled at age	Credits needed
31 through 42	20
43	21
44	22
45	23
46	24
47	25
48	26
49	27
50	28
51	29
52	30
53	31
54	32
55	33
56	34
57	35
58	36
59	37
60	38
61	39
62 or older	40

In addition, at least 20 of the credits must be earned during the past 10 years immediately before you became disabled.

Workers younger than age 31 can acquire a disability-insured status with fewer credits. For *ages 24 through* 30, you must have worked half the time between age 21 and the time you become disabled. For example, a worker disabled at age 27 needs credit for three years of work out of the past six years.

If you become *disabled before age 24*, you must have earned six credits during the three-year period ending when your disability begins. Finally, blind persons are required only to have a fully insured status. They are not required to meet the recent-work test requirement that applies to other disability applicants.

TYPES OF BENEFITS

The total program consists of Social Security (OASDI) and Medicare. The OASDI program pays monthly retirement, survivor, and disability benefits to eligible beneficiaries. The Medicare program covers the medical expenses of almost all persons aged 65 and older and certain disabled beneficiaries younger than age 65. We discuss only OASDI cash benefits at this point; Medicare is covered later in the chapter.

Retirement Benefits

Social Security retirement benefits are an important source of income to most retired workers. Without these benefits, poverty and economic insecurity among the aged would be substantially increased.

Full Retirement Age The **full retirement age** (also called the normal retirement age) for full benefits is currently age 65. However, the full retirement age will gradually increase in the future to age 67 to improve the financial solvency of the OASDI program and to allow for the increase in life expectancy.

Exhibit 24.1 shows the increase in the full retirement age. For persons attaining age 62 in 2000, the normal retirement age will be increased to age 65 and two months. In each succeeding year, the full

EXHIBIT 24.1
Social Security Retirement Age at a Glance

The "normal retirement age" will gradually rise from 65 to 66, and then later from 66 to 67. Early benefits will still be available at age 62, but the reduction in benefits will be larger. The following table shows how these changes will phase in.

Who Is Affected by Increases in Social Security's Normal Retirement Age?

People born in:	And reaching age 62 in:	Can claim unreduced benefits at age:	At age 62, benefits will be reduced by:
1937 or earlier	1999 or earlier	65, 0 months	20.0 percent
1938	2000	65, 2 months	20.8 percent
1939	2001	65, 4 months	21.7 percent
1940	2002	65, 6 months	22.5 percent
1941	2003	65, 8 months	23.3 percent
1942	2004	65, 10 months	24.2 percent
1943–1954	2005–2016	66, 0 months	25.0 percent
1955	2017	66, 2 months	25.8 percent
1956	2018	66, 4 months	26.7 percent
1957	2019	66, 6 months	27.5 percent
1958	2020	66, 8 months	28.3 percent
1959	2021	66, 10 months	29.2 percent
1960 and later	2022 and later	67, 0 months	30.0 percent

SOURCE: National Academy of Social Insurance (www.nasi.org).

retirement age will be increased by two additional months until it reaches age 66 for persons attaining age 62 in 2005. The full retirement age will then be maintained at age 66 through 2016. Beginning in 2017, for persons attaining age 62, the full retirement age will again be increased two months each year until it reaches age 67 for persons attaining age 62 in 2022 and later.

Early Retirement Age Workers and their spouses can retire as early as age 62 with actuarially reduced benefits. The benefit payable at the full retirement age is reduced ⁵⁄₉ of 1 percent per month for each of the first 36 months that the person is below the normal retirement age at the time of retirement, and by ⁵⁄₁₂ of 1 percent for additional months as the retirement age increases. Thus, at present, when the full retirement age is 65, a worker retiring at age 62 has a 20 percent reduction in benefits.

The actuarial reduction in benefits for early retirement at age 62 will gradually increase to 30 percent in the future when the higher full retirement age provisions become fully effective.

Monthly Retirement Benefits Monthly retirement benefits can be paid to retired workers and their dependents. Eligible persons include the following:

1. *Retired worker.* Monthly retirement benefits can be paid at the full retirement age to a fully insured worker. Reduced benefits can be paid as early as age 62.
2. *Spouse of a retired worker.* The spouse of a retired worker can also receive monthly benefits if she or he is at least age 62 and has been married to the retired worker for at least one year. A divorced spouse is also eligible for benefits based on the retired worker's earnings if she or he is at least age 62, and the marriage lasted at least 10 years.
3. *Unmarried children younger than age 18.* Monthly benefits can also be paid to unmarried children of a retired worker who are younger than age 18 (or 19 if full-time elementary or high school students).
4. *Unmarried disabled children.* Unmarried disabled children age 18 or older are also eligible for benefits based on the retired worker's earnings if they were severely disabled before age 22 and continue to remain disabled.

5. *Spouse with dependent children younger than age 16.* A spouse at any age can receive a monthly benefit if the spouse is caring for an eligible child younger than age 16 (or is caring for a child of any age who was disabled before age 22) who is receiving a benefit based on the retired worker's earnings. The mother's or father's benefit terminates when the youngest child attains age 16 (unless the mother or father is caring for a child disabled before age 22).

Retirement Benefit Amount The monthly retirement benefit is based on the worker's **primary insurance amount (PIA)**, which is the monthly amount paid to a retired worker at the full retirement age or to a disabled worker. The PIA, in turn, is based on the worker's **average indexed monthly earnings (AIME)**, which is a method that updates the worker's earnings based on increases in the average wage in the national economy. The indexing of covered wages results in a relatively constant replacement rate so that workers retiring today and in the future will have about the same proportion of their work earnings replaced by OASDI benefits.

Earnings are indexed by taking into account changes in average wages in the national economy since the worker actually earned the money. The indexing year is the second year before the worker reaches age 62, becomes disabled, or dies, whichever occurs first. For example, assume that Vicki is a registered nurse who retired at age 62 in 1999. The critical year for setting the index factor is the second year before she attained age 62 (1997). To illustrate the method for one year, assume that Vicki's earnings in 1970 were $7800. If her actual earnings in 1970 are multiplied by the index factor for that year (4.43339), her indexed earnings are $34,580.44. This procedure is carried out for each year during the measurement period, which begins with 1951, except that actual dollar amounts are counted for and after the indexing year. The index factors change each year as average wages in the national economy change.

For persons born after 1928, the highest 35 years of indexed earnings are used to calculate the worker's AIME for retirement benefits. (For those born earlier, fewer years are counted.) The AIME is then used to determine the worker's primary insurance amount. A weighted benefit formula is used, which reflects the social adequacy principle discussed earlier.

Exhibit 24.2 provides examples of monthly OASDI retirement benefits for selected beneficiary designations.

Delayed Retirement Credit To encourage working beyond the full retirement age, a delayed retirement credit is available. The delayed retirement credit applies to the period beyond the full retirement age and up to age 70. For people attaining age

65 in 2000, the primary insurance amount is increased 6 percent for each year of delayed retirement (prorated monthly). The credit will gradually increase to a maximum of 8 percent in the future for workers who were born in 1943 or later.

Automatic Cost-of-Living Adjustment The monthly cash benefits are automatically adjusted each year for changes in the cost of living, which maintains the real purchasing power of the benefits during periods of inflation. Whenever the consumer

---

EXHIBIT 24.2
Examples of Monthly OASDI Retirement Benefits at the Full Retirement Age

The following table shows approximate monthly benefits at the full retirement age for you and your spouse. It is assumed that you have worked steadily and received pay raises at a rate equal to the U.S. average throughout your working career. It is also assumed that your earnings, and the general level of wages and salaries in the country, will stay the same until you retire. This way, **the table shows the value of your benefits in today's dollars.**

Your spouse may, instead, qualify for a higher retirement benefit based on her or his own work record.

Age in 2000	Who receives benefits	$20,000	$30,000	$45,000	$60,000	$76,200 and higher
		Your present annual earnings				
65	You	$742	$ 973	$1246	$1354	$1433
	Spouse	371	486	623	677	716
64	You	761	999	1283	1398	1484
	Spouse	380	499	641	699	742
63	You	794	1041	1340	1465	1560
	Spouse	397	520	670	732	780
62	You	813	1067	1377	1509	1612
	Spouse	406	533	688	754	806
61	You	814	1068	1380	1518	1626
	Spouse	407	534	690	759	813
55	You	820	1077	1393	1564	1713
	Spouse	410	538	696	782	856
50	You	825	1083	1397	1579	1756
	Spouse	412	541	698	789	878
45	You	829	1090	1402	1585	1774
	Spouse	414	545	701	792	887
40	You	834	1098	1407	1593	1790
	Spouse	417	549	703	796	895
35	You	838	1104	1412	1599	1800
	Spouse	419	552	706	799	900

Source: *2000 Guide to Social Security and Medicare* (Louisville, KY: William M. Mercer, November 1999), p. 12.

price index for all urban wage earners and clerical workers on a quarterly basis increases from the third quarter of the previous year to the third quarter of the present year, the benefits are automatically increased by the same percentage for the December benefits (payable in January). The cost-of-living increase for benefits payable in January 2000 was 2.4 percent.

Earnings Test The OASDI program has an **earnings test (retirement test)** that can result in a reduction or loss of monthly benefits for workers with earned incomes above certain annual limits. The earnings test has been changed several times. The most recent change occurred in 2000, which eliminated the earnings test for beneficiaries who attain the full retirement age (currently 65 but is scheduled to increase). As a result, hundreds of thousands of older workers can continue to work without losing any benefits.

1. **Beneficiary under the full retirement age.** If a beneficiary is under the full retirement age (currently age 65), $1 in benefits will be deducted for each $2 of earnings in excess of the annual limit. For 2000, the annual limit is $10,080. The annual limit is increased annually based on increases in average wages in the national economy.
2. **Calendar year in which the beneficiary attains the full retirement age.** The earnings test is liberalized for this age group. In the calendar year in which the beneficiary attains the full retirement age, $1 in benefits will be deducted for each $3 of earnings above the annual limit. For 2000, the annual limit is $17,000. *However, only earnings before the month in which the beneficiary attains the full retirement age are counted.* For example, assume that Jason attains the full retirement age in May 2000. During the first four months of 2000, Jason earned $20,000. Because his earnings are $3000 over the annual limit, he will lose $1000 in benefits.

   The annual limit for this age group will increase to $25,000 in 2001, $30,000 in 2002, and thereafter will increase based on increases in average wages in the national economy.
3. **Earnings test eliminated after attainment of the full retirement age.** The new legislation eliminates the earnings test in and after the month the beneficiary attains the full retirement age. *Beneficiaries who have attained the full retirement age or beyond can now earn any amount and receive full OASDI benefits.* As an alternative, beneficiaries who continue working beyond the full retirement age can elect to receive a delayed retirement credit instead of monthly cash benefits.

The earnings test does not apply to investment income, dividends, interest, rents, or annuity payments. The purpose of this exception is to encourage private savings and investments to supplement OASDI benefits.

Survivor Benefits

Survivor benefits can be paid to the dependents of a deceased worker who is either fully or currently insured. For certain survivor benefits, a fully insured status is required.

1. *Unmarried children younger than age 18.* Survivor benefits can be paid to unmarried children younger than age 18 (younger than 19 if full-time elementary or high school students).
2. *Unmarried disabled children.* Unmarried children age 18 or older who become severely disabled before age 22 are eligible for survivor benefits based on the deceased parent's earnings.
3. *Surviving spouse with children younger than age 16.* A widow, widower, or surviving divorced spouse is entitled to a monthly benefit if she or he is caring for an eligible child who is younger than age 16 (or who is disabled) and is receiving a benefit based on the deceased worker's earnings. The benefits terminate for the surviving spouse when the youngest child reaches age 16, or the disabled child dies, marries, or is no longer disabled.
4. *Surviving spouse age 60 or older.* A surviving spouse age 60 or older is also eligible for survivor benefits. The deceased worker must be fully insured. A surviving divorced spouse age 60 or older is also eligible for survivor benefits if the marriage lasted at least 10 years.
5. *Disabled widow or widower, ages 50 through 59.* A disabled widow, widower, or surviving divorced spouse who is age 50 or older can receive survivor benefits under certain conditions. The person must be disabled at the time of the worker's death or become disabled no later than

seven years after the mother's or father's benefits end. The deceased must be fully insured.

6. *Dependent parents.* Dependent parents age 62 and older can also receive survivor benefits based on the deceased's earnings. The deceased worker must be fully insured.

7. *Lump-sum death benefit.* A lump-sum death benefit of $255 can be paid when a worker dies. The benefit, however, can be paid only if there is an eligible surviving widow, widower, or entitled child.

The value of Social Security survivor benefits is substantial. For an average wage earner with a family, the value of the survivor benefits is equivalent to $354,000 of private life insurance.[5] The benefits, however, are paid monthly and not in a lump sum.

Disability Benefits

Disability-income benefits can be paid to disabled workers who meet certain eligibility requirements, including the following:

- Be disability insured
- Meet a five-month waiting period
- Satisfy the definition of disability

A disabled worker must be disability insured and must also meet a five-month waiting period. Benefits begin after a waiting period of five full calendar months. Therefore, the first payment is for the sixth full month of disability.

The definition of disability stated in the law must also be met. A strict definition of disability is used in the program: *The worker must have a physical or mental condition that prevents him or her from doing any substantial gainful work and is expected to last (or has lasted) at least 12 months or is expected to result in death.* The impairment must be so severe that the worker is prevented from doing any substantial gainful work in the national economy. In determining whether a person can do substantial gainful work, his or her age, education, training, and work experience can be taken into consideration. If the disabled person cannot work at his or her own occupation but can engage in other substantial gainful work, the disability claim will not be allowed.[6]

The major groups eligible to receive OASDI disability-income benefits are as follows:

1. *Disabled worker.* A disabled worker under the full retirement age receives a benefit equal to 100 percent of the primary insurance amount. The worker must meet the definition of disability, be disability insured, and satisfy a full five-month waiting period.

2. *Spouse of a disabled worker.* Benefits can be paid to the spouse of a disabled worker at any age if she or he is caring for a child younger than age 16 or a child who became disabled before age 22 and is receiving benefits based on the disabled worker's earnings. If no eligible children are present, the spouse must be at least age 62 to receive benefits.

3. *Unmarried children younger than age 18.* Disability benefits can be paid to unmarried children younger than age 18 (or younger than 19 if a full-time elementary or high school student).

4. *Unmarried disabled children.* Unmarried children age 18 or older who became severely disabled before age 22 are also eligible for benefits, based on the disabled worker's earnings.

In summary, the OASDI program provides valuable retirement, survivor, and disability benefits to eligible beneficiaries. To help workers plan better for their retirement, the Social Security Administration sends to people age 25 and older an annual statement showing projected benefits. The statement enables covered persons to check for errors; projects the monthly retirement benefits at the early and full retirement age, and at age 70; and projects the amount of disability and survivor benefits that would be paid if the worker becomes disabled or dies (see Insight 24.1).

Medicare Benefits

The fourth principal benefit is Medicare. **Medicare** covers the medical expenses of almost all persons age 65 and older. Medicare also covers disabled persons younger than age 65 who have been entitled to disability benefits for at least 24 months (they need not be continuous). In addition, the program covers persons younger than age 65 who need long-term kidney dialysis treatment or a kidney transplant.

The Medicare program has been changed several times since its inception in 1965. The present program consists of the following coverages: (1)

Insight 24.1

Get the Picture on Your Social Security Benefits

The Social Security Administration has begun sending annual estimated benefits statements to U.S. workers. By reading your statement, you'll find out how much you can expect in benefits—and that you'll probably need to save more to meet your retirement goals.

Your retirement might be far off, but the Social Security Administration (SSA) wants you to start thinking about your financial future now. To help you better plan, the SSA has begun mailing individualized statements that contain your earnings history, a projection of the monthly retirement benefit you'll receive at age 62 (the first year for which you're eligible to receive Social Security retirement benefits), at your full retirement age, and at age 70, as well as information on disability and survivor benefits. The statement will help you realize that Social Security will provide only a part of your retirement income, and that you'll probably need to save additional funds on your own. It also gives you the opportunity to check the completeness and accuracy of the SSA records of your work history and Social Security contributions.

"The Social Security Statement is a valuable tool that will help Americans prepare for their long-term financial security," says Kenneth Apfel, Social Security Commissioner.

The annual Social Security Statement is the result of efforts by Senator Daniel Moynihan to establish in law the requirement that all Americans receive an annual statement of their potential Social Security benefits. Under this initiative, you can expect to receive your statement three months before your birthday if you are 25 years old or older and not yet receiving Social Security benefits. The SSA began sending these statements automatically to individuals age 60 and over in 1995, and workers have been able to receive the statement by request since 1988.

A recent Gallup poll shows that receipt of a Social Security Statement has played a significant role in increasing Americans' understanding of Social Security. According to the survey, individuals who received their statement were more likely to know that the amount of their Social Security retirement benefits depends on how much they have earned; that Social Security pays benefits to workers who become disabled and to dependents of workers who die; and that Social Security was designed to provide only part of their total retirement income.

About the Statement

The four-page statement will be sent to 125 million workers. On the first page, Commissioner Apfel dis-

---

Hospital Insurance (Part A), (2) **Supplementary Medical Insurance (Part B)**, and (3) **Medicare + Choice.**

Hospital Insurance (Part A) *Inpatient hospital care* is covered for up to 90 days for each benefit period. A benefit period starts when the patient first enters the hospital and ends when the patient has been out of the hospital or skilled nursing facility for 60 consecutive days. For the first 60 days, Medicare pays all covered costs except for an initial hospital deductible ($776 in 2000). The deductible is paid only once during the benefit period no matter how many times the patient goes to a hospital. For the 61st through 90th day, Medicare pays all covered costs except for a daily coinsurance charge ($194 in 2000). If the patient is still in the hospital after 90

days, a *lifetime reserve* of 60 additional days can be used. Lifetime reserve days are subject to a daily coinsurance charge ($388 in 2000). The hospital deductible and coinsurance charges are adjusted each year to reflect changes in hospital costs.

Inpatient care in a *skilled nursing facility* is also covered up to a maximum of 100 days in a benefit period. The first 20 days of covered services are paid in full. For the next 80 days, the patient must pay a daily coinsurance insurance charge ($97 in 2000). To be eligible for coverage, the patient must be hospitalized first for at least three days and must require skilled nursing care. Intermediate care and custodial care are not covered.

Home health care services in the patient's home are covered if the patient requires skilled care and meets certain conditions. Covered services include

cusses the important role of Social Security, but also stresses the need to save more for retirement: "Social Security benefits were not intended to be the only source of income for you and your family when you retire. You'll need to supplement your benefits with income from a pension plan, savings, or investments."

On page two, you'll find a description of how your benefits are calculated, as will as a statement of your estimated retirement, disability, and survivor benefits. Page three lists your earnings record from the first year you began working and paying into Social Security. On page four, you'll find facts on Social Security and Medicare that will help you determine when you become eligible for benefits.

Here's what to do with the statement when you receive it:

Check for errors. The statement contains an annual breakdown of your earnings to date and a total of the Social Security taxes paid by you and your employer(s) over your working career. This is important information that you should ensure is accurate. An employer may have made a mistake, or, if you're a woman, earnings may be listed under both your married name and your maiden name. You can correct errors by calling the SSA at 800-772-1213.

Estimate when you'd like to retire. Since your statement will give you three projected monthly benefits (for retiring at age 62, your full retirement age, or 70), you will be able to better plan for retirement. Remember, if you retire at age 62, you will receive reduced benefits. This is because the amount of your monthly Social Security check corresponds to a total lifetime amount allotted base on average life expectancy and time of retirement. People who start collecting retirement benefits earlier receive smaller monthly income benefits since payments are expected to be made over a longer period of time.

Check your disability and survivor benefits. One out of every three Social Security beneficiaries is not a retiree but a disabled worker, a member of a disabled worker's family, or a survivor of a worker who has died. The Social Security Statement gives you a projected amount of the monthly disability benefit you could be entitled to should you become disabled, and an estimate of the monthly benefit your family would receive if you died.

SOURCE: Adapted from TIAA-CREF, "Get the Picture on Your Social Security Benefits," *Participant* (February 2000), pp. 20–21.

skilled nursing care, physical therapy, home health aide services, and speech language therapy. Durable medical equipment is covered as well. No cost-sharing provisions apply to covered services, but the patient must pay 20 percent of the approved amount for durable medical equipment.

Hospice care for terminally ill beneficiaries is covered for up to 210 days if the care is provided by a hospice certified by Medicare. Hospice care beyond 210 days is covered if a physician certifies that the beneficiary is still terminally ill. A hospice program is a program that provides inpatient, outpatient, and home care services to terminally ill patients, such as cancer patients.

Finally, Part A pays for the cost of inpatient *blood transfusions* furnished by a hospital or skilled nursing facility during a covered stay, except for the first three pints of blood per year. However, the patient cannot be charged for the first three pints if the blood is replaced, or the cost of the blood is covered under Part B.

Hospitals are reimbursed for inpatient services provided to Medicare beneficiaries under a prospective payment system. Under this system, hospital care is classified into **diagnosis-related groups (DRGs)**, and a flat amount is paid for each type of care depending on the diagnosis group in which the case is placed. Thus, a flat, uniform amount is paid to each hospital for the same type of care or treatment. However, the amount paid varies among different geographical locations and by urban and rural facilities.

The purpose of the DRG system is to create a financial incentive to encourage hospitals to operate more efficiently. Hospitals are allowed to keep payment amounts that exceed their costs, but they must absorb any costs in excess of the DRG flat amounts.

Supplementary Medical Insurance (Part B)

Part B of Medicare is a voluntary program that covers physician's fees and other related medical services. Persons covered under Part A on the basis of covered earnings are automatically covered under Part B unless they voluntarily decline the coverage.

Part B pays for several types of services that are medically necessary. *Physician's services* are covered in the doctor's office, hospital, or elsewhere. Medical supplies furnished by a doctor in the office, services of the office nurse, and drugs administered by a doctor are also covered.

Outpatient hospital services for diagnosis and treatment are covered, such as care in an emergency room or outpatient clinic in a hospital. Laboratory tests, X rays, and diagnostic hospital services as an outpatient are also covered.

Home health care services are also provided by Part B. Such services are similar to those provided by Part A.

Finally, *other medical and health care services* are covered, including diagnostic tests, X rays and radiation treatment, limited ambulance services, prosthetic devices, and durable medical equipment used at home.

Part B excludes numerous medical services and items, including routine physicals, most dental care, dentures, routine foot care, hearing aids, and most prescription drugs. Eye glasses are covered only if the patient needs corrective lenses after a cataract operation.

Part B pays 80 percent of the approved charges for most covered services after a calendar-year deductible is met. However, some covered services have higher co-payments. For example, if the beneficiary receives outpatient mental services, only 50 percent of the Medicare-approved amount is paid.

- *Reimbursement of Physicians.* As stated earlier, Part B generally pays only 80 percent of the Medicare-approved amount, which is usually less than the physician's actual fee. The approved amount is based on a complex relative-value fee schedule that determines payment based on the time, skill, and intensity of the services provided;

the cost of practicing medicine; and medical malpractice costs. Geographical variations in the cost of practicing medicine are also considered.

Medicare payments to physicians are made on an assigned or nonassigned basis. By accepting an assignment, a physician agrees to accept the Medicare-approved amount as payment in full. The patient is not liable for any additional out-of-pocket costs other than the calendar-year deductible and coinsurance payments. However, physicians who do not accept an assignment of a Medicare claim cannot charge more than 115 percent of the Medicare approved fee for such physicians.

- *Part B Monthly Premium.* Part B beneficiaries must pay a monthly premium for the benefits provided ($45.50 in 2000), which is supplemented by the federal government out of general revenues. In calendar-year 1999, general revenues accounted for about 73 percent of all Part B income; enrollee premiums accounted for about 23 percent, and interest income on the trust fund assets accounted for about 4 percent.[7]

Medicare + Choice

The Balanced Budget Act of 1997 created a new Medicare + Choice program (also called Part C) as an alternative to Parts A and B of Medicare. Medicare beneficiaries can now choose among the following options:[8]

- *Original Medicare Plan.* Beneficiaries can elect the original Medicare plan, which is the traditional system run by the federal government that provides Part A and Part B services. Beneficiaries can elect any provider that accepts Medicare patients. Medicare pays its share of the bill, and the beneficiary pays the balance. Some services are not covered.

- *Original Medicare Plan with a Supplemental Policy.* Beneficiaries can elect coverage under the original Medicare plan and purchase any one of ten standard policies (also called Medigap insurance, as discussed later). The benefits provided depend on the plan selected. There is coverage for at least some deductible and coinsurance costs. Depending on the plan, additional benefits not provided by Medicare may be available.

- *Managed Care Plan.* Beneficiaries can elect a managed care plan, which is an approved network of doctors, hospitals, and other providers who agree to provide care for a fixed monthly fee. Managed care plans include approved health maintenance organizations (HMOs), health maintenance organizations with a point-of-service option (POS), preferred provider organizations (PPOs), and provider-sponsored organizations (PSOs). A PSO is a closed network operated by health care providers, such as a group of physicians.

- *Private Fee-for-Service Plan.* Beneficiaries can elect a private fee-for-service plan that accepts Medicare beneficiaries. Patients can go to any physician or hospital participating in the plan. The private plan, rather than Medicare, determines the amounts paid for covered services, however. Patients can be billed for amounts in excess of what Medicare pays (up to a certain limit). Patients must pay the difference between the provider's full fee and the Medicare payment. Some private plans may offer additional benefits not provided by Medicare.

- *Medicare Medical Savings Account.* This test program is currently available to no more than 390,000 eligible Medicare beneficiaries. Beneficiaries can elect to be covered under a medical savings account (MSA), which is a major medical policy with a high deductible. Medicare pays the premium for the MSA plan and makes a deposit into the MSA plan for medical expenses. Money can be withdrawn to pay for the insured's medical expenses. If the beneficiary does not use all of the money in the MSA, next year's deposit will be added to the balance. Money can also be withdrawn from the MSA for nonmedical expenses, although that amount is subject to taxation. There are no limits on the amounts that providers can charge beneficiaries above what is paid by the MSA plan. Beneficiaries can enroll in an MSA plan each year in November and must remain in the plan for a full year.

Medigap Insurance   Because of numerous exclusions, deductibles, cost-sharing provisions, and limitations on approved charges, Medicare does not pay all medical expenses. As a result, most Medicare beneficiaries either have post-retirement health benefits from their former employers or have purchased a **Medigap policy** or Medicare supplement policy that

pays part or all of the covered charges not paid by Medicare.

Medigap policies are sold by private insurers and are strictly regulated by federal law. There are ten standard policies, each of which offers a different combination of benefits. The basic policy has a core package of benefits. The remaining policies have a different combination of benefits, but they all include the core package. Each policy has a letter designation ranging from A through J (see Exhibit 24.3). Insurers are not allowed to change the various combinations of benefits or the letter designations.

Insurers must provide an open enrollment period of six months from the date the applicant first enrolls in Medicare Part B and is age 65 or older. Applicants cannot be turned down or charged higher premiums because of poor health if they buy a policy during that period. Once the Medigap open enrollment period ends, beneficiaries may not be able to buy a policy of their choice but may have to accept whatever an insurer is willing to provide.

Insurers and agents are subject to criminal charges and fines if they engage in deceptive sales practices. Certain practices are forbidden, including the sale of a policy that duplicates Medicare coverage, selling a policy that is not an approved standard policy, and making a false statement that the policy meets legal standards when it does not.

Financing Social Security Benefits

OASDI benefits are financed by a payroll tax paid by employees, employers, and the self-employed; interest income on the trust-fund investments; and revenues derived from taxation of part of the monthly cash benefits.

In 2000, the worker paid a tax contribution rate of 7.65 percent on a maximum taxable earnings base of $76,200, and 1.45 percent on all earned income in excess of that amount. The employee's contribution is matched by an identical contribution from the employer. The self-employed pay a tax rate of 15.3 percent on the same earnings base, and 2.9 percent on all earnings in excess of that amount. However, the self-employed are allowed certain deductions, which reduce the effective tax rate.[9] The maximum taxable earnings base will automatically increase in the future if average wages in the national economy increase.

EXHIBIT 24.3
Chart of Ten Standard Medigap Policies

Medigap can be sold only in ten standardized plans. This chart shows the benefits included in each plan. Every company offers Plan A. Companies may have some, all, or none of the other plans. Some plans may not be available in every state.

Basic Benefits: Included in All Plans
- Hospitalization: Part A coinsurance plus coverage for 365 additional days during your lifetime after Medicare benefits end.
- Medical Expenses: Part B coinsurance (generally 20% of Medicare-approved expenses).
- Blood: First three pints of blood each year.

Medigap benefits	A	B	C	D	E	F*	G	H	I	J*
Basic Benefits	✓	✓	✓	✓	✓	✓	✓	✓	✓	✓
Part A: Inpatient Hospital Deductible		✓	✓	✓	✓	✓	✓	✓	✓	✓
Part A: Skilled-Nursing Facility Co-Insurance			✓	✓	✓	✓	✓	✓	✓	✓
Part B: Deductible			✓			✓				✓
Foreign Travel Emergency			✓	✓	✓	✓	✓	✓	✓	✓
At-Home Recovery				✓			✓		✓	✓
Part B: Excess Charges						100%	80%		100%	100%
Preventive Care					✓					✓
Prescription Drugs								Basic ✓ coverage	Basic ✓ coverage	Extended ✓ coverage

*Plans F and J also have a high deductible option.

SOURCE: Health Care Financing Administration.

Hospital Insurance (Part A) of Medicare is financed largely by a payroll tax of 1.45 percent on all earned income, including earnings in excess of the OASDI taxable earnings base. (The 1.45 percent is part of the 7.65 percent mentioned earlier.) The self-employed pay 2.9 percent on all earned income. Finally, as noted earlier, Supplementary Medical Insurance (Part B) is financed by monthly premiums and by general revenues of the federal government.

Taxation of Benefits

About 26 percent of all beneficiaries who receive monthly cash benefits must pay an income tax on part of the benefits. The amount of benefits subject to taxation depends on your total combined income. *Combined income* includes earnings, pension income, dividends, and taxable interest from investments and other sources *plus* tax-exempt interest *plus* one-half of your Social Security benefits. If you file a federal tax return as an individual and your combined income is between $25,000 and $34,000, up to 50 percent of your benefits is subject to taxation. If your combined income exceeds $34,000, up to 85 percent of your benefits is subject to taxation.

If you file a joint return and you and your spouse have a combined income between $32,000 and $44,000, up to 50 percent of the benefits are subject to taxation. If your combined income exceeds $44,000, up to 85 percent of the benefits are subject to taxation.

At the end of each year, you will receive a form from the Social Security Administration that shows the amount of Social Security benefits received. The Internal Revenue Service has prepared a detailed worksheet to determine the amount of the benefits, if any, to include in your taxable income.

PROBLEMS AND ISSUES

Social Security and Medicare are currently faced with serious problems and issues. Three timely issues include (1) the long-range OASDI actuarial deficit, (2) the Medicare financial crisis, and (3) coverage of outpatient prescription drugs under Medicare.

Long-Range OASDI Actuarial Deficit

Based on the 2000 Board of Trustees Report and the intermediate cost estimate, the OASDI trust funds will experience serious financial problems in the future. *The combined OASDI trust funds are projected to be adequately financed until 2037. At that time, annual tax income to the combined trust funds is projected to equal only about 72 percent of the cost of benefits.* The OASI trust fund, which pays retirement and survivor benefits, is projected to be able to pay full benefits until 2039. The DI trust fund, which pays disability benefits, should be able to pay full benefits until 2023.[10]

In addition, the combined OASDI trust fund is projected to incur a long-range actuarial deficit of 1.89 percent of taxable payroll over a 75-year period. However, little support exists today for increasing payroll tax rates by 1.89 percentage points to eliminate this actuarial deficit.

The primary reason why future OASDI costs will increase more rapidly than income is that the number of beneficiaries will increase more rapidly as the "baby boom" generation retires, whereas the number of workers paying payroll taxes will increase more slowly. The number of workers per OASDI beneficiary is expected to decline from 3.4 in 2000 to 1.9 in 2075.[11] As a result, relatively fewer workers will be working to support an increasing number of beneficiaries.

Numerous proposals have been made to eliminate the long-range deficit. Other proposals would seek to reform the OASDI program. For sake of simplicity, the various proposals can be grouped into the following categories: (1) maintaining the present program, (2) establishing individual accounts, and (3) using the projected budget surplus to save Social Security.

Maintaining the Present Program Under this approach, the present OASDI program would be maintained with certain changes and modifications. The changes would reduce costs and increase revenues. Proposed changes include the following:

- Extend Social Security coverage to new state and local government employees.
- Increase the number of years used in calculating benefits from 35 to 38.
- Speed up the increase in the normal retirement age under present law, or increase it beyond age 67.
- Reduce benefits for future retirees across the board.
- Reduce or eliminate benefits for workers with higher incomes.
- Increase the Social Security taxable wage base to cover a larger percentage of earnings.
- Increase the percentage of Social Security benefits subject to the federal income tax.

Another proposal would allow the trust funds to invest up to 40 percent of their assets in common stocks.

The preceding proposals are controversial. However, discussion of them is beyond the scope of the text. Congressional debate on these proposals undoubtedly will be intense.

Establishing Individual Accounts Under this approach, each worker would have an individual retirement account. The OASDI payroll tax would be reduced by 2 percentage points (or by some other amount), which would be used to fund the worker's retirement benefits. If the worker died before retirement, the deceased worker's spouse or beneficiary would inherit the assets.

A major criticism of the present program is the relatively low return that younger workers will receive on the OASDI taxes paid. The Advisory Council on Social Security estimates that the *internal real rate of return* on OASDI payroll taxes paid by average and upper-income single workers in the future will be less than 2 percent.[12] The projected rates of return are relatively low compared with those available from other investments in the economy. Proponents believe that individual accounts will allow younger workers to earn substantially higher real rates of return, especially if the funds are invested in common stocks.

The establishment of individual accounts is a controversial issue. Critics argue that the risk to the workers will increase. Workers would have to bear any investment losses, and the present program with its safety net and income guarantees would be dramatically altered.

Using the Projected Budget Surplus to Save Social Security Thanks to the robust economy and low unemployment, the federal budget is projected to incur a surplus in excess of $1.9 trillion over the next ten years. As discussed earlier, part of this surplus could be used to fund the OASDI program. Thus, general revenue financing would help fund the program under this proposal. At present, the OASDI program is funded largely by earmarked payroll taxes, and general revenue financing is not the major source of revenue.

Using the surplus to save Social Security is controversial. Although the long-range solvency of the OASDI trust funds would be substantially improved, at least two objections to this proposal have been made. First, the expected surplus may not materialize if the nation experiences a recession, and federal tax revenues decline. Second, general revenue financing represents a dramatic departure from the present principle of a financially self-supporting program

based largely on payroll taxes. The present financing system encourages a more responsible attitude on the part of elected representatives, which could be lost by relying on general revenue financing.

Medicare Financial Crisis

Part A of Medicare will also experience a serious financial crisis in the future. *The 2000 Board of Trustees report showed that the Hospital Insurance (HI) trust fund will be exhausted in 2023.*

This unsatisfactory financial condition is due to several factors, including an increase in the number of Medicare beneficiaries, inflation in hospital costs exceeding the overall rate of inflation, fraud and abuse by health care providers, substantial increases in home health care costs, and an inefficient and inflationary fee-for-service method of reimbursement.

To hold down Medicare costs, Congress has reduced payments to hospitals and physicians, placed spending limits on specified services, limited fees paid to physicians, implemented the diagnosis-related group method in which flat amounts are paid to hospitals for each specific case, and enacted other cost-reduction measurers. Despite these efforts, Medicare costs continue to increase.

More recently, the National Bipartisan Commission on the Future of Medicare has made several recommendations to improve the solvency of Medicare and modernize the program.[14] Major recommendations include the following: (1) increasing gradually the Medicare eligibility age from age 65 to 67 to match the scheduled increase for OASDI; (2) increasing competition by allowing beneficiaries to enroll in private health insurance plans that would compete with the traditional fee-for-service Medicare plan; (3) combining the Part A and Part B trust funds into a single Medicare trust fund. These recommendations remain controversial. At the time of this writing, Congress had not enacted any of these recommendations into law.

Outpatient Prescription Drugs Under Medicare

Another important issue is coverage of outpatient prescription drugs under the Medicare program.

Medicare does not presently cover prescription drugs outside the hospital. The elderly spend a relatively larger proportion of their annual incomes on health care, and prescription drug costs are a major expenditure. *In 1999, Medicare beneficiaries, on average, paid estimated out-of-pocket expenditures of $2430 on health care, or 19 percent of their annual income.*[15] Long-term care costs are not included in that total. Spending on prescription drugs represented 17 percent of the elderly's out-of-pocket spending on health care, which is the largest single spending component after Medicare premium payments.[16]

Another study projected that, in 1999, an estimated 14 percent of Medicare beneficiaries would pay out-of-pocket expenses of $1000 or more for outpatient prescription drugs—a substantial amount for low-income beneficiaries with no insurance.[17]

In 1996, approximately one-third of all Medicare beneficiaries had no coverage for prescription drugs.[18] The remaining two-thirds had some drug coverage from other sources, including employer-sponsored health plans, Medicare + Choice plans, and Medigap plans. However, Medigap plans with drug coverage are expensive, impose significant deductible and coinsurance requirements, and have relatively low annual limits. In addition, premiums have been increasing in recent years.

The National Bipartisan Commission on the Future of Medicare has recommended an immediate drug benefit for low-income seniors with incomes below 135 percent of the poverty line (about $11,000 for an individual in 1999). In addition, all private and public Medicare plans would be required to offer a standard benefits package that would include prescription drug coverage.

The preceding recommendation has inspired considerable debate. Although substantial numbers of low-income beneficiaries would be helped, Medicare costs would increase substantially. Also, critics fear that the federal government would eventually impose price controls on drugs to hold down Medicare costs.

UNEMPLOYMENT INSURANCE

Unemployment insurance programs are federal-state programs that pay weekly cash benefits to workers who are involuntarily unemployed. Each state has its own unemployment insurance program. The various state programs arose out of the unemployment insurance provisions of the Social Security Act of 1935.

Unemployment insurance has several basic objectives:[19]

- Provide cash income during involuntary unemployment
- Help unemployed workers find jobs
- Encourage employers to stabilize employment
- Help stabilize the economy

Weekly cash benefits are paid to unemployed workers during periods of **short-term involuntary unemployment**, thus helping them maintain their economic security. A second objective is to help unemployed workers find jobs; applicants for benefits must register for work at local employment offices, and officials provide assistance in finding suitable jobs. A third objective is to encourage employers to stabilize their employment through experience rating (discussed later). Finally, unemployment benefits help stabilize the economy during recessionary periods.

Coverage

Most private firms, state and local governments, and nonprofit organizations are covered for unemployment benefits. A *private firm* is subject to the federal unemployment tax if it employs one or more employees in each of at least 20 weeks during the calendar year (or preceding calendar year), or it pays wages of $1500 or more during a calendar quarter of either year. Most jobs in *state and local government* are also covered for unemployment insurance benefits. However, state and local governments are not required to pay the federal unemployment tax but instead may elect to reimburse the system for the benefits paid to government employees. In addition, *nonprofit charitable, educational, or religious organizations* are covered if they employ four or more workers for at least one day in each of 20 different weeks during the current or prior year. The nonprofit organization has the right either to pay the unemployment tax or to reimburse the states for the benefits paid.

Agricultural firms are covered if they have a quarterly payroll of at least $20,000 or employ ten or more workers in at least 20 weeks during the current or prior year. *Domestic employment* in a private household is covered if the employer pays domestic wages of $1000 or more in a calendar quarter during the current or prior year.

Eligibility Requirements

An unemployed worker must meet the following eligibility requirements:

- Have qualifying wages and employment during the base year
- Be able and available for work
- Actively seek work
- Be free from disqualification
- Serve a one-week waiting period

The applicant must earn qualifying wages of a specified amount during his or her base year. In most states, the base year is the first four of the last five calendar quarters preceding the unemployed worker's claim for benefits. Most states also require employment in at least two calendar quarters during the base year. The purpose of this requirement is to limit benefits to workers with a current attachment to the labor force.

The applicant must be physically and mentally capable of working and must be available for work. The claimant must register for work at a public employment office and actively seek work.

The applicant must not be disqualified from receiving benefits. Disqualifying acts include voluntarily quitting his or her job without good cause, direct participation in a labor dispute, being discharged for misconduct, or refusing suitable work.

Finally, a one-week waiting period must be satisfied in most states. The waiting period eliminates short-term claims, holds down costs, and provides time to obtain the claimant's wage record and process the claim.

Benefits

A weekly cash benefit is paid for each week of total unemployment. The benefit paid varies with the worker's past wages, within certain minimum and maximum dollar amounts. Most states use a formula that pays weekly benefits based on a fraction of the worker's high quarter wages. For example, a fraction of $1/26$ results in the payment of benefits equal to 50 percent of the worker's full-time wage in the highest quarter (subject to minimum and maximum amounts). For instance, assume that Jennifer earns $400 weekly or $5200 during her highest quarter. Applying the fraction of $1/26$ to this amount produces a weekly unemployment benefit of $200, or 50 percent of her full-time weekly wage. Several states also pay a dependent's allowance for certain dependents.

During the third quarter of calendar 1999, the average weekly benefit amount ranged from $152.79 in Mississippi to $276.85 in Washington. The average weekly benefit for the United States was $209.54 during the same period.[20] In virtually all jurisdictions, the maximum duration of regular benefits is limited to 26 weeks.

During periods of high unemployment, some workers exhaust their regular unemployment benefits. A permanent federal-state program of extended benefits pays additional benefits to unemployed workers who exhaust their regular benefits during periods of high unemployment in individual states. Under the **extended-benefits program**, claimants can receive up to 13 additional weeks of benefits or one-half the total amount of regular benefits, whichever is less. There is an overall limit of 39 weeks for both regular and extended benefits. The costs of the extended benefits are shared equally by the federal government and the states.

Financing

State unemployment insurance programs are financed largely by payroll taxes paid by employers on the covered wages of employees. A few states also require the employees to contribute. All tax contributions are deposited in the Federal Unemployment Trust Fund. Each state has a separate account, which is credited with the unemployment-tax contributions and the state's share of investment income. Unemployment benefits are paid out of each state's account.

For 2000, covered employers paid a federal payroll tax of 6.2 percent on the first $7000 of annual wages paid to each covered employee. Employers can credit toward the federal tax any contributions paid under an approved unemployment insurance program and any tax savings under an approved experience-rating plan. The total employer credit is limited to a maximum of 5.4 percent. The remaining 0.8 percent is paid to the federal government and used for state and federal administrative expenses, for financing the federal government's share of the extended-benefits program, and for maintaining a loan fund from which states can temporarily borrow when their accounts are depleted.

Because of a desire to strengthen their unemployment reserves and maintain fund solvency, the majority of states have a taxable wage base that exceeds $7000.

Experience rating is also used, by which firms with favorable employment records pay reduced tax rates. The major argument in support of experience rating is that firms have a financial incentive to stabilize their employment. However, some cyclical and seasonal firms have little control over their employment, and experience rating provides little financial incentive for them to stabilize employment. Also, labor unions are opposed to experience rating, because some business firms may resist benefit increases and contest some valid claims.

Problems and Issues

State unemployment insurance programs have numerous problems. Some important problems are summarized as follows:

1. *Decline in the proportion of unemployed who receive benefits.* Only a relatively small proportion of the total unemployed at any time receive unemployment benefits. On average, only 36 percent of unemployed workers received unemployment insurance benefits in 1996. This figure compares with a peak of 81 percent of the unemployed who received benefits in April 1975 and a low point of 26 percent in October 1987.[21]

   Several factors help explain the long-term decline in the proportion of unemployed workers who receive benefits: (1) a decline in the proportion of unemployed individuals in the manufacturing sector where unemployment insurance claims have been historically high; (2) geographic shifts in the composition of the unemployed in different regions in the country; (3) more stringent state eligibility requirements, including an increase in the base-period earnings requirement, an increase in income denials for unemployment benefits, and tighter nonmonetary eligibility requirements; (4) changes in federal policy, such as the taxation of unemployment compensation benefits; and (5) changes in unemployment as measured by the Current Population Survey (CPS).[22]

2. *Inadequate reserves.* Some state unemployment insurance programs have relatively low reserve accounts. During previous recessions, many states found their reserve funds inadequate for meeting the increased cost of benefits due to high unemployment and a longer duration of payments. States are permitted to borrow from the federal unemployment account if their accounts decline to a level where benefit obligations cannot be met.

   One widely used measure to estimate the adequacy of a state's unemployment reserve account is known as the "high-cost multiple."[23] A value of 1 means that the state's current reserve account could pay 12 months of unemployment benefits at the highest unemployment rate historically experienced. The Interstate Commission of Employment Security Administrators has recommended a high-cost multiple of 1.5, which would enable a state to pay benefits for 18 months during a recession without borrowing. *However, in 1996, only five jurisdictions had a high-cost multiple of 1.5 or higher, and only 15 jurisdictions had a high-cost multiple of one or higher.*[24]

   In the past, many states with high-cost multiples that were lower than 1 experienced serious financial problems during recessions. If the U.S. economy should experience a severe recession, many states once again will exhaust their unemployment reserves and be forced to borrow from the federal government to pay benefits.

3. *Imperfect experience-rating formulas.* Unemployment insurance tax rates are experience rated, which encourages employers to reduce layoffs, gives employers an incentive to police fraudulent claims, and allocates the cost of unemployment to those firms that are responsible for the unemployment.

In reality, these objectives have not been completely met because of "imperfect" experience-rating formulas. That is, the employers responsible for the unemployment are not charged for all benefits paid to former employees. Employers are often not charged the full cost of benefit payments because of numerous reasons, such as partial forgiveness of charges for employers with negative balances in their reserve accounts, payments made on behalf of firms going out of business, special industry tax rates, caps on changes in annual employer tax rates, and low state-taxable wage bases.

In addition, employers that pay maximum tax rates because of layoffs are incurring benefit costs that must be funded by other employers. Under the present system, low-cost firms with positive balances in their reserve accounts subsidize high-cost firms with negative balances in their account. This subsidy is unfair to low-cost firms, and it reduces the incentive for high-cost firms that pay maximum tax rates to reduce their unemployment.

The Advisory Council on Unemployment Compensation has prepared an experience rating index (ERI) that measures the degree of experience rating in a state. It takes into account the percentage of benefits charged to individual employers. *Between 1988 and 1994, the ERI declined in the majority of states. In addition, between 1988 and 1992, the U.S. average for all jurisdictions declined from 63 to 56.*[25] Thus, firms that are now paying maximum unemployment insurance tax rates have little financial incentive to reduce unemployment.

WORKERS COMPENSATION

Millions of workers are injured or become sick each year because of job-related accidents or disease. In addition to pain and suffering, disabled workers must deal with the loss of earned income, payment of medical bills, partial or permanent loss of bodily functions or limbs, and job separation.

Workers compensation is a social insurance program that provides medical care, cash benefits, and rehabilitation services to workers who are disabled from job-related accidents or disease. The benefits are extremely important in reducing the economic insecurity that may result from a job-related disability.[26]

Development of Workers Compensation

Under the *common law of industrial accidents*, dating back to 1837, workers injured on the job had to sue their employers and prove negligence before they could collect damages. However, an employer could use three common law defenses to block lawsuits from injured workers:

- Contributory negligence doctrine
- Fellow-servant doctrine
- Assumption-of-risk doctrine

Under the **contributory negligence doctrine**, an injured worker could not collect damages if he or she contributed in any way to the injury. Under the **fellow-servant doctrine**, the injured worker could not collect if the injury resulted from the negligence of a fellow worker. And under the **assumption-of-risk doctrine**, the injured worker could not collect if he or she had advance knowledge of the dangers inherent in a particular occupation. As a result of the harsh common law, relatively few disabled workers collected adequate amounts for their injuries.

The enactment of *employer liability laws* between 1885 and 1910 was the next step in the development of workers compensation. These laws reduced the effectiveness of the common law defenses, improved the legal position of injured workers, and required employers to provide safe working conditions for their employees. However, injured workers were still required to sue their employers and prove negligence before they could collect for their injuries.

Finally, the states passed *workers compensation laws* as a solution to the growing problem of work-related accidents. In 1908, the federal government passed a workers compensation law covering certain federal employees, and by 1920, most states had passed similar laws. All states today have workers compensation laws.

Workers compensation is based on the fundamental principle of **liability without fault**. *The employer is held absolutely liable for job-related injuries or disease suffered by the workers, regardless* *of who is at fault.* Disabled workers are paid for their injuries according to a schedule of benefits established by law. The workers are not required to sue their employers to collect benefits. The laws provide for the prompt payment of benefits to disabled workers regardless of fault and with a minimum of legal formality. The costs of workers compensation benefits are therefore considered to be a normal cost of production, which is included in the price of the product.

Objectives of Workers Compensation

State workers compensation laws have several basic objectives:[27]

- Broad coverage of employees for job-related accidents and disease
- Substantial protection against the loss of income
- Sufficient medical care and rehabilitation services
- Encouragement of safety
- Reduction in litigation

A fundamental objective is to provide broad coverage of employees for job-related accidents and disease. That is, workers compensation laws should cover most occupations or job-related accidents and disease.

A second objective is to provide substantial protection against the loss of income. The cash benefits are designed to restore a substantial proportion of the disabled worker's lost earnings, so that the disabled worker's previous standard of living can be maintained.

A third objective is to provide sufficient medical care and rehabilitation services to injured workers. Workers compensation laws require employers to pay hospital, surgical, and other medical costs incurred by injured workers. Also, the laws provide for rehabilitation services to disabled employees so they can be restored to productive employment.

Another objective is to encourage firms to reduce job-related accidents and to develop effective safety programs. Experience rating is used to encourage firms to reduce job-related accidents and disease, because firms with superior accident records pay relatively lower workers compensation premiums.

Finally, workers compensation laws are designed to reduce litigation. The benefits are paid promptly to disabled workers without requiring them to sue their employers. The objective is to reduce or eliminate the payment of legal fees to attorneys, and time-consuming and expensive trials and appeals.

Types of Laws

State workers compensation laws are either compulsory or elective. Almost all states have compulsory laws that require covered employers to provide specified benefits to workers who become disabled from a job-related accident or disease.

Two states (New Jersey and Texas) have elective laws that permit employers either to elect or reject the workers compensation law. If the employer rejects the law and the injured employee sues for damages based on the employer's negligence, the employer is deprived of the three common-law defenses. In such a case, the injured worker has only to establish the employer's negligence to collect damages.

Complying with the Law

Employers can comply with state law by purchasing a workers compensation policy, by self-insuring, or by obtaining insurance from a monopoly or competitive state fund.

Most firms purchase a workers compensation policy from a private insurer. The policy pays the benefits that the employer must legally provide to workers who have a job-related accident or disease.

Self-insurance is allowed in most states. Many large firms self-insure their workers compensation losses to save money. In addition, group self-insurance is often available to smaller firms that pool their risks and liabilities.

Finally, workers compensation insurance can be purchased from a state fund in certain states. In eight jurisdictions, covered employers generally must purchase workers compensation insurance from a **monopoly state fund.** Nineteen states have **competitive state funds** that compete with private insurers.[28]

Covered Occupations

Although most occupations are covered by workers compensation laws, certain occupations are excluded or have incomplete coverage. Because of the nature of the work, most states exclude or provide incomplete coverage for farm workers, domestic servants, and casual employees. Some states have numerical exemptions, by which small firms with fewer than a specified number of employees (typically three to five) are not required to provide workers compensation benefits. However, employers can voluntarily cover employees in an exempted class. Finally, some states exclude professional athletes from workers compensation (see Insight 24.2).

Eligibility Requirements

Two principal eligibility requirements must be met to receive workers compensation benefits. First, the disabled person must work in a covered occupation. Second, the worker must have a job-related accident or disease. *This means the injury or disease must arise out of and in the course of employment.* The courts have gradually broadened the meaning of this term over time. The following situations are usually covered under a typical workers compensation law:

- An employee who travels is injured while engaging in activities that benefit the employer.
- The employee is injured while performing specified duties at a specified location.
- The employee is on the premises and is injured going to the work area.
- The employee has a heart attack while lifting some heavy materials.

Workers Compensation Benefits

Workers compensation laws provide four principal benefits:

- Unlimited medical care
- Disability income
- Death benefits
- Rehabilitation services

Unlimited Medical Care Medical care generally is covered in full in all states. However, the majority of states have medical fee schedules that limit the amounts paid for certain medical procedures.

Medical care is expensive. To hold down medical costs, many states allow employers to use managed care arrangements to treat injured employees. The use of health maintenance organizations (HMOs) and preferred provider organizations (PPOs) has also increased over time.

Disability Income Disability-income benefits can be paid after the disabled worker satisfies a waiting period that usually ranges from three to seven days. If the injured worker is still disabled after a certain number of days or weeks, most states pay disability benefits retroactively to the date of injury.

The weekly cash benefit is based on a percentage of the injured worker's weekly wage, typically two-thirds, and is subject to minimum and maximum payments. There are four classifications of disability: (1) temporary total, (2) permanent total, (3) temporary partial, and (4) permanent partial. Temporary total disability claims are the most common and account for the majority of all cash claims. For example, a worker in Nebraska may break a leg and be totally disabled for three months. After a one-week waiting period, the disabled worker would receive two-thirds of his or her weekly wage up to a maximum of $444 weekly.

Death Benefits Death benefits can be paid to eligible survivors if the worker dies as a result of a job-related accident or disease. Two types of benefits are paid. First, a burial allowance is paid. Second, weekly income benefits can be paid to eligible surviving dependents. The weekly benefit is based on a proportion of the deceased worker's wages (typically two-thirds) and is usually paid to a surviving spouse for life or until she or he remarries. Upon remarriage, the widow or widower typically gets one or two years of payments in a lump sum. A weekly benefit can also be paid to each dependent child until a specified age, such as age 18 or later.

Rehabilitation Services All states provide rehabilitation services to restore disabled workers to productive employment. In addition to weekly disability benefits, workers who are being rehabilitated are compensated for board and room, travel, books, and equipment. Training allowances may also be paid in some states.

Insight 24.2

Are Professional Football and Baseball Players Eligible for Workers Compensation?

Don't think sports superstars file workers compensation claims? Think again. Among the more high-profile professional athletes to file for workers comp is Joe Montana, former quarterback of the San Francisco 49ers and the Kansas City Chiefs, who has reportedly filed a workers compensation permanent total claim due to his accumulated injuries.

Professional athletes are generally covered under the workers compensation laws of the various states unless there is specific excepting statute or case law. Some states have statutory provisions negatively affecting workers comp for professional athletes. Florida, Massachusetts, Maryland, Michigan, Pennsylvania, and Texas are just a few states with these statutes.

These statutes vary from a complete exclusion of benefits in Florida to a specific exception in Massachusetts for professional athletes if their contract provides for the payment of wages during the period of disability resulting from such employment to an election of benefits between contract benefits or workers compensation after injury in Texas. There also is some case law on professional athletes and workers compensation, with the most frequently reported case being *Palmer v. Kansas City Chiefs Football Club*. The claimant, a professional football player, was injured executing a trap block.

The court held that the injury was not accidental because, as a matter of judicial notice, football is a dangerous sport fraught with the expectation of injury. The court said "that the act simply does not contemplate that the deliberate collision between human bodies constitutes an accident or the injury in the usual course of such an occupation caused by an unexpected event."

In the state of Maryland, the law was amended in 1982 with a view to preventing a similar decision. The law provided that "compensation may not be denied to an employee because of the degree of risk associated with the employment." Professional athletes in Maryland may receive benefits if the injury is a departure from their usual sport activity such as, for example, when a fan throws a bottle and hits and injures a player.

The *Palmer* case has been criticized for several reasons. First, the employees were covered by the workers compensation law but not protected when doing their job. Secondly, inadvertent traumatic injuries were held to be nonaccidental. Finally, the court reintroduced the assumption of risk doctrine even though it was not permitted by statute.

There are basically two major arguments that have been used to avoid awarding workers compensation benefits to professional athletes:

1. *Accidental versus intentional.* Here we are dealing with football and baseball players with classical traumatic injuries: broken ankles, smashed knees, and torn shoulders. Their type of injury is not uncommon in workers compensation. But the frequency may be significant for professional athletes. A 1990 study by the NFL Players Association reported that more than one-third of the 645 players with careers between 1940 and 1986 retired with disability injuries. Apparently, two out of three retired NFL players live with a permanent injury.

*The athletes' injuries, however, are not intentional—*that is, they use protective gear that is constantly being improved and certain dangerous activities are discouraged, such as football face-masking, spearing, unnecessary roughing, and clipping.

2. *Assumption of risk*, which is one of the common law defenses that made workers compensation statutes necessary in the first place. Assumption of risk is the concept that there should be no damages for injury when you assume the risk of, for example, a fan at a hockey game who is hit by a puck.

The classic assumption-of-risk defense has no place in workers compensation law or the world's most dangerous jobs would not get done. In fact, the workers compensation laws when enacted eliminated the three common law defenses of assumption of risk, fellow servant, and contributory negligence.

The public perception that highly paid individuals such as professional athletes should not receive workers compensation benefits is wrong. *Corporations are subject to workers compensation laws to cover their employees. Athletes also should be covered.*

SOURCE: Adapted from Donald T. Decarlo, "Athletic Disability," *Risk & Insurance* (April 15, 1998).

Second-Injury Funds

Most states have provisions for a **second-injury fund**. The purpose is to encourage employers to hire handicapped workers. If a second-injury fund did not exist, employers would be reluctant to hire handicapped workers because of the higher benefits that might have to be paid if a second injury occurs.

For example, assume that a worker with a preexisting injury or handicap is injured in a job-related accident. When combined with the first injury, the second injury produces a disability more severe than that caused by the second injury alone. Thus, the workers compensation benefits that must be paid are higher than if only the second injury had occurred. The employer pays only for the second injury, and the second-injury fund pays the additional benefits that are required.

Problems and Issues

Numerous problems and issues are associated with current workers compensation programs. Some important problems are summarized as follows.

1. *Increase in workplace violence.* Thousands of workers are killed or assaulted each year while at work. Workers are often killed or injured because of robbery and other business crimes, domestic quarrels that spill over into the workplace, actions by angry and disgruntled employees toward employers, and terrorism and hate crimes. Workers who are more likely to be assaulted or killed include employees in fast-food stores, liquor stores, and gas stations; cab drivers; teachers; police officers; bartenders; and nurses.

   Statistics on workplace violence tell a harrowing tale:[29]

   - In 1995, 1024 workers were murdered on the job, which represented 16 percent of all job fatalities.
   - An employee is almost twice as likely to be killed by coworkers, former coworkers, or clients than is a police officer in the line of duty.
   - One million individuals are victims of violent crime at work each year.
   - Six million employees are threatened at a work site each year.

   - The chance of being attacked, threatened, or harassed on the job is one in four.

   To deal with the problem of workplace violence, some companies have formed in-house threat assessment or crisis management teams, which provide a way for employees to report potentially violent behavior.

2. *Carpal tunnel syndrome.* Carpal tunnel syndrome injuries have increased substantially in recent years, and the claims related to this condition are more costly than workers compensation claims. Carpal tunnel syndrome is an occupational disease that results from repeated motions in the hand, wrist, and shoulder. Highly repetitive motions can cause severe nerve damage and a crippling of the wrist, hands, and arms. Workers employed in food preparation, meat packing, construction, product fabrication, and clerical positions, such as computer operators, frequently experience this type of injury.

   Carpal tunnel syndrome claims account for a high proportion of total claims and are more costly to settle. The time lost from work is also much longer than the time lost from other injuries. National Council on Compensation Insurance (NCCI) claims data show that *for 1994 and 1995, the median cost of carpal tunnel claims was more than double the median cost of all other claims. The median duration of lost-time claims for this disease was more than four times the median duration for all other claims.*[30]

   Employers are now using a number of approaches to reduce carpal tunnel claims. These measures include a redesign of work stations and special chairs for computer operators to reduce stress, instruction on the correct use of tools, and improved work habits.

3. *Increased litigation.* Although a fundamental objective of workers compensation is to reduce lawsuits, attorneys are involved in a substantial percentage of claims, especially high-cost claims. A study of claims in 13 states by the National Council on Compensation Insurance revealed that 80 to 90 percent of the high-cost claims involved attorneys. High-cost claims included permanent total disability cases, permanent partial disability cases, and negotiated awards.[31]

   The increased litigation is due to (1) suits by injured workers who are dissatisfied with their workers compensation awards and then sue for higher amounts; (2) denial of claims by some employers, which results in lawsuits by the injured workers; and (3) court decisions that have eroded the **exclusive remedy doctrine**. This doctrine states that workers compensation benefits should be the sole and exclusive remedy for injured workers; workers have a statutory right to receive benefits without proving negligence, but in turn, they give up the right to sue the employer. This doctrine has been eroded by court decisions in recent years. As a result, injured employees often can receive both workers compensation benefits and a tort damage award based on negligence.

SUMMARY

- Social insurance programs are compulsory insurance programs with certain characteristics that distinguish them from other government insurance programs. Social insurance programs in the United States have the following characteristics:

  Compulsory programs

  Floor of income

  Emphasis on social adequacy rather than individual equity

  Benefits loosely related to earnings

  Benefits prescribed by law

  No means test

  Full funding unnecessary

  Financially self-supporting

- The Old-Age Survivors, and Disability Insurance (OASDI) program, commonly called Social Security, is the most important social insurance program in the United States. The program pays monthly cash benefits to eligible beneficiaries who retire or become disabled. The program also pays survivor benefits to eligible surviving family members.

- The current Medicare program consists of (1) Hospital Insurance (Part A), (2) Supplementary Medical Insurance (Part B), and (3) Medicare + Choice.

- Unemployment insurance programs are federal-state programs that pay weekly cash benefits to workers who are involuntarily unemployed. Unemployment programs have several objectives:

  Provide cash income to unemployed workers during periods of involuntary unemployment

  Help unemployed workers find jobs

  Encourage employers to stabilize employment

  Help stabilize the economy

- Unemployed workers must meet certain eligibility requirements to receive weekly cash benefits:

  Have qualifying wages and employment during the base year

  Be able and available for work

  Actively seek work

  Be free from disqualification

  Serve a one-week waiting period in most states

- Workers compensation is a social insurance program that provides medical care, cash benefits, and rehabilitation services to workers who become disabled from job-related accidents or disease. Workers compensation laws have the following objectives:

  Broad coverage of employees for job-related injuries and disease

  Substantial protection against the loss of income

  Sufficient medical care and rehabilitation services

  Encouragement of safety

  Reduction in litigation

- State workers compensation laws typically pay the following benefits:

  Unlimited medical care

  Weekly disability-income benefits

  Death benefits to survivors

  Rehabilitation services

KEY CONCEPTS AND TERMS

Assumption-of-risk doctrine

Average indexed monthly earnings (AIME)

Competitive state fund

Contributory negligence doctrine

Credit (quarter of coverage)

Currently insured

Diagnosis-related groups (DRGs)

Disability insured

Earnings test (retirement test)

Exclusive remedy doctrine

Experience rating

Extended-benefits program

Fellow-servant doctrine

Full retirement age

Fully funded program
Fully insured
Hospital Insurance
 (Part A)
Individual equity
Liability without fault
Means test
Medicare
Medicare + Choice
Medigap policy
Monopoly state fund

Primary insurance amount
 (PIA)
Second-injury fund
Short-term involuntary
 unemployment
Social adequacy
Social Security (OASDI)
Supplementary Medical
 Insurance (Part B)
Unemployment insurance
Workers compensation

REVIEW QUESTIONS

1. Why are social insurance programs necessary?

2. Describe the basic characteristics of social insurance programs.

3. Explain the meaning of fully insured, currently insured, and disability insured under the OASDI program.

4. Describe briefly the major benefits under the OASDI program.

5. Explain the definition of disability used in the OASDI program.

6. Describe briefly the major benefits under the Medicare program.

7. Describe the basic objectives of unemployment insurance programs.

8. Explain the eligibility requirements for receiving unemployment insurance benefits.

9. Describe the basic objectives of workers compensation laws.

10. Identify the major benefits under a typical workers compensation law.

APPLICATION QUESTIONS

1. The Social Security (OASDI) program is expected to experience severe financial problems in the future. Numerous proposals have been made to save Social Security.
   a. Why is the Social Security program expected to experience severe financial problems in the future?
   b. Explain the various proposals for dealing with the future financial problems that the Social Security program may encounter.

2. The Medicare program is also expected to experience severe financial problems in the future. Numerous proposals have been made to reform Medicare.
   a. Why is the Medicare program expected to experience severe financial problems in the future?
   b. Explain the various proposals for reforming the Medicare program.

3. A critic of unemployment insurance stated that "unemployment insurance programs are designed to maintain the economic security of unemployed workers, but several critical problems must be resolved."
   a. Are all types of unemployment covered under the state unemployment insurance programs? Explain.
   b. Describe some situations that may disqualify a worker for unemployment benefits.
   c. Are all unemployed persons receiving unemployment insurance benefits at the present time? Explain your answer.

4. Workers compensation laws provide considerable financial protection to workers who have a job-related injury or disease.
   a. Explain the fundamental principle on which workers compensation laws are based.
   b. Explain the eligibility requirements for collecting workers compensation benefits.
   c. Explain the problem of workplace violence as it relates to workers compensation insurance.

SELECTED REFERENCES

Advisory Council on Social Security. *Report of the 1994–1996 Advisory Council on Social Security*, Vols. I and II. Washington, DC: U.S. Government Printing Office, 1997.

Advisory Council on Unemployment Compensation. *Reports and Recommendations*. Washington, DC: Advisory Council on Unemployment Compensation, 1994.

———. *Unemployment Insurance in the United States: Benefits, Financing, Coverage*. Washington, DC: Advisory Council on Unemployment Compensation, 1995.

———. *Collected Findings and Recommendations: 1994–1996*. Washington, DC: Advisory Council on Unemployment Compensation, 1996.

Case Application

Simon, age 35, and Andrea, age 33, are married and have a son, age 1. Simon is employed as an accountant and earns $50,000 annually. Andrea is an associate professor of finance at a local university and earns $80,000 annually. Both are currently and fully insured under the OASDI program. Assume you are a financial planner who is asked to give them advice concerning OASDI and other social insurance programs. Answer each of the following questions based on the following situations. Treat each situation separately.

a. Simon is killed in an automobile accident. To what extent, if any, would the surviving family members be eligible to receive OASDI survivor benefits?

b. Andrea has laryngitis that damaged her vocal cords. As a result, she can no longer teach. She is offered a research position in the business research bureau of the university where she is employed. To what extent, if any, would Andrea be eligible to receive OASDI disability benefits?

c. A deranged student fired a handgun at Andrea because she gave him a grade of D+. As a result, Andrea was seriously injured and is expected to be off work for at least one year while she is recovering. To what extent, if any, would existing social insurance programs in the United States provide income during the period of temporary disability?

d. Simon would like to retire at age 62 and still work part-time as an accountant. He has been informed that the OASDI earnings test would be relevant in his case. Explain how the earnings test might affect his decision to work part-time after retirement.

e. Simon resigned from his job to find a higher-paying position. Explain whether Simon could receive unemployment insurance benefits during the period of temporary unemployment before he finds a new job.

Gluck, Michael E. "A Medicare Prescription Drug Benefit," *Medicare Brief*, National Academy of Social Insurance (April 1999), No. 1.

Myers, Robert J. *Social Security*. 4th ed. Philadelphia: Pension Research Council and University of Pennsylvania Press, 1993.

National Bipartison Commission on the Future of Medicare. *Building a Better Medicare for Today and Tomorrow*, Washington, DC, Final Version, March 16, 1999.

1999 Analysis of Workers Compensation Laws. Washington, DC: U.S. Chamber of Commerce, 1999.

Rejda, George E. *Social Insurance and Economic Security*, sixth edition. Upper Saddle River, NJ: Prentice-Hall, 1999.

————. "Unemployment Compensation Programs," in Jerry D. Rosenbloom, ed., *The Handbook of Employee Benefits, Design, Funding, Administration*, fourth edition. Burr Ridge, IL: Irwin Professional Publishing, 1996, Chapter 28.

Social Security Advisory Board. *The 1999 Technical Panel on Assumptions and Methods, Report to the Social Security Advisory Board. Washington*, DC: Social Security Advisory Board, November 1999.

————. *Social Security, Why Action Should Be Taken Soon*. Washington, DC: Social Security Advisory Board, July 1998.

Social Security and Medicare Board of Trustees. *Status of the Social Security and Medicare Programs, A Summary of the 2000 Annual Report*. Washington, DC: March 2000.

United States General Accounting Office. *Medicare Beneficiaries' Prescription Drug Coverage* (GAO/T-HEHS-99-198). Statement of Laura A. Dummit, Associate Director, Health Financing and Public Health Issues, Health, Education, and Human Services Division. Washington, DC: September 28, 1999.

————. *Medicare Reform, Ensuring Fiscal Sustainability While Modernizing the Program Will Be Challenging* (GAO/T-HEHS/AIMD-99-294). Statement of David M. Walker, Comptroller General of the United States. Washington, DC: September 22, 1999.

————. *Social Security, Evaluating Reform Proposals* (GAO/AIMD/HEHS-00-29). Washington, DC: United States General Accounting Office, November 1999.

NOTES

1. *2000 Guide to Social Security and Medicare* (Louisville, KY: William M. Mercer, November 1999), p. 30.

2. George E. Rejda, *Social Insurance and Economic Security*, sixth edition (Upper Saddle River, NJ: Prentice-Hall, 1999), pp. 18–25.

3. Data supplied to the author by Robert J. Myers, former chief actuary, Social Security Administration.

4. This section is based largely on Rejda, Chapters 5 and 6.

5. Social Security Administration, SSA Publication no. 05–10055, April 2000.

6. A more liberal rule applies to blind workers. A blind worker age 55 or older must be unable to perform work that requires skills or abilities comparable to those required by the work that he or she did regularly before age 55 (or before he or she became blind, if later than age 55).

7. *2000 Annual Report of the Board of Trustees of the Federal Supplementary Medical Insurance Trust Fund* (March 2000).

8. This section is based on *Medicare & You* (Baltimore, MD: Health Care Financing Administration, 1999).

9. The self-employed are allowed two deductions that reduce the effective tax rate. First, net earnings from self-employment are reduced by an amount approximately equal to one-half of the total self-employment tax, which reflects the fact that the employer's share of the total Social Security tax is not considered taxable income to the employee. Second, for income-tax purposes, half of the self-employment tax is deductible as a business expense, which reflects the fact that employers are allowed to deduct the Social Security taxes paid on behalf of their employees.

10. Social Security and Medicare Board of Trustees, *Status of Social Security and Medicare Programs, A Summary of the 2000 Annual Reports* (March 2000).

11. *The 2000 Annual Report, Board of Trustees, The Federal Old-Age and Survivors Insurance and Disability Insurance Trust Funds* (March 2000).

12. *Report of the 1994–1996 Advisory Council on Social Security, Volume I: Findings and Recommendations* (Washington, DC: 1994–1996 Advisory Council on Social Security, 1997), p. 41.

13. Social Security and Medicare Board of Trustees, *Status of Social Security and Medicare Programs, A Summary of the 2000 Annual Reports* (March 2000).

14. See National Bipartisan Commission on the Future of Medicare, *Building a Better Medicare for Today and Tomorrow*, Washington, DC, Final Version, March 16, 1999.

15. Laurie McGinley, "AARP Report to Fuel Debate on Health Costs," *The Wall Street Journal*, December 9, 1999, p. A28.

16. *Ibid.*

17. Michael E. Gluck, "A Medicare Prescription Drug Benefit," *Medicare Brief*, National Academy of Social Insurance (April 1999), No. 1, Table 1, p. 2.

18. United States General Accounting Office, *Medicare Beneficiaries' Prescription Drug Coverage* (GAO/T-HEHS-99-198), Statement of Laura A. Dummit, Associate Director, Health Financing and Public Health Issues, Health, Education, and Human Services Division, Washington, DC, September 28, 1999, p. 6.

19. The material on unemployment insurance in this chapter is based on Rejda, Chapters 14 and 15.

20. Data obtained from U.S. Department of Labor, Employment and Training Division at http://www.doleta.gov/. See UI Data & Statistics.

21. Committee on Ways and Means, U.S. House of Representatives, *1998 Green Book* (Washington, DC: U.S. Government Printing Office, 1998), p. 331.

22. *Ibid.*

23. The high-cost multiple is calculated by comparing two ratios: (1) the ratio of current net trust-fund reserves to current-year total wages earned in insured employment divided by (2) the ratio of the highest amount of total state benefit payments experienced in any 12 consecutive months to the total wages in insured employment during those 12 months.

24. *1998 Green Book*, Table 4-8, pp. 348–349.

25. *Defining Federal and State Roles in Unemployment, A Report to the President and Congress* (Washington, DC: Advisory Council on Unemployment Compensation, 1996), Table 7-1, pp. 102–103.

26. The material on workers compensation in this chapter is based on Rejda, Chapter 12.

27. Rejda, pp. 259–262.

28. Exclusive or monopoly funds exist in Nevada, North Dakota, Ohio, Washington, West Virginia, Wyoming, Puerto Rico, and the Virgin Islands. In January 1997, competitive state funds existed in Arizona, California, Colorado, Hawaii, Idaho, Kentucky, Louisiana, Maine, Maryland, Michigan, Minnesota, Montana, New York, Oklahoma, Oregon, Pennsylvania, Tennessee, Texas, and Utah.

29. Russ Banham, "Defusing Workplace Violence," *1997 Issues Report, Vital Workers Compensation Information* (Boca Raton, FL: National Council on Compensation Insurance, 1997), p. 75.

30. Rejda, p. 249.

31. "Attorneys Involved in Most High-Cost Workers Compensation Claims," *1996 Issues Report, Vital Workers Compensation Information* (Boca Raton, FL: National Council on Compensation Insurance, 1996), p. 47.

 Students may take a self-administered test on this chapter at www.awlonline.com/rejda

Part Six

The Insurance Industry

Chapter 25

Types of Insurers and Marketing Systems

"Insurers are increasingly using multiple distribution channels to sell their products."

Insurance Information Institute

Learning Objectives

After studying this chapter, you should be able to:

▲ Describe the major types of private insurers, including the following:

   Stock insurers
   Mutual insurers
   Reciprocal exchanges
   Lloyd's Associations
   Blue Cross and Blue Shield plans
   Health maintenance organizations

▲ Explain why some life insurers have demutualized or formed holding companies in recent years.

▲ Explain the difference between a building agency and a nonbuilding agency as marketing systems in life insurance.

▲ Describe the direct response system for selling life insurance.

▲ Describe the different marketing systems in property and liability insurance, including the following:

   Independent agency system
   Exclusive agency system
   Direct writer
   Direct response system
   Mixed systems

▲ Access an Internet site and obtain consumer information about life insurance and property and liability insurance.

Internet Resources

- The **American Council of Life Insurance (ACLI)** represents the life insurance industry on issues dealing with legislation and regulation. ACLI also publishes statistics on the life insurance industry in an annual fact book. Visit the site at:

  http://www.acli.com

- The **American Insurance Association (AIA)** is an important property and casualty trade association that represents more than 375 companies writing more than $60 billion annually in premiums. The site lists available publications, position papers on important issues in property and casualty insurance, press releases, insurance-related links, and names of state insurance commissioners. Visit the site at:

http://www.aiadc.org

- The **Insurance Information Institute (III)** is an excellent site for obtaining information on the property and liability insurance industry. It provides timely consumer information on auto, homeowners, and business insurance, and other types of property and liability insurance. Visit the site at:

http://www.iii.org/

- The **Life Office Management Association** provides extensive information dealing with the management and operations of life insurers and financial services companies. Visit the site at:

http://www.loma.org/

- **LIMRA International, Inc.**, is the principal source of industry sales and marketing statistics in life insurance. Its site provides news and information about LIMRA and the financial services field, conducts research, and produces a wide range of publications. Visit the site at:

http://www.limra.com

- The **National Association of Mutual Insurance Companies** is a trade association that represents mutual insurance companies in property and casualty insurance. Visit this site at:

http://www.namic.org

*A*ndrew, age 35, is a single parent with two sons, ages 5 and 2. His wife was recently killed in an auto accident. The amount of life insurance on her life was insufficient for paying the funeral costs. After reassessing his situation, Andrew believes he should purchase additional life insurance. A friend recommends the purchase of insurance from a mutual insurer because policyowners may receive dividends. Andrew has no idea what a mutual insurer is and how one differs from other insurers. He is not alone in his confusion. Many consumers also do not understand the differences among insurers.

This chapter deals with the insurance industry. Thousands of life and health, and property and liability insurers are doing business in the United States today. The insurance industry has a profound effect on the American economy. It sells various financial and insurance products that enable individuals and families to attain a high degree of economic security. In addition, it provides millions of jobs for American workers and is an important source of capital for the business community. Indemnification for losses is one of the most important economic functions performed by insurers; it ensures that insureds are restored partly or completely to their previous financial position, thereby maintaining their economic security.

This chapter discusses the basic characteristics of the private insurance industry. Topics discussed include the major types of insurers, the various methods for marketing insurance, and the role of agents and brokers in the sales process.

TYPES OF PRIVATE INSURERS

A large number of private insurers are currently doing business in the United States. At the end of 1998, 1563 U.S. life insurers were operating in various states. These insurers make available a wide variety of life and health products, private pension plans, and related financial products. In addition, in 1997, 3366 property and liability insurers were doing business in the United States.[1] These insurers sell some form of property and liability insurance and related lines, including inland marine coverages and surety and fidelity bonds.

In terms of legal organization and ownership, the major types of private insurers can be classified as follows:

- Stock insurers
- Mutual insurers
- Reciprocal exchanges
- Lloyd's Associations
- Blue Cross and Blue Shield plans
- Health maintenance organizations (HMOs)

Stock Insurers

A **stock insurer** *is a corporation owned by stockholders who participate in the profits and losses of the insurer.* The stockholders elect a board of directors, who in turn appoint executive officers to manage the corporation. The board of directors has the ultimate responsibility for the corporation's financial success.

The types of insurance that a stock insurer can write are determined by its charter. In property and liability insurance, the majority of stock insurers are multiple-line insurers that write most types of insurance, with the exception of life and health insurance. Some states also permit the writing of life and health insurance.

A stock insurer cannot issue an assessable policy. As assessable policy permits the insurer to assess the policyowners additional premiums if losses are excessive. Instead, the stockholders must bear all losses. But they also share in the profits: if the business is profitable, dividends can be declared and paid to the stockholders. The value of the stock may also increase if the business is profitable.

Mutual Insurers

A **mutual insurer** *is a corporation owned by the policyowners.* The policyowners elect the board of directors, who appoint the executives who manage the corporation. Because relatively few policyowners bother to vote, the board of directors has effective management control of the company.

A mutual insurer may pay a dividend or give a rate reduction in advance. In life insurance, a dividend is largely a refund of a redundant premium that can be paid if the mortality, investment, and operating experience is favorable. However, because the mortality and investment experience cannot be guaranteed, the dividends legally cannot be guaranteed by insurers.

There are several types of mutual insurers, including the following:

- Assessment mutual
- Advance premium mutual
- Factory mutual
- Fraternal insurer

Assessment Mutual An **assessment mutual** *is an insurer that has the right to assess policyowners an additional amount if the experience is unfavorable.* Relatively few assessment mutuals are in existence today, partly because of the practical problem of collecting the assessments. Those insurers still doing business are smaller insurers that operate in limited geographical areas and write only a limited number of lines of insurance.

Advance Premium Mutual An **advance premium mutual** *is owned by the policyowners, but it does not issue an assessable policy.* Once the insurer's surplus (difference between assets and liabilities) exceeds a certain amount, the states will not permit a mutual insurer to issue an assessable policy. The advance premium mutual is generally larger and financially stronger than the assessment mutual described earlier. The premiums charged are expected to be sufficient to pay all claims and expenses. Any additional costs because of poor experience are paid out of the company's surplus.

In life insurance, most mutual insurers pay dividends annually to the policyowners. In property and liability insurance, dividends to policyowners are not paid on a regular basis. Property and liability insurers instead may charge lower initial premiums that are closer to the actual amount needed for claims and expenses.

Factory Mutual A **factory mutual** *is a specialized insurer that insures only superior properties.* There is great emphasis on loss prevention, and before a factory can be insured, it must meet stringent underwriting standards. The factory typically must be of superior construction, have an approved sprinkler system, and meet other requirements.

A factory mutual provides periodic inspection and engineering services to its insureds. Because the costs of these loss-control services are high, only the larger risks are eligible for the insurance.

Fraternal Insurer A **fraternal insurer** *is a mutual insurer that provides life and health insurance to members of a social or religious organization.* To qualify as a fraternal insurer under a state's insurance code, the insurer must have some type of social or religious organization in existence, such as a lodge or a religious, charitable, or benevolent society. Examples of fraternals are the Knights of Columbus, Catholic Workmen, and Aid Association for Lutherans.

Fraternal insurers sell only life and health insurance to their members. The assessment principle was originally used to pay death claims. Today, most fraternals operate on the basis of the level premium and legal reserve system that is used by commercial life insurers. Fraternal insurers also sell term life insurance.

Because fraternals are nonprofit or charitable organizations, they receive favorable tax treatment.

Changing Corporate Structure of Mutual Insurers The corporate structure of mutual insurers—especially life insurers—is changing dramatically. Three trends are clearly evident: (1) an increase in company mergers, (2) demutualization, and (3) formation of mutual holding companies.

1. *Company Mergers.* The number of active life insurers has declined sharply in recent years, from 2150 insurers in 1994 to 1563 in 1998, or a decrease of 27 percent.[2] Most of the decline is due to company mergers and consolidation. A merger means that one insurer is absorbed by another insurer or that two or more existing insurers are merged into an entirely new company. Mergers occur because insurers with to reduce their operating costs and general overhead costs. They also occur because some insurers wish to acquire a line of new insurance or enter a new area of business.

2. *Demutualization.* **Demutualization** means that a mutual insurer is converted into a stock insurer. Some mutual insurers have become stock insurers for the following reasons: (1) the ability to raise new capital is increased; (2) stock insurers have greater flexibility to expand by acquiring new companies or by diversification; (3) stock options can be offered to attract and retain key employees; and (4) conversion to a stock insurer may provide tax advantages.[3]

There are three principal methods by which a mutual insurer can convert to a stock insurer—pure conversion, merger, or bulk reinsurance.[4] In a *pure conversion*, a mutual insurer amends its articles of incorporation and is reorganized as a stock insurer. In a *merger*, a mutual insurer and stock insurer are joined together as a single company, and the stock insurer is the surviving company. In *bulk reinsurance*, a mutual insurer cedes all of its assets and liabilities to a stock company, and the mutual insurer is then dissolved (see Exhibit 25.1).

3. *Mutual Holding Company.* Demutualization is cumbersome, expensive, and slow, and it requires the approval of regulatory authorities. As an alternative, many states have enacted legislation that allows a mutual insurer to form a holding company. A **holding company** is a company that directly or indirectly controls an authorized insurer. A mutual insurer is reorganized as a holding company that owns or acquires control of stock insurance companies that could issue common stock (see Exhibit 25.2). The mutual holding company would own at least 51 percent of the subsidiary stock insurer if the latter issues common stock.

Mutual holding companies are highly controversial. Proponents argue that they offer numerous advantages: (1) insurers have an easier and less expensive way to raise new capital to expand

EXHIBIT 25.1
Alternative Modes of Demutualization

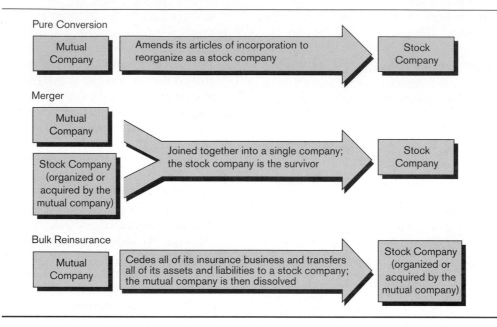

EXHIBIT 25.2
Mutual Holding Company Illustration

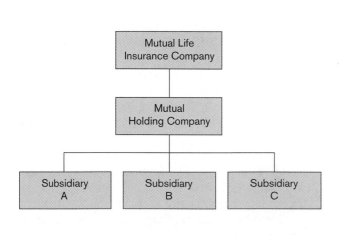

or remain competitive; (2) insurers can enter new areas of insurance more easily, such as a life insurer acquiring a property and liability insurer; and (3) stock options can be given to attract and retain key employees.

Critics of mutual holding companies, however, argue that policyowners may be financially hurt by the change; the mutual holding structure could result in a reduction of dividends to policyowners and other financial benefits. Critics also argue that a conflict of interest may arise between top management and the policyowners. For example, top management may be given company stock or stock options for earning higher operating profits, which could result in lower dividends or higher premiums for policyowners.

Reciprocal Exchanges

A reciprocal exchange is another type of private insurer. A **reciprocal exchange** (*also called an* **interin-**

surance exchange) *can be defined as an unincorporated mutual.* A reciprocal insurer has several distinct characteristics. *First, in its purest form, insurance is exchanged among the members; each member of the reciprocal insures the other members and, in turn, is insured by them.* Thus, there is an exchange of insurance promises—hence the name reciprocal exchange.

Second, a reciprocal is managed by an attorney-in-fact. The attorney-in-fact is usually a corporation that is authorized by the subscribers to seek new members, pay losses, collect premiums, handle reinsurance arrangements, invest the funds, and perform other administrative duties. However, the attorney-in-fact is not personally liable for the payment of claims and is not the insurer. The reciprocal exchange is the insurer.

Third, from a historical perspective, reciprocals can be classified as pure or modified. Historically, the reciprocals that operated earlier were of the pure type. A separate account was kept for each member. The account was credited with the member's premiums and share of investment earnings and debited for the member's share of losses and expenses. The balance in the account could be paid to a terminating member. Thus, in its purest form, insurance was provided "at cost" to the member.

Most reciprocals today are of the modified type. In the modified form, a reciprocal is similar to an advance premium mutual. Individual accounts are not set up for each member to reflect the profit or losses of the reciprocal. In effect, the financial operations of the reciprocal are similar to a mutual insurer, with the exception of management by an attorney-in-fact.

Most reciprocals are relatively small and account for only a small percentage of the total property and liability insurance premiums written. In addition, most reciprocals specialize in a limited number of lines of insurance. However, a few reciprocals are multiple-line insurers and can be large.

Lloyd's Associations

Insurance can also be purchased from a Lloyd's Association. There are two basic types of **Lloyd's Associations:** (1) Lloyd's of London, and (2) American Lloyds.

Lloyd's of London Lloyd's of London is a major worldwide ocean marine insurer that writes a wide variety of risks and is extremely important as a professional reinsurer. Lloyd's is also famous for writing insurance on diverse exposure units such as a pianist's fingers, a Kentucky Derby winner's legs, and a hole-in-one at a professional golf tournament.

Lloyd's of London has several important characteristics. *First, Lloyd's technically is not an insurance company, but is an association that provides physical facilities and services to the members for selling insurance.* Lloyd's by itself does not write insurance; the insurance is written by the syndicates that belong to Lloyd's. In this respect, Lloyd's is similar to the New York Stock Exchange, which does not buy or sell securities, but provides a marketplace and other services to the members.

Second, the insurance is actually written by the various syndicates that belong to Lloyd's. The syndicates are managed by an underwriting agent who is responsible for appointing a professional underwriter for each major type of business. The syndicates tend to specialize in marine, aviation, automobile, and other property and liability insurance lines. The unusual exposure units that have made Lloyd's famous account for only a small part of the total business. Likewise, life insurance accounts only for a small fraction of the total business and is limited to short term contracts.

Third, the individual members (called Names) who belong to the various syndicates have unlimited liability with respect to insurance written as individuals. Names pledge their personal fortunes to pay their agreed-upon share of the insurance written as individuals and have unlimited liability.

Prior to 1993, Lloyd's experienced severe underwriting losses. These losses were due largely to natural disasters, asbestos liability claims, and mismanagement. Because of unlimited liability, many individual Names could not pay their share of claims and were financially ruined.

Another characteristic is that corporations with limited liability can join Lloyd's of London. Because of the underwriting losses mentioned earlier and the need to raise new capital, corporations are now permitted to join Lloyd's of London. Unlike the individual Names, however, corporations have limited liability. The infusion of new capital from corporations has substantially increased the ability of Lloyd's to write new business.

Individual members must also meet stringent financial requirements. Each member must make a substantial underwriting deposit. All premiums are deposited into a premium trust fund, and withdrawals are allowed only for claims and expenses. A central guarantee fund pays the loss if an individual member is financially insolvent.

Finally, Lloyd's is licensed only in a small number of jurisdictions in the United States. In the other states, Lloyd's must operate as a nonadmitted insurer. This means that a surplus lines broker or agent can place business with Lloyd's, but only if the insurance cannot be obtained from an admitted insurer in the state. Despite the lack of licensing, Lloyd's does a considerable amount of business in the United States. In particular, Lloyd's of London reinsures a large number of American insurers and is an important professional reinsurer.

American Lloyds Private underwriters in the United States have formed associations similar to Lloyd's of London. The American Lloyds associations, however, differ from Lloyd's of London in many respects. First, the number of individual underwriters is smaller. Second, the liability of an individual underwriter is limited. Each underwriter is responsible only for his or her share of the loss and not that of any insolvent member. Third, the personal net worth and financial strength of an underwriter are considerably lower than that of a Lloyd's of London member. Fourth, an American Lloyds association does not operate through a syndicate, but is managed by an attorney-in-fact. Finally, the financial reputation of an American Lloyds association is not as good as that of Lloyd's of London. Several associations have failed, and some states, such as New York, forbid the formation of new associations.

Blue Cross and Blue Shield Plans

Blue Cross and Blue Shield plans are another type of insurer organization. In most states, Blue Cross plans typically are organized as nonprofit, community-oriented prepayment plans that provide coverage primarily for hospital services. Blue Shield plans generally are nonprofit, prepayment plans that provide payment for physicians' and surgeons' fees and other

medical services. In recent years, the majority of Blue Cross and Blue Shield plans have merged into single entities. In early 1997, 49 plans jointly wrote Blue Cross and Blue Shield benefits. However, six separate Blue Cross plans and four Blue Shield plans were in operation.

Although most members are insured through group plans, individual and family coverages are also available. Blue Cross and Blue Shield plans also sponsor health maintenance organizations (HMOs) and preferred provider organizations (PPOs).

In the majority of states, Blue Cross and Blue Shield plans are nonprofit organizations that receive favorable tax treatment and are regulated under special legislation. However, to raise capital and become more competitive, a few Blue Cross and Blue Shield plans have converted to a for-profit status with stockholders and a board of directors. In addition, many nonprofit Blue Cross and Blue Shield plans own profit-seeking affiliates.

Health Maintenance Organizations

HMOs are organized plans of health care that provide comprehensive health care services to their members. HMOs provide broad health care services to a specified group for a fixed prepaid fee; cost control is emphasized; choice of health care providers may be restricted; and less costly forms of treatment are often provided. The characteristics of HMOs have already been discussed in Chapter 22, so additional treatment is not needed here.

AGENTS AND BROKERS

A successful sales force is the key to the company's financial success. Most policies today are sold by agents and brokers.

Agents

An **agent** *is someone who legally represents the insurer and has the authority to act on the insurer's behalf.* As we noted in Chapter 5, an agent can bind the principal by expressed powers, by implied powers, and by apparent authority. If you buy insurance, you will probably purchase the insurance from an agent. However, there is an important difference between a life insurance agent and a property and liability insurance agent. A life insurance agent usually does not have the authority to bind the company. He or she is merely a soliciting agent who induces persons to apply for life insurance. The applicant for life insurance must be approved by the company before the insurance becomes effective.

In contrast, a property and liability insurance agent typically has the power to bind the company immediately with respect to certain types of coverage. *This relationship is normally created by a binder, which is temporary evidence of insurance until the policy is actually issued.* Binders can be oral or written. For example, if you telephone an agent and request insurance on your motorcycle, the insurance can become effective immediately.

Brokers

In contrast to an agent who represents the insurer, a **broker** *is someone who legally represents the insured.* A broker legally does not have the authority to bind the insurer. Instead, he or she can solicit or accept applications for insurance and then attempt to place the coverage with an appropriate insurer. But the insurance is not in force until the insurer accepts the business.

A broker is paid a commission from the insurers where the business is placed. Many brokers are also licensed as agents, so that they have the authority to bind their companies as agents.

Brokers are extremely important in property and liability insurance at the present time. Large brokerage firms have knowledge of highly specialized insurance markets, provide risk management and loss control services, and control the accounts of large corporate insurance buyers.

Brokers are also important in the surplus lines markets. *Surplus lines refer to any type of insurance for which there is no available market within the state, and the coverage must be placed with a nonadmitted insurer.* A **nonadmitted insurer** *is an insurer not licensed to do business in the state.* A **surplus lines broker** *is a special type of broker who is licensed to place business with a nonadmitted insurer.* An individual may be unable to obtain the coverage from an admitted insurer because the loss exposure is too great, or the required amount of insurance is too large. A surplus lines broker has the authority to place the business with a surplus lines insurer if the coverage cannot be obtained in the state from an admitted company.

Finally, brokers are important in the area of employee benefits, especially for larger employers. Large employers often obtain their group life and medical expense coverages through brokers.

TYPES OF MARKETING SYSTEMS

Marketing systems refer to the various methods for selling insurance. Insurers employ actuaries, claims adjusters, underwriters, and other home office personnel, but unless insurance policies are profitably sold, the insurer's financial survival is unlikely. Thus, an efficient marketing system is essential to an insurance company's survival.

Life Insurance Marketing Systems

Marketing systems for the sale of life insurance have changed dramatically over time. Traditional methods for selling life insurance have been substantially modified, and new marketing models have emerged. At the time of this writing, the major life insurance marketing systems can be classified as follows.[5]

- Agency building system
- Nonbuilding agency system
- Direct response system

Agency Building System An **agency building system** is a system by which an insurer builds its own agency force by recruiting, financing, training, and supervising new agents. The new agents generally represent only the insurer.

Several types of agency building systems exist. Two basic types are the general agency system and managerial system.

1. *General Agency System.* Under the **general agency system**, the general agent is an independent contractor who represents only one insurer. The general agent is in charge of a territory and is responsible for recruiting, training, and motivating new agents. The general agent receives a commission based on the amount of business produced.

Insight 25.1

When Internet Selling Falls Short

No one can know the potential for selling insurance on the Internet, but it is clear that some types of products are just not suited for sale in this electronic medium. The Internet has great potential as a worldwide source of information that consumers can access for insurance products.

For sales, however, it lends itself to the less complicated products such as term life insurance or auto/homeowners insurance. These products have differences, but are easier to compare side-by-side.

Assuming consumers have some idea of their need for the product, they can access a tremendous amount of comparative information on the Internet.

In the case of auto/homeowners products, the need is demand driven. Either state law requires purchase or a lending institution makes it a requirement for a loan. Term insurance is not as frequently mandated, but can be required as part of a divorce decree.

On the other hand, permanent life insurance is not a demand product and has many more "moving parts" that need to be understood.

There is an old saying that life insurance is not bought, but rather is sold. In most permanent life insurance sales and many term insurance sales, prospects need a face-to-face discussion with a qualified producer.

This professional needs to be able to qualify the buyer and to assess the needs to determine exactly what product should be recommended and how that product will fit into an overall plan.

Buyers today are much more sophisticated and want to purchase a product or service from someone they trust and respect.

Without a professional there may also be no assurance that a sale complies with tougher industry standards. In virtually every sale, carriers want to know that a "needs analysis" has been done and that the client clearly understands the nuances of the policy to be purchased.

The large number of class-action suits against insurance carriers and other regulatory investigations have forced companies to completely reevaluate the way their products are marketed.

Licensing differences among states are an issue as well. Licensing rules vary and can even be product-specific. Some states have different licensing requirements for the sale of variable products versus traditional or general-account products.

Most insurers provide some financial assistance to the general agent. For example, the insurer may pay part or all of the expenses of hiring and training new agents, and it therefore has considerable control over the selection of agents and their training. The insurer may also provide an allowance for agency office expenses and other expenses.

2. *Managerial System.* The **managerial system** is another type of agency building system. Under this system, branch offices are established in various areas. The branch manager is an employee of the company who has the responsibility for hiring and training new agents. In some companies, sales by the manager are not allowed or are discouraged; in other companies, sales are allowed but are usually not expected.

The manager is paid a salary and commission based on the volume and quality of the insurance sold and the number of productive agents hired Under this system, the company pays the expenses of the branch office, including the financing of new agents.

Nonbuilding Agency System A **nonbuilding agency system** is a marketing system by which an insurer sells its products through established agents who are already engaged in selling life insurance. Under this system, an insurer enters into contracts with successful agents who agree to sell the insurer's products.

Examples of these nonbuilding agency systems abound. Only one of them—the personal-producing general agent—is discussed here.

Today, a considerable amount of new life insurance is sold by personal-producing general agents. A **personal-producing general agent** is a successful agent who is hired primarily to sell insurance under a

For example, a producer licensed in California for traditional or general-account products could sell a traditional policy to a nonresident of California as long as the application is signed in California. Conversely, a California producer who wants to write variable life business on an Arizona resident would have to be securities and nonresident licensed in Arizona.

If a variable life client of a California producer moved to Nebraska, the producer would need to be nonresident licensed in Nebraska in order to service that business.

Servicing the business that has been sold is certainly a necessity, and trying to do this exclusively over the Internet could prove challenging.

This is not to say that certain companies are not doing well selling products directly to the consumer, but they represent a very small percentage of the total life insurance sold.

These sales tend to be simpler, basic family-need cases in which no sophisticated selling is involved. The more complex business and estate-planing sales tend to take more time and require the application of more planning and tax-law considerations.

These sales involve the accountant and attorney and certainly call for more knowledge on the part of the producer. The professional agent spends a great deal of time keeping up on the latest product and tax-law changes so as to be of great service to clients.

The Internet may be used to attract the buyer to a particular idea or product, but the sale normally will be made in the one-on-one environment.

Anyone who is spending a substantial amount of money on insurance products wants and deserves the kind of one-on-one discussion and advice that only can be delivered in person.

It could be argued that the Internet can be a service vehicle for the producer, but that presumes that a trust level has already been established by personal contact. Sophisticated buyers want to look salespeople in the eye and to measure them to see if their actions live up to their words.

As the Internet becomes even more pervasive, more insurance will be purchased through that medium. But it will never be a substitute for the professional advice and counsel that a well-trained producer can deliver in person.

SOURCE: Terry M. Kaltenbach, "When Internet Selling Falls Short," *Best's Review*, Life & Health ed. (August 1998), p. 74. Copyrighted by A. M. Best Company. Used with permission.

---

contract that provides both direct and overriding commissions. A personal-producing general agent is an above-average salesperson or "super-producer" with a proven sales record. He or she is hired to sell insurance and not to recruit and train new agents. The personal-producing general agent usually receives higher commissions than the typical agent. In return, he or she is expected to sell a certain amount of insurance for a particular insurer. In addition, a personal-producing general agent may have contracts with more than one insurer. Finally, such agents typically pay their own expenses.

Direct Response System The **direct response system** is a marketing system by which life and health insurance is sold directly to customers without the services of an agent. Potential customers are solicited by television radio, mail, newspapers, and other media. Some insurers use *telemarketing* to sell their products. Many insurers also have Web sites through which life and health insurance can be sold directly to the customer.

Direct response insurers engage heavily in market research and testing. New computer technology enables them to gather relevant information about consumers and to maintain extensive records.

The direct response system has several advantages. It enables insurers to gain access to large markets; acquisition costs can be held down; and uncomplicated products can be sold effectively. One disadvantage, however, is that complex products are often difficult to sell because an agent's services may be required. In particular, some marketing experts believe that selling life insurance on the Internet will never become a substitute for professional advice from competent agents (see Insight 25.1).

Finally, in addition to the preceding methods, substantial amounts of new individual life insurance, annuities, long-term care insurance, and other financial products are now being sold to employees in group insurance plans. Premiums are deducted from the employee's wages. Workers who are no longer employed can keep the insurance in force by paying premiums directly to the insurance company.

Property and Liability Insurance Marketing Systems

The major methods for marketing property and liability insurance include the following:

- Independent agency system
- Exclusive agency system
- Direct writer
- Direct response system
- Multiple distribution systems

Independent Agency System The **independent agency system**, which is sometimes called the American agency system, has several basic characteristics. First, *the independent agency is a firm that usually represents several unrelated insurers*. Agents are authorized to write business on behalf of these insurers and in turn are paid a commission based on the amount of business produced.

Second, the agency owns the *expirations or renewal rights to the business*. If a policy comes up for renewal, the agency can place the business with another insurer if it chooses to do so. Likewise, if the contract with an insurer is terminated, the agency can place the business with other insurers.

Third, the independent agent is *compensated by commissions that vary by line of insurance*. The commission rate on renewal business typically is the same as that paid on new business. If a lower renewal rate is paid, the insurer would lose business, because the agent would place the insurance with another insurer. A second commission called a *contingent or profit-sharing commission* (or bonus) may also be paid to the agent based on a favorable loss ratio.

In addition to selling, independent agents perform other functions. They are frequently authorized to adjust small claims. The larger agencies may also provide loss control services to the insureds, such as accident prevention and fire control engineers. Also, for some lines, the agency may bill the policyowners and collect the premiums. However, most insurers have resorted to *direct billing*, by which the policyowner is billed directly by the insurer and then remits the premium to the company. This is particularly true of personal lines of insurance, such as auto and homeowners.

Exclusive Agency System *Under the* **exclusive agency system**, *the agent represents only one insurer or group of insurers under common ownership*. The agent is generally prohibited by contract from representing other insurers.

Agents under the exclusive agency system do not usually own the expirations or renewal rights to the policies. There is some variation, however, in this regard. Some insurers do not give their agents any ownership rights in the expirations. Other insurers may grant limited ownership of expirations while the agency contract is in force, but this interest terminates when the agency contract is terminated.[6] In contrast, under the independent agency system, the agency has complete ownership of the expirations.

Another difference is the payment of commissions. Exclusive agency insurers generally pay a lower commission rate on renewal business than on new business. This approach results in a strong financial incentive for the agent to write new business and is one factor that helps explain the rapid growth of exclusive agency insurers. In contrast, as noted earlier, insurers using the independent agency system typically pay the same commission rate on new and renewal business.

Also, exclusive agency insurers provide strong supportive services to the new agent. The new agent usually starts as an employee during a training period to learn the business. After the training period, the agent becomes an independent contractor who is then paid on a commission basis.

The functions performed by exclusive agents vary among insurers. Some insurers limit exclusive agents to selling insurance, while others permit them to adjust small first-party claims as well. Virtually all exclusive agency insurers use the direct billing method and are responsible for issuance of the policy.

Direct Writer A direct writer is often erroneously confused with an exclusive agency insurer. A **direct writer** *is an insurer in which the salesperson is an employee, not an independent contractor*. The insurer pays all the selling expenses, including the employee's salary and Social Security taxes. Similar to exclusive agents, an employee of a direct writer represents only one insurer.

Employees of direct writers are usually compensated on a "salary plus" arrangement. Some companies pay a basic salary plus a commission directly related to the amount of insurance sold. Others pay a salary and a bonus that represent both selling and service activities of the employee.

Direct Response System Property and liability insurers also use the direct response system to sell insurance. As noted earlier, a direct response insurer sells directly to the public by television, telephone, mail, newspapers, and other media. Many property and liability insurers also operate Web sites that provide information and premium quotes.

The direct response system is used primarily to sell personal lines of insurance, such as auto and homeowners insurance. However, it is not as effective in the marketing of commercial property and liability coverages because of their complexity and rating considerations.

Multiple Distribution Systems The distinctions between the traditional marketing systems are breaking down as insurers search for new ways to sell insurance. To increase their profits, many property and liability insurers are using more than one distribution system to sell insurance. These systems are referred to as **multiple distribution systems**. For example, some insurers that have traditionally used the independent agency system are now selling insurance directly to consumers over the Internet or by television and mail advertising. Other insurers that have used only exclusive agents (also called captive agents) in the past to sell insurance are now using independent agents as well. Other insurers are marketing property and liability insurance through banks and to consumer groups through employers and through professional and business associations. The lines between the traditional distribution systems will continue to blur in the future as insurers develop new systems to sell insurance.

Market Shares Exclusive agency insurers, direct writers, and direct response insurers as a group dominate the personal lines market. In 1995, this group

accounted for about 68 percent of the net premiums written in the personal lines market. In contrast, the independent agency companies dominate the commercial lines market. In 1995, this group accounted for approximately 71 percent of the net premiums written in the commercial lines market.[7]

Several reasons help explain the dominance of exclusive agency companies, direct writers, and direct response insurers in the personal lines market.[8] Initially, this group focused on auto insurance, which is the largest market in the personal lines field. The combined effect of the large size of the auto insurance market and its relative simplicity enabled the companies to build up large agency forces with minimal delay and financial expense. The same companies also sold homeowners insurance to the same customers, which resulted in additional growth in the personal lines market.

In addition, exclusive agency companies paid relatively lower commissions, which enabled them to compete effectively based on price. As noted earlier, exclusive agency companies pay lower commission rates on renewal business than do the independent agency insurers.

Finally, these companies were among the first to use direct billing, mechanization of policy writing, and other internal service functions. This approach enabled them to reduce their underwriting expenses and created efficiencies that independent agencies had difficulty in matching.

In contrast, independent agencies dominate the commercial lines market. The commercial lines markets are highly specialized markets that require a great deal of skill and knowledge in providing proper insurance coverages and risk management services to business firms. Independent agency insurers have highly specialized agents and loss-control specialists to service this market effectively. Although exclusive agency insurers and direct writers have made some inroads into the commercial lines market, the independent agency insurers as a group still continue to dominate this market.

MASS MERCHANDISING

Some property and liability insurers use mass merchandising to market their insurance. **Mass merchandising** *is a plan for insuring individuals in a group*

Insight 25.2

Payroll Plan Lets Workers Save Money and Checks

When Kenneth Kraut's auto insurance comes due four times a year, he writes a check and mails it.

He may soon be free of the bother, thanks to his employer.

Kraut, a flavor chemist in Somerset, New Jersey, now can have the insurance payments deducted a bit at a time from his biweekly paychecks. In addition to removing a worry, he saves 5 percent off the top of his premium.

"It's a great convenience. It's kind of like a forced savings," Kraut said. "It's small amounts per paycheck. This way you're not hit all at once with a big bill."

Kraut's company, Flavor Dynamics Inc., is among a growing number of small businesses around the country now able to offer discounts on optional employee benefits through automatic payroll deductions. The offerings aren't new, but in the past they've generally been available only to large companies able to negotiate volume discounts.

The program was introduced by Ceridian Corp., a Minnesota-based payroll services company that joined with RewardsPlus of America Corp. in Baltimore to develop the plan for small business clients.

Flavor Dynamics, a family-owned business with 20 employees, that makes flavorings for the food industry, jumped at the chance to sign up, said Marilyn De Rovira, a company vice president.

The program give employees convenience and price breaks on services they might be buying elsewhere, De Rovira said. Companies like Flavor Dynamics are able to offer benefits that attract employees, she said.

The program from Ceridian's Small Business Solutions unit includes auto, homeowners, pet, life and long-term care insurance, home security, mortgages, and home equity loans at prices 5 percent to 15 percent below what individuals would pay on their own. There are no startup fees or administrative expenses.

"The program enables us to assist small business owners in retaining their most valuable asset—their employees—by providing them with optional benefits at a low cost," said Robert Digby, senior vice president of marketing for Bloomington, Minnesota-based Ceridian.

For Flavor Dynamics, the program helps De Rovira and her husband, Dolf, who own the business, compete for employees.

"There's such stiff competition with employees and trying to make them happy," Mrs. De Rovira said. "I thought this would be something that would be very interesting for them."

SOURCE: Adapted from Karren Mills, "Payroll Plan Lets Workers Save Money and Checks," *Lincoln Journal Star*, May 16, 1999, p. 3D. Reprinted with permission from the Associated Press.

---

under a single program of insurance at reduced premiums. Property and liability insurance is sold on a group basis to employers, labor unions, trade associations, and other groups.

Mass-merchandising plans have several distinct characteristics. First, property and liability insurance is sold to individual members of a group; auto and homeowners insurance are popular lines that have been used in such plans. Second, individual underwriting is used; individuals applying for coverage must meet the insurer's underwriting standards. Third, rate reductions of 5 to 15 percent are typically given because of a lower commission scale for agents and savings in administrative expenses. In addition, premiums are paid by payroll deduction. Finally, employers usually do not contribute to the plans; any employer contributions result in taxable income to the employees.

Insight 25.2 provides a practical illustration of a mass-merchandising plan that allows employees to pay for various types of insurance through convenient payroll deduction.

SUMMARY

- There are several basic types of insurers:

  Stock insurers

  Mutual insurers

  Reciprocal exchanges

Lloyd's Associations

Blue Cross and Blue Shield Plans

Health maintenance organizations (HMOs)

- An agent is someone who legally represents the insurer and has the authority to act on the insurer's behalf. In contrast, a broker is someone who legally represents the insured.

- *Surplus lines* refer to any type of insurance for which there is no available market within the state, and the coverage must be placed with a nonadmitted insurer. A *nonadmitted insurer* is a company not licensed to do business in the state. A *surplus lines broker* is a special type of broker who is licensed to place business with a nonadmitted insurer.

- In life insurance, several basic marketing methods are used:

    Agency building system

    Nonbuilding agency system

    Direct response system

- In property and liability insurance, a number of marketing systems are used:

    Independent agency system

    Exclusive agency system

    Direct writer

    Direct response system

    Multiple distribution systems

- Mass merchandising is a plan by which property and liability insurance is sold on a group basis. Individual members of a group are insured under a single program of insurance at reduced premiums. There is, however, individual underwriting.

KEY CONCEPTS AND TERMS

Advance premium mutual	rights to business
Agency building system	Factory mutual
Agent	Fraternal insurer
Assessment mutual	General agency system
Broker	Holding company
Contingent or profit-sharing commission	Independent agency system
Demutualization	Lloyd's Associations
Direct response system	Lloyd's of London
Direct writer	Managerial system
Exclusive agency system	Mass merchandising
Expirations or renewal	Multiple distribution systems

Mutual insurer	Reciprocal exchange (interinsurance exchange)
Nonadmitted insurer	Stock insurer
Nonbuilding agency system	Surplus lines broker
Personal-producing general agent	

REVIEW QUESTIONS

1. Identify the major characteristics of a stock insurer.
2. Describe the major features of a mutual insurer. Identify the basic types of mutual insurers.
3. Describe the major features of Lloyd's of London.
4. Describe the basic characteristics of a reciprocal exchange.
5. What is a fraternal insurer? Explain your answer.
6. What is the legal distinction between an agent and a broker?
7. Explain briefly the basic characteristics of the following marketing systems in life and health insurance:
   a. Agency building system
   b. Nonbuilding agency system
   c. Direct response system
8. Explain briefly the basic characteristics of the following marketing systems in property and liability insurance:
   a. Independent agency system
   b. Exclusive agency system
   c. Direct writer
   d. Direct response system
   e. Multiple distribution systems
9. Who owns the policy expirations or renewal rights to the business under the independent agency system?
10. Describe the characteristics of a mass-merchandising plan in property and liability insurance.

APPLICATION QUESTIONS

1. Compare a stock insurer with a mutual insurer with respect to each of the following:
   a. Legal ownership of the company
   b. Right to assess policyowners
   c. Payment of dividends
2. An insurance author stated that "Lloyd's of London is an association that provides physical facilities and services to the members for selling insurance. The insur-

ance is underwritten by the various syndicates who belong to Lloyd's." Describe Lloyd's of London with respect to each of the following:

a. Nature of the operation

b. Types of insurance written

c. Financial safeguards to protect insureds

3. Property and liability insurance can be marketed under different marketing systems. Compare the independent agency system with the exclusive agency system with respect to each of the following:

a. Legal status of the agents

b. Number of insurers represented

c. Ownership of policy expirations

4. Market share is extremely important in the profitability of insurers. Independent agency companies tend to dominate the commercial lines market, while exclusive agency companies account for a relatively large share of the personal lines market.

a. Explain the factors that account for the relatively high market share of the personal lines market by exclusive agency companies.

b. Why do independent agency companies continue to dominate the commercial lines market?

SELECTED REFERENCES

ACLI Life Insurance Fact Book 1999. Washington, DC: American Council of Life Insurance, 1999.

Black, Kenneth, Jr., and Harold D. Skipper, Jr. *Life Insurance*, 13th edition. Upper Saddle River, NJ: Prentice-Hall, 2000, Chapters 23-24.

The Fact Book 2000, Insurance Information Institute, New York, NY: Insurance Information Institute, 1999.

Graves, Edward E., ed. *McGill's Life Insurance*, 2nd ed. Bryn Mawr, PA: The American College, 1998, Chapters 28–29.

Webb, Bernard L., et al. *Insurance Operations*, 2nd ed., Vol. 1. Malvern, PA: American Institute for Chartered Property Casualty Underwriters, 1997, Chapters 1–3.

NOTES

1. *ACLI Life Insurance Fact Book 1999* (Washington, DC: American Council of Life Insurance, 1999), p. 78; *The Fact Book 2000, Insurance Information Institute* (New York, NY: Insurance Information Institute, 1999), p. 1.6.

Case Application

Acme Insurance is a medium-sized stock property and liability insurer that specializes in the writing of commercial lines of insurance. The board of directors has appointed a committee to determine the feasibility of forming a new subsidiary insurer that would sell only personal lines of insurance, primarily homeowners and auto insurance. The new insurance company would have to meet certain management objectives. One member of the board of directors believes the new insurer should be legally organized as a mutual insurer. Assume you are an insurance consultant who is asked to serve on the committee. To what extent, if any, would each of the following objectives of the board of directors be met by formation of a mutual property and liability insurer? Treat each objective separately.

a. Acme Insurance must legally own the new insurer.

b. The new insurer must be able to raise additional capital for expansion in the future.

c. The policies sold should pay dividends to the policyowners.

d. The new insurer should be licensed to do business in all states.

2. *ACLI Life Insurance Fact Book 1999*, p. 78.

3. Edward E. Graves, ed., *McGill's Life Insurance* (Bryn Mawr, PA: The American College, 1998), pp. 707–708.

4. *Ibid.*, pp. 709–710.

5. This section is based on Graves, pp. 737–741, 747.

6. Bernard L. Webb, et al., *Insurance Operations*, 2nd ed., Vol. 1 (Malvern, PA: American Institute for Chartered Property and Casualty Underwriters, 1997), p. 91.

7. *Ibid.*, pp. 114–115.

8. *Ibid.*, p. 114.

9. *Ibid.*, p. 104.

Students may take a self-administered test on this chapter at www.awlonline.com/rejda

Chapter 26

Insurance Company Operations

> *"People who work for insurance companies do a lot more than sell insurance."*
>
> Insurance Information Institute

Learning Objectives

After studying this chapter, you should be able to:

▲ Explain the rate-making function of insurers.

▲ Define underwriting and explain the steps in the underwriting process.

▲ Describe the objectives of claim settlement and the steps in the process of settling a claim.

▲ Explain the reasons for reinsurance and the various types of reinsurance treaties.

▲ Explain the importance of insurance company investments and identify the various types of investments of insurers.

▲ Access an Internet site and obtain information about job opportunities in the insurance industry.

Internet Resources

- The **American Council of Life Insurance (ACLI)** represents the life insurance industry on issues dealing with legislation and regulation. ACLI also publishes statistics on the life insurance industry in an annual fact book. Visit the site at:

  http://www.acli.com/

- The **American Insurance Association (AIA)** is an important property and casualty trade association that represent more than 375 companies writing more than $60 billion annually in premiums. The site lists available publications, position papers on important issues in property and casualty insurance, press releases, insurance-related links, and names of state insurance commissioners. Visit the site at:

  http://www.aiadc.org/

- The **Insurance Information Institute (III)** is an excellent site for obtaining information on the property and liability insurance industry. It provides timely consumer information on auto, homeowners, and business insurance, and other types of property and liability insurance. Visit the site at:

  http://www.iii.org/

ristin, age 23, is a senior at the large Eastern university. The university is sponsoring a job fair where recruiters from major corporations will interview students for a possible employment. Kristin has signed up for interviews with several insurance companies to learn about job opportunities in that industry. One recruiter explains that insurers hire new employees with a variety of educational backgrounds, and that a wide variety of jobs are available in the industry today. Kristin is surprised to learn of the wide diversity of employment opportunities in the insurance industry. Jobs currently exist in rate making, underwriting, sales, claims, finance, information technology, accounting, legal, and numerous other areas.

This chapter deals with these occupational areas in the insurance industry. To make insurance available to the public, insurers must engage in a wide variety of specialized functions or operations. This chapter discusses the major functional operations of insurers.

INSURANCE COMPANY OPERATIONS

The most important insurance company operations consist of the following:

- Rate making
- Underwriting
- Production
- Claim settlement
- Reinsurance
- Investments

Insurers also engage in other operations, such as accounting, legal services, loss control, and data processing.

The following section discusses each of these functional areas in some detail.

RATE MAKING

Rate making *refers to the pricing of insurance.* Insurance pricing differs considerably from the pricing of other products. When other products are sold, the company generally knows in advance what its costs of production are, so that a price can be established to cover all costs and yield a profit. However, the insurance company does not know in advance what its actual costs are going to be. The premium charged for the insurance may be inadequate for paying all claims and expenses during the policy period, because it is only after the period of protection has expired that an insurer can determine its actual losses and expenses. Of course, the insurer hopes that the premium paid in advance will be sufficient to pay all claims and expenses and yield a profit.

The person who determines the rates is known as an **actuary**. An actuary is a highly skilled mathematician who is involved in all phases of insurance company operations, including planning, pricing, and research. In life insurance, the actuary studies important statistical data on births, deaths, marriages, disease, employment, retirement, and accidents. Based on this information, the actuary determines the rates for life and health insurance policies. The objectives are to calculate premiums that will make the business profitable, enable it to compete effectively with other insurers, and allow it to pay claims and expenses as they occur. A life insurance actuary must also determine the legal reserves a company needs for future obligations.[1]

Professional certification as an actuary is attained by passing a series of examinations administered by the Society of Actuaries, which qualifies the actuary as a Fellow of the Society of Actuaries.

In property and liability insurance, actuaries also determine the rates for different lines of insurance. Rates are based on the company's past loss experience and industry statistics. Statistics on hurricanes, tornadoes, fires, diseases, crime rates, traffic accidents, and the cost of living are also carefully analyzed. Many companies use their own loss data in establishing the rates. Other companies obtain loss data from rating organizations, such as the Insurance Services Office (ISO). These organizations calculate historical or prospective loss costs that individual companies can use in calculating their rates.

Actuaries in property and liability insurance also determine the adequacy of loss reserves,[2] allocate expenses, and compile statistics for company management and for state regulatory officials. Also, actuaries help resolve management problems in underwriting, sales, claims, and product development.

To become a certified actuary in property and liability insurance, the individual must pass a series of examinations administered by the Casualty Actuarial Society. Successful completion of the examinations enables the actuary to become a Fellow of the Casualty Actuarial Society.

UNDERWRITING

Underwriting *refers to the process of selecting and classifying applicants for insurance.* The underwriter is the person who decides to accept or reject an application. The fundamental objective of underwriting is to produce a profitable book of business. The underwriter constantly strives to select certain types of applicants and to reject others so as to obtain a profitable portfolio of insurable risks.

Statement of Underwriting Policy

Underwriting starts with a clear statement of underwriting policy. An insurer must establish an underwriting policy that is consistent with company objectives. The objective may be a large volume of business with low unit profits or a smaller volume with a larger unit of profit. Classes of business that are acceptable, borderline, or prohibited must be clearly stated. The amounts of insurance that can be written on acceptable and borderline business must also be determined.

The insurer's underwriting policy is determined by top-level management in charge of underwriting. The **line underwriters**—persons who make daily decisions concerning the acceptance or rejection of business—are expected to follow official company policy. The underwriting policy is stated in detail in an *underwriting guide* that specifies the lines of insurance to be written; territories to be developed; forms and rating plans to be used; acceptable, borderline, and prohibited business; amounts of insurance to be written; business that requires approval by a senior underwriter; and other underwriting details.

Basic Underwriting Principles

As noted earlier, the goal of underwriting is to produce a profitable volume of business. To achieve this goal, certain underwriting principles are followed. Three important principles are as follows:

- Selection of insureds according to the company's underwriting standards
- Proper balance within each rate classification
- Equity among policyowners

The first principle is that the underwriter must select prospective insureds according to the company's underwriting standards. This means that the underwriters should select only those insureds whose actual loss experience will not exceed the loss experience assumed in the rating structure. For example, a factory mutual may wish to insure only high-grade factories, and expects that its actual loss experience will be well below average. Underwriting standards are established with respect to eligible factories, and a rate is established based on a relatively low loss ratio.[3] Assume that the expected loss ratio is established at 30 percent, and the rate is set accordingly. The underwriters ideally should insure only those factories that can meet the stringent underwriting requirements, so that the actual loss ratio for the group will not exceed 30 percent.

The purpose of the underwriting standards is to reduce adverse selection against the insurer. There is an old saying in underwriting, "select or be selected against." Adverse selection is the tendency of people with a higher-than-average chance of loss to seek insurance at standard (average) rates, which if not controlled by underwriting, will result in higher-than-expected loss levels.

The second underwriting principle is to have a proper balance within each rate classification. This means that a below-average insured in an underwriting class should be offset by an above-average insured, so that on balance, the class or manual rate for the group as a whole will be adequate for paying all claims and expenses. For example, much of the underwriting today is **class underwriting**, especially for personal lines of insurance. Exposure units with similar loss-producing characteristics are grouped together and placed in the same underwriting class. Each exposure unit within the class is charged the same rate. However, all exposure units are not completely identical. Some will be above average for the class as a whole, while others will be below average. The underwriter must select a proper balance of insureds so that the class rate (average rate) will be adequate for paying all claims and expenses.

A final underwriting principle is equity among the policyowners. This means that equitable rates should be charged, and that each group of policyowners should pay its own way in terms of losses and expenses. Stated differently, one group of policyowners should not unduly subsidize another group.

For example, a group of 20-year-old persons and a group of 80-year-old persons should not pay the same premium rate for individual life insurance. If identical rates were charged to both groups, younger persons would be subsidizing older persons. This would be inequitable. Once the younger persons became aware that they were being overcharged, they would seek other insurers whose classification systems are more equitable. The first insurer would then end up with a disproportionate number of older, unhealthy persons, and the underwriting results would be unprofitable. Thus, because of competition, there must be rate equity among the policyowners.

Steps in Underwriting

After the insurer's underwriting policy is established, it must be communicated to the sales force. Initial underwriting starts with the agent in the field.

Agent as First Underwriter This step is often called field underwriting. The agent is told what types of applicants are acceptable, borderline, or prohibited. For example, in auto insurance, an agent may be told not to solicit applicants who have been convicted for drunk driving, who are single drivers under age 21, or who are young drivers who own high-powered sports cars. In property insurance, certain exposures, such as bowling alleys and restaurants, may have to be submitted to a company underwriter for approval.

In property and liability insurance, the agent often has authority to bind the company immediately, subject to subsequent disapproval of the application and cancellation by a company underwriter. Thus, it is important that the agent follow company policy when soliciting applicants for insurance. To encourage a submission of only profitable business, a *contingent or profit-sharing commission* is often paid based on the agent's favorable loss experience.

In life insurance, the agent must also solicit applicants in accordance with the company's underwriting policy. The agent may be told not to solicit applicants who are drug addicts, active alcoholics, or persons who work in hazardous occupations.

Sources of Underwriting Information The underwriter requires certain types of information in deciding whether to accept or reject an applicant for insurance. The type of information varies by type of insurance. In property insurance, both the physical features of the property and personal characteristics of the applicant must be considered. Physical features include the type of construction, occupancy of the building, quality of fire protection, water supply, and exposure from surrounding buildings.

With respect to personal characteristics of the applicant, information that reveals the presence of *moral hazard* is particularly important. The underwriter wants to screen out applicants who may intentionally cause a loss or inflate a claim beyond its actual value. Thus, the applicant's present financial condition, past loss record, living habits, and moral character are especially important in the underwriting process.

Underwriting information can be obtained from a wide variety of sources. The most important sources include the following:

- Application
- Agent's report
- Inspection report
- Physical inspection
- Physical examination and attending physician's report
- Medical Information Bureau (MIB)

The **application** is a basic source of underwriting information. It varies depending on the type of insurance. For example, in life insurance, the application will show the individual's age, gender, weight, occupation, personal and family health history, and any hazardous hobbies, such as sky diving.

An **agent's report** is another source of information. Most companies require the agent to give an evaluation of the prospective insured. For example, in life insurance, the agent may be asked to state how long he or she has known the applicant, to estimate the applicant's annual income and net worth, to judge whether the applicant plans to lapse or surrender existing life insurance, and to determine whether the application is the result of the agent's solicitation.

An **inspection report** may be required, especially if the underwriter suspects moral hazard. An outside firm investigates the applicant for insurance and makes a detailed report to the company. The report may include the applicant's present financial condi-

tion, drinking habits, marital status, amount of outstanding debts, delinquent bills, policy record, felony convictions, and additional information, such as whether the applicant has ever declared bankruptcy.

A **physical inspection** may also be required before an application for property and liability insurance is approved. The agent or company representative may physically inspect the building or plant to be insured and then submit a report to the underwriter. For example, in workers compensation insurance, an inspection may reveal unsafe working conditions, such as dangerous machinery; violation of safety rules, such as not wearing goggles when a grinding machine is used; and an excessively dusty or toxic plant.

Especially important for life insurance, a physical examination will reveal whether the applicant is overweight, has high blood pressure, or has any abnormalities in the heart, respiratory system, urinary system, or other parts of the body. An **attending physician's report** may also be required, which is a report from a physician who has treated the applicant in the past.

A final source of underwriting information in life insurance is a **Medical Information Bureau (MIB) report**. Companies that belong to the bureau report any health impairments, which are then recorded and made available to member companies. For example, if an applicant for life insurance has high blood pressure, this information would be recorded in the MIB files, which are coded and do not reveal the decision made by the submitting company.

Insurers are continually seeking new sources of information that will enable underwriters to screen applicants more carefully. One of the most controversial questions today is whether insurers should be allowed to use genetic testing in underwriting (see Insight 26.1).

Making an Underwriting Decision After the underwriter evaluates the information, an underwriting decision must be made. There are three basic underwriting decisions with respect to an initial application for insurance:

- Accept the application
- Accept the application subject to certain restrictions or modifications
- Reject the application

First, the underwriter can accept the application and recommend that the policy be issued. A second option is to accept the application subject to certain restrictions or modifications. Several examples illustrate this second type of decision. Before a crime insurance policy is issued, the applicant may be required to place iron bars on windows or install an approved central station burglar alarm system; the applicant may be refused a homeowners policy and offered a more limited dwelling and contents policy; a large deductible may be inserted in a property insurance policy; or a higher rate for life insurance may be charged if the applicant is substandard in health. If the applicant agrees to the modifications or restrictions, the policy is then issued.

The third decision is to reject the application. However, excessive and unjustified rejection of applications reduces the insurer's profitability and alienates the agents who solicited the business. If an application is rejected, the rejection should be based on a clear failure to meet the insurer's underwriting standards.

Many insurers now use computerized underwriting for certain personal lines of insurance that can be standardized, such as automobile and homeowners insurance. As a result, underwriting decisions can be expedited.

Other Underwriting Considerations

Other factors are also considered in underwriting. They include the following:

1. *Rate adequacy and underwriting.* When rates are considered adequate for a class, insurers are more willing to underwrite new business. However, if rates are inadequate, prudent underwriting requires a more conservative approach to the acceptance of new business. If moral hazard is excessive, the business generally cannot be insured at any rate.

   In addition, in commercial property and liability insurance, the underwriters have a considerable impact on the price of the product. A great deal of negotiation over price takes place between the line underwriter and the agent concerning the proper pricing of a commercial risk.

   Finally, the critical relationship between adequate rates and underwriting profits or losses results in periodic underwriting cycles in certain lines of insurance, such as commercial general liability and commercial multiperil insurance. If rates are adequate, underwriting profits are higher, and underwriting is more liberal. Conversely, when rates are inadequate, underwriting losses occur, and underwriting becomes more restrictive.

2. *Reinsurance and underwriting.* Availability of reinsurance facilities may result in more liberal underwriting. However, if reinsurance cannot be obtained on favorable terms, the underwriting may be more restrictive.

3. *Renewal underwriting.* In life insurance, policies are not cancelable. In property and liability insurance, most policies can be canceled or not renewed. If the loss experience is unfavorable, the insurer may either cancel or not renew the policy. Most states have placed restrictions on the insurer's right to cancel.

PRODUCTION

The term **production** refers to the sales and marketing activities of insurers. Agents who sell insurance are frequently referred to as **producers**. This word is used because an insurance company can be legally chartered, personnel can be hired, and policy forms printed, but nothing is produced until a policy is sold. The key to the insurer's financial success is an effective sales force.

Agency Department

Life insurers have an agency or sales department. This department is responsible for recruiting and training new agents and for the supervision of general agents, branch office managers, and local agents.

Property and liability insurers have marketing departments. To assist agents in the field, special agents may also be appointed. A *special agent* is a highly specialized technician who provides local agents in the field with technical help and assistance with their marketing problems. For example, a special agent may explain a new policy form or a special rating plan to agents in the field.

In addition to development of an effective sales force, an insurance company engages in a wide vari-

Insight 26.1

Genetic Testing Threatens to Fundamentally Alter the Whole Notion of Insurance

Over the next ten years, advances in genetic testing will have a profound impact on medical care. But they also may have an equally huge effect in another area: insurance.

Already, people are undergoing genetic testing for susceptibility to breast, colon, and ovarian cancer. And researchers are pushing ahead in their endeavors to discover genetic mutations that may predispose people to heart disease, other types of cancer, diabetes, and other illnesses.

But a future of routine genetic testing may also be a future in which the very nature of insurance is fundamentally altered.

The concept of a preexisting condition, which many insurers use to weed out bad health risks, could come to encompass *potential illnesses* as well as actual ones. People with unlucky genetic legacies could be deemed uninsurable, or at least subject to sky-high premiums. Meanwhile, people with "clean" genetic profiles could find themselves courted by insurers.

The result: People who need coverage the most might not get it—or they could eschew genetic tests altogether, for fear of how the results could be used against them.

"A trend which is very positive from a scientific point of view has some very frightening ramifications from an insurance point of view," says J. Robert Hunter, director of insurance for the Consumer Federation of America, a consumer advocacy group in Washington.

Insurers dispute the bleak scenarios, but some experts believe that genetic testing will become such a fixture—and deprive so many people of coverage—that it may eventually bring about a huge backlash. In fact, some say, it may even lead to the creation of a system that has been resisted in this country for years: national health coverage.

The grim scenarios are plausible, consumer advocates say, because of how insurance works. The whole concept of insurance is based upon spreading risk. In the case of health insurance, for example, those risks are the potential medical costs for the broad range of illnesses that can befall both healthy and less healthy people. In the individual insurance market, insurers try to minimize risk and make profits by covering as many good risks—younger, healthy people—as possible to balance out the bad risks.

They try to improve their chances by separating or weeding out less-healthy people with preexisting conditions, such as heart disease or cancer, by raising premiums, imposing waiting periods before coverage begins, excluding them from coverage for their particular illness—or denying them coverage altogether. In the group market, insurers spread risk by charging higher rates to companies with older, sicker work forces, raising premiums for everyone in that work force.

Genetic testing, if it becomes cheap and widely done, could offer insurers a powerful new tool to know ahead of time which people are the greatest health risks for which particular illnesses—and, consumer advocates fear, to weed

---

ety of marketing activities. These activities include the development of a marketing philosophy and the company's perception of its role in the marketplace; identification of short-run and long-run production goals; marketing research; development of new products to meet the changing needs of consumers and business firms; development of new marketing strategies; and advertising of the insurer's products.

Professionalism in Selling

The marketing of insurance has been characterized by

a distinct trend toward professionalism in recent years. This means that the modern agent should be a competent professional who has a high degree of technical knowledge in a particular area of insurance and who also places the needs of his or her clients first. The professional agent identifies potential insureds, analyzes their insurance needs, and recommends the best solution to the problem. After the sale, the agent has the responsibility of providing follow-up service to clients to keep their insurance programs up to date. Finally, a professional agent abides by a code of ethics.

them out of coverage accordingly. At the same time, insurers probably would aggressively court people with clean genetic profiles by offering them cheaper policies, just as insurers now in the individual market try to attract younger, healthier people with cheaper rates, Mr. Hunter says.

Finding Nonfilers

"The ideal dream of any insurer is to find people who won't file claims, and they'll be more able to do that with this sort of information," Mr. Hunter says. For people who have done well in the genetic lottery, those policies would be very attractive because of their low prices.

The other upshot of such genetic risk-classification would be some very strange-looking policies. For example, an insurer might offer a bare-bones policy at the lowest rate that covered only routine procedures such as checkups and emergency hospitalization. The policy would come with riders that people could buy separately to get coverage for each disease, such as heart disease, colon cancer, diabetes, and Alzheimer's disease. Those genetically predisposed to a particular disease might be charged a much higher rate to get that additional coverage than someone at average risk—or they might be denied that coverage altogether if the insurer deemed them too great a risk.

Another possibility is that insurers might offer several different types of policies, ranging from minimal to a deluxe policy covering most illnesses. But, as has sometimes happened with homeowners' insurance, insurers might engage in a sort of medical redlining,

denying Cadillac policies to inhabitants of bad genetic "neighborhoods," Mr. Hunter says. For example, "there would be a 'breast cancer ghetto' in the minds of the insurance companies," Mr. Hunter says.

Right now, insurers face few legal barriers to entering the brave new world of genetic testing. A 1996 federal law on health-insurance portability for job-switchers provides some minimal protection by preventing group health plans from considering the results of a genetic test alone to be a preexisting condition that could delay eligibility for coverage.

Several proposals in Congress would go much further in limiting insurers' ability to require or ask for genetic testing, and such a provision is part of the Republican patient bill of rights recently passed by the Senate. More than 30 states have passed some type of law limiting health insurers' use of genetic testing. But these laws vary widely in the protection they provide and don't apply to self-insured health plans, which cover about a third of people with private, workplace health insurance.

Health insurers oppose such legislation because they fear it is overly broad and would interfere with some of the questions they currently ask when issuing individual policies, such as inquiring about a person's family medical history or the results of a cholesterol test. Even more than health insurers, life insurers have fiercely lobbied against proposals that would limit their access to genetic information and have successfully defeated such efforts in many states.

Source: Adapted from Nancy Ann Jeffrey, "A Change in Policy, Genetic Testing Threatens to Fundamentally Alter the Whole Notion of Insurance," *The Wall Street Journal,* October 18, 1999, p. R15.

Several organizations have developed professional programs for agents and other personnel in the insurance industry. In life and health insurance, the American College has established the **Chartered Life Underwriter (CLU)** program. An individual must pass ten professional examinations to receive the CLU designation.

The American College also awards the **Chartered Financial Consultant (ChFC)** designation for professionals who are working in the financial services industry. To earn the ChFC designation, students must pass ten professional examinations.

A similar professional program exists in property and liability insurance. The American Institute for CPCU has established the **Chartered Property Casualty Underwriter (CPCU)** program. The CPCU program also requires an individual to pass ten examinations.

Other professionals are also important in the insurance industry. Many financial planners are also licensed as insurance agents. The **Certified Financial Planner (CFP)** designation is granted by the Certified Financial Planner Board of Standards, Inc. Many agents in property and liability insurance have been awarded the **Certified Insurance Counselor (CIC)** designation sponsored by the Society of Certified Insurance Counselors.

CLAIM SETTLEMENT

Every insurance company has a claims division or department for settling claims. This section examines the basic objectives in settling claims, the different types of claim adjusters, and the various steps in the claim-settlement process.

Basic Objectives in Claim Settlement

From the insurer's viewpoint, there are several basic objectives in settling claims.[4]

- Verification of a covered loss
- Fair and prompt payment of claims
- Personal assistance to the insured

The first objective in settling claims is to verify that a covered loss has occurred. This step involves determining whether a specific person or property is covered under the policy, and the extent of the coverage. This objective is discussed in greater detail later in the chapter.

The second objective is the fair and prompt payment of claims. If a valid claim is denied, the fundamental social and contractual purpose of protecting the insured is defeated. Also, the insurer's reputation may be harmed, and the sales of new policies may be adversely affected. Fair payment means that the insurer should avoid excessive claim settlements and should resist the payment of fraudulent claims, because they will ultimately result in higher premiums. If the insurer follows a liberal claims policy, all policyowners will suffer because a rate increase will become necessary.

The states have passed laws that prohibit unfair claim practices. These laws are patterned after the National Association of Insurance Commissioners' Model Act. Some unfair claim practices prohibited by these laws include the following:[5]

1. Refusing to pay claims without conducting a reasonable investigation.
2. Not attempting in good faith to effectuate prompt, fair, and equitable settlements of claims in which liability has become reasonably clear.

3. Compelling insureds or beneficiaries to institute lawsuits to recover amounts due under its policies by offering substantially less than the amounts ultimately recovered in suits brought by them.

A third objective is to provide personal assistance to the insured after a covered loss occurs. Aside from any contractual obligations, the insurer should also provide personal assistance after a loss occurs. For example, the claims adjustor could assist the agent in helping a family find temporary housing after a fire occurs.

Types of Claims Adjustors

The person who adjusts a claim is known as a **claims adjustor**. The major types of adjustors include the following:

- Agent
- Company adjustor
- Independent adjustor
- Adjustment bureau
- Public adjustor

An **agent** often has authority to settle small first-party claims up to some maximum limit.[6] The insured submits the claim directly to the agent, who has the authority to pay up to some specified amount. This approach to claim settlement has several advantages: it is speedy, it reduces adjustment expenses, and it preserves the policyowner's good will.

A **company adjustor** can settle a claim. The adjustor is usually a salaried employee who represents only one company. After notice of the loss is received, the company adjustor will investigate the claim, determine the amount of loss, and arrange for payment.

An **independent adjustor** can also be used to settle claims. An independent adjustor is a person who offers his or her services to insurance companies and is compensated by a fee. The company may use an independent adjustor in certain geographical areas where the volume of claims is too low to justify a branch office with a staff of full-time adjustors. An independent adjustor may also be used in highly specialized areas where a company adjustor with the necessary technical skills and knowledge is not available.

An **adjustment bureau** can be used to settle claims. An adjustment bureau is an organization for adjusting claims that is supported by insurers that use its services. Claims personnel employed by an adjustment bureau are highly trained individuals who adjust claims on a full-time basis. An adjustment bureau is frequently used when a catastrophic loss, such as a hurricane, occurs in a given geographical area, and a large number of claims are submitted at the same time.

A **public adjustor** can be involved in settling a claim. *A public adjustor, however, represents the insured rather than the insurance company and is paid a fee based on the amount of the claim settlement.* A public adjustor may be employed by the insured if a complex loss situation occurs and technical assistance is needed, and also in those cases where the insured and insurer cannot resolve a dispute over a claim.

Steps in Settlement of a Claim

There are several important steps in settling a claim:

- Notice of loss must be given.
- The claim is investigated.
- A proof of loss may be required.
- A decision is made concerning payment.

Notice of Loss The first step is to notify the insurer of a loss. A provision concerning notice of loss is usually stated in the policy. A typical provision requires the insured to give notice immediately or as soon as possible after the loss has occurred. For example, the homeowners policy requires the insured to give immediate notice; a medical expense policy may require the insured to give notice within 30 days after the occurrence of a loss, or as soon afterward as is reasonably possible; and the personal auto policy requires that the insurer must be notified promptly of how, when, and where the accident or loss happened. The notice must also include the names and addresses of any injured persons and of witnesses.

Investigation of the Claim After notice is received, the next step is to investigate the claim. An adjustor must determine that a covered loss has occurred and must also determine the amount of the loss. A series of questions must be answered before the claim is approved. The most important questions include the following:[7]

- Did the loss occur while the policy was in force?

- Does the policy cover the peril that caused the loss?
- Does the policy cover the property destroyed or damaged in the loss?
- Is the claimant entitled to recover?
- Did the loss occur at an insured location?
- Is the type of loss covered?
- Is the claim fraudulent?

The last question dealing with fraudulent claims is especially important. Insurance fraud is widespread, especially in auto and health insurance. Dishonest people frequently submit claims for bodily injuries that have never occurred.

Filing a Proof of Loss A proof of loss may be required before the claim is paid. A proof of loss is a sworn statement by the insured that substantiates the loss. For example, under the homeowners policy, the insured may be required to file a proof of loss that indicates the time and cause of the loss, interest of the insured and others in the damaged property, other insurance that may cover the loss, and any change in title or occupancy of the property during the term of the policy.

Decision Concerning Payment After the claim is investigated, the adjustor must make a decision concerning payment. There are three possible decisions. *The claim can be paid.* In most cases, the claim is paid promptly according to the terms of the policy. *The claim can be denied.* The adjustor may believe that the policy does not cover the loss or that the claim is fraudulent. Finally, the claim may be valid, but there may be a dispute between the insured and insurer over the amount to be paid. *In the case of a dispute, a policy provision may specify how the dispute is to be resolved.* For example, if a dispute arises under the homeowners policy, both the insured and insurer select a competent appraiser. The two appraisers select an umpire. If the appraisers cannot agree on an umpire, a court of law will appoint one. An agreement by any two of the three is then binding on all parties.

REINSURANCE

Reinsurance is another important insurance operation. This section discusses the meaning of reinsurance, the reasons for reinsurance, and the different types of reinsurance contracts.

Definitions

Reinsurance *is the shifting of part or all of the insurance originally written by one insurer to another insurer.* The insurer that initially writes the business is called the **ceding company**. The insurer that accepts part or all of the insurance from the ceding company is called the **reinsurer**. The amount of insurance retained by the ceding company for its own account is called the **net retention** or **retention limit**. The amount of the insurance ceded to the reinsurer is known as the **cession**. Finally, the reinsurer in turn may obtain reinsurance from another insurer. This is known as a **retrocession**.

Reasons for Reinsurance

Reinsurance is used for several reasons. The most important reasons include the following:

- Increase underwriting capacity
- Stabilize profits
- Reduce the unearned premium reserve
- Provide protection against a catastrophic loss

Reinsurance also enables an insurer to retire from a territory or class of business and to obtain underwriting advice from the reinsurer.

Increase Underwriting Capacity Reinsurance can be used to increase the insurance company's underwriting capacity to write new business. The company may be asked to assume liability for losses in excess of its retention limit. Without reinsurance, the agent would have to place large amounts of insurance with several companies or not accept the risk. This is awkward and may create ill will on behalf of the policyowner. Reinsurance permits the primary company to issue a single policy in excess of its retention limit for the full amount of insurance.

Stabilize Profits Reinsurance can be used to stabilize profits. An insurer may wish to avoid large fluctuations in annual financial results. Loss experience can fluctuate widely because of social and economic conditions, natural disasters, and chance. Reinsurance can be used to level out the effects of poor loss experience. For example, reinsurance may be used to cover a large exposure. If a large, unexpected loss occurs, the reinsurer would pay the portion of the loss in excess of some specified limit. Another arrangement would be to have the reinsurer reimburse the ceding insurer for losses that exceed a specified loss ratio during a given year. For example, an insurer may wish to stabilize its loss ratio at 70 percent. The reinsurer then agrees to reimburse the ceding insurer for part or all the losses in excess of 70 percent up to some maximum limit.

Reduce the Unearned Premium Reserve Reinsurance can be used to reduce the unearned premium reserve. For some insurers, especially newer and smaller ones, the ability to write large amounts of new insurance may be restricted by the unearned premium reserve requirement. The **unearned premium reserve** *is a liability item on the insurer's balance sheet that represents the unearned portion of gross premiums on all outstanding policies at the time of valuation.* In effect, the unearned premium reserve reflects the fact that premiums are paid in advance, but the period of protection has not yet expired. As time goes on, part of the premium is considered earned, while the remainder is unearned. It is only after the period of protection has expired that the premium is fully earned.

As noted earlier, an insurer's ability to grow may be restricted by the unearned premium reserve requirement. This is because the entire gross premium must be placed in the unearned premium reserve when the policy is first written. The insurer also incurs relatively heavy first-year acquisition expenses in the form of commissions, state premium taxes, underwriting expenses, expenses in issuing the policy, and other expenses. In determining the size of the unearned premium reserve, there is no allowance for these first-year acquisition expenses, and the insurer must pay them out of its surplus. (Policyholders' surplus is the difference between assets and liabilities.[8])

For example, a one-year property insurance policy with an annual premium of $1200 may be written on January 1. The entire $1200 must be placed in the unearned premium reserve. At the end of each month, one-twelfth of the premium, or $100, is earned and the remainder is unearned. On December 31, the entire premium is fully earned. However, assume that first-year acquisition expenses are 30 percent of the gross premium, or $360. This amount will come out of the insurer's surplus up front. Thus, the more business it writes, the greater is the short-term drain on its surplus. A rapidly growing insurer's ability to write new business could eventually be impaired.

Reinsurance reduces the level of the unearned premium reserve required by law and temporarily increases the insurer's surplus position. As a result, the ratio of policyholders' surplus to net written premiums is improved, which permits the insurer to continue to grow.

Provide Protection Against a Catastrophic Loss

Reinsurance also provides financial protection against a catastrophic loss. Insurers experience catastrophic losses because of natural disasters, industrial explosions, commercial airline disasters, and similar events. Reinsurance can provide considerable protection to the ceding company that experiences a catastrophic loss. The reinsurer pays part or all of the losses that exceed the ceding company's retention up to some specified maximum limit.

Other Reasons for Reinsurance

An insurer can use reinsurance to retire from the business or from a given line of insurance or territory. Reinsurance permits the insurer's liabilities for existing insurance to be transferred to another carrier; thus, the policyowner's coverage remains undisturbed.

Finally, reinsurance can enable an insurer to obtain the underwriting advice and assistance of the reinsurer. An insurer may wish to write a new line of insurance, but it may have little experience with respect to underwriting the line. The reinsurer can often provide valuable assistance with respect to rating, retention limits, policy coverages, and other underwriting details.

Types of Reinsurance

There are two principal forms of reinsurance: (1) facultative and (2) treaty.

Facultative Reinsurance

Facultative reinsurance *is an optional, case-by-case method that is used when the ceding company receives an application for insurance that exceeds its retention limit*. Before the policy is issued, the primary insurer shops around for reinsurance and contacts several reinsurers. The primary insurer is under no obligation to cede insurance, and the reinsurer is under no obligation to accept the insurance. But if a willing reinsurer can be found, the primary insurer and reinsurer can then enter into a valid contract.

Facultative reinsurance is frequently used when a large amount of insurance is desired. Before the application is accepted, the primary insurer determines whether reinsurance can be obtained. If available, the policy can then be written.

Facultative reinsurance has the advantage of flexibility, because a reinsurance contract can be arranged to fit any kind of case. It can increase the insurer's capacity to write large amounts of insurance. The reinsurance tends to stabilize the insurer's operations by shifting large losses to the reinsurer.

The major disadvantage of facultative reinsurance is that it is uncertain. The ceding insurer does not know in advance if a reinsurer will accept any part of the insurance. There is also a further disadvantage of delay, because the policy will not be issued until reinsurance is obtained. In times of bad loss experience, the reinsurance market tends to dry up. Therefore, facultative reinsurance has the further disadvantage of being unreliable.

Treaty Reinsurance

Treaty reinsurance *means the primary insurer has agreed to cede insurance to the reinsurer, and the reinsurer has agreed to accept the business*. All business that falls within the scope of the agreement is automatically reinsured according to the terms of the treaty.

Treaty reinsurance has several advantages to the primary insurer. It is automatic, and no uncertainty or delay is involved. It is also economical, because it is not necessary to shop around for reinsurance before the policy is written.

Treaty reinsurance could be unprofitable to the reinsurer. The reinsurer generally has no knowledge about the individual applicant and must rely on the underwriting judgment of the primary insurer. The primary insurer may write bad business and then reinsure it. Also, the premium received by the reinsurer may be inadequate. Thus, if the primary insurer has a poor selection of risks or charges inadequate rates, the reinsurer could incur a loss. However, if the primary insurer consistently cedes unprofitable business to its reinsurers, the ceding insurer will find it difficult to operate because reinsurers will not want to do business with it.

There are several types of reinsurance treaties and arrangements, including the following:

- Quota-share treaty
- Surplus-share treaty
- Excess-of-loss treaty
- Reinsurance pool

QUOTA-SHARE TREATY Under a **quota-share treaty**, the ceding insurer and reinsurer agree to share premiums and losses based on some proportion. *The ceding insurer's retention limit is stated as a percentage rather than as a dollar amount.* For example, Apex Fire and Geneva Re may enter into a quota-share treaty by which premiums and losses are shared 50 percent and 50 percent. Thus, if a $12,000 loss occurs, Apex Fire pays $12,000 to the insured but is reimbursed by Geneva Re for $6000.

Premiums are also shared based on the same agreed-on percentages. However, the reinsurer pays a **ceding commission** to the primary insurer to help compensate for the expenses incurred in writing the business. Thus, in the previous example, Geneva Re would receive 50 percent of the premium less a ceding commission that is paid to Apex Fire.

The major advantage of quota-share reinsurance is that the unearned premium reserve is reduced. For smaller insurers and other insurers that wish to reduce a surplus drain, a quota-share treaty can be especially effective. The principal disadvantage is that a large share of potentially profitable business is ceded to the reinsurer.

SURPLUS-SHARE TREATY Under a **surplus-share treaty**, the reinsurer agrees to accept insurance in excess of the ceding insurer's retention limit, up to some maximum amount. *The retention limit is referred to as a line and is stated as a dollar amount.* If the amount of insurance on a given policy exceeds the retention limit, the excess insurance is ceded to the reinsurer up to some maximum limit. The primary insurer and reinsurer then share premiums and losses based on the fraction of total insurance retained by each party.

Each party pays its respective share of any loss regardless of its size.

For example, assume that Apex Fire has a retention limit of $200,000 (called a line) for a single policy, and that four lines, or $800,000, are ceded to Geneva Re. Apex Fire now has a total underwriting capacity of $1 million on any single exposure. Assume that a $500,000 property insurance policy is issued. Apex Fire takes the first $200,000 of insurance, or two-fifths, and Geneva Re takes the remaining $300,000, or three-fifths. These fractions then determine the amount of loss paid by each party. If a $5000 loss occurs, Apex Fire pays $2000 (two-fifths), and Geneva Re pays the remaining $3000 (three-fifths). This situation can be summarized as follows:

Apex Fire	$ 200,000	(one line)
Geneva Re	800,000	(four lines)
Total underwriting capacity	$1,000,000	
$500,000 policy		
Apex Fire	$200,000	(2/5)
Geneva Re	$300,000	(3/5)
$5000 loss		
Apex Fire	$2000	(2/5)
Geneva Re	$3000	(3/5)

Under a surplus-share treaty, premiums are also shared based on the fraction of total insurance retained by each party. However, the reinsurer pays a ceding commission to the primary insurer to help compensate for the acquisition expenses.

The principal advantage of a surplus-share treaty is that the primary insurer's underwriting capacity is increased. The major disadvantage is the increase in administrative expenses. The surplus-share treaty is more complex and requires greater record keeping.

EXCESS-OF-LOSS TREATY An **excess-of-loss treaty** is designed largely for catastrophic protection. Losses in excess of the retention limit are paid by the reinsurer up to some maximum limit. The excess-of-loss treaty can be written to cover (1) a single exposure, (2) a single occurrence, such as a catastrophic loss from a tornado, or (3) excess losses when the primary insurer's cumulative losses exceed a certain amount during some stated time period, such as a year. For example, assume that Apex Fire wants protection for all windstorm losses in excess of $1 million. Assume that an excess-of-loss treaty is written with Franklin Re to cover single occurrences during a specified time period. Franklin Re agrees to pay all losses exceeding $1 million but only to a maximum of $10 million. If a $5 million hurricane loss occurs, Franklin Re would pay $4 million.

REINSURANCE POOL Reinsurance can also be provided by a reinsurance pool. A **reinsurance pool** *is an organization of insurers that underwrites insurance on a joint basis.* Reinsurance pools have been formed because a single insurer alone may not have the financial capacity to write large amounts of insurance, but the insurers as a group can combine their financial resources to obtain the necessary capacity. For example, the combined hull and liability loss exposures on a commercial jet can exceed $500 million if the jet should crash. Such high limits are usually beyond the financial capability of a single insurer. However, a reinsurance pool for aviation insurance can provide the necessary capacity. Reinsurance pools also exist for nuclear energy exposures, oil refineries, marine insurance, insurance in foreign countries, and numerous other types of exposures.

The method for sharing losses and premiums varies depending on the type of reinsurance pool. Pools work in two ways.[9] First, each pool member agrees to pay a certain percentage of every loss. For example, if one insurer has a policyowner that incurs a $100,000 loss, and there are 50 members in the pool, each insurer would pay 2 percent, or $2000 of the loss, depending on the agreement.

A second arrangement is similar to the excess-of-loss reinsurance treaty. Each pool member is responsible for its own losses below a certain amount. Losses exceeding that amount are shared by all members in the pool.

Other Approaches to Catastrophe Losses

As an alternative to traditional reinsurance, new financial instruments have been developed in the capital markets to help insurers pay catastrophe losses. They include cat bonds and catastrophe future options.

Cat bonds (catastrophe bonds) are special bonds issued by insurers to help them pay for natural disaster losses, such as losses from hurricanes and earthquakes. The bonds are usually rated below investment grade (junk bonds) and pay relatively high yields, such as 10 percent. If catastrophe losses are below a certain level during some specified time period—such as one year—bond investors receive back their principal plus interest. However, if catastrophe losses exceed that level, bond investors forfeit part or all of the interest or principal, or payment of the principal is deferred, depending on how the transaction is structured. Cat bonds are typically purchased by institutional investors seeking higher-yielding, fixed-income securities.

Insurers can also pay catastrophe claims by purchasing catastrophe insurance options on the Chicago Board of Trade (CBOT). *Catastrophe insurance options* are standard, exchange-traded contracts that track catastrophe loss indices developed by Property Claim Services (PCS). PCS provides nine loss indices each day to the CBOT based on estimates of insured catastrophe losses in different parts of the United States. Because of this geographic diversity, catastrophe options can help meet the financing needs of insurers and reinsurers regardless of their geographic risk exposure.

For example, an insurer may be overexposed to hurricanes in Florida during the hurricane season (third quarter of the year). Assume the insurer buys catastrophe options for the third quarter that pay off if insured industry losses in Florida are between $6 billion and $8 billion. If insured industry losses are less than $6 billion, the options expire worthless, and nothing is paid. However, if insured industry losses are between $6 billion and $8 billion, the options increase in value, and the insurer earns a positive net return. The funds can then be used to pay catastrophe claims.

INVESTMENTS

The investment function is an extremely important function in the overall operations of insurance companies. Because premiums are paid in advance, they can be invested until needed to pay claims and expenses.

Life Insurance Investments

At the end of 1998, U.S. life insurers held assets of $2.8 trillion.[10] The funds available for investment are derived primarily from premium income, investment earnings, and maturing investments that must be reinvested.

Life insurance investments have an important economic and social impact on the nation. First, life insurance contracts are long-term in nature, and the liabilities of life insurers extend over long periods of time, such as 50 or 60 years. Most life insurance investments are therefore long-term in nature, and the primary investment objective is safety of principal. Thus, at year end 1998, about 54 percent of the assets were invested in corporate and government bonds. Only about 27 percent of the assets were invested in stocks, which fluctuate widely in value. The remaining assets were invested in mortgages, real estate, policy loans, and miscellaneous assets.[11]

Investment income is extremely important in reducing the cost of insurance to policyowners because the premiums can be invested and earn interest. The interest earned on investments is reflected in the payment of dividends to policyowners, which reduces the cost of life insurance.

Life insurance premiums also are an important source of capital funds to the economy. These funds are invested in shopping centers, housing developments, office buildings, hospitals, new plants, and other economic and social ventures.

Property and Liability Insurance Investments

In 1998, property and liability insurance company investments totaled about $797 billion.[12] Most assets are invested in securities that can be quickly sold to pay claims if a major catastrophe occurs—primarily stocks and bonds rather than real estate.

In addition, in 1998, net premiums written for all lines totaled about $282 billion.[13] Premiums are typically paid in advance, so they can be invested until needed for claims and expenses.

Two important points must be stressed when the investments of property and liability insurers are analyzed. *First, in contrast to life insurance, property and liability insurance contracts are short-term in nature.* The policy period in most contracts is one year or less, and property claims are usually settled quickly. Also, in contrast to life insurance claims, which are generally fixed in amount, property and liability claim payments can vary widely depending on catastrophic losses, inflation, medical costs, construction costs, automobile repair costs, economic conditions, and changing value judgments by society. For these reasons, the investment objective of liquidity is extremely important to property and liability insurers.

Second, investment income is extremely important in offsetting unfavorable underwriting experience. The investment of capital and surplus funds, along with the funds set aside for loss reserves and the unearned premium reserve, generate investment earnings that usually permit an insurer to continue its insurance operations despite an underwriting deficit. For example, in 1998, property and liability insurers incurred an underwriting loss of $16.8 billion. However, net investment income totaled $39.9 billion.[14] Thus, despite an underwriting loss, the business overall was still profitable.

OTHER INSURANCE COMPANY FUNCTIONS

Insurers also perform other functions. They include accounting, legal, loss control services, and data processing.

Accounting

The **accounting department** is responsible for the financial accounting operations of an insurer. Accountants prepare financial statements, develop budgets, analyze the company's financial operations, and keep track of the millions of dollars that flow into and out of a typical company each year. Periodic reports are prepared dealing with premium income, operating expenses, claims, investment income, and dividends to policyowners. Accountants also prepare statutory annual statements that must be filed with state insurance departments. If the company is publicly traded, accountants must also prepare accounting statements based on Generally Accepted Accounting Principles (GAAP).

Legal Function

Another important function of insurance companies is the **legal function**. In life insurance, attorneys are widely used in advanced underwriting and estate planning. Attorneys also draft the legal language and policy provisions in insurance policies and review all new policies before they are marketed to the public. Other activities include providing legal assistance to actuarial personnel who testify at rate hearings; reviewing advertising and other published materials; providing general legal advice concerning taxation, marketing, investments, and insurance laws; and lobbying for legislation favorable to the insurance industry.

Finally, attorneys must keep abreast of the frequent changes in state and federal laws that affect the company and its policyowners. These include laws on consumerism, cost disclosure, affirmative action programs, truth in advertising, and similar legislation.

Loss-Control Services

Loss control is an important part of risk management, and a typical property and liability insurer provides numerous loss-control services. These services include advice on alarm systems, automatic sprinkler systems, fire prevention, occupational safety and health, prevention of boiler explosions, and other loss-prevention activities. In addition, loss-control specialists can provide valuable advice on the construction of a new building or plant to make it safer and more resistive to damage, which can result in a substantial rate reduction.

Data Processing

Another important functional area is **data processing** (**EDP**). Use of the computer has revolutionized the insurance industry by speeding up the processing of information and by eliminating many routine tasks. The computer is now used in accounting, policy processing, premium notices, information retrieval, telecommunications, simulation studies, market analysis, training and education, sales, and policyowner services. Information can quickly be obtained on premium volume, claims, loss ratios, investments, and underwriting results.

SUMMARY

- Rate making refers to the pricing of insurance. Insurance rates are determined by persons called actuaries.

- Underwriting refers to the process of selecting and classifying applicants for insurance. There are several important underwriting principles:

    Selection of insureds according to the company's underwriting standards

    Proper balance within each rate classification

    Equity among policyowners

- In determining whether to accept or reject an applicant for insurance, underwriters have several sources of information. They include the application, agent's report, inspection report, physical inspection, physical examination, attending physician's report, and the Medical Information Bureau.

- Production refers to the sales and marketing activities of insurers. Agents who sell insurance are called producers.

- From the insurer's viewpoint, there are several basic objectives in settling claims:

    Verification of a covered loss

    Fair and prompt payment of claims

    Personal assistance to the insured

- The person who adjusts a claim is known as a claims adjustor. The major types of adjustors are as follows:

    Agent

    Company adjustor

    Independent adjustor

    Adjustment bureau

    Public adjustor

- Several steps are involved in settling a claim:

    Notice of loss must be given to the company.

    The claim is investigated by the company.

    A proof of loss must be filed.

    A decision is made concerning payment.

- Reinsurance is the shifting of part or all of the insurance originally written by one insurer to another insurer. Reinsurance is used for several reasons:

    To increase the company's underwriting capacity

    To stabilize profits

    To reduce the unearned premium reserve

    To provide protection against a catastrophic loss

■ Facultative reinsurance means the primary company shops around for reinsurance. The primary company is under no obligation to reinsure, and the reinsurer is under no obligation to accept the insurance. But if the primary company and reinsurer enter into a valid contract, it is known as a facultative treaty. In contrast, under treaty reinsurance, if the business falls within the scope of the agreement, the primary company must cede insurance to the reinsurer, and the reinsurer must accept.

■ The most important types of automatic reinsurance treaties are as follows:

  Quota-share treaty

  Surplus-share treaty

  Excess-of-loss treaty

  Reinsurance pool

■ Other important insurance company operations include investments, accounting, legal services, loss-control services, and data processing.

KEY CONCEPTS AND TERMS

Accounting department	Independent adjustor
Actuary	Inspection report
Adjustment bureau	Line underwriter
Agent's report	Loss control
Attending physician's report	Medical Information Bureau (MIB) report
Ceding commission	Producers
Ceding company	Production
Certified Financial Planner (CFP)	Public adjustor
	Quota-share treaty
Certified Insurance Counselor (CIC)	Rate making
	Reinsurance
Cession	Reinsurance pool
Chartered Financial Consultant (ChFC)	Reinsurer
	Retention limit (net retention)
Chartered Life Underwriter (CLU)	Retrocession
Chartered Property Casualty Underwriter (CPCU)	Surplus-share treaty
	Treaty reinsurance
	Underwriting
Claims adjustor	Unearned premium reserve
Class underwriting	
Company adjustor	
Data processing (EDP)	
Excess-of-loss treaty	
Facultative reinsurance	

REVIEW QUESTIONS

1. Briefly describe the rate-making function.

2. Define underwriting. Explain several important underwriting principles.

3. Describe the sources of information available to underwriters.

4. Explain the meaning of production.

5. What are the objectives in the settlement of claims?

6. Describe the steps in the claim settlement process.

7. Define reinsurance. Why is reinsurance used?

8. Distinguish between facultative reinsurance and treaty reinsurance.

9. Describe the following types of reinsurance treaties:
   a. Quota-share treaty
   b. Surplus-share treaty
   c. Excess-of-loss treaty
   d. Reinsurance pool

10. Briefly describe the following insurance company operations:
    a. Accounting
    b. Legal services
    c. Loss control
    d. Data processing

APPLICATION QUESTIONS

1. a. The underwriting function is often misunderstood by the public. Explain the basic objectives of the underwriting function.
   b. How does the underwriting department handle the problem of adverse selection?

2. a. If loss occurs, the claims adjustor must determine whether the loss is covered by the policy. Explain the items of coverage that the claims adjustor must check to make this decision.
   b. Explain the difference between a public adjustor and claims adjustor employed by an insurance company.

3. a. Explain the nature and purpose of a special agent.
   b. Describe the various marketing activities of insurance companies.

4. Apex Fire enters into a surplus-share reinsurance treaty with Geneva Re. Apex Fire has a retention limit of $100,000 and four lines of insurance are ceded to

Geneva Re. A building is insured with Apex Fire in the amount of $300,000. If a $30,000 loss occurs, how much will the ceding company and reinsurer pay? Explain your answer.

5. Explain the major differences between life insurance company investments and property and liability insurance company investments.

SELECTED REFERENCES

Alliance of American Insurers. *Careers in Insurance.* Schaumburg, IL: Alliance of American Insurers, 1996.

Black Kenneth, Jr., and Harold D. Skipper, Jr. *Life Insurance,* thirteenth edition. Upper Saddle River, NJ: Prentice-Hall, Inc., 2000, Chapters 25–26.

Constance M. Luthardt, et al. *Property and Liability Insurance Principles,* third edition. Malvern, PA: Insurance Institute of America, 1999.

Graves, Edward E., ed. *McGill's Life Insurance,* second edition. Bryn Mawr, PA: The American College, 1998, Chapters 21–22, 29, 32.

Webb, Bernard L., Connor M. Harrison, and James J. Markham. *Insurance Operations,* second edition, Vols. 1 and 2. Malvern, PA: American Institute for Chartered Property Casualty Underwriters, 1997.

NOTES

1. A legal reserve is a liability item on a company's balance sheet that measures the insurer's obligations to its policyowners. State laws require a company to maintain policy reserves at a level that is sufficient to pay all policy obligations as they fall due.

2. In property and liability insurance, a loss reserve is an estimated liability item that represents an amount for claims reported but not yet paid, claims in the process of settlement, and claims that have already occurred but have not been reported. See Chapter 27 for a further discussion of loss reserves.

3. A loss ratio is the ratio of incurred losses to earned premiums. For example, if incurred losses are $70 and earned premiums are $100, the loss ratio is 0.70, or 70 percent.

4. For additional information on claim settlement, see Bernard L. Webb, Connor M. Harrison, and James J. Markham, *Insurance Operations,* second edition, Vol. 2 (American Institute for Chartered Property Casualty Underwriters, 1997), Chapters 13–15.

5. Webb et al., p. 249.

6. A first-party claim is a claim submitted by the insured to the insurer, such as fire damage to property owned by the insured.

7. Robert I. Mehr, Emerson Cammack, and Terry Rose, *Principles of Insurance,* 8th ed. (Homewood, IL: Richard D. Irwin, 1985), pp. 616–617.

8. Technically, for a stock insurer, policyholders' surplus is the sum of capital stock (value of the contributions of original stockholders), plus surplus (the amount

Case Application

Reinsurance can be used by an insurer to solve several problems. Assume you are an insurance consultant who is asked to give recommendations concerning the type of reinsurance plan or arrangement to use. For each of the following situations, indicate the type of reinsurance plan or arrangement that the ceding insurer should use, and explain the reasons for your answer.

a. Company A is an established insurer and is primarily interested in having protection against a catastrophic loss arising out of a single occurrence.

b. Company B is rapidly growing and desires a plan of reinsurance that will reduce the drain on its surplus from writing a large volume of new business.

c. Company C has received an application to write a $25 million life insurance policy on the life of the chief executive officer of a major corporation. Before the policy is issued, the life insurer wants to make certain that adequate reinsurance is available.

d. Company D would like to increase its underwriting capacity to underwrite new business.

paid in by the organizers in excess of the par value of the stock), plus any retained earnings. In the case of a mutual insurer, there is no capital account. Policy-holders' surplus is the excess of assets over liabilities.

9. *Sharing the Risk,* Revised, third edition (New York: Insurance Information Institute, 1989), pp. 119–120.

10. *ACLI Life Insurance Fact Book 1999* (Washington, DC: American Council of Life Insurance, 1999), p. 113.

11. *Ibid.,* Table 8.2, pp. 116–117.

12. *The Fact Book 2000, Insurance Information Institute* (New York, NY: Insurance Information Institute), p. 1.15.

13. *Ibid.,* p. 1.10.

14. *Ibid.,* p. 1.11.

Students may take a self-administered test on this chapter at www.awlonline.com/rejda

Chapter 27

Insurance
Pricing

" Actuaries hold an insurance company's profits in their hands. "

Insurance Careers

Learning Objectives

After studying this chapter, you should be able to:

▲ Explain the major objectives of rate making.

▲ Describe the basic methods for determining rates in property and liability insurance, including the following:
  Judgment rating
  Class rating
  Merit rating

▲ Explain how an underwriting profit or loss for a property and liability insurer is determined.

▲ Explain the basic concepts used in life insurance, including the following:
  Net single premium
  Net level premium
  Gross premium

▲ Identify the various reserves that insurers must maintain by law.

▲ Access an Internet site and obtain premium quotes for auto insurance and life insurance.

Internet Resources

- The **American Academy of Actuaries** is a public policy and communications organization that represents actuaries in all practice specialties. It develops standards of practice through the Actuarial Standards Board. Visit the site at:

  www.actuary.org

- The **American Society of Pension Actuaries** is an organization formed to educate pension actuaries, consultants, and other professionals in the employee benefits field. Visit the site at:

  www.aspa.org

- The **Casualty Actuarial Society** is a professional organization that promotes education in actuarial science and statistics in property and casualty insurance. Visit the site at:

  http://www.casact.org

- The **Conference of Consulting Actuaries** is an organization that consists of consulting actuaries in all disciplines. Visit the site at:

  www.ccactuaries.org

*J*ason, age 32, is an actuary for a large global property and liability insurer. A high school counselor asked him to speak to a senior class about career opportunities in actuarial science. Jason explained that insurance pricing, or rate making, is one of the most important functions of an insurance company. Actuaries hold the profits of an insurance company in their hands and must determine the correct rates to charge, expenses that will be incurred, and potential profits. As Jason also explained, actuaries must analyze vast amounts of statistics and loss data to determine the correct rates to charge. The actual rates charged must be high enough to pay all losses and expenses and still earn a profit for the insurer. However, if the rates are too high, the insurer may find itself at a competitive disadvantage.

This chapter discusses the important rate-making function of insurers. Major topics covered include the objectives of rate making, the basic rating methods used in property and liability insurance and life insurance, and the various reserves that insurers must maintain by law.

OBJECTIVES OF RATE MAKING

Rate making, or insurance pricing, has several basic objectives. Because insurance rates—primarily property and liability rates—are regulated by the states, certain statutory or regulatory requirements must be satisfied. Also, due to the overall goal of profitability, certain business objectives must be stressed in rate making. Thus, rate-making goals can be classified into two basic categories—regulatory objectives and business objectives.

Regulatory Objectives

The goal of insurance regulation is to protect the public. The states have rating laws that require insurance rates to meet certain standards. In general, rates charged by insurers must be adequate, not excessive, and not unfairly discriminatory.

Adequate Rates The first regulatory requirement is that rates must be adequate. *This means the rates charged by insurers should be high enough to pay all* *losses and expenses.* If rates are inadequate, an insurer may become insolvent and fail. As a result, policyowners, beneficiaries, and third-party claimants may be financially harmed if their claims are not paid. However, rate adequacy is complicated by the fact that the insurer does not know its actual costs when the policy is first sold. The premium is paid in advance, but it may not be sufficient to pay all claims and expenses during the policy period. It is only after the period of protection has expired that an insurer can determine its actual costs.

Not Excessive The second regulatory requirement is that the rates must not be excessive. *This means that the rates should not be so high that policyowners are paying more than the actual value of their protection.* Exorbitant prices are not in the public interest.

Not Unfairly Discriminatory The third regulatory requirement is that the rates must not be unfairly discriminatory. *This means that exposures that are similar with respect to losses and expenses should not be charged substantially different rates.*[1] For example, if two healthy males, age 30, buy the same type and amount of life insurance from the same insurer, they should not be charged two different rates. However, if the loss exposures are substantially different, it is not unfair rate discrimination to charge different rates. Thus, if two males, age 30 and age 65, apply for the same type and amount of life insurance, it is not unfair to charge the older male a higher rate because of the higher probability of death.

Business Objectives

Insurers are also guided by certain business objectives in designing a rating system. The rating system should also meet the following objectives:[2]

- Simplicity
- Stability
- Responsiveness
- Encouragement of loss control

Simplicity The rating system should be easy to understand so that producers can quote premiums with a minimum amount of time and expense. This is especially important in the personal lines market, where the relatively small premiums do not justify a large amount of time and expense in the preparation of premium quotations. In addition, commercial insurance purchasers should understand how their premiums are determined so that they can take active steps to reduce their insurance costs.

Stability Rates should be stable over short periods so that consumer satisfaction can be maintained. If rates change rapidly, insurance consumers may become irritated and dissatisfied. They may then look to government to control the rates or to enact a government insurance program.

Responsiveness The rates should also be responsive over time to changing loss exposures and changing economic conditions. To meet the objective of rate adequacy, the rates should increase when loss exposures increase. For example, as a city grows, auto insurance rates should increase to reflect the greater traffic and increased frequency of automobile accidents. Likewise, the rates should reflect changing economic conditions. Thus, if inflation causes liability awards to increase, liability insurance rates should be increased to reflect this trend.

Encouragement of Loss Control The rating system should also encourage loss-control activities that reduce both loss frequency and severity. This point is important because loss control tends to keep insurance affordable. Profits are also stabilized. As you will see later, certain rating systems provide a strong financial incentive to the insured to engage in loss control.

BASIC DEFINITIONS IN RATE MAKING

Before proceeding, you should be familiar with some basic terms that are widely used in rate making. A **rate** is the price per unit of insurance. An **exposure unit** is the unit of measurement used in insurance pricing. It varies by line of insurance. For example, in fire insurance, the exposure unit is $100 of coverage; in products liability insurance, it is $1000 of sales; and in auto collision insurance, it is one car-year, which is one car insured for a year.

The **pure premium** refers to that portion of the rate needed to pay losses and loss-adjustment expenses. **Loading** refers to the amount that must be added to the pure premium for other expenses, profit, and a margin for contingencies. The **gross rate** consists of the pure premium and a loading element. Finally, the **gross premium** paid by the insured consists of the gross rate multiplied by the number of exposure units. Thus, if the gross rate is 10 cents per $100 of property insurance, the gross premium for a $500,000 building would be $500.

RATE MAKING IN PROPERTY AND LIABILITY INSURANCE

There are three basic rate-making methods in property and liability insurance—judgment, class, and merit rating. Merit rating in turn can be broken down into schedule rating, experience rating, and retrospective rating. Thus, the basic rating methods can be conveniently classified as follows:[3]

- Judgment rating
- Class rating
- Merit rating
    Schedule rating
    Experience rating
    Retrospective rating

Judgment Rating

Judgment rating *means that each exposure is individually evaluated, and the rate is determined largely by the underwriter's judgment.* This method is used when the loss exposures are so diverse that a class rate cannot be calculated, or when credible loss statistics are not available.

Judgment rating is widely used in ocean marine insurance and in some lines of inland marine insurance. Because the various ocean-going vessels, ports of destination, cargoes carried, and dangerous waters are so diverse, ocean marine rates are determined largely by judgment.

Class Rating

The second type of rating method is class rating. Most rates used today are class rates. **Class rating** *means exposures with similar characteristics are placed in the same underwriting class, and each is charged the same rate.* The rate charged reflects the *average loss experience* for the class as a whole. Class rating is based on the assumption that future losses to insureds will be determined largely by the same set of factors. For example, major classification factors in life insurance include age, gender, health, and whether the applicant smokes or is a nonsmoker. Accordingly, healthy persons who are the same age and gender and do not smoke are placed in the same underwriting class and charged the same rate for life insurance. Smokers are placed in a different underwriting class and charged higher rates.

The major advantage of class rating is that it is simple to apply. Also, premium quotations can be quickly obtained. As such, it is ideal for the personal lines market.

Class rating is also called *manual rating*, because the various rates are published in a rating manual. Class rating is widely used in homeowners insurance, private passenger auto insurance, workers compensation, and life and health insurance.

There are two basic methods for determining class rates: the pure premium and loss ratio methods.

As stated earlier, the pure premium is that portion of the gross rate needed to pay losses and loss-adjustment expenses. The **pure premium** *can be determined by dividing the dollar amount of incurred losses and loss-adjustment expenses by the number of exposure units.* Incurred losses include all losses paid during the accounting period, plus amounts held as reserves for the future payment of losses that have already occurred during the same period. Thus, incurred losses include all losses that occur during the accounting period whether or not they have been paid by the end of the period. Loss-adjustment expenses are the expenses incurred by the company in adjusting losses during the same accounting period.

To illustrate how a pure premium can be derived, assume that in auto collision insurance, 500,000 automobiles in a given underwriting class generate incurred losses and loss-adjustment expenses of $30 million over a one-year period. The pure premium is $60. This can be illustrated by the following:

Pure premium =

$$\frac{\text{Incurred losses and loss-adjustment expenses}}{\text{Number of exposure units}}$$

$$= \frac{\$30,000,000}{500,000}$$

$$= \$60$$

The final step is to add a loading for expenses, underwriting profit, and a margin for contingencies. The expense loading is usually expressed as percentage of the gross rate and is called the expense ratio. The **expense ratio** *is that proportion of the gross rate available for expenses and profit.* The final gross rate can be determined by dividing the pure premium by 1 minus the expense ratio. For example, if expenses are 40 percent of the gross rate, the final gross rate is $100. This can be illustrated by the following:[4]

$$\text{Gross rate} = \frac{\text{Pure premium}}{1 - \text{Expense ratio}}$$

$$= \frac{\$60}{1 - 0.40}$$

$$= \$100$$

Under the loss ratio method, the actual loss ratio is compared with the expected loss ratio, and the rate is adjusted accordingly. The **actual loss ratio** *is the ratio of incurred losses and loss-adjustment expenses to* **earned premiums**.[5] The **expected loss ratio** *is the percentage of the premiums that is expected to be used to pay losses.* For example, assume that a line of insurance has incurred losses and loss-adjustment expenses in the amount of $800,000, and earned premiums are $1 million. The actual loss ratio is 0.80, or 80 percent. If the expected loss ratio is 0.70, or 70 percent, the rate must be increased 14.3 percent. This can be illustrated by the following:

$$\text{Rate change} = \frac{A - E}{E}$$

where A = Actual loss ratio
E = Expected loss ratio

$$= \frac{0.80 - 0.70}{0.70}$$

$$= 0.143, \text{ or } 14.3\%$$

Merit Rating

The third principal type of rating method is merit rating. **Merit rating** *is a rating plan by which class rates (manual rates) are adjusted upward or downward based on individual loss experience.* Merit rating is based on the assumption that the loss experience of a particular insured will differ substantially from the loss experience of other insureds. Thus, class rates are modified upward or downward depending on individual loss experience.

There are several different types of merit rating plans:

- Schedule rating
- Experience rating
- Retrospective rating

Schedule Rating Under a **schedule rating** *plan, each exposure is individually rated. A basis rate is determined for each exposure, which is then modified by debits or credits for undesirable or desirable physical features.* Schedule rating is based on the assumption that certain physical characteristics of the insured's operations will influence the insured's future loss experience. Thus, the physical characteristics of the exposure to be insured are extremely important in schedule rating.

Schedule rating is used in commercial property insurance for large, complex buildings, such as an industrial plant. Each building is individually rated based on the following factors:

- Construction
- Occupancy
- Protection
- Exposure
- Maintenance

Construction refers to the physical characteristics of the building. A building may be constructed with frame, brick, fire-resistive, or fire-proof materials. A frame building is charged a higher rate than a brick or fire-resistive building. Also, tall buildings and buildings with large open areas may receive debits because of the greater difficulty of extinguishing or containing a fire.

Occupancy refers to use of the building. The probability of a fire is greatly influenced by its use. For example, open flames and sparks from torches and welding can quickly cause a fire. Also, if highly combustible materials or chemicals are stored in the building, the fire will be more difficult to contain.

Protection refers to the quality of the city's water supply and fire department. It also includes protective devices installed in the insured building. Rate credits are given for a fire alarm system, security guard, automatic sprinkler system, fire extinguishers, and similar protective devices.

Exposure refers to the possibility that the insured building will be damaged or destroyed from a fire that starts in an adjacent building and spreads to the insured building. The greater the exposure from surrounding buildings, the greater are the charges applied.

Finally, *maintenance* refers to the housekeeping and overall maintenance of the building. Debits are applied for poor housekeeping and maintenance. Thus, debits may be given if oily rags are scattered about.

Experience Rating Experience rating is another form of merit rating. Under an **experience rating** plan, *the class, or manual, rate is adjusted upward or downward based on past loss experience.* The most distinctive characteristic of experience rating is that *the insured's past loss experience is used to determine the premium for the next policy period.* The loss experience over the past three years is typically used to determine the premium for the next policy year. If the insured's loss experience is better than the average for the class as a whole, the class rate is reduced. If the loss experience is worse than the class average, the rate is increased. In determining the magnitude of the rate change, the actual loss experience is modified by a *credibility factor*[6] based on the volume of experience.

For example, assume that a retail firm has a general liability insurance policy that is experience rated. Annual premiums are $30,000, and the expected loss ratio is 30 percent. If the actual loss ratio over the past three years is 20 percent, and the credibility factor (C) is 0.29, the firm will receive a premium reduction of 9.7 percent. This can be illustrated by the following:

$$\text{Premium change} = \frac{A - E}{E} \times C$$

$$= \frac{0.20 - 0.30}{0.30} \times 0.29$$

$$= -9.7\%$$

Thus, the new premium for the next policy period is $27,090. As you can see, experience rating provides a financial incentive to reduce losses, because premiums can be reduced by favorable loss experience.

Experience rating is generally limited only to larger firms that generate a sufficiently high volume of premiums and more credible experience. Smaller firms are normally ineligible for experience rating. This rating system is frequently used in general liability insurance, workers compensation, commercial auto liability insurance, and group health insurance.

Retrospective Rating The final form of merit rating is retrospective rating. Under a **retrospective rating** plan, *the insured's loss experience during the current policy period determines the actual premium paid for that period.* Under this rating plan, there is a minimum and a maximum premium. If actual losses during the current policy period are small, the minimum premium is paid. If losses are large, the maximum premium is paid. The actual premium paid generally will fall somewhere between the minimum and maximum premium, depending on the insured's loss experience during the current policy period. Retrospective rating is widely used by large firms in workers compensation insurance, general liability insurance, auto liability and physical damage insurance, and burglary and glass insurance.

RATE MAKING IN LIFE INSURANCE

Our discussion of rate making so far has applied largely to property and liability insurance. This section briefly examines the fundamental of life insurance rate making.[7]

Net Single Premium

Life insurance policies can be purchased with a single premium, or with annual, semiannual, quarterly, or monthly premiums. Although most policies are not purchased with a single premium, the net single premium forms the foundation for the calculation of all life insurance premiums.

The **net single premium (NSP)** *can be defined as the present value of the future death benefit.* It is that sum that, together with compound interest, will be sufficient to pay all death claims. In calculating the NSP, only mortality and investment income are considered. Insurance company expenses or the loading element are considered later, when the gross premium is calculated.

The NSP is based on three basic assumptions: (1) premiums are paid at the beginning of the policy year, (2) death claims are paid at the end of the policy year, and (3) the death rate is uniform throughout the year.

Certain assumptions must also be made concerning the probability of death at each attained age. Although life insurers generally develop their own mortality data, we will use the Commissioners 1980 Standard Ordinary Mortality Table in our illustrations (see Exhibit 27.1).

Also, since we are assuming that premiums are paid in advance, and that death claims are paid at the end of the policy year, the amount needed to pay death benefits is discounted for compound interest. It is assumed that the amounts needed for death claims can be discounted annually at 5 percent compound interest.

Term Insurance The NSP for term insurance can be calculated easily. The period of protection is only for a specified period or to a stated age. The face amount is paid if the insured dies within the specified period, but nothing is paid if the insured dies after the period of protection expires.

The NSP for *yearly renewable term insurance* is considered first. Assume that a $1000 yearly renewable term insurance policy is issued to a male age 45. *The cost of each year's insurance is determined by multiplying the probability of death by the amount of insurance multiplied by the present value of $1 for the time period the funds are held.* By referring to the 1980 CSO mortality chart in Exhibit 27.1, we see that out of 10 million males alive at age zero, 9,210,289 are still alive at the beginning of age 45. Of this number, 41,907 persons will die during the year. Therefore, the probability that a person age 45 will die during the year is 41,907/9,210,289. This fraction is then multiplied by $1000 to determine the amount of money the insurer must have on hand from each policyowner at the end of the year to pay death claims. However, because premiums are paid in advance, and death claims are paid at the end of the year, the amount needed can be discounted for one year of interest. From Exhibit 27.2, we see that the present value of $1 at 5 percent interest is 0.9524. Thus, if the probability of death at age 45 is multiplied by $1000, and the sum is discounted for one year's interest, the resulting net single premium is $4.33. This calculation is summarized as follows:

Age 45, NSP

$$\frac{41,907}{9,210,289} \times \$1000 \times 0.9524 = \$4.33$$

If $4.33 is collected in advance from each of the 9,210,289 persons who are alive at age 45, this amount together with compound interest will be sufficient to pay all death claims.

If the policy is renewed for another year, the NSP at age 46 would be calculated as follows:

Age 46, NSP

$$\frac{45,108}{9,168,382} \times \$1000 \times 0.9524 = \$4.69$$

The NSP for a yearly renewable term insurance policy issued at age 46 is $4.69. Premiums for subsequent years are calculated in the same manner.

Now consider the NSP for a *five-year term insurance policy* in the amount of $1000 issued to a person age 45. In this case, the company must pay the

EXHIBIT 27.1
Commissioners 1980 Standard Ordinary Mortality Table, Male Lives

Age at beginning of year	Number living at beginning of designated year	Number dying during designated year	Age at beginning of year	Number living at beginning of designated year	Number dying during designated year
0	10,000,000	41,800	25	9,663,007	17,104
1	9,958,200	10,655	26	9,645,903	16,687
2	9,947,545	9,848	27	9,629,216	16,466
3	9,937,697	9,739	28	9,612,750	16,342
4	9,927,958	9,432	29	9,596,408	16,410
5	9,918,526	8,927	30	9,579,998	16,573
6	9,909,599	8,522	31	9,563,425	17,023
7	9,901,077	7,921	32	9,546,402	17,470
8	9,893,156	7,519	33	9,328,932	18,200
9	9,885,637	7,315	34	9,510,732	19,021
10	9,878,322	7,211	35	9,491,711	20,028
11	9,871,111	7,601	36	9,471,683	21,217
12	9,863,510	8,384	37	9,450,466	22,681
13	9,855,126	9,757	38	9,427,785	24,324
14	9,845,369	11,322	39	9,403,461	26,236
15	9,834,047	13,079	40	9,377,225	28,319
16	9,820,968	14,830	41	9,348,906	30,758
17	9,806,138	16,376	42	9,318,148	33,173
18	9,789,762	17,426	43	9,284,975	35,933
19	9,772,336	18,177	44	9,249,042	38,753
20	9,754,159	18,533	45	9,210,289	41,907
21	9,735,626	18,595	46	9,168,382	45,108
22	9,717,031	18,365	47	9,123,274	48,536
23	9,698,666	18,040	48	9,074,738	52,089
24	9,680,626	17,619	49	9,022,649	56,031

SOURCE: Black/Skipper, *Life Insurance*, 12th ed., 1994, pp. 518–519. Reprinted by permission of Prentice-Hall, Inc., Englewood Cliffs, NJ.

death claim if the insured dies any time within the five-year period. However, any death claims are paid at the end of the year in which they occur, not at the end of the five-year period. Consequently, the cost of each year's mortality must be computed separately and then added together to determine the net single premium.

The cost of insurance for the first year is determined exactly as before, when we calculated the net single premium for yearly renewable term insurance. Thus, we have the following equation:

Age 45, first-year insurance cost

$$\frac{41,907}{9,210,289} \times \$1000 \times 0.9524 = \$4.33$$

The next step is to determine the cost of insurance for the second year. Referring back to Exhibit 27.1, we see that at age 46, 45,108 people will die during the year. Thus, for the 9,210,289 persons who are alive at age 45, the probability of dying during age 46 is 45,108/9,210,289. Note that the de-

Age at beginning of year	Number living at beginning of designated year	Number dying during designated year	Age at beginning of year	Number living at beginning of designated year	Number dying during designated year
50	8,966,618	60,166	75	4,898,907	314,461
51	8,906,452	65,017	76	4,584,446	323,341
52	8,841,435	70,378	77	4,261,105	328,616
53	8,771,057	76,396	78	3,932,489	329,936
54	8,694,661	83,121	79	3,602,553	328,012
55	8,611,540	90,163	80	3,274,541	323,656
56	8,521,377	97,655	81	2,950,885	317,161
57	8,423,722	105,212	82	2,633,724	308,804
58	8,318,510	113,049	83	2,324,920	298,194
59	8,205,461	121,195	84	2,026,726	284,248
60	8,084,266	129,995	85	1,742,478	266,512
61	7,954,271	139,518	86	1,475,966	245,143
62	7,814,753	149,965	87	1,230,823	220,994
63	7,664,788	161,420	88	1,009,829	195,170
64	7,503,368	173,628	89	814,659	168,871
65	7,329,740	186,322	90	645,788	143,216
66	7,143,418	198,944	91	502,572	119,110
67	6,944,474	211,390	92	383,472	97,191
68	6,773,084	223,471	93	286,281	77,900
69	6,509,613	235,453	94	208,381	61,660
70	6,274,160	247,892	95	146,721	48,412
71	6,026,268	260,937	96	98,309	37,805
72	5,765,331	274,718	97	60,504	29,054
73	5,490,613	289,026	98	31,450	20,693
74	5,201,587	302,680	99	10,757	10,757

nominator does not change but remains the same for each probability fraction. Because the amount needed to pay second-year death claims will not be needed for two years, it can be discounted for two years at 5 percent interest. Thus, for the second year, we have the following calculation:

Age 46, second-year insurance cost

$$\frac{45,108}{9,210,289} \times \$1000 \times 0.9070 = \$4.44$$

For each of the remaining three years, we follow the same procedure (see Exhibit 27.3). If the insurer collects $22.74 in a single premium from each of the 9,210,289 persons who are alive at age 45, that sum together with compound interest will be sufficient to pay all death claims during the five-year period.

Ordinary Life Insurance In calculating the NSP for an ordinary life policy, the same method described earlier for the five-year term policy is used except

EXHIBIT 27.2
Present Value of $1 at 5 Percent Rate of Compound Interest

Number of years	5%	Number of years	5%
1	0.9524	21	0.3589
2	0.9070	22	0.3418
3	0.8638	23	0.3256
4	0.8227	24	0.3101
5	0.7835	25	0.2953
6	0.7462	26	0.2812
7	0.7107	27	0.2678
8	0.6768	28	0.2551
9	0.6446	29	0.2429
10	0.6139	30	0.2314
11	0.5847	35	0.1813
12	0.5568	40	0.1420
13	0.5303	45	0.1113
14	0.5051	50	0.0872
15	0.4810	53	0.0753
		54	0.0717
16	0.4581	55	0.0683
17	0.4363		
18	0.4155		
19	0.3957		
20	0.3769		

SOURCE: Alan Gart and David J. Nye, "Present Value of $1," *Insurance Company Finance*. Copyright © 1986 Insurance Institute of America, Inc. Reprinted by permission.

that the calculations are carried out to the end of the mortality table (age 99). Thus, in our illustration, the NSP for a $1000 ordinary life insurance policy issued at age 45 would be $270.84.

Net Annual Level Premium

Most life insurance policies are not purchased with a single premium because of the large amount of cash that is required. Consumers generally find it more convenient to pay for their insurance in installment payments. If premiums are paid annually, the net single premium must be converted into a net annual level premium, which must be the mathematical equivalent of the net single premium. The net annual level premium cannot be determined by simply dividing the net single premium by the number of years over which the premiums are to be paid. Such a division would produce an insufficient premium, for two reasons. First, the net single premium is based on the assumption that the entire premium is paid in advance at the beginning of the period. If premiums are paid in installments, and some persons die prematurely, the insurer would suffer the loss of future premiums.

Second, installment payments result in the loss of interest income because of the smaller amounts that are invested. Thus, the mathematical adjustment for the loss of premiums and interest is accomplished by dividing the net single premium by the present value of an appropriate life annuity due of $1. To be more precise, the **net annual level premium (NALP)** *is determined by dividing the net single premium by the present value of a life annuity due (PVLAD) of $1 for the premium-paying period.* Thus, we obtain the following:

$$ \text{NALP} = \frac{\text{NSP}}{\text{PVLAD of \$1 for the premium-paying period}} $$

The concept of a life annuity due requires a brief explanation. The annual premium payments can be viewed as being similar to a life annuity, except that the payments flow from the insured to the insurer. Both life annuity payments and premium payments are similar in that both are paid during the lifetime of a specified individual, or for a stated period of time. Both cease on death (unless the annuity has a refund feature), and both are discounted for compound interest. The major exception is that the first premium is due immediately (because premiums are paid in advance), while the first annuity payment is due one payment interval from the date of purchase.[8] Thus, the annual payments are the equivalent of a regular life annuity plus one payment that is made immediately. However, to distinguish the premium payments from the annuity payments, we refer to the series of premium payments as a *life annuity due*. If the annual level premiums are to be paid for life— such as in an ordinary life policy—the premium is called a *whole life annuity due*. If the annual premi-

EXHIBIT 27.3

Figuring the NSP for a Five-Year Term Insurance Policy

Age	Probability of death		Amount of insurance		Present value of $1 at 5%		Cost of insurance
45	$\dfrac{41,907}{9,210,289}$	×	$1000	×	0.9524	=	$ 4.33 (year 1)
46	$\dfrac{45,108}{9,210,289}$	×	$1000	×	0.9070	=	4.44 (year 2)
47	$\dfrac{48,536}{9,210,289}$	×	$1000	×	0.8638	=	4.55 (year 3)
48	$\dfrac{52,089}{9,210,289}$	×	$1000	×	0.8227	=	4.65 (year 4)
49	$\dfrac{56,031}{9,210,289}$	×	$1000	×	0.7835	=	4.77 (year 5)
						NSP =	$22.74

ums are to be paid for only a temporary period—such as in the case of term insurance or limited payments policies—the premium is called a *temporary life annuity due.*[9]

Term Insurance Consider the net annual level premium for a five-year term insurance policy in the amount of $1000 issued at age 45. Recall that the net single premium for a five-year term insurance policy at age 45 is $22.74. This sum must be divided by the present value of a five-year *temporary life annuity due of $1.* For the first year, a $1 payment is due immediately. For the second year, the probability that a person age 45 will still be *alive* at age 46 to make the second payment of $1 must be determined. Referring back to Exhibit 27.1, 9,210,289 persons are alive at age 45. Of this number, 9,168,382 are still alive at age 46. Thus, the probability of survival is 9,168,382/9,210,289. This fraction is multiplied by $1, and the resulting sum is then discounted for one year's interest. Thus, the present value of the second payment is $0.948. Similar calculations are performed for the remaining three years. The various calculations are summarized as follows:

Age 45 $1 due immediately   = $1.000

Age 46 $\dfrac{9,168,382}{9,210,289}$ × $1 × 0.9524 = 0.948

Age 47 $\dfrac{9,123,274}{9,210,289}$ × $1 × 0.9070 = 0.898

Age 48 $\dfrac{9,074,738}{9,210,289}$ × $1 × 0.8638 = 0.851

Age 49 $\dfrac{9,022,649}{9,210,289}$ × $1 × 0.8227 = 0.806

PVLAD of $1 = $4.503

The present value of a five-year temporary life annuity due of $1 at age 45 is $4.50. If the net single premium of $22.74 is divided by $4.50, the net annual level premium is $5.05.

$$\text{NALP} = \frac{\text{NSP}}{\text{PVLAD of \$1}} = \frac{\$22.74}{\$4.50} = \$5.05$$

Ordinary Life Insurance The net annual level premium for a $1000 ordinary life insurance policy issued at age 45 is calculated in a similar manner. The same procedure is used except that the calculations are extended to the end of the mortality table. Thus, the present value of a *whole life annuity due of $1* for ages 45 through 99 must be calculated. If the calculations are performed, the present value of a whole life annuity due of $1 at age 45 is $15.312. The net single premium ($270.84) is then divided by the present value of a whole life annuity due of $1 at age 45 ($15.312), and the net annual level premium is $17.69.

Gross Premium The gross premium is determined by adding a loading allowance to the net annual level premium. The loading must cover all operating expenses, provide a margin for contingencies, and, in the case of stock life insurers, provide for a contribution to profits. If the policy is a participating policy, the loading must also reflect a margin for dividends.

Three major types of expenses are reflected in the loading allowance: (1) production expenses, (2) distribution expenses, and (3) maintenance expenses.[10] Production expenses are the expenses incurred before the agent delivers the policy, such as policy printing costs, underwriting expenses, and the cost of the medical examination. Distribution expenses are largely selling expenses, such as the first-year commission, advertising, and agency allowances. Maintenance expenses are the expenses incurred after the policy is issued, such as renewal commissions, costs of collecting renewal premiums, and state premium taxes.

RESERVES IN PROPERTY AND LIABILITY INSURANCE

The remainder of this chapter focuses largely on the various financial reserves of insurance companies. Insurers are required by law to maintain minimum reserves on their balance sheets. Because premiums are paid in advance, but the period of protection extends into the future, insurers must establish certain reserves to assure that the premiums collected in advance will be available to pay future losses.

Property and liability insurers are required to maintain two principal types of financial reserves:

- Unearned premium reserve
- Loss reserves

Unearned Premium Reserve

The **unearned premium reserve** *is a liability item that represents the unearned portion of gross premiums on all outstanding policies at the time of valuation.* An insurer is required by law to place the entire gross premium in the unearned premium reserve when the policy is first written, and renewal premiums must be placed in the same reserve.

Reasons for the Unearned Premium Reserve
The fundamental purpose of the unearned premium reserve is to pay for losses that occur during the policy period. Premiums are paid in advance, but the period of protection extends into the future. To assure policyowners that future losses will be paid, the unearned premium reserve is required.

The unearned premium reserve is also needed so that premium refunds can be paid to the policyowners in the event of cancellation. If the insurer cancels the policy, a full pro rata premium refund based on the unexpired portion of the policy term must be paid to the policyowner. Thus, the unearned premium reserve must be adequate so the premium refunds can be made in the event of cancellation.

Finally, if the business is reinsured, the unearned premium reserve serves as the basis for determining the amount that must be paid to the reinsurer for carrying the reinsured policies to the end of their terms. In practice, however, the amount paid to the reinsurer may be considerably less than the unearned premium reserve, because the reinsurer does not incur heavy first-year acquisition expenses in acquiring the reinsured policies.

Methods of Calculation Several methods can be used to calculate the unearned premium reserve. Only one of them is described here. Under the **annual pro rata method**, it is assumed that the policies are written uniformly throughout the year. For purposes of determining the unearned premium reserve, it is assumed that all policies are issued on July 1, which is the average issue date. Therefore, on December 31, the unearned premium reserve for all one-year policies is one-half of the premium income attributable to these policies. For two-year policies, the unearned premium reserve is three-fourths of the premium income, and for three-year policies, it is five-sixths of the premium income.

Equity in Unearned Premium Reserve

The law requires an insurer to place the entire gross premium in the unearned premium reserve. As will be shown later, this results in a redundant or excessive reserve, because most of the expenses incurred in writing the business are incurred when the policy is first written. Relatively lower expenses are incurred after the policy is issued. However, because of its emphasis on insurer solvency, the law prohibits an insurer from taking credit in advance for these prepaid expenses. Although the premium is being earned gradually over the policy period, the initial acquisition and underwriting expenses cannot be amortized over the same period. Instead, they are treated as cash expenses, to be charged off immediately. Therefore, because the unearned premium reserve must be established on the basis of a gross premium rather than a net premium, it is substantially overstated. *This overstatement or redundancy in the unearned premium reserve is called the* **equity in the unearned premium reserve**. Authorities estimate that the unearned premium reserve may be overstated by 20 to 40 percent, with 35 percent being a typical or average estimate of the equity in this reserve.

Effect on Underwriting Profit or Loss

The equity in the unearned premium reserve is extremely important in determining the true underwriting profit or loss of a property-liability insurer. For example, assume that a new property insurance company begins operating on January 1. It plans to sell only one-year property insurance policies. In establishing the rates, the insurer has an expected loss ratio of 60 percent, an expected expense ratio of 35 percent, and expects to earn an underwriting profit of 5 percent.[11] Also assume that the business is written uniformly throughout the year, and the annual pro rata method is used to determine the unearned premium reserve. During the year, $10 million of property insurance premiums are written. Losses and loss adjustment expenses incurred total $3 million,

and expenses incurred are $3.5 million.[12] On December 31, what is the insurer's underwriting profit or loss? The law requires the company to use a *statutory underwriting formula* to determine its underwriting results. Investment gains or losses are not considered in the formula. The statutory formula is as follows:

Statutory underwriting profit or loss =

$$\text{Earned premiums} - \begin{array}{c}\text{Losses incurred and}\\\text{loss-adjustment}\\\text{expenses incurred}\end{array} - \begin{array}{c}\text{Expenses}\\\text{incurred}\end{array}$$

In our illustration, the company has a statutory underwriting loss of $1.5 million. This can be illustrated as follows:

($000 omitted)

Premiums written		$10,000
Deduct unearned premiums		−5,000
Earned premiums		$ 5,000
Losses incurred	$3,000	
Expenses incurred	$3,500	
Total losses and expenses		−6,500
Statutory underwriting loss		($ 1,500)

Although the insurer's actual loss and expense experience conforms exactly to the experience anticipated in the rating structure, it has a statutory underwriting loss rather than a 5 percent underwriting profit. This result is due to the statutory method for determining a profit or loss. As noted earlier, the first-year acquisition expenses cannot be amortized over the policy term but must be immediately charged off as a cash expense. This requirement produces a statutory underwriting loss in our example.

The statutory underwriting loss of $1.5 million is a charge against the insurer's surplus. Thus, a rapidly growing insurer will experience a surplus drain because of a continuous increase in the unearned premium reserve. The opposite is true for an insurer whose premium volume is declining. The insurer will have a gain in its surplus account as the business runs off the books. The equity in the unearned premium reserve will flow into the insurer's surplus with the passage of time as the policy terms run off. Thus, to correct for the distortion that may result from the statutory formula, an *adjusted underwriting profit or loss* (called a trade profit or loss) is often used by financial analysts to determine the true underwriting results.

One method for determining the insurer's adjusted underwriting profit or loss is to consider the equity in the unearned premium reserve. The increased equity in the unearned premium reserve can be added to the statutory profit or loss to determine the adjusted underwriting profit or loss. Returning to our earlier illustration, assume that the insurer experienced an increase of $5 million in the unearned premium reserve. If an estimated equity of 35 percent in the unearned premium reserve is also assumed, the insurer has an adjusted underwriting profit rather than a loss. This can be illustrated as follows:

($000 omitted)

Statutory underwriting loss	$−1500
Equity in the unearned premium reserve	1750
Adjusted underwriting profit	$ 250

After adjusting the statutory formula for the equity in the unearned premium reserve, the insurer has an adjusted underwriting profit of $250,000, which is exactly 5 percent of earned premiums.

Based on the statutory formula method for determining underwriting profits, the property and liability industry is not highly profitable. The annual rate of return is generally lower than in other industries (see Insight 27.1).

Loss Reserves

The loss reserve is another important liability reserve for property-liability insurers. A loss reserve is the estimated cost of settling claims that have already occurred but have not been paid as of the valuation date. More specifically, the **loss reserve** *is an estimated amount for (1) claims reported and adjusted but not yet paid, (2) claims reported and filed but not yet adjusted, and (3) claims incurred but not yet reported to the company.* The loss reserve is especially important to casualty insurers because bodily injury and property damage liability lawsuits may take a long time to settle—often several years. In contrast, property insurance claims, auto collision and comprehensive losses, and other first-party insurance claims are settled more quickly; hence loss reserves are relatively small for property insurers.

Loss reserves generally can be classified into two major categories: case reserves and incurred-but-not reported reserves.

Case reserves are loss reserves that are established for each individual claim when it is reported. The major types of case reserves include the following:[13]

- Judgment method
- Average value method
- Loss ratio method
- Tabular method

Under the *judgment method*, a claim reserve is established for each individual claim. The amount of the loss reserve can be based on the judgment of someone in the claims department, or it can be estimated by a computer program. Many insurers now use computer programs that apply certain rules to calculate the size of the loss reserve. The details of an individual claim are entered into the computer, and the computer program estimates the size of the required loss reserve.

Under the *average value method*, an average value is assigned to each claim. This method is used when the number of claims is large, the average claim amount is relatively small, and the claims are quickly settled. For example, loss reserves for auto physical damage claims are often based on this method.

Under the *loss ratio method*, a formula based on the expected loss ratio is used to estimate the loss reserve. The expected loss ratio is multiplied by premiums earned during some time period. Losses and loss-adjustment expenses paid to date are then subtracted from the ultimate loss figure to determine the current loss reserve. This method is required by law for certain lines of insurance, such as workers compensation.

Insight 27.1

Comparison of Annual Rate of Return for Property and Casualty Insurance Industry with Other Industries

- In 1998, the property/casualty insurance industry's rate of return, as computed by Generally Accepted Accounting Principles (GAAP), was 8.4 percent, down from 11.6 percent in 1997.
- According to the Insurance Services Office, the return on net worth of the property/casualty insurance business on a GAAP accounting basis has been lower than the adjusted rate of return for the Fortune 500 in 14 out of the last 16 years.

Annual Rate of Return: Net Income After Taxes as a Percent of Equity

Year	Property/casualty insurance		Other industries[4]			
	Statutory accounting[1]	GAAP accounting[2]	Diversified financial[3]	Commercial banks	Utilities	Fortune 500[5]
1989	9.1%	10.5%	13.0%	13.6%	12.4%	15.0%
1990	8.5	8.8	12.7	9.9	11.5	13.0
1991	8.9	9.6	13.9	11.9	11.5	10.2
1992	4.4	4.5	12.8	12.2	9.4	9.0

Year	Statutory accounting[1]	GAAP accounting[2]	Diversified financial[3]	Commercial banks	Electric & gas utilities	Fortune 500 combined industrial service[5]
1993	10.6	11.0	17.1	14.9	11.1	11.9
1994	5.6	5.6	18.4	15.6	11.3	13.7
1995	9.0	8.7	18.2	15.6	11.9	14.0
1996	9.5	9.3	18.5	16.5	11.5	14.1
1997	11.9	11.6	14.9	16.9	10.4	13.9
1998	9.2	8.4	19.8	16.0	10.2	13.4

1. Net income after taxes, divided by year-end policyholders' surplus. Calculated by the Insurance Information Institute from A.M. Best Company data. Used by insurers when preparing the annual statements they submit to regulators.
2. Return on average net worth, Insurance Services Office, Inc.
3. Companies whose major source of revenue is from providing diversified financial services. They are not specifically chartered as insurance companies, banks or savings institutions, or brokerage or securities companies, although they may earn revenue from these sources.
4. Return on equity on a GAAP accounting basis, *Fortune Magazine*.
5. *Fortune* 500 Combined Industrial and Service Businesses median return on equity.

NOTE: Data from A.M. Best Company, Inc., Insurance Services Office, Inc., *Fortune Magazine*.

SOURCE: *The I.I.I. Fact Book 2000* (New York, NY: Insurance Information Institute), p. 1.14. Reprinted with permission.

Under the *tabular value method,* loss reserves are determined for certain claims for which the amounts paid depend on the length of life, duration of disability, remarriage of the beneficiary, and similar factors. This method is often used to establish loss reserves involving total permanent disability, partial permanent disability, survivor benefits, and similar claims. The loss reserve is called a *tabular reserve* because the duration of the benefit period is based on data derived from mortality, morbidity, and remarriage tables.

The **incurred-but-not-reported (IBNR) reserve** is a loss reserve that must be established for claims that have already occurred but have not yet been reported. For example, on December 31, a certain number of claims have already occurred but have not been reported to the insurer. Loss reserves must be established for such claims.

LIFE INSURANCE POLICY RESERVES

Policy reserves are the major liability item of life insurers. This section briefly examines the nature, purposes, and types of life insurance policy reserves.[14]

Nature of the Reserve

Under a level-premium plan of life insurance, the premiums paid during the early years of the contract are higher than are necessary to pay death claims, while those paid during the later years are insufficient to pay death claims. The excess premiums collected during the early years of the contract must be accounted for and held for future payment to the policyowners' beneficiary. The excess premiums paid during the early years result in the creation of a policy reserve. *Policy reserves are a liability item on the company's balance sheet that must be offset by assets equal to that amount.* Policy reserves are considered a liability item because they represent an obligation by the insurer to pay future policy benefits to policyowners. The policy reserves held by the insurer plus future premiums and future interest earnings will enable the insurer to pay all future policy benefits if the actual experience conforms to the actuarial assumptions used in calculating the reserve. Policy reserves are often called *legal reserves,* because state insur-

ance laws specify the minimum basis for calculating them.

Purposes of the Reserve

The policy reserve has two fundamental purposes. *First, it is a formal recognition of the insurer's obligation to pay future benefits.* The policy reserve plus future premiums and interest earnings must be sufficient to pay all future policy benefits.

Second, the reserve is a legal test of the insurer's solvency. The insurer must hold assets equal to its legal reserves and other liabilities. This requirement is the legal test of the insurer's ability to meet its present and future obligations to its policyowners. Policy reserves should not, therefore, be viewed as a fund. Rather, they are a liability item that must be offset by "funds" or assets. About 80 percent of the insurer's assets are needed to offset its reserve liabilities.

Definition of the Reserve

The **policy reserve** *can be defined as the difference between the present value of future benefits and the present value of future net premiums.* The net single premium is equal to the present value of future benefits. At the inception of the policy, the net single premium is also equal to the present value of future net premiums. The net single premium can be converted into a series of annual installment payments without changing this relationship. However, once the first installment premium payment is made, this statement is no longer true. The present value of future benefits and the present value of future net premiums are no longer equal to each other. The present value of future benefits will increase over time, because the date of death is drawing closer, while the present value of future net premiums will decline, because fewer premiums will be paid. Thus, the difference between the two is the policy reserve.

This situation is illustrated in Exhibit 27.4, which shows the prospective reserve (defined later) for an ordinary life policy issued at age 45. At the inception of the policy, the net single premium is equal to the present value of future benefits and the present value of future net premiums.

EXHIBIT 27.4
Prospective Reserve—Ordinary Life Insurance

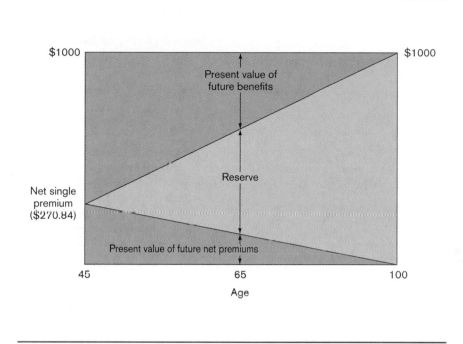

The present value of future benefits increases over time, while the present value of future net premiums declines, and the reserve is the difference between them. At age 100, the reserve is equal to the policy face amount. If the insured is still alive at that time, the face amount of insurance is paid to the policyowner.

Types of Reserves

The reserve can be viewed either retrospectively or prospectively. If we refer to the past experience, the reserve is known as a retrospective reserve. The **retrospective reserve** *represents the net premiums collected by the insurer for a particular block of policies, plus interest earnings at an assumed rate, less the amounts paid out as death claims.*[15] Thus, the retrospective reserve is the excess of the net premiums accumulated at interest over the death claims paid out.

The reserve can also be viewed prospectively when we look to the future. The **prospective reserve** *is the difference between the present value of future benefits and the present value of future net premiums.* The retrospective and prospective methods are the mathematical equivalent of each other. Both methods will produce the same level of reserves at the end of any given year if the same set of actuarial assumptions is used.

Reserves can also be classified based on the time of valuation. At the time the reserves are valued, they can be classified as terminal, initial, and mean. A **terminal reserve** *is the reserve at the end of any given policy year.* It is used by companies to determine cash surrender values as well as the net amount at risk for purposes of determining dividends. The **initial reserve** *is the reserve at the beginning of any policy year.* It is equal to the preceding terminal reserve plus the net level annual premium for the current year. The initial reserve is also used by insurers to determine dividends. Finally, the **mean reserve** *is the* *average of the terminal and initial reserves.* It is used to indicate the insurer's reserve liabilities on its annual statement.

SUMMARY

- State rating laws require insurance rates to meet certain standards. The rates charged by insurers must be adequate, not excessive, and not unfairly discriminatory.

- The rating system should also meet certain business objectives. The rates should be simple, stable, and responsive, and should encourage loss prevention.

- Three major rating methods are used in property and liability insurance: judgment, class, and merit rating.

- Judgment rating means that each exposure is individually evaluated, and the rate is determined largely by the underwriter's judgment.

- Class rating means that exposures with similar characteristics are placed in the same underwriting class, and each is charged the same rate. The rate charged reflects the average loss experience for the class as a whole. Most personal lines of insurance are class rated.

- Merit rating is a rating plan by which class rates are adjusted upward or downward based on individual loss experience. It is based on the assumption that the loss experience of a particular insured will differ substantially from the loss experience of other insureds.

- There are three principal types of merit rating plans:

  Schedule rating

  Experience rating

  Retrospective rating

- Under *schedule rating*, each exposure is individually rated, and debits and credits are applied based on the physical characteristics of the exposure to be insured. *Experience rating* means that the insured's past loss experience is used to determine the premium for the next policy period. *Retrospective rating* means the insured's loss experience during the current policy period determines the actual premium paid for that period.

- In life insurance rate making, the *net single premium* is the present value of the future death benefit. The *net annual level premium* must be the mathematical equivalent of the net single premium. The net annual level premium is determined by dividing the net single premium by the present value of a life annuity due of $1 for the premium-paying period. A loading for expenses must be added to the net annual level premium to determine the gross premium.

- The unearned premium reserve in property and liability insurance is a liability reserve that represents the unearned portion of gross premiums on all outstanding policies at the time of valuation. The fundamental purpose of the unearned premium reserve is to pay for losses that occur during the policy period.

- A loss reserve is the estimated cost of settling claims that have already occurred but have not been paid as of the valuation date.

- In life insurance, a policy reserve is defined as the difference between the present value of future benefits and the present value of future net premiums. Policy reserves or legal reserves are a formal recognition of the insurer's obligation to pay future benefits. Also, the reserve is a legal test of an insurer's solvency, because the insurer must hold assets equal to its legal reserves and other liabilities.

KEY CONCEPTS AND TERMS

Actual loss ratio	Judgment rating
Adjusted underwriting profit or loss	Loading
Annual pro rata method	Loss reserve
Case reserves	Mean reserve
Class rating (manual rating)	Merit rating
Earned premiums	Net annual level premium (NALP)
Equity in the unearned premium reserve	Net single premium (NSP)
Expected loss ratio	Policy reserve
Expense ratio	Prospective reserve
Experience rating	Pure premium
Exposure unit	Rate
Gross premium	Retrospective rating
Gross rate	Retrospective reserve
Incurred-but-not-reported (IBNR) reserve	Schedule rating
Initial reserve	Temporary life annuity due
	Terminal reserve
	Unearned premium reserve
	Whole life annuity due

REVIEW QUESTIONS

1. Describe the major objectives of rate making.

2. Explain the meaning of judgment rating.

3. What is class rating?

4. What is merit rating? Describe the three principal types of merit-rating plans.

5. Explain the concept of the net single premium in life insurance.

6. How is the net annual level premium computed?

7. What is the gross premium and how is it determined?

8. Explain the nature and purposes of unearned premium reserve in property and liability insurance.

9. What is a loss reserve? Describe the various types of loss reserves in property and liability insurance.

10. Describe the nature of a policy reserve (legal reserve) in life insurance.

APPLICATION QUESTIONS

1. Class rates (manual rates) are widely used in personal lines of insurance.
   a. Briefly describe the principal methods of determining class rates.
   b. Explain the advantages of class rating to insurers.

2. Merit rating is used in property and liability insurance where the final premium paid depends at least partly on the loss experience of the individual insured. Describe the major features of each of the following types of merit-rating plans:
   a. Schedule rating
   b. Experience rating
   c. Retrospective rating

3. A property and liability insurer has a redundancy or equity in its unearned premium reserve.
   a. Explain the reasons for the unearned premium reserve in property and liability insurance.
   b. Explain how the redundancy or equity in the unearned premium reserve arises.

4. Property and liability insurers are required to maintain certain types of loss reserves.
   a. Explain the nature of a loss reserve in property and liability insurance.
   b. Briefly describe the following types of case reserves:
      (1) Judgment method
      (2) Average value method
   c. What is an incurred-but-not-reported (IBNR) loss reserve?

SELECTED REFERENCES

Black, Kenneth, Jr., and Harold D. Skipper, Jr. *Life Insurance*, thirteenth edition (Upper Saddle River, NJ: Prentice-Hall, Inc., 2000), Chapters 27–30.

Graves, Edward E., ed. *McGill's Life Insurance*, second edition. Bryn Mawr, PA: The American College, 1998, Chapters 15–17.

Marshal, David H., et al. *Accounting and Finance for Insurance Professionals*, first edition. Malvern, PA: American Institute for CPCU, 1997.

Webb, Bernard L., Connor M. Harrison, and James J. Markham. *Insurance Operations*, second edition, Vols. 1 and 2. Malvern, PA: American Institute for Chartered Property Casualty Underwriters, 1997.

NOTES

1. Robert J. Gibbons, George E. Rejda, and Michael W. Elliott, *Insurance Perspectives* (Malvern, PA: American Institute for Chartered Property Casualty Underwriters, 1992), p. 119.

2. Bernard L. Webb, Connor M. Harrison, and James J. Markam, *Insurance Operations*, second edition, Vol. 2 (Malvern, PA: American Institute for Chartered Property Casualty Underwriters, 1997), pp. 89–90.

3. The basic rate-making methods are discussed in some detail in Webb et al., Chapter 10. See also Bernard L. Webb, J. J. Launie, Willis Park Rokes, and Norman A. Baglini, *Insurance Company Operations*, third edition, Vol. II (Malvern, PA: American Institute for Property and Liability Underwriters, 1984), Chapters 9 and 10.

4. An equivalent method for determining the final rate is to divide the pure premium by the permissible loss ratio. The *permissible loss ratio* is the same as the expected loss ratio. If the expense ratio is 0.40, the permissible loss ratio is 1 – 0.40, or 0.60. Thus, if the pure premium of $60 is divided by the permissible loss ratio of 0.60, the resulting gross rate is also $100.

$$\text{Gross rate} = \frac{\text{Pure premium}}{\text{Permissable loss ratio}} = \frac{\$60}{0.60} = \$100$$

5. Earned premiums are the premiums actually earned by a company during the accounting period, rather than the premiums written during the same period.

6. The credibility factor (C) refers to the statistical relia-bility of the data. It ranges from a value of 0 to 1 and increases as the number of claims increases. If the ac-tuary believes that the data are highly reliable and can accurately predict future losses, a credibility factor of 1 can be used. However, if the data are not completely reliable as a predictor of future losses, a credibility factor of less than 1 is used.

7. This section is based on Kenneth Black, Jr., and Harold D. Skipper, Jr., *Life Insurance*, twelfth edition (Englewood Cliffs, NJ: Prentice Hall, 1994), pp. 530–543, 552–554; and Dan M. McGill, *Life Insur-ance*, Revised Edition (Homewood, IL: Richard D. Irwin, 1967), pp. 182–275. The author drew heavily on these sources in preparing this section.

8. For example, if an immediate life annuity is purchased with annual payments, the first payment would be due one year from the purchase date.

9. Black and Skipper, p. 553.

10. McGill, pp. 247–248.

11. The loss ratio is the ratio of losses and loss-adjustment expenses to *earned premiums*. The expense ratio is the ratio of expenses incurred to *written premiums*.

12. Expenses incurred of $3.5 million are based on writ-ten premiums. Remember that the expense ratio is the ratio of expenses incurred to written premiums ($3,500,000/$10,000,000 = 35%).

13. For a detailed explanation of loss reserves, see Webb, et al., *Insurance Operations*, pp. 148–152.

14. Life insurance reserves are discussed in greater detail in Black and Skipper, Chapter 20, and McGill, pp. 218–245.

15. McGill, p. 219.

Case Application

Assume that you are asked to explain how premi-ums in a life insurance policy are calculated. Based on the following information, answer the questions below.

a. Compute the net single premium for a five-year term insurance policy in the amount of $1000 issued at age 40.

b. Compute the net annual level premium for the same policy as in part (a).

c. Is the net annual level premium the actual pre-mium paid by the policyowner? Explain your answer.

Age at beginning of year	Number living at beginning of designated year	Number dying during designated year	Present value of $1 at 5%	
			Year	Factor
40	9,377,225	28,319	1	0.9524
41	9,348,906	30,758	2	0.9070
42	9,318,148	33,173	3	0.8638
43	9,284,975	35,933	4	0.8227
44	9,249,042	38,753	5	0.7835

Students may take a self-administered test on this chapter at www.awlonline.com/rejda

Chapter 28

Government Regulation of Insurance

> *"There are serious shortcomings in state laws and regulatory activities with respect to protecting the interests of insurance consumers."*
>
> U.S. General Accounting Office

Learning Objectives

After studying this chapter, you should be able to:

▲ Explain the major reasons why insurers are regulated.

▲ Identify key legal cases and legislation that have had an important impact on insurance regulation.

▲ Identify the areas that are regulated.

▲ Explain the objectives of rate regulation and the different types of rating laws.

▲ Explain the major arguments for and against state regulation of insurance.

▲ Access the Web site of the state insurance department in your state and obtain consumer information about insurance products and laws.

Internet Resources

- The **Insurance Regulatory Examiners Society** is a nonprofit professional and educational association for insurance company examiners and other professionals working in insurance regulation. Visit the site at:

  http://www.go-ires.org

- The **National Association of Insurance Commissioners (NAIC)** is an organization of state insurance commissioners that promotes uniformity in state insurance laws and recommends legislation to state legislatures. The Web site for each state insurance department (except New Mexico) can be accessed through the NAIC Web site. Visit the site at:

  www.naic.org

- The **National Conference of Insurance Guaranty Funds** is an advisory organization to state guaranty funds. It gathers and disseminates information regarding insurer insolvencies. Visit the site at:

  http://www.ncigf.org

■ The **National Conference of Insurance Legislators** is an organization of chairpersons of state legislative committees dealing with insurance-related matters. Visit the site at:

http://www.ncoil.org

egan, age 26, was involved in an auto accident where she was at fault. Her car was damaged beyond repair. Megan carried collision insurance on the car. She is upset because her insurer denied payment of the collision claim on the grounds that a policy provision has been violated. A friend suggested that Megan contact the state insurance department for assistance. After conducting an investigation, the state insurance department representative concluded that the claim should be paid. The claim was later settled to Megan's satisfaction.

One important activity of state insurance departments is the protection of consumers. In the preceding case, the state insurance department helped Megan resolve her claim dispute with the insurance company. To protect consumers, the states regulate the activities of insurers. Certain federal laws also apply to private insureres.

This chapter discusses the fundamentals of insurance regulation. Topics covered include the reasons why insurers are regulated, the various methods for regulating insurers, and the specific areas that are regulated. The chapter concludes with a discussion of current issues in insurance regulation.

REASONS FOR INSURANCE REGULATION

Insurers are regulated by the states for several reasons, including the following:

■ Maintain insurer solvency
■ Compensate for inadequate consumer knowledge
■ Ensure reasonable rates
■ Make insurance available

Maintain Insurer Solvency

Insurance regulation is necessary to maintain the solvency of insurers. Solvency is important for several reasons. First, premiums are paid in advance, but the period of protection extends into the future. If an insurer goes bankrupt and a future claim is not paid, the insurance protection paid for in advance is worthless. Therefore, to ensure that claims will be paid, the financial strength of insurers must be carefully monitored.

A second reason for stressing solvency is that individuals can be exposed to great financial insecurity if insurers fail and claims are not paid. For example, if the insured's home is totally destroyed by a tornado and the loss is not paid, he or she may be financially ruined. Thus, because of the possibility of great financial hardship to insureds, beneficiaries, and third-party claimants, regulation must stress insurer solvency.

Finally, when insurers become insolvent, certain social and economic costs are incurred. Examples include the loss of jobs by insurance company employees, a reduction in premium taxes paid to the states, and a "freeze" on the withdrawal of cash values by life insurance policyowners. These costs can be minimized if insolvencies are prevented.

Insurer solvency is an important issue that is discussed in greater detail later in the chapter.

Compensate for Inadequate Consumer Knowledge

Regulation is also necessary because of inadequate consumer knowledge. Insurance contracts are technical, legal documents that contain complex clauses and provisions. Without regulation, an unscrupulous insurer could draft a contract so restrictive and legalistic that it would be worthless.

Also, most consumers do not have sufficient information for comparing and determining the monetary value of different insurance contracts. It is difficult to compare dissimilar policies with different premiums because the necessary price and policy information is not readily available. For example, individual health insurance policies vary widely by cost, coverages, and benefits. The average consumer would find it difficult to evaluate a particular policy based on the premium alone.

Without good information, consumers cannot select the best insurance product. This failure can reduce the impact that consumers have on insurance markets as well as the competitive incentive of insurers to improve product quality and lower price. Thus, regulation is needed to produce the same market effect that results from knowledgeable consumers who are purchasing products in highly competitive markets.

Finally, some agents are unethical, and state licensing requirements are minimal. Thus, regulation is needed to protect consumers against unscrupulous agents.

Ensure Reasonable Rates

Regulation is also necessary to ensure reasonable rates. Rates should not be so high that consumers are being charged excessive prices. Nor should they be so low that the solvency of insurers is threatened. In most insurance markets, competition among insurers results in rates that are not excessive. Unfortunately, this result is not always the case. In some insurance markets with relatively few insurers, such as credit and title insurance, rate regulation is needed to protect consumers against excessive rates. Regulation also protects consumers against some insurers who may attempt to increase rates to exorbitant levels after a natural disaster occurs so as to recoup their underwriting losses.

Make Insurance Available

Another regulatory goal is to make insurance available to all persons who need it. Insurers are often unwilling to insure all applicants for a given type of insurance because of underwriting losses, inadequate rates, adverse selection, and a host of additional factors. However, the public interest may require regulators to take actions that expand private insurance markets so as to make insurance more readily available. If private insurers are unable or unwilling to supply the needed coverages, then government insurance programs may be necessary.

HISTORICAL DEVELOPMENT OF INSURANCE REGULATION

In this section, the development of insurance regulation by the states is briefly reviewed. You should pay careful attention to certain landmark legal decisions and legislative acts that have had a profound impact on insurance regulation.

Early Regulatory Efforts

Insurance regulation first began when state legislatures granted charters to new insurers, which authorized their formation and operation. The new insurers were initially subject to few regulatory controls. The charters required only that the companies issue periodic reports and provide public information concerning their financial conditions.

The creation of state insurance commissions was the next step in insurance regulation. In 1851, New Hampshire became the first state to create a separate insurance commission to regulate insurers. Other states followed suit. In 1859, New York created a separate administrative agency headed by a single superintendent who was given broad licensing and investigative powers. Thus, initial insurance regulation developed under the jurisdiction and supervision of the states.

Paul v. Virginia

The case of *Paul v. Virginia* in 1868 was a landmark legal decision that established the right of the states to regulate insurance.[1] Samuel Paul was an agent in Virginia who represented several New York insurers. Paul was fined for selling fire insurance in Virginia without a license. He appealed the case on the grounds that Virginia's law was unconstitutional. He argued that because insurance was interstate commerce, only the federal government had the right to regulate insurance under the commerce clause of the U.S. Constitution. The Supreme Court disagreed. The Court ruled that issuance of an insurance policy was not interstate commerce. Therefore, the insurance industry was not subject to the commerce clause of the Constitution. *Thus, the legal significance of* Paul v. Virginia *was that insurance was not interstate commerce, and that the states rather than the federal government had the right to regulate the insurance industry.*

South-Eastern Underwriters Association Case

The precedent set in *Paul v. Virginia*, which held that insurance is not interstate commerce, was overturned by the Supreme Court in 1944. The **South-Eastern Underwriters Association (SEUA)** was a cooperative rating bureau that was found guilty of price fixing and other violations of the Sherman Antitrust Act. *In the landmark case of* U.S. v. South-Eastern Underwriters Association, *the Supreme Court ruled that insurance was interstate commerce when conducted across state lines and was subject to federal regulation.*[2] The Court's decision that insurance was interstate commerce and subject to federal antitrust laws caused considerable turmoil for the industry and state regulators. The decision raised serious doubts concerning the legality of private rating bureaus, and

the power of the states to regulate and tax the insurance industry.

McCarran-Ferguson Act

To resolve the confusion and doubt that existed after the SEUA decision, Congress passed the **McCarran-Ferguson Act** (Public Law 15) in 1945. *The McCarran-Ferguson Act states that continued regulation and taxation of the insurance industry by the states are in the public interest. It also states that federal antitrust laws apply to insurance only to the extent that the insurance industry is not regulated by state law.* Therefore, as long as state regulation is in effect, federal antitrust laws will not apply to insurance. However, the exemption from antitrust laws is not absolute. The Sherman Act forbids any acts or agreements to boycott, coerce, or intimidate. In these areas, insurers are still subject to federal law.

At present, the states still have the primary responsibility for regulating insurance. However, Congress can repeal the McCarran-Ferguson Act, which would then give the federal government primary authority over the insurance industry. There have been strong pressures from some politicians and consumer groups to repeal the McCarran-Ferguson Act, but Congress to date has not done so. This important issue is explained later in the chapter.

METHODS FOR REGULATING INSURERS

Three principal methods are used to regulate insurers: legislation, courts, and state insurance departments.

Legislation

All states have insurance laws that regulate the operations of insurers. These laws regulate (1) formation of insurance companies, (2) licensing of agents and brokers, (3) financial requirements for maintaining solvency, (4) insurance rates, (5) sales and claim practices, (6) taxation, and (7) rehabilitation or liquidation of insurers. Also, laws have been passed to protect the rights of consumers, such as laws restricting the right of insurers to terminate insurance contracts and laws making insurance more widely available.

Insurers are also subject to regulation by certain federal agencies and laws. Only a few are mentioned here. The Federal Trade Commission has authority to regulate mail-order insurers in those states where they are not licensed to do business. The Securities and Exchange Commission has created regulations concerning the sale of variable annuities and has jurisdiction over the sale of insurance company securities to the public. The Employee Retirement Income Security Act of 1974 (ERISA) applies to the private pension plans of insurers.

Courts

State and federal courts periodically hand down decisions concerning the constitutionality of state insurance laws, the interpretation of policy clauses and provisions, and the legality of administrative actions by state insurance departments. As such, the various court decisions can affect the market conduct and operations of insurers in an important way.

State Insurance Departments

All states, the District of Columbia, and U.S. territories have a separate insurance department or bureau. An insurance commissioner, who is elected or appointed by the governor, has the responsibility to administer state insurance laws. Through administrative rulings, the state insurance commissioner wields considerable power over insurers doing business in the state. The insurance commissioner has the power to hold hearings, issue cease-and-desist orders, and revoke or suspend an insurer's license to do business.

The state insurance commissioners belong to an important organization known as the **National Association of Insurance Commissioners (NAIC)**. The NAIC, founded in 1871, meets periodically to discuss industry problems that might require legislation or regulation. The NAIC has drafted model laws in various areas and has recommended adoption of these proposals by state legislatures. Although the NAIC has no legal authority to force the states to adopt the recommendations, most states have accepted all or part of them.

WHAT AREAS ARE REGULATED?

Insurers are subject to numerous laws and regulations. The principal areas regulated include the following:

- Formation and licensing of insurers
- Financial regulation
- Rate regulation
- Policy forms
- Sales practices and consumer protection

Formation and Licensing of Insurers

All states have requirements for the formation and licensing of insurers. A new insurer is typically formed by incorporation. The insurer receives a charter or certificate of incorporation from the state, which authorizes its formation and legal existence.

After being formed, insurers must be licensed before they can do business. The licensing requirements for insurers are more stringent than those imposed on other new firms. If the insurer is a capital stock insurer, it must meet certain minimum capital and surplus requirements, which vary by state and by line of insurance. A new mutual insurer must meet a minimum surplus requirement (rather than capital and surplus, as there are no stockholders), and other requirements.

A license can be issued to a domestic, foreign, or alien insurer. A **domestic insurer** is an insurer domiciled in the state; it must be licensed in the state as well as in other states where it does business. A **foreign insurer** is an out-of-state insurer that is chartered by another state; it must be licensed to do business in the state. An **alien insurer** is an insurer chartered by a foreign country. It must also meet certain licensing requirements to operate in the state.

Financial Regulation

In addition to minimum capital and surplus requirements, insurers are subject to other financial regulations. These financial regulations are designed to maintain solvency.

Admitted Assets An insurer must have sufficient assets to offset its liabilities. Only admitted assets can be shown on the insurer's balance sheet. **Admitted assets** *are assets that an insurer can show on its statutory balance sheet in determining its financial condition.* All other assets are nonadmitted.

Most assets are classified as admitted assets. These assets include cash, bonds, common and preferred stocks, mortgages, real estate, and other legal investments. Nonadmitted assets include premiums overdue by 90 or more days, office furniture and supplies, and certain investments or amounts that exceed statutory limits for certain types of securities. Nonadmitted assets are excluded because their liquidity is uncertain. As a result, policyholders' statutory surplus is decreased by an increase in nonadmitted assets.

Reserves Reserves *are liability items on an insurer's balance sheet and reflect obligations that must be met in the future.* The states have regulations for the calculation of reserves. The various methods for calculating reserves were discussed in Chapter 27

Surplus The surplus position is also carefully monitored. **Policyowners' surplus** *is the difference between an insurer's assets and its liabilities.* The surplus of a capital stock insurer consists of two items: (1) a capital stock account that represents the value of the shares issued to the stockholders, and (2) paid-in surplus that represents amounts paid in by stockholders in excess of the par value of the stock. Both items together represent policyowners' surplus. Because a mutual insurer has no stockholders, policyowners' surplus is simply the difference between assets and liabilities.

In property and liability insurance, policyowners' surplus is important for several reasons. First, the amount of new business an insurer can write is limited by the amount of policyowners' surplus. One conservative rule is the **Kenney rule**, by which a property insurer can safely write $2 of new net premiums for each $1 of policyowners' surplus.[3] Second, policyowners' surplus is necessary to offset any substantial underwriting or investment losses. Finally, policyowners' surplus is required to offset any deficiency in loss reserves that may occur over time.

In life insurance, policyowners' surplus is less important because of the substantial safety margins in the calculation of premiums and dividends, conservative interest assumptions used in calculating legal reserves, conservative valuation of investments, greater stability in operations over time, and less likelihood of a catastrophic loss.

Risk-based Capital To reduce the risk of insolvency, life and health insurers must meet certain risk-based capital standards based on a model law developed by the NAIC. The NAIC has drafted a similar model law for property and liability insurers. Only the standards for life and health insurers are discussed here.

Risk-based capital *means that insurers must have a certain amount of capital, depending on the riskiness of their investments and insurance operations. Insurers are monitored by regulators based on how much capital they have relative to their risk-based capital requirements.* For example, insurers that invest in less-than-investment-grade corporate bonds ("junk bonds") must set aside more capital than if Treasury bonds were purchased.

The risk-based capital requirements in life insurance are based on a formula that considers four types of risk—asset default risk, insurance risk, interest rate risk, and general business risk. Asset default risk is the risk of default of specific assets and a market decline in the insurer's investment portfolio. Insurance risk is the risk that premiums and reserves may be inadequate for paying benefits. Interest rate risk reflects possible losses due to changing interest rates. Examples include a decline in the market value of assets supporting contractual obligations and liquidity problems arising from disintermediation because of changing interest rates. Finally, business risk refers to other risks that insurers face, such as guaranty fund assessments and insolvency because of bad management.

The NAIC model act requires a comparison of the company's total adjusted capital with the amount of required risk-based capital (RBC). *Total adjusted capital* is the company's net worth (assets minus liabilities) with certain adjustments.

The model act specifies certain regulatory and company actions that must be taken if an insurer's total adjusted capital falls below its RBC level. There are four action levels based on the follwing RBC ratios:[4]

Action level	RBC ratio	Required action
Company action level	200%	Insurer must file a comprehensive plan.
Regulatory action level	150%	Regulator must examine insurer; insurer files a comprehensive plan
Authorized control level	100%	Regulator is authorized to seize insurer.
Mandatory control level	70%	Regulator is required to seize insurer.

An insurer with an RBC ratio between the first and second thresholds (company action level and regulatory action level) must file a plan with regulators to increase its risk-based capital. If the RBC ratio falls below the second threshold (regulatory action level), regulators must examine the insurer and take corrective action if necessary; the insurer must also file a corrective plan. If the RBC ratio is between the third and fourth thresholds (authorized control level and mandatory control level), regulators are authorized to seize the insurer and take control of its operations. If the ratio falls below the mandatory control level, regulators are required to seize the insurer and place it under regulatory control.

The effect of the RBC requirements is to raise the minimum amount of capital for many insurers and decrease the chance that a failing insurer will exhaust its capital before it can be seized by regulators. Thus, the overall result is to limit an insurer's financial risk and reduce the cost of insolvency.

As a practical matter, the vast majority of insurers have total adjusted capital that exceeds their risk-based capital requirements. In 1996, approximately 97 percent of life and health insurers and 94 percent of property and liability insurers had RBC ratios of 250 percent or higher.[5]

Investments Insurance company investments are regulated with respect to types, quality, and percentage of total assets or surplus that can be invested in different investments. The basic purpose of these regulations is to prevent insurers from making unsound investments that could threaten the company's solvency and harm the policyowners.

Life insurers typically invest in common and preferred stocks, bonds, mortgages, real estate, and policy loans. The laws generally place maximum limits on each type of investment based on a percentage of assets or surplus. For example, a state may specify that common stock investments are limited to a maximum of 10 percent of total assets.

Property and liability insurers are subject to fewer restrictions in their investments than life insurers. The actual restrictions vary among the states, and only two general comments are made here.[6] First, with respect to minimum capital requirements, the funds must usually be invested in federal, state, or municipal bonds, or bonds and notes secured by mortgages and trust deeds on improved real estate. In some states, certain public utility or high-quality corporate bonds can be used to meet this requirement. In addition, assets equal to a specified percentage of the unearned premium and loss reserves must also be invested in restricted securities with the same high quality.

Second, any excess funds over the minimum capital requirements and reserve liabilities can be invested in the common stock of solvent corporations or in real estate the company can legally hold. There are restrictions, however, on the proportion of assets that can be invested in any single corporation.

Dividend Policy In life insurance, the annual gain from operations can be distributed in the form of dividends to policyowners, or it can be added to the insurer's surplus for present and future needs. Many states limit the amount of surplus a participating life insurer can accumulate to a maximum of 10 percent of policy reserves. The purpose of this limitation is to prevent life insurers from accumulating a substantial surplus at the expense of dividends to policyowners.

Reports and Examinations Annual reports and examinations are used to maintain insurer solvency. Each insurer must file an annual report with the state insurance department in states where it does business. The annual report provides detailed financial information to regulatory officials with respect to assets, liabilities, reserves, investments, claim payments, risk-based capital, and other information.

Insurance companies are also periodically examined by the states. Depending on the state, domestic insurers are examined every three to five years by the state insurance department. However, state regulations have the authority to conduct an examination at any time when considered necessary. Licensed out-of-state insurers are also periodically examined.

Liquidation of Insurers If an insurer is financially impaired, the state insurance department assumes control of the company. With proper management, the insurer may be successfully rehabilitated. If the insurer cannot be rehabilitated, it is liquidated according to the state's insurance code.

Most states have adopted the Insurers Supervision, Rehabilitation, and Liquidation Model Act drafted by the NAIC in 1977 or similar types of legislation. The Act is designed to achieve uniformity among the states in the liquidation of assets and payment of claims of a defunct insurer and provides for a comprehensive system for rehabilitation and liquidation.

If an insurer becomes insolvent, some claims may still be unpaid. All states have **guaranty funds** that provide for the payment of unpaid claims of insolvent property and liability insurers. In life insurance, all states have enacted guaranty laws and guarantee associations to pay the claims of policyowners of insolvent life and health insurers.

The **assessment method** is the major method used to raise the necessary funds to pay unpaid claims. Insurers are generally assessed after an insolvency occurs. New York is an exception because it maintains a permanent preassessment solvency fund, which assesses property and liability insurers prior to any insolvency. Insurers can recoup part or all of the assessments paid by special state premium tax credits, refunds from the state guaranty funds, and higher insurance premiums. The result is that taxpayers and the general public indirectly pay the claims of insolvent insurers.

The guaranty funds limit the amount that policyowners can collect if an insurer goes broke. For example, in life insurance the guaranty funds may place

a limit of $100,000 on cash values and $300,000 on the combined benefits from all policies. Some state funds also do not protect out-of-state residents when an insurer domiciled in the state goes broke.

Rate Regulation

All states except Illinois have rating laws that require property and liability insurance rates to meet certain statutory standards. As noted in Chapter 27, rates must be adequate, reasonable (not excessive), and not unfairly discriminatory. However, there are wide variations among states with respect to implementation of these objectives.

Rate regulation is far from uniform. Some states have more than one rating law, depending on the type of insurance. The principal types of rating laws are the following:

- Prior-approval laws
- File-and-use laws
- Open-competition laws
- Flex-rating laws

Prior-Approval Laws The majority of states have some type of prior-approval law for regulating rates. Under a **prior-approval law**, rates must be filed and approved by the state insurance department before they can be used. In most states, if the rates are not disapproved within a certain period, such as 30 or 60 days, they are deemed to be approved.

Insurance companies have criticized prior-approval laws on several grounds. There is often considerable delay in obtaining a needed rate increase, because state insurance departments are often understaffed. The rate increase that is granted may be inadequate, and needed rate increases can be denied for political purposes. In addition, the statistical data required by the state insurance department to support a rate increase may not be readily available.

File-and-Use Laws This type of law is more liberal than the laws discussed earlier. Under a **file-and-use law**, insurers are required only to file the rates with the state insurance department, and the rates can be used immediately. Regulatory authorities have the authority to disapprove the rates later if they violate state law. This type of rating law overcomes the problem of delay that exists under a prior-approval law.

A variation of file and use is a **use-and-file law.** Under this law, insurers can put into effect rate changes, but the rates must be filed with the regulatory authorities within a certain period after first being used, such as 15 or 60 days.

Open-Competition Laws Open-competition laws (also called no-filing laws) are the most liberal of all rating laws. Under an open-competition law, insurers are not required to file their rates with the state insurance department. However, insurers may be required to furnish rate schedules and supporting data to state officials. The fundamental assumption underlying an open-competition law is that market forces will determine the price and availability of insurance rather than the discretionary acts of regulatory officials.

Flex-Rating Laws Some states have enacted an innovative rating law known as flex rating. Under a **flex-rating law,** prior approval of rates is required only if the rate increase or decrease exceeds a specific predetermined range. Rates changes of up to 10 to 25 percent are typically permitted without prior approval. The purpose of a flex-rating law is to allow insurers to make rate changes more rapidly in response to changing market conditions.

Life Insurance Rate Regulation Life insurance rates are not directly regulated by the states.[7] Rate adequacy in life insurance is indirectly achieved by regulations that require legal reserves to be at least a minimum size. Minimum legal reserve requirements affect the rates that must be charged to pay death claims and expenses.

Policy Forms

The regulation of new policy forms is another important area of insurance regulation. Because insurance contracts are technical and complex, the state insurance commissioner has the authority to approve or disapprove new policy forms before the contracts are sold to the public. The purpose is to protect the public from misleading, deceptive, and unfair provisions.

Sales Practices and Consumer Protection

The sales practices of insurers are regulated by laws concerning the licensing of agents and brokers, and by laws prohibiting twisting, rebating, and unfair trade practices.

Licensing of Agents and Brokers All states require agents and brokers to be licensed. Depending on the type of insurance sold, applicants must pass one or more written examinations. The purpose is to ensure that agents have knowledge of the state insurance laws and the contracts they intend to sell. If the agent is incompetent or dishonest, the state insurance commissioner has the authority to suspend or revoke the agent's license.

All states have legislation requiring the continuing education of agents. The continuing education requirements are designed to upgrade an agent's knowledge and skills.

Twisting All states forbid twisting. **Twisting** *is the inducement of a policyowner to drop an existing policy in another company due to misrepresentation or incomplete information.* Twisting laws apply largely to life insurance policies; the objective here is to prevent policyowners from being financially harmed by replacing one life insurance policy with another.

All states have replacement regulations so that policyowners can make an informed decision concerning the replacement of an existing life insurance policy. These laws are based on the premise that replacement of an existing life insurance policy generally is not in the policyowner's best interest. For example, a new front-end load for commissions and expenses must be paid; a new incontestable clause and suicide clause must be satisfied; and higher premiums based on the policyowner's higher attained age may have to be paid. *However, in some cases, switching policies can be financially justified.* One earlier study of life insurance policy replacements found that the majority of the replacements were acceptable; that is, there were cost savings to policyowners. The authors concluded that their data provided no support for the commonly held viewpoint of state insurance commissioners that replacements are generally undesirable.[8] However, more recently, deceptive sales practices by agents in certain insurers have resulted in the replacement of life insurance policies that were financially harmful to the policyowners.

Rebating Most state insurance codes also forbid rebating. **Rebating** *is giving to an individual a premium reduction or some other financial advantage not stated in the policy as an inducement to purchase the policy.* One obvious example is a partial refund of the agent's commission to the policyowner. The basic purpose of antirebate laws is to ensure fair and equitable treatment of all policyowners by preventing one insured from obtaining an unfair price advantage over another.

Consumer groups, however, believe that antirebating laws are harmful to consumers. Critics argue that (1) rebating will increase price competition and lower insurance rates; (2) present antirebating laws protect the incomes of agents rather than consumers; and (3) insurance purchasers are denied the right to negotiate price with insurance agents.

Unfair Trade Practices Insurance laws prohibit a wide variety of *unfair trade practices*, including misrepresentation, twisting, rebating, deceptive or false advertising, inequitable claim settlement, and unfair discrimination. The state insurance commissioner has the legal authority to stop insurers from engaging in unfair trade practices and deceptive advertising. Insurers can be fined, an injunction can be obtained, or, in serious cases, the insurer's license can be suspended or revoked.

Complaint Division State insurance departments typically have a complaint division or department for handling consumer complaints. The department or individual will investigate the complaint and try to obtain a response from the offending insurer or agency. Most consumer complaints involve claims. An insurer may refuse to pay a claim, or it may dispute the amount payable. Although state insurance departments respond to individual complaints, the departments generally lack direct authority to order insurers to pay disputed claims where factual questions are an issue. *However, you should phone or write your state insurance department if you feel you are being treated unfairly by your insurer or agent.*

This consideration is especially true for auto insurance disputes where certain insurers have significantly higher complaint ratios than others (see Insight 28.1).

Readable Policies Greater protection of the consumer is also evidenced by the trend toward more *readable policies*. To make insurance contracts more understandable, the states have approved policies in which the language is less technical and is therefore simpler and easier to understand. The development of more readable policies will undoubtedly benefit most consumers.

Shopper's Guides Some states publish *shoppers' guides* for insurance consumers. The guides typically show the premiums charged by insurers for auto insurance and homeowners insurance, so that consumers can make meaningful cost comparisons. As a result, consumers may be able to purchase auto and homeowners insurance from low-cost insurers.

Taxation of Insurers

Insurers pay numerous local, state, and federal taxes. Two important taxes are the federal income tax and the state premium tax. Insurers pay federal income taxes based on complex formulas and rules established by federal legislation and the Internal Revenue Service. The states also levy a premium tax on gross premiums received from policyowners, such as 2 percent of the premium paid.

The primary purpose of the premium tax is to raise revenues for the states, not to provide funds for insurance regulation. However, many state insurance departments are underfunded and receive only a small fraction of the premium taxes collected. Critics of state regulation argue that if state regulation is to become more effective, more money must be spent on insurance regulation.

Most states also have **retaliatory tax laws** that affect premium taxes and other taxes. For example, assume that the premium tax is 2 percent in Nebraska and 3 percent in Iowa. If insurers domiciled in Nebraska are required to pay a 3 percent premium tax on business written in Iowa, then domestic insurers in Iowa doing business in Nebraska must also pay 3 percent even though Nebraska's rate is 2 percent. The purpose of a retaliatory tax law is to protect domestic insurers in the state from excessive taxation by other states where they do business.

STATE VERSUS FEDERAL REGULATION

Critics of state regulation argue that the McCarran-Ferguson Act should be repealed and replaced by federal regulation. Certain advantages are claimed for federal regulation.

Advantages of Federal Regulation

The following arguments are offered in support of federal regulation of insurance:

- *Uniformity of laws.* Federal regulation can provide greater uniformity of laws. Under state regulation, insurers doing business in more than one state must observe different state laws. Under federal regulation, the laws would be uniform.
- *Greater efficiency.* It is argued that federal regulation would be more efficient. Insurers doing business nationally would deal with only one federal agency rather than with numerous insurance departments. Also, the federal agency would be less likely to yield to industry pressures, especially those reflecting the views of local insurers. Federal regulation would also be less expensive to administer.
- *More competent regulators.* Federal regulation would attract higher-quality personnel who would do a superior job of regulating the insurance industry. The higher salaries and prestige would attract more highly talented and skilled individuals.

Advantages of State Regulation

Supporters of state regulation also offer convincing arguments for continued regulation of insurance by the states. The major advantages claimed for state regulation are as follows:

- *Greater responsiveness to local needs.* Local needs vary widely and state regulators can respond more quickly to local needs. In contrast, under federal regula-

tion, "red tape" and government bureaucracy would result in considerable delay in solving problems at the local level.
- *Promotion of uniform laws by NAIC.* Uniformity of laws can be achieved by the model laws and proposals of the NAIC. Thus, there is reasonable uniformity of state laws in important areas at the present time.
- *Greater opportunity for innovation.* State regulation provides greater opportunities for innovation in regulation. An individual state can experiment, and if the innovation fails, only that state is affected. In contrast, poor federal legislation would affect all states.
- *Unknown consequences of federal regulation.* State regulation is already in existence, and its strengths and weaknesses are well known. In contrast, the consequences of federal regulation on consumers and the insurance industry are unknown.
- *Decentralization of political power.* State regulation results in a decentralization of political power. Federal regulation would result in further encroachment of the federal government on the economy and a corresponding dilution of states' rights.

Shortcomings of State Regulation

Congressional committees and the General Accounting Office (GAO) have assessed the effectiveness of state regulation of insurance and have found serious shortcomings, including the following:[9]

- *Inadequate protection against insolvency.* Because the insurance industry operates globally, existing state regulatory systems are considered dangerously inadequate for supervising the solvency of insurers, which depend substantially on offshore companies to pay claims. State governments do not have sufficient resources, legal powers, or determination to protect policyowners from mismanagement and fraud by some insurers here and abroad. In addition, some property and liability insurers have been licensed to do business when they were undercapitalized, and state insurance departments have not carefully checked the background or monitored the activities of persons running the companies.
- *Inadequate protection of consumers.* Critics argue that state insurance departments do not have systematic procedures for determining whether

Insight 28.1

Auto Insurance Complaints in New York State

The New York State Insurance Department makes available annual rankings of auto insurers doing business in New York. The 1998 rankings shown here are based on the complaint ratios of 51 insurance companies or groups of companies.

The *complaint ratio* represents the number of private passenger auto insurance complaints upheld against an insurer as a percentage of its average 1997–

1998 New York State private passenger auto insurance premiums. *The insurer with the lowest ratio is ranked first in the report; the insurer with the highest ratio is ranked last. The lower the ratio, the better is the insurer's performance.* Insurers with the lowest and highest ratios for 1998 are shown below. Data for 1996 and 1997 are shown for comparison purposes.

Lowest Complaint Ratios—Top 25 in 1998

Company or Group	1998 Complaint Ratio	1998 Ranking	1997 Ranking	1996 Ranking
Aegon USA Inc.[1]	0.00	1	26	37
Erie Insurance Exchange	0.00	2	—[2]	—[2]
GRE[3]	0.03	3	4	5
Amica Mutual	0.04	4	2	4
Allianz	0.04	5	19	6
Atlantic	0.05	6	10	18
Eagle	0.06	7	14	42
Tri-State Consumer	0.06	8	8	9
USAA	0.06	9	3	12
Chubb & Son	0.08	10	13	7
Berkshire-Hathaway (GEICO)	0.08	11	9	11
Utica National	0.10	12	42	25
Farm Family	0.10	13	7	36
NY Central Mutual Fire	0.10	14	17	22
Electric	0.11	15	21	29
Travelers	0.12	16	28	16
CNA	0.12	17	33	35
Metropolitan	0.13	18	11	13
Interboro Mutual Indemnity	0.13	19	40	49
Allmerica Financial[4]	0.13	20	6	20
Liberty Mutual	0.14	21	15	8
US Fidelity & Guaranty	0.14	22	16	17
Hartford F & C	0.14	23	27	19
AMEX Assurance	0.15	24	46	32
Progressive	0.15	25	32	31

1. Was Capital Holding Corporation Group in 1996 ranking.
2. Not ranked in that year due to low premium volume.
3. Was Netherlands Group in 1996 & 1997 ranking.
4. Was America Group in 1996 ranking.

Highest Complaint Ratios, 1998

Company or Group	1998 Complaint Ratio	1998 Ranking	1997 Ranking	1996 Ranking
Leucadia	0.57	51	50[1]	50[1]
Eveready	0.38	50	44	2
Zurich-American	0.34	49	38	45
General Electric	0.34	48	50[1]	49[1]
Reliance	0.30	47	—[2]	—[2]
American Financial	0.28	46	23	15
SAFECO	0.27	45	—[2]	—[2]
Lumbermans Mutual	0.25	44	22	30
Nationwide Group	0.24	43	31	21
Merchants Mutual	0.23	42	47	46

1. In 1996 and 1997, Leucadia and General Electric comprised one group.
2. Did not appear in that year's ranking.

Complaint Ratios—Ten Largest Auto Insurers

Company or Group	1998 Complaint Ratio	1998 Ranking	1997–1998 Average Premium (in millions)	Approximate Market Share
Allstate	0.17	30	$1,589.3	19.5%
State Farm	0.16	29	1,033.9	12.7
Berkshire-Hathaway (GEICO)	0.08	11	791.9	9.7
Travelers	0.12	16	491.0	6.0
Progressive	0.15	25	466.6	5.7
Nationwide	0.24	43	405.2	5.0
Liberty Mutual	0.14	21	320.4	3.9
CGU	0.18	32	289.8	3.6
New York Central Mutual	0.10	14	256.7	3.1
Metropolitan	0.13	18	151.7	1.9
Top Ten			$5,796.6	71.1%

SOURCE: Adapted from New York State Insurance Department, *1998 Annual Ranking of Automobile Insurance Complaints.*

consumers are being treated properly with respect to claim payments, rate setting, and protection from unfair discrimination.

- *Improvements needed in handling complaints.* Although many states prepare complaint ratios (ratio of complaints to premiums) for each company, few states publicize those ratios.
- *Inadequate market conduct examinations.* Market conduct examinations refer to insurance department examinations of consumer matters such as claims handling, underwriting, advertising, and other trade practices. Serious deficiencies have been found in many market conduct examination reports. The most serious defect is the lack of explicit standards in evaluating the market conduct of insurers.
- *Insurance availability.* Many states have not conducted current studies to determine whether property and liability insurance availability is a serious problem in their states.
- *Regulators overly responsive to insurance industry.* State insurance departments are overly responsive to the insurance industry at the expense of consumers. Insurance regulation is not characterized by an "arm's-length" relationship between regulators and the regulated. Many state insurance commissioners were previously employed in the insurance industry, and many return to the industry after leaving office.

Repeal of the McCarran-Ferguson Act

As noted earlier, the McCarran-Ferguson Act gives the states primary responsibility for regulation of the insurance industry and also provides limited exemption from federal antitrust laws. Because of the shortcomings of state regulation, there is considerable public and political support for repeal of the McCarran-Ferguson Act. Because of the trend toward deregulation and greater price competition, critics also argue that insurers should not be exempt from federal antitrust laws that prohibit price fixing, collusion, and other activities harmful to consumers.

Critics of state regulation present several arguments for repeal of the McCarran Act. They include the following:

- *The insurance industry no longer needs broad antitrust exemption.* Critics argue that the "state ac-

tion doctrine" has been fully developed and clarified by the Supreme Court. The state action doctrine defines certain activities required by state law that are exempt from federal antitrust activities. Because permissible actions of insurers have been clarified, exemption from the antitrust laws is no longer needed. In addition, it is argued that other industries are not exempt from antitrust laws, and the same should also be true for insurers.

- *Price collusion among insurers may create a problem of insurance affordability and availability.* Critics argue that collusive price fixing among insurers under the present system created the crisis in commercial liability insurance in the mid-1980s in which rates soared and availability of insurance was reduced.
- *Federal regulation is needed because of the defects in state regulation.* Critics argue that federal minimum standards are needed to ensure nondiscrimination in insurance pricing, full availability of essential property and liability coverages, and elimination of unfair and excessive rate differentials among insureds.

The insurance industry, however, has strongly opposed any legislation that would repeal the McCarran-Ferguson Act. The industry believes that substantial harm to both insurers and the public will result from repeal of the act. The following arguments are presented in support of the industry's position:

- *The insurance industry is already competitive.* More than 3300 property and liability insurers and more than 1500 life insurers now compete for business.
- *Small insurers would be harmed.* Smaller insurers would be unable to compete because they cannot develop accurate rates based on their limited loss and expense experience. Thus, smaller insurers may go out of business or be taken over by larger insurers. Hence a small number of large insurers will ultimately control the business, a result exactly opposite of that intended by repeal of the McCarran-Ferguson Act.
- *Insurers may be prevented from developing common coverage forms.* This problem could lead to costly gaps in coverage for insurance buyers and increased litigation between insurers and policyowners. Also, it would be difficult for insureds to

know what is covered and excluded if nonstandard forms are used.

- *Dual regulation may result from repeal of the McCarran-Ferguson Act.* However, the past record of federal regulation is poor. Federal regulators have done a poor job in regulating the savings and loan industry, which resulted in the insolvency of hundreds of thrifts with a cost to taxpayers of billions of dollars. Also, critics argue that federal regulation of railroads, airlines, and trucking has been destructive to competition. Federal regulation has also obstructed entry into an industry, entrenched the market power of large companies, and resulted in a cozy relationship between the regulators and the regulated.

Numerous federal proposals have been introduced during the past 20 years to repeal or modify the McCarran-Ferguson Act. In general, these proposals would prohibit certain activities of insurers, including price fixing, tying the sale of one product to another, attempting to monopolize, and dividing up territories with competitors.

CURRENT ISSUES IN INSURANCE REGULATION

Several timely issues are important in insurance regulation. They include the following:

- Convergence of financial services
- Increase in mergers and acquisitions
- Growth of the Internet and e-commerce
- Insolvency of insurers
- Quality of insurance regulation
- Deregulation of commercial lines

Convergence of Financial Services

One of the most important regulatory issues today is the convergence of financial services. *A single financial institution can now sell a wide variety of financial products and services that were sold earlier by separate financial institutions.* Financial institutions include commercial banks, savings and loan institutions, insurance companies, stock brokerage firms, investment companies, real estate firms, and other financial institutions. In the past, because of legal and regulatory restrictions, the activities of financial in-

stitutions were limited to specific areas. For example, commercial banks provided banking services and generally did not sell insurance. In contrast, insurance companies sold insurance products and generally did not engage in banking. Investment firms sold investment products and generally did not engage in banking or insurance activities.

Because of court decisions, changes in banking laws and regulatory decisions, and new federal legislation, the distinction between banking, insurance, and investments has largely disappeared. Financial institutions can now provide banking services; sell life insurance, auto, homeowners, and other insurance contracts; offer annuities and other investments; and make real estate loans.

In particular, because of favorable court decisions, commercial banks are deeply entrenched in the insurance business and have become major competitors to traditional insurers. Commercial banks now sell term life insurance, universal life insurance, auto and homeowners insurance, long-term care insurance, disability insurance, group health insurance, annuities, and other investments. Likewise, several large insurers have acquired commercial banks or have announced plans to do so.

Financial Modernization Act of 1999 In 1999, Congress enacted legislation that eliminated provisions in the Glass-Steagall Act that prevented banks, insurers, and investment firms from making full entry into one another's markets. New legislation was considered necessary to allow financial institutions in the United States greater freedom to compete domestically and internationally in the financial markets and to provide better service to consumers. Insurers can now buy banks; banks can underwrite insurance and securities; and a company that wants to provide banking, insurance, and investment services through a single entity can form a new holding company for that purpose. As a result, the traditional lines that once separated types of financial institutions are disappearing (see Insight 28.2).

Impact on State Insurance Regulation The new legislation provides for several areas of regulation. State insurance departments will regulate the insurance industry and insurance activities of other financial institutions. State and federal banking agencies will regulate banks and thrifts. The Securities and

Insight 28.2

Boundaries Blurring for Financial Services

Some day soon, you might buy fire insurance for your boat, take $80 out of an ATM, and invest your retirement nest egg in the Sure Thing Mutual Fund, all from the same company.

It's called one-stop financial shopping, and it's the result of a new federal law that promises to change the way people handle their finances.

But you say that's already happening? Well, yes and no.

Financial services—banking, insurance, and investment brokerages—have been edging closer and closer together over the past decade. Through one loophole or another, many banks could offer insurance products, insurers could affiliate with banks, and brokerages could join up with either one or both.

But the 1933 Glass-Steagall Act was still a roadblock, with government regulators trying hard to keep banks out of general commerce as a way to prevent intense financial concentration, which many people blamed for the Great Depression.

And government regulation of the various financial businesses was still handled by a widely separated set of powerful agencies—U.S. Securities and Exchange Commission, the U.S. Comptroller of the Currency, and 50 state insurance departments, especially.

Then a series of court decisions and actions by the Comptroller's office in recent years brought the issue to a head: unless Congress did something to make its intent clear, the regulators and the industry would simply battle it out on their own.

So in November [1999], ending more than 20 years of debate, Congress passed the Financial Services Modernization Act, setting up a system that makes it easier for the financial companies to venture into each others' realms and, at the same time, clarifying who will be in charge of each segment.

As a result, said Judith Owen, president of Norwest Bank Nebraska, a part of Wells Fargo & Co., consumer-influencing changes are on the way.

"There certainly will be some benefits in the future," Owen said. "We're excited about the opportunity."

Large financial companies are the most likely to take advantage of the new law first. *A scenario might work like this:*

XYZ Bancorp acquires ABC Life Insurance Co. and MNOP Investment Services, uniting them under the new A2Z Financial Services Holding Co. (The bank does the acquiring because it has the most capital.)

While the three divisions operate separately, customers of all three companies begin hearing more about products that the others offer. That's called cross-selling, with the idea of creating two, three, or more product relationships with each customer—say, checking account, a life insurance policy, a brokerage account, and an estate plan.

Take Omaha's First National of Nebraska Inc., parent of First National Bank of Omaha.

J. William Henry, executive vice president, said the bank has 27 executives in a division called Investment One, which it started nearly three years ago in Nebraska, Colorado, Kansas, and South Dakota. The 27 act as agents for an investment company that actually carries out the investment transactions.

Now, under the Financial Services Modernization Act, First National could open its own brokerage or acquire one, but Henry said the company has no such plans yet. Nor has the company decided whether to form a financial services holding company and offer broader products.

But already, First National is testing an annuity product in North Platte, Nebraska. Sold at the bank and "wrapped" as a First National product, the annuities are actually issued by a separate insurance company. The bank does not take the insurance risk.

Insurers, too, are evaluating the new law. Mutual of Omaha has a team of executives examining its potential impact, spokesman Jim Nolan said.

The company's mutual structure—it is owned by its policyholders, rather than by stockholders—would make it difficult if not impossible to become part of a financial services holding company with broader financial powers, Nolan said. But there's no proposal in the works to change that structure, he said.

"We're glad Congress passed the law," Nolan said. "It should give consumers more flexibility in the financial arena. But our goal is not to rush into any changes, to make sure that what we do fits with our business strategy and our long-term goals."

Provisions of the Financial Modernization Act

Major provisions of the Financial Modernization Act of 1999

- **Privacy of financial information**

  Stung by recent incidents of people's financial information apparently being shared with outside marketing companies, Congress ordered banks and other financial companies to tell people their privacy policies and let customers choose to not let their information be shared. Information could still be exchanged between divisions of the same financial services holding company, within limits.

- **Financial services holding companies**

  Companies that want to combine banking, insurance, and brokerage services under one company can form new holding companies for that purpose. Affiliates can work together, within some limits, to cross-market products to customers.

- **Mergers and acquisitions**

  The new structure and powers are likely to result in even more mergers in the financial industry, mostly likely with big banks acquiring insurers and brokerages. But the law bars companies outside the financial industry from merging with them.

- **Regulations**

  The law basically preserves the status quo—banks supervised mostly by the U.S. Comptroller of the Currency and other federal agencies, brokers by the Securities and Exchange Commission and insurers by state insurance departments, at least initially. The regulatory power could shift with time, however, at the direction of Congress.

- **New financial products**

  Some new financial services companies will develop hybrid products that will give some consumers new choices for investing their money. Some may combine properties of insurance, investments, and banking, possibly customized to fit each consumer's needs.

- **Federal Home Loan Bank**

  To balance the benefits that big financial companies expect from the new law, Congress changed the rules for the Federal Home Loan Bank system to benefit small banks by providing them a new source of capital for lending.

- **Mutual insurance holding companies**

  Mutual insurance holding companies, which are owned by their policyholders, will now be able to convert to a new structure that provides more financial flexibility by allowing the sale of stock and other pathways to increased capital for growth.

SOURCE: Adapted from Steve Jordon, "Boundaries Blurring for Financial Services," *Sunday World-Herald*, January 2, 2000, p. 6-R.

Exchange Commission will regulate the sale of securities. The Federal Reserve will have umbrella authority over bank affiliates that engage in risky activities such as underwriting insurance and developing real estate.

The new law will have a substantial impact on state insurance regulation.[10] Possible effects include the following: (1) competition between insurers and banks and other financial institutions may increase; (2) state insurance departments will regulate the sale of insurance by noninsurance companies, such as banks, that are not subject to the full scope of their authority in certain areas such as financial solvency; (3) mergers and acquisitions between insurers and other financial institutions will continue; (4) small insurers are more likely to be absorbed by large insurers; (5) state insurance departments will be pressured to maintain a level playing field so that no financial institution will be disadvantaged in the sale of insurance; (6) some financial institutions may attempt to tie the sale of other financial products to the sale of insurance, which could harm consumers; and

(7) considerable coordination and cooperation between the different regulators of financial institutions will be required.

The ability of state insurance departments to regulate effectively may be severely tested, especially for departments with limited budgets. Conflicts between state insurance commissioners and federal banking regulators are also likely to occur.

Increase in Mergers and Acquisitions

In Chapter 25, we noted that mergers and acquisitions in the insurance industry have increased, especially among life insurers (see Exhibit 28.1). Also, numerous mutual insurers have demutualized, formed mutual holding companies, or announced plans to do so. This trend is likely to continue.

The increase in mergers and acquisitions has both advantages and disadvantages for regulatory officials. On the positive side, regulators will be responsible for regulating a smaller group of larger and

EXHIBIT 28.1
Total Insurance-Related Reported Mergers and Acquisitions, 1989–1998

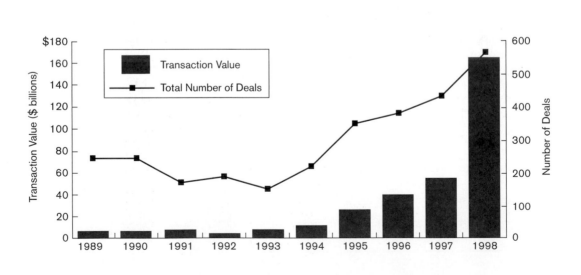

NOTE: The data include property/casualty, life, health/managed care, service, and distribution companies.
SOURCE: *The I.I.I. Fact Book 2000* (New York, NY: Insurance Information Institute), p. 1.4.

more sophisticated insurers, which should require less oversight and supervision.[11] Also, financially weaker insurers are more likely to be absorbed by stronger insurers, which should improve the regulatory environment.

On the negative side, mergers and acquisitions may result in highly leveraged insurers with complex financial structures; thus, the risk of insolvency will still be present.[12]

Also, regulators will have the additional burden of protecting existing policyowners if a mutual company demutualizes or forms a mutual holding company because of a possible conflict of interest between the policyowners and stockholders. For example, top-level management may receive company stock or stock options, which could reduce the company's operating profits. As a result, dividends to policyowners could decrease.

Finally, in the health insurance field, mergers and acquisitions may give health maintenance organizations (HMOs) too much power and leverage in dealing with patients and physicians. For example,

the American Medical Association (AMA) expressed some concern over the recent merger between Aetna, Inc., and Prudential Health Care, which allowed Aetna to become the nation's largest HMO.

Growth of the Internet and E-Commerce

Another timely issue centers on the rapid growth of the Internet and electronic commerce (e-commerce). Insurers increasingly are establishing Web sites to sell insurance. These sites provide consumers with information and premium quotes on a wide variety of insurance and investment products, including annuities and mutual funds; life insurance; auto and homeowners insurance; long-term care insurance; and other individual health insurance plans. In particular, sales of term insurance on the Internet are expected to grow rapidly in the future (see Exhibit 28.2).

The rapid growth of the Internet has created several problems for regulators. First, opportunities for

EXHIBIT 28.2
Forecast of Internet Individual Life Insurance Sales

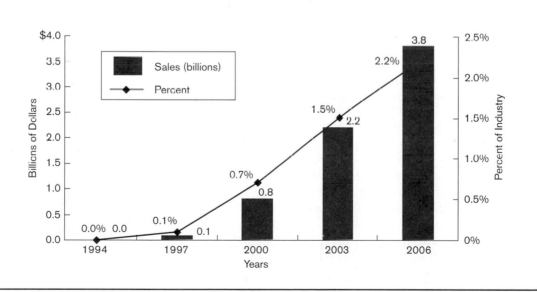

SOURCE: Robert W. Klein, *A Regulator's Introduction to the Insurance Industry* (Kansas City, MO: NAIC Education and Research Foundation, 1999), Figure 12.3, p. 12-12. Reprinted with permission.

unethical insurers to engage in deceptive sales practices have increased. In the sixth edition of this book, we noted that the life insurance industry was being rocked by scandals related to deceptive sales practices, including misrepresentation, churning of policies, and lies and fraud by agents. Since then, rapid growth of the Internet has provided even more opportunities for unethical insurers to engage in deceptive sales practices. In addition, some information provided to insurance consumers on the Internet can be technically incorrect. As a result, insurance consumers can be misled. State insurance departments with limited financial resources will find it more difficult to monitor the vast amount of insurance information available on the Internet.

Second, state regulation of insurance becomes less meaningful when the global nature of the insurance industry is considered. Major insurers operate worldwide—not only at the state level. As a result, regulators may find it more difficult to regulate the market conduct of alien insurers. As noted earlier, an alien insurer is a company domiciled in a foreign country. For example, the Nebraska Department of Insurance may find it difficult to regulate the market conduct of an insurer domiciled in the United Kingdom if a Nebraska resident purchases the insurance on the Internet.

Finally, new computer technology enables insurers to gather important information about consumers and to maintain extensive records. This information can include income, occupation, credit history, claim records, and detailed information from applicants for life and health insurance. It is used for purposes of marketing, underwriting, and pricing. Some regulators believe that consumers can be adversely affected by the dissemination of the new information.[13] For example, some applicants for auto insurance may pay higher premiums because they have poor credit histories. Regulators will have the problem of regulating the use of new databases by insurers in a manner that is fair to consumers.

Insolvency of Insurers

Insolvency of insurers remains an important regulatory problem. Between 1991 and 1998, 305 insurers were liquidated (see Exhibit 28.3). During this same period, there were 344 conservations and rehabilitations (see Exhibit 28.4). However, in recent years, the number of liquidations, conservations, and rehabilitations has declined.

Reasons for Insolvencies Insurers fail for several reasons. Major causes of failure include charging of inadequate rates, rapid growth and inadequate surplus, problems with affiliates, overstatement of assets, alleged fraud, failure of reinsurers to pay claims, mismanagement, and catastrophe losses.

When an insurer becomes insolvent or financially impaired, state regulators must take appropriate action. With proper management, the insurer may be rehabilitated. If rehabilitation is not feasible, the insurer may be involuntarily liquidated. Other possible regulatory actions include license revocation, cease-and-desist orders, and other actions that restrict an insurer's freedom to do business.

What happens to your policy or unpaid claim if your insurer becomes insolvent? Your policy may be sold to another insurer, and an unpaid claim may be paid by the state's guaranty fund. However, failure of a large insurer may result in delay of several years before all claims are paid.

Methods of Ensuring Solvency The principal methods of ensuring solvency are the following:

- *Financial requirements.* Insurers must meet certain financial requirements that vary among the states, such as minimum capital and surplus requirements, restrictions on investments, and valuation of loss reserves.
- *Risk-based capital standards.* As we noted earlier, life and health insurers must meet the risk-based capital standards based on a model law developed by the NAIC. The increased capital requirements help to prevent insolvency.
- *Annual financial statements.* Certain annual financial statements must be submitted to state insurance departments in a prescribed manner to provide information on premiums written, expenses, losses, investments, and other information. The financial statements are then reviewed by regulatory officials.
- *Field examinations.* State laws require that insurers must be examined every three to five years. The NAIC coordinates the examination of insurers that do business in several states.

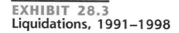

EXHIBIT 28.3
Liquidations, 1991–1998

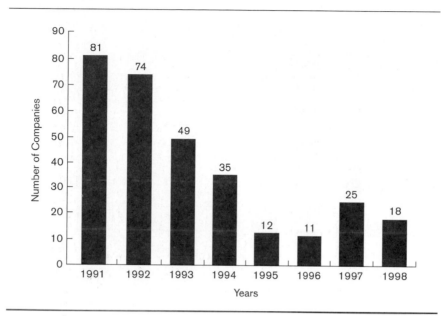

SOURCE: National Association of Insurance Commissioners, 1999. Reprinted with permission.

- *Early warning system.* The NAIC administers an early warning system called the Insurance Regulatory Information System (IRIS). Financial ratios and other reports are developed based on information in the annual statement (see Exhibit 28.5). Based on a review of this information, insurers may be designated for immediate review or targeted for regulatory attention. The system, however, is not perfect. The financial ratios may not identify all troubled insurers. The system also has identified an increasing number of insurers, some of which do not require immediate regulatory attention.

In addition, the NAIC employs a solvency screening system called FAST (Financial Analysis Solvency Tracking) that prioritizes insurers for additional analysis. Different point values are assigned for the various ranges of financial ratio results. The points are then summed to determine a FAST score for each insurer. Based on their FAST scores, certain insurers are considered priority insurers for regulatory action. Exhibit 28.6 shows the different financial ratios for determining FAST scores.

Quality of Insurance Regulation

Improving the quality of insurance regulation remains an important issue. As noted earlier, studies by Congressional committees and the U.S. General Accounting Office have pointed out numerous defects in state insurance regulation. More recently, consumer groups have criticized state insurance departments on the grounds that they provide inadequate insurance information to consumers.

The Consumer Federation of America has graded 51 jurisdictions on the types and usefulness of insurance information available to consumers, such as premium data, shopping guides, complaint data, and information on the major types of insurance consumers buy. The majority of jurisdictions received grades of "C" or higher (see Insight 28.3) However, seven jurisdictions received below-average grades of "D+" to "D–." Five jurisdictions received

EXHIBIT 28.4
Conservations/Rehabilitations, 1991–1998

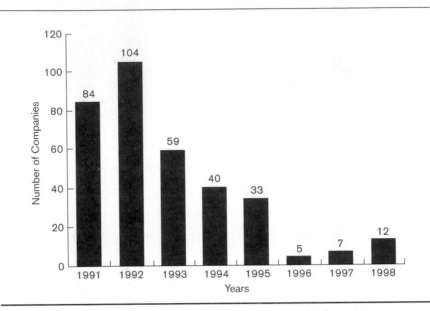

SOURCE: National Association of Insurance Commissioners, 1999. Reprinted with permission.

grades of "F." Seven jurisdictions received an incomplete (I) because they did not respond to requests for material. The NAIC blasted the study as flawed and incomplete because it presented a distorted picture of consumer activities and capabilities of state insurance departments.[14] Nevertheless, it is clear that the negative perceptions of state insurance departments by consumer groups are not likely to go away soon.

Improving the Efficiency of State Regulation

State insurance regulators and the NAIC have identified several areas that require reexamination and review to promote greater competition and to protect consumers. Areas under review include company admission and licensing requirements, rate and form review, special deposit requirements, countersignature requirements, and regulation of commercial lines.[15] In addition, some states have streamlined their insurance regulations by removing obsolete and unnecessary regulations.

Accreditation Program of NAIC To upgrade the quality of state regulation, the NAIC has also enacted certain financial regulation standards. States meeting

those standards are accredited by the NAIC. At the time of this writing, the vast majority of states have been accredited.

Deregulation of Commercial Lines

Another timely issue is the deregulation of commercial lines for large commercial accounts. At the time of this writing, at least eight states have passed legislation that exempts insurers from filing rates and forms for large commercial accounts with the state insurance department for approval.[16] Other states are considering similar legislation. In most states, the legislation applies to commercial auto, general liability, and commercial multiperil lines. Most states exclude workers compensation.

Deregulation of commercial lines is highly controversial. Large commercial accounts and risk managers generally support such legislation. Surplus lines insurers and agents' association are generally opposed.

Arguments for Deregulation of Commercial Lines Arguments for deregulation include the following:[17]

EXHIBIT 28.5
IRIS Ratios

Property/Liability		Unusual value equal to/or*	
		Over	Under
1.	Gross premium to surplus	900	–
1A.	Net premium to surplus	300	–
2.	Change in net writings	33	–33
3.	Surplus aid to surplus	15	–
4.	Two-year overall operating ratio	100	–
5.	Investment yield	10	4.5
6.	Change in surplus	50	–10
7.	Liabilities to liquid assets	105	–
8.	Agents' balances to surplus	40	–
9.	One-year reserve development to surplus	20	–
10.	Two-year reserve development to surplus	20	–
11.	Estimated current reserve deficiency to surplus	25	–
Life/Health		Range	
1.	Net change in capital and surplus	50	–10
1A.	Gross change in capital and surplus	50	–10
2.	Net income to total income (including realized capital gains and losses)	–	0
3.	Commissions and expenses to premiums and deposits (discontinued)		
4.	Adequacy of investment income	900	125
5.	Nonadmitted to admitted assets	10	–
6.	Total real estate and total mortgage loans to cash and invested assets	30	–
7.	Total affiliated investments to capital and surplus	100	–
8.	Surplus relief		
	(More than $5 million capital and surplus)	30	–99
	($5 million or less capital and surplus)	10	–10
9.	Change in premium	50	–10
10.	Change in product mix	5	–
11.	Change in asset mix	5	–
12.	Change in reserving ratio	20	–20

*Values defining the normal value range for each ratio are expressed as a percentage.
SOURCE: Robert W. Klein, *A Regulator's Introduction to the Insurance Industry* (Kansas City, MO: NAIC Education and Research Foundation, 1999), pp. 10–14. Reprinted with permission.

- *Insurers can customize and design innovative products to meet the insurance needs of large corporations in a timely fashion.* Insurers can design specific products that large commercial buyers need, and rate and form filings would not require approval. Large corporations are sophisticated enough to negotiate price and to understand the assumptions underlying the coverages requested.

EXHIBIT 28.6
FAST Ratios

Property/Casualty

1. Investment yield
2. Change in combined ratio
3. Gross expenses and commissions to gross premiums
4. Change in gross expenses and commissions
5. Gross premiums to surplus
6. Net premiums to surplus
7. Change in gross premiums written
8. Change in net premiums written
9. Surplus aid to surplus
10. Reinsurance recoverable on paid losses to surplus
11. Reinsurance recoverable on unpaid losses to surplus
12. Reserves to surplus
13. Two-year reserve development to surplus
14. Affiliated investments to surplus
15. Affiliated receivables to surplus
16. Miscellaneous recoverables to surplus
17. Noninvestment grade bond exposure
18. Other invested assets to surplus
19. Change in liquid assets
20. Change in agents balances
21. Cash flow from operations
22. Change in policyholders surplus

Life

1. Change in capital and surplus
2. Surplus relief
3. Change in net premiums and annuity cons. and deposit-type funds
4. A&H bus. to net premiums and annuity cons. and deposit type funds
5. Change in dir. and ass. annuities and deposit type funds
6. Change in net income
7. Trend of net income
8. Surrenders to premiums and deposit type funds
9. Grp. surr. to grp. premiums and grp. dept. type funds
10. Change in liquid assets
11. Affiliated investments to capital and surplus
12. Non inv. gr. bonds and st. inv. to capital and surplus and AVR
13. Collateralized mortgage obligations to capital and surplus and AVR
14. Problem real estate and mortgages to capital and surplus and AVR
15. Sch. BA assets to capital and surplus and AVR
16. Total real estate and mortgages to capital and surplus and AVR

Health

1. Change in capital and surplus
2. Surplus relief
3. Gross A&H premiums to capital and surplus
4. Net A&H premiums to capital and surplus
5. Gross A&H res. to capital and surplus
6. A&H reserve deficiency
7. Change in net prems. and annuity cons. and deposit type funds
8. Stockholders divs. to prior-year capital and surplus
9. Change in net income
10. Trending of net income
11. Comm. and incurred exp. to prem. and ann. dep.
12. Change in liquid assets
13. A&H reserves/liquid assets
14. Affiliated investments to capital and surplus
15. Sch. BA assets to capital and surplus and AVR
16. Total R.E. and mortgages to capital and surplus and AVR

SOURCE: Robert W. Klein, *A Regulator's Introduction to the Insurance Industry* (Kansas City, MO: NAIC Education and Research Foundation, 1999), p. 10-17. Reprinted with permission.

Insight 28.3

Insurance Department Report Card

The Consumer Federation of America (CFA) has released a study grading each state's insurance department on the basis of informational brochures that each department has available. After reviewing the materials, the CFA awarded each department a letter grade.

State	Grade	State	Grade
Alabama	I	Montana	C–
Alaska	B+	Nebraska	C+
Arizona	C+	Nevada	B+
Arkansas	I	New Hampshire	I
California	B+	New Jersey	D–
Colorado	A	New Mexico	D
Connecticut	B–	New York	B
Delaware	C+	North Carolina	D+
District of Columbia	I	North Dakota	D+
Florida	A	Ohio	A–
Georgia	F	Oklahoma	C–
Hawaii	C	Oregon	B–
Idaho	F	Pennsylvania	B–
Illinois	B+	Rhode Island	F
Indiana	C+	South Carolina	B–
Iowa	B–	South Dakota	F
Kansas	A	Tennessee	F
Kentucky	C+	Texas	A+
Louisiana	C	Utah	C
Maine	B	Vermont	C–
Maryland	I	Virginia	B
Massachusetts	D	Washington	C+
Michigan	I	West Virginia	D+
Minnesota	I	Wisconsin	A+
Mississippi	D+	Wyoming	C
Missouri	A		

Source: Excerpted from *Insurance Department Report Card*, Consumer Federation of America, March 24, 1999.

- *Insurers would save money because rates and forms would not have to be filed for a commercial account with offices in several states.* Under current regulation, an insurer may not be able to write the coverage because rates and forms must be approved in each state in which the corporation does business.
- *Risk managers can get the specific coverages needed more quickly.* Risk managers in different industries often face problems because of the time required to get approval of the rates and forms in several states. Deregulation would avoid this problem.

Arguments Against Deregulation of Commercial Lines
Arguments against deregulation include the following:

- *Surplus lines carriers would be at a competitive disadvantage.* Surplus lines carriers are companies not licensed to do business in the state. They insure risks that are difficult to insure in the normal (admitted) markets, charging substantially higher rates for the coverage provided. However, before such risks can be insured, the surplus lines carrier generally must show that coverage is not available in the normal or admitted markets—for example, by showing that three admitted insurers have declined coverage. Under deregulation, admitted commercial insurers would not have to meet this requirement. Also, because admitted insurers do not have to file rates for large commercial accounts, surplus lines carriers would find it more difficult to charge a correct rate.

- *There is disagreement concerning the size of commercial accounts for which rate and form filings would not be required.* Many agents believe deregulation should not apply to smaller commercial accounts. Insurance purchase decisions for smaller firms may be made by unsophisticated buyers who are motivated primarily by price and do not understand any limitations on coverage. Agents also believe that, under deregulation, insurers will draft different policy forms, which will present problems for smaller firms that may not have the expertise to understand the technical language in the policy.

- *Consumer advocates believe that deregulation for commercial lines could result in pressure by insurers to subsequently deregulate personal lines.* Consumers who buy auto and homeowners insurance generally do not read and understand the coverages and laws. As a result, they could be financially hurt by deregulation.

SUMMARY

- The insurance industry is regulated for several reasons:
    - To maintain insurer solvency
    - To compensate for inadequate consumer knowledge
    - To insure reasonable rates
    - To make insurance available

- The insurance industry is regulated by the states. The McCarran-Ferguson Act states that continued regulation and taxation of the insurance industry by the states are in the public interest.

- Three principal methods are used to regulate the insurance industry:
    - Legislation
    - Courts
    - State insurance departments

- The principal areas that are regulated include the following:
    - Formation and licensing of insurers
    - Financial regulation
    - Rate regulation
    - Policy forms
    - Sales practices and consumer protection

- The states have rating laws that require rates to be adequate, reasonable (not excessive), and not unfairly discriminatory. The principal types of rating laws are as follows:
    - Prior-approval laws
    - File-and-use laws
    - Open-competition laws
    - Flex-rating laws

- Insurers must pay a state premium tax on gross premiums. The primary purpose is to raise revenues for the state, not to provide funds for insurance regulation.

- State versus federal regulation is an issue that has evoked considerable debate. The alleged advantages of federal regulation include the following:
    - Uniformity of laws
    - Greater efficiency
    - More competent regulation

- The advantages of state regulation include the following:
    - Greater responsiveness to local needs
    - Promotion of uniform laws by the NAIC
    - Greater opportunity for innovation
    - Unknown consequences of federal regulation
    - Decentralization of political power

- Critics argue that state regulation of insurance has serious shortcomings, including the following:
    - Inadequate regulation
    - Inadequate protection of consumers
    - Defects in financial regulation
    - Improvements needed in handling complaints
    - Inadequate market conduct examinations

Insurance availability studies conducted only in a minority of states

Regulators overly responsive to the insurance industry

- Several current issues in insurance regulation include the following:

    Convergence of financial services

    Increase in mergers and consolidations

    Growth of the Internet and e-commerce

    Insolvency of insurers

    Quality of insurance regulation

    Deregulation of commercial lines

KEY CONCEPTS AND TERMS

Admitted assets	Open-competition laws
Alien insurer	*Paul v. Virginia*
Assessment method	Policyowners' surplus
Domestic insurer	Prior-approval law
File-and-use law	Rebating
Flex-rating law	Reserves
Foreign insurer	Retaliatory tax laws
Guaranty funds	Risk-based capital
Kenney rule	South-Eastern Underwriters
McCarran-Ferguson Act	Association
National Association of	Twisting
Insurance Commissioners	Use-and-file law
(NAIC)	

REVIEW QUESTIONS

1. Explain the reasons why insurance companies are regulated.

2. Describe briefly the historical development of insurance regulation by the states. Point out some important legal decisions in your answer.

3. What methods are used to regulate insurance companies?

4. Identify the areas of insurance company operations that are regulated by the states.

5. Explain the different types of rating laws.

6. Explain the principal arguments for federal regulation of the insurance industry. What are the major arguments in support of state regulation?

7. Explain the major arguments for and against repeal of the McCarran-Ferguson Act.

8. Identify the major techniques that regulators use to ensure insurance company solvency.

9. Describe the risk-based capital standards that insurers must meet.

10. Briefly explain some current issues in insurance regulation.

APPLICATION QUESTIONS

1. Certain legal cases are significant in insurance regulation. Explain the legal significance of each of the following U.S. Supreme Court decisions and legislative acts with respect to regulation of the insurance industry by the states:
   a. *Paul v. Virginia*
   b. South-Eastern Underwriters Association case
   c. McCarran-Ferguson Act

2. State rating laws vary. Some states have file-and-use laws, while others have prior-approval laws and open-competition laws. Explain how a file-and-use law differs from the following:
   a. prior-approval law
   b. open-competition law

3. a. One important goal of insurance regulation is to maintain the solvency of insurers. Describe the specific financial areas of operations that are regulated by the states.
   b. Describe some specific areas of regulation or activities of state insurance departments that aim directly at protecting the consumer.
   c. Explain the major reasons for the insolvency of insurers.

4. The insurance industry contends that smaller insurers may become insolvent or may be merged with larger companies if the McCarran-Ferguson Act is repealed.
   a. Do you agree or disagree with this statement? Explain your answer.
   b. Some observers maintain that the development of common coverage forms and standard forms will be accelerated if the McCarran-Ferguson Act is repealed. Do you agree or disagree with the statement? Explain your answer.

SELECTED REFERENCES

"After the Sale, Special Report Excerpt: Mergers & Acquisitions, The Myth & the Reality," *Best's Review*, Life/Health Edition (February 1999), pp. 31–34.

Brady, Justin L., et al. *The Regulation of Insurance*, first edition. Malvern, PA: Insurance Institute of America, 1995.

Ettlinger, Kathleen Heald, et al. *State Insurance Regulation*, first edition. Malvern, PA: Insurance Institute of America, 1995.

Hamilton, Karen L. *The Changing Nature of Insurance Regulation*, second edition. Malvern, PA: Insurance Institute of America, 1996.

Klein, Robert W. *A Regulator's Introduction to the Insurance Industry*. Kansas City, MO: NAIC Education and Research Foundation, 1999.

Tate, Christine. "Spelling Out Reform," *Best's Review*, Life/Health Edition (May 1999), pp. 53–57.

Whitney, Sally. "Commercial Lines Unshackled," *Best's Review*, Property/Casualty Edition (May 1999), pp. 28–34.

NOTES

1. 8 Wall 168, 183 (1869).

2. 322 U.S. 533 (1944).

3. See Roger Kenney, *Fundamentals of Fire and Casualty Insurance Strength*, 4th ed. (Dedham, MA: Kenney Insurance Studies, 1967).

4. Robert W. Klein, *A Regulator's Introduction to the Insurance Industry* (Kansas City, MO: NAIC Education and Research Foundation, 1999), Box 10.1, p. 10-5.

5. *Ibid*. Table 10.1, p. 10-5.

6. S. S. Huebner, Kenneth Black, Jr., and Bernard L. Webb, *Property and Liability Insurance*, fourth edition (Upper Saddle River, NJ: Prentice-Hall), pp. 653–654.

7. There are exceptions. Maximum credit life insurance rates are regulated by the states.

8. William C. Scheel and Jack VanDerhei, "Replacement of Life Insurance: Its Regulation and Current Activity," *Journal of Risk and Insurance*, Vol. 45, No. 2 (June 1978).

9. See U.S. Congress, House, and Subcommittee on Oversight and Investigations of the Committee on Energy and Commerce, *Wishful Thinking, A World View of Insurance Solvency Regulation* (Washington, DC: U.S. Government Printing Office, 1994), and *Failed Promises: Insurance Company Insolvencies* (Washington, DC: U.S. Government Printing Office,

Case Application

Ashley is an actuary who is employed by the Nebraska Department of Insurance. Her duties include monitoring the financial position of insurance companies doing business in Nebraska. Based on an analysis of annual financial statements that insurers are required to submit, she discovered that Mutual Insurance has a risk-based capital ratio of 175 percent. Based on this information, answer the following questions.

a. What is the purpose of requiring insurers to meet risk-based capital requirements?

b. What regulatory action, if any, should the Nebraska Department of Insurance take with respect to Mutual Insurance?

c. Would your answer to part (b) change if the risk-based capital ratio for Mutual Insurance fell to 65 percent? Explain your answer.

d. Mutual Insurance has 25 percent of its assets invested in common stocks. Assume the stocks are sold, and the proceeds are invested in U.S. government bonds. What effect, if any, will this investment change have on the risk-based capital ratio of Mutual Insurance? Explain your answer.

1990). See also United States General Accounting Office, *Health Insurance Regulation, Wide Variation in States' Authority, Oversight, and Resources* (Washington, DC: United States General Accounting Office, 1993); and Comptroller General of the United States, *Issues and Needed Improvements in State Regulation of the Insurance Business (Executive Summary)* (Washington, DC: United States General Accounting Office, 1979).

10. Klein, *A Regulator's Introduction to the Insurance Industry*, p. 12-5.

11. *Ibid.*, p. 12-3.

12. *Ibid.*

13. *Ibid.*, p 12-10.

14. Steven Brostoff, "Consumer Group Grades Insurance Departments," *National Underwriter*, Property & Casualty/Risk and Benefits Management Edition, March 15, 1999, p. 8.

15. Klein, p. 12-13.

16. Arkansas, Colorado, Indiana, Kansas, Louisiana, Maine, Oklahoma, and Rhode Island.

17. This section is based on Sally Whitney, "Commercial Lines Unshackled," *Best's Review*, Property/Casualty Edition (May 1999), pp. 28–34; and Alex Maurice, "Dereg Effort Faces Agent Fight," *National Underwriter*, Property & Casualty/Risk & Benefits Management Edition, July 19, 1999, pp. 2, 22–24.

Homeowners 3 (Special Form)

Homeowners Policy Declarations

POLICYHOLDER: David M. and Joan G. Smith   **POLICY NUMBER:**   296 H 578661
(Named Insured)   216 Brookside Drive
                          Anytown, USA 40000

POLICY PERIOD: **Inception:**   March 30, 2000   Policy period begins 12:01 A.M. standard time
                      Expiration: March 30, 2001   at the residence premises.

FIRST MORTGAGEE AND MAILING ADDRESS:

Federal National Mortgage Assn.
C/O Mortgagee, Inc.
P.O. Box 5000
Businesstown, USA 55000

We will provide the insurance described in this policy in return for the premium and compliance with all applicable
policy provisions.

SECTION I COVERAGES	LIMIT	
A—Dwelling	$ 120,000	**SECTION I DEDUCTIBLE:** $ 250
B—Other Structures	$ 12,000	(In case of loss under Section I, we cover
C—Personal Property	$ 60,000	only that part of the loss over the
D—Loss of Use	$ 36,000	deductible amount shown above.)

SECTION II COVERAGES	LIMIT	
E—Personal Liability	$ 300,000	Each Occurrence
F—Medical Payments to Others	$ 1,000	Each Person

CONSTRUCTION: Masonry Veneer   **NO. FAMILIES:** One   **TYPE ROOF:** Approved

YEAR BUILT: 1970   **PROTECTION CLASS:** 7   **FIRE DISTRICT:** Cook Township

NOT MORE THAN 1000 FEET FROM HYDRANT

NOT MORE THAN 5 MILES FROM FIRE DEPT.

FORMS AND ENDORSEMENTS IN POLICY: HO 00 03, HO 04 61

POLICY PREMIUM: $ 350.00   **COUNTERSIGNATURE DATE:** March 1, 2000   **AGENT:** A.M. Abel

HOMEOWNERS 3 – SPECIAL FORM

AGREEMENT

We will provide the insurance described in this policy in return for the premium and compliance with all applicable provisions of this policy.

DEFINITIONS

A. In this policy, "you" and "your" refer to the "named insured" shown in the Declarations and the spouse if a resident of the same household. "We", "us" and "our" refer to the Company providing this insurance.

B. In addition, certain words and phrases are defined as follows:

1. "Aircraft Liability", "Hovercraft Liability", "Motor Vehicle Liability" and "Watercraft Liability", subject to the provisions in **b.** below, mean the following:

   a. Liability for "bodily injury" or "property damage" arising out of the:

      (1) Ownership of such vehicle or craft by an "insured";

      (2) Maintenance, occupancy, operation, use, loading or unloading of such vehicle or craft by any person;

      (3) Entrustment of such vehicle or craft by an "insured" to any person;

      (4) Failure to supervise or negligent supervision of any person involving such vehicle or craft by an "insured"; and

      (5) Vicarious liability, whether or not imposed by law, for the actions of a child or minor involving such vehicle or craft.

   b. For the purpose of this definition:

      (1) Aircraft means any contrivance used or designed for flight except model or hobby aircraft not used or designed to carry people or cargo;

      (2) Hovercraft means a self-propelled motorized ground effect vehicle and includes, but is not limited to, flarecraft and air cushion vehicles; and

      (3) Watercraft means a craft principally designed to be propelled on or in water by wind, engine power or electric motor.

      (4) Motor vehicle means a "motor vehicle" as defined in **7.** below.

2. "Bodily injury" means bodily harm, sickness or disease, including required care, loss of services and death that results.

3. "Business" means:

   a. A trade, profession or occupation engaged in on a full-time, part-time or occasional basis; or

   b. Any other activity engaged in for money or other compensation, except the following:

      (1) One or more activities, not described in **(2)** through **(4)** below, for which no "insured" receives more than $2,000 in total compensation for the 12 months before the inception date of the policy;

      (2) Volunteer activities for which no money is received other than payment for expenses incurred to perform the activity;

      (3) Providing home day care services for which no compensation is received, other than the mutual exchange of such services; or

      (4) The rendering of home day care services to a relative of an "insured".

4. "Employee" means an employee of an "insured", or an employee leased to an "insured" by a labor leasing firm under an agreement between an "insured" and the labor leasing firm, whose duties are other than those performed by a "residence employee".

5. "Insured" means:

   a. You and residents of your household who are:

      (1) Your relatives; or

      (2) Other persons under the age of 21 and in the care of any person named above;

   b. A student enrolled in school full time, as defined by the school, who was a resident of your household before moving out to attend school, provided the student is under the age of:

      (1) 24 and your relative; or

      (2) 21 and in your care or the care of a person described in **a.(1)** above; or

N
E
W

c. Under Section **II**:

(1) With respect to animals or watercraft to which this policy applies, any person or organization legally responsible for these animals or watercraft which are owned by you or any person included in **a.** or **b.** above. "Insured" does not mean a person or organization using or having custody of these animals or watercraft in the course of any "business" or without consent of the owner; or

(2) With respect to a "motor vehicle" to which this policy applies:

(a) Persons while engaged in your employ or that of any person included in **a.** or **b.** above; or

(b) Other persons using the vehicle on an "insured location" with your consent.

Under both Sections **I** and **II,** when the word an immediately precedes the word "insured", the words an "insured" together mean one or more "insureds".

6. "Insured location" means:

a. The "residence premises";

b. The part of other premises, other structures and grounds used by you as a residence; and

(1) Which is shown in the Declarations; or

(2) Which is acquired by you during the policy period for your use as a residence;

c. Any premises used by you in connection with a premises described in **a.** and **b.** above;

d. Any part of a premises:

(1) Not owned by an "insured"; and

(2) Where an "insured" is temporarily residing;

e. Vacant land, other than farm land, owned by or rented to an "insured";

f. Land owned by or rented to an "insured" on which a one, two, three or four family dwelling is being built as a residence for an "insured";

g. Individual or family cemetery plots or burial vaults of an "insured"; or

h. Any part of a premises occasionally rented to an "insured" for other than "business" use.

7. "Motor vehicle" means:

a. A self-propelled land or amphibious vehicle; or

b. Any trailer or semitrailer which is being carried on, towed by or hitched for towing by a vehicle described in **a.** above.

8. "Occurrence" means an accident, including continuous or repeated exposure to substantially the same general harmful conditions, which results, during the policy period, in:

a. "Bodily injury"; or

b. "Property damage".

9. "Property damage" means physical injury to, destruction of, or loss of use of tangible property.

10. "Residence employee" means:

a. An employee of an "insured", or an employee leased to an "insured" by a labor leasing firm, under an agreement between an "insured" and the labor leasing firm, whose duties are related to the maintenance or use of the "residence premises", including household or domestic services; or

b. One who performs similar duties elsewhere not related to the "business" of an "insured".

A "residence employee" does not include a temporary employee who is furnished to an "insured" to substitute for a permanent "residence employee" on leave or to meet seasonal or short-term workload conditions.

11. "Residence premises" means:

a. The one family dwelling where you reside;

b. The two, three or four family dwelling where you reside in at least one of the family units; or

c. That part of any other building where you reside;

and which is shown as the "residence premises" in the Declarations.

"Residence premises" also includes other structures and grounds at that location.

N

E

W

DEDUCTIBLE

Unless otherwise noted in this policy, the following deductible provision applies:

Subject to the policy limits that apply, we will pay only that part of the total of all loss payable under Section I that exceeds the deductible amount shown in the Declarations.

SECTION I – PROPERTY COVERAGES

A. Coverage A – Dwelling

1. We cover:

   a. The dwelling on the "residence premises" shown in the Declarations, including structures attached to the dwelling; and

   b. Materials and supplies located on or next to the "residence premises" used to construct, alter or repair the dwelling or other structures on the "residence premises".

2. We do not cover land, including land on which the dwelling is located.

B. Coverage B – Other Structures

1. We cover other structures on the "residence premises" set apart from the dwelling by clear space. This includes structures connected to the dwelling by only a fence, utility line, or similar connection.

2. We do not cover:

   a. Land, including land on which the other structures are located;

   b. Other structures rented or held for rental to any person not a tenant of the dwelling, unless used solely as a private garage;

   c. Other structures from which any "business" is conducted; or

   d. Other structures used to store "business" property. However, we do cover a structure that contains "business" property solely owned by an "insured" or a tenant of the dwelling provided that "business" property does not include gaseous or liquid fuel, other than fuel in a permanently installed fuel tank of a vehicle or craft parked or stored in the structure.

3. The limit of liability for this coverage will not be more than 10% of the limit of liability that applies to Coverage **A**. Use of this coverage does not reduce the Coverage **A** limit of liability.

C. Coverage C – Personal Property

1. **Covered Property**

   We cover personal property owned or used by an "insured" while it is anywhere in the world. After a loss and at your request, we will cover personal property owned by:

   a. Others while the property is on the part of the "residence premises" occupied by an "insured"; or

   b. A guest or a "residence employee", while the property is in any residence occupied by an "insured".

2. **Limit For Property At Other Residences**

   Our limit of liability for personal property usually located at an "insured's" residence, other than the "residence premises", is 10% of the limit of liability for Coverage **C,** or $1,000, whichever is greater. However, this limitation does not apply to personal property:

   a. Moved from the "residence premises" because it is being repaired, renovated or rebuilt and is not fit to live in or store property in; or

   b. In a newly acquired principal residence for 30 days from the time you begin to move the property there.

3. **Special Limits Of Liability**

   The special limit for each category shown below is the total limit for each loss for all property in that category. These special limits do not increase the Coverage **C** limit of liability.

   a. $200 on money, bank notes, bullion, gold other than goldware, silver other than silverware, platinum other than platinumware, coins, medals, scrip, stored value cards and smart cards.

   b. $1,500 on securities, accounts, deeds, evidences of debt, letters of credit, notes other than bank notes, manuscripts, personal records, passports, tickets and stamps. This dollar limit applies to these categories regardless of the medium (such as paper or computer software) on which the material exists.

   This limit includes the cost to research, replace or restore the information from the lost or damaged material.

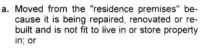

c. $1,500 on watercraft of all types, including their trailers, furnishings, equipment and outboard engines or motors.

d. $1,500 on trailers or semitrailers not used with watercraft of all types.

e. $1,500 for loss by theft of jewelry, watches, furs, precious and semiprecious stones.

f. $2,500 for loss by theft of firearms and related equipment.

g. $2,500 for loss by theft of silverware, silver-plated ware, goldware, gold-plated ware, platinumware, platinum-plated ware and pewterware. This includes flatware, hollow-ware, tea sets, trays and trophies made of or including silver, gold or pewter.

h. $2,500 on property, on the "residence premises", used primarily for "business" purposes.

i. $500 on property, away from the "residence premises", used primarily for "business" purposes. However, this limit does not apply to loss to electronic apparatus and other property described in Categories **j.** and **k.** below.

j. $1,500 on electronic apparatus and accessories, while in or upon a "motor vehicle", but only if the apparatus is equipped to be operated by power from the "motor vehicle's" electrical system while still capable of being operated by other power sources.

Accessories include antennas, tapes, wires, records, discs or other media that can be used with any apparatus described in this Category **j.**

k. $1,500 on electronic apparatus and accessories used primarily for "business" while away from the "residence premises" and not in or upon a "motor vehicle". The apparatus must be equipped to be operated by power from the "motor vehicle's" electrical system while still capable of being operated by other power sources.

Accessories include antennas, tapes, wires, records, discs or other media that can be used with any apparatus described in this Category **k.**

4. Property Not Covered

We do not cover:

a. Articles separately described and specifically insured, regardless of the limit for which they are insured, in this or other insurance;

b. Animals, birds or fish;

c. "Motor vehicles".

  (1) This includes:

    (a) Their accessories, equipment and parts; or

    (b) Electronic apparatus and accessories designed to be operated solely by power from the electrical system of the "motor vehicle", but only while such property is in or upon the "motor vehicle". Accessories include antennas, tapes, wires, records, discs or other media that can be used with any apparatus described above, but only while such property is in or upon the "motor vehicle".

  (2) We do cover "motor vehicles" not required to be registered for use on public roads or property which are:

    (a) Used solely to service an "insured's" residence; or

    (b) Designed to assist the handicapped;

d. Aircraft meaning any contrivance used or designed for flight including any parts whether or not attached to the aircraft;

We do cover model or hobby aircraft not used or designed to carry people or cargo;

e. Hovercraft and parts. Hovercraft means a self-propelled motorized ground effect vehicle and includes, but is not limited to, flare-craft and air cushion vehicles;

f. Property of roomers, boarders and other tenants, except property of roomers and boarders related to an "insured";

g. Property in an apartment regularly rented or held for rental to others by an "insured", except as provided in **E.10.** Landlord's Furnishings under Section I – Property Coverages;

h. Property rented or held for rental to others off the "residence premises";

i. "Business" data, including such data stored in:

  (1) Books of account, drawings or other paper records; or

  (2) Computers and related equipment.

We do cover the cost of blank recording or storage media, and of prerecorded computer programs available on the retail market;

j. Credit cards, electronic fund transfer cards or access devices used solely for deposit, withdrawal or transfer of funds except as provided in **E.6.** Credit Card, Electronic Fund Transfer Card Or Access Device, Forgery And Counterfeit Money under Section **I** – Property Coverages; or

k. Water or steam.

D. Coverage D – Loss Of Use

The limit of liability for Coverage **D** is the total limit for the coverages in **1.** Additional Living Expense, **2.** Fair Rental Value and **3.** Civil Authority Prohibits Use below.

1. Additional Living Expense

If a loss covered under Section **I** makes that part of the "residence premises" where you reside not fit to live in, we cover any necessary increase in living expenses incurred by you so that your household can maintain its normal standard of living.

Payment will be for the shortest time required to repair or replace the damage or, if you permanently relocate, the shortest time required for your household to settle elsewhere.

2. Fair Rental Value

If a loss covered under Section **I** makes that part of the "residence premises" rented to others or held for rental by you not fit to live in, we cover the fair rental value of such premises less any expenses that do not continue while it is not fit to live in.

Payment will be for the shortest time required to repair or replace that part of the premises rented or held for rental.

3. Civil Authority Prohibits Use

If a civil authority prohibits you from use of the "residence premises" as a result of direct damage to neighboring premises by a Peril Insured Against, we cover the loss as provided in **1.** Additional Living Expense and **2.** Fair Rental Value above for no more than two weeks.

4. Loss Or Expense Not Covered

We do not cover loss or expense due to cancellation of a lease or agreement.

The periods of time under **1.** Additional Living Expense, **2.** Fair Rental Value and **3.** Civil Authority Prohibits Use above are not limited by expiration of this policy.

E. Additional Coverages

1. Debris Removal

a. We will pay your reasonable expense for the removal of:

(1) Debris of covered property if a Peril Insured Against that applies to the damaged property causes the loss; or

(2) Ash, dust or particles from a volcanic eruption that has caused direct loss to a building or property contained in a building.

This expense is included in the limit of liability that applies to the damaged property. If the amount to be paid for the actual damage to the property plus the debris removal expense is more than the limit of liability for the damaged property, an additional 5% of that limit is available for such expense.

b. We will also pay your reasonable expense, up to $1,000, for the removal from the "residence premises" of:

(1) Your tree(s) felled by the peril of Windstorm or Hail or Weight of Ice, Snow or Sleet; or

(2) A neighbor's tree(s) felled by a Peril Insured Against under Coverage **C;**

provided the tree(s):

(3) Damage(s) a covered structure; or

(4) Does not damage a covered structure, but:

(a) Block(s) a driveway on the "residence premises" which prevent(s) a "motor vehicle", that is registered for use on public roads or property, from entering or leaving the "residence premises"; or

(b) Block(s) a ramp or other fixture designed to assist a handicapped person to enter or leave the dwelling building.

The $1,000 limit is the most we will pay in any one loss regardless of the number of fallen trees. No more than $500 of this limit will be paid for the removal of any one tree.

This coverage is additional insurance.

2. Reasonable Repairs

a. We will pay the reasonable cost incurred by you for the necessary measures taken solely to protect covered property that is damaged by a Peril Insured Against from further damage.

b. If the measures taken involve repair to other damaged property, we will only pay if that property is covered under this policy and the damage is caused by a Peril Insured Against. This coverage does not:

(1) Increase the limit of liability that applies to the covered property; or

(2) Relieve you of your duties, in case of a loss to covered property, described in **B.4.** under Section I – Conditions.

3. Trees, Shrubs And Other Plants

We cover trees, shrubs, plants or lawns, on the "residence premises", for loss caused by the following Perils Insured Against:

a. Fire or Lightning;

b. Explosion;

c. Riot or Civil Commotion;

d. Aircraft;

e. Vehicles not owned or operated by a resident of the "residence premises";

f. Vandalism or Malicious Mischief; or

g. Theft.

We will pay up to 5% of the limit of liability that applies to the dwelling for all trees, shrubs, plants or lawns. No more than $500 of this limit will be paid for any one tree, shrub or plant. We do not cover property grown for "business" purposes.

This coverage is additional insurance.

4. Fire Department Service Charge

We will pay up to $500 for your liability assumed by contract or agreement for fire department charges incurred when the fire department is called to save or protect covered property from a Peril Insured Against. We do not cover fire department service charges if the property is located within the limits of the city, municipality or protection district furnishing the fire department response.

This coverage is additional insurance. No deductible applies to this coverage.

5. Property Removed

We insure covered property against direct loss from any cause while being removed from a premises endangered by a Peril Insured Against and for no more than 30 days while removed.

This coverage does not change the limit of liability that applies to the property being removed.

6. Credit Card, Electronic Fund Transfer Card Or Access Device, Forgery And Counterfeit Money

a. We will pay up to $500 for:

(1) The legal obligation of an "insured" to pay because of the theft or unauthorized use of credit cards issued to or registered in an "insured's" name;

(2) Loss resulting from theft or unauthorized use of an electronic fund transfer card or access device used for deposit, withdrawal or transfer of funds, issued to or registered in an "insured's" name;

(3) Loss to an "insured" caused by forgery or alteration of any check or negotiable instrument; and

(4) Loss to an "insured" through acceptance in good faith of counterfeit United States or Canadian paper currency.

All loss resulting from a series of acts committed by any one person or in which any one person is concerned or implicated is considered to be one loss.

This coverage is additional insurance. No deductible applies to this coverage.

b. We do not cover:

(1) Use of a credit card, electronic fund transfer card or access device:

(a) By a resident of your household;

(b) By a person who has been entrusted with either type of card or access device; or

(c) If an "insured" has not complied with all terms and conditions under which the cards are issued or the devices accessed; or

(2) Loss arising out of "business" use or dishonesty of an "insured".

c. If the coverage in **a.** above applies, the following defense provisions also apply:

(1) We may investigate and settle any claim or suit that we decide is appropriate. Our duty to defend a claim or suit ends when the amount we pay for the loss equals our limit of liability.

(2) If a suit is brought against an "insured" for liability under **a.(1)** or **(2)** above, we will provide a defense at our expense by counsel of our choice.

(3) We have the option to defend at our expense an "insured" or an "insured's" bank against any suit for the enforcement of payment under **a.(3)** above.

7. **Loss Assessment**

   a. We will pay up to $1,000 for your share of loss assessment charged during the policy period against you, as owner or tenant of the "residence premises", by a corporation or association of property owners. The assessment must be made as a result of direct loss to property, owned by all members collectively, of the type that would be covered by this policy if owned by you, caused by a Peril Insured Against under Coverage **A**, other than:

      (1) Earthquake; or

      (2) Land shock waves or tremors before, during or after a volcanic eruption.

      The limit of $1,000 is the most we will pay with respect to any one loss, regardless of the number of assessments. We will only apply one deductible, per unit, to the total amount of any one loss to the property described above, regardless of the number of assessments.

   b. We do not cover assessments charged against you or a corporation or association of property owners by any governmental body.

   c. Paragraph **P.** Policy Period under Section **I** – Conditions does not apply to this coverage.

   This coverage is additional insurance.

8. **Collapse**

   a. With respect to this Additional Coverage:

      (1) Collapse means an abrupt falling down or caving in of a building or any part of a building with the result that the building or part of the building cannot be occupied for its current intended purpose.

      (2) A building or any part of a building that is in danger of falling down or caving in is not considered to be in a state of collapse.

      (3) A part of a building that is standing is not considered to be in a state of collapse even if it has separated from another part of the building.

      (4) A building or any part of a building that is standing is not considered to be in a state of collapse even if it shows evidence of cracking, bulging, sagging, bending, leaning, settling, shrinkage or expansion.

   b. We insure for direct physical loss to covered property involving collapse of a building or any part of a building if the collapse was caused by one or more of the following:

      (1) The Perils Insured Against named under Coverage **C**;

      (2) Decay that is hidden from view, unless the presence of such decay is known to an "insured" prior to collapse;

      (3) Insect or vermin damage that is hidden from view, unless the presence of such damage is known to an "insured" prior to collapse;

      (4) Weight of contents, equipment, animals or people;

      (5) Weight of rain which collects on a roof; or

      (6) Use of defective material or methods in construction, remodeling or renovation if the collapse occurs during the course of the construction, remodeling or renovation.

   c. Loss to an awning, fence, patio, deck, pavement, swimming pool, underground pipe, flue, drain, cesspool, septic tank, foundation, retaining wall, bulkhead, pier, wharf or dock is not included under **b.(2)** through **(6)** above, unless the loss is a direct result of the collapse of a building or any part of a building.

   d. This coverage does not increase the limit of liability that applies to the damaged covered property.

9. **Glass Or Safety Glazing Material**

   a. We cover:

      (1) The breakage of glass or safety glazing material which is part of a covered building, storm door or storm window;

      (2) The breakage of glass or safety glazing material which is part of a covered building, storm door or storm window when caused directly by earth movement; and

      (3) The direct physical loss to covered property caused solely by the pieces, fragments or splinters of broken glass or safety glazing material which is part of a building, storm door or storm window.

b. This coverage does not include loss:

(1) To covered property which results because the glass or safety glazing material has been broken, except as provided in **a.(3)** above; or

(2) On the "residence premises" if the dwelling has been vacant for more than 60 consecutive days immediately before the loss, except when the breakage results directly from earth movement as provided in **a.(2)** above. A dwelling being constructed is not considered vacant.

c. This coverage does not increase the limit of liability that applies to the damaged property.

10. Landlord's Furnishings

We will pay up to $2,500 for your appliances, carpeting and other household furnishings, in each apartment on the "residence premises" regularly rented or held for rental to others by an "insured", for loss caused by a Peril Insured Against in Coverage **C**, other than Theft.

This limit is the most we will pay in any one loss regardless of the number of appliances, carpeting or other household furnishings involved in the loss.

This coverage does not increase the limit of liability applying to the damaged property.

11. Ordinance Or Law

a. You may use up to 10% of the limit of liability that applies to Coverage **A** for the increased costs you incur due to the enforcement of any ordinance or law which requires or regulates:

(1) The construction, demolition, remodeling, renovation or repair of that part of a covered building or other structure damaged by a Peril Insured Against;

(2) The demolition and reconstruction of the undamaged part of a covered building or other structure, when that building or other structure must be totally demolished because of damage by a Peril Insured Against to another part of that covered building or other structure; or

(3) The remodeling, removal or replacement of the portion of the undamaged part of a covered building or other structure necessary to complete the remodeling, repair or replacement of that part of the covered building or other structure damaged by a Peril Insured Against.

b. You may use all or part of this ordinance or law coverage to pay for the increased costs you incur to remove debris resulting from the construction, demolition, remodeling, renovation, repair or replacement of property as stated in **a.** above.

c. We do not cover:

(1) The loss in value to any covered building or other structure due to the requirements of any ordinance or law; or

(2) The costs to comply with any ordinance or law which requires any "insured" or others to test for, monitor, clean up, remove, contain, treat, detoxify or neutralize, or in any way respond to, or assess the effects of, pollutants in or on any covered building or other structure.

Pollutants means any solid, liquid, gaseous or thermal irritant or contaminant, including smoke, vapor, soot, fumes, acids, alkalis, chemicals and waste. Waste includes materials to be recycled, reconditioned or reclaimed.

This coverage is additional insurance.

12. Grave Markers

We will pay up to $5,000 for grave markers, including mausoleums, on or away from the "residence premises" for loss caused by a Peril Insured Against under Coverage **C.**

This coverage does not increase the limits of liability that apply to the damaged covered property.

SECTION I – PERILS INSURED AGAINST

A. Coverage A – Dwelling And Coverage B – Other Structures

1. We insure against risk of direct physical loss to property described in Coverages **A** and **B**.

2. We do not insure, however, for loss:

a. Excluded under Section I – Exclusions;

b. Involving collapse, except as provided in **E.8.** Collapse under Section I – Property Coverages; and

c. Caused by:

(1) Freezing of a plumbing, heating, air conditioning or automatic fire protective sprinkler system or of a household appliance, or by discharge, leakage or overflow from within the system or appliance caused by freezing. This provision does not apply if you have used reasonable care to:

(a) Maintain heat in the building; or

(b) Shut off the water supply and drain all systems and appliances of water.

However, if the building is protected by an automatic fire protective sprinkler system, you must use reasonable care to continue the water supply and maintain heat in the building for coverage to apply.

For purposes of this provision a plumbing system or household appliance does not include a sump, sump pump or related equipment or a roof drain, gutter, downspout or similar fixtures or equipment;

(2) Freezing, thawing, pressure or weight of water or ice, whether driven by wind or not, to a:

(a) Fence, pavement, patio or swimming pool;

(b) Footing, foundation, bulkhead, wall, or any other structure or device that supports all or part of a building, or other structure;

(c) Retaining wall or bulkhead that does not support all or part of a building or other structure; or

(d) Pier, wharf or dock;

(3) Theft in or to a dwelling under construction, or of materials and supplies for use in the construction until the dwelling is finished and occupied;

(4) Vandalism and malicious mischief, and any ensuing loss caused by any intentional and wrongful act committed in the course of the vandalism or malicious mischief, if the dwelling has been vacant for more than 60 consecutive days immediately before the loss. A dwelling being constructed is not considered vacant;

(5) Mold, fungus or wet rot. However, we do insure for loss caused by mold, fungus or wet rot that is hidden within the walls or ceilings or beneath the floors or above the ceilings of a structure if such loss results from the accidental discharge or overflow of water or steam from within:

(a) A plumbing, heating, air conditioning or automatic fire protective sprinkler system, or a household appliance, on the "residence premises"; or

(b) A storm drain, or water, steam or sewer pipes, off the "residence premises".

For purposes of this provision, a plumbing system or household appliance does not include a sump, sump pump or related equipment or a roof drain, gutter, downspout or similar fixtures or equipment; or

(6) Any of the following:

(a) Wear and tear, marring, deterioration;

(b) Mechanical breakdown, latent defect, inherent vice, or any quality in property that causes it to damage or destroy itself;

(c) Smog, rust or other corrosion, or dry rot;

(d) Smoke from agricultural smudging or industrial operations;

(e) Discharge, dispersal, seepage, migration, release or escape of pollutants unless the discharge, dispersal, seepage, migration, release or escape is itself caused by a Peril Insured Against named under Coverage **C**.

Pollutants means any solid, liquid, gaseous or thermal irritant or contaminant, including smoke, vapor, soot, fumes, acids, alkalis, chemicals and waste. Waste includes materials to be recycled, reconditioned or reclaimed;

(f) Settling, shrinking, bulging or expansion, including resultant cracking, of bulkheads, pavements, patios, footings, foundations, walls, floors, roofs or ceilings;

(g) Birds, vermin, rodents, or insects; or

(h) Animals owned or kept by an "insured".

Exception To c.(6)

Unless the loss is otherwise excluded, we cover loss to property covered under Coverage **A** or **B** resulting from an accidental discharge or overflow of water or steam from within a:

(i) Storm drain, or water, steam or sewer pipe, off the "residence premises"; or

(ii) Plumbing, heating, air conditioning or automatic fire protective sprinkler system or household appliance on the "residence premises". This includes the cost to tear out and replace any part of a building, or other structure, on the "residence premises", but only when necessary to repair the system or appliance. However, such tear out and replacement coverage only applies to other structures if the water or steam causes actual damage to a building on the "residence premises".

We do not cover loss to the system or appliance from which this water or steam escaped.

For purposes of this provision, a plumbing system or household appliance does not include a sump, sump pump or related equipment or a roof drain, gutter, down spout or similar fixtures or equipment.

Section I – Exclusion **A.3.** Water Damage, Paragraphs **a.** and **c.** that apply to surface water and water below the surface of the ground do not apply to loss by water covered under **c.(5)** and **(6)** above.

Under **2.b.** and **c.** above, any ensuing loss to property described in Coverages **A** and **B** not precluded by any other provision in this policy is covered.

B. Coverage C – Personal Property

We insure for direct physical loss to the property described in Coverage **C** caused by any of the following perils unless the loss is excluded in Section I – Exclusions.

1. Fire Or Lightning

2. Windstorm Or Hail

This peril includes loss to watercraft of all types and their trailers, furnishings, equipment, and outboard engines or motors, only while inside a fully enclosed building.

This peril does not include loss to the property contained in a building caused by rain, snow, sleet, sand or dust unless the direct force of wind or hail damages the building causing an opening in a roof or wall and the rain, snow, sleet, sand or dust enters through this opening.

3. Explosion

4. Riot Or Civil Commotion

5. Aircraft

This peril includes self-propelled missiles and spacecraft.

6. Vehicles

7. Smoke

This peril means sudden and accidental damage from smoke, including the emission or puffback of smoke, soot, fumes or vapors from a boiler, furnace or related equipment.

This peril does not include loss caused by smoke from agricultural smudging or industrial operations.

8. Vandalism Or Malicious Mischief

9. Theft

a. This peril includes attempted theft and loss of property from a known place when it is likely that the property has been stolen.

b. This peril does not include loss caused by theft:

(1) Committed by an "insured";

(2) In or to a dwelling under construction, or of materials and supplies for use in the construction until the dwelling is finished and occupied;

(3) From that part of a "residence premises" rented by an "insured" to someone other than another "insured"; or

(4) That occurs off the "residence premises" of:

(a) Trailers, semitrailers and campers;

(b) Watercraft of all types, and their furnishings, equipment and outboard engines or motors; or

(c) Property while at any other residence owned by, rented to, or occupied by an "insured", except while an "insured" is temporarily living there. Property of an "insured" who is a student is covered while at the residence the student occupies to attend school as long as the student has been there at any time during the 60 days immediately before the loss.

10. Falling Objects

This peril does not include loss to property contained in a building unless the roof or an outside wall of the building is first damaged by a falling object. Damage to the falling object itself is not included.

11. Weight Of Ice, Snow Or Sleet

This peril means weight of ice, snow or sleet which causes damage to property contained in a building.

Copyright, Insurance Services Office, Inc., 1999   HO 00 03 10 00

12. **Accidental Discharge Or Overflow Of Water Or Steam**

   a. This peril means accidental discharge or overflow of water or steam from within a plumbing, heating, air conditioning or automatic fire protective sprinkler system or from within a household appliance.

   b. This peril does not include loss:

   (1) To the system or appliance from which the water or steam escaped;

   (2) Caused by or resulting from freezing except as provided in Peril Insured Against **14.** Freezing;

   (3) On the "residence premises" caused by accidental discharge or overflow which occurs off the "residence premises"; or

   (4) Caused by mold, fungus or wet rot unless hidden within the walls or ceilings or beneath the floors or above the ceilings of a structure.

   c. In this peril, a plumbing system or household appliance does not include a sump, sump pump or related equipment or a roof drain, gutter, downspout or similar fixtures or equipment.

   d. Section I – Exclusion **A.3.** Water Damage, Paragraphs **a.** and **c.** that apply to surface water and water below the surface of the ground do not apply to loss by water covered under this peril.

13. **Sudden And Accidental Tearing Apart, Cracking, Burning Or Bulging**

   This peril means sudden and accidental tearing apart, cracking, burning or bulging of a steam or hot water heating system, an air conditioning or automatic fire protective sprinkler system, or an appliance for heating water.

   We do not cover loss caused by or resulting from freezing under this peril.

14. **Freezing**

   a. This peril means freezing of a plumbing, heating, air conditioning or automatic fire protective sprinkler system or of a household appliance but only if you have used reasonable care to:

   (1) Maintain heat in the building; or

   (2) Shut off the water supply and drain all systems and appliances of water.

   However, if the building is protected by an automatic fire protective sprinkler system, you must use reasonable care to continue the water supply and maintain heat in the building for coverage to apply.

   b. In this peril, a plumbing system or household appliance does not include a sump, sump pump or related equipment or a roof drain, gutter, downspout or similar fixtures or equipment.

15. **Sudden And Accidental Damage From Artificially Generated Electrical Current**

   This peril does not include loss to tubes, transistors, electronic components or circuitry that are a part of appliances, fixtures, computers, home entertainment units or other types of electronic apparatus.

16. **Volcanic Eruption**

   This peril does not include loss caused by earthquake, land shock waves or tremors.

SECTION I – EXCLUSIONS

A. We do not insure for loss caused directly or indirectly by any of the following. Such loss is excluded regardless of any other cause or event contributing concurrently or in any sequence to the loss. These exclusions apply whether or not the loss event results in widespread damage or affects a substantial area.

   1. **Ordinance Or Law**

   Ordinance Or Law means any ordinance or law:

   a. Requiring or regulating the construction, demolition, remodeling, renovation or repair of property, including removal of any resulting debris. This Exclusion **A.1.a.** does not apply to the amount of coverage that may be provided for in **E.11.** Ordinance Or Law under Section I – Property Coverages;

   b. The requirements of which result in a loss in value to property; or

   c. Requiring any "insured" or others to test for, monitor, clean up, remove, contain, treat, detoxify or neutralize, or in any way respond to, or assess the effects of, pollutants.

   Pollutants means any solid, liquid, gaseous or thermal irritant or contaminant, including smoke, vapor, soot, fumes, acids, alkalis, chemicals and waste. Waste includes materials to be recycled, reconditioned or reclaimed.

   This Exclusion **1.** applies whether or not the property has been physically damaged.

   2. **Earth Movement**

   Earth Movement means:

   a. Earthquake, including land shock waves or tremors before, during or after a volcanic eruption;

b. Landslide, mudslide or mudflow;

c. Subsidence or sinkhole; or

d. Any other earth movement including earth sinking, rising or shifting;

caused by or resulting from human or animal forces or any act of nature unless direct loss by fire or explosion ensues and then we will pay only for the ensuing loss.

This Exclusion **2.** does not apply to loss by theft.

3. Water Damage

Water Damage means:

a. Flood, surface water, waves, tidal water, overflow of a body of water, or spray from any of these, whether or not driven by wind;

b. Water or water-borne material which backs up through sewers or drains or which overflows or is discharged from a sump, sump pump or related equipment; or

c. Water or water-borne material below the surface of the ground, including water which exerts pressure on or seeps or leaks through a building, sidewalk, driveway, foundation, swimming pool or other structure;

caused by or resulting from human or animal forces or any act of nature.

Direct loss by fire, explosion or theft resulting from water damage is covered.

4. Power Failure

Power Failure means the failure of power or other utility service if the failure takes place off the "residence premises". But if the failure results in a loss, from a Peril Insured Against on the "residence premises", we will pay for the loss caused by that peril.

5. Neglect

Neglect means neglect of an "insured" to use all reasonable means to save and preserve property at and after the time of a loss.

6. War

War includes the following and any consequence of any of the following:

a. Undeclared war, civil war, insurrection, rebellion or revolution;

b. Warlike act by a military force or military personnel; or

c. Destruction, seizure or use for a military purpose.

Discharge of a nuclear weapon will be deemed a warlike act even if accidental.

7. Nuclear Hazard

This Exclusion **7.** pertains to Nuclear Hazard to the extent set forth in **M.** Nuclear Hazard Clause under Section I – Conditions.

8. Intentional Loss

Intentional Loss means any loss arising out of any act an "insured" commits or conspires to commit with the intent to cause a loss.

In the event of such loss, no "insured" is entitled to coverage, even "insureds" who did not commit or conspire to commit the act causing the loss.

9. Governmental Action

Governmental Action means the destruction, confiscation or seizure of property described in Coverage **A**, **B** or **C** by order of any governmental or public authority.

This exclusion does not apply to such acts ordered by any governmental or public authority that are taken at the time of a fire to prevent its spread, if the loss caused by fire would be covered under this policy.

B. We do not insure for loss to property described in Coverages **A** and **B** caused by any of the following. However, any ensuing loss to property described in Coverages **A** and **B** not precluded by any other provision in this policy is covered.

1. Weather conditions. However, this exclusion only applies if weather conditions contribute in any way with a cause or event excluded in **A.** above to produce the loss.

2. Acts or decisions, including the failure to act or decide, of any person, group, organization or governmental body.

3. Faulty, inadequate or defective:

a. Planning, zoning, development, surveying, siting;

b. Design, specifications, workmanship, repair, construction, renovation, remodeling, grading, compaction;

c. Materials used in repair, construction, renovation or remodeling; or

d. Maintenance;

of part or all of any property whether on or off the "residence premises".

SECTION I – CONDITIONS

A. Insurable Interest And Limit Of Liability

Even if more than one person has an insurable interest in the property covered, we will not be liable in any one loss:

1. To an "insured" for more than the amount of such "insured's" interest at the time of loss; or

2. For more than the applicable limit of liability.

B. Duties After Loss

In case of a loss to covered property, we have no duty to provide coverage under this policy if the failure to comply with the following duties is prejudicial to us. These duties must be performed either by you, an "insured" seeking coverage, or a representative of either:

1. Give prompt notice to us or our agent;

2. Notify the police in case of loss by theft;

3. Notify the credit card or electronic fund transfer card or access device company in case of loss as provided for in **E.6.** Credit Card, Electronic Fund Transfer Card Or Access Device, Forgery And Counterfeit Money under Section I – Property Coverages;

4. Protect the property from further damage. If repairs to the property are required, you must:

   a. Make reasonable and necessary repairs to protect the property; and

   b. Keep an accurate record of repair expenses;

5. Cooperate with us in the investigation of a claim;

6. Prepare an inventory of damaged personal property showing the quantity, description, actual cash value and amount of loss. Attach all bills, receipts and related documents that justify the figures in the inventory;

7. As often as we reasonably require:

   a. Show the damaged property;

   b. Provide us with records and documents we request and permit us to make copies; and

   c. Submit to examination under oath, while not in the presence of another "insured", and sign the same;

8. Send to us, within 60 days after our request, your signed, sworn proof of loss which sets forth, to the best of your knowledge and belief:

   a. The time and cause of loss;

   b. The interests of all "insureds" and all others in the property involved and all liens on the property;

   c. Other insurance which may cover the loss;

d. Changes in title or occupancy of the property during the term of the policy;

e. Specifications of damaged buildings and detailed repair estimates;

f. The inventory of damaged personal property described in **6.** above;

g. Receipts for additional living expenses incurred and records that support the fair rental value loss; and

h. Evidence or affidavit that supports a claim under **E.6.** Credit Card, Electronic Fund Transfer Card Or Access Device, Forgery And Counterfeit Money under Section I – Property Coverages, stating the amount and cause of loss.

C. Loss Settlement

In this Condition **C.**, the terms "cost to repair or replace" and "replacement cost" do not include the increased costs incurred to comply with the enforcement of any ordinance or law, except to the extent that coverage for these increased costs is provided in **E.11.** Ordinance Or Law under Section I – Property Coverages. Covered property losses are settled as follows:

1. Property of the following types:

   a. Personal property;

   b. Awnings, carpeting, household appliances, outdoor antennas and outdoor equipment, whether or not attached to buildings;

   c. Structures that are not buildings; and

   d. Grave markers, including mausoleums;

   at actual cash value at the time of loss but not more than the amount required to repair or replace.

2. Buildings covered under Coverage **A** or **B** at replacement cost without deduction for depreciation, subject to the following:

   a. If, at the time of loss, the amount of insurance in this policy on the damaged building is 80% or more of the full replacement cost of the building immediately before the loss, we will pay the cost to repair or replace, after application of any deductible and without deduction for depreciation, but not more than the least of the following amounts:

   (1) The limit of liability under this policy that applies to the building;

   (2) The replacement cost of that part of the building damaged with material of like kind and quality and for like use; or

   (3) The necessary amount actually spent to repair or replace the damaged building.

N
E
W

If the building is rebuilt at a new premises, the cost described in **(2)** above is limited to the cost which would have been incurred if the building had been built at the original premises.

b. If, at the time of loss, the amount of insurance in this policy on the damaged building is less than 80% of the full replacement cost of the building immediately before the loss, we will pay the greater of the following amounts, but not more than the limit of liability under this policy that applies to the building:

   (1) The actual cash value of that part of the building damaged; or

   (2) That proportion of the cost to repair or replace, after application of any deductible and without deduction for depreciation, that part of the building damaged, which the total amount of insurance in this policy on the damaged building bears to 80% of the replacement cost of the building.

c. To determine the amount of insurance required to equal 80% of the full replacement cost of the building immediately before the loss, do not include the value of:

   (1) Excavations, footings, foundations, piers, or any other structures or devices that support all or part of the building, which are below the undersurface of the lowest basement floor;

   (2) Those supports described in **(1)** above which are below the surface of the ground inside the foundation walls, if there is no basement; and

   (3) Underground flues, pipes, wiring and drains.

d. We will pay no more than the actual cash value of the damage until actual repair or replacement is complete. Once actual repair or replacement is complete, we will settle the loss as noted in **2.a.** and **b.** above.

   However, if the cost to repair or replace the damage is both:

   (1) Less than 5% of the amount of insurance in this policy on the building; and

   (2) Less than $2,500;

   we will settle the loss as noted in **2.a.** and **b.** above whether or not actual repair or replacement is complete.

e. You may disregard the replacement cost loss settlement provisions and make claim under this policy for loss to buildings on an actual cash value basis. You may then make claim for any additional liability according to the provisions of this Condition **C. Loss Settlement**, provided you notify us of your intent to do so within 180 days after the date of loss.

D. Loss To A Pair Or Set

In case of loss to a pair or set we may elect to:

   1. Repair or replace any part to restore the pair or set to its value before the loss; or

   2. Pay the difference between actual cash value of the property before and after the loss.

E. Appraisal

If you and we fail to agree on the amount of loss, either may demand an appraisal of the loss. In this event, each party will choose a competent and impartial appraiser within 20 days after receiving a written request from the other. The two appraisers will choose an umpire. If they cannot agree upon an umpire within 15 days, you or we may request that the choice be made by a judge of a court of record in the state where the "residence premises" is located. The appraisers will separately set the amount of loss. If the appraisers submit a written report of an agreement to us, the amount agreed upon will be the amount of loss. If they fail to agree, they will submit their differences to the umpire. A decision agreed to by any two will set the amount of loss.

Each party will:

   1. Pay its own appraiser; and

   2. Bear the other expenses of the appraisal and umpire equally.

F. Other Insurance And Service Agreement

If a loss covered by this policy is also covered by:

   1. Other insurance, we will pay only the proportion of the loss that the limit of liability that applies under this policy bears to the total amount of insurance covering the loss; or

   2. A service agreement, this insurance is excess over any amounts payable under any such agreement. Service agreement means a service plan, property restoration plan, home warranty or other similar service warranty agreement, even if it is characterized as insurance.

G. Suit Against Us

No action can be brought against us unless there has been full compliance with all of the terms under Section I of this policy and the action is started within two years after the date of loss.

H. Our Option

If we give you written notice within 30 days after we receive your signed, sworn proof of loss, we may repair or replace any part of the damaged property with material or property of like kind and quality.

I. Loss Payment

We will adjust all losses with you. We will pay you unless some other person is named in the policy or is legally entitled to receive payment. Loss will be payable 60 days after we receive your proof of loss and:

1. Reach an agreement with you;

2. There is an entry of a final judgment; or

3. There is a filing of an appraisal award with us.

J. Abandonment Of Property

We need not accept any property abandoned by an "insured".

K. Mortgage Clause

1. If a mortgagee is named in this policy, any loss payable under Coverage **A** or **B** will be paid to the mortgagee and you, as interests appear. If more than one mortgagee is named, the order of payment will be the same as the order of precedence of the mortgages.

2. If we deny your claim, that denial will not apply to a valid claim of the mortgagee, if the mortgagee:

   a. Notifies us of any change in ownership, occupancy or substantial change in risk of which the mortgagee is aware;

   b. Pays any premium due under this policy on demand if you have neglected to pay the premium; and

   c. Submits a signed, sworn statement of loss within 60 days after receiving notice from us of your failure to do so. Paragraphs **E.** Appraisal, **G.** Suit Against Us and **I.** Loss Payment under Section I – Conditions also apply to the mortgagee.

3. If we decide to cancel or not to renew this policy, the mortgagee will be notified at least 10 days before the date cancellation or nonrenewal takes effect.

4. If we pay the mortgagee for any loss and deny payment to you:

   a. We are subrogated to all the rights of the mortgagee granted under the mortgage on the property; or

   b. At our option, we may pay to the mortgagee the whole principal on the mortgage plus any accrued interest. In this event, we will receive a full assignment and transfer of the mortgage and all securities held as collateral to the mortgage debt.

5. Subrogation will not impair the right of the mortgagee to recover the full amount of the mortgagee's claim.

L. No Benefit To Bailee

We will not recognize any assignment or grant any coverage that benefits a person or organization holding, storing or moving property for a fee regardless of any other provision of this policy.

M. Nuclear Hazard Clause

1. "Nuclear Hazard" means any nuclear reaction, radiation, or radioactive contamination, all whether controlled or uncontrolled or however caused, or any consequence of any of these.

2. Loss caused by the nuclear hazard will not be considered loss caused by fire, explosion, or smoke, whether these perils are specifically named in or otherwise included within the Perils Insured Against.

3. This policy does not apply under Section I to loss caused directly or indirectly by nuclear hazard, except that direct loss by fire resulting from the nuclear hazard is covered.

N. Recovered Property

If you or we recover any property for which we have made payment under this policy, you or we will notify the other of the recovery. At your option, the property will be returned to or retained by you or it will become our property. If the recovered property is returned to or retained by you, the loss payment will be adjusted based on the amount you received for the recovered property.

O. Volcanic Eruption Period

One or more volcanic eruptions that occur within a 72 hour period will be considered as one volcanic eruption.

P. Policy Period

This policy applies only to loss which occurs during the policy period.

Q. Concealment Or Fraud

We provide coverage to no "insureds" under this policy if, whether before or after a loss, an "insured" has:

1. Intentionally concealed or misrepresented any material fact or circumstance;

2. Engaged in fraudulent conduct; or

3. Made false statements;

relating to this insurance.

R. Loss Payable Clause

If the Declarations show a loss payee for certain listed insured personal property, the definition of "insured" is changed to include that loss payee with respect to that property.

If we decide to cancel or not renew this policy, that loss payee will be notified in writing.

SECTION II – LIABILITY COVERAGES

A. Coverage E – Personal Liability

If a claim is made or a suit is brought against an "insured" for damages because of "bodily injury" or "property damage" caused by an "occurrence" to which this coverage applies, we will:

1. Pay up to our limit of liability for the damages for which an "insured" is legally liable. Damages include prejudgment interest awarded against an "insured"; and

2. Provide a defense at our expense by counsel of our choice, even if the suit is groundless, false or fraudulent. We may investigate and settle any claim or suit that we decide is appropriate. Our duty to settle or defend ends when our limit of liability for the "occurrence" has been exhausted by payment of a judgment or settlement.

B. Coverage F – Medical Payments To Others

We will pay the necessary medical expenses that are incurred or medically ascertained within three years from the date of an accident causing "bodily injury". Medical expenses means reasonable charges for medical, surgical, x-ray, dental, ambulance, hospital, professional nursing, prosthetic devices and funeral services. This coverage does not apply to you or regular residents of your household except "residence employees". As to others, this coverage applies only:

1. To a person on the "insured location" with the permission of an "insured"; or

2. To a person off the "insured location", if the "bodily injury":

a. Arises out of a condition on the "insured location" or the ways immediately adjoining;

b. Is caused by the activities of an "insured";

c. Is caused by a "residence employee" in the course of the "residence employee's" employment by an "insured"; or

d. Is caused by an animal owned by or in the care of an "insured".

SECTION II – EXCLUSIONS

A. "Motor Vehicle Liability"

1. Coverages **E** and **F** do not apply to any "motor vehicle liability" if, at the time and place of an "occurrence", the involved "motor vehicle":

a. Is registered for use on public roads or property;

b. Is not registered for use on public roads or property, but such registration is required by a law, or regulation issued by a government agency, for it to be used at the place of the "occurrence"; or

c. Is being:

(1) Operated in, or practicing for, any prearranged or organized race, speed contest or other competition;

(2) Rented to others;

(3) Used to carry persons or cargo for a charge; or

(4) Used for any "business" purpose except for a motorized golf cart while on a golfing facility.

2. If Exclusion **A.1.** does not apply, there is still no coverage for "motor vehicle liability" unless the "motor vehicle" is:

a. In dead storage on an "insured location";

b. Used solely to service an "insured's" residence;

c. Designed to assist the handicapped and, at the time of an "occurrence", it is:

(1) Being used to assist a handicapped person, or

(2) Parked on an "insured location";

d. Designed for recreational use off public roads and:

(1) Not owned by an "insured"; or

(2) Owned by an "insured" provided the "occurrence" takes place on an "insured location" as defined in Definitions **B. 6.a., b., d., e.** or **h.;** or

e. A motorized golf cart that is owned by an "insured", designed to carry up to 4 persons, not built or modified after manufacture to exceed a speed of 25 miles per hour on level ground and, at the time of an "occurrence", is within the legal boundaries of:

(1) A golfing facility and is parked or stored there, or being used by an "insured" to:

(a) Play the game of golf or for other recreational or leisure activity allowed by the facility;

N
E
W

(b) Travel to or from an area where "motor vehicles" or golf carts are parked or stored; or

(c) Cross public roads at designated points to access other parts of the golfing facility; or

(2) A private residential community, including its public roads upon which a motorized golf cart can legally travel, which is subject to the authority of a property owners association and contains an "insured's" residence.

B. "Watercraft Liability"

1. Coverages **E** and **F** do not apply to any "watercraft liability" if, at the time of an "occurrence", the involved watercraft is being:

   a. Operated in, or practicing for, any prearranged or organized race, speed contest or other competition. This exclusion does not apply to a sailing vessel or a predicted log cruise;

   b. Rented to others;

   c. Used to carry persons or cargo for a charge; or

   d. Used for any "business" purpose.

2. If Exclusion **B.1.** does not apply, there is still no coverage for "watercraft liability" unless, at the time of the "occurrence", the watercraft:

   a. Is stored;

   b. Is a sailing vessel, with or without auxiliary power that is:

      (1) Less than 26 feet in overall length; or

      (2) 26 feet or more in overall length and not owned by or rented to an "insured"; or

   c. Is not a sailing vessel and is powered by:

      (1) An inboard or inboard-outdrive engine or motor, including those that power a water jet pump, of:

         (a) 50 horsepower or less and not owned by an "insured"; or

         (b) More than 50 horsepower and not owned by or rented to an "insured"; or

      (2) One or more outboard engines or motors with:

         (a) 25 total horsepower or less;

         (b) More than 25 horsepower if the outboard engine or motor is not owned by an "insured";

         (c) More than 25 horsepower if the outboard engine or motor is owned by an "insured" who acquired it during the policy period; or

(d) More than 25 horsepower if the outboard engine or motor is owned by an "insured" who acquired it before the policy period, but only if:

   (i) You declare them at policy inception; or

   (ii) Your intent to insure them is reported to us in writing within 45 days after you acquire them.

The coverages in **(c)** and **(d)** above apply for the policy period.

Horsepower means the maximum power rating assigned to the engine or motor by the manufacturer.

C. "Aircraft Liability"

This policy does not cover "aircraft liability".

D. "Hovercraft Liability"

This policy does not cover "hovercraft liability".

E. Coverage E – Personal Liability And Coverage F – Medical Payments To Others

Coverages **E** and **F** do not apply to the following:

1. **Expected Or Intended Injury**

   "Bodily injury" or "property damage" which is expected or intended by an "insured" even if the resulting "bodily injury" or "property damage":

   a. Is of a different kind, quality or degree than initially expected or intended; or

   b. Is sustained by a different person, entity, real or personal property, than initially expected or intended.

   However, this Exclusion **E.1.** does not apply to "bodily injury" resulting from the use of reasonable force by an "insured" to protect persons or property;

2. **"Business"**

   a. "Bodily injury" or "property damage" arising out of or in connection with a "business" conducted from an "insured location" or engaged in by an "insured", whether or not the "business" is owned or operated by an "insured" or employs an "insured".

   This Exclusion **E.2.** applies but is not limited to an act or omission, regardless of its nature or circumstance, involving a service or duty rendered, promised, owed, or implied to be provided because of the nature of the "business".

   b. This Exclusion **E.2.** does not apply to:

      (1) The rental or holding for rental of an "insured location";

N

E

W

(a) On an occasional basis if used only as a residence;

(b) In part for use only as a residence, unless a single family unit is intended for use by the occupying family to lodge more than two roomers or boarders; or

(c) In part, as an office, school, studio or private garage; and

(2) An "insured" under the age of 21 years involved in a part-time or occasional, self-employed "business" with no employees;

3. Professional Services

"Bodily injury" or "property damage" arising out of the rendering of or failure to render professional services;

4. "Insured's" Premises Not An "Insured Location"

"Bodily injury" or "property damage" arising out of a premises:

a. Owned by an "insured";

b. Rented to an "insured"; or

c. Rented to others by an "insured";

that is not an "insured location";

5. War

"Bodily injury" or "property damage" caused directly or indirectly by war, including the following and any consequence of any of the following:

a. Undeclared war, civil war, insurrection, rebellion or revolution;

b. Warlike act by a military force or military personnel; or

c. Destruction, seizure or use for a military purpose.

Discharge of a nuclear weapon will be deemed a warlike act even if accidental;

6. Communicable Disease

"Bodily injury" or "property damage" which arises out of the transmission of a communicable disease by an "insured";

7. Sexual Molestation, Corporal Punishment Or Physical Or Mental Abuse

"Bodily injury" or "property damage" arising out of sexual molestation, corporal punishment or physical or mental abuse; or

8. Controlled Substance

"Bodily injury" or "property damage" arising out of the use, sale, manufacture, delivery, transfer or possession by any person of a Controlled Substance as defined by the Federal Food and Drug Law at 21 U.S.C.A. Sections 811 and 812. Controlled Substances include but are not limited to cocaine, LSD, marijuana and all narcotic drugs. However, this exclusion does not apply to the legitimate use of prescription drugs by a person following the orders of a licensed physician.

Exclusions **A.** "Motor Vehicle Liability", **B.** "Watercraft Liability", **C.** "Aircraft Liability", **D.** "Hovercraft Liability", and **E.4.** "Insured's" Premises Not An "Insured Location" do not apply to "bodily injury" to a "residence employee" arising out of and in the course of the "residence employee's" employment by an "insured".

F. Coverage E – Personal Liability

Coverage **E** does not apply to:

1. Liability:

a. For any loss assessment charged against you as a member of an association, corporation or community of property owners, except as provided in **D.** Loss Assessment under Section II – Additional Coverages;

b. Under any contract or agreement entered into by an "insured". However, this exclusion does not apply to written contracts:

(1) That directly relate to the ownership, maintenance or use of an "insured location"; or

(2) Where the liability of others is assumed by you prior to an "occurrence";

unless excluded in **a.** above or elsewhere in this policy;

2. "Property damage" to property owned by an "insured". This includes costs or expenses incurred by an "insured" or others to repair, replace, enhance, restore or maintain such property to prevent injury to a person or damage to property of others, whether on or away from an "insured location";

3. "Property damage" to property rented to, occupied or used by or in the care of an "insured". This exclusion does not apply to "property damage" caused by fire, smoke or explosion;

4. "Bodily injury" to any person eligible to receive any benefits voluntarily provided or required to be provided by an "insured" under any:

a. Workers' compensation law;

N
E
W

     HO 00 03 10 00

b. Non-occupational disability law; or

c. Occupational disease law;

5. "Bodily injury" or "property damage" for which an "insured" under this policy:

   a. Is also an insured under a nuclear energy liability policy issued by the:

     (1) Nuclear Energy Liability Insurance Association;

     (2) Mutual Atomic Energy Liability Underwriters;

     (3) Nuclear Insurance Association of Canada;

     or any of their successors; or

   b. Would be an insured under such a policy but for the exhaustion of its limit of liability; or

6. "Bodily injury" to you or an "insured" as defined under Definitions **5.a.** or **b.**

   This exclusion also applies to any claim made or suit brought against you or an "insured":

     (1) To repay; or

     (2) Share damages with;

     another person who may be obligated to pay damages because of "bodily injury" to an "insured".

G. Coverage F – Medical Payments To Others

Coverage **F** does not apply to "bodily injury":

1. To a "residence employee" if the "bodily injury":

   a. Occurs off the "insured location"; and

   b. Does not arise out of or in the course of the "residence employee's" employment by an "insured";

2. To any person eligible to receive benefits voluntarily provided or required to be provided under any:

   a. Workers' compensation law;

   b. Non-occupational disability law; or

   c. Occupational disease law;

3. From any:

   a. Nuclear reaction;

   b. Nuclear radiation; or

   c. Radioactive contamination;

   all whether controlled or uncontrolled or however caused; or

   d. Any consequence of any of these; or

4. To any person, other than a "residence employee" of an "insured", regularly residing on any part of the "insured location".

SECTION II – ADDITIONAL COVERAGES

We cover the following in addition to the limits of liability:

A. Claim Expenses

We pay:

1. Expenses we incur and costs taxed against an "insured" in any suit we defend;

2. Premiums on bonds required in a suit we defend, but not for bond amounts more than the Coverage **E** limit of liability. We need not apply for or furnish any bond;

3. Reasonable expenses incurred by an "insured" at our request, including actual loss of earnings (but not loss of other income) up to $250 per day, for assisting us in the investigation or defense of a claim or suit; and

4. Interest on the entire judgment which accrues after entry of the judgment and before we pay or tender, or deposit in court that part of the judgment which does not exceed the limit of liability that applies.

B. First Aid Expenses

We will pay expenses for first aid to others incurred by an "insured" for "bodily injury" covered under this policy. We will not pay for first aid to an "insured".

C. Damage To Property Of Others

1. We will pay, at replacement cost, up to $1,000 per "occurrence" for "property damage" to property of others caused by an "insured".

2. We will not pay for "property damage":

   a. To the extent of any amount recoverable under Section **I**;

   b. Caused intentionally by an "insured" who is 13 years of age or older;

   c. To property owned by an "insured";

   d. To property owned by or rented to a tenant of an "insured" or a resident in your household; or

   e. Arising out of:

     (1) A "business" engaged in by an "insured";

     (2) Any act or omission in connection with a premises owned, rented or controlled by an "insured", other than the "insured location"; or

     (3) The ownership, maintenance, occupancy, operation, use, loading or unloading of aircraft, hovercraft, watercraft or "motor vehicles".

N

E

W

This exclusion **e.(3)** does not apply to a "motor vehicle" that:

(a) Is designed for recreational use off public roads;

(b) Is not owned by an "insured"; and

(c) At the time of the "occurrence", is not required by law, or regulation issued by a government agency, to have been registered for it to be used on public roads or property.

D. Loss Assessment

1. We will pay up to $1,000 for your share of loss assessment charged against you, as owner or tenant of the "residence premises", during the policy period by a corporation or association of property owners, when the assessment is made as a result of:

   a. "Bodily injury" or "property damage" not excluded from coverage under Section II – Exclusions; or

   b. Liability for an act of a director, officer or trustee in the capacity as a director, officer or trustee, provided such person:

      (1) Is elected by the members of a corporation or association of property owners; and

      (2) Serves without deriving any income from the exercise of duties which are solely on behalf of a corporation or association of property owners.

2. Paragraph **I.** Policy Period under Section II – Conditions does not apply to this Loss Assessment Coverage.

3. Regardless of the number of assessments, the limit of $1,000 is the most we will pay for loss arising out of:

   a. One accident, including continuous or repeated exposure to substantially the same general harmful condition; or

   b. A covered act of a director, officer or trustee. An act involving more than one director, officer or trustee is considered to be a single act.

4. We do not cover assessments charged against you or a corporation or association of property owners by any governmental body.

SECTION II – CONDITIONS

A. Limit Of Liability

Our total liability under Coverage **E** for all damages resulting from any one "occurrence" will not be more than the Coverage **E** limit of liability shown in the Declarations. This limit is the same regardless of the number of "insureds", claims made or persons injured. All "bodily injury" and "property damage" resulting from any one accident or from continuous or repeated exposure to substantially the same general harmful conditions shall be considered to be the result of one "occurrence".

Our total liability under Coverage **F** for all medical expense payable for "bodily injury" to one person as the result of one accident will not be more than the Coverage **F** limit of liability shown in the Declarations.

B. Severability Of Insurance

This insurance applies separately to each "insured". This condition will not increase our limit of liability for any one "occurrence".

C. Duties After "Occurrence"

In case of an "occurrence", you or another "insured" will perform the following duties that apply. We have no duty to provide coverage under this policy if your failure to comply with the following duties is prejudicial to us. You will help us by seeing that these duties are performed:

1. Give written notice to us or our agent as soon as is practical, which sets forth:

   a. The identity of the policy and the "named insured" shown in the Declarations;

   b. Reasonably available information on the time, place and circumstances of the "occurrence"; and

   c. Names and addresses of any claimants and witnesses;

2. Cooperate with us in the investigation, settlement or defense of any claim or suit;

3. Promptly forward to us every notice, demand, summons or other process relating to the "occurrence";

4. At our request, help us:

   a. To make settlement;

   b. To enforce any right of contribution or indemnity against any person or organization who may be liable to an "insured";

   c. With the conduct of suits and attend hearings and trials; and

   d. To secure and give evidence and obtain the attendance of witnesses;

5. With respect to **C.** Damage To Property Of Others under Section **II** – Additional Coverages, submit to us within 60 days after the loss, a sworn statement of loss and show the damaged property, if in an "insured's" control;

6. No "insured" shall, except at such "insured's" own cost, voluntarily make payment, assume obligation or incur expense other than for first aid to others at the time of the "bodily injury".

D. Duties Of An Injured Person – Coverage F – Medical Payments To Others

1. The injured person or someone acting for the injured person will:

   a. Give us written proof of claim, under oath if required, as soon as is practical; and

   b. Authorize us to obtain copies of medical reports and records.

2. The injured person will submit to a physical exam by a doctor of our choice when and as often as we reasonably require.

E. Payment Of Claim – Coverage F – Medical Payments To Others

Payment under this coverage is not an admission of liability by an "insured" or us.

F. Suit Against Us

1. No action can be brought against us unless there has been full compliance with all of the terms under this Section **II**.

2. No one will have the right to join us as a party to any action against an "insured".

3. Also, no action with respect to Coverage **E** can be brought against us until the obligation of such "insured" has been determined by final judgment or agreement signed by us.

G. Bankruptcy Of An "Insured"

Bankruptcy or insolvency of an "insured" will not relieve us of our obligations under this policy.

H. Other Insurance

This insurance is excess over other valid and collectible insurance except insurance written specifically to cover as excess over the limits of liability that apply in this policy.

I. Policy Period

This policy applies only to "bodily injury" or "property damage" which occurs during the policy period.

J. Concealment Or Fraud

We do not provide coverage to an "insured" who, whether before or after a loss, has:

1. Intentionally concealed or misrepresented any material fact or circumstance;

2. Engaged in fraudulent conduct; or

3. Made false statements;

relating to this insurance.

SECTIONS I AND II – CONDITIONS

A. Liberalization Clause

If we make a change which broadens coverage under this edition of our policy without additional premium charge, that change will automatically apply to your insurance as of the date we implement the change in your state, provided that this implementation date falls within 60 days prior to or during the policy period stated in the Declarations.

This Liberalization Clause does not apply to changes implemented with a general program revision that includes both broadenings and restrictions in coverage, whether that general program revision is implemented through introduction of:

1. A subsequent edition of this policy; or

2. An amendatory endorsement.

B. Waiver Or Change Of Policy Provisions

A waiver or change of a provision of this policy must be in writing by us to be valid. Our request for an appraisal or examination will not waive any of our rights.

C. Cancellation

1. You may cancel this policy at any time by returning it to us or by letting us know in writing of the date cancellation is to take effect.

2. We may cancel this policy only for the reasons stated below by letting you know in writing of the date cancellation takes effect. This cancellation notice may be delivered to you, or mailed to you at your mailing address shown in the Declarations. Proof of mailing will be sufficient proof of notice.

   a. When you have not paid the premium, we may cancel at any time by letting you know at least 10 days before the date cancellation takes effect.

   b. When this policy has been in effect for less than 60 days and is not a renewal with us, we may cancel for any reason by letting you know at least 10 days before the date cancellation takes effect.

N E W

c. When this policy has been in effect for 60 days or more, or at any time if it is a renewal with us, we may cancel:

   (1) If there has been a material misrepresentation of fact which if known to us would have caused us not to issue the policy; or

   (2) If the risk has changed substantially since the policy was issued.

   This can be done by letting you know at least 30 days before the date cancellation takes effect.

d. When this policy is written for a period of more than one year, we may cancel for any reason at anniversary by letting you know at least 30 days before the date cancellation takes effect.

3. When this policy is canceled, the premium for the period from the date of cancellation to the expiration date will be refunded pro rata.

4. If the return premium is not refunded with the notice of cancellation or when this policy is returned to us, we will refund it within a reasonable time after the date cancellation takes effect.

D. Nonrenewal

We may elect not to renew this policy. We may do so by delivering to you, or mailing to you at your mailing address shown in the Declarations, written notice at least 30 days before the expiration date of this policy. Proof of mailing will be sufficient proof of notice.

E. Assignment

Assignment of this policy will not be valid unless we give our written consent.

F. Subrogation

An "insured" may waive in writing before a loss all rights of recovery against any person. If not waived, we may require an assignment of rights of recovery for a loss to the extent that payment is made by us.

If an assignment is sought, an "insured" must sign and deliver all related papers and cooperate with us.

Subrogation does not apply to Coverage F or Paragraph **C.** Damage To Property Of Others under Section II – Additional Coverages.

G. Death

If any person named in the Declarations or the spouse, if a resident of the same household, dies, the following apply:

1. We insure the legal representative of the deceased but only with respect to the premises and property of the deceased covered under the policy at the time of death; and

2. "Insured" includes:

   a. An "insured" who is a member of your household at the time of your death, but only while a resident of the "residence premises"; and

   b. With respect to your property, the person having proper temporary custody of the property until appointment and qualification of a legal representative.

N E W

Personal Auto Policy

Personal Auto Policy Declarations

POLICYHOLDER:
(Named Insured)
David M. and Joan G. Smith
216 Brookside Drive
Anytown, USA 40000

POLICY NUMBER: 296 S 468211

POLICY PERIOD: **FROM:** December 25, 2000
TO: June 25, 2001

But only if the required premium for this period has been paid, and for six-month renewal periods if renewal premiums are paid as required. Each period begins and ends at 12:01 A.M. standard time at the address of the policyholder.

INSURED VEHICLES AND
SCHEDULE OF COVERAGES

VEHICLE	COVERAGES	LIMITS OF INSURANCE		PREMIUM
1	1988 Toyota Tercel	ID #JT2AL21E8B3306553		
	Coverage A—Liability	$ 300,000	Each Occurrence	$ 101.50
	Coverage B—Medical Payments	$ 5,000	Each Person	$ 18.00
	Coverage C—Uninsured Motorists	$ 300,000	Each Occurrence	$ 30.90
			TOTAL	$ 150.40
2	1997 Ford Taurus	ID #1FABP3OU7GG212619		
	Coverage A—Liability	$ 300,000	Each Occurrence	$ 101.50
	Coverage B—Medical Payments	$ 5,000	Each Person	$ 18.00
	Coverage C—Uninsured Motorists	$ 300,000	Each Occurrence	$ 30.90
	Coverage D—Other Than Collision	Actual Cash Value Less $ 100		$ 20.80
	—Collision	Actual Cash Value Less $ 250		$ 115.50
			TOTAL	$ 286.70

POLICY FORM AND ENDORSEMENTS: PP 00 01, PP 03 06

COUNTERSIGNATURE DATE: December 1, 2000

AGENT: A.M. Abel

PERSONAL AUTO
PP 00 01 06 98

PERSONAL AUTO POLICY

AGREEMENT

In return for payment of the premium and subject to all the terms of this policy, we agree with you as follows:

DEFINITIONS

A. Throughout this policy, "you" and "your" refer to:

1. The "named insured" shown in the Declarations; and

2. The spouse if a resident of the same household.

If the spouse ceases to be a resident of the same household during the policy period or prior to the inception of this policy, the spouse will be considered "you" and "your" under this policy but only until the earlier of:

1. The end of 90 days following the spouse's change of residency;

2. The effective date of another policy listing the spouse as a named insured; or

3. The end of the policy period.

B. "We", "us" and "our" refer to the Company providing this insurance.

C. For purposes of this policy, a private passenger type auto, pickup or van shall be deemed to be owned by a person if leased:

1. Under a written agreement to that person; and

2. For a continuous period of at least 6 months.

Other words and phrases are defined. They are in quotation marks when used.

D. "Bodily injury" means bodily harm, sickness or disease, including death that results.

E. "Business" includes trade, profession or occupation.

F. "Family member" means a person related to you by blood, marriage or adoption who is a resident of your household. This includes a ward or foster child.

G. "Occupying" means in, upon, getting in, on, out or off.

H. "Property damage" means physical injury to, destruction of or loss of use of tangible property.

I. "Trailer" means a vehicle designed to be pulled by a:

1. Private passenger auto; or

2. Pickup or van.

It also means a farm wagon or farm implement while towed by a vehicle listed in **1.** or **2.** above.

J. "Your covered auto" means:

1. Any vehicle shown in the Declarations.

2. A "newly acquired auto".

3. Any "trailer" you own.

4. Any auto or "trailer" you do not own while used as a temporary substitute for any other vehicle described in this definition which is out of normal use because of its:

a. Breakdown;

b. Repair;

c. Servicing;

d. Loss; or

e. Destruction.

This Provision **(J.4.)** does not apply to Coverage For Damage To Your Auto.

K. "Newly acquired auto":

1. "Newly acquired auto" means any of the following types of vehicles you become the owner of during the policy period:

a. A private passenger auto; or

b. A pickup or van, for which no other insurance policy provides coverage, that:

(1) Has a Gross Vehicle Weight of less than 10,000 lbs.; and

(2) Is not used for the delivery or transportation of goods and materials unless such use is:

(a) Incidental to your "business" of installing, maintaining or repairing furnishings or equipment; or

(b) For farming or ranching.

2. Coverage for a "newly acquired auto" is provided as described below. If you ask us to insure a "newly acquired auto" after a specified time period described below has elapsed, any coverage we provide for a "newly acquired auto" will begin at the time you request the coverage.

a. For any coverage provided in this policy except Coverage For Damage To Your Auto, a "newly acquired auto" will have the broadest coverage we now provide for any vehicle shown in the Declarations. Coverage begins on the date you become the owner. However, for this coverage to apply to a "newly acquired auto" which is in addition to any vehicle shown in the Declarations, you must ask us to insure it within 14 days after you become the owner.

If a "newly acquired auto" replaces a vehicle shown in the Declarations, coverage is provided for this vehicle without your having to ask us to insure it.

b. Collision Coverage for a "newly acquired auto" begins on the date you become the owner. However, for this coverage to apply, you must ask us to insure it within:

(1) 14 days after you become the owner if the Declarations indicate that Collision Coverage applies to at least one auto. In this case, the "newly acquired auto" will have the broadest coverage we now provide for any auto shown in the Declarations.

(2) Four days after you become the owner if the Declarations do not indicate that Collision Coverage applies to at least one auto. If you comply with the 4 day requirement and a loss occurred before you asked us to insure the "newly acquired auto", a Collision deductible of $500 will apply.

c. Other Than Collision Coverage for a "newly acquired auto" begins on the date you become the owner. However, for this coverage to apply, you must ask us to insure it within:

(1) 14 days after you become the owner if the Declarations indicate that Other Than Collision Coverage applies to at least one auto. In this case, the "newly acquired auto" will have the broadest coverage we now provide for any auto shown in the Declarations.

(2) Four days after you become the owner if the Declarations do not indicate that Other Than Collision Coverage applies to at least one auto. If you comply with the 4 day requirement and a loss occurred before you asked us to insure the "newly acquired auto", an Other Than Collision deductible of $500 will apply.

PART A – LIABILITY COVERAGE

INSURING AGREEMENT

A. We will pay damages for "bodily injury" or "property damage" for which any "insured" becomes legally responsible because of an auto accident. Damages include prejudgment interest awarded against the "insured". We will settle or defend, as we consider appropriate, any claim or suit asking for these damages. In addition to our limit of liability, we will pay all defense costs we incur. Our duty to settle or defend ends when our limit of liability for this coverage has been exhausted by payment of judgments or settlements. We have no duty to defend any suit or settle any claim for "bodily injury" or "property damage" not covered under this policy.

B. "Insured" as used in this Part means:

1. You or any "family member" for the ownership, maintenance or use of any auto or "trailer".

2. Any person using "your covered auto".

3. For "your covered auto", any person or organization but only with respect to legal responsibility for acts or omissions of a person for whom coverage is afforded under this Part.

4. For any auto or "trailer", other than "your covered auto", any other person or organization but only with respect to legal responsibility for acts or omissions of you or any "family member" for whom coverage is afforded under this Part. This Provision (**B.4.**) applies only if the person or organization does not own or hire the auto or "trailer".

SUPPLEMENTARY PAYMENTS

In addition to our limit of liability, we will pay on behalf of an "insured":

1. Up to $250 for the cost of bail bonds required because of an accident, including related traffic law violations. The accident must result in "bodily injury" or "property damage" covered under this policy.

2. Premiums on appeal bonds and bonds to release attachments in any suit we defend.

3. Interest accruing after a judgment is entered in any suit we defend. Our duty to pay interest ends when we offer to pay that part of the judgment which does not exceed our limit of liability for this coverage.

4. Up to $200 a day for loss of earnings, but not other income, because of attendance at hearings or trials at our request.

5. Other reasonable expenses incurred at our request.

EXCLUSIONS

A. We do not provide Liability Coverage for any "insured":

1. Who intentionally causes "bodily injury" or "property damage".

2. For "property damage" to property owned or being transported by that "insured".

3. For "property damage" to property:
   a. Rented to;
   b. Used by; or
   c. In the care of;
   that "insured".

   This Exclusion **(A.3.)** does not apply to "property damage" to a residence or private garage.

4. For "bodily injury" to an employee of that "insured" during the course of employment. This Exclusion **(A.4.)** does not apply to "bodily injury" to a domestic employee unless workers' compensation benefits are required or available for that domestic employee.

5. For that "insured's" liability arising out of the ownership or operation of a vehicle while it is being used as a public or livery conveyance. This Exclusion **(A.5.)** does not apply to a share-the-expense car pool.

6. While employed or otherwise engaged in the "business" of:
   a. Selling;
   b. Repairing;
   c. Servicing;
   d. Storing; or
   e. Parking;

   vehicles designed for use mainly on public highways. This includes road testing and delivery. This Exclusion **(A.6.)** does not apply to the ownership, maintenance or use of "your covered auto" by:
   a. You;
   b. Any "family member"; or
   c. Any partner, agent or employee of you or any "family member".

7. Maintaining or using any vehicle while that "insured" is employed or otherwise engaged in any "business" (other than farming or ranching) not described in Exclusion **A.6.**

   This Exclusion **(A.7.)** does not apply to the maintenance or use of a:
   a. Private passenger auto;
   b. Pickup or van; or
   c. "Trailer" used with a vehicle described in **a.** or **b.** above.

8. Using a vehicle without a reasonable belief that that "insured" is entitled to do so. This Exclusion **(A.8.)** does not apply to a "family member" using "your covered auto" which is owned by you.

9. For "bodily injury" or "property damage" for which that "insured":
   a. Is an insured under a nuclear energy liability policy; or
   b. Would be an insured under a nuclear energy liability policy but for its termination upon exhaustion of its limit of liability.

   A nuclear energy liability policy is a policy issued by any of the following or their successors:
   a. Nuclear Energy Liability Insurance Association;
   b. Mutual Atomic Energy Liability Underwriters; or
   c. Nuclear Insurance Association of Canada.

B. We do not provide Liability Coverage for the ownership, maintenance or use of:

1. Any vehicle which:
   a. Has fewer than four wheels; or
   b. Is designed mainly for use off public roads.

   This Exclusion **(B.1.)** does not apply:
   a. While such vehicle is being used by an "insured" in a medical emergency;
   b. To any "trailer"; or
   c. To any non-owned golf cart.

2. Any vehicle, other than "your covered auto", which is:
   a. Owned by you; or
   b. Furnished or available for your regular use.

3. Any vehicle, other than "your covered auto", which is:
   a. Owned by any "family member"; or
   b. Furnished or available for the regular use of any "family member".

   However, this Exclusion **(B.3.)** does not apply to you while you are maintaining or "occupying" any vehicle which is:
   a. Owned by a "family member"; or
   b. Furnished or available for the regular use of a "family member".

4. Any vehicle, located inside a facility designed for racing, for the purpose of:
   a. Competing in; or
   b. Practicing or preparing for;

   any prearranged or organized racing or speed contest.

LIMIT OF LIABILITY

A. The limit of liability shown in the Declarations for each person for Bodily Injury Liability is our maximum limit of liability for all damages, including damages for care, loss of services or death, arising out of "bodily injury" sustained by any one person in any one auto accident. Subject to this limit for each person, the limit of liability shown in the Declarations for each accident for Bodily Injury Liability is our maximum limit of liability for all damages for "bodily injury" resulting from any one auto accident.

The limit of liability shown in the Declarations for each accident for Property Damage Liability is our maximum limit of liability for all "property damage" resulting from any one auto accident.

This is the most we will pay regardless of the number of:

1. "Insureds";

2. Claims made;

3. Vehicles or premiums shown in the Declarations; or

4. Vehicles involved in the auto accident.

B. No one will be entitled to receive duplicate payments for the same elements of loss under this coverage and:

1. Part **B** or Part **C** of this policy; or

2. Any Underinsured Motorists Coverage provided by this policy.

OUT OF STATE COVERAGE

If an auto accident to which this policy applies occurs in any state or province other than the one in which "your covered auto" is principally garaged, we will interpret your policy for that accident as follows:

A. If the state or province has:

1. A financial responsibility or similar law specifying limits of liability for "bodily injury" or "property damage" higher than the limit shown in the Declarations, your policy will provide the higher specified limit.

2. A compulsory insurance or similar law requiring a nonresident to maintain insurance whenever the nonresident uses a vehicle in that state or province, your policy will provide at least the required minimum amounts and types of coverage.

B. No one will be entitled to duplicate payments for the same elements of loss.

FINANCIAL RESPONSIBILITY

When this policy is certified as future proof of financial responsibility, this policy shall comply with the law to the extent required.

OTHER INSURANCE

If there is other applicable liability insurance we will pay only our share of the loss. Our share is the proportion that our limit of liability bears to the total of all applicable limits. However, any insurance we provide for a vehicle you do not own shall be excess over any other collectible insurance.

PART B – MEDICAL PAYMENTS COVERAGE

INSURING AGREEMENT

A. We will pay reasonable expenses incurred for necessary medical and funeral services because of "bodily injury":

1. Caused by accident; and

2. Sustained by an "insured".

We will pay only those expenses incurred for services rendered within 3 years from the date of the accident.

B. "Insured" as used in this Part means:

1. You or any "family member":

   a. While "occupying"; or

   b. As a pedestrian when struck by;

   a motor vehicle designed for use mainly on public roads or a trailer of any type.

2. Any other person while "occupying" "your covered auto".

EXCLUSIONS

We do not provide Medical Payments Coverage for any "insured" for "bodily injury":

1. Sustained while "occupying" any motorized vehicle having fewer than four wheels.

2. Sustained while "occupying" "your covered auto" when it is being used as a public or livery conveyance. This Exclusion (**2.**) does not apply to a share-the-expense car pool.

3. Sustained while "occupying" any vehicle located for use as a residence or premises.

4. Occurring during the course of employment if workers' compensation benefits are required or available for the "bodily injury".

5. Sustained while "occupying", or when struck by, any vehicle (other than "your covered auto") which is:

   a. Owned by you; or

   b. Furnished or available for your regular use.

6. Sustained while "occupying", or when struck by, any vehicle (other than "your covered auto") which is:

   a. Owned by any "family member"; or

   b. Furnished or available for the regular use of any "family member".

   However, this Exclusion (**6.**) does not apply to you.

7. Sustained while "occupying" a vehicle without a reasonable belief that that "insured" is entitled to do so. This Exclusion **(7.)** does not apply to a "family member" using "your covered auto" which is owned by you.

8. Sustained while "occupying" a vehicle when it is being used in the "business" of an "insured". This Exclusion **(8.)** does not apply to "bodily injury" sustained while "occupying" a:

   a. Private passenger auto;

   b. Pickup or van that you own; or

   c. "Trailer" used with a vehicle described in **a.** or **b.** above.

9. Caused by or as a consequence of:

   a. Discharge of a nuclear weapon (even if accidental);

   b. War (declared or undeclared);

   c. Civil war;

   d. Insurrection; or

   e. Rebellion or revolution.

10. From or as a consequence of the following, whether controlled or uncontrolled or however caused:

    a. Nuclear reaction;

    b. Radiation; or

    c. Radioactive contamination.

11. Sustained while "occupying" any vehicle located inside a facility designed for racing, for the purpose of:

    a. Competing in; or

    b. Practicing or preparing for;

    any prearranged or organized racing or speed contest.

LIMIT OF LIABILITY

A. The limit of liability shown in the Declarations for this coverage is our maximum limit of liability for each person injured in any one accident. This is the most we will pay regardless of the number of:

1. "Insureds";

2. Claims made;

3. Vehicles or premiums shown in the Declarations; or

4. Vehicles involved in the accident.

B. No one will be entitled to receive duplicate payments for the same elements of loss under this coverage and:

1. Part **A** or Part **C** of this policy; or

2. Any Underinsured Motorists Coverage provided by this policy.

OTHER INSURANCE

If there is other applicable auto medical payments insurance we will pay only our share of the loss. Our share is the proportion that our limit of liability bears to the total of all applicable limits. However, any insurance we provide with respect to a vehicle you do not own shall be excess over any other collectible auto insurance providing payments for medical or funeral expenses.

PART C – UNINSURED MOTORISTS COVERAGE

INSURING AGREEMENT

A. We will pay compensatory damages which an "insured" is legally entitled to recover from the owner or operator of an "uninsured motor vehicle" because of "bodily injury":

1. Sustained by an "insured"; and

2. Caused by an accident.

The owner's or operator's liability for these damages must arise out of the ownership, maintenance or use of the "uninsured motor vehicle".

Any judgment for damages arising out of a suit brought without our written consent is not binding on us.

B. "Insured" as used in this Part means:

1. You or any "family member".

2. Any other person "occupying" "your covered auto".

3. Any person for damages that person is entitled to recover because of "bodily injury" to which this coverage applies sustained by a person described in **1.** or **2.** above.

C. "Uninsured motor vehicle" means a land motor vehicle or trailer of any type:

1. To which no bodily injury liability bond or policy applies at the time of the accident.

2. To which a bodily injury liability bond or policy applies at the time of the accident. In this case its limit for bodily injury liability must be less than the minimum limit for bodily injury liability specified by the financial responsibility law of the state in which "your covered auto" is principally garaged.

3. Which is a hit-and-run vehicle whose operator or owner cannot be identified and which hits:

   a. You or any "family member";

   b. A vehicle which you or any "family member" are "occupying"; or

   c. "Your covered auto".

4. To which a bodily injury liability bond or policy applies at the time of the accident but the bonding or insuring company:

   a. Denies coverage; or

   b. Is or becomes insolvent.

However, "uninsured motor vehicle" does not include any vehicle or equipment:

1. Owned by or furnished or available for the regular use of you or any "family member".

2. Owned or operated by a self-insurer under any applicable motor vehicle law, except a self-insurer which is or becomes insolvent.

3. Owned by any governmental unit or agency.

4. Operated on rails or crawler treads.

5. Designed mainly for use off public roads while not on public roads.

6. While located for use as a residence or premises.

EXCLUSIONS

A. We do not provide Uninsured Motorists Coverage for "bodily injury" sustained:

   1. By an "insured" while "occupying", or when struck by, any motor vehicle owned by that "insured" which is not insured for this coverage under this policy. This includes a trailer of any type used with that vehicle.

   2. By any "family member" while "occupying", or when struck by, any motor vehicle you own which is insured for this coverage on a primary basis under any other policy.

B. We do not provide Uninsured Motorists Coverage for "bodily injury" sustained by any "insured":

   1. If that "insured" or the legal representative settles the "bodily injury" claim without our consent.

   2. While "occupying" "your covered auto" when it is being used as a public or livery conveyance. This Exclusion (**B.2.**) does not apply to a share-the-expense car pool.

   3. Using a vehicle without a reasonable belief that that "insured" is entitled to do so. This Exclusion (**B.3.**) does not apply to a "family member" using "your covered auto" which is owned by you.

C. This coverage shall not apply directly or indirectly to benefit any insurer or self-insurer under any of the following or similar law:

   1. Workers' compensation law; or

2. Disability benefits law.

D. We do not provide Uninsured Motorists Coverage for punitive or exemplary damages.

LIMIT OF LIABILITY

A. The limit of liability shown in the Declarations for each person for Uninsured Motorists Coverage is our maximum limit of liability for all damages, including damages for care, loss of services or death, arising out of "bodily injury" sustained by any one person in any one accident. Subject to this limit for each person, the limit of liability shown in the Declarations for each accident for Uninsured Motorists Coverage is our maximum limit of liability for all damages for "bodily injury" resulting from any one accident.

This is the most we will pay regardless of the number of:

1. "Insureds";

2. Claims made;

3. Vehicles or premiums shown in the Declarations; or

4. Vehicles involved in the accident.

B. No one will be entitled to receive duplicate payments for the same elements of loss under this coverage and:

   1. Part **A.** or Part **B.** of this policy; or

   2. Any Underinsured Motorists Coverage provided by this policy.

C. We will not make a duplicate payment under this coverage for any element of loss for which payment has been made by or on behalf of persons or organizations who may be legally responsible.

D. We will not pay for any element of loss if a person is entitled to receive payment for the same element of loss under any of the following or similar law:

   1. Workers' compensation law; or

   2. Disability benefits law.

OTHER INSURANCE

If there is other applicable insurance available under one or more policies or provisions of coverage that is similar to the insurance provided under this Part of the policy:

1. Any recovery for damages under all such policies or provisions of coverage may equal but not exceed the highest applicable limit for any one vehicle under any insurance providing coverage on either a primary or excess basis.

2. Any insurance we provide with respect to a vehicle you do not own shall be excess over any collectible insurance providing such coverage on a primary basis.

     PP 00 01 06 98

3. If the coverage under this policy is provided:

a. On a primary basis, we will pay only our share of the loss that must be paid under insurance providing coverage on a primary basis. Our share is the proportion that our limit of liability bears to the total of all applicable limits of liability for coverage provided on a primary basis.

b. On an excess basis, we will pay only our share of the loss that must be paid under insurance providing coverage on an excess basis. Our share is the proportion that our limit of liability bears to the total of all applicable limits of liability for coverage provided on an excess basis.

ARBITRATION

A. If we and an "insured" do not agree:

1. Whether that "insured" is legally entitled to recover damages; or

2. As to the amount of damages which are recoverable by that "insured";

from the owner or operator of an "uninsured motor vehicle", then the matter may be arbitrated. However, disputes concerning coverage under this Part may not be arbitrated.

Both parties must agree to arbitration. If so agreed, each party will select an arbitrator. The two arbitrators will select a third. If they cannot agree within 30 days, either may request that selection be made by a judge of a court having jurisdiction.

B. Each party will:

1. Pay the expenses it incurs; and

2. Bear the expenses of the third arbitrator equally.

C. Unless both parties agree otherwise, arbitration will take place in the county in which the "insured" lives. Local rules of law as to procedure and evidence will apply. A decision agreed to by two of the arbitrators will be binding as to:

1. Whether the "insured" is legally entitled to recover damages; and

2. The amount of damages. This applies only if the amount does not exceed the minimum limit for bodily injury liability specified by the financial responsibility law of the state in which "your covered auto" is principally garaged. If the amount exceeds that limit, either party may demand the right to a trial. This demand must be made within 60 days of the arbitrators' decision. If this demand is not made, the amount of damages agreed to by the arbitrators will be binding.

PART D – COVERAGE FOR DAMAGE TO YOUR AUTO

INSURING AGREEMENT

A. We will pay for direct and accidental loss to "your covered auto" or any "non-owned auto", including their equipment, minus any applicable deductible shown in the Declarations. If loss to more than one "your covered auto" or "non-owned auto" results from the same "collision", only the highest applicable deductible will apply. We will pay for loss to "your covered auto" caused by:

1. Other than "collision" only if the Declarations indicate that Other Than Collision Coverage is provided for that auto.

2. "Collision" only if the Declarations indicate that Collision Coverage is provided for that auto.

If there is a loss to a "non-owned auto", we will provide the broadest coverage applicable to any "your covered auto" shown in the Declarations.

B. "Collision" means the upset of "your covered auto" or a "non-owned auto" or their impact with another vehicle or object.

Loss caused by the following is considered other than "collision":

1. Missiles or falling objects;

2. Fire;

3. Theft or larceny;

4. Explosion or earthquake;

5. Windstorm;

6. Hail, water or flood;

7. Malicious mischief or vandalism;

8. Riot or civil commotion;

9. Contact with bird or animal; or

10. Breakage of glass.

If breakage of glass is caused by a "collision", you may elect to have it considered a loss caused by "collision".

C. "Non-owned auto" means:

1. Any private passenger auto, pickup, van or "trailer" not owned by or furnished or available for the regular use of you or any "family member" while in the custody of or being operated by you or any "family member"; or

2. Any auto or "trailer" you do not own while used as a temporary substitute for "your covered auto" which is out of normal use because of its:

a. Breakdown,

b. Repair;

c. Servicing;

d. Loss; or

e. Destruction.

TRANSPORTATION EXPENSES

A. In addition, we will pay, without application of a deductible, up to a maximum of $600 for:

1. Temporary transportation expenses not exceeding $20 per day incurred by you in the event of a loss to "your covered auto". We will pay for such expenses if the loss is caused by:

   a. Other than "collision" only if the Declarations indicate that Other Than Collision Coverage is provided for that auto.

   b. "Collision" only if the Declarations indicate that Collision Coverage is provided for that auto.

2. Expenses for which you become legally responsible in the event of loss to a "non-owned auto". We will pay for such expenses if the loss is caused by:

   a. Other than "collision" only if the Declarations indicate that Other Than Collision Coverage is provided for any "your covered auto".

   b. "Collision" only if the Declarations indicate that Collision Coverage is provided for any "your covered auto".

   However, the most we will pay for any expenses for loss of use is $20 per day.

B. If the loss is caused by:

1. A total theft of "your covered auto" or a "non-owned auto", we will pay only expenses incurred during the period:

   a. Beginning 48 hours after the theft; and

   b. Ending when "your covered auto" or the "non-owned auto" is returned to use or we pay for its loss.

2. Other than theft of a "your covered auto" or a "non-owned auto", we will pay only expenses beginning when the auto is withdrawn from use for more than 24 hours.

C. Our payment will be limited to that period of time reasonably required to repair or replace the "your covered auto" or the "non-owned auto".

EXCLUSIONS

We will not pay for:

1. Loss to "your covered auto" or any "non-owned auto" which occurs while it is being used as a public or livery conveyance. This Exclusion (1.) does not apply to a share-the-expense car pool.

2. Damage due and confined to:

   a. Wear and tear;

   b. Freezing;

   c. Mechanical or electrical breakdown or failure; or

   d. Road damage to tires.

This Exclusion (2.) does not apply if the damage results from the total theft of "your covered auto" or any "non-owned auto".

3. Loss due to or as a consequence of:

   a. Radioactive contamination;

   b. Discharge of any nuclear weapon (even if accidental);

   c. War (declared or undeclared);

   d. Civil war;

   e. Insurrection; or

   f. Rebellion or revolution.

4. Loss to any electronic equipment designed for the reproduction of sound and any accessories used with such equipment. This includes but is not limited to:

   a. Radios and stereos;

   b. Tape decks; or

   c. Compact disc players.

This Exclusion (4.) does not apply to equipment designed solely for the reproduction of sound and accessories used with such equipment, provided:

   a. The equipment is permanently installed in "your covered auto" or any "non-owned auto"; or

   b. The equipment is:

   (1) Removable from a housing unit which is permanently installed in the auto;

   (2) Designed to be solely operated by use of the power from the auto's electrical system; and

   (3) In or upon "your covered auto" or any "non-owned auto" at the time of loss.

5. Loss to any electronic equipment that receives or transmits audio, visual or data signals and any accessories used with such equipment. This includes but is not limited to:

   a. Citizens band radios;

   b. Telephones;

   c. Two-way mobile radios;

   d. Scanning monitor receivers;

   e. Television monitor receivers;

   f. Video cassette recorders;

   g. Audio cassette recorders; or

   h. Personal computers.

This Exclusion (5.) does not apply to:

   a. Any electronic equipment that is necessary for the normal operation of the auto or the monitoring of the auto's operating systems; or

         PP 00 01 06 98

b. A permanently installed telephone designed to be operated by use of the power from the auto's electrical system and any accessories used with the telephone.

6. Loss to tapes, records, discs or other media used with equipment described in Exclusions **4.** and **5.**

7. A total loss to "your covered auto" or any "non-owned auto" due to destruction or confiscation by governmental or civil authorities.

This Exclusion **(7.)** does not apply to the interests of Loss Payees in "your covered auto".

8. Loss to:

a. A "trailer", camper body, or motor home, which is not shown in the Declarations; or

b. Facilities or equipment used with such "trailer", camper body or motor home. Facilities or equipment include but are not limited to:

(1) Cooking, dining, plumbing or refrigeration facilities;

(2) Awnings or cabanas; or

(3) Any other facilities or equipment used with a "trailer", camper body, or motor home.

This Exclusion **(8.)** does not apply to a:

a. "Trailer", and its facilities or equipment, which you do not own; or

b. "Trailer", camper body, or the facilities or equipment in or attached to the "trailer" or camper body, which you:

(1) Acquire during the policy period; and

(2) Ask us to insure within 14 days after you become the owner.

9. Loss to any "non-owned auto" when used by you or any "family member" without a reasonable belief that you or that "family member" are entitled to do so.

10. Loss to equipment designed or used for the detection or location of radar or laser.

11. Loss to any custom furnishings or equipment in or upon any pickup or van. Custom furnishings or equipment include but are not limited to:

a. Special carpeting or insulation;

b. Furniture or bars;

c. Height-extending roofs; or

d. Custom murals, paintings or other decals or graphics.

This Exclusion **(11.)** does not apply to a cap, cover or bedliner in or upon any "your covered auto" which is a pickup.

12. Loss to any "non-owned auto" being maintained or used by any person while employed or otherwise engaged in the "business" of:

a. Selling;

b. Repairing;

c. Servicing;

d. Storing; or

e. Parking;

vehicles designed for use on public highways. This includes road testing and delivery.

13. Loss to "your covered auto" or any "non-owned auto", located inside a facility designed for racing, for the purpose of:

a. Competing in; or

b. Practicing or preparing for;

any prearranged or organized racing or speed contest.

14. Loss to, or loss of use of, a "non-owned auto" rented by:

a. You; or

b. Any "family member";

if a rental vehicle company is precluded from recovering such loss or loss of use, from you or that "family member", pursuant to the provisions of any applicable rental agreement or state law.

LIMIT OF LIABILITY

A. Our limit of liability for loss will be the lesser of the:

1. Actual cash value of the stolen or damaged property; or

2. Amount necessary to repair or replace the property with other property of like kind and quality.

However, the most we will pay for loss to:

1. Any "non-owned auto" which is a trailer is $500.

2. Equipment designed solely for the reproduction of sound, including any accessories used with such equipment, which is installed in locations not used by the auto manufacturer for installation of such equipment or accessories, is $1,000.

B. An adjustment for depreciation and physical condition will be made in determining actual cash value in the event of a total loss.

C. If a repair or replacement results in better than like kind or quality, we will not pay for the amount of the betterment.

PAYMENT OF LOSS

We may pay for loss in money or repair or replace the damaged or stolen property. We may, at our expense, return any stolen property to:

1. You; or
2. The address shown in this policy.

If we return stolen property we will pay for any damage resulting from the theft. We may keep all or part of the property at an agreed or appraised value.

If we pay for loss in money, our payment will include the applicable sales tax for the damaged or stolen property.

NO BENEFIT TO BAILEE

This insurance shall not directly or indirectly benefit any carrier or other bailee for hire.

OTHER SOURCES OF RECOVERY

if other sources of recovery also cover the loss, we will pay only our share of the loss. Our share is the proportion that our limit of liability bears to the total of all applicable limits. However, any insurance we pro-vide with respect to a "non-owned auto" shall be ex-.ess over any other collectible source of recovery including, but not limited to:

1. Any coverage provided by the owner of the "non-owned auto";
2. Any other applicable physical damage insurance;
3. Any other source of recovery applicable to the loss.

APPRAISAL

A. If we and you do not agree on the amount of loss, either may demand an appraisal of the loss. In this event, each party will select a competent appraiser. The two appraisers will select an umpire. The appraisers will state separately the actual cash value and the amount of loss. If they fail to agree, they will submit their differences to the umpire. A decision agreed to by any two will be binding. Each party will:

1. Pay its chosen appraiser; and
2. Bear the expenses of the appraisal and umpire equally.

B. We do not waive any of our rights under this policy by agreeing to an appraisal.

PART E – DUTIES AFTER AN ACCIDENT OR LOSS

We have no duty to provide coverage under this policy unless there has been full compliance with the following duties:

A. We must be notified promptly of how, when and where the accident or loss happened. Notice should also include the names and addresses of any injured persons and of any witnesses.

B. A person seeking any coverage must:

1. Cooperate with us in the investigation, settlement or defense of any claim or suit.
2. Promptly send us copies of any notices or legal papers received in connection with the accident or loss.
3. Submit, as often as we reasonably require:
   a. To physical exams by physicians we select. We will pay for these exams.
   b. To examination under oath and subscribe the same.
4. Authorize us to obtain:
   a. Medical reports; and
   b. Other pertinent records.
5. Submit a proof of loss when required by us.

C. A person seeking Uninsured Motorists Coverage must also:

1. Promptly notify the police if a hit-and-run driver is involved.
2. Promptly send us copies of the legal papers if a suit is brought.

D. A person seeking Coverage For Damage To Your Auto must also:

1. Take reasonable steps after loss to protect "your covered auto" or any "non-owned auto" and their equipment from further loss. We will pay reasonable expenses incurred to do this.
2. Promptly notify the police if "your covered auto" or any "non-owned auto" is stolen.
3. Permit us to inspect and appraise the damaged property before its repair or disposal.

PART F – GENERAL PROVISIONS

BANKRUPTCY

Bankruptcy or insolvency of the "insured" shall not relieve us of any obligations under this policy.

CHANGES

A. This policy contains all the agreements between you and us. Its terms may not be changed or waived except by endorsement issued by us.

B. If there is a change to the information used to develop the policy premium, we may adjust your premium. Changes during the policy term that may result in a premium increase or decrease include, but are not limited to, changes in:

   1. The number, type or use classification of insured vehicles;

   2. Operators using insured vehicles;

   3. The place of principal garaging of insured vehicles;

   4. Coverage, deductible or limits.

If a change resulting from **A.** or **B.** requires a premium adjustment, we will make the premium adjustment in accordance with our manual rules.

C. If we make a change which broadens coverage under this edition of your policy without additional premium charge, that change will automatically apply to your policy as of the date we implement the change in your state. This Paragraph (**C.**) does not apply to changes implemented with a general program revision that includes both broadenings and restrictions in coverage, whether that general program revision is implemented through introduction of:

   1. A subsequent edition of your policy; or

   2. An Amendatory Endorsement.

FRAUD

We do not provide coverage for any "insured" who has made fraudulent statements or engaged in fraudulent conduct in connection with any accident or loss for which coverage is sought under this policy.

LEGAL ACTION AGAINST US

A. No legal action may be brought against us until there has been full compliance with all the terms of this policy. In addition, under Part **A**, no legal action may be brought against us until:

   1. We agree in writing that the "insured" has an obligation to pay; or

   2. The amount of that obligation has been finally determined by judgment after trial.

B. No person or organization has any right under this policy to bring us into any action to determine the liability of an "insured".

OUR RIGHT TO RECOVER PAYMENT

A. If we make a payment under this policy and the person to or for whom payment was made has a right to recover damages from another we shall be subrogated to that right. That person shall do:

   1. Whatever is necessary to enable us to exercise our rights; and

   2. Nothing after loss to prejudice them.

However, our rights in this Paragraph (**A.**) do not apply under Part **D**, against any person using "your covered auto" with a reasonable belief that that person is entitled to do so.

B. If we make a payment under this policy and the person to or for whom payment is made recovers damages from another, that person shall:

   1. Hold in trust for us the proceeds of the recovery; and

   2. Reimburse us to the extent of our payment.

POLICY PERIOD AND TERRITORY

A. This policy applies only to accidents and losses which occur:

   1. During the policy period as shown in the Declarations; and

   2. Within the policy territory.

B. The policy territory is:

   1. The United States of America, its territories or possessions;

   2. Puerto Rico; or

   3. Canada.

This policy also applies to loss to, or accidents involving, "your covered auto" while being transported between their ports.

TERMINATION

A. Cancellation

This policy may be cancelled during the policy period as follows:

   1. The named insured shown in the Declarations may cancel by:

     a. Returning this policy to us; or

     b. Giving us advance written notice of the date cancellation is to take effect.

   2. We may cancel by mailing to the named insured shown in the Declarations at the address shown in this policy:

     a. At least 10 days notice:

       (1) If cancellation is for nonpayment of premium; or

(2) If notice is mailed during the first 60 days this policy is in effect and this is not a renewal or continuation policy; or

b. At least 20 days notice in all other cases.

3. After this policy is in effect for 60 days, or if this is a renewal or continuation policy, we will cancel only:

a. For nonpayment of premium; or

b. If your driver's license or that of:

(1) Any driver who lives with you; or

(2) Any driver who customarily uses "your covered auto";

has been suspended or revoked. This must have occurred:

(1) During the policy period; or

(2) Since the last anniversary of the original effective date if the policy period is other than 1 year; or

c. If the policy was obtained through material misrepresentation.

B. Nonrenewal

If we decide not to renew or continue this policy, we will mail notice to the named insured shown in the Declarations at the address shown in this policy. Notice will be mailed at least 20 days before the end of the policy period. Subject to this notice requirement, if the policy period is:

1. Less than 6 months, we will have the right not to renew or continue this policy every 6 months, beginning 6 months after its original effective date.

2. 6 months or longer, but less than one year, we will have the right not to renew or continue this policy at the end of the policy period.

3. 1 year or longer, we will have the right not to renew or continue this policy at each anniversary of its original effective date.

C. Automatic Termination

If we offer to renew or continue and you or your representative do not accept, this policy will automatically terminate at the end of the current policy period. Failure to pay the required renewal or continuation premium when due shall mean that you have not accepted our offer.

If you obtain other insurance on "your covered auto", any similar insurance provided by this policy will terminate as to that auto on the effective date of the other insurance.

D. Other Termination Provisions

1. We may deliver any notice instead of mailing it. Proof of mailing of any notice shall be sufficient proof of notice.

2. If this policy is cancelled, you may be entitled to a premium refund. If so, we will send you the refund. The premium refund, if any, will be computed according to our manuals. However, making or offering to make the refund is not a condition of cancellation.

3. The effective date of cancellation stated in the notice shall become the end of the policy period.

TRANSFER OF YOUR INTEREST IN THIS POLICY

A. Your rights and duties under this policy may not be assigned without our written consent. However, if a named insured shown in the Declarations dies, coverage will be provided for:

1. The surviving spouse if resident in the same household at the time of death. Coverage applies to the spouse as if a named insured shown in the Declarations; and

2. The legal representative of the deceased person as if a named insured shown in the Declarations. This applies only with respect to the representative's legal responsibility to maintain or use "your covered auto".

B. Coverage will only be provided until the end of the policy period.

TWO OR MORE AUTO POLICIES

If this policy and any other auto insurance policy issued to you by us apply to the same accident, the maximum limit of our liability under all the policies shall not exceed the highest applicable limit of liability under any one policy.

Appendix C

Whole Life Policy

29-3854-01(1-86) WHOLE LIFE
I/R 4400.00

This is a representative sample of Mutual Life's NN series Whole Life Policy. Policy benefits and wording may vary to comply with state regulations. The notations are to guide you through provisions of the policy. They do not modify the policy terms.

Our promise to you. ——————————————— Mutual Life Insurance Company agrees to pay the benefits prov In this policy, subject to its terms and conditions.

PRESIDENT AND C.E.O.   *SECRETARY*

WHOLE LIFE POLICY

Eligible For Annual Dividends.

Insurance payable on death of Insured. Premiums payable for p shown on page 3.

Return the policy ———————————— **Right to Return Policy** — Please read this policy carefully. The p
within ten days if you   may be returned by the Owner for any reason within ten days a
don't like it, and your   was received. The policy may be returned to your agent or to th
money will be   Home Office of the Company at 720 East Wisconsin Avenue,
refunded.   Milwaukee, WI 53202. If returned, the policy will be considered
from the beginning. Any premium paid will then be refunded.

NN 1

You, as a policyowner,
are also an owner of ——————————— **Mutual Life** ●
this mutual company.

"Whole Life Policy" reprinted with permission from Northwestern Mutual Life.

This policy is a legal contract between the Owner and Mutual Life Insurance Company.
Read your policy carefully.

Table of Contents. ———————————————————— GUIDE TO POLICY PROVISIONS

NN 1, 4

Page 4 shows our ━━━━━━━━━━━━━━━━BENEFITS AND PREMIUMS
minimum guarantees.
DATE OF ISSUE - JANUARY 1, 1986

PLAN AND ADDITIONAL BENEFITS	AMOUNT	ANNUAL PREMIUM	PAYABLE FOR
WHOLE LIFE PAID-UP AT 90	$ 100,000	$ 1,533.00	55 YEARS

A PREMIUM IS PAYABLE ON JANUARY 1, 1986 AND EVERY JANUARY 1 AFTER THAT.
THE FIRST PREMIUM IS $1,533.00.

THE OWNER MAY ELECT THE SPECIFIED RATE OR THE VARIABLE RATE LOAN INTEREST
OPTION. SEE SECTIONS 8.4 THROUGH 8.6 OF THE POLICY. THE VARIABLE RATE
LOAN INTEREST OPTION WAS ELECTED ON THE APPLICATION.

THIS POLICY IS ISSUED IN A SELECT PREMIUM CLASS.

DIRECT BENEFICIARY   JANE M DOE, WIFE OF THE INSURED

OWNER   JOHN J DOE, THE INSURED

INSURED	JOHN J DOE	AGE AND SEX	35 MALE
POLICY DATE	JANUARY 1, 1986	POLICY NUMBER	1 000 001
PLAN	WHOLE LIFE PAID-UP AT 90	AMOUNT	$ 100,000
NN 1		PAGE 3	

Type of policy you
bought.

Your policy's "I.D."

TABLE OF GUARANTEED VALUES

END OF POLICY YEAR	JANUARY 1,	CASH VALUE	PAID-UP INSURANCE	$100,000 EXTENDED TERM INSURANCE TO
1	1987	$ 0	$ 0	JUN 15, 1991
2	1988	1,078	5,000	APR 29, 1995
3	1989	2,261	9,800	SEP 14, 1998
4	1990	3,421	14,400	SEP 14, 1998
5	1991	4,568	18,700	SEP 26, 2001
6	1992	5,852	22,900	JUN 12, 2004
7	1993	7,125	26,800	FEB 7, 2007
8	1994	8,528	30,500	OCT 12, 2009
9	1995	9,942	34,100	FEB 15, 2012
10	1996	11,411	37,400	MAR 14, 2014
11	1997	12,933	40,600	JAN 14, 2016
12	1998	14,515	43,700	SEP 18, 2017
13	1999	16,156	46,600	MAR 12, 2019
14	2000	17,860	49,300	AUG 12, 2020
15	2001	19,629	51,900	NOV 18, 2021
16	2002	21,466	54,400	FEB 1, 2023
17	2003	23,370	56,800	MAR 19, 2024
18	2004	25,341	59,000	APR 7, 2025
19	2005	27,380	61,100	APR 3, 2026
20	2006	29,486	63,100	MAR 12, 2029
AGE 60	2011	38,328	71,800	OCT 30, 2030
AGE 65	2016	47,545	78,800	FEB 16, 2034
AGE 70	2021	56,741	84,400	FEB 18, 2037

VALUES ARE INCREASED BY PAID-UP ADDITIONS AND DIVIDEND ACCUMULATIONS
AND DECREASED BY POLICY DEBT. VALUES SHOWN AT END OF POLICY YEAR
DO NOT REFLECT ANY PREMIUM DUE ON THAT POLICY ANNIVERSARY.

INSURED	JOHN J DOE	AGE AND SEX	35 MALE
POLICY DATE	JANUARY 1, 1986	POLICY NUMBER	1 000 001
PLAN	WHOLE LIFE PAID-UP AT 90	AMOUNT	$ 100,000
NN 1		PAGE 4	

SECTION 1. THE CONTRACT

The contract is made up of the policy and the application.

1.1 LIFE INSURANCE BENEFIT

The Northwestern Mutual Life Insurance Company will pay a benefit on the death of the Insured. Subject to the terms and conditions of the policy:

- payment of the death proceeds will be made after proof of the death of the Insured is received at the Home Office; and
- payment will be made to the beneficiary or other payee under Sections 8 and 9.

The company's defense against misrepresentation ends two years after the policy is issued if the insured is still alive.

The amount of the death proceeds when all premiums due have been paid will be:

- the plan Amount shown on page 3; plus
- the amount of any paid-up additions then in force (Section 4.2); plus
- the amount of any dividend accumulations (Section 4.2); plus
- the amount of any premium refund (Section 3.1) and any dividend at death (Section 4.4); less
- the amount of any policy debt (Section 6.3).

The company's defense against suicide ends one year after the policy is issued if the insured is still alive.

These amounts will be determined as of the date of death.

The amount of the death proceeds when the Insured dies during the grace period following the due date of any unpaid premium will be:

- the amount determined above assuming the overdue premium has been paid; less
- the amount of the unpaid premium.

The amount of the death proceeds when the Insured dies while the policy is in force as extended term or paid-up insurance will be determined under Sections 5.2 or 5.3.

1.2 ENTIRE CONTRACT; CHANGES

This policy with the attached application is the entire contract. Statements in the application are representations and not warranties. A change in the policy is valid only if it is approved by an officer of the Company. The Company may require that the policy be sent to it for endorsement to show a change. No agent has the authority to change the policy or to waive any of its terms.

1.3 INCONTESTABILITY

The Company will not contest this policy after it has been in force during the lifetime of the Insured for two years from the Date of Issue. In issuing the policy, the Company has relied on the application. While the policy is contestable, the Company, on the basis of a misstatement in the application, may rescind the policy or deny a claim.

1.4 SUICIDE

If the Insured dies by suicide within one year from the Date of Issue, the amount payable by the Company will be limited to the premiums paid, less the amount of any policy debt.

1.5 DATES

The contestable and suicide periods begin with the Date of Issue. Policy months, years and anniversaries are computed from the Policy Date. Both dates are shown on page 3.

1.6 MISSTATEMENT OF AGE OR SEX

If the age or sex of the Insured has been misstated, the amount payable will be the amount which the premiums paid would have purchased at the correct age and sex.

1.7 PAYMENTS BY THE COMPANY

All payments by the Company under this policy are payable at its Home Office.

SECTION 2. OWNERSHIP

2.1 THE OWNER

The Owner is named on page 3. The Owner, his successor or his transferee may exercise policy rights without the consent of any beneficiary. After the death of the Insured, policy rights may be exercised only as provided in Sections 8 and 9.

The policy can have a new owner.

2.2 TRANSFER OF OWNERSHIP

The Owner may transfer the ownership of this policy. Written proof of transfer satisfactory to the Company must be received at its Home Office. The transfer will then take effect as of the date that it was signed. The Company may require that the policy be sent to it for endorsement to show the transfer.

NN 1,4

5

2.3 COLLATERAL ASSIGNMENT

The Owner may assign this policy as collateral security. The Company is not responsible for the validity or effect of a collateral assignment. The Company will not be responsible to an assignee for any payment or other action taken by the Company before receipt of the assignment in writing at its Home Office.

The interest of any beneficiary will be subject to any collateral assignment made either before or after the beneficiary is named.

A collateral assignee is not an Owner. A collateral assignment is not a transfer of ownership. Ownership can be transferred only by complying with Section 2.2.

The policy may be assigned as security for a loan.

SECTION 3. PREMIUMS AND REINSTATEMENT

3.1 PREMIUM PAYMENT

Payment. All premiums after the first are payable at the Home Office or to an authorized agent. A receipt signed by an officer of the Company will be furnished on request. A premium must be paid on or before its due date. The date when each premium is due and the number of years for which premiums are payable are described on page 3.

Frequency. Premiums may be paid every 3, 6 or 12 months at the published rates of the Company. A change in premium frequency will take effect when the Company accepts a premium on a new frequency. Premiums may be paid on any other frequency approved by the Company.

You have 31 days beyond the due date to pay your premium.

Grace Period. A grace period of 31 days will be allowed to pay a premium that is not paid on its due date. The policy will be in full force during this period. If the Insured dies during the grace period, any overdue premium will be paid from the proceeds of the policy.

If the premium is not paid within the grace period, the policy will terminate as of the due date unless it continues as extended term or paid-up insurance under Section 5.2 or 5.3.

Premium Refund At Death. The Company will refund a portion of a premium paid for the period beyond the date of the Insured's death. The refund will be part of the policy proceeds.

3.2 REINSTATEMENT

The policy may be reinstated within five years after the due date of the overdue premium. All unpaid premiums (and interest as required below) must be received by the Company while the Insured is alive. The policy may not be reinstated if the policy was surrendered for its cash surrender value. Any policy debt on the due date of the overdue premium, with interest from that date, must be repaid or reinstated.

In addition, for the policy to be reinstated more than 31 days after the end of the grace period:

- evidence of insurability must be given that is satisfactory to the Company; and
- all unpaid premiums must be paid with interest from the due date of each premium. Interest is at an annual effective rate of 6%.

How to reinstate your policy.

SECTION 4. DIVIDENDS

You may receive dividends annually.

4.1 ANNUAL DIVIDENDS

This policy will share in the divisible surplus of the Company. This surplus is determined each year. This policy's share will be credited as a dividend on the policy anniversary. The dividend will reflect the mortality, expense and investment experience of the Company and will be affected by any policy debt during the policy year.

4.2 USE OF DIVIDENDS

Annual dividends may be paid in cash or used for one of the following:

This popular way to use dividends provides additional insurance.

- **Paid-up Additions.** Dividends will purchase paid-up additional insurance. Paid-up additions share in the divisible surplus.

- **Dividend Accumulations.** Dividends will accumulate at interest. Interest is credited at an annual effective rate of 3 1/2%. The Company may set a higher rate.

Another popular way to use dividends is to reduce premiums.

- **Premium Payment.** Dividends will be used to reduce premiums. If the balance of a premium is

not paid, or if this policy is in force as paid-up insurance, the dividend will purchase paid-up additions.

Other uses of dividends may be made available by the Company.

If no direction is given for the use of dividends, they will purchase paid-up additions.

4.3 ADDITIONS AND ACCUMULATIONS

Paid-up additions and dividend accumulations increase the policy's cash value. They are payable as part of the policy proceeds. Additions may be surrendered and accumulations may be withdrawn unless they are used for a loan, for extended term insurance or for paid-up insurance.

4.4 DIVIDEND AT DEATH

A dividend for the period from the beginning of the policy year to the date of the Insured's death will be payable as part of the policy proceeds.

NN 1,4

6

The rights you have if you no longer want to pay premiums.

SECTION 5. CASH VALUES, EXTENDED TERM INSURANCE
AND PAID-UP INSURANCE

5.1 CASH VALUE

The cash value for this policy, when all premiums due have been paid, will be the sum of:

- the cash value from the Table of Guaranteed Values;
- the cash value of any paid-up additions; and
- the amount of any dividend accumulations.

The cash value within three months after the due date of any unpaid premium will be the cash value on that due date reduced by any later surrender of paid-up additions and by any later withdrawal of dividend accumulations. After that, the cash value will be the cash value of the insurance then in force, including any paid-up additions and any dividend accumulations.

The cash value of any extended term insurance, paid-up insurance or paid-up additions will be the net single premium for that insurance at the attained age of the Insured.

You can have term insurance for a period of time determined by the cash surrender value.

5.2 EXTENDED TERM INSURANCE

If any premium is unpaid at the end of the grace period, this policy will be in force as extended term insurance. The amount of the death proceeds under this term insurance will be:

- the plan Amount shown on page 3; plus
- the amount of any paid-up additions in force (Section 4.2); plus
- the amount of any dividend accumulations (Section 4.2); less
- the amount of any policy debt (Section 6.3).

These amounts will be determined as of the due date of the unpaid premium. The term insurance will start as of the due date of the unpaid premium. The period of term insurance will be determined by using the cash surrender value as a net single premium at the attained age of the Insured. If the term insurance would extend to or beyond age 100, paid-up insurance will be provided instead. Extended term insurance does not share in divisible surplus.

If the extended term insurance is surrendered within 31 days after a policy anniversary, the cash value will not be less than the cash value on that anniversary.

You can take a dividend paying policy, good for life, requiring no further premium payment, in an amount determined by the cash value.

5.3 PAID-UP INSURANCE

Paid-up insurance may be selected in place of extended term insurance. A written request must be received at the Home Office no later than three months after the due date of an unpaid premium. The amount of insurance will be determined by using the cash value as a net single premium at the attained age of the Insured. Any policy debt will continue. Paid-up insurance will share in divisible surplus.

The amount of the death proceeds when this policy is in force as paid-up insurance will be:

- the amount of paid-up insurance determined above, plus

NN 1

- the amount of any in force paid-up additions purchased by dividends after the policy has become paid-up insurance (Section 4.2); plus
- the amount of any existing dividend accumulations (Section 4.2); plus
- the amount of any dividend at death (Section 4.4); less
- the amount of any policy debt (Section 6.3).

These amounts will be determined as of the date of death.

If paid-up insurance is surrendered within 31 days after a policy anniversary, the cash value will not be less than the cash value on that anniversary reduced by any later surrender of paid-up additions and by any later withdrawal of dividend accumulations.

5.4 CASH SURRENDER

The Owner may surrender this policy for its cash surrender value. The cash surrender value is the cash value less any policy debt. A written surrender of all claims, satisfactory to the Company, will be required. The date of surrender will be the date of receipt at the Home Office of the written surrender. The policy will terminate and the cash surrender value will be determined as of the date of surrender. The Company may require that the policy be sent to it.

5.5 TABLE OF GUARANTEED VALUES

Cash values, paid-up insurance and extended term insurance are shown on page 4 for the end of the policy years indicated. These values assume that all premiums due have been paid for the number of years stated. They do not reflect paid-up additions, dividend accumulations or policy debt. Values during a policy year will reflect any portion of the year's premium paid and the time elapsed in that year.

Values for policy years not shown are calculated on the same basis as those on page 4. A list of these values will be furnished on request. A detailed statement of the method of calculation of all values has been filed with the insurance supervisory official of the state in which this policy is delivered. The Company will furnish this statement at the request of the Owner. All values are at least as great as those required by that state.

5.6 BASIS OF VALUES

The cash value for each policy year not shown on page 4 equals the reserve for that year calculated on the Commissioners Reserve Valuation Method. Net single premiums are based on the Commissioners 1980 Standard Ordinary Mortality Table for the sex of the Insured; except that for extended term insurance, the Commissioners 1980 Extended Term Insurance Table for the sex of the Insured is used for the first 20 policy years. Interest is based on an annual effective rate of 5 1/2% for the first 20 policy years and 4% after that. Calculations assume the continuous payment of premiums and the immediate payment of claims.

7

You can take out all of your cash value, less any policy debt.

SECTION 6. LOANS

You can borrow money from the company, the maximum amount to be determined by the loan value.

6.1 POLICY AND PREMIUM LOANS

The Owner may obtain a loan from the Company in an amount that is not more than the loan value.

Policy Loan. The loan may be obtained on written request. No loan will be made if the policy is in force as extended term insurance. The Company may defer making the loan for up to six months unless the loan is to be used to pay premiums due the Company.

Premium Loan. If the premium loan provision is in effect on this policy, a loan will be made to pay an overdue premium. If the loan value is not large enough to pay the overdue premium, a premium will be paid for any other frequency permitted by this policy for which the loan value is large enough. The Owner may elect or revoke the premium loan provision by written request received at the Home Office.

6.2 LOAN VALUE

The loan value is the smaller of a. or b., less any policy debt and any premium then due or billed; a. and b. are defined as:

a. the cash value one year after the date of the loan, assuming all premiums due within that year are paid, less interest to one year from the date of the loan.

b. the cash value on the due date of the first premium not yet billed that is due after the date of the loan, less interest from the date of the loan to that premium due date.

Two important facts about loans: Indebtedness is subtracted at death from the insurance proceeds. Despite the loan, the cash value continues to grow as guaranteed, and the policy continues to be eligible for dividends.

6.3 POLICY DEBT

Policy debt consists of all outstanding loans and accrued interest. It may be paid to the Company at any time. Policy debt affects dividends under Section 4.1. Any policy debt will be deducted from the policy proceeds.

If the policy debt equals or exceeds the cash value, this policy will terminate. Termination occurs 31 days after a notice has been mailed to the Owner and to any assignee on record at the Home Office.

You can choose between a fixed or a variable loan rate and you may be able to change your option once a year.

6.4 LOAN INTEREST

Interest accrues and is payable on a daily basis from the date of the loan on policy loans and from the premium due date on premium loans. Unpaid interest is added to the loan.

The Specified Rate loan interest option or the Variable Rate loan interest option is elected on the application.

Change To Variable Rate Loan Interest Option. The Owner may request a change to the Variable Rate loan interest option at any time, with the change to take effect on the January 1st following receipt of a written request at the Company's Home Office.

Change To Specified Rate Loan Interest Option. The Owner may request a change to the Specified Rate loan interest option if the interest rate set by the Company under Section 6.6 for the year beginning on the next January 1st is less than 8%. The written request to change must be received at the Home Office between November 15th and the last business day of the calendar year; the change will take effect on the January 1st following receipt of the request at the Home Office.

6.5 SPECIFIED RATE LOAN INTEREST OPTION

Interest is payable at an annual effective rate of 8%.

6.6 VARIABLE RATE LOAN INTEREST OPTION

Interest is payable at an annual effective rate that is set by the Company annually and applied to new or outstanding policy debt during the year beginning each January 1st. The highest loan interest rate that may be set by the Company is the greater of (i) 6 1/2% for the first 20 policy years and 5% after that or (ii) a rate based on the Moody's Corporate Bond Yield Averages-Monthly Average Corporates for the immediately preceding October. This Average is published by Moody's Investor's Service, Inc. If it is no longer published, the highest loan rate will be based on some other similar average established by the insurance supervisory official of the state in which this policy is delivered.

The loan interest rate set by the Company will not exceed the maximum rate permitted by the laws of the state in which this policy is delivered. The loan interest rate may be increased only if the increase in the annual effective rate is at least 1/2%. The loan interest rate will be decreased if the decrease in the annual effective rate is at least 1/2%.

The Company will give notice:
- of the initial loan interest rate in effect at the time a policy or premium loan is made.
- of an increase in loan interest rate on outstanding policy debt no later than 30 days before the January 1st on which the increase takes effect.

This policy will not terminate during a policy year as the sole result of an increase in the loan interest rate during that policy year.

The fixed loan rate is 8%. The variable loan rate is based on Moody's Corporate Bond Yield Averages - Monthly Average Corporates.

NN 1,4,9

8

SECTION 7. CHANGE OF POLICY

You can change the plan, keeping the original issue age.

7.1 CHANGE OF PLAN

The Owner may change this policy to any permanent life insurance plan agreed to by the Owner and the Company by:

- paying the required costs; and
- meeting any other conditions set by the Company.

You can change the policy to insure the life of another person, e.g., wife to husband, one business partner to another.

7.2 CHANGE OF INSURED

Change. The Owner may change the insured under this policy by:

- paying the required costs; and
- meeting any other conditions set by the Company, including the following:

    a. on the date of change, the new insured's age may not be more than 75;

    b. the new insured must have been born on or before the Policy Date of this policy;

c. the new insured must be insurable; and

d. the Owner must have an insurable interest in the life of the new insured.

Date Of Change. The date of change will be the later of:

- the date of the request to change; or
- the date of the medical examination (or the non-medical application).

Terms Of Policy After Change. The policy will cover the new insured starting on the date of change. When coverage on the new insured starts, coverage on the prior insured will terminate.

The contestable and suicide periods for the new insured start on the date of change.

The amount of insurance on the new insured will be set so that there will be no change in the cash value of the policy at the time of change. If the policy has no cash value, the amount will be set so that premiums do not change.

Any policy debt or assignment will continue after the change.

NN 1,4,9

9

SECTION 8. BENEFICIARIES

8.1 DEFINITION OF BENEFICIARIES

The term "beneficiaries" as used in this policy includes direct beneficiaries, contingent beneficiaries and further payees.

8.2 NAMING AND CHANGE OF BENEFICIARIES

By Owner. The Owner may name and change the beneficiaries of death proceeds:

- while the Insured is living.
- during the first 60 days after the date of death of the Insured, if the Insured just before his death was not the Owner. No one may change this naming of a direct beneficiary during this 60 days.

By Direct Beneficiary. A direct beneficiary may name and change the contingent beneficiaries and further payees of his share of the proceeds:

- if the direct beneficiary is the Owner;
- if, at any time after the death of the Insured, no contingent beneficiary or further payee of that share is living; or
- if, after the death of the Insured, the direct beneficiary elects a payment plan. The interest of any other beneficiary in the share of that direct beneficiary will end.

These direct beneficiary rights are subject to the Owner's rights during the 60 days after the date of death of the Insured.

By Spouse (Marital Deduction Provision).

- **Power To Appoint.** The spouse of the Insured will have the power alone and in all events to appoint all amounts payable to the spouse under the policy if:

  a. the Insured just before his death was the Owner; and

  b. the spouse is a direct beneficiary; and

  c. the spouse survives the Insured.

- **To Whom Spouse Can Appoint.** Under this power, the spouse can appoint:

  a. to the estate of the spouse; or

  b. to any other persons as contingent beneficiaries and further payees.

- **Effect Of Exercise.** As to the amounts appointed, the exercise of this power will:

  a. revoke any other designation of beneficiaries;

  b. revoke any election of payment plan as it applies to them; and

  c. cause any provision to the contrary in Section 8 or 9 of this policy to be of no effect.

NN 1,2,4,6,8,9

Effective Date. A naming or change of a beneficiary will be made on receipt at the Home Office of a written request that is acceptable to the Company. The request will then take effect as of the date that it was signed. The Company is not responsible for any payment or other action that is taken by it before the receipt of the request. The Company may require that the policy be sent to it it to be endorsed to show the naming or change.

8.3 SUCCESSION IN INTEREST OF BENEFICIARIES

Direct Beneficiaries. The proceeds of this policy will be payable in equal shares to the direct beneficiaries who survive and receive payment. If a direct beneficiary dies before he receives all or part of his full share, the unpaid part of his share will be payable in equal shares to the other direct beneficiaries who survive and receive payment.

Contingent Beneficiaries. At the death of all of the direct beneficiaries, the proceeds, or the present value of any unpaid payments under a payment plan, will be payable in equal shares to the contingent beneficiaries who survive and receive payment. If a contingent beneficiary dies before he receives all or part of his full share, the unpaid part of his share will be payable in equal shares to the other contingent beneficiaries who survive and receive payment.

Further Payees. At the death of all of the direct and contingent beneficiaries, the proceeds, or the present value of any unpaid payments under a payment plan, will be paid in one sum:

- in equal shares to the further payees who survive and receive payment; or
- if no further payees survive and receive payment, to the estate of the last to die of all of the direct and contingent beneficiaries.

Owner Or His Estate. If no beneficiaries are alive when the Insured dies, the proceeds will be paid to the Owner or to his estate.

8.4 GENERAL

Transfer Of Ownership. A transfer of ownership of itself will not change the interest of a beneficiary.

Claims Of Creditors. So far as allowed by law, no amount payable under this policy will be subject to the claims of creditors of a beneficiary.

Succession Under Payment Plans. A direct or contingent beneficiary who succeeds to an interest in a payment plan will continue under the terms of the plan.

10

As an aid to estate and tax planning, a third-party policyowner can change beneficiaries after the death of the insured.

The marital deduction provision is valuable in cases in which the spouse is the direct beneficiary.

Living successor beneficiaries can be provided for by contract.

This clause may safeguard policy proceeds.

A wide range of payment plans is available.

SECTION 9. PAYMENT OF POLICY BENEFITS

9.1 PAYMENT OF PROCEEDS

Interest is paid on policy proceeds from the date of death.

Death proceeds will be paid under the payment plan that takes effect on the date of death of the insured. The Interest Income Plan (Option A) will be in effect if no payment plan has been elected. Interest will accumulate from the date of death until a payment plan is elected or the proceeds are withdrawn in cash.

Surrender proceeds will be the cash surrender value as of the date of surrender. These proceeds will be paid in cash or under a payment plan that is elected. The Company may defer paying the surrender proceeds for up to six months from the date of surrender. If payment is deferred for 30 days or more, interest will be paid on the surrender proceeds from the date of surrender to the date of payment. Interest will be at an annual effective rate of 5 1/2% during the first 20 policy years and 4% after that.

9.2 PAYMENT PLANS

Interest Income Plan (Option A). The proceeds will earn interest which may be received each month or accumulated. The first payment is due one month after the date on which the plan takes effect. Interest that has accumulated may be withdrawn at any time. Part or all of the proceeds may be withdrawn at any time.

Beneficiaries, who have the right to withdraw from the chosen payment plan, can change payment plans.

Installment Income Plans. Payments will be made each month on the terms of the plan that is elected. The first payment is due on the date that the plan takes effect.

- **Specified Period (Option B).** The proceeds with interest will be paid over a period of from one to 30 years. The present value of any unpaid installments may be withdrawn at any time.

- **Specified Amount (Option D).** Payments of not less than $10.00 per $1,000 of proceeds will be made until all of the proceeds with interest have been paid. The balance may be withdrawn at any time.

Proceeds under these payment plans continue to earn interest.

Life Income Plans. Payments will be made each month on the terms of the plan that is elected. The first payment is due on the date that the plan takes effect. Proof of the date of birth, acceptable to the Company, must be furnished for each person on whose life the payments are based.

- **Single Life Income (Option C).** Payments will be made for a chosen period and, after that, for the life of the person on whose life the payments are based. The choices for the period are:

  a. zero years;

  b. 10 years;

  c. 20 years; or

  d. a refund period which continues until the sum of the payments that have been made is equal to the proceeds that were placed under the plan.

NN 1.2.4.6.9

11

- **Joint And Survivor Life Income (Option E).** Payments are based on the lives of two persons. Level payments will be made for a period of 10 years and, after that, for as long as one or both of the persons are living.

- **Other Selections.** The Company may offer other selections under the Life Income Plans.

- **Withdrawal.** The present value of any unpaid payments that are to be made for the chosen period (Option C) or the 10 year period (Option E) may be withdrawn only after the death of all of the persons on whose lives the payments are based.

- **Limitations.** A direct or contingent beneficiary who is a natural person may be paid under a Life Income Plan only if the payments depend on his life. A corporation may be paid under a Life Income Plan only if the payments depend on the life of the insured or, after the death of the insured, on the life of his spouse or his dependent.

Payment Frequency. On request, payments will be made once every 3, 6 or 12 months instead of each month.

Transfer Between Payment Plans. A beneficiary who is receiving payment under a plan which includes the right to withdraw may transfer the amount withdrawable to any other plan that is available.

Minimum Payment. The Company may limit the election of a payment plan to one that results in payments of at least $50.

If payments under a payment plan are or become less than $50, the Company may change the frequency of payments. If the payments are being made once every 12 months and are less than $50, the Company may pay the present value or the balance of the payment plan.

9.3 PAYMENT PLAN RATES

Interest Income And Installment Income Plans. Proceeds will earn interest at rates declared each year by the Company. None of these rates will be less than an annual effective rate of 3 1/2%. Interest of more than 3 1/2% will increase the amount of the payments or, for the Specified Amount Plan (Option D), increase the number of payments. The present value of any unpaid installments will be based on the 3 1/2% rate of interest.

The Company may offer guaranteed rates of interest higher than 3 1/2% with conditions on withdrawal.

Life Income Plans. Payments will be based on rates declared by the Company. These rates will provide at least as much income as would the Company's rates, on the date that the payment plan takes effect, for a single premium immediate annuity contract, with no charge for issue expenses. Payments under these rates will not be less than the amounts that are described in Minimum Payment Rates.

Life income rates vary with investment conditions, but a minimum rate is guaranteed. Once a payment plan takes effect, that rate is assured thereafter.

Minimum Payment Rates. The minimum payment rates for the Installment Income Plans (Options B and D) and the Life Income Plans (Options C and E) are shown in the Minimum Payment Rate Tables.

The Life Income Plan payment rates in those tables depend on the sex and on the adjusted age of each person on whose life the payments are based. The adjusted age is:

- the age on the birthday that is nearest to the date on which the payment plan takes effect; plus

- the age adjustment shown below for the number of policy years that have elapsed from the Policy Date to the date that the payment plan takes effect. A part of a policy year is counted as a full year.

POLICY YEARS ELAPSED	AGE ADJUSTMENT	POLICY YEARS ELAPSED	AGE ADJUSTMENT
1 to 5	+ 8	31 to 35	-2
6 to 10	+ 6	36 to 40	-3
11 to 15	+ 4	41 to 45	-4
16 to 20	+ 2	46 to 50	-5
21 to 25	0	51 or more	-6
26 to 30	-1		

9.4 EFFECTIVE DATE FOR PAYMENT PLAN

A payment plan that is elected for death proceeds will take effect on the date of death of the Insured if:

- the plan is elected by the Owner; and

- the election is received at the Home Office while the Insured is living.

In all other cases, a payment plan that is elected will take effect:

- on the date the election is received at the Home Office; or

- on a later date, if requested.

9.5 PAYMENT PLAN ELECTIONS

For Death Proceeds By Owner. The Owner may elect payment plans for death proceeds:

- while the Insured is living.

- during the first 60 days after the date of death of the Insured, if the Insured just before his death was not the Owner. No one may change this election made during those 60 days.

For Death Proceeds By Direct Or Contingent Beneficiary. A direct or contingent beneficiary may elect payment plans for death proceeds payable to him if no payment plan that has been elected is in effect. This right is subject to the Owner's rights during the 60 days after the date of death of the Insured.

For Surrender Proceeds. The Owner may elect payment plans for surrender proceeds. The Owner will be the direct beneficiary.

9.6 INCREASE OF MONTHLY INCOME

A direct beneficiary who is to receive proceeds under a payment plan may increase the amount of the monthly payments. This is done by the payment of an annuity premium to the Company at the time the payment plan elected under Section 9.5 takes effect. The amount that will be applied under the payment plan will be the net premium. The net premium is the annuity premium less a charge of not more than 2% and less any premium tax. The net premium will be applied under the same payment plan and at the same rates as the proceeds. The Company may limit this net premium to an amount that is equal to the direct beneficiary's share of the proceeds payable under this policy.

Beneficiaries can add funds to a payment plan when it takes effect.

Our minimum guarantees for installment income plans.

MINIMUM PAYMENT RATE TABLE

Minimum Monthly Income Payments Per $1,000 Proceeds

INSTALLMENT INCOME PLANS (Options B and D)

PERIOD (YEARS)	MONTHLY PAYMENT	PERIOD (YEARS)	MONTHLY PAYMENT	PERIOD (YEARS)	MONTHLY PAYMENT
1	$84.65	11	$ 9.09	21	$ 5.56
2	43.05	12	8.46	22	5.39
3	29.19	13	7.94	23	5.24
4	22.27	14	7.49	24	5.09
5	18.12	15	7.10	25	4.96
6	15.35	16	6.76	26	4.84
7	13.38	17	6.47	27	4.73
8	11.90	18	6.20	28	4.63
9	10.75	19	5.97	29	4.53
10	9.83	20	5.75	30	4.45

NN 1,2,4,6,9

12

MINIMUM PAYMENT RATE TABLES
Minimum Monthly Income Payments Per $1,000 Proceeds

Our minimum guarantees for life income plans. LIFE INCOME PLAN (Option C)

SINGLE LIFE MONTHLY PAYMENTS									
MALE ADJUSTED AGE*	CHOSEN PERIOD (YEARS)				FEMALE ADJUSTED AGE*	CHOSEN PERIOD (YEARS)			
	ZERO	10	20	REFUND		ZERO	10	20	REFUND
55	$ 4.99	$ 4.91	$ 4.66	$ 4.73	55	$ 4.54	$ 4.51	$ 4.38	$ 4.40
56	5.09	5.00	4.72	4.81	56	4.62	4.58	4.44	4.47
57	5.20	5.10	4.78	4.90	57	4.71	4.66	4.51	4.54
58	5.32	5.20	4.85	4.99	58	4.80	4.75	4.57	4.62
59	5.44	5.31	4.91	5.08	59	4.90	4.84	4.64	4.70
60	5.57	5.42	4.97	5.18	60	5.00	4.93	4.70	4.78
61	5.71	5.54	5.04	5.29	61	5.11	5.03	4.77	4.87
62	5.86	5.67	5.10	5.40	62	5.23	5.14	4.84	4.96
63	6.02	5.80	5.16	5.51	63	5.36	5.25	4.91	5.06
64	6.20	5.94	5.22	5.63	64	5.49	5.37	4.98	5.17
65	6.38	6.08	5.28	5.76	65	5.64	5.50	5.05	5.28
66	6.54	6.23	5.33	5.90	66	5.79	5.63	5.12	5.39
67	6.70	6.38	5.38	6.04	67	5.94	5.77	5.19	5.52
68	6.87	6.54	5.43	6.19	68	6.09	5.91	5.25	5.65
69	7.05	6.71	5.48	6.35	69	6.25	6.07	5.32	5.79
70	7.21	6.87	5.52	6.52	70	6.42	6.23	5.37	5.94
71	7.40	7.05	5.55	6.69	71	6.59	6.40	5.43	6.09
72	7.58	7.21	5.59	6.88	72	6.78	6.58	5.48	6.26
73	7.77	7.40	5.62	7.07	73	6.96	6.76	5.52	6.44
74	7.95	7.57	5.64	7.28	74	7.16	6.95	5.57	6.63
75	8.14	7.75	5.66	7.49	75	7.35	7.14	5.60	6.83
76	8.32	7.92	5.68	7.72	76	7.56	7.34	5.63	7.04
77	8.49	8.09	5.70	7.96	77	7.77	7.54	5.66	7.26
78	8.84	8.26	5.71	8.21	78	7.97	7.74	5.68	7.51
79	9.18	8.42	5.72	8.47	79	8.18	7.94	5.70	7.76
80	9.51	8.57	5.73	8.74	80	8.37	8.13	5.71	8.03
81	9.84	8.71	5.74	9.04	81	8.57	8.32	5.72	8.32
82	10.18	8.85	5.74	9.34	82	8.93	8.50	5.73	8.61
83	10.49	8.97	5.75	9.65	83	9.28	8.67	5.74	8.93
84	10.82	9.09	5.75	9.98	84	9.62	8.83	5.74	9.27
85 and over	11.13	9.20	5.75	10.34	85 and over	9.96	8.97	5.75	9.62

LIFE INCOME PLAN (OPTION E)

MALE ADJUSTED AGE*	JOINT AND SURVIVOR MONTHLY PAYMENTS						
	FEMALE ADJUSTED AGE*						
	55	60	65	70	75	80	85 and over
55	$4.16	$4.34	$4.51	$4.65	$4.76	$4.84	$4.88
60	4.26	4.51	4.75	4.98	5.16	5.29	5.37
65	4.35	4.65	4.98	5.31	5.61	5.84	5.98
70	4.41	4.76	5.17	5.62	6.07	6.44	6.68
75	4.46	4.84	5.32	5.88	6.48	7.03	7.42
80	4.48	4.89	5.41	6.05	6.79	7.52	8.07
85 and over	4.50	4.92	5.46	6.15	6.99	7.85	8.53

*See Section 9.3.

NN 1,2,4,6,8,9

13

WAIVER OF PREMIUM BENEFIT (LIFE & TERM)

1. THE BENEFIT

Disability Before Age 60. If total disability of the Insured starts on or before the policy anniversary nearest his 60th birthday, the Company will waive all premiums that come due on the policy as long as the total disability continues.

Disability After Age 60. If total disability of the Insured starts after the policy anniversary nearest his 60th birthday, the Company will waive those premiums that come due on the policy as long as the total disability continues, but only to the policy anniversary that is nearest his 65th birthday.

Premium Waived On An Annual Basis. Even if premiums have been paid more often than every 12 months, a premium waived on a policy anniversary will be an annual premium.

Refund Of Premium. The Company will refund that portion of a premium paid which applies to a period beyond the policy month in which the total disability began.

Premium For Benefit. The premium for this Benefit is shown on page 3.

2. TOTAL DISABILITY

Definition Of Total Disability. A total disability is one which prevents the Insured from engaging in an occupation. For the first 24 months of total disability, an occupation is the one that the Insured had at the time he became disabled. After 24 months, an occupation is one for which the Insured is qualified by education, training or experience. Due regard will be given to his vocation and earnings before he became disabled.

Disabilities Covered By This Benefit. Premiums are waived for total disability only if:

- the Insured becomes disabled while this Benefit is in force;

- the disability results from an accident or sickness; and

- the disability lasts for at least six months.

Presumptive Total Disability. Even if the Insured is able to work, he will be considered totally disabled if he incurs the total and irrecoverable loss of:

- sight of both eyes;
- use of both hands;
- use of both feet;
- use of one hand and one foot;
- speech; or
- hearing in both ears.

The loss must be the result of an accident that occurs, or from a sickness that first appears, while this Benefit is in force.

3. PROOF OF DISABILITY

Before any premium is waived, proof of total disability must be given to the Company within one year from the start of disability. However, the claim will not be affected if the proof is given as soon as reasonably possible.

4. PROOF THAT DISABILITY HAS CONTINUED

Proof that the total disability has continued may be required once a year. If the proof is not given when it is required, no more premiums will be waived. The Company will not require proof that the disability continues beyond the policy anniversary that is nearest the 65th birthday of the Insured.

5. PAYMENT OF PREMIUM

A premium that comes due while the Insured is disabled, but before the Company has approved the claim, is payable and should be paid. A premium that is paid and later waived will be refunded. A premium that is not paid will be waived if the total disability began before the end of the grace period.

6. TERMINATION OF BENEFIT

This Benefit will terminate on the policy anniversary that is nearest the 65th birthday of the Insured, unless he has been totally disabled since the policy anniversary that is nearest his 60th birthday. It will terminate earlier:

- when the policy terminates.
- when the policy becomes extended term or paid-up insurance.
- when the Owner's written request is received at the Home Office.

I/R 4400.00
29-3855-07 (12-85)

NN 1,2,4,5 WP

SPECIMEN
COPY
**PROVISIONS MAY VARY SLIGHTLY
IN CERTAIN STATES**

ADDITIONAL PURCHASE BENEFIT

1. THE BENEFIT

The Company will issue additional permanent life insurance policies on the Insured, with no evidence of insurability, subject to the terms and conditions below.

The term "new policy" means each additional policy issued under this Benefit.

The premium for this Benefit is shown on page 3.

2. PURCHASE DATES

The Owner may purchase a new policy as of each Purchase Date. There is a Purchase Date on each policy anniversary that is nearest the 22nd, 25th, 28th, 31st, 34th, 37th, and 40th birthdays of the Insured.

The Company must receive an application and the first premium for each new policy:

- while the Insured is living; and
- not more than 60 days before, nor more than 30 days after, a Purchase Date

The Owner of the new policy must have an insurable interest in the life of the Insured.

3. ADVANCE PURCHASE

A new policy may be purchased before a Purchase Date each time one of these events occurs:

- the marriage of the Insured.
- the birth of a child of the Insured.
- the completion, by the Insured, of the legal adoption of a child.

The event must occur while this policy is in force. To make an advance purchase of a new policy, there must be a future Purchase Date that has not been used. An advance purchase of a new policy cancels the next unused Purchase Date.

The Company must receive an application and the first premium for each new policy:

- while the Insured is living; and
- not more than 90 days after the marriage, birth or adoption.

The Company may require proof of the marriage, birth or adoption.

The Owner of the new policy must have an insurable interest in the life of the Insured.

4. AUTOMATIC TERM INSURANCE

The Company will provide term insurance on the life of the Insured during each 90 day period in which the Owner may purchase a new policy. The amount of the term insurance will be the largest amount of insurance which could have been purchased as a new policy under this Benefit. The proceeds of the term insurance are payable on the death of the Insured only if:

- a new policy was not purchased within that period; or
- a new policy purchased within that period is surrendered to the Company for a refund of premiums.

The proceeds of the term insurance will be payable to the beneficiary and subject to the terms of this policy.

5. TERMS OF NEW POLICY

Plan. Each new policy will be on a level premium permanent life insurance plan being issued by the Company on the date of purchase of the new policy. An additional benefit that is made a part of the new policy will contain the provisions of that benefit as it is being issued by the Company on the date of issue of the new policy.

Amount. The minimum amount of each new policy on the Whole Life Paid Up at 90 plan will be $20,000. The amount of each new policy on any other plan must be at least the Company's minimum for policies being issued on that plan at that time. The maximum amount of each policy will be the Amount of the Additional Purchase Benefit shown on page 3. However, in the event of a multiple birth, the maximum amount which may be purchased as an advance purchase will be the Amount of this Benefit multiplied by the number of children of the birth.

Waiver Of Premium Benefit. If the Waiver of Premium Benefit is in force on this policy at the time that the Owner has the right to purchase a new policy:

- a new policy on a plan with a level death benefit on which premiums are payable to age 90 or later may be issued with the Waiver of Premium Benefit. If premiums are being waived for this policy at the time the new policy is purchased, premiums will also be waived for the new policy for as long as they are waived for this policy.
- a new policy on a plan with a nonlevel death benefit or a plan on which all premiums are payable before age 90 may be issued with the Waiver of Premium Benefit only if premiums are not then being waived for this policy. If the Waiver of Premium Benefit is a part of the new policy, it will apply only to a disability that starts after the new policy takes effect.

NN 1 Life APB

I/R 4400.00
29-3855-02 (12-85)

(Continued on reverse side)

Accidental Death Benefit. Each new policy may be issued with the Accidental Death Benefit, provided that:

- the Accidental Death Benefit is a part of this policy when the new policy is issued; and
- the Accidental Death Benefit amount is not more than the amount of the new policy. However, the total amount of Accidental Death Benefit in force with the Company on the life of the Insured may not be more than the Company's published limits.

Provisions. The Suicide and Incontestability provisions in each new policy will be in effect from the Date of Issue of this policy. Each new policy will contain any exclusion provision which is a part of this policy.

Premiums. The premium for each new policy, including any additional benefits, will be determined as of its date of issue based on:

- the Company's premium rates then in effect;
- the plan and amount of the new policy and any additional benefits; and
- the Insured's age on the policy date of the new policy.

If the Insured was age 18 or more on the Policy Date of this policy, the premium for the new policy will be based on the classification of risk of this policy. If the Insured was age 17 or less on the Policy Date of this policy, the premium for the new policy will be based on the classification of risk of this policy adjusted to reflect the Insured's cigarette smoking habits.

Effective Date. Each new policy will take effect on the later of:

- the date the Company receives the application; or
- the date the Company receives the first premium.

6. TERMINATION OF BENEFIT

This Benefit will terminate on the policy anniversary that is nearest the 40th birthday of the Insured. It will terminate earlier:

- when this policy terminates.
- when this policy becomes extended term or paid-up insurance.
- on the use of the final Purchase Date by an advance purchase.
- when the Owner's written request is received at the Home Office.

ACCIDENTAL DEATH BENEFIT

1. THE BENEFIT

The Company will pay an Accidental Death Benefit upon receipt of proof that the Insured's death:

- resulted, directly and independently of all other causes, from accidental bodily injury; and
- occurred while this Benefit was in force.

2. PREMIUM AND AMOUNT OF BENEFIT

The premium for and the amount of this Benefit are shown on page 3. The Benefit will be payable as part of the policy proceeds.

3. RISKS NOT ASSUMED

This Benefit will not be payable if the Insured's death resulted from or was contributed to by:

- suicide.
- bodily or mental infirmity or disease.

- an act or incident of war, declared or undeclared.
- riding in any kind of aircraft:
  a. as a passenger in any aircraft operated by or for the armed forces.
  b. as a pilot, as a participant in training, or as a crew member. The term "crew member" includes anyone who has any duties at any time on the flight with respect to either the flight or the aircraft.

4. TERMINATION OF BENEFIT

This Benefit will terminate on the policy anniversary that is nearest the 70th birthday of the Insured. It will terminate earlier:

- when the policy terminates.
- when the policy becomes extended term or paid-up insurance.
- when the Owner's written request is received at the Home Office.

Universal Life Policy

FLEXIBLE-PREMIUM (UNIVERSAL) LIFE INSURANCE POLICY

Flexible-Premium Life Insurance Policy

Life insurance payable if the insured dies before the Final Date of Policy. Accumulation Fund payable on the Final Date.

Adjustable death benefit.

Premiums payable while the insured is alive and before the Final Date of Policy. Premiums must be sufficient to keep the policy in force.

Not eligible for dividends.

10-Day Right to Examine Policy—Please read this policy. You may return this policy to us or to the sales representative through whom you bought it within 10 days from the date you receive it. If you return it within the 10-day period, the policy will be void from the beginning. We will refund any premium paid.

See Table of Contents and Company address on back cover.

POLICY SPECIFICATIONS

DATE OF POLICY..............................

INSURED'S AGE AND SEX....................

FINAL DATE OF POLICY.....................POLICY ANNIVERSARY AT AGE 95

DEATH BENEFIT ....OPTION   (SEE PAGE 5)

OWNER ....SEE APPLICATION

BENEFICIARY AND
CONTINGENT BENEFICIARY...................SEE APPLICATION

POLICY CLASSIFICATION......................

INSURED

SPECIFIED
FACE AMOUNT
OF INSURANCE .....   —AS OF DATE OF POLICY   ..POLICY NUMBER

PLAN ....FLEXIBLE-PREMIUM LIFE

THIS POLICY PROVIDES LIFE INSURANCE COVERAGE UNTIL THE FINAL DATE IF SUFFICIENT PREMIUMS ARE PAID. THE PLANNED PREMIUM SHOWN BELOW MAY NEED TO BE INCREASED TO KEEP THIS POLICY AND COVERAGE IN FORCE.

PLANNED PREMIUM OF   —PAYABLE

(TOTAL PREMIUM FOR LIFE INSURANCE BENEFIT, ANY SUPPLEMENTAL RATING AND ANY ADDITIONAL BENEFITS LISTED BELOW)

ADDITIONAL BENEFITS

FORM 7-82 MIAC   401. 402. 403. 404.

"Flexible-Premium (Universal) Life Insurance Policy" from *Policy Kit for Students of Insurance*. Reprinted with permission from Alliance of American Insurers.

Table of Guaranteed Maximum Rates For Each $1,000 of Term Insurance
(See "Cost of Term Insurance" Provision on page 6.)

Age Male	Age Female	Monthly Rate*	Age Male	Age Female	Monthly Rate*	Age Male	Age Female	Monthly Rate*
0	—	.370	33	36	.196	79	82	9.320
1	—	.136	34	37	.204	80	83	10.174
2	—	.124	35	38	.214	81	84	11.088
3	—	.119	36	39	.227	82	85	12.053
4	—	.114	37	40	.242	83	86	13.070
5	—	.110	38	41	.261	84	87	14.146
6	—	.106	39	42	.283	85	88	15.289
7	—	.103	40	43	.307	86	89	16.509
8	—	.101	41	44	.334	87	90	17.822
9	—	.100	42	45	.363	88	91	19.256
10	—	.101	43	46	.394	89	92	20.852
11	—	.103	44	47	.429	90	93	22.665
—	0	.329	45	48	.467	91	94	24.769
—	1	.128	46	49	.509	92	—	27.258
—	2	.115	47	50	.556	93	—	30.251
—	3	.110	48	51	.608	94	—	34.025
—	4	.105	49	52	.666			
—	5	.101	50	53	.729			
—	6	.097	51	54	.798			
—	7	.094	52	55	.873			
—	8	.092	53	56	.955			
—	9	.092	54	57	1.044			
—	10	.092	55	58	1.141			
—	11	.094	56	59	1.249			
—	12	.096	57	60	1.367			
—	13	.099	58	61	1.496			
—	14	.102	59	62	1.638			
12	15	.107	60	63	1.794			
13	16	.113	61	64	1.963			
14	17	.118	62	65	2.148			
15	18	.125	63	66	2.351			
16	19	.131	64	67	2.573			
17	20	.138	65	68	2.819			
18	21	.143	66	69	3.091			
19	22	.147	67	70	3.392			
20	23	.151	68	71	3.722			
21	24	.153	69	72	4.076			
22	25	.156	70	73	4.452			
23	26	.158	71	74	4.843			
24	27	.160	72	75	5.248			
25	28	.162	73	76	5.671			
26	29	.164	74	77	6.124			
27	30	.167	75	78	6.623			
28	31	.171	76	79	7.183			
29	32	.175	77	80	7.817			
30	33	.180	78	81	8.532			
31	34	.185						
32	35	.190						

*If there is a supplemental rating for the life insurance benefit, as shown on page 3, the monthly deduction for such supplemental rating must be added to the monthly rate determined from this table.

401-82

Understanding This Policy

"You" and "your" refer to the owner of this policy.

"We", "us" and "our" refer to Metropolitan Insurance and Annuity Company.

The "insured" named on page 3 is the person at whose death the insurance proceeds will be payable.

The "Specified Face Amount of Insurance" as of the date of policy is shown on page 3. A new page 3 will be issued to show any change in the Specified Face Amount of Insurance that has occurred at your request.

The "Date of Policy" is shown on page 3.

The "Final Date of Policy" is the policy anniversary on which the insured is age 95.

Policy years and months are measured from the date of policy. For example, if the date of policy is May 5, 1990, the first policy month ends June 4, 1990, and the first policy year ends May 4, 1991. Similarly, the first monthly anniversary is June 5, 1990, and the first policy anniversary is May 5, 1991.

The "accumulation fund" forms the basis for the benefits provided under your policy. Computation of the accumulation fund is described on page 6.

The "Designated Office" is our Executive Office at One Madison Avenue, New York, N. Y. 10010. We may, by written notice, name other offices within the United States to serve as Designated Offices.

To make this policy clear and easy to read, we have left out many cross-references and conditional statements. Therefore, the provisions of the policy must be read as a whole. For example, our payment of the insurance proceeds (see page 5) depends upon the payment of sufficient premiums (see page 7).

To exercise your rights, you should follow the procedures stated in this policy. If you want to request a payment, adjust the death benefit, change a beneficiary, change an address or request any other action by us, you should do so on the forms prepared for each purpose. You can get these forms from your sales representative or our Designated Office.

Payment When Insured Dies

Insurance Proceeds—If the insured dies before the Final Date of Policy, an amount of money, called the insurance proceeds, will be payable to the beneficiary. The insurance proceeds are the sum of:

- The death benefit described below.

   PLUS

- Any insurance on the insured's life that may be provided by riders to this policy.

   MINUS

- Any policy loan and loan interest.

We will pay the insurance proceeds to the beneficiary after we receive proof of death and a proper written claim.

Death Benefit—The death benefit under the policy will be either (1) or (2) below, whichever is chosen and is in effect on the date of death:

1. Under Option A, the greater of:

   (a) the Specified Face Amount of Insurance;

      or

   (b) 110% of the accumulation fund on the date of death.

2. Under Option B:

   The Specified Face Amount of Insurance;

      PLUS

   The accumulation fund on the date of death.

402-82

Death Benefit Adjustment—At any time after the first policy year while this policy is in force, you may change the death benefit option or change (either increase or decrease) the Specified Face Amount of Insurance, subject to the following.

1. In the event of a change in the death benefit option, we will change the Specified Face Amount of Insurance as needed.

2. The Specified Face Amount of Insurance may not be reduced to less than $50,000 during the first 5 policy years or to less than $25,000 after the 5th policy year.

3. For any change which would increase the death benefit, you must provide evidence satisfactory to us of the insurability of the insured. Also, the increased death benefit will be subject to a charge of $3 for each $1,000 of insurance increase. We will deduct this charge from the accumulation fund as of the date the increase takes effect.

4. No change in the death benefit will take effect unless the accumulation fund, after the change, is sufficient to keep this policy in force for at least 2 months. Subject to this condition, a request for a change in the death benefit will take effect on the monthly anniversary which coincides with or next follows: (a) if evidence of insurability is required, the date we approve the request; or (b) if not, the date of the request.

5. We will issue a new page 3 for this policy showing the change. We may require that you send us this policy to make the change.

Computation of Accumulation Fund

Accumulation Fund—The value of the accumulation fund is as follows:

- On the date of policy—91% of the first premium;

  MINUS

  The monthly deduction for the first month.

- On any monthly anniversary—The value on the last monthly anniversary;

  PLUS

  One month's interest on such value at the currently applicable rates;

  PLUS

  91% of the premiums received since the last monthly anniversary;

  MINUS

  The monthly deduction for the month beginning on the current monthly anniversary.

- On other than a monthly anniversary—The value on the last monthly anniversary;

  PLUS

  91% of the premiums received since the last monthly anniversary.

Note: The 9% deduction from premiums is an expense charge.

If you make a partial cash withdrawal (see page 7), the accumulation fund defined above will be reduced by the amount of such withdrawal.

Monthly Deduction—The deduction for any policy month is the sum of the following amounts, determined as of the beginning of that month:

- The monthly cost of the term insurance (See Cost of Term Insurance on page 6).
- The monthly cost of any benefits provided by riders.
- For each of the first 12 policy months only, a charge of $35 plus $.25 for each $1,000 of Specified Face Amount of Insurance.

Interest Rate—The guaranteed interest rate used to determine the accumulation fund is .32737% a month, compounded monthly. This is equivalent to a rate of 4% a year, compounded annually.

Interest will be credited to the accumulation fund each month as follows:

- At the guaranteed interest rate on the first $1,000 in the accumulation fund.
- In the manner and at the rate we set from time to time, on amounts in excess of $1,000 in the accumulation fund. The rate we set will never be less than the guaranteed interest rate.
- If there is a loan against this policy, interest on that portion of the accumulation fund in excess of $1,000 that equals the loan will be at a rate we set. The rate with respect to the amount of the loan will never be less than the guaranteed interest rate.

Example—Suppose the accumulation fund is $10,000 and there is a policy loan of $2,000. If we set the annual interest rates at 10% for amounts over $1,000 in the accumulation fund and at 6% for the amount of any loan, then interest would be credited: at the rate of 4% on the first $1,000; at the rate of 6% on the next $2,000 representing the amount of the loan; and at the rate of 10% on the remaining $7,000.

Cost of Term Insurance—Under either death benefit option, the amount of term insurance for any policy month is equal to:

- The death benefit divided by 1.0032737;

  MINUS

- The accumulation fund.

The accumulation fund used in this calculation is the accumulation fund at the beginning of the policy month before the deduction for the monthly cost of term insurance, but after the deductions for riders and any other charges.

The cost of the term insurance for any policy month is equal to the amount of term insurance multiplied by the monthly term insurance rate. Monthly term insurance rates will be set by us from time to time, based on the insured's age, sex, and underwriting class. But these rates will never be more than the maximum rates shown in the table on page 4.

402-82

Payments During Insured's Lifetime

Payment on Final Date of Policy—If the insured is alive on the Final Date of Policy, we will pay you the accumulation fund minus any policy loan and loan interest. Coverage under this policy will then end.

Cash Value—Your policy has a cash value while the insured is alive.

The cash value at any time during the first policy year will equal:

- The accumulation fund;

    MINUS

- $35 times the number of full policy months left in that year;

    MINUS

- Any policy loan and loan interest.

After the first policy year, the cash value at any time will

- he accumulation fund;

    MINUS

- The interest in excess of the guaranteed rate credited to the fund during the last 12 policy months;

    MINUS

- Any policy loan and loan interest.

Full and Partial Cash Withdrawal—We will pay you all or part of the cash value after we receive your request at our Designated Office. The cash value will be determined as of the date we receive your request. If you request and are paid the full cash value, this policy and all our obligations under it will end. We may require surrender of this policy before we pay you the full cash value.

Each partial withdrawal of cash value must be at least $250. When a partial withdrawal is made, we will reduce the accumulation fund by the amount of the partial withdrawal. If Option A is in effect, we will also reduce the Specified Face Amount of Insurance by the amount of the partial withdrawal; and a new page 3 will then be issued. We may require that you send us this policy to make the change.

If you request a partial withdrawal which would reduce the cash value to less than $500, we will treat it as a request for a full cash withdrawal. Also, if Option A is in effect and the Specified Face Amount of Insurance would be reduced to less than $50,000 during the first 5 policy years, or to less than $25,000 thereafter, we will treat your request as a request for a full cash withdrawal.

Policy Loan—You may also get cash from us by taking a policy loan. If there is an existing loan you can increase it. The most you can borrow at any time is the cash value on the next monthly anniversary, less the monthly deduction for the following month.

Loan interest is charged daily at the rate of 8% a year, and is due at the end of each policy year. Interest not paid within 31 days after it is due will be added to the amount of the loan. It will be added as of the due date and will bear interest at the same rate as the rest of the loan.

A loan will affect the interest rate we credit to amounts over $1,000 in the accumulation fund (see "Interest Rate" on page 6).

Loan Repayment—You may repay all or part (but not less than $25) of a policy loan at any time while the insured is alive and this policy is in force. If any payment you make to us is intended as a loan repayment, rather than a premium payment, you must tell us this when you make the payment.

Failure to repay a policy loan or to pay loan interest will not terminate this policy unless the accumulation fund, minus the policy loan and loan interest, is insufficient to pay the monthly deduction due on a monthly anniversary. In that case, the Grace Period provision will apply (see page 8).

Deferment—We may delay paying a full or partial cash withdrawal for up to 6 months from the date we receive a request for payment. If we delay for 30 days or more, interest will be paid from the date we receive the request at a rate not less than 3% a year.

We also may delay making a policy loan, except for a loan to pay a premium, for up to 6 months from the date you request the loan.

Premiums

Premium Payments—Premiums may be paid at our Designated Office or to our sales representative. A receipt signed by our President or Secretary and countersigned by the sales representative will be given for a premium paid to the sales representative.

The first premium is due on the date of policy and will be credited as of that date. No insurance will take effect before the first premium is paid. Other premiums may be paid at

any time while the policy is in force and before the Final Date of Policy and in any amount and subject to the limits described below.

We will send premium notices, if you request in writing, according to the planned premium shown on page 3. You may skip planned premium payments or change their frequency and amount if the accumulation fund is large enough to keep your policy in force.

402-82

Premiums (Continued)

Limits—The first premium may not be less than the planned premium shown on page 3. Each premium payment after the first must be at least $250 ($50 for a Check-O-Matic payment).

We may increase these minimum premium limits. No increase will take effect until 90 days after notice is sent

The total premiums paid in a policy year may not exceed the maximum we set for that year.

Grace Period—If the accumulation fund on any monthly anniversary, minus any policy loan and loan interest, is less than the monthly deduction for that month, there will be a grace period of 61 days after that anniversary to pay an amount that will cover the monthly deduction. We will send you a notice at the start of the grace period. We will also send a notice to any assignee on our records.

If we do not receive a sufficient amount by the end of the grace period, your policy will then end without value.

If the insured dies during the grace period, we will pay the insurance proceeds minus any overdue monthly deduction.

Reinstatement—If the grace period has ended and you have not paid the required premium and have not surrendered your policy for its cash value, you may reinstate this policy while the insured is alive if you:

1. Ask for reinstatement within 3 years after the end of the grace period;

2. Provide evidence of insurability satisfactory to us;

3. Pay a sufficient amount to keep the policy in force for at least 2 months after the date of reinstatement;

4. If the grace period began during the first policy year, pay: (a) an amount sufficient to cover the unpaid portion of the charges applicable during the first 12 policy months; plus (b) interest on such amount to the date of reinstatement at the rate of 6% a year.

The effective date of the reinstated policy will be the monthly anniversary following the date we approve the reinstatement application. If we approve it on a monthly anniversary, the effective date will be that anniversary.

Ownership and Beneficiary

Owner—As owner, you may exercise all rights under your policy while the insured is alive. You may name a contingent owner who would become the owner if you should die before the insured.

Change of Ownership—You may name a new owner at any time. If a new owner is named, any earlier choice of a contingent owner, beneficiary, contingent beneficiary or optional income plan will be canceled, unless you specify otherwise.

Beneficiary—The beneficiary is the person or persons to whom the insurance proceeds are payable when the insured dies. You may name a contingent beneficiary to become the beneficiary if all the beneficiaries die while the insured is alive. If no beneficiary or contingent beneficiary is named, or if none is alive when the insured dies, the owner (or the owner's estate) will be the beneficiary. While the insured is alive, the owner may change any beneficiary or contingent beneficiary.

If more than one beneficiary is alive when the insured dies, we will pay them in equal shares, unless you have chosen otherwise.

How to Change the Owner or the Beneficiary—You may change the owner, contingent owner, beneficiary or contingent beneficiary of this policy by written notice or assignment of the policy. No change is binding on us until it is recorded at our Designated Office. Once recorded, the change binds us as of the date you signed it. The change will not apply to any payment made by us before we recorded your request. We may require that you send us this policy to make the change.

Collateral Assignment—Your policy may be assigned as collateral. All rights under the policy will be transferred to the extent of the assignee's interest. We are not bound by any assignment unless it is in writing and is recorded at our Designated Office. We are not responsible for the validity of any assignment.

402-82

General Provisions

The Contract—This policy includes any riders and, with the application attached when the policy is issued, makes up the entire contract. All statements in the application will be representations and not warranties. No statement will be used to contest the policy unless it appears in the application.

Limitation on Sales Representative's Authority—No sales representative or other person except our President, a Vice-President, or the Secretary may (a) make or change any contract of insurance; or (b) make any binding promises about policy benefits; or (c) change or waive any of the terms of this policy. Any change is valid only if made in writing and signed by our President, a Vice-President, or the Secretary.

Incontestability—We will not contest the validity of your policy after it has been in force during the insured's lifetime for 2 years from the date of policy. We will not contest the validity of any increase in the death benefit after such increase has been in force during the insured's lifetime for 2 years from its effective date.

Suicide—The insurance proceeds will not be paid if the insured commits suicide, while sane or insane, within 2 years from the date of policy. Instead we will pay the beneficiary an amount equal to all premiums paid, without interest, less any policy loan and loan interest and less any partial cash withdrawals. If the insured commits suicide, while sane or insane, more than 2 years after the date of this policy but within 2 years from the effective date of any increase in the death benefit, our liability with respect to such increase will be limited to its cost.

Age and Sex—If the insured's age or sex on the date of the policy is not correct as shown on page 3, we will adjust the benefits under this policy. The adjusted benefits will be those that the premiums paid would have provided at the correct age and sex.

Nonparticipation—This policy is not eligible for dividends; it does not participate in any distribution of our surplus.

Computation of Values—The minimum accumulation fund and policy reserves are computed using interest at the rate of 4% a year. These values and the maximum term insurance rates shown on page 4 are based on the 1958 Commissioners Standard Ordinary Mortality Table, age last birthday for male lives. For female lives, they are based on that table set back 3 years at ages 15 and older and on the female extension of that table at ages under 15.

We have filed a detailed statement of the method of computation with the insurance supervisory official of the state in which this policy is delivered. The values under this policy are equal to or greater than those required by the law of that state.

Annual Reports—Each year we will send you a report showing the current death benefit, accumulation fund and cash value for this policy.

It will also show the amount and type of credits to and deductions from the accumulation fund during the past policy year.

The report will also include any other information required by state laws and regulations.

Illustration of Future Benefits—At any time, we will provide an illustration of the future benefits and values under your policy. You must ask in writing for this illustration and pay the service fee set by us.

403-82

Optional Income Plans

The insurance proceeds when the insured dies, or the amount payable on the Final Date of Policy, instead of being paid in one sum may be applied under one or more of the following income plans. Also, at any time before the Final Date and while the insured is alive, you may ask us to:

(a) Apply the full cash value of this policy under a non-life income plan;

or

(b) Apply the accumulation fund of this policy, minus any policy loan and loan interest, under a life income plan.

Non-Life Income Plans

Option 1. *Interest Income*
The amount applied will earn interest which will be paid monthly. Withdrawals of at least $500 each may be made at any time by written request.

Option 2. *Instalment Income for a Stated Period*
Monthly instalment payments will be made so that the amount applied, with interest, will be paid over the period chosen (from 1 to 30 years).

Option 2A. *Instalment Income of a Stated Amount*
Monthly instalment payments of a chosen amount will be made until the entire amount applied, with interest, is paid.

Life Income Plans

Option 3. *Single Life Income—Guaranteed Payment Period*

Monthly payments will be made during the lifetime of the payee with a chosen guaranteed payment period of 10, 15 or 20 years.

Option 3A. *Single Life Income—Guaranteed Return*
Monthly payments will be made during the lifetime of the payee. If the payee dies before the total amount applied under this plan has been paid, the remainder will be paid in one sum as a death benefit.

Option 4. *Joint and Survivor Life Income*
Monthly payments will be made jointly to two persons while they are both alive and will continue during the remaining lifetime of the survivor. A total payment period of 10 years is guaranteed.

Other Frequencies and Plans—Instead of monthly payments, you may choose to have payments made quarterly, semiannually or annually. Other income plans may be arranged with us.

Choice of Income Plans—A choice of an income plan for insurance proceeds made by you in writing and recorded by us while the insured is alive will take effect when the insured dies. A choice of an income plan for the amount payable on the Final Date of Policy will take effect on such date. All other choices of income plans will take effect when recorded by us or later, if requested. When an income plan starts, we will issue a contract that will describe the terms of the plan. We may require that you send us this policy. We may also require proof of the payee's age

Income plans for insurance proceeds may be chosen

1. By you during the lifetime of the insured.

2. By the beneficiary, within one year after the date the insured died and before any payment has been made, if no election was in effect on the date of death.

Income plans for the amount payable on the Final Date of Policy may be chosen by you:

1. On or before the Final Date of Policy.

2. Within one year after the Final Date of Policy and before any payment has been made.

A choice of an income plan will not become effective unless each payment under the plan would be at least $50.

Limitations—If the payee is not a natural person, the choice of an income plan will be subject to our approval An assignment for a loan will modify a prior choice of income plan. The amount due the assignee will be payable in one sum and the balance will be applied under the income plan.

Income plan payments may not be assigned and, to the extent permitted by law, will not be subject to the claims of creditors.

Income Plan Rates—Amounts applied under non-life income plans will earn interest at a rate we set from time to time. That rate will never be less than 3% a year.

Life income plan payments will be based on a rate set by us and in effect on the date the amount to be applied becomes payable.

404-82

Optional Income Plans (Continued)

Minimum Payments under Optional Income Plans—Monthly payments under Options 2, 3, 3A and 4 for each $1,000 applied will not be less than the amounts shown in the following Tables.

Option 2. *Instalment Income for a Stated Period*
Monthly Payments for each $1,000 Applied

Years Chosen	Minimum Amount of Each Monthly Payment	Years Chosen	Minimum Amount of Each Monthly Payment	Years Chosen	Minimum Amount of Each Monthly Payment
1	$84.47	11	$8.86	21	$5.32
2	42.86	12	8.24	22	5.15
3	28.99	13	7.71	23	4.99
4	22.06	14	7.20	24	4.84
5	17.91	15	6.87	25	4.71
6	15.14	16	6.53	26	4.59
7	13.16	17	6.23	27	4.47
8	11.68	18	5.96	28	4.37
9	10.53	19	5.73	29	4.27
10	9.61	20	5.51	30	4.18

To determine the minimum amount for quarterly payment, multiply the above monthly payment by 2.99; for semiannual by 5.96; and for annual by 11.84.

Option 3. *Single Life Income*—Guaranteed Payment Period
Minimum Amount of each Monthly Payment for each $1,000 Applied

Option 3A.
Single Life Income—Guaranteed Return
Minimum Amount of each Monthly Payment for each $1,000 Applied

Payee's Age	Guaranteed Payment Period							
	10 years		15 years		20 years			
	Male	Female	Male	Female	Male	Female	Male	Female
50	$4.50	$4.09	$4.40	$4.05	$4.28	$3.99	$4.24	$3.96
55	4.96	4.49	4.80	4.41	4.58	4.31	4.61	4.29
60	5.53	4.99	5.25	4.86	4.90	4.67	5.07	4.72
65	6.25	5.67	5.75	5.40	5.18	5.03	5.67	5.28
70	7.11	6.55	6.23	5.99	5.39	5.31	6.46	6.04
75	8.03	7.60	6.61	6.48	5.49	5.45	7.54	7.06
80	8.87	8.60	6.81	6.74	5.51	5.50	9.01	8.44
85 and over	9.40	9.22	6.86	6.84	5.51	5.51	11.14	10.26

Option 4. *Joint and Survivor Life Income*—Guaranteed Period of 10 years
Minimum Amount of each Monthly Payment for each $1,000 Applied

Age of Both Payees	One Male and One Female	Two Males	Two Females
50	$3.77	$3.92	$3.67
55	4.09	4.27	3.97
60	4.52	4.73	4.37
65	5.10	5.35	4.91
70	5.90	6.18	5.68
75	6.95	7.21	6.72

On request, we will provide additional information about amounts of minimum payments.

404-82

Glossary

Absolute liability Liability for damages even though fault or negligence cannot be proven, for example, in such situations as occupational injury of employees under a workers compensation law.

Accelerated death benefits rider A rider that allows insureds who are terminally ill or who suffer from certain catastrophic diseases to collect part or all of their life insurance benefits before they die, primarily to pay for the care they require.

Accident A loss-causing event that is sudden, unforeseen, and unintentional. *See also* **Occurrence**.

Accidental bodily injury Bodily injury resulting from an act whose result was accidental or unexpected.

Actual cash value Value of property at the time of its damage or loss, determined by subtracting depreciation of the item from its replacement cost.

Actual loss ratio The ratio of incurred losses and loss-adjustment expenses to earned premiums.

Add-on plan Pays benefits to an accident victim without regard to fault, but the injured person still has the right to sue the negligent driver who caused the accident.

Adjustment bureau Organization for adjusting insurance claims that is supported by insurers using the bureau's services.

Advance funding Pension-funding method in which the employer systematically and periodically sets aside funds prior to the employee's retirement.

Advance premium mutual Mutual insurance company owned by the policyowners that does not issue assessable policies but charges premiums expected to be sufficient to pay all claims and expenses.

Adverse selection Tendency of persons with a higher-than-average chance of loss to seek insurance at standard (average) rates, which, if not controlled by underwriting, results in higher-than-expected loss levels.

Agency building system Marketing system in life insurance by which an insurer builds its own agency force by recruiting, financing, training, and supervising new agents.

Agent Someone who legally represents the insurer, has the authority to act on the insurer's behalf, and can bind the principal by expressed powers, by implied powers, and by apparent authority.

Aggregate deductible Deductible in some property and health insurance contracts in which all covered losses during a year are added together and the insurer pays only when the aggregate deductible amount is exceeded.

Aleatory contract One in which the values exchanged may not be equal but depend on an uncertain event.

Alien insurer Insurance company chartered by a foreign country and meeting certain licensing requirements.

"All-risks" policy Coverage by an insurance contract that promises to cover all losses except those losses specifically excluded in the policy. *See also* **Risk of direct loss to property**.

Alternative dispute resolution (ADR) techniques Techniques to resolve a legal dispute without litigation.

Annuitant Person who receives the periodic payment of an annuity.

Annuity Periodic payment to an individual that continues for a fixed period or for the duration of a designated life or lives.

Appraisal clause Used when the insured and insurer agree that the loss is covered, but the amount of the loss is in dispute.

Assessment mutual Mutual insurance company that has the right to assess policyowners for losses and expenses.

Assumption-of-risk Defense against a negligence claim that bars recovery for damages if a person understands and recognizes the danger inherent in a particular activity or occupation.

Attractive nuisance Condition that can attract and injure children. Occupants of land on which such a condition exists are liable for injuries to children.

Automatic premium loan Cash borrowed from a life insurance policy's cash value to pay an overdue premium after the grace period for paying the premium has expired.

Automobile insurance plan Formerly called assigned risk plan. Method for providing automobile insurance to persons considered to be high-risk drivers who cannot obtain protection in the voluntary markets. All automobile insurers in the state are assigned their share of such drivers based on the volume of automobile insurance business written in the state.

Average indexed monthly earnings (AIME) Under the OASDI program, the person's actual earnings are indexed to determine his or her primary insurance amount (PIA).

Avoidance *See* **Loss avoidance**.

Bailee's customer policy Policy that covers the loss or damage to property of customers regardless of a bailee's legal liability.

Basic form *See* **Dwelling Property 1**.

Benefit period A period of time, typically one to three years, during which major medical benefits are paid after the deductible is satisfied. When the benefit period ends, the insured must then satisfy a new deductible in order to establish a new benefit period.

Binder Authorization of coverage by an agent given before the company has formally approved a policy. Provides evidence that the insurance is in force.

Blackout period The period during which Social Security benefits are not paid to a surviving spouse—between the time the youngest child reaches age 16 and the surviving spouse's sixtieth birthday.

Blue Cross plans Typically nonprofit, community-oriented prepayment plans that provide health insurance coverage primarily for hospital services.

Blue Shield plans Typically nonprofit prepayment plans that provide health insurance coverage mainly for physicians's services.

Boat owners package policy A special package policy for boat owners that combines physical damage insurance, medical expense insurance, liability insurance, and other coverages in one contract.

Broad form *See* **Dwelling Property 2; Homeowners 2 policy.**

Broker Someone who legally represents the insured, soliciting or accepting applications for insurance that are not in force until the company accepts the business.

Burglary Taking of property from within the premises by someone who unlawfully enters or leaves the premises, with marks of forcible entry or exit.

Business income coverage form Business income form drafted by the Insurance Services Office to cover the loss of business income regardless of whether the income is derived from retail or service operations, manufacturing, or rents.

Businessowners policy Package policy specifically designed to meet the basic property and liability insurance needs of smaller business firms in one contract.

Cafeteria plan Generic term for an employee benefit plan that allows employees to select among the various group life, medical expense, disability, dental, and other plans that best meet their specific needs. Also called flexible benefit plans.

Calendar-year deductible Amount payable by an insured during a calendar year before a group or individual health insurance policy begins to pay for medical expenses.

Capacity Term used in the property and liability insurance industry that refers to the relative level of surplus; the greater the industry's surplus position, the more willing underwriters will write new business or reduce premiums.

Capital budgeting Method of determining which capital investment projects a company should undertake based on the time value of money.

Capital retention approach A method used to estimate the amount of life insurance to own. Under this method, the insurance proceeds are retained and are not liquidated.

Captive insurer Insurance company established and owned by a parent firm in order to insure its loss exposures while reducing premium costs, providing easier access to a reinsurer, and perhaps easing tax burdens.

Cargo insurance Type of ocean marine insurance that protects the shipper of the goods against financial loss if the goods are damaged or lost.

Cash refund annuity The balance is paid in one lump sum to the beneficiary after the death of the annuitant, if total payments not completed.

Cash surrender value Amount payable to the owner of a life insurance policy should he or she decide it is no longer wanted. Calculated separately from the legal reserve.

Casualty insurance Field of insurance that covers whatever is not covered by fire, marine, and life insurance. Includes automobile, liability, burglary and theft, workers compensation, glass, and health insurance.

Causes-of-loss form Form added to commercial property insurance policy that indicates the causes of loss that are covered. There are four causes-of-loss forms: basic, broad, special, and earthquake.

Ceding company Insurer that writes the policy initially and later shifts part or all of the coverage to a reinsurer.

Certified Financial Planner (CFP) Professional who has attained a high degree of technical competency in financial planning and has passed a series of professional examinations by the College for Financial Planning.

Certified Insurance Counselor (CIC) Professional in property and liability insurance who has passed a series of examinations sponsored by the Society of Certified Insurance Counselors.

Chance of loss The probability that an event will occur.

Change-of-plan provision Allows policyowners to exchange their present policies for different contracts, provides flexibility.

Chartered Financial Consultant (ChFC) An individual who has attained a high degree of technical competency in the fields of financial planning, investments, and life and health insurance and has passed ten professional examinations administered by The American College.

Chartered Life Underwriter (CLU) An individual who has attained a high degree of technical competency in the fields of life and health insurance and who is expected to abide by a code of ethics. Must have minimum of three years of experience in life or health insurance sales and have passed ten professional examinations administered by The American College.

Chartered Property Casualty Underwriter (CPCU) Professional who has attained a high degree of technical competency in property and liability insurance and has passed ten professional examinations administered by the American Institute for Chartered Property Casualty Underwriters.

Chief risk officer (CRO) Person responsible for the treatment of pure and speculative risks faced by an organization.

Choice no-fault plans Motorists can elect to be covered under the state's no-fault law with lower premiums or can retain the right to sue under the tort liability system with higher premiums.

Claims adjustor Person who settles claims: an agent, company adjustor, independent adjustor, adjustment bureau, or public adjustor.

Claims-made policy A liability insurance policy that only covers claims that are first reported during the policy period, provided the event occurred after the retroactive date (if any) stated in the policy.

Class rating Rate-making method in which similar insureds are placed in the same underwriting class and each is charged the same rate. Also called manual rating.

CLU *See* **Chartered Life Underwriter.**

Coinsurance provision Common provision in commercial property insurance contracts that requires the insured to maintain insurance on the property at a stated percentage of its actual cash value. Payment for a loss is determined by multiplying the amount of the loss by the fraction derived from the amount of insurance required. If the coinsurance requirement is not met at the time of loss, the insured will be penalized. Coinsurance is also used to refer to the percentage participation clause in health insurance. *See also* **Percentage participation clause.**

Collateral source rule Under this rule, the defendant cannot introduce any evidence that shows the injured party has received compensation from other collateral sources.

Collision loss Damages to an automobile caused by the upset of the automobile or its impact with another vehicle or object. Collision losses are paid by the insurer regardless of fault.

Commercial general liability policy (CGL) Commercial liability policy drafted by the Insurance Services Office containing two coverage forms—an occurrence form and a claims-made form.

Commercial package policy (CPP) A commercial policy that can be designed to meet the specific insurance needs of business firms. Property and liability coverage forms are combined to form a single policy.

Commodity price risk Risk of losing money if the price of a commodity changes.

Commutative contract One in which the values exchanged by both parties are theoretically even.

Company adjustor Claims adjustor who is a salaried employee representing only one company.

Comparative negligence laws Laws enacted by many jurisdictions permitting an injured person to recover damages even though he or she may have contributed to the accident. The financial burden is shared by both parties according to their respective degrees of fault.

Completed operations Liability arising out of faulty work performed away from the premises after the work or operations are completed; applicable to contractors, plumbers, electricians, repair shops, and similar firms.

Comprehensive major medical insurance Type of group plan combining basic plan benefits and major medical insurance in one policy.

Compulsory insurance law Law protecting accident victims against irresponsible motorists by requiring owners and operators of automobiles to carry certain amounts of liability insurance in order to license the vehicle and drive legally within the state.

Concealment Deliberate failure of an applicant for insurance to reveal a material fact to the insurer.

Conditions Provisions inserted in an insurance contract that qualify or place limitations on the insurer's promise to perform.

Consequential loss Financial loss occurring as the consequence of some other loss. Often called an indirect loss.

Consolidation Combining of business organizations through mergers and acquisitions.

Contingent beneficiary Beneficiary of a life insurance policy who is entitled to receive the policy proceeds on the insured's death if the primary beneficiary dies before the insured; or the beneficiary who receives the remaining payments if the primary beneficiary dies before receiving the guaranteed number of payments.

Contingent liability Liability arising out of work done by independent contractors for a firm. A firm may be liable for the work done by an independent contractor if the activity is illegal, the situation does not permit delegation of authority, or the work is inherently dangerous.

Contract bond Type of surety bond guaranteeing that the principal will fulfill all contractual obligations.

Contract of adhesion The insured must accept the entire contract, with all of its terms and conditions.

Contractual liability Legal liability of another party that the business firm agrees to assume by a written or oral contract.

Contribution by equal shares Type of other-insurance provision often found in liability insurance contracts that requires each company to share equally in the loss until the share of each insurer equals the lowest limit of liability under any policy or until the full amount of loss is paid.

Contributory negligence Common law defense blocking an injured person from recovering damages if he or she has contributed in any way to the accident.

Contributory plan Group life, health, or pension plan in which the employees pay part of the premiums.

Coordination-of-benefits provision Provision of a group medical expense plan that prevents over-insurance and duplication of benefits when one person is covered under more than one group plan.

Corridor deductible Major medical plan deductible that integrates a basic plan with a supplemental group major medical expense policy.

Cost-of-living rider Benefit that can be added to a life insurance policy under which the policyowner can purchase one-year term insurance equal to the percentage change in the consumer price index with no evidence of insurability.

Coverage for damage to your auto That part of the personal auto policy insuring payment for damage or theft of the insured automobile. This optional coverage can be used to insure both collision and other-than-collision losses.

CPCU *See* **Chartered Property Casualty Underwriter.**

Credit insurance Protects a firm against abnormal credit losses because of customer insolvency or past due accounts when they are filed for collection within a specified time stated in the policy.

Currency exchange rate risk Risk of loss of value caused by changes in exchange rates between countries.

Current assumption whole life insurance Nonparticipating whole life policy in which the cash values are based on the insurer's current mortality, investment, and expense experience. An accumulation account is credited with a current interest rate that changes over time. Also called interest-sensitive whole life insurance.

Currently insured Status of a covered person under the Old-Age, Survivors, and Disability Insurance (OASDI) program who has at least six quarters of coverage out of the last thirteen quarters, ending with the quarter of death, disability, or entitlement to retirement benefits.

Damage to property of others Damage covered up to $1000 per occurrence for an insured who damages another's property. Payment is made despite the lack of legal liability. Coverage is included in Section II of the homeowners policy.

Declarations Statements in an insurance contract that provide information about the property to be insured and used for underwriting and rating purposes and identification of the property to be insured.

Deductible A provision by which a specified amount is subtracted from the total loss payment that would otherwise be paid.

Deferred annuity A retirement annuity that provides benefits at some future date.

Defined-benefit plan Type of pension plan in which the retirement benefit is known in advance but the contributions vary depending on the amount necessary to fund the desired benefit.

Defined-contribution plan Type of pension plan in which the contribution rate is fixed but the retirement benefit is variable.

Demutualization A term to describe the conversion of a mutual insurer into a stock insurer.

Dependency period Period of time following the readjustment period during which the surviving spouse's children are under eighteen and therefore dependent on the parent.

Deposit-administration plan Type of pension plan in which all pension contributions are deposited in an unallocated fund. An annuity is purchased only when the employee retires.

Diagnosis-related groups (DRGs) Method for reimbursing hospitals under the Medicare program. Under this system, a flat, uniform amount is paid to each hospital for the same type of medical care or treatment.

Difference in conditions insurance (DIC) "All-risks" policy that covers other perils not insured by basic property insurance contracts, supplemental to and excluding the coverage provided by underlying contracts.

Direct loss Financial loss that results directly from an insured peril.

Direct-response system A marketing method where insurance is sold without the services of an agent. Potential customers are solicited by advertising in the mails, newspapers, magazines, television, radio, and other media.

Direct writer Insurance company in which the salesperson is an employee of the insurer, not an independent contractor, and which pays all selling expenses, including salary.

Disability-insured Status of an individual who is insured for disability benefits under the Old-Age, Survivors, and Disability Insurance (OASDI) program. The covered person must be disability-insured and have at least twenty quarters of coverage out of the last forty, ending with the quarter in which the disability occurs. Fewer quarters are required for persons under age thirty.

Domestic insurer Insurance company domiciled and licensed in the state in which it does business.

Double indemnity rider Benefit that can be added to a life insurance policy doubling the face amount of life insurance if death occurs as the result of an accident.

Dram shop law Law that imputes negligence to the owner of a business that sells liquor in the event that an intoxicated customer causes injury or property damage to another person; usually excluded from general liability policies.

Driver education credit Student discount or reduction in premium amount for which young drivers become eligible on completion of a driver education course.

Dwelling Property 1 Property insurance policy that insures the dwelling, structures, personal property, fair rental value, and certain other coverages; covers a limited number of perils.

Dwelling Property 2 Property insurance policy that insures the dwelling and other structures at replacement cost. It adds additional coverages and has a greater list of covered perils than the Dwelling Property 1 policy.

Dwelling Property 3 Property insurance policy that covers the dwelling and other structures against direct physical loss from any peril except for those perils otherwise excluded. However, personal property is covered on a named-perils basis.

Earnings test (retirement test) Test under the Old-Age, Survivors, and Disability Insurance (OASDI) program that reduces monthly benefits to those persons who have annual earned income in excess of the maximum allowed.

Education IRA A saving plan that allows taxpayers to make nondeductible contributions to an IRA to help pay for qualified higher education expenses for their children. Qualified distributions generally are not subject to income taxes.

Eligibility period Brief period of time during which an employee can sign up for group insurance without furnishing evidence of insurability.

Elimination period (waiting period) Waiting period in health insurance during which benefits are not paid. Also a period of time that must be met before benefits are actually payable.

Employee dishonesty coverage form Commercial crime insurance form drafted by the Insurance Services Office that covers the loss of money, securities, and other covered property because of any dishonest act of a covered employee or employees.

Employee Retirement Income Security Act (ERISA) Legislation passed in 1974 applying to most private pension and welfare plans that requires certain standards to protect participating employees.

Employers liability insurance Covers employers against lawsuits by employees who are injured in the course of employment, but whose injuries (or disease) are not compensable under the state's workers compensation law.

Endorsement Written provision that adds to, deletes, or modifies the provisions in the original contract. See also **Rider**.

Endowment insurance Type of life insurance that pays the face amount of insurance to the beneficiary if the insured dies within a specified period or to the policyowner if the insured survives to the end of the period.

Enterprise risk management Comprehensive risk management program that considers an organization's pure risks, speculative risks, strategic risks, and operational risks.

Entire-contract clause Provision in life insurance policies stating that the life insurance policy and attached application constitute the entire contract between the parties.

Equity in the unearned premium reserve Amount by which an unearned premium reserve is overstated because it is established on the basis of gross premium rather than net premium.

Equity indexed annuity A fixed, deferred annuity that allows participation in the stock market but guarantees the principal against loss if the contract is held to term.

ERISA See **Employee Retirement Income Security Act**.

Errors and omissions insurance Liability insurance policy that provides protection against loss incurred by a client because of some negligent act, error, or omission by the insured.

Estate planning Process designed to conserve estate assets before and after death, distribute property according to the individual's wishes, minimize federal estate and state inheritance taxes, provide estate liquidity to meet costs of estate settlement, and provide for the family's financial needs.

Estoppel Legal doctrine that prevents a person from denying the truth of a previous representation of fact, especially when such representation has been relied on by the one to whom the statement was made.

Excess insurance Under an excess insurance plan, the insurer does not participate in the loss until the actual loss exceeds a certain amount.

Exclusion ratio Calculation to determine the taxable and nontaxable portions of annuity payments, which is determined by dividing the investment in the contract by the expected return.

Exclusions Listing in an insurance contract of the perils, losses, and property excluded from coverage.

Exclusive agency system Type of insurance marketing system under which the agent represents only one company or group of companies under common ownership.

Exclusive provider organization (EPO) A plan that does not cover medical care received outside of a network of preferred providers.

Exclusive remedy doctrine Doctrine in workers compensation insurance that states that workers compensation benefits should be the exclusive or sole source of recovery for workers who have a job-related accident or disease; doctrine has been eroded by legal decisions.

Expense loading *See* **Loading**.

Expense ratio That proportion of the gross rate available for expenses and profit. Ratio of expenses incurred to premiums written.

Experience rating (1) Method of rating group life and health insurance plans that uses the loss experience of the group to determine the premiums to be charged. (2) As applied to property and liability insurance, the class or manual rate is adjusted upward or downward based on past loss experience. (3) As applied to state unemployment insurance programs, firms with favorable employment records pay lower tax rates.

Exposure unit Unit of measurement used in insurance pricing.

Extended nonowned coverage Endorsement that can be added to an automobile liability insurance policy that covers the insured while driving any nonowned automobile on a regular basis.

Extra expense coverage form A separate form that can be used to cover the extra expenses incurred by a firm to continue operations during a period of restoration.

Factory mutual Mutual insurance company insuring only properties that meet high underwriting standards; emphasizes loss prevention.

Facultative reinsurance Optional, case-by-case method of reinsurance used when the ceding company receives an application for insurance that exceeds its retention limit.

Fair Access to Insurance Requirements (FAIR plan) Property insurance plan that provides basic property insurance to property owners in areas where they are unable to obtain insurance in the normal markets. Each state with such a plan has a central placement facility.

Fair rental value Amount payable to an insured homeowner for loss of rental income due to damage that makes the premises uninhabitable.

Family purpose doctrine Concept that imputes negligence committed by immediate family members while operating a family car to the owner of the car.

Federal crop insurance Federal insurance program that provides coverage for unavoidable crop losses, such as hail, wind, drought, and plant disease.

Federal surety bond Type of surety bond required by federal agencies that regulates the actions of business firms. It guarantees that the bonded party will comply with federal standards, pay all taxes or duties accrued, or pay any penalty if the bondholder fails to pay.

File-and-use law Law for regulating insurance rates under which companies are required only to file the rates with the state insurance department before putting them into effect.

Financial responsibility law Law that requires persons involved in automobile accidents under certain circumstances to furnish proof of financial responsibility up to a minimum dollar limit or face having driving privileges revoked or suspended.

Fire legal liability Liability of a firm or person for fire damage caused by negligence and damage to property of others.

Fixed-amount option Life insurance settlement option in which the policy proceeds are paid out in fixed amounts.

Fixed annuity Annuity whose periodic payment is a guaranteed fixed amount.

Fixed-period option Life insurance settlement option in which the policy proceeds are paid out over a fixed period of time.

Flexible-premium annuity An annuity contract that permits the owner to vary the size and frequency of premium payments. The amount of retirement income depends on the accumulated sum in the annuity at retirement.

Flexible-spending account An arrangement by which the employee agrees to a salary reduction, which can be used to pay for plan benefits, unreimbursed medical and dental expenses, and other expenses permitted by the Internal Revenue Code.

Flex-rating law Type of rating law in which prior approval of the rates is required only if the rates exceed a certain percentage above and below the rates previously filed.

Foreign insurer Insurance company chartered by one state but licensed to do business in another.

Fortuitous loss Unforeseen and unexpected loss that occurs as a result of chance.

Franchise deductible Deductible found in some marine insurance contracts in which the insurer has no liability if the loss is under a certain amount, but once this amount is exceeded, the entire loss is paid in full.

Fraternal insurer Mutual insurance company that provides life and health insurance to members of a social organization.

Fully insured Insured status of a covered person under the Old-Age, Survivors, and Disability Insurance (OASDI) program. You must have one quarter of coverage for each year after 1950 (or after the year you attain age twenty-one, if later) up to the year of death, disability, or attainment of age sixty-two. A minimum of six quarters and a maximum of forty quarters are required.

Fundamental risk A risk that affects the entire economy or large numbers of persons or groups within the economy.

Funding agency A financial institution or individual that provides for the accumulation or administration of the pension contributions that will be used to pay pension benefits.

Funding instrument An insurance contract or trust agreement that states the terms under which the funding agency will accumulate, administer, and disburse the pension funds.

General agency system Type of life insurance marketing system in which the general agent is an independent businessperson who represents only one insurer, is in charge of a territory, and is responsible for hiring, training, and motivating new agents.

General aggregate limit The maximum amount the insurer will pay for the sum of the following—damages under Coverage A, B, and medical expenses under Coverage C.

General average In ocean marine insurance, a loss incurred for the common good that is shared by all parties to the venture.

Good student discount Reduction of automobile premium for a young driver at least sixteen who ranks in the upper 20 percent of his or her class, has a B or 3.0 average, or is on the Dean's list or honor roll. It is based on the premise that good students are better drivers.

Grace period Period of time during which a policyowner may pay an overdue life insurance premium without causing the policy to lapse.

Gross estate The value of the property that you own when you die. Also includes value of jointly-owned property, life insurance, death proceeds, and certain other items.

Gross premium Amount paid by the insured, consisting of the gross rate multiplied by the number of exposure units.

Gross rate The sum of the pure premium and a loading element.

Group deferred annuity Type of allocated pension plan in which a single-premium deferred annuity is purchased each year and is equal to the retirement benefit for that year.

Group life insurance Life insurance provided on a number of persons in a single master contract. Physical examinations are not required, and certificates of insurance are issued to members of the group as evidence of insurance.

Group term life insurance Most common form of group life insurance. Yearly renewable term insurance on employees during their working careers.

Group universal life products (GULP) Universal life insurance plans sold to members of a group, such as individual employees of an employer. There are some differences between GULP plans and individual universal life plans; for instance, GULP expense charges are generally lower than those assessed against individual policies.

Guaranteed investment contract An investment contract with an insurer in which the insurer guarantees both principal and interest on a pension contribution.

Guaranteed purchase option Benefit that can be added to a life insurance policy permitting the insured to purchase additional amounts of life insurance at specified times in the future without requiring evidence of insurability.

Guaranteed renewable Continuance provision of a health insurance policy under which the company guarantees to renew the policy to a stated age, and whose renewal is at the insured's option. Premiums can be increased for broad classes of insureds.

Guaranteed replacement cost In the event of a total loss, the insurer agrees to replace the home exactly as it was before the loss even though the replacement cost exceeds the amount of insurance stated in the policy.

Hard insurance market A period in the underwriting cycle during which underwriting standards are strict and premiums are high. *See also* **soft insurance market** and **underwriting cycle**.

Hazard Condition that creates or increases the chance of loss.

Health maintenance organization (HMO) Organized system of health care that provides comprehensive health services to its members for a fixed prepaid fee.

Hedging Technique for transferring the risk of unfavorable price fluctuations to a speculator by purchasing and selling options and futures contracts on an organized exchange.

HMO See Health maintenance organization.

Hold-harmless clause Clause written into a contract by which one party agrees to release another party from all legal liability, such as a retailer who agrees to release the manufacturer from legal liability if the product injures someone.

Home service life insurance Industrial life insurance and monthly debit ordinary life insurance contracts that are serviced by agents who call on the policyowners at their homes to collect the premiums.

Homeowners 2 policy (broad form) Homeowners insurance policy that provides coverage on a named-perils basis on the dwelling, other structures, and personal property. Personal liability insurance is also provided.

Homeowners 3 policy (special form) Homeowners insurance policy that covers the dwelling and other structures on a risk-of-direct-loss basis and personal property on a named-perils basis. Personal liability insurance is also provided.

Homeowners 4 policy (contents broad form) Homeowners insurance policy that applies to tenants renting a home or apartment. Covers the tenant's personal property and provides personal liability insurance.

Homeowners 5 policy (comprehensive form) Homeowners insurance policy that provides open perils coverage ("all risks coverage") on both the building and personal property. The dwelling, other structures, and personal property are insured against the risk of direct physical loss to property; all losses are covered except those losses specifically excluded.

Homeowners 6 policy (unit-owners form) Homeowners insurance policy that covers personal property of insured owners of condominium units and cooperative apartments on a broad form, named-perils basis. Personal liability insurance is also provided.

Homeowners 8 policy (modified coverage form) Homeowner policy that is designed for older homes. Dwelling and other structures are indemnified on the basis of repair cost using common construction materials and methods. Personal liability insurance is also provided.

Hospital expense insurance Individual health insurance that pays for medical expenses incurred while in a hospital.

Hospital Insurance (Part A) Part A of Medicare that covers inpatient hospital care, skilled nursing facility care, home health care services, and hospice care for Medicare beneficiaries.

Hospital-surgical insurance Medical expense plan that provides hospital and surgical benefits and other ancillary benefits.

HR-10 plan *See* **Keogh plan for the self-employed**.

Hull insurance (1) Class of ocean marine insurance that covers physical damage to the ship or vessel insured. Typically written on an "all-risks" basis. (2) Physical damage insurance on aircraft—similar to collision insurance in an automobile policy.

Human life value For purposes of life insurance, the present value of the family's share of the deceased breadwinner's future earnings.

Immediate annuity An annuity where the first payment is due one payment interval from the date of purchase.

Immediate-participation guarantee plan (IPG) Type of pension plan in which all pension contributions are deposited in an unallocated fund and used directly to pay benefits to retirees.

Imputed negligence Case in which responsibility for damage can be transferred from the negligent party to another person, such as an employer.

Incontestable clause Contractual provision in a life insurance policy stating that the insurer cannot contest the policy after it has been in force two years during the insured's lifetime.

Indemnification Compensation to the victim of a loss, in whole or in part, by payment, repair, or replacement.

Independent adjustor Claims adjustor who offers his or her services to insurance companies and is compensated by a fee.

Independent agency system Type of property and liability insurance marketing system, sometimes called the American agency system, in which the agent is an independent businessperson representing several insurers. The agency owns the expirations or renewal rights to the business, and the agent is compensated by commissions that vary by line of insurance.

Indeterminate-premium whole life insurance Nonparticipating whole life policy that permits the insurer to adjust premiums based on anticipated future experience. Initial premiums are guaranteed for a certain period. After the initial guaranteed period expires, the insurer can increase premiums up to some maximum limit.

Indirect loss *See* **Consequential loss.**

Individual Retirement Account (IRA) Individual retirement plan that can be established by a person with earned income. An IRA plan enjoys favorable income tax advantages.

Industrial life insurance Type of life insurance in which policies are sold in small amounts and the premiums are collected weekly or monthly by a debit agent at the policyowner's home.

Inflation-guard endorsement Endorsement added at the insured's request to a homeowners policy to increase periodically the face amount of insurance on the dwelling and other policy coverages by a specified percentage.

Initial reserve In life insurance, the reserve at the beginning of any policy year.

Inland marine insurance Transportation insurance that provides protection for goods shipped on land including imports, exports, domestic shipments, means of transportation, personal property floater risks, and commercial property floater risks.

Installment refund annuity Pays the annuitant a lifetime income, but if death occurs before receiving payments equal to the purchase price, the income payments continue to the beneficiary.

Insurance Pooling of fortuitous losses by transfer of risks to insurers who agree to indemnify insureds for such losses, to provide other pecuniary benefits on their occurrence, or to render services connected with the risk.

Insurance guaranty funds State funds that provide for the payment of unpaid claims of insolvent insurers.

Insurance Services Office (ISO) Major rating organization in property and liability insurance that drafts policy forms for personal and commercial lines of insurance and provides rate data on loss costs for property and liability insurance lines.

Insuring agreement That part of an insurance contract that states the promises of the insurer.

Integrated risk management A risk management technique that combines coverage for pure and speculative risks in the same insurance contract.

Interest-adjusted method Method of determining cost to an insured of a life insurance policy that considers the time cost of money by applying an interest factor to each element of cost. *See also* **Net payment cost index; Surrender cost index.**

Interest option Life insurance settlement option in which the principal is retained by the insurer and interest is paid periodically.

Interest rate risk Risk of loss caused by adverse interest rate movements.

Invitee Someone who is invited onto the premises for the benefit of the occupant.

IPG plan *See* **Immediate-participation guarantee plan.**

IRA *See* **Individual Retirement Account.**

Irrevocable beneficiary Beneficiary designation allowing no change to be made in the beneficiary of an insurance policy without the beneficiary's consent.

ISO *See* **Insurance Services Office.**

Joint and several liability rule Under which several people may be responsible for the injury, but a defendant who is only slightly responsible may be required to pay the full amount of damages.

Joint-and-survivor annuity Annuity based on the lives of two or more annuitants. The annuity income (either the full amount of the original income or only two-thirds or one-half of the original income when the first annuitant dies) is paid until the death of the last annuitant.

Joint underwriting association (JUA) Organization of automobile insurers operating in a state that makes automobile insurance available to high-risk drivers. All underwriting losses are proportionately shared by insurers on the basis of premiums written in the state.

Judgment rating Rate-making method for which each exposure is individually evaluated and the rate is determined largely by the underwriter's judgment.

Judicial bond Type of surety bond used for court proceedings and guaranteeing that the party bonded will fulfill certain obligations specified by law, for example, fiduciary responsibilities.

Juvenile insurance Life insurance purchased by parents for children under a specified age.

Keogh plan for the self-employed (HR-10 plan) Retirement plan individually adopted by self-employed persons that allows a tax-deductible contribution to a deferred-contribution or defined-benefit plan.

Lapsed policy One that is not in force because premiums have not been paid.

Last clear chance rule Statutory modification of the contributory negligence law allowing the claimant endangered by his or her own negligence to recover damages from a defendant if the defendant has a last clear chance to avoid the accident but fails to do so.

Law of large numbers Concept that the greater the number of exposures, the more closely will actual results approach the probable results expected from an infinite number of exposures.

Legal reserve Liability item on a life insurer's balance sheet representing the redundant or excessive premiums paid under the level-premium method during the early years. Assets must be accumulated to offset the legal reserve liability. Purpose of the legal reserve is to provide lifetime protection.

Liability coverage That part of the personal auto policy that protects a covered person against a suit or claim for bodily injury or property damage arising out of negligent ownership or operation of an automobile. A single or split limit for bodily injury and property damage liability is applied on a per accident basis. Liability coverage is also included in the homeowner's policy, which provides coverage for bodily injury and property damage liability.

Liability without fault Principle on which workers compensation is based, holding the employer absolutely liable for occupational injuries or disease suffered by workers, regardless of who is at fault.

License and permit bond Type of surety bond guaranteeing that the person bonded will comply with all laws and regulations that govern his or her activities.

Licensee Someone who enters or remains on the premises with the occupant's expressed or implied permission.

Life annuity with guaranteed payments Pays a life income to the annuitant with a certain number of guaranteed payments.

Life income option Life insurance settlement option in which the policy proceeds are paid during the lifetime of the beneficiary. A certain number of guaranteed payments may also be payable.

Life insurance planning Systematic method of determining the insured's financial goals, which are translated into specific amounts of life insurance, then periodically reviewed for possible changes.

Limited-payment policy Type of whole life insurance providing protection throughout the insured's lifetime and for which relatively high premiums are paid only for a limited period.

Liquor liability law *See* **Dram shop law.**

Loading The amount that must be added to the pure premium for expenses, profit, and a margin for contingencies.

Long-term-care insurance A form of health insurance that pays a daily or monthly benefit for medical or custodial care received in a nursing facility or hospital.

Loss control Risk management activities that reduce both the frequency and severity of losses for a firm or organization.

Loss frequency The probable number of losses that may occur during some given time period.

Loss ratio *See* **Actual loss ratio.**

Loss reserve Amount set aside by property and liability insurers for claims reported and adjusted but not yet paid, claims reported and filed but not yet adjusted, and claims incurred but not yet reported to the insurer.

Loss severity The probable size of the losses that may occur.

McCarran-Ferguson Act Federal law passed in 1945 stating that continued regulation of the insurance industry by the states is in the public interest and that federal antitrust laws apply to insurance only to the extent that the industry is not regulated by state law.

Major medical insurance Health insurance designed to pay a large proportion of the covered expenses of a catastrophic illness or injury.

Malpractice liability insurance Covers acts of malpractice resulting in harm or injury to patients.

Managed care A generic name for medical expense plans that provide covered services to the members in a cost-effective manner.

Manual rating *See* **Class rating.**

Manuscript policy Policy designed for a firm's specific needs and requirements.

Mass merchandising Plan for insuring individual members of a group, such as employees of firms or members of labor unions, under a single program of insurance at reduced premiums. Property and liability insurance is sold to individual members using group insurance marketing methods.

Master contract Formed between the insurer and group policyowner for the benefit of the individual members.

Maximum possible loss Worst loss that could possibly happen to a firm during its lifetime.

Maximum probable loss Worst loss that is likely to happen to a firm during its lifetime.

Mean reserve In life insurance, the average of the terminal and initial reserves.

Medical Information Bureau (MIB) Bureau whose purpose is to supply underwriting information in life insurance to member companies, which report any health impairments of an applicant for insurance.

Medical payments coverage That part of the personal auto policy that pays all reasonable medical and funeral expenses incurred by a covered person within three years from the date of an accident.

Medical payments to others Pays for medical expenses of others under the homeowners policy in the event that a person (not an insured) is accidentally injured on the premises, or by the activities of an insured, resident employee, or animal owned by or in the care of an insured.

Medicare Part of the total Social Security program that covers the medical expenses of most people age 65 and older and certain disabled people under age 65.

Medicare + Choice A term to describe alternatives to Parts A and B of Medicare, such as managed care plans, private fee-for-service plans, and medical savings accounts; also called Part C of Medicare.

Merit rating Rate-making method in which class rates are adjusted upward or downward based on individual loss experience.

MIB *See* **Medical Information Bureau.**

Minimum coverage requirement A test that must be met to prevent employers from establishing a qualified pension plan that covers only the highly compensated. *See also* **Ratio percentage test.**

Misstatement of age or sex clause Contractual provision in an insurance policy stating that if the insured's age or sex is misstated, the amount payable is the amount that the premium would have purchased at the correct age.

Mobilehome insurance A package policy that provides property insurance and personal liability insurance to the owners of mobile homes. A special endorsement is added to HO-2 or HO-3.

Modified life policy Whole life policy for which premiums are reduced for the first three to five years and are higher thereafter.

Modified no-fault plan An injured person has the right to sue a negligent driver only if the bodily injury claim exceeds the dollar or verbal threshold.

Monetary threshold An injured motorist would not be permitted to sue but would collect from his or her insurer, unless the claim exceeded the threshold amount.

Moral hazard Dishonesty or character defects in an individual that increase the chance of loss.

Morale hazard Carelessness or indifference to a loss because of the existence of insurance.

Multicar discount Reduction in automobile insurance premium for insured who owns two or more automobiles, on the assumption that two such autos owned by the same person will not be driven as frequently as only one.

Multiple distribution systems Insurance marketing method that refers to the use of several distribution systems by an insurer; for example, a property and liability insurer may use the independent agency method and direct response system to sell insurance.

Multiple-line insurance Type of insurance that combines several lines of insurance into one contract, for example, property insurance and casualty insurance.

Mutual insurer Insurance corporation owned by the policyowners, who elect the board of directors. The board appoints managing executives, and the company may pay a dividend or give a rate reduction in advance to insureds.

NAIC *See* **National Association of Insurance Commissioners.**

NALP *See* **Net annual level premium.**

Named insured The person or persons named in the declarations section of the policy, as opposed to someone who may have an interest in the policy but is not named as an insured.

Named-perils policy Coverage by an insurance contract that promises to pay only for those losses caused by perils specifically listed in the policy.

National Association of Insurance Commissioners (NAIC) Group founded in 1871 that meets periodically to discuss industry problems and draft model laws in various areas and recommends adoption of these proposals by state legislatures.

Needs approach Method for estimating amount of life insurance appropriate for a family by analyzing various family needs that must be met if the family head should die and converting them into specific amounts of life insurance. Financial assets are considered in determining the amount of life insurance needed.

Negligence Failure to exercise the standard of care required by law to protect others from harm.

Net amount at risk Concept associated with a level-premium life insurance policy. Calculated as the difference between the face amount of the policy and the legal reserve.

Net annual level premium (NALP) Annual level premium for a life insurance policy with no expense loading. Mathematically equivalent to the net single premium.

Net payment cost index Method of measuring the cost of an insurance policy to an insured if death occurs at the end of some specified time period. The time value of money is taken into consideration.

Net present value Used in capital budgeting and is the sum of the present values of the future cash flows minus the cost of the project. A positive net present value represents an increase in value for the firm.

Net retention *See* **Retention limit.**

Net single premium (NSP) Present value of the future death benefit of a life insurance policy.

No-fault insurance A tort reform proposal in which the injured person would collect benefits from his or her insurer and would not have to sue a negligent third party who caused the accident and establish legal liability.

Nonbuilding agency system Life insurance marketing system by which an insurer sells its products through established agents who are already engaged in selling life insurance.

Noncancellable Continuance provision of a health insurance policy stipulating that the policy cannot be cancelled, that the renewal is guaranteed to a stated age, and that the premium rates cannot be increased.

Noncontributory plan Employer pays the entire cost of a group insurance or private pension plan. All eligible employees are covered.

Nonforfeiture law State law requiring insurance companies to provide at least a minimum nonforfeiture value to policyowners who surrender their cash value life insurance policies.

Noninsurance transfers Various methods other than insurance by which a pure risk and its potential financial consequences can be transferred to another party, for example, contracts, leases, and hold-harmless agreements.

Nonoccupational disability The accident or illness must occur off the job.

Nonparticipating policy Term used to describe a life insurance policy that does not pay dividends.

Objective risk Relative variation of actual loss from expected loss, which varies inversely with the square root of the number of cases under observation.

Obligee The party to a surety bond who is reimbursed for damages if the principal to the bond fails to perform.

Occurrence An accident, including continuous or repeated exposure to substantially the same general, harmful conditions, which results in bodily injury or property damage during the policy period. *See also* **Accident.**

Occurrence policy A liability insurance policy that covers claims arising out of occurrences that take place during the policy period, regardless of when the claim is made. *See also* **Claims-made policy.**

Ocean marine insurance Type of insurance that provides protection for all types of oceangoing vessels and their cargoes as well as legal liability of owners and shippers.

Open-competition law Law for regulating insurance rates under which insurers are not required to file rates at all with the state insurance department but may be required to furnish rate schedules and supporting data to state officials.

Optionally renewable policy The insurer has the right to terminate a policy on any anniversary date, or in some cases, on a premium date.

Ordinary life insurance Type of whole life insurance providing protection throughout the insured's lifetime and for which premiums are paid throughout the insured's lifetime.

Other-insurance provisions Provisions whose purpose is to prevent profiting from insurance and violation of the principle of indemnity.

Other-than-collision loss Part of the coverage available under Part D: Coverage for Damage to Your Auto in the personal auto policy. All physical damage losses to an insured vehicle are covered except collision losses and those losses specifically excluded.

Ownership clause Provision in life insurance policies under which the policyowner possesses all contractual rights in the policy while the insured is living. These rights can generally be exercised without the beneficiary's consent.

P&I Insurance *See* **Protection and indemnity insurance.**

Package policy Policy that combines two or more separate contracts of insurance in one policy, for example, homeowners insurance.

Partial disability Inability of the insured to perform one or more important duties of his or her occupation.

Participating policy Life insurance policy that pays dividends to the policyowners.

Particular average An ocean marine loss that falls entirely on a particular interest as contrasted with a general average loss that falls on all parties to the voyage.

Particular risk A risk that affects only individuals and not the entire community.

Past-service credits Pension benefits awarded to employees based on service with the employer prior to the inception of the plan.

Paul v. Virginia Landmark legal decision of 1869 establishing the right of the states, and not the federal government, to regulate insurance. Ruled that insurance was not interstate commerce.

Pension accrual benefit A disability income benefit that makes a pension contribution so that the disabled employee's pension benefit remains intact.

Pension Benefit Guaranty Corporation (PBGC) A federal corporation that guarantees the payment of vested or nonforfeitable benefits up to certain limits if a private pension plan is terminated.

Percentage participation clause Provision in a health insurance policy that requires the insured to pay a certain percentage of eligible medical expenses in excess of the deductible. Also called coinsurance.

Peril Cause or source of loss.

Personal injury Injury for which legal liability arises (such as for false arrest, detention or imprisonment, malicious prosecution, libel, slander, defamation of character, violation of the right of privacy, and unlawful entry or eviction) and which may be covered by an endorsement to the homeowners policy.

Personal liability insurance Liability insurance that protects the insured for an amount up to policy limits against a claim or suit for damages because of bodily injury or property damage caused by the insured's negligence. This coverage is provided by Section II of the homeowners policy.

Personal-producing general agent Term used to describe an above-average salesperson with a proven sales record who is hired primarily to sell life insurance under a contract that provides both direct and overriding commissions.

Personal umbrella policy Policy designed to provide protection against a catastrophic lawsuit or judgment, whose coverage ranges generally from $1 million to $10 million and extends to the entire family anywhere in the world. Insurance is excess over underlying coverages.

Physical hazard Physical condition that increases the chance of loss.

PIA *See* **Primary insurance amount.**

Point-of-service plan (POS) Establishes a network of preferred providers. If patients see a preferred provider, they pay little or nothing. Outside provider care is covered, but at a substantially higher deductible and copayment.

Policy loan Cash value of a life insurance policy that can be borrowed by the policyowner in lieu of surrendering the policy.

Policyowners' surplus Difference between an insurance company's assets and its liabilities.

Pooling Spreading of losses incurred by the few over the entire group, so that in the process, average loss is substituted for actual loss.

Preexisting condition Physical or mental condition of an insured that existed prior to issuance of a policy.

Preexisting-conditions clause Contractual provision in a health insurance policy stating that preexisting conditions are not covered or are covered only after the policy has been in force for a specified period.

Preferred risks Individuals whose mortality experience is expected to be lower than average.

Premises burglary coverage form Commercial crime insurance form by the Insurance Services Office that provides coverage for premises burglary and robbery of a guard.

Primary and excess insurance Type of other-insurance provision that requires the primary insurer to pay first in the case of a loss; when the policy limits under the primary policy are exhausted, the excess insurer pays.

Primary beneficiary Beneficiary of a life insurance policy who is first entitled to receive the policy proceeds on the insured's death.

Primary insurance amount (PIA) Monthly cash benefit paid to a retired worker at the full retirement age, or to a disabled worker eligible for benefits under the Old-Age, Survivors, and Disability Insurance (OASDI) program.

Principal The bonded party in the purchase of a surety bond who agrees to perform certain acts or fulfill certain obligations.

Principal of indemnity States that the insurer agrees to pay no more than the actual amount of the loss. The insured should not profit from a covered loss but should be restored to approximately the same financial position that existed prior to the loss.

Prior-approval law Law for regulating insurance rates under which the rates must be filed and approved by the state insurance department before they can be used.

Pro rata liability clause Clause in a property insurance policy that makes each company insuring the same interest in a property liable according to the proportion that its insurance bears to the total amount of insurance on the property.

Probationary period Waiting period of one to six months required of an employee before he or she is allowed to participate in a group insurance plan.

Products-completed operations hazard Liability losses that occur away from the premises and arise out of the insured's product or work after the insured has relinquished possession of the product, or the work has been completed.

Products liability The legal liability of manufacturers, wholesalers, and retailers to persons who are injured or who incur property damage from defective products.

Prospective reserve In life insurance, the difference between the present value of future benefits and the present value of future net premiums.

Protection and indemnity insurance (P&I) Coverage that can be added to an ocean marine insurance policy to provide broad, comprehensive liability insurance on an indemnity basis for property damage and bodily injury to third parties.

Proximate cause Factor causing damage to property for which there is an unbroken chain of events between the occurrence of an insured peril and damage or destruction of the property.

Public adjustor Claims adjustor who represents the insured rather than the insurance company and is paid a fee based on the amount of the claim settlement. A public adjustor may be employed in those cases where the insured and insurer cannot resolve a dispute over a claim, or if the insured needs technical assistance in a complex loss situation.

Public official bond Type of surety bond guaranteeing that public officials will faithfully perform their duties for the protection of the public.

Pure no-fault plan The injured person cannot sue at all, regardless of the seriousness of the claim, and no payments are made for pain and suffering.

Pure premium That portion of the insurance rate needed to pay losses and loss-adjustment expenses.

Pure risk Situation in which there are only the possibilities of loss or no loss.

Rate Price per unit of insurance.

Rate making Process by which insurance pricing or premium rates are determined for an insurance company.

Ratio percentage test A test that a qualified pension plan must meet to receive favorable income tax treatment. The pension plan must benefit a percentage of employees that is at least 70 percent of the highly compensated employees covered by the plan.

Readjustment period One- to two-year period immediately following the breadwinner's death during which time the family should receive approximately the same amount of income it received while the breadwinner was alive.

Reasonable and customary charges Payment of physicians' normal fees if they are reasonable and customary, such as a fee that does not exceed the 80th or 90th percentile for a similar procedure performed by physicians in the area.

Rebating A practice—illegal in virtually all states—of giving a premium reduction or some other financial advantage to an individual as an inducement to purchase the policy.

Reciprocal exchange Unincorporated mutual insuring organization in which insurance is exchanged among members and which is managed by an attorney-in-fact.

Regression analysis Method of characterizing the relationship between two or more variables, and then using this characterization as a predictor.

Reinstatement clause Contractual provision in a life insurance policy that permits the owner to reinstate a lapsed policy within five years if certain requirements are fulfilled; for example, evidence of insurability is required and overdue premiums plus interest must be paid.

Reinstatement provision Provision of a health insurance policy that allows the insured to reinstate a lapsed policy by payment of premium either without an application or with an application.

Reinsurance The shifting of part or all of the insurance originally written by one insurer to another insurer.

Reinsurance facility Pool for placing high-risk automobile drivers that arranges for an insurer to accept all applicants for insurance. Underwriting losses are shared by all automobile insurers in the state.

Relative-value schedule Variation of the schedule approach in which units or points are assigned to each surgical operation on the basis of degree of difficulty, and a conversion factor is used to convert the relative value into a dollar amount paid to the surgeon.

Replacement-cost insurance Property insurance by which the insured is indemnified on the basis of replacement cost with no deduction for depreciation.

Reporting form Coverage for commercial property insurance that requires the insured to report monthly or quarterly the value of the insured inventory, with automatic adjustment of insurance amount to cover the accurately reported inventory.

Representations Statements made by an applicant for insurance regarding, for example, occupation, state of health, and family history.

Residual disability Residual disability means that a proportionate disability-income benefit is paid to an insured whose earned income is reduced because of an accident or illness.

Residual market The residual market refers to plans in which automobile insurers participate to make insurance available to high-risk drivers who are unable to obtain coverage in the standard markets. Examples include an automobile insurance plan, joint underwriting association, and reinsurance facility. Also called the shared market.

Res ipsa loquitur Literally, the thing speaks for itself. Under this doctrine, the very fact that the event occurred establishes a presumption of negligence on behalf of the defendant.

Retained limit Term found in an umbrella policy (also known as self-insured retention). If the loss is covered by the umbrella policy but not by any underlying contract, the insured must retain or pay a certain amount of the loss.

Retention Risk management technique in which the firm retains part or all of the losses resulting from a given loss exposure. Used when no other method is available, the worst possible loss is not serious, and losses are highly predictable.

Retention limit Amount of insurance retained by a ceding company for its own account in a reinsurance operation.

Retirement test *See* **Earnings test**.

Retrocession Process by which a reinsurer obtains reinsurance from another company.

Retrospective rating Type of merit-rating method in which the insured's loss experience during the current policy period determines the actual premium paid for that period.

Retrospective reserve In life insurance, the net premiums collected by the insurer for a particular block of policies, plus interest earnings at an assumed rate, less the amounts paid out as death claims.

Revocable beneficiary Beneficiary designation allowing the policyowner the right to change the beneficiary without consent of the beneficiary.

Rider Term used in insurance contracts to describe a document that amends or changes the original policy. *See also* **Endorsement.**

Risk Uncertainty concerning the occurrence of a loss.

Risk-based capital Under NAIC standards, insurers are required to have a certain amount of capital that is based on the riskiness of their investments and operations.

Risk control Risk management techniques that reduce the frequency and severity of losses, such as avoidance, loss prevention, and an automatic sprinkler system.

Risk financing Risk management techniques that provide for the funding of losses after they occur, such as retention, noninsurance transfers, and commercial insurance.

Risk management Systematic process for the identification and evaluation of loss exposures faced by an organization or individual, and for the selection and implementation of the most appropriate techniques for treating such exposures.

Risk management information system Computerized data base that permits the risk manager to store and analyze risk management data and to use such data to predict future loss levels.

Risk map Map used in risk management that shows grids detailing the potential frequency and severity of risks faced by the organization.

Robbery Taking of property from a person by someone who has (1) caused or threatens to cause bodily harm to that person, or (2) committed an obviously unlawful act witnessed by that person.

Roth IRA An IRA in which the contributions are not income-tax deductible but distributions are received income-tax free if certain conditions are met.

Safe driver plan Plan in which the automobile premiums paid are based on the insured's driving record and on the records of those living with the insured.

Savings bank life insurance Life insurance sold by mutual savings banks in Massachusetts, New York, and Connecticut, and certain surrounding states.

Scheduled personal property endorsement Special coverage added at the insured's request to a homeowners policy to insure items specifically listed. Used to insure valuable property such as jewelry, furs, and paintings.

Schedule rating Type of merit-rating method in which each exposure is individually rated and given a basis rate that is then modified by debits or credits for undesirable or desirable physical features.

Second-injury fund State funds paying the excess amount of benefit awarded an employee for a second injury if the disability is greater than that caused by the second injury alone. Its purpose is to encourage employers to hire handicapped workers.

Section 401(k) plan A qualified profit-sharing or thrift plan that allows participants the option of putting money into the plan or receiving the funds as cash. The employee can voluntarily elect to have his or her salary reduced up to some maximum limit, which is then invested in the employer's Section 401(k) plan.

Self-insurance Retention program in which the employer self-funds or pays part or all of its losses.

Self-insured retention *See* **Retained limit.**

SEP *See* **Simplified Employee Pension.**

Separate account Variation of the deposit administration pension plan arrangement in which pension funds are segregated so that account assets are not commingled with insurance company's general assets and can be invested separately.

Service benefits Health insurance benefits that pay hospital charges or payment for care received by the insured directly to the hospital or providers of care. The plan provides service rather than cash benefits to the insured.

Settlement options Ways in which life insurance policy proceeds can be paid other than in a lump sum, including interest, fixed period, fixed amount, and life income options.

SEUA case *See* **South-Eastern Underwriters Association (SEUA) case.**

Shared market *See* **Residual market.**

Short-rate table Schedule used by insurers to refund premiums on policy cancelation. It refunds less than a pro rata amount to cover insurer's expenses in issuing and printing the policy and to offset adverse selection.

SIMPLE retirement plan A qualified retirement plan for smaller employers who are exempt from most nondiscrimination and administrative rules. Employees can elect to contribute up to $6000 annually. The employer has the option of (1) matching the employee's contribution on a dollar-for-dollar basis up to 3 percent of salary, or (2) making a nonelective contribution of 2 percent of salary for all eligible employees.

Simplified Employee Pension (SEP) An employer-sponsored individual retirement account that meets certain requirements. Paperwork is reduced for employers who wish to cover employees in a retirement plan.

Single limit The total amount of insurance applies to the entire accident without a separate limit for each person.

Single-premium deferred annuity A retirement annuity that is purchased with a single premium with benefits to start at some future date.

Single-premium whole life insurance A whole life policy that provides lifetime protection with a single premium payment.

Social insurance Government insurance programs with certain characteristics that distinguish them from other government insurance programs. Programs are generally compulsory; specific earmarked taxes fund the programs; benefits are heavily weighted in favor of low-income groups; and programs are designed to achieve certain social goals.

Soft insurance market A period during which underwriting standards are more liberal and premiums are relatively low. *See also* **hard insurance market** and **underwriting cycle.**

South-Eastern Underwriters Association (SEUA) case Legal landmark decision of 1944 overruling the Paul v. Virginia ruling and finding that insurance was interstate commerce when conducted across state lines and was subject to federal regulation.

Speculative risk Situation in which either profit or loss are clear possibilities.

Split limits The amounts of insurance for bodily injury liability and property damage liability are stated separately.

Stop-loss limit Modification of the coinsurance provision in major medical plans that places a dollar limit on the maximum amount that an individual must pay rather than requiring that the insured pay 20 percent of all expenses in excess of deductible.

Straight deductible Deductible in an insurance contract by which the insured must pay a certain number of dollars of loss before the insurer is required to make a payment.

Subjective risk Uncertainty based on one's mental condition or state of mind.

Subrogation Substitution of the insurer in place of the insured for the purpose of claiming indemnity from a negligent third party for a loss covered by insurance.

Suicide clause Contractual provision in a life insurance policy stating that if the insured commits suicide within two years after the policy is issued, the face amount of insurance will not be paid; only premiums paid will be refunded.

Supplemental major medical insurance Group health insurance plan that supplements the benefits provided by a basic medical expense plan. It provides more comprehensive benefits with higher limits and is designed for a catastrophic loss.

Supplementary Medical Insurance Part B of the Medicare program that covers physicians' fees and other related medical services. Most eligible Medicare recipients are automatically included unless they voluntarily refuse this coverage.

Surety Party who agrees to answer for the debt, default, or obligation of another in the purchase of a bond.

Surety bond Bond that provides monetary compensation if the bonded party fails to perform certain acts.

Surgical expense insurance Health insurance that provides for payment of physicians' fees for surgical operations performed in a hospital or elsewhere.

Surplus line broker Specialized insurance broker licensed to place business with a nonadmitted insurer (a company not licensed to do business in the state).

Surrender cost index Method of measuring the cost of an insurance policy to an insured if the policy is surrendered at the end of some specified time period. The time value of money is taken into consideration.

Survivor income benefits Monthly benefits paid to an eligible surviving spouse or children for a limited period following the disabled worker's death.

Term insurance Type of life insurance that provides temporary protection for a specified number of years. It is usually renewable and convertible.

Terminal reserve In life insurance, the reserve at the end of any given policy year.

Theft Any act of stealing; includes burglary, robbery. *See also* **Burglary; Robbery.**

Time limit on certain defenses provision Provision in a health insurance policy that prohibits the company from canceling the policy or denying a claim on the basis of a preexisting condition or misstatement in the application after the policy has been in force for two or three years, with the exception of fraudulent misstatement.

Total disability Condition of an insured that makes him or her completely unable to perform all duties of the insured's own occupation or unable to perform the duties of any occupation for which the insured is reasonably fitted by training, education, and experience.

Traditional IRA An IRA that allows workers to deduct part or all of their IRA contributions if taxable compensation is under a certain limit. Distributions are taxed as ordinary income.

Traditional net cost method Traditional method of determining cost to an insured of a life insurance policy, determined by subtracting the total dividends received and cash value at the end of a period from the total premiums paid during that period.

Treaty reinsurance Type of reinsurance in which the primary company must cede insurance to the reinsurer and the reinsurer must accept. The ceding company is automatically reinsured according to the terms of the reinsurance contract.

Trespasser A person who enters or remains on the owner's property without the owner's consent.

Trust Arrangement in which property is legally transferred to a trustee who manages it for the benefit of named beneficiaries for their security and to insure competent management of estate property.

Trust-fund plan Type of pension plan in which all pension contributions are deposited with a trustee who invests the funds according to a trust agreement between employer and trustee. Benefits are paid directly out of the trust fund.

Twisting Illegal practice of inducing a policyowner to drop an existing policy in one company and take out a new policy in another through misrepresentation or incomplete information.

Ultimate net loss The total amount that the insured is legally obligated to pay.

Underinsured motorists coverage Coverage that can be added to the personal auto policy. Coverage pays damages for a bodily injury to an insured caused by the ownership or operation of an underinsured vehicle by another driver. The negligent driver may have insurance that meets the state's financial responsibility or compulsory insurance law requirement, but the amount carried is insufficient to cover the loss sustained by the insured.

Underwriting The selection and classification of applicants for insurance through a clearly stated company policy consistent with company objectives.

Underwriting cycle A term to describe the cyclical pattern in underwriting standards, premium levels, and profitability. *See also* **Hard insurance market; Soft insurance market.**

Unearned premium reserve Liability reserve of an insurance company that represents the unearned part of gross premiums on all outstanding policies at the time of valuation.

Unified tax credit Tax credit that can be used to reduce the amount of the federal estate or gift tax.

Unilateral contract Only one party makes a legally enforceable promise.

Uninsured motorists coverage That part of the personal auto policy designed to insure against bodily injury caused by an uninsured motorist, a hit-and-run driver, or a driver whose company is insolvent.

Unisex rating A rating system in which the pooled loss experience of both sexes is used to determine the rates charged.

Unit-owners form *See* **Homeowners 6 policy.**

Universal life insurance A flexible-premium whole life policy that provides lifetime protection under a contract that separates the protection and saving components. The contract is an interest-sensitive product that unbundles the protection, saving, and expense components.

Unsatisfied judgment fund Fund established by a small number of states to compensate accident victims who have exhausted all other means of recovery.

Utmost good faith That a higher degree of honesty is imposed on both parties to an insurance contract than is imposed on parties to other contracts.

Valued policy Policy that pays the face amount of insurance, regardless of actual cash value, if a total loss occurs.

Valued policy laws Laws requiring payment to an insured of the face amount of insurance if a total loss to real property occurs from a peril specified in the law, even though the policy may state that only actual cash value will be paid.

Vanishing-premium policy A whole life policy in which the premium vanishes or disappears after a number of years.

Variable annuity Annuity whose periodic lifetime payments vary depending on the level of common stock prices (or other investments), based on the assumption that cost of living and common stock prices are correlated in the long run. Its purpose is to provide an inflation hedge.

Variable life insurance Life insurance policy in which the death benefit and cash surrender values vary according to the investment experience of a separate account maintained by the insurer.

Verbal threshold A suit for damages is allowed only in serious cases, such as those involving death, dismemberment, etc.

Vesting Characteristic of pension plans guaranteeing the employee's right to part or all of the benefits attributable to the employer's contributions if employment terminates prior to retirement.

Vicarious liability Responsibility for damage done by the driver of an automobile that is imputed to the vehicle's owner.

Waiver Voluntary relinquishment of a known legal right.

Waiver-of-premium provision Benefit that can be added to a life insurance policy providing for waiver of all premiums coming due during a period of total disability of the insured.

War clause Restriction in a life insurance policy that excludes payment if the insured dies as a direct result of war.

Warranty Statement of fact or a promise made by the insured, which is part of the insurance contract and which must be true if the insurer is to be liable under the contract.

Workers compensation insurance Insurance that covers payment of all workers compensation and other benefits that the employer must legally provide to covered employees who are occupationally disabled.

Index